Cemeteries of Grundy County, Tennessee

and More

Volume 3

A Transcription Project of the
Tennessee Consolidated Coal Company Library
A Division of the
Grundy County Historical Society
Grundy County, Tennessee
Editors
Janelle Layne Taylor & Joan Bishop Nasso

WALDENHOUSE PUBLISHERS, INC.
WALDEN, TENNESSEE

Cemeteries of Grundy County, Tennessee and More – Volume 3
Copyright ©2023 Grundy County Historical Society. All rights reserved. Permission to reproduce information regarding individual grave markers and obituary information is granted provided attribution is given. Requests to reproduce more extensive portions of Cemeteries should be directed to:

Editor, Janelle L. Taylor

Grundy County Historical Society Publications

P.O. Box 1422

Tracy City, TN 37387

Edited by Janelle Layne Taylor and Joan Bishop Nasso
Published by Waldenhouse Publishers, Inc.
100 Clegg Street, Signal Mountain, Tennessee 37377 USA
www.Waldenhouse.com   423-886-2721
Printed in the United States of America
ISBN: 978-1-947589-81-0
REF013000 REFERENCE/Genealogy & Heraldry
REF020000 REFERENCE/Research
HIS036120 HISTORY/United States/State & Local/South
Library of Congress Control Number: 2024937242

Burials of individuals with Grundy County, Tennessee, connections; locations; parents' names; spouse's name; military service. Some corrections and additions from previous volumes. Newly located cemeteries and new cemeteries started more recently and located by description or GPS.
– Provided by Publisher

Cemeteries of Grundy County, Tennessee & More, Volume 3 is issued by the Grundy County Historical Society; P.O. Box 1422; Tracy City, TN 37387. Copies are available through the Society whose street location is at the Grundy County Heritage Center; 465 Railroad Ave; Tracy City, TN 37387. It may also be obtained through our Facebook site at Grundy County Tennessee History & Genealogy or the website at www.grundycountyhistory.org.

Illustrations on the front and back covers are from Warren "Red Hill" Cemetery in Pelham, TN.

Grundy County Historical Society

November 2023, First Edition

This publication is dedicated to the loyal workers in the Tennessee Consolidated Coal Company Library & Research Center who have given their time, talent, and resources to preserve the history and heritage of Grundy County. Their work will be an important part of their legacy and a lasting impact that their lives have made on our county.

Front l-r: Jan (Rulison) Canfield, Joan (Bishop) Nasso, Barbara (Mooney) Myers

Back l-r: Gabriela (Gomez) Crabtree, Janelle (Layne) Taylor, Frankie Jean Pattie

In Remembrance of

Willene (Nunley) Campbell

December 7, 1946 – May 24, 2024

Willene was a loyal supporter of the Grundy County Historical Society and the Tennessee Consolidated Coal Company Library through the years serving on the board and co-editing several of our publications. She will be dearly missed.

Acknowledgements

We are very thankful for those who have gone over and above to help with this project, whether it was to search out information, keep up with obituaries on a weekly basis, type names, dates, and information to go in the book, answer questions about who is buried where, or a hundred other jobs that went into the compiling of *Cemeteries of Grundy County Tennessee and More, Volume 3*. Of course, our dedicated library staff has been invaluable. They are Jan Canfield, Gabby Crabtree, Barbara Myers, Joan Nasso, Jean Pattie and Janelle Taylor to whom this book is dedicated. Others who have contributed are Megan Coats Benton, Faye Church Bonner, John W. Campbell (deceased), Willene Nunley Campbell (deceased), Kirby Crabtree, Patrick Dean, Phyllis Dent, Jean Garrett, Dana Gilliam, Sue Bouldin Parrott, Wanda Turner Kilgore, John Franklin "Squirrel" Layne, Jackie Layne Partin, Claire Proudfoot, Brenda Sanders Ruehling, Ralph Rieben (deceased), Deb Scissom, Gerald Sitz, Kenneth & Vickie Stoner, Theresa Gilliam Utz, & Boyce Wanamaker. Cumberland Funeral Home, Layne Funeral Home at Tracy City and Palmer, as well as Moore Cortner in Winchester have also been helpful in our searches. We want to thank you all.

Explanations and Abbreviations

A few abbreviations have been used in this publication. They are as follows:

ca – about

cem – abbreviation for cemetery

cert - certificate

co – abbreviation for county

dau – abbreviation for daughter

m – married

An underlined word indicates that it may seem to be misused or misspelled, but that is the word intended because it may be an unusual use or a changed spelling.

Introduction

Work on collecting the names of individuals to be included in *Cemeteries of Grundy County TN and More, Volume 3* began as soon as the last names were added to Volumes 1 & 2 before their publication in 2013. This work is ongoing.

Cemeteries of Grundy County and More, Volume 3 is different from the previous two volumes in that it is not organized by cemeteries located in or near Grundy County, but by names of individuals who have some connection to Grundy County. These people are not necessarily buried in the county.

Some persons listed are those who have information corrections from previously published books as well as those who were missed or who have died since the last *Cemeteries of Grundy County Tennessee* publications in 2013. We collected names up through June 30, 2022. This was done largely by obituaries and information reported to us by family members. Those who have died since the end of June 2022 are included in *The Pathfinder*, our quarterly publication from the Grundy County Historical Society. In some instances, those who are more recently deceased are included in this publication since they had a tombstone already in place when the previous books were published.

We apologize for any missed deaths or burials. We urge you to report information about anyone not included in this volume so that we can add them to our *Pathfinder* publication as the names come to our attention. We also ask that you report any corrections or additions to the information we have here. Those will also be recorded in *The Pathfinder* on an ongoing basis. The information we need is as follows: Name of the deceased, date of birth, date of death, place of burial or indicate if cremated, names of parents including mother's maiden name, name of spouse with maiden name and military service branch if applicable.

We hope to publish newly collected names on our website, **www.grundycountyhistory.org** in the future.

There are references in this volume back to Volumes 1 & 2 of *Cemeteries of Grundy County TN*, which also give the page reference in the previous publications. We hope that you will find them useful.

With the advent of privacy laws, people have been more reluctant to provide obituaries and relevant information about deceased family members. In some cases, there were no obituaries at all other than, perhaps, the name of the deceased. Modern day information is much more difficult to obtain.

Send your information to us at Grundy County Historical Society; P.O. Box 1422; Tracy City, TN 37387 or email to heritagelibrary@benlomand.net or jantay641@gmail.com.

We hope that you will find Volume 3 helpful in your genealogical research. Thank you for your support.

Cemeteries Found Since the Publication of Cemeteries of Grundy County Volumes 1 & 2

African American Cemetery at Rutledge Hill

An African American Cemetery, the name of which is unknown, was located near Owen & Lisa (Meeks) Campbell's homeplace in Rutledge Hill Community, which is in Coffee County, but near the Grundy County line. The cemetery is reputed to have had about 100 graves of slaves. None of the graves which were marked by fieldstones in the past had names attached to the graves, but in more recent years all the fieldstones have been removed, so the location of individual graves is not discernable anymore.

Barks, Daryl Cemetery in Beersheba Springs

The Barks Cemetery is located at 1375 Bess Town Rd. and was created June 5, 2022, with the burial of Darrell Ray Barks on his own land. Barks was born Nov 2, 1953, and died June 5, 2022.

As of September 30, 2023, Daryl's is the only burial there.

Gibbs Bend Family Cemetery in Coalmont

Gibbs Bend Cemetery is reported to be at the old G.W. Gibbs homeplace near the TVA power line. We never found the graves, but they are reputed to be there.

These are the children of James & Hanna Gibbs

Gibbs, Louisiana "Louise	b. ca 1831
Gibbs, John	b. 1833
Gibbs, William J.	b. 1836
Gibbs, Mary "Polly"	b. ca 1838
Gibbs, Nancy	b. 1839

Gibbs, Adam, a Civil War soldier is said to be buried at Gibbs Bend as well, per Kelly Gibbs, a family descendant. We found nothing other than oral history to locate this burial ground called Gibbs Bend.

Gibbs, James Odom "J.O." (born, Sep 18, 1867- died 1950), was married to Nancy Gibbs. J.O.'s father is unidentified. J.O. Gibbs is buried at Hobbs Hill, however. He married Sarah "Sallie" (Hobbs) Argo. They were the parents of Lucy Bell Argo (1867-1931) J.O. Hollow is the hollow behind the Elijah & Kitt Meeks' burial site across from the church in the Sweeton Hill area of Coalmont. This is also a possible location of the burial place of the Gibbses. If you have more information about their burial place, please let us know at heritagelibrary@benlomand.net.

Goodman/Moran Cemetery in Valley Home

The Goodman/ Moran site has been completely destroyed with no trace left behind. It is said to have been located on Goodman Lane in the Valley Home Community in the barnyard of the Moran place, which is now the farm belonging to Butch & Linda (Dykes) Goodman. No names of those buried there remain, but it is said that the graves were of the slaves who lived and worked on the farm there for the most part with members of the families who owned the land and also lived there.

Hobbs, Wesley "Scat" Cemetery is located at 35°30' 26" N 85° 44' 54" W, off the Northcutt's Cove Rd. It is remote and has no road leading to the cemetery. There are only two marked graves there, that of Wesley "Scat" Hobbs and of a baby, Mary Rhea, who was born and died in 1801. There are several more graves there, but they only have rocks to mark their location.

Dry Shave Mountain Cemetery on the Grundy/Warren County Line

The Dry Shave Mountain Cemetery has no known name, but we are calling it Dry Shave Mountain Cemetery because of its location which is at 35° 31' 52" N and 85° 42' 56" W. Although it is very near the Warren County line, it is in Grundy County. It is remote with no road access, gated where one is coming into the private property that is owned by the heirs of Leonard Smartt. There is evidence that people lived around where the cemetery is located, since there are remains of homes nearby and an old well. Cattle are grazed in the area and nursery property owned by Anthony Wanamaker adjoins the cemetery property. No names of those buried there are remembered from this cemetery located on what is now known as the Jay Hobbs place. The cemetery itself has not been bulldozed. Information from Chassity Bell & Anthony Wanamaker

Magourik Family "Boot's Garden" Cemetery on Cagle Mountain in Sequatchie County

The cemetery was begun July 1, 2003, at 232 Thompson Rd; Dunlap, TN, by the Magourik family and currently as of October 10, 2023, has two graves, those of Betty Sue (Thompson) Magourik and her daughter Tammy Jeanice Magourik, b. Nov 24, 1962; d. Dec 14, 2021.

Magouirk is the normal spelling of this surname, but when the patriarch of this branch of the family was in the Army, there was a clerical error which caused the spelling to be changed to Ray "Magourik", and, apparently, it was just easier to let the incorrect spelling stay as it was. Subsequent generations were born with the same spelling, and so, it continues to be spelled that way. The people who use the Magouirk and the people who use the Magourik spelling are of the same origins. This family was introduced into the area in Pelham Valley, but moved to the plateau for work in coal and timber and is now commonly in the Palmer area.

Meeks, Elijah & Kitt Hollow Cemetery in Coalmont

Elijah & Kitt Meeks Hollow Cem; location of grave is 39 19' 39" N and 85 40' 38" W; Located a few miles behind the pumping station on County Farm Road in Coalmont. Only Ruthy Jane Fults grave is marked in this very remote area.

Buried there are Ruthy Jane Fults, Jul 18, 1882 – Sep 20, 1920; Dau. of Jesse & Mary A. (Haskins) Fults (1850-1930) and 4 more individuals in unmarked graves. Some believe that two of them are her parents. Ruthy had children Maggie Marie Fults Roberts (1901-1989) who married Francis Roberts and Myrtle Ellen Fults Byers (1904-1956), who is buried at Warren "Red Hill" Cemetery in Pelham, so neither of her children are buried here.

Meeks Family Cemetery at Flat Branch

35°. 3100860 N   85°.7033350 W is the GPS location with the street address being 2572 Flat Branch Spur Road, Tracy City, TN 37387

Directions for driving: From State Route 56 in Coalmont, TN, turn on Q Switch Rd, and continue until that road intersects with Flat Branch Rd. Turn right on Flat Branch Road and follow it until you see Flat Branch Spur Road on the left. Turn onto Flat Branch Spur and follow it until you reach 2572 Flat Branch Spur. You will be at the Randall Meeks residence. At that point you will need to ask permission to go onto his private property since the cemetery is a distance out in his field with only a dirt road access.

The cemetery was established by Randall Meeks, Sr. and his son Randall Meeks, Jr. and wife Amy. An additional adjoining acre has also been given by Zach Meeks, grandson of Billy Meeks, in January of 2019. The cemetery was begun December 9, 2011, with the burial of Felicia Lynn Meeks, Randall Meeks, Sr.'s daughter. Those buried there are listed in the body of this book.

Nunley Oaks Cemetery at Altamont

Nunley Oaks is located on Old Burroughs' Cove Rd. in Altamont at the residence of George & Ann (Higgins) Nunley. Only George Edward Nunley is buried as of October 10, 2023.

Richardson Cemetery in Beersheba Springs area

When traveling from Altamont, turn left at Cumberland Baptist Church (brown building). Go one mile on Bess Town Rd. Turn right onto John Richardson Rd. to a single wide trailer on your left. Go behind trailer into field. 3 or 4 buried there currently. (October 10, 2023).

Rural Cemetery at Easter Knob

We do not know the original name of this cemetery, but we have given it the name Rural Cemetery at Easter Knob because it has been posted in some places simply as Rural Cemetery. It overlooks Savage Cove Creek. We have also called this cemetery the William Houston "Bud" and Sally (Nunley) Stoner Cemetery because they are the two known graves there.

For those of you who are more familiar with the area you may know local names in the area, so for those of you who are familiar, the cemetery is located between the Cal Place and Easter Knob, just inside the Grundy

County line that adjoins Warren County. The GPS location is 35° 30' 40" N   85° 43' 18.0" W. There are 11 identifiable graves in this burial site, but there may have been many more since it is obvious that the area has been dozed.

This remote cemetery is located just east of Easter Knob in an area that is 80' to 100' wide and then drops off to both sides.

Known to be buried there are the following:

William Houston "Bud" Stoner

1822-before 1891
Parents: Peter Countiss, IV and Lavinia Stoner

Sarah "Sally" Nunley

1827-1894
Parents: William & Jean (Miller) Nunley

Seagroves Cemetery in Coalmont

Seagroves Cemetery is located at 175 Freemont Rd. As of September 30, 2023, Cynthia Seagroves is the only burial there.

Stoner Cemetery at Stella Bottom and Other Graves

The Stoner Cemetery at Dry Shave is just inside the Warren County Line   GPS: 35.53060N 85.72190W.

To reach this cemetery, which is difficult to find, travel on State Route 56 to the Warren/Grundy County line. Turn on Dry Shave Road and travel to the end of the road. At that point one must walk or use an ATV to go on to the cemetery which is about ¼ mile further. Use the GPS to find the location.

According to Price Scott and his wife Joyce, the Stella Bottom Cemetery was given the name for Stella Stoner who, as a child, was hoeing corn nearby the cemetery when her father observed that she was chopping as much corn as she was Johnson Grass. Her stepfather, T.J. Nunley, ordered her home to save the corn! From that time forward the field where Stella was chopping and the nearby cemetery was given the name, Stella Bottom. This explanation was given directly to Price Scott by Stella (Stoner) Bartlett herself, who was, at the time, 97 years old and living in Texas, and it was confirmed by Jack Nunley, her brother, 93, then living in Oklahoma, who escorted the Scotts to visit with Stella at the time. Stella and Jack moved west with their family from Dry Shave at the ages of 12 & 8 respectively.

Susan A. Nunley initially married John Stoner, who built the Stoner home in Dry Shave. After John's death, she married Thomas Jefferson "T.J." Nunley (1865-1952). The James "Jim" Clendenon family lived about a quarter of a mile away in the area where residents lived in almost exclusively log homes, but the Clendenons lived in the distinctive home that was the first board house in the area. Boards became available when Burl

Killian located a sawmill in a nearby hollow. Maybe this new style house had something to do with prompting the Stoners to realize that there were new possibilities for their lives. At any rate, they made the decision to move West – to Texas. Sometime after their move West, a tornado took the old homes away on April 3, 1974, leaving no clue that the Stoners or the Clendenons had ever lived there. The area is now (2020) abandoned to settlement and is owned by Dianne Smartt, daughter of Leonard & Lottie Smartt, and the land is currently rented by Verble Wanamaker for cattle grazing.

Mr. Price remembered that there were two graves on up in the gulf from the Clendenon place, not at Stella Bottom, but he never knew of anyone who could identify those who were buried there. In addition to these graves, there are two more unidentified graves at the head of the hollow at Dry Shave. These burials are lost to history, but they give evidence of the many families who lived in the area on the sides of the mountains away from the banks of Collins River in their quest to avoid mosquito borne diseases. This cemetery is said to have graves of members of the Smartt, Fults and Stoner families. Known graves at Stella Bottom follow in bold print:

Samuel M. Stoner   Apr 1850   June 19, 1905   Son of William H. & Sarah "Sally" (Nunley) Stoner. This grave is marked by a fieldstone.

Vina (Stoner) Myers   Sept 9, 1800   June 24, 1886   m. 1) Peter Countiss, IV & had a son, William Houston "Bud" Stoner. No marriage record was found for Vina Stoner & Peter Countiss. (2) Vina's second marriage was to Johnny Myers. Vina's grave has a tombstone.

Andrew J. Stoner   June 12, 1886   Apr 16, 1895   Son of John & Susan A. (Nunley) Stoner; struck by lightning. This grave has a tombstone.

John Stoner   1847   1890   Son of William Houston Sarah "Sally" (Nunley) Stoner   Fieldstone marker only (According to death records, John is buried in Stoner Cemetery which is thought to be this Stoner Cemetery at Stella Bottom.)

A baby who was named **Carrie** is also said to be buried in this cemetery, but no surname is remembered for the baby.

"Thank you" to Kenneth Stoner & wife Vickie & Price Scott & wife Joyce for help with the information collected about this cemetery. Price Scott passed away in March of 2021.

Yokley Family Cemetery

The Yokley Family Cemetery is located at 17715 South Pittsburg Mt. Rd. in Sewanee inside Marion County.

Name	Born	Died	Details
Abrahamson, Doris Ann	Oct 19, 1949	Mar 20, 2011	Swiss Colony Cem.; Dau. of Barney & Joyce Layne; addition to Cemeteries of Grundy Co.Vol. 2, p. 798
Acevedo, Antonio	Jun 12, 1934	Jul 24, 2017	Little Johnny Myers Cem.; Son of Steven & Delphenia (Cabereras) Acevedo of Puerto Rico; m. Francis Acevedo
Adams, Aaron Matthew	Oct 21, 1972	Mar 12, 2016	Coalmont Cem.; Son of Alfred & Myrtis Adams, his adoptive parents, & biological parents, Larry Anderson & Lydeth (O'Dear) Hardbarger
Adams, Albert Dewey	Jan 25, 1919	Nov 05, 1977	Hobbs Hill Cem.; Son of Charles F. Adams & Dolly A. Tate; m. Kitty Estelle Agan; Army WWII
Adams, Alford A.	May 06, 1951	May 17, 1951	Bonny Oak Cem.; Son of Henry & Ruby Corin (Hobbs) Adams; addition to Cemeteries of Grundy Co, Vol. 1, p. 86
Adams, Alfred Thompson, Jr.	Aug 01, 1927	May 21, 2013	Grace Chapel Cem.; Son of Alfred Thompson, Sr. & Karin (Hughes) Adams; m. 1) Peggy Joyce Keylon 2) Patricia Riley Fleming; US Navy
Adams, Alice Carrie (Pack)	Mar 09, 1903	Dec 01, 1972	Monteagle Cem.; Dau. of John & Mary Ellen (Elliot) Pack; m. Lewis D. Adams, Dec 10, 1929; addition to Cemeteries of Grundy County, Vol. 1, p. 429
Adams, Barney	Feb 29, 1896	Apr 26, 1970	Monteagle Cem.; Son of John H. & Lou Ann (Long) Adams; correction to Grundy County Cemetery Book, Vol. 1, p. 420
Adams, Benjamin Harrison	Jun 4, 1820	Dec 9, 1898	B.H. Adams Gravesite; Son of John & Martha Matilda (Ashlin) Adams; m. 1) Nancy Crosslin 2) Elizabeth Crossland; addition to Grundy Co. Cemeteries, Vol. 1, p. 2
Adams, David Porterfield, Jr.	1931	Jan 26, 2019	Body donated to Emory Univ. School of Medicine; Son of David Porterfield Adams & Mildred Goodpasture; m. Wendy Oehlert; U.S. Marine
Adams, Emma (Smith)	Apr 26, 1875	Nov 08, 1973	Wesley Chapel Cem.; Dau. of Henry & Allice (Cookston) Smith; m. Samuel Henry Adams, son of Benjamin Harrison & Elizabeth (Crosslin) Adams, Sr.; Addition to Cemeteries of Grundy Co.Vol. 2, p. 975
Adams, Franklin D	Sep 09, 1939	May 27, 2019	Monteagle Cem.; Son of Lloyd Adams & Doris Barnes; m. Opal Thomas
Adams, Levina J. (Lindsey)	Jul 27, 1861	Nov 5, 1889	Monteagle Cem.; Dau. of William David & Mary Elizabeth "Eliza" (Weaver) Lindsey; addition to Cemeteries of Grundy Co. Vol. 1, p. 385

Name	Born	Died	Notes
Adams, Lewis Davis	Jun 24, 1894	Jan 04, 1957	Monteagle Cem.; Son of Charles Allison Woodville & Malone Elizabeth (Crownover) Adams; m. Alice Carrie Pack; addition to Cemeteries of Grundy Co. Vol. 1, p. 429
Adams, Madeline (Reynolds)	Feb 03, 1934	Nov 21, 2020	Cremated; Dau. of John Rook & Edith (Horn) Reynolds; m. Howell Elliot Adams, Jr.; Madeline had a home in Beersheba.
Adams, Pherbia (Nunley)	Oct 1, 1852	May 10, 1941	Orange Hill Cem.; m. Pink Adams; no marker; addition to Cemeteries of Grundy Co.Vol. 2, p. 547
Adams, Richard Lambert	Nov 04, 1926	Feb 22, 2020	Tracy City Cem.; Son of Charles Wesley & Olivia "Livy" (Petty) Adams; m. Ella Rose Fults; U.S. Navy
Adams, William Edward	Nov 03, 1918	May 01, 1974	Oak Grove Cem.; Son of Jefferson Fabian "Jeff" & Ida Mae (Davis) Adams; PFC US Army; addition to Cemeteries of Grundy Co.Vol. 1, p 511
Adkins, Orlena Marie	Nov 24, 1971	Mar 01, 2018	Cremated; Dau. of Lucille Dockham; m. Robert Adkins
Agee, Kimberly Diane (Terry)	Oct 23, 1968	Mar 29, 2016	Clouse Hill Cem.; Dau. of Earl & Rena Terry; m. Steve Agee
Akins, Kara	Feb 15, 1990	Dec 17, 2015	Coalmont Cem.; Dau. of Kenneth W. & Tabitha (Irvin) Akins
Akins, Lorene Nannie (Holt)	Dec 23, 1907	Dec 09, 2002	Palmer Cem.; Dau. of Oscar Lee & Amanda Elizabeth (Parson) Holt; m. 1) Chester M. Tate 2) Rupert Tate on Nov 23, 1927, 3) Allen S. Akins on Sep 21, 1933; correction of marriages to include her first husband, Chester M. Tate. Rupert Tate was 2nd husband, & Allen S. Akins her third. Addition to Cemeteries of Grundy Co.Vol. 2, p. 572
Akins, Whitney Kala	Feb 15, 1990	Dec 17, 2015	Coalmont Cem.; Dau of Kenneth W. & Tabitha (Irvin) Akins
Albritton, Daniel Lake	Jan 06, 1904	Sep 25, 1996	Airview Cem.; Son of John Thomas & Ethel Theodosia (Moore) Albritton; m. Etta Lee Morgan; addition to Cemeteries of Grundy County; Vol. 1, p. 5
Albritton, Etta Lee (Morgan)	Apr 21, 1910	Oct 06, 1977	Airview Cem.; Dau. of Edmund & Callie (Bynum) Morgan; m. Daniel Lake Albritton, Oct 2, 1927, Bradley Co TN; addition to Cemeteries of Grundy Co.Vol. 1, p. 5
Albritton, Ruby Jo (McCuiston)	May 09, 1932	Jun 28, 1998	Airview Cem.; Dau. of Ralph & Mary (Snyder) McCuiston; m. Charles Ray Albritton; addition to Cemeteries of Grundy Co, Vol. 1, p 5
Alexander, Allen Chester, Sr.	Jan 22, 1888	May 11, 1905	Burns Cem.; Son of Allen Crockett & Mary Rosetta (Roop) Alexander; m. Nellie Foster; addition to Cemeteries of Grundy Co.Vol. 1, p. 134

Name	Born	Died	Notes
Alexander, Neva June (Sherrill)	Dec 20, 1947	May 10, 2020	Rutledge Hill Cem.; Dau. of Howard & Verbie Sherrill; m. Johnny Alexander
Alexander, William Robert	1885	Dec 02, 1951	Monteagle Cem.; m. Elizabeth Kilgore, Sep 8, 1918, in Grundy Co; born in Scotland
Allan, Henry Stanley	Oct 14, 1891	Apr 21, 1963	Burns Cem.; Son of James Millard & Nettie Mae (McGill) Allan; m. Ruth Foster; addition to Cemeteries of Grundy Co.Vol. 1, p. 134
Allen, Ashley Karan	Feb 28, 1995	Mar 02, 1995	Palmer Cem.; Dau. of Jennifer Allen; addition to Cemeteries of Grundy Co.Vol. 2, p. 577
Allen, Carol Olive	Dec 11, 1958	Sep 01, 2021	Fall Creek Cem.; Dau. of John Henry & Nellie Irene (Layne) McBee
Allen, Courtney Rebeccah	Mar 17, 1989	Aug 21, 2021	Fall Creek Cem.; Dau. of Carol Allen; fiance, Gregory "AJ" Hester
Allen, Geneva (Meeks)	Dec 18, 1938	Sep 16, 2021	Coalmont Cem.; Dau. of Lee & Mollie Pearl (Brown) Meeks; m. John Edward Allen
Allen, Howard C.	Jan 03, 1921	Dec 02, 2011	Homeland Acres Cem.; Son of Iulus & Bonnie Ree (Huffmaster) Allen; m. Evola Jones
Allen, Kobe Bryant	May 09, 1988	Feb 18, 2020	DeKalb Cem.; Son of Tommy & Patsy (Hobbs) Basham; m. Amanda Allen
Allen, Margie Faith (Fulfer)	Oct 04, 1955	Dec 17, 2020	Cremated; Dau. of Bill Sam & Shirley (McCurry) Fulfer; m. Keith Gipson
Allred, Charles Edward	Nov 06, 1939	Feb 17, 1973	Plainview Cem.; Son of William Curtis & Treava L. Allred; m. Ruby May Miller; addition to Cemeteries of Grundy Co.Vol. 2, p. 672
Allred, Tava Lucille	Feb 05, 1921	Jul 10, 1966	Plainview Cem.; Dau. of Erman & Annie (Meeks) Meeks; m. William Curtis Allred; addition to Cemeteries of Grundy Co, Vol. 2, p. 672
Allred, Tava N.	Jan 16, 1970	Feb 25, 1973	Plainview Cem.; Dau. of Charles Edward & Willie Mae (Miller) Allred; addition to Cemeteries of Grundy Co., Vol. 1, p. 672
Almany, F.M.	ca. 1843	May 06, 1915	Burns Cem.; Son of Nathan & Sarah "Sallie" (Hicks) Almany; m. Mary Catherine "Kate" Myers; CSA
Almany, James Francis	May 24, 1925	May 24, 1925	Tracy City Cem.; Son of Wiley Francis Marion & Mamie Beatrice (Manley) Almany; no tombstone, buried near his grandparents James & Sally (Phipps) Manley, per family
Andelson, Bonny Johnson	Jun 24, 1923	Oct 30, 2014	Orange Hill Cem.; Dau of Barney William & Pearl Lilly (Orange) Johnson; m. Robert Vernon Andelson
Anderson, Agnes Inez	Sep 20, 1949	Aug 21, 2012	Gregg Cem.; Dau. of Mack C. & Rachel Elizabeth (Robertson) Bennett; m. Roy L. Anderson; correction to Cemeteries of Grundy Co.; Vol. 1, p. 307

Name	Born	Died	Notes
Anderson, Amos Phillip	Mar 30, 1963	Jan 18, 2022	Tate Cem. in Martin Springs; Son of Elbert Hubert & Ruby (Shrum) Anderson; m. Carol Anderson
Anderson, C. L.	1949	Jan 25, 2022	Plainview Cem.; Son of Elisha & Dorothy Anderson; m. Mary Jo Parsons
Anderson, Carl Edward	Oct 18, 1963	Feb 08, 2022	Brown's Chapel Cem.; Son of Howell Edward & Carolyn Ann (Wideman) Anderson
Anderson, Carter Hayden Elisha	Nov 16, 2021	Mar 05, 2022	Plainview Cem.; Son of Kirsten Fults & Robert Anderson
Anderson, Charles E.	Apr 24, 1937	May 20, 1937	Gregg Cem.; Son of Elisha & Dorothy (Collins) Anderson
Anderson, Claude Leon	Jan 16, 1945	Apr 23, 2014	Swiss Colony Cem.; Son of George Washington Anderson & Ella Mae Rust; m. Sylvia Kay Anderson
Anderson, Dale	Mar 26, 1949	Feb 07, 2021	Fults Cem.; Son of John & Louise (Hodge) Anderson; m. Edna Fults
Anderson, David Ray	Jun 10, 1985	Dec 10, 2020	Plainview Cem.; Son of Floy & Patricia (Wallace) Anderson
Anderson, Douglas Elisha	1955	Jun 15, 2014	Coalmont Cem.; Son of Elisha & Dorothy Anderson
Anderson, Emily Elizabeth Paige	Sep 28, 2018	Sep 28, 2018	Plainview Cem.
Anderson, Evalena "Inez"	Sep 15, 1974	Oct 26, 2017	Plainview Cem.; Dau. of Floyd Ray, Sr. & Patricia (Wallace) Anderson; m. Jimmy Tressler
Anderson, Fannie (Caldwell)	Aug 22, 1889	Oct 02, 1984	Altamont Cem.; Dau. of William & Sarah J. (Thurman) Caldwell; addition to Cemeteries of Grundy Co. Vol. 1, p. 30
Anderson, Gladys Margaret	Jan 17, 1902	Mar 20, 1969	Altamont Cem.; Dau. of Edward E. & Harriet (Davenport) Armstrong; m. Joseph Dewey Anderson; addition to Cemeteries of Grundy Co., Vol. 1, p. 10
Anderson, Guy Richard	Jul 28, 1952	Jul 28, 2021	Swiss Colony Cem.; Son of George Allen & Bessie Lou (Hale) Anderson; m. Clair Slatton
Anderson, Hershel Eugene	Mar 22, 1925	Nov 06, 1977	Oak Grove Cem.; Son of George Washington "Wash" & Araminda "Mindy" (Braden) Anderson; m. Minnie Green; addition to Cemeteries of Grundy Co., Vol. 1, p. 511
Anderson, Infant			Infant of Wash & Ella (Campbell) Anderson; buried near the farm pond on the old Partin's Dairy Farm on Pigeon Springs Rd.
Anderson, Infant		Oct 01, 1915	Gregg Cem.; Child of Tom Anderson; Source, *Mrs. Grundy,* Oct 28, 1915
Anderson, Jacob Lee	Mar 14, 1854	Aug 06, 1939	Palmer Cem.; Son of William Riley Anderson & Nancy Headrick
Anderson, James Henry "Q Ball"	Jun 20, 1947	Dec 31, 2015	Plainview Cem.; Son of James Robert & Juanita (Dyer) Anderson; m. Brenda Ann Hodge; US Army

Name	Birth	Death	Details
Anderson, James Mitchell "Rust"	Jan 16, 1957	Nov 23, 2018	Plainview Cem.; Son of Ernest R. Anderson, Jr. & Betty L. Parson; m. Barbara Amelia Coffey
Anderson, James Neely "Nelia"	Feb 01, 1913	Jan 24, 1938	White Cem.; Son of Sam & Margaret "Maggie" (Smedley) Anderson; m. Maude L. Shrum on Feb 19, 1932; addition to Cemeteries of Grundy Co., Vol. 2, p. 1007
Anderson, James Richard "Ricky"	Feb 12, 1980	Apr 01, 2014	Warren "Red Hill" Cem.; Son of Raymond Leslie & Pamela (Meeks) Anderson
Anderson, James Robert "Bo"	Jan 04, 1935	Mar 22, 2013	Plainview Cem.; Son of John Henry & Jessie (Nunley) Anderson; m. Helen Levan
Anderson, James Thomas	Oct 25, 1909	Mar 09, 1965	Palmer Cem.; Son of Jacob Lee Anderson & Mary Anderson; m. Elvie Ellen Nolan
Anderson, Jerry Don	Sep 24, 1972	Mar 27, 2022	Unknown cem.; Son of David Ray & Linda Ann (Layne) Anderson
Anderson, Judy (Geary)	Nov 22, 1938	Jan 23, 2019	Chattanooga National Cem.; Dau. of Carl T. and Nellie Dee Geary; m. Ray Anderson
Anderson, Justin Don	Oct 22, 1990	Aug 22, 2021	Plainview Cem.; Son of Jerry Don Anderson & Tina Michelle Meadows
Anderson, Kenitha M.	Nov 13, 1959	Jan 26, 1960	Brown's Chapel Cem.; Dau. of James L. & Carmenell (Wideman) Anderson; addition to Cemeteries of Grundy Co, Vol. 1, p. 110
Anderson, Larry W	Apr 26, 1949	Jul 01, 2018	Cremated; Son of Hershel & Verna (Byers) Anderson; m. Deborah Gipson
Anderson, Leonard Edward	Nov 22, 1960	Jun 09, 2019	Palmer Cem.; Son of Billy Bice & Brenda Cassidy; m. Helen Hoffmann
Anderson, Leslie	Jul 28, 1900	Jan 28, 1901	Tracy City Cem. (unmarked); Son of Charles W. Anderson & Mary Ellen (King) Anderson
Anderson, Linda Ann (Layne)	Aug 19, 1952	Oct 12, 2020	Plainview Cem.; Dau. of Oliver Dentrell "O.D." & Margaret (Nunley) Layne; m. David Ray Anderson; addition to Cemeteries of Grundy Co.Vol. 2, p. 700
Anderson, Loulene (Thomas)	Aug 19, 1940	May 17, 2019	Cremated; Dau. of Hamp Bernest Thomas & Tressie Mae Ellen Meeks; m. Herbert Anderson on Jun 5, 1965
Anderson, Mary Ann (Crocker)	Jun 07, 1943	Jan 01, 2015	Wiser Bluff Cem in Coffee Co TN; Dau. J.C. & Annie Rose Zella (West) Crocker; m. Nolan Anderson
Anderson, Mary Elizabeth	May 2, 1877	Jun 10, 1927	Palmer Cem.; Dau. of William Simon Doss Anderson & Catherine Jane Clark; m. Jacob Lee Anderson
Anderson, Mary Jo (Parsons)	Apr 29, 1956	Nov 23, 2021	Plainview Cem.; Dau. of Roy & Clara Parsons; m. C. L. Anderson
Anderson, Otsie June (Partin)	Sep 19, 1937	Sep 02, 2013	Brown's Chapel Cem.; Dau. of Benjamin & Ollie Jackson (Cagle) Partin; m. Alvin T. "Tom" Anderson
Anderson, Pamela Rose (Meeks)	Nov 01, 1959	Mar 15, 2013	Plainview Cem.; Dau. of James Buford & Edna Meeks; m. Leslie Raymond Anderson

Anderson, Ricky Leon	Oct 13, 1958	Feb 12, 2022	Brown's Chapel Cem.; Son of Alvin Thomas & June (Partin) Anderson; m. Kathy Jones
Anderson, Robert Kenneth	Feb 25, 1932	Mar 17, 2015	Wesley Chapel Cem.; Son of Abb & Willie Jane (Phillips) Anderson; m. Helen Maxine Adams; addition to Cemeteries of Grundy Co.Vol. 2, p. 993
Anderson, Robert Lee	Oct 09, 1963	Sep 11, 2013	Plainview Cem.; Son of Sam & Brenda Gayle (Nunley) Anderson; m. 1) Laurie Allison Lewis 2) Tasha Anderson
Anderson, Robert Nelson, Sr.	Sep 01, 1935	Jul 05, 2016	Clouse Hill Cem.; Son of Elisha & Dorothy Anderson; m. Mary E. Anderson
Anderson, Sam	Nov 20, 1874	Feb 11, 1931	White Cem in Palmer; Son of A.P. & Annie (Dove) Anderson; correction of birth date & death date (from death certificate) to Cemeteries of Grundy Co., Vol. 2, p. 1007
Anderson, Sam Watson	Aug 20, 1915	Dec 25, 1989	Plainview Cem.; Son of Ramie & Nancy C. Bell (Robertson) Anderson; m. Rosa Lee Braden
Anderson, Sam Watson, Jr.	Oct 27, 1942	Mar 09, 2022	Plainview Cem.; Son of Sam & Rosa Lee (Braden) Anderson; m. Brenda Gayle Nunley
Anderson, Sandra Dee	Nov 19, 1970	Apr 24 2013	Swiss Colony Cem.; Dau. of Jimmy & Donna Jo Layne; m. Dennis Anderson
Anderson, T.A.	Nov 6, 1898	Jan 2, 1899	Tracy City Cem.; Son of Charles W. & Mary Ellen (King) Anderson; Cemeteries of Grundy Co.Vol. 1, p. 876
Anderson, Teresia (Irvin)	Nov 21, 1950	Aug 09, 2016	Coalmont Cem.; Dau. of Carl David & Ophelia (Burnett) Irvin; m. Edd F. Anderson
Anderson, Ubert Tony	1940	Sep 30, 2018	Gregg Cem.; Son of Elisha Anderson & Dorothy Collins; US Army
Anderson, Virgie Lee (Meeks)	Oct 26, 1923	Jul 11, 2018	Tracy City Cem.; Dau. of Arthur & Fannie (Nunley) Meeks; m. Frances Lee "Buster" Anderson on Feb 24, 1941; addition to Cemeteries of Grundy Co., Vol. 2, p. 834
Anderson, Willie Mae (Fults)	Aug 31, 1897	Aug 31, 1931	Tracy City Cem.; Dau. of Dock & Della (Lockhart) Fults; Grundy County Cemeteries, Vol. 2, p. 852
Andy, Leo Leonard, Jr.	1938	Oct 25, 2019	Chattanooga National Cemetery; Son of Leo Leonard Andy, Jr. & Thelma Wright; m. Brenda Layman; U. S. Army - Vietnam
Anglian, John Huston	Mar 23, 1883	May 13, 1965	Plainview Cem.; Son of Adrian Thomas & Mary Emeline (Stotts) Anglin (Spelling of surname varies, and is "Anglin" in many records); m. Daisy Dean Turner on Dec 24, 1901; addition to Cemeteries of Grundy Co, Vol. 2, p. 673

Name	Birth	Death	Notes
Anglin, J.D.	Possibly 1793 see comment	Sep 27, 1861	Altamont Cemetery; Possibly the grave of Jonathan Anglin, husband of Sabrina "Sabra" Tipton; addition to Cemeteries of Grundy Co, Vol. 1, p. 13
Anthony, Amzi	Dec 11, 1808	Dec 31, 1888	Wesley Chapel Cem.; Moved from Coulson Cemetery across Hwy 108 to Wesley Chapel Cem by Red Sanders and Morris King per Mae King Wilhelm; m. 1) Harriet Gowen 2) Amanda "Mandy" Parks Aug 7, 1842, Lincoln Co. TN. His mother Nancy Anthony is listed on his tombstone; addition to Cemeteries of Grundy Co., Vol. 2, p. 962
Anthony, Nancy	ca. 1777 per 1860 census	Aug 26, 1870	Wesley Chapel Cem.; Moved from Coulson Cemetery across Hwy. 108 to Wesley Chapel Cem by Red Sanders & Morris King per Mae King Wilhelm; possibly the wife of Nicholas Anthony per Gammons Family Tree on Ancestry; The inscription referenced above is on Amzi Anthony's tombstone; addition to Cemeteries of Grundy Co.Vol. 2, p. 962
Archey, Kelly Jo	Mar 25, 1993	Sep 25, 2013	Palmer Cem.; Dau. of Dennis Rheal & Beatrice (Archey) Hampton
Argo or Rhea children possibly, Unidentified			Northcutt's Cove Road burials; 4.7 miles from Altamont on left with white picket fence around 2 of the graves indicating that they were probably from the same family.
Argo, Ada (Scott)	Oct 9, 1874	Apr 20, 1959	Bonny Oak Cem.; Dau. of Spuder & Martha (Freeman) Scott; m. Carrol Argo; addition to Cemeteries of Grundy Co. Vol. 1, p. 88
Argo, Beuna Vista (Fults)	Aug 20, 1872	Mar 19, 1958	Altamont Cem.; Dau. of Hiram & Mary (Smartt) Argo; m. Abner "Dock" Argo; addition to Cemeteries of Grundy Co, Vol. 1, p. 37
Argo, Carrol	Sep 2, 1852	Jan 03, 1950	Bonny Oak Cem.; Son of John Josiah & Sarah (Hobbs) Argo; m. Ada Scott; addition to Cemeteries of Grundy Co.Vol. 1, p.88
Argo, Dean	1956	Nov 12, 2018	Coalmont Cem.; Son of Dewey Barney & Jennie Argo.
Argo, Dewey Barney	Jun 26, 1933	Feb 13, 2014	Coalmont Cem.; Son of Dewey Doston & Sally Ann (Nunley) Argo; m. Jennie Argo; US Army
Argo, Dillard Henry	Apr 01, 1948	Aug 30, 2015	Bethel Cem.; Son of Earl & Stella (Sartain) Argo; m. Billie Jean Meeks on Aug 5, 1984; addition to Cemeteries of Grundy Co, Vol. 1, p. 67
Argo, Elma (Perry)	Dec 25, 1930	Oct 05, 1996	Fall Creek Cem.; Dau. of Manuel Perry & Hannah Jassels; m. Jack Willis Argo

Argo, Evelyn Gearlean	Apr 09, 1928	Oct 08, 1929	Bonny Oak Cem.; probably Dau. of Carrol & Ada (Scott) Argo; correction to spelling of name; Cemeteries of Grundy Co, Vol. 1, p. 88
Argo, Fannie (Madewell)	1881	1961	Plainview Cem.; Dau. of James & Nancy (Fults) Madewell; m. Willis Argo, Jan 22, 1895; addition to Cemeteries of Grundy Co., Vol. 2, p 697
Argo, Hettie (Frazier)	Feb 22, 1912	Jul 17, 1988	Coalmont Cem.; Dau. of Frank & Lillie Frazier; m. Loyd Argo; correction to Cemeteries of Grundy Co, Vol. 1, p. 183
Argo, Irving	Nov 01, 1848	1910	Argo Knob area near Dry Shave; Son of John Josiah & Sally Sarah (Hobbs) Argo; m. Mary Fults; Asked to be buried beside his son Melchizedek "Dick" Argo; from *New Era* newspaper
Argo, Melchizedek "Dick"	ca. 1875	Dec 04, 1887	Argo Knob area near Dry Shave; Son of Irving Argo; killed by a falling limb during a storm; from *New Era* newspaper
Argo, Melvin J	Sep 14, 1927	Nov 30, 1974	Airview Cem.; Son of Arcy Lee & Ora (Fults) Argo; m. Ruth Albritton; addition to Cemeteries of Grundy Co.Vol. 1, p. 5
Argo, Ruth (Albritton)	Jun 12, 1932	Apr 01, 1984	Airview Cem.; Dau. of Daniel Lake & Etta Lee (Morgan) Albritton; m. Melvin Argo; addition to Cemeteries of Grundy Co., Vol. 1, p. 5
Argo, Thomas Dale	Mar 31, 1950	Nov 19, 2017	Airview Cem.; Son of Thomas Melvin Argo & Mary Ruth (Albritton) Tittsworth
Argo, Thomas Ervin	May 03, 1971	Feb 08, 2022	Clouse Hill Cem.; Son of Thomas Dale & Edith (Dennis) Argo
Argo, Twins (Earl & Estella)			Bonny Oak Cem.; Son & Dau. of Earl & Stella (Sartain) Argo; addition to Cemeteries of Grundy Co., Vol. 1, p. 83
Argo, William John "Bill"	Aug 21, 1935	Jul 28, 2015	Mt. Garner Cem.; Son of Dewey Doston & Sally Ann (Nunley) Argo; m. Earlene Harris
Armentrout, Sue Ellen (Gray)	Jan 30, 1940	Sep 01, 2013	Cremated; Dau. of William H. & Lucille (Whitlock) Gray; m. Donald Smith Armentrout
Arnet, Gladys Creighton	May 24, 1913	May 02, 2014	Southern Memorial Cem.; in North Miami, FL; Dau of Morgan & Elizabeth Creighton; m. Robert M. Arnet
Arnold, Anthony Lynn	Apr 27, 1963	Dec 10, 2021	Cremated; Son of Riley Hershel, Sr. & Lillian Louise (Crocker) Arnold Meeks & stepson of Jackie Meeks of Pelham
Arp, Eddie Glenn	Jan 19, 1962	Nov 22, 2017	Bethel Cem.; Son of Paul & Rose (Chester) Arp
Ashburn, Carol Dannette	Oct 19, 1971	Aug 26, 2021	Cremated; Dau. of Hattie Demetro Nunley; Carol grew up in Payne's Cove.

Name	Born	Died	Details
Ashby, Leatrice	Mar 22, 1928	Jan 31, 2017	Swiss Cem.; Dau. of Floyd & Bea Wright; m. Yancy Barton Ashby
Ashby, Yancy Barton, Jr.	Mar 03, 1921	Nov 03, 2013	Swiss Cem.; Son of Yancy Barton, Sr. & Nettie (Crutchfield) Ashby; m. Leatrice Wright
Asher, Edward Clay, Jr.	Jul 25, 1942	Jun 23, 2016	Cremated; Son of Edward Clay, Sr. & Lois (King) Asher; m. Myra Maria Ward – He was born in Monteagle.
Ashley, Bertha (Shulze)	Aug 22, 1908	May 19, 2013	Rose Hill Memorial Gardens Cem.; Dau. of Oscar & Emma (Hunziker) Schulze; m. Joe Ashley
Atha, Betty Sue (Scott)	Jun 20, 1941	Mar 02, 2018	Mt. Zion Cem.; Dau. of William Bryan Scott & Mary Daisy Howard; m. 1) James Claudie Northcutt 2) Earl J. Atha
Austell, Jane (Petty)	1806	1842	Willis Cemetery; Dau. of Charles & Mary "Polly" (Leak) Petty; m. William Austell Dec 14, 1831, Spartanburg, SC; addition to Cemeteries of Grundy Co.Vol. 2.
Austin, Joseph Adam	Dec 14, 1994	Aug 26, 2020	Homeland Acres Cem.; Son of Adam Austin & Gail Wanamaker; m. Shea Ashlyn Pickett; U.S. Army - Afghanistan
Ax, Hazel Elva Belle (Duncan)	Aug 15, 1902	Oct 25, 1990	Homeland Acres Cem.; Dau. of Harry E. & Nellie (Craig) Duncan; m. Clarence "Jum" Ax on Oct 4, 1919; addition to Cemeteries of Grundy Co, Vol. l, p. 340
Ayers, Marilyn Kay (Clendenon)	Oct 26, 1950	May 06, 2018	Cremated; Dau. of Harlie Everett Clendenon & Etta Bea Nunley; m. Earl Ayers
Aylor, Boyd	Apr 29, 1928	Nov 11, 2018	Watson-North Memorial Park; Son of Clyde & Dessie (Wooten) Aylor; m. Lela Patterson; U.S. Navy
Aylor, Priscilla Ruth	Jan 19, 1943	Jan 09, 2022	Cremated; Dau. of Emmett & Tressie (McFarland) Aylor of Monteagle; lived in New Bern, NC
Babineau, Louise (Green)	Jul 25, 1952	Oct 12, 2015	Cremated; Dau. of William Ernest & Veller Green; m. Charles L. Babineau III
Baerg, "Betty Jo" Elizabeth Joanne (Gaitens)	Sep 04, 1936	Aug 15, 1999	Cumberland Heights Cem.; Dau. of James C. & Anna P. (Hartwell) Gaitens; m. Freberin Parker "Bernie" Baerg; addition to Cemeteries of Grundy Co.Vol. 1, p. 197
Baggenstoss, Ann Edwene	Oct 14, 1949	May 09, 2022	Tracy City Cem.; Dau. of Charles W. & Edwene (Curtis) Baggenstoss
Baggenstoss, Pauline (Brawley)	Feb 06, 1917	Jul 24, 2013	Plainview Cem.; Dau. of Norman & Lou Ermine (Henley) Brawley; m. Albert Baggenstoss
Bailey, Allen Pickett	Jan 10, 1943	Aug 01, 2018	Fall Creek Cem.; Son of John Lillard Pickett & Helen Beatrice Caldwell; m. Barbara Joan Eastridge; US Navy

Name	Birth	Death	Details
Bailey, John	Aug 1826	Nov 22, 1913	Tracy City Cem.; Son of Henry & Cynthia (Singleton) Bailey; m. Sarah A. Turner; no tombstone; information from family, Marty Ogelvie
Bailey, Michael Shane "Mikey"	Jun 28, 1973	Jul 21, 1998	Plainview Cem.; Son of Mary Layne and stepfather Charles E. Born; m. Shannon Gay (Layne) Bailey; addition to Cemeteries of Grundy Co. Vol. 3, p. 690
Bailey, Sarah A. (Turner)	1830	1900	Tracy City Cem.; m. John Bailey; no tombstone
Bain, Willadean (Gilliam)	1937	Jun 13, 2021	Hillsboro Presbyterian Cem.; Dau. of Wilson & Lizzy Mae (Cox) Gilliam; m. James Frank Bain
Baker, Annette (Crittenden)	Feb 14, 1948	Feb 03, 2021	Bonnie Oak Cem.; Dau. of James & Rendy Crittenden
Baker, Christine	1941	May 12, 2014	Fall Creek Cem.; Dau of Arthur & Clemmie (Hobbs) Sanders; m. Billy Baker
Baker, Frances Juanita (Rhea)	Mar 02, 1936	Apr 30, 2015	Philadelphia Cem.; Dau. of Oscar & Laura Ether (Scott) Rhea; m. William Hardin Baker; addition to Cemeteries of Grundy Co. Vol. 2, p. 629
Baker, Jessica Susan	Feb 11, 1977	Sep 14, 2021	Palmer Cem.; Dau. of Deborah Baker; m. Danny Charles Tate
Baker, Johnnie Mae (Garner) Bonner	Sep 20, 1935	Mar 03, 2022	Warren "Red Hill" Cem.; Dau. of John & Lottie Garner; m. 1) Glenn William Bonner 2) Curtis Baker
Baker, Malcolm Jackson, Sr.	Mar 21, 1914	Apr 26, 1996	Plainview Cem.; Son of Leona Baker; m. Mary Ellen Pattie; addition to Cemeteries of Grundy Co, Vol. 2, p 659
Baker, Michael Vernon	May 02, 1954	Apr 24, 2021	Mt. Garner Cem.; Son of Vernon Crownover & Eva Bell (Meeks) Baker; m. Teresa Ballew
Baker, Robert	Sep 14, 1937	Aug 13, 1995	Burns Cem.; Son of David & Elvah (Huffar) Baker; m. Edna Kilgore; addition to Cemeteries of Grundy Co., Vol. 1, p. 130
Baker, Thomas Gene	Jun 20, 1943	Apr 07, 2015	Fall Creek Cem.; Son of Jesse Edward & Laura Bell (Wright) Baker m. Linda Gipson
Baker, William Hardin	Nov 17, 1931	May 12, 2015	Philadelphia Cem.; Son of Clyde & Edith (Keyt) Baker; m. Frances Juanita Rhea Oct 17, 1958, addition to Cemeteries of Grundy Co., Vol. 2, p. 629
Bale, Annie	ca. 1854	Feb 8. 1931	Swiss Colony Cem.; Dau. of Jacob & Annie (Miller) Schoenmann; born in Switzerland
Balkenende, Robert	Jan 12, 1946	May 11, 2019	St. Mary's Catholic Church Cem. Roseville, IA; Son of William & Christine Balkenende; m. Betty Darter; U.S. Army

Name	Birth	Death	Details
Banholzer, Katherina geb (Von Bergen)	Aug 29, 1833	Aug 17, 1880	Swiss Colony Cem.; Dau. of Johannes & Sara (Dahler) Von Bergen; m. Andreas Banholzer; Addition to Cemeteries of Grundy Co.Vol. 2, p. 785
Banks, James L.	Aug 24, 1877	Nov 25, 1942	Brown's Chapel Cem.; Son of Richard Harrison & Barbara (Tollett) Banks; m. Mary L. Cagle; addition to Cemeteries of Grundy Co. Vol, 1, p. 111
Bankston, Vivian Lee (Shepherd)	Aug 10, 1955	Oct 11, 2018	Pine Grove United Methodist Church Cem, High Point, AL; Dau. of Edward Freeman Shepherd & Erma Faye Berry; m. Robert Bankston
Barker, Elizabeth "Betey" (Hudson)	Nov 5, 1814	Jul 1, 1891	Brown's Chapel Cem.; Dau. of John Hudson; m. Howel B. Barker; addition to Cemeteries of Grundy Co.Vol. 1, p. 111
Barker, Gilliam B.	May 16, 1850	Apr 29, 1932	Brown's Chapel Cem.; Son of Howell & Elizabeth (Hudson) Barker; m. Ruth Stone; addition to Cemeteries of Grundy Co. Vol. 1, p. 110
Barker, Naomi (Miller)	Oct 04, 1928	Aug 22, 2018	Chapel Hill Cem.; Dau. of R.E. & Naomi Miller; m. Flavius Barker
Barks, Phillip Harold	Oct 30, 1959	Jul 31, 2014	Whitman - King - Bess Cemetery; Son of James Ed & Euphema (King) Barks; m. Roxanne Campbell
Barksdale, Virginia Hyman (Hoosier)	Jul 22, 1936	Mar 24, 2020	Cremated: Dau. of Tom & Mildred Hoosier; m. Julin Wallace Barksdale
Barnard, Donald Howard	Apr 21, 1935	Jun 03, 2004	Coalmont Cem.; Son of Howard Russell & Nellie Irene (Davis) Barnard; m. Elsie Marie Scissom; correction to Cemeteries of Grundy Co. Tennessee, Vol. 1, p. 180
Barnard, Elsie (Scissom)	Jul 26, 1928	Dec 09, 1997	Coalmont Cem.; m. James Alford Smith; correction to Cemeteries of Grundy Co. Tennessee, Vol. 1, p. 180
Barnes, Alvin Lee	Apr 10, 1957	Feb 15, 2014	Condra Cem in Whitwell; Son of James & Georgia Barnes; m. Rhonda Denise Barnes
Barnes, Grady "Buck"	Jan 01, 1943	Apr 01, 2019	Cremated; Son of Jesse & Gracie (Steel) Barnes; m. Maybelle Ogelvie
Barnes, Thomas Bruce	Feb 27, 1948	Sep 27, 2019	Plainview Cem.; Son of Harry Richard & Marylou (Bookout) Barnes; m. 1) Louise "Bumble" Meeks 2) Rena Griswold; US Army – Vietnam; addition to Cemeteries of Grundy Co, Vol. 2, p 663
Barnett, Elsie Holt (Ramsey-Wright)	Apr 27, 1928	Aug 27, 2020	Spring Hill Cem.; Dau. of Elbert & Mary Ramsey-Wright; m. Sam Holt
Barnett, James L.	Sep 3, 1832	Nov 15, 1904	Tracy City Cem.; Son of David & Nancy Ann (Schnebly) Barnett; m. Mary Elizabeth Linton; addition to Cemeteries of Grundy Co, Vol. 2, p. 909

Barnett, Lafayette George "Pepe", Jr.	Jun 22, 1943	Oct 30, 2018	Orange Hill Cem.; Son of Lafayette G. & Clara (Griffin) Barnett; m. Mary Lockhart; U.S. Navy
Barnett, Lorna Mae	Mar 17, 1961	Jul 24, 2015	Cremated; Dau. of William W. Barnett & Geraldine (Short) Walker; m. Roy Ellis Durham, Jr.
Barrett, Charles Thomas	Jul 16, 1956	May 08, 2023	Warren "Red Hill" Cem: Son of Marvin Eugene & Sue Ellen (Jaynes) Barrett; m, Patricia "Patti" Medley, dau of Johnny "Shorty" & Mary (Henley) Medley
Barrett, Chastity A. (Cunningham)	Dec 15. 1975		Airview Cem.; Dau. of Rick & Debbie (Bess) Cunningham; m. Jarron G. Barrett; addition to Cemeteries of Grundy Co, Vol. 1, p. 8
Barrett, Cord Montana	Jul 17, 1996	Jun 30, 2019	Bonnie Oak Cem.; Son of Jeff & Twilla Nichole (Hall) Barrett
Barrett, Deanny Marie (Hawk)	Feb 24, 1938	Jun 18, 2015	Bethel Cem.; Dau. of Hubert Arvin & Hazel (Sartain) Hawk; m. Joseph Leo Barrett, Jr.; She died in sun City, AZ, and was not brought back for burial in Bethel.
Barrett, Irene (Kelly)	Aug 20, 1931		Airview Cem.; Dau. of Elford & Charlcie (Mahan) Kelly; m. Alford Ray Barrett; addition to Cemeteries of Grundy Co.Vol. 1, p. 8
Barrett, Jo	May 22, 1946	Mar 11, 2018	Airview Cem.; Dau. of Eugene & Lois E. (Dendy) Hampton; m. Jack Barrett, Oct 7, 1960; addition to Cemeteries of Grundy Co., Vol. 1, p. 9
Barrett, Lorene (Fitch)	Jul 19, 1933	Aug 11, 2014	Altamont Cem.; Dau. of Floyd & Ollie Faye (Sanders) Fitch; m. Wayne Barrett
Barrett, Mae (Myers)	Jun 08, 1951	Mar 08, 2017	Airview Cem.; Dau. of Vernon & Mary E. "Totie" Myers; m. Keith Barrett
Barrett, Mamie Ione	Apr 01, 1927	Dec 29, 2017	Airview Cem.; Dau. of Eugene Dalvern & Lois E. (Dendy) Hampton; m. James Thomas Barrett; addition to Cemeteries of Grundy Co; Vol. 1, p. 9.
Barrett, Ola Jo (Hampton)	May 21, 1946	Mar 11, 2018	Airview Cem.; Dau. of Eugene Dalvern & Lois Elizabeth (Dendy) Hampton; m. Jackie Barrett
Barrett, Thomas	Dec 08, 1872	Dec 16, 1945	Airview Cem.; Son of William & Susanah "Annie" Minerva "Mexico" (Scott) Barrett; m Louisa Myers; addition to Cemeteries of Grundy; Vol. 1, p. 9
Barrett, Twilla Nichole	Aug 07, 1971	Dec 11, 2018	Bonnie Oak Cem.; Dau. of Harold & Prudance Hall; m. 1) Jeff Barrett 2) companion Ed Nichols
Barry, Ross Thomas	Dec. 20, 1932	Feb 26, 2015	Eastern Star Cem.; Son of Arthur Collier & Sarah Ann (Long) Barry; m. Sylvia Ann Ricketts; U.S. Army

Name	Born	Died	Details
Barry, Thelma Juanita (Martin)	Apr 12, 1931	Jun 22, 2019	Lappin Cem.; Dau. of Samuel Cecil & Bertha Emma Jean (Lappin) Martin; m. William Edward Barry
Barry, William Edward	Aug 03, 1927	Sep 18, 1990	Lappin Cem.; Son of Arthur Collier & Sarah Ann (Long) Barry; m. Thelma Juanita Martin
Basham, Patsy Ann	Jul 11, 1968	Jan 25, 2017	Cremated; Dau. of Elmer Francis & Oma Lee (Wrisner) Hobbs; m. Tommy Basham
Baxter, Don Houston	Sep 09, 1953	Apr 13, 2021	Son of Martha Lou Hampton; m. Kathy Baxter
Bean, Annie Katherine	Aug 03, 1936	Jan 31, 1937	Bonny Oak Cem.; Dau. of Raymond & Dora (Nunley) Bean; addition to Cemeteries of Grundy Co.Vol. 1, p. 88
Bean, Clyde	Mar 06, 1929	Apr 09, 2017	Fall Creek Cem.; Dau. of William Matthew & Mary (Mitchell) Bean
Bean, James Edward	Jun 07, 1959	Jan 23, 2021	Bonnie Oak Cem.; Son of Stanford & Mildred (Campbell) Bean; m. Wilma Bean
Bean, James Edward	Dec 05, 1921	Apr 01, 1992	Rutledge Hill Cem.; Son of Lloyd Owen & Jennie Earmie (Sartain) Bean;
Bean, Joe Lloyd	May 30, 1952	Feb 26, 2011	Mt. Garner Cem.; Son of Leonard Owne & Anna Bell (Payne) Bean; m. Nancy Elain Davis
Bean, John William	Aug 23, 1936	Nov 13, 2020	Rutledge Hill Cem.; Son of Lloyd & Jennie (Sartain) Bean; m. Zora Elizabeth Parks
Bean, Lillie (Meeks)	Apr 30, 1880	Oct 02, 1905	Payne's Cove Cem.; Dau. of Benjamin Franklin & Martha "Mattie" (Davis) Meeks, m. Jay Boyd Bean; correction & addition to Cemeteries of Grundy Co., Vol. 2, p. 596
Bean, Mildred (Campbell)	Dec 03, 1938	Jul 05, 2015	Bonny Oak Cem.; Dau. of Edward & Della Campbell; m. Stanford Bean
Bean, Raymond, Jr.	1931	1935	Bonny Oak Cem.; Son of Rymond & Dora (Nunley) Bean; addition to Cemeteries of Grundy Co.Vol. 1, p. 88
Bean, Ronnie	1961	Oct 16, 2021	Cremated; Son of Stanford & Mildred Bean; m. Jackie Bean
Beasley, Marion Catherin (Goedjen)	Apr 17, 1921	Feb 28, 2018	Elm Wood Cem in Memphis; Dau. of Albert J & Eugenie Goedjen; m. William Boddie Rogers Beasley, Jr.
Becker, Mannie (Smith)	Feb 14, 1927	Nov 30, 2018	Cumberland Heights Cem.; Dau. of Willie Beckham & Maude (Wilhoite) Smith; m. 1) Raymond Earl Becker, Sr. 2) Robert McKenzie Brown; addition to Cemeteries of Grundy Co, Vol. 1, p. 197
Becker, Raymond Earl, Sr.	Mar 15, 1920	Dec 05, 1997	Cumberland Heights Cem.; Son of Leon R. & Lydia (Schroeder) Becker; m. Mannie Smith; addition to Cemeteries of Grundy Co.Vol. 1, p. 197
Beetch, Dorothy Mae (Roeder)	Mar 21, 1925	Sep 03, 2013	Cremated; Dau. of John William & Murtle (Donham) Roeder; m. Charles Beetch

Name	Born	Died	Notes
Bekurs, Suzanne (Walden)	Oct 20, 1944	May 19, 2017	Cremated; Dau. of Charles & Annie Sue (Moon) Walden; m. Henry Gray Bekurs
Bell, Cathleen (Harris)	1924	Aug 28, 2018	Forest Hill Cem.; Dau. of Jay C. & Johnnie Harris; m. Eugene R. Bell
Bell, James Franklin	Sep 11, 1846	May 23 1913	Rowe Cemetery in edge of Franklin Co; Son of Harrison "Harris" & Rachel (Laxson) Bell. Erroneously reported to have been in the Bell Cemetery in Bell's Cove; m. 1) Sarah (Rowe) Bell (1846-1877) who is also buried in Rowe Cem. along with their daughter Effie Eugenia Bell Clemmons (1876-1957). James also married 2) Emma Cotnam Hinton; correction to Cemeteries of Grundy Co.Vol. 1, p. 43
Bell, James Frederick, Jr.	Dec 15, 1942	Sep 20, 2013	Valhalla Memory Gardens Cem in Huntsville, AL; Son of James F., Sr. & Charlotte "Lottie" (Partin) Bell; m. Carolyn Connell; US Army
Bell, Lisa Kay	Apr 18, 1967	Dec 19, 2017	Tracy City Cem.; Dau. of William & Maxine Jordon Bell
Bender, Nana (Rothwell)	Sep 24, 1877	Jul 01, 1965	Altamont Cem.; Dau. of William Willis & Harriet E. (Haywood) Rothwell; m. Elder Urbanus Bender; correction of father's name & addition to Cemeteries of Grundy Co., Vol. 1, p. 31
Bendyna, Alexander, Sr.	Mar 03, 1930	Jul 31, 2015	Homeland Acres Cem.; Son of George & Michilena (Rayback) Bendyna; m. Mary Alexander
Bennett, Charles Jackson	Dec 05, 1942	Feb 25, 2010	Monteagle Cem.; Son of Mack Stephen & Clara Belle (Tate) Bennett; m. 1) Margaret Inez Musgrove 2) Luz Bennett; addition to Cemeteries of Grundy Co.Vol. 1, p. 422
Bennett, Daisy Katherine	Feb 19, 1944	Feb 18, 2017	Monteagle Cem.; Dau. of Hudson Melroy Flippin & Ruby Lillian Newcomb; m. John Bennett
Bennett, David Darl	Oct 08, 1938	May 17, 2018	Monteagle Cem.; Son of Dave & Alma Jean Bennett; m. Lynda Kay Bennett
Bennett, Dorthy Leslie	Jan 08, 1934	Oct 31, 1999	Hobbs Hill Cem.; Dau. of David Leslie & Minnie Lee (Campbell) Dykes; addition to Cemeteries of Grundy Co., Vol. 1, p. 331
Bennett, Ella Adea	Sep 12, 1922	Apr 22, 1990	Bonny Oak Cem.; Dau. of George W. & Mary Jane (Kelly) Bennett; addition to Cemeteries of Grundy Co.Vol. 1, p. 93
Bennett, James W., Sr.	Dec 21, 1927	Dec 26, 2015	Monteagle Cem.; Son of Mack & Clara B. Bennett; m. Becky Bennett; US Army
Bennett, Robert	Aug 19, 1929	Jun 04, 2019	Cremated; Son of Ad Young Bennett & Irene Thompson; m. Ruth Rhinehart; U.S. Air Force

Name	Birth	Death	Notes
Bennett, Ruth Carlie (Shoemake)	1908	1993	Monteagle Cem.; Dau. of George Washington & Hattie (Jones) Shoemake; m. Clyde William Bennett; Correction of spelling of maiden name & mother's maiden name; Cemeteries of Grundy Co.Vol. 1, p. 414
Benson, Effie (Brendle)	Jul 11, 1912	Aug 16, 1976	Altamont Cem.; Dau. of Jon Harmon & Hetie E. (Petty) Brendle; m. Ira Nisbitte "Benny" Benson; addition to Cemeteries of Grundy Co.Vol. 1, p. 14
Benton, Lot markers	2022	2022	Warren "Red Hill" Cem.; Lot markers installed for graves spots between Nora Lee (Hooper) Maze & her grandson Thomas Eugene Coats, Jr. and the foot of Mary Elsie Payne & husband Joseph Elbert Layne's graves out to the access road.
Bergholt, Edward Sanford	May 12, 1934	Jul 30, 2013	Altamont Cem.; Son of Edward Sanford, Sr. & Alice (Funglie) Bergholt
Berry, Glenn Hampton	Jun 01, 1908	Aug 7, 1968 Los Angeles, CA	Tracy City Cem.; Son of Henry Edward & Myrtle (Thomas) Berry US Army, WWII; no tombstone, buried beside his parents
Berry, Marcella Mildred	Mar 31, 1914	Sep 07, 2000	Homeland Acres Cem.; Dau. of Charles Leroy & Ethel M (Pray) Berry; addition to Cemeteries of Grundy Co.Vol. 1, p. 342
Berry, Sue	ca 1885	Aug 28, 1922	Oak Grove Cem.; Dau. of Will & Susan (Graham) Meeks; m. Charlie Berry; no tombstone; Addition to Cemeteries of Grundy Co., Vol. 1
Bess, Anna Christine (Borne)	Jan 28, 1938	Apr 04, 2021	Fall Creek Cem.; Dau. of Lawrence & Maude Victoria (Woodlee) Borne; m. George Cope Bess
Bess, Aubrey	May 22, 1901-death cert. says 1898	Oct 29, 1962	Monteagle Cem.; Dau. of Arthur Watley, m. Charlie Bess; correction to birth date and addition to p. 459; Cemeteries of Grundy Co., Vol. 1, p. 459
Bess, Clayton Gerald	Sep 06, 1950	Jan 08, 2022	Altamont Cem.; Son of Clifford Iola & Therisa Gladys Bess
Bess, Clint Bodie	Jun 22, 1957	Oct 15, 2021	Altamont Cem.; Son of Basil & Mary Elizabeth (Lockhart) Bess; m. Diane Meeks
Bess, Dusty Cole "Korn"	Apr 12, 1983	Apr 08, 2008	Altamont Cem.; Son of Cyndi Bess & Robert Lynn Christian; addition to Cemeteries of Grundy Co.Vol. 1, p. 16
Bess, Elizabeth Louise (Phillips)	Sep 27, 1935	Jun 23, 2014	Altamont Cem.; Dau. of Joe & Arizona (Middlebrock) Phillips; m. Edgar L. Bess; addition to Cemeteries of Grundy Co.Vol. 1, p. 19
Bess, Heber Earl	Oct 02, 1919	Jan 14, 2014	Bess, King, Whitman Cem.; Son of Venus & Lettie (Whitman) Bess; m. Esther L. Bouldin, Jun 15, 1939; addition to Cemeteries of Grundy Co.Vol. 1, p. 46

Name	Born	Died	Details
Bess, Homer Douglas	Mar 06, 1948	Oct 04, 1964	Altamont Cem.; Son of Clifford Iola & Thersia Gladys (Bess) Bess; addition to Cemeteries of Grundy Co.Vol. 1, p. 20
Bess, John Henry "Nookum"	Feb 08, 1936	Feb 07, 2001	Monteagle Cem.; Son of Charlie & Aubrey (Watley) Bess; m. Sarah Bell, addition to Cemeteries of Grundy Co.Vol. 1, p. 455
Bess, Mary Elizabeth "Shorty" (Lockhart)	Sep 15, 1930	Oct 20, 2021	Altamont Cem.; Dau. of Fred & Lela (Tate) Lockhart; m. Basil Bess
Bess, Oliver	Oct 01, 1914	Dec 25, 1914	Fults Cem.; Son of Oliver Bess; from *Grundy Co. Times*, Mar 25, 1915; Cemeteries of Grundy Co., Vol. 1, p. 279
Bess, Roger Dale	Feb 01, 1952	Jul 27, 2020	Altamont Cem.; Son of Basil Bess & Mary Elizabeth Lockhart
Bess, Sandra Jean (Nunley)	Jan 10, 1950	Oct 02, 2013	Plainview Cem.; Dau. of Paul Louis & Edna (Meeks) Nunley; m. Dale Bess
Bess, Sarah Bell	Feb 23, 1939	Jan 25, 2008	Monteagle Cem.; Dau. of Simon C. & Bertha E. (McClure) Evans; m. John Henry Bess; addition to Cemeteries of Grundy Co.Vol. 1, p. 455
Bess, Wiley	1844	Aug 15. 1893	Bess, King, Whitman Cem.; Son of Eli & Lear (Killian) Bess; m. Tennessee Webb; Co, H, 16th TN Inf. CSA; addition to Cemeteries of Grundy Co.Vol. 1, p. 46
Bess, Woodrow Coleman	Jul 01, 1944	Jan 19, 2021	Altamont Cem.; Son of Clifford & Gladys Bess
Bezoid, Mildred Pauline (Wise)	Nov 10, 1921	Mar 10, 2013	Monteagle Cem.; Dau. of Tom Norris & Ruby Lee (Weathers) Wise
Bice, Billy Ronald	May 08, 1941	Sep 13, 2018	Palmer Cem.; Son of Oscar & Sarah Penny Bice; m. Brenda Gail Cassidy
Birdwell, Kendra Lynette	Aug 02, 1968	Apr 17, 2022	Fall Creek Cem.; Dau. of Walter David & Audrey (Gravitt) Birdwell
Birdwell, Roy Lee	May 29, 1946	Sep 01, 2021	Fall Creek Cem.; Son of Mose & Almeta (Stocker) Birdwell; m. Pat Meeks; U.S. Navy
Birdwell, Walter David	Oct 18, 1942	Mar 30, 2018	Fall Creek Cem.; Son of Laude Leonard Birdwell & Willette Brewer; m. Audrey Gravitt
Bishop, Charles Edwin	Sep 17, 1929	May 27, 2013	Collegedale Memorial Park Cem.; Son of James Lafayette & Lula Permelia (Tatum) Bishop m. Charlene Grace Bishop
Bishop, Juanita Marie (Patrick)	Feb 04, 1924	Dec 1, 1998	Fall Creek Cem.; Dau. of Charles Francis & Veola (Hampton) Patrick; m. 1) Jacob Monroe Bishop, Jr. 2) Gary Bishop
Bivens, Donald Eugene	Oct 28, 1949	Jul 11, 2016	Burkett's Chapel Cem.; Son of William T. & Mae A. (Brown) Bivens; m. Brenda Bivens
Bivens, Elizabeth Fay (Nance)	Jan 07, 1949	Jun 20, 2018	Burkett's Chapel Cem.; Dau. of Mitchel Nance & Margaret Fay Knowlan; m. Charles Bivens
Bivens, Evelyn Denise (O'Brien)	Jan 29, 1959	Nov 11, 2020	Burkett's Chapel Cem.; Dau. of Marshall & Doris (Carrick) O'Brien

Name	Born	Died	Notes
Bivens, Jonathan	Dec 04, 1952	Apr 18, 2015	Burkett's Chapel Cem.; Son of Marshall & Doris (Carrick) Bivens; m. Dellene Keener
Bivens, Mae Arlene	Aug 23, 1923	Aug 04, 2014	Fall Creek Cem.; Dau of Hershel & Minnie (Johnson) Brown; m. William T. Bivens
Black, Celende (Taylor)	Jul 25, 1963	Jun 30, 2021	Cremated; Dau. of Jon Monson & Janice Jane (Tolman) Taylor; m. Charles Loyd Black
Blackburn, Carolyn Janet (Pack)	Sep 09, 1944	Dec 09, 2017	Harrison Cem.; Dau. of Ernest William & Beulah May (Gilliam) Pack
Blackwell, Marian Louise	Sep 12, 1911	Jun 09, 2003	Cumberland Heights Cem.; Dau. of Charles Winchester & Mary Magdalene (Strong) Miller; m. Nicholas Officer Blackwell; "In Memory" footstone at Helen M. Miller grave; addition to Cemeteries of Grundy Co., Vol, 1, p. 196
Blackwood, Clara Etta (Wooten)	Oct 6, 1898	Nov 15, 1898	Monteagle Cem.; Dau. of Benjamin Franklin & Cynthia J. (Lawson) Wooten; 2nd wife fo James Thomas Blackwood, Rev. correction to Grundy County Cemetery Book Vol. 1, p. 414
Blake, Lilah A.	Jul 06, 1902	Jun 06, 1984	Altamont Cem.; Dau. of John & Minnie Beamer; m. Owen Andrew Blake; addition to Cemeteries of Grundy Co.Vol. 1, p. 17
Blake, Owen A.	May 06, 1905	Dec 02, 1974	Altamont Cem.; Son of Walter & Mary Alice (Owen) Blake; m. Lilah A. Beamer; addition to Cemeteries of Grundy Co., Vol. 1, p. 17
Blakley, Deborah (Hobbs)	Dec 10, 1962	Jun 03, 2015	Little Johnny Myers Cem.; Dau. of Delbert & Grace Hobbs, m. Darrell Blakley
Blanton, Anna (Lowe)	Apr 5, 1878	Oct 26, 1955	Monteagle Cem.; Dau. of William E & Mary A. (Prater) Lowe; correction to Cemeteries of Grundy County Vol. 1, p. 389
Blaylock K.M.	May 05, 1914	Dec 05, 2000	Brown's Chapel Cem.; Son of Nathaniel William Andrew & Sally H. (Savage) Westfall Blaylock; m. Margaret Elizabeth (Andrews) Wideman; addition to Cemeteries of Grundy Co.Vol. 1, p. 110
Blaylock, Betty C. (White)	1934	Jan 08, 2020	Cremated; Dau. of J.T. & Pearl (Glisson) Bryant White; m. Robert Hal Blaylock
Blaylock, James Echerd "Eck"	Apr 01, 1958	Jul 19, 1990	Brown's Chapel Cem.; Son of James Nimrod & Kathryn C. Blaylock; addition to Cemeteries of Grundy Co.Vol. 1, p. 110
Blaylock, Margaret Elizabeth (Andrews) Wideman	May 20, 1922	Jan 04, 1997	Brown's Chapel Cem.; Dau. of Jesse Richard & Tabitha Anabel (Ingle) Andrews; m. 1) Manuel Wideman 2) K.M. Blaylock; addition to Cemeteries of Grundy Co., Vol. 1, p. 110
Blaylock, Nora (Prater)	Oct 25, 1919	May 13, 2018	Raincy-Dill Cem.; Dau. of Arthur Young Prater & Emma Johnson; m. K. M. Blaylock

Name	Born	Died	Details
Blaylock, Ollie (Prater)	Aug 19, 1888	Dec 31, 1931	Wesley Chapel Cem.; Dau. of Simps & Sally (Roberts) Prater; m. Jim Blaylock on Jan 1, 1830; addition to Cemeteries of Grundy Co, Vol, 2, p. 970
Blaylock, Robert "Bob"	Feb 20, 1899	Jul 22, 1967	Brown's Chapel Cem.; Son of William Nathaniel "Blue" & Sally Ann (Savage) Blaylock; m. Allie C. Cagle; PVT BTRY Co 68k Field Art; WWII; addition to Cemeteries of Grundy Co. Vol, 1, p 110
Blaylock, Robert H.	Aug 20, 1935	Oct 01, 2016	Cremated; Son of James Robert & Allie (Cagle) Blaylock; m. Betty Blaylock
Blaylock, Una Mae (Walker)	Apr 03, 1919	Jul 25, 2001	Brown's Chapel Cem.; Dau. of Grover H. & Sissan (Smith) Walker; m. John Henry Blaylock; addition to Cemeteries of Grundy Co.Vol. 1, p. 114
Blevins, John Truman	Aug 19, 1938	Feb 10, 2021	Brown's Chapel Cem.; Son of Ike & Martie (Conatser) Blevins; m. Wilma Pemberton
Blum, Eva Jeannette (Johnson)	Aug 05, 1947	May 04, 2015	Blum Family Cem.; Dau. of Lee & Emma Johnson; m. James Edgar Blum
Boggess, Leo Edward	Mar 05, 1941	Dec 07, 2021	Palmer Cem.; Son of Cecil Woodrow & Fay (Mahan) Boggess
Boggs, Cora (Pearson)	Ca 1853	Oct 26, 1915	Tracy City Cem.; Dau. of Catherine Pearson; m. William Simms Boggs; Source - death certificate
Boggs, William Simms	Mar 2, 1866	Apr 20, 1952	Tracy City Cem.; Son of Pleasant D. & Permelia Ann (Hays) Boggs; m. 1) Cora Pearson on Mar 8, 1888, Lincoln Co. TN, 2) Fannie Law, Jan 28, 1935; Source death certificate & marriage records
Bohr, Dagmar (Plumacher)	1866	1958	Hunerwadel Cem.; Dau. of Eugene H. & Olga Marie Pauline (Hunerwadel) Plumacher; m. Fred Bohr; Cemeteries of Grundy Co., Vol. 1, p. 42 correction, Delte her from this page and add her to the Hunerwadel Cem. p. 347
Bolinger, Carrie Lee (Magness)	Aug 23, 1917	Nov 21, 1987	Burns Cem.; Dau. of L.P. & Bettie Magnus; m. Delno Leeotis "Dale" Bolinger; addition to Cemeteries of Grundy Co, Vol. 1, p. 129
Bolinger, Delno Leeotis "Dale"	Jul 19, 1907	Nov. 20, 1987	Burns Cem.; Son of Milburn Paris & Malda (Pace) Bolinger; m. Carrie Lee Magness; addition to Cemeteries of Grundy Co., Vol. 1, p. 129
Bolinger, John Neal	Jan 15, 1945	Oct 20, 2018	Cremated; Son of Delno Leeotis "Dale" & Carrie Lee (Magnes) Bolinger
Bone, Duke "Sam"	Jun 28, 1934	Mar 31, 2019	Bonny Oak Cemetery; Son of Samuel Bone & Lillian Mooney; m. Mae Ellen McCreary
Bone, Male stillborn	Sep 9, 1938	Sep 09, 1938	Tracy City Cem.; Son of Martin Luther & Mary Elizabeth (Owens) Bone; no tombstone; cornerstones with "B" on them; information from family – Maty Ogelvie

Name	Born	Died	Notes
Bone, Mary Elizabeth (Owens)	Dec 25, 1911	Sep 02, 1967	Monteagle Cem.; Dau. of James Harvey & Leota "Lee" (Thorpe) Owens; m. Martin Luther Bone, Sr.; addition to Cemeteries of Grundy Co., Vol. 1, p. 428
Bone, Mary Eva	Oct 20, 1932	Sep 03, 1933	Tracy City Cem.; Dau. of Martin Luther & Mary Elizabeth (Owens) Bone; unmarked grave except for cornerstones with a "B" on them; information from family, Marty Ogelvie
Bone, Sammy Duke, Jr.	Nov 17, 1954	Nov 26, 1954	Bonny Oak Cem.; Son of Sammy Duke Sr. & Mae Ellen (McCreary) Bone; addition to Cemeteries of Grundy Co.Vol. 1, p. 85
Bone, Sammy Duke, Sr.	Jun 28, 1938	Mar 31, 2019	Bonny Oak Cem.; Son of Samuel & Lillian (Mooney) Bone; m; Mae Ellen McCurry who will also be buried at Bonny Oak. Mae Ellen is the dau of Gerald & Mae Elvie McCurry
Bone, Sharon	Jan 17, 1958	Jan 18, 1958	Bonny Oak Cem.; Dau. of Sammy Duke, Sr. & Mae Ellen (McCreary) Bone; addition to Cemeteries of Grundy Co.Vol. 1, p. 85
Bonner, Clifton	Jun 17, 1942	Feb 20, 2013	Franklin Memorial Cem.; Son of Morgan Haskell & Bethie D. (Hawk) Bonner; m. Linda Church; US Army
Bonner, Wayne Oddist	Sep 27, 1928	Nov 01, 2016	Bethel Cem.; Son of Morgan Haskel & Bethie Dillon (Hawk) Bonner; m. Pauline (Nunley) Myers Aug 8, 1957; addition to Cemeteries of Grundy Co.Vol. 1, p. 68
Booker, Carl Frank	Feb 15, 1944	Jun 27, 2020	Cremated; Son of Carl & Rochelle Booker; m. Bettye Brown
Bookout, Cecil C.	May 04, 1942	Sep 12, 2017	Rutledge Hill Cem.; Son of Lizzie R. Bookout; m. Anna Jean Sherrill
Boren, Judy Ann (Tate)	May 07, 1943	Aug 13, 2021	Altamont Cem.; Dau. of Arnold Eugene & Mary Lou (Fults) Tate; m. George Boren
Born, Frederick Theodore	1875	Aug 31, 1953	Swiss Colony Cem.; Son of Fred & Anna Mary (Studer) Born; m. Elizabeth Lisette Ruch
Borne, Abbie Mary Ellen (Anderson)	Apr 14, 1939	Aug 06, 2020	Fall Creek Cem.; Dau. of George Washington & Ella Mae (Rust) Anderson; m. Lonnie Borne
Borne, Bonnie Lorrine (Sweeton)	Jul 12, 1928	May 05, 2022	Fall Creek Cem.; Dau. of J.D. & Irene (Meeks) Sweeton; m. Howard Borne
Borne, Carl Edward	Aug 25, 1940	Apr 03, 2020	Fall Creek Cem.; Son of George Washington Borne & Della Frances Collins
Borne, Labrina Kay (McDaniel)	Sep 30, 1977	Oct 31, 2019	Cremated: Dau. of Charles & Rita (Dennis) McDaniel
Borne, Virgil Marie (Green)	Mar 27, 1931	Mar 21, 2016	Burkett's Chapel Cem.; Dau. of Virgil & Rena B. (Higgins) Green; m. Melvin "Snood" Borne
Boscaino, Vincent Frank	Apr 18. 1926	Jan 24, 1996	Plainview Cem.; Son of Vincinzo Francisco & Catherine A (Cincotta) Boscanino; m. Bertha Fay Dove; addition to Cemeteries of Grundy Co., Vol. 2, p 673

Name	Born	Died	Notes
Boston, Barbara Nell (Mowdry)	Dec 23, 1938	Oct 17, 2013	Bonnie Oak Cem.; Dau. of Mike & Mamie Mowdry; m. Bill Boston
Boswell, Mary Nell "Nello"	Apr 17, 1960	Jul 03, 2018	Cremated; Dau. of Charles William Boswell & Linda Anderson; m. Franck Viez
Bouldin, Elizabeth Ann (Schoenmann)	Aug 08, 1959	Jul 29, 2021	Palmer Cem.; Dau. of Alvin Tony & Argie Earlene (Scissom) Schoenmann
Bouldin, Gary Lee	Mar 10, 1955	May 23, 2018	Swiss Colony Cem.; Son of Wade Crawford Bouldin & Cornelia Mae Wiley
Bouldin, James Allan	Feb 07, 1930	Jun 04, 2019	Chattanooga National Cemetery; Son of Leander Bouldin & Anna Margaret Schild; m. Jane Armstrong; U.S. Navy
Bouldin, James Larry	Apr 03, 1947	Nov 13, 2019	Armstrong Cem.; Son of James Parker Bouldin & Ruby Carter; m. Deborah Sue Jordan; U.S. Navy - Vietnam
Bouldin, Ralph E.	Dec. 12, 1933	Sep 8. 2013	Swiss Colony Cem.; Son of Leander & Anna (Schild) Bouldin
Bouldin, Roy Lyn	Apr 14, 1950	Jan 07, 2016	Cremated; Son of Willard & Cleo (Richardson) Bouldin; m. Karen Hansen
Bowling, Ralph Richard	Oct 6. 1927	Sep 23, 2002	Plainview Cem.; Son of Elmer Earnest & Carrie John (Thomas) Bowling; m. Mary Imogene "Jean" Dempsy; US Navy, addition to Cemeteries of Grundy Co., Vol. 2, p. 673
Bowman, Roger Wilson	Mar 15, 1947	Aug 21, 2018	R.W. Bowman Family Cem. in Dekalb County; Son of Mary Christine West & Wilson James Tucker; M. Lori Jo Paulsen
Boyd, Attie Lee (Higdon)	Aug 29, 1890	Jul 29, 1962	Oak Grove Cem.; Dau. of David & Para Lee (Kilgore) Boyd; m. Joe Higdon; addition to Cemeteries of Grundy Co., Vol. 1, p. 509
Boyd, Fannie Ardella	Dec 4, 1877	Jun 03, 1918	Altamont Cem.; Dau. of Christopher Columbus & Martha Rebecca (Faucett) Williams; m. George Dibrell Boyd; addition to Cemeteries of Grundy Co., Vol. 1, p. 29
Boyd, Martha Sue (Thorpe)	Jun 08, 1934	Sep 22, 2021	Franklin Memorial Gardens; Dau. of Edwin Austin & Catherine Thorpe
Boyer, Margaret Neil (Brooksher)	Dec 24, 1932	Aug 22, 1913	Monteagle Cem.; Dau. of Audie Lee & Lela Dixie (McNeil) Brooksher, m. Malcomb Emmet Boyer; addition to Cemeteries of Grundy Co, Vol. 1, p 446,
Boyette, Barbara Ann (Givens)	Dec 15, 1947	Jun 08, 2015	Cremated; Dau. of Howard L. & Melonee (Crowell) Givens, m. Clyde Boyette
Braden, Denver Wayne	Jan 06, 1935	May 19, 1958	Oak Grove Cem.; Son of Claude Hobart & Lillie Mae (Bussell) Braden; addition to Cemeteries of Grundy Co.Vol. 1, p. 492
Braden, Geneva Edna	Sep 04, 1924	Aug 24, 2014	Swiss Colony Cem.; Dau of Elbert Patrick & Ethel Swearengen; m. Harley Braden
Braden, Hester Mae (James)	ca. 1939	Feb 07, 2014	Fall Creek Cem.; Dau. of Ralph & Ines (Givens) James; m. Bernice "Bones" Brewer

Name	Birth	Death	Details
Braden, Isaac Michael	Jun 1855	Sep 27, 1929	Pigeon Springs Cem.; Son of James Mitchell & Sarah "Sallie" (Johnson) Braden; m. Tabitha Louvisa "Bicie" Anderson – no tombstone
Braden, Jeremy Louis	Mar 26, 1986	Oct 19, 2014	Fall Creek Cem.; Son of Buster & Diane (Burnett) Braden; Companion, Glenda Sue White
Braden, Kirk	Mar 31, 1972	Sep 25, 2019	Coalmont Cem.; Son of Randy & Mary Rebecca (Burrows) Braden
Braden, Margie Marie (Layne)	Mar 14, 1946	Jul 17, 2017	Fall Creek Cem.; Dau. of Bass & Pearlie (Doss) Layne
Braden, Richard Lee	Dec 26, 1969	Feb 08, 2018	Fall Creek Cem.; Son of Tommy Eugene Braden & Shirley May Cox; m. Lisa Layne
Braden, Tabitha "Bicie" Louvisa	May 1859	Jan 17, 1933	Oak Grove Cem.; Dau. of Hezekiah Carr & Nancy (Smith) Anderson; m. Isaac Michael Braden; addition to Grundy Co. Cemeteries
Bradford, Quinton, Jr.	Feb 22, 1965	Apr 15, 2016	Bradford/Layne Cem.; Son of Quinton & Zada Elizabeth (Bouldin) Bradford
Brady, Billiefaye Lee (Burnette)	Sep 20, 1980	Sep 01, 2021	Altamont Cem.; Dau. of Carl David & Vesta Ann (Rose) Burnette; m. Kevin Brady
Brady, Hazel Louise (Campbell)	Jun 10, 1928	Nov 08, 1996	Little Johnny Myers Cem.; Buried there with her birth family as Hazel L. Caldwell even though she has a stone in Wesley Chapel Cem. (See p. 990 Cemeteries of Grundy Co., Vol. 2) Dau. of Buford Hollis & Louvenia (Hobbs) Campbell; m. 1) Hershel Glenn Brady 2) Paul Tate 3) Leonard Caldwell
Brady, Hershell Glenn	Sep 15, 1953	Jul 26, 2020	Altamont Cem.; Son of Clyde & Novella (Nunley) Brady; m. Vesta Ann Rose
Brady, James Colonel	Aug 06, 1904	Dec 01, 1970	Wesley Chapel Cem.; Son of Johnny & Addie (Wilson) Brady; m. Lillie May Myers; addition to Cemeteries of Grundy Co., Vol. 2, p. 989
Brannan, Helen Joyce (Partin)	Aug 26, 1939	Dec 21, 2014	Franklin Memorial Gardens; Dau of Orville Patrick Partin & Allie Blair Goodman; m. Rev. Marvin Brannan
Brannan, Johnsie Katherine	Jul 03, 1932	Jun 18, 2013	Monteagle Cem.; Dau. of Charles & Mary Elisabeth Myers; m. Johnny C. Brannan
Brannan, Marvin	Apr 10, 1937	Jan 25, 2015	Franklin Memorial Gardens Cem.; Son of Sol & Clara Bell (Crownover) Brannon; m. Helen Joyce (Partin) Richmond
Brannan, Mary Ann E. (Hessey)	Sep 11, 1878	Jun 06, 1960	Monteagle Cem.; Dau. of Robert Hatton & Eliza Mary (Doney) Hessey; addition to Cemeteries of Grundy Co.Vol. 2, p. 410
Braseel-Davis, Imojean (Nunley)	Dec 26, 1940	Oct 19, 2020	Bethel Cem.; Dau. of Graham & May Ellen (Campbell) Nunley; m. 1) Clyde Leo Braseel 2) Andrew Davis, Sr.; addition to Cemeteries of Grundy Co., Vol. 1, p. 5

Name	Birth	Death	Details
Braseel, Selma Joyce (King)	Jan 04, 1941	Apr 19, 1919	Bethel Cem.; Dau. of Richard H. & Lucille (Knight) King; m. Tommy Ray Braseel; addition to Cemeteries of Grundy Co, Vol, 1, p. 52
Brawley, Vera Jean (Sartin)	1921	Nov 12, 2014	United Methodist Church Cem in Hillsboro, TN; Dau of Hervie Lee Sartin & Leora Patra Spears; m. J.D. Brawley
Braxton, James	Apr 1860	1927	Altamont Cem.; Son of Lacy & Lugina Lazina "Lizzie" (Tripp) Braxton; m. Bannie Sullivan; correction and addition to Cemeteries of Grundy Co.Vol. 1, p. 19
Bray, Clarice Virginia	Feb 08, 1936	Jul 25, 2016	Plainview Cem.; Dau. of William Clarence & Mearl "Minnie" (Pettit) Jones; m. 1) Leonard Benedict Runge 2) Johnny Whitman, 3) Ronald Bray
Bray, Jerome	Nov 13, 1950	Jun 02, 2020	Unknown Cem.; Son of Epps Bray & Ethel Smith; m. Sherry Dempsey; U.S. Army
Brazier, Chad	1975	Jan 11, 2022	Cremated; Son of Danny Lee & Margaret "Peggy" (Clay) Brazier; Chad lived in Clarks Hill SC, but his father taught at Grundy Co. High and his mother was from Pelham.
Brazier, Jona Mae	Nov 28, 1939	Dec 22, 2021	Watson-North Memorial Park in Winchester; Dau. of Berry Luke & Alice Elizabeth (Neal) Brazier; mother of Gary Brazier of Pelham, TN
Bretz, Jaxson Case	Aug 18, 2017	Aug 18, 2017	Monteagle Cem.; probably John & Ashley (Mahaffey) Bretz
Bretz, John Walker	Jun 22, 2016	Jul 26, 2016	Monteagle Cem.; John & Ashley (Mahaffey) Bretz
Brewer, Clifford H. "Buck"	Apr 30, 1930	Sep 27, 2014	Orange Hill Cem.; Son of Walter Brewer & Dona Cagle; m. Mary Catherine Coffelt
Brewer, Edna (Layne)	Mar 12, 1926	Jul 06, 2013	Coalmont Cem.; Dau. of Aylor & Maudie (Morrison) Layne; m. James Echerd Brewer
Brewer, Eugene N.	Nov 21, 1929	Nov 29, 1948	Fall Creek Cem.; Son of Jesse L. & Ida Lee (Hale) Brewer; drowned per death cert. addition
Brewer, Evelyn Dean (Taylor)	Apr 25, 1942	Jan 03, 2021	Brown's Chapel Cem.; Dau. of Corbett & Pauline (Sartain) Taylor; m. Charles Brewer
Brewer, Kenneth	1943	Nov 27, 2015	Brown's Chapel Cem.; Son of Grady & Marie (Crabtree) Brewer
Brewer, Linda F. "Little Red" (Murphy)	Sep 17, 1944	Nov 15, 2009	Fall Creek Cem.; Dau. of Floyd & Noma Beatrice (Powell) Murphy; m. J. Ronny Brewer
Brewer, Mark Dwain	Dec 22, 1952	Jul 16, 2014	Brown's Chapel Cem.; Son of Grady & Edna Marie (Crabtree) Brewer; m. Glenda Morrison

Name	Born	Died	Details
Brewer, Mary Catherine (Coffelt)	Dec 24, 1934	Aug 08, 2021	Brown's Chapel Cem.; Dau. of Walter & Tilda (Roberts) Coffelt; m. Clifford Howell "Buck" Brewer
Brewer, Randall Ralph	May 29, 1943	Dec 26, 2013	Brown's Chapel Cem.; Son of Ralph Otto Brewer & Emma Lorene Goforth; companion Rachel E. Nodine
Brewer, Terry Ernest	Dec 07, 1947	Mar 22, 2017	Chattanooga National Cem.; Son of Grady & Edna Marie (Crabtree) Brewer; m. Vanessa Sue Walters; U.S. Navy Vietnam
Bridgers-Carlos, Jane Bennett	Apr 05, 1966	Dec 02, 2020	Cremated; Dau. of Ben & Sue Ellen Bridgers
Britton, Buddie	Feb 26, 1934	Feb 26, 1934	Fall Creek Cem.; Son of Gilliam Ernest & Martha Belle (Henry) Britton
Britton, Chasten Ryean	Apr 26, 1999	Jul 04, 2019	Airview Cem.; Dau. of Tony Britton & Chasity Britton Barrett & stepfather Jarron Barrett
Britton, Hilda (Brazier)	Dec 14, 1937	Sep 29, 2020	Unknown Cem.; Dau. of Berry Luke & Alice Elizabeth (Neal) Brazier; m. Wilson "Shorty" Britton
Britton, J. Raymond	Jul 21, 1917	Dec 01, 1967	Fall Creek Cem.; Son of Gilliam Ernest & Martha Belle (Henry) Britton; m. Doris Brewer
Brock, Marzella Marcie (Morrison)	Oct 01, 1955	Jan 10, 2021	Cremated; Dau. of Claude Wesley & Clarine (Pollard) Morrison; m. James Alton Brock
Brock, Walter	Mar 04, 1935	Aug 30, 2013	Pryor Ridge Cem./cremated; Son of John & Sarah Brock; m. Juanita (Shell) Caldwell
Brodt, Andrew Jacob	Mar 04, 1935	Oct 31, 2003	Cumberland Heights Cem.; Son of Andrew & Pauline (Ishcum) Brodt; m. Josephine Darlene Tavares; addition to Cemeteries of Grundy Co, Vol. 1, p. 198
Bronstetter, Walton Lee	Mar 03, 1922	Jul 12, 2015	Monteagle Cem.; Son of William Eli & Ruth Bronstetter; m. Margaret Guyear; U.S. Army
Brookman, Jennie E. (Downam)	1886	Jun 01, 1970	Plainview Cem.; Dau. of Daniel B. & Eliza (Statum) Downam; m. Andrew Jackson Brookman; addition and correction to Cemeteries of Grundy Co, Vol. 2, p. 662
Brookman, Keith Allen	Sep 27, 1960	Nov 24, 1960	Fall Creek Cem.; Son of Allen & Shirley (Smith) Brookman
Brookman, Shirley (Smith)	1938	Nov 20, 2020	Cremated; Dau of Thomas Lee "Polite" & Harlie Ophelia (Haynes) Smith; m. Allen Brookman; lived in Tracy City
Brooks, Charles Bailey	Mar 26, 1939	Feb 02, 2016	Coalmont Cem; Son of Charles Eugene Brooks & Christine (Martin) Brooks Reeves; m. 1) Mary Tate 2) Linda Geary
Brooks, James Albert	Dec 10, 1937	Aug 20, 2018	Palmer Cem.; Son of James Calvin "Flop" Brooks & Elsie Kathleen Nunley; m. Darlene Huffman; US Army
Brooks, William Lyndal	Jul 17, 1940	Sep 28, 2021	Welch Chapel Cem.; Son of James & Flossie (Nichols) Brooks

Name	Birth	Death	Details
Brothers, Elsie Harlan	Oct 20, 1925	Nov 30, 2011	Hillsboro United Methodist Cem.; Dau. of B.B. & Tillman Rosamond (Critz) Harlan; m. James Robert Brothers
Brothers, Fred Newton	May 27, 1936	Jan 28, 2016	Hillsboro United Methodist Cem.; Son of Matthew Talley & Maude H. (Roberts) Brothers
Brothers, James Robert "Bob"	Sep 22, 1922	Feb 15, 1994	Hillsboro United Methodist Cem.; Son of Matthew Talley & Maude H. (Roberts) Brothers; m. Elsie Harlan; U.S. Army Air Corps, WWII
Brown, Anthony Lynn	Feb 21, 1961	Sep 05, 2019	Cremated; Son of Lewis Wayne Brown & Jane Roberta O'Neal; m. Marilenea Brown; US Army
Brown, Bessie Lee (Burnett)	Dec 03, 1938	May 12, 2018	Fall Creek Cem.; Dau. of John Francis Burnett & Mary Ann Hargis; m. Hershel Douglas Brown
Brown, Carl R.	Dec 02, 1934	Feb 19, 2013	Summerfield Cem.; Son of Ulysses Grant & Miriam (Lautzenhouser) Brown; m. Violet King
Brown, Connie Darlene (Paradise)	1957	Oct 09, 2019	Unknown Cem.; Dau. of James & Louvenia Paradise; m. Allan Brown
Brown, Deborah Marie (Campbell)	Dec 06, 1958	Sep 18, 2015	Palmer Cem.; Dau. of Rod & Nornia Mae (Slatton) Campbell; partner: Bo Layman
Brown, Dwight Lee	Jan 30, 1945	Jun 02, 2017	Wesley Chapel Cem.; Son of Buford, Sr. & Ann (Cunningham) Brown
Brown, Edgar Louis	Nov 3, 1893	Apr 04, 1977	Brown's Chapel Cem.; Son of Stephen & Elizabeth (Rever) Brown; m. Rosey Rhea; addition to Cemeteries of Grundy Co.; Vol. 1, p.113
Brown, Eleanor Elizabeth (Brooks)	Nov 09, 1914	Jun 28, 1994	Cumberland Heights Cem.; Dau. of Walter W. & Cora (Devine) Brooks; m. Robert McKenzie Brown; addition to Cemeteries of Grundy Co.Vol. 1, p. 197
Brown, Elmer Benson	Aug 19, 1902	Dec 22, 1976	White Cem.; Son of James Knox Polk & Elizabeth (Smith) Brown; m. Anna Evelyn Bowers; Pvt. US Army WWII; addition to Cemeteries of Grundy Co.Vol. 2, p. 1008
Brown, Frank	Jan 15, 1939	Nov 18, 2015	Coalmont Cem.; Son of Rudolph & Clara Brown; m. Nellie Shrum; US Army
Brown, George Daryl	Sep 12, 1948	Oct 07, 2017	Jones Cem, Livingston, TN; Son of Louis Bud Brown & Dean Sullivan; m. Judith Ledford; US Army
Brown, Hazel (Floyd)	Mar 29, 1941	Dec 02, 2017	Franklin Memorial Gardens; Dau. of L.B. & Elsie Irene (Garrison) Floyd; m. Bill Brown
Brown, Helen E.	Sep 15, 1925	Mar 24, 2016	Plainview Cem.; Dau. of James W & Unis (Allen) Austin; m. Roy E. Brown on Oct 31, 1955; addition to Cemeteries of Grundy Co.Vol. 2, p. 666

Name	Born	Died	Details
Brown, Helen E.	Oct 19, 1942	Dec 03, 1984	Summerfield Cem.; Dau. of Roy & Leslie Jane (Scott) Watson; m. Roddy Brown
Brown, Henry L	Dec 15, 1885	Mar 08, 1959	Fall Creek Cem.; Son of Leander Virgil & Malvina (Cornelison) Brown; m. Anna Medley; correction of Cemeteries of Grundy Co., Vol. 1, p. 248
Brown, Ida Pearl (Johnson)	Nov 26, 1935	Dec 05, 2019	Condra Cem.; Dau. of Bill Johnson & Loucinda Tate; m. Paul David Brown
Brown, James Albert, Jr. "Chief Brown"	Aug 13, 1935	Jan 29, 2013	Guam Veterans Cemetery in Piti, Guam; Son of James Albert, Sr. & Rebecca Marguerite (Geary) Brown; m. Rosita Salas; US Navy Vietnam
Brown, James Allen	Jun 27, 1951	Jun 28, 2013	Cremated; Son of Willis Eston & Anna Bell (Savage) Brown
Brown, James William	Jun 08, 1928	Jul 21, 2019	Chattanooga National Cemetery; Son of William Cecil Brown & Martha Cleo Givens; m. Nellie Ford; U.S. Army
Brown, Jane Roberta (O'Neal)	May 06, 1938	Mar 13, 2019	Grace Chapel Cem.; Dau. of Johnny & Mabel (King) O'Neal; m. Lewis Wayne Brown
Brown, John	1918	1918	Hobbs Hill Cem.; Son of John B. & Mary Etta (Sweeton) Brown
Brown, John H.	Nov 26, 1939	Mar 03, 2006	Plainview Cem.; Son of Claude & Dessie (Gasaway) Brown – last residence Ft. Oglethorpe, GA
Brown, Joshua Darrell	Oct 13, 1979	Oct 13, 1979	Plainview Cem.; Son of Darrell Hembry & Sarah Ann (Sanders) Brown; addition to Cemeteries of Grundy Co,Vol. 2, p. 686
Brown, Juanita (Layne)	Ca 1943	Dec 05, 2015	Fall Creek Cem.; Dau. of Bass & Pearlie (Doss) Layne; m. Preston Brown
Brown, Kelley	Aug 08, 1987	Apr 05, 2022	Grace Chapel Cem.; Son of Anthony Lynn & Marilena Brown; partner: Mesha Borne; US Marine Corps
Brown, Leona M. (McCubbins)	Feb 12, 1912	Dec 09, 1996	Fall Creek Cem.; Dau. of Charlie & Jessie McCubbins; m. Harvey E. Brown
Brown, Lula (Wooten)	Apr 21, 1904	Nov 11, 1954	Monteagle Cem.; Dau. of Benjamin Anderson & Martha Naomi (Summers) Wooten; m. Ben Tilman Brown; addition to Cemeteries of Grundy Co.Vol. 1, p. 459
Brown, Mannie Becker (Smith)	Feb 14, 1927	Nov 30, 2018	Cumberland Heights Cem.; Dau. of Willis & Maudie (Wilhoit) Smith; m. 1) Raymond Earl Becker 2) Robert Brown
Brown, Marshall E.	Jun 20, 1936	Apr 13, 1967	Fall Creek Cem.; Son of Robert & Rose Lee (Pocus) Brown; TN Vietnam TSGT 4 Mil Air Lift SQ AF
Brown, Martha Josephine (Johnson)	Dec 31, 1850	Jan 16, 1923	Hobbs Hill Cem.; Dau. of Jonathan Tolliver & Margaret A. (Davis) Johnson; m. Rev. Norris Burr Brown, Aug 14, 1870; addition to Cemeteries of Grundy Co., Vol. 1, p. 330

Name	Born	Died	Notes
Brown, Marvin Stanley	Jan 03, 1913	Jul 29, 1988	Grace Chapel Cem.; Son of B. Marvin & Timmie H. (Smith) Brown; m. Dorothy Beck; Cemeteries of Grundy Co. Vol. 1, p. 300 correction
Brown, Mary (Fults)	1864	May 5, 1898	Stoner Cem.; Dau. of Alfred & Anna Fults, m. William Brown 1882 at 36 years old. She was the sister of Daniel Fults
Brown, Mildred T (Dyer)	Sep 23, 1921	Apr 13, 2020	Coalmont Cem.; Dau. of George Winfield & Margaret Dyer; m. Clarence "Tobe" Brown
Brown, Nancy Elizabeth (Gross)	Jul 9, 1851	May 05, 1935	Hobbs Hill Cem.; Dau. of Asa & Sarah Louise (Bost) Gross
Brown, Paul Douglas "Tree"	Apr 13, 1971	Sep 19, 2020	Fall Creek Cem.; Son of Paul David & Ida Pearl (Johnson) Brown; m. LeAnn Carpenter
Brown, Penelope "Neppie or P.J." (Saint)	Nov 28, 1848	Jan 03, 1907	Grace Chapel Cem.; Dau. of ___ Saint; m. William Almond Brown;Cemeteries of Grundy County, Vol 1, p. 300 addition
Brown, Phyllis (Tate)	Mar 04, 1947	Oct 09, 2020	Chattanooga National Cem.; Dau. of Harley & Omalee Tate; m. John R. Brown
Brown, Quinton Silas	Sep 28, 1901	Oct 16, 1998	Oak Grove Cem.; Son of Silas James & Carrie Melinda (Baker) Brown; m. Alma Rosalinde Christina Meyer; addition to Cemeteries of Grundy Co.,Vol. 1, p. 491
Brown, Rosa (Meyer)	Jun 17, 1902	Sep 02, 1986	Oak Grove Cem.; Dau. of John H. & Bertha (Lindermann) Meyer; correction of maiden name & addition to Cemeteries of Grundy Co., Vol. 1, p, 492
Brown, Stanley Wade "Stan"	Jan 21, 1954	Oct 13, 2021	Warren "Red Hill" Cem.; Son of Ulysses S. Grant, Jr. & Mary Lou (Smith) Brown; m. Doris "Dot" Owens
Brown, Tammy Lee	Aug 06, 1974	Jan 22, 2014	Airview Cem.; Dau of Nora Ryan; m. David Brown
Brown, Ulysses S. Grant, Jr.	Jun 26, 1932	Oct 06, 2014	Warren "Red Hill" Cem.; Son of Ulysses S. & Miriam (Lautzenheiser) Brown; m. Mary Lee Smith; addition to Cemeteries of Grundy Co.Vol. 2, p. 956
Brown, Violet I.	Feb 13, 1914	Jul 13, 2001	Dau. of Ruthie Jane Fults; m. Lindsay Leonard Brown; addition to Cemeteries of Grundy Co.,Vol. 2, p. 668
Brown, William Almond "W.A."	May 23, 1847	Jul 04, 1926	Grace Chapel Cem.; Son of William Sanford & Nancy (Dykes) Brown; m. Penelope Saint; Cemeteries of Grundy Co., Vol 1, p. 300 addition
Brown, William Duke	May 16, 1933	Jun 23, 2018	Coalmont Cem.; Son of Burt Brown & Nellie Frederick; m. Mary Sue Brown
Brown, William Robert "Bob"	Apr 27, 1883	Apr 11, 1927	Fall Creek Cem.; Son of Thomas Richard & Mary Frances (Teal) Brown; m. Leanna "Lettie" Lockhart

Name	Born	Died	Details
Brownell, Ross Thomas	Apr 15, 1938	May 28, 2019	Canada; Son of Walter Brownell & Frances Jennings
Bryan, Dale McGregor	Dec 25, 1957	May 21, 2018	Franklin Memorial Gardens; Son of Oakley Willis & Vernice (McGregor) Bryan; m. Holly Lisbeth Hayes
Bryan, Lorene (Gilliam)	Oct 03, 1924	Aug 08, 2014	Rose Hill Memorial Garden; Dau of James William "Billy" Gilliam & Mattie May Hill; m. 1) Lancen Gilliam 2) Thomas M. Bryan
Bryant, Eva (Sinks)	1903	Mar 04, 1926	Fall Creek Cem.; Dau of William M & Amanda Jane (Bullard) Sinks; m. Pat Bryant; buried with her baby
Bryant, Garret	Jan 13, 1996	May 11, 2018	Pryor Ridge Cem.; Son of Troy & Cindy Bryant; m. Whitney Bryant
Bryant, Hazel Edith (Thomas)	Aug 25, 1929	Jan 04, 2020	Plainview Cem.; Dau. of Roy & Esther Elizabeth Thomas; m. Elmer Jackson Bryant
Bryant, Jerry William	Jul 27, 1959	Jan 15, 2016	Plainview Cem.; Son of W.R. & Faye (Anderson) Bryant; m. Dorie Sanders
Bryant, Millie (Smith)	May 17, 1885	Mar 29, 1935	Fall Creek Cem.; Dau. of William & Rachael (Anderson) Smith; m. George Ferrell Bryant; addition to Cemeteries of Grundy Co., Vol 1, p. 213
Bryant, William "Houston"	Nov 12, 1940	Mar 27, 2016	Pryor Ridge Cem.; Son of Jesse Lawrence & Ethel Bryant; m. Ruth Nunley
Buckner, Allie Mae (Hawk)	Nov 18, 1935	Nov 20, 2020	Rose Hill Memorial Gardens; Dau. of Hubert & Hazel (Sartain) Hawk; m. Finis Buckner
Buckner, Carl Junior	Oct 02, 1932	May 27, 2017	Bonny Oak Cem.; Son of Carl & Mary Buckner; m. Betty Mae Sweeton; addition to Cemeteries of Grundy Co.,Vol. 1, p. 87
Buckner, Dustin Wade	May 16, 1984	Oct 22, 2019	Bethel Cem.; Son of Dennis Wade Buckner & Bonnie L. Nunley; m.1) Autumn Gilliam 2) Jamie Grein; U. S. Air Force
Buckner, Howard Don	1939	Oct 17, 2018	Rose Hill Memorial Gardens Cem.; Son of Clayton Buckner & Rosetta Lindsey; m. Joann Whitman; US Air Force
Buckner, Jean Ann (Gallagher)	Mar 22, 1944	Jan 04, 2021	Cremated; Dau. of Tom & Vergie (Payne) Gallagher; m. Joe Buckner
Buckner, Mary Opal (Bonner)	Aug 09, 1926	May 02, 2014	Bethel Cem.; Dau. of Morgan Haskel & Bethie Dillon (Hawk) Bonner; m. Benjamin Franklin "B.F." Buckner; addition to Cemeteries of Grundy Co.Vol. 1, p. 69
Buckner, Terri Jane (Chambers)	Dec 06, 1958	Jun 10, 2021	Rose Hill Memorial Gardens Cem.; Dau. of Johnny Wayne & Thelma "Jane" (Bryan) Chambers; m. Finis "Randy" Buckner

Buckner, William Bluford	1824	After 1900 census	Buckner Gravesite, Son of John & Melinda (Runion) Buckner, possibly; m.1) Martha Jane Nevill on Jan 22, 1852, 2) Sarah Rebecca Parks (1824-1886) no marriage date found; 3) Mary Melinda (West) Knight on Jan 28, 1892, Franklin Co. TN; addition to Cemeteries of Grundy Co. Vol. 1, p. 117
Buehler, Jack Alton	Apr 03, 1933	Sep 07, 1999	Fall Creek Cem.; Son of Alton J & Juliana M (Debusschere) Buehler
Buffington, Martha Louise "Marty"	Jun 13, 1946	Aug 05, 2014	Monteagle Sunday School Assembly Cem.; Dau. of Ray A. & Ellen D. (Earthman) Cates; m. Ronald Paul Buffington, Mar. 1967, Marion Co. FL
Bunch, Tracy Laverne (Sartain)	Jun 18, 1958	Jul 17, 2016	Sartain Cem. (behind Bethel Church); Dau. of Charles Harold & Barbara LaVerne (Davenport) Sartain; m. Michael Branch; addition to Cemeteries of Grundy Co.
Bunde, Matthew Wayne	1974	Sep 16, 2019	Cremated; Son of Marvin Bunde & Ruth Lafary; m. Lisa Meeks
Burdick, Alfred Burnell	May 21, 1906	Sep 01, 1986	Altamont Cem.; Son of Alfred William & Ina Elvina (Poole) Burdick; m. Mary Emmogene Bartle; addition to Cemeteries of Grundy Co,Vol. 1, p. 17
Burdick, Mary Emmogene	Apr 29, 1908	Oct 01, 2005	Altamont Cem.; Dau. of Fred Wilcox & Mary Camilla (Hovey) Bartle; m. Alfred Burnell Burdick; addition to Cemeteries of Grundy Co,Vol. 1, p. 17
Burge, Martha (Page)	May 04, 1947	May 22, 2016	Cremated; Dau. of Luther E. & Mary Agnes (Colvin) Page; m. Rev. John E. Burge; died in Suriname while on a mission
Burkhalter, Emma (Lyda)	Apr 18, 1929	Feb 16, 2016	Flatrock United Methodist Cem.; Dau. of Virgil & Ora (Medlin) Lyda; m. James C. Burkhalter
Burnet, William Bromwell II	Jun 06, 1914	Mar 28, 1978	Monteagle Cem.; Son of David & Agnes McClung (West) Burnet; m. 1) Frances Peronneau Martin 2) Betsy (Cox) Weems; addition to Cemeteries of Grundy Co. Vol. 1, p. 418
Burnett, Angela A. "Angie"	Jan 26, 1961		Warren "Red Hill" Cem.; Dau. of Grady W. & Helen (Scott) Northcutt; m. Carlton H. Burnett; Dec 31, 1979; Our Children Amanda Jean & Nathaniel Hoyt Burnett; addition to Cemeteries of Grundy Co.,Vol. 2, new tombstone planned
Burnett, Barbara Ann	Jan 08, 1942	Oct 02, 2013	Orange Hill Cem.; Dau. of Elmer & Rose Brown
Burnett, Betty (Meeks)	Aug 14, 1938	Dec 16, 2015	Fall Creek Cem.; Dau. of Hollis & Ida (Tate) Meeks; m. James Burnett

Name	Birth	Death	Details
Burnett, Billy Garner	Sep 15, 1936	Oct 07, 2013	Pelham Church of Christ Cem.; Son of Willie & Johnnie Vera (Patton) Burnett; m. Marguerite Sartain; addition to Cemeteries of Grundy Co,Vol. 2, p. 605
Burnett, Carl David	Apr 12, 1960	Jan 06, 2016	Summerfield Cem.; Son of John David "J.D.". & Flona Lee (Brown) Burnett; m. 1)Vesta Ann Rose 2) Kim Burnett
Burnett, Carlton H.	Jun 03, 1955		Warren "Red Hill" Cem.; Son of Leburn Hoyt "L.H." & Gladys (Crabtree) Burnett; m. Angela A. Northcutt, Dec 31, 1979; Our children Amanda Jean & Nathaniel Hoyt Burnett; addition to Cemeteries of Grundy Co,Vol. 2, new tombstone planned
Burnett, Charles Benny	Nov 01, 1935	Dec 19, 2021	Fall Creek Cem.; Son of Grover Cleveland & Ola (Grooms) Burnett; m. Rachel Payne; U.S. Army
Burnett, Edna Jewell (White)	Nov 15, 1913	Jan 04, 1999	Palmer Cem.; Dau. of Dock & Myrtle (Tate) White; m. Frank Savage Burnett; Correction to Cemeteries of Grundy Co,Vol. 2, p. 562
Burnett, Evelyn Marie (Nix)	Oct 17, 1917	Dec 14, 1999	Coalmont Cem.; Dau. of William Bedford & Sophia (Deitz) Nix; m. Edward Melvin Burnett
Burnett, Frank Savage	Dec 03, 1911	Sep 02, 1973	Palmer Cem.; Son of Elisha & Mary Ellen (Byers) Burnett; m. Edna Jewell White; addition to Cemeteries of Grundy Co.Vol. 2, p. 562
Burnett, Frankie E.	Dec 08, 1918	Jan 24, 2014	Coalmont Cem.; Dau of Laden & Tampico Golston; m. Carl David Burnett
Burnett, Leburn Hoyt "L.H."	Mar 13, 1919	Jun 05, 2013	Warren "Red Hill" Cem.; Son of John & Jennie (Wilson) Burnett; m. Gladys Crabtree
Burnett, Lula Mae (Corn)	Oct 08, 1940	Nov 07, 2019	Winchester Memorial Park Cem.; Dau. of William & Alberta (Taylor) Corn; m. James Corn
Burnett, Margaret W. (Coffelt)	Jun 16, 1928	Jul 26, 2016	Palmer Cem.; Dau. of John Wesley & Mattie (Roberts) Coffelt; m. Aug 9, 1952 to Walter R. Burnett; addition to Cemetries of Grundy Co,Vol. 2, p. 577
Burnett, Mary (Byers)	Sept 16, 1890	May 14, 1959	Warren "Red Hill" Cem.; Dau. of William Monroe & Isabell (Crowe) Byers; m. Elisha "Lish" Burnett
Burnett, Ralph Edwin	Sep 19, 1926	Jun 10, 2023	Fall Creek Cem.; Son of Albert Cleveland & Ola Rebecca (Grooms) Burnett; m. Doris O. McBee on Feb 11, 1945; addition to Cemeteries of Grundy Co. Vol 1, p. 209
Burnette, Brittany Aaron	Mar 18, 1991	Mar 11, 2020	Cremated; Dau. of Tommy Harmon & Melody Burnette
Burnette, Flona Lee (Brown)	Sep 18, 1939	Oct 06, 2021	Summerfield Cem.; Dau. of Ulysses & Miriam (Lautzenhauser) Brown; m. John David "J. D." Burnette

Name	Born	Died	Details
Burnette, Jeffery Allen	May 07, 1964	Sep 17, 2021	Pelham Church of Christ Cem.; Son of Johnny & Judy (Carrick) Burnett; m. 1) Shanna Meeks 2) Carrie Elsea
Burney, Linda (Matheson)	Nov 16, 1948	Sep 06, 2020	Summerfield Cem.; Dau. of Kenneth Matheson & Hazel Tedder; m. Gene Burney
Burr, Jno.	Sep 01, 1915	Dec 04, 1915	Hobbs Hill Cem.; Son of J.B. Brown; Source *Mrs. Grundy*, Dec 9, 1915
Burrell, Dorothey (Ward)	Jan 19, 1928	Aug 16, 2000	Monteagle Cem.; Dau. of Luther D. & Dorothy Ward; Correction of mother's name in Cemeteries of Grundy Co.Vol. 1, p. 436
Burroughs/Burrows, Josie Josephine (Campbell)	Oct 29, 1873	Feb 17, 1917	Buried in Burroughs' Cove from *Mrs. Grundy* (Bethel Cem); Dau. of Lemuel & Jenny Campbell; m. J. Burrows
Burrows, Kathleen	Feb 08, 1961	Jan 06, 2013	Coalmont Cem.; Dau. of Drew & Bessie (Roberts) Campbell; m. Jack Burrows
Burrows, Scott Brannon	Mar 04, 1969	Jul 17, 2018	Coalmont Cem.; Son of Jack & Kathleen Burrows
Burrows, Shelby Jean (Brown)	Jan 02, 1939	Oct 11, 2021	Coalmont Cem.; Dau. of Hembree & Dorothy (Haynes) Brown; m. Stanley Burrows
Bush, Betty Jean (Finch)	Nov 23, 1931	Mar 14, 2018	Palmer Cem.; Dau. of Herschel Lee & Ruby Lee (Gifford) Finch; m. 1) Johnnie Morgan Hill 2) William Miller "Bill" Bush
Bush, William Miller	Jun 25, 1927	Oct 03, 1987	Palmer Cem.; Son of William H, & Louise V. (Johnson) Bush; m. Betty Jean Finch; U.S. Navy, WW II; addition to Cemeteries of Grundy County,Vol. 2, p. 565
Bussard, Christy	Jul 09, 1975	Mar 18, 2017	Loudon Memory Garden Cem.; Dau. of Mike & Cindy Brannan; m. Casey Bussard
Butler , George Parker	Apr 11, 1947	Dec 14, 2021	Franklin Memorial Gardens; Son of Claude & Pauline (Novak) Butler; m. Sharon Butler
Butler, Marjorie Claudette	Dec 08, 1946		Monteagle Cem.; Dau. of Nellie Blanche Rediker; addition to Cemeteries of Grundy Co.Vol. 1, p 443
Butler, Timothy Joseph	1965	Jul 13, 2018	Plainview Cem.; Son of William & Kathleen (Clark) Butler; m. Pearl Butler
Butler, Walter, Sr.		Feb 21, 2015	No information found
Butner, Clarentine T. (Green)	Feb 12, 1857	Jul 16, 1899	Tracy City Cem.; Dau. of Bethel & Mary Green; m. Noah Butner; addition to Cemeteries of Grundy Co, Vol. 2, p. 907
Byars, "Joe" William	Sep 02, 1903	Jun 09, 1951	Gregg Cem.; Son of Joab Lambirth & Minda A. (Teague) Byars; m. Maude E. Taylor; Cemeteries of Grundy Co,Vol. 1, p. 306 correction
Byars, Annie Frances (McDaniel)	Jun 19, 1934	Dec 15, 2003	Bonny Oak Cem.; Dau. of Henry Clay & Edith Louise (Bone) McDaniel; m. George David Byars; correction of surname erroneously listed as Annie Myers in Cemeteries of Grundy Co.Vol. 1, p. 94.

Name	Birth	Death	Details
Byars, Archie D. "Oscar"	Mar 24, 1892	Oct 05, 1916	Coalmont Area; Son of Charles Frank "Charlie" & Rosa (Martin) Byers; killed in slate fall in C Mine in Coalmont; Source *Mrs. Grundy*
Byars, Donald Wayne	May 16, 1933	Jun 01, 1963	Gregg Cem.; Son of Joe William "Joab" & Maude Elizabeth (Taylor) Byars; m. Willie Mae McDaniel; addition to Cemeteries of Grundy Co.Vol. 1, p. 306
Byars, Floyd Mitchell	Feb 08, 1929	Jan 26, 2015	Gregg Cem.; Son of "Joe" William Joab & Maude Elizabeth (Taylor) Byars; m. 1) Marie Byars from Germany 2) Patsy Geary Tucker
Byars, Herbert Henry	Jan 14, 1892	Nov 18, 1914	Gregg Cem.; Son of Joab Lambirth & Minda A. (Teague) Byars; addition to Cemeteries of Grundy Co.Vol. 1, p. 306
Byars, Infant	1921	Jul 19, 1921	Oak Grove Cem.; Son of Oscar & Myrtle (Boggs) Byars
Byars, Joab Lambirth	Feb 15, 1867	Jun 13, 1931	Gregg Cem.; Son of John W. & Sarah J. (Morgan) Byars; Cemeteries of Grundy County,Vol. 1, p. 306 correction
Byars, Joe William "Joab"	Sep 02, 1903	Jun 09, 1951	Gregg Cem.; Son of Joab Lambirth & Minda A. (Teague) Byars; m. Maude Elizabeth Taylor; correction of death year by family to Cemeteries of Grundy Co.Vol. 1, p. 306
Byars, John Wayne	Oct 03, 1906	Apr 25, 1927	Gregg Cem.; Son of Jacob Lambirth & Amanda (Teague) Byars; addition to Cemeteries of Grundy Co.,Vol. 1, p. 306
Byars, Malinda A. (Teague)	Mar 8, 1874	Oct 10, 1944	Gregg Cem.; Dau. of Henry & Rhonda (Beene) Teague; Cemeteries of Grundy County,Vol. 1, p. 306 correction
Byers, Augusta (Smith)	May 26, 1839	1919	Tracy City Cem.; Dau. of Samuel & Amarillys (Peat) Smith; m. William E. Byers; born in OH; addition to Cemeteries of Grundy Co, Vol. 2, p. 843
Byers, Charles William "Frosty"	Aug 21, 1924	Jun 30, 2017	Plainview Cem.; Son of William Monroe & Lena (Stump) Byers; m. Della Mae Gross
Byers, Donna Jo	Apr 20, 1955	Sep 26, 2013	Gregg Cem.; Dau. of Donald Wayne & Willie Mae (McDaniel) Byers
Byers, Dustin "Big Country"	Feb 25, 1984	Jan 21, 2020	Plainview Cem.; Son of Kenny Seagroves & Mary Byers
Byers, Floyd Mitchel	Feb 08, 1929	Jan 26, 2015	Cremated; Son of William J. & Maude E. (Taylor) Byars; m. Maria Patsy R (Geary) Tucker; U.S. Army- Changed spelling of his name from Byars to Byers
Bycrs, G.C.	May 22, 1951	Feb 05, 2017	Lappin Cem.; Son of Bill & Hattie Mae Byers

Byers, George David	Feb 13, 1930	Feb 25, 1979	Bonny Oak Cem.; Son of John & Myrtle (Fults) Byers; m. Annie Frances McDaniel; correction of name which was ereneously listed as George Myers and an addition to Cemeteries of Grundy Co.Vol. 1, p. 94
Byers, Grace Evelyn	Oct 22, 1926	Jan 29, 2013	Plainview Cem.; Dau. of George P. & Willie Ann (Reid) Anderson; m. James Byers
Byers, James William	Oct 19, 1957	Feb 28, 2022	Plainview Cem.; Son of James & Evelyn (Anderson) Byers
Byers, Jason	Jan 24, 1971	May 20, 2017	Burns Cem.; Son of Charles & Sue (Shrum) Byers; m. Kristi Wise
Byers, Jimmy Ray	1936	May 14, 2014	Cremated;Son of John Berry Byers & Mattie Ethel Davis; m. Barbara Byers
Byers, Johnnie B.	Aug 29, 1943	Aug 03, 2016	Monteagle Cem.; Cremated; Son of Willie D. "Bill" Bookman & Mary Jennings; m. Becky Meeks
Byers, Johnny Billy	Aug 29, 1943	Aug 03, 2016	Cremated; Son of Mary (Byers) Jennings m. Rebecca "Becky" Meeks
Byers, Lena Rivers (Stump)	Jun 03, 1884	May 03, 1984	Plainview Cem.; Dau. of William Michael & Senie (Tate) Stump; m. William Monroe Byers; addition to Cemeteries of Grundy Co.Vol. 2, p. 692
Byers, Lisa Ellen (Fredrick)	Feb 21, 1965	Jul 01, 2018	Monteagle Cem.; Dau. of Paul Austin Fredrick & Jean Ellen Campbell; m. Daniel Byers
Byers, Mary Ann	Aug 25, 1841	Mar 17, 1892	Providence Methodist Cem.; Dau. of William Morrison & Malena (McCown) Byers; m. Isaac Washington Sullivan, Jr. in Lincoln Co. TN, on Mar 3, 1868; addition & correction to Cemeteries of Grundy Co, Vol. 2, p. 711
Byers, Maude Elizabeth (Taylor)	Jun 05, 1901	Oct 20, 1991	Gregg Cem.; Dau of Bevley B. Taylor & Gwennie Estella Mae Fowler; m. 1) John Wayne Byers 2) "Joe" William Byers; addition to Cemeteries of Grundy Co., Vol 1, p. 506.
Byers, Payton Elizabeth Clarity	Apr 05, 2005	Apr 28, 2020	Plainview Cem: Dau. of Billy & Kerry (Metcalfe) Byers
Byers, Rodney	Jun 06, 1945	Feb 03, 2013	Cremated; Son of William & Clara (Anderson) Byers; m. Clara Meeks
Byers, William Monroe	Feb 15, 1888	Feb 11, 1962	Plainview Cem.; Son of Charles William & Amanda Roseann (Martin) Byers; m Lena Rivers Stump; addition to Cemeteries of Grundy Co.Vol. 2, p. 692
Byrd, Jeffrey Lee	Jul 03, 1983	Nov 23, 2020	Plainview Cem.; Son of Harold & Anna Ruth (Byrd) Green; m. Tabitha Byrd
Cagle, David Wade	Aug 27, 1950	Oct 01, 2016	Summerfield Cem.; Son of James & Robena (Thomas) Cagle
Cagle, Donnie Ray	Dec 23, 1959	Sep 26, 2016	Swiss Colony Cem.; Son of Billy R. & Judy (Turley) Cagle; m. Wavie Layne

Name	Born	Died	Notes
Cagle, Gladys Marie	Jul 19, 1928	Aug 16, 2008	Cremated; died in Las Crusas, NM, native of Tracy City; Dau of Thomas Lee "Polite" Smith & Harlie Ophelia Haynes; m. 1) James Cagle 2) Glenn Thomas
Cagle, James A	May 17, 1925	Jan 12, 1969	Coalmont Cem.; Son of Albert A. Cagle & Minnie Tabor (later Kilgore); m. Gladys Marie Smith; killed while a law enforcement officer in Tracy City; Navy WWII
Cagle, James Larry "Jim"	Sep 28, 1948	May 29, 2014	Ft. Bliss National Cem. El Paso, TX; Son of James Cagle & Gladys Marie Smith; companion; Lissa Gardner; Army
Cagle, Jerry Albert	Sep 24, 1952	Oct 09, 1980	Rosewood Cem; Humble, TX; Son of James A. & Marie (Smith) Cagle of Tracy City; m. Candyce Lynn Beasley
Cagle, Larry Randall	Mar 03, 1951	Mar 22, 2020	Brown's Chapel Cem.; Son of Dexter & Velma (Green) Cagle
Cagle, Michael Douglas	Jan 29, 1956	May 01, 2010	Cremated in New Mexico; Son of James A. & Gladys Marie (Smith) Cagle
Cagle, Wavie Lillie Mae (Layne)	Jul 13, 1939	Jun 29, 2017	Swiss Colony Cem.; Dau. of Frank & Gertrude Layne; m. Billy Ray Cagle
Caldwell, Billy Eugene	Jan 08, 1949		Palmer Cem.; Son of Hillard & Ruby (Worley) Caldwell; m. Juanita Green; addition to Cemeteries of Grundy Co.Vol. 2, p. 73
Caldwell, Brenda Lorene (Woodward)	Apr 17, 1953	Aug 16, 2017	Palmer Cem.; Dau. of Richard & Virginia (Halfacre) Woodward; m. Ricky Caldwell
Caldwell, Bruce Wayne	Mar 23, 1970	Mar 06, 2022	Burkett's Chapel Cem.; Son of Joyce (Caldwell) Smith Nunley; m. Carrie Hamilton
Caldwell, Carl Junior	Aug 08, 1947	Nov 29, 2014	Fall Creek Cem.; Son of Marcus Caldwell & Myra Jeanetta Layman" US Army Vietnam
Caldwell, Carolyn	Sep 25, 1956	Dec 16, 2017	Cremated; Dau. of Charles T, "Chick" & Alice (Hart) Caldwell
Caldwell, Carrie Etta (Layne)	Jul 25, 1887	Jan 25, 1977	Coalmont Cem.; Dau. of William Harrison & Mary Isabella (Tate) Layne; m. Frank H. Caldwell; Correction to Cemeteries of Grundy Co. ,Vol. 1, p. 175
Caldwell, Christine	Apr 03, 1947	Apr 12, 2022	Cremated; Dau. of Clay & Alice (Layne) McDaniel; m. Lee Franklin Caldwell
Caldwell, Craig Alton	Jul 19, 1972	Aug 30, 2014	Burkett's Chapel Cem.; Son of Alton Caldwell & Grace McDaniel; m. Crystal Overturf
Caldwell, Denise Linette (Long)	Apr 30, 1958	Mar 01, 2022	Eastern Star Cem.; Dau. of Harry & Alma Jean (McBee) Long
Caldwell, Grace E. (McDaniel)	Oct 27, 1952	Sep 18, 2019	Cremated; Dau. of Clay & Edith (Bone) Mc Daniel; m. Willis Alton Caldwell
Caldwell, Hazel Louise (Campbell)	Jun 10, 1928	Nov 08, 1996	Little Johnny Myers Cem; Dau of Hollis Buford & Louvinia Elizabeth (Hobbs) Campbell; m. 1) Leonard Farrell Cladwell , 2) Paul Henderson Tate 3) Hershel Glenn Brady

Name	Birth	Death	Details
Caldwell, Helen Dean (Hayes)	Apr 19, 1951	Feb 18, 1922	Plainview Cem.; Dau. of William & Pauline (Kirk) Hayes; m. Carl Caldwell
Caldwell, Helen Lena (Knowlan)	Sep 27, 1934	Feb 22, 2014	Fall Creek Cem.; Dau. of Fate & Maggie Knowlan; m. 1) James Ralph Givens 2) ____Caldwell
Caldwell, Herbert Edward	Mar 26, 1930	Jun 27, 2013	White Cem.; Son of Calvin B. & Ida Mae (Nunley) Caldwell; m. Bonnie Cook
Caldwell, Hilda Naomi (Meeks)	Aug 22, 1912	Jun 16, 1999	Orange Hill Cem.; Dau. of Baxter & Lillie (Nunley) Meeks; Herbert Caldwell
Caldwell, Kenneth Ray	Apr 21, 1963	Mar 22, 2021	Douglas Flynn Cem.; Son of Billy Ray & Rena Ann (Flynn) Caldwell ; m. Carrie Leigh Wooten
Caldwell, Larry Dean	Apr 04, 1958	Jul 02, 2013	Cremated; Son of Stanley, Jr. & Christine (Anderson) Caldwell; m. Tammy Godfrey
Caldwell, Lillie Mae (Sanders)	Nov 12, 1926	Apr 22, 2015	Coalmont Cem.; Dau. of John William & Maggie (Sweeton) Sanders; m. 1) Robert Eugene Sweeton 2) William Howard "Soll" Caldwell
Caldwell, Ophelia (Myers)	Jun 10, 1910	Jun 01, 1991	Plainview Cem.; Dau. of Everette B. & Renee (Tooney) Myers; m. Charles Edward Caldwell, Sr.; addition to Cemeteries of Grundy Co .Vol. 2, p. 688
Caldwell, Pamela Jo (Dent)	Jan 30, 1954	Feb 26, 2019	Palmer Cem.; Dau. of J.D. & Faye (Smith) Dent; m. Gene Caldwell
Caldwell, Patricia Ann (Anderson)	Aug 12, 1941	Sep 12, 2013	Monteagle Cem.; Dau. of Morris & Georgia (Wilson) Anderson; m. Jim Caldwell
Caldwell, Polly Ann (Brown)	May 10, 1929	Dec 29, 1984	Fall Creek Cem.; Dau. of William & Jenna Mae Brown
Caldwell, Ruth Sarah (Jackson)	Sep 29, 1917	Jul 25, 2001	Palmer Cem.; Dau. of Charles William & Annie Lee (Linley) Jackson; m. Grover H. Caldwell; addition to Cemeteries of Grundy Co.Vol. 2, p. 553
Caldwell, Stephen Edward	May 24, 1961	Oct 16, 2017	Bethel Cem.; Son of Charles Edward Caldwell, Jr. & Joann (Thompson) Givens
Campbell, Bob Alton	1954	May 25, 2014	Coalmont Cem.; Son of Edward & Della Campbell; m. Dorothy Campbell
Campbell, Catherine		before 1908	Parson's Graveyard/now Bonny Oak; Dau of Hugh Campbell & Elizabeth "Betty" Campbell
Campbell, Charles Wayne	1943	Nov 27, 2014	Red Hill Cem.; Son of Alex & Jessie Low Campbell; Dianne Campbell
Campbell, Elizabeth "Betty" (Nunley)	1832	ca. 1905	Parson's Graveyard/now Bonny Oak; Dau. of Emanuel & Catherine Ellis (Coulston) Nunley; m. Hugh Campbell; no stone, per relatives
Campbell, Hugh	May 1835	Apr 25, 1917	Parson's Graveyard/now Bonny Oak; Son of James C. & Malinda C. (Roberson) Campbell; m Elizabeth "Betty" Nunley; no stone, per relatives

Name	Birth	Death	Details
Campbell, Louisa/Louiza (Phipps)	Mar 16, 1866	Mar 24, 1948	Bonny Oak Cem.; Dau. of David & Elizabeth (Sweeton) Phipps; m. Alexander W. Campbell on Feb 22, 1896; addition to Cemeteries of Grundy Co.
Campbell, Lucille "Lucy" Bell	Jan 7, 1897	May 01, 1973	Monteagle Cem.; daughter of Norris Martin & Fannie Ellen (Smith) Campbell; granddaughter of Mortimer B & Virginia Lovette; m. Douglas John Campbell on Dec 19, 1920; addition to Cemeteries of Grundy County Vol. 1, p. 425
Campbell, Lucille (Stacy)	Jan 20, 1946	Oct 27, 2020	Coalmont Cem.; Dau. of Lawson & Ocie Ruth (Stiltner) Stacy; m. Larry Campbell
Campbell, Lucy (Smith)	Sep 20, 1899	Mar 14, 1971	Bonny Oak Cem.; Dau. of Henry L & Mae (Nunley) Smith; m. Tobe Campbell, Sr. on Dec 25, 1910; addition to Cemeteries of Grundy Co.Vol. 1, p.90
Campbell, Malcolm "Dickie"	Sep 10, 1939	Jun 21, 2014	Eastern Star Cem.; Son of Melvin & Hazel Campbell; m. Imogene Yokley
Campbell, Martin	Mar 19, 1905	1918	Monteagle Cem.; Dau. of Norris Martin & Fannie Ellen (Smith) Campbell; correction of Cemeteries of Grundy County, Vol. 1, p.424, errenously listed as a daughter.
Campbell, Melvin F.	1936	2012	Little Johnny Myers Cem.; Son of Hollis & LouVenia (Hobbs) Campbell; m. 1) Willene Phillips 2) Sylvia Beatrice Campbell; addition to Cemeteries of Grundy Co. Vol. 1, p. 367
Campbell, Moss	May 07, 1934	Oct 17, 2019	Altamont Cem.; Son of Oddist Campbell & Kate Nunley; m. Alene Killian
Campbell, Myrtle (Reynolds)	Aug 06, 1925	Mar 26, 2020	Palmer Cem.; Dau. of John Reynolds & Eva Sergent; m Watson Campbell
Campbell, Naomi (Meeks)	Mar 03, 1936	Jan 19, 2017	Clouse Hill Cem.; Dau. of Jackson Hiles, Sr. & Peggy Cleo (Cox) Meeks; addition to Cemeteries of Grundy Co.,Vol. 1, p. 152
Campbell, Norris Martin, Jr.		Early 1900's	Monteagle Cem.; Fieldstone in Section 2 West listed at the top of page Cemeteries of Grundy Co., Vol 1, p. 424. Died as a baby- years unknown.
Campbell, Ola May	Sep 04, 1903	Mar 17, 1941	Bethel Cem.; Dau. of William Enoch & Lucy D. (Meeks) Campbell per death certificate; correction of father's name & addition to Cemeteries of Grundy Co.,Vol. 1, p. 48
Campbell, Patrick Claiborne	1870	ca 1905	Parson's Graveyard/now Bonny Oak Cem.; Son of Hugh Campbell & Elizabeth "Betty" Nunley - no stone per family
Campbell, Paula Marie (Perry)	Sep 03, 1956	Aug 01, 2020	Cremated; Dau. of George & Virginia Perry- died in Ringgold, GA
Campbell, Randolph	Sep 22, 1932	May 02, 2018	Fall Creek Cem.; Son of Johnny Campbell & Lucille Sweeton

Name	Birth	Death	Details
Campbell, Robert Roscoe	Aug 10, 1937	Apr 15, 2021	Nunley/Campbell Cem.; Son of Harris & Nora (Sweeton) Campbell
Campbell, Rocky Dwight	Nov 27, 1954	Jan 23, 2008	Bonny Oak Cem.; Son of Allen Campbell & Bonnie Meeks
Campbell, Roger Vaughn	Jul 28, 1947	Dec 06, 2017	Plainview Cem.; Son of James M. & Margaret (Sanders) Campbell; m. Shirley Campbell; US Navy
Campbell, Ronald Lee	Oct 14, 1953	Sep 12, 1974	Swiss Colony Cem.; Son of John Homer & Alice Mae (Nussbaum) Campbell; addition to Cemeteries of Grundy Co.Vol. 2, p. 792
Campbell, Sarah Ann (Scott)	Jan 13, 1861	Jul 25, 1952 death cert. says Jul 21st	Bonny Oak Cem.; Dau. of John & Martha (Bond) Scott; m. James Enoch "Jim" Campbell Jan 5, 1880; addition to Cemeteries of Grundy Co.,Vol. 1, p. 90
Campbell, Shawn Edward	Jan 02, 1963	Nov 06, 2021	Cremated; Son of Edward & Naomi (Meeks) Campbell, Jr.; m. Stacey Campbell
Campbell, Sheila Marie (Westman)	Jul 22, 1941	Jul 12, 2020	Hillsboro Cumberland Presbyterian Cem.; Dau. of Andrew & Margaret Westman; m. Johnny Campbell
Campbell, Shirley "Sherry" (Nunley)	Apr 05, 1962	Aug 31, 2020	Plainview Cem.; Dau. of Lewis & Edna Nunley; m. Steve Campbell
Campbell, Steven	Jul 28, 1948	Oct 17, 2015	Clouse Hill Cem.; Son of Brossie & Mary Lillian (Nunley) Campbell ; m. Cerena D. Campbell
Campbell, Susan Matilda (DeLeeuw)	Jan 01, 1947		Coalmont Cem.; m. Harry Damon Campbell; addition to Cemeteries of Grundy County,Vol. 1, p. 178
Campbell, Sylvia Beatrice (Jones) Frisbee	ca 1940	Dec 31, 2014	Little Johnny Myers Cem.; Dau. of Clarence & Millie M. (Pettit) Jones; m. 1) Harvey Lee Frisbee 2) Melvin Campbell
Campbell, Tierra E. (Nunley)	Sep 24, 1895	Jun 09, 1905	Hobbs Hill Cem.; Dau. of William Carroll & Lydia Parelee (Parsons) Nunley; m. Alexander W. Campbell; addition to Cemeteries of Grundy Co.Vol. 1, p. 338
Campbell, Timothy Lee	Aug 06, 1959	Dec 14, 2018	Coalmont Cem.; Son of Lillard Campbell & Betty Jean Curtis
Campbell, Tony Lamar	Jun 04, 1949	Jul 10, 2020	Cremated; Son of Thomas "Bud" Campbell & Nancy Mae Cotham; m. Anita Caldwell; lived in Altamont; U.S. Navy
Campbell, Vance "Toby"	Jan 18, 1950	Oct 26, 2015	Add Smith Cem.; Son of Brosie & Lillian Campbell ; m. Faye Garret
Campbell, Violet H.	1922	Aug 14, 2014	Hobbs Hill Cem.; Dau of Ben C. Hampton, Sr. & Meddie Crick; m. Stanley A. Campbell
Campbell, Virginia Juanita (Stevens)	Oct 21, 1944	Feb 19, 2022	Summerfield Cem.; Dau. of John Clark & Irene E. Stevens
Campbell, Wade Preston	May 04, 1959	Jun 23, 2020	Altamont Cem.; Son of Moss Campbell & Alene Killian; m. Patricia Dykes

Name	Birth	Death	Details
Campbell, William Deloe	Mar 15, 1971	Mar 15, 1971	Fall Creek Cem.; Son of William Howard & DeLaura (Hiatt) Campbell; addition to Cemeteries of Grundy Co.Vol. 1, p. 265
Campbell, William Frank	Jun 16, 1889	Dec 03, 1925	Bonny Oak Cem.; Son of Arch H. & Mary (Leverton) Campbell; TH PVT 163 Inf 43 Div. WWI; correction of death date & addition to Cemeteries of Grundy Co.Vol. 1, p. 79
Campbell, William Harrison	Jul 22, 1864	Oct 05, 1928	Bethel Cem.; Son of Lemuel J., Sr. & Jincy Jane (Meeks) Campbell; m. Ida Woodlee
Campbell, William Oscar	1939	Mar 10, 2016	Summerfield Cem.; Son of Tom & Minnie Mae (Thomas) Campbell
Campbell, William Ray "Pudgy"	May 10, 1947	Feb 18, 2021	Coalmont Cem.; Son of Brosie & Lillian (Nunley) Campbell; m. Marsha Caldwell
Campbell, William Wayne	Feb 22, 1950	Apr 06, 2015	Hobbs Hill Cem.; Son of Stanley & Violet (Hampton) Campbell; m. Rose Nunley
Cannon, Archie D. "Oscar"	Mar 24, 1892	Oct 05, 1916	Coalmont Cem.; Son of Charles Frank & Rosa (Martin) Byers;; Killed in C mine in Coalmont in slate fall, source *Mrs. Grundy*
Cannon, Freddie Morgan	Mar 25, 1896	Jan 22, 1975	Palmer Cem.; Son of Taylor Lavater & Mari Ida Ella (Dishroon) Cannon; m. Agnes Marguerite Henley; Cemeteries of Grundy Co., Vol. 2, page 551
Cannon, Jerry	Sep 09, 1936	Feb 17, 2017	Fall Creek Cem.; Son of Leon & Rosa Lee (McBee) Cannon; m. Charlotte Long, Nov. 23, 1963
Cannon, Martha (Burnette)	Nov 13, 1927	Aug 13, 2001	Monteagle Cem.; Dau. of Elisha & Mary E. (Byers) Burnett; m. Howard G. Cannon, addition to Cemeteries of Grundy Co.Vol. 1, p. 447
Cannon, Theodore L.	Jul 13, 1966		Palmer Cem.; Son of Jerry & Charlotte (Long) Cannon; m. Jerri D. Harrison; addition to Cemeteries of Grundy Co,Vol. 2, p. 567.
Cantrell-Daly, Elizabeth	Apr 07, 1942	Dec 05, 2014	Eastern Star Cem.; Dau of Walter & Arlie Parker Cantrell; m. Lavern E. Daly
Cantrell, Alice "Allie" (Sweeton)	Sep 19, 1880	Jun 19, 1906	Tracy City Cem.; Dau. of John & Manerva (Gipson) Sweeton; m. Newton "Nute" Cantrell on Nov 15, 1900; addition to Cemeteries of Grundy Co,Vol. 2, p. 839
Cantrell, Billie Marie (Jones)	Jun 16, 1943	May 04, 2021	Garden of Memory Cem.; Dau. of Wesley Born & Maudie Earline (Jaco) Jones; m. 1) John Roy Weddington 2) ____Cantrell
Cantrell, Claude Jackson "C.J."	Jan 4, 1896	Jun 10, 1968	Monteagle Cem.; Son of George Washington & Malinda (Saville) Cantrell; m. Margaret Emily Stone; US Navy WWI; addition to Cemeteries of Grundy Co,Vol. 1, p 455
Cantrell, Claudia Seals Roberts	Apr 07, 1912	Jan 17, 1961	Fall Creek Cem.; Dau. of James & Nellie B. Cantrell ; m. George Roberts

Name	Born	Died	Notes
Cantrell, Georgia H. (Adams)	Jan 06, 1900	Oct 18, 1968	Plainview Cem.; Dau. of Charles Francis & Dorothy "Dolly" (Tate) Adams; m. James Erskine Cantrell; addition to Cemeteries of Grundy Co,Vol. A, p. 685
Cantrell, Jackson Venus	Jun 12, 1938	Sep 06, 2019	Cowan Montgomery Cem.; Son of Ernest Lee Cantrell & Grace Katherine Walker; m. Mary "Meme" Cantrell
Cantrell, Margaret Emily (Stone)	Jul 4, 1897	Feb 01, 1978	Monteagle Cem.; Dau. of Fletcher Richardson & Tullulah Mae Stone; m. Claude J. "C.J." Cantrell; addition to Cemeteries of Grundy Co,Vol. 1, p 455
Capel, Virginia Anne (Boulton)	Aug 23, 1942	Jul 03, 2020	Cremated; Dau. of Robert Boulton & Alice Delaney
Carden, Roy W.	Apr 11, 1898	Oct 11, 1962	Warren "Red Hill" Cem.; Son of Dr. Lynn Adolphus & Cleopatra "Cleo" (Cook) Carden; m. Thelma E. (McClendon) Blassingame; correction of wife's maiden name; Cemeteries of Grundy Co.Vol. 2, p. 929
Carden, Thelma E. (McClendon)	1900	1981	Warren " Red Hill" Cemetery; Dau. of James T. & Alice (Markham) McClendon m. 1) Max Blassingame 2) Roy W. Carden; addition and correction to Cemeteries of Grundy Co.Vol. 2, p. 929
Carlson, Marie Ann (Myers)	Oct 19, 1952	Sep 27, 2019	Cremated; Dau. of Luther Myers & Deamie Fults; m. David Carlson
Carpenter, April Renee	Jun 03, 1905	Sep 24, 2021	Pryor Ridge Cem.; Dau. of Clay & Karla (Greene) Carpenter
Carpenter, Velma Pauline "Polly" (Gass)	Nov 23, 1938	Jun 30, 2015	Franklin County Memorial Gardens Cem.; Dau. of Jay C. & Pressie (Gudger) Gass; m. Ambrose Carpenter
Carr, Josephine	1887	Oct 02, 1920	Orange Hill Cem.; Dau. of Patrick & Eliza Caroline (Martin) Carr; m. Samuel Emmett Orange; addition to Cemeteries of Grundy Co.;Vol. 2, p. 537
Carrick, Naomi M.	Jul 07, 1921	Sep 18, 1986	Plainview Cem.; Dau. of Dillard Dee Tillman & Betty (Roberts) Brown; m. Charles Mariman Carrick; addition to Cemeteries of Grundy Co,Vol. 2, p. 667
Carrick, Patricia "Patsy" (Lambert)	1936	Nov 07, 2015	Oak Hill Memorial Park, Kingsport, TN; Dau. of John & Ginger Lambert; m. Herman Carrick
Carrick, Phyllis J (Sitz)	Oct 22, 1949	Dec 09, 2021	Gregg Cem.; Dau. of James & Thelma (Coppinger) Sitz; m. Benny Carrick
Carrick, Robert Jackson	Mar 02, 1936	Mar 06, 2022	Orange Hill Cem.; Son of Joe Wheeler & Maggie Hazel (Nunley) Carrick; U.S. Army
Carter, Grace (Tucker)	Dec 13, 1907	May 04, 1994	Monteagle Cem.; Dau. of Silas & Frances A. (Sherrill) Tucker;; correction to parents' names; Cemeteries of Grundy Co.Vol. 1, p. 446

Name	Born	Died	Details
Carter, Harold Gordon	Aug 18, 1938	Oct 22, 2018	Philadelphia Cem.; Son of Casto Carter & Gladys Delong; U.S. Army
Carter, Mary Elizabeth (Gober)	Jul 10, 1939	Oct 04, 2020	Unknown Cem.; Dau. of Alfred & Alice Gober; m. C.D. Carter
Carter, Richmond	Feb 15, 1949	Nov 23, 2021	Cremated; Son of Arthur Richmond & Agnes Grace (Lowe) Carter; m. Geraldine Hackworth; US Army
Cash, David Binkley	Oct 14, 1965	May 19, 2013	Eastern Star Cem.; Son of Billy Joe & Faye Cash
Cashen, Nancy Jane (Dove) Shadrick	Jan 29, 1859	Apr 26, 1944	Orange Hill Cem.; Dau. of James & Nancy (Ridge) Dove; m. 1) Anderson Shadrick 2) John Cashen; no tombstone; information from family & Find A Grave
Cashion, Melvin G.	Sep 18, 1941	Jun 03, 2015	Old Orchard Cem.; Son of James & Annie Lee (Gibson) Cashion
Casseday, Lynn Hampton	Oct 05, 1932	Mar 09, 2022	Sequatchie Valley Memorial Gardens Cem.; Son of Roy Dale & Josephine Burell (Molissee) Casseday; m. Martha Kathleen Pope
Cassidy, Christopher James	1993	Aug 20, 2021	Oak Grove Cem.; Son of Joey & Donna Beth Nolan
Catildo, Robert Francis		Mar 18, 2012	Hunerwadel Cem.; Son of Richard & Theresa M. Catildo
Caudle, Mike	Jan 21, 1924	Sep 23, 1980	Coalmont Cem.; Son of John Fulton & Ellen Priscilla (Anderton) Caudle; PFC US Army WWII; correction to Cemeteries of Grundy Co Vol. 1, p. 172
Causey, Rose H. (Hayes)	Mar 25, 1930	Oct. 21, 2015	Cremated; Dau. of A.H. & Elma (Tyler) Hayes; m. John W. Causey
Cauthen, Mary Elizabeth (Aylor)	Apr 05, 1926	Jan 02, 2014	Plainview Cem.; Dau. of Sylvester "Bud" & Georgia Lee (Bradford) Aylor; m. Coy Cauthen; addition to Cemeteries of Grundy Co., Vol. 2, p. 670
Cawley, Charles Robert	Mar 05, 1932	Oct 11, 2020	Fall Creek Cem.; Son of Charles Raymond & Emma (Hoskins) Cawley; m. Joyce Sweeton
Cecil, Charles Walter	Aug 2, 1889	Jun 06, 1981	Airview Cem.; Son of Elbert Bisson & Helena "Lennie" (Hurst) Cecil; m. Matilda Belle Bolen; addition to Cemeteries of Grundy Co, Vol. 1, p. 7
Cecil, Matilda Belle (Bolen)	Oct 21, 1886	Sep 08, 1964	Airview Cem.; Dau. of Franklin & Matilda (Fuller) Bolen; m. Charles Walter Cecil; addition to Cemeteries of Grundy Co, Vol. 1, p. 7
Chambers, Alma (Fults)	1919	Jun 13, 2014	Cremated; Dau of Jefferson Davis & Annie Fults; m. William W. Chambers
Chambers, Barbara Jean (Meeks)	Sep 04, 1941	Oct 05, 2019	Mt. View Cem.; Dau. of John & Eula Mae Meeks; m. 1) Tigue 2) Chambers

Name	Born	Died	Notes
Champion, Benjamin			Monteagle Cem.; possible Gordon Champion family member; correction of Grundy County Cemetery Book Vol. 1; name
Champion, Danny Ray	1956	Oct 16, 2021	Cremated; Son of Jimmy & Ruth Champion
Champion, Scott			Monteagle Cem.; possible William Champion family member; Cemeteries of Grundy County Vol. 1
Chapman, William R.	Jun 14, 1916	Jan 04, 1973	Monteagle Cem.; Son of John Rosco & Maurine Chapman; m. Helen Elizabeth Austin; Florida Pvt Co B Inf WWII; addition to Cemeteries of Grundy Co.Vol. 1, p. 447
Chatham, Sharan Claudette (Riddle)	Jun 24, 1956	Jul 11, 2020	Warren "Red Hill" Cem.; Dau. of Billy Reid & Jayne Carolyn (Patterson) Riddle; m. Steve Chatham; lived in Huntsville, AL
Chatham, Steve	living when information was gathered Oct. 28, 2023		Warren "Red Hill" Cem.; m. Sharon Claudette Riddle
Cheek, Eric Carter	Oct 01, 1973	Jul 18, 2018	Tracy City Cem.; Son of James & LaNea (Geary) Cheek
Chester, Samuel Hall, Jr. (born III)	Dec 16, 1927	Dec 29, 2017	Cremated; Son of Samuel Hall, Sr. & Temperance Ransom Hudson Chester; m. Bettie Martin Thomas
Childers, Alton Thomas	Sep 08, 1970	May 24, 2016	Gardens of Memory; Son of Lois & Mary (Keener) Childers; m. Tina Melson
Childers, Annie Myrtle (Richardson)	May 29, 1928	Apr 28, 2014	Altamont Cem.; Dau. of McKinley & Elease (Walker) Richardson
Childers, Charles Edwin	Jul 30, 1952	Jul 26, 2019	Altamont Cem.; Son of Gordon & Marzee (Dickerson) Childers; m. Linda Sue Hobbs
Childers, Edna May (Smith)	Jul 15, 1920	Apr 27, 1990	Bonny Oak Cem.; Dau. of Robert Taylor & Mary Jane "Mollie" (Church) Smith; m. Raymond L. Childers; addition to Cemeteries of Grundy Co.Vol. 1, p. 82
Childers, George S.	1880	1954	Bonny Oak Cem.; died of malnutrition among other things; m. Ida Pickett; Source *Mrs. Grundy* Jan 6, 1916
Childers, Infant	1918	1918	Buried at home near Coalmont; Child of Robert Lee Childers & Tressie Powell
Childers, Irene (Hodges)	Jul 11, 1932	May 11, 2017	Airview Cem.; Dau. of Gurna Daniel & Nellie Laura (Hollars) Hodges of NC; addition to Cemeteries of Grundy Co,Vol. 1, p. 4
Childers, James Eric	1972	Aug 03, 2014	Gregg Cem.; Son of Bill & Glenda Childers; Army
Childers, Jason Roland	1975	Sep 01, 2019	Plainview Cem.; Son of Jack & Mae Childers; m. Veda M. Childers

Name	Born	Died	Notes
Childers, Maggie (Henley)	Jan 29, 1900	Feb 21, 1989	Warren "Red Hill" Cem.; Dau. of James Campbell & Estella (Parks) Henley; m. Perry Childers; Cemeteries of Grundy County, Vol 2, p. 946
Childers, Marguerite (Dickerson)	Jun 30, 1936	Feb 22, 2019	Bonnie Oak Cem.; Dau. of Ame Dickerson & Sally Givens; m. Golan Childe
Childers, Martha	1964	Aug 18, 2019	Bonny Oak Cem.; Dau. of Golan & Marguerite (Dickerson) Childers
Childers, Richard Gwinn	Sep 04, 1952	Jan 14, 2018	Cremated; Son of Richard Henry Childers & Annie Myrtle Richardson; m. Pok Cha Kim; US Army
Childers, Richard Henry	Jun 25, 1931	Aug 19, 1994	Altamont Cem.; Son of Thomas Edward & Lena (King) Childers; m. Annie Myrtle Richardson; Correction of parents' names; addition to Cemeteries of Grundy Co.,Vol. 1, p. 18
Childers, Susie M. (Brown)	Sep 15, 1924	Jun 14, 2013	Bonny Oak Cem.; Dau. of Burton & Nellie (Frederick) Brown; m. Louis Woodrow Childers; addition to Cemeteries of Grundy Co. Vol. 1, p. 94
Childers, Synthia A.	Dec 13, 1877	May 13, 1902	Bonny Oak Cem.; Dau. of John & Margaret (Meeks) Sweeton; m. Ed Childers on Aug 30, 1896; correction of parents' names by family & addition to Cemeteries of Grundy Co.,Vol. 1, p. 75
Childers, William Rufus, Sr.	Jun 24, 1897	Jul 04, 1973	Altamont Cem.; Son of Ed & Synthia (Sweeton) Childers; m. Lily May Woodlee; correction of mother's name; addition to Cemeteries of Grundy Co.Vol. 1, p. 18
Childress or Childers, Infant		Jan 02, 1916	Parson Graveyard/Bonny Oak Cem.; Child of George & Ida Childers/Childress; source *Mrs. Grundy*, Jan 6, 1916
Christian, Linda Mae	Sep 20, 1949	Aug 14, 2016	Palmer Cem.; Dau. of Jack Jones & Margaret (Simpson) Dishroom; m. Mitchell Christian
Christian, Lisa Dawn (King)	May 19, 1970	Feb 02, 2015	Mt. Carmel Cem.; Dau. of Dwight & Myrna (Tate) King; m. David Christian
Christian, Rachel B. (Beitia)	Nov 27, 1923	Nov 01, 2013	Wesley Chapel Cem.; Dau. of Cosme & Julia (Aroyo) Beitia; m. Vaughn Worth Christian; children Roddy, Susie, Sandy, Sonia, Fletcher, Charlotte; addition to Cemeteries of Grundy Co,Vol. 2, p. 991
Christian, Vaughn Worth	Feb 05, 1920	Mar 19, 2009	Wesley Chapel Cem.; Son of Doyle Worth & Kate (Bonner) Christian; m. Rachel Beitia; addition to Cemeteries of Grundy Co,Vol. 2, p. 991
Christman, William Melvin	Ca 1947	Jun 02, 2013	Little Creek Cem.; Son of Earl & Kate Christman; m. Patricia Holt

Name	Born	Died	Notes
Church, Iva Jean	May 23, 1931	Sep 16, 2017	Cumberland View Cem.; Dau. of Spencer Burton & Nellie (Fredrick) Brown; m. Martin Church, Jr.
Church, Nervie Louisa Adaline Jane (Parsons)	Aug 4, 1880	Oct 22, 1957	Plainview Cem.; Dau. of Lewis Elsbery & Mary Adaline (Boland) Parsons; m. John Henry O. Church; addition to Cemeteries of Grundy Co, Vol. 2, p.682
Church, Sydney (Layne)	Dec 01, 1932	Mar 16, 2013	Plainview Cem.; Dau. of Leander & Francis (Tate) Layne; m. John Kenneth "Buc" Church; addition to Cemeteries of Grundy Co. Vol. 2, p. 703
Clark, Ada Florence (Leak)	May 09, 1938	Oct 19, 2017	Airview Cem.; Dau. of George & Maxine (Large) Leak; m. Donald R. Clark; addition to Cemeteries of Grundy Co, Vol. 1, p. 8
Clark, Brenda Joyce (Johnson)	Feb 04, 1950	Jan 01, 2016	Cremated; Dau. of Claude & Goldie (Payne) Johnson; companion 38 yrs. Evalardo "Joe" Ortiz
Clark, Donald R.	Nov 22, 1927	Oct 06, 2015	Airview Cem.; Son of Claude & Earle (Hanson) Clark; m. Ada Florence Leak; Navy WW II, & Korea; addition to Cemeteries of Grundy Co. Vol. 1, p. 8
Clark, Doris (Pearson)	May 30, 1930	Oct 11, 2004	Plainview Cem.; Dau. of Bennie & Grace Estella (Scott) Pearson; m. John Ray Clark on Jan 17, 1947; addition to Cemeteries of Grundy Co., Vol. 2, p. 701
Clark, Earl Wayne	Dec 05, 1938	May 18, 2019	Body donated to Vanderbilt Medical Center; Son of John Overton & Edna Earl (Turner) Clark; m. Peggy Carol Henshaw
Clark, Gerald "Jerry" Wayne	Jun 18, 1952	Feb 17, 2020	Pelham Church of Christ Cem.; Son of Riley Clark & Lorraine Owens; m. Nancy O'Neal Brandon
Clark, H.		infant	Pelham Church of Christ Cem.; Son of Martin B. & Mary Ethel (Gallagher) Clark
Clark, James William	Apr 20, 1930	Mar 06, 2017	Plainview Cem.; Son of James & Allie Clark; never married
Clark, Logan James Brock	Nov 04, 2018	Jan 19, 2019	Cremated; Son of Brandon Ferrell & Lades Campbell
Clark, Nancy O'Neal (Brandon)	May 01, 1956	Apr 21, 2017	Pelham Church of Christ Cem.; Dau. of O'Neal & Josephine Elizabeth (Keel) Brandon; m. Gerald "Jerry" Wayne Clark
Clay, George Harris, Jr.	Feb 13, 1958	Jan 15, 2015	Orange Hill Cem.; Son of George Harris "G.H.", Sr. & Elizabeth (Bouldin) Clay; m. Susan Thompson from KY; U.S. Army
Clay, Kenneth Ray	Sep 06, 1983	Feb 27, 2018	Cremated; Son of Wayne Clay & Lottie Meeks
Clay, Ralph C	Jun 06, 1935	Feb 12, 2018	Cremated; Son of Garnett Clay & Hilda Hazel Campbell; m Deloris Clay

Name	Born	Died	Notes
Clay, Selby (Henley)	Jun 12, 1923	Jan 10, 2015	Warren "Red Hill" Cem.; Dau. of Clarence H. & Dessie (Sanders) Henley; m. Elston Clay; Aug 12, 1939; addition to Cemeteries of Grundy Co,Vol. 2, p. 957
Clay, Wayne	Dec 11, 1942	Apr 16, 2015	Warren "Red Hill" Cem.; Son of Elston & Selby (Henley) Clay; m. Lottie Meeks
Cleek, Alpha Gay (Dishroon)	Apr 12, 1935	Mar 24, 2018	Palmer Cem.; Dau. of Ernest B. Dishroon & Hazel Graham; m. Gene Cleek
Cleek, Arnold	Aug 27, 1936	Jun 14, 2019	Palmer Cem.; Son of John Cleek, Jr. & Louvine Elizabeth Shrum; m. Patricia Marie Scissom
Cleek, Bill Falls	Mar 27, 1929	May 20, 2017	Fall Creek Cem.; Son of Hearl & Lillie L (Ross) Cleek; m. Helen Caldwell
Cleek, Charles Clayton	Mar 25, 1926	Mar 20, 1999	Palmer Cem.; Son of Hearl F. & Lillie L (Ross) Cleek; m. Venova M. Cannon; S1 US Navy, WWII; addition to Cemeteries of Grundy Co,Vol. 2, p. 566
Cleek, Gene	Apr 30, 1936	Jul 25, 2013	Palmer City Cem.; Son of Hearl & Lillie L (Ross) Cleek ; m. Alpha Gay Dishroon
Cleek, Hazel Ruth (Crisp)	Apr 12, 1939	Aug 26, 2016	Palmer Cem.; Dau. of Fred & Lennie Bell (Weir) Crisp; m. Marion Mitchell Crisp Aug 15, 1980; addition to Cemeteries of Grundy Co.,Vol. 2, p. 567
Cleek, Kollins Ryann	May 01, 2020	May 01, 2020	Palmer Cem.; Dau. of Charles Dakota Cleek & Keon Shiann Summers
Cleek, Leon Carl	Mar 11, 1930	Nov 11, 2016	Hicksite Cem. in Greensburg, IN; Son of John & Lizzie (Shrum) Cleek; m. Louise Nunley
Cleek, Melanie Ann	Sep 15, 1961	Jul 06, 2009	Palmer Cem.; Dau. of Billy Ed & Mildred (McDaniel) Phillips; addition to Cemeteries of Grundy Co.Vol. 2, p. 572
Cleek, Tammy Lou (Dent)	Oct 17, 1957	Jan 13, 2020	Palmer Cem.; Dau. of J.D. Dent & Nelson Faye Smith; m. Lonnie Cleek
Clemens, Patricia Faye "Pati" (Wolford)	May 21, 1930	Dec 15, 2019	Cremated; Dau. of Orville William & Ida Faye M. (Northstine) Wolford; m. Pat Clemens
Clements, Paul Raymond	Feb 17, 1913	Feb 03, 1990	Monteagle Cem.; Son of Ernest B. & Carol Bernice (Black) Clements; m. Vera Ruth Houpert; Correction to parents' names; Cemeteries of Grundy Co.;Vol. 1, p. 433
Clements, Vera Ruth (Houpert)	Sep 28, 1914	Mar 25, 1988	Monteagle Cem.; Dau. of Henry C. & Lora M. (Rader) Houpert; m. Paul Raymond Clements; correction to mother's name; Cemeteries of Grundy Co.Vol. 1, p. 433
Clemons, Cindy (Rackar)	Sep 09, 1955	Feb 13, 2022	Coalmont Cem.; Dau. of John Steve & Evie (Woodlee) Rackar; m. Jerry Wayne Clemons
Clemons, Leslie Clay	Jul 22, 1929	May 20, 2015	Palmer Cem.; Son of James and Rebecca (Peeks) Clemons; US Army

Name	Born	Died	Notes
Clendenon James Wiley	Jul 23, 1931	Apr 29, 2008	Altamont Cem.; Son of Ova Wiser & Lassie (Coppinger) Clendenon; m. Victoria Dickerson; addition to Cemeteries of Grundy Co.Vol. 1, p. 22
Clendenon, Jerry	Sep 01, 1961	Aug 14, 2016	Altamont Cem.; Son of J.W. & Victoria (Dickerson) Clendenon
Clendenon, Lucille (Sanders)	Jul 22, 1944	Apr 24, 2013	Palmer Cem.; Dau. of Henry James & Ethel Mae (Scott) Sanders; m. Junior Clendenon
Clepper, Rebecca "Beck"	1875	Feb 20, 1922	Warren "Red Hill" Cem.; Dau. of Thomas W. Clepper & Martha Jane Gilliam; from *Mrs. Grundy*
Cleveland, Susan Joyce (Douglas)	Jun 10, 1957	Oct 14, 2018	Cremated; Dau. of Charles Mitchell Douglas & Ruth Clydene Gross; from Tracy City; m. Richard Cleveland
Click, Pamela Sue	Aug 11, 1958	May 11, 2021	Cremated; Dau. of Paul Ronald & Nancy Ocie Olla (Meeks) Click; her parents from Payne's Cove
Coalson, David	Dec 25, 1771	Aug 12, 1840	Coulson/Wesley Chapel Cem.; Son of James Coulson; m. Sarah Cox
Coalson, Sarah (Cox)	Feb 26, 1778	Apr 21, 1840	Coulson/Wesley Chapel Cem.; Dau. of William Cox
Coats, Thomas Eugene, Jr.	Oct 22, 1945	May 20, 2016	Warren "Red Hill" Cem.askes buried; Son of Thomas Eugene, Sr., & Flora Louise (Moore) Coats; m. Linda Janelle Layne; US Air Force
Cofer, Mary Helen (Garrett)	Dec 17, 1923	Oct 15, 2015	Mt. Garner Cem.; Dau. of Olvy J. & Otha Dale (Smith) Garrett
Coffelt, Bessie Ann	Feb 13, 1934	Feb 13, 1934	Palmer Cem.; Dau. of Crip Wesley & Mattie (Roberts) Coffelt; addition to Cemeteries of Grundy Co,Vol. 2, p. 570
Coffelt, Betty Ruth (Creighton)	Nov 22, 1927	May 04, 2016	Palmer Cem.; Dau. of John A. & Mable (Hobbs) Creighton; m. Francis Marvin Lee "Leck" Coffelt
Coffelt, Bruce	Oct 07, 1948	Jul 27, 2013	Fall Creek Cem.; Son of Daniel & Rosa Nell (Brewer) Coffelt; m. Gail Coffelt; US Army Vietnam
Coffelt, Christina Leigh Danelle	Jul 19, 1992	May 05, 2020	Palmer Cem.; Dau. of James Allen Coffelt & Erica Caldwell
Coffelt, Dorcas (Shadrick)	Nov 11, 1946	Jul 27, 2021	Griffiths Creek Cem.; Dau. of Carl Alton & Gracie Mae (Green) Shadrick; m. John Henry Coffelt
Coffelt, Francis Marvin Lee "Leck"	Mar 06, 1924	May 04, 2016	Palmer Cem.; Son of Crip Wesley & Mattie (Roberts) Coffelt; m. Betty Ruth Creighton; US Army WWII
Coffelt, Frankie Mae	Oct 23, 1914	Nov 21, 1989	Palmer Cem.; Dau. of Crip Wesley & Mattie (Roberts) Coffelt; Correction to Cemeteries of Grundy Co.,Vol. 2, p. 570

Name	Birth	Death	Notes
Coffelt, James H. "Cork"	Apr 27, 1958	Jul 20, 2014	Swiss Colony Cem; Son of Amos Henry Coffelt & Violet Lucille Smith; m. Sandra Sue Caldwell
Coffelt, Louie Hershel	Apr 17, 1927	Sep 25, 2007	Palmer Cem.; Son of Crip Wesley & Mattie (Roberts) Coffelt; CPL USAAF WWII; correction to parents' names in Cemeteries of Grundy Co. Vol. 2, p. 570
Coffelt, Luelda	Oct 26, 1919	Apr 28, 1924	Bonny Oak Cem.; Dau. of Crip Wesley & Mattie (Roberts) Coffelt; correction of parents' names by family; Cemeteries of Grundy Co. ,Vol. 1, p. 72
Coffelt, Mattie (Roberts)	Apr 07, 1892	Apr 29, 1991	Palmer Cem.; Dau. of Amos & Mollie (Anderson) Roberts; Cemeteries of Grundy County,Vol. 2, p. 570 correction
Coffelt, Patricia Ann "Pat" (Shaffer)	Feb 13, 1942	living May 9, 2023	Palmer Cem.; Dau. of Harley Wayne & Edna (Halstead) Shaffer from Indiana; m. Bob Coffelt; addition to Cemeteries of Grundy Co,Vol. 2, p. 571
Coffelt, Robbie Wayne	Jul 19, 1961	Jan 26, 2020	Cremated; Son of Robert Edward Coffelt & Patricia Ann Shaffer
Coffelt, Violet (Smith)	May 30, 1921	Oct 08, 2001	Palmer Cem.; Dau. of John & Minnie (Nunley) Smith; m. Amos Coffelt; addition to Cemeteries of Grundy Co.,Vol. 2, p. 570
Coggle, Judy Tessa	May 14, 1934	Dec 26, 2015	Cumberland Mennonite Fellowship Cem.; Dau. of Kenneth & Phyllis (Anstey) Coggle; m. Michael J.R. Clayton in Jul 1956
Cole, Arthur Carman, DD	1869	May 07, 1941	Cremated; buried in front of DuBose School in Monteagle; Son of Daniel H, & Celia (Francis) Cole; m. Ada Cole, a professor
Coll, Albert George	Nov 04, 1920	Aug 18, 2002	Plainview Cem.; Son of Hugh Aloysius & Nellie Elizabeth (Stacey) Coll, m. Charlotte Maybell Sartain; US NAVY WWII; correction and addition to Cemeteries of Grundy Co.Vol. 2, p. 695
Collier, Rosa Beatrice (Rosendaul)	Feb 05, 1921	Sep 02, 1999	Cumberlanad Heights Cem.; Dau. of Albert Ellsworth & Arminta Estella (Gnagey) Rosendaul; m. Roscoe Ivan Collier; addition to Cemeteries of Grundy Co.Vol. 1, p. 196
Collier, Wiley Carter, Jr.	Nov 22, 1953	Mar 01, 2016	Cremated; Son of Wiley Carter, Sr. & Joan Collier; m. Ruth Ann Collier; US Navy
Collings, Joshua David	Ca 1995	Dec 15, 2015	Cremated; Son of Daniel & Stephanie (Rowland) Collings
Collins, Carl Leon	May 19, 1920	Nov 17, 1951	Coalmont Cem.; Son of John B. & Sarah Elizabeth "Lizzie" (Godsby) Collins; TN PFC 562 AAA AW BN CAC WWII; addition to Vol. 1, p. 187
Collins, Edward Rayburn, Sr.	Apr 12, 1942	Jul 11, 2002	Palmer Cem.; Son of Eunice Collins; m. Jerel "Judy" James; US Army, Cemeteries of Grundy Co.Vol. 2, p. 563

Collins, Girlie (Sims)	Mar 01, 1904	Jul 09, 1994	Airview Cem.; Dau. of James Albert & Missouri Cordelia (Lawson) Sims; m. Eunice Colling; addition to Cemeteries of Grundy Co,Vol. 1, p. 5
Collins, Harold Lee	Mar 06, 1943	Dec 09, 2020	Plainview Cem.; Son of Eunice & Girlie (Sims) Collins; m. Linda "Sue" Collins
Collins, Isaac M.	Apr 24, 1824	Jul 9, 1899	Unidentified Cem.; m. Elizabeth Davidson; father of Maria Evelyn (Collins) Mabee; no stone
Collins, Jeffery Glenn	Nov 14, 1974	Jul 15, 2021	AirView Cem.; Son of James Lionell "Hard Knot" and Martha A. Collins
Collins, Jennifer Rae	Apr 01, 1973	May 09, 2013	Cremated; Dau. of James Ray & Bobbie (Gilliam) Collins ; comp. Joey Jackson
Collins, Jewel "Judy" (James)	Oct 25, 1939		Palmer Cem.; Dau. of Marvin & Vinnie (Crabtree) James; addition to Cemeteries of Grundy Co, Vol, 2, p. 563
Collins, John E.	Ca 1943	Nov 10, 2016	Cremated; Son of John & Annie Collins; m. Carol Collins; US Army
Collins, Johnny B.	Sep 1, 1880	Oct 11, 1880	Coalmont Cem.;Son of William D & Sally A (Gipson) Collins; correction to Cemeteries of Grundy County, Vol.1, p. 187
Collins, Johnny Ray	Mar 16, 1935	Feb 20, 1974	Coalmont Cem.; Son of Johnny B & Lizzie (Godsby) Collins; correction to Cemeteries of Grundy County,Vol. 1, p. 186
Collins, Joshua David	Ca 1995	Dec 15, 2015	Cremated; Son of Daniel & Stephanie (Rowland) Collins
Collins, Maryon Virginia	Dec 12, 1925	Nov 28, 2017	Univ of the South Cem.; Dau. of Lionel Moise & Maryon Mounts; m. David Browning Collins
Collins, William H.	Mar 4, 1862	Apr 29, 1937	Providence Methodist Cem.; Son of Thomas C. & Sarah A Collins; m. Ida Patterson Nov 5, 1913, in Grundy Co.; Addition to Cemeteries of Grundy Co,Vol. 2, p. 710
Comer, Shelby LeAnn	Oct 23, 1997	Dec 23, 2017	Grace Chapel Cem.; Dau. of Ray Comer & Mary Nabors
Comfort, Misty Carol	Feb 11, 1977	Feb 11, 2022	Philadelphia Cem.; Dau. of William & Lola Mae Comfort
Comfort, William Conway	Aug 21, 1929	Sep 26, 2021	Philadelphia Cem.; Son of James & Grace (Tate) Comfort; m. Lola Mae Fults; U.S. Air Force
Comstock, Harriet June (Hagelbarger)	1921	Apr 01, 2019	Union Grove Cem. Gambier, OH; Dau. of Walter J. Hagelbarger & Cora Jane Workman; m. Lester Ray Comstock
Comstock, Lester Ray	Sep 08, 1923	Jan 11, 2016	Union Grove Cem. Gambier, OH; Son of Lewis Raymond & Oddie (Dailey) Comstock; m. Harriet June Hagelbarger; US Army WWII
Condra, Alvin D.	Sep 04, 1950	Jul 09, 1974	Coalmont Cem.; Son of John Douglas & Shirley Ruth (Meeks) Condra

Name	Born	Died	Details
Condra, Carl Eugene	Jan 22, 1947	Jul 11, 2021	Monteagle Cem.; Son of Charles & Grace Condra; m. Carolyn Jane Wesley
Condra, Thurman Eugene	Sep 20, 1922	Aug 15, 1923	Monteagle Cem.; Son of Edward Lafayette "Fate" Condra & Rhoda Lee O'Dear; Vol. 1, p. 400; addition of middle name
Conn, A.M. "Jack"	Nov 06, 1927	May 30, 2013	Mt. Garner Cem.; Son Mark G & Ethel (Brazier) Conn; m. Edna Brazile; USMC
Connell, Earl Stanley	Sep 14, 1922	May 02, 1999	Swiss Memorial Cem.; Son of Thomas Nathaniel & Bessie (Coggins) Connell; m. Minnie Stampfli on Nov 17, 1946; CPL US Army Air Force; addition to Cemeteries of Grundy Co,Vol. 2, p.791
Conner, Frank	Feb 02, 1913	Sep 15, 1994	Coalmont Cem.; Son of Whitt & Elzora Conner; correction to Cemeteries of Grundy County,Vol. 1, p. 175
Conry, Carl William	Jul 26, 1939	Aug 28, 2020	Plainview Cem.; Son of Carl Eugene Conry & Willie Mae Anderson; m. 1) Ameda Lawrence 2) Dalpha Meeks 3) Polly Layne; USMC
Conry, Daniel Campbell "Cam"	Mar 29, 1899	Feb 24, 1962	Warren "Red Hill" Cem.; Son of James R. & Margaret (Hargis) Conry; m. Lorene Wilson; Correction to Cemeteries of Grundy County,Vol. 2, p. 936
Conry, Danny Brice	Jun 30, 1953	Mar 07, 1963	Fall Creek Cem.; Son of Duncan & Luella (Brown) Conry
Conry, Ernest James, Sr.	Aug 27, 1923	Jan 17, 1987	Monteagle Cem.; Son of Oscar Franklin & Mary Agnes (Meeks) Aylor; m. Elwanda Louise Aylor ; Cemeteries of Grundy Co. ,Vol. 1 correction; p. 461
Conry, Ernest, Jr.	Jun 05, 1947	Jul 12, 2021	East Tennessee Veterans Cem.; Son of Ernest & Elwanda (Aylor) Conry; m. Tammy Jo Conry; U.S. Air Force
Conry, Mike E., Jr.	Apr 14, 1927	Oct 01, 2021	Hamilton Memorial Gardens; Son of Mike & Allie Conry; m. Bessie Conry
Conry, Mike Emmett	Apr 27, 1891	Mar 09, 1957	Warren "Red Hill" Cem.; Son of James R. & Margaret (Hargis) Conry; m. Allie White (Caldwell); correction of Margaret's surname & addition to Cemeteries of Grundy Co,Vol. 2, p. 936
Cook, Sara Josephine (Sain)	Sep 30, 1850	Mar 23, 1903	Wesley Chapel Cem.; Dau. of Thomas Finneran & Mary Ann (Adams) Sain; m. Henry C. Cook, Sep 24, 1868; addition to Cemeteries of Grundy Co.,Vol. 2, p. 983
Cook, Wanda Lee (Nunley)	Jul 25, 1936	Apr 17, 2019	Plainview Cem.; Dau. of Alvin Nunley & Maggie Caldwell; m. Charles M. Cook
Cooke, Paul Gene	Sep 23, 1939	Oct 08, 2016	Cremated; Son of Arthur & Edna C. Cooke; m. Barbara Meeks; US Marine Corps

Name	Birth	Death	Details
Cookston, Emmett Kelly	Jun 23, 1925	Jun 23, 1925	White Cem.; Son of George Washington & Josephine (White) Cookston; addition to Cemeteries of Grundy Co.Vol. 2, p. 1012
Cookston, George Washington	Feb 2, 1870	Feb 08, 1938	White Cem.; Son of Leonard & Martha (Killian) Cookston; m Josephine White; addition to Cemeteries of Grundy Co.Vol. 2, p. 1012
Cookston, Opal (Rogers)	Apr 10, 1905	Jun 15, 1905	White Cem.; Dau. of Bert B. & Mildred (Higdon) Rogers; m.1) Joe Seagroves 2) William Stone "Buck" Cookston; addition to Cemeteries of Gundy Co.Vol. 2, p. 1013
Cooper, Barry Bradley	May 11, 1951	Oct 16, 2020	Cremated; Son of John Nathan & Jane (Bradley) Cooper; m. Vickie Lynn Martin
Cooper, Donnie Edwin "Duck"	Jun 30, 1973	Apr 29, 2022	Fall Creek Cem.; Son of Danny & Ann (Burnett) Cooper; m. Cristal Pickett
Cooper, Herbert Chris, Jr.	Sep 27, 1967	Jan 23, 2022	Coalmont Cem.; Son of Herbie & Christine (Nunley) Cooper
Cooper, Jannie D. (Dickinson)	Sep 28, 1893	May 18, 1966	Fall Creek Cem.; Dau. of Joe & Dorothy (Marshall) Dickinson
Cooper, Jerry Wayne	Aug 06, 1948	Mar 21, 2020	Gardens of Memory Cem.; Son of J.W. Cooper & Theonia Ruth LeFevers; m. Lisa Powers; Tennessee National Guard
Cooper, Molt B.	Sep 24, 1889	Jun 24, 1964	Fall Creek Cem.; Son of Alex & Claria (Shepherd) Cooper; m. Jamie Dickinson
Cope, Martin	Feb 28, 1866	Sep 25, 1894	Tracy City Cem.; Son of William & Piney Angeline (Sanders) Cope; m. Mollie Gilley, who is buried in Section 6.; Addition to Cemeteries of Grundy Co.Vol. 2, p. 898
Copeland, Archie	Nov 30, 1896	Feb 15, 1971	Plainview Cem.; Son of Campbell Washington & Ludora (Sevier) Copeland m. Nora White; addition to Cemeteries of Grundy Co,Vol. 2, p. 685
Copeland, Charlotte Darlene (O'Neal)	Feb 14, 1973	Feb 07, 2022	Cremated; Dau. of Elbert & Bettie Sue O'Neal; m. Ronnie Copeland
Copeland, Jason Lee	Jan 01, 1986	Jan 15, 2022	Cremated; Son of Bill & Rose Copeland & Charlie Anderson; m. Sheila Copeland
Copeland, Jim	Aug 1934	Dec 13, 2014	Plainview Cem; Son of Archie & Nora (White) Copeland; m. Lillie Mae Parsons
Copeland, Lillie Mae (Parsons)	1927	Sep 02, 2018	Plainview Cem.; Dau. of Elmer Parsons & Mozella Hampton; m. Jim Copeland
Copeland, Nora (White)	Nov 15, 1898	Oct 17, 1986	Plainview Cem.; Dau. of Christopher C. & Selina Vestina (Gunnels) White; m. Archie Copeland; addition to Cemeteries of Grundy Co, Vol. 2, p. 685
Copeland, Skyler Gauge	Dec 07, 2001	Jun 01, 2019	Plainview Cem.; Son of Jason Lee & Jamie Copeland

Name	Birth	Death	Details
Copeland, Walter Garfield	May 28, 1928	May 25, 1998	Lappin Cem.; Son of John M. & Beatrice (Byrd) Copeland; m. Alva Pauline Yokely; addition to Cemeteries of Grundy Co.Vol. 1, p. 359
Coppinger, Benny Eugene	Sep 08, 1943	Jun 01, 2020	Palmer Cem.; Son of James Paul Coppinger & Mary Catherine Tate; m. Linda Hobbs
Coppinger, Dollie Etta (Foster)	May 21, 1872	Mar 04, 1945	Gregg Cem.; Dau. of James F. & Martha (Sellars) Foster; m. George Anthony Coppinger; addition to Cemeteries of Grundy Co.;Vol. 1; p 304
Coppinger, Faye (Johnson)	Apr 20, 1944	Jun 26, 2020	Gregg Cem.; Dau. of Roy & Hazel Johnson; m. George Coppinger
Coppinger, Frank Marshall, Jr.	Jun 12, 1943	Jan 01, 2018	Philadelphia Cem.; Son of Frank Marshall & Stella Margie Gross; m. Gloria Caudill
Coppinger, Gene	Feb 02, 1951	Jul 27, 2020	Fults Cem.; Son of Bobby Coppinger & Julie Myers; m. Evelyn Scott
Coppinger, Margaret E. "Maggie" (Meadows)	Jan 24, 1903	Dec 15, 1995	Gregg Cem.; Dau. of William Henry & Maudie (Sanders) "Maggie" Meadows; m. Clarence G. Coppinger; addition to Cemeteries of Grundy Co.Vol. 1, p. 308
Coppinger, Mary "Molly" (Purdom)	Sep 1848	Jul 01, 1904	Savage Gulf Schoolhouse Cem.; Dau. of Wilson & Lydia (Fults) Purdom; wife of David Coppinger and is presumed to be buried next to her husband, but there is not a tombstone naming her. Addition to Cemeteries of Grundy Co.Vol. 2, p. 741
Coppinger, Wanda L	1963	Sep 03, 2018	Gregg Cem.; Dau. of George A Willard & Faye Coppinger
Corbaley, Ida M. (Garner)	Dec 21, 1871	Mar 04, 1954	Altamont Cem.; Dau. of David Smith & Martha (Wall) Garner; m. Elder F.M. Corbaley; addition to Cemeteries of Grundy Co,Vol. 1, p. 18
Cordell, Joe Laster	Oct 16, 1881	Dec 01, 1920	Brown's Chapel Cem.; Son of John Cross & Ada (Hicks) Cordell; m. Clara Matilda Fisher; addition to Cemeteries of Grundy Co. Vol, 1, p. 109
Cordell, Joyce	Jan 24, 1932	Sep 18, 2015	Brown's Chapel Cem.; Dau. of Herman & Maudie (Sehorne) Brown; m. Charles Clifford Cordell
Cordova, April Dawn (Guess)	Apr 17, 1967	Dec 14, 2013	Cremated; Dau. of Ed Gullie & Mildred "Mickie" Guess; m: Thomas Cordova
Cottrell, Kenneth F. "Ken"	Aug 12, 1954	Dec 13, 1995	Fall Creek Cem.; Son of Velma Hawkins
Coulson, Alexander	1806	1872	Burkett's Chapel Cem.; Son of of David C & Sarah (Cox) Coulson; m. Margaret Abigail Myers; known to be buried here, but there is no tombstone; addition to Cemeteries of Grundy Co. ,Vol. 1, p. 125

Name	Born	Died	Notes
Coutu, Richard Brian	Apr 17, 1972	Dec 09, 1978	Palmer Cem.; Son of Euclid & Mary (Thebault) Coutu; m. Ethel Loraine Flake; died in a fire with wife; addition to Cemeteries of Grundy Co, Vol. 2 p. 571
Cowan, Michael, DDS	May 23, 1948	Mar 26, 2016	National Cemetery Chattanooga, TN; Son of Leland & Francis Cowan; m. Marsha Cowan
Cox, Amanda M.	Jan 26, 1974	May 11, 1986	Swiss Colony Cem.; Dau. of Grady Lockhart & Bonnie Cox; addition to Cemeteries of Grundy Co. Vol. 2, p. 791
Cox, Carol Ann	Dec 17, 1964	May 01, 2013	Fults Cem.; Dau. of Richard & Sally (Knapp) Dodge; m. William Cox
Cox, Daisy Mae (Crabtree)	1950	Feb 20, 2020	Humphrey's Cem., Ft. Oglethorpe; Dau. of Duck Crabtree & Minnie Guffey; m. Charles Daniel Cox
Cox, Eddie Junior "Dickie"	Sep 25, 1957	Nov 09, 2013	Swiss Cem.; Son of Carolyn Sue (Morrison) Cox; m. Kathy Borne; TN Air National Guard
Cox, Elsie (McCormack)	Feb 18, 1936	Jul 24, 2019	Mt. Zion Cem.; Dau. of Tommie Lester McCormack & Elisa Ophia Womack; m. Seabert Price
Cox, Estil Kelly (Dove)	May 29, 1928	Feb 15, 2015	Dove/Harris Cem.; Dau. of Avery Jordan, Sr. & Callie Estil (Dove) Cox; m. Ferrell Dean Cox; addition to Cemeteries of Grundy Co., Vol, 1, p. 201
Cox, Ferrell Dean	Aug 01, 1926	Apr 12, 2010	Dove/Harris Cem.; Son of Charles E. & Helen Jeanette (Furlong) Cox; m Estil Kelly Dove; PHM3 US Navy WWII; addition to Cemeteries of Grundy Co. Vol. 1, p. 201
Cox, Frank Vestal	Jun 20, 1937	Nov 16, 2007	Altamont Cem.; Son of William Warfield & Catherine (Stevenson) Cox; addition to Cemeteries of Grundy Co, Vol, 1, p. 15
Cox, George William	Dec 01, 1867	Aug 05, 1952	Monteagle Cem.; Son of James Arnold & Mary Jane Cox
Cox, Hallie Mae (Doss)	Apr 25, 1937	Mar 10, 2017	Griffith's Creek Cem.; Dau. of Sydney & Rosie (Layne) Doss; m. 1) Robert Slatton 2) Clyde Reagan 3) Wiley Cox
Cox, James Alex "Jamie"	ca 1907	Apr 12, 1956	Tracy City Cem.; Son of John Hardy & Susie Eller (Smith) Cox; m. Lucille Henley; no tombstone; addition to Cemeteries of Grundy Co. Vol. 2, p. 890
Cox, Jeffery Thomas	Jul 16, 1956	Sep 15, 2018	Palmer Cem.; Son of William Paul Cox & Mildred Tate Yarworth
Cox, John Edward	Mar 20, 1937	Aug 31, 2019	Swiss Colony Cem.; Son of James Cox and Edith Box; m. Charlestine Rogers
Cox, Lucille (Henley)	1909	1954	Tracy City Cem.; Dau. of Jacob & Rose (Scott) Henley; m. James Alex Cox; no tombstone ; addition to Cemeteries of Grundy Co. Vol. 2, p. 890

Name	Birth	Death	Details
Cox, Mary Albertine (Richmond)	Sep 23, 1868	Apr 27, 1933	Monteagle Cem.; Dau. of James H & Asbury Phoebe Anders (Steaman) Richmond; m. William Rush Cox; Nov 6, 1895; fieldstone marker only; addition to Cemeteries of Grundy Co.Vol. 1, p. 415
Cox, Mary E. (Sanders)		Oct 04, 1942	Palmer Cem.; Dau. of Henry James & Ethel (Scott) Sanders; m. Hoyt Cox; addition to Cemeteries of Grundy Co,Vol. 2, p. 561.
Crabtree, Anita June (Finch)	Jun 25, 1936	Jun 16, 2019	Palmer Cem.; Dau. of Hershel & Ruby (Gifford) Finch; m. L.B. "Noel" Finch; addition to Cemeteries of Grundy Co;Vol. 2, p. 567
Crabtree, Charles Edman	Jul 29, 1955	May 26, 2018	Palmer Cem.; Son of Alfred Edman Crabtree & Edna Gipson; m. Rita Smartt
Crabtree, Charles W.	Jun 10, 1896	Jul 20, 1981	Palmer Cem.; Son of Henry Simpson & Martha "Mattie" (Sanders) Crabtree; addition to Cemeteries of Grundy Co,Vol. 2, p. 571
Crabtree, Gabriela (Gomez)	Mar 31, 1980		Clouse Hill Cem.; Dau. of Gregorio & Graciela (Garza) Gomez; m. Kirby Earl Crabtree, Oct 31, 2010
Crabtree, Grace (Smartt)	Apr 20, 1908	Apr 18, 1996	Palmer Cem.; Dau. of James & Mary Estells Estora Leona (Sanders) Smartt; m. William Henry Crabtree, Sr.; addition & correction to Cemeteries of Grundy Co.,Vol. 2, p. 568
Crabtree, Johnny S.	Aug 06, 1954	Jul 08, 2016	Plainview Cem.; Son of Bruce & Lucretia (Thomas) Crabtree; US Navy
Crabtree, Kirby Earl	Nov 02, 1990		Clouse Hill Cem.; Son of Roxanne Crabtree & Daniel Wade Brown; m. Gabriela Gomez, Oct 31, 2010
Crabtree, Margaret (Summers)	Dec 29, 1936	Mar 20, 2012	Palmer Cem.; Dau. of Robert T. & Gladys (Barnett) Summers; m. William "Jip" Crabtree; addition to Cemeteries of Grundy Co,Vol. 2, p. 574
Crabtree, Roxanne	Jul 18, 1962	Aug 04, 2016	Coalmont Cem.; Dau. of Walter Earl & Rachel (Burrows) Crabtree
Crabtree, Walter Earl	Jan 27, 1941	Nov 01, 2007	Coalmont Cem.; Son of Walter Reed & Winnie Ella (Campbell) Crabtree; correction to Cemeteries of Grundy County, Vol. 1, p. 188
Crabtree, William E.	May 18, 1924	May 16, 1927	Bonny Oak Cem.; Son of Jerome Wilson & Lydia Frances (Scruggs) Crabtree; addition to Cemeteries of Grundy Co.,Vol. 1, p. 83
Crabtree, William Henry, Sr.	Nov 7, 1891	Oct 29, 2003	Palmer Cem.; Son of William Simpson, Sr. & Martha S. (Campbell) Crabtree; m. 1) May Smith on May 30, 1926; 2) Grace Smartt; addition correction to Cemeteries of Grundy Co.Vol. 2, p. 568
Creighton, Anna Polk	Feb 22, 1923	Dec 19, 2017	Chattanooga National Cem.; Dau. of James Polk & Anna Grace Rieder Conry; m. Earl Franklin Creighton

Name	Born	Died	Details
Creighton, Barbara Mae (Meeks)	Nov 03, 1941	Sep 20, 2021	Palmer Cem.; Dau. of Mart Clinton & Mary Juanita (Henderson) Meeks; m. Ralph Taylor Creighton
Creighton, Danny Steven	Oct 09, 1948	Jan 02, 2016	Summerfield Cem.; Son of Leona Creighton; m. Mary Creighton
Creighton, Ernestine "Tine" (Ross)	Jul 03, 1927	Jun 15, 2015	Coalmont Cem.; Dau. of John William "Bill" & True Ernestine Ross; m. Robert M. Creighton; Cemeteries of Grundy Co.,Vol. 1, p. 167 correction per informant
Creighton, Ethleen Gladys (Brown)	Mar 15, 1899	May 01, 1977	Coalmont Cem.; Dau. of Isaac Sanford & Maggie (Nunley) Brown; m. Robert Asa Creighton
Creighton, John A.	Apr 01, 1933	Mar 20, 2017	Palmer Cem.; Son of John & Mable (Hobbs) Creighton; m. Sue Pocus
Creighton, John Isaiah	Jul 02, 1930	Jan 21, 2022	Chattanooga National Cem.; Son of Morgan & Elizabeth (Perry) Creighton; m. Wanda Creighton; U.S. Navy
Creighton, Juanita Joan	Feb 21, 1937	Dec 29, 2016	Summerfield Cem.; Cremated Dau. of James Lee "Jim: & Elma/Elmo Lee (Vinson) Crawford; m. William David Creighton; Addition to Cemeteries of Grundy Co.,Vol. 2, p, 768
Creighton, Loretta (Sanders)	May 07, 1946	Sep 29, 2018	Fall Creek Cem.; Dau. of Secil Sanders & Ethel Johnson; m. Dick Creighton
Creighton, Lydia Leona (Brewer)	Aug 30, 1927	May 08, 2019	Summerfield Cem.; Dau. of Walter & Dona (Cagle) Brewer; m. Billy Jo Creighton; addition to Cemeteries of Grundy Co. Vol, 2, p 768
Creighton, Margaret L. (Cleek)	Apr 26, 1921	Feb 04, 2016	Plainview Cem.; Dau. of Dee & Susie (Tucker) Cleek; m. Tom Creighton
Creighton, Nicky Mason	Jan 22, 1937	Feb 06, 2020	Brown's Chapel Cem.; Son of Frank Earl Creighton & Myrtle Edith Brown; m. Darla Creighton
Creighton, Robert Asa	Mar 4, 1894	Nov 04, 1975	Coalmont Cem.; Son of William Morton & Susan (Killian) Creighton; m. Ethleen Gladys Brown
Creighton, Sherry Lois (Dills)	Feb 23, 1964	Feb 26, 2019	Fall Creek Cem.; Dau. of Buddy Ray Dills & Mary L. Dills; m. Keith Creighton
Creighton, Stacy D.	May 08, 1968	Mar 05, 2013	Fall Creek Cem.; Son of Dick & Loretta (Sanders) Creighton
Cribbs, Mollie (Meeks)	Feb 28, 1890	Feb 19, 1981	Bonny Oak Cem.; Dau. of James Donald "Don" & Sarah Lottie (Sanders) Meeks; m. 1) James Cribbs 2) Will Curtis; correction of surname spelling & addition to Cemeteries of Grundy Co.Vol. 1, p. 84

Name	Born	Died	Notes
Crick, Mary C. (Butler)	Apr 14, 1846	Nov 15, 1907	Tracy City Cem.; Dau. of David & Emily Butler; m. Jocob Powell Crick Feb 25, 1867, in Coffee Co, TN; addition to Cemeteries of Grundy Co.Vol. 2, p. 844
Crisp, Amelia (Stone)	Nov 28, 1855	Sep 03, 1918	Oak Grove Cem.; Dau. of William & Amanda (Brown) Stone; m. Thomas William Crisp; no tombstone- addition to Cemeteries of Grundy Co.Vol. 1, p. 512
Crisp, Bertha Elizabeth (Shrum)	Sep 20, 1933	Dec 10, 2018	Burns Cem.; Dau. of Oscar Shrum & Louella Caldwell; m. Frankie Crisp
Crisp, Carl "Squat"	Sep 16, 1926	Mar 18, 2015	Plainview Cem.; Son of Green Benny & Jennie Crisp; m. 1) Ida Mae Street 2) Joan Patterson
Crisp, Linda Carol	Apr 14, 1950	Aug 25, 2020	Pryor Ridge Cem.; Dau. of Lucille Worley Shrum; m. Lloyd Crisp
Crisp, W. Leon	Nov 30, 1924	Oct 20, 2015	Oak Grove Cem.; Son of Thomas & Lizzie (Nunley) Crisp; m. Hazel Kilgore
Crittenden, Harry Blake	Aug 22, 1959	Jan 20, 2018	Bonny Oak Cem.; Son of James Crittenden & Rendy Crittenden
Cronan, Vickie Rae	Apr 25, 1951	Dec 29, 2013	Cremated; Dau. of Vernon Ross & Jacqueline Mellen
Crosslin, Amy Celeste	1981	Sep 18, 2020	Cremated; Dau. of Dennis & Reba (Howell) Crosslin
Crosslin, Melanie Joyce	1959	May 28, 2017	Wesley Chapel Cem.; Son of John M. & Alma (Smartt) Collins; m. Ronald Crosslin
Crosslin, Richard	1949	Oct 01, 2019	Hillsboro Memorial Cem.; Son of Hoyt Cleve Crosslin & Alta Cordelia Wilson; m. Linda Willis
Crouch, Elizabeth "Betty" (White)	May 4, 1843	Nov 02, 1925	Warren "Red Hill" Cem.; Dau. of Robert Gilbert & Malines (Lowe) White, Sr.; m: Easter Mosley Crouch per death certificate; correction of parents' names & addition to Cemeteries of Grundy Co,Vol. 2, p. 926
Crouch, Feraby	1842	1888	Wesley Chapel Cem.; Dau. of William & Sarah (Fults) Crouch; Correction of name; Cemeteries of Grundy Co., Vol. 2, p. 1004
Crouch, Orin White, Sr.	Jul 22, 1925	Aug 08, 2017	Franklin Memorial Gardens Cem.; Son of Robert Lee & Mae Belle (Cole) Crouch; m. Betty Lynn; US Army
Crownover, Mary Anita "Ann"	Oct 08, 1935	Aug 23, 2018	Mt. Garner Cem.; Dau. of Robert Wilson Ashby & Ella Pearl Walker; m. Carl Edward Crownover; Ann was Pelham's Postmaster.
Crozier, Walter	Sep 1880	Jul 24, 1906	Oak Grove Cem.; Son of George & Ninnie Pauline (Baker) Crozier; shot by John Byers, a striking miner; no tombstone; Ancestry & newspaper source
Crutchfield, Joan "Bunny" (Nunley)	Jul 11, 1938	Dec 26, 2018	Cremated; Dau. of John Beecher & Abbye (Bryant) Nunley; m. Ward Crutchfield

Name	Birth	Death	Details
Cullinder, George D., Dr.	Jul 8, 1819	Oct 5, 1899	Old Baptist Cem.; Son of Henry & Mary Jane (Pile) Cullender; m. Mary C. Cullinder; died of typhoid fever; addition to Cemeteries of Grundy Co.Vol. 2, p. 518
Cullom, Robert Martin	1952	Feb 21, 2021	Cremated; Son of John & Wanda (McMahan) Cullum; m. Lynn Womble; U.S. Marines
Cunningham, Allen Howard	Oct 07, 1952	Jul 27, 2016	Fall Creek Cem.; Son of Shirley & Virginia (Burnett) Cunningham
Cunningham, Brandy Lynn	Jul 25, 1979	Apr 25, 2016	Clouse Hill Cem.; Dau. of Lanny & Brenda (Murray) Campbell
Cunningham, Cecil W.	Oct 01, 1923	Apr 17, 2016	Plainview Cem.; Son of Emmett & Ida (Brown) Cuningham; m. 1) Johnnie Marie Johnson 2) Minnie Murray; addition to Cemeteries of Grundy Co.,Vol. 2, p. 680
Cunningham, Infant			Clouse Hill Cem.; Dau. of Porter & Annie Lee (Gibbs) Cunningham
Cunningham, Minnie (Murray)	Jun 26, 1938	Dec 12, 2015	Plainview Cem.; Dau. of Thomas & Maude (Thorpe) Murray; m. Cecil Cunningham
Cunningham, Shirley	Jan 05, 1925	Nov 27, 2016	Fall Creek Cem.; Son of Webb & Sarah (Gipson) Cunningham; m. Virginia Burnett; US Navy, WWII
Cunningham, Toby James	Nov 23, 1971	Aug 28, 2020	Plainview Cem.; Son of Porter & Geneva Cunningham
Curtis, Arthur David	Mar 14, 1942	Aug 19, 2017	Palmer Cem.; Son of Arthur Roy & Estella (Woodlee) Curtis; m. Gertrude Campbell; USMC
Curtis, Audra Jewel (Brewer)	Oct 16, 1935	Sep 22, 2021	Brown's Chapel Cem.; Dau. of Walter & Dona (Cagle) Brewer; m. Jimmy Curtis
Curtis, Bessie Mae	Apr 15, 1932	May 05, 1933	Oak Grove Cem.; Dau. of Jerry Dewitt & Martha Rose "Mattie" (Green) Curtis; addition to Cemeteries of Grundy Co,Vol. 1, p. 500
Curtis, Darrell Gregory	1951	Sep 11, 2014	Orange Hill Cem.; Son of James Mitchell Curtis & Pauline Keel; Deborah Hampton
Curtis, David Wesley	1920	1922	Oak Grove Cem.; Son of Jerry Dewitt & Martha Rose "Mattie" (Green) Curtis; addition to Cemeteries of Grundy Co,Vol. 1, p. 500
Curtis, Haley Denise	Nov 02, 1993	Jun 18, 2017	Coalmont Cem.; Dau. of Kevin Wise & Shannon Curtis; never married
Curtis, Hershel	May 17, 1917	Nov 18, 2016	Oak Grove Cem.; Son of Dee & Mattie Cutis; m. Louise Nunley; US Army, WWII
Curtis, Jackie Wade	May 24, 1954	May 16, 1978	Fall Creek Cem.; Son of Paul Wesley & Billie Evelyn (Layne) Curtis; U. S. Air Force
Curtis, James Henry	Mar 13, 1932	Nov 23, 2016	Franklin Memorial Gardens; Son of Charlie & Frances Curtis; m. Virginia S. Curtis; US Army, Korea
Curtis, James Ray	May 30, 1945	Jun 11, 2017	Pryor Ridge Cem.; Son of Mitchell & Pauline (Braden) Curtis; m. Judy Ann Layne; addition to Cemeteries of Grundy Co,Vol. 2, p. 718

Name	Born	Died	Details
Curtis, Jerry	Feb 26, 1926	Jan 12, 2015	Tracy City Cem.; Son of Dee & Mattie Curtis; m. Ruth Layne ; U.S. Navy
Curtis, John David	Oct 21, 1940	Feb 16, 2018	Burns Cem.; Son of Will Curtis & Kate; m. Carolyn
Curtis, Juanita Carol	Jul 20, 1931	Aug 04, 2015	Meeks Cem.; Dau. of Herschel & Ruby (Pruitt) Harlan; m. Robert Murphy
Curtis, Linda Faye	1967	May 07, 2014	Cremated; Dau of James Walter & Freida Porter, Jr. & step father Cecil Nelson
Curtis, Linda Gail	Oct 07, 1957	Oct 08, 1957	Oak Grove Cem.; Dau. of James Mitchell & Frances Pauline (Keel) Curtis; addition to Cemeteries of Grundy Co.Vol. 1, p. 488
Curtis, Lola Bell (Keener)	May 02, 1936	Jun 22, 2017	Brown's Chapel Cem.; Dau. of Luther C. & Gracie Lea (Kilgore) Keener; m. William Howard Curtis; addition to Cemeteries of Grundy Co.Vol. 1, p. 104
Curtis, Noah Chase	Oct 16, 2014	Feb 07, 2015	Fall Creek Cem.; Son of Jeremiah & Felicia (Northcutt) Curtis
Curtis, Robert Alan	Aug 10, 1952	Dec 02, 2009	Oak Grove Cem.; Son of Herschel & Ruby (Myers) Curtis; US Navy; addition to Cemeteries of Grundy Co,Vol. 1, p. 500
Curtis, Robert Kelly	Jul 21, 1943	Mar 04, 2019	Franklin Memorial Gardens Cem.; Son of William Robert Curtis & Henrietta Rieder
Curtis, Steven Jeffery	May 27, 1962	Apr 30, 1977	Fall Creek Cem.; Son of Paul Wesley& Billie Evelyn (Layne) Curtis
Curtis, William Harold	May 18, 1927	Jul 18, 1998	Brown's Chapel Cem.; Son of William R. & Bytha (Prater) Curtis; m. Lola Bell Keener; US Navy, WWII; Addition to Cemeteries of Grundy Co.Vol. 1, p. 104
Curtis, William Robert	Jan 22, 1924	Sep 26, 2018	Coalmont Cem.; Son of Arthur & Minnie Curtis; m. Henrietta Rieder; US Army
Curtiss, Barbara Jean (Grayson)	Aug 09, 1954	Feb 18, 2021	Rose Hill Memorial Gardens; Dau. of Walter Crawford & Ada Mae (Holloway) Grayson; m. Fred Neal Curtiss
Curtiss, Fred Neil	Aug 26, 1944	Jul 16, 2017	Cremated; Son of Fred & Virginia Curtis; m. Barbara Jean
Custer, Silas Lafayette, Jr.	May 20, 1940	Dec 18, 2021	Monteagle Cem.; Son of Silas Lafayette & Nora Custer; m. Margaret Custer
Da Costa, Gloria (Martin)	Jan 18, 1925	Feb 03, 2016	Philadelphia Cem.; Dau. of Elijah Depew "Lige" and Myrtle (Hall) Cain Martin; m. Richard Da Costa; addition & correction to Cemeteries of Grundy Co.Vol. 2; p. 639
Daily, Timothy S.	Sep 14, 1972	Dec 14, 2021	Mt. Olivet Baptist Church Cemetery in Raleigh, NC; Son of Terry & Anita R. Daily; m. Virginia Ann Jacobs
Daley, Angela Marie (Arthur)	May 10, 1963	Sep 15, 2019	Cremated; Dau. of Francis Douglas & Alice Arthur
Daniel, Sanada Elizabeth	Oct 30, 1938	Nov 06, 2016	Shiloh Cem.; Dau. of Ralph & Katherine (Young) Oyler; m. Glenn Willis Daniel, Sr.

Name	Born	Died	Details
Darland, Mary (Myers)	Jan 06, 1950	Apr 24, 2020	Mt. Zion Cem.; Dau. of Calvin Myers & Geneva Caldwell; m. Eugene Dale Darland
Darnell, Miriam Catherine "Kay"	Aug 09, 1920	Feb 28, 2006	Palmer Cem.; Dau. of Michael H. & Genevive Edwards; m. Harold Darnell; addition to Cemeteries of Grundy Co, Vol. 2, p. 564
Davidson, Margaret Jane (Hudson)	Oct 13, 1820	Jan 8, 1892	Old Baptist Cem.; Dau. of John & Mary (Muse) Hudson; m. Thomas Jefferson Davidson, Dec 13, 1838, Lincoln Co. TN; addition to Cemeteries of Grundy Co.Vol. 2, p. 518.
Davis, Dorothy Orleen (Taylor)	Nov 03, 1933	Jul 10, 1995	Swiss Colony Cem.; Dau. of Emory W. & Esther (Daniels) Taylor; m. Amuel T. Davis, Sr. on Dec 27, 1957; addition to Cemeteries of Grundy Co.Vol. 2, p. 785
Davis, Edith Griffy "Edie"	Apr 03, 1935	Jan 16, 2017	Fall Creek Cem.; Dau. of George H. & Mary E. (Thomas) Lemons; m. Alfred B. Davis
Davis, George Washington	May 11, 1861	Mar 29, 1911	Oak Grove Cem.; Son of Benjamin & Rhoda Jane (Graham) Davis; m. Julia A. Coker; addition to Cemeteries of Grundy Co,Vol. 1, p. 496
Davis, Grady Lester "Lurch"	Feb 28, 1952	Oct 05, 2019	Cremated; Son of William Davis & Myrtle Dishroon; m. Rebecca Lynn Green; U.S. Air Force
Davis, Imojean "Jean" (Nunley)	Dec 26, 1940	Oct 19, 2020	Dau. of Graham & Mae Ellen (Campbell) Nunley; m. 1) Clyde Leo "C.L." Braseel 2) Andrew Davis
Davis, Linda Irene (Fults)	May 05, 1905	Dec 12, 2020	King Cem.; Dau. of Ruben & Velma Irene (King) Fults; m. Roy Levan Davis
Davis, Nancy Sue (Camp)	Sep 20, 1936	Mar 30, 2019	Keith Springs Cem.; Dau. of Noel Loner Camp & Edna Earl Young; m. Odell Jackson Davis
Davis, Norman	1935	Dec 16, 2015	Cagle Cem.; Son of Matt Scott Davis & Georgia (Payne) Davis; m. Frances Carol Bickford; US Army
Davis, Reba Mae	Jul 21, 1951	Apr 05, 2020	Cremated; Dau. of Burt & June (Cowin) Davis; m. Charles Washington Corbin
Davis, Rebecca Lynn (Green)	Apr 28, 1960	Mar 21, 2022	Palmer Cem.; Dau. of William "Red" & Shirley Faye (Ashburn) Green; m. Grady Lester "Lurch" Davis
Davis, Wanda (Hart)	Dec 15, 1921	Aug 14, 1998	Cumberland Heights Cem.; Dau. of Roy Rainey & Ada Ellen (Murr) Hart; m. John Pershing Davis; correction & addition to Cemeteries of Grundy Co,Vol. 1, p. 197
Davis, William Levi	Mar 20, 1864	Aug 24, 1922	Bonny Oak Cem.; Son of William & Frances (Hilburn) Davis; addition to Cemeteries of Grundy Co., Vol. 1, p. 7
Davis, Willis Polk Macklin, Sr.	Ca. 1947	Oct 16, 2017	Plainview Cem.; Son of Lawrence M. & Clementine Davis; m. Lisa Davis

Name	Born	Died	Notes
Dawson, Samuel Benner	Dec 13, 1938	Aug 09, 2020	Plainview Cem.; Son of Johnny Theodore Dawson & Ruth A. Davis; m. Jerrie Jeanette Rosa; U.S. Air Force
Dean, Virginia Lee	Oct 15, 1932	Feb 03, 2016	Payne Cem. in Trenton, GA; Dau. of James & Bertha (Smith) Mahan
DeBruyn, Leonard Gary, Sr.	Jan 16, 1944	Apr 14, 2022	Bethel Cem.; Son of Addren & Hazel (Johnson) DeBruyn of Rochester, NY; m. Barbara Ann Argo; US Air Force
Dempsey, James Ray	Nov 07, 1932	Jan 14, 2022	Cremated; Son of Hubert & Jessie (White) Dempsey; m. Pat Tate; Herbert was from Whitwell.
Dempsey, Sariah Louise	Sep 09, 1941	Apr 07, 2018	Pryor Ridge Cem.; Dau. of Dillard & Lillian Virginia (Smartt) Sanders; m. Robert Lee Dempsey
DenBesten, John	Jul 24, 1903	Dec 23, 1971	Homeland Acres Cem.; Son of Gilbert & Clara DenBesten; m. Lillian Bennett; addition to Cemeteries of Grundy Co., Vol, 1, p. 342
DenBesten, Lillian (Fugate)	Aug 24, 1902	Jul 19, 1984	Homeland Acres Cem.; Dau. of Bruce & Amanda Fugate; m. 1) Cadwaldar Price Bennett 2) John DenBesten; correction & addition to Cemeteries of Grundy Co; Vol. 1, p. 342
Dent, Scotty Walter	Apr 06, 1970	Jan 14, 2016	Palmer Cem.; Son of J.D. Dent & Faye Dent Hoosier; m. Joanie Green
Derry, Doris (Meadows)	Aug 31, 1938	Jun 21, 2020	Hobbs Hill Cem.; Dau. of Thomas Jefferson Meadows & Bertha Lee Hazel Howard
Derryberry, John Eddie	Aug 03, 1933	Feb 03, 2016	Lone Oak Cem. in Lewisburg, TN; Son of George & Elizabeth (Andrews) Derryberry; m. Dorothy Jean Harrison; US Navy
Desmarias, Raymond "Skip"	Jun 02, 1945	Aug 31, 2013	Coalmont Cem.; Son of Wallace & Florence (Flanders) Desmarais; m. Wanda Burrows
Desmaris, Wanda (Burrows)	1955	Apr 30, 2014	Coalmont Cem.; Dau of Melvin Burrows & Frankie Mae Hobbs; m. Raymond "Skip" Desmaris
Devine, Sarah "Sally"	1845	1925	Monteagle Cem.; Her nephew Felix Carr of Blytheville, Arkansas, is mentioned in her will; She was born in MS; Vol. 1, p. 396,
DeWitt, Danielle Elizabeth	Jun 22, 1947	Dec 22, 2020	Cremated; Dau. of Daniel & Elizabeth DeWitt
Dickerson, Betty (Sherman)	Apr 29, 1947	Dec 23, 2020	Altamont Cem.; Dau. of I.B, & Bertha Pauline (King) Sherman; m. Robert Allen Dickerson; addition to Cemeteries of Grundy Co. Vol. 1, p. 22
Dickerson, Clifford		infant	Bethel Cem.; Son of Mint (female) Dickerson; Cemeteries of Grundy Co.Vol. 1, p. 50 addition

Name	Birth	Death	Details
Dickerson, Dorothy Eva Ruth (Hutchison)		Mar 16, 1993	Altamont Cem.; Dau. of William H. & Julia Virginia (Williams) Hutchison; Solie Dee Dickerson; addition to Cemeteries of Grundy Co, Vol. 1, p. 11
Dickerson, John	Feb 01, 1887	Ca 1930	Dickerson Family Cem in Burroughs' Cove; Son of Soloman & Amanda (Foster) Dickerson; never married, unmarked grave
Dickerson, Mary Elizabeth	Feb 26, 1941	Dec 04, 2017	Rose Hill Memorial Gardens; Dau. of Paul & Ethel Richie Cook; m. Joseph Carl Dickerson
Dickerson, Robert Allen	Aug 19, 1945	Apr 11, 2014	Altamont Cem.; Son of Clarence L & Alma (Scott) Dickerson; m. Betty Sherman, Feb 28, 1967; addition to Cemeteries of Grundy Co. Vol, 1, p. 22
Dickey, John David	Apr 07, 1940	Jul 04, 2021	Hamilton Mem. Gardens; Son of John William & Opal Pauline (Veal) Dickey; m. Linda Longley
Dickinson, Rick Lee	Dec 08, 1962	Feb 20, 2016	Summerfield Cem.; Son of Arthur & Barbara Dickinson; m. Donna Dickinson
Dickson, Elizabeth Ann (Yates)	Sep 27, 1945	Jun 30, 2020	Eastern Star Cem.; Dau. of Edward Yates & Mary Grace McBee; m. Thomas L. Dickson
Dies, Janette (Givens)	Nov 05, 1949	Jun 21, 2017	Wilson County Memorial Gardens Cem.; Dau. of Hershel O. & Rilla Mae (Crowell) Givens; m. 1) Bobby Henley 2) Wayne Dies
Dillon, Mary Craigmiles	May 15, 1854	Nov 30, 1938	Tracy City Cem.; Dau. of William H. & Francis Adeline (Foute) Craigmiles; m. William George Dillon; no tombstone
Dillon, William George	Dec 12, 1850	Sep 07, 1917	Tracy City Cem.; Son of Daniel D. & Rebecca A. Dillon; m. 1) Louisa Binkley 2) Mary Craigmiles in Bradley Co. TN, Jan 18, 1885; Professor 16 years at Shook School, huge marker bought by former students; According to *Chattanooga Daily Times,* Dec 2, 1938, p. 13, Mary Craigmiles was also interred in Tracy City Cem, but there is no tombstone. Addition to Cemeteries of Grundy Co. Vol. 2, p. 852
Dills, Phillip Wayne	Jun 05, 1944	Jun 07, 2019	Plainview Cem.; Son of Woodrow & Carmel (Barillaro) Dills; m. Phyllis Cunningham
Disheroon, Imogene Elizabeth (Schoenmann)	Nov 14, 1927	Ma 22, 2009	Plainview Cem.; Dau. of Walter Douglas & Annie (McCarver) Schoenmann; m. George E. Disheroon; addition to Cemeteries of Grundy Co. Vol. 2, p. 696
Disheroon, Jimmie Lee (Sanders)	Aug 10, 1929	Jan 12, 2018	Chattanooga Memorial Park Cem.; Dau. of Theo & Jennie Sanders; m. Preston Disheroon
Dishroom, Benny Hayes	Sep 08, 1930	Feb 19, 2015	Hampton Cove Cem.; Son of Ernest & Hazel Dishroom; m. Nancy Manley; U.S. Air Force
Dishroom, John Wayne	Oct 30, 1949	Dec 21, 2013	Rutledge Hill Cem.; Son of Fred & Letha (Morrison) Dishroom; m. Pat Dishroom

Dishroon, Fred D.	Feb 08, 1914	Feb 16, 1986	Palmer Cem.; Son of Hollis S. & Edna (Haynes) Dishroom; addition to Cemeteries of Grundy Co.,Vol. 2, p. 565
Dishroon, Georgia Fletcher (Tate)	Nov 25, 1923	Nov 15, 2018	Bonnie Oak; Dau. of George Tate & Margaret Dyer; m. 1) Alvin Fletcher 2) Herschel Dishroon
Dishroon, John Wayne	1949	Dec 21, 2013	Rutledge Hill Cem.; Son of Fred & Letha (Morrison) Dishroom; m. Pat Sheeks; Army
Dishroon, Louann Mary (Farmer)	Jan 08, 1945	Nov 30, 2021	Palmer Cem.; Dau. of Oscar Lloyd & Marilyn Margaret (Shields) Farmer; m. Jim Dishroon
Dishroon, Margaret Irene (Simpson)	Nov 23, 1923	Mar 05, 2002	Palmer Cem.; Dau. of Albert Benton & Dovie Mae (Lewis) Buchanan Simpson; m 1) Jack Jones 2) Bill D. Dishroon; addition to Cemeteries of Grundy Co,Vol. 2, p. 567
Dishroon, Ruth Ann	Oct 16, 1922	Jan 25. 1976	Palmer Cem.; Dau. of Thomas H. & Susie (Peden) Brown; m. Bill D. Dishroon; addition to Cemeteries of Grundy Co,Vol. 2, p. 564
Dixon, Hilda Louise	Apr 10, 1956	Nov 11, 2016	Pryor Ridge Cem.; Dau. of Charles A. & Jennie (Layne) Shrum; m. Arnold Lee "Fat" Dixon
Dixon, Juanita Jones (Roberts)	Feb 28, 1941	Oct 14, 2018	Philadelphia Cem.; Dau. of Tom Roberts & Annalee King; m. 1) Willie Lee Jones 2) Billy Joe Dixon
Dixon, Vernon Newton	1954	Sep 28, 2019	Cremated; Son of Newton & Annie L Dixon
Doak, Christian Calvin	Mar 21, 1966	Sep 15, 2018	East Tennessee State Cem.; Son of E. Dale & Anna Marie Doak; Tennessee National Guard
Dobroff, Mike		Jan 26, 1927	Parson's Graveyard (old section of Bonny Oak Cem); Young miner from Bulgaria, recently living in West Frankfort, IL, who was to marry Bob Gibbs' daughter; killed by falling slate while gathering coal with his intended. Source- Newspaper article
Dodd, Harvey, Jr.	Dec 20, 1930	Jul 05, 2020	Clouse Hill Cem.; Son of Harvey Dodd & Edna Mae Wooten; m. Ruth Meeks
Dodd, Ruth M. (Meeks)	Feb 01, 1940	Apr 25, 2015	Clouse Hill Cem.; Dau. of John & Allie Meeks; m. Harvey Dodd, Jr.
Dodson, Barbara Joette (Pickett)	Jul 29, 1968	May 16, 2021	Fall Creek Cem.; Dau. of Bailey Allen & Barbara Joan (Eastridge) Pickett
Dodson, Caroll "Toby"	May 19, 1854	Feb 26, 1940	Wesley Chapel Cem.; Son of Samuel & Elizabeth Margaret (Tucker) Dodson; m. Elizabeth Boyd Aug 30, 1871; addition to Cemeteries of Grundy Co,Vol. 2, p. 970
Dooley, Berry Lee, Jr.	1939	Oct 30, 2014	Orange Hill Cem.; Son of Berry Lee Dooley & Lois Anderson; m. Rosemary "Patty" Dooley
Doran, John David	Jan 11, 1946	Nov 21, 2020	Cremated; Son of Phillip & Phyllis Doran

Doss, Clyde A.	Feb 21, 1935	Jul 29, 1989	Palmer Cem.; Son of Fred & Opal (Matthews) Doss; m. Margie Janie Kilgore; addition to Cemeteries of Grundy County, Vol. 2, p. 56
Doss, Margie Janie (Kilgore)	Oct 05, 1935	Feb 10, 2012	Palmer Cem.; Dau. of Earl & Janie (Bone) Kilgore; m. Clyde A. Doss; addition & correction to Cemeteries of Grundy Co., Vol. 2; p. 563
Doss, Mary Katherine (King)	Dec 25, 1935	May 02, 2018	Griffith's Creek Cem.; Dau. of Byron King & Mary Thompson; m. Hayden Edward Doss
Dotson, Cinthia Melvina "Molly" (Meeks)	Apr 1850	Apr 27, 1914	Summerfield Cem.; m. Nicholas "Nick" M.A. Dotson; no tombstone; Death notice from *Mrs. Grundy*, Apr 30, 1914
Dotson, George Edward, Jr.	1952	Dec 22, 2013	Cremated ashes at Eastern Star Cem; Son of George Edward "Buddy" Dotson, Sr. & Sammie June Finney; m. Krista Dotson; US Navy
Douglas, Robert "Bob"	Ca. 1937	Jan 01, 2021	Monteagle Cem.; cremated; Son of Pete & Hazel (Francis) Douglas; m. Jane Creasman.
Dove, Charles Edward	Apr 13, 1926	Mar 21, 1962	Rose Hill Memorial Garden, Tullahoma, TN; Son of Avery, Sr. & Estil (Sweeton) Dove; Charles was listed as being buried at Dove/Harris Cem, but he is not; correction to Cemeteries of Grundy Co. Vol. 1, p. 202
Dove, Clarence Roscoe	May 18, 1915	Mar 05, 1964	Speed Hensley Cem in Molus, KY; Son of Avery, Sr, & Callie Estil (Sweeton) Dove; m. Elizabeth "Teat" Saylor; correction of burial location which is in Molus, Ky & not in Dove/Harris Cem. as reported in Cemeteries of Grundy Co, Vol. 1, p. 202
Dove, Clayton Dean	Mar 17, 1939	Jul 14, 2014	Davidson Memorial Garden in Floyd Co. KY; Son of Avery Sr. & Callie Estil (Sweeton) Dove; m. Mildred Louise Smith; Clayton was listed as being buried at the Dove/Harris Cem.; in Coalmont, but he is not. Correction to Cemeteries of Grundy Co, Vol. 1, p. 202
Dove, David	Sep 18, 1873	Feb 17, 1917	Tracy City Cem.; Son of Benjamin & Virginia (Dykes) Dove; m. Mary Ella Headrick; Cemeteries of Grundy Co. Vol. 2, p. 824 addition
Dove, James Willard	Nov 08, 1935	Sep 25, 2021	Plainview Cem.; Son of Thomas & Emma Dove; m. Sally Sanders
Dove, John David	1950	Nov 01, 2018	Shrum Family Cem.; Son of Arnold & Susie Dove; m. Mavis Lillian Shrum
Dove, Johnny	Sep 13, 1923	Jun 05, 2000	Chicago, IL; Son of Avery Sr. & Callie Estle (Sweeton) Dove; m. Beatrice Arlene Hammond; Correction of burial location. He is not buried at Dove/Harris Cem in Coalmont; Cemeteries of Grundy Co. Vol. 1, p. 202

Name	Birth	Death	Notes
Dove, Jordan B.	May 12, 1858	Feb 17, 1917	Dove /Harris Cem.; Son of James & Nancy Dove; m. Virginia Dykes; from *Mrs. Grundy* Feb 22, 1917
Dove, Lola (Howard)	Mar 15, 1921	Jun 08, 1993	Dove/Harris Cem.; Dau. of Noah & Johnnie (Saylor) Howard; m. Walter Clayton Dove, Aug 2, 1941; addition to Cemeteries of Grundy Co,Vol. 1, p. 201
Dove, Mavis Lillian (Shrum)	Feb 27, 1954	Jun 27, 2020	Shrum Family Cem.; Dau of Fred Lee Shrum & Sarah Sweeton; m. John David Dove
Dove, Sally Ann (Sanders)	Jun 22, 1941	Aug 30, 2021	Plainview Cem.; Dau. of Lloyd & Louella Sanders; m. Willard Dove
Dove, William Henry	Jan 13, 1983	Jan 12, 2021	Orange Hill Cem.; Son of Charles Robert & Christine (Adam) Dove, Jr.; m. Gail Campbell
Dove, Willie Carl	Jun 03, 1922	Aug 29, 1948	Molus, KY; Son of Avery & Margaret Dove; m. Lucille Brock; per death certificate; correction of wife's name & burial location in Cemeteries of Grundy Co,Vol. 1, p. 202
Drake, Laura A. (Parsons)	1875 on stone, records say 1864	1949 on stone, records say Dec 2, 1937	Bonny Oak Cem.; Dau. of Jess & Mandy (Sanders) Parsons; m. Berry Drake; correction & addition to Cemeteries of Grundy Co, Vol, 1, p.75
Drinkard, Keith	May 24, 1966	Apr 21, 2005	Plainview Cem.; b. Chicago, Il, died in Riverbend Maximum Security, Nashville, TN
Driver, Evelyn Donna (Tate)	Oct 01, 1944	Feb 20, 2019	Bascom Cem.; Dau. of Joe Bradford Tate & Kathryn Iola Driver
Dudley, Charles Edward	Jun 18, 1938		Airview Cem.; Son of Homer F. & Nancy Jane (Goad) Dudley; m. Elizabeth Pearl Weaver; addition to Cemeteries of Grundy Co,Vol. 1, p. 5
Dudley, Elizabeth Pearl (Weaver)	Dec 28, 1946	Apr 15, 2003	Airview Cem.; Dau. of Henry Herbert & Lilly Mae (Hodge) Warner; m. Charles Edward Dudley Apr 24, 1982; addition to Cemeteries of Grundy Co,Vol. 1, p. 5
Dudley, Margaret	Ca. 1930	Jan 24, 2017	Lynchburg Cem.; Dau. of Charles & Mary Pierce; m. Ed Dudley
Dugger, Tommie Mae (Parks)	Sep 04, 1925	Mar 18,2017	Warren "Red Hill" Cem.; Dau. of Frederick Allen & Grace (Payne) Parks; m. Paul Dugger
Duke, Diane (Winton)	Jun 17, 1950	Dec 05, 2022	Cremated in Fernandina Beach, FL; Dau. of Col. Marshal & Elizzabeth (King) Winton
Dunn, Ronald Joseph	1949	Oct 02, 2014	Plainview Cem.; Son of Joseph Leenn & Evora McClellan; m. Laura Jean Dunn; US Army wounded permanently in Vietnam
Dunn, William	Nov 23, 1962	Sep 16, 2017	Chattanooga National Cem.; Son of Melvin Eugene Dunn & Bonnie Harvey; m. Carmen Dunn; US Army
Dunwoody, Georgie E. (Meeks)	Feb 11, 1922	Apr 17, 2013	Tracy City Cem.; Dau. of Edgar & Cleo (Myers) Meeks; m. Jim Dunwoody

Name	Born	Died	Details
Dunwoody, William Thatcher	Dec 10, 1955	Jun 22, 2019	Tracy City Cem.; Son of Jim Dunwoody & Georgia Meeks
Dutton, Henry Griffith	Jun 9, 1889	Aug 13, 1978	Altamont Cem.; Son of Joel Marion & Martha Helen M. (Jackson) Dutton; m. Ruby Marie Jessee; addition to Cemeteries of Grundy Co.Vol. 1, p. 16
Dycus, Nina G. (Sanders) Tate	Jul 10, 1948	Sep 04, 2008	Altamont Cem.; Dau. of Leonard "Little Red"& Nellie (Campbell) Sanders; m: 1) Roger Dwight Tate 2) ___Dycus
Dye, Michael Sean	Mar 17, 1966	Jan 10, 2013	Cremated/Plainview Cem.; Son of Ben & Jean (Anderson) Dye
Dyer, Anita Louise	1960	Dec 04, 2020	Summerfield Cem.; Dau. of Henry "Buck", Jr. & Barbara (Metcalfe) Dyer; m. Doyle Searcy
Dyer, Harold	Mar 07, 1939	Mar 05, 2018	Franklin Memorial Gardens Cem.; Son of James Dyer & Harlie Scott; m. Barbara Dyer
Dyer, Henry "Buck", Jr.	May 14, 1936	Apr 04, 2014	Summerfield Cem.; Son of Henry, Sr. & Lillian (Johnson) Dyer; m. Barbara Metcalf; addition to Cemeteries of Grundy Co.,Vol. 2, p. 771
Dyer, J.C.	Jan 17, 1924	Mar 21, 2001	Cumberland Heights Cem.; Son of Henry, Sr & Lillian (Johnson) Dyer; m. Willie Mae Birdwell; addition to Cemeteries of Grundy Co.Vol. 1, p. 197
Dykes, Beatrice G. (Yarworth)	Jan 01, 1916	Jun 30, 2005	Orange Hill Cem.; Dau. of Edward John & Louisa Jane (Hargis) Yarworth; m. Arnold Dykes on Mar 22, 1941
Dykes, Bennie	Sep 25, 1928	Dec 07, 2015	Gregg Cem.; Son of Andy & Hallie (Sanders) Dykes; m. Delores Dykes
Dykes, Byrtle M. (Byers)	Mar 29, 1924	Oct 26, 2000	Gregg Cem.; Dau. of John Wayne & Maude Elizabeth (Taylor) Byers; m. Clifford Eugene Dykes; addition & correction to Cemeteries of Grundy Co.Vol. 1, p. 306
Dykes, Carl Elmer	Oct 22, 1926	Jan 05, 2017	Tracy City Cem.; Son of Clinton & Nancy Dykes
Dykes, Charles W.	Mar 29, 1931	Nov 01, 2015	Plainview Cem.; Son of Andy & Hallie (Sanders) Dykes; m. Claudine McDaniel
Dykes, Claudene (McDaniel)	Mar 02, 1936	Jan 21, 2019	Plainview Cem.; Dau. of Bill & Tressie McDaniel; m. Charles W. Dykes
Dykes, Clfford Eugene	Feb 14, 1924	Dec 10, 2012	Gregg Cem.; Son of Andy & Hallie (Sanders) Dykes; m. Byrtle M. Byers: addition to Cemeteries of Grundy Co.Vol. 1, p. 306 – different from Clifford Eugene Dykes buried at Hobbs Hill Cem.;
Dykes, Clifford Eugene	Feb 14, 1924	Dec 10, 2012	Gregg Cem.; Son of Andy & Hallie (Sanders) Dykes

Name	Birth	Death	Details
Dykes, Clifford Eugene	Jan 13, 1935	Dec 03, 1981	Hobbs Hill Cem.; Son of Marvin L. Roberts & Edna M. Dykes per Ancestry.com records; addition to Cemeteries of Grundy Co.Vol. 1, p. 334
Dykes, David A	May 09, 1946		Hobbs Hill Cem.; Son of David Leslie & Minnie Lee (Campbell) Dykes; m. Rose Edna Coppinger; addition to Cemeteries of Grundy Co. Vol. 1, p. 331
Dykes, Delores (Byers)	1931		Gregg Cem.; Dau. of Joe William "Joab" & Maude Elizabeth (Taylor) Byars/Byers
Dykes, Elsie W (Williams)	Jan 06, 1928	Jan 26, 2021	Brown's Chapel Cem.; Dau. of Daniel & Charlotte Williams; m. Robert J. Dykes, Feb 13, 1945; b. in Hollybush, England; naturalized Nov 17, 1955; addition to Cemeteries of Grundy Co.Vol. 1, p. 108
Dykes, Helen Marie (Parson)	Oct 23, 1941	Sep 25, 2020	Hobbs Hill Community Church Cem.; Dau. of Hershel & Berta "Birdie" Parson; m. Grady Dykes
Dykes, Hoyt G.	Nov 19, 1937	Mar 27, 2013	Hobbs Hill Cem.; Son of Calvin & Nancy (O'Neal) Dykes; m. Helen Parson
Dykes, J (Possibly John Dykes)	1819 see comment	Dec 1858	Altamont Cem.; probably John Dykes, son of Martin & Mary Jane (Sanders) Dykes; m. Dolly Dykes; addition to Cemeteries of Grundy Co. Vol, 1, p. 13
Dykes, Lewis	Dec 20, 1953	Aug 04, 2015	Plainview Cem.; Son of Lonnie & Susie Dykes
Dykes, Melissa G. (Brady)	Jan 20, 1974	Sep 06, 2012	Coalmont Cem.; Dau. of James Mitchell & Brenda Faye (Pickett) Brady; m. Thomas Dykes; correction to Cemeteries of Grundy County,Vol. 1, p. 179
Dykes, Minnie Lee (Campbell)	Sep 05, 1909	Mar 14, 1973	Hobbs Hill Cem.; Dau. of Alexander William & Tierra Elizabeth (Nunley) Campbell; m. David Leslie Dykes; addition to Cemeteries of Grundy Co.,Vol. 1, p. 331
Dykes, Samantha Marie (Brown)	Sep 03, 1991	Jun 03, 2020	Pryor Ridge Cem.; Dau. of Russell & Tammy (O'Dear) Brown
Dykes, Stanley Franklin "Bowzer"	1932	May 27, 2014	Orange Hill Cem.; Son of Clinton & Nancy (O'Neal) Dykes; US Army Korea
Dykes, Susie	Jan 30, 1936	Feb 03, 2013	Plainview Cem.; Dau. of Melton & Irene Lockhart; m. Lonnie Dykes
Dykes, Taylor Rosalee	Dec 31, 1999	Dec 31, 1999	Palmer Cem.; Dau. of Jody & Jamie (Morrison) Dykes; addition to Cemeteries of Grundy Co.,Vol. 2, p. 579
Early, Glenn Dale	Oct 03, 1965	Oct 01, 2021	Leaning-E Cem.; Son of Albert & Jeanette Early; m. Patricia Lynn Early
Eckard, Vida (Williams)	May 25, 1899	Mar 09, 1974	Homeland Acres Cem.; Dau. of Frank & Ada (Swingle) Williams; m. Gail Philbrook Eckard; addition to Cemeteries of Grundy Co.,Vol. 1, p. 341

Edmister, Elfa Irene (Lillie)	Jul 09, 1920	Jun 26, 2008	Altamont Cem.; Dau. of Charles Phelps & Catherine Ellen (Philbrick) Lillie; m. Arthur Leon Edmister; addition to Cemeteries of Grundy Co, Vol. 1, p. 31
Edmister, Mattie Ann (Jessee)	May 10, 1920	Jan 25, 1984	Altamont Cem.; Dau. of Henry Dobbin & Laura Catherine (Wallace) Jessee; m. Wilfred Homer Edmister; addition to Cemeteries of Grundy Co.Vol. 1, p. 33
Edwards, Juanita (Garner)	Dec 31, 1941	Oct 13, 2018	Palmer Cem.; Dau. of Hobert Garner & Myrtle Sissom
Eldridge, Carlene (Haynes)	Apr 11, 1928	Oct 07, 2013	Oak Grove Cem.; Dau. of Vernon & Edith Haynes; m. Herschel Eldridge; no tombstone
Eldridge, Stephan Wayne	Jul 24, 1947	Mar 05, 1963	Oak Grove Cem.; Son of Herschel & Carlene (Haynes) Eldridge; m. Ophelia Crisp; addition to Cemeteries of Grundy Co.Vol. 1, p. 510
Eller, Martha "Mattie" (McCurdy)	Ca. 1875	Jan 06, 1914	Tracy City Cem.; Dau. of William Alexander & Elizabeth A. (Crichlow) McCurdy; m. Wiley Harrison Eller; Cemeteries of Grundy Co.Vol. 2, p. 875 addition from *Mrs. Grundy*, Jan 1, 1914
Elliott, Martha Alice (Wooten)	1937	May 10, 2022	Cremated; Dau. of Hughie, Sr. & Lillie Katherine (King) Wooten; m. Mickey Elliott; She was from Monteagle, TN.
Ellis, Daisy Jo (Custer)	Dec 12, 1942	Feb 26, 2022	Tennessee-Georgia Memorial Park; Dau. of Silas & Nora Custer; m. David F. Ellis
Ellis, Eula Mae (Layne)	Apr 11, 1936	Feb 19,1965	Fall Creek Falls Cem.; Dau. of Ples & Maggie Myrtle (Panter) Layne
Ellis, Lou (Sanson)	Mar 25, 1873	Nov 11, 1918	Tracy City Cem.; Dau. of Green F. & Caldonia "Callie" (Morris) Sanson; m. William M. Ellis, Jun 13, 1889; addition to Cemeteries of Grundy Co.Vol. 2, p. 817
Ellison, Earl Austin, Sr.	Aug 09, 1923	Dec 29, 1994	Clouse Hill Cem.; Son of Walter Lee & Maude C. (Lawrence) Ellison;1) Bonnie Gaynell Thomas 2) Mary Elizabeth Foreman; addition to Cemeteries of Grundy Co.Vol. 1, p. 150
Engdahl, Eugene R	Dec 20, 1931	Oct 05, 2020	Son of Herbert & Hazel Ann Engdahl; m. Frances Elizabeth Sobczak; U.S. Army - Korea
England, Alexander Calvin	Oct 16, 1845	Apr 01, 1929	Wesley Chapel Cem.; Son of Landy Holloway & Martha Ann (Barnes) England; m. Mary Purcell on Sep 1, 1867; addition to Cemeteries of Grundy Co. Vol. 2, p. 975
Engle, Elzie Lee "Brown"	Dec 28, 1941	Dec 02, 2005	Coalmont Cem.; Son of Joseph Edgar & Maxine (Kilgore) Engle; grandson of Josie & Tom Kilgore; funeral home marker; Army Vietnam; Navy Persian Gulf; addition to Cemeteries of Grundy Co.,Vol. 1, p. 169

Name	Born	Died	Notes
Eubanks, Glenda Mae (Huntley)	Jul 25, 1960	Mar 03, 2021	Schild-Tate Cem.; Dau. of Edward & Melba (McGee) Huntley; m. William Drobesh Huntley
Eubanks, Josephine (King)	Nov 08, 1921	Jul 09, 2012	Grace Chapel Cem.; Dau. of Aubrey Hill & Callie Dora (Hale) King; m. Raymond Carl Eubanks, Sr.
Eubanks, William Drobesh	May 30, 1954	Mar 16, 2018	Schild-Tate Cem.; Son of Raymond Carl Eubanks & Josephine King; m. Glenda Huntley
Evans, Ada (Fisher)	Jan 27, 1854	Mar 21, 1953	Altamont Cem.; Dau. of Samuel & Elizabeth (Black) Fisher; m. 1) Lee M. Trees on Jun 29, 1899, in Indiana 2) Walter Lee Evans Feb 27, 1902 in Indiana; addition to Cemeteries of Grundy Co, Vol. 1, p. 18
Evans, Deborah Ann	Feb 26, 1968	Jun 13, 2020	Cremated; Dau. of John Ernest and Della Faye (Collins) Evans
Evans, Della Faye (Collins)	Jun 13, 1941*	Jul 23, 1978	Airview Cem.; Dau. of Eunice & Girlie (Sims) Collins; m. John Ernest Evans; * census records indicate she was born in 1931 even though her tombstone states 1941. Addition to Cemeteries of Grundy Co, Vol. 1, p. 5
Evans, Dorothy "Dot" (Hiett)	Oct 13, 1940	Oct 22, 2018	Ft. Myers, FL Cem.; Dau. of Wallace Samuel Hiett, Sr. & Florence Margaret Brown; m. Wirt Thomas Evans
Evans, John Ernest	Aug 22, 1914	Apr 05, 1991	Airview Cem.; Son of Charles Edward & Lily (Overby) Evans; m. Della Faye Collins; addition to Cemeteries of Grundy Co, Vol. 1, p. 5
Evans, Joyce Jean (Miller)	Mar 20, 1937	May 08, 2019	Cremated: Dau. of Royal Miller & Mary Iva Goff; m. Bobby Franklin Evans; She lived in Skymont.
Evans, Stephen Michael	Apr 15, 1952	Feb 16, 2021	Cremated; Son of Alfred & Martha Evans; m. Vickie Medley; Mike lived in Pelham.
Everett, Bonnie Angalee	Oct 31, 1930	Apr 16, 1997	Plainview Cem.; Dau. of Lucy S. Everett; born in Rhea Co, TN; Died at Haven of Rest Nursing Home; addition to Cemeteries of Grundy Co, Vol. 2, p. 673
Faharry, James	Ca 1931	Dec 3, 1891	Altamont Cem.; appointed postmaster at Beersheba Jan 20, 1886; Correction of birth date (Stone says 60 years) & addition of information for Cemeteries of Grundy Co, Vol. 1, p. 28
Fanshaw, Hazel Marie (Hunziker)	Jun 01, 1918	Mar 01, 2020	Cremated; Dau. of Edward J & Susie Swann Hunziker; m. Caleb G. Fanshaw; Hazel was born in Tracy City.
Farmer, Belmont "Belle" (Wilbanks)	Feb 2, 1862	Feb 22, 1950	Monteagle Cem.; Dau. of William Henry & Charlotta Wilbanks; m. William Henry "Bill" Farmer, addition to Cemeteries of Grundy Co; Vol. 1, p. 427

Name	Birth	Death	Notes
Farmer, Samuel	Jun 1888	1974	Monteagle Cem.; Son of William Henry & Belmont "Belle" (Wilbanks) Farmer, addition to Cemeteries of Grundy Co, Vol. 1, p. 428
Farr, Carl Allen "Jack"	Nov 19, 1880	Jan 06, 1961	Altamont Cem.; Son of Joseph & Martha (King) Farr; m. Effie Cordelia Tanner; addition to Cemeteries of Grundy Co.Vol. 1, p. 27
Farr, Effie Cordelia (Tanner)	Oct 3, 1877	Feb 07, 1965	Altamont Cem.; Dau. of William & Sarah (Thompson) Tanner; m. Carl Allen "Jack" Farr; addition to Cemeteries of Grundy Co.Vol. 1, p. 27
Farr, Jackie	Feb 09, 1942	Mar 03, 1999	Coalmont Cem.; Son of Carl Allen "Jack" & Effie (Tanner) Farr; correction to Cemeteries of Grundy Co, Vol. 1, p. 173
Farrar, Janice Ruth (Anderson)	Sep 21, 1943	Jul 26, 2020	Gregg Cem. broken stone; Dau. of Herschel & Verna Louise (Byers) Anderson; m. 1) Albert Coppinger 2) Neil Farrar; addition; She is actually buried in Nashville, TN at Mt. Olivet Cem.
Farris, Lena Grace (Brewer)	Jan 07, 1939	Apr 12, 2019	Brown's Chapel Cem.; Dau. of Walter & Donna (Cagle) Brewer; m. George H. Farris; addition to Cemeteries of Grundy Co.,Vol. 1, p. 104
Feldman, Ronald A.	Oct 06, 1943	Sep 14, 2021	Cremated; Son of Adolf & Mae (Geier) Feldman; m. Carol Ortel; U.S. Air Force
Felton, Margie E. (Johnson)	Feb 21, 1930	Nov 12, 2013	Bonny Oak Cem.; Dau. of Luther Bryan & Della (Caldwell) Johnson; m. Henry Paul Felton
Ferguson, Alexandria Ann	Jan 20, 1992	Jan 02, 2006	Summerfield Cem.; Dau. of Deborah Layne adopted by James Ferguson, husband of Deborah; grand dau of Billy Layne of Layne's Cove; addition to Cemeteries of Grundy Co,Vol. 2, p. 767
Ferguson, Celia Naomi	Jan 25, 1906	Mar 02, 1964	Monteagle Cem.; Dau. of Frank & Ora (Rich) Dyke; addition to Cemeteries of Grundy Co.Vol. 1, p. 448
Fero, June Irene	Jun 22, 1922	Nov 10, 2016	Cremated; Dau. of Fred & Minnie (Pomrenting) Fero; June died in Beersheba Springs.
Ferrell, Larry "Dude"	Mar 29, 1946	Oct 18, 2019	Eastern Star Cem. of Sewanee; Son of Alma Jean Ferrell & Eldred Anderson; U.S. Air Force
Ferrell, Steven Joe	1957	May 25, 2014	Little Johnny Myers Cem.; Son of William Ferrell & Betty Joann Veal Hayes; m. Amy Hobbs; USMC
Ferriss, Maria Judson	Dec 12, 1894	Feb 01, 1964	Hunerwadel Cem.; Dau. of Andrew Caldwell & Nettie C. (Judson) Ferriss; Judson is not Maria's maiden name. Correction addition to Cemeteries of Grundy Co. Vol. 1, p.344

Finch, Benjamine	Oct 30, 1855	Jan 2, 1889	Tracy City Cem.; Son of George M. & Martha Ann (Wilson) Finch; m. Ellen Leverton on Jun 9, 1882; addition to Cemeteries of Grundy Co. Vol, 2, p. 902
Finch, Herschel Lee	Apr 08, 1957	Dec 26, 2020	Palmer Cem.; Son of Herschel Lee & Jeanetta (Tate) Finch; m. Maria Finch
Finch, Herschel, Jr.	Oct 14, 1929	Oct 16, 2015	Palmer Cem.; Son of Herschel & Ruby (Gifford) Finch; m. Jeanetta Tate; US Navy, Korea & Vietnam
Finch, Jeffrey Thomas "Jeff"	Oct 4, 1975	Jul 08, 2014	Cremated; Son of Larry Thomas & Sheila Regina (Akins) Finch; m. Misty (Layne) Lawrence ; from Palmer died in Alberta Canada
Finch, Margie Joan	Jan 11, 1954	Aug 10, 2014	White Cem.; Dau of Howard Wideman & Stella Andrews; m. Jimmy Dale Finch
Finch, Mary Etta	Ca 1897	Jan 25, 1917	Tracy City Cem.; Dau. of George Elbert & Annie (Goodman) Finch; from *Mrs. Grundy*, Feb 1, 1917, edition
Finch, Sandra Lee	Jul 05, 1960	Nov 11, 1997	Swiss Colony Cem.; Dau. of Ronnie Finch & Eva Cecile Holiday; m. Kevin J. Goehler; addition to Cemeteries of Grundy Co.Vol. 2, p. 798
Finch, Sheila Regina (Akins)	Sep 18, 1948	Jan 06, 2015	Coalmont Cem.; Dau. of Allen & Lorene (Holt) Akins; m. Larry Thomas Finch
Finch, Tecia Laverne (Bellflower)	Jan 01, 1936	Jul 14, 2000	Fall Creek Cem.; Dau. of Bill Bellflower & William Donaldson (step father) & June C. Floyd; m. Charles E. Finch, Sr.
Fincher, Hubert Allen	Mar 02, 1946	Sep 30, 2021	Walker Cem.; Son of Allen Gussie & Margie (Kilgore) Fincher; m. Dean Richardson; U.S. Army
Fincher, Paul David	May 10, 1947	Mar 20, 2021	Walker Cem.; Son of Allen G. and Marie (Kilgore) Fincher; m. Emma Forsyth
Finchum, Mary Evelyn (Geary)	Aug 17, 1934	May 09, 2018	Dau. of Willie Hayes Geary & Minnie Bell Lockhart; m. Roland Finchum
Finchum, Roland	1941	Dec 20, 2017	Willow Mount Cem.; Son of John Robert & Jessie May Finchum; m. Mary Geary; US Army – Vietnam
Finchum, Troy Allen	Sep 28, 1967	Nov 21, 2017	Cremated; Son of John H. Finchum & Elizabeth Daly
Finnell, Le Alice (Clay)	Oct 01, 1921	Aug 24, 2017	Forest Park Cem Shreveport. LA; Dau. of Charles & Juanita (Holland) Clay; m. Lewis Roscoe Finnell
Finney, Herbert G.	Jul 07, 1906	Feb 24, 1931	Fall Creek Cem.; Son of Henry Finney & Carrie Tate; m. Minnie Nussbaum
Finney, Richard G.	Apr 14, 1931	Apr 16, 1931	Fall Creek Cem.; Son of Herbert G. & Minnie (Nussbaum) Finney

Name	Born	Died	Notes
Fisher, Adalphash	May 21, 1910	May 30, 1985	Palmer Cem.; Son of Robert Taylor & Cora Della (Smith) Fisher; m. Ophelia Weaver; addition to Cemeteries of Grundy Co,Vol. 2, p 566.
Fisher, Dorothy Amy (Edwards)	Sep 15, 1926	Oct 27, 2021	Chattanooga National Cem.; Dau. of Richard & Amy Eugenia (Wilson) Edwards; m. Richard Leroy Fisher, Jr.
Fisher, Ophelia W.	Jul 06, 1917	Aug 11, 1996	Palmer Cem.; Dau. of Andrew Jackson & Annie (Bedford) Weaver; m Adalphash Fisher; addition to Cemeteries of Grundy County, Vol. 2, p. 566
Fisher, Richard Leroy, Jr.	Jul 28, 1930	Jun 12, 2013	Chattanooga National Cem.; Son of Richard Leroy, Sr. & DeVera (Bauldauf) Fisher; m. Dorothy Amy Edwards; USMC
Fitch, Bernice Margaret (Schreiber)	Feb 16, 1931	Feb 18, 2007	Altamont Cem.; Dau. of John & Mary (Stiehl) Schreiber; m. Lewis Fitch; addition to Cemeteries of Grundy Co, Vol. 1, p. 15
Fitch, Douglas	May 31, 1942	Jul 28, 2014	Altamont Cem.; Son of Floyd & Ollie Faye (Sanders) Fitch
Fitch, Ethel	Aug 16, 1929	Mar 22, 2006	Altamont Cem.; Dau. of Doug & Betty (Nunley) Dickerson; m. John Wilson Fitch
Fitch, Michael Stephen	Dec 27, 1976	Jul 17, 2008	Altamont Cem.; Son of Michel Stephen & Linda (Basham) Fitch; addition to Cemeteries of Grundy Co, Vol. 1, p. 15
Fitch, Ronald Dean	infant	infant	Altamont Cem.; Son of John Wilson & Ethel (Dickerson) Fitch
Fitch, Shirley Jean (Turner)	Nov 27, 1951	Feb 29, 2020	Altamont Cem.; Dau. of Warner Turner & Jessie R. McCormick; m. Douglas Fitch
Fitch, Stephen	Apr 01, 1952	Apr 15, 2020	Altamont Cem.; Son of John Wilson Fitch & Ethel Dickerson; m. Linda Henderson
Fitch, Susie (Cannon)	Sep 17, 1878	Sep 19, 1960	Altamont Cem.; Dau. of James M. & Rececca (Sims) Cannon; m. Henry Harris Fitch; addition to Cemeteries of Grundy Co.,Vol. 1, p. 35
Fitch, Teresa Ann (Johnson)	May 06, 1958		Altamont Cem.; Dau. of Pauline Johnson; addition to Cemeteries of Grundy Co.,Vol. 1, p. 37
Flanagan, John D.	Aug 16, 1828	Jun 05, 1913	Tracy City Cem.; Son of James & Mary (Keeregan) Flanagan; m. Mary (Dunn) Mason; addition to Cemeteries of Grundy Co.Vol. 2, p. 863
Flanagan, Mary (Dunn)	Nov 28, 1938	Aug 21. 1912	Tracy City Cem.; Dau of William P. & Patience (Johnston) Dunn; m. 1) Walter Ballard Mason 2) John D. Flanagan; addition and correction to Cemeteries of Grundy Co. Vol. 2, p. 863

Name	Birth	Death	Details
Fletcher Disheroon, Georgia (Tate)	Nov 25, 1923	Nov 15, 2018	Bonny Oak Cem.; Dau. of George Winfield & Margaret Katherine (Dyer) Tate; m. 1) Alvin Tate 2) Herschel Disheroon 3) Alvin L. Fletcher; addition to Cemeteries of Grundy Co. vol, 1, p. 85
Fletcher, Alvin L.	Apr 15, 1916	Jun 28, 1989	Bonny Oak Cem.; Son of Charles Marion & Mina (Sanders) Fletcher; m. Georgia Tate Disheroon; addition to Cemeteries of Grundy Co.Vol. 1, p. 85
Fletcher, Dale Ray	Oct 17, 1961	Oct 30, 2021	Middle TN Veterans Cem in Nashville; Son of Kyle Ray & Lana Fletcher; Step- father John Holt; m. Bobbie Fletcher; US Army
Fletcher, Preston Eugene	Feb 28, 1923	Jul 20, 1924	White Cem in Palmer; Son of John Reese "Renzi" & Corinne (Pocus) Fletcher; addition to Cemeteries of Grundy Co.,Vol. 2, p. 1007
Floyd, Douglas Andrew	Mar 20, 1973	Jul 30, 2020	Griffiths Creek Cem.; Son of Hugh Ellis Floyd & Virginia Ramsey; m. Dana Henderson; Ohio Army National Guard
Floyd, Hester (Slatton)	Oct 22, 1932	Apr 22, 2018	Swiss Colony Cem.; Dau. of Luther Slatton & Mae Ellen Bivens; m. 1) Amos Howard Layne 2) Herbert Grimes 3) Hugh E Floyd
Floyd, Hugh Ellis "Bit"	Apr 06, 1934	Feb 07, 2020	Griffiths Creek Cem.; Son of Amos A. Floyd & Edith Cordelia Morrison; m. Virgie V. Floyd
Floyd, Mary M.	1931	2007	Oak Grove Cem.; Dau. of Samson & Lizzie (Knight) Martin; addition to Cemeteries of Grundy Co.,Vol. 1, p. 505
Floyd, Minnie C.	Jul 16, 1908	Aug 05, 2002	Summerfield Cem.; Dau. of Thomas F. & Elizabeth (Thomas) Cooke; 94 years. Died in FL; addition to Cemeteries of Grundy Co.,Vol. 2, p. 774
Floyd, Nancy	Nov 01, 1840	May 02, 1940	Oak Grove Cem.; Dau of James Jackson & Ellen Nellie Coffelt; m. Silas Preston Floyd
Floyd, Wendell Charles	Dec 31, 1974	Oct 05, 2021	Blue's Hill Cem.; Son of Charles & Betty Floyd; m. Serena Martin
Flury, Catherine Bell	Mar 30, 1923	Sep 20, 2016	Tracy City Cem.; Dau. of Clarence E. & Theona (Haynes) Kilgore; m. Fritz L. Flury
Flury, Elizabeth (Von Rohr)	Aug 14, 1841	Mar 17, 1907	Swiss Colony Cem.; Dau. of Leonhard & Elisabeth (Schoenemann) Von Rohr; m. 1) Fidel "Fred" Studer 2) Henrich J. "Henry" Flury; addition & correction to Cemeteries of Grundy Co.Vol. 2, p. 785
Flury, Frances (Arbuckle)	Jul 11, 1918	Apr 06, 2014	Tracy City Cem.; Dau. of Jasper William & Ethel Gordon (Summers) Arbuckle; m. Henry Stocker Flury
Flury, Henry	Oct 15, 1843	Mar 29, 1907	Swiss Colony Cem.; Son of Frank J. Flury; m. Elizabeth Von Rohr; Correction of spelling of surname and addition to Cemeteries of Grundy Co.Vol. 2, p. 785

Name	Birth	Death	Details
Flury, Mary Elwyn (Reid)	Dec 19, 1919	Jun 12, 2021	Tracy City Cem.; Dau. of Robert Caldwell & Mary (Eads) Reid; m. Sammy Louis Flury
Flynn, Elizabeth "Eliza" (Keeling)	Jan 3, 1849	Jul 4, 1899	Tracy City Cem.; Dau. of James Lowery & Charlotte (McGraw) Keeling; m. Michael "Mike" Flynn, Sr. on Nov 10, 1858; correction to birth year & additional information to Cemeteries of Grundy Co, Vol, 2, p. 899
Flynn, George	Feb 12, 1869	Dec 25, 1942	Tracy City Cem.; Son of Michael & Elizabeth (Keeling) Flynn; m. Lina Caroline Hall; addition to Cemeteries of Grundy Co, Vol. 2, p. 900
Flynn, George Walter	Apr 19, 1901	Oct 14, 1981	Tracy City Cem.; Son of George & Linna Caroline (Hall) Flynn; m. Martha Irene Goodman; addition to Cemeteries of Grundy Co, Vol. 2, p. 900
Flynn, Grace Sherbonne (Barnes)	Jan 04, 1935	Oct 19, 2017	Coalmont Cem.; Dau. of Fred & Dorothy (Gallagher) Barnes; m. William Henry "Red" Flynn
Flynn, James Henry	Dec 6, 1879	Oct 29, 1923	White Cem.; Son of Michael Joseph, Sr. & Elizabeth (Keeling) Flynn; m. Willie Myrtle Meeks; addition to Cemeteries of Grundy Co, Vol. 2, p. 1010
Flynn, Michael "Mike", Sr.	Apr 11, 1830	Feb 3, 1896	Tracy City Cem.; Son of John & Bridget (Sullivan) Flynn; born in Belfast, Ireland; m. Elizabeth Keeling; addition to Cemeteries of Grundy Co., Vol. 2, p. 899
Flynn, Patrick Sheehan	Jul 07, 1929	Sep 24, 2005	Coalmont Cem.; Son of Michael R & Kathleen M (Sheehan) Flynn; correction to Cemeteries of Grundy County, Vol. 1, p 185
Flynn, Willie Myrtle (Meeks)	Dec 4, 1883	Sep 17, 1979	White Cem.; Dau. of Willis Benson & Nancy Jane (Ragsdale) Meeks; m. James Henry Flynn; addition to Cemeteries of Grundy Co., Vol. 2, p. 1010
Fogle, Linda Roxanne (Ferrell)	Jun 20, 1959	Nov 14, 2021	Cremated; Dau. of Vance & Cherie (Eller) Ferrell; m. Alan Fogle
Ford, Ella Faye (Knox)	Jul 21, 1936	Aug 30, 1970	Palmer Cem.; Dau. of Fred Earl & Pearl M. (Henry) Knox; m. Russell Ford; addition to Grundy Co. Cemeteries, Vol. 2; p. 555.
Ford, John R.	Jan 9, 1888	Jan 20, 1965	Wesley Chapel Cem.; Son of William R. & Mary (Wilson) Ford; m. Myrtle Virgil "Mirtie" Goodwin; addition to Cemeteries of Grundy Co, Vol. 2, p. 975
Ford, Russell	Oct 06, 1931	Jun 11, 1978	Palmer Cem.; Son of Sherman & Gertie (Moore) Ford; m. Ella Faye Knox; addition to Cemeteries of Grundy Co, Vol. 2, p. 555
Forsyth, Arter Clinton	Mar 23, 1941	May 25, 2018	Walker Cem.; Son of Joseph Thomas Forsyth & Sarah Rhevena Baker; m. Brenda King

Name	Born	Died	Details
Forsyth, James Robert	Mar 14, 1947	Feb 28, 2022	Walker Cem.; Son of Joseph Thomas & Sarah Rhevena (Baker) Forsyth; m. Mildred McCormick; U.S. Army - Vietnam
Forsyth, Vanessa Kay (Green)	Sep 05, 1965	Oct 05, 2018	Philadelphia Cem.; Dau. of George Earl Green & Carrie Louise King; m. Roy G. Forsyth, Jr.
Foster, Bettye Jean (Charles)	Mar 19, 1926	Jan 14, 2016	Philadelphia Cem.; Dau. of Jennings & Anna V. (Roddy) Charles; m. Robert Hill Foster
Foster, John Robert	1902	Feb 28, 1920	Foster Falls Cem.; Son of Robert & Margarita (Almany) Foster per Ralph Shrum
Foster, Mary Frances (Magouirk)	Dec 04, 1935	May 09, 2019	Gnat Hill Cem.; Dau. of James William & Mary Etta Magouirk; m. Richard Foster
Foster, William	1895	Jun 24, 1948	Foster Falls Cem.; Son of Robert & Margarerita (Almany) Foster per Ralph Shrum
Foutch, Carolyn Fay (Crisp)	Dec 12, 1941	Jul 16, 2015	Monteagle Cem.; Dau. of Haskel & Leta (Rollins) Crisp; m. Garland Foutch
Fowler, Jerry Lynn	Feb 29, 1952	Jan 01, 2015	Cremated; Son of Melvin G & Virginia (Cates) Fowler; US Army; lived in Altamont
Fox, Sally Virginia (Willis)	Jul 2, 1862	Sep 8, 1891	Tracy City Cem.; Dau. of William & Sarah (Merett) Vaughn; m. Thomas W. Fox; on May 4, 1879; addition to Cemeteries of Grundy Co.,Vol. 2, p. 889
Frame, George W.	Jan 05, 1937	Jul 27, 2015	Cremated; Son of George Abner & Ethel May (Daum) Frame; m. Nancy Louise Medley
Franklin, James Rodman	Jul 19, 1930	Oct 10, 2013	Cremated; Son of Selmon T. Franklin
Franklin, Kenneth Jason	Mar 08, 1972	Sep 20, 2021	Palmer Cem.; Son of K.R. & Janice Franklin; m. Tammy May Franklin
Frederick, Cecil Nortn	1929	Sep 27, 2014	Orange Hill Cem.; Son of Isaac Jessie Frederick & Fronia Novella Sanders; m. Mary E. Frederick
Frederick, Kathy	Nov 02, 1958	Jan 31, 2017	Hilltop Cem. Centerville, TN; Dau. of Vernon & Janice (Tarzi) Smartt; m. Howell Jeffrey Frederick
Frederick, Mary Kathleen "Bet"	Jun 09, 1940	Apr 13, 2016	Bonny Oak Cem.; Dau. of Harvey & Edna Vera (Morgan) Nunley; m. Edward "Pat" Frederick; addition to Cemeteries of Grundy Co.Vol. 1, p. 95
Fredrick, John Dewey	Jul 23, 1933	Jan 14, 2019	Shady Grove Cem.; Son of Jessie Fredrick & Fronie Sanders; m. Louise Gibbs
Fredrick, Mary Kathleen "Bet" (Nunley)	Jun 09, 1940	Apr 13, 2016	Bonny Oak Cem.; Dau. of Harvey & Edna Vera (Morgan) Nunley; m. Edward Ernest "Pat" Fredrick, Mar 24, 1956
French, Earldene Metcalfe	1940	May 16, 2014	Summerfield Cem.; Dau of Jim Earl Thomas & Clara Irene Layne; m. Joseph Maurice Metcalfe
French, Violet O. "Vi"	Jul 07, 1923	Feb 13, 2010	Monteagle Cem.; m. Edgar French; addition to Cemeteries of Grundy Co.Vol. 1, p 444

Name	Birth	Death	Details
Frisbee, Crimson Wade	Apr 10, 2017	Jul 23, 2018	Palmer Cem.; Son of William H "Bill" Frisbee & Lauren Rochelle Garner
Frisbee, James Ray	Nov 27, 1966	Sep 08, 2021	Little Johnny Myers Cem.; Son of Harvey Lee & Sylvia Beatrice (Jones) Frisbee; m. Diane Skinner
Frisbee, Willow Brooke	Jan 18, 2016	Jul 23, 2018	Palmer Cem.; Dau. of William H "Bill" Frisbee & Lauren Rochelle Garner
Fry, John	Jun 13, 1939	Apr 26, 2021	Chattanooga National Cem.; Son of Dan J. & Lydia (Helmuth) Fry; U.S. Army
Fulton, Danice N. Pierce	ca. 1950	Sep 21 2015	Cremated; He was from Tullahoma, TN. no further information was located
Fulton, Irene "Reenie" Lewisy Bean	Nov 14, 1947	Aug 01, 2015	Cremation; Dau. of George & Dorothea Jeanne Lewisy
Fults - Kilgore, Mary Jo	Jun 30, 1929	Jul 24, 2016	Plainview Cem.; Dau. of James O & Margie (Nunley) Fults; m. Clarence Kilgore, Jr.
Fults, Adell (Campbell)	Jan 22, 1940	Aug 12, 2008	Fults Cem. Northcutt's Cove; Dau. of Andrew Jackson & Ola M. Campbell; m. Johnny Fults; addition to Cemeteries of Grundy Co.Vol. 1, p. 284
Fults, Amy Lou	Jan 15, 1950	Jul 18, 2017	Fall Creek Cem.; Dau. of Paul Cleek & Edith Turner Minton; m. Hoyt Fults
Fults, Anna Viola "Annie" (Oliver)	Aug 01, 1893	Oct 28, 1928	Warren "Red Hill" Cemetery; Dau. of Robert "Bob" & Mary Myrtle "Myrt" (Meeks) Oliver; m. Jay Fults; no tombstone; information from death certificate
Fults, Annie Beatrice (Elkins)	Aug 02, 1931	Dec 04, 2020	Hebron Cem.; Dau. of James & Violet (Johnson) Elkins; m. John Henry Russell Fults
Fults, Betty (Rollins)	Oct 14, 1938	Feb 18, 2013	Brown's Chapel Cem.; Dau. of James & Lucy (Burnett) Rollins
Fults, Boyd	Jul 30, 1945	Nov 12, 2016	Palmer Cem.; Son of Wesley & Parthenia (McHone) Fults; m. Linda Van Hoosier
Fults, Brenda Corean	Feb 10, 1958	Feb 22, 1958	Brown's Chapel Cem.; Dau. of Ether Loren & Martha J. (King) Fults; addition to Cemeteries of Grundy Co.,Vol. 1, p. 103
Fults, Caroline Brown	Apr 23, 1850	Oct 02, 1909	Hobbs Hill Cem.; Dau. of Alexander William & Rachael (Austin) Brown; m. 1) John Hobbs 2) Lawson F. Fults; correction of birthdate per tombstone & addition to Cemeteries of Grundy Co.,Vol. 1, p. 330
Fults, Carolyn Denise (Hill)	Feb 23, 1961	Apr 10, 2014	Fults Cem.; Dau. of Marvin Dennis Hill & Mary Lee (Owenby) Farmer; m. Kent Fults
Fults, Clara Marie (Tate)	Oct 08, 1926	Sep 13, 2014	Altamont Cem.; Dau. of Leo & Ollie Bell (Gross) Tate; m. Hugh Willard "Dutch" Fults; addition to Cemeteries of Grundy Co.Vol. 1, p. 24
Fults, Clarence Fults	Mar 28, 1946	Aug 29, 2021	Old Bybee Chapel Cem.; Son of Ruben & Velma Irene (King) Fults; m. Carolyn Sue Fisher

Name	Birth	Death	Details
Fults, Clifford	Jul 12, 1934	Dec 28, 2014	Fults, Clifford Gravesite; Son of Oris & Emma (Layne) Fults; m. Esther May Perry; addition to Cemeteries of Grundy Co, Vol. 1, p. 274
Fults, Cynthia Joan	Sep 24, 1960	Jan 16, 2018	Fults Cem.; Dau. of Johnny Earl Fults & Adell Campbell
Fults, Daisy Lee	Aug 11, 1884	Jan 07, 1968	Hobbs Hill Cem.; Dau. of John & Emma Suttle; m. John Bell Fults on Nov 30, 1902; addition to Cemeteries of Grundy Co. Vol. 1, p. 330
Fults, Dave	Nov 18, 1872	Dec 01, 1929	Swiss Colony Cem.; Son of James & Sophronia Ann (Cope) Fults; m. Belle Smartt; addition Cemeteries Grundy Co, Vol. 2, p. 785
Fults, Dorothy Jean (Tate)	Sep 08, 1931	Dec 11, 2020	Altamont Cem.; Dau. of Buford & Sarah (Scott) Tate
Fults, Earl F.	Jan 10, 1936	Nov 08, 2009	Brown's Chapel Cem.; Son of Jay & Ola Idella (Meeks) Fults; m. Betty Rollins; addition to Cemeteries of Grundy Co.Vol. 1, p. 103
Fults, Edith Jane (Whitman)	Jan 30, 1944	Dec 19, 2018	Fults Family Cem.; Dau. of Lecil Whitman & Sarah Jane Anderson; m. Boyd Stanton Fults
Fults, Elihu	Jul 4, 1880	Jan 03, 1965	Hobbs Hill Cem.; Son of George & Mary (Smartt) Fults; m. 1)Sarah Elizabeth Argo 2) Anna Selina Harris; addition to Cemeteries of Grundy Co.Vol. 1, p. 328
Fults, Ferlin James "Archie"	Jul 20, 1956	Oct 09, 2020	Palmer Cem.; Son of Clifford & Esther Mae (Perry) Fults; m. Jan Fults
Fults, Gordon	Apr 02, 1931	Dec 16, 2017	Mt. Zion Cem.; Son of Tom & Alkie Scott Fults; m. Linda Wallace Fults
Fults, Helen Ruth	Jan 19, 1942	May 29, 2020	Airview Cem.; Dau. of B.F. & Wilma Dovie (Fisher) Yates; m. Larry Parker Fults; addition to Cemeteries of Grundy Co,Vol. 1, p. 7
Fults, Hester Mae (Meeks)	Mar 21, 1925	Nov 23, 2016	Plainview Cem.; Dau. of Newt A. & Flora Mae (McWain) Meeks; m. Raymond "Cotton" Fults on Nov.18, 1944; addition to Cemeteries of Grundy Co,Vol. 2, p. 668
Fults, Hollis McDonald "Mack"	Feb 14, 1922	Dec 12, 2013	Fults Cem.; Son of Albert Hannar & Margaret Ann (Gross) Fults
Fults, Infant			Clouse Hill Cem.; child of Kenny & Pamela (Miller) Fults
Fults, Irean	Jul 04, 1924	Jul 21, 1925	Bonny Oak Cem.; Dau. of Martin VanBuren Jackson & Lilly Belle (Nunley) Fults; name is on the same tombstone as her sister Margret Fults; addition to Cemeteries of Grundy Co,Vol. 1, p. 82
Fults, James E	Feb 09, 1930	Jul 04, 2018	Sunset Memorial Gardens, Odessa, TX; Son of Charlie Fults & Louise Cannon; m. Bobbye Tennis; US Air Force; Korea
Fults, James Marvin	Feb 13, 1950	Dec 28, 2015	Plainview Cem.; Son of Wesley Earl & Perrie Ula (Myers) Fults

Fults, Jannie Robin (Edwards)	Feb 11, 1962	Feb 23, 2022	Palmer Cem.; Son of Floyd A. & Verdie Marie (Reed) Edwards; m. Ferlin J. "Archie" Fults
Fults, Jay F	Jun 18, 1886	Jun 19, 1967	Fall Creek Cem.; Son of John Carroll & Sarah Jane (Brown) Fults
Fults, Joe Monroe	May 26, 1945	Jun 26, 2013	Brown's Chapel Cem.; Son of Ether & Martha (King) Fults; Companion, Linda Taylor
Fults, Joe Willard	Sep 17, 1927	Sep 25, 2017	Palmer Cem.; Son of Theron & Josephine E. (Brown) Fults; m. Jul 17, 1946, to Emma Jean Worley; US Navy WWII; addition to Cemeteries of Grundy Co.,Vol. 2, p. 577
Fults, John Mason	Oct 04, 1993	Sep 15, 2018	Cremated; Son of John & Hope (Root) Fults; grandparents Clay & Vivian (Henley) Fults; grandparents from Pelham
Fults, Johnny Earl	Mar 22, 1900	Jul 18, 2013	Fults Cem.; Son of Bob & Pearl (Payne) Fults; m. Adell Campbell; US Army
Fults, Josephine E. (Brown)	Dec 09, 1908	Feb 26, 1988	Swiss Colony Cem.; Dau. of Edward H. & Georgia H. (Eckles) Brown; m. Theron Elmore Fults on July 22, 1926; addition to Cemeteries of Grundy Co.Vol. 2, p. 793
Fults, Joyce Marie (Nunley)	Jun 19, 2939	Feb 05, 2022	Cremated; Dau. of Gordon & Jessie (Trussell) Nunley
Fults, Julie A. (McCormick)	Jun 9, 1888	Feb 16, 1961	Wesley Chapel Cem.; Dau. of William B. & Mary (Tallent) McCormick; m. 1) Dave Fults 2) John King O'Neal 3) Hother Roberts; Addition to Cemeteries of Grundy Co.,Vol. 2, p. 984
Fults, Kenneth Dale	1951	Dec 31, 2013	Palmer Cem.; Son of Willie Carl & Beatrice Franklin "Bootsie" (Nunley) Fults; m. Carolyn Scissom
Fults, Lawson	Jan 25, 1905	Mar 05, 1920	Hobbs Hill Cem.; Son of David & Arminta (Patrick) Fults; addition to Cemeteries of Grundy Co.,Vol. 1, p. 338
Fults, Lillie Carlyon (Bates)	Sep 14, 1942	Sep 11, 2021	Mount Zion Cem.; Dau. of Clarence & Eta Pearl (Scott) Bates; m. Fred A. Fults, Jr.
Fults, Linda Joyce (VanHooser)	Apr 01, 1947	Oct 14, 2021	Palmer Cem.; Dau. of Isaac & Nora (Layne) VanHooser; m. Boyd Fults
Fults, Luther Don	Sep 05, 1950	Mar 26, 2021	Wesley Chapel Cem.; Son of France Hill & Martha Myrtle Fults; m. Martha Wimberly; U.S. Army
Fults, Margret Lucille	Nov 30, 1919	Nov 30, 1919	Bonny Oak Cem.; Dau. of Martin VanBuren Jackson & Lilly Belle (Nunley) Fults; sister Irean Fults is on the same tombstone; addition to Cemeteries of Grundy Co,Vol. 1, p. 82
Fults, Marjorie (Gardner)	Feb 26, 1923	Oct 14, 2000	Altamont Cem.; Dau. of Frank Threlfell & Ada Emiley (Hickman) Gardner; m. Chester Lawrence Fults; Addition to Cemeteries of Grundy Co.,Vol. 1, p. 28

Fults, Marke Kevin	Dec 07, 1973	Aug 24, 2015	Fall Creek Cem.; Son of Hoyt & Amie (Cleek) Fults
Fults, Martha Jane (King)	Apr 07, 1916	Jun 14, 1994	Brown's Chapel Cem.; Dau. of Thomas & Martha Jane (Myers) King; m. Ether Loren Fults; addition to Cemeteries of Grundy Co.Vol. 1, p. 102
Fults, Melissa Ann	Sep 27, 1966	Jan 11, 2015	Fults Cem.; Dau. of Denver Yarworth & Patricia Myers; m. Fred Fults, Jr.
Fults, Melvin Levern	Ca 1937	Dec 08, 2017	Palmer City Cem.; Son of Wesley & Parthenia (McHone) Fults; m. Violet Faye VanHoosier
Fults, Michael Dale	Jul 08, 1967	Dec 05, 2015	Swiss Cem.; Son of Ray & Wanda (Scissom) Fults; m. Tammy Fults
Fults, Nola Jean	Jul 17, 1955	Jun 20, 2018	King Cem.; Dau. of Nathaniel Tate & Lola Roberts; m. Edwin Fults
Fults, Ophelia (Dickerson)	Jul 16, 1917	Dec 19, 2016	Altamont Cem.; Dau. of Jim & Nina (Givens) Dickerson; m. Kermit R. Fults; addition to Cemeteries of Grundy Co.Vol. 1, p. 21
Fults, Parthenia L. (McHone)	Aug 25, 1918	Jul 01, 2013	Palmer Cem.; Dau. of Harley & Mattie (Shoemake) McHone; m. Wesley A. Fults; addition to Cemeteries of Grundy Co.Vol. 2, p. 560
Fults, Perrie Ula (Myers)	Jan 15, 1923	Apr 23, 1965	Plainview Cem.; Dau. of Myles Benson & Nancy Kate (Campbell) Myers; m. Richard W. Fults; addition to Cemeteries of Grundy Co,Vol. 2, p. 698
Fults, Ray Jackson	Jun 19, 1939	Feb 14, 2014	Swiss Colony Cem.; Son of Lawrence & Emma (McHone) Fults; m. Joy Lee Carpenter
Fults, Ronald Dean	Mar 15, 1945	Jan 19, 2019	Fults Cem.; Son of Hollis Macdonald Fults & Clara Evangeline Campbell; m. Kathryn Sanders
Fults, Ruthy Jane	Jul 11, 1882	Sep 20, 1920	Elijah & Kitt Meeks Hollow Cem.; location of grave is 39 19' 39" N and 85 40' 38" W; remote; Dau. of Jesse & Mary A. (Haskins) Fults (1850-1930); 4 more unmarked graves are here also. Some believe that two of them are her parents. Ruthy had children Maggie Marie Fults Roberts (1901-1989) who married Francis Roberts and Myrtle Ellen Fults Byers (1904-1956), who is buried at Warren "Red Hill" Cemetery in Pelham.
Fults, Sarah Louise (Scott)	Jul 7, 1869 per records	Mar 13, 1905	Altamont Cem.; Dau. of John & Sarah (Smartt) Scott; addition to Cemeteries of Grundy Co.Vol. 1, p. 34
Fults, Sheryl Lynn "Sherri" (Sherwood)	Dec 17, 1962	May 10, 2020	Wesley Chapel Cem.; Dau. of James Robert Sherwood & Bettye Lou Wooten; m. Randy Fults
Fults, Tade	Sep 15, 1841	Jun 06, 1916	Gruetli Community; Son of Andrew Jackson "Andy" & Nancy (Hobbs) Fults; from *Mrs. Grundy* Jun 8, 1916

Name	Birth	Death	Details
Fults, Tennessee	1854	Jan 16, 1929	Swiss Colony Cem.; Dau of Tade Fults & Nancy Lucinda Pickett; Died at her home near Gruetli, information from newspaper
Fults, Thomas Bryan	Jan 24, 1886	Jun 03, 1961	Coalmont Cem.; Son of John Wesley & Lucretia (Campbell) Fults per birth certificate; m: Mary Nunnley; correction to Cemeteries of Grundy County, Vol. 1, p.189
Fults, Tiffany Rhea	Nov 22, 1979	Mar 19, 2017	Shellsford Cem.; Dau. of Eddie Sullivan & Nelda Jodi Cantrell; m. Andrew Lee Fults
Fults, Tresa Gail	Apr 22, 1966	Jul 21, 2013	Fults Family Cem. at Stoner Mountain; Dau. of Boyd Stanton & Edith Jane Fults
Fults, Vernon Lee	Apr 29, 1927	Sep 30, 2017	Fults Cem.; Son of Robert Lee "Bob" & Pearl Layne Fults, m. Brenda Newby Fults
Fults, Violet Faye (VanHooser)	Jul 28, 1940	Apr 22, 2021	Palmer Cem.; Dau. of Isaac & Nora (Layne) VanHooser; m. Melvin Fults
Fults, Virginia Lucille "Susie"	Apr 03, 1958	Oct 25, 1997	Fall Creek Cem.; Dau. of Clifford Fults & Ester Perry; m. 1) Danny Lee Layne 2) Kenneth Walton Bowman
Fults, Wayne "Smiley"	Ca 1948	Nov 17, 2017	Orange Hill Cem.; Son of Wesley Nunley & Perrie Fults m. Nila Nunley
Fults, Wendell Edward	Dec 15, 1944	Jan 10, 2021	Griffiths Creek Cem.; Son of Oris & Emma (Layne) Fults; m. Lou Ella Sanders
Fultz, Hester Mae	Mar 21, 1925	Nov 23, 2016	Plainview Cem.; Dau. of Newt & Flora (McWain) Meeks; m. Raymond "Cotton" Fultz
Fultz, Thomas Edward	Jan 19, 1922	Dec 31, 2010	Plainview Cem.; Son of Charley Jesse & Florence (Smith) Fultz; m. Mary Irvin; addition to Cemeteries of Grundy Co. Vol. 2, p. 665
Fultz, Willie Mae (Patrick)	Sep 25, 1940	Jun 07, 2016	Plainview Cem.; Dau. of Millard Fletcher & Cora Elizabeth (Nunley) Patrick; m. Johnny L. Fultz; addition to Cemeteries of Grundy Co, Vol. 2, p. 702
Gaitens, Anna Pearl (Hartwell)	Oct 11, 1904	Mar 16, 1993	Cumberland Heights Cem.; Dau. of Herbert Clifton & Sarah Elizabeth "Sadie" (Jones) Hartwell; m. James Clyde Gaitens; addition to Cemeteries of Grundy Co. Vol. 1, p.197
Gaitens, James Clyde	Jun 29, 1907	Nov 29, 1976	Cumberland Herights Cem.; Son of Rae Clyde & Helen Stewart (McEwan) Gaitens; m. Anna Pearl Hartwell; addition to Cemeteries of Grundy Co. Vol. 1, p. 198
Gallagher, Jerry Dale	Jan 16, 1954	Dec 24, 2017	Cremated; Son of Benton Clay & Cleora (Wilson) Gallagher; m. Karen Barnes; lived in Pelham
Gallagher, Mary Frances (Prince)	Oct 08, 1929	Dec 06, 2018	Franklin Memorial Gardens; Dau. of J.D. Prince & Irene Hawkins; m. Joseph Clark Gallagher

Name	Birth	Death	Details
Gallagher, Willodean "Dean"	May 24, 1928	Feb 02, 2016	Franklin Memorial Gardens; Dau. of Joseph Edmond & Aubrey Lellis (Patton) Gallagher; never married
Gamble, Carrie Grace	Mar 19, 1922	Apr 06, 1988	Oak Grove Cem.; Dau. of William A. & Mildred (Kilgore) Green; m. Orby Gamble; addition Cemeteries of Grundy Co.Vol. 1. p 499
Gamble, Orby	Nov 21, 1917	Oct 01, 1990	Oak Grove Cem.; Son of John J. Gamble of Whitwell, TN m. Carrie Grace Green; addition to Cemeteries of Grundy Co,Vol. 1, p. 499
Garner, Billy Ed	Mar 27, 1938	Dec 29, 2020	Montgomery-Cowan Cem.; Son of Ed Monroe & Martha Lee Garner
Garner, Clarence W	Jan 09, 1928	Apr 16, 2016	Pelham Church of Christ Cem.; Son of Oscar S. & Ella (Long) Garner; m. Faye Moran; Our children Dennis & Marcia and grandson Matthew Garner; addition to Cemeteries of Grundy Co.Vol. 2, p. 606
Garner, Dorothy	May 11, 1921	Jun 20, 2016	Palmer Cem.; Dau. of Ben & Rene Morrison; Herbert Garner
Garner, Fay (Moran)	Jan 28, 1932	Oct 01, 2018	Pelham Church of Christ Cem.; Dau. of Wiley & Vivian (Henley) Moran; m. Clarence W. Garner; addition to Cemeteries of Grundy Co,Vol. 2, p. 606
Garner, Jeffrey Douglas "Pottsie"	Mar 16, 1958	Oct 23, 2021	Cremated; Son of Billy Douglas & Bertha Mae Garner
Garner, Lauren Rochelle	Jan 22, 1988	Jul 23, 2018	Palmer Cem.; Dau. of Don Carlos Garner & Rochelle Meeks
Garner, Louis Stanley	ca. 1937	Jan 28, 2014	Chattanooga Memorial Gardens; Son of Henry & Ora Garner; m. Niccoa Ann Charles; US Marine Corps
Garner, Wanda Faye (Nunley)	May 11, 1943	Nov 18, 2020	Coalmont Cem.; Dau. of Lee & Rachel (Nunley) Green; m. Floyd Garner
Garretson, Frances A	Oct 6, 1806	Sep 15, 1871	Coulson/Wesley Chapel Churh Cem.; m. Isaac Garretson
Garretson, Mary E	Aug 10, 1840	Nov 9, 1860	Coulson/Wesley Chapel Churh Cem.; Dau. of Isaac & Frances Garretson
Garretson, Robert W	Dec 27, 1838	Dec 7, 1860	Coulson/Wesley Chapel Church Cem.; Son of Isaac & Frances Garretson
Gates, Roy Leon	Mar 19, 1956	Aug 14, 2015	Cremated; Son of Fred & Sandra Gates; m Susan Gates
Gatewood, Joseph Rodney	Dec 25, 1938	Oct 10, 2001	Cumberland Heights Cem.; Son of Guy Percy & Irene Stella (Stewart) Gatewood; m. Reba Ann Slater; US Army; addition to Cemeteries of Grundy Co,Vol. 1, p.198
Gattis, Betty (Roberts)	Sep 16, 1943	May 30, 2020	Franklin Memorial Gardens Cem.; Dau. of Marvin Roberts & Edna Dykes; m. Charles Gattis

Gattis, Nell (Dickerson)	Mar 07, 1915	Apr 07, 2000	Altamont Cem.; Dau. of Ame David & Sally (Givens) Dickerson; m. C.F. Gattis; even though she has a tombstone in Altamont, she is buried at Franklin Memorial Gardens in Winchester, TN.
Geary, Carson Dennis	Jun 14, 2002	Mar 23, 2020	Geary Family Gravesite a.k.a. Tabernacle of the Lord Cem in Tracy City; Son of Clayton Geary & Candace Sanders
Geary, Dennis Clayton	Sep 02, 1928	Sept 18, 2013	Geary Family Gravesite a.k.a Tabernacle of the Lord in Tracy City; Son of Everett & Winnie Davis (Carrick) Geary
Geary, Dennis Clayton	Sep 02, 1928	Sep 18, 2013	Geary Family Gravesite a.k.a. Tabernacle of the Lord Cem.; Son of Everett & Winnie Davis (Carrick) Geary; m. William Mae Thomas; addition to Cemeteries of Grundy Co.Vol. 1, p. 287
Geary, Ima Jean (Shrum)	Dec 10, 1935	Feb 01, 2022	Fall Creek Cem.; Dau. of James & Mary Ellen (Tate) Shrum; m. Robert Lee Geary
Geary, Johnnie Marie (Johnson)	Oct 15, 1928	Dec 12, 2017	Orange Hill Cem.; Dau. of Barney William & Lillie Pearl (Orange) Johnson; m. 1) Cecil Cunningham 2) Earl Geary, Sr.
Geary, Max Douglas, Sr.	Mar 08, 1926	May 21, 2016	Plainview Cem.; Son of William Robert "W.R." & Lillie (Myers) Geary; m. Helen June Taulbee; addition to Cemeteries of Grundy Co.Vol. 2, p. 660
Geary, Roy Clayton	1965	Jun 10, 2017	Tabernacle of the Lord Cem.; Son of Dennis & Willie Mae (Thomas) Geary; m. Candace Sanders; US Army
Geary, Thelma Arlean (Shrum)	Mar 08, 1929	Mar 14, 2019	Palmer Cem.; Dau. of Rev. Joe Bailey & Grace Leona (Dishroon) Shrum; m. Alvin Oats Geary Jul 2, 1949; addition to Cemeteries of Grundy Co,Vol. 2, p 552
Geary, Thomas Jaefferson	Aug 25, 1880	Feb 10, 1950	Plainview Cem.; Son of Thomas & Texas (Dixon) Geary; m. Ferby Sweeton
Geary, Willie Mae (Thomas)	Feb 12, 1933	Nov 02, 2009	Geary Family Cem.; a.k.a. Tabernacle of the Lord Tracy City Cem.; Dau. of Roy Hillman "Judd" & Esther Elizabeth "Beth" Thomas; m. Dennis Clayton Geary
Geil, Elizabeth geb (Claus)	Mar 10, 1863	Mar 9, 1884	Swiss Colony Cem.; possibly Dau. of Jordan & Barbara Claus; "geb" means "born" in the German language; addition to Cemeteries of Grundy Co,Vol. 2, p. 785
Geil, Elizabeth geb (Glaus)	Mar 10, 1863	Mar 9, 1884	Swiss Colony Cem.; Born in Switzerland Dau. of Nicholaus Glaus; m. Jacob Geil in NY
Gentry, Madella (Beebe)	Mar 16, 1930	Sep 26, 2016	Pleaseant View Cem.; Dau. of Walter & Liby (Coble) Beebe

Name	Birth	Death	Details
Gholston, Sam, Jr.	Sep 09, 1927	Jul 07, 2005	White Cem.; Son of Sam & Ellen Beatrice (Turner) Gholston; m. Mona Lee Worley; addition to Cemeteries of Grundy Co., Vol. 2, p. 1007
Gibbons, Tommy Louis	Nov 07, 1965	Apr 21, 2008	White Cem.; Son of Walton Lee & Rebecca "Reba" (Long) Gibbons; m. Leslie Modschiedler; addition to Cemeteries of Grundy Co., Vol. 2, p. 1013
Gibbs, Everett R.	Feb 22, 1932	Jan 03, 2021	Plainview Cem.; Son of Luke & Jessie (Parsons) Gibbs; m. Nell Rose Gibbs
Gibbs, Frances Cordelia "Puss"	Sep 18, 1860	Jun 30, 1911	Clouse Hill Cem.; Dau. of Virginia Vincent & Mary Elizabeth "Polly" (Sanders) Gibbs; mother of Annie Lee (Gibbs) Cunningham; never married; info. source Faye (Church) Bonner
Gibbs, Gordon H.	Jun 05, 1934	Jan 17, 2016	Mt. Moriah Cem in Troy, AL; Son of Luke Grady & Jessie Beatrice (Parsons) Gibbs; m. Audrey Gibbs
Gibbs, Homer, Jr.	Feb 05, 1927	Apr 14, 2014	Plainview Cem.; Son of Luke Grady & Jessie Beatrice (Parsons) Gibbs; m. 1) Clara Louise Burnett on Nov 27, 1968 2) Willie Mae McDaniel Feb 5, 1982; WWII
Gibbs, James Odom	Sep 18, 1867	Mar 23, 1950	Hobbs Hill Cem.; Son of Nancy Gibbs per death certificate; m. Lucy B. Argo, Sep 20, 1889; addition to Cemeterieis of Grundy Co, Vol. 1, p. 329
Gibbs, Lindel Joseph	Jun 03, 1945	Apr 10, 2018	Fall Creek Cem.; Son of Johnny Dillard Gibbs & June Borne
Gibbs, Lucy B. (Argo)	1867	1931	Hobbs Hill Cem.; Dau. of John & Sallie Argo; m. James Odom Gibbs, Sep 20, 1889; addition to Cemeteries of Grundy Co., Vol. 1, p 329
Gibbs, Tedd K.	Mar 05, 1936	Jun 06, 2015	Plainview Cem.; Son of Paul & Ida Mae (Thomas) Gibbs
Giblin, Sandi Diane	Aug 28, 1950	Oct 03, 2013	Palmer Nazarene Church Cem.; Dau. of Harley & Opal (Stephenson) Fulghum
Gibson, Martha Ann (Newman)	Apr 18, 1928	Mar 11, 2015	Orange Hill Cem.; Dau. of George Martin & Lillian Lucille (Denton) Newman; addition to Cemeteries of Grundy Co, TN, Vol. 2, p. 525
Gibson, William Dean	Aug 08, 1927	Sep 06, 2019	Mt. Garner Cem.; Son of William Oscar Gipson & Emma Crystal Wintrow; m. Bettye Young; U.S. Army
Gifford, Gary Eugene III	Apr 24, 1989	Apr 09, 2020	Palmer Cem.; Son of Gary E. Gifford, Jr. & Tammy Dale Gifford
Gifford, Hannah (James)	Sep 12, 1894	Oct 01, 1977	Palmer Cem.; Dau. of William "Bill & Sarah "Sally" (Pelham) James; m. 1) Manuel Perry 2) Russ Gifford; addition to Cemeteries of Grundy Co. Vol. 2, p 553

Gilbert, Ernestine (Roberts)	Feb 18, 1939	Jun 13, 2013	Fall Creek Cem.; Dau. of Francis M. & Maggie (Fults) Roberts; m. John Thomas Gilbert
Gillespie, David Wayne	Jul 16, 1958	Jun 27, 2020	Cremated; Son of William Harold Gillespie & Aiko Kikuchi; m. Daisie Layne
Gillespie, Gordon R	Nov 16, 1940	Feb 21, 2018	Cremated; Son of Thomas E. Gillespie & Vera Roberts
Gillespie, James Ray	Jan 14, 1943	Oct 28, 2019	Gardens of Memory Cem.; Son of David Daniel & Soledad Gillespie
Gilley, Benjamin	ca. 1844	Dec 16, 1909	Tracy City area; Son of Gideon & Edy (Morris) Gilley; m. Elizabeth Cope; Killed by falling slate Reid Hill Mine- newspaper
Gilley, Ella (Disheroon)	Oct 10, 1885	Dec 10, 1955	Plainview Cem.; Dau. of James & Elizabeth (Thompson) Disheroon; m. William Henry Gilley; addition to Cemeteries of Grudy Co,Vol. 2, p. 685
Gilley, William Henry	Sep 8, 1867	Mar 31, 1958	Plainview Cem.; Son of Benjamin Franklin & Elizabeth (Phipps) Gilley; m. Ella Disheroon; addition to Cemeteries of Grundy Co.,Vol. 2, p. 685
Gilliam Edna Jane	Jan 20, 1946	Mar 10, 2018	Summerfield Cem.; Dau. of Fred & Letha Dishroom; m. Lewis Wright Gilliam
Gilliam, Alma Christine (Williams)	Dec. 17, 1933	Apr 25, 2015	Rose Hill Memorial Gardens Cem.; Dau. of Walter & Lucy (Meeks) Williams; m. Gerald Edward "Bud" Gilliam
Gilliam, Barbara "Bobbie" (Graves)	Feb 16, 1951	Feb 25, 2021	Harrison Chapel Cem.; Dau. of James & Mignone Graves; m. Sandy Gilliam
Gilliam, Bunia (Nunley)	Aug 25, 1927	Jan 27, 2015	Mt. Olivet Cemetery in Parkersburg WV.; Dau. of Louis Jefferson & Bunia (Dickerson) Nunley; m. Billy Gilliam, Jr.
Gilliam, Charles Hayden, Sr.	Jan 27, 1951	Jul 26, 2007	Burns Cem.; Son of Gordon & Gladys (Medley) Gilliam; m. Pauline (Privett) Harris; funeral home marker; addition to Cemeteries of Grundy Co.Vol. 1, p. 128
Gilliam, Charles Henry	Jan 27, 1940	Jan 24, 2013	Harrison Cem.; Son of Charles E & Alma (Long) Gilliam; m. Helen Hill
Gilliam, Denny Martin	Nov 11, 1966	May 07, 2020	Warren"Red Hill" Cem.; Son of John Grady & Freda Louise (Anderson) Gilliam; m. Amanda Marr; Army & Air Force
Gilliam, Glen A.	1939	Mar 14, 2019	Harrison Cem.; Son of James E. Gilliam & Bertha Green
Gilliam, James Harold	1958	Mar 09, 2019	New Hope Cem.; Son of Robert Gilliam & Clarsie Mae Meeks; m. Linda Faye Luttrell
Gilliam, Jimmy	Mar 21, 1947	May 31, 2014	Hill Cem.; Son of Robert "Bob Mitch" Gilliam & Clercie Mae Meeks; m. Mary Ann Gilliam
Gilliam, Margie Mae (Bain)	1936	Aug 26, 2021	Greene Lawn Memory Gardens, Greenville, TN; Dau. of Frank & Ova Mae Bain; m. Burwell Gilliam

Name	Birth	Death	Details
Gilliam, Minnie Pearl (Elliott)	1944	Aug 29, 2019	Red Hill Cem Rutledge Ford; Dau. of John Thomas Elliott & Minnie Lou Presley; m. Robert Gilliam, Jr.
Gilliam, Nancy M.	Mar 19, 1934	Mar 30, 2013	Eastern Star Cem.; Dau. of Fred O. & Maude (Garner) Hughes ; m. Frank Gilliam
Gilliam, Pauline (Privett) Harris	Dec 11, 1943	Jun 22, 2006	Burns Cem.; Dau. of Harley & Estelle (Caskett) Privett; m. 1) Gilbert B. Harris 2) Charles Hayden Gilliam, Sr. ;addition to Cemeteries of Grundy Co.,Vol. 1, p. 128
Gilliam, Robert, Jr.	Apr 07, 1942	Sep 22, 2015	Red Hill Cem. at Rutledge Ford; Son of Robert "Bob Mitch" & Clercy "Sis" (Meeks) Gilliam; m. Minnie Gilliam
Gilliam, Samuel	Dec 30, 1842	Mar 11, 1923	Bostick Place (possibly in Roberts'Cove, now Hawk Hollow or possibly Bostick Family Cem in Franklin Co. behind Henry Cox's house just below Penile Hill on the Winchester side on State Route 50); Son of Harris & Nancy (Reed) Gilliam
Gilliam, Thelma (Turner)	Jan 17, 1942	Feb 20, 2022	Mt. Garner Cem.; Dau. of Margie Sweeton; m. Cordell Hull Gilliam
Gipson, Eugene Burdith	1923	Sep 22, 1923	Tracy City Cem.; Son of Joe C. & Nellie Pearl (Poff) Gipson; no tombstone, location of grave in the cemetery is unknown
Gipson, Franklin Delano Roosevelt	Oct 01, 1935	Jul 19, 2017	Summerfield Cem.; Son of Robert Lee, Sr. & Dauntie Elizabeth Layne; m. Peggy Joyce Worley
Gipson, James Elbert	Jun 09, 1943	Nov 24, 2016	Wilson County Memorial Gardens; Son of Robert Lee, Sr. & Dauntie (Layne) Gipson; m. Vernice Mae Campbell
Gipson, Joshua Kane	Apr 21, 1978	Aug 10, 2020	Hamilton Memorial Gardens; Son of Michael Anthony Gipson & Kathy Ilene Trotter
Gipson, Mary (Sherrill)	Mar 06, 1956	Mar 28, 2019	Eastern Star Cem.; Dau. of James William Sherrill & Cleo Dotson; m. Paul Collis Gipson
Gipson, Pamela	ca 1953	Feb 18, 2013	Brown's Chapel Cem.; Dau. of Earnest & Margaret Dotson; m. Richard Gipson
Gipson, Stanley	Apr 25, 1942	Jan 09, 2020	Winchester Memorial Park Cem.; Son of Elbert Gipson & Harley Gilliam; m. Clarice Spray
Gipson, Vernice Mae (Campbell)	Apr 06, 1943	Jan 14, 2013	Wilson County Memorial Gardens; Dau. of Taft & Georgia Lee (Smartt) Campbell Walker; step father Howard Walker; m. James Elbert Gipson
Givens, Eliza A. (Nichols)	1818	1911	Altamont Cem.; Dau. of William & Sarah (Wallace) Nichols; m. William Anderson Givens; addition to Cemeteries of Grundy Co,Vol. 1, p. 12
Givens, Helen K.	Sep 27, 1934	Feb 22, 2014	Fall Creek Cem.; Dau of Fate & Maggie Knowlan; m. James Ralph Givens

Name	Birth	Death	Details
Givens, Jeffery Rodney "Bogart"	Jul 14, 1958	Aug 22, 2020	Fall Creek Cem.; Son of Ralph Givens & Helen Nolan; m. Stacy Kilgore
Givens, Rondal Owen	Nov 03, 1946	Jan 05, 2017	Bethel Cem.; Son of Hershel Owen & Rilla Mae (Crowell) Givens; m. 1. Edna McCallie 2. Joan (Thompson) Caldwell; US Army Vietnam
Goforth, Anna (Griswold)	Jan 01, 1917	Jan 20, 2017	Tracy City Cem.; Dau. of David M & Anna (Dykes) Griswold; m. 1) Carl Sweeton 2) Doug Goforth
Goins, Clarence, Jr.	Ca. 1948	Sep 11, 2016	Cremated; Son of Clarence & Mary (Cline) Goins; m. Linda Goins
Goins, Hattie Louise (Bombailey)	Apr 12, 1925	May 30, 2008	Cumberland Heights Cem.; Dau. of Starnes Frederick & Gertrude "Gertie" (Thacker) Bombailey; m. Clinton Goins; addition to Cemeteries of Grundy Co.Vol. 1, p. 197
Goldey, Bobby Elizabeth (Singleton)	Jul 15, 1934	May 06, 2019	Cremated; Dau. of Albert Singleton & Mildred Harris
Golston, Louis Donald	Feb 25. 1939		No information; Son of Barton & Josie Golston
Good, Hattie & Mattie (twins)	After 1930	After 1930	Warren "Red Hill" Cem.; no marker; Daus. of Lewis B. & Margie (Layne) Good; stillborn twins; addition to Cemeteries of Grundy Co.,Vol. 2, p. 958
Goodman, Alace	Oct 01, 1880	Feb 23, 1924	Goodman Cem.; Dau of William & Unk. (Haley) Tucker
Goodman, Dorothy Nell	Jun 28, 1929	Apr 28, 2016	Swiss Cem.; Dau. of Harris & Nora (Sweeton) Campbell
Goodman, Eula Gaynell (Booker)	Oct 02, 1913	Jan 13, 2003	Coalmont Cem.; Dau. of Ode H & Josie (Hall) Booker; correction to Cemeteries of Grundy County, Vol. 1, p. 182
Goodman, Harold Franklin	Sep 23, 1915	May 07, 1990	Coalmont Cem.; Son of James Tolbert & Bessie Myrtle (Royal) Goodman; correction to Cemeteries of Grundy County, Vol. 1 p. 182
Goodman, James Ralph	Aug 23, 1921	Feb 12, 2018	Warren "Red Hill" Cem.; Son of James Elbert Goodman and Elizabeth "Bettie" Turner; m. Genevieve Conry
Goodman, Jewell (Hamby)	Jul 06, 1918	May 18, 2014	Bethel Cem.; Dau. of Grover Cleveland "Cleve" & Bessie L. (Meeks) Hamby; m. Lude Carroll Goodman; addition to Cemeteries of Grundy Co. Vol. 1, p. 49
Goodman, Mark Andrew	Oct 04, 1971	Jul 04, 2017	Eastern Star Cem.; Son of William L. & Linda Goodman; m. Tonya Sons
Goodman, Martha A	1854	broken	Warren "Red Hill" Cem.; probably Dau. of Solomon P. & Julia A Goodman; stone broken and mostly buried; addition to Cemeteries of Grundy Co.Vol. 2, p. 958

Goodman, Robert Harleth	Mar 04, 1930	Nov 09, 1939	Warren "Red Hill" Cem.; Son of Lillard Harleth & Lucille (Henley) Goodman; correction to Cemeteries of Grundy Co. Vol. 2, p. 941
Goodman, Sally Carole	1934	Apr 19, 2014	Robertson Co. Memorial Gardens; Dau of Ingram Parmley & Rebecca Cannon; m. Cliff Goodman
Goodman, Thomas S.	Jan 25, 1843	Oct 29, 1874	Warren "Red Hill" Cem.; Son of Solomon & Julia A. Goodman; CSA First Turney's Unit; displaced stone set inside rock surround under cedar tree; addition to Cemeteries of Grundy Co,Vol. 2, p. 958
Goodman, William L.	Jul 20, 1874	Aug 28, 1921	Goodman Cem.; Son of W.M. & Mary Alice (Tucker) Goodman
Goodman, William Larry	Sep 03, 1946	Feb 24, 2021	Eastern Star Cem.; Son of Ward and Frances Goodman; m. Linda Goodman; U.S. Navy
Goodson, Ewing Marshall, II, Dr.	Aug 15, 1935	Dec 11, 2020	Philadelphia Cem.; Son of Robert Jerome & Lois (Boyles) Goodson; m. Katharine Pearsall Jul 11, 1963, in Grundy Co,; Addition to Cemeteries of Grundy Co.Vol. 2, p. 633
Goodwin, Francis Marion	Sep 17, 1852	Aug 09, 1926	Wesley Chapel Cem.; Son of Richard Jackson & Eliza J. (Bullard) Goodwin; m. Lavinia Dale, Mar 15, 1873, in Dekalb Co, TN; correction of birth year and addition to Cemeteries of Grundy Co.Vol. 2, p. 975
Goolsby, Marie (Wooten)	Jun 23, 1938	Mar 15, 2018	Wesley Chapel Cem.; Dau. of Lois & Hester (Henley) Wooten; m. William Alex Goolsby
Gorby, Joyce (Myers) Tuck	Aug 29, 1943	Apr 12, 2015	Prairie Plains Church Cem.; Dau. of William Floyd & Eloise (Campbell) Myers; m. 1) Charles Tuck 2) Ken Gorby
Gordon, Robert Louis	Jan 15, 1937	Aug 03, 2019	Chattanooga National Cemetery; Son of Arthur A. Gordon & Muriel Frizinger; U.S. Army
Goss, Sophia Christine	Nov 21, 1874	Jun 27, 1959	Altamont Cem.; Dau. of Johann Goss; not married per death certificate; Correction of name & addition to Cemeteries of Grundy Co,Vol. 1, p. 18
Graham, Donna Gayle (Watley)	Dec 17, 1957	Dec 20, 2018	Cremated; Dau. of Grady Watley & Thelma Meeks; from Monteagle
Graham, Earl William	Aug 28, 1949	Jan 17, 2016	Hixson Cem in Bledsoe County, TN; Son of Earl Graham & Dortha (Kilgore) Brown
Graham, Homer, Jr.	Mar 06, 1934	Jul 22, 2019	Rose Hill Memorial Gardens Cem.; Son of Homer & Renice Graham; m. Dalpha Meeks
Graham, James Walter	May 18, 1930	Jan 05, 2019	Sequatchie Memorial Gardens Cem.; Son of Homer, Sr. & Renice Graham; m. Delores Beard

Name	Born	Died	Notes
Graham, Martha "Patsy" (Stamback)	Mar 3, 1842	Aug 18, 1903	Oak Grove Cem.; Dau. of Benjamin & Margaret "Peggy" (Payne) Stamback; addition to Cemeteries of Grundy Co.,Vol. 1, p. 502
Graham, Martha Jane "Mattie" (Davis)	Nov 29, 1871	Apr 07, 1910	Oak Grove Cem.; Dau. of William & Lucinda Davis; addition, Cemeteries of Grundy Co.,Vol. 1, p. 502
Graham, Ralph James	Dec 16, 1953	Feb 16, 2018	Chattanooga National Cem.; Son of Ralph J. Graham & Irene; US Army
Graham, Simmon Peter	Aug 17, 1834	Feb 20, 1898	Oak Grove Cem.; Son of John H. & Elizabeth G. Graham; CSA; addition to Cemeteries of Grundy Co.Vol. 1, p. 502
Grant, Charlestine F. (Flynn)	Mar 30, 1928	Dec 24, 2018	Lakewood Memory Gardens South; Dau. of Charles & Addie Mae Flynn; m. James S. Grant
Grantham, Cynthia Ann (Castleberry)	Feb 14, 1829	Feb 03, 1904	Tracy City Cem; Dau. of William & Susannah (Wilson) Castleberry; however, she married John Grantham as Cynthia Anna Huffer on Aug 25, 1843, in McMinn Co. TN; addition to Cemeteries of Grundy Co,Vol. 2, p. 905
Grantham, Pleasant A.	Jun 22, 1846	Feb 06, 1915	Tracy City Cem.; Son of John & Cynthia Anna (Castleberry) Grantham; m. 1) Dorothea Shriever 2) Dorcus Sweeton; addition to Cemeteries of Grundy County.Vol. 2, p. 883; quote from *Mrs. Grundy*, Feb 11, 1915 addition: "…he remained loyal to the Union, serving in the 10th TN Cavalry, and had a most enviable war record…"
Gratigny, Frances E. (Sitz)	Apr 14, 1923	Jun 01, 2018	Fall Creek Cem.; Dau. of Virgil & Maggie (Levan) Sitz; m. Melvin Gratigny
Gray, Horace Ann (Cleek)	Dec 17, 1945	May 22, 2020	Cremated; Dau. of Mitchell Cleek & Oma Lee Cannnon; m. Jimmy Wayne Gray
Gray, Jimmy Wayne	Sep 13, 1951	Aug 31, 2021	Cremated; Son of Bill & Josephine (Dunn) Gray; m. Horace Ann Cleek
Gray, Joe D.	Jul 26, 1931	Dec 27, 2015	Altamont Cem.; Son of Daniel Clifford & Bertie Mae (Hagewood) Gray; m. Harriette Dickerson; addition to Cemeteries of Grundy Co.,Vol. 1, p. 22
Green, Anita Celeste (Culbertson)	Aug 03, 1967	Jul 18, 2020	Derryberry Cem in Columbia, TN.; Dau. of Robert Culbertson & Edith Culbertson; m. Charles "Tony" Green
Green, Barbara Jo	Nov 21, 1948		Hunerwadel Cem.; Dau. of Howard & Opal Turner; m. Parker H. Green; Addition to Cemeteries of Grundy Co.,Vol. 1, p. 349
Green, Billy Ray	May 04, 1959	Apr 02, 2013	Fall Creek Cem.; Son of Scott & Mary Edna (Walker) Green; no tombstone
Green, Charles Edward	Dec 24, 1944	Apr 18, 2021	Plainview Cem.; Son of Dortha & Beuna Green

Name	Birth	Death	Details
Green, Charles Wesley, Sr.	Jul 22, 1932	Mar 18, 2020	Palmer Cem.; Son of Dave Wesley & Pearl (Nunley) Green; m. Juanita Campbell on Dec 28, 1957; US Army, Korea; addition to Cemeteries of Grundy County, Vol. 2, p. 561
Green, Columbus James	May 03, 1943	Apr 08, 2020	Cremated; Son of Columbus and Sallie Green; m. Janice Johnson; Tennessee Army National Guard – Vietnam, Desert Storm, Iraqi Freedom; lived in Sewanee
Green, Daisy Irene	Sep 23, 1937	Jan 15, 1939	Brown's Chapel Cem.; Dau. of William Jody, Sr. & Bell (King) Green; addition to Cemeteries of Grundy Co. Vol. 1, p. 106
Green, Elmer L.	Aug 09, 1940	Jun 06, 2017	Cremated; Son of Dortha & Beuna Green; m. Josephine Meeks
Green, Gloria Willene (Collins)	Aug 08, 1945	Feb 25, 2018	Coalmont Cem.; Dau. of John Clinton Collins & Annie Esther Short
Green, Henry Cleston	Dec 15, 1932	Sep 03, 2020	Cremated; Son of James Author & Lena Mae Green; m. Diana Thomas
Green, James A.	Sep 03, 1928	Apr 01, 2016	Cremated; Son of James & Lena Green; m. Betty Ray Campbell; US Navy, Korea
Green, James "Bill", Jr.	Nov 27, 1948	Dec 16, 2020	Cremated: Son of James & Anna Mae Green; m. Debra Green; Bill lived in Tracy City.
Green, Jimmy Ray	May 08, 1954	Mar 30, 2018	Orange Hill Cem.; Son of Benton J. Green & Allene Meeks; m. Roxanne Meeks; US Army
Green, John Harold	Nov 11, 1950	Jan 03, 2021	Cumberland Heights. Memorial Cem.; Son of Clyde & Sue (Nance) Green; m. Cynthia K. Caldwell
Green, Katie E.	Oct 22, 1898	Oct 17, 1901	Oak Grove Cem.; Dau. of James Alexander & Sarah Elizabeth "Betty" (Long) Green, Addition to Cemeteries of Grundy Co, Vol. 1, p. 506
Green, Kelsey Lynn	Sep 08, 1993	Jun 04, 2020	Coalmont Cem.; Dau. of Richard Lee Green & Buffy Lynn Campbell
Green, Kenneth	Apr 23, 1939	Jan 13, 2013	Plainview Cem.; Son of Dan & Amanda (O'Neal) Green; m. Phyllis Green.
Green, Leona Marie	Jan 12, 1950	Dec 26, 2013	Plainview Cem.; George D. & Ruby (Land) Henry; m. Paul L. Green
Green, Lilly Artie Mishie	Feb 18, 1911	Sep 11, 1911	Oak Grove Cem.; Dau. of James Alexander & Sarah Elizabeth "Betty" (Long) Green, Addition to Cemeteries of Grundy Co, Vol. 1, p. 506
Green, Marie (Parsons)	Mar 31, 1906	Oct 23, 1931	Fall Creek Cem.; Dau. of William Joseph & Dolly Ann (Ellis) Parsons; m. Teddy Estel Green
Green, Mary C.	Nov 23, 1933	Oct 17, 1934	Oak Grove Cem.; Dau. of Norman Lemuel & Milda Mary "Mildie" (Nolan) Green; addition to Cemeteries of Grundy Co. Vol. 1, p. 508
Green, Mary Elizabeth (Haynes)	Sep 05, 1933	Jul 15, 2018	Cremated; Dau. of Joe Haynes & Louise Jordan; m. W.C. Green

Name	Birth	Death	Details
Green, Millie L. (Melton)	Feb 2, 1884	Apr 14, 1964	Brown's Chapel Cem.; Dau of Rice & Betsy Melton; m. Hayes Green on Jan 7, 1902; addition to Cemeteries of Grundy Co., Vol. 1, p. 106
Green, Mordica	Dec 14, 1829	Jan 10, 1903	Burkett's Chapel Cem.; Son of Samuel & Esther Alice (Miller) Green; m. Elizabeth Jane "Elsie" Reed; addition to Cemeteries of Grundy Co. Vol. 1, p. 121
Green, Nancy	1827	Oct 10, 1887	Wesley Chapel Cem.; Dau. of James & Mary Polly Smith; aged about 60 years; addition to Cemeteries of Grundy Co, Vol. 2, p. 972
Green, Norman "Wesley"	Oct 02, 1943	Apr 03, 2021	Orange Hill Cem.; Son of Norman L. & Mildie Green; m. Mary "Jane" Green
Green, Ola Iowa	May 26, 1912	Sep 17, 1989	Fults Cem. Northcutt's Cove; Dau. of William Martin & Julia P. (Carter) Totherow; m. Thomas Haywood Green; addition to Cemeteries of Grundy Co. Vol. 1, p. 284
Green, Parker H.	Feb 02, 1949		Hunerwadel Cem.; Son of Parker I & Vernie (Knight) Green; m. Barbara Joe Turner; addition to Vol. 1, p. 349
Green, Paul Lesley	May 29, 1949	Mar 23, 2019	Plainview Cem.; Son of Dortha Green & Buena Johnson; m. Leona Marie Henry
Green, Paul Richard	Oct 18, 1935	Mar 15, 2016	Plainview Cem.; Son of Paul & Rosie (Shrum) Green
Green, Ralph Edward	Sep 29, 1963	Nov 18, 2021	Plainview Cem.; Son of Charles & Glenda Green; m. Rose Meeks
Green, Robert Jackson	Mar 27, 1896	Jan 02, 1929	White Cem.; Son of John David & Mary Ann (Burns) Green; m. Florence Clemmons; addition to Cemeteries of Grundy Co. Vol. 2, p. 1006
Green, Shirley F. "Shirl"	Oct 06, 1941	Mar 09, 2013	Palmer Cem.; m. William Alexander "Red" Green; addition to Cemeteries of Grundy Co., Vol. 2, p. 559
Green, Shirley Faye	Oct 06, 1941	Mar 09, 2013	Palmer Cem.; Dau. of Joe & Clara (Griffith) Ashburn; m. William "Red" Green
Green, Shirley Jeanette (Jones)	Jul 27, 1931	Nov 01, 2018	Fall Creek Cem.; Dau. of William Arthur Jones & Margaret Helenthal; m. James Frank Green
Green, Thomas Haywood	Jan 9, 1882	Apr 02, 1958	Fults Cem Northcutt's Cove; Son of John William & Sarah Ann (Baker) Green; m. Ola Iowa Green; addition to Cemeteries of Grundy Co, Vol. 1, p. 284
Green, William George	Jan 25, 1925	Mar 2, 1942	Brown's Chapel Cem.; Son of Hayes & Millie (Melton) Green; no stone- death certificate
Greene, Billy Ray	May 04, 1959	Apr 02, 2013	Fall Creek Cem.; Son of Scott & Mary Edna (Walker) Green

Name	Born	Died	Notes
Greene, Bobby Lloyd	Aug 11, 1933	Sep 26, 2018	Palmer Cem.; Son of Virgil Franklin & Lena Belle (Higgins) Greene; m. Faye "Perkie" Cannon; addition to Cemeteries of Grundy Co.,Vol. 2, p. 564
Greene, Dorothy Elizabeth (Park)	Mar 28, 1916	Dec 18, 1977	Cumberland Heights Cem.; Dau. of T. Blake & Katie (Krueger) Park; m. Joseph Charles Greene; addition to Cemeteries of Grundy Co.Vol. 1, p. 196
Greene, Fay "Perkie" (Cannon)	Oct 21, 1942		Palmer Cem.; Dau. of Scott & Velma Louise (White) Cannon; m. Bobby Lloyd Greene; correction to spelling of surname in Cemeteries of Grundy Co.,Vol. 2, p. 564
Greene, Joseph Charles	Jan 05, 1916	Nov 05, 2002	Cumberland Heights Cem.; Son of Peter L. & Edith E. (Sprears) Greene; addition to Cemeteries of Grundy Co.,Vol. 1, p. 196
Greene, Julia Virginia (Williams)	Aug 15, 1897	Mar 06, 1972	Altamont Cem.; Dau. of Julius Bennett & Nancy Eglatine "Nannie" (Phelps) Williams; m. 1) William Henry Hutchison 2) Clayborn William Greene on Sep 8, 1968; correction of maiden name and addition to Cemeteries of Grundy Co.,Vol. 1, p. 23
Greene, Lensia (Rhea)	Jul 26, 1899	Jan 01, 1965	Fall Creek Cem.; Dau. of Robert & Ruth (Fults) Rhea; m. Claborn Greene
Greenlee, Mary Frances (Downum)	Aug 17, 1874	Apr 10, 1956	Hobbs Hill Cem.; Dau. of Daniel Boone & Eliza Jane (Statum) Downum; m. William James Greenlee; addition to Cemeteris of Grundy Co.,Vol. 1, p. 332
Greenlee, William James	Feb 6, 1870	Mar 31, 1930	Hobbs Hill Cem.; Son of Henderson & Amanda (McWhirter) Greenlee, m. Mary Frances Downum on Nov 19, 1896; addition to Cemeteries of Grundy Co.,Vol. 1, p. 332
Greeter, Christine (Worley)	Aug 10, 1843	Jul 24, 1932	Altamont Cem.; Dau. of Unk. Worley & Unk. Killian per death certificate; m. John J. Greeter; correction of maiden name & addition to Cemeteries of Grundy Co.,Vol. 1, p.37
Greeter, Elizabeth	Oct 1798	Mar 1883	Swiss Colony Cem.; b. in Switzerland m. Jacob Greeter/Gruetter b. 1795; Her maiden name was Bechart; addition to Cemeteries of Grundy Co.Vol. 2, p 783
Greeter, John J.	Jan 8, 1830	Jan 17, 1896	Altamont Cem.; Son of Jacob & Elizabeth (Becker) Grutter; m. Christine Worley; correction of Christine's last name and addition to Cemeteries of Grundy Co. Vol, 1, p. 37
Greeter, John W.	Sep 14, 1935	Mar 13, 2021	Monteagle Cem.; Son of Harvey & Ethel (Roberson) Greeter; m. Lois Bradley; Tennessee Army National Guard

Name	Birth	Death	Details
Greeter, Marguerite (Walker)	Oct 14, 1902	May 29, 1993	Altamont Cem.; Dau. of William & Grace (Cain) Walker; m. Werner E. Greeter; addition to Cemeteries of Grundy Co. Vol. 1, p. 36
Gregory, Aurella Dell	Apr 20, 1921	Jul 07, 2013	Cremated; Dau. of Silas & Mattie Gregory; m. Ernest Hoyt Smith; died in CA.
Gregory, Lula Virginia (Corliss)	Mar 21, 1877	Sep 17, 1965	Altamont Cem.; Dau. of John Orr & Julia Ann (Burgess) Corliss; m. Abel Landers Gregory; addition to Cemeteries of Grundy Co. Vol. 1, p. 17
Gregory, Vivian Marie (Ladd)	Feb 14, 1928	Feb 28, 2016	Cremated; Dau. of Jack & Charlotte Rebecca (Danzey) Dolar; m. George Ladd
Griffin, Don Edwin	Jul 23, 1933	Jun 15, 2015	New Hope Cem.; Son of Perry & Audrey Pearl (Stanley) Griffin; m. Sandra Cornett
Griffin, Floyd	Aug 27, 1913	Oct 11, 1990	Burns Cem.; Son of Andrew V. & Heather (Gosnell) Griffin; m. Gertie Mae Rogers; addition to Cemeteries of Grundy Co., Vol. 1, p. 136
Griffin, Gertie Mae (Rogers)	Sep 23, 1921	Jan 31, 1993	Burns Cem.; Dau. of George Daniel & Cordie Belle (Clark) Rogers; m. Floyd Griffin; addition to Cemeteries of Grundy Co., Vol. 1, p. 136
Griffis, Martha (Brandt)	Jan 26, 1920	Dec 31, 2020	Cremated: Dau. of Julius & Josephine Brandt; m. James Griffith
Griffith, Billy Ray	Dec 15, 1954	Sep 27, 2020	Pryor Ridge Cem.; Son of William & Pauline (Sanders) Griffith
Griffith, Janice Faye (Layne)	Apr 07, 1951	Aug 08, 2016	Swiss Colony Cem.; Dau. of Amos & Hester Layne
Griffith, Juanita Marjorie (Grimes)	Jan 13, 1947	Nov 15, 2016	Burkett's Chapel Cem.; Dau. of Hershel & Ethel (Vaughn) Grimes; m. Larry Dean Griffith
Griffith, Kay (Eldridge)	Dec 27, 1945	Mar 19, 2022	Plainview Cem.; Dau. of Carlene Haynes Eldridge; m. 1) Jimmy Jordan 2) Billy Griffith
Griffith, Maxie Leann	Sep 12, 1988	Jul 08, 2014	Palmer Cem.; Dau of Mark Thompson & Pamela O'Brien; m. Michael Griffith
Griffith, Nancy Ann "Susie" (Campbell)	Apr 28, 1952	Feb 18, 2020	Palmer Cem.; Dau. of Raymond Campbell & Hazel Dishroon
Griffith, Rachel (Slatton)	Jun 21, 1932	Nov 09, 2014	Griffith's Creek Cem.; Dau of Huke Slatton & Bertha Kilgore; m. William Griffith, Jr.
Griffith, William, Jr.	Jan 27, 1927	Oct 23, 2014	Griffith's Creek Cem.; Son of William Griffith, Sr. & Mattie McGowan; m. Rachel Slatton
Grimes, Brenda Rogers	Ca 1946		Palmer Cem.; Dau. of Benjamin Hade & Pauline Marie (Ward) Rogers; m. Earl Wesley Grimes
Grimes, Charles P.	Aug 20, 1952	Sep 23, 2013	Burkett's Chapel Cem.; Son of Hershel & Ethel (Vaughn) Grimes; m. Carol Lynn Burnett
Grimes, Dale	Jan 07, 1956	Jul 30, 2021	Fall Creek Cem.; Son of James Edward & Beatrice (LeCroy) Grimes; m. Marcella Jordan

Name	Born	Died	Details
Grimes, Earl Wesley	Jun 19, 1945	Dec 29, 2018	Palmer Cem.; Son of Herschel Grimes & Ethel Juanita Vaughn; m. Brenda Rogers
Grimes, Gregory Lee	Oct 15, 1978	May 10, 2019	Burkett's Chapel Cem.; Son of Herbert Lee Grimes & Claudette Grimes
Grimes, James William	Dec 07, 1950	Feb 06, 2021	Swiss Colony Cem.; Son of Herschel & Ethel Juanita (Vaughn) Grimes; m. Connie Roach
Grimes, Robert "Bud", Jr.	Ca. 1928	Apr 11, 2016	Lakewood Memorial Garden in Rossville; Son of Robert, Sr. & Eunice Grimes; m. Elouise Grimes
Grimm, Mary Elizabeth	Jan 09, 1964	May 30, 2014	Cremated; Dau of Frank Edward Frye & Mary Ann McElderry; m. Richard Grimm
Grissom, Shawn Cameron	Mar 27, 1973	Oct 04, 2019	Smyrna Cem.; Son of Harry Grissom & Diane Turner; m. LeAnne Jones
Griswold, Ellene	Oct 04, 1907	Jun 30, 1921	Altamont Cem.; Dau. of David Murphy & Anna Belle (Dykes) Griswold; addition to Cemeteries of Grundy Co.Vol. 1, p. 28
Griswold, Martha "Mattie"	Nov 14, 1856	Dec 19, 1902	Altamont Cem.; Dau. of Eli Harlan & Harriet Elizabeth (Arnold) Bennett; m. G.G. Griswold; addition to Cemeteries of Grundy Co.Vol. 1, p. 27
Griswold, Willie	Nov 1897	May 03, 1924	Altamont Cem.; Son of George Gilbert & Martha Jane Griswold; Pvt 1st Class; 114 Engineers, Arkansas; addition to Cemeteries of Grundy Co,Vol. 1, p. 26
Grooms, Elbert Ronald "Lad"	May 28, 1935	Apr 29, 2019	Fall Creek Cem.; Son of Elbert B. Grooms & Willie Mae Fults; m. Nellie C. Overturf; U.S. Navy
Grooms, Keith Jackson "Budge"	May 05, 1930	Nov 12, 2020	Brown's Chapel Cem.; Son of Elbert & Willie Mae (Fults) Grooms; m. Lou Kenner
Gross, Johnny Floyd	Jan 04, 1950	Jun 16, 2021	Grace Chapel Cem.; Son of Leonard Floyd & Loretta (Walker) Gross; m. Diane Tate
Gross, Leonard Floyd	Apr 07, 1921	May 12, 2014	Grace Chapel Cem; Son of John Cleveland & Frances (King) Gross; m. Loretta Walker
Gross, Lillie Mae (Smith)	Jun 22,1869	Jan 04, 1933	Hobbs Hill Cem.; Dau. of John Calvin & Sarah Almeda (Scruggs) Smith; m. Floyd Lawson Gross; addition to Cemeteries of Grundy Co.,Vol. 1, p. 326
Gross, Stanley Uvohn	Jan 02, 1946	Mar 03, 1971	Philadelphia Cem.; Son of Fred Cleveland & Margie Frances (Perry) Gross; m. Diane Sneed
Guess, Ricky Darrell	Jun 25, 1960	Sep 21, 2015	Summerfield Cem.; Son of Thomas & Una Guess; m. Rita Guess
Guffy, Rebecca (Coffelt)	Apr 26, 1942	Oct 05, 2015	Palmer Cem.; Dau. of Ervine & Agnes (Roberts) Coffelt; m. Billy Carl Guffey
Gugliemotto, Anna Fay (King)	Jan 30, 1950		Altamont Cem.; Dau. of Hershel Coy & Minnie Lee (Scruggs) King; m. Joseph Jack Gugliemotto; addition to Cemeteries of Grundy Co,Vol. 1, p. 15

Name	Born	Died	Notes
Guin, Matthew Allen	Dec 22, 1984	May 01, 2013	Cremated; Son of Gene & Terry Guin
Guinn, Hobert N.	Mar 11, 1905	Apr 24, 1899	Tate Cem.; Son of Tennie Guinn; 1 yr. 8 mos 4 days; grandson of Thomas C. (Reynolds) Willis
Gulas, Stewart Anton "Stu"	Jul 24, 1951	Oct 27, 2013	Altamont Cem.; Son of Anton Adams & Nadine (Brookshire) Gulas; m. Jane Lorraine Gray; Addition to Cemeteries of Grundy Co.Vol. 1, p. 22
Gunn, Bernard M.	Jun 11, 1843	Oct 05, 1925	Altamont Cem.; From Ireland, farmer, lived in Beersheba; found dead; a single man; Willie Greeter was his administrator, Cemeteries of Grundy Co. Vol. 1, p. 28
Gunn, Patricia Ann (Lowrie)	Mar 16, 1944	Mar 30, 2022	Church of Christ Cem. Pelham; Dau. of Harold & Anna Lee (Gossett) Lowrie; m. Thomas Edgar Gunn
Gunn, Thomas Edgar	Dec 24, 1939		Pelham Church of Christ Cem.; Son of Roscoe & Georgia (Wilson) Gunn; m. Patricia Lowrie
Guy, Margaret Estel	Feb 25, 1930	Dec 06, 1993	Plainview Cem.; Dau. of Jesse H. & Arizona (Levan) Johnson; addition to Cemeteries of Grundy Co.,Vol. 2, p. 695
Guyear, Marion	1880	1923	Presbyterian Church Cem. no longer exists. (located across US 41 from Dutch Maid Bakery behind Citizens Tri County Bank); Dau. of Susan Catherine Guyear (per Barbara Mooney Myers)
Guyear, Nancy (Stanback)	Sep 26, 1843	Dec 04, 1923	Oak Grove Cem.; m. Marion Phillip Guyear, Oct 5, 1871in Lincoln Co. TN; no tombstone; addition to Cemeteries of Grundy Co.Vol. 1, p. 512
Guyear, Paul Newton	Feb 15, 1978	Apr 02, 2021	Eastern Star Cem.; Son of Willie Ray & Catherine Jane Guyear
Guyer, Thomas	no info	Jun 15, 1904	Old Baptist Cem.; m. Mary Richie; Source *Mrs. Grundy* Jun 23, 1904
Hain, Adela A.	Jul 18, 1869	Apr 22, 1891	Summerfield Cem.; apparently has a stone at Swiss Colony Cem, but reported has a record of being buried at Summerfield; correction and addition to Cemeteries of Grundy Co.Vol. 2, p. 783
Hale, Fred C.	Jan 08, 1942	Jan 07, 2020	Cremated; Son of Aubrey F. Hale & Rebecca Charles Carrick; m. Sandra Rieder
Hall, Alton Floyd	Jul 6, 1943	Dec 23, 2016	Clouse Hill Cem.; Son of Charlie & Carrie Ola (McWain) Hall; m. Willie Mae Meeks
Hall, Bruce Cullen	Ca. 1954	Jul 18, 2015	Middle TN Veterans' Cem.; Son of Larry & Elinor Hall; US Army
Hall, Carrie Ola (McWain)	Dec 10, 1910	Jan 11, 1993	Bonny Oak Cem.; Dau. of Benjamin Franklin "Frank" & Nancy (Meeks) McWain; 1) Pascal Keel 2) Charlie Hall; addition to Cemeteries of Grundy Co.Vol. 1, p. 90

Name	Born	Died	Details
Hall, Eddie Dean	Dec 26, 1949	Apr 05, 2022	Bonny Oak Cem.; Son of Charlie & Ola (McWain) Hall; m. Cheryl Smartt
Hall, Glenn H.	Oct 23, 1939	Jun 08, 2020	Warren "Red Hill" Cem.; Son of Elbert H. & Vivian Inez Hall; m. Judy Roper
Hall, Howard E.	Dec 27, 1910	Aug 06, 1972	Monteagle Cem.; Son of Edward E. & Emma Florence (Clements) Hall; Virginia PVT US Army; addition to Cemeteries of Grundy Co., Vol. 1, p. 411
Hall, James N.	Sep 17, 1939	Oct 16, 2018	Fults Cem.; Son of Van & Myrtle Hall; m. Janice Whitman
Hall, James O. "Red"	Dec 21, 1944	Jan 20, 2017	Bonnie Oak Cem.; Son of Charlie & Ola Hall; never married
Hall, John Douglas	Sep 30, 1914	Jun 06, 1944	National Cemetery in Chattanooga, TN; Son of Benjamin Franklin "Bee" & Lou (Latham) Hall; m. Evelyn Davis; US Army Paratrooper; WWII – plane shot down – KIA – France- body returned to US & buried Dec 8, 1948; from Tracy City, TN.
Hall, John Solomon	1859	Jan 12, 1909	Tracy City Cem.; m. Martha "Mattie" Hansel on Apr 30, 1879, in Rockcastle, KY; addition & correction to Cemeteries of Grundy Co, Vol. 2, p. 859
Hall, Kimberly Renae (Melton)	Aug 25, 1964	Jul 08, 2022	Cremated; Dau. of Delbert Carlton "Bolley" & Mildred "Micki" (Lowe) Melton; m. 1) David Richie 2) Marlon "Marty" Hall
Hall, Lucille (Kilgore)	Jul 30, 1923	Jun 04, 2013	Oak Grove Cem.; Dau. of Walter B & Katie (Shrum) Kilgore; addition to Cemeteries of Grundy Co., Vol. 1, p. 487
Hall, Margaret	Mar 24, 1940	Jan 12, 2004	Homeland Acres Cem.; Dau. of George & Alda M. Franke; addition to Cemeteries of Grundy Co. Vol. 1, p. 340
Hall, Ray Edward	Jun 04, 1955	Mar 03, 2015	Oak Grove Cem.; Son of Harvey & Lucille (Kilgore) Hall
Hall, Sherrie Ellen (Brannon)	May 13, 1955	Mar 29, 2017	Bonnie Oak Cem.; Dau. of Marshall & Louella (Headrick) Brannon; m. Willis Robert Hall; no tombstone
Hall, Willis Robert	Feb 19, 1950	Dec 20, 2019	Bonny Oak Cem.; m. Sherrie Ellen Brannon; US Marine Corps; lived in Decatur, TN, no tombstone
Hallbert, Madeleine (Slaick)	Jun 04, 1927	Mar 08, 2007	Palmer Cem.; Dau. of John & Madeline R. Slaick; m. John Betzel "Jack" Hallberg; addition to Cemeteries of Grundy Co, Vol. 2, p. 565
Hallman, Mark Omar	Aug 27, 1930	Feb 11, 1985	Palmer Cem.; Son of James Samuel & Rhonda (Price) Hallman; m. 1) Agnes Cotton 2) Louise Kathleen (Slatton) Kilgore; addition to Cemeteries of Grundy Co. Vol. 2, p. 576

Name	Born	Died	Notes
Hamby, Billy Mitchell	Oct 22, 1955	Mar 16, 2019	Cremated; Son of Horace Mitchell Hamby & Evelyn Brannan; m. Martha Jane Hamby
Hamby, Billy Wayne "Blue"	Mar 5, 1932	Oct 25, 2014	Monteagle Cem.; Son of Robert Hamby & Ezella Thomas; m. Jo Ann Hamby; Army ; Bronze star, Korea
Hamby, Catherine (Calhoun)	1825	1887	Hamby Family Cem.; Dau. of William Calhoun & Elizabeth Ross; m. Ephraim L. Hamby
Hamby, Eli Washington	1826	1884	Eli Washington "Wash" Hamby Family Cem.; Son of Eli William Hamby & Sarah Lewis; m. Rachel Arkansas (Sartain) Bost
Hamby, Eli William	1791	1862	Eli Washington "Wash" Hamby Family Cem.; m. Sarah Lewis
Hamby, Elizabeth Dianne	Oct 23, 1948	Jun 05, 2016	Cremated; Dau. of Herbert & Lula Mae (Powers) Hill; m. David Hamby
Hamby, Ephraim L.	1816	1878	Hamby Family Cem.; Son of Eli William Hamby & Sarah Lewis
Hamby, Ernestine (Meeks)	Jan 17, 1945	Oct 28, 2015	Cremated; Dau. of W.D. & Georgia Mae (Nunley) Meeks; m. Doyle Hamby
Hamby, Mary Leona (Johnson)	1939	Mar 30, 2022	Monteagle Cem.; Dau. of Embrey & Mary Johnson; m. Grady Hamby
Hamby, Robert Lee	1939	Nov 13, 1953	Monteagle Cem.; Son of Jesse Ransom & Mary "Mary Jess" (Hawk) Hamby; m. Vandrene Ezella Thomas; correction to Cemeteries of Grundy Co.Vol. 1, p. 454 of his mother's maiden name
Hamby, Sarah Lewis	1790	1875	Eli Washington "Wash" Hamby Family Cem.; Dau. of William & Jean Lewis; m. Eli William Hamby
Hamilton, Brenda (Bonner)	Oct 14, 1944	Mar 21, 2022	West Miller's Cove Cem., Walland, TN.; Dau. of Charlie Vernon & Louella (Davidson) Bonner; m. James Gordon Hamilton
Hamilton, Emma Jeanette	Jul 01, 1927	Jul 29, 2016	Cremated; Dau. of Luther & Zula (Perry) Harrell; m. William John Hamilton
Hamilton, Judith (Holiday)	Jan 16, 1936	Mar 04, 2015	Cremated; Dau. of LaDue & Evelyn (McCurdy) Holiday; m. 1) Frank Emmett Clay 2) Paul Hamilton
Hamlin, Nicholas Allen	Nov 18, 1989	Feb 18, 2016	Cremated; Son of Ricky & Paula (Magouirk) Hamlin
Hammers, Huey Dale	Feb 19, 1961	Nov 10, 2020	Clouse Hill Cem.; Son of Hubert & Rosal Nell Hammers; m. Kathy Jane Hammers
Hammond, Elvin Wayne, Sr.	Sep 28, 1936	Nov 12, 2012	Altamont Cem.; Son of James Hines & Mary Alice (Laramore) Hammond; m. Earlene Y. (Evans) Speer; addition to Cemeteries of Grundy Co,Vol. 1, p. 22

Name	Birth	Death	Details
Hammond, Mittie Jane	Jul 05, 1931	Aug 28, 2001	Monteagle Cem.; Dau. of Percy C. & Elizabeth M. (Edge) Soape; m. Charles Edward Hammond; addition to Cemeteries of Grundy Co, Vol. 1, p. 446
Hammons, Arvile Edward	Aug 13, 1946	Jan 09, 2017	Cremated; Son of Robert L & Nannie Hammons; m. Linda Darlene Stoup
Hampton, Beatrice Ann (Archey)	May 04, 1976	Jan 04, 2019	Cremated; Dau. of Lawson Timothy Archer & Charcie Dean Nolan
Hampton, Betty Jean	Aug 05, 1935	Jun 7, 2023	Orange Hill Cem.; Dau. of Milton & Lillie (Nunley) Hampton; m. 1) James Edward Lockhart 2) James Edward Hampton on Jul 21, 1956
Hampton, Charles Edward "Buck"	Feb 04, 1947	Jul 25, 2017	Plainview Cem.; Son of Thomas E. & Edna Mae (Fultz) Hampton: m. 1) Rachel Hampton 2) Connie Hampton
Hampton, Christopher Shane	May 15, 1979	May 29, 1979	Son of David & Debbie (Tate) Hampton; correction of mother's given name; Cemeteries of Grundy Co, Vol. 1, p. 10
Hampton, Cora (Womble)	Mar , 1901	Sep 07, 1983	Fall Creek Cem.; Dau. of Benjamin & Hattie Lou (Ona) Womble; m. Mark C. Hampton
Hampton, Glenn "Rip", Jr.	Jan 08, 1943	Nov 21, 2015	Plainview Cem.; Son of Glenn & Leona (Brazille) Hampton, Sr.; m. Lucyle Pirtle
Hampton, Helen Marie (Nunley)	May 05, 1934	Dec 05, 2017	Airview Cem.; Dau. of Robert Kelly & Eula Augusta Pickett Nunley
Hampton, Jennie Elizabeth	Nov 19, 1914	Jan 18, 1914	Hobbs Hill Cem.; Dau. of Phineas "Finas" & Lillie Bell (Harrison) Hampton
Hampton, Johnnie Ruth	Feb 27, 1937	Aug 08, 2014	Brown's Chapel Cem.; Dau of John A. & Nellie (Dykes) Cordell
Hampton, Lula Emma (Taylor)	Jan 07, 1900	Feb 11, 2006	Hobbs Hill Cem.; Dau. of Bob & Dena (Hall) Taylor; m. Fines H. Hampton; addition to Cemeteries of Grundy Co. Vol. 1, p. 337
Hampton, Melvin	Feb 24, 1937	May 02, 2013	Sequatchie Valley Memorial Gardens Cem.; Son of Melvin C. "Bud" & Elizabeth Hampton; m. 1) Johnnie Ruth Cordell 2) Kathy Hampton
Hampton, Otis	May 10, 1933	Apr 17, 2015	Airview Cem.; Son of Eugene & Lois (Dendy) Hampton; m. Ann Thompson
Hampton, Phineas H. "Fines"	Mar 18, 1896	Feb 10, 1983	Hobbs Hill Cem.; Son of Smartt L & Mary Emma (Nunley) Hampton; m. 1) Lillie Bell Harrison 2) Lula Emma Taylor; Pvt US Army, WWI; addition & correction to father's name; Cemeteries of Grundy Co., Vol. 1, p. 337
Hampton, William H.	Aug 26, 1942	Dec 26, 1942	Airview Cem.; Son of J.C. & Cecil (Miller) Hampton – dau of Henry Miller- both she and her baby died. Addition to Cemeteries of Grundy Co., Vol. 1, p. 6
Hancock, Warren O'Dell	Oct 18, 1944	Sep 30, 2019	Palmer Cem: Son of Wagner Warren Hancock & Genevea Ruth Umbarger; m. Sylvia Henry

Hankins, John William	Oct 21, 1926	Feb 15, 2014	Eastern Star Cem.; Son of Horace B,. & Katie Fay (Anderson) Hankins; m. Peggy Rose Cowan; WWII vet
Hankins, Peggy Rose C.	Jul 17, 1929	Aug 06, 2013	Eastern Star Cem.; Dau. of Ed Pratt & Cullie Agnes (Rose) Cowan; m. John William Hankins
Hanna, Earl Mark	Ca 1891	Nov 29,1918	Bonny Oak Cem.; Son of Jim & Lula Hannah; addition to Cemeteries of Grundy Co.,Vol. 1, p. 95
Hannah, Carolyn (Arnold)	Jan 23, 1929	Feb 10, 2016	Mt. Garner Cem.; Dau. of Bunn Francis & Nancy (Willis) Arnold; m. James Edward Hannah
Hanner, Thomas Huel	Jan 31, 1946	Jan 25, 2015	Altamont Cem.; Son of Thomas H. & Mary Lou Hanner
Hanner, Thomas Jeffery	Jan 05, 1966	Mar 07, 2019	Altamont Cem.; Son of Thomas Huel Hanner & Jewel Dean Walker
Hanson, Howard Sidney	Feb 08, 1932	Jan 22, 2014	Mt. Zion Cem.; Son of Sidney R. Hanson & Lucille Luebeck; m. Willis Mae Argo; USAF Korea & Vietnam
Hanson, Margaret (Layne)	Oct 17, 1935	May 01, 2015	Chattanooga National Cem.; Dau. of Roy David & Louise (Geary) Layne; m. Donald Hanson
Harbolt, Byron David, MD	Jul 30, 1923	Aug 21, 2017	Cumberland Heights Cem.; Son of Willima Henry "Hallie" & Ethel Amy (Cummings) Harbolt; m. Genevieve Donaker
Harbolt, Genevieve L. (Donaker)	Feb 19, 1924	Jun 16, 2006	Cumberland Heights Cem.; Dau. of John Martin & Reva May (Ellis) Donaker; m. Byron David Harbolt, MD; addition to Cemeteries of Grundy County,Vol 1, p. 197
Harbutt, Charles, Jr.	Jul 29, 1935	Jun 30, 2015	Died in Monteagle, TN, - burial place not known; Son of Charles Harbutt, Sr. & Catharine McMahon; m. 1) Alberta Steves 2) Joan Liftin
Harden, Elisha T.	Mar 7, 1868	May 20, 1887	Tracy City Cem.; Son of Peter & Sarah (Hefner) Hardin; addition to Cemeteries of Grundy Co. Vol, 2, p. 891
Hardin, Dickie Lee "Buckey"	Dec 21, 1958	Jul 24, 2017	O'Dear Cem.; Son of Joe Allen Pack & Frances Louise Adams Hardin
Hardin, Henry	Ca. 1875	Dec 01, 1913	Tracy City Cem; Son of Peter & Sarah Catherine (Hefner) Hardin; m. Alice Arbuckle; Source *Mrs. Grundy*, Jan 1, 1914; died in Hartford, AK; Hardin family moved back to Grundy Co.
Hardy, Carrie (Buckner)	Apr 26, 1967	Sep 26, 2019	Hamilton Memorial Gardens; Dau. of Joe & Jean Buckner; m. 1) Unk. Benson 2) Unk. Hardy
Hargis, Alfreda "Susie"	Oct 16, 1949	Jan 31, 2021	Collier Cem.; Dau. of Claude & Lorene Jo (Smith) Hargis

Name	Born	Died	Notes
Hargis, Anna (Adkins)	1858	Nov 14, 1933	Swiss Colony Cem.; m. James Gable Hargis, Jr. on Nov 5, 1874; no tombstone, but according to family members she is buried here; addition to Cemeteries of Grundy Co.,Vol. 2, p. 798
Hargis, Carol Anne (Isaac)	Jun 26, 1932	Jul 15, 2011	Fall Creek Cem.; Dau. of George Isaac & Mary Christy; m. Allen R Hargis
Hargis, Clayton D.	Jul 15, 1932	Jan 24, 2015	Fall Creek Cem.; Son of Carmon & Allie (Adams) Hargis; m. Joyce Roberts; U.S. Air Force
Hargis, Delbert Lee	Mar 10, 1920	Sep 15, 2015	Swiss Colony Cem.; Son of Robert & Rose (Wichser) Hargis; m. Carlene Givens; addition to Cemeteries of Grundy Co,Vol. 2, p. 797
Hargis, Doris Allene (Nunley)	Feb 03, 1929	Dec 19, 2015	Fall Creek Cem.; Dau. of Graham & Sarah (Cannon) Nunley; m. Clayton Ray Hargis
Hargis, Dorothy (Wiggins)	May 23, 1940	Jan 16, 2017	Orange Hill Cem.; Dau. of Robert & Dot Wiggins; m. Billy Hargis
Hargis, Julia (Kirk)	Mar 18, 1919	Jun 27, 2019	Orange Hill Cem.; Dau. of Willie & Pearlie (Dykes) Kirk; m. Dolph Hargis; addition to Grundy Co Cemeteries,Vol. 2, p. 530
Hargis, Larry Dale	Oct 13, 1955	Oct 27, 2019	Fall Creek Cem.; Son of James Hargis & Mary Ethelene Bean
Hargis, Margaret Joyce (Roberts)	Feb 12, 1934	Nov 13, 2013	Fall Creek Cem.; Dau. of Henry & Oda (James) Roberts; m. Clayton Hargis
Hargis, Mary Ethlene	Oct 26, 1925	Sep 25, 2013	Fall Creek Cem.; Dau. of Willie & Mary (Mitchell) Bean; m. Jimmy Hargis
Hargis, Minnie Frances (Fults)	May 20, 1942	Oct 24, 2020	Fall Creek Cem.; Dau. of Charlie & Louise (Cannon) Fults; m. Glenn"Bill" Hargis
Hargis, William		1906	Pigeon Springs Cem.; Son of Thomas & Mary (Gunter) Hargis; reported by family
Hargis, William Raymond	Feb 10, 1928	Nov 21, 2018	Swiss Colony Cem.; Son of William Lee & Thelma (Troxler) Hargis; m. Doris Brown; addition to Cemeteries of Grundy Co., Vol., 2, p. 794
Harless, James "Jim" Ronald	Sep 19, 1932	Dec 25, 2002	Plainview Cem.; Son of Chester Thomas & Gracie (Cooksey) Harless
Harrell, Winona Elizabeth (Flury)	1948	Feb 24, 2021	Tracy City Cem.; Dau. of Henry & Frances Flury; m. Jerry Oscar Harrell
Harriman, Michael	1957	Jul 15, 2018	Orange Hill Cem.; Son of Paul & Marion Harriman; m. Linda Harriman
Harris, Barbara Gail	Oct 13, 1943	May 13, 2015	Monteagle Cem.; Dau. of John & Agnes (Foutch) Metcalfe; m. Wendell Harris
Harris, Ben Easley Wilson, Sr.	Nov 16, 1855	Oct 09, 1923	Burns Cem.; Son of Martin & Orphie (Wilson) Harris; m. Mary Jane Foster, Oct 16, 1884; addition to Cemeteries of Grundy Co.Vol. 1, p.132
Harris, Charlie Edward	Sep 27, 1900	Oct 06, 1978	Gregg Cem.; Son of Jessie Miles Harris & Nannie Woody; m. Kate Anderson

Name	Born	Died	Details
Harris, Donnie Edward	Dec 30, 1956	Sep 05, 2017	Mt. View Cem.; Son of Robert & Pauline (Williams) Harris; m. Rhonda (Hampton) Harris
Harris, Ellen (Dykes)	Feb. 1890	Dec 2. 1960	Burns Cem.; Dau. of Gilbert Preston & Julia Elizabeth (Scott) Dykes; m. 1) Albert Shrum 2) Foster Harris; addition to Cemeteries of Grundy Co.Vol. 1, p. 132
Harris, Gilbert B.	May 26, 1932	Jan 23, 1990	Burns Cem.; Son of Charles R & Ilene Louise (Manley) Harris; m. Pauline Privett; correction to Cemeteries of Grundy Co.,Vol. 1, p. 128
Harris, Harold Edsel	Mar 26, 1930	May 01, 1996	Altamont Cem.; Son of Elbert L. & Leona (Russell) Harris; m. Marian Chancey; TSgt. USAF Korea, Vietnam; addition to Cemeteries of Grundy Co.Vol. 1, p. 21
Harris, Helen Caroline (Kruzewski)	Jan 15, 1913	Mar 04, 2005	Cumberland Heights Cem.; Dau. of Andrew & Felicia (Suwalski) Kruzewski; addition to Cemeteries of Grundy Co.Vol. 1, p. 197
Harris, Herbert Spencer	Mar 14, 1909	Jun 25, 1987	Cumberland Heights Cem.; Son of William Edwin, Sr. & Rosetta Annetta (Force) Harris; addition to Cemeteries of Grundy Co.Vol. 1, p. 198
Harris, Howard	ca 1977	Apr 13, 1985	Oak Grove Cem.; Son of Albert Calloway Jackson & Bertha Jane (Nolan) Harris; m. Rebha Rust Dec 21, 1940; no tombstone; addition Cemeteries of Grundy Co.Vol. 1
Harris, Inez	Jan 22, 1940	Feb 09, 2014	Mt. Garner Cem.; Dau. of Preston Lee & Mattie Cleo (Meeks) Tate; m. James W. Harris
Harris, Jessie Miles	1896	1976	Hobbs Hill Cem.; Son of Elic Harris; m. Lillie Foster; PVT US Army WWI; addition to Cemeteries of Grundy Co.Vol. 1, p. 338
Harris, John Bradford	Feb 24, 1920	May 20, 1942	Tracy City Cem.; Son of Jay Cleveland & Johnnie Marler (Gates) Harris
Harris, Kathryn "Kate"	Jun 11, 1885	Oct 18, 1961	Gregg Cem (Death Certificate says Coppinger Cem); Dau. of Matt & Rachel (Anderson) Robertson
Harris, Lorenza B.	Sep 05, 1950	Oct 22, 2019	Airview Cem.; born in Philippines; m. James W Harris
Harris, Margaret	Feb 14, 1870	Nov 10, 1870	Coulson/Wesley Chapel Church Cem.; Dau. of Samuel J Harris & Jane Parks
Harris, Margaret (Thomas)	Jun 15, 1925	May 04, 1997	Monteagle Cem.; Dau. of Marvin W & Alice (McFarland) Thomas; m. Sory E. Harris, Jul 1, 1943; addition to Cemeteries of Grundy Co.Vol. 1, p. 447
Harris, Mary (Sitz)	Mar 11, 1887	Sep 11, 1951	Fall Creek Cem.; Dau of George Washington Sitz & Sarah Jane Richmond; m. William Carroll Harris in 1903; correction to Cemeteries of Grundy Co. Vol 1, p. 208

Name	Birth	Death	Details
Harris, Minnie Ada	Aug 04, 1915	Aug 19, 2007	Airview Cem.; Dau. of Dan & Elizabeth (Bondurant) Simmons from NC; m. Willis Franklin Harris; addition to Cemeteries of Grundy Co.Vol. 1, p. 6
Harris, Sherry Dene (Layne)	Mar 12, 1953	Feb 25, 2020	Orange Hill Cem.; Dau. of Homer Lewis & Wilma Layne; m. Nat Harris
Harris, Willis Franklin	May 07, 1913	Apr 03, 1987	Airview Cem.; Son of Thomas & Susan (Clark) Harris from KY; m. Minnie Ada Simmons; addition to Cemeteries of Grundy Co.,Vol. 1, p. 6
Harrison, Clarence	Dec 09, 1933	Mar 14, 2015	Eastern Star Cem.; Son of Hayes & Eleanor (Garner) Harrison; m. Shirley Hanson; U.S. Army
Harrison, Jennie (King)	Jun 11, 1874	Jan 10, 1934	Hobbs Hill Cem.; Dau. of George & Elizabeth (Rose) King; m. James Andrew Harrison Sep 17, 1893, in Franklin Co TN; addition to Cemeteries of Grundy Co.Vol. 1, p. 337
Harrison, Jennie Elizabeth	Nov 19, 1914	Jan 18, 1915	Hobbs Hill Cem.; Dau. of Phineas H. "Fines" & Lillie Bell (Harrison) Hampton; addition to Cemeteries of Grundy Co.,Vol. 1, p. 337
Harrison, Lillie Belle	Mar 1898	1914 or 1915	Hobbs Hill Cem.; Dau. of James Andrew & Jennie Harrison, m. Phineas H. "Fines" Hampton; addition to Cemeteries of Grundy Co.,Vol. 1, p. 337
Harrison, Nancy (Pack)			Roberts Cove Cem.; m. Thomas Harrison in 1784, Lincoln Co. NC: from research of Judy Harrison Vaughn
Harrison, Thomas	1760 in Maryland	Nov 4, 1839	Roberts Cove Cem.; m. Nancy Pack in 1784 in Lincoln Co. NC, was a Revolutionary War soldier in the NC line. Known to have lived in Roberts Cove Grundy Co. daughter was Susannah Harrison Sartain; obituary published in *Huntsville Democrat*.
Harrison, William Randal	Oct 28, 1947	Oct 14, 2020	Palmer Cem.; Son of Hershel & Willie Mae (Scissom) Harrison; m. Glenda Britton; U.S. Army - Vietnam
Harshman, Dale Lee	Sep 03, 1937	Feb 16, 2015	Bethel Cem.; Son of Glenn & Ruth (Slick) Harshman; m. Melvia Ruth Nunley; Children: Dale Lee, Jr.; Timothy R; Anthony W; Brian L; Stacy C.; addition to Cemeteries of Grundy Co.Vol. 1, p.68
Harshman, Timothy Ray	May 20, 1960	Jul 16, 1960	Bethel Cem.; Son of Dale Lee & Melvia Ruth (Nunley) Harshman; body moved from Indiana to Bethel
Hart, O'lean	Apr 17, 1931	Mar 22, 2013	Palmer Cem.; Dau. of Hearl & Lillie (Ross) Cleek; m.1) Coleman Layne 2) J.B. Hart
Hartsel, Doris	Feb 14, 1944	Mar 12, 2012	Coalmont Cem.; Dau. of Richard & Ruby (Cameron) Hale; m. 1)___Sisk 2) Thomas Hartsel

Name	Birth	Death	Details
Hartsel, Wolbun (Chang) "Joanne"	Mar 30, 1940	Dec 11, 1997	Coalmont Cem.; Dau. of Chang J Sok & Ani Ke; m. Thomas Hartsel; correction to Cemeteries of Grundy County, Vol. 1, p. 181
Hartwell, Vernon Dwight	Dec 08, 1931	Feb 26, 2020	Palmer Cem.; Son of Russell Vernon & Cleta Ione Hartwell; m. 1) Jessie Ruth Sissom 2) Beverly Hartwell; US Army & US Navy; addition to Cemeteries of Grundy County, Vol. 1, p. 552
Haskins, Franz	1891	May 09, 1921	Hobbs Hill Cem.; Son of Abe & Biddie (Nunley) Haskins
Hassebrock, Fermenda (Hill)	Dec 07, 1922	Nov 12, 2017	Summerfield Cem.; Dau. of William & Hattie (Partin) Hill; m. Fred Hassebrock
Hassebrock, Freddie Wayne	Nov 06, 1944	Jan 28, 2013	Summerfield Cem.; Son of Fred & Ferminda (Hill) Hassebrock; m. Cathy Thomas
Hastings, Billy Wayne	Apr 08, 1961	Mar 23, 2018	Burns Cem.; Son of Robert Hastings & Irene Stephens; m. Nelda Shrum
Hastings, Nelda	Apr 15, 1964	Oct 23, 2017	Burns Cem.; Dau. of Rev. Stanley E. & Katie M. Shrum; m. Billy Wayne Hastings
Haston, Jerry Dean	Feb 02, 1932	Jan 25, 2018	Armstrong Cemetery; Son of Herbert L Haston & Jessie White; m. Bettye Claire Woodlee; Tennessee Army National Guard
Hatfield, Emily Dell (Bolinger)	Jun 04, 1943	Oct 16, 2021	Cremated; Dau. of Delno & Carrie Bolinger; m. Perry Shelton Hatfield
Hatfield, Mary Ethel	Jul 31, 1939	Mar 14, 2014	Orange Hill Cem.; Dau. of Virgel & Ruth Fincher; m. Martin Hatfield
Hatfield, Perry Shelton	Mar 29, 1947	Feb 13, 2014	Cremated; Son of Curt & Ida Hatfield; m. Emily Dell Bolinger; Vietnam - Black Horse Armored Cavalry, Troup L
Havens, Walter Sherman	Jan 19, 1858	Oct 12, 1933	Altamont Cem.; Son of Jesse & Rebecca (Berry) Havens; addition to Cemeteries of Grundy Co. Vol. 1, p. 31
Hawes, Rosie Gearldean (Shrum)	Dec 12, 1972	Jan 25, 2022	Sequatchie Valley Memorial Gardens; Dau. of Paul & Gearldean Shrum; m. Al Hawes
Hawk, Ruby (Rieder)	Aug 03, 1913	Dec 20, 2015	Warren "Red Hill" Cem.; Dau. of Henry J. & Lillie (Moran) Rieder; m. Dillon Hawk; addition to Cemeteries of Grundy Co, Vol. 2, p. 942
Hawkings, Jeannine	Jul 29, 1943	Jul 19, 2010	Homeland Acres Cem.; Dau. of George & Alda M. (Franke) Scullin; m. A.J. Hawkins; addition to Cemeteries of Grundy Co., Vol, 1, p. 340
Hawkins Ernestine P. (Peyton)	Apr 30, 1928	Mar 31, 2021	Eastern Star Cem.; Dau. of Ernest & Dorcas Peyton; m. John Ross Hawkins
Hawkins, Deborah	Feb 19, 1900	Jun 06, 2013	King Cem.; Dau. of Carl & Catherine (Pease) Hobbs; m. Ricky Hawkins
Hawkins, James Marshall, Sr.	1939	Jun 19, 2014	Cremated; Son of Jack Horace & Kathryn Hawkins; m. Hazek M. Hawkins

Name	Birth	Death	Details
Hawkins, Marion Inez	Sep 01, 1930	Jul 31, 2015	Eastern Star Cem.; Dau. of Thelma Brooks; m. Glen H. Hawkins
Hay, Sarah Barnwell Elliot (Howe)	1943	Dec 10, 2021	Cremated; Dau. of Raymond Reed & Isabelle (Puckette) Howe; m. Robert Donald Hay
Hayes, William W	1871	1961	Coalmont Cem.; Son of John P. & Elizabeth (Yates) Hayes; m. Minnie Brady
Haynes, Bobby Edwin, Jr.	Mar 02, 1960	Jan 27, 1962	Oak Grove Cem.; Son of Bobby Edwin, Sr. & Mary Helen (Meeks) Haynes; addition to Cemeteries of Grundy Co.,Vol. 1, p. 494
Haynes, Diane Marie (Brittin)	Nov 28, 1953	Feb 19, 2015	Fall Creek Cem.; Dau. of Charles Ray & Patsy Joan (Brittin) Gipson
Haynes, Donald D	1931	Apr 15, 2018	Hamilton Memorial Gardens Cem.; Son of Harvey Chester Haynes & Ollie Mae Argo; m. Julia
Haynes, Doris Ophelia	May 15, 1914	Aug 08, 2015	Plainview Cem.; Dau. of Levator & Ella Cannon; m. Paul Haynes
Haynes, Elizabeth Orme (Raulston)	Dec 08, 1932	Jun 16, 2015	Monteagle Cem.; Dau. of Jefferson Jones & Mary Orme (Sayles) Raulston; m. George Haynes; addition to Cemeteries of Grundy Co.,Vol. 1, p. 417
Haynes, Ephraim Madison	Sep 16, 1820	Oct 01, 1901	Summerfield Cem.; Age 79 years; Son of Eli & Elizabeth (Cook) Haynes; m. Clariss Eveline "Clercy" Wooten; addition to Cemeteries of Grundy Co.,Vol. 2, p. 765
Haynes, Ernest Alfred	Jun 09, 1926	Sep 11, 1983	Gregg Cem.; Son of Huch Allen & Gladys Lee (Johnson) Haynes; m. Zelma M. Johnson; PFC US Army WWII
Haynes, Ernest Joel	Jun 4,1946	Jan 01, 2013	Pine Grove Cem. Jasper, TN; Son of Howard & Vesta Haynes; m. Mary Adams
Haynes, Eugene "Gene"	Aug 21, 1930	Dec 14, 2011	Pryor Ridge Cem.; Son of Vernon E. & Edith (Kilgore) Haynes; m. 1) Eva L. Hernandes 2) Rena J. (Shrum) King
Haynes, George Holbert "Big George" III	ca 1953	Dec 27, 2021	Allen Cem in Caney Springs Community near Chapel Hill; Son of George Holbert Haynes II & Elizabeth Raulston
Haynes, George Holbert IV	May 26, 1979	Jun 18, 2021	Allen Cem. in Caney Springs Commmunity near Chapel Hill; Son of George Holbert III & Sonya Haynes
Haynes, Henry		Aug 16, 1914	Orange Hill Cem.
Haynes, Henry Francis	Sep 27, 1853	Jul 31, 1915	Oak Grove Cem.; Son of Ephraim Madison Haynes & Clarissa Evaline Wooten ; m. Harriet Ellen Dennis
Haynes, Hettie Juanita (Lockhart)	Sep 01, 1940		Warren "Red Hill" Cem.; Dau. of Earl & Minnie Lee (Nunley) Lockhart; m. James Hollinsworth "Jim" Haynes
Haynes, James Hollingsworth	Nov 23, 1939	May 30, 2019	Warren "Red Hill" Cem.; Son of George Holbert Haynes & Mary Magdalene "Maggie" Kennedy; m. Hettie Juanita Lockhart

Name	Birth	Death	Details
Haynes, Kenneth	Mar 12, 1936	Aug 01, 2017	Pryor Ridge Cem.; Son of Vernon & Edith Haynes; m. Anna M. Haynes
Haynes, Larry Lewis	Sep 25, 1946	Jan 18, 2013	Pelham Church of Christ Cem.; Son of Holbert & Maggie (Kennedy) Haynes; m. 1) Linda Bohannan 2) Martha Haynes
Haynes, Lula (Rollins)	Apr 19, 1918	Jun 09, 2005	Monteagle Cem.; Dau. of James "Jim" & Mary (Lemons) Rollins; m. James Buford Haynes; correction – even though she has Rollins as her last name on her tombstone, she was Lula Rollins Haynes; She is buried beside her brother John Thomas Rollins; addition to Cemeteries of Grundy Co., Vol. 1, p. 459
Haynes, Mary (Meeks)	May 08, 1947	Jul 23, 2019	Plainview Cemetery; Dau. of Claude Meeks & Mary Louise Cantrell; m. Larry Haynes
Haynes, Ophelia (Cannon)	May 15, 1914	Aug 08, 2015	Plainview Cem.; Dau. of Lavator & Ella (Scruggs) Cannon; m. Paul Haynes
Haynes, Perry Lee	May 08, 1947	Nov 22, 1986	Plainview Cem.; Son of Vernon E. & Edith (Kilgore) Haynes; m. Theresa Darlene Crisp on Mar 12, 1965
Haynes, Rachel N. (Campell)	Jan 15, 1952	Jan 10, 2018	Monteagle Cem.; Dau. of Tom Albert & Minnie Mae (Thomas) Campbell; m. John W. Haynes; Rachel has a tombstone in Warren "Red Hill" Cemetery with her husband John Haynes, but she is actually buried in the Monteagle Cem. Addition to Cemeteries of Grundy Co.Vol. 2, p. 925
Haynes, Randall E.	Feb 16, 1940	Nov 08, 1992	Orange Cem.; Son of Vernon C. & Edith (Kilgore) Haynes; m. Sylvia Carrick; correction to Cemeteries of Grundy Co.Vol. 2, p. 668
Haynes, Sylvia (Carrick)	Apr 21, 1905	Nov 05, 2018	Orange Hill Cem.; Dau. of Bob & Vilda Carrick; m. Randale Haynes
Haynes, Terry Blake	Dec 23, 1982	Apr 07, 2021	Monteagle Cem.; Son of Terry Dee & Cheryl Haynes
Haynes, Theresa Darlene	Aug 20, 1948		Plainview Cem.; Dau. of Leon Crisp; m. Perry Lee Haynes on Mar 12, 1965
Haynes, Virginia Marie (Lewis)	May 23, 1934	Jun 20, 2020	Pryor Ridge Cem.; Dau. of Allison Lewis & Mary Ducker; m. Paul Edward Haynes
Hayostek, Alton	1934	Feb 20, 2021	Cremated, burial later in MI; Son of Andrew & Betty J Hayostek; m. Sondra Hayostek
Hayse, Vernon "Gabby"	1931	Dec 13, 2015	Orange Hill Cem.; Son of Willie & Maybelle Hayes; m. Tericia Hayse; Korea & Vietnam vet
Hazen, Brooke	living at time of survey		Warren "Red Hill" Cem.; Dau. of William R.H. & Sherry Fay (Mayes) Hazen; grave place holder -no information on stone

Name	Birth	Death	Notes
Hazen, Sherry Fay (Mayes)	Jun 28, 1950		Warren "Red Hill" Cem.; Dau. of Blantford & Dorothy (Meeks) Mayes; m 1) Raymond Shimmin 2) William R.H. Hazen
Hazen, William R.H. "Bill"	Nov 29, 1935	Aug 16, 2016	Warren "Red Hill" Cem.; Son of Harold Russell & Irene (Martin) Hazen; m. Sherry (Mayes) Shimmin; USMC & USAF; addition
Headrick, James Edward	Feb 14, 1881	after 1920	Oak Grove Cem.; Son of William R. Headrick; m. Hattie Rust Dec 23, 1916; no tombstone; addition to Cemeteries of Grundy Co.Vol. 1, p. 512
Headrick, Lemuel J.	June 1858	May 11, 1957	Tracy City Cem.; no marker; Son of Thomas & Flora (Anderson) Headrick; addition
Headrick, Louisa "Liza" (Anderson)	1854	1889	Pigeon Springs Cem.; no monument- death certificate; addition to Cemeteries of Grundy County,Vol. 2
Headrick, William Henry	1908	1959	Bonny Oak Cem.; Son of William R & Sarah Headrick (possibly)
Hedges, Joseph B. W.	Aug 26, 1932	Feb 26, 2020	Camp Butler National Cem.; Son of Sydney Hedges and Lois Mullins; m. Earlene Hedges
Hedges, Milton Leland, Jr.	Jan 20, 1940	Feb 19, 2014	Monteagle Cem.; Son of Milford & Rev. Lilian (Gibbs) Hedges; m. Susan Hedges
Hediger, Arnold	Feb 4, 1882	Aug 03, 1970	Swiss Colony Cem.; Son of Arnold (1852-1934) & Anna Marie (Brugger) Hediger; m. Lydia Richner
Heer, Heinrich "John Henry"	Jan 24, 1830	Oct 17, 1913	Tracy City Cem.; Son of Hilarius & Anna Susanna (Kundert) Heer; born in Switzerland; m. 1) Anna Hagman 2) Eliza "Ettie" Werner; addition to Cemeteries of Grundy Co.Vol. 2, p. 877
Henderson, Albert	Ca 1892	Nov 15, 1933	Tracy City Cem.; Son of John & Mary (Smartt) Henderson; death certificate; addition to Cemeteries of Grundy Co.,Vol. 2
Henderson, Charles E.	Feb 18, 1929	Jul 16, 2015	Palmer Cem.; Son of Jasper & Dollie (Banks) Henderson; m. Frances ; US Army
Henderson, Rosa (McGovern)	Apr 1873	Nov 21, 1911	Hobbs Hill Cem.; Dau. of James & Rosa McGovern; m. George Henderson; addition to Cemeteries of Grundy Co.,Vol. 1, p. 335
Henderson, Willie Lee	Jul 16, 1925	Jun 14, 2002	Plainview Cem.; Son of Charley & Louise (Thompson) Henderson; addition to Cemeteries of Grundy Co., Vol. 2, p. 707
Hendrickson, Loda Jean	Ca. 1960	Nov 10, 2016	Cremated; Dau. of Theopolis & Peggy Perry; m. Conrad Hendrickson
Henley, Adolphis	Apr 24, 1928	Aug 09, 2019	Cremated; Son of General Joe Henley & Grace Marie Layne; m. Lillian Graves

Henley, Allen C.	May 18, 1872	Nov 12, 1941	Tracy City Cem.; Son of James "Jim" & Margaret (Garner) Henley; m. 1) Rosa Hobbs Jackson, Jul 3,1898, Grundy Co, TN, 2) Edmonia "Mona" Patton, addition to Cemeteries of Grundy Co. Vol, 2, p. 890
Henley, Bill	Ca. 1837	Feb 01, 1921	Monteagle Cem.; Found murdered in woods near Monteagle; missing 3 weeks; source: *Mrs. Grundy*, Mar 4, 1921; found by fortune teller, Kitt Meeks
Henley, Boris Stephen	Jan 05, 1961	May 04, 2016	Summerfield Cem.; Son of Adolphus & Lillian Henley; m. Heidi Johnson
Henley, Claude Willis	Apr 16, 1905	Nov 03, 2013	Mt. Garner Cem.; Son of Claude C. & Fannie (Willis) Henly; m. Joyce Greeter
Henley, Dorothy "Dottie" Jean (Keller)	Jun 14, 1937	Dec 21, 2018	Providence Methodist Cem.; Dau. of Daniel Crawford & Clara Mildred (Laxson) Keller; Children Beckye, Millie, William; m. William Samuel "Sam" Henley; addition to Cemeteries of Grundy Co,Vol. 2, p.709
Henley, Dorothy Mae (Fults)	Sep 29, 194	May 23, 2021	Franklin Memorial Gardens Cem.; Dau. of Alfred & Vincy Lee (Meeks) Fults; m. Buford Henley
Henley, Evelyn (Russell)	Dec 13, 1927	Mar 04, 2021	Fall Creek Cem.; Dau. of Fred & Billie Russell; m. William "Buddy" Brooks Henley
Henley, John Burwell	Sep 16, 1926	Jul 21, 2020	Marshall Memorial Cem in Arab, AL; Son of Horace & Alma (Brashear) Henley; m. Dorothy Ray
Henley, John Edward, Jr.	Jul 13, 1952	Feb 01, 2014	Tracy City Cem.; Son of John Edward Henley & Loadema F. Thompson; m. Judy Dianne Meadows
Henley, John Patrick	Sep 30, 1836	Sep 10, 1905	Henley, John Patrick family Cem.; Son of James Campbell & Malinda Abigail (Thompson) Henley; correction to Grundy County Cemetery book Vol. 1, p. 321
Henley, Marvin F.	Jun 11, 1938	Apr 16, 1979	Fall Creek Cem.; Son of Marvin L. & Louis (Brooks) Henley; m. Virginia Jo Scoggins
Henley, Nora Agnes (Armstrong)	Jan 9, 1886	Apr 25, 1952	Tracy City Cem.; Dau. of Jim Northcutt & Flora Armstrong; g-dau of Martin & Mary Caroline (Goodman) Armstrong
Henley, Parker Dean	Oct 29, 1937	Sep 09, 2016	Summerfield Cem.; Son of General Joseph & Grace (Layne) Henley; m. Marilyn N. Long
Henley, Rosa Hobbs Jackson	Mar 06, 1881	Jan 22, 1914	Tracy City Cem.; m. Allen C. Henley
Henley, Sybil Lee (Partin)	Jan 20, 1945	Mar 02, 2015	Warren "Red Hill" Cem.; Dau. of Bryan & Emma (Bramblett) Partin; m. 1) David Bean from Chattanooga 2) Kenneth Kilgore 3) _____ Henley
Henley, Thelma Corrine (Woodlee)	Feb 16, 1933	Aug 07, 2019	Fall Creek Cem.; Dau. of Douglas Woodlee & Arrie Hayes; m. John Lewis Henley

Name	Born	Died	Notes
Henley, William Everett "Bill"	Jul 04, 1936	Jul 12, 2018	Cremated; Son of Horace & Alma (Brashear) Henley; m. 1) Arlene Partin 2) Fay Layne
Hennessee, Berry Gwenel	Oct 14, 1950	Jul 24, 2021	Hunerwadel Cem.; Son of Grover & Gladys (Bisop) Hennessee; U.S. Air Force
Henninger, Frances E.	Oct 13, 1876	Nov 23, 1968	Fall Creek Cem.; Dau. of Marcus Aurelius & Eliza Emmaline (Thurmon) Henninger
Henry, Douglas Selph	May 18, 1926	Mar 01, 2017	Mt. Olivet Cemetery, Nashville; Son of Douglas & Kathryn Henry; m. Loiette "Lolly" Hume; U.S. Army
Henry, Georgia Ruth	Aug 20, 1951	Aug 30, 2015	Fall Creek Cem.; Dau. of Warner & Virginia (Anderson) Troxler; m. 1) Harvey Nolan 2) Rodney Henry
Henry, Herman "Whick"	Jan 15, 1927	Nov 28, 2021	Whitwell Memorial Cem.; Son of Oscar & Mollie Henry; m. Patricia Sue Caldwell; U.S. Navy
Henry, Hubert H.	Mar 03, 1915	Apr 04, 1998	Palmer Cem.; Son of Marion Alexander & Rena B. (Howard) Henry; m. Gladys Irene Davis; Nov. 11, 1934; addition to Cemeteries of Grundy Co, Vol. 2, p 569
Henry, Loiette "Lolly" (Hume)	Oct 18, 1927	Dec. 12, 2016	Mt. Olivet Cemetery, Nashville; Dau. of Foster & Loiette Hume; m. Senator Douglas Selph Henry
Hereford, Kenneth Michael	Aug , 1948	Dec 20, 2019	Stewart Cem., Fayetville, TN; Son of Richard Kenneth Hereford & Nell Gray; m. Sandra Tate
Herman, William	Aug 31, 1943	Nov 13, 2020	Bonny Oak Cem.; Son of William & Daisy (McAlexander) Herman; m. Carol Herman
Herriford, Sarah (Coalson)	Oct 16, 1815	May 1, 1847	Burial location unknown; Dau. of David Coalson & Sarah Cox; m. John Herriford
Hess, Nellie Mae	Mar 02, 1919	May 22, 2013	Sequatchie Valley Memorial Gardens Cem.; Dau of John Lewis & Martha Tennessee Smith; m. Glyn Hess
Heubi, Austin Hayden	May 09, 1911	Sep 02, 1989	Plainview Cem.; Son of John Jacob & Emily Amelie (Fehr) Heubi; m. Nellie Christine Nunley; addition & correction to Cemeteries of Grundy Co., Vol. 2, p. 698
Heubi, Ryan Austin	Feb 17, 2003	Mar 01, 2017	Cremated; Son of Jeremiah & Stephanie (Gilbert) Heubi
Hickey, Brenda Lee (Yokley)	Nov 10, 1960	Nov 17, 2021	Fall Creek Cem.; Dau. of Jerry Donald & Virginia Fay (Cleek) Yokley; m. Donald E. Hickey
Hickey, John Wesley	Jan 08, 1900	Sep 08, 1981	White Cem.; Son of John Sterling & Maggie Ann (Lowe) Hickey; m. Mary E. Layne; addition to Cemeteries of Grundy Co., Vol. 2, p.1006
Hicks, George	Nov 18, 1893	Jan 18, 1959	Fall Creek Cem.; Son of Isaac & Elizabeth (Cordell) Hicks

Name	Birth	Death	Details
Hicks, Glendon Farrell	Nov 03, 1944	Mar 12, 2022	Fall Creek Cem.; Son of James Martin & Mable Venear (Tate) Hicks; m. Eunice Ann Shoemaker; U.S. Army
Hiers, Kathleen (Veal)	Sep 10, 1941	Oct 06, 2015	Cremated; Dau. of Robert & Kate (Hutchinson) Veal; m. Tony Hiers
Hiett, Marion	Sep 21, 1938	Nov 30, 2015	Coalmont Cem.; Dau. of Cecil & Sylvia Gregory; m. William Hiett
Hiett, William Eugene	Mar 17, 1934	Aug 26, 2013	Coalmont Cem.; Son of Wallace & Florence (Brown) Hiett; m. Marion Gregory
Higginbotham, Jane	May 05, 1930	Jun 07, 2021	Dau. of James Robert & Virginia Mae Dean (Brown) Higginbotham
Higgins, Donnie Ellen (Shrum)	Dec 09, 1948	Sep 26, 2020	Shrum Family Cem.; Dau. of Fred & Sarah Shrum; m. Daniel Higgins
Higgins, Kelly Amos	Apr 01, 1933	Nov 19, 2017	Brown's Chapel Cem.; Son of Wiley Amos & Carrie Layne Higgins; m. Patsy Creighton; US Army - Korea
Hill, Josephine C.	1931	Sep 26, 2014	Summerfield Cem.; Dau of Howard & Elizabeth Cox; m. Joe Lannie Hill
Hill, Brenda Ann	Nov 10, 1953	Mar 19, 2013	Cremated; Dau. of Russell & Regina Aebi
Hill, Charles D. "Big Don", Sr.	Mar 17, 1939	Apr 19, 2015	Schild-Tate Cem.; Son of Richard Harding & Thelma Ruth (Rollings) Hill; m. 1) Jo Ann Sanders 2) Fay Layne 3) Reba Evelyn King 4) Ruby Lee Bush; addition to Cemeteries of Grundy Co. Vol. 2, p. 742
Hill, Charles Edward "Charlie"	Feb 22, 1942	Jul 18, 2017	Rutledge Hill Cem.; Son of Marvin Wilson & Ethel Mae (Church) Hill; m. Deborah Cawthorn
Hill, James Franklin	Oct 29, 2008	Dec 31, 2015	Rutledge Hill Cem.; Son of Aaron & Lynetta (Bunde) Hill
Hill, James Marvin "Slick"	Apr 05, 1941	Jun 28, 2020	Cremated; Son of Will Hill & Annie Edith Jackson
Hill, Linda Lee	Aug 06, 1946	Aug 02, 2015	Rose Hill Memorial Gardens; Dau. of Alf & Vivian (Byers) Anderson; m. 1) Harold Collins 2) Grover Hill
Hill, Lucy Jane (Sears)	Oct 08, 1953	Jul 22, 2021	Warren "Red Hill" Cem.; Dau. of Buddy & Elsie Sears; m. Billy Joe Hill
Hill, Marcus Hayes, Jr.	May 15, 1928	May 30, 2018	Hunerwadel Cem.; Son of Marcus Hayes Hill & Robbye Etta Hobbs; m. Verise Virginia Smith
Hill, Morris Richard	Aug 15, 1900	Apr 01, 1948	Summerfield Cem.; Son of John "Jack" & Nera (Woodson) Hill. Per his descendants, his surname is really Johnson, but he was raised by the Hill family; m. Leora Merritt Layne; correction to Cemeteries of Grundy Co., Vol. 2, p. 777

Name	Born	Died	Notes
Hill, Nancy Pauline (Shetters)	Dec 29, 1929	Jun 17, 2017	Summerfield Cem.; Dau. of Elijah, Sr. & Annie Elizabeth (Lynch) Shetters; m. William Hamilton "Hamp" Hill; addition to Cemeteries of Grundy Co.Vol. 2, p. 779
Hill, Nellie Katherine	Mar 19, 1945	Nov 02, 2013	Cremated; Dau. of Harvey & Edna Nunley; m. Larry Hill
Hill, Norma Marie	Jun 28, 1950	Jan 13, 2016	Hill Cem.; Dau. of Thomas & Thelma (Cook) Marlow; m. Francis Hill
Hill, Reba Evelyn	Oct 15, 1945	Oct 21, 2020	Hunerwadel Cem.; Dau. of Richard & Lucille (Knight) King; m. Charles D. Hill, Sr.
Hill, Richard Harding	Oct 12, 1920	Sep 15, 2008	Schild/Tate Cem.; Son of Benjamin Jefferson & Minnie Bell (Clendenon) Hill; m. Thelma Ruth Rollings
Hill, Ruby Lee (Bush)	Jun 28, 1942	Dec 24, 2017	Schild-Tate Cem.; Dau. of Wayne & Mildred (Westfall) Bush; m. Charles D. "Big Don" Hill; addition to Cemeteries of Grundy Co.,Vol. 2, p. 742
Hill, Susan Pauline	Jan 11, 1918	Nov 09, 2013	Shiloh Cem.; Dau. of Benjamin J. & Minnie Belle (Clendenen) Hill
Hill, Virginia Louise (Cox)	Aug 06, 1948	Dec 23, 2018	Mt. Garner Cem.; Dau. of James H Cox & Lula Mae Gilliam; m. Rayburn Hill
Hillard, Caroly Faye (Clark)	Jul 06, 1942	Feb 26, 2014	Hunerwaldel Cem.; Dau. of Thurman & Mary (Tucker) Clark; m. Stanley Gene "Duke" Hillard; addition to Cemeteries of Grundy Co.,Vol. 1, p. 344
Hillis, Hershel Leon	Nov 21, 1942	Oct 26, 2020	Philadelphia Cem.; Son of Willie Hazel & Audrey B Hillis; m. Nadine Rogers; Army National Guard; Correction of death date in Cemeteries of Grundy Co.Vol. 2, p. 646
Hillis, Linda "Kaye" (Johnson)	Nov 28, 1946		Philadelphia Cem.; Dau. of James Freeman & Oma Lee (Dykes) Johnson; m. Edwin Carroll "E.C." Hillis; addition to Cemeteries of Grundy Co.,Vol. 2, p. 653
Hindman, Marjorie (Stockwell)	May 24, 1927	Mar 14, 2015	Brown's Chapel Cem.; Dau. of John Willard & Minnie (McGovern) Stockwell; m. 1) J.L. Payne 2) Joseph B. Hindman
Hinerman, Sharon (Katona) "Sherry"	Dec 30, 1938	May 16, 2020	Body donated to science; Dau. of William & Alida Katona
Hines, Janie Belle (Gallagher)	Apr 02, 1915	Mar 10, 2016	Pelham Church of Christ Cem.; Dau. of John & Belle (Patton) Gallagher; m. Raymond Glenn "Ray" Hines
Hinkle, Ruby Inez (Gilliam)	1929	Nov 28, 2015	Pinehaven Cem.; Hollywood, AL; Dau. of L.M. & Ethel (Talley) Gilliam; m. Charles L. Hinkle
Hoback, Claudia L.	Jul 15, 1922	Mar 3, 2013	Eastern Star Cem.; Dau. of Claude & Myrtle Hopkins; m. Charles Hoback, Jr.
Hoback, Dorothy Louvinia (Sisk)	Sep 26, 1931	Jun 27, 2019	Eastern Star Cem.; Dau. of Joseph Sisk & Myrtle Jackson; m. Robert Lee Hoback

Name	Born	Died	Details
Hoback, Johnny Wendell	Mar 08, 1950	Jun 22, 2019	Clouse Hill Cem.; Son of Robert Lee Hoback & Dorothy Louvinia Sisk; m. Donna Jo Hoback; U.S. Army
Hobbs, Billy	Apr 12, 1960	Jan 05, 2017	Fults Cem.; Son of James Hobbs & Freda Cantrell
Hobbs, Bobby Franklin	Mar 12, 1933	Jan 20, 2020	Little Johnny Myers Cem.; Son of Doc Albert Hobbs & Lucy Myers; m. Ketherine Hampton
Hobbs, Bryan	Jul 31, 1978	Feb 17, 2015	Little Johnny Myers Cem.; Son of Oma Lee Hobbs
Hobbs, Clyne Alan	Jul 26, 1948	Feb 19, 2021	Fall Creek Cem.; Son of Isham & Agnes (Reagan) Hobbs
Hobbs, Earl Edward	Oct 13, 1934	Jan 17, 2015	Altamont Cem.; Son of Odie & Lyda (Myers) Hobbs; m. Grace Johnson
Hobbs, Eddie Leon	Sep 09, 1950	Oct 05, 2016	Palmer Cem.; Son of Leonard & Polly (Johnson) Myers; m. Judith Coffelt
Hobbs, Franklin Eugene	Oct 31, 1954	May 21, 2021	Fall Creek Cem.; Son of Isham & Agnes (Reagan) Hobbs
Hobbs, Gary Adam	Nov 22, 1977	Feb 13, 2000	Brown's Chapel Cem.; Son of Jimmy Lester & Marcella (Nolan) Hobbs; brother of Roger Hobbs
Hobbs, Helen Virgina "Sue"	Apr 14, 1931	Jan 26, 2006	Bonny Oak Cem.; Dau. of Stanley Earl & Carrie K (Havner) Esser; m. Alvin E. Hobbs; addition to Cemeteries of Grundy Co., Vol. 1, p. 90
Hobbs, Henry Haskell, Jr.	Oct 23, 1934	Mar 02, 2020	Sequatchie Valley Memory Gardens; Son of Henry Haskell Hobbs & Emma Roberts; m. Carrie Dockery
Hobbs, Infant			Clouse Hill Cem.; Son of J.N. & Lou Ella "Yell" (Gibbs) Hobbs who were married Jan 16, 1926
Hobbs, Jerry Frances	Jun 01, 1959	May 22, 2018	Little Johnny Myers Cem.; Son of Elmer Frances & Oma Lee Hobbs
Hobbs, Judith Marcella	Nov 25, 1953	Aug 08, 2003	Palmer Cem.; Dau. of Amos Henry & Violet (Smith) Coffelt; m. 1) Gary Edward McBee 2) Eddie L. Hobbs; addition to Cemeteries of Grundy Co, Vol. 2, p. 571
Hobbs, Patricia Irene (Ooley)	May 03, 1905	Apr 12, 2018	Little Johnny Myers Cem.; Dau. of James Bert Ooley & Frances Maries Vest; m. Billy Charles Hobbs: addition to Cemeteries of Grundy Co., Vol. 1, p. 363
Hobbs, Sandra D. (Cole)	Jun 12, 1951		Little Johnny Myers Cem.; Dau. of George & Joan Cole; m. 1) Randel Knight 2) E.J. Richardson 3) Danny Lee Hobbs; addition to Cemeteries of Grundy Co., Vol. 1, p. 364
Hobbs, Sarah	1848	Jul 09, 1918	Bonny Oak Cem.; Dau. of Abraham & Elizabeth (Nunley) Hobbs; addition to Cemeteries of Grundy Co. Vol. 1, p. 95

Name	Birth	Death	Notes
Hobbs, Sharon Denise	Feb 23, 1952	Nov 08, 2019	Fall Creek Cem.; Dau. of Isham Hobbs & Agnes Reagan
Hobbs, Thomas William "Tom"	Oct 3, 1867	Nov 16, 1948	Bonny Oak Cem.; Son of Wesley "Scat" & Lucindy (Lowe) Hobbs per death certificate; m. Martha Campbell; correction to Cemeteries of Grundy Co. Vol. 1, p. 89
Hobbs, Wesley J. "Scat"	1824	1896	Wesley "Scat" Hobbs Cemetery in Northcutt's Cove; Son of Christopher Hobbs & Elizabeth Nunley; m. Lucinda Lowe
Hobbs, William Douglas	Mar 04, 1936	Feb 24, 2019	Airview Cem.; Son of William Horton Hobbs & Ida Mai Fults; m. Joyce Miller
Hodge, M. Janice (infant dau)	Jan 29, 1931	Jan 29, 1931	Grace Chapel Cem.; Dau. of Harmon & Myrtle (Brown) Hodge; addition to Cemeteries of Grundy County, Vol. 1, p. 300
Hoffman, Doris Elaine	Mar 07, 1942	Jul 12, 2017	Cremated; Dau. of Albert Michael & Roberta Ellen (Bogart) Witt; m. 1) Dennis Zeman 2) Bill Hoffman
Hoffman, Joseph Durward	1948	Oct 04, 2019	Summerfield Cem.; Son of William Graham "Red" & Verdie (Aylor) Hoffman; US Army
Hoffman, Sherry	Ca. 1952	Dec 03, 2015	Cremated; Dau. of Bill & Helen (Nunley) Byers; m. J.C. Hoffman
Hoffs, Hester Orange	1878		Orange Hill Cem.; Dau. of John William & Nancy J. (Lockhart) Orange; m. W.L. "Willie" Hoffs. Mistakenly listed as Hester Orange King in Cemeteries of Grundy Co., Vol. 2, p. 357
Hogan, Harry III	Mar 04, 1940	Oct 02, 1998	Swiss Colony Cem.; Son of Harry D. Francis & Iva G. (Van Meter) Hogan; PFC USMC; correction of spelling of last name and addition to Cemeteries of Grundy Co; Vol. 2, p. 793
Hogan, Traci Ann	Dec 22, 1968	Dec 31, 1997	Swiss Colony Cem.; cremated; Dau. of Harry D. Francis & Iva G. (VanMeter) Hogan; correction of last name spelling; addition to Cemeteries of Grundy Co, Vol. 2, p. 793
Holder, Melrose (Hamby)	Dec 15, 1918	Aug 03, 2010	Bethel Cem.; Dau of Grover Cleveland & Bessie (Meeks) Hamby; m. Edward H. Holder
Holland, Dorothy (Fletcher)	Jan 16, 1925	Jan 25, 2021	Mount Garner Cem.; Dau. of Reece & Corine (Pocus) Fletcher; m. Dean Murray Holland
Holland, Steve Allan	1948	Jan 09, 2020	Summerfield Cem.; Son of Caril Preston Holland & Eva Green
Holland, William M.	1879	1960	Orange Hill Cem.; Son of Alexander & Thomasetta (Dove) Holland; m. Sallie Crowe; addition to Cemeteries of Grundy Co. Vol. 2, p. 539
Hollon, Charles O., Jr. "Bones"	Nov 01, 1935	Jul 23, 2014	Cremated; Son of Charles O. Hollon, Sr. & Minnie Mae Morris; born in Jackson, KY

Holmes, Minnie Mae	Feb 20, 1920	Feb 15, 1985	Monteagle Cem.; Dau. of John Witt & Flossie (Smith) Elliott; m.1) Ralph Herman Delaney 2) Earl A. Holmes 3) James L. Clark; addition to Cemeteries of Grundy Co.,Vol. 1. p. 450
Holt, James Earl "Bud"	Mar 15, 1931	Aug 10, 2013	Hunerwadel Cem.; Son of Arvis Milburn & Ruthie (Jackson) Holt; m. Fran Griffith; US Army
Holt, John Milburn	Feb 24, 1945	Dec 17, 2020	Mt. View Cem., Sherwood; Son of Arvis & Ruthie Jane (Jackson) Holt; m. Lana Haddon
Holt, Michael	Apr 14, 1956	Aug 15, 2021	Smith Chapel Cem.; Son of Charles & Mary Lou Holt; m. Mary Okuly
Holt, Ula Alvia	May 24, 1892	Sep 28, 1924	Bonny Oak Cem.; Son of Granville & Lucinda (Woods) Holt; m. Margie Cannon, Apr 27, 1913; addition to Cemeteries of Grundy Co.,Vol. 1, p. 82
Hood, Andrea F.	1964	Feb 23, 2014	Cremated; Dau. of Margaret & Lloyd Veit; m. Bob Hood
Hookey, Ruth (Bunch)	Nov 24, 1930	Mar 28, 2019	Cumberland View Cemetery in Kimball, TN.; Dau. of Warren Otto & Gladie Marguerite (Walter) Bunch; m. Ted Hookey; addition to Cemeteries of Grundy Co.,Vol. 1. Visiting Bible teacher to Grundy Co. Schools along with her sister Doris (Bunch) Sargent who is buried in Lappin Cemetery in Monteagle (See Vol. 2)
Hooper, Bobby Gene	Mar 30, 1945	Feb 09, 2013	Hooper Cem.; Son of Zach & Ruby (Rickman) Hooper; m. Zelda Deitz; USMC
Hoosier, Fay (Smith) Dent	Dec 25, 1931	Jul 15, 2016	Palmer Cem.; Dau. of Lester B. & Iva B. (Frizell) Smith; m. 1) J.D. Dent 2) Jones Hoosier
Hoosier, Nell Rose	May 18, 1936	Aug 20, 1989	Fall Creek Cem.; Dau. of Otis & Orpha E (Meeks) Magouirk
Hoosier, Scotty Ray	Oct 04, 1973	Feb 27, 2021	Altamont Cem.; Son of Billy Ray & Connie Louise (Seagroves) Hoosier
Hooten, Estell (Dick)	Nov 02, 1918	Dec 08, 2015	Fall Creek Cem.; Dau. of Malcom & Della (Knight) Dick; m. 1) William Tate 2) Roy Hooten
Hopkins, Michael John	Oct 12, 1932	Jan 01, 2014	Cremated; Son of William John & Carolyn (King) Hopkins
Hopper, Troy Lee, Jr.	Sep 27, 1989	Jun 05, 2016	Griffith's Creek Cem.; Son of Troy L. & Lisa G. (Fults) Hopper
Hornbuckle, Carl Douglas	Apr 05, 1938	Jul 11, 2015	Palmer Cem.; Son of Charles & Hazel (Roberts) Hornbuckle; m. Patricia LeCroy; U.S. Navy
Hornbuckle, Hazel Irene (Roberts)	May 10, 1919	Nov 22, 2012	Palmer Cem.; Dau. of Isham & Bessie (Tate) Roberts; m. Charles Hornbuckle Apr 23, 1936, in Welch, WV; addition to Cemeteries of Grundy Co.,Vol. 2, p. 574

Name	Birth	Death	Details
Horton, Anna Mae (Nunley)	Jul 14, 1931	Mar 29, 2019	Rose Hill Memorial Gardens; Dau. of Graham Nunley & Mae Ellen Campbell; m. 1) Cordell Gilliam 2) Nathan Deon Pool 3) Hallie O'Neal Horton
Horton, David Allen	Jul 24, 2004	Jan 31, 2017	Cremated; Son of David & Amanda Gail (Meeks) Horton
Horton, Kathleen Marie (Smail)	Apr 14, 1949	Oct 09, 2019	Plainview Cem.; Dau. of Herbert Smail & Dorothy Kelley; m. Wilston T. Horton
Horton, Mordica Pinkney "Pink"	1852	1936	Summerfield Cem.; Son of William & Irena Horton; m. Louisa Jane Reaves; addition to Cemeteries of Grundy Co., Vol. 2, p. 768
Hostetler, Thomas Daniel	Jan 14, 1932	Nov 26, 2021	Cumberland Mennonite Fellowship Cem.; Son of Daniel & Nancy Hostetler; m. Esther Bawel
Howard, Allie May (Haley)	1948	Nov 29, 2019	Gilliam Cemetery; Dau. of Jimmy Paul Haley & Rose Marie Bratcher
Howard, John Gilliland	Oct 28, 1833	Jan 30, 1914	Sims Cem.; Son of John Phillip & Sarah (Gilliland) Howard; m. Sarah Lucinda Nevill; Confederate veteran per *Mrs. Grundy*, Feb 21, 1914
Howell, Mary Elizabeth	Oct 16, 1917	May 16, 2016	Bonnie Oak Cem.; Dau. of George & Margaret (Dyer) Tate; m. Harvey L. Howell
Huelbig, Martin Keith	Nov 17, 1954	Aug 18, 2009	Fall Creek Cem.; Son of Martin Gerald & Edith Alice (McFarland) Huelbig
Hughes, Doris Emily (Graham)	Feb 19, 1928	Apr 03, 2020	Burns Cem.; Dau. of James Homer Graham & Renice Myers; m. 1) Arvill Elihue Roberts 2) Herschel Hughes
Huling, Walter, Dr.	Feb 05, 1925	Jun 19, 1979	Brown's Chapel Cem.; Son of Arthur Mourfield & Georgia (Byrd) Huling; m. Mary Jo Garrett; AMM2, US Navy, WWII; addition to Cemeteries of Grundy Co. Vol. 1, p. 114
Hull, Joshua Cly	Nov 05, 1989	Sep 01, 2018	Cremated; Son of Rodney & Susan Ann Hull; US Army
Humphreys, Judy Elaine (Brewer)	Dec 05, 1944	Feb 03, 2018	Brown's Chapel Cem.; Dau. of Burnes E. "Tooter Bill" Brewer & Ila Lee Layne
Hunerwadel, Beulah Mae (Turner)	Jun 11, 1928	Feb 08, 2004	Hunerwadel Cem.; Dau. of Mark T. & Nora (Walker) Turner; m. 1) James McKamey Parkinson 2) Robert Alexander Hunerwadel; addition to Cemeteries of Grundy Co. Vol. 1, p. 345
Hunerwadel, Robert Alexander	May 10, 1917	Feb 28, 2004	Hunerwadel Cem.; Son of Alexander P & Laura (Barnes) Hunerwadel; m Beulah Mae (Turner) Parkinson; addition to Cemeteries of Grundy Co. Vol. 1, p. 345
Hunt, Mary Jane (Metcalf)	Ca 1871	Feb 01, 1921	Monteagle Cem.; Dau. of Stephen & Sarah (Smith) Metcalfe; m. Abraham Lincoln Hunt on Sep 24, 1905; Source Grundy Co. TN Tidbits, Vol. 3 & death cert. no tombstone

Hunt, Richard Mark	Oct 28, 1981	Dec 16, 2013	Cumberland Heights Memorial Cem.; Son of Elwood Mark & Phyllis Ann (Mullins) Hunt
Huntley, George Alvin, Jr.	May 25, 1938	Mar 11, 2022	Fults Cem.; Son of George "Peck" & Ethelene (King) Huntley; m. Edith McGee
Hunziker, Dorothy Rita (Torres)	Jun 27, 1926	Oct 10, 1996	Monteagle Cem.; Dau. of Quintin & Rosie (Castro) Torres from Hawaii; m. Edward John "E.J." Hunziker, Jr.; addition to Cemeteries of Grundy Co.,Vol. 1, p. 433
Hunziker, Jacob	Nov 8, 1840	Nov 25, 1914	Swiss Colony Cem.; Son of Andreas Andrew & Marie (Bentz) Hunziker; m. Elizabeth Hess; addition to Cemeteries of Grundy Co.Vol. 2, p. 786
Hunziker, Mary Cella "Boots"	Jun 20, 1924	May 11, 2015	Sequatchie Memorial Gardens Cem.; Dau. of James M. & Bessie Tate ; m. James D. Hunziker
Hunziker, Susie (Swann)	May 7, 1895	May 03, 1966	Monteagle Cem.; Dau. of John Wesley & Nettie (Cunningham) Swann; m. Edward John Hunziker, Sr.; addition and correction to Cemeteries of Grundy Co.Vol. 1, p. 433
Hurst, Arbie Inez (Falls)	Nov 28, 1877	Sep 01, 1978	Summerfield Cem.; Dau. of Daniel & Mary Ann (Maddox) Falls; m. William Sterling Hurst; addition to Cemeteries of Grundy Co. Vol. 2, p. 768
Hutchins, Peggy Evelyn (Tate)	May 21, 1929	Oct 08, 2019	Gardens of Memory Memorial Cem.; Dau. of Haskell Tate & Ada Scruggs; m. Orbin Latton Hutchins
Hutchison, Howard Bennett	Dec 23, 1922	Aug 23, 1963	Altamont Cem.; Son of William Henry & Julia Virginia (Williams) Hutchison; m. Anita Lillian Jenne; addition to Cemeteries of Grundy Co,Vol. 1, p. 24
Ikard, Betty Wiles (Lucas)	Sep 25, 1930	Jul 08, 2021	Mt. Garner Cem.; Dau. of William Orville & Lena Rivers (Wiles) Lucas; m. Lannie Looney Ikard
Ikard, Lannie	Jan 03, 1927	Jan 10, 2018	Mt. Garner Cem.; Son of J.L. Ikard & Gladys May Looney; m. Betty Lucas
Ingle, Jack	Nov 08, 1943	Jul 23, 2016	Cowan Montgomery Cem.; Son of Newton Dowell & Mary H. (Goodrich) Ingle; m. Bobbie Lee Rogers
Ingle, Roger Neal	1967	Nov 23, 2021	Cremated; Son of Newton Dowell & Sadie (Harris) Ingle
Inman, Lela Mae (Hickey)	Mar 24, 1943	Feb 21, 2020	Chattanooga National Cem.; Dau. of Joh Wesley Hickey & Mary Elizabeth Layne; m. David Andrew Inman
Irvin, Betty Ann (Collins)	Apr 16, 1889	Mar 24, 1975	Bonny Oak Cem.; Dau. of William & Sarah Collins; m. Jack Irvin; addition to Cemeteries of Grundy Co.Vol. 1, p. 75

Name	Birth	Death	Details
Irvin, David E	Apr 23, 1905	Jan 28, 2021	Bonny Oak Cem.; Son of Robert Clark & Susie Ann (Nunley) Irvin; m. Katherine Elaine Irvin; U. S. Navy
Irvin, Dorothy Jewel (Hobbs)	Oct 15, 1928	Dec 11, 2015	Coalmont Cem.; Dau. of Herman & Carlena (Rubley) Hobbs; m. Freeman Irvin
Irvin, Gail Evelyn	Dec 05, 1946	Aug 08, 2015	Coalmont Cem.; Dau. of Dave & Pearl (Nunley) Green; m. Johnny Irvin
Irvin, George Eugene	Oct 08, 1962	Feb 05, 2021	Bonny Oak Cem.; Son of George & Myrtle Irvin
Irvin, Jane (Payne)	Ca 1823	Aug 04, 1913	Tracy City Cem.; Mother of sons Clabe, Mike, Joe, Kirb, & Jim Irvin & daughters Mesdames Lige (Kit) Meeks, Fate Sweeton, & Sally Flynn from *Mrs. Grundy* Aug 7, 1913
Irvin, Ophelia (Burnett) "Totsie"	Oct 17, 1930	Feb 16, 2022	Coalmont Cem.; Dau. of Morgan & Myrtle (Hammers) Burnett; m. Carl David "Copie" Irvin
Irvin, Russell	Apr 30, 1905	Sep 24, 2021	Coalmont Cem.; Son of William & Hilda Grace (Bretze) Irvin; m. Brenda Nance; U.S. Army
Irvin, Wanda Jane (Garner)	Apr 21, 1955	Sep 27, 2019	Bonnie Oak Cem.; Dau. of Billy Douglas Garner & Bertha Mae McBee; m. Paul Irvin
Irwin, Kenneth	May 17, 1952	May 29, 2021	Cremated; ashes thrown over Fiery Gizzard Gulf near old White Hotel on Pigeon Springs Rd.; Son of Doris Henderlight & step father James David Henderlight
Isbell, Wanda Carol (Thomas)	May 12, 1948	Dec 16, 2018	Summerfiel Cem.; Dau. of Charles E. & Odell Thomas; m. Larry Isbell
Ison, Aliene Frances	Jun 02, 1934	Mar 12, 1994	Oak Grove Cem.; Dau. of George Washington & Cora (Earps) Kilgore; addition to Cemeteries of Grundy Co.,Vol. 1, p. 490
Jablonski, Edith (Gilley)	May 30, 1906	Feb 15, 2000	Plainview Cem.; Dau. of William H. & Ella (Disheroon) Gilley; m. John Jablonski; addition to Cemeteries of Grundy Co, Vol. 2, p. 666
Jacks, Reatha (Henry)	Aug 16, 1939	Nov 28, 2014	Palmer Cem.; Dau. of Hubert H. & Gladys I (Davis) Henry; m. James K. Jacks, Sr; correction of birth date and addition of information to Grundy Co. Cemeteries,Vol. 1, p. 577
Jackson Florence I. (Miller)	Jun 15, 1939	Nov 16, 2018	Fall Creek Cem.; Dau. of Louis Miller & Helen Beazilius; m. Samuel L. Jackson
Jackson, Andrew David	Nov 02, 1951	Aug 08, 2020	Plainview Cem.; Son of William Jackson & Dorothy Woods; m. Donna Jackson
Jackson, Charles Thomas	Feb 13, 1900	Jan 07, 2016	Evergreen Cem.; Son of Billie & Sharon Jackson
Jackson, Charles W.	Mar 16, 1945	Jun 08, 1960	Fall Creek Cem.; Son of David Jackson & Esper Dishroon

Name	Birth	Death	Details
Jackson, Doris "Dot" (Owens)	Dec 28, 1954		Warren "Red Hill" Cem.; Dau. of Thomas Earl & Alma Brewer Owens; m. 1) Wade Stanley Brown 2) Larry Kilgore 3) Harold Jackson
Jackson, James Lincoln Reed	Jan 30, 2020	Feb 29, 2020	Plainview Cem.; Son of Jamie Ray Jackson & Miriah Donielle LaShaey Jackson
Jackson, Paul Andrew	Oct 12, 1923	May 06, 2015	Franklin Memorial Gardens Cem.; Son of Paul & Rebecca (Wilson) Jackson; m. Ida May Sherrill
Jackson, Tommy	Jan 03, 1946	Jan 07, 2019	Cowan Montgomery Cem.; Son of Ed Jackson & Bessie Morris; m. Joyce Davis
Jackson, William		Apr 07, 2013	Mountain View Cem. in Sherwood; Son of John William & Elizabeth Jackson
Jacobs, Angela	Jun 10, 1977	Oct 20, 2016	Harrison Cem.; Dau. of Leon & Charlene Guess; m. Jim Jacobs
Jacobs, Evelyn Ann (Barry)	Apr 12, 1905	Dec 10, 2021	Harrison Cem.; Dau. of Arthur C. & Sarah Ann Barry; m. Clyde E. Jacobs
Jacobs, Gary Wayne	Jun 14, 1957	Mar 10, 2017	Cremated; Son of Bertha Louise Jacobs; m. Jean Green
Jacobs, Joyce (Layne)	Jun 14, 1954	Jan 20, 2020	Gnat Hill Cem.; Dau. of Homer Layne & Wilma Haynes; m. Don Jacobs
James, Jeanne (Roberts)	1969	Feb 01, 2022	Cremated; Dau. of Billy Hagan & Donna (Meeks) Roberts; m. 1) Paul David James 2) ____Leaderman; from Payne's Cove
James, Agnes A. (Banks)	Dec 28, 1911	Nov 12, 2011	Brown's Chapel Cem.; Dau. of James L, & Mary L (Cagle) Banks; m. Gordon Lee Banks; addition to Cemeteries of Grundy Co.Vol. 1, p. 104
James, Amanda Opal	Apr 12, 1914	Dec 29, 2020	Harpeth Hills Cem.; Dau. of Willie & Vernie (Creighton) Hobbs
James, Arnold E.	Jan 16, 1947	Dec 03, 2021	Farrah Hill Cem.; Son of Elbert & Thelma James; m. Pamela Jane Kurtzenger; His son is Patrick James, who married Susan Wilson, lives in Pelham.
James, Carl	Nov 19, 1932	Nov 19, 1932	Brown's Chapel Cem.; Son of Fred Jackson & Rosa (Schonemann) James; addition to Cemeteries of Grundy Co,Vol. 1, p. 111
James, Christopher Columbus "Lum"	1857	Nov 07, 1917	Hobbs Hill Cem.; Son of Richard M. "Dick" & his 1st wife Eliza Jane (Taylor) James, but raised by 2nd wife Rebecca Jane (Crabtree) James per family; correction & addition to Cemeteries of Grundy Co.,Vol. 1, p. 339
James, Edna Parthenia	May 07, 1941	Jul 05, 1997	Oak Grove Cem.; Dau. of William E. & Cora (Patton) James; addition to Cemeteries of Grundy Co.,Vol. 1, p. 488
James, Jeffery Harold	Mar 01, 1970	Mar 01, 1970	Palmer Cem.; Son of Oscar Howell & Martha M. (Knowland) James; Correction to Cemeteries of Grundy Co.,Vol. 2, p. 563

Name	Birth	Death	Notes
James, Johnny E.	Jul 12, 1942	Mar 14, 1960	Palmer Cem.; Son of Marvin D. & Janie (Crabtree) James; addition to Cemeteries of Grundy Co.,Vol. 2, p. 562
James, Josh Logan	Dec 21, 1990	Oct 13, 2019	Cremated; Son of Paul David James, Sr. & Jeanne (Roberts) James Leaderman
James, Lum Christopher Columbus	1857	Nov 07, 1917	Hobbs Hill Cem.; Son of Richard M. "Dick" & Eliza Jane (Taylor) James, but Richard's 2nd wife Rebecca (Crabtree) James raised him per family. Information from death certificate, no tombstone
James, Madge A. (Tate)	Jun 04, 1933	Apr 14, 2012	Palmer Cem.; Dau. of John Harrison & Elva Arlene (Street) Tate; m. Neal Richard James; Correction & addition to Cemeteries of Grundy Co.Vol. 2, p. 563
James, Marshall F.	Aug 03, 1948	Oct 08, 2017	Brown's Chapel Cem.; Son of Gordon Lee & Agnes (Banks) James; m. Neva Joyce Smith; addition to Cemeteries of Grundy Co.Vol. 1, p. 104
James, Mary Lou (Fulfer)	May 15, 1881	Jun 02, 1943	Brown's Chapel Cem.; Dau. of Houston & Mary Elizabeth (Vaughn) Fulfer; m. Jessie Jackson "Jack" James; correction of spelling of surname and addition to Cemeteries of Grundy Co.,Vol. 1, p. 104
James, Melvin	ca 1845	Jul 23, 1915	Hobbs Hill Cem (likely); Son of Christopher Columbus "Lum" James; no stone; lived in Hunt Co. TX in 1860 census but died in Grundy Co., TN
James, Nancy Dee (Nunley)	Dec 10, 1882	Nov 19, 1918	Bonny Oak Cem.; Dau. of Francis Marion & Martha Elizabeth (Campbell) Nunley; m. William Emmett James; correction of parents' names & addition to Cemeteries of Grundy Co.,Vol. 1, p. 86
James, Oscar Howell	Apr 22, 1935	Nov 10, 2017	Palmer Cem.; Son of Albert M. & Ruby I (Anderson) James; m. Martha M. Knowland; Addition to Cemeteries of Grundy Co.,Vol. 2
James, Pamela Jane (Kurtsinger)	Aug 22, 1946	Apr 11, 2018	Farrar Hill Cem. in Coffee Co; Dau. of Michael Kurtsinger & Doris Gill; m. Arnold James
James, Randel Hoyt	Jun 04, 1943	Dec 09, 2016	Palmer Cem.; Son of Albert & Ruby (Anderson) James; m. Claudia "Sissy" Burnett
James, Richard M. "Dick"	Mar 9, 1826	Aug 13, 1889	Old Baptist Cem.; Son of Thomas & Martha James; m. 1) Eliza Jane Taylor 2) Sarah Jane Rebecca Crabtree per family; addition of first wife to Cemeteries of Grundy Co.,Vol. 2, p. 519
James, Ruby Nell (Shrum)	Sep 23, 1932	Dec 03, 2021	Palmer Cem.; Dau. of Joseph Bailey & Grace Leona (Dishroon) Shrum; m. Malery Eugene James

Name	Born	Died	Notes
James, Ruth (Vandergriff)	Nov 22, 1940	Jan 14, 1988	Palmer Cem.; Dau. of Spearman & Ella (Smith) Vandergriff; m. Kenneth D. James; correction & addition to Cemeteries of Grundy Co.Vol. 2, p. 562
James, Shelvy	Nov 17, 1936	Feb 21, 1938	Brown's Chapel Cem.; Dau. of Fred Jackson & Rosa (Schoenmann) James; addition to Cemeteries of Grundy Co.,Vol. 1, p. 111
James, Steven Howell	Oct 14, 1968	Oct 16, 1968	Palmer Cem.; Son of Oscar Howell & Martha M. (Knowland) James; addition to Cemeteries of Grundy Co.,Vol. 2, p. 563
James, Vinnie L. (Crabtree)	Dec 28, 1909	Apr 23, 2005	Palmer Cem.; Dau. of Henry & Martha (Sanders) Crabtree; m. Marvin D. "Red" James; addition to Cemeteries of Grundy Co.,Vol. 2 p. 562.
James, William Emmett "Floose"	Jul 03, 1906	Mar 23, 1962	Palmer Cem.; Son of Will & Nancy D. (Nunley) James; m. Cora Patton; addition Cemeteries of Grundy Co.Vol. 2
Jarrell, Ruby Louise (Owen)	Apr 06, 1924	Jun 29, 2013	Homeland Acres Cem.; m. Ed Jarrell
Jarrett, Tommy D.	Sep 16, 1939	Sep 24, 2016	Cremated; Son of Talley Davis & Rose M. (Taylor) Jarrett; US Navy
Jean, Carl Reese	Sep 08, 1913	Oct 08, 1975	Coalmont Cem.; Son of Thomas Kurtis Jean & Ada Honey; PFC US Army, WWII; addition to Cemeteries of Grundy County; Vol. 1, p. 172
Jean, Margaret Elizabeth (Pollack)	Mar 10, 1910	Apr 16, 1977	Coalmont Cem.; Dau. of John & Ellen Pollack; m. Carl R Jean; correction to Cemeteries of Grundy County, Vol. 1, p 172
Jenkins, Julia Catherine (Gipson)	Jul 20, 1941	Oct 22, 2019	Monteagle Cem.; Dau. of Elmer Gipson & Dicie Jane Rollins
Jennings, Mary E.	1925	Dec 19, 2014	Cremated; Dau of John Byers & Ethel Davis
Jennings, Wendell Ward	Apr 15, 1933	Aug 14, 1933	Brown's Chapel Cem.; Son of James Berger & Pauline (Cordell) Jennings; addition to Cemeteries of Grundy Co., Vol., 1, p.109
Jensen, Roger Eric	Feb 5. 1950	Apr 08, 2014	Cremated; Son of Ozzie M & Mary H Jensen
Jervis, Jean (McKee)	Sep 18, 1937	Dec 29, 2021	Monteagle Sunday School Assembly Cem.; Dau. of Wallace F & Ruth (Pohlman) McKee; m. Oliver Wheeler Jervis
Jessing, Shirley "Susie" (Teeters)	Apr 29, 1937	Aug 19, 2017	Caney Branch Cem.; Dau. of Gordon & Eugenia Teeters
Johnson Harris, Lassie Arizona	Aug 14, 1912	Feb 02, 1989	Plainview Cem.; Dau. of Hence & Tim (Fults) Levan; m 1) Jesse H. Johnson 2) ___Harris; addition to Cemeteries of Grundy Co.,Vol. 2, p. 694
Johnson, Aaron Huling	Jan 12, 1997	Jan 12, 1997	Palmer Cem.; Son of Huling Eugene "Buddy" & Mary M. (Anderson) Johnson; addition to Cemeteries of Grundy Co.,Vol. 2, p. 568

Name	Birth	Death	Notes
Johnson, Allie Angeline (Cookston) Smith	Mar 28, 1848	May 01, 1928	Wesley Chapel Cem. no stone, but unmarked grave beside her husband; Dau. of Leonard & Martha (Robison) Cookston per death cert; m. 1) Henry Clay Smith 2) James R. Johnson
Johnson, Annie (Scott)	Feb 26, 1905	May 05, 1905	Palmer Cem.; Dau. of Steve & Ellen E. (Childers) Scott; m. 1) John T. Johnson 2) ____ VanHooser; addition to Cemeteries of Grundy Co.,Vol. 2, p. 571
Johnson, Billy Levon	Jun 26, 1950	Jul 06, 2018	Plainview Memorial Cem.; Son of Leo & Virginia Johnson; m. Pat Johnson
Johnson, Boyd	Dec 24, 1952	Feb 08, 2022	Cremated; Son of Ora & Lucy (Isom) Johnson; m. Ruth Johnson
Johnson, Byrtle Arminda Way Echols	Oct 14, 1923	Nov 06, 2005	Oak Grove Cem.; Dau. of Charles Hayes & Millie (Shrum) Way; m.1) Martin Eugene "Gene" Echols 2) Pascal Johnson; addition to Cemeteries of Grundy Co.,Vol. 1, p. 499
Johnson, Cody Garrett	Dec 20, 1991	Jul 20, 2020	Gregg Cem.; Son of Phillip & Susan Johnson
Johnson, Daniel Seigfried	Feb 25, 1885	Jun 23, 1969	Altamont Cem.; Son of Wilhelm & Anna Elizabeth (Beckman) Johansson; m. Anna Elizabeth Olin; born in Sweden; correction of death date & addition to Cemeteries of Grundy Co., Vol. 1, p. 33
Johnson, Danny Timothy "Tim"	Jul 22, 1961	Aug 20, 2020	Son of James Freeman Johnson & Oma Lee Dykes; m. Tracey Prater
Johnson, David Jerome "Buckey"	Aug 06, 1955	Mar 20, 2019	Airview Cem.; Son of Jarvis Johnson & Thelma P. Barrett
Johnson, David Walter	May 27, 1939	Jan 29, 2022	Plainview Cem.; Son of Pascal & Edna (Nolan) Johnson; m. Edwene Meeks
Johnson, Delbert Wayne	May 07, 1905	Jun 04, 2018	Cremated; Son of Leon Johnson and Sarah Nunley
Johnson, Dora S.	May 16, 1905	May 08, 1982	Oak Grove Cem.; Dau. of John James & Martha J (Smith) Johnson; addition to Cemeteries of Grundy Co.,Vol. 1, p. 496
Johnson, Dustin Cody Boyd	Nov 03, 1993	Apr 28, 2020	Coalmont Cem.; Son of Robert Johnson & Shannon Johnson; m. Eliza Gibbs
Johnson, Francis "Frank" Clarke	Sep 29, 1906	Nov 21, 1982	Oak Grove Cem.; Son of John Clark & Marjorie V. (McDuffie) Johnson; addition to Cemeteries of Grundy Co., Vol. 1, p. 496
Johnson, Francis "Frank" J.	Apr 20, 1862	Feb 12, 1946	White Cem.; Son of William Henry & Harriet (Heard) Johnson; m. Martha Elizabeth Cheek; correction & addition to Cemeteries of Grundy Co.Vol. 2, p.1006
Johnson, Geraldine (O'Dear) Nunley	Jun 12, 1928	Nov 23, 2003	Plainview Cem.; Dau. of Herman & Rosa (Killman) O'Dear; addition to Cemeteries of Grundy Co., Vol. 2, p. 663
Johnson, Grady Eugene	Jul 10, 1941	Jan 09, 2021	Plainview Cem.; Son of James & Loma Lea Johnson; m. Joan Johnson

Name	Born	Died	Notes
Johnson, Hammon Val	Jun 21, 1927	Dec 06, 1926	Bonny Oak Cem.; Son of Luther Bryan & "Dellar" Opehelia Della (Caldwell) Johnson; correction of given name spelling in Cemeteries of Grundy Co., Vol. 1, p. 95
Johnson, Harvey	Nov 17, 1931	Jul 03, 2003	Plainview Cem.; Son of Lewis B. & Theresa D. Johnson; addition to Cemeteries of Grundy Co., Vol. 2, p. 707
Johnson, Hazel Lorene (Sweeton)	Apr 03, 1945	Nov 03, 2019	Coalmont Cem.; Dau. of Lillard Sweeton & Gladys Caldwell; m. John Wesley Johnson
Johnson, Henry Frank	Nov 30, 1887	May 07, 1933	Tracy City Cem.; Son of William Walter & Sarah Virginia (Ramey) Johnson/Johnston; m. Daisy Meeks Walker; no tombstone
Johnson, Hilda Daphine (Roberts)	May 21, 1949	Sep 10, 2013	Roberts Family Cem.; Dau. of Charlie Bradford & Gladys (Woodlee) Roberts; m. Gene Johnson
Johnson, Huling Eugene "Buddy"	Jul 20, 1958	Aug 15, 2006	Palmer Cem.; Son of Louie & Betty Joyce (Johnson) Roberts; m. Mary Marie Anderson; addition to Cemeteries of Grundy Co., Vol. 2, p. 568
Johnson, Infant	Jul 21, 1921	Jul 21, 1921	Burkett Chapel Cem.; Dau. of Albert & Julia (Hillis) Johnson
Johnson, James Franklin	Oct 26, 1940	Jun 10, 2019	Wesley Chapel Cem.; Son of James Calvin Johnson & Mabel Fults; m. Mildred Hobbs; U.S. Army
Johnson, James K	Jun 28, 1962	May 22, 1982	Palmer Cem.; Son of James & Irmgard (Klien) Johnson; addition to Cemeteries of Grundy Co., Vol. 2, p. 567
Johnson, James R.	Oct 1845	Nov 26, 1909	Wesley Chapel Cem.; m. Allie Angeline (Cookston) Smith; addition to Cemeteries of Grundy Co.
Johnson, Jeff		Jul 31, 2016	Plainview Cem.; Son of Jack & Alene (Gipson) Johnson; m. Roxann Johnson
Johnson, Jerlene "Jerry" (Braseel)	Feb 23, 1930	Apr 17, 2013	Monteagle Cem.; Dau. of Ethridge "Bud" & Alma (Harrison) Braseel; m. Jack Johnson
Johnson, Jess	Jun 25, 1908	Jul 30, 1953	Hobbs Hill Cem.; Son of Eddie M. & Lillie (Nunley) Johnson; Killed in a train accident which severed his head & legs from his body per Find A Grave; addition to Cemeteries of Grundy Co. Vol. 1 p. 335
Johnson, Jimmy Ray	Sep 21, 1951	Feb 05, 2018	Coalmont Cem.; Son of Pascal Johnson & Edna Nolan; m. Linda Tate; US Army
Johnson, John	Aug 11, 1925	Dec 01, 2006	Gardens of Memory Cem in McMinnville, TN is his place of burial even though he has a stone at Wesley Chapel Cem. with his wife, Mabel M. Fults; Son of Will & Mattie (Bohannon) Johnson; m. Mable M. Fults; Bm2 US Navy WWII; Correction & addition to Cemeteries of Grundy Co., Vol. 2, p. 1001

Johnson, Johnnie	Oct 23, 1901	Aug 01, 1972	Palmer Cem.; Son of John T & Annie (Scott) Johnson; m. Elizabeth Crabtree; addition to Cemeteries of Grundy Co.,Vol. 2, p. 571
Johnson, Joseph M.	Mar 14, 1900	Jun 12, 2017	Gum Creek Cem in Franklin Co; Son of Claude & Goldie (Payne) Johnson; m. Willie Mae McMahan
Johnson, Joyce Ann (Burnett)	Feb 15, 1935	Jun 05, 1989	Gregg Cem.; Dau. of Melvin & Evelyn Mae (Nix) Burnett; addition to Cemeteries of Grundy County,Vol. 1, p. 305
Johnson, Julie Travis	Dec 5, 1886	Sep 15, 1942	Oak Grove Cem.; Dau. of Joseph Snyder & Nancy "Nannie" Lile; m. Jacob Floyd Ray, Feb 1, 1903 in Rhea County TN., addition to Cemeteries of Grundy Co.,Vol. 1, p. 487.
Johnson, L. Jerelene "Jerry" (Braseel)	Feb 23, 1930	Mar 17, 2013	Monteagle Cem.; Dau. of Ethridge "Bud" & Alma F (Harrison) Braseel; m. John T. "Jack" Johnson, Jr.; correction to death date and addition to Cemeteries of Grundy Co.Vol. 1, p. 452
Johnson, Lassie Arizona Harris	Aug 14, 1912	Feb 02, 1989	Plainview Cem.; Dau. of Hence & Tim (Fults) Levan; m. 1) Jesse H. Johnson 2) ___ Harris;
Johnson, Luther Bryan	Aug 06, 1897	Jan 16, 1963	Bonny Oak Cem.; Son of William Johnson & Tennessee Fults; m. Della Ophelia Johnson
Johnson, Mabel Ruth (Hobbs)	Jan 25, 1946	Dec 08, 2019	Little Johhny Myers Cem.; Dau. of Odie Hobbs & Lyda Myers
Johnson, Margaret Elizabeth (Summers)	Feb 07, 1926	Jul 16, 2021	Plainview Cem.; Dau. of Clarence Walden & Bessie Lea (McCreary) Summers; m. Loyd Richard Johnson
Johnson, Martha Elizabeth "Mattie" (Cheek)	Mar 7, 1870	Jan 05, 1943	White Cem.; Dau. of William & Jemima (Mansfield) Cheek; m. Francis "Frank" J. Johnson; addition to Cemeteries of Grundy Co.,Vol. 2, p. 1006
Johnson, Mary (Thomas)	Jun 05, 1922	May 17, 2016	Monteagle Cem.; Dau. of James Earl "Jim Earl" & Irene (Layne) Thomas; m. Embry Johnson; addition to Cemeteries of Grundy Co.,Vol. 1. p. 447
Johnson, Mary Lee (Hill)	Oct 05, 1929	Feb 06, 2022	Summerfield Cem.; Dau. of William & Hattie (Partin) Hill; m. Alton "Bear" Johnson
Johnson, Mary M.	Jun 05, 1922	May 17, 2016	Cremated; Dau. of Jim Earl & Clara Irene (Layne) Thomas; m. Embrey Johnson
Johnson, Maxie Ray	Apr 29 1942	Oct 26, 2019	Mt. View Cem.; Son of William Johnson & Lillie Mae Meeks; m. Mary Johnson
Johnson, Mildred M.	Oct 21, 1915	Jun 01, 1997	Palmer Cem.; Dau. of Andrew Jackson & Annie (Bedford) Weaver; Addition to Cemeteries of Grundy Co.,Vol. 2, p. 566
Johnson, Mona	Jun 24, 1940	May 18, 2016	Bonny Oak Cem.; Dau. of Celo & Pearl (Sweeton) Campbell; m. Dennis Clayton "Butch" Johnson

Name	Birth	Death	Details
Johnson, Morgan "Jack"	May 09, 1933	Nov 06, 2014	Gregg Cemetery; Son of George Morgan & Beulah Sidney (Carrick) Johnson; m. Alene Gibson; addition to Cemeteries of Grundy Co. Vol. 1, p. 303
Johnson, Pauline (Sanders)	Aug 21, 1923	Mar 25, 1979	Orange Hill Cem.; Dau. of Willie James & Ida Mae (Nunley) Sanders; m. Loys Leo Johnson; addition to Cemeteries of Grundy Co.Vol. 2; p. 542
Johnson, Pearl Dollie (Powers)	Oct 24, 1924	Oct 16, 2004	Orange Hill Cem.; Dau. of Granville and Mary Powers; m. Jan 24, 1944, to Elbert S. Johnson
Johnson, Phinis	Aug 15, 1894	Oct 01, 1938	White Cem.; Son of Frances "Frank" J. & Martha Elizabeth "Mattie" (Cheek) Johnson; m. Myrtle Hardiwood; correction & addition to Cemeteries of Grundy Co., Vol. 2, p. 1006
Johnson, Sally (Kilgore)	Ca 1853	After 1880 census	Bonny Oak Cem.; m. William Riley Johnson on Dec 25, 1869, in Grundy Co. and is most likely buried at Bonny Oak. No tombstone, but her husband and his 2nd wife are at Bonny Oak.
Johnson, Samuel Clay	Aug 19, 1996	Jan 05, 2017	Palmer Cem.; Son of Miles & Fatima (Kostiverejac) Johnson
Johnson, Samuel Green	Oct 13, 1842	Mar 01, 1915	Wesley Chapel Cem.; Son of John Albert & Nancy Southdown (Young) Johnson; addition to Cemeteries of Grundy Co.,Vol. 2, p. 977
Johnson, Sara Hall	Aug 26, 1848	Sep 16, 1924	Monteagle Cem.; Dau. of Alfred & Drusilla (Hall) Johnson; correction to Cemeteries of Grundy Co., Vol. 1, p. 400
Johnson, Steve Allan	Jun 06, 1961	Jun 12, 1984	Palmer Cem.; Son of Vernon Eugene & Zora M. (Campbell) Johnson; addition to Cemeteries of Grundy Co.,Vol. 2, p. 568
Johnson, Tennessee Palestine (Fults)	Aug 5, 1865	Mar 29, 1950	Bonny Oak Cem.; Dau. of Smith & Tinny (Sanders) Fults; m. William Riley Johnson; no tombstone; information from death certificate
Johnson, Thelma Pauline (Barrett)	Sep 28, 1922	Sep 26, 2019	AirView Cem.; Dau. of Charles Barrett & Edna McCarver; m. Jarvis Johnson
Johnson, Wayne Clark	Jul 06, 1942	Dec 05, 2016	Oak Grove Cem.; Exceptional Enterprise Bachelor (inscription on tombstone) obituary states his survivor is Vallery Griffith Shannon Courtney & husband Bruce.
Johnson, William Riley	Nov 2, 1850	Oct 17, 1925	Bonny Oak Cem.; Son of Thomas & Jane (Nunley) Johnson; m. 1) Sarah Kilgore 2) Tennessee Palestine Fults; no tombstone; information from death certificate
Jones, Annilee (McDonald)	Oct 28, 1903	Dec 04, 1979	Plainview Cem.; Dau. of William Wilbur & Malissa C. (Montgomery) McDonald; m. Jay Rucker Fathergill Jones

Name	Born	Died	Details
Jones, Arlington "Bumpus"	Apr 26, 1905	Feb 04, 2009	Cumberland Heights Cem.; Son of Boyd & Martha (Hughes) Jones; m. Linda Fults; addition to Cemeteries of Grundy Co. Vol. 1, p. 194
Jones, Beatrice (Franklin)	Apr 27, 1937	Apr 01, 2018	Franklin Memorial Gardens Cem.; Dau. of Marion Isaac Franklin & Myrtle Tucker Sweeton; m. Thurman Jones
Jones, Boyd	Jan 27, 1911	Aug 12, 1985	Cumberland Heights Cem.; Son of Adelbert Ira & Zella V. (Francis) Jones; m. Martha L. Hughes; addition to Cemeteries of Grundy Co.,Vol. 1, p. 195
Jones, Connie (Keel)	Jun 29, 1947	Nov 05, 2013	Cremated; Dau. of William F. & Jean James Keel; m. L.J. Jones
Jones, Connie (Sweeton)	De 23, 1953	Nov 15, 2019	Cremated; Dau. of J.C. & Dottie Sweeton
Jones, Floyd Burton	Mar 03, 1940	Jul 22, 2021	Palmer City Cem.; Son of Jack & Margaret (Simpson) Jones; m. Brenda Shrum
Jones, Jay Rucker Fothergill	Dec 1895	Nov 01, 1963	Plainview Cem.; Son of William Wilbur & Bell (Fothergill) Jones; m. Annilee McDonald; TN MMI US NAVY WWI NC; Correction to father's name in Cemeteries of Grundy Co.,Vol. 2, p. 687
Jones, Linda Marie	Apr 29, 1944	Aug 04, 2017	Palmer Cem.; Dau. of Wesley & Parthenia (McHone) Fults; m. Arlington Boyd "Bumps" Jones
Jones, Martha (Hughes)	Nov 03, 1909	Jun 22, 1991	Cumberland Heights Cem.; Dau. of John Arlington & Rosalea Regina (Poulton) Hughes; m. Boyd Jones; addition to Cemeteries of Grundy Co., Vol, 1, p. 195
Jones, Mary Ethel (Burnett)	Sep 22, 1940	Jul 08, 2015	Pelham Church of Christ Cem.; Dau. of Willie & Johnnie Vera (Patton) Burnett; m. 1) Kenneth Magouirk 2) Ronald Evan Jones; addition to Cemeteries of Grundy Co.,Vol. 2, p. 610
Jones, Naomi Ruth	Jun 24, 1931	Sep 28, 1993	Homeland Acres Cem.; Dau. of Clarence W. & Hazel (Duncan) Ax; addition to Cemeteries of Grundy Co., Vol. 1, p. 340
Jones, Ronald Evan	Aug 25, 1937	Jun 13, 2006	Pelham Church of Christ Cem.; Son of Evan B. & Retha Mae (Hurt) Jones; m. Mary Ethel Burnett; addition & correction to Cemeteries of Grundy Co.,Vol. 2, p. 610
Jones, Timothy Boyd	Aug 30, 1967	Jan 29, 2015	Cremated; Son of Arlington Boyd & Linda M. (Fults) Jones
Jones, Twila	Sep 15, 1954	Oct 26, 2014	Cremated; Dau of Ulys Clayton Miller & Lorene Lecroy; m. Marshall Jones
Jones, Willard Coleman	Feb 24, 1926	Sep 28, 1993	Homeland Acres Cem.; Son of Sylvester & Josephine Floyd (Phillips) Jones; addition to Cemeteries of Grundy Co.,Vol. 1, p. 340

Name	Birth	Death	Notes
Jones, William Emmett	Jul 03, 1906	Mar 23, 1962	Palmer Cem.; Layne funeral home; no information found
Jones, William Kenneth	Feb 23, 1925	Jul 09, 1962	Tracy City Cem.; Son of J. Rucker & Anna Lee (McDonald) Jones; TN TECH 4 582 AMB MOTOR DIV WWII; m. Katie Helen Garner; addition to Cemeteries of Grundy Co.,Vol. 2, p. 850
Jordan, John A.	Apr 23, 1929	Mar 14, 2001	Fall Creek Cem.; Son of Emmett & Rose Lee (Robinson) Jordan
Jossi, Ulrich	Nov 11, 1818	Jun 14, 1883	Tracy City Cem.; Son of Ulrich (1788-1880) & Margritha (Huber) Jossi; m. Feb 8, 1876, to Marie C. Spreiht; addition to Cemeteries of Grundy Co,Vol. 2, p. 892
Jossi, William Lecil	Feb 14, 1908	Jul 12, 1945	Tracy City Cem.; Son of William James & Mary (Bobo) Jossi; TM1 US NAVY; correction to death date Cemeteries of Grundy Co.,Vol. 2, p. 811
Judge, Katie Mae (Johnson)	Jan 06, 1955	Dec 23, 2020	Dau. of Claude & Goldie (Payne) Johnson; m. Kenneth Judge
Kaldaras - Parks, Adeline (Argo)	Apr 29, 1925	Feb 06, 2016	Warren "Red Hill" Cem.; Dau. of Doston & Sally Ann (Nunley) Argo; m. 1) Jonas H. Parks 2) ____ Kaldaras
Kalmar, Dorothy	Jan 16, 1945	Apr 22, 2013	Clouse Hill Cem.; Dau. of Andrew Westman & Margaret (Smartt) Bouldin; m. Jenoe Kalmar
Kalmar, Joshua Lee	Jun 23, 1983	Dec 02, 2013	Clouse Hill Cem.; Son of Bunny Stiefel & Jackie Shultz; grandmother was Dorothy Kalmar
Kania, Paul	1963	Sep 23, 2014	Cremated; Son of Ralph R. Kania & Bette Burnett; m. Tracy Yvette Tolar
Kashola, Ernest Ralph, Jr.	Nov 19, 1960	Jun 23, 2017	Cremated; Son of Ernest R., Sr. & Margaret M. (Bowles) Kashola
Kearn, Daniel Leroy	Jul 22, 1951	Jan 04, 2007	Plainview Cem; Son of David Daniel & Lucille Mae (Granlee) Kern
Keel, Jean (James)	Sep 15, 1927	Sep 19, 2007	Palmer Cem.; Dau. of William Emmett & Cora (Patten) James; m. William F. Keel; addition to Cemeteries of Grundy Co.,Vol. 2, p. 550
Keel, Mildred Marie	Oct 01, 1932	May 23, 1933	Oak Grove Cem.; Dau. of Jake & Nellie (Green) Keel; death certificate; addition to Cemeteries of Grundy Co.,Vol. 1
Keel, Randal	Jul 13, 1947	Oct 14, 2017	Plainview Cem.; Son of Pascal & Florence Keel; m. Betty Keel; US Army
Keel, Ronnie	Jun 29, 1947	Sep 24, 2008	Palmer Cem.; Son of William F. & Jean (James) Keel; addition to Cemeteries of Grundy Co,.Vol. 2, p. 550
Keel, Ruth Lourine	Sep 09, 1936	Oct 01, 2019	Hamilton Memorial Gardens Cem.; Lived in Monteagle- no other information; m. Pascal Keel

Name	Born	Died	Details
Keel, William F.	May 07, 1927	Dec 08, 1969	Palmer Cem.; Son of Pascal & Ola Mae (Hall) Keel; m. Jean James; addition to Cemeteries of Grundy Co.,Vol. 2, p. 550
Keele, Dorothy Jean	Sep 19, 1943	Apr 12, 2020	Rose Hill Memorial Gardens; Dau. of Lansing & Lorene Gilliam; m. Marvin E. Keele
Keele, Robert Larry	May 16, 1934	Nov 25, 2017	Cremated; Son of Hon. Robert Levi & Amarilla Sullivan Keele; m. Karen Schwante
Keener, Clayton Casto	Oct 25, 1953	Jul 04, 2018	Brown's Chapel Cem.; Son of Calvin Keener & Alice Lockhart; m. Wanda Mayfield
Keener, Dakota "Cody"	Sep 23, 1997	Aug 17, 2015	Smith Cem.; Son of Randy Keener & JoAnne Johnson
Keener, Gracie Lea (Kilgore)	Feb 10, 1908	Jan 08, 1976	Brown's Chapel Cem.; Dau. of Calvin Calhoun & Pearly (Dove) Kilgore; m. Luther C. Keener; addition to Cemeteries of Grundy Co.,Vol. 1, p. 104
Keener, Ricky Lewis	May 16, 1955	Oct 19, 2014	Cremated; Son of Joann Keener m. Janice Rose
Keener, Rita Faye (Roles)	Feb 04, 1963	Feb 18, 2012	Brown's Chapel Cem.; Dau. of Morris Hugh Arrington & Mollie Roles
Keener, Rosie Virginia (Hammers)	Jul 27, 1932	Jul 17, 1993	Fall Creek Falls Cem.; Dau. of Alex L & Susie (Meeks) Hammers; m. Ervin Pete Keener
Keener, Wilburn "Bud"	Apr 10, 1943	Jul 31, 2013	Brown's Chapel Cem.; Son of Luther & Grace (Kilgore) Keener; m. Rita Fults
Keever, Linda Gail	Dec 03, 1949	Nov 22, 2019	Oak Ridge Memorial Park; Dau. of Ray Keever & Mildred Ada Neal; m. Brad Weibert
Keller, David	Oct 05, 1938	Mar 16, 2022	Franklin Memorial Gardens; Son of Harold A. & Anna Bernadine (Bordenet) Keller; m. Emma Jean Hawk; U.S. Marines
Keller, William Albert	Dec 30, 1940	Sep 12, 2020	Cremated; Son of Harold & Anna Bernardine (Bordenet) Keller; m. Isabel Anders; USMC
Kelley, Dennis Eugene	May 07, 1948	Oct 29, 2021	Palmer Cem.; Son of James & Mildred (Goodwin) Kelley; m. Judy Kelley
Kelley, Dora Edith	Aug 04, 1918	Feb 07, 2015	Coalmont Cem.; Dau. of Noah A. & Nancy Jane (Scruggs) Kelley; m. 1) Robert Hargis, 2) Roy Gilmer, 3) James Kelley
Kelley, Judy Ann (Morrison)	Dec 05, 1945	Mar 30, 2015	Palmer Cem.; Son of Ben, Jr. & Jessie (Tate) Morrison; m. Dennis Kelley
Kelley, Michael Wayne	Sep 05, 1967	Jan 19, 2021	Cremated; Son of Keith "Budge" & Lou Grooms
Kelso, Jimmy Ray	Aug 07, 1928	Dec 07, 2018	Monteagle Cem.; Son of James Moffitt & Leda G. (Pirtle) Kelso; m. Paula Rae Clements; addition to Cemeteries of Grundy Co.,Vol. 1, p. 433
Kelso, Paula R.	Apr 20, 1945	Jan 13, 2017	Monteagle Cem.; Dau. of Paul & Vera Ruth (Houppert) Clements; m. Jimmy Ray Kelso; cremated in FL.; addition to Cemeteries of Grundy Co.,Vol. 1, p. 433

Kemmerly, Virginia Maxine	Feb 18, 1934	Feb 18, 2014	Mt. Olivet Cem. Nashville, TN; Dau. of Dewey & Lottie Whitaker; m. Dr. Paul C. Kemmerly
Kennedy, Delitha Jennie (Scissom)	May 1877		Hobbs Hill Cem.; Dau. of George Thomas & Sarah Ann (Steele) Scissom; m. Walter Kennedy, information from relative, John D. Sissom
Kennedy, John Charles	Dec 02, 1953	May 24, 2020	Cremated; Son of Charles Wesley Kennedy & Wilma Mari Johnson; m. Tressie Jo Gallagher
Kennedy, Tressie Jo	May 04, 1945	Oct 19, 2018	Franklin Memorial Gardens; Dau. of Benton Clay Gallagher & Cleora Wilson; m. 1) Joey Magouirk 2) John Charles Kennedy
Kennerly, Ora Lee	Sep 13, 1934	Sep 13, 2015	Thorgood Cem.; Dau. of Jerry & Bernice Swain; m. John Kennerly
Kent, Herbert Leo	Mar 14, 1935	Dec 07, 2013	Burns Cem.; Son of Herbert Leo & Grace (Moore) Kent
Kerley, Mary Elizabeth (Smith)	Mar 11, 1871	Dec 07, 1968	Hobbs Hill Cem.; m. Thomas Newton Kerley
Kerley, Thomas Newton	May 2, 1861	Oct 20, 1925	Hobbs Hill Cem.; Son of Joshua & Margie J (Graham) Kerley; m. 1) Fanny Ann Moody 2) Mary Elizabeth Smith; addition to Cemeteries of Grundy Co., Vol. 1, p. 333
Kern, Jeffrey Allen	Mar 13, 1961	Mar 08, 2013	Monteagle Cem.; Jim & Charlene (Hayes) Kern; m. Marsha Kern
Kilby, John Edward	Jun 05, 1923	Mar 29, 2013	Plainview Cem.; Son of C.H. & Mary (Pratt) Kilby; m. Maudie Haston
Kilby, Maudie Bell (Lewis)	Sep 23, 1942	Sep 17, 2013	Plainview Cem.; Dau. of Dudley & Lillie Mae (Haston) Lewis; m. John Edward Kilby
Kilgore Pearlie Mae (Nunley)	Oct 20, 1927	Mar 24, 2018	Oak Grove Cem.; Dau. of Murph Nunley & Melinda Meeks; m. 1) Joe Allen Nunley 2) Harold Kilgore
Kilgore, Allen Richard	1957	Apr 05, 2020	Plainview Cem.; Son of Roy "Moe" & Frances Kilgore; m. Joy Alfreda Kilgore
Kilgore, Andrew Elmer	May 08, 1912	Ooct 26, 1999	Plainview Cem.; Son of Craven & Anna (Turner) Kilgore; m. Martha Myrtle Meeks; addition to Cemeteries of Grundy Co.,Vol. 2, p. 698
Kilgore, Arla Sue (North)	Aug 18, 1927	Oct 10, 2004	Burns Cem.; Dau. of John Lee & Vera North; m. Joseph G. Kilgore; addition to Cemeteries of Grundy Co., Vol. 1, p. 127
Kilgore, Bertha	Oct 19, 1897	May 15, 1898	Gregg Cemetery; Dau. of George Morgan & Beulah Sidney (Carrick) Johnson; m. Alene Gibson; addition to Cemeteries of Grundy Co., Vol. 1, p. 303
Kilgore, Bertie	Apr 10, 1899	Dec 10, 1899	Gregg Cemetery; Dau. of George Morgan & Beulah Sidney (Carrick) Johnson; m. Alene Gibson; addition to Cemeteries of Grundy Co. Vol. 1, p. 303

Name	Born	Died	Notes
Kilgore, Betty (Grimes)	Jun 23, 1934	Apr 25, 2019	Palmer Cem.; Dau. of Fred & Mila (Green) Grimes; m. William Harold Kilgore; addition to Cemeteries of Grundy Co.,Vol. 2, p. 264
Kilgore, Billy Joe "Flashlight"	Sep 26, 1936	Apr 14, 2021	Burns Cem.; Son of Wash & Serena Kilgore; m. Delphia Carroll
Kilgore, Blanton	Jan 20, 1928	Oct 25, 2015	Summitville Cem.; Son of Emmitt & Estie (Dickerson) Kilgore; m. Willie Ruth Kilgore
Kilgore, Carl H.	May 14, 1956	Mar 14, 2017	Sequatchie Valley Memorial Gardens Cem.; Son of Carl P. & Beatrice (Green) Kilgore; m, Vicki Middleton
Kilgore, Carl H.	Ca. 1957	Mar 14, 2017	Sequatchie Valley Memorial Gardens Cem.; Son of Carl P. & Beatrice (Green) Kilgore; m. Vicki Middleton
Kilgore, Cecelia Fay (Watson)	May 12, 1905	Jul 27, 2018	Clouse Hill Cem.; Dau. of Helen Watson; m. Daniel Kilgore
Kilgore, Clarence Edward, Jr.	Feb 14, 1928	Jan 06, 2015	Tracy City Cem.; Son of Clarence E. & Theona N. (Haynes) Kilgore; m. Mary Jo Fults
Kilgore, Danny Ray "Skinny"	1951	Dec 09, 2014	Eastern Star Cem.; Son of Barney Glenn Kilgore & Clara Elvia Marie Caldwell; m. Patricia Ann Kilgore
Kilgore, David C	Mar 08, 1944	Mar 19, 2018	Burns Cem.; Son of John & Abba Jean Kilgore; m. JoAnn
Kilgore, Edna (Schoenmann)	Aug 08, 1929	Dec 14, 2019	Browns Chapel Cem.; Dau. of William Elbert Schoenmann & Minnie Agnes Tate; m. Billy Jackson Kilgore
Kilgore, Edward	Jul 25, 1901	Aug 12, 1902	Orange Hill Cem.; Son of Frank & Matilda (Shadrick) Kilgore; addition to Cemeteries of Grundy Co.,Vol. 2, p. 539
Kilgore, Elizabeth (Gipson)	Nov 27, 1951	Oct 18, 2019	Cremated; Dau. of Albert Preston & Beatrice Gipson; m. Jim Kilgore
Kilgore, Erlene	Oct 10, 1951		Palmer Cem.; Dau. of Wesley Earl & Bertha (Layne) Kilgore; m. Jerry E. Kilgore; addition to Cemeteries of Grundy Co.,Vol. 2, p. 578
Kilgore, Ernest Ray	Oct 16, 1922	Oct 26, 1999	Plainview Cem.; Son of Andrew Kilgore & Dovie Seagroves per correction sent by family for Cemeteries of Grundy County,Vol. 2, p. 698
Kilgore, Essel	Jan 21, 1930	Oct 19, 2017	Fall Creek Cem.; Son of Rufus & Essie (Slatton) Kilgore; m. Essie Ross; US Army - Korea
Kilgore, Frank Emmitt	Jul 27, 1937	Mar 25, 2020	Fults Cem.; Son of Emmitt Kilgore & Estella Dickerson; m. Mildred Myers
Kilgore, George C.	Ca. 1945	Oct 04, 2015	Burns Cem.; Son of Barney & Elvia (Caldwell) Kilgore; m. Janice Kilgore

Name	Birth	Death	Details
Kilgore, Glen Ernest "Lucky 7"	Aug 18, 1942	Nov 17, 2021	Plainview Cem.; Son of Andrew & Martha Kilgore; m. Sarah Layne
Kilgore, Harold E	May 10, 1942	Jun 07, 2020	Oak Grove Cem.; Son of Spence Kilgore & Daisy Nunley; m. Pearlie Mae Kilgore
Kilgore, Harold Wayne	May 02, 1933	Jul 04, 2021	Fults Cem.; Son of Emmitt & Estella (Dickerson) Kilgore; m. Ruby Myers
Kilgore, Hershel Franklin "Frank"	Dec 15, 1930	Jul 29, 2017	Burns Cem.; Son of Amos & Minnie E. (Harris) Kilgore; m. Anna Cleo Green; US Army- Korea & Vietnam
Kilgore, Hershel Franklin "Frank"	Dec 15, 1930	Jul 29, 2017	Burns Cem.; Son of Amos & Minnie E. (Harris) Kilgore; m. Anna Cleo Green; US Army- Korea & Vietnam
Kilgore, Hobart Lee	Sep 16, 1938	Jan 12 1939	Clouse Hill Cem.; Son of Kethley & Fronie (Meeks) Kilgore- no marker
Kilgore, James Olen	Oct 01, 1947	Aug 09, 1948	Clouse Hill Cem.; Son of Kethley & Fronie (Meeks) Kilgore; no marker
Kilgore, Jane Katherine "Katie" (Shrum)	Dec 07, 1902	Jan 27, 1977	Plainview Cem.; Dau. of Joe David & Bessie Leona (Almany) Shrum; m. Walter Benjamin Kilgore
Kilgore, Jewell Yvonne (Nunley)	Apr 24, 1929	Dec 27, 2019	Plainview Cem.; Dau. of Frank P. & Jenny Mae (Bess) Nunley; m. Joe E. Kilgore; addition to Cemeteries of Grundy Co. Vol. 2, p. 668
Kilgore, Joe Anner	May 24, 1905	Mar 18, 1915	Bonny Oak Cem.; Son of Joseph Elishey & T. Cora (Myers) Kilgore; addition to Cemeteries of Grundy Co. Vol. 1, p. 80
Kilgore, Joseph Elishey	Jul 25, 1881	Dec 08, 1950	Bonny Oak Cem.; Son of Levi Marion & Elizabeth (Campbell) Kilgore; m. T. Cora Myers; addition to Cemeteries of Grundy Co., Vol. 1, p. 80
Kilgore, Katherine Fults (Thomas)	Nov 24, 1963	Oct 27, 2021	Fults Cem.; Dau. of James Herman & Mary Lou (Tate) Thomas ; m. Scottie Dale Kilgore
Kilgore, Leonard	Oct 27, 1904	Nov 09, 1924	Gregg Cemetery; Son of George Morgan & Beulah Sidney (Carrick) Johnson; m. Alene Gibson; addition to Cemeteries of Grundy Co., Vol. 1, p. 303
Kilgore, Linda Sue (Reel)	1952	Apr 28, 2020	Burns Cem.; Dau. of Ira Reel & Virginia Dove; m. Thomas Kilgore
Kilgore, Lou Rebecca (Starling)	Mar 4, 1872	Apr 04, 1950	Monteagle Cem.; Dau. of George & Elizabeth (Sanders) Starling; correction to parents' names Cemeteries of Grundy Co. Vol. 1, p. 441
Kilgore, Maggie Mae (James)	Aug 9, 1896	Jan 04, 1975	Palmer Cem.; Dau. of William "Bill" & Sarah L. "Sally" (Pelham) James; m. Bill Kilgore; addition to Cemeteries of Grundy Co., Vol. 2, p. 553

Name	Birth	Death	Notes
Kilgore, Margaret (probably maiden named Scott)	Jan 01, 1860	Oct 25, 1915	Tracy City Cem.; probably married Houston "Uncle Gab" Kilgore; Margaret died of stroke; Source *Mrs. Grundy* newspaper, 1900 census of Grundy Co.
Kilgore, Martha Myrtle (Meeks)	Oct 01, 1905	Nov 01, 1996	Plainview Cem.; Dau. of George C. & Mary Elizabeth (Sanders) Meeks; m. Andrew Elmer Kilgore
Kilgore, Mary E. (Griffith)	May 15, 1944	Feb 05, 2009	Burns Cem.; Dau. of Alvis & Alace (Meeks) Griffith; m. Roger Dale Kilgore; m. Jul 26, 1986; Correction to Cemeteries of Grundy Co., Vol. 1, p. 129
Kilgore, Mary Magalene (Meeks)	Jul 17, 1939	Jul 25, 2017	Clouse Hill Cem.; Dau. of George Mack & Maggie Myrtle (Smartt) Meeks; m. James Riley Kilgore
Kilgore, Mildred Mae (Myers)	Jul 28, 1939	Apr 17, 2022	Fults Cem.; Dau. of Cheatum & Lena (Risner) Myers; m. Frank Emmitt Kilgore
Kilgore, Nancy Elizabeth "Liz"	1849	Apr 15, 1921	Liz Kilgore Hollow Cem.; Dau. of Bird Campbell & Bettie Myers; died at Roddy Springs; m. Levi Marion Kilgore
Kilgore, Orin Winfred	Apr 01, 1937	May 08, 2022	Plainview Cem.; Son of Walter B. & Katie (Shrum) Kilgore; m. Debbie Kilgore; U.S. Navy – Vietnam
Kilgore, Patrick	1957	Nov 18, 2014	Presnell Cem.; Son of J.W. & Ann Kilgore; m. Paige Mitchell
Kilgore, Pauline H. "Polly"	Feb 02, 1923	Sep 21, 2014	Monteagle Cem.; Dau. of Thomas Hunziker; addition to Cemeteries of Grundy Co., Vol. 1, p. 441
Kilgore, Pearly (Dove)	Mar 22, 1887	Dec 21, 1918	Orange Hill Cem.; Dau. of Jordan & Virginia (Dykes) Dove; m. Calvin Kilgore; no tombstone, added by family
Kilgore, Ramon	Aug 18, 1910	Feb 01, 1912	Oak Grove Cem.; Son of Charles Wesley & Roda Lee (Cope) Kilgore; addition to Cemeteries of Grundy Co., Vol. 1, p. 494
Kilgore, Richard Joseph "Bud"	May 10, 1863	Jan 10, 1946	Oak Grove Cem.; Son of Matison Monroe "Mat" & Nancy (Layne) Kilgore; addition to Cemeteries of Grundy Co., Vol. 1, p. 499
Kilgore, Robbie Crawford	Aug 08, 1972	Jul 04, 2019	Burns Cem.; Son of David C. & JoAnn Kilgore; m. Valerie Kilgore
Kilgore, Roy "Moe"	Apr 6. 1941	Mar 16, 2014	Plainview Cem.; Son of Roy & Cretty (Meeks) Kilgore; m. Frances M. Kilgore
Kilgore, Roy Laverne	Nov 28, 1930	Dec 17, 2016	Cremated; Son of Ernest Kilgore & Mattie Osborn; m. Kaity Laverne; US Army
Kilgore, Shane Leon "Gory"	Mar 04, 1977	Aug 02, 1993	Palmer Cem.; Son of Leon & Jeanne Kilgore; addition to Cemeteries of Grundy Co., Vol. 2, p. 573

Name	Born	Died	Details
Kilgore, T. Cora	May 12, 1882	Mar 16, 1955	Bonny Oak Cem.; Dau. of Christopher C. & Mary Sophrona "Fronie" (Brown) Myers; m. Joseph Elishey Kilgore; information from death certificate; no tombstone; died in Walker Co, AL.
Kilgore, Timothy Mark	Jan 10, 1959	Oct 04, 2018	Cremation; Son of LaVoy Kilgore & Erma Colleen Thomas
Kilgore, William Allen	Jul 18, 1964	Mar 09, 2022	Browns Chapel Cem.; Son of Billy Jackson & Edna (Schoenmann) Kilgore
Kilgore, William Eugene	Jun 02, 1934	Aug 28, 2000	Oak Grove Cem.; Son of Washington Monroe & Serena E. (Newsome) Kilgore; m. Barbara Lee Burgos; addition to Cemeteries of Grundy Co.,Vol. 1, p. 490
Kilgore, William Harold	Oct 19, 1931	Apr 29, 2012	Palmer Cem.; Son of Earl & Janie (Bone) Kilgore; m. Betty Grimes; addition to Cemeteries of Grundy Co.,Vol. 2, p 564
Killian, Betty Sue	Feb 26, 1948	Oct 11, 2016	Altamont Cem.; Dau. of Marshall O. & E. Iola (Green) King; m. Jerry Killian
Killian, Chad	Jul 16, 1971	Sep 27, 2015	Altamont Cem.; Son of Arthur & Geraldine (Smartt) Killian; m. Melinda Tate
Killian, Jesse	Dec 3, 1871	Auf 20, 1947	Altamont Cem.; Son of Jeremiah & Mary Ann (Coppinger) Killian; m. Lou Tate; correction of mother's name & addition to Cemeteries of Grundy Co.,Vol. 1, p. 29
Killian, Paul Raymond	Sep 07, 1927	Feb 13, 2018	Plainview Cem.; Son of Vernon Frank & Estelle (Fults) Killian; addition to Cemeteries of Grundy Co.,Vol. 2, p. 689
Killian, Scotty	Aug 29, 1983	Dec 30, 2015	Altamont Cem.; Son of Arthur D. & Geraldine (Smartt) Killian
Killian, Stanley Earl "Snip"	Mar 29, 1936	Feb 19, 2020	Cremated: Son of J.B. "Babe" & Dora Killian; m. Sue Patrick; Korean War veteran from Altamont
Killian, Vera Mildred	Sep 14, 1906	Dec 24, 1987	Altamont Cem.; Dau. of Edward & Hattie (Stugeon) Armstrong; m. George W. Killian; addition to Cemteries of Grundy Co.,Vol. 1, p. 10
Killian, Waynie Morris	Oct 26, 1941	May 15, 2018	Philadelphia Cem.; Son of Willie Morris Killian & Emma Lee Hobbs; m. Elsie Perry
Killian, Wilber	Nov 05, 1903	Aug 14, 1906	Philadelphia Cem.; Son of Jeremian Daniel & Linnie Lee (Ware) Killian; addition to Cemeteries of Grundy Co.,Vol. 2, p. 645
Kimble, Jessie Mae	Dec 22, 1890	Aug 11, 1962	Altamont Cem.; Dau. of Carrie Estep; m. Ray Kimble; addition to Cemeteries of Grundy Co., Vol. 1, p. 18
Kinary, Doris Laverna (James)	Jan 07, 1912	Jun 12, 1988	Palmer Cem.; Dau. of Alexander James & Ethel M. (Threehouse) James; addition to Cemeteries of Grundy Co.,Vol. 2, p. 576

Name	Birth	Death	Notes
King, Alice (Orange)	1876		Orange Hill Cem.; Dau. of John William & Nancy J. (Lockhart) Orange; m. W.L. "Willie" King; addition to Cemeteries of Grundy Co.,Vol. 2 , p. 537
King, Allen Anthony	Jul 08, 1951	Jan 15, 2022	Palmer Cem.; Son of Edna Ruth King; m. Barbara June Fults
King, Alma Lorene (Lockhart)	Sep 01, 1938	Jan 13, 2018	Orange Hill Cem.; Dau. of James Leonard Lockhart & Lillie May Layne; m. Billy H. King
King, Annie D.	May 18, 1881	Aug 23, 1887	King Cem.; correction for death date Cemeteries of Grundy Co., Vol 1, p. 353
King, Arminda	Apr 10, 1887	Mar 22, 1905	Monteagle Cem.; Dau. of Stephen N. & Sarah Catherine (Perry) King (likely) ; no stone, source King Bible
King, Bill Monroe	Mar 23, 1947	Jun 04, 2021	King Cem.; Son of Monroe & Sara Bonita (Fults) King
King, Billy Joe	May 23, 1954	Sep 17, 2021	Brown's Chapel Cem.; Son of Walter & Bessie Lee (Partin) King; m. Sandy King
King, Calbert Lee	Jun 02, 1927	Oct 19, 2019	King Cem.; Son of Aubrey Hill King & Callie Hale; m. 1) Thelma Nunley 2) Marie Bain 3) Barbara King
King, Carmen Ford	Apr 13, 1911	Oct 21, 1972	Monteagle Cem.; m. 2) Dorothy Ward; correction to Cemeteries of Grundy Co., Vol. 1, p. 436
King, Derek Edward	Mar 12, 1977	Jan 23, 2015	Cremated/White Cem.; Son of Morris & Shirley King; m. Jennifer Brunett
King, Edna Jean	May 25, 1940	Jul 08, 2017	Hunerwadel Cem.; Dau. of Johnny Wesley & Alvilda (King) Perry; m. Elmer Cline King
King, Elmer Cline	Dec 23, 1938	Sep 24, 2014	Hunerwadel Cem; Son of Marshall O & E. Iola (Green) King; m. Edna Jean Perry; addition to Cemeteries of Grundy Co.,Vol. 1, p. 348
King, Eloise	Apr 29, 1930	Sep 29, 2016	Fall Creek Cem.; Dau. of Sam & Ophelia (Green) Walker; m. Elzie Martin King
King, Elsie Ailene (Anderson)	1933	May 15, 2022	Brown's Chapel Cem.; Dau. of Maude Anderson; m. Clyde Bean
King, Emmett Edwin	Sep 18, 1944	Oct 16, 2017	O'Dear Cem.; Son of Emmett Edward & Eliza Catherine (Dodson) King; m. Martha King
King, Etta Mae (Finch)	Mar 24, 1908	Jul 22, 1974	Palmer Cem.; Dau. of John Henry & Carrie E. (Partin) Finch; m. Ira L. King; addition to Cemeteries of Grundy County, Vol. 2, p. 569
King, Fernando Edward "Tony"	Oct 16, 1922	Jan 22, 2019	Grace Chapel Cem.; Son of Jess King & Dora Perry; m. Mary Edith Layne; US Army WWII
King, Gary Richard	Jul 18, 1938		Monteagle Cem.; Son of Carmen Ford & Dorothy (Ward) King; Correction to Cemeteries of Grundy Co.Vol. 1, p. 436
King, Glema Ann (Sailors)	1956	Apr 16, 2015	King Cem.; Dau. of Oscar & Nellie (Braswell) Sailors; m. Eddie Lee King

Name	Birth	Death	Notes
King, Glenn Edward	Mar 12, 1960	May 09, 2018	King Cem.; Son of Monroe King & Sara Bonita Fults; m. Loretta Nolan
King, Herbert William	Jun 16, 1934 Soc Sec. says birth 1935	Sep 30, 2007	Burkett Chapel Cem.; Son of John Wesley & Sarah Ellen (Dennis) King; m Annie Bell Borne; addition to Cemeteries of Grundy Co.,Vol. 1, p. 124
King, Herbert William, Jr.	Nov 03, 1955	Jan 05, 2020	Burkett's Chapel Cem. Son of Herbert William King, Sr. & Annie Bell Borne
King, Hester (Orange)	1878		Orange Hill Cem.; Dau. of John William & Nancy J. (Lockhart) Orange. Her name should be Hester (Orange) Hoffs. Correction, Cemeteries of Grundy Co.,Vol. 2, p. 357
King, Heual Denzil	Oct 06, 1937	Feb 14, 2020	O'Dear Cem.; Son of Emmett Edward King & Eliza Catherine Dodson; U.S. Army
King, Ira L.	Oct 30, 1909	Nov 18, 2004	Palmer Cem.; Son of Jesse Stokes & Martha Frances (Camp) King; m. Etta Mae Finch; addition to Cemeteries of Grundy Co.,Vol. 2, p. 569
King, Isabelle Margaret	Mar 30, 1916	Sep 10, 2007	Homeland Acres Cem.; Dau. of Charles Leroy & Ethel M. (Pray) Berry; addition to Cemeteries of Grundy Co.,Vol. 1, p. 342
King, Jennifer Ann (Byers)	Oct 25, 1975	Jan 19, 2022	Bonny Oak Cem.; Dau. of George & Lena Byers; m. Michael Alton King
King, Jeremy Wayne	Nov 07, 1982	Aug 21, 2011	Homeland Acres Cem.; Son of Jerry King & Karen (Ax) King of Kansas City, MO.; addition to Cemeteries of Grundy Co.,Vol. 1, p. 340
King, Jessica Lee (Pickett)	Jun 19, 1986	Apr 25, 2020	O'Dear Cem.; Dau. of Donnie Pickett & Mary J. Pickett
King, Jimmy Dean	Aug 04, 1940	Jan 05, 2015	Palmer Cem.; Son of Robert & Katie (Watts) King
King, Lee Rev.	May 09, 1913	Sep 11, 1996	Palmer Cem.; Son of Jesse Stokes & Martha Frances (Camp) King; m. Leona Finch; addition to Cemeteries of Grundy Co.,Vol. 2, p. 569
King, Leroy	Mar 20, 1876	Mar 23, 1931	Morton Memorial/Tarlton Cem.; Son of Sarah King; information from death certificate; no tombstone
King, Loretta M (Minton)	Aug 24, 1948		Brown's Chapel Cem.; Dau. of S.T. & Josephine Minton; m. Ronald L. "Bud" King; addition to Cemeteries of Grundy Co.,Vol. 1, p. 106
King, Lucille	1927	1930	King Cem.; Dau. of Jess & Dora (Perry) King; addition to Cemeteries of Grundy Co.,Vol. 1, p. 356
King, Lucille	1927	1930	King Cem.; Dau. of Jess & Dora (Perry) King; addition to Cemeteries of Grundy Co,Vol. 1, p. 356

Name	Born	Died	Details
King, Mamie (Martin)	Feb 22, 1892	Mar 19, 1966	Fall Creek Cem.; Dau. of James Isham Martin & Ellen Wiseman; m. Harley King on Mar. 29, 1923
King, Marlene	Aug 04, 1958	Sep 25, 2014	Philadelphia Cem.; Dau of Glen & Nellie Gladys King
King, Melanie Jean (Smith)	Nov 20, 1960		Hunerwadel Cem.; Dau. of George Preston & Ruth Mable (Kilgore) Smith; m. Rev. Billy Dione King; addition to Cemeteries of Grundy Co., Vol. 1, p. 346
King, Michael Allen	Dec 01, 1975	May 01, 2020	O'Dear Cem.; Son of Ricky Morrison & Kathy Morrison
King, Minnie Emaline Payne (Anderson)	Mar 12, 1926	Aug 11, 1996	Oak Grove Cem.; Dau. of George Washington "Wash" & Araminda "Mindy" (Braden) Anderson; m. Teddy Ray King; Correction and addition to Cemeteries of Grundy Co., Vol. 1, p. 511
King, Minnie Lee	Apr 10, 1933	Oct 23, 1974	Fall Creek Cem.; Dau. of Oscar B & Lola (Sanders) King
King, Morris E.	Jun 02, 1945	Feb 04, 1990	Palmer Cem.; Son of Fernando "Tony" & Mary Edith King; m. Shirley White; addition to Cemeteries of Grundy Co., Vol. 2, p. 576
King, Newton Everett	Apr 17, 1952	Feb 24, 2019	Center Hill Cem.; Son of Newton & Rosalee King
King, Nora	May 27, 1895	Apr 03, 1961	Brown's Chapel Cem.; Dau. of Tom & Martha (Mays) King; m. William King; addition to Cemeteries of Grundy Co., Vol. 1, p. 103
King, Norman Lee	Jan 31, 1939	Nov 29, 2017	Bess-Whitman-King Cem.; Son of Frank C. & Elizabeth Bess King; m. Annie Mae Tate
King, Ora (Mitchell)	Dec 26, 1898	May 18, 1982	Fall Creek Cem.; Dau. of Henry Newton & Susannah (Roberts) Mitchell; m. Ray E. King
King, Paul Edward	1939	Oct 02, 2014	Plainview Cem.; Son of Dillard King & Elizabeth Dishroon; m. Patsy King; US Army
King, Percy Glenn	Jun 02, 1925	Jun 24, 2013	Cremated/Middle TN Veterans Cem.; Son of Charles & Mary Myrtle (Huie) King; m. Betty Mae; US Army
King, Regina G. (Irvin)	Apr 16, 1963	Dec 08, 2020	Cremated; Dau. of William & Donna Lou (Meeks) Irvin; m. Dale King
King, Rev. Lee	May 09, 1913	Sep 11, 1996	Palmer Cem.; Son of Jesse Stokes & Martha Frances (Camp) King; m. Leona Finch; addition to Cemeteries of Grundy Co., Vol. 2, p. 569
King, Rickie Lee	Mar 18, 1997	Nov 25, 2021	King Cem.; Son of Jodie King
King, Ricky E.	Jun 26, 1956	Jun 26, 1956	Fall Creek Cem.; Son of Robert E. King & Lois Christian
King, Roy Douglas	Sep 11, 1947	Oct 01, 2020	Cremated; Son of Richard Howell & Hassie Lucille (Knight) King; m. 1) Patricia Winton 2) Tina Marie Ritchie

Name	Born	Died	Notes
King, Roy Lee	Dec 12, 1962	Nov 12, 2017	Fults Cem.; Son of Leroy Venus King & Roberta Pike Rowe; m. Melissa Stone
King, Sandra Leigh (Bennett)	Jul 31, 1955	Dec 05, 2021	Gudger Family Cem.; Joseph & Virginia (McBee) Bennett; m. Houston King
King, Stanley Thomas	Aug 11, 1956	Nov 18 2013	Pleasant Hill Cem.; Son of Eugene & Ovie (Fults) King
King, Steve Allen	Jun 12, 1955	Aug 15, 2000	Palmer Cem.; Son, Adopted by Walter & Bessie King; m. Sherry Kay Cleek; addition to Cemeteries of Grundy Co., Vol. 2, p. 566
King, Steven Shane	Jun 16, 1973	Jul 28, 2003	Palmer Cem.; Son of Steve A. & Sherry Kay (Cleek) King; Addition to Cemeteries of Grundy Co., Vol. 2, p. 566
King, Thelma S. (Perry)	Feb 09, 1945	Apr 09, 1998	Hunerwadel Cem.; Dau. of Johnny Wesley & Almeda (King) Perry; m. Glen Edward King; addition to Cemeteries of Grundy Co., Vol. 1, p. 343
King, Tomothy Jacob "Voo Doo"	1965	Sep 14, 2014	Fall Creek Cem.; Son of Esther Wood; companion, Katina Needham
King, Wilborn Ray	Mar 25, 1962	Dec 12, 2018	King Cem.; Son of Clarence Glenn King & Mary Ledbetter
Kinsey, Aleta Lee (Thomas)	Oct 09, 1955	May 25, 2021	Hamilton Memorial Gardens; Dau. of Barbara Thomas; m. Bennie Kinsey, Jr.
Kirby, Robert Ray	Oct 25, 1936	Dec 03, 2003	Airview Cem.; Son of Louis & Audia Mae Kirby; m. Betty J. Hampton; addition to Cemeteries of Grundy Co., Vol. 1, p. 6
Kirk, Eliza Belle (Stephens)	Dec 8, 1871	Feb 05, 1908	Tracy City Cem.; Possibly dau of Samuel & Mary Jane (Parker) Stephens; 1st wife of Rufus L. Kirk; Correction by family to Cemeteries of Grundy Co., Vol. 2, p. 839
Kirk, Georgia Helen (Tate)	Nov 15, 1930	Oct 12, 2020	Fall Creek Cem.; Dau. of Arthur & Mary Jane (Knox) Tate; m. Charles "Buddy" Kirk
Kirk, Helen Myers	Nov 06, 1927	Oct 02, 2016	Tracy City Cem; Dau. of Claude & Angie (Ingram) Myers; m. Tom Ed Kirk
Kirk, Rufus L.	Apr 9, 1861	Sep 08, 1946	Tracy City Cem.; Son of James B & Frances "Fannie" Laura (Creek) Kirk; m. Eliza Belle Stephens; per additional information provided by family; no marker
Kissling, Johann	Feb 22, 1827	May 26, 1892	Swiss Colony Cem.; born in Kant, Bern, Switzerland; m. Margritha "Margaret" Balsiger; addition to Cemeteries of Grundy Co., Vol. 2, p. 784
Kissling, Margritha "Margaret" (Balsiger)	1837	1897	Swiss Colony Cem.; Dau. of Magdalena Balsiger; m. Johann Kissling; addition to Cemeteries of Grundy Co. Vol. 2, p. 784
Kitchens, Alex Shields	Sep 15, 1945	Mar 07, 2015	Cremated; Son of Sterling Bert & Montyne (Shield) Kitchens; m. Judy Rinehart; US. Marie Corps

Name	Birth	Death	Notes
Kitts, Isabella	Dec. 12, 1866	Nov. 23, 1959	Tracy City Cem.; Dau. of Reason O. & Susannah (Layne) Kitts; never married
Knight, Albert "Hooty"	May 23, 1930	Nov 21, 2016	Hunerwadel Cem.; Son of Albert & Bernice (Miller) Knight; m. Imogene Smartt
Knight, Bruce Edward	Nov 23, 1951	Dec 18, 2020	Brown's Chapel Cem.; Son of Edwin & Hallie (James) Knight; m. Shannon Chesser
Knight, Charles Ronnie	Jul 04, 1943	Oct 08, 2018	Fall Creek Cem,; Son of Charles Raymond Knight & Dorothy Cleo Givens; m. Rosalyn Cannon
Knight, Clifford Wayne	Aug 02, 1957	Jan 02, 2022	Son of Horace & Hallie Knight; m. Linda Schiller
Knight, Georgia N. (Nunley)	Nov 27, 1930	Jul 01, 2022	Hunerwadel Cem.; Dau. of George Franklin & Lyla (Shadrick) Nunley; m. Dennis Knight; addition to Cemeteries of Grundy Co.,Vol. 1, p. 347
Knight, Gus	Dec 20, 1939	Oct 25, 1941	Bonny Oak Cem.; Son of Jack B. & Lydia Sue (Nunley) Knight; addition to Cemeteries of Grundy Co.,Vol. 1, p. 82
Knight, Hallie F. (James)	Apr 16, 1932	May 10, 2014	Brown's Chapel Cem.; Dau. of Gordon Lee & Agnes A (Banks) James; m. Horace E. "Gid" Knight; addition to Cemeteries of Grundy Co.,Vol. 1, p. 104
Knight, Horace Newton, Jr.	Jun 14, 1969	Jun 14, 1969	Hunerwadel Cem.; Son of Horace Newton, Sr. & Esther (King) Knight; He is actually buried at Philadelphia Cem.; See Cemeteries of Grundy Co.Vol. 2, p 651. This is a memorial stone only; addition to Cemeteries of Grundy Co.,Vol. 1, p. 344
Knight, Jimmie Carolyn (Jones)	Sep 28, 1952	Mar 22, 2020	Smyrna Cem.; Dau. of James Paul Jones & Georgia Mae Hale; m. Elton Knight
Knight, Mahaley "Haley" (O'Rear)	Oct 1857	Jan 04, 1922	Orange Hill Cem.; Dau. of Calvin & Eda (Webb) O'Rear; m. Starling Knight on Aug 4, 1877, in Grundy Co., no tombstone
Knight, Pearly Mae (Childers)	Apr 19, 1899	Feb 01, 1988	Bonny Oak Cem.; Dau. of Ed & Synthia A. (Sweeton) Childers; m. George William Knight; correction of mother's name and addition to Cemeteries of Grundy Co.,Vol. 1, p. 75
Knight, Phoeba Ann (James)	Apr 13, 1873	Mar 12, 1950	Bonny Oak Cem.; Dau. of Richard & Bessie (Crabtree) James; m. Levander Knight; addition to Cemeteries of Grundy Co. Vol. 1, p. 75
Knight, Robert	1917	1925	Bonny Oak Cem.; Son of Levander & Phoeba Ann (James) Knight; addition to Cemeteries of Grundy Co.,Vol. 1, p. 75
Knight, Ronald Colby	Jan 01, 1970	Dec 15, 2015	Fall Creek Cem.; Son of Charles Ronnie & Rosalyn (Cannon) Knight

Name	Born	Died	Details
Knight, Timothy Randall	Jan 13, 1958	Jul 11, 2014	Fall Creek Cem.; Son of Charles Raymond "Babe" Knight & Dorothy Cleo "Dude" Givens
Knight, William Harris	Sep 4, 1868	Apr 14, 1939	Fall Creek Cem.; Son of Starling & Manerva (Hobbs) Knight
Knott, Alfred A.	May 2, 1827	Jun 27, 1899	Wesley Chapel Cem.; Son of Willis & Mary B. Knott, m. Elvira Jane McNew; addition to Cemeteries of Grundy Co., Vol. 2, p. 977
Knott, Katherine (Rollins)	Jul 02, 1924	Jul 20, 2015	Clouse Hill Cem.; Dau. of Bob & Levester (Thomas) Rollins; m. 1) Gene Williams 2) Francis Lee Knott
Knott, Manuel Melvin	May 23, 1922	Mar 31, 2013	Eastern Star Cem.; Son of Oscar Luck & Carrie (Long) Knott; m. Savannah Smith; US Marine Corps
Knowlan, Annie (Davis)	ca. 1889	1906	Oak Grove Cem.; Dau. of G.W. Davis; m. Fred Knowlan; no tombstone; newspaper article in *Sequachee Valley News*. She was 17 years old, married
Knowlan, Charles Ray	Nov 09, 1936	May 28, 2019	National Cem. in Chattanooga, but has a tombstone at Palmer; Son of John Lafayette "Fate" & Katie Maggie (Davis) Knowlan; m. Yoshiko Ito from Japan. Yoshiko will also be buried at the National Cemetery in Chattanooga even though she has a tombstone in Palmer Cem.; Correction & addition to Cemeteries of Grundy Co.Vol. 2, p. 560
Knowlan, Ottis Preston	Jun 29, 1946		Palmer Cem.; Son of John Lafayette "Fate" & Katie Maggie Plumber (Davis) Knowlan; m. Willene Bivens; addition to Cemeteries of Grundy Co.,Vol. 2; p. 560
Knowlan, Willene (Bivens)	Nov 28, 1945		Palmer Cem.; Dau. of William T. & Mae Arlene (Johnson) Bivens; m. Ottis Preston Bivens; addition to Cemeteries of Grundy Co.,Vol. 2, p. 560
Knowlan, Yoshiko (Ito)	Feb 10, 1933	Feb 18, 2022	Chattanooga National Cem.; born in Japan; m. Charles Ray Knowlan
Knowland, Franklen Hershel	Apr 26, 1915	Nov 26, 1995	Palmer Cem.; Son of Fate & Mary Jane (Davis) Knowland; m. Ina Ruth Green; correction to spelling of name according to tombstone for Cemeteries of Grundy Co.,Vol. 2, p. 563.
Knowland, Ina Ruth (Green)	Feb 03, 1920	Dec 24, 2002	Palmer Cem.; Dau. of James Arthur & Lena May (Land) Green; m. Franklin Hershel Knowland; addition to Cemeteries of Grundy Co.,Vol. 2, p. 563
Knox, Albert Edward	Feb 2, 1898	Feb 28, 1972	Palmer Cem.; Son of George Leonard & Bertha L. (Payne) Knox; m. Mabel Meeks; addition to Cemeteries of Grundy Co.,Vol. 2, p. 555

Name	Born	Died	Notes
Knox, Mabel (Meeks)	Feb 17, 1915	Jan 20, 2006	Warren "Red Hill" Cemetery; cremated; Dau. of George & Ozella (Magouirk) Meeks; m. Albert Edward Knox; Addition to Cemeteries of Grundy Co., Vol. 2.
Knox, Pearl M. (Henry)	1904	Mar 11, 1967	Palmer Cem.; Dau. of Billie & Sally (Troutman) Henry; m. Fred Earl Knox; addition to Cemeteries of Grundy Co.,Vol. 2, p. 555.
Koeppel, Emma Catherine (Schlageter)	1892	1971	Swiss Colony Cem.; Dau. of Ignatz & Elizabeth (Schild) Schlageter; m. John Severin Koeppel in 1923; addition to Cemeteries of Grundy Co.,Vol. 2, p. 788
Kopek, Lawrence David	Jan 28, 1958	Oct 06, 2013	Cremated; Son of Larry & Arlene Kopek
Kopp, Elizabeth (Fults) Winton	Nov 30, 1918	Jan 11, 2018	Tracy City Cem.; m. 1) Leonard Dale Winton 2) William Hayes Kopp
Kosack, Roberta Virginia	May 13, 1925	Aug 25, 1996	Monteagle Cem.; Dau. of Robert & Mae (Johnson) Schneider; addition to Cemeteries of Grundy Co.,Vol. 1, p. 456
Kovacs, Irene (Myers)	Nov 20, 1904	Apr 29, 1981	Oak Grove Cem.; Dau. of Miles Benson & Mary "Mollie" Caroline Davis; m. Samuel Kovacs; addition to Cemeteries of Grundy Co.,Vol. 1, p. 497
Kraft, Virginia Ann (Roberts)	Nov 28, 1928	Jul 29, 2022	Monteagle Cem.; Dau. of Blaine E. & Violet Blanche (Schlasner) Roberts; m. Ralph Kraft; p. 446 correction to maiden name and addition to Cemeteries of Grundy Co.,Vol. 1
Krahenbuhl, Jacob W.	Jan 17, 1842	Dec 22, 1889	Tracy City Cem.; Son of Samuel Krahenbuhl; m. Sophie M. Werren; addition to Cemeteries of Grundy Co.,Vol. 2, p. 891
Kunz, Homer Bernard	Jul 28, 1913	Dec 20, 2012	Tracy City Cem.; Son of John & Marie Magdaline (Stamm) Kunz; m. June Mildred Borrensen on Jul 5, 1942; Swiss flag on tombstone
Kunz, June Mildred (Borrensen)	Jun 11, 1921	Apr 04, 2008	Cremated, ashes at Tracy City Cem.; Dau. of Olaf & Anna Borrensen; Ashes placed in Homer Bernard Kunz's (husband) coffin;Cemeteries of Grundy Co., Vol. 2, p. 883 correction
Kunzle, George	Aug 27, 1847	Dec 31, 1886	Swiss Colony Cem.; Son of George Kunzle & Katherine Zimmermann; addition to Cemeteries of Grundy Co.,Vol. 2, p. 784
Kustos, Rafael "Ralph"	Dec 23, 1938	Jun 14, 2019	Bethel Cem.; Born in Budapest, Hungary; companion of Violet (Crabtree) Anderson
Laager, Burkhardt	Apr 27, 1851	Jan 13, 1907	Swiss Colony Cem.; Son of Johann Jacob & Regula Laager; addition to Cemeteries of Grundy Co.,Vol. 2, p. 785

Name	Birth	Death	Details
Lacy, Alice Pauline (Smith) "Polly"	Apr 27, 1907	Apr 17, 1990	Monteagle Cem.; Dau. of Alexander H. & Margaret (Chapin) Smith; m. Virgil Ward Lacy Nov. 13, 1931 in Overton Co.; correction to Cemeteries of Grundy Co., Volume 1, p. 396
Ladd, Betty Louise	Mar 22, 1932	Nov 04, 2013	Monteagle Cem.; Dau. of William F. & Adeline Garner; m. John Henry Ladd
Ladd, Charles Dwight	Nov 12, 1974	Jan 26, 2017	Monteagle Cem.; Son of John David & Virginia Lucille (Westerfield) Ladd; never married
Ladd, Delbert Lamar	Jun 06, 1953	May 09, 2015	Burns Cem. Ashes; Son of John W. & Jessie (Caldwell) Collins; partrner Bridgett B. Scott
Ladd, Estelle (Anderson)	May 04, 1932	Mar 09, 2020	Monteagle Cem.; Dau. of Morris Anderson & Georgia Ann Wilson; m. James Bufford Ladd
Ladd, Fannie Della (Armstrong) no tombstone, rock marker only			Monteagle Cem.; possible grave of Fannie Della (Armstrong) Ladd; m. 1) J. W. White 2). John W. Ladd; Cemeteries of Grundy Co., Vol. 1, p. 404 addition
Ladd, Gwendolyn Kay	Jan 31, 1957	Jul 16, 2013	Monteagle Cem.; Dau. of Lawrence & Joyce (Kunz) Ladd
Ladd, James Bufford	Dec 06, 1928	Jan 16, 2020	Monteagle Cemetery; Son of George W. Ladd & Rosie Lee Norwood; m. Estelle Anderson
Ladd, Patricia Sue (Rector)	Nov 13, 1946	Sep 24, 2006	Burns Cem.; Dau. of Edna Jo White; m. Delbert Lamar Ladd; addition to Cemeteries of Grundy Co.,Vol. 1, p. 129
Ladd, Virginia Lucille	1943	May 09, 2014	Monteagle Cem.; Dau of Johnny Bear Westerfield & Frances Marie Rollins
Ladd, William "Willie" Kennetth	Jul 13, 1954	Sep 17, 2021	Cremated; Son of John Henry & Betty (Garner) Ladd; m. Jo Ladd
Ladewig, Bettie Mae (Sanders)	Jul 22, 1946	Oct 03, 2018	Monteagle Cem.; Dau. of Willie Edward & Margaret Louise (McFarland) Sanders; m. John G. Ladewig
Ladewig, John G.	Apr 21, 1932	Mar 27, 2017	Cremated; Son of George William & Eva Nancy (Goletz) Ladewig of Chicago, IL, m. 1) Judy Ried, May 5, 1930 IN; 2) Bettie Mae Sanders
Lamz, Jonathan Troy	Jan 22, 1969	Mar 04, 2021	Cremated: Son of Larry & Joan (Crabtree) Lamz; m. 1) Denise Lamz 2) Brandy Moser
Lamz, Kylee Leanna	Jun 01, 1993	Apr 14, 2019	Cremated; Dau. of Jonathan Troy & Denise Lamz; companion Justin Wayne Sheppard
Land, Jesse Jane	Dec 08, 1919	Jul 12, 2013	Fall Creek Cem.; Dau. of Jim & Rosie (Tate) Shrum; m. Doug "Monk" Land
Land, William Bishop	Mar 29, 1954	Dec 17, 2017	Plainview Cem.; Son of Howard Willard & Mary (Cunningham) Land; m. 1) Kathy Stevens 2) Carolyn Johnson
Landon, Clara Augusta (Bone)	Aug 20, 1920	Mar 13, 2015	Coalmont Cem.; Dau. of Samuel & Lillian (Mooney) Bone; m. George Landon

Name	Birth	Death	Details
Landrum, Barbara Jane (Partin)	Feb 27, 1940	Aug 13, 2019	Warren "Red Hill" Cem.; Dau. of Bryan & Emma (Bramblett) Partin
Lane, John Franklin III	Sep 05, 1960	May 10, 2014	Hunerwadel Cem.; Son of Clemit & Shirley (Shoemaker) Lane; 2nd husband of Melanie Jean (Lanoie) King Lane Goins
Lane, Margaret L.	Dec 01, 1927	Jun 30, 2015	Monteagle Cem.; Dau. of Yancy & Clara (Worley) Nunley; m. Oliver D. Layne
Lanford-Simmons, James A.	Aug 15, 2013	Aug 15, 2013	White Cem.; Son of Jennifer Lanford & Allen Simmons
Lanford, William Davis "Bill"	Mar 15, 1919	Aug 23, 2004	White Cem.; Son of William Henry & Emma Glenn (Osborne) Lanford: m. Hallie Gean White; addition to Cemeteries of Grundy Co., Vol. 2, p. 1010
Lang, Edward Joseph	Oct 14, 1946	Nov 29, 2019	Airview Cem.; Son of Edward William Lang & Rita Josephine Foley
Langer, Larry Joe, Jr.	Dec 29, 1970	Oct 19, 1974	Palmer Cem.; Son of Larry Joe, Sr. & Shelby (Davis) Langer; addition to Cemeteries of Grundy Co., Vol. 1, p. 567
Lankford, Beersheba B. (Thompson)	May 17, 1861	Oct 21, 1912	Tracy City Cem.; per *Mrs. Grundy*; m. Thomas Benjamin Lankford Jul 29, 1877; correction to Cemeteries of Grundy Co., Vol. 2, p. 549; She was reported to have been buried at Orange Hill, but is actually buried in Tracy City Cem.
Lankford, Charles Rogers	Jan 22, 1931	May 02, 2022	Plainview Cem.; Son of Charles Douglas & Arvilla (Perry) Lankford; m. Clara Louise Rose; Army
Lankford, Earl L.	Apr 06, 1908	1908	Orange Hill Cem.; Son of Albert Lee Levi & Matilda (Hatfield) Lankford; addition to Cemeteries of Grundy Co., Vol. 2, p. 547
Lankford, Elsie (Kilgore)	1900	1990	Fall Creek Cem.; Dau. of Houston & Margaret (Scott) Kilgore; m. Robert Mark DeWitt Lankford
Lankford, Elsie Iona	May 04, 1928	1928	Orange Hill Cem.; Dau. of Albert Lee & Matilda (Hatfield) Lankford
Lankford, Gilliam	May 11, 1907	1907	Orange Hill Cem.; Son of Albert Lee Levi & Matilda (Hatfield) Lankford; addition Cemeteries of Grundy Co., Vol. 2, p. 547
Lankford, Harley D	Aug 04, 1923	Jul 01, 1924	Orange Hill Cem.; Son of Albert Lee & Matilda (Hatfield) Lankford
Lankford, Herbert Newell	Feb 01, 1930	1930	Orange Hill Cem.; Son of Albert Lee & Matilda (Hatfield) Lankford
Lankford, James W "Bo John", Sr.	1925	2014	Cremated; Son of Newton Johnston Lankford & Eunice Estelle Lovelace; m. Jennifer Lankford

Lankford, James Wesley	May 24, 1935	Aug 18, 2014	Summerfield Cem.; Son of Neutra & Genice Estell (Lovlace) Lankford m. 1) Shirley C. Fults, Dec 7, 1966; 2) Jennifer Lynn Totherow; Nov 5, 1985; He is actually buried in Monteagle Cem.; addition to Cemeteries of Grundy Co.,Vol. 2, p. 769
Lankford, Leslie	Feb 08, 1917	Sep 01, 1917	Orange Hill Cem.; Dau. of Albert Lee & Matilda (Hatfield) Lankford
Lankford, Reta Beth (LaFollette)	Jun 29, 1940	Sep 21, 2020	Monteagle Cem.; Dau. of Ivan Kermit & Luster Beatrice (Ottinger) LaFollette; m. James Loyd "Bub" Lankford; addition to Cemeteries of Grundy Co.,Vol. 1, p. 452
Lankford, Vachel (Mrs.)		Mar 01, 1885	Philadelphia Cem.; She died in Tracy City, but was buried at Philadelphia per *The Southern Standard*, Mar 28, 1885
Lappin, Charles		Nov 20, 1899	Unidentified Cem.; Son of J.B. Lappin; no stone
Lappin, Frances Caroline (Seeley)	May 23, 1834	Jun 09, 1913	Lappin Cem.; Dau. of Jesse & Prudence (Brown) Seeley; m. Wellington William Lappin; stone and remains moved from Monteagle Cemetery; correction of death year
Lappin, Martha Sue	Dec 02, 1937	Feb 06, 2014	Tate Cem.; Dau. of Thomas & Gladys (Mooney) Green; m. Roger Lappin
Lappin, Nell Beauty (Sartain)	Apr 29, 1929	Oct 16, 2017	Coalmont Cem.; Dau. of Louis & Betty (Dickerson) Sartain; m. Ralph M. Lappin, Sr.
Lappin, Wellington William	Aug 31, 1831	Apr 25, 1882	Lappin Cem.; Son of Robert & Elizabeth "Betsy" (Stewart) Lappin; stone & remains moved from Monteagle Cemetery
Lasater, Randy E.	Jun 21, 1954		Warren "Red Hill" Cem.; Son of David C. & Ruth Laurenen (Shaddoack) Lasater; m. 1) Vickie Walls 2) Lana Harris 3) Susan Shmitt
Laskowske, Phillip William	Jun 05, 1929	Jul 05, 2005	Altamont Cem.; Son of Otto Ernest & Mary (Seipp) Laskowske; m. Betty Frances Beech; TSgt. USAF addition to Cemeteries of Grundy Co.,Vol. 1, p. 22
Lathum, John G.	May 4, 1861	Aug 04, 1902	Fall Creek Cem.; Son of John & Jennie "June" Lathum
Lautzenheiser, Elliott, Geneva Bell "Bluie" (Gregory)	Apr 20, 1921	Jul 27, 2015	Monteagle Cem.; Dau. of Silas Samuel & Mattie L (Thomas) Gregory; m. 1) Ernest Glen "Hunkie" Lautzenheiser 2) Bill Elliott; correction to birth date and additional information to Cemeteries of Grundy Co.,Vol. 1, p. 451
Laviner, Henry Thomas, Jr.	Oct 12, 1945	Oct 04, 2017	Cremated; Son of Henry Thomas & Catherine Laviner, Sr.; lived in Pelham was from SC
Lawhorn, Willie Edward	May 12, 1928	Nov 07, 2016	Cremated; Son of Jess & Una (Linder) Lawhorn; m. Mary Ann Lawhorn

Name	Born	Died	Notes
Lawrence, Misty Shea (Layne)	Aug 15, 1978	Apr 08, 2022	Cremated; Dau. of Harold Wayne & Doris (Pollard) Layne; m. Jeff Finch
Lawson, Allan	Dec 20, 1984	Sep 19, 2001	Orange Hill Cem.; Son of Phillip A. Lawson & Paula Nunley
Lawson, Andrew	Sep 9, 1854	Feb 24, 1935	Monteagle Cem.; Son of William & Elizabeth (Tucker) Lawson; no stone
Lawson, Carrie Francis (Layne)	Jun 21, 1921	Oct 21, 2014	Plainview Cem.; Dau. of Roy & Alice (Russell) Layne; m. Henry Jackson Lawson; addition to Cemeteries of Grundy Co., Vol. 1, p. 676
Lawson, Charles A., Jr.	Mar 11, 1933	Apr 22, 2013	Orange Hill Cem.; Son of Charles A. & Mildred E. Lawson; m. Annette; US Army
Lawson, Coy "Gene"	Dec 20, 1941	Mar 05, 2022	Son of Coy Washington & Minnie (Davis) Lawson; m. Martha Lawson
Lawson, Mildred Annette (Allison)	Jan 06, 1934	Sep 19, 2018	Orange Hill Cem.; Dau. of Henry O. & Nannie Mae Allison; m. Charles Alfred Lawson, Jr.
Lawson, Phillip A.	Oct 24, 1959	Dec 07, 2016	Orange Hill Cem.; Son of Phillip Oscar Lawson & Betty (Meeks) O'Neal; m. Paula Nunley
Lawson, Phillip Oscoe	Jun 20, 1928	Apr 15, 1967	Tracy City Cem.; Son of Henry Jackson & Buelah Edna (Walter) Roddy; m. Margaret Sue Roddy; US Army WWII
Lawson, Rubye Lee (Robinson)	Dec 09, 1943	Mar 06, 2020	Shockley Cem.; Dau. of Hebron & Nina Mae Robinson; m. Kenneth Wayne Lawson
Lawson, Samuel W. "Sammy"	Ca 1944	Dec 15, 2017	Lusk Cem.; Son of Lester & Mildred Lawson
Laxson, Charles "Josh"	Jun 18, 1929	May 04, 2020	Providence Methodist Cem.; Son of John Guinn Laxson & Rebecca Idella Eudora Sanders; addition to Cemeteries of Grundy Co, Vol. 2, p. 709
Laxson, Charles Edwin "Josh"	Jun 18, 1929	May 04, 2020	Providence Methodist Church Cem.; Son of Jessie Cecil Laxson & Mary Grooms; m. Lowanda Maxwell
Laxson, Sandra Lee (Griggs)	Jan 08, 1943	Jan 11, 2020	Warren "Red Hill" Cem.; Dau. of Henry Samuel Griggs & Beulah Jean McMillan; m. Herbie Laxson
Lay, Alma Jean (Borne)	Jul 30, 1935	Feb 12, 2015	Fall Creek Cem. Dau. of Lawrence & Maude (Woodlee) Borne; m. Clifford Lay, Jr.
Lay, Peter Edgar	Dec 5, 1896	Dec 26, 1979	Swiss Colony Cem.; Son of William Leslie & Lelon (Rogers) Lay; m. Aug 3, 1919, to Emma Myers; addition to Cemeteries of Grundy Co., Vol. 2, p. 793
Layman, Alton E.	May 07, 1954	Apr 19, 2014	Fall Creek Cem.; Son of Everett Layman & Kathryn Sanders; m. Pam Layman
Layman, Alicia Cheyenne	Jul 20, 2002	May 14, 2017	Turner-Layman Cem.; Dau. of Billy Ray & Andrea L. (Turner) Layman
Layman, Arrietta Elois (James)	Nov 05, 1938	May 26, 2022	Brown's Chapel Cem.; Dau. of Fred & Rosa (Schoenmann) James; m. Ralph Layman

Name	Born	Died	Notes
Layman, Charles Vernon	Oct 13, 1941	May 16, 2015	Homeland Acres Cem.; Son of Clyde & Jean (Walton) Layman; m. Beverly Irene Brown Rankhorn
Layman, David Allen "Big Al"	Feb 04, 1964	Nov 21, 2017	Griffiths Creek Cem.; Son of John & Elsie Griffith Layman;
Layman, Dorothy Irene	Dec 14, 1927	Aug 26, 1999	White Cem.; Dau. of Taylor W. & Stella (Harris) Pry; m. Tommy Leon Layman; addition to Cemeteries of Grundy Co., Vol. 2, p. 1009
Layman, Edna (Scott)	Dec 08, 1938	Nov 06, 2018	White Cem.; Dau. of William Bryan Scott & Mary Daisy Howard; m. Joe Ray Layman
Layman, Elsie Marie (Griffith)	Apr 11, 1937	Mar 02, 2022	Griffiths Creek Cem.; Son of George David & Emma N. (Layne) Griffith; m. John Adam Layman
Layman, J. C.	Sep 30, 1967	Apr 07, 2019	J. C. Layman Cem.; Son of John Layman & Elsie Griffith
Layman, James Clyde	Apr 11, 1937	Aug 03, 2002	White Cem.; Son of George Washington & Virgie (Layne) Layman; addition to Cemeteries of Grundy Co., Vol. 2, p. 1009
Layman, Joe Ray	Oct 11, 1936	Mar 25, 2018	White Cem.; Son of Homer Layman & Ola White; m. Edna Scott
Layman, Nancy	Jun 27, 1965	Jun 30, 1965	Fall Creek Cem.; Dau. of Everett J. & Katherine (Sanders) Layman; no tombstone
Layman, Pamela Kay	Mar 04, 1955	Oct 26, 2016	Fall Creek Cem.; Dau. of Jerry & Lena Mae (Haynes) McTaggart; m. Alton E. Layman
Layman, Tom	Apr 7, 1877	Jun 17, 1920	White Cem.; Son of Mitchell Michael & Elizabeth Jane (Cheek) Layman; m. Alice White; addition to Cemeteries of Grundy Co., Vol. 2, p. 1009
Layman, Tommy Leon	Apar 11, 1921	Jan 13, 2000	White Cem.; Son of George Washington & Virgie (Layne) Layman; m. Dorothy Irene Pry; addition to Cemeteries of Grundy Co., Vol. 2, p. 1009
Layman, Tommy Leon, Jr.	Oct 29, 1949	Dec 31, 2020	Brown's Chapel Cem.; Son of Tommy Leon & Dorothy Irene (Pryor) Layman; m. Molly O. Layman
Layman, Virgie (Layne)	Nov 8, 1899	Apr 29, 1964	White Cem.; Dau. of Andrew Jackson & Sally (Dykes) Layne; m. 1) George Washington Layman 2) Gilbert Overturf; addition to Cemeteries of Grundy Co., Vol. 2, p. 1009
Laymon, Homer W.	Oct 21, 1911	Nov 20, 2000	White Cem.; Son of George Washington & Virgie (Layne) Laymon; m. Ola H. White, Sep 23, 1933; addition to Cemeteries of Grundy Co., Vol. 2, p. 1011
Laymon, Percy Ezell	Sep 03, 1934	Apr 21, 2022	White Cem.; Son of Homer & Ola (White) Laymon

Name	Birth	Death	Notes
Layne - Shirley, Edith Irene (Hill)	Oct 30, 1911	Apr 25, 2014	Summerfield Cem.; Dau. of William Thomas "Bill" & Hattie Huetta "Etta" (Partin) Hill; m. 1) Abraham Kelly "Little Abe" Layne 2) Hudson Robert "Bob" Shirley of OK; in Grundy Co. Jul 4, 1985
Layne child			Monteagle Cem.; Dau. of Preston Franklin & Elizabeth (Hopkins) Layne; fieldstone
Layne, Aberham	Sep 9, 1924	Feb 15, 1907	Burkett's Chapel Cem; Son of Isaac "Doc" Layne & Mary "Polly" Mayhew Steele; m. Matieal Layne/census records say Margaret Layne; dates and wife are listed on old tombstone;
Layne, Abraham	Not on tombstone	1863	Burkett's Chapel Cem.; Son of David Stephen & Esther (Stephens) Layne; hanged by Confederates for being Union sympathizer per the tombstone, but *Layne, Lain, Lane Genealogy* by Floyd Benjamin Layne says he was hanged by the Union for supporting the Confederacy; modern day tombstone; addition to Cemeteries of Grundy Co., Vol, 1, p.118
Layne, Alexander Benson "Dude"	1930	Jan 09, 2014	Ft. Huachuca Cem. in AZ; Son of Arthur Alexander Layne & Emma Rose King; m. Mary Sue Church; Army Korea
Layne, Alfred Leemon	Aug 21, 1928	May 03, 2022	Plainview Cem.; Son of John & Myrtle (Dykes) Layne; m. Betty Jean Layne
Layne, Aylor "A.J."	May 22, 1928	Mar 08, 2017	Hamilton Memorial Gardens Cem.; Son of Aylor & Maudie Layne; m. Jo Ann Layne
Layne, Billy Ray	1931	Dec 17, 2014	Monteagle Cem.; Son of John & Myrtle (Dykes) Layne; m. Delores (Campbell) Layne
Layne, Bobby Joe	Feb 25, 1965	May 10, 2012	Burkett's Chapel Cem.; Son of Robert Joe & Nina Faye (White) Layne; m. Tammy Shadrick
Layne, Brenda J.	Aug 19, 1942		Warren "Red Hill" Cem.; Dau of Willie Arvell Koger & Nola Magdalene Davis; m. Dillard Harold Layne, Jr.
Layne, Charles "Boy"	Jan 17, 1972	Sep 01, 2015	Griffith's Creek Cem.; Son of Albert Layne & Irene Nunley
Layne, Charles Doyle	Oct 27, 1943	Oct 18, 2016	Springfield Memorial Gardens; Son of Dillard H. "Dill" & Corene (Cox) Layne; m. 1) Linda Gibson 2) Louise Drake; US Air Force
Layne, Charles Edward	May 19, 1947	Oct 03, 2021	Cagle Mount Pleasant Cem.; Son of Coleman & Joyce Olean (Cleek) Layne; m. Joyce Sherman
Layne, Chester Earl	Nov 16, 1942	Sep 10, 2019	Catoosa Memorial Gardens; Son of Roy David Layne & Mary Louise Geary; m. Linda Darlene Layne
Layne, Claude Elmer	May 15, 1936	Oct 23, 2018	Swiss Colony Cem.; Son of Ike & Lillie (Fults) Layne; m. Alene Grimes; addition to Cemeteries of Grundy Co.,Vol. 2, p. 798

Layne, Clell Lendon	May 23, 1964	Sep 30, 2019	King Cem.; Son of Thomas Jackson Layne & Margie King; m. Laura Frances Nolan
Layne, Coleman	Mar 03, 1925	Aug 21, 1947	Fall Creek Cem.; Son of Frank McKinley & Edith (Morton) Layne;
Layne, Danny Lee	Jan 24, 1959	Jul 01, 2016	Swiss Cem.; Son of Claude & Loretta (Smartt) Layne; m. Tammy McDaniel
Layne, Darrell	Jul 20, 1952	Aug 27, 2013	Pryor Ridge Cem.; Son of Alfred L & Betty (Haynes) Layne
Layne, Dereda Joyce	May 22, 1929	Apr 26, 2014	Palmer Cem.; Dau of Arthur Tate & Mary Jane Knox; m. James Layne
Layne, Devin James	Sep 10, 1995	Aug 09, 1996	Burkett Chapel Cem.; Son of John Jacob & Melissa (Corbisier) Layne; addition to Cemeteries of Grundy Co., Vol, 1, p. 125
Layne, Dillard Harold, Jr.	Apr 16, 1938	Mar 19, 2020	Warren "Red Hill" Cem.; Son of Dillard H. Layne, Sr. & Anna Corene Cox; m. Brenda Koger, Jul 1, 1961; U.S. Air Force
Layne, Dorothy Arlene (Mainord)	Sep 08, 1956	Oct 11, 2021	Swiss Colony Cem.; Dau. of Louis Waymond & Etheleen (Schieser) Mainord; m. Rex Allen Layne
Layne, Dorothy L. (Rollins)	Sep 04, 1937	Mar 18, 2015	Summerfield Cem.; Dau. of Robert Jackson & Lee Vester (Thomas) Rollins; m. John William "Johnny" Layne; addition to Cemeteries of Grundy Co.Vol. 2, p. 775
Layne, Douglas Dewayne	Aug 13, 1967	Dec 23, 2018	Swiss Colony Cem.; Son of Scottie Douglas Layne & Judy Lynn Taylor; m. Tammy Caldwell
Layne, E.W.	Dec 17, 1931	May 21, 2014	Cremated; Son of Robert Dewitt Layne & Esper Woodlee; m. Lucretia "Sissy" Cannon; Army
Layne, Earline (O'Neal)	Sep 22, 1933	Mar 27, 2021	Summerfield Cem.; Dau. of Early & Nina (Bouldin) O'Neal; m. Lonnie Layne
Layne, Emma Jean (Meeks)	Aug 18, 1932	Aug 08, 1995	Fall Creek Cem.; Dau. of Earnest & Mary Meeks
Layne, Etta (Slatton)	Jul 22, 1916	Aug 08, 2005	White Cem.; Dau. of Enoch & Timmie (Layne) Slatton, m. John Wesley Layne; addition to Cemeteris of Grundy Co.,Vol. 2, p. 1013
Layne, Fannie Clair	Nov 10, 1919	Feb 11, 2013	Griffith's Creek Cem.; Dau. of Isier & Frances (Bowman) Layne
Layne, Frank	Oct 3, 1887	Apr 23, 1926	White Cem.; Son of Henry Miller & Martha C. (Pickett) Layne; m. Minnie Thompson; TN PVT Co. G2. DV BN WWI; addition to Cemeteries of Grundy Co.,Vol. 2, p. 1006
Layne, Franklin Parks, Jr.	Oct 03, 1924	Jul 13, 2017	Palmer Cem.; Son of Franklin Parks, Sr. & Dixie Lee (Nunley) Layne

Name	Birth	Death	Details
Layne, Fred	Feb 18, 1896	Dec. 1971	Palmer Cem.; Son of Jack & Harriet (Bryant) Layne; m. Mittie Kilgore (1896-Jan 12,1965); no tombstone; addition to Cemeteries of Grundy Co.Vol. 2.
Layne, Fred Anthony	Mar 04, 1938	Mar 17, 2014	Shelby Memorial Garden, OH; Son of William Jennings Bryan "Jay" & Huetta "Etta" (Gilliam) Layne; m. Marlene Moses
Layne, George Coleman	Nov 26, 1947	Apr 08, 2014	Anderson Cem. Sewanee; Son of Clyde & Elsie (Meeks) Layne; m. Nina Sue Rollins
Layne, Gilbert	Jul 24, 1933	Dec 08, 2016	Chattanooga Memorial Park Cem.; Son of Henry & Bettie (Crisp) Layne; m. Carolinda ; US Army
Layne, Grady	Dec 28, 1938	May 19, 2020	Oak Lawn Memorial Gardens Cem.; Son of Edd & Beulah Layne; m. Katherine Layne; U.S. Army
Layne, Harold Franklin	Aug 14, 1948	May 15, 2021	Burns Cem.; Son of Edd & Mary Beulah Layne; Kaye Curtis
Layne, Ida Ellen (Cantrell)	Apr 19, 1982	Feb 14, 2021	Fall Creek Cem.; Dau. of Herbert & Lisa Cantrell; m. Jason Layne
Layne, Imogene (Jones)	Oct 30, 1933	Mar 13, 2018	Rose Hill Memorial Gardens; Dau. of Herbert Jones & Lucille Parker; m. W.T. Layne
Layne, Jackie	Jan 29, 1940	Aug 15, 1991	Palmer Cem.; Son of Roy D. & Louise (Geary) Layne; m. Nan Ruth Magouirk; addition to Cemeteries of Grundy Co.,Vol. 2, p. 570
Layne, Jackson Reid	Jan 08, 2014	Jan 08, 2014	Warren "Red Hill" Cem.; Son of Johnathan Layne & Kara Campbell
Layne, James Duane "Jim"	Spe 20, 1964	Apr 23, 2020	Fall Creek Cem.; Son of James Ed Layne & Irene Braden "Renie" ; m. Karen Burnett
Layne, James Walter	Jan 25, 1932	Aug 30, 2021	Gregg Cem.; Son of Bartley & Almedia Layne; m. Margaret Layne
Layne, Jennifer Leann (Roddy)	Jul 19, 1991	Feb 21, 2016	Eastern Star Cem.; Dau. of Joseph Roddy & Jenna (Cash) Roddy Myers; m. Russell Layne
Layne, Jerry Hayes	Jan 07, 1943	Jul 16, 2020	Son of Jack Watson & Elsie Levona (Bennett) Layne
Layne, Jim Washington	Feb 05, 1905	Apr 06, 1905	White Cem: Son of Stephen & Nancy E. (Kilgore) Layne; m. Lila Melton; addition to Cemeteries of Grundy Co.,Vol. 2, p. 1006
Layne, Joe Edward	Apr 16, 1969	Oct 09, 2021	Cagle Mountain Cem.; Son of Charles Edward & Joyce (Sherman) Layne; m. Jane Cunningham
Layne, John Dave	Sep 23, 1929	May 09, 2014	Gregg Cem.; Son of Bartley Layne & Almedia Newsome; m. Margaret Coppinger
Layne, John Henry	Jan 16, 1939	Jan 10, 2021	Cremated; Son of Robert & Willie Layne; m. Susie Ellen Smartt
Layne, John Henry, Jr.	Oct 20, 1961	Dec 22, 2018	Cremated; Son of John Henry Layne & Susie Smartt; m. Darlene Beene

Layne, John Wesley	Jan 23, 1910	Dec 07, 1980	White Cem.; Son of Benjamin Etwell & Dannie Ella (Graves) Layne; m. Ella Slatton; PFC US Army WWII; addition to Cemeteries of Grundy Co, Vol. 2, p. 1013
Layne, Johnnie	May 10, 1907	Aug 10, 1962	Fall Creek Falls Cem.; Son of William Anderson & Sarah Layne
Layne, Johnny Ray	Jan 05, 1954	Apr 13, 2018	Pryor Ridge Cem.; Son of Alfred L & Betty J Layne
Layne, Joyce (Kilgore)	May 23, 1932	Aug 01, 2016	Swiss Colony Cem.; Dau. of Ernest & Gertrude Kilgore, m. Barney H. Layne; addition to Cemeteries of Grundy Co., Vol. 2, p. 786
Layne, Judy Lynn	Jun 26, 1944	Apr 01, 2013	Swiss Cem.; Dau. of Emory W. & Ester (Daniel) Taylor; m. Scottie Douglas Layne
Layne, Kenneth Owen	May 29, 1943	Jul 20, 2020	Bethel Cem.; Son of William Jennings Bryan "Jay" Layne & Huetta Gilliam; m. Bunia Nunley
Layne, Kent A. "Bear"	Sep 02, 1936	Jan 25, 2014	Fall Creek Cem.; Son of Joe C. Layne & Hazel Morrison ; m. Doris Sanders
Layne, Kimberly Michelle	Jun 18, 1976	Sep 26, 2021	Palmer Cem.; Dau. of Charles & Nancy Ann "Susie" (Campbell) Layne
Layne, Larry Dean	May 06, 1949	Jan 15, 2017	Fall Creek Cem.; Son of Joe T. & Elsie A. (McHone) Layne; US Air Force
Layne, Leonard	Dec 19, 1932	Mar 18, 2013	Palmer Cem.; Son of Frank & Edith (Morton) Layne; m. Troas (Knowlan) Layne
Layne, Lila (Melton)	Mar 5, 1874	May 09, 1950	White Cem.; Dau. of Dave & Martha (Rutherford) Melton; m. Jim Washington Layne; addition to Cemeteries of Grundy Co., Vol. 2, p. 1006
Layne, Linda Janelle	Jan 06, 1947		Warren "Red Hill" Cem.; Dau. of Joseph Elbert & Mary Elsie (Payne) Layne; m. 1) Thomas Eugene Coats, Jr. 2) David Richard Taylor; tombstone back: Mary Megan Coats Benton, dau; Riley & Ryan Benton, grandsons; addition & change to Cemeteries of Grundy Co., Vol. 2, p. 924
Layne, Lonnie	Nov 21, 1928	Mar 06, 2014	Summerfield Cem.; Son of William Jennings Bryan "Jay" & Huetta "Etta" (Gilliam) Layne; m. Earline Harris
Layne, Louise (Geary)	Feb 26, 2011	Mar 03, 2006	Palmer Cem.; Dau. of Joseph S. & Emma (Nunley) Geary; m. Roy David Layne; addition to Cemeteries of Grundy Co., Vol. 2, p. 570
Layne, Margaret Aleene (Turner)	Oct 15, 1923	Mar 17, 2015	Summerfield Cem.; Dau. of William Polk & Laura Mae (Smith) Turner; m. Emiel Dewey Layne

Layne, Margie Elizabeth (Green)	Jul 19, 1924	Nov 16, 1965	Oak Grove Cem.; Dau. of James Arthur, Jr. & Lena May (Land) Green; m. Oscar F. Layne; addition, Cemeteries of Grundy Co.,Vol. 1, p. 789
Layne, Mark Anthony	Oct. 11, 1962	May 27, 2015	Palmer Cem.; Son of Harvey Raymond & Betty May (Perry) Layne; m. Patricia Cox
Layne, Martin Eugene	Aug 29, 1928	Dec 02, 2018	Palmer Cem.; Son of Franklin Parks Layne & Dixie Lee Nunley; m. Bonnie Finch; U.S. Army
Layne, Mary (Crowe)	Sep 21, 1900	Jan 22, 1976	Oak Grove Cem.; Dau. of Robert & Edna (Howell) Crowe m. Robert Overton Layne; addition to Cemeteries of Grundy Co.,Vol. 1, p. 511
Layne, Mary M. (Lockhart)	Feb 19, 1867	Apr 29, 1906	Altamont Cem.; Dau. of William & Jane (Baly) Lockhart; m. Samuel Layne; addition to Cemeteries of Grundy Co.,Vol. 1, p. 14
Layne, Mary Sue (Church)	Mar 08, 1934	Jan 28, 2023	Fr. Huachuca Cem., AZ; Dau of Desmer Church & Dorothy Cunningham; m. Alexander Benson "Dude" Layne
Layne, Melinda Carol	Jun 05, 1961	Dec 27, 2013	Palmer Cem.; Dau. of Theodore & Carol (Meeks) Long
Layne, Melinda Carol "Lindy"	Jun 05, 1961	Dec 27, 2013	Palmer Cem.; Dau of Theodore Lindley Long, Jr. & Carol Meeks
Layne, Mildred Pollard (Johnson)	Jun 07, 1936	May 05, 2021	Griffith's Creek Cem.; Dau. of Ivor Lee & Lena Mae (Norris) Johnson; m. Paul Edward Layne
Layne, Nan Ruth (Magouirk)	May 07, 1945		Palmer Cem.; Dau. of Rex & Mary Eunice (Shrum) Magouirk; m. 1) Jackie Layne 2) Arnold Cleek; addition to Cemeteries of Grundy Co.,Vol. 2, p. 570
Layne, Nellie Ruth	Aug 11, 1942	Dec 17, 2017	Palmer Cem.; Dau. of Fred J. & Rosa Schoenmann James; m. Charles D. "Steamboat" Layne
Layne, Nelson	Apr 30, 1949	Jan 18, 2021	Hobbs Hill Cem.; Son of Ford Ray & Ruby Edna (Shrum) Layne; m. Joan Spithaler
Layne, Nicholas Cole "Bird"	Dec 30, 1986	Feb 17, 2020	Palmer Cem.; Son of Mark Anthony Layne & Patricia Cox
Layne, Novella	Oct 16, 1949	Jan 06, 2015	Warren "Red Hill" Cem.; Dau. of Clyde & Elsie (Meeks) Layne; companion; Carl Ellis Bryan
Layne, Patricia Carole (Vangaasbeck)	May 05, 1942	Apr 27, 2015	Swiss Cem.; Dau. of James Burton & Katherine (Sheeley) Vangaasbeck; m. 1) James Phillip Martin 2) Ricky Layne
Layne, Paul Edward	Jun 14, 1945	Oct 08, 2020	Griffith Creek Cem.; Son of Harley & Roxie (Graham) Layne; m. Mildred Johnson; U.S. Army
Layne, Rickey Gene	Jul 09, 1987	Apr 19, 2015	Fall Creek Cem.; Dau. of Rick Layne & Shona Basham

Layne, Rita Faye	Jul 03, 1970	Feb 08, 2019	Summerfield Cem.; Dau. of Yancie & Hilda Layne; m.____Bailey
Layne, Robert	Jun 2, 1898	Feb 25, 1952	Oak Grove Cem.; Son of Simeon Glover & Josephine (Summers) Layne; m. Mary Crowe; PVT 45 Infantry 9 Div TN WWII; correction of father's name & addition to Cemeteries of Grundy Co.,Vol. 1, p. 491
Layne, Robert Bradford	Dec 09, 1947	Apr 18, 2022	Plainview Cem.; Son of Bradford & Lora Lee (Hargis) Layne; m. Mary Erma Brookman
Layne, Rodney Gerald	Jul 22, 1944	Sep 02, 2018	Cremated; Son of Andrew Layne & Willie May Brown; m. Faye Cash
Layne, Ronnie Dwayne	Dec 29, 1950	Jul 18, 2017	Mt. View Cem. McMinnville, TN; Son of Robert Earl, Sr. & Clara O'Dell Layne; m. Karon Layne
Layne, Roy David	Jan 29, 1940	Aug 15, 1991	Palmer Cem.; Son of Jay Hugh & Emma (Lathrum) Layne; m. Louise Geary; Jan 22, 1933; addition to Cemeteries of Grundy Co.,Vol. 2, p. 570
Layne, Sherman	Dec 05, 1936	Sep 24, 2016	Cremated; Son of Abraham K. "Little Abe", Jr. & Edith (Hill) Layne Shirley; m. Patricia Dickerson
Layne, Tammy E.	Apr 03, 1971	Aug 13, 2006	Swiss Colony Cem.; Dau. of Grady & Linda (Morrison) Layne; correction to Cemeteries of Grundy Co.,Vol. 2, p. 795
Layne, William Harrison "Little Britches"	1812	1863	Burkett's Chapel Cem.; Son of David Stephen & Esther (Stephens) Layne; hanged by Confederates for being Union sympathizer per tombstone, but *Layne, Lain, Lane Genealogy* by Floyd Benjamin Layne says he was hanged by Union troops for supporting Confederates. addition to Cemeteries of Grundy Co.,Vol. 1, p. 118
Layne, William Kinnard "Kenny"	Sep 10, 1937	Jan 06, 2021	Fall Creek Cem.; Son of Daniel Leander & Hazel Ann (Tate) Layne; m. Dorma Doepel
Layne, William Lee	Jun 03, 1899	Jul 22, 1899	Burkett's Chapel Cem.; Son of Spencer & Mary J. (Smith) Layne
Layne, William Leonard	Feb 14, 1945	May 09, 2017	Cremated in Hillsboro,TX; Son of William Virgil & Rachel (Tidwell) Layne; m. 1) Margaret Loretta Hassebrock 2) Donna Jones
Layne, William Wayne	Jun 21, 1952	Dec 20, 2017	Swiss Colony Cem.; Son of Raymond & Thelma Summers Layne; m. Rhonda (Meeks) Layne
Layne, Willie Mae (Borne)	Apr 29, 1927	Oct 18, 2014	Fall Creek Cem.; Dau. of Jessie Arthur & Ada Bell (Nunley) Borne; m. Carl David Layne
Layne, Willie Mae (Brown)	Jul 24, 1922	Jul 14, 2017	Griffith's Creek Cem.; Dau. of Thomas & Aletha (Bell) Brown; m. Andrew Layne

Name	Born	Died	Notes
Lea Bailey, Mary Anna (Knight)	Oct 11, 1935	Oct 16, 2015	Hunerwadel Cem.; Dau. of Geroge William & Pearly Mae (Childers) Knight; m. Gerald Dean Lea 2) ____ Bailey
Lea, Gerald Dean "Poppie"	Feb 28, 1936	Jun 07, 1995	Hunerwadel Cem.; Son of Dan & Louise (Overton) Lea; m. Anna Knight; masonic symbol; addition to Cemeteries of Grundy Co., Vol. 1, p. 348
Leach, Henry Grady	Jul 04, 1924	Jul 11, 1991	Lappin Cem.; Son of Henry Grady, Sr. & Bessie Lee (Alexander) Leach; m. Alberta Lappin; addition to Cemeteries of Grundy Co., Vol. 1, p. 358
Leaird, Alfred	1840	Nov 23, 1871	Wesley Chapel Cem.; Son of William & Elva McLeard; m. Susan L. Christian; addition to Cemeteries of Grundy Co., Vol. 2, p. 979
Lecroy, Donna Elizabeth (Shadrick)	Sep 15, 1942	May 17, 2015	Fall Creek Cem.; Dau. of Barney & Estell (Brown) Shadrick; m. Larry T. Lecroy
Lecroy, Jeffrey "Darin"	Nov 22, 1965	Sep 09, 2013	Palmer Cem.; Son of Larry Thomas & Donna Elizabeth (Shadrick) Lecroy; m. Rhonda (Caldwell) McCory
LeCroy, Mamie Kathleen (Layne)	Apr 15, 1919	Nov 30, 2017	Fall Creek Cem.; Dau. of Mark & Bell Layne; m. Samuel Duke LeCroy
Ledbetter, Billy J.	May 30, 1944	Sep 25, 2017	Cremated; Son of Virgil & Ester (McFarland) Ledbetter; m. Margaret Ledbetter; US Marine Vietnam
Ledford, Billy Ray	Jan 28, 1936	Mar 24, 2013	Summerfield Cem.; Son of Thomas Franklin & Bessie (Lowhorn) Ledford
Lee, Banster	Jun 16, 1916	Jul 27, 2004	Altamont Cem.; Son of B.L. & Fannie Mae (Beard) Lee; m. Beulah Jane Cupp; Tec 5 US Army WWII; Addition to Cemeteries of Grundy Co., Vol. 1, p. 22
Lee, Ellen (Ahlstrom)	Apr 24, 1896	Jan 06, 1991	Altamont Cem.; Dau. of Klas Emil Andersson & Marie Kajsa (Danilesdotter) Ahlstrom; m. Harold Ellsworth Lee; addition to Cemeteries of Grundy Co., Vol. 1, p. 19
Lee, Harold Ellsworth	Feb 8, 1898	Jun 06, 1991	Altamont Cem.; Son of Peter Elbert & Katie E. (Higgins) Lee; m. Ellen Ahlstrom; addition to Cemeteries of Grundy Co, Vol. 1, p. 19
Lee, Nancy Clay	Jul 29, 1938	Jan 12, 2018	Gamaliel KY Cem.; Dau. of Paul D. Hughes & Ella P. Downing.; m. Paul R. Lee
Leedy, Harold S. III	Sep 06, 1963	Apr 14, 2022	Cremated; Son of Harold S., Jr. & Ruth (Tilghman) Leedy; m. Melissa "Missy" Rogers
Leiderman, Mitchell Bryan	Mar 30, 1977	Aug 25, 2021	Cremated; Son of Hoyt & Charlene Leiderman and step father, Stanley Floyd
Leiderman, Mitchell Hoyt	Jun 09, 1954	Aug 12, 2021	Cremated, ashes at Plainview Cem.; Son of Homer Mitchell Leiderman & Lily Oneida Barbee; m. Patti Nunley
Leiderman, Nita "Granny"	Jan 22, 1935	Oct 09, 2015	Plainview Cem.; unable to find information

Leitsinger, Henry	May 23, 1836	Feb 22, 1906	Swiss Colony Cem.; Son of Johann Heinrich & Agatha (Knobel) Leitseinger; m. Margaret Kubli; addition to Cemeteries of Grundy Co.,Vol. 2, p. 785
Leitsinger, Lydia Margaret (Smith)	Feb 1887	Jul 01, 1932	Swiss Colony Cem.; Dau. of Simon Peter & Irene Jane (Williams) Smith; m. Gabriel Leitsinger; addition to Cemeteries of Grundy Co.,Vol. 2, p. 789
Leitsinger, Margaret (Kubli)	Nov 20, 1836	Dec 07, 1913	Swiss Colony Cem.; Dau. of Gabriel & Mary Magdalenen Kubli; m. Henry Leitsinger; addition to Cemeteries of Grundy Co.,Vol. 2, p. 785
Leitzel, Jessie Robert	Sep 12, 1942	Jan 24, 2014	Cremated; Son of Donald & Bessie Leitzel; m. Jan Leitzel; USMC
Lenox, Betty (Rollings)	Jul 1, ,1930	Oct 2, 2020	Altamont Cem.; Dau. of Frank E. & Timmie L. (Scruggs) Rollings; m. John Gordon Lenox; addition to Cemeteries of Grundy Co.,Vol. 1, p. 23
Lenox, John Gordon	Feb 15, 1930	Oct 29, 2016	Altamont Cem.; Son of G. Merrill & Lydia (Frakenfield) Lenox; m. Betty Rollings; US Navy; addition to Cemeteries of Grundy Co.,Vol. 1, p. 23
Lenox, Stephen Rollings	Nov 27, 1965		Altamont Cem.; Son of John Gordon & Betty (Rollings) Lennox; addition to Cemeteries of Grundy Co.,Vol. 1, p. 23
Lentz, Geraldine (Conry)	1924	Oct 7, 2014	Athens City Cem. AL; Dau of Cam & Lorena (Wilson) Conry; m. Bill Lentz
Leonard, Joyce Inez (Upchurch)	1942	Jan 07, 2021	Roselawn Memorial Gardems, Murfreesboro; Dau. of Charlie & Ruby (Scantland) Upchurch; m. Floyd James "Nehi" Leonard
Levan, Daniel	1961	Aug 15, 2018	Plainview Cem.; Son of James Alton Levan & Lena Mae Scott; m. Celia "Sis" Levan
Levan, Fannie Elizabeth (Tate)	Sep 17, 1875	Jul 14, 1964	Oak Grove Cem.; Dau. of James & Tennessee (Layne) Levan; addition to Cemeteries of Grundy Co.,Vol. 1, p. 506
Levan, Frances (Bostain)	Feb 8, 1892	Dec 09, 1972	Fall Creek Cem.; Dau. of James M & Elizabeth (Whitehead) Bostain; m. Charles Oscar Levan
Levan, Hence	Jan 10, 1885	Died by 1930	Plainview Cem.; Son of Annie Levan ; m. Feb 15, 1903 to Timmie Fults; addition to Cemeteries of Grundy Co.
Levan, James Alton, Sr.	Apr 15, 1925	Feb 04, 2000	Plainview Cem.; Son of Hence & Timmie (Fults) Levan; m. Lena Mae Scott; US ARMY WWII; Addition to Cemeteries of Grundy Co,Vol. 2, p 699
Levan, Ressie Paul (Turner)	Mar 06, 1927	Jan 13, 2011	Fall Creek Cem.; Dau. of Robert Turner & Ester Morrison; m. Martin E. Levan

Name	Birth	Death	Details
Levan, Timmie (Fults)	May 22, 1886	Apr 15, 1968	Plainview Cem.; Dau. of Daniel & Evaline (Argo) Fults; m. Hence Levan; addition to Cemeteries of Grundy Co.,Vol. 2, p. 688
Lewis Oma Lee (Boyd)	Jul 05, 1924	Jan 13, 2019	Palmer Cem.; Dau. of Clyde Boyd & Pearl Worley; m. William Howard Lewis
Lewis, Priscilla Fay (Caldwell)	Feb 28, 1961	Nov 14, 2014	Cremated; Dau of Melvin Ray Caldwell & Floye Green; m. Phillip Lewis
Lewis, Billy Wayne	Apr 28, 1939	Dec 22, 1989	Plainview Cem.; Son of Phillip s. & Alma (Sons) Lewis; SGT US ARMY
Lewis, Carlos Everett	Oct 31, 1944	Apr 29, 2013	Giles Memory Gardens; Son of George Herbert & Della (Brown) Lewis; m. Deborah Kirkendoll; US Army
Lewis, Cheryl Lynn (Shook)	Jul 31, 1948	Aug 01, 1987	Pryor Ridge Cem.; Dau. of Leonard Clint & Reba Bernice (Jenness) Shook; m. Joe Allison Lewis, Jr.; addition to Cemeteries of Grundy Co.,Vol. 2, p. 716
Lewis, George Herbert	Feb 1, 1897	Jul 21, 1981	White Cem.; Son of George Washington & Lydia Ellen (Murray) Lewis; m. Flora (White) Cook; addition to Cemeteries of Grundy Co.,Vol. 2, p. 1011
Lewis, Gloria	Sep 01, 1927	Dec 11, 2016	Cremated; m. Edward Lewis
Lewis, Jimmy Don	Apr 28, 1940	Jul 11, 2017	Summerfield Cem.; Son of Hobart & Willie (Green) Lewis; m. Jo Anne Anderson
Lewis, Oma Lee (Boyd)	Jul 05, 1924	Jan 13, 2019	Palmer Cem.; Dau. of Clyde & Pearl (Worley) Boyd; m. Dec 19, 1941, to William Howard Lewis; addition to Cemeteries of Grundy Co.,Vol. 2, p. 578
Lewis, Thomas Howard	Sep 15, 1964	Apr 06, 2015	Cremated; Son of Howard Creig & Linda Faye (Pyburn) Lewis; m. Bonnie Pritchett; U.S. Navy
Lewis, Tim Joe	Mar 08, 1968	May 02, 2021	Cremated; Son of Joe A. & Cheryl Lynn (Shook) Lewis; m. Francine Lewis
Lewis, Timothy Dan	May 19, 1959	Mar 17, 2014	Franklin Memorial; Son of Danny "Jughead" & Virginia (Garner) Lewis; m. Barbara Payne; US Army
Lewis, William Austin	Jul 29, 1938	Jan 04, 2016	Palmer Cem.; Son of Hayden & Susie Lewis; m. Shelva Jean Cleek; US Navy
Lewis, William Howard	Apr 05, 1923	Oct 24, 2018	Palmer Cem.; Son of Hubert W. & Lela (Tate) Lewis; m. Oma Lee Boyd, Dec 19, 1941; addition to Cemeteries of Grundy Co.,Vol. 2, p. 578
Lillie, Catherine Ellen	Jan 6, 1884	Apr 09, 1976	Altamont Cem.; Dau. of William F. & Katie Isabell (DeMaranville) Philbrick; m. Charles Phelps Lillie; addition to Cemeteries of Grundy Co.,Vol. 1, p. 30
Lincoln, Miriam Illsey	Nov 18, 1920	Feb 04, 2016	Eastern Star Cem.; Dau. of Edward & Emma Illsey; m. 1) Alexander Benton Lincoln 2) Roy Jack Sarver

Name	Birth	Death	Details
Lind, John Hilding	Dec 05, 1947	May 13, 2006	Fults Cem Northcutt's Cove; Son of Hilding & Gladys Violet (Rundquist) Lind; m. 1) Sally Hamilton 2) Deborah Annette (Smartt) Wanamaker; m. Aug 13, 1983; addition to Cemeteries of Grundy Co.,Vol. 1, p. 284
Linkous, Anna J.	Jul 28, 1969	Feb 07, 2014	Burkett's Chapel Cem.; Dau. of Robert Leo & Brenda Sue Linkous
Linton, Charles Jones	May 3, 1814	May 9, 1871	Tracy City Cem.; b. England; served in CSA 1st Infantry; m. Mary Jane Walker who was b. in England; addition to Cemeteries of Grundy Co.,Vol. 2, p. 890
Little, Patricia Ann (Campbell)	May 12, 1955	Dec 11, 2007	Little Johnny Myers Cem.; Dau. of Melvin Franklin & Willene (Phillips) Campbell; m. Lawrence Merrill Perkins of WV 2) Dennis Castleman of CA 3) James Little; addition to Cemeteries of Grundy Co., information per family; Vol. 1, p. 366
Ljungblad, Inga Thuridor (Gohl)	Mar 11, 1894	Mar 01, 1983	Altamont Cem.; Dau. of Hampas Fritsof & Josefa Christina (Lungblad) Gohl; m. Jonas Emanuel Ljungblad; addition to Cemeteries of Grundy Co.,Vol. 1, p. 34
Ljungblad, Jonas Emanuel	Nov 10, 1894	Jul 17, 1974	Altamont Cem.; Son of Carl August & Amelia (Gustafsdotter) Ljungblad; m. Inga Thuridor Gohl; addition to Cemeteries of Grundy Co.,Vol. 1, p. 34
Lobdell, Minnie Ctherine	May 15, 1870	May 23, 1963	Tracy City Cem.; Dau. of Peter A. & Ruth Miller; m. Frank W. Lobdell; addition to Cemeteries of Grundy Co.,Vol. 2, p. 856
Locke, Emma Clara (Wooten)	Ca. Jul 1870	Sep 04, 1927	Tracy City Cem.; Dau. of Thomas Benton & Susan Anna (Vaughn) Wooten; m. William Setliffe Locke, ca. 1894; no marker; addition to Cemeteries of Grundy Co.,Vol. 2, p. 844
Lockhart, Alta Josephine	Nov 07, 1934	May 15, 1966	Orange Hill Cem.; Dau. of Herbert "Louis" & Lillie Irene (Roach) Frye; m. Paul Eugene Lockhart; addition to Cemeteries of Grundy Co.Vol. 2, p. 532
Lockhart, Andy	Jan 26, 1933	Jun 09, 2019	Altamont Cem.; Son of Allen Lockhart & Octa Whitman; m. Edith Blondell Northcutt; U.S. Air Force
Lockhart, Bettie	Ca. 1844	Jun 02, 1916	Tracy City area; died in Dykes Hollow; source *Mrs. Grundy* Jun 8, 2016
Lockhart, Bobby Eugene	Dec 30, 1939	Oct 20, 2019	Orange Hill Cem.; Son of William Henry Lockhart & Veola Christine O'Neal; U.S. Army
Lockhart, Buford William	Jul 25, 1902	May 12, 1946	Altamont Cem.; Son of William Condit & Elizabeth "Bettie" (Summers) Lockhart; addition to Cemeteries of Grundy Co.,Vol. 1, p. 34

Name	Birth	Death	Notes
Lockhart, Edgar Monroe	Apr 22, 1883	Dec 14, 1883	Brown's Chapel Cem.; Son of James Monroe & Sarah Jane (Brown) Lockhart; addition to Cemeteries of Grundy Co., Vol. 1, p. 109
Lockhart, Elizabeth "Bettie" (Summers)	Dec 25, 1871	Mar 16, 1957	Altamont Cem.; Dau. of John W. & Martha Elizabeth (Guess) Summers; m. Willie Condit Lockhart; addition to Cemeteries of Grundy Co., Vol. 1, p. 33
Lockhart, George C.	Jun 22, 1879	Jun 22, 1879	Brown's Chapel Cem.; Son of James Monroe & Sarah Jane (Brown) Lockhart; addition to Cemeteries of Grundy Co., Vol. 1, p. 109
Lockhart, Hester (Ross)	Nov 02, 1908	Apr 03, 1975	Ross Mountain Cem.; Back of stone says In Memory of Hester (Ross) Lockhart, dau of Samuel & Nellie Gertrude Ross; Hester is buried at Orange Hill Cem.; m. Oscar Lockhart; addition to Cemeteries of Grundy Co., Vol. 2, p. 726
Lockhart, James Leonard "Sandy"	Feb 15, 1912	Oct 28, 1965	White Cem.; Son of Milton Dixon & Winnie (Sutton) Lockhart; m. Margaret Andrews Wideman on Sep 5, 1958; correction and addition to Cemeteries of Grundy Co. Vol. 2, p. 1006
Lockhart, Jason Wallice	Dec 16, 1979	Jun 12, 2014	Palmer Cem.; Son of Jerry Lockhart & Dianne Cherry; m. Sarah Lockhart
Lockhart, John Willie	May 09, 1929	Jan 10, 2013	Altamont Cem.; Son of Allen & Octa (Whitman) Lockhart; m. Margaret McCutcheon
Lockhart, Lucy (Hunter)	Apr 8, 1848	Mar 03, 1936	Altamont Cem.; Dau. of Squire & Elizabeth Hunter; m. Joseph S. Lockhart; addition to Cemeteries of Grundy Co., Vol. 1, p. 34
Lockhart, Margaret (McCutchen)	Sep 05, 1936	Mar 28, 2015	Altamont Cem.; Dau. of Merzy & Lillian (Greene) McCutchen ; m. John Willie Lockhart
Lockhart, May Belle (Shadrick)	Sep 11, 1888	Sep 3, 1986	Bonny Oak Cem.; Dau. of Anderson & Nancy (Dove) Shadrick; m. Roy Lee Shadrick; addition to Cemeteries of Grundy Co., Vol. 1, p. 88
Lockhart, Minnie (Nunley)	Jun 02, 1914	Apr 02, 2014	Bonny Oak Cem.; Dau. of Joe & Lydia (Woodlee) Nunley; m. Earl Lockhart; correction and addition to Cemeteries of Grundy Co. Vol. 1, p. 85
Lockhart, Stephen Allen	May 10, 1966	May 10, 1966	Oak Grove Cem.; Son of Paul Eugene & Alta Josephine Lockhart; addition to Cemeteries of Grundy Co., Vol. 2, p. 532
Lockhart, Toby Bradford	Oct 13, 1987	Sep 23, 2013	Plainview Cem.; Son of Troy Lockhart & Rhonda Kay Roddy; m. Whitney Parson
Lockhart, Violet Marie (Garner)	Aug 28, 1929	Aug 19, 2019	Brown's Chapel Cem.; Dau. of Hobert & Myrtle (Sissom) Garner; m. Willie "Elder" Lockhart; addition to Cemeteries of Grundy Co., Vol. 1, p.108

Lockhart, William E.	Jul 06, 1947	Feb 02, 1974	Altamont Cem.; Son of Mary Nell Dove; addition to Cemeteries of Grundy Co.Vol. 1, p. 27
Logan, Bobby Lee	Jan 17, 1938	Jun 12, 2008	Plainview Cem.; Son of Johnny Foy & Hattie Mae Kelly; addition to Cemeteries of Grundy Co.,Vol. 2, p. 704
Lohman, Evelyn M. (Smith)	Dec 08, 1915	Apr 06, 2015	Cumberland Heights Cem.; Dau. of Merrill & Bessie (Bower) Smith; m. Melvin Lohman
Long, Abram Wallace	Nov 30, 1877	Dec 04, 1933	Palmer Cem.; Son of James Riley & Louisa Ann "Lucy" (Cotton) Long; m. Myrtle Ova Owen; addition to Cemeteries of Grundy Co.,Vol. 2, p. 571
Long, Carol Lee (Meeks)	Aug 22, 1942	Sep 30, 2020	Palmer Cem.; Dau. of Elihugh & Alma Jean (Givens) Meeks; m. Theodore Lindley Long, Jr.
Long, Charles Edward	Oct 18, 1942	Mar 20, 2018	Cremated; Son of William Houston Long & Orphia Carlee Bouldin; m. Bennie Kay Grissom
Long, Colleene "Cookie" (Burnette)	Dec 25, 1938 other sources 1935	Dec 27, 1997	Monteagle Cem.; Dau. of James C. & Emma (Hargis) Burnette; m. Bill D. Long; addition to Cemeteries of Grundy Co.,Vol. 1, p. 419
Long, Joyce Winona	Jul 04, 1928	Apr 27, 2013	Fall Creek Cem.; Dau. of Doug & Mabel (Henley) Sweeton; m. James E. "Jim" Long
Long, June Ann (Smith)	Jun 06, 1927	Mar 12, 2013	Cremated; Dau. of George & Myrtle (McFarland) Smith; m. Kenneth Long
Long, Lloyd Raymond	Sep 12, 1948	Apr 22, 2019	Franklin Memorial Gardens Cem.; Son of Lloyd "Dean" Palmer Long & Ruby Anna Mae Partin
Long, Lula Ann "Lou"	1870	1896	Monteagle Cem.; Dau. of Cornelius & Lourany (Skillin) Long
Long, Margaret Pearson (Marks)	Jan 15, 1924	May 23, 2020	Paririe Plains Church of Christ Cem.; Dau. of Felix Marks & Lou Alma Cash; m. William Albro Long
Long, Myrtle Ova (Owen)	Dec 19, 1896	Jan 10, 1995	Palmer Cem.; Day of John Savage & Geraldine (Farrar) Owens; m. Abram Wallace Long; addition to Cemeteries of Grundy Co.,Vol. 2, p. 571
Long, Sue Ann	Apr 03, 1940	Sep 29, 2016	Palmer Cem.; Dau. of Arthur & Jessie (Shrum) Land; m. 1) Gene Cleek 2) Kelso Long
Long, William Bertram	Jan 15, 1930	Aug 15, 2017	Eastern Star Cem.; Son of William & Berthe (Garner) Long
Lovett, Mark William	Jul 01, 1953	Jan 18, 2018	Son of Joseph William Lovett, Jr. & Arlyn Ruth Ende; m. Claire Reggio
Lowe, John Wesley	Nov 1, 1876	Aug 25, 1941	Oak Gruove Cem.; Son of William Patterson & Faithy (Sitz) Lowe; no marker; death certificate
Lowe, Velma (Turner) "Little Un"	Jan 17, 1942	Apr 11, 2016	Plainview Cem.; Dau. of Marllin & Margie (Sweeton) Turner; m. Kenny Lowe

Name	Birth	Death	Details
Lowrie, Charlene A. (Thomas)	Jul 29, 1924	Aug 10, 2015	Monteagle Cem.; Dau. of Charlie & Nettie (Holder) Thomas; m. Wm. David "Bill" Lowrie
Lowrie, James William	Oct 07, 1940	Mar 18, 2021	Monteagle Cem.; Son of Harold Lappin & Anna Lee (Gossett) Lowrie; m. Tana Terrill
Loyd, Jack Williams "Bill Jack"	Sep 01, 1934	Aug 16, 2017	Plainview Cem.; Son of Cecil & Esther (Williams) Loyd; m. 1) Jeanette Griffith 2) Mary Conry ; USMC
Luchsinger, Hilarius	Oct 28, 1834	Oct 23, 1883	Swiss Colony Cem.; Son of Jackob & Anna (Blumer) Luchsinger; m. Barbara Trumpy; addition to Cemeteries of Grundy Co.,Vol. 2, p. 784
Luchsinger, John B.	Aug 1, 1857	Jan 12, 1944	Swiss Colony Cem.; Son of Hilbrey & Fannie Luchsinger; m. Verena Leuzi; addition to Cemeteries of Grundy Co.,Vol. 2, p. 789
Luchsinger, Verena (Leuzi)	Dec 10, 1861	Jan 31, 1941	Swiss Colony Cem.; Dau. of Kaspar & Verena (Weber) Luchsinger; m. John B. Luchsinger; addition to Cemeteries of Grundy Co.,Vol. 2, p. 789
Ludwig, Alfred II "Big Al"	May 21, 1950	Apr 19, 2021	Cremated; Son of Tom & Veda Ludwig; m. Mary Ludwig; lived in Monteagle, TN.
Lusk, Bessie Bolen (Cecil)	Mar 15, 1925	May 07, 2015	Airview Cem.; Dau. of Charles Walter & Matilda Belle (Bolen) Cecil; m. Earl T. Lusk; addition to Cemeteries of Grundy Co.,Vol. 1, p. 7
Lusk, Clarron Delton	Feb 20, 1943	May 22, 2020	AirView Cem.; Son of Thomas Clinton Lusk & Cora Lee Beaird; m. Phyllis Housley
Lusk, Opal (McCuiston)	May 10, 1931	Apr 14, 2016	Airview Cem.; Dau. of Ralph & Mary (Snyder) McCuiston. m. Byron Hugh Lusk; addition to Cemeteries of Grundy Co.,Vol. 1, p. 6
Lyle, Sadie Anastasia	Jan 21, 2009	Jul 01, 2018	Cremated; Dau. of Steven Matt & Sarah Lyle; lived in Tracy City
Lynch, Earl Edison	Jan 05, 1919	Aug 01, 1976	Plainview Cem.; Son of Justice James Gable & Laura Elizabeth (Bryant) Lynch; m. Mary Kathleen Layne; PFC US ARMY WWII; addition to Cemeteries of Grundy Co.Vol. 2, p. 673
Lynch, Mary Kathleen (Layne)	Jun 28, 1929	Apr 07, 1993	Plainview Cem.; Dau. of Fred & Mittie Rutellie (Kilgore) Layne; m. Earl Edison Lynch; addition to Cemeteries of Grundy Co.,Vol. 2, p. 673
Lynn, Helen Northcutt	Oct 14, 1945	Jan 05, 2016	Mt. Zion Cem in Viola, TN; Dau. of Clarence & Lydia Mae (Fults) Northcutt; m. Clark Lynn
Machen, Nina (Christa)	Oct 09, 1933	Apr 27, 2021	Sequatchie Valley Memorial Gardens; Dau. of Jesse & Florence (Miles) Christa; m. 1) Kenneth Eugene Tanner 2) James Machen
Madewell, Ray	Jan 12, 1947	Jun 06, 2020	Spencer Town Cem.; Son of Elbert Madewell & Gladys Simmons; m. Shirley Jean Rigsby

Name	Born	Died	Details
Maeder, Elizabeth	May 22, 1866	Jul 16, 1881	Swiss Colony Cem.; Dau. of Jacob & Katharina Aplanalp; m. Jacob Maeder; addition to Cemeteries of Grundy Co. Vol. 2, p. 784
Magouirk, Annie Alberta "Bertie"	Aug 21, 1920	Nov 21, 2018	Payne's Cove Cem.; Dau. of Lanson O'Dell "Dellie" & Annie (Layne) Gilliam; m. Dorcie Allen Magouirk; addition to Cemeteries of Grundy Co., Vol. 2, p. 594
Magouirk, DJ, Jr.	Nov 15, 1958	Jun 25, 2020	Plainview Cem.; Son of D J & Bertie Mae Magouirk; m. Cindy Magouirk
Magouirk, Don Allen	Jul 22, 1945	Feb 05, 2021	Palmer Cem.; Son of Paul V. & Amelia (Payne) Magouirk; m. Doris Layne
Magouirk, George Washington	Apr 6, 1834	Feb 09, 1917	Payne's Cove Cem.; Son of John & Annie (Coldwell) Magouirk, both born in VA; m. Martha Elizabeth Ooley; Thought to be buried here. Source *Mrs. Grundy*, Feb 15, 1917
Magouirk, James William, Jr.	Jan 27, 1933	May 21, 2020	Summerfield Cem.; Son of James William, Sr. & Mary Etta (Watley) Magouirk; m. Robena Thomas; addition to Cemeteries of Grundy Co., Vol. 2, p. 775
Magouirk, James William, Sr.	Jul 10, 1910	Apr 01, 1973	Rhea Co. Memory Gardens in Dayton, TN; Raised by grandmother Martha (Ooley) Magouirk; m.1) Mary Etta Watley 2) Edna E. Magouirk
Magouirk, Kenneth Wayne	Dec 20, 1938	Sep 27, 2018	Gnat Hill Cem.; Son of James William Magouirk & Mary Etta (Watley) Magouirk; m. Shirley Jacobs
Magouirk, Nacole Church	Jun 04, 1975	Jul 04, 2018	Plainview Cem.; Dau. of D J & Cindy Magouirk & Bobby & Teresa Church- both couples listed as parents in her obituary.
Magouirk, Ruth (Pemberton)	Apr 26, 1948	Sep 30, 2020	Brown's Chapel Cem.; Clarence & Geneva (Blaylock) Pemberton; m. Jerry Magouirk
Magouirk, Thermon B.	Jan 09, 1939	Nov 09, 2016	Brown's Chapel Cem.; Son of Francis & Lena (Smith) Magouirk; m. Eleanor Ross
Magourik, Betty Sue (Thompson)	May 11, 1940	Jul 01, 2003	Boot's Garden, the Magourik Family Cemetery; Dau of Wilburn & Berniect Thompson; m. Ray Magourik Same family as Magouirk, but spelling was changed when he was in the military
Magourik, Tammy Jeanice	Nov 24, 1962	Dec 14, 2021	Magourik Family "Boot's Garden" Cem.; Dau. of Ray & Betty Sue (Thompson) Magourik; companion, Alton King
Mainord, Tegan Brooke	Apr 20, 2021	Dec 05, 2021	Fall Creek Cem.; Dau. of Trinton & Terra Mainord
Malde, Motichand	Apr 14, 1925	Oct 10, 2020	Cremated; Son of Lakha Jerual & Lathi Ladhiben Malde; m. Bhanu Malde ; born in India

Name	Birth	Death	Details
Malone, Edith M.	Aug 02, 1933	Apr 20, 1998	Palmer Cem.; Dau. of James Henry & Mamie Lee (Cope) Lankford; addition to Cemeteries of Grundy Co., Vol. 2, p. 554
Manders, Solomon W.	Mar 21, 1841	Jul 11, 1913	Unidentified Cem.; Son of John & Ellen Manders; m. NJ Manders; Military L 5th TN Cavalry Civil War; source *Mrs Grundy*, Jul 22, 1913
Manders, Young	Ca 1886	Jul 31, 1913	Unidentified Cem.; m. Julia Tate on Jan 10, 1907; source *Mrs Grundy* Aug 7, 1913
Mankin, Mrs. Erp		Mar 11, 1903	Unidentified Cem.; Mother of Brown Mankin; newspaper death notice
Mankin, Sarah Jane (Long) "Sallie"	Jun 26, 1963	Dec 17, 1952	Monteagle Cem.; Dau. of Cornelius & Lourany (Skillin) Long; m. 1) Henry Schaerer 2) Brown H. Mankin; correction of birth date, maiden name & parents to Cemeteries of Grundy Co., Vol. 1, p. 387
Manley, Dennis W.	Jul 31, 1943	Mar 01, 2021	Plainview Cem.; Son of James H. "Son" & Helen F. (O'Neal) Manley; m. Ella Virginia "Dolly" Lynch on Jan 1, 1963; addition to Cemeteries of Grundy Co.
Manley, Ella Virginia "Dolly" (Lynch)	Jul 16, 1948	Apr 07, 2015	Plainview Cem.; Dau. of Earl & Tootsie (Layne) Lynch; m. Dennis W. Manley; addition to Cemeteries of Grundy Co., Vol. 2, p. 701
Manley, James Galen "Shim"	Feb 09, 1963	Jan 01, 2011	Coalmont Cem.; Son of Hayden Francis & Hazel (Scissom) Manley; m. Regina Kay Jackson
Manley, Robert Ray	Jun 21, 1937	Jul 01, 1938	Oak Grove Cem.; Son of James Henry & Helen Frankie (O'Neal) Manley; addition to Cemeteries of Grundy Co., Vol. 1
Manning, Marie (Dickerson)	Jun 01, 1922	Dec 12, 2012	Altamont Cem.; Dau. of Ame David & Sallie (Givens) Dickerson; m. Benny Manning; addition to Cemeteries of Grundy Co., Vol. 1, p. 21
Mansfield, Jonathan "Noodle"	May 13, 1960	Dec 19, 2020	Cremated; Son of Jerry & Juanita (Mooney) Mansfield; m. Patty (Winton) Milner
Mansfield, Laura (Smith)	Ca. 1850	Feb 15, 1883	Wesley Chapel Cem.; Dau. of Rebecca Smith; m. John William Mansfield; aged 32y, 3m, 15d; addition to Cemeteries of Grundy Co., Vol. 2, p. 977
Manus, Wilma Tate	Dec 12, 1944	May 22, 2016	Grace Chapel Cem.; Dau. of Nathaniel & Lola (Roberts) Tate; m. Gene Manus
Martin, Corinne H.	Jan 25, 1931	Jul 13, 2010	Cumberland Mennonite Fellowship Cem.; Dau. of Aaron H. & Amanda (Horst) Martin; m. Lehman Martin
Martin, Estie (Crouch)	Nov 29, 1866	Nov 28, 1923	Wesley Chapel Cem.; Dau. of Isaac & Elizabeth (Lovelace) Crouch; correction to Cemeteries of Grundy Co., Vol. 2, p. 960

Name	Born	Died	Notes
Martin, Hilda Marie (Nunley)	Mar 03, 1972	Jul 28, 2020	Gardens of Memory Cem.; Dau. of William Carol Nunley & Barbara Grace Scheisser; m. Willis Edwin Martin
Martin, Jack Andrew	Mar 06, 1987	Nov 06, 2021	Clouse Hill Cem.; Son of Stephen & Jill (Shelnut) Martin
Martin, James Phillip	Dec 13, 1940	Mar 03, 2006	Swiss Colony Cem.; Son of William James & Mary Delores (Longendyke) Martin; m. Patricia C. Vangaasbek; addition to Cemeteries of Grundy Co., Vol. 2, p. 792
Martin, Lehman	Apr 16, 1931	Apr 09, 2017	Cumberland Mennonite Fellowship Cem.; Son of Isaac Eby & Susan (Hedge) Martin; m. Corinne Horst
Martin, Mildred (Ray)	Oct 15, 1931	Apr 30, 2002	Lappin Cem.; Dau. of Hobert & Annie (Hawkins) Ray; m. Halson Wooten Martin; addition to Cemeteries of Grundy Co., Vol. 1, p. 358
Martin, Patricia C. (Van Gaasbek)	May 05, 1942	Apr 27, 2015	Swiss Colony Cem.; Dau. of James Burton & Kathryn (Sheeley) VanGaasbek; m. James Phillip Martin; addition to Cemeteries of Grundy Co., Vol. 2, p. 792
Martin, Thomas	Aug 18, 1836	Aug 17, 1911	Wesley Chapel Cem.; Son of Evan & Mary Martin; correction to Cemeteries of Grundy Co; Vol. 2 , p. 960
Martin, Wanda K. (Gilliam)	Jun 25, 1945	Jan 22, 2021	Cremated in Florida; Dau. of Austin & Mary Kathleen (Bennett) Gilliam; m. Thomas A. Martin
Masingill, Charles Edward	Apr 09, 1928	May 02, 2021	Chattanooga National Veterans Cem.; Son of William & Mary Kelly (Harlow) Masingill; m. Carolyn Sitz; U.S. Navy , U.S. Marine Corps.
Mason, Barbara Reave	Oct 05, 1964	Jan 04, 2021	Mount Carmel Cem., Bridgeport; Dau. of Howard Price & Freda (Jones) Mason
Mason, Jerry Q	Jan 28, 1933	May 12, 2013	Cremated; Son of Walter Scott & Flora Mae (Garner) Mason; m. Elsie Jean Tate
Mason, Nancy Jane (Farrell)	Mar 25, 1857	Oct 8, 1877	Tracy City Cem.; Dau. of Patrick & Margaret (Jenkins) Farrell; m. Daniel Mason; stone not found, but was in Charles Sherrill's book in 1988; addition to Cemeteries of Grundy Co., Vol. 2, p. 890
Mason, Thurman Lee	Aug 19, 1935		Hunerwadel Cem: Son of Waymon & Joann (Halterman) Mason; m. Sylvia Jane Hill; addition to Cemeteries of Grundy Co. Vol. 1, p. 344
Massey, Bessie Mae (Layne)	Jul 12, 1898	Apr 03, 1946	Monteagle Cem.; Dau. of Preston Franklin & Elizabeth (Hopkins) Layne ; m. George Massey; correction to Grundy County Cemetery Book Vol. 1, p. 422
Mathews, Steve Allen	Oct 22, 1953	Dec 18, 2017	Cremated; Son of Bill & Dorothy (Luttrel) Mathews; companion, Carolyn (Click) Conry

Name	Born	Died	Details
Matney, Issic Lee	May 18, 2009	Apr 27, 2019	Fall Creek Cem.; Son of Jeffery Lee Matney & Nellie Singleton
May, Judy	Jul 04, 1943	Aug 07, 2017	Cremated; Dau. of Willie Winton & Louella (Crabtree) Tucker; m. Ernest R. May
Mayes, Diane M (Meeks)	Apr 10, 1957	Feb 16, 2021	Winton Cem.; Dau. of Fred & Marlee Meeks; m. Billy Mayes
Mayes, Gary W.	May 13, 1946		Warren "Red Hill" Cem.; Son of Blantford "B.F"& Dorothy (Meeks) Mayes; US Army
Mayes, Glenn A.	Mar 26, 1940	Aug 17, 2015	Monteagle Cem.; Son of Roy & Veola (Patrick) Mayes; m. Maxine Layne
Mayes, Johnnie Maxine (Layne)	Sep 22, 1941	Jan 22, 2019	Monteagle Cem.; Dau. of Cleveland & Clara Mai Layne; m. Glenn Mayes
Mayes, Kenneth L	Dec 01, 1940		Warren "Red Hill" Cem.; Son of Blantford & Dorothy (Meeks) Mayes; m. Linda Gayle Rieder, May 28,1960
Mayes, Linda Gayle (Rieder)	Mar 01, 1940		Warren "Red Hill" Cem.; Dau. of Lloyd & Georgia Fay (Garner) Rieder; m. Kenneth Mayes
Maynard, Ova (Moore)	Feb 18, 1881	Feb 20, 1962	Fall Creek Cem.; Dau. of George W. & Darthula Moore; m. Waymon L. Maynard
Maynard, Waymon, L.	May 13, 1881	Feb 26, 1956	Fall Creek Cem.; Son of Kendrick & Dorthena (Haston) Maynard; m. Ova Moore
Mc Daniel, Bunia Lee (Argo)	May 31, 1922	Jun 09, 2000	Coalmont Cem.; Dau of Doston & Sally Ann (Nunley) Argo; m William Eugene McDaniel
Mc Farland, Lillie Myrtle "Daisy" (Tucker)	1888	1967	Monteagle Cem.; Dau. of David Thomas "Dan" & Isabelle "Belle" (Ragsdale) Tucker; m. James N. McFarland, Feb 16, 1901; addition to Cemeteries of Grundy Co., Vol. 1, p. 398
Mc Govern, Phillip H.	May 8, 1887	May 16, 1953	Hobbs Hill Cem.; Son of John & Vina (Sanders) McGovern; m. Nancy Kilgore; addition to Cemeteries of Grundy Co., Vol. 1, p. 336
McAfee, Sharon (Dodd)	Nov 08, 1957	Oct 21, 2020	Soddy Presbyterian Cem.; Dau. of F.L. "Hokey" & Vera Louise (Reynolds) Dodd; m. Danny McAfee
McAlpine, Susan (Gilliam)	Nov 04, 1957	Aug 28, 2019	Monteagle Cem.; Dau. of George Louise (Turner) Gilliam & Louise Turner; m. Davis A. McAlpine
McAmis, Jean Hobbs	Aug 27, 1958	Mar 30, 2019	Fults Cem.; Dau. of Clyde James & Imogene (Hobbs) McAmis
McBee, Aylene L. (Layne)	Dec 22, 1932	Feb 02, 2020	Palmer Cem.; Dau. of Pat Layne & Cleo (Sanders) Harvey; m. Jim Dave McBee, Dec 24, 1955; addition to Cemeteries of Grundy Co., Vol. 2, p. 566

Name	Born	Died	Details
McBee, Edgar William	Nov 21, 1891	Dec 08, 1964	Lappin Cem: Son of Churchwell & Malinda (Hill) McBee; m Lora Bertha Sherrill on Apr 7, 1910; addition to Cemeteries of Grundy Co., Vol. 1, p. 359
McBee, Etta Mae (Braden)	Dec 16, 1937	Dec 21, 2018	Hamilton Memorial Gardens Cem.; Dau. of William & Bessie Braden; m. James N. McBee
McBee, Frances Louise (Pace)	Dec 20, 1926	Oct 17, 2013	Monteagle Cem.; Dau. of Henry & Irene Pace; m. Paul McBee
McBee, James Edward	Jun 09, 1956	Mar 29, 2018	Mtn. View Cem.; Son of William Edward McBee & Bertha Hill
Mcbee, Julie Ann	Nov 01, 1959	Jun 17, 2018	Cremated; Dau. of William Edward McBee & Bertha Lee Hill; companion, James "Punkin" Shetters
McBee, Leona (Rose) Hawk	Jul 15, 1922	Jan 31, 2015	Franklin County Memorial Gardens Cem.; Dau. of Dick & Emma Rose; m. 1) D. C. Hawk 2) Lawrence McBee
McBee, Terrell Keith	Sep 28, 1958	Mar 18, 2020	Palmer Cem.; Son of James David "Jim Dave" McBee & Alyene Layne; m. Renee Hart
McCampbell, Jaime Elizabeth	Jan 11, 1977	Jul 07, 2020	Plainview Cem.; Dau. of James "Peanut" & Terri Yvonne Campbell; companion Shane Meeks
McCanless, Paulette	Jun 24, 1930	Jan 05, 2017	Oak Grove Cem.; Dau. of Foster & Ethel (Crowe) Stevens; m. Willie Earl McCanless
McCanless, Willie Earl	Oct 16, 1928	Aug 20, 1989	Oak Grove Cem.; Son of William Edward & Katie (Smith) McCanless; m. Paulette Stevens; U.S. Navy WWII; addition to Cemeteries of Grundy Co., Vol. 1, p. 511
McCann, Elizabeth (Duncan)	Dec 20, 1921	Jul 12, 1999	Oak Grove Cem.; Dau. of Robert S. & Virginia O. (Sherrill) Duncan; m. Dallas Porter McCann; addition to Cemeteries of Grundy Co., Vol. 1, p. 501
McCarver, Rosie Nell	Jun 27, 1946	Aug 23, 2015	Mt. Pleasant Cem. in Cagle; Dau. of Harvey & Elizabeth (Tate) Howell; m. David McCarver
McClain, Richard Lee	Aug 27, 1941	Aug 19, 2021	Cremated; Son of Charles Edward & Marie (Rogers) McClain; m. Bernice Sanders
McClure, Fannie	Mar 23, 1879	May 06, 1946	Altamont Cem.; Dau. of James & Sallie (Fults) McClure; addition to Cemeteries of Grundy Co., Vol. 1, p. 24
McClure, James Madison	Dec 15, 1833	Apr 27, 1919	Altamont Cem.; Son of William & Margaret Jane (White) McClure; m. Sallie Fults; Pvt. Co 1 TN Inf. CSA; addition to Cemeteries of Grundy Co., Vol. 1, p. 24
McClure, Sallie (Fults)	May 10, 1854	Feb 06, 1932	Altamont Cem.; Dau. of Joseph & Jenny Fults; m. James McClure; addition to Cemeteries of Grundy Co., Vol. 1, p. 24

Name	Birth	Death	Details
McCord, Anna (Smith)	1869	1941	Tracy City Cem.; Dau. of James Albert & Mary Alice (Williams) Smith; wife of Samuel B. McCord; addition to Cemeteries of Grundy Co., Vol. 2, p. 828
McCormick, Ann (Rhea)	Sep 30, 1943	May 26, 2022	Mount Zion Cem.; Dau. of Russ & Mae Rhea
McCormick, Clifford Levander	Apr 01, 1900	Oct 17, 2014	Jerico Cem, in White County; Son of Bransford Levander & Mary "Molly" (Holder) McCormick ; m. 1) Evelyn Kilgore 2) Mary Alice Causey
McCormick, Nelson Wayne	Sep 09, 1954	Jan 12, 2014	Tracy City Cem.; Son of Clifford L. & Mary Evelyn (Kilgore) McCormick; m. Debbie Ann Waldo
McCormick, Raymond E.	Jul 13,1933	Apr 07, 2015	Wesley Chapel Cem.; Son of Jim & Minnie (Sanders) McCormick; m. Tressie Myers
McCormick, Raymond Earl	Jul 13, 1933	Apr 07, 2015	Wesley Chapel Cem;Son of Jim & Minnie (Sanders) McCormick; addition to Cemeteries of Grundy Co., Vol. 2, p. 984
McCormick, Rosie Della (Dickerson)	Dec 13, 1929	Jun 25, 2002	Wesley Chapel Cem.; Dau. of Tom & Mary (Brown) Dickerson; m. William Ace McCormick; addition to Cemeteries of Grundy Co., Vol. 2, p. 984
McCoy, Brenda Mai (Hollis)	Jul 27, 1948	Jan 14, 2021	King Cem.; Dau. of Gilmer & Fannie Mai (Williams) Hollis; m. Arlis Wayne McCoy
McCoy, Sally Ann	ca 1897	Jun 18, 1899	Wm. Well's Farm Family Cem. in Monteagle, TN; Dau. of Sherman & Caroline McCoy. From newspaper
McCraw, Susan Laura	Feb 29, 1844	Jun 21, 1895	Altamont Cem.; Dau. of William & Martha (Armstrong) McCraw; m. Harrison James Campbell; addition to Cemeteries of Grundy Co., Vol. 1, p. 14
McCullough, Danny Lavaughn	Oct 10, 1970	Oct 01, 2020	Fall Creek Cem.; Son of Danny L. & Betty (Carrick) McCullough; m. 1) Kathy Hargis 2) Latienne Cole
McCurry, Barney	May 25, 1934	Nov 17, 2010	Bonny Oak Cem.; Son of Jewarl Louis & Mae Elvin (Nunley) McCurry; addition to Cemeteries of Grundy Co., Vol. 1, p. 88
McCurry, Carleton G., Jr.	Apr 05, 1943	Dec 25, 2017	Cremated; Son of Carleton G., Sr. & Fan Jordan McCurry; m. Kathryn McCurry; US Army – Vietnam (Purple Heart & Bronze Star)
McCurry, Charles W.	Jan 7, 1930	Jan 19, 1930	Bonny Oak Cem.; Probable son of Barney McCurry; buried next to Barney; Sealie Nunley b. & d. 1933 is on the same stone; addition to Cemeteries of Grundy Co. Vol. 1, p. 88
McCurry, Mae Elvin (Nunley)	Oct 18, 1909	Oct 15, 1996	Bonny Oak Cem.; Dau. of Murphy & Nancy "Nannie" (Woodlee) Nunley; m. Barney McCurry; addition to Cemeteries of Grundy Co., Vol. 1, p. 88

Name	Born	Died	Notes
McCutcheon, Edward Troy	May 05, 1935	Aug 05, 2015	White Chapel Cem in Troy, MI; Son of Mersey & Lillian (Green) McCutcheon; US Army
McDaniel, Anna Lee	Oct 14, 1939	Apr 02, 2016	Palmer Cem.; Dau. of Floyd & Mary Louise (Cunningham) Tate; m. Jack McDaniel
McDaniel, Charles Ray	May 21, 1954	Mar 05, 2020	Plainview Cem.; Son of James Franklin "Buzz" & Stella Lucille (Seagroves) McDaniel; m. Rita McDaniel
McDaniel, Eddie L.	Aug 11, 1964	Sep 10, 2013	Fults Cem.; Son of Oscar Howell & Kate (Campbell) McDaniel; m. Donna Huntley
McDaniel, Eulice	Mar 11, 1945	Aug 10, 2020	Bonny Oak Cem.; Son of Clay & Alice (Layne) McDaniel; m. Joyce Layne
McDaniel, Henry Clay "Reggie"	Jul 08, 1942	Jun 17, 1987	Bonny Oak Cem.; Son of Horace G. & Julia Ann (Price) McDaniel; m. 1) Alice Layne 2) Edith Louise Bone; addition to Cemeteries of Grundy Co., Vol. 1, p. 84
McDaniel, James Carlton, Sr.	Sep 10, 1944	Apr 12, 2014	Plainview Cem.; Son of James Franklin "Buzz" & Stella Lucille (Segroves) McDaniel; m. Katherine Marie Nunley
McDaniel, James Franklin "Buzz"	May 19, 1907	May 19, 1964	Plainview Cem.; Son of Horace G & Julia Ann (Price) McDaniel; m. Stella Lucille Seagroves; addition to Cemeteries of Grundy Co., Vol. 2, p. 698
McDaniel, Jamey Mae (Kilgore)	Jan 27, 1974	Apr 01, 2022	Fall Creek Cem.; Dau. of Ronnie Eugene & Ruth Ann Kilgore; m. Richard Lee McDaniel
McDaniel, Jimmy Dewayne	Jul 02, 1969	May 29, 2021	Cremated; Son of James & Catherine (Nunley) McDaniel; Lived in Altamont, TN.
McDaniel, Katie Mae (Campbell)	May 01, 1936	Sep 23, 2021	Palmer Cem.; Dau. of Louie & Mazie (Graham) Campbell; m. Oscar Howell McDaniel
McDaniel, Linda (Ruehling)	Jul 27, 1943	Oct 25, 2011	Fall Creek Cem.; Dau. of Hurl G & Willie M (Woodlee) Ruehling; m. Randall McDaniel
McDaniel, Melissa M (White)	Oct 10, 1951	Aug 28, 2018	Monteagle Cem.; Dau. of R.L. & Essie White
McDaniel, Nadine P.	Aug 23, 1949	Sep 05, 2013	Cremated; Dau of James Franklin "Buzz" & Stella Lucille (Seagroves) McDaniel; m. Melvin Richard Phillips
McDaniel, Oscar Howell	Jul 25, 1934	Dec 19, 2021	Cremated; Son of Frank & Leila (Banks) McDaniel Tate; m. Katie Campbell
McDaniel, Randall "Buck"	Aug 11, 1980	Oct 01, 2005	Bonny Oak Cem.; Son of Randy Carl & Tina (Bean) McDaniel; Grandson of Carl Ladue McDaniel
McDaniel, Rickey Dewayne "Gomer"	May 21, 1953	Apr 18, 2016	Bonny Oak Cem.; Son of Charles & Joyce Avis (Bess) McDaniel
McDaniel, Rose Ann (Rogers)	Oct 11, 1976	Jun 06, 2021	Plainview Cem.; Dau. of Gary Joel Rogers & Anna Ruth McDaniel
McDaniel, Wanda J	May 25, 1905	May 22, 2019	Cremated; Dau. of James McDaniel & Marie Nunley; m. Jimmy Ryan

Name	Birth	Death	Details
McDaniel, William Eugene	May 31, 1924	Sep 20, 1989	Coalmont Cem.; Son of Crawford & Margaret (Williams) McDaniel; m. Bunia Lee Argo
McDonald, Melissa Carlie (Montgomery)	Oct 1870	Dec 01, 1957	Tracy City Cem.; Dau. of John A. & Clara (Crick) Montomery; m. John S. McDonald; addition to Cemeteries of Grundy Co., Vol. 2, p. 895
McDowell, Brian	Apr 03, 1951	Dec 25, 2016	Plainview Cem.; Son of David McDowell & Mara Grodzicki; m. Ciela McDowell
McElhaney, Georgia (Snyder)	Feb 13, 1870	Jul 05, 1966	Altamont Cem.; Dau. of John & Lorenda (Mell) Snyder; m. Norman M McElhenie; addition to Cemeteries of Grundy Co., Vol. 1, p. 17
McElhaney, Leoni Kate	Sep 3, 1880	Feb 23, 1923	Orange Hill Cem.; Dau. of Nathan Thomas & Louisa "Eliza" (Rogers) McElhaney; m. George William James Graham; addition to Cemeteries of Grundy Co. Vol. 2, p. 534
McElhaney, Maude	Sep 1882	Apr 08, 1905	Orange Hill Cem.; Dau. of Nathan Thomas & Louisa "Eliza" (Rogers) McElhaney; m. Joseph Bailey Haynes; addition to Cemeteries of Grundy Co., Vol. 2, p. 534
McFarland, Angie Marie	Jul 03, 1971	Nov 08, 2021	Monteagle Cem.; Dau. of William E. "Scooter Bill" & Margaret McFarland
McFarland, Daisy (Tucker)	Mar 02, 1905	May 20, 1905	Monteagle Cem.; Dau. of David Thomas "Dan" & Isabelle "Belle" (Ragsdale) Tucker; Her real name was Lillie Myrtle Tucker; addition to Vol. 1, p. 398
McFarland, Elijah	Apr 30, 1914	Apr 30, 1914	Monteagle Cem.; Son of George Carter & Ella Mae (Cox) McFarland; no stone
McFarland, Fred	Jan 2, 1888	Dec 07, 1918	Monteagle Cem.; Son of John & Elizabeth (Sales) McFarland, m. Minnie Belle Price; addition to Cemeteries of Grundy Co., Vol. 1, p. 464
McFarland, George Carter	May 10, 1850	Jan 17, 1926	Monteagle Cem.; Son of James Washington Lafayette Benjamin & Sarah (Johnson) McFarland; m 1) Amanda Caroline Trussell 4) Ella Mae Cox; Cemeteries of Grundy County; Vol. 1, p. 418 correction
McFarland, James B. "JB"	Jun 18, 1918	Oct 24, 1944	Monteagle Cem.; Son of George Carter & Ella Mae (Cox) McFarland; memorial stone; went down on Japanese POW ship in South China Sea; Purple Heart; S Sgt.
McFarland, James Cecil "JC"	Sep 14, 1989	May 11, 2020	Monteagle Cem.; Son of James Cecil & Karen Renee McFarland; U.S. Army
McFarland, Lillie Myrtle "Daisy" (Tucker)	Oct 8, 1888 but Oct 1884 in census	May 15, 1967	Monteagle Cem.; Dau. of Silas Leon & Orpha (Levan) Tucker: Her mother changed her name to "Daisy" after seeing a cute little girl of that name in Monteagle.

Name	Born	Died	Details
McFarland, Thomas Edgar "Ed"	Feb 11, 1893	Apr 20, 1924	Monteagle Cem.; Son of William Edward & Rue Cassander "Cassie" (Crabtree) McFarland; m. Orpha Gertrude "Gertie" Tucker, Oct 2, 1910; correction of spouse's name; Cemeteries of Grundy Co, Vol. 1, p. 463
McFarland, William Henry	Feb 01, 1917	Mar 01, 1918	Monteagle Cem.; Son of Thomas Edgar & Orpha Gertrude (Tucker) McFarland; Cemeteries of Grundy Co., Vol. 1, p. 462
McGee, Eva Rosy (Hamby)	Mar 18, 1933	Jan 17, 2020	Claridon Cem., Claridon, OH.; Dau. of Horace & Nila (Parsons) Hamby; m. 1) Bill Winton 2) Hubert McGee
McGee, Nelma Dean (Wanamaker)	May 18, 1929	Dec 01, 2013	Philadelphia Cem.; Dau. of Beecher & Ollie Mary (Coppinger) Wanamaker; m. G.W. McGee; addition to Cemeteries of Grundy Co., Vol. 2, p. 628
McGee, Stephanie Leigh-Ann (Hall)	Jun 03, 1982	Jan 21, 2021	Clouse Hill Cem.; Dau. of Michael Hall & Maria Gibbs; m. Josh McGee
McGee, Thelma Ruth (Tate)	Jan 27, 1934	Jan 19, 2021	Fults Cem.; Dau. of Buford & Sarah (Scott) Tate; m. Loyd McGee
McGhee, Martha Jewell	Feb 09, 1945	Sep 03, 2016	Plainview Cem.; Dau of John W. & Eddie Clara Newman
McGinnis, Patsy Ruth (Meeks)	Jul 27, 1941	May 31, 2021	AirView Cem.; Dau. of Donald Henderson & Mildred Irene (Brown) Meeks; m. Richard McGinnis
McGovern, Alice (Brown)	Jan 13, 1890	Feb 23, 1978	Plainview Cem.; Dau. of Norris B. & Josephine (Johnson) Brown; m. James Leonard "Jim" Magouirk; addition to Cemeteries of Grundy Co., Vol. 2, p. 672
McGovern, Betty E. (Elliott)	Apr 21, 1905	Jun 13, 2018	Cremated; Dau. of William Estill & Lena (Edwards) Elliott; m. 1) Benjamin McCeney 2) Bill McGovern
McGovern, Charles L.	Apr 27, 1919	Jan 25, 1958	Fall Creek Cem.; Son of Thomas B. McGovern & Sula Brown; TN PFC COC 86 ENGR AVNBN WWII
McGovern, James	Ca 1900	Nov 06, 1918	Hobbs Hill Cem.; Son of Pete & Anna Lee (Roberts) McGovern; addition to Cemeteries of Grundy Co., Vol. 1, p. 339; source – death certificate
McGovern, John	Ca 1860	Oct 02, 1916	Hobbs Hill Cem.; Son of James & Eliza Jane (Myers) McGovern; addition to Cemeteries of Grundy Co., Vol. 1, p. 339 ; source *Mrs. Grundy* Oct 5, 1916
McGovern, Nancy (Kilgroe)	Jan 24, 1888	Feb 01, 1962	Hobbs Hill Cem.; Dau. of Craven & Tennessee (Pennington) Kilgore; m. Phillip H. McGovern; addition to Cemeteries of Grundy Co., Vol. 1, p. 336

Name	Birth	Death	Details
McGraw, Dorothy Louise (Stucker)	Sep 01, 1916	Feb 28, 2006	Summerfield Cem.; Dau. of Samuel & Stella (Flint) Stucker; m. 1) __Newman 2) Howard Wessner 3) ___ McIntire 4) Samuel B. McGraw, Nov 2, 1984; addition to Cemeteries of Grundy Co., Vol. 2, p. 776
McGregor, Sarah (Green)	Feb 07, 1932	Jul 29, 2016	Monteagle Cem.; Dau. of Columbus & Sally (Jacobs) Green; m. Jesse Howard McGregor
McHone, Edward	Sep 23, 1949	Sep 03, 2019	Palmer Cem.; Son of Billy McHone & Kathleene L. Slatton; m. Betty Campbell
McIntosh, Ernest John	Apr 22, 1941	Jan 16, 2020	Cremated; Son of Floyd C. McIntosh & Ann Margaret Gaston; m. Wanda Daniel; U.S. Army - Vietnam
McIntyre, Susan (Raney)	May 10, 1946	Jul 02, 2019	Monteagle Assembly Cem.; Dau. of William Andrew Raney & Jane Moore; m. William Henry McIntyre
McKenzie, Estel Guthrie	Sep 15, 1913	Feb 03, 1991	Airview Cem.; Son of John W. & Thenia O. (Boring) McKenzie; m. Louetta Miller; addition to Cemeteries of Grundy Co., Vol. 1, p. 6
McKenzie, Harold F.	Mar 04, 1910	Apr 30, 1995	Airview Cem.; Son of John W. & Thenia O (Boring) McKenzie; Tech 3 US Army WWII; addition to Cemeteries of Grundy Co., Vol. 1, p.6
McKnigh, Lois Ann (Ondrizek)	Aug 12, 1915	Sep 22, 2014	Cumberland Heights Cem.; Dau. of Joseph & Bertha (Patterson) Ondrizek; m. Melvin Theodore McKnight; addition to Cemeteries of Grundy Co., Vol. 1, p. 197
McKnight, Frieda Lucille (Dickerson)	Mar 26, 1924	Jan 10, 2021	Altamont Cem.; Dau. of Ame & Sallie (Givens) Dickerson; m. Grady H. McKnight
McKnight, Katherine K.	Apr 05, 1924	Jul 19, 2017	Cumberland Heights Memorial Gardens; Dau. of Joseph & Hedwig (Kopnitsky) Korpits; m. Ronald Leroy McKnight
McLain, Richard Lee	Aug 27, 1941	Aug 19, 2021	Cremated: Son of Charles Edward & Marie (Rogers) McLain; m. Bernice Sanders
McNabb, Ethleen	Sep 30, 1916	Jan 27, 2014	Sequatchie Valley Memorial Gardens; Dau of Virgil Henry Sitz & Maggie Lou Levan; m. William Crandel McNabb
McNabb, Oma Louise (James)	Jul 23, 1917	Oct 25, 2013	Palmer Cem.; Dau. of William Eli "Jesse" & Nancy Dee (Nunley) James; m. Obid Marion "Soap" McNabb; addition to Cemeteries of Grundy Co., Vol. 2, p. 560
McNabb, William Crandle	Jun 09, 1937	Jan 28, 2015	Sequatchie Valley Memorial Cem.; Son of Thomas Crawford & Florence (Knight) McNabb; m. Ethleen Sitz
McNeece, Edna M. (Huckabee)	Feb 1, 1889	Jan 16, 1959	Burns Cem.; Dau. of John & Edna (Deen) McNeece; m. Virgil Huckabee; addition to Cemeteries of Grundy Co., Vol. 1, p. 130

Name	Born	Died	Notes
McPherson, Arnold M., Jr.	Oct 29, 1971	Oct 29, 1971	White Cem.; Son of Arnold M McPherson, Sr.; addition to Cemeteries of Grundy Co., Vol. 2, p. 1012
McPherson, Mamie Lee (Cox)	Sep 29, 1950	May 18, 2021	Cremated; Dau. of Herman Dallas & Mamie Esther (Nolan) Cox; m. Arnold McPherson
McQuiston, Clarence W.	Apr 25, 1920	Jun 30, 2008	Plainveiw Cem.; Son of Joseph Emery & Lily Ann (Ward) McQuiston; PFC US ARMY, WWII; addition to Cemeteries of Grundy County, Vol. 2, p. 704
McRae, Ruby (Layne)	Apr 19, 1935	Sep 28, 2018	Tracy City Cem.; Dau. of R.D. Layne & Esper Woodlee; m. John D. McRae
McWain, Buford Larry	Dec 07, 1947	Dec 09, 2021	Palmer Cem.; Son of Buford & Myrtle Marie (Cagle) McWain; m. Nadine Anderson
McWain, Hazel (Sloan)	Jan 08, 1900	Nov 05, 1993	Bonny Oak Cem.; Dau. of Robert & Mattie Sloan; m. 1) Joe Mooney 2) Thomas Franklin McWain; correction to Cemeteries of Grundy Co., Vol. 1, p. 74
McWilliams, James E	Dec 12, 1958	Dec 28, 2020	Clouse Hill Cem.; Son of William McWilliams & Marie Roysden; m. Melinda McWilliams
Meade, Norman Cline	Apr 17, 1939	Mar 22, 2004	Plainview Cem.; Son of Conley & Geneva Jane (Fulton) Meade
Meadows, Cecil Udell (Byers)	Aug 11, 1911	Apr 26, 1945	Hobbs Hill Cem.; Dau. of Joab Lambirth & Minda A. (Teague) Byars
Meadows, John Mitchell	May 23, 1905	Nov 19, 1963	Hobbs Hill Cem; Son of William H. & Maudie (Sanders) Meadows; m. Nov 25, 1928
Meadows, Lloyd Edward "George"	Sep 09, 1963	Aug 24, 2021	Hobbs Hill Cem.; Son of Lloyd Ray & Ida Mae Meadows; m. Starr
Meadows, Loyd Ray	Nov 21 1941	Nov 30, 2007	Hobbs Hill Cem.; Son of Johan Mitchell & Cecil Udell (Byars) Meadows
Meadows, Thomas Eugene, Jr. "Red"	Jun 20, 1952	Dec 15, 2021	Summerfield Cem.; Son of Thomas Eugene, Sr. & Virginia Meadows; m. Babette Meadows; U. S. Marine Corps
Meadows, Tommy Eugene	Nov 21, 1931	Jul 29, 1973	Hobbs Hill Cem.; Son of John Mitchell & Cecil Udell (Byars) Meadows
Meadows, William Henry "Bill"	Aug 02, 1935	Jul 16, 2014	Coalmont Cem.; Son of Charlie Meadows & Cora Kilgore; m. Daphine " Posie" Meadows
Meadows, William Henry Harrison "Hatton", Jr.	Apr 15, 1892	Sep 23, 1924	Tracy City Cem.; Son of William Henry Harrison, Sr. & Maude Josephine (Sanders) Meadows; m. Dessie Mae Allen, Jun 10, 1910; death date correction by family; correction to Cemeteries of Grundy Co., Vol. 2, p. 832
Medley, Claude "Pork Chop"	Feb 26, 1963	Jan 09, 2021	Cremated; Son of Edward & Ruth (Tucker) Medley; m. Angela Medley
Medley, Danny Pascal	Jul 12, 1955		New Brick Church Cem.; Son of Pascal "Pack" & Willie Jo (Sitz) Medley; m. 1) Wanda Merritt 2) Deborah Gilmer 3) Shawn Derosett

Name	Birth	Death	Details
Medley, Deborah Kaye (Gilmer)	Aug 17, 1967	Feb 26, 2008	New Brick Church Cem.; Dau of Jim & Evelyn (Finney) Gilmer; m. Danny Pascal Medley
Medley, Edward Lee "Edd"	Nov 27, 1931	May 16, 2015	New Brick Church Cem. in Coffee Co.; Son of Rufus Emmett "Dock" & Virginia Isabel (Rust) Medley; m. Margie Ruth Tucker
Medley, James Isaac	Apr 11, 1883	Aug 28, 1954	Coalmont Cem.; Son of Isaac & Emily (Howard) Medley; addition of name to Cemeteries of Grundy Co., Vol. 1, p. 187
Medley, John Albert	Feb 23, 1948	Jun 12, 1964	Coalmont Cem.; Son of Albert J & Frances (Rees) Medley; correction to Cemeteries of Grundy County, Vol. 1, p. 186
Medley, Margie Ruth (Tucker)	Jul 07, 1939	Oct 18, 2019	New Brick Church Cem in Coffee Co.; Dau. of Johnnie & Lottie Tucker; m. Edward Medley
Medley, Willie Jo	Jun 16, 1937	Aug 28, 2021	Warren "Red Hill" Cem.; Dau. of Dan & Ovie (Nunley) Sitz; m. Pascal Medley
Meek, Marvin Vester, Rev.	Oct 12, 1902	Jul 28, 1960	Orange Hill Cem.; Son of George Mac & Mary Elizabeth (Bean) Meeks; m. Agnes Jane Sanders
Meeks, Thomas "Tommie"	May 11, 1913	Nov 04, 1995	Brown's Chapel Cem.; Son of George C."Banty" & Mary Elizabeth "Lizzie" (Sanders) Meeks; m. Edna "Eddie" Scott; addition to Cemeteries of Grundy Co., Vol. 1, p. 115
Meeks, "Denny" Mitchell Meeks	Dec 17, 1954	Oct 03, 2019	Coalmont Cem.; Son of Horace David & Colleen C. Meeks
Meeks, Adam Shane	Feb 15, 1978	Sep 22, 2019	Pryor Ridge Cem.; Son of Paul Meeks & Linda Thomas; m. Charlene Harris
Meeks, Agnes Jane (Sanders)	Aug 29, 1905	Aug 01, 1965	Orange Hill Cem.; Dau. of Alex Houston & Birdie (Meeks) Sanders; m. Rev. Martin Vester Meeks
Meeks, Alice Ladean	Apr 23, 1905	Jan 01, 2018	Plainview Cem.; Dau. of Jackson Hiles & Cleo (Cox) Meeks
Meeks, Allen	Dec 17, 1912	May 07, 1990	Bonnie Oak Cem.; Son of John Vester & Nancy "Dollie" (Meeks) Meeks; m. Lorene Nunley; addition to Cemeteries of Grundy Co., Vol. 1, p. 86
Meeks, Allie (Smartt)	Ca 1906 . The 1940 census does not agree, but others do	May 28, 1905	Clouse Hill Cem.; Dau of John C. & Hallie (Green) Smartt; m. John Meeks, Jr. on Jan 23, 1920; death date from family
Meeks, Alma (Smartt)	Jul 10, 1910	Sep 18, 1993	Orange Hill Cem.; Dau. of Steven A. & Lucy (Nunley) Smartt; m. Wiley C. Meeks; addition to Cemeteries of Grundy Co., Vol. 2, p. 526
Meeks, Arthur Edward	ca 1917	Mar 04, 1940	Tracy City Cem.; Son of George Cope Meeks & Lizzie Sanders; no tombstone, info from death certificate #11556

Meeks, Belle	Jan 30, 1905	Jun 10, 1921	Oak Grove Cem.; Dau. of Isaac Crabtree; m. Thomas Meeks on Dec. 25, 1889 in Grundy Co.
Meeks, Billie Louie "Bill"	Oct 21, 1933	Aug 18, 2010	Hobbs Hill Cem.; Son of William Grover & Bonnie Mae (Campbell) Meeks; actually buried at Guam Veterans Cemetery in Piti, but has a tombstone at Hobbs Hill; correction of death date and addition of parents' names to Cemeteries of Grundy Co., Vol. 1, p. 338
Meeks, Bobby Dewayne	Apr 15, 1964	Jul 12, 2013	Fall Creek Cem.; Son of Tommy & Mary (Braden) Meeks
Meeks, Bobby Levoid	May 08, 1905	Nov 24, 2021	Mt. Pleasant Cem.; Son of Tom & Anna Dorean Meeks
Meeks, Bonnie Mae (Campbell)	May 27, 1914	Feb 10, 1999	Hobbs Hill Cem.; Dau. of Alexander W. & Tierra Ellizabeth (Nunley) Campbell; m. William Grover Meeks on Jan 25, 1930; addition to Cemeteries of Grundy Co. Vol. 1, p.338
Meeks, Bradford Orion	Jul 21, 1980	Feb 10, 2019	Bonny Oak Cem.; Son of Bradford Meeks & Darlene Pickett
Meeks, Brady Wayne	May 17, 1978	Mar 09, 2022	Cremated; Son of Larry & Marilyn (Tate) Meeks
Meeks, Buddy	Mar 07, 1951	Nov 29, 2018	Plainview Cem.; Son of Jess & Sue Meeks; m. Kathy Meeks
Meeks, Buford Eldridge	Apr 10, 1924	Dec 07, 1990	Palmer Cemetery; Son of Norman M. & Mary Elizabeth "Lizzie" (Smith) Meeks; m. Nadine Cannon on May 8, 1943; S1 US Navy; WWII. addition to Cemeteries of Grundy Co., Vol. 2 p. 551
Meeks, Buford Howard "Mousey"	Jan 04, 1944	Jul 11, 2017	Palmer Cem.; Son of Buford E. & Nadine (Cannon) Meeks; m. Christine "Tina" Harrison
Meeks, Chandra Gayle	Aug 13, 1980	Mar 28, 2014	Orange Hill Cem.; Dau. of Grady & Mary Jo (Meeks) Lockhart
Meeks, Charles E.	Apr 12, 1907	Feb 16, 1987	Palmer Cem.; Son of Jerry Riley & Sophronia A (Glowner) Meeks; m. Janie A. (Bone); addition to Cemeteries of Grundy Co. Vol. 2; p. 564
Meeks, Charles Martin	Oct 02, 1947	Mar 13, 2020	Body donated to science; Son of James Meeks & Delia Sanders; m. Virginia Katherine Miller
Meeks, Charlotte Main (Layne)	Feb 18, 1937	Mar 02, 2021	Fall Creek Cem.; Dau. of Frank Parks & Dixie Lee (Nunley) Layne; m. Willie Dee Meeks
Meeks, Chester "Bug", Jr.	Apr 11, 1954	Dec 17, 2013	Plainview Cem.; Son of Chester "Chet" & Joann (Braziel) Meeks; addition to Cemeteries of Grundy Co., Vol. 2, p. 694
Meeks, Child	Ca 1910	Nov 01, 1915	Gregg Cem.; Son of Dave Meeks buried last week – reported in *Mrs. Grundy* Nov. 25, 1915
Meeks, Child		Jul 20, 1916	Sweeton Hill area; Child of John Meeks; from *Sweeton Hill News*

Name	Birth	Death	Details
Meeks, Claude	Feb 22, 1927	Jan 07, 1974	Plainview Cem.; Son of Francis "France" & Ethel D. (Price) Meeks; m. Mary Louise "Ladybug" Cantrell; TN BUL 2 US NAVY WWII; addition to Cemeteries of Grundy Co., Vol. 2, p. 673
Meeks, Cleracy	Jun 01, 1909	Feb 24, 1910	Bonny Oak Cem.; death certificate; born in Meeks, TN, now Flat Branch- no other information; name was supposed to be Clercy
Meeks, Clyde Junior	Aug 03, 1951	Nov 30, 2002	Plainview Cem.; Son of James Isaac & Margaret Louise (Meeks) Meeks; m. Judy Ann Levan; m. Jan 19, 1974; addition to Cemeteries of Grundy Co., Vol. 2, p. 676
Meeks, Connie (Levan)	Oct 06, 1958	Apr 30, 2018	Pryor Ridge Cem.; Dau. of James Alton Levan & Lena Mae Scott; m. Danny F Meeks
Meeks, Creasie Eldridge (Green)	Feb 04, 1931	Jul 10, 2012	Meeks Family Cemetery at Flat Branch; Dau. of Dortha & Buena (Johnson) Green m. Ray Meeks
Meeks, David Jerome Wiley	Dec 19, 1892	Jun 05, 1941	Orange Hill Cem; Son of Wiley & Sarah Agnes (Anderson) Meeks; m. Celia Myers; He died in Harlan, KY.
Meeks, David's little son	Ca 1910	Nov. 25, 1915	Gregg Cemetery; Son of Dave Meeks; from *Mrs. Grundy*
Meeks, Delma Inez (Forsyth)	Jun 25, 1939	Nov 26, 2019	Burns Cem.; Dau. of J.T. Forsyth & Sarah Rhevena Baker; m. Clyde Meeks
Meeks, Diana M.	Aug 08, 1948	Jun 04, 2009	Palmer Cem.; Dau. of John Vester, Jr. & Mable Marie (Higgins) Meeks; addition to Cemeteries of Grundy Co., Vol. 2, p. 567
Meeks, Diane (Sanders)	Jun 26, 1956	May 27, 2022	Cremated; Dau. of Melvin & Pauline (Jones) Sanders; m. Steven Darrell Meeks
Meeks, Donald Ray	Mar 28, 1960	Nov 15, 2016	Pryor Ridge Cem.; Son of Oscar Franklin & Geraldine (Nunley) Meeks
Meeks, Dora Kay (Treat)	Dec 01, 1958	Feb 15, 2019	Clouse Hill Cem.; Dau. of William Cebis Treat & Sarah Jane Reagan; m. Benton Meeks
Meeks, Earnest Dwayne	Nov 20, 1959	Mar 20, 2015	Palmer Cem.; Son of Richard & Gladys (Ross) Meeks; m. Pamela Henry
Meeks, Edna "Eddie" (Scott)	Sep 04, 1914	Jun 11, 2007	Brown's Chapel Cem.; Dau of Amos J. & Martha Jane "Jennie" (Savage) Scott; m. Thomas "Tommie" Meeks
Meeks, Ernest R.	Oct 31, 1923	Dec 30, 1923	Payne's Cove Cem.; Son of Norman M. & Mary Elizabeth (Smith) Meeks; addition to Cemeteries of Grundy Co., Vol. 2, p. 597
Meeks, Ernie Sue (Dishman)	Dec 29, 1947	Jul 15, 2018	Cremated; Dau. of Ted Dishman & Zola Byrd; m. Douglas Meeks
Meeks, Evelyn Bell (Meeks)	Feb 03, 1931	Apr 16, 2017	Payne's Cove Cem.; Dau. of Sam & Leona (Holt) Meeks; m. Billy Leonard Meeks; addition to Cemeteries of Grundy Co., Vol. 2, p. 593

Meeks, Faye Barrett	Dec 19, 1940	Nov 15, 2013	Pryor Ridge Cem.; Dau. of Ethridge & Mildred (Rymer) Barrett
Meeks, Felicia Lynn	Mar 07, 1988	Dec 09, 2011	Meeks Family Cemetery at Flat Branch; Dau. of Randall E. & Hazel (Frederick) Meeks
Meeks, Floyd Clayton	Nov 29, 1942	Apr 12, 2012	Gregg Cem.; Son of James & Delia (Sanders) Meeks; m. Dessie Nix , Aug 11, 1965; correction & addition to Cemeteries of Grundy Co., Vol. 1, p. 305
Meeks, Frank Ray	May 31, 1928	Dec 24, 2013	Plainview Cem.; Son of George Cope "Banty" & Mary Elizabeth "Lizzie" (Sanders) Meeks; m. Hassie L. Smartt; addition to Cemeteries of Grundy Co., Vol. 2, p. 685
Meeks, George	1928	Apr 19, 2021	Orange Hill Cem.; Son of Wiley Clinton & Alma (Smartt) Meeks
Meeks, George Cope "Banty"	Sep 1, 1873 or Oct. 1877	before 1929	Orange Hill Cem.; Son of Wiley Meeks & Sarah Agnes Anderson; no tombstone; m. Lizzie Sanders Jan 1, 1899; George C "Banty" Meeks and his wife are buried beside William "Bill" & Carol Nunley per family
Meeks, Georgia Mae (Nunley)	Jun 12, 1926	Mar 24, 2005	Plainview Cem.; Dau. of Francis Lee & Hattie "Crick" (Nunley) Meeks; m. W. D. "Jack" Meeks; addition & correction to Cemeteries of Grundy Co., Vol. 2, p. 690
Meeks, Gladys Faye	Dec 23, 1924	May 17, 2016	Plainview Cem.; Dau of Richard & Perry (Fults) Meeks; m. James A. Meeks
Meeks, Glenda Sue (Nunley)	Apr 20, 1951	Dec 12, 2018	Coalmont Cem.; Dau. of Taylor Nunley & Frances Napier; m. Larry B. Meeks
Meeks, Gordon Vince	Sep 25, 1930	Feb 20, 1995	Brown's Chapel Cem.; Son of Newt A. & Flora (McWain) Meeks; m. Viney Sarah Meeks; addition to Cemeteries of Grundy Co., Vol. 1, p. 115
Meeks, Harvey Sonny	Feb 12, 1940	Sep 12, 2014	Palmer Cem.; Son of Alvin "Jack" & Ellen (Magouirk) Meeks; m. Mary Elizabeth Garner; addition to Cemeteries of Grundy Co., Vol. 2, p. 574
Meeks, Hazel Darlene (Frederick)	May 06, 1958	Feb 07, 2016	Meeks Family Cemetery at Flat Branch; Dau. of Ernest "Pat" & Mary Kathleen (Nunley) Frederick; m. Randall E. Meeks
Meeks, Henry Benton	Nov 16, 1930	Sep 01, 2018	Bethel Cem.; Son of William Francis "France" Meeks & Bettie Isabel Sartain; m. Melva Rogers; US Army; addition to Cemeteries of Grundy Co., Vol 1, p. 65
Meeks, Hollis Melton	Apr 12, 1908	Jul 31, 1988	White Cem.; Son of William & Nancy E. Meeks; m. Ida Mae Tate; addition to Cemeteries of Grundy Co., Vol. 2, p. 1011
Meeks, Infant	None stated	Jul 16, 1918	Gregg Cem.; Son of Taylor & Bell (Braden) Meeks; addition to Cemeteries of Grundy Co. TN, Vol. 1

Meeks, Infant		Feb 15, 1917	Coalmont Cem.; Son of Arthur Meeks of Coalmont; *Mrs. Grundy* Feb 22, 1919
Meeks, Infant	None stated	Jul 16, 1918	Gregg Cem.; Son of Taylor & Bell (Braden) Meeks; addition to Cemeteries of Grundy Co., Vol. 1, p. 308
Meeks, Infant	May 12, 1918	May 12, 1918	Clouse Hill Cem.; Son of William F. & Rachel Oma "Omie" (Robertson) Meeks
Meeks, Infant	Sep 17, 1924	Sep 17, 1924	Clouse Hill Cem.; Son of Charlie & Tressie (Fults) Meeks; from death certificate
Meeks, Infant	None stated	Jul 16, 1918	Gregg Cem.; Son of Taylor & Bell (Braden) Meeks; addition to Cemeteries of Grundy Co., Vol. 1, p. 308
Meeks, Jackson			No information found
Meeks, James Edward	Nov 12, 1965	Feb 15, 1966	Fall Creek Cem.; Son of Marvin H & Martha Josephine (Tabors) Meeks
Meeks, James Gregory	Apr 07, 1966	Jun 16, 2013	Clouse Hill Cem.; Son of James David & Ruth Meeks
Meeks, James Lee	Aug 12, 1944	Jun 03, 2018	Bethel Cem.; Son of Clyde Meeks & Oma Lee Kilgore; m. Rona Lee (Givens) Patton
Meeks, James Leonard	Jul 06, 1930	May 30, 2000	Plainview Cem.; Son of James Frank & Emma Marie (Reed) Meeks; m.Virginia Pearl Green; addition to Cemeteries of Grundy Co., Vol. 2, p. 697
Meeks, James Malcolm	May 25, 1936	Mar 25, 1998	Pryor Ridge Cem.; Son of James Dee & Lora Louise (Nunley) Meeks; m. Josephine Meeks; US ARMY; addition to Cemeteries of Grundy Co., Vol. 2, p. 716
Meeks, Jason Peter	Mar 31, 1975	Jan 14, 2014	Bethel Cem.; Son of Ronald F. & Laura (Bernard) Meeks
Meeks, Jeffrey L.	Jun 24, 1962	Sep 10, 1985	Fall Creek Cem.; Son of Frances H & Johnnie Ruth (Henry) Meeks
Meeks, Jewell Virginia "Sissy"	Aor 8, 1925	Feb 25, 1997	Palmer Cem.; Dau. of Robert James & Mary Savannah (Sweeton) Meeks; addition to Cemeteries of Grundy Co., Vol. 2, p. 577
Meeks, Joann (Braziel)	Jun 26, 1938		Plainview Cem.; Dau. of James Franklin & Martha Katherine (Tigue) Braziel; m. Chester "Bug" Meeks, Jr.; addition to Cemeteries of Grundy Co., Vol. 2, p. 694
Meeks, Joe Lester	Aug 12, 1918	Jan 22, 2011	Bonny Oak Cem.; Son of John Vester & Dollie (Meeks) Meeks; m. Arizona Campbell; addition to Cemeteries of Grundy Co., Vol, 1, p. 76
Meeks, John Henderson	Jul 2, 1880	Nov 03, 1953	Monteagle Cem.; Son of George & Mary E (Crabtree) Meeks; correction to Cemeteries of Grundy Co., Vol. 1, p. 451

Name	Birth	Death	Details
Meeks, John Vester, Jr.	Jul 22, 1919	Mar 26, 1976	Palmer Cem.; Son of John Vester, Sr. & Nancy "Dolly" (Meeks) Meeks; m. Mable Marie Higgins; addition to Cemeteries of Grundy Co., Vol. 2, p. 567
Meeks, John Wesley	Jul 22, 1913	Apr 29, 1963	Coalmont Cem.; Son of Jack & Nancy (Pendergrass) Meeks; m. Lucy Bean; correction to Cemeteries of Grundy Co., Vol. 1, p. 173
Meeks, Johnny R. (Henry)	Dec 17, 1936	Oct 14, 1989	Fall Creek Cem.; Dau. of Roy Lee & Oma Lee (Meeks) Henry; m. Frances H Meeks; m. Jul 9, 1954
Meeks, Joyce Charlene	Nov 08, 1956	Jan 06, 2014	Plainview Cem.; Dau of Frank Ray Meeks & Hassie Smartt; m. Danny Ray Meeks
Meeks, Judy Ann (Levan)	Sep 08, 1954	Jul 08, 2014	Plainview Cem.; Dau. of James Alton & Lena Mae (Scott) Levan; Clyde Junior Meeks
Meeks, Kathleen M.	Mar 23, 1927	Dec 14, 2020	Meeks Family Cem.; Dau. of Carl H & Jean (Frederick) Sitz
Meeks, Kenneth O	Dec 12, 1943	Aug 30, 2021	Cumberland Cem. in Kimball; Son of Arthur & Agnes Meeks; m. Linda Meeks; Veteran
Meeks, Laura	Oct 17, 1948	Feb 17, 2016	Bethel Cem.; Dau of Raymond & Rose Bernard; m. Ronald F. Meeks
Meeks, Laura (Nelson)	Jun 19, 1927	Apr 06, 2006	Dau. of John & Myrtle E (Sims) Nelson; m. Marvin A. Meeks
Meeks, Laura M. (Bernard)	Oct 17, 1948	Feb 17, 2015	Bethel Cem.; Dau. of Raymond & Rose (Verde) Bernard; m. Ronald F. Meeks; addition to Cemeteries of Grundy Co., Vol. 1, p. 68
Meeks, Lizzie (Sanders)	Mar 14, 1882	Aug 31, 1948	Orange Hill Cem.; Dau of Harrison Sanders & Leddy Parmley; m. George Cope "Banty" Meeks
Meeks, Lois Elizabeth	Nov 22, 1939	Jun 13, 2013	Monteagle Cem.; Dau of Henry "Bud" & Helen (Smith) Melton; m. James "Danny" Meeks
Meeks, Lorene (Nunley)	Mar 11, 1918	Dec 23, 1996	Bonny Oak Cem.; Dau. of Russell & Nancy (Ward) Nunley; m. Allen Meeks; addition to Cemeteries of Grundy Co., Vol. 1, p. 86
Meeks, Margaret (Rose)	Jun 19, 1878	Jan 22, 1963	Clouse Hill Cem.; Dau. of John & Margaret (Rose) Meeks; m. John T. Meeks, Sr. per death certificate; addition to Cemeteries of Grundy Co., Vol. 1, p. 151
Meeks, Margaret Louise	1926	1964	Plainview Cem.; Dau. of George C. & Mary Elizabeth "Lizzie" (Sanders) Meeks; m. James Isaac Meeks; addition to Cemeteries of Grundy Co., Vol. 2, p. 697
Meeks, Martha Ellen (Shortridge)	Dec 23, 1925	Jun 24, 2014	Bethel Cem.; Dau. of Granville & Maudie (Street) Shortridge; m. Uliss Meeks Jul 30, 1955; addition to Cemeteries of Grundy Co., Vol. 1, p. 65

Name	Birth	Death	Details
Meeks, Marvin Vester, Rev.	Oct 12, 1902	Jul 28, 1960	Orange Hill Cem.; Son of George Mac & Mary Elizabeth (Bean) Meeks; m. Agnes Jane Sanders
Meeks, Mary <u>Cathrine</u> (May)	Mar 13, 1924	Sep 25, 1983	Clouse Hill Cem.; Dau. of Beverly Marcus & Doshia (Blanton) May; m. Carl David Meeks; addition to Cemeteries of Grundy Co, Vol. 1, p. 156.
Meeks, Mary Elizabeth "Lizzie" (Sanders)	Mar 14, 1882	Aug 31, 1948	Orange Hill Cem.; Dau. of Harrison & Lydia "Leddy" (Parmley) Sanders, no tombstone
Meeks, Mary Ellen	Aug 01, 1923	Feb 15, 2016	Coalmont Cem.; Dau. of Doc & Gertrude (Anderson) Brown; m. Paul David Meeks
Meeks, Mary Jo	Apr 14, 1953	Mar 27, 2020	Orange Hill Cem.; Dau. of Wiley & Alma Meeks
Meeks, Mary Louise	Feb 05, 1927	Jun 02, 2016	Plainview Cem.; Dau. of Alvin & Vivian (Tigue) Cantrell; m. Claude Meeks, Sr.
Meeks, Mary Magdalene	Feb 02, 1911	Oct 21, 1973	Fall Creek Cem.; Dau. of Riley & Alice Meeks
Meeks, Mary Ruth (Nunley)	May 07, 1937	Jun 09, 2018	Pryor Ridge Cem.; Dau. of Howard & Elsie (Dykes) Nunley; m. Walter Felix Meeks, Jr.; addition to Cemeteries of Grundy Co., Vol. 2, p. 716
Meeks, Mary Savannah	Mar 29, 1884	Jan 03, 1975	Hobbs Hill Cem.; Dau. of Lafayette & Mary Ellen (Irvin) Sweeton; m. Robert James Meeks; addition to Cemeteries of Grundy Co., Vol. 1, p. 331
Meeks, Melissa Faye (Brewer)	Nov 28, 1941	Jul 11, 2021	Rose Hill Memorial Gardens; Dau. of Earl & Ila Lee (Layne) Brewer; m. Kenneth Marshal Meeks
Meeks, Melvin Frank	Jul 13, 1949	Feb 16, 2017	Clouse Hill Cem.; Son of James Frank & Emma Mae (Reed) Meeks
Meeks, Michael Anthony	Jul 01, 1970	Jun 19, 2020	Cremated; Son of William C. & Candy (Weatherup) Meeks
Meeks, Mickey Virgil	Aug 24, 1967	May 10, 2022	Bethel Cem.; Son of Henry Benton & Melva (Rogers) Meeks; m. Lori Baker
Meeks, Nadine (Cannon)	Jun 24, 1928	May 07, 1972	Palmer Cem.; Dau. of Freddie Morgan & Agnes Marguerite (Henley) Cannon; m. Buford Eldridge Meeks; addition to Cemeteries of Grundy Co., Vol. 2, p.551
Meeks, Nancy Jo	Sep 27, 1930		No information found
Meeks, Nancy L.	Jul 26, 1946	Jan 09, 1987	Dick Meeks' Family Cem in Payne's Cove; Dau. of Cheatom Clinton & Mattie F. (James) Meeks; correction to birth year in Cemeteries of Grundy Co., Vol. 2, p. 375
Mccks, Norman, Jr. "Junebug"	Jul 03, 1937	Sep 26, 2017	Fall Creek Cem.; Son of Norman & Elizabeth (Smith) Meeks, Sr.; m. Carolyn Sweeton
Meeks, Oscar Franklin	Jan 20, 1935	Aug 19, 2012	Pryor Ridge Cem.; Son of Joe Vernon & Cora (Layne) Meeks; m. Geraldine Nunley; addition to Cemeteries of Grundy Co., Vol. 2, p. 716

Name	Birth	Death	Details
Meeks, Paul Ray	May 19, 1934	Feb 15, 2015	Pryor Ridge Cem.; Son of Sam & Leona (Holt) Meeks; m. Fay Barrett
Meeks, Paulette (Johnson)	Oct 22, 1948	Feb 15, 2021	Orange Hill Cem.; Dau. of Loys & Pauline (Sanders) Johnson
Meeks, Pearl M. (Tate)	May 2, 1888	May 25, 1981	Plainview Cem.; Dau. of Davidson & Mary (Layne) Tate; m. Will Meeks; addition to Cemeteries of Grundy Co., Vol. 2, p. 677
Meeks, Peggy Sue	Mar 08, 1954	Mar 16, 1984	Plainview Cem.; Dau. of James Isaac & Margaret Louise (Meeks) Meeks; addition to Cemeteries of Grundy Co., Vol. 2, p. 697
Meeks, Phillip Douglas	Aug 26, 1947	Oct 10, 2014	Clouse Hill Cem.; Son of Jessie Meeks & Henrietta Campbell; m. Judith Anderson
Meeks, Phillip Doyle	Dec 12, 1930	Oct 19, 1955	Orange Hill Cem.; Son of Rev. Marvin Vester & Agnes Jane (Sanders) Meeks
Meeks, Polly (Cope)	Sep 01, 1841	May 12, 1913	Payne's Cove Cem.; Dau. of Stephen & Comfort Cope; m. John "Crip John" Meeks; died at her home per Mrs. Grundy Newspaper, May 15, 1913 edition; birth date from census; addition to Grundy Co. Cemeteries, Vol. 2, no tombstone
Meeks, Quarrels Sutton	Dec 19, 1897	Mar 22, 1972	Hobbs Hill Cem.; Son of John William & Doris "Dosie" (Harrison) Meeks; correction of name listing & addition to Cemeteries of Grundy Co., Vol. 1, p. 338
Meeks, Ralph Adams	Jul 25, 1930	Jan 09, 2016	Macon County Memorial Gardens; Son of Ralph Meeks; m. Shirley Lockhart
Meeks, Ralph Clinton	Jun 30, 1936	Jun 01, 2020	Church of Christ Cem. Pelham; Son of Cheatum Clinton & Mattie (James) Meeks; m. Helen Ruth Medley
Meeks, Ray	Mar 08, 1935	Apr 05, 2014	Meeks Family Cemetery at Flat Branch; Son of Newton Alexander & Flora Mae (McWain) Meeks; m. Creasie Eldridge Green
Meeks, Ray Edward	Oct 02, 1953	Jul 14, 2020	Bethel Cem.; Son of Billy & Evelyn (Meeks) Meeks; m. Mary Ann Hoagland; addition to Cemeteries of Grundy Co., Vol. 1, p. 68
Meeks, Richard N.	Mar 01, 1938	Jun 12, 2017	Cremated; Son of Norman Meeks, Sr. & Mary E. Smith; m. Gladys Tate Ross
Meeks, Ricky Allen	Apr 03, 1961	May 05, 2002	Fall Creek Cem.; Son of Cecil Thomas & Mary Louise (Braden) Meeks; m. Kelli Lea Wilkerson
Meeks, Ricky Allen	Jan 16, 1958	Mar 20, 2013	Cremated; ashes at Plainview Cem.; Son of Claude Meeks & Mary O'Dear
Meeks, Riley D. "Dee"	Mar 10, 1889	Mar 23, 1920	Orange Hill Cem.; Son of Wiley D. Meeks & Sarah Agnes Anderson; m. Alice Northcutt; information from death certificate
Meeks, Robert Franklin "Bobby"	Sep 23, 1929	Aug 5, 2016	Hendersonville Memory Gardens; Son of James "Jim" Houston & Zora Belle (Parks) Meeks; m. Shirley Franks

Name	Birth	Death	Notes
Meeks, Roberta Jo (Dills)	Jan 14, 1971	Mar 21, 2019	Cremated: Dau. of Philip Wayne Dills & Kitty Woodward
Meeks, Ronald F.	Nov 07, 1944	Apr 30, 2017	Bethel Cem.; Son of Ellis & Clara (Dupree) Meeks; m. Laura M. Bernard; children: Jason, Ryan, Jacqueline, Nathan, Darren; US ARMY;
Meeks, Rosa Lee (Kilgore)	Apr 16, 1921	Aug 31, 2013	Coalmont Cem.; Dau. of Roy & Crede (Meeks) Kilgore; m. France Meeks
Meeks, Sally R.	Jan 25, 1936	Apr 01, 2003	Palmer Cem.; Dau. of Elmer Elbert & Gladys Louella (Blaylock) Smith; m. 1) Gilliam Baxter Nolan 2) ____ Meeks; addition to Cemeteries of Grundy Co., Vol. 2, p. 564
Meeks, Sarah Agnes (Anderson)	Nov 26, 1865	Jul 07, 1950	Orange Hill; No tombstone; Find a Grave says that her son Newt Meeks listed the wrong parents on her death certificate; m. Wiley D. Meeks
Meeks, Sarah Charlotte "Lottie"	Mar 11, 1860	Jan 05, 1931	Bonny Oak Cem.; Dau. of Andrew Jacob & Louisa W. (Cope) Sanders; m. James Donald Meeks; no tombstone; info. from Brian Cribbs
Meeks, Sarah J. (Morgan) Byars	Nov 21, 1844	Sep 05, 1903	Clouse Hill Cem.; Dau. of William M. & Rebecca (Moore) Morgan; m. 1) John Wayne Byars; m. 2) Thomas Meeks, Apr 5, 1873; He is buried beside her, but has no tombstone. correction of middle name of father, Cemeteries of Grundy Co., Vol. 1, p. 151
Meeks, Shalonda (Gallagher)	Oct 07, 1974	Feb 13, 2021	Coalmont Cem.; Dau. of Jerry Dale & Karen (Barnes) Gallagher; m. 1) Billy Braden 2) Monte Meeks
Meeks, Sherry Oleta	Jul 24, 1948	May 26, 2022	Fall Creek Cem.; Dau. of Pascal & Lillie Bell (Rust) Meeks
Meeks, Shirley (Meeks)	Mar 27, 1937	Apr 19, 2015	Plainview Cem.; Dau. of Wallace Sanders & Hester Gibbs; m. Alfred D. Meeks
Meeks, Shirley M. (Franks)	Sep 14, 1936	Jun 06, 2022	Hendersonville Memory Gardens; Dau of Lawrence & Stella Franks; m. Robert Franklin "Bobby" Meeks
Meeks, Shirley Mae (Gibbs)	Dec 13, 1948	May 26, 2011	Bonny Oak Cem.; Dau. of Lois Lindsay & Etta Mae (Burnett) Gibbs; addition to Cemeteries of Grundy Co., Vol. 1, p. 95
Meeks, Siebert	Dec 26, 1935	May 25, 2020	Coalmont Cem.; Son of France Meeks & Ethel Price; m. Florence M. Smith
Meeks, Sue E. (Dishman)	Dec 29, 1947	Jul 15, 2018	Plainview Cem.; cremated; Dau. of Ted & Zola (Byrd) Dishman; m. Douglas Meeks; correction & addition to Cemeteries of Grundy Co., Vol. 2, p. 690
Meeks, Theresa (Robak) Mayo	Oct 08, 1903	Sep 09, 1992	Plainview Cem.; Dau. of Ralph & Hattie (Kuzak) Robak; m. William E. Meeks; addition to Cemeteries of Grundy Co., Vol. 2, p. 688

Name	Birth	Death	Notes
Meeks, Thomas		ca 1900	Clouse Hill Cem.; m. Sarah Morgan Byars, buried beside her, but he has no tombstone; info from family Michael Morgan
Meeks, Thomas "Tommie"	May 11, 1913	Nov 04, 1995	Brown's Chapel Cem; Son of George Cope "Banty" Meeks & Mary Elizabeth "Lizzie" Sanders; m. Edna "Eddie" Scott
Meeks, Virginia Carol	Jan 30, 1963	Dec 21, 2019	Plainview Cem.; Dau. of James L. Meeks & Virginia Green; m. Eddie Wayne Meeks
Meeks, Virginia Louise (Nunley)	Apr 11, 1905	Nov 04, 2019	Cremated: Dau of George & Lila Shadrick; m. Vester Meeks
Meeks, Virginia Pearl (Green)	Aug 26, 1935	Jun 03, 2019	Plainview Cem.; Dau. of Norman L. & Mildie M (Nolan) Green; m. James Leonard Meeks; addition to Cemeteries of Grundy Co., Vol. 2, p. 697
Meeks, Wanda June (Hampton)	Jan 05, 1929	Jul 24, 2021	Fall Creek Cem.; Dau. of Melvin C. "Bud" & Elizabeth (Creighton) Hampton; m. J.T. Meeks
Meeks, Wiley D.	Nov 26, 1865	Jul 07, 1950	Orange Hill Cem.;
Meeks, William	ca 1881	Aug 26, 1934	Bonny Oak Cem.; Son of Nathan & Fannie (Burroughs) Meeks; no stone; death certificate
Meeks, William Allan	Mar 26, 1964	Apr 11, 2020	Clouse Hill Cem.; Son of Homer "Cotton" Meeks & JoAnn L. Meeks
Meeks, William C.	1856 inTX	Dec 12, 1919	Oak Grove Cem.; Son of Riley (1831- before 1869) & Hatty "Hessie" Jane Cope (1830-1882) Meeks; died in mining accident; no tombstone, but buried next to to his wife; m. Susie Graham; information reported by family; addition to Cemeteries of Grundy Co., Vol. 1, p. 486 fieldstone next to his wife,
Meeks, William Grover	Sep 19, 1908	Feb 14, 1973	Hobbs Hill Cem.; Son of John & Margaret (Rose) Meeks; m. Bonnie Mae Campbell; addition to Cemeteries of Grundy Co. Vol. 1, p. 338
Meeks, William Ray "Billy"	Oct 14, 1944	Jan 01, 2019	Meeks Family Cemetery at Flat Branch; Son of Alfred James & Agnes Lillian (Coppinger) Meeks; m. 1) Betty Nunley 2) Shirley Tipton
Meeks, William Ray C	1856	Dec 01, 1919	Oak Grove Cem.; Son of Riley & Hetty Jane (Cope) Meeks; m. Mary Susan Graham
Meeks, Willie "Tate"	Jul 24, 1941	Jan 23, 2020	White Cem.; Son of Hollis Melton Meeks & Ida Mae Tate; m. Joyce Meeks
Meeks, Willie Dee	Mar 27, 1936	Jan 11, 2013	Fall Creek Cem.; Son of Elihugh & Alma Jean Meeks; m. Charlotte Layne
Meeks, Wilson Alexander	Nov 22, 1956	May 21, 2017	Clouse Hill Cem.; Son of James Britton & Dellia Emma Meeks
Meenen, Peter Martin, Jr.	Aug 10, 1946	Mar 20, 2020	Swiss Colony Cem.; Son of Peter Martin Meenen & Marie Elizabeth DeBoer; m. Francine Wiersma

Name	Birth	Death	Notes
Meimbresse, Carol	Dec 01, 1946		Orange Hill Cem.; Dau. of Frederick & Mary B. (Wierik) Meimbresse of PA.; addition to Cemeteries of Grundy Co., Vol. 2, p. 537; Her name is on the Orange family stone.
Meleen, Evelyn Estella (Gibson) Carman	May 05, 1896	Jun 22, 1980	Cumberland Heights Cem.; Dau. of John William & Flora Ella (Holland) Gibson; m. 1) Ernest E. Carman 2) Eric Martin Meleen; correction of maiden name spelling and addition to Cemeteries of Grundy Co., Vol. 1, p. 195
Mell, Hildegard Margaret (Jensen)	Jun 06, 1914	Sep 11, 2001	Swiss Colony Cem.; Dau. of Jacob V. & Fredia (Klingel) Jensen; m. George Washington Mell; addition to Cemeteries of Grundy Co., Vol. 2, p. 795
Melton, Bryan Uriah	Dec 24, 1920	Apr 21, 2013	Chattanooga National Cem.; Son of Dyke H & Hattie M. Melton; m. Maude Roddy; US Army
Melton, Connie Marie (Parsons)	Sep 16, 1971	Jan 11, 2014	Clouse Hill Cem.; Dau of Randel & Janice Parsons; m. Michael Melton
Melton, Dave	Jan 03, 1945	Oct 25, 2013	Cremated; Son of C.D. & Jessie Pauline (Parson) Melton; m. Sue Rankin
Melton, Dawn Marie	Mar 04, 1975	Nov 22, 2013	Cremated; Dau. of Bill & Darlene (Childers) Melton
Melton, Delbert Carlton "Bolley"	Sep 26, 1938	Feb 06, 2017	Clouse Hill Cem.; Son of Joseph Elbert Layne & Thelma Lucille Meeks; step father, Carl David Melton; m. Mildred "Mickey" Lowe
Melton, Floyd C	1927	1930	Brown's Chapel Cem.; Son of Wiley B. & Vennie A. (Perry) Melton; addition to Cemeteries of Grundy Co., Vol. 1, p. 106
Melton, Harvey E	Jun 16, 1909	May 13, 1980	Coalmont Cem.; Son of Harvey Houston & Patricia Laeria (Standifer) Melton; correction to Cemeteries of Grundy Co., Vol 1, p. 183
Melton, Helen Louise	Mar 02, 1931	Jun 02, 2018	Tracy City Cem.; Dau. of Tom Melton & Maude Shrum
Melton, Jack Foster	Aug 27, 1923	Sep 27. 2016	Philadelphia Cem.; Son of Robert & Bertha A (Foster) Melton; m. Taskah L. Madewell; addition to Cemeteries of Grundy Co., Vol. 2, p. 651
Merrell, Hassie M. "Pebbles" (Hill)	Nov 02, 1963	Aug 18, 2020	Dau. of Joe Lannie Hill & Josephine Cox; m. Jimmy Merrell
Merrell, Juanita	Jul 29, 1935	Apr 11, 2023	Brown's Chapel Cem.; Dau. of Albert E. & Margaret D. (Nunley) Merrell
Metrolis, George Eric	Feb 02, 1930	Oct 05, 2018	Mississippi Veterans Memorial Cem.; Son of George J. Metrolis & Mildred Woods; m. Sandy Sharp; US Navy
Meyer, Herman Eduard	May 2, 1884	May 11, 1969	Palmer Cem.; immigrant from Germany; m. Franziska Margareta Groh 15 Nov 1928 Frankfort, Ger; addition to Cemeteries of Grundy Co., Vol. 2, p.555

Name	Born	Died	Notes
Milbrath, Mary Lou Shook	Feb 14, 1919	Sep 22, 2013	Cremated; Dau. of Alan & Buena (Cannon) Shook; m, Ralph E. Milbrath
Miller, Anna Mae (Messer)	Apr 28, 1897	Jan 16, 1987	Airview Cem.; Dau. of Doc Lewis & Louthenia Caldonia (Whaley) Messer; m. Henry L. Miller; addition to Cemeteries of Grundy Co., Vol. 1, p. 5
Miller, Colton James	Oct 16, 1995	Feb 25, 2018	Franklin Memorial Gardens Cem.; Son of Clinton Miller & Angelia Stevens
Miller, Goldie Lee (Meeks)	Dec 24, 1935	Oct 02, 2021	Coalmont Cem.; Dau. of Lee & Mollie Pearl (Brown) Meeks; m. Marvin Miller
Miller, Harry R.	Jul 9, 1898	Jan 23, 1971	Homeland Acres Cem.; minister born in PA; not married; addition to Cemeteries of Grundy Co., Vol. 1, p. 341
Miller, Henry L.	Nov 21, 1891	Nov 08, 1970	Airview Cem.; Son of Alden & Martha (Hooper) Miller; m. Anna Mae Messer on Sept 14, 1913 in Bradley Co, TN; addition to Cemeteries of Grundy Co., Vol. 1, p. 5
Miller, Marie A (Fales)	Oct 06, 1947	Feb 18, 2018	Plainview Cem.; Dau. of Varsal Fales & Donnabelle Livingston Kissinger; m. Robert G. Miller, Jr.
Miller, Michael D.	Apr 30, 1977	Feb 17, 2016	Palmer Cem.; Son of Billy Wayne Miller & Tammy Campbell
Miller, Randall "Randy"	Jun 21, 1956	Oct 11, 2013	Pelham Church of Christ Cem.; Son of Don & Shirley (Roark) Miller; m. Doris Parks; USMC
Miller, Robert G, Jr.	Oct 03, 1943	Aug 22, 2018	Plainview Cem.; Son of Robert G. Sr. & Georgia M. (Flynn) Miller m. Marie Miller; US Army
Miller, Ronald "Ronney" Campbell	Mar 18, 1949	Aug 11, 1997	Burns Cem.; Son of Lee & Frankie Miller; m. Cathy Miller; US Army; addition to Cemeteries of Grundy Co., Vol. 1, p. 135
Miller, Roy Alton	May 16, 1904	Oct 22, 1971	Coalmont Cem.; Son of Jacob Thomas & Sarah Annette (Dent) Miller; m. Sallie Mae Young on Jun 8, 1929; correction to Cemeteries of Grundy Co., Vol. 1, p. 176
Miller, Ruth (Eckard)	Oct 15, 1915	Jul 30, 1981	Homeland Acres Cem.; Dau. of <u>Gail</u> P. & Vida Margaret (Williams) Eckard; addition to Cemeteries of Grundy Co., Vol. 1, p. 341
Miller, Sallie Mae (Young)	Jun 01, 1910	May 31, 1994	Coalmont Cem.; Dau. of Benjamin Franklin & Sarah Jane (Burdett) Young; m. Roy Alton Miller; correction to Cemeteries of Grundy Co., Vol. 1, p. 176
Miller, Tammy Rae (Fults)	Mar 05, 1966	Jan 22, 2018	Coalmont Cem.; Dau. of Ray Jackson Fults & Wanda Sue Scissom Layne
Millirons, Robert Raymond	Feb 05, 1958	May 29, 2020	Cremated; Son of Robert R. Millirons & Edith Player; m. Tammy Millirons
Millraney, Tennie Sue	Jan 16, 1940	Aug 15, 2015	Rose Hill Memorial Gardens; Dau. of Rufus & Pauline (Reed) Phillips; m. Wayne Millrany

Name	Born	Died	Details
Millsaps, Larry Newton	Oct 07, 1952	Mar 13, 2018	Christ Church Monteagle Cem.; Son of Silas & Ruby Mae Millsaps; m. Linda Matherly; US Army
Milner, Joseph Hartwell	Apr 11, 1905	Jul 24, 2014	Eastern Star Cem.; Son of Oscar Allen & Ethel (Blake) Milner; m Naomi Brandon; US Army
Milner, Naomi (Brandon)	Apr 16, 1905	Oct 24, 2014	Eastern Star Cem.; Dau. of Carl Jack Brandon & Mattie Coleman Frost; m. Joseph Hartwell Milner
Milstead, Forrest Eugene	Feb 03, 1945	Sep 16, 2021	Armstrong Cem.; Son of Charlie & Gertie (Roberts) Milstead; US Army
Mince, Jimmy M.	Feb 26, 1944	Dec 06, 2018	Cremated; Son of James Earl Mince & Tippie Louise Wheeler; m. Mary Guyear
Minkler, Ray Ingman	Aug 17, 1952	Aug 18, 2021	Cremated; Son of Jackson Dwight & Dorothy (Ingman) Minkler; m. April Minkler
Minor, Donald Eugene "Gene", Sr.	Nov 22, 1931	Dec 17, 2016	Summerfield Cem.; Son of Euless Mose & Mary Leota (Foster) Minor; m. 1) Huetta Gipson 2) Carolyn (Sweeton) Bolin; addition to Cemeteries of Grundy Co., Vol. 2, p. 776
Minor, Huetta Jean	Apr 16, 1931	Nov 22, 2005	Summerfield Cem.; Dau. of Hugh & Lucille (Hill) Gipson; m. Donald Eugene Minor, Sr.; addition to Cemeteries of Grundy Co., Vol. 2, p. 776
Mitchell, Emmett Estle	Mar 04, 1904	May 17, 2001	White Cem.; Son of Henry Newton & Susan Elizabeth (Roberts) Mitchell; m Gertrude Leona (Dobbs) Ward; addition & correction to Cemeteries of Grundy Co., Vol. 2, p. 1005
Mitchell, Gertrude Leona (Dobbs)	Jul 01, 1904	Aug 28, 1993	White Cem.; Dau. of James D. & Samantha Dobbs; m. 1) Oscar Lee Ward 2) Emmett Estle Mitchell; addition and correction to Cemeteries of Grundy Co., Vol. 2, p.1005
Mitchell, H. Mattie (House)	Mar 19, 1902	Jul 24, 1926	Hobbs Hill Cem.; Dau. of James & Evelyn (Hoffman) House; m. Willie B. Mitchell; addition to Cemeteries of Grundy Co., Vol. 1, p. 325
Mitchell, Henry Newton	Jan 9, 1856	May 31, 1921	Hobbs Hill Cem.; Son of John & Mary Ann (Tipton) Mitchell; m. Susan Roberts; addition to Cemeteries of Grundy Co., Vol. 1, p. 325
Mitchell, Kelsey H.	Feb 09, 1920	Apr 05, 1966	Fall Creek Cem.; Son of Willie B. & Mattie (House) Mitchell; TN BMC US Navy WWII
Mitchell, Mattie (White)	Dec 10, 1910	Jul 13, 1998	White Cem.; Dau. of Charles Logan & Rachel Louisa (Hennessee) White; m. Pasgal Marvin Mitchell; addition to Cemeteries of Grundy Co., Vol. 2, p. 1010.
Mitchell, Pasgal Marvin	Mar 27, 1900	Jun 20, 1978	White Cem.; Son of Henry Newton & Susannah Elizabeth (Roberts) Mitchell; m. Mattie Loraine White on Aug 16, 1931; addition to Cemeteries of Grundy Co., Vol. 2, p. 1010

Name	Born	Died	Details
Modschiedler, Larry L.	Feb 09, 1943	Sep 13, 2016	White Cem.; Son of John & Dorothy (Myrick) Modschiedler; m. Reba White; US Navy
Moneyheffer, Bertha (Henegar)	Jun 14, 1897	Apr 23, 1984	Fall Creek Cem.; Dau. of Marion & Emma E Henegar; m. William H. Moneyheffer
Moon, Frances Marie	Jun 02, 1935	Oct 03, 2017	Swiss Colony Cem.; Dau. of Barney & Delia (Graham) Partin; m. Austin D. Moon
Mooney, Albert Lucis	Apr 05, 1915	Oct 26, 1918	St. Andrews Cem.; Son of James & Julie (Scott) Mooney; grave unmarked
Mooney, Buddy	1913	Oct 27, 1918	Harrison Cem.; Son of James & Julie (Scott) Mooney; grave unmarked
Mooney, Georgia Goodman	Aug 27, 1914	Dec 07, 2017	Eastern Star Cem.; Dau. of Elbert & Betty (Turner) Goodman; m. Paul W. Mooney
Mooney, Willie Belle	Jun 07, 1921	Aug 25, 1998	Pryor Ridge Cem.; Dau. of Christopher C. & Mattie M. (Poteet) Standridge; m. 1)___Dills 2) ___Matthews 3) Joe Mooney; supposedly cremated by Marsh Family in GA, but her body was tossed into a concrete crypt outside on the property. Two years later, still dressed in her hospital clothes, she was brought back to Pryor Ridge to be buried. Addition to Cemeteries of Grundy Co., Vol. 2, p. 717
Mooneyham, Douglas E., Jr.	Aug 15, 1963	Sep 02, 2019	Greene Lawn Memory Gardens; Son of Douglas E. Mooneyham, Sr.
Moore, Charles Donald	Apr 29, 1942	Oct 21, 2000	Plainview Cem.; Son of James Willard & Eula (Fossett) Moore; Pharmacist; m. Mary Wynn on Apr 6, 1963; addition to Cemeteries of Grundy Co., Vol. 2, p. 669
Moore, Janet Lou (Sternkopf)	Feb 23, 1948	Jan 18, 2022	Warren "Red Hill" Cem.; Dau. of Robert Henry & Virginia Edith (Smith) Sternkopf; m. John Carroll Moore
Moore, Jessy Howard	Mar 24, 1939	Jan 12, 2002	Clouse Hill Cem.; Son of Lynwood & Mary V. (Jarvis) Moore; m. Ruth Hazel (Meeks) Parsons; He was born in VA; addition to Cemeteries of Grundy Co., Vol. 1, p. 154
Moore, John Carroll	Feb 16, 1940		Warren "Red Hill" Cem.; Son of Silas Alton "Tom" & Helen Virginia (Snavely) Moore; m. Janet Lou Sternkopf
Moore, Novella (Hargis)	Mar 05, 1927	Sep 03, 2021	University of the South Cem.; Dau. of Alfred & Irene (Troxler) Hargis; m. 1) Robert Henley 2) J. Horace Moore, Jr.
Moore, Terry Lee	Apr 29, 1905	Dec 19, 2014	Franklin Memorial Gardens; Son of Burlin Lee & Dorothy Moore; caregiver Wanda Estes
Moore, Thomas Davis, Jr.	Nov 30, 1958	Oct 04, 2021	Fall Creek Cem.; Son of Thomas Moore & Mona Sweeton
Moorehead, Stephanie	Jun 28, 1976	Jun 19, 2014	Cremated; No other infromation found

Name	Born	Died	Notes
Moran, Bessie Elizabeth "Bet"	Nov 27, 1946	Nov 04, 2017	Warren "Red Hill" Cem.; Dau of Carl & Ollie (Scott) Phillips of South Pittsburg, TN,; m. Mark Moran II: See Mark Wilson Moran for children & grandchildren
Moran, James	Jul 04, 1863	Feb 01, 1909	Tracy City Cem.; Son of Peter & Bridgett Moran; deaf; froze to death per newspaper article
Moran, Mark Wilson	Aug 03, 1944	Jan 12, 2022	Warren "Red Hill" Cem.; Son of Franklin Peter & Martha Faye "Willie" (Meeks) Moran; m. Bessie Elizabeth "Bet" Phillips; Family: Terri, Jerri, Karen, Mark III; Grandchildren: Dino, Talisha, Austin, Kayla, Kera, Tera, Kati
Moran, Patrick Ellis	Jul 14, 1956	Oct 06, 2018	Cremated; Son of Tom Moran & Jean Galligan; m. Rhonda Newby
Moreland, Mona Griswold (Sweeton)	Dec 10, 1937	Jan 22, 2018	Tracy City Cem.; Dau. of Carl P. Sweeton & Anna Griswold; m. Karl Phillip Moreland
Morgan, Appielona O'Neal	Oct 11, 1875	Feb 03, 1913	Oak Grove Cem.; Dau. of John Wilburn & Nancy Jane (Burnett) Neal, Sr.; wife of John Lonzo Morgan; Addition to Cemeteries of Grundy Co., Vol. 1, p.105
Morgan, Betty Jean "Mary Lou"	May 01, 1941	Jun 08, 2014	Burns Cem.; Dau. of Daniel Wesley Green & Amanda Matilda " Mandy" O'Neal; m. Franklin Morgan
Morgan, Charles William	Jul 30, 1930	Dec 29, 2014	Coalmont Cem.; Son of David Garvin & Flora E. (Mooney) Morgan; m. Jewell Rosanell "Ann" Meadows; US Army; addition to Cemteries of Grundy Co., Vol. 1, p. 173
Morgan, Craig Franklin	Feb 13, 1967	Oct 19, 2013	Burns Cem.; Son of Franklin D. & Betty Morgan; m. Allison Goodman
Morgan, Dorothy Mae	May 01, 1920	Jun 20, 1921	Oak Grove Cem.; in an unmarked grave beside Josie (Nunley) Morgan; probably Dau. Of George W. & Josie (Nunley) Morgan; addition to Cemeteries of Grundy Co., Vol. 1, p. 490
Morgan, Franklin D.	Sep 29, 1885	Jul 29, 1973	Plainview Cem.; Son of John Lonzo Morgan & Ethel Virginia Caldwell; m. Betty Morgan; US Army
Morgan, George Washington "Judge"	Sep 7, 1878	Mar 08, 1932	Bonny Oak Cem.; Son of David Jackson & Arcadia Jane (Stephens) Morgan; m. Mary Louise "Lula" Hill; correction by relative Mike Morgan to death date in Cemeteries of Grundy Co., Vol. 1, p. 83
Morgan, Jackie Ray	May 19, 1944	Jan 29, 2013	Cremated; Son of John A. & Ethel Morgan
Morgan, Lorene (Campbell)	Sep 28, 1913	Jan 21, 2003	Airview Cem.; Dau. of Andrew Jackson & Christine (Johnson) Campbell; m. Walter Orene Morgan; Oct 8, 1932; addition to Cemeteries of Grundy Co., Vol. 1, p. 8

Name	Born	Died	Details
Morgan, Nell (Nunley)	Jan 17, 1907	Mar 01, 1977	Bonny Oak Cem.; Dau. of Albert Carroll & Ada (Nunley) Nunley; m. J.T. Morgan; addition to Cemeteries of Grundy Co., Vol. 1, p. 91
Morgan, Patsy Louise	Apr 24, 1947	Oct 29, 2014	Plainview Cem.; Dau of Andrew Bass Payne & Minnie Anderson;
Morgan, Phyllis Ann	Feb 27, 1951	Jul 07, 2021	Dau. of Charles & Bertie Morgan; never married
Morgan, Rose Marie "Rosie" (Dykes)	Ca. 1951	Oct 05, 2015	Brown's Chapel Cem.; Dau. of Robert J. & Elsie Dykes
Morgan, Rudy Lee	Oct 16, 1949	Nat 12, 1950	Bonny Oak Cem.; Son of Charles J. & Ethel (Way) Morgan; addition to Cemeteries of Grundy Co., Vol. 1, p. 89
Morgan, Shawn Lisa	Jun 29, 1962	Mar 11, 2022	Morgan Memorial Gardens in Gainesboro, TN; Dau. of Charles Eugene, Sr. & Sarah LaVerna (Fish) Kimming; Her sons Zac & Zeb Morgan live in Grundy Co.
Morgan, Tom Ray	Apr 16, 1948	May 12, 1949	Bonny Oak Cem.; Son of Charles J. & Ethel (Way) Morgan; addition to Cemeteries of Grundy Co., Vol. 1, p. 89
Morgan, Walter Orene	Apr 28, 1904	Dec 14, 1998	Airview Cem.; Son of Thomas A. & Fannie (Taylor) Morgan; m. Lorene Campbell; addition to Cemeteries of Grundy Co., Vol. 1, p. 8
Morris, Christopher	Dec 12, 1974	Aug 27, 2019	Cowan-Montgomery Cem.; Son of Franklin Taylor Morris & Annette Matthews & step father Troy Matthews; m. Kim Morris
Morris, Johnny Lee	Mar 17, 1960	Mar 05, 2022	Payne's Cove Cem.; Son of Jessie & Maymie Morris; m. Wanda Morris
Morris, Lee Roy	Feb 18, 1944	Feb 04, 2022	Franklin Memorial Gardens; Son of Elbert T & Minnie P. (Roberts) Morris; m. Darlene Kennerly
Morris, Mary Elizabeth (Henry)	Aug 06, 1943	Sep 02, 2021	Brown's Chapel Cem.; Dau. of Roy Lee & Oma Lee (King) Henry
Morris, Rita T.	Aug 31, 1980	Dec 04, 2020	Palmer Cem.; Dau. of Ricky & Kathy Morrison
Morris, Timothy Wade	Sep 20, 1971	Sep 30, 2020	Cremated; Son of Kenneth & Barbara (Morris) Morris; m. Melissa Morris
Morrison, Allen Eugene	1951	Jun 09, 2021	Cremated; Son of Lonnie & Ethel Morrison; m. Linda Carol Rogers; U.S. Army Vietnam
Morrison, Allie Edith (Glisson)	Jul 05, 1903	Mar 05, 1967	Palmer Cem.; Dau. of John W. & Nannie J. (Reed) Glisson; addition of Cemeteries of Grundy Co., Vol. 2, p. 568
Morrison, Arnold Theodore	Sep 19, 1933	Aug 10, 2022	Oak Grove Cem.; Son of Adam Theodore Mitchell & Elsie Harriet (Nolan) Morrison; m. 1) Kathleen Nunley 2) Eda (Sanders) Anderson; addition to Cemeteries of Grundy Co., Vol. 1, p. 510

Name	Born	Died	Details
Morrison, Ben	Feb 12, 1916	Mar 28, 1979	Palmer Cem.; Son of David Alfred & Martha E. (Blevins) Morrison; m. Jessie Lee Tate; addition to Cemeteries of Grundy Co., Vol. 1, p. 567
Morrison, Benjamin H.	Nov 15, 1889	Mar 06, 1977	Palmer Cem.; Son of Zachary Taylor & Delilah Jane (Sanders) Morrison; addition to Cemeteries of Grundy Co., Vol. 2, p. 568
Morrison, Betty Jean (Dishroom)	Mar 24, 1941	Feb 11, 2018	Summerfield Cem.; Dau. of Freddy Dishroom & Letha Morrison; m. George Morrison
Morrison, Billy Keith	Sep 27, 1991	Jun 06, 2008	Palmer Cem.; Son of Randy & Kelly (Burrel) Morrison
Morrison, Charlene "Char" (Jacobs)	Jun 24, 1937	Oct 23, 2018	Woodlawn Memorial Park Cem. Nashville, TN; Dau. of Charles & Rachel (Bonner) Jacobs; m. 1) Charles Nunley 2) William "Bill" Morrison
Morrison, Claude Edward	Nov 19, 1958	Nov 21, 2018	Son of Claude Wesley Morrison & Clarine Pollard
Morrison, Dan Stanford	Dec 25, 1960	Nov 30, 2021	Coalmont Cem.; Son of Huch Elmer & Ruthie Jane (Moore) Morrison; m. Teresa Stevens
Morrison, Danny Ray	Nov 14, 1962	Feb 18, 2015	Palmer Cem.; Son of Ben & Jessie Lee (Tate) Morrison, Jr.
Morrison, Elsia (Nolan)	Feb 05, 1915	May 28, 1990	Oak Grove Cem.; Dau. of James & Louise Elizabeth (Higdon) Nolan; m. Mitchell Morrison; addition to Cemeteries of Grundy Co., Vol. 1, p. 508
Morrison, Elsie Lee (Johnson)	Jan 09, 1930	Jun 15, 2000	Plainview Cem.; Dau. of Willie & Flora (Lockhart) Johnson; m. John C. Morrison; addition to Cemeteries of Grundy Co.
Morrison, Hunter Hobbs	Jul 18, 2020	Jul 18, 2020	AirView Cem.; Son of Paul & Mandy Morrison
Morrison, Jerry E.	Jun 15, 1938	Jul 30, 1994	Swiss Colony Cem;Sonof Lonnie Norman & Ethel Tresie (Turner) Morrison; addition to Cemeteries of Grundy Co., Vol. 2, p. 795
Morrison, Jerry R.	1939	1986	Palmer Cem.; Son of Benjamin H. & Addie E. (Glisson) Morrison; Cemeteries of Grundy Co., Vol 2, p.568
Morrison, John C.	Mar 22, 1927	Nov 16, 1967	Plainview Cem.; Son of Isom Moses & Josie Lee (Way) Morrison; m. Elsie Lee Johnson; addition to Cemeteries of Grundy Co., Vol. 2, p. 686
Morrison, Johnny Kenneth	Aug 08, 1965	Sep 11, 2020	Cremated; Son of Alfred Morrison, Jr. & Nellie D. Tate
Morrison, Kathleen (Nunley)	Jun 29, 1934	Dec 06, 1996	Oak Grove Cem: Dau. of Yancy & Clara G. (Worley) Nunley; m. Arnold T. Morrison; addition to Cemeteries of Grundy Co., Vol. 1, p. 510
Morrison, Martin Charles	Feb 09, 1934	Jan 30, 2014	Cremated; Son of Lee Robert Morrison & Pearl Layne; m. Dorothy Privett

Name	Birth	Death	Details
Morrison, Nellie D.	Dec 16, 1927	Dec 28, 2015	Palmer Cem.; Dau. of Martha D. Brown; m. Alfred Morrison, Jr.
Morrison, Oma Lee (Meeks)	Nov 24, 1935	Oct 10, 2020	Plainview Cem.; Dau. of James Frank & Emma Mae (Reed) Meeks; m Ozia Bonnal "O.B." Morrison; addition to Cemeteries of Grundy Co., Vol. 2, p. 697
Morrison, Robert Lee	Jan 08, 1966	Oct 16, 1992	Palmer Cem.; Son of Martin Charles & Dorothy Carol (Privett) Morrison; addition to Cemeteries of Grundy Co., Vol. 2, p. 579
Morrison, Ronald	Jun 03, 2016	Jun 03, 2016	Coalmont Cem.; Son of Cyrus Morrison & Hayley Huntley; premature baby
Morrison, Ruthie Jane	Jul 05, 1922	Mar 22, 2012	Coalmont Cem.; m. Hugh L Morrison; correction to Cemeteries of Grundy Co., Vol. 1, p.187
Morrison, Teresa (Stevens)	Dec 10, 1962	Jun 22, 2021	Coalmont Cem.; Dau. of Harold James & Verna Mae (Gipson) Stevens; m. Dan Stanford Morrison
Morrison, William Daniel	Nov 11, 1961	Aug 13, 2013	Palmer Cem.; Son of Alfred & Nellie D. Morrison; m. Stephany Morrison
Morrison, Wilma Grace	Jun 10, 1938	Nov 22, 2017	Palmer Cem.; Dau. of James Benjamin & Rebecca (Peeks) Clemons; m. Lonnie Harold Morrison; addition to Cemeteries of Grundy Co., Vol. 2, p. 569
Morrow, Betty (Carrick)	Jul 29, 1942	Feb 06, 2015	Jacksonville National Cem in FL; Dau. of Robert & Vilda Corinne (Kirk) Carrick; m. Willie Edward "Bill" Morrow; Cpl. US Army Korea
Mosier, Charles	Mar 07, 1941	Sep 22, 2016	Burkett's Chapel Cem.; Son of Raymond Mosier & Alice (Layne) McDaniel
Mosley, Mildred Christine (O'Neal) Sanders	May 07, 1938		Oak Grove Cem.; Dau. of Elbert Willis & Dora Lee (Braden) O'Neal; m. 1) Joe Reggie Sanders 2)____ Mosley; addition to Cemeteries of Grundy Co., Vol. 1, p. 510
Moss, Gisela Alwine Karla (Kropp)	Nov 28, 1928	Dec 24, 1986	Monteagle Cem.; Dau. of Karl & Johanne (Reimers) Kropp; m. William Lee Moss, Jr.; addition to Cemeteries of Grundy Co., Vol. 1, p. 432
Moss, Thomas Wesbury	Aug 03, 1928	May 24, 2018	Memory Hill Cem. Dothan, AL; Son of John Grover & Mary Shilo Moss
Moss, Virginia A.	Jan 10, 1907	Oct 14, 1994	Monteagle Cem.; Dau. of James David & Virginia (Ladd) Moss; m. William Lee Moss; addition to Cemeteries of Grundy Co., Vol. 1, p. 449
Moss, William Lee, Jr.	Sep 27, 1932	Mar 02, 1993	Monteagle Cem.; Son of William Asa & Virginia A. (Smith) Moss; m. Gislea A. Moss; TSGT US AIR FORCE VIETNAM; addition to Cemeteries of Grundy Co., Vol. 1, p. 432

Name	Born	Died	Details
Mott, Claudie	Dec 11, 1934	Feb 10, 2014	Coalmont Cem Son of Floyd & Hazel (Lockhart) Mott; m. Willie Kate Campbell
Mott, Linda Rose (Ware)	Feb 14, 1941	Feb 17, 2019	Coalmont Cem.; Dau. of John Ware & Lucille Brown; m. Tommy Mott
Mottern, Lorene (Patterson)	Jun 06, 1920	Jun 15, 2013	Providence Methodist Cem.; Dau. of Daniel B. & Rosa Ellen (Conry) Patterson; m. Jack Henderson Mottern; addition to Cemeteries of Grundy Co., Vol. 2, p. 713
Mullican, James Arthur	Feb 25, 1945	Jun 28, 1990	White Cem.; Son of Arthur Gyle & Minnie Ruth (Simmons) Mullican; m. Sonya J. Cookston; addition to Cemeteries of Grundy Co., Vol. 2, p. 1012
Murphy, Crista Jane (Cornelison)	Jan 18, 1952	Jul 11, 2021	Chattanooga National Cem.; Dau. of James Paul & June Gloria (Braly) Cornelison; m. Charles Austin Murphy, III
Murphy, Dorothy Ella (McNeece)	May 29, 1918	Jan 11, 1997	Burns Cem.; Dau. of Virgil N & Edna N. (Huckabee) McNeece; addition to Cemeteries of Grundy Co., Vol, 1, p. 130
Murphy, Juanita Carol (Harlan)	Jul 30, 1931	Aug 4 2015	Meeks Family Cem at Flat Branch; Dau. of Friend S. & Emma Theodosia (LeMasters) Harlan; m. Robert Murphy
Murphy, Morris V.	Nov 22, 1910	Aug 14, 1931	Fall Creek Cem.; Son of Paul Silas & Minnie (Ransome) Murphy
Murray, Adam Troy "Scoobie"	Aug 21, 1964	Jul 18, 2005	Palmer Cem.; Son of Bill & Faye Murray; correction to Cemeteries of Grundy Co. Vol. 2, p. 561
Murray, David Vincent	Jun 03, 1945		Warren "Red Hill" Cem.; Son of adoptive parents: Joseph & Margaret (Holland) Murray. Born in Dorchester, MA, but no idea of who real parents were. David and his sister were adopted together.; m. Mattie M. (Layne) Lawyer; military
Murray, Keith Allen, Sr.	Mar 12, 1956	May 13, 2019	Cremated; Son of George & Gladys Murray; m. Sharon Murray
Murray, Mattie M. (Layne)	Aug 15, 1946	Feb 12, 2020	Warren "Red Hill" Cem.; Dau. of Clyde & Elsie (Meeks) Layne: m. 1)_____ Lawyer 2) David Murray
Murray, Opal R. (Meeks)	Apr 13, 1905	Jun 21, 2016	Plainview Cem.; Dau. of Jim King & Mary Blaylock; m. 1) R.M. McFalls 2) John K. "Buck" Meeks 3) Bill Murray
Murvin, Theoren J., Jr.	Oct 22, 1929	Jan 03, 2017	City of Pompano Beach Cem.; Son of Theoren & Lillian (Barwick) Murvin; US Air Force
Muthling, Waldermar Friedrick	Apr 22, 1932	1999	Monteagle Cem.; b. in Hamburg, Germany; m 1) Peggie L McCarty, Jan 1958 in FL 2) Helen Jewel Shook, Apr 19, 1980; Army Wpns Co. 3rd Inf. WWII, addition to Cemeteries of Grundy Co., Vol. 1, p. 461

Name	Birth	Death	Details
Myers, Altalene "Tiny" (Sissom)	Feb 16, 1931	Mar 24, 2014	Coalmont Cem.; Dau. of Alton & Bertha Louise (Melton) Sissom; m. John Myers
Myers, Bernie Robert	Jun 16, 1950	May 10, 1971	Palmer Cem.; Son of James W. & Georgia M. (Knox) Myers; grave moved to cem. from a residence; addition to Cemeteries of Grundy Co., Vol. 2, p. 555
Myers, Billie Faye (Hampton)	Mar 13, 1932	Feb 27, 2022	Plainview Cem.; Dau. of George H & Mattie (Griswold) Hampton; m. John K. Myers
Myers, Bonnie Ozell (Patterson)	Mar 06, 1922	Jan 11, 2010	Warren "Red Hill" Cem.; Dau. of Daniel M. & Annie (Jacobs) Patterson; m. Carmon Myers; addition to Cemeteries of Grundy Co., Vol. 2, p. 945
Myers, Brent	Jan 16, 1974	Jan 01, 2020	Eastern Star Cemetery; Son of David Myers & Jennie Lee Griswold; m. Jeana Myers; U.S. Army
Myers, Carmon Ernest, Sr	Jun 11, 1922	Aug 15, 2014	Bethel Cem.; Son of Lonnie & Alice (Campbell) Myers; m. 1) Bonnie Patterson 2) Ruth (Shaddock) Lasater; addition to Cemeteries of Grundy Co., Vol. 1, p. 53
Myers, Cebert C.	Oct 05, 1905	Jul 07, 1961	Altamont Cem.; Son of Claude Eugene & Laura Louella (Owen) Myers; m. Alva M. Smartt; addition to Cemeteries of Grundy Co., Vol. 1, p. 25
Myers, David Allen	Jun 09, 1945	Jul 09, 2021	Payne's Cove Cem.; Son of Edgar & Nell Ruth (Oliver) Myers; 1) Wanda Sue Marilyn Arp on Oct 8, 1966 2) Kathy Myers
Myers, Delbert "Delva"	Jul 27, 1932	Sep 20, 2017	Wesley Chapel Cem.; Son of Calvin & Grace (Hobbs) Myers; m. Betty Sue Brady
Myers, Donald "Catfish"	Nov 17, 1972	Jun 01, 2021	Clouse Hill Cem.; Son of Donald Ray & Debra Jane (Thomas) Myers; m. Beth Steedley
Myers, Donald Edward "Donnie"	May 21, 1946	Jan 01, 2021	Cremated; Son of Clifton & Abbie (Schiesser) Myers
Myers, Donald Ray	May 07, 1905	Dec 23, 2015	Cremated; Son of Charlie & Mildred Jewel Myers; m. Debra Myers
Myers, Emma B. (Holt)	Jun 19, 1872	Mar 24, 1946	Tracy City Cem.; Dau of David S. Holt & Mary Ann Polston; m. John Will Myers; no tombstone
Myers, Ethel Aileen (Meeks)	1929	Feb 16, 2021	Coalmont Cem.; Dau. of France & Ethel (Price) Meeks; m. Vance Myers
Myers, Evelyn D (Bates)	May 26, 1953	Aug 27, 2019	Cremated; Dau. of Charles Bates & Joyce Roberts
Myers, Franklin S.	Jun 20, 1956	Mar 19, 1961	Fall Creek Cem.; Son of Calvin & Geneva (Caldwell) Myers; information from death certificate – no tombstone
Myers, Gene D	1938	May 12, 2020	Prairie Plains Church of Christ Cem.; Son of Floyd & Elloise (Campbell) Myers; m. Judith Wolff

Name	Birth	Death	Notes
Myers, Georgia M. (Knox)	Oct 28, 1930	May 08, 2011	Palmer Cem.; Dau. of Fred Earl & Pearl (Henry) Knox; m. James W. Myers; addition to Cemeteries of Grundy Co., Vol. 2, p. 555
Myers, Ina Myers	Oct 19, 1927	Dec 22, 2021	Cremated; Dau. of William Cecil & Elsie (Campbell) Myers
Myers, James	Nov 28, 1949	Feb 16, 2019	Coalmont Cem.; Son of Vance Myers & Aileen Meeks; m. Loretta Kay Wood
Myers, James Herman	May 04, 1940	Oct 01, 2020	Bethel Cem.; Son of James Merrell & Vela Lucille (Hawk) Myers; m. Betsy Barton
Myers, James Lee	Apr 06, 1975	May 02, 1991	Plainview Cem.; Son of William Douglas & Alma Lee (Nunley) Myers; addition to Cemeteries of Grundy Co., Vol. 2, p. 697
Myers, John Kenneth "Duck"	Sep 04, 1924	Mar 14, 2019	Plainview Cem.; Son of Claude & Argie (Ingram) Myers; m. Billie Fay Hampton; US Navy WWII
Myers, John Will	1869	Dec 01, 1922	Tracy City Cem.; Son of Bill Myers & Sally Nunley; m. Emma B. Holt; no tombstone
Myers, Keith R.	Feb 13, 1956	Feb 18, 2015	Bethel Cem.; Son of Pascal & Juanita (Oliver) Myers; m. Nadine Nunley
Myers, Kenneth Dewayne	Oct 18, 1960	Feb 20, 2021	Hunerwadel Cem.; Son of Speeker & Shirley (Whitman) Myers
Myers, Lavina "Vina" (Stoner)	Sep 9, 1800	Jun 24, 1886	Stoner Cem at Stella Bottom; Dau. of Henry, Jr. & Elizabeth (Wilson) Stoner; m. 1) Peter Countiss, IV 2) Johnny Myers
Myers, Lettie Lucille	Sep 10, 1920	Mar 02, 2013	Bonny Oak Cem.; Day of Johnnie & Jennie (Argo) Fults; m. Leonard Myers
Myers, Lillie Frances (Davis)	1876	1959	Plainview Cem.; Dau. of John R. & Elizabeth A. (Holmes) Davis; m. John J. Myers; addition to Cemeteries of Grundy Co., Vol. 2, p. 673
Myers, Mae Wanda (McFarland)	1943	Nov 26, 2021	Monteagle Cem.; Dau. of R.C. & Kate McFarland; m. Buddy Myers
Myers, Mancil Perry	Sep 19, 1920	Aug 16, 1977	Franklin Memorial Gardens Cem.; Son of Alton & Clara (Bryant) Myers; m. Ruby Jewel Curtis; WWII
Myers, Marshall E.	Aug 16, 1959	Apr 09, 1979	Palmer Cem.; Son of James W. & Georgia M. (Knox) Myers; grave moved to cemetery from a residence; addition to Cemeteries of Grundy Co., Vol. 2, p. 555
Myers, Marshall E.	Aug 16, 1959	Apr 09, 1979	Palmer Cem.; Son of James W. & Georgia M. (Knox) Myers – grave moved from a residence
Myers, Martha Katherine (Tigue) Brazile	Jan 21, 1921	Jul 27, 2008	Tracy City Cem.; Dau of Leonard Norton & Daisy Bell Tigue; m. 1) James Franklin Brazile 2) Denver Alton Myers; correction to Cemeteries of Grundy Co., Vol. 2, p. 837
Myers, Mary Belle (King)	Mar 10, 1943	Dec 13, 2021	Altamont Cem.; Dau. of Harvey & Lela (Fitch) King; m. Kermit Ray Denton
Myers, Mary Ellen "Toodie" (Hobbs)	Oct 17, 1932	Jan 02, 2019	Little Johnny Myers Cem.; Dau. of Odie Hobbs & Lydia Myers; m. Vernon Myers

Name	Born	Died	Details
Myers, Michael Hardy	Aug 20, 1956	Jun 05, 2021	Swiss Colony Cem.; Son of Glenn Hardy & Lela Mae (Crabtree) Myers
Myers, Mollie (Davis)	Nov 3, 1868	Mar 03, 1952	Oak Grove Cem.; Dau. of John R. & Elizabeth (Holmes) Davis; addition to Cemeteries of Grundy Co., Vol. 1, p. 497
Myers, Orpha Jean (Griffith)	Jul 24, 1932	Mar 12, 2021	Oak Grove Cem.; Jesse Griffith & Julia Harris; m. 1) Waldo Myers 2) John Russell Buchan
Myers, Pamela G. (Conry)	Nov 07, 1962	Nov 22, 2020	Plainview Cem.; Dau. of Conald Conry & Bertha Lowe; m. Mitchel Myers
Myers, Paul Jacob	Aug 15, 1977	Aug 15, 1977	Oak Grove Cem.; Son of Jim W. Myers; addition to Cemeteries of Grundy Co., Vol. 1, p. 488
Myers, Ruby Jewel	Sep 11, 1931	Feb 27, 2016	Franklin Memorial Gardens; m. Mancel Perry Myers
Myers, Rudy Wendell	May 19, 1952	Aug 18, 2013	Swiss Cem.; Son of Clifton & Abbie (Schiesser) Myers; m.1) Cora Jean Sanders 2) Nancy Ann Layne
Myers, Teresa Ann	Jul 31, 1953	Apr 27, 2017	Clouse Hill Cem.; Dau. of L.B. & Anita Crabtree; m. Stanley Myers
Myers, Thomas L.	Oct 16, 1932	Feb 04, 2013	Cremated; Son of Henry Clay & Cecil Etheleen (Tate) Myers; US Army
Myers, Vance "Tubby"	Oct 23, 1926	Apr 24, 2022	Coalmont Cem.; Son of Benson & Nancy (Campbell) Myers; m. Ethel Aileen Meeks
Myers, Wendell Matthew	Oct 09, 1975	Apr 04, 2014	Palmer Cem.; Son of Wendell Myers & Nancy (Campbell) Griffith
Myers, William	Mar 26, 1832	Oct 17, 1895	Tracy City Cem.; Son of Jacob & Dorcus (Lynn) Myers, m. Celia Nunley Aug 1, 1857; addition to Cemeteries of Grundy Co., Vol. 2, p. 903
Nance, Kayla Leigh Ann	Jan 09, 2008	Jan 09, 2008	Swiss Colony Cem.; Dau. of Curtis & Christie (Rollins) Nance
Nance, Leonard Curtis	Jan 09, 2008	Jan 09, 2008	Swiss Colony Cem.; Son of Curtis & Christie (Rollins) Nance
Nance, Margaret Fay	Jan 03, 1931	Jun 03, 2016	Burkett's Chapel Cem.; Dau. of John Lafayette & Katie M. Plumer Davis Knowlen Nance m. Mitchel G. Nance
Nance, Mayna Rose (Avent)	Jun 17, 1932	May 13, 2020	Cremated; Dau. of James Avent & Jeanette Nelson; m. Walter Nance
Nance, Michael Lonnie	Jul 18, 1965	May 02, 2022	Swiss Colony Cem.; Son of Lonnie B. & Jewelene (Sanders) Nance; m. Sherri Lynn Caldwell
Neal, James Robert	May 12, 1877	May 11, 1954	Monteagle Cem.; Son of William & Lizzie Neal; m. Sally Neal
Neal, Jerry W.	1963	Feb 01, 2014	Lexi Cross Roads Cem.; Son of James David Neal & Margaret Smith; m. Bessie Jane Reed

Name	Birth	Death	Notes
Neal, Roy	Jul 18, 1929	Oct 17, 2013	Fall Creek Cem.; Son of Fred & Adeline (McDaniel) Neal; m. 1) Lily Mae Neal 2) Hazel Tate
Nearn, Mary L.	Feb 17, 1905	Mar 03, 1905	Altamont Cem.; Dau. of Mansfield Lafayette & Virginia T. (Soward) Nearn; addition to Cemeteries of Grundy Co., Vol. 1, p. 29
Nearn, Nellie P.	1880	1880	Altamont Cem.; Dau. of Mansfield Lafayette & Virginia T. (Soward) Nearn; addition to Cemeteries of Grundy Co., Vol. 1, p. 29
Nelson, George Edward	Aug 12, 1932	Jun 09, 2015	Gilliam Cem in Kimball; Son of Dennis & Pearl (Nichols) Nelson; m. JoAnne Merriman
Nelson, Theodore Ray	Jun 28, 1947	Jan 31, 2022	Cremated; Son of Harvey & Margaret (Jennings) Nelson; m. Sharon Hurst; Naval Reserve
Nester, Honor Eda Nettie (Dockum)	Jun 02, 1905	Mar 25, 1999	Homeland Acres Cem.; Dau. of John Sinclair & Hulda Ellen (Wilson) Dockum; m. Harvey Wilson Nester; addition to Cemeteries of Grundy Co., Vol. 1, p. 341
Newbern, Helen	Ca. 1961	Oct 04, 2015	Cremated; Dau. of James & Anna Faye (Campbell) Petty
Newsome, Buford Eugene	May 11, 1944	May 20, 2016	Cremated; Son of Charles A. & Gladys (Brown) Newsome; m. Irene O'Dea Clardy
Newsome, James Henry	1858	Feb 27, 1937	Orange Hill; no info on tombstone, probable son of Grover W & Elizabeth (McGraw) Newsome; addition to Cemeteries of Grundy Co., Vol. 2, p. 533
Newson, Laura Jean (Willoughby)	Apr 13, 1963	Jan 21, 2022	Cremated: Dau. of James Willoughby & Barbara Jean (Leon) Nolan; m. Tonny W. Newson
Newson, Tonny Wilkie	Jul 21, 1961	Feb 14, 2020	Cremated; Son of Charles Wilkie Newson & Velma Louise Norris; m. Laura Willoughby; U.S. Navy – Desert Storm
Nicholson, James L, III	Dec 28, 1934	Jan 05, 2020	Cremated; Son of James Nicholson, Jr. & Charlene Thomasson
Nigg, Joseph	Mar 11, 1858	Aug 18, 1931	Swiss Cem.; born Switzerland; from death certificate, He was a baker.
Nivison, Lois Leta Rutherford	Mar 05, 1914	Apr 27, 1997	Monteagle Cem.; Dau. of Arthur L. & Daisy L. (Paris) Hall m. 1) LeRoy Nivison 2) Edgar L. Rutherford; addition to Cemeteries of Grundy Co., Vol. 1, p. 457
Nivison, Wilhelmina (Weber)	May 16, 1888	Jun 27, 1960	Fall Creek Cem.; Dau. of Ernest Weber & Wilhelmina Buckholz; m. Leroy N. Nivison
Nix, George Ray	Sep 16, 1945	Apr 15, 2020	Chattanooga National Cem.; Son of Luther & Nina Mae (Byars) Nix; m. Irmgard Nix; U.S. Army
Nix, Infant	Apr 29, 1905	Apr 29, 1905	Gregg Cem.; Son of Luther G. & Nina Mae (Byars) Nix; correction to Cemeteries of Grundy Co., Vol. 1, p. 306

Name	Birth	Death	Notes
Nix, Mildred L. (Smartt)	Sep 14, 1943	Aug 24, 2010	Gregg Cem.; Dau. of Carl David Smartt; m. Henry Joel Nix; correction & addition to Cemeteries of Grundy Co., Vol. 1, p. 305
Nixon, Martha Louise (Kilgore)	Mar 19, 1952	Sep 16, 2018	Cremated; Dau. of James Alton & Nancy Jean Kilgore; m. John Edwin Nixon
Noel, Cynthia Lee (White)	Sep 23, 1956	Feb 06, 2019	Cremated; tombstone at Stoghill Cem. in Jackson, GA; Dau of Dorothy Tribble; m. Dean Noel
Nolan, Alpha Neoma (Meeks)	Oct 03, 1922	Oct 10, 2003	Palmer Cem.; Dau. of Benjamin Franklin & Nancy (Meeks) McWain; m. Freeman Douglas Nolan; addition to Cemeteries of Grundy Co., Vol. 2, p. 563
Nolan, Annie Ruth	Dec 18, 1958	Feb 08, 1959	Oak Grove Cem.; Dau. of Gilliam Baxter & Sally Ruth (Smith) Nolan; addition to Cemeteries of Grundy Co., Vol. 1, p. 499
Nolan, Barbara Jean (Leon)	Aug 23, 1943	May 25, 2020	Fall Creek Cem.; Dau. of Theodore Leon & Grace Demo; m. Jimmy Nolan
Nolan, Clyde Allen	Jul 27, 1940	Nov 21, 2017	Palmer Cem.; Son of John & Gladys Pickett Nolan
Nolan, Dee Jay	Jul 27, 1994	Nov 02, 2015	Palmer Cem.; Son of Donnie & Rhonda (Cox) Nolan
Nolan, Edward Louis	Jan 25, 1957	Mar 23, 2017	Palmer Cem.; Son of Gilliam & Sally Ruth (Smith) Nolan
Nolan, Elsie (Nunley)	Oct 02, 1942	May 20, 2022	Palmer Cem.; Dau. of Wesley Earl Nunley & Elizabeth Bertha Louise (Layne) Nunley; m. Raymond Charleston Nolan
Nolan, Gaberial (Hillis)	Jan 19, 1964	Feb 04, 2021	Palmer Cem.; Dau. of J.D. & Betty Marie (Kenner) Hillis; m. Eugene "Rudy" Nolan
Nolan, Herman	Dec 12, 1937	Nov 21, 2015	Palmer Cem.; Son of Claude & Ruby (Hayes) Nolan; m. Ola Mae Nolan; US Army
Nolan, James Jerome	Jan 16, 1969	Dec 16, 2013	Palmer Cem.; Son of Clyde Nolan & Bonnie (Brady) Shultz
Nolan, Jimmy Dale	Jan 29, 1971	Dec 06, 2021	Palmer Cem.; Son of Dale Baxter & Christine Nolan
Nolan, Jimmy Leefayette	Jan 02, 1936	Dec 12, 2019	Fall Creek Cem.; Son of John Jerome Nolan & Gladys Tennessee Pickett; m. Barbara Jean Leon
Nolan, Katherine Lucille (Kilgore)	Dec 23, 1946	Aug 10, 2014	Presnell Cem in Marion Co.; Dau of John W. & Tiny Ann Kilgore; m. Clyde Allen Nolan
Nolan, Maggie Marie (Curtis)	Jan 30, 1924	Dec 10, 2019	Oak Grove Cem.; Dau. of Dee & Mattie Curtis; m. Oscar Edward Nolan
Nolan, Marvin	Mar 05, 1939	May 26, 2020	Palmer Cem.; Son of Claude Nolan & Ruby Haynes; m. Donna Nolan
Nolan, Mary Louise "Molley" (Partin)	Aug 16, 1886	Mar 11, 1909	Orange Hill Cem.; Dau. of John Louis & Thomas Etta (Dove) Partin; m. William Edward "Ed" Nolan; addition to Cemeteries of Grundy Co., Vol. 1, p. 539

Name	Birth	Death	Details
Nolan, Naomi (McWain)	Oct 03, 1922	Oct 10, 2015	Palmer Cem.; Dau. of Frank & Nancy (Meeks) McWain; m. Freeman Doug Nolan; Cemeteries of Grundy Co., Vol 2, p.563
Nolan, Shelia Faye (Campbell)	Jan 31, 1977	Jul 10, 2018	Fall Creek Cem.; Dau. of Estes & Frances Sue Campbell
Nolan, Shirley Jean (Ward)	Sep 21, 1937	Oct 31, 1907	Brown's Chapel Cem.; Dau. of William F. & Velma (Berry) Ward; m. Alvin Lee Nolan, Sr.; addition to Cemeteries of Grundy Co., Vol. 1, p. 110
Nolan, Stone Garrett	Feb 14, 1996	Jun 05, 2020	Cremated; Son of Dale & Sudonna Nolan
Nolan, Thelma	Mar 21, 1927	Oct 16, 2015	Palmer Cem.; Dau. of Will & Rosa (Caldwell) Bone; m. Alfred "Buddy" Nolan
Norman, Dwayne Fulton	Dec 14, 1961	Apr 30, 2002	Monteagle Cem.; Son of Henry & Betty Jean (Boot) Norman; m. Alice Cantrell; addition to Cemeteries of Grundy Co., Vol. 1, p. 447
Norman, William Franklin, Rev.	Jun 15, 1868	Aug 23, 1947	Monteagle Cem.; Son of Newton & Christine Norman; m. 1) Lela Banks 2) Lucy Gregory; minister in the Nazarene and Methodist Churches; correction to Cemeteries of Grundy Co., Vol. 1
Norris, Arene	Jun 01, 1935	May 17, 2013	Griffith Creek Cem.; Dau. of William & Mattie (McGowan) Griffith; m. Billy J. Norris
Norris, Bobby Eugene	Oct 15, 1945	Jan 31, 2014	Fults Cem.; Son of Arwin Eugene Norris & Rebecca Faye Smartt; m. Teresa Carol Braseel
Norris, Clarence E.	Jul 04, 1915	May 25, 1973	Altamont Cem.; Son of Sam & Edith Norris; m. Charity Whitman; addition to Cemeteries of Grundy Co., Vol. 1, p. 20
Norris, Louella (Grimes)	Jun 13, 1924	Apr 26, 1995	Fall Creek Cem.; Dau. of Robert & Mary E (Land) Grimes; m. Elmer Lee Norris
Norris, Melissa Carol (Prater)	Jul 22, 1964	Jun 17, 2021	Walker Cemetery; Dau. of Melvin & Virginia (Henderson) Prater; m. Kevin Norris
Northcut, Fannie Louise (McCraw)	Jan 4, 1839	Feb 17, 1907	Altamont Cem.; Dau. of William & Martha (Armstrong) McCraw; m. Harris Bradford Northcut; addition to Cemeteries of Grundy Co., Vol. 1, p. 30
Northcut, Mary Elizabeth (Myers)	Jan 10, 1851	Dec 28, 1923	Altamont Cem.; Dau. of Thomas Snoddy & Martha Jane (Billingsly) Myers; m. Lawson Hill Northcut; addition to Cemeteries of Grundy Co., Vol. 1, p. 36
Northcut, William E.	1872	Mar 8, 1882	Altamont Cem.; Son of Stephen Adrian & Sarah E. (Winton) Northcut; addition to Cemeteries of Grundy Co., Vol. 1, p. 26
Northcut, William Elihu	May 24, 1859	Jan 12, 1880	Altamont Cem.; Son of William Elihu & Mary Ann Susannah (Griswold) Northcut; m. Elizabeth "Lizzie" McGovern; addition and correction to mother's maiden name, Cemeteries of Grundy Co., Vol. 1, p. 26

Name	Birth	Death	Notes
Northcutt, Crystal Eddie	Sep 16, 1971	Nov 16, 2017	Palmer Cem.; Dau. of Joseph Northcutt & Evelyn Tate
Northcutt, Hunter Andrew	Feb 21, 2002	Sep 18, 2017	Bethel Cem.; Son of Marty & Diana (Clark) Northcutt
Northcutt, Jo Nathan	Jun 06, 1985	Jun 27, 2016	Fults Cem.; Son of Lynngail Northcutt
Northcutt, Mrs. Spencer		Aug. 25, 1913	Tracy City Cem.; m. Spencer Northcutt
Northcutt, Nadine (Hampton)	May 22, 1943	Dec 23, 2021	Bethel Cem.; Dau. of Edward Fultz & Edna Mae Hampton m. George Benson Northcutt; Used mother's surname and had a half sister also named Nadene Fultz.
Northcutt, Robby Dwayne	Jul 27, 1965	Jan 05, 2022	Cremated: Son of George Benson & Nadine (Hampton) Northcutt; m. Myrtle Ann Corley
Northcutt, William Earl	Feb 26, 1943	Dec 02, 2021	Bethel Cem.; Son of Stanley & Willie Mae Northcutt; m. Donna Davidson
Northcutt, Willie Mae (Payne)	Jun 21, 1921	Apr 28, 2016	Bethel Cem.; Dau. of Willie Wilson "Will" & Thursa (Hamby) Payne; m. George Stanley Northcutt
Norwood, Donald Wade	May 10, 1965	Nov 12, 2016	Orange Hill Cem.; Son of Wilburn C. & Shirley (Carter) Norwood
Norwood, Lizzie (Keel)	May 06, 1901	Jun 23, 1922	Monteagle Cem.; Dau. of James Bell & Nancy (Coffelt) Keel; m. James "Jim" Norwood; source death certificate
Norwood, Samuel Henry, Sr.	Ca 1838	Jul 03, 1910	Unknown Cem.; newspaper notice
Nunely, Mary Elizabeth	Dec 26, 1904	Jan 14, 1966	Hobbs Hill Cem.; Dau. of William Edward & Martha Ada (Tate) Nunley; m. Mark Howard Nunley; addition to Cemeteries of Grundy Co., Vol. 1, p. 326
Nunley Smartt, Janie Elizabeth (Nunley)	Dec 17, 1939	Feb 07, 2016	Coalmont Cem: Dau. of James Hobart "Mutt" & May Magdalene "Duck" (Johnson) Nunley; m. 1) Phillip D. Nunley and has a tombstone at Orange Hill, but is buried in Coalmont Cem. where her 2nd husband Wayne L. Smartt will be buried; addition to Cemeteries of Grundy Co., Vol. 2, p. 527
Nunley, Albert Douglas	May 28, 1949	Dec 08, 2016	Nunley Cem.; Son of Harvey & Edna (Morgan) Nunley; m. Carol Tressie Frederick
Nunley, Amelia Faith	Jun 24, 2019	Jun 24, 2019	Monteagle Cem.; Dau. of Cory Nunley & Hope Sartain
Nunley, Anthony Dean	Nov 27, 1956	Apr 22, 2013	Palmer Cem.; Son of Donald Ray Nunley & Clara (Hart) Partin; m. 1) Melinda Hiett 2) Shirley (Elliott) Nunley
Nunley, Audrey Lea (McBee)	Sep 26, 1974	Mar 02, 2016	Fall Creek Cem.; Dau. of Charllie & Angela (Coffelt) McBee; m. Keith Alan Nunley
Nunley, Barbara Jean (Roberts)	Jun 16, 1939	Sep 19, 2020	Coalmont Cem.; Dau. of James & Flora Roberts; m. Barney Nunley

Name	Birth	Death	Details
Nunley, Barbara Jean (Roberts)	Jun 16, 1939	Sep 18, 2020	Coalmont Cem.; Dau. of Henry & Flora Roberts; m. Barney Jasper Nunley Oct 6, 1956; addition to Cemeteries of Grundy Co., Vol. 1, p. 173
Nunley, Barney Jasper	Jun 13, 1937	Jul 31, 2015	Coalmont Cem.; Son of William Perry & Lillie (Drake) Nunley; m. Barbara Jean Roberts; Addition to Cemeteries of Grundy Co., Vol. 1, p. 173
Nunley, Beatrice (Whitt)	Dec 31, 1920	Jun 17, 1970	Hobbs Hill Cem.; Dau. of George Mack & Nora Evelyn (Roberts) Whitt; m. William Grady Nunley; addition to Cemeteries of Grundy Co., Vol. 1, p. 325
Nunley, Betty Loulene "Tarp" (Short)	Jan 01, 1943	Aug 01, 2018	Coalmont Cem.; Dau. of George Short & Gladys Marie Smartt; m. Maxie Bruce Nunley
Nunley, Beverly Jo	Sep 21, 1961	Aug 28, 2017	Coalmont Cem.; Dau. Billy Joe & Alice Faye (Owen) Cash; m. Ronnie "Bud" Nunley
Nunley, Billy D.	Nar 23, 1941	Mar 22, 2000	Bonny Oak Cem.; Son of Alvin & Esther (Lockhart) Nunley; m. Mary Nunley; addition to Cemeteries of Grundy Co., Vol. 1, p. 93
Nunley, Billy Earl	Mar 20, 1933	Mar 11, 1962	Bonny Oak Cem.; Son of Charlie D. & Fannie (Nunley) Nunley; m. Shirley Nunley; addition to Cemeteries of Grundy Co., Vol. 1, p. 91
Nunley, Billy Joe	Nov 06, 1946	Oct 04, 1962	Oak Grove Cem.; Son of James Douglas & Otsia (Teague) Nunley; addition to Cemeteries of Grundy Co., Vol. 1, p. 495
Nunley, Billy Ray	Apr 22, 1933	Feb 28, 2021	Cremated; Son of Graham & Sarah (Cannon) Nunley; m. 1) Shirley Ketola 2) Ruth Nunley
Nunley, Bobby Allen	Jul 04, 1946	Mar 15, 2017	Oak Grove Cem.; Son of Bob & Pearl (Nunley) Nunley; m. Irene Nunley
Nunley, Bobby C.	Feb 17, 1936	Feb 22, 2017	Bethel Cem.; Son of Lish & Mildred (Kilgore) Nunley; m. Magdaline "Dale" A. Nunley
Nunley, Bobby D.	Apr 14, 1905	Apr 16, 1905	Bonny Oak Cem.; Son of Yancy & Clara (Worley) Nunley; addition to Cemeteries of Grundy Co., Vol. 1, p. 77
Nunley, Bobby Gene "Bob"	Apr 10, 2013	Apr 02, 2014	Pryor Ridge Cem.; Son of Buford & Birtia "Birdie" (Layne) Nunley; m. Bobbie Jean Lewis
Nunley, Bonaill B.	Jun 03, 1936	May 23, 2017	Pryor Ridge Cem.; Son of Buford & Berta Nunley; m. Dortha Jean "Dot" Shell
Nunley, Bruce Edward	Jul 13, 1957	Dec 11, 2021	Walker Cem.; Son of Henry Howard & Mary Frances (Baker) Nunley; m. Sherry Lynn Holt
Nunley, Caldonia (Bost)	Aug 08, 1957	Mar 01, 1937	Fall Creek Cem.; Dau. of Noah & Abigail (Moffett) Nunley; m. 1) Henderson Pleasant Nunley 2) C Carroll Nunley
Nunley, Carl Edward, Jr.	Jun 13, 1964	Aug 02, 2019	Cremated; Son of Carl Edward Nunley & Delores Morrison
Nunley, Carol			Orange Hill Cem.; from FL m. William Nunley

Name	Birth	Death	Details
Nunley, Carrie Bell (Parsons)	Sep 5, 1899	Dec 07, 1985	Bonny Oak Cem.; Dau. of Isaac & Ann (Gilliam) Parsons; m. Charles Edward Nunley; addition to Cemeteries of Grundy Co., Vol. 1, p. 89
Nunley, Charles Edward	Nov 11, 1922	Sep 29, 2013	Gregg Cem.; Son of John Franklin & Sarah Louise (Hatfield) Nunley; m. 1) Jewel Turner 2) Grace O. Price; US Navy
Nunley, Charles N. "Shot"	Jul 26, 1937	Sep 07, 2020	Mt. Zion Cem.; Son of J.L. Nunley & Fannie Belle Newman; m. Patricia Strick
Nunley, Charlie D.	Feb 8, 1895	Jul 25, 1970	Bonny Oak Cem.; Son of Albert Carroll & Ada (Nunley) Nunley; PVT. Co M 52 Inf WWI
Nunley, Charlie, Jr.	Mar 21, 1937	Feb 27, 2015	Bonny Oak Cem.; Son of Charles & Fannie Nunley, Sr.; m. Elizabeth Janie Sanders; U.S. Navy
Nunley, Christeen (Ruckweed)	May 1, 1864	Jul 09, 1945	Burkett Chapel Cem.; Dau. of Christopher & Mary Ann (Bone) Ruckweed; m. Lawson Nunley; addition to Cemeteries of Grundy Co., Vol. 1, p. 124
Nunley, Clifford Leroy	Feb 26, 1941	Mar 07, 1972	Plainview Cem.; Son of James Calvin & Lucy Viola (Baters) Nunley; addition to Cemeteries of Grundy Co., Vol. 2, p. 680
Nunley, Clytus	Apr 08, 1927	May 12, 1983	Bonny Oak Cem.; Son of William Norman & Lucy Emeline "Bell" (Parsons) Nunley; m. Stella F. Scaggs; correction of spouse's name & addition to Cemeteries of Grundy Co. Vol. 1, p. 76
Nunley, Connie Ray	Jun 12, 1949	Jun 20, 1949	Bonny Oak Cem.; Son of Lawrence Edward, Sr. & Dorothy (Meeks) Nunley; addition to Cemeteries of Grundy Co.,Vol, 1, p. 79
Nunley, Connie Ray	Jun 12, 1949	Jun 20, 1949	Bonny Oak Cem.; Son of Lawrence Edward, Sr. & Dorothy (Meeks) Nunley; addition to Cemeteries of Grundy Co. Vol, 1, p. 79
Nunley, Cora Jean (Kilgore)	Jan 22, 1942	Jan 01, 2018	Oak Grove Cem.; Dau. of John E. Kilgore & Abba Jean Layne; m. Stanley Nunley
Nunley, Daryl G.	Sep 16, 1950	Nov 24, 2020	Coalmont, Cem.; Son of James & Frances (Campbell) Nunley; m. Elaine Nunley
Nunley, David Abraham	Aug 23, 1944	Mar 01, 2018	Hunerwadel Cem.; Son of William Carroll Nunley and Barbara Grace Schiesser; m. Georgia Knight
Nunley, Deloris Janie May (Harris)	Nov 30, 1941	Feb 10, 2018	Plainview Cem.; Dau. of Howard Harris & Reba Rust Bouldin; m. Joe Bailey Nunley
Nunley, Donnie Lee	Jun 13, 1958	May 04, 1959	Coalmont Cem.; Son of Clarence & Judy (Smartt) Nunley
Nunley, Earl Dean	Aug 27, 1943	May 22, 2022	Son of Robert & Grace (Hoback) Nunley; m. Kathryn Nunley

Name	Birth	Death	Notes
Nunley, Edna Josephine (Meeks)	Jan 10, 1950	Oct 02, 2013	Plainview Cem.; Dau. of Jackson Hiles "Jack" Meeks, Sr. & Peggy Cleo Cox ; m. Paul Louis Nunley
Nunley, Edna Mae	Jul 16, 1922	Sep 10, 2016	Oak Grove Cem.; Dau. of William H. & Laura (Armstrong) Sanders; m. Ernest Nunley
Nunley, Edwin	Dec 07, 1948	Apr 03, 2020	Body donated to science; Son of Graham & Mae Ellen (Campbell) Nunley; divorced, wife was from Indiana
Nunley, Elizabeth Jane (Sanders)	Sep 11, 1945	Aug 11, 2019	Bonnie Oak Cem.; Dau. of Arthur Lee Sanders & Mildred Frances Morgan; m. Charlie Nunley, Jr.
Nunley, Emaline (Phipps)	Jan 31, 1880	Dec 19, 1903	Bonny Oak Cem.; Dau. of John & Martha (Dickerson) Phipps; m. Norman Nunley on Sep. 25, 1954; addition to Cemeteries of Grundy Co., Vol. 1, p. 76
Nunley, Fannie	Feb 21, 1902	Jun 18, 1991	Bonny Oak Cem.; Dau. of Rev Gilliam & Dillie Ann (Argo) Nunley; m. Charles D. Nunley; addition to Cemeteries of Grundy Co. Vol. 1, p. 91
Nunley, Faye (Hill)	Sep 10, 1929	Nov 03, 1986	Bonny Oak Cem.; Dau. of Alvin Murphy & Esther (Lockhart) Nunley. m. ___ Hill; Correction of maiden name from Hall to Hill. It is Hill on the tombstone. Addition to Cemeteries of Grundy Co., Vol. 1, p. 90
Nunley, Freddy Allen	Aug 23, 1947	Oct 05, 2013	Plainview Cem.; Son of Bailey & Margie (Meeks) Nunley; m. Judith E. "Judy" Dishroom
Nunley, George	Ca 1851	Mar 30, 1916	Hobbs Hill Cem.; Son of David & Sarah (Brown) Nunley; probably m. Mollie Phipps; Some information from *Mrs. Grundy;* addition to Cemeteries of Grundy Co., Vol. 1, p, 339
Nunley, George Edward	Mar 05, 1952	May 24, 2016	Nunley Oaks Cem on Old Burroughs' Cove Rd. in Altamont behind his house; Son of James Nunley & Frances Schiesser; m. Ann Higgins
Nunley, Grace Josephine (Sartain)	May 19, 1933	Sep 11, 2018	Plainview Cem.; Dau. of Ike Washington Sartain & Grace Thomas; m. W.H. Nunley
Nunley, Harley Dee	Jan 18, 1933	Jan 18, 1982	Bonny Oak Cem.; Son of Charlie D & Fannie (Nunley) Nunley; m. Janice Lawson; addition to Cemeteries of Grundy Co., Vol. 1, p. 91
Nunley, Harriett (Smith)	Jan 29, 1905	Mar 24, 1905	Burkett Chapel Cem.; Dau. of Anderson & Martha (Thurman) Smith; m. William Elihu Nunley on Apr 3, 1873; addition to Cemeteries of Grundy Co., Vol. 1, p. 120
Nunley, Helen Marie	Mar 06, 1929	Feb 04, 2013	Palmer Cem.; Dau. of Paul & Jessie (Thompson) Worley; m. Stanley Nunley

Nunley, Henry Gordon	Oct 28, 1915	Mar 31, 1954	Hobbs Hill Cem.; Son of Marvin "Mark" & Rebecca (Geary) Nunley; m. Jessie Trussell; addition to Cemeteries of Grundy Co., Vol. 1, p. 325
Nunley, Henry Newton	May 09, 1932	Sep 05, 2018	Orange Hill Cem.; Son of Henry & Clara Louise (Meeks) Nunley; m. Mae Dean Caldwell; addition to Cemeteries of Grundy Co., Vol. 2, p. 528
Nunley, Houston	Aug 25, 1969	Dec 08, 2019	Coalmont Cem.; Son of James David & Phyllis (Morrison) Nunley
Nunley, Infant	Dec 01, 1920	Aug 14, 1921	Orange Hill Cem.; Dau. of Ed & Lettie Jane (Hattfield) Nunley
Nunley, Jacqueline Patricia (Sanders)	Mar 01, 1935	Apr 18, 2018	Providence United Methodist Church Cem.; Dau. of Emmitt Sanders & Elizabeth Moore; m. Jimmy Nunley
Nunley, James Howard "Red"	Nov 03, 1932	Dec 15, 1991	Coalmont Cem.; Son of Matt Nunley & Nora Rogers; correction to Cemeteries of Grundy Co., Vol. 1, p. 181
Nunley, James Oscar	Oct 13, 1895	Mar 23, 1936	Bonny Oak Cem.; Son of Isaac Murphy Nunley & Nancy Woodlee; m, Ruby Eleanor Myers
Nunley, Janie Elizabeth	Dec 17, 1939	Feb 07, 2016	Orange Hill; Dau. of James Hobart "Mutt" Nunley & Mary Magdalin "Duck" Johnson; m. Phillip Nunley
Nunley, Jason Edward	Dec 18, 1975	Aug 27, 2021	Fall Creek Cem.; Son of Keith & Charlene (Perry) Nunley; m. Patti Morrison
Nunley, Jay C.	1874	Mar 06, 1924	Altamont Cem.; m. Flora Fults; he has no marker, but there is an unmarked grave next to his wife. It is assumed to be him.
Nunley, Jean (Lewis)	Jan 10, 1936	Nov 22, 2019	Pryor Ridge Cem.; Dau. of Joe Allison & Mary Etta (Ducker) Lewis; m. Bob Nunley
Nunley, Jeffery Lynn	Jun 18, 1959	Oct 29, 1975	Oak Grove Cem.; Son of Ernest & Edna Mae (Sanders) Nunley; addition Cemeteries of Grundy Co., Vol. 1 , p. 495
Nunley, Jeffery Newton	1976	Apr 22, 2018	Orange Hill Cem.; Son of Henry Newton Nunley & Mae Dean Nunley
Nunley, Jeremy	Sep 19, 1971	Feb 05, 2018	Cremated; Son of Bobby Joe "Jody" & Edith (Carrick) Nunley m. Marti Watson
Nunley, Jeri Lynn	May 12, 1958	Apr 04, 2021	Fall Creek Cem.; Dau. of Carl Ed Nunley & Charlotte (Long) Nunley Cannon; m 1). Jeremy Campbell; 2) Walter Bourne
Nunley, Jerry Louise (Spencer)	Nov 02, 1947	Sep 15, 2019	Hebron Cem.; Dau. of Jese David Spencer & Jeriah Beatrice Jones; m. Jim Nunley
Nunley, Jim	Jan 1, 1872	Oct 30, 1905	Hobbs Hill Cem.; Son of Jesse & Elizabeth Nunley; Baby Charles William Nunley is buried on top of Jim; addition to Cemeteries of Grundy Co., Vol. 1, p. 337

Name	Birth	Death	Notes
Nunley, Jimmie "Boots" (Finch)	Jan 29, 1934	Sep 15, 1991	Palmer Cem.; Dau. of Hershel & Ruby Lee (Gifford) Finch; correction to Cemeteries of Grundy Co., Vol. 2, p. 551
Nunley, Jimmy Allen	Jul 28, 1944	Apr 07, 2009	Bonny Oak Cem.; Son of Charlie D. & Fannie (Nunley) Nunley; correction to mother's maiden name in Cemeteries of Grundy Co., Vol. 1, p. 91
Nunley, Joe	Ca 1895	Mar 17, 1917	Parsons' Graveyard old part of Bonny Oak Cem.; Son of Kelley & Manerva (Haskins) Nunley; m. Liddy Woodlee, Mar 4, 1906; information about burial from death certificate; no stone; addition to Cemeteries of Grundy Co., Vol. 1, p. 77
Nunley, Joe Edwin, Jr.	Jan 30, 1946	Apr 23, 2021	Mt. Zion Cem.; Son of Joe & Jessie (DePriest) Nunley; m. Anna McDaris; US Army
Nunley, John W.	Nov 03, 1919	Nov 1, 1998	Palmer Cem.; Son of William A & Lue G (McGuffey) Nunley; m. E. Ster Nolan; addition to Cemeteries of Grundy Co., Vol. 2, p. 559
Nunley, Juanita	Jan 13, 1943	Feb 17, 2013	Pine Hill Cem in the Pocket; Dau. of Edward & Della Campbell; m. Carl David Nunley
Nunley, Judith "Judy" Elaine	ca 1953	Dec 07, 2014	Cremated; Dau of James Everette Dishroon & Bessie Nunley; m. Freddy Nunley; Judy gathered names for the original Cemeteries of Grundy County
Nunley, Kelly Carroll	Sep 23, 1988	Sep 23, 1988	Airview Cem.; Son of Kelly Leon Nunley
Nunley, Kelly Greenberry	1861	Ca. 1915	Bonny Oak Cem.; Son of Hiram & Ann Nunley; m. Minerva Haskins on Aug 26, 1883
Nunley, Kenneth Douglas	Aug 10, 1944	Aug 14, 2013	Oak Grove Cem.; Son of James D. & Otsie Naomi (Tigue) Nunley
Nunley, Kenneth Paul	Aug 06, 1944	Jul 02, 1992	Bonny Oak Cem.; Son of Alvin Murphy & Esther (Lockhart) Nunley; addition to Cemeteries of Grundy Co. Vol, 1, p. 87
Nunley, Kermit Ray	May 03, 1936	Oct 16, 2006	Airview Cem.; Son of William & Barbara (Schiesser) Nunley; m. Opal Faye Hobbs Mar 30, 1957; correction of death date in Cemeteries of Grundy Co., Vol. 1, p. 4
Nunley, Kirstin Nicole (McDole)	May 13, 1999	Feb 18, 2021	Burkett's Chapel Cem.; Dau. of Chris & Cathy (McDole) Mays; m. Matthew Dean Nunley
Nunley, Lavonna	Ca 1958	Feb 24, 2013	Cremated; Monteagle Cem.; Dau. of Grady & Thelma (Meeks) Watley; m. William T. Nunley
Nunley, Lawrence Edward, Sr.	Aug 04, 1926	Nov 20, 1971	Bonnie Oak Cem.; Son of Samuel & Lily Pearl (Reeves) Nunley; m. Dorothy Meeks; addition to Cemeteries of Grundy Co., Vol. 1, p. 79
Nunley, Lee Roy	Apr 10, 1949	Oct 11, 2016	Orange Hill Cem.; Son of Howard & Elsie Nunley; m. Rita Nunley

Nunley, Leona Holt	Mar 26, 1903	Aug 05, 2000	Payne's Cove Cem.; Dau. of William Bennett & Mary Sue (Haggenmacher) Holt; m. 1) Samuel James Meeks, Mar 19, 1927 Madison Co, AL 2) Leonard "Pood" Nunley; m. Mar 4, 1940; Grundy Co. TN; correction to Cemeteries of Grundy Co., Vol. 2, p. 593
Nunley, Leslie H.	Jul 07, 1938	Oct 29, 2003	Plainview Cem.; Son of Charley & Fannie (Green) Nunley; US Navy Vietnam, Silver Star, Purple Heart; addition to Cemeteries of Grundy Co, Vol. 2. p. 671
Nunley, Linda Sue (Sanders)	Jul 02, 1945	Oct 19, 2020	Tracy City Cem.; Dau. of Ernest Milton & Ola (Meeks) Sanders; m. Justin Nunley
Nunley, Lloyd Allen, Sr.	Mar 21, 1947	Mar 14, 2014	Clouse Hill Cem.; Son of Harvey & Edna (Morgan) Nunley; m. Willie Mae Nunley
Nunley, Louis Donald "Grey Fox"	Feb 25, 1939	Apr 11, 2014	Cremated; Son of Barton & Josie (Golston) Nunley; m. Patricia Page Nunley
Nunley, Lucy Viola (Bates)	Apr 02, 1900	Jan 23, 1960	Plainview Cem.; Dau. of John William & Lula Mae (Cagle) Bates; m. James Calvin Nunley; addition to Cemeteries of Grundy Co, Vol. 2, p. 689
Nunley, Lydia (Woodlee)	Nov 29, 1889	Nov 08, 1918	Bonnie Oak Cem.; Dau. of Leonard Patton Woodlee & Jennie Sophronia Nunley; m. Joe Nunley
Nunley, Mable Sandra	Mar 31, 1924	Dec 26, 1972	Bonny Oak Cem.; Dau. of James Oscar & Ruby Eleanor (Myers) Nunley; addition to Cemeteries of Grundy Co., Vol. 1, p. 82
Nunley, Magdalene (Lawson)	Jul 20, 1924	Oct 01, 1979	Bonny Oak Cem.; Dau. of Henry Jackson & Eula Edna (Walter) Lawson; m. Charles William Nunley; correction to surname of parents; Cemeteries of Grundy Co. Vol. 1, p. 89
Nunley, Mamie Florene (Campbell)	Mar 28, 1937	Jul 13, 2020	Eastern Sar Cem.; Dau. of James William Campbell & Florence Laurene Yates; m. Robert Eugene Nunley
Nunley, Marcus DeShawn	2000	May 17, 2018	Cremated: Son of Kenneth Douglas Nunley, Jr. & Ola Ann Cowan
Nunley, Mark Douglas	Sep 07, 1953	Mar 03, 2017	Orange Hill Cem.; Son of Alvin & Violet Nunley; m. Shirley Nunley
Nunley, Martha Ada (Tate)	Oct 1857	Sep 20, 1927	Hobbs Hill Cem.; Dau. of Francis Marion & Mary Sarah (Bost) Tate; m. William E. Nunley; addition to Cemeteries of Grundy Co., Vol, 1, p. 333
Nunley, Mary Alyce (Fletcher)	Jan 02, 1934	Jul 23, 2013	Orange Hill Cem.; Dau. of James Henry & Dorothy Irene (Huffine) Fletcher; m. Clarence Nunley

Name	Born	Died	Notes
Nunley, Mary Emaleene (Sanders)	ca 1829	Jul 15, 1916	Bonny Oak Cem: Dau. of Southerland "Southy" or "Suddy" & Nancy (Summers) Sanders; m. James Mattison or Madison Nunley; No tombstone; addition to Cemeteries of Grundy Co., Vol. 1, p. 96
Nunley, Mary Lillie "Lil"	May 5, 1898	Jul 22, 1947	Payne's Cove Cem.; Dau. of Clouse L & Minnie (Stokes) Meeks; m. Ed Nunley on 23 Dec 1917; addition to Cemeteries of Grundy Co., Vol. 2, p. 595
Nunley, Mary Magdalene "Duck" Johnson	Apr 22, 1914	Mar 03, 2017	Orange Hill Cem.; Dau. of George Morgan & Beulah (Carrick) Johnson; m. James H. Nunley
Nunley, Melissa Ann	Oct 11, 1967	Sep 11, 2020	Clouse Hill Cem.; Dau. of Louis A. Nunley & Mary Christine Shrum
Nunley, Michael "Mody"	Jul 28, 1961	Dec 03, 2016	Coalmont Cem.; Son of Clarence & Judy (Smartt) Nunley; m. Brooke Nunley
Nunley, Michael William	Jun 14, 1963	Jul 07, 1963	Oak Grove Cem.; Son of Bonell & Dorothy (Shell) Nunley; addition to, Cemeteries of Grundy Co., Vol. 1, p. 495
Nunley, Mildred "Millie"	ca 1846	not in census after 1910	Burkett's Chapel Cem.; Dau. of Wilford & Rachel (Green) Nunley; addition to Cemeteries of Grundy Co., Vol. 1, p. 121
Nunley, Mrs. Roy		Jul 15, 1916	Dick Sanders Schoolhouse Cem.; source *Mrs. Grundy*, Jul 20, 1916
Nunley, Murphy	Mar 16, 1978	May 02, 2021	Bonny Oak Cem.; Son of Michael & Patricia (Curtis) Nunley
Nunley, Nancy Ann Matilda (Ward)	Jan 6, 1875	Oct 04, 1959	Bonny Oak Cem.; Dau. of William Hudson Ward & Lucy A. Neighbors; m. Hiram Russell Nunley on Nov 12, 1922; addition to Cemeteries of Grundy Co., Vol. 1, p. 89
Nunley, Nancy Louisa	Mar 08, 1923	Apr 11, 1923	Bonny Oak Cem.; Dau. of James Oscar & Ruby (Myers) Nunley; addition to Cemeteries of Grundy Co., Vol. 1, p. 82
Nunley, Naomi Ruth (Layne)	Aug 08, 1951	Jan 16, 2017	Cremated; Dau. of Rev. Daniel Leander & Hazel (Tate) Layne; m. Danny James Nunley
Nunley, Neal Edward	Mar 29, 1949	Feb 04, 2022	Bonny Oak Cem.; Dau. of Clarence Edward & Elsie (Sweeton) Nunley; m. Carolyn Nunley
Nunley, Nevaeh	Dec 07, 2019	Feb 24, 2021	Burkett's Chapel Cem.; Dau. of Matthew Dean & Kirstin (McDole) Nunley
Nunley, Opal Faye (Hobbs)	Mar 13, 1941	Feb 14, 2017	Airview Cem.; Dau. of Horton & Ida (Fults) Hobbs; m. Kermit Ray Fults; addition to Cemeteries of Grundy Co., Vol. 1, p. 4
Nunley, Otsie (Tigue)	Jul 02, 1923	Jun 29, 1948	Tracy City Cem.; Dau. of Leonard Norton & Daisy Bell (Worley) Nunley; m. James Douglas Nunley
Nunley, Patricia	Oct 13, 1957	May 29, 2016	Airview Cem.; Dau. of James & Virginia (Green) Meeks; m. Carl Dewayne Nunley

Name	Birth	Death	Details
Nunley, Patty Laverne (McClearen)	Aug 23, 1937	May 13, 1972	Bethel Cem.; Dau. of Charlie & Pauline McClearen; She was from Farmers Exchange, TN, in Hickman County; Killed in Greyhound bus wreck; correction to Cemeteries of Grundy Co., Vol. 1, p. 61
Nunley, Pearl (Reeves)	Jan 01, 1904	Aug 27, 1970	Bonny Oak Cem.; Dau. of James Franklin & Della (Cunningham) Reeves; m. Samuel Nunley; addition to Cemeteries of Grundy Co., Vol. 1, p. 90
Nunley, Rachel (Green)	ca 1815	Jul 27, 1874	Burkett Chapel Cem: Dau. of Samuel & Esther Alice (Miller) Green; m. Wilford Nunley
Nunley, Randil E.	Aug 31, 1937	Apr 28, 2017	Bethel Cem.; Son of Webster & Mamie Lee (Givens) Nunley; m. 1) Bonnie Harris 2) Sue Fults 3) Clara Huntley
Nunley, Rhoda Allen		Apr 01, 1916	Tracy City Cem.; m. John Nunley 14 July 1868; from *Mrs. Grundy*, Apr 6, 1916
Nunley, Robert E.	Sep 08, 1940		Plainview Cem.; Son of Yancy & Clara (Worley) Nunley
Nunley, Robert G.	ca 1961	Feb 29, 2016	Cremated; Son of William L & Lottie Lena (Pavlak) Nunley
Nunley, Robert K.	Dec 02, 1904	Nov 19, 1973	Bonny Oak Cem.; Son of Kelly & Nervie (Haskins) Nunley; m. Eula A. Pickett; addition to Cemeteries of Grundy Co., Vol. 1, p. 91
Nunley, Robert Vernon	Apr 07, 1935	Jun 14, 2014	Plainview Cem.; Son of Vernon N. & Anna Mae (Meeks) Nunley; m. Betty L. "Nell" Hand on Jan 1, 1955; addition to Cemeteries of Grundy Co., Vol. 2, p. 699
Nunley, Robin B	Aug 16, 1959	Jan 23, 2020	Cremation; Son of Charles William & Donna Nunley; m. Sabrina Lockhart
Nunley, Roger Dale	1961	Aug 28, 2018	Bonny Oak Cem.; Son of John Henry & Shirley Nunley
Nunley, Roger William	May 24, 1962	May 24, 1962	Oak Grove Cem; Son of William & Hazel (McCann) Nunley; addition to Cemeteries of Grundy Co., Vol. 1, p. 501
Nunley, Rose (Diebold)	May 17, 1940	Feb 11, 2022	Coalmont Cem.; Dau. of Peter & Marie Diebold; m. James Howard Nunley
Nunley, Roy Wayne	Apr 07, 1952	Apr 02, 2016	Bonnie Oak Cem.; Son of Herbert & Nellie (Morgan) Nunley; m. Mary L. Pickett
Nunley, Ruby Eleanor (Myers)	Jul 01, 1902	Feb 15, 1988	Bonny Oak Cem.; Dau. of Robert Elijah & Ella Louise (Sanders) Myers; m. James Oscar Nunley; addition to Cemeteries of Grundy Co., Vol. 1, p. 82
Nunley, Sally M. (Haskins)	1868	1899	Dick Sanders Cem.; Dau. of Joseph & Betty (Myers) Haskins; m. Lewis Jefferson "Jeff" Nunley; no tombstone; Correction of name listing & addition to Cemeteries of Grundy Co., Vol. 2, p. 731

Name	Birth	Death	Notes
Nunley, Sealie	Mar 20, 1933	Mar 20, 1933	Bonny Oak Cem.; Name is on the same tombstone as Charles W. Nunley & next to Barney McCurry, so she is probably his daughter; addition to Cemeteries of Grundy Co., Vol. 1, p. 88
Nunley, Sharon Maxine (Duncan)	Sep 14, 1955	Aug 22, 2013	Altamont Cem.; Dau. of Max & Mina (Mancroft) Duncan; m. Clark Nunley
Nunley, Sheila Jean (McFalls)	Jun 28, 1959	May 29, 2022	Cremated: Dau. of R. M. & Opal (King) McFalls; m. Marcus D. Nunley
Nunley, Shirley (Short)	Feb 12, 1940	Mar 08, 2013	Coalmont Cem.; Dau. of Jim & Faye (Goff) Short; m. James Reuben Short
Nunley, Sonja Gail (Lawson)	Mar 08, 1948	Jan 08, 2013	Plainview Cem.; Dau. of William & Reba (Partin) Lawson; m. Leslie H. Nunley
Nunley, Stella F. (Scaggs)	Dec 09, 1935	Nov 04, 2006	Bonny Oak Cem.; Dau. of Robert Thomas & Ruby (Perkins) Scaggs; m. Clytus Nunley; addition to Cemeteries of Grundy Co. Vol. 1, p. 76
Nunley, Stephen Chad	Dec 07, 1973	Dec 02, 2017	Plainview Cem.; Son of Robert & Betty Lou Saint Nunley; m. Angela Griffith Darby
Nunley, Ted Allen	Jun 03, 1932	Mar 01, 2016	Palmer Cem.; Son of Simon & Elizabeth "Lizzie" (Henley) Nunley; m. Hazel Scott; Cemeteries of Grundy Co., Vol. 2, p. 571
Nunley, Teddy Reece	Apr 28, 1939	Mar 16, 2022	Florida National Cem.; Son of Melvin Reece & Irene Holt (Phipps) Nunley; m. Helen Bass; U.S. Army
Nunley, Tommye Sue	Jan 07, 1941	May 30, 2021	Philadelphia Cem.; Dau. of Helen Louise Patrick; m. Avery Willis Nunley
Nunley, Tracy Scott	Oct 18, 1972	Mar 22, 1976	Bonny Oak Cem.; Son of Kenneth Nunley; addition to Cemeteries of Grundy Co. Vol 1, p. 90
Nunley, Valentine (Church)	Feb 14, 1903	Oct 06, 1919	Bonny Oak Cem.; Dau. of John Henry O. & Minerva Louise Aseltine (Parsons) Church; Twin to William Perry Church; m. Charley Nunley; addition to Cemeteries of Grundy Co., Vol. 1, p. 78
Nunley, Wilburn Haggard	Jun 01, 1921	Jul 02, 1921	Hobbs Hill Cem.; Son of Hollis & Lorrine (Tate) Nunley
Nunley, Wilford	1824	1885	Burkett's Chapel; Son of Elias & Margaret (Fults) Nunley; m. Rachel Green
Nunley, Will	Sep 17, 1899	Jun 19, 1976	Coalmont Cem.; Son of Gilliam & Dillie Nunley; m. Pearl Anglin; no tombstone
Nunley, William	no information	no information	Orange Hill Cem.; Son of James Hobart "Jim Mutt" Nunley & Anna Bryant; m. Carol Nunley
Nunley, William Carroll	Apr 28, 1892	Feb 20, 1966	Bonny Oak Cem.; Son of Kelly & Manervia (Haskins) Nunley; correction by family, Cemeteries of Grundy Co., Vol. 1

Name	Birth	Death	Details
Nunley, William Charles	Aug 26, 1941	May 25, 1971	Bonny Oak Cem.; Son of Clarence & Elsie Nunley; m. Margie Ann Myers; addition to Cemeteries of Grundy Co., Vol. 1, p. 92
Nunley, William Elihu	Sep 17, 1854	1935	Burkett's Chapel Cem.; Son of Wilford & Rachel (Green) Nunley; m. Harriett Smith; addition to Cemeteries of Grundy Co., Vol, 1, p. 120
Nunn, Novella (Layne)	Oct 16, 1949	Jan 05, 2015	Warren "Red Hill" Cem.; Dau. of Clyde & Elsie (Meeks) Layne
Nussbaum, Francis Richard	Mar 22, 1872	Aug 20, 1913	Swiss Colony Cem.; adopted son (per census) of Henry & Julia (Kellog) Nussbaum; m. Rosina Scholer on Jul 21, 1895; addition to Cemeteries of Grundy Co., Vol. 2, p.786
O'Brien, Aileen (Fitzgerald)	May 24, 1931	Oct 14, 2019	Monteagle Assembly Cem.; Dau. of Frank & Ethel Fitzgerald
O'Brien, Carlotta Leigh (Yarrington)	Oct 19, 1935	Oct 26, 2020	Burkett's Chapel Cem.; Dau. of Alfred & Dorothy (Wilson) Yarrington
O'Dear, Esther Louise (Sitz)	Jan 25, 1951	May 30, 2018	Watson-North Funeral Home Cem.; Dau. of Charles Harvey Sitz & Ovie Nunley; m. Dennis W. O'Dear
O'Dear, James Herman	Feb 14, 1927	May 22, 2001	Plainview Cem.; Son of Herman & Rosa B. (Killman) O'Dear; addition to Cemeteries of Grundy Co., Vol. 2, p. 663
O'Dear, Mary (Nunley)	Mar 11, 1918	Apr 01, 1986	Bonnie Oak Cem.; Dau. of Albert Carroll & Ada (Nunley) Nunley; m. Elbert O'Dear; addition to Cemeteries of Grundy Co., Vol. 1, p. 92
O'Neal, Early Peyton	Ca 1903	Sep 06, 1933	Oak Grove Cem.; Son of John Wilburn & Amanda (Caldwell) O'Neal; no tombstone
O'Neal, Infant	Mar 29, 1905	Oct 01, 1915	Oak Grove Cem.; Son of Lawrence & Daisy (King) O'Neal; Source *Mrs. Grundy* Oct 28, 1915
O'Neal, J.D.	Sep 29, 1925	Feb 05, 2013	Brown's Chapel Cem.; Son of Jim & Dora (Kilgore) O'Neal; m. Billie Anderson; US Army
O'Neal, John Wilburn, Jr.	Jul 1, 1863	Sep 16, 1922	Oak Grove Cem.; Son of John & Nancy Jane (Burnett) O'Neal; m. 1) Amanda Caldwell 2) Lelia Hayes; addition to Cemeteries of Grundy Co., Vol. 1, p. 505
O'Neal, Jonathan Corbett, Jr. "Jay"	Apr 19, 1935	Feb 12, 2018	Monteagle Cem.; Son of Jonathan Corbett O'Neal,Sr. & Allie Jean Parker
O'Neal, Kenneth	Sep 04, 1952	Dec 22, 2020	Summerfield Cem.; Son of Charles & Hazel Rurh O'Neal; m. Linda O'Neal
O'Neal, Marlene (Layne)	Dec 16, 1951	Jan 21, 2015	Summerfield Cem.; Dau. of William Jennings Bryan "Jay" & Huetta (Gilliam) Layne; m. 1) Earnest Nunley 2) Kenny O'Neal

Name	Birth	Death	Details
O'Neal, Robert B.	Ca 1890	May 14, 1933	Oak Grove Cem.; Son of John & Amanda (Caldwell) O'Neal; addition by death certificate – no marker; Cemeteries of Grundy Co. Vol. 1
O'Neal, William P "Sonny"	Feb 04, 1947	Mar 31, 2020	Cremated; obit. states "private burial"; Son of William Perry O'Neal & Ruth Gipson; m. Stella O'Neal; U.S. Air Force – Vietnam
Oblander, Ada Hart	Oct 18, 1900	Nov 21, 1995	Cumberland Heights Cem.; Dau. of Albert Bailey & Sabrah Ann (Good) Murr; m. John Fred Oblander, Oct 31, 1965; addition to Cemeteries of Grundy Co., Vol. 1, p. 197
Oblander, Rosamond Rachel (Hintz)	Mar 10, 1898	May 08, 1964	Fall Creek Cem.; Dau. of Johann Herman & Emma Alice (Auld) Hintz
Odom, Anna Bell (King)	Oct 28, 1934	Feb 12, 2013	Altamont Cem.; Dau. of Fred & Virginia (Smartt) King ; m. Joe Odom
Ogelvie, Cynthia Caroline (Bailey)	Jan 25, 1905	Dec 16, 1902	Tracy City Cem.; Dau. of John & Sarah A. (Turner) Bailey; m. John Washington Ogelvie; no tombstone; information from Marty Ogelvie & Ancestry.com
Ogelvie, Essie Mae (Thomas)	Jul 27, 1917	May 20, 2013	Monteagle Cem.; Dau. of Roy Dunn & Frances Ann (Todd) Thomas
Olgiati, Annie (Wichser)	Sep 18, 1878	Mar 17, 1963	Swiss Colony Cem.; Dau. of Frederic & Barbara (Wild) Wichser; m. Roman A. Olgiati, addition to Cemeteries of Grundy Co. Vol. 2, p. 789
Olgiati, Roman Anton	Oct 15, 1867	Jul 28, 1907	Swiss Colony Cem.; Son of Pietro Rodolfo & Ursula (Franconi) Olgiati; m. Anna Wichser; addition to Cemeteries of Grundy Co., Vol. 2, p. 786
Olinger, Cheryl	1946		Wesley Chapel Cem.; probably Dau. of Leroy Elbert & Sarah Lorene (Lusk) Olinger; name is on a tombstone with them.
Olinger, Leroy Elbert	Jan 16, 1920	Sep 26, 2014	Wesley Chapel Cem.; Son of Elbert & Eva (Williams) Olinger; m. Sarah Lorene Lusk; addition to Cemeteries of Grundy Co; Vol. 2, p. 1001
Olinger, Sarah Lorene (Lusk)	Oct 28, 1918	Jul 29, 1983	Cremated; Wesley Chapel Cem.; Dau. of Amos & Erier A. (Griswold) Lusk; m. Leroy Elbert Olinger; correction and addition to Cemeteries of Grundy Co., Vol. 2, p. 1001.
Oliver, Altha	1917	Sep 15, 1923	Oliver Cem.; Dau. of Arthur Lee "Yock" and Stella Mae (Payne) Oliver; tombstone now in place; correction to Cemeteries of Grundy Co., Vol. 2, p. 521
Oliver, Asa	Apr 18, 1761	Apr 18, 1823	Caldwell Cem.; Son of John & Elizabeth (Forrest) Oliver; tombstone is present in cemetery; addition to Cemeteries of Grundy Co., Vol. 1, p. 142

Name	Birth	Death	Notes
Oliver, Danita Renea (Campbell)	Mar 29, 1957	Apr 17, 2019	Clouse Hill Cem.; Dau. of Edward "Duxie" & Naomi Campbell
Oliver, George	Feb 01, 1921	Oct 13, 1923	Oliver Cem.; Son of Arthur Lee "Yock" & Stella Mae (Payne) Oliver; Tombstone now in place; correction to Cemeteries of Grundy Co., Vol. 2, p. 520
Oliver, Martha Jane (Hobbs)	Mar 11, 1948	Mar 08, 2020	Oliver Family Cem.; Dau. of Jay Hobbs & Lassie Clendenon; m. Paul Oliver
Oliver, Paul William	Mar 17, 1940	May 03, 2020	Philadelphia Cem.; Son of Johnny Oliver & Lorene Sanders; m. Martha Jane Hobbs
Oliver, Ruben Eugene	1938	Jul 22, 2021	Plainview Cem.; Son of Alfred & Edna Allene (Nunley) Oliver; m. Nancy Oliver
Olmstead, James Glenwood	Apr 1, 1885	Mar 29, 1883	Cumberland Heights Cem.; Son of Earl LeVant & Mary J. (Humphrey) Olmstead; m. 1) Etta Lena Reader 2) Olive Alda Peterson; addition to Cemeteries of Grundy Co., Vol. 1, p. 195
Olmstead, Olive Alda (Peterson)	Jan 8, 1892	Jan 12, 1980	Cumberland Heights Cem.; Dau. of Daniel S. & Kate Emma (Rollins) Paterson; m. James G. Olmstead; addition to Cemeteries of Grundy Co, Vol, 1, p. 195
Olney, Arthur Hamilton	Nov 09, 1929	Jul 07, 1905	Unknown Cem in CA; Son of Arthur Cain Olney & Leona Ellen Hartzell; m. Mary Emma Lamb
Olney, Mary Emma	Aug 03, 1942	Mar 21, 2009	Altamont Cem.; Dau. of James Clayton Sisk & Ruby (Rowe) Lamb; m. Arthur Olney; addition to Cemeteries of Grundy Co., Vol. 1, p. 17
Orange, Alvin Lee	1864		Orange Hill Cem.; Son of John William & Nancy Jane (Lockhart) Orange; m. Angie Lockhart, correction of parents listed in Cemeteries of Grundy Co., Vol. 2, p. 537
Orange, Edward Ray	Sep 14, 1955	May 05, 2016	Orange Hill Cem.; Son of James & Johnnie (Ray) Orange; m. Donna Ray Tate
Orange, Emmett Sylvester	Apr 18, 1908	Jul 10 1997	Orange Hill Cem.; Son of Samuel Emmett & Josephine (Carr) Orange; m. Rose Lese; memorial stone; actually buried in Riverside National Cem in CA.; WWII; correction to Cemeteries of Grundy Co., Vol 2, p. 537
Orange, Fred George	May 25, 1873	Sep 30, 1934	Orange Hill Cem.; Son of John William Frederick & Nancy Jane (Lockhart) Orange; m. Delilah Mary Parmley; addition to Cemeteries of Grundy Co., Vol. 2, p. 536
Orange, George Stanford	Jun 05, 1941	Feb 16, 2018	George Orange Cem.; Son of Buford Orange & Minnie Sanders; m. Stella Frederick
Orange, James Douglas "Big O"	Dec 09, 1953	Oct 19, 2020	Cremated; Son of James & Johnnie Mae Orange; m. Angelia West

Name	Born	Died	Notes
Orange, James Emmett	Jan 19, 1933	Nov 19, 2005	Orange Hill Cem.; Son of James Emmett Orange; addition Cemeteries of Grundy Co. Vol. 2, p. 537
Orange, Josephine (Carr)	Feb 1, 1889	Oct 02, 1920	Orange Hill Cem.; p. 537; Dau. of Patrick & Eliza (Martin) Carr; m. Samuel Emmett Orange; memorial stone
Orange, Rosa (Lese)	Feb 21, 1914	Sep 01, 1980	Orange Hill Cem.; Dau. of ___Lese & ___ Servidia; m. Emmett Sylvester Orange; addition to Cemeteries of Grundy Co., Vol. 2, p. 537; She is actually buried in Riverside National Cem. Riverside, CA, but her name is on the tombstone at Orange Hill as Lese, Rosa.
Orange, Samuel Emmett	Dec 23, 1886	Mar 10, 1915	Orange Hill Cem.; Son of John William Frederick & Nancy Jane Lockhart; m. Josephine Carr; Cemeteries of Grundy Co., Vol 2, p. 537 memorial stone
Orange, William	None on stone	None given	Orange Hill Cem.; Correction; parents not known- not as stated in Cemeteries of Grundy Co., Vol. 2. p. 536
Orr, Margaret (Donohue)	Jun 18, 1948	Nov 06, 2020	University of the South Cem.; Dau. of John T. & Hannah Aldridge (Hardie) Donohue; m. John W Orr
Orrell, Royce A	Aug 20, 1924	Nov 29, 1964	Fall Creek Cem.; Dau. of Robert & Annie (Lehman) Ackerman
Ortiz, Evalardo "Joe"	Aug 18, 1953	Jan 27, 2016	Cremated; companion of Brenda Joyce (Johnson) Clark
Osborne, Martha Ann (Mansfield)	1874	1937	Wesley Chapel Cem.; Dau. of William & Laura (Smith) Mansfield; m. John Osborn on Mar 27, 1901, in Coffee Co, TN; addition to Cemeteries of Grundy Co., Vol. 2, p. 977
Ostertag, Madison Miller	Nov 14, 1997	Nov 25, 2016	Cremated; Dau. of Michael Ostertag & Iva Michelle Russell
Overturf, Jerry Edward	Oct 13, 1946	Dec 15, 2016	Cremated; Son of Clifton & Magdaline (Smith) Overturf; m. Mary Morrison
Overturf, Junior	Dec 24, 1929	Dec 24, 1929	White Cem.; Son of Edgar & Ora (Thompson) Overturf; addition to Cemeteries of Grundy Co., Vol. 2, p.1006
Overturf, Mary Magdelene (Smith)	Aug 12, 1930	May 31, 2019	Chattanooga National Cem.; Dau. of Alonzo & Josie Evelina Smith; m. Henry Clifton Overturf
Overturf, Williadean Brock	Jul 03, 1926	Dec 21, 2007	Fall Creek Cem.; Dau. of Hobert & Virgie (Bedwell) Brock; m. Oscar Darrell Overturf
Overturff, Edwin Lee	1895	May 05, 1959	Philadelphia Cem.; Son of William b. & Martha "Mattie" (Hayes) Overturff; m. Sarah Lawson in Lincoln Co, Oct 9, 1917; addition to Cemeteries of Grundy Co., Vol. 2, p. 635

Name	Birth	Death	Details
Overturff, Mary Virginia	Jan 12, 1919	May 15, 2000	Philadelphia Cem.; Dau. of Charles & Julia (Herington) Beazley; m. Ben H. Overturff; addition to Cemeteries of Grundy Co., Vol 2, p. 635
Owenby, Dorothy L.	Jul 01, 1915	Jun 15, 2005	Burns Cem.; Dau. of Charlie & Fanny H. (Riding) Robinson; m. Lawrence R. Owenby; addition to Cemeteries of Grundy Co., Vol. 1, p. 136
Owenby, Lawrence Robert	Feb 18, 1913	May 02, 1995	Burns Cem.; Son of Edward J. & Rose M. (Burnett) Owenby; m. Dorothy Lee Robinson; addition to Cemeteries of Grundy Co., Vol. 1, p. 136
Owens, David	Jul 31, 1948	Oct 21, 2021	Plainview Cem.; Son of William Robert & Tressie Leona Owens; m. Elsie Owens
Owens, Henrietta (Myers) "Tiny"	Nov 18, 1939	Dec 17, 2012	Tracy City Cemetery; Dau. of Denver & Katherine Myers; m. William Owens
Owens, Roy Allen	Apr 01, 1958	Sep 03, 2019	Owens Chapel Cem.; Son of Thomas Earl Owens & Pearlie Alma Brewer
Owens, William Thomas	Apr 28, 1934	Mar 13, 2006	Tracy City Cem.; Son of William George & Georgia Evelin (Thomas) Owens; m. Henrietta Bazile, Jul 23, 1965; US ARMY, NAVY KOREA; addition to Cemeteries of Grundy Co, Vol. 2, p. 836
Owings Family Plot			Tracy City Cem.; Plot empty as of November 2022; Cemeteries of Grundy Co., Vol. 2, p. 835 correction of spelling of surname; Graves planned for the location are Jon Michael Owings, b. Nov, 28, 1937 and wife Sally Marie (Carrick) Owings, b. 2/20/1939
Pack, Allan Foster	Sep 27, 1955	Jun 18, 2019	Hunerwadel Cem.; Son of Robert R. Pack & Barbara Anne Hill; m. Lois Deborah Banker; U.S. Army
Pack, Brooks Kennedy Hayes	Jan 14, 1965	Aug 18, 2020	Fults Cem.; Son of Robert Pack & Barbara Ann Bloodworth; m. Shelia Smartt
Pack, Jefferson Davis	Oct 21, 1919	Feb 21, 1993	Monteagle Cem.; Son of Edward David "Edd" & Nellie (Lowery) Pack; m. Ortense Wilson; US Navy WWII; addition to Cemeteries of Grundy Co., Vol. 1, p. 433
Pack, Jesse Earl, Jr.	Feb 10, 1947	Apr 23, 2020	Monteagle Cem.; Son of Jesse & Willie Mae Pack; m. Donna Mae Pack; US Navy
Pack, Ortense W.	Sep 17, 1921	Oct 18, 2001	Monteagle Cem.; Dau. of George Leonard & Alma (Holder) Wilson; m. Jefferson Davis Pack; addition to Cemeteries of Grundy Co. Vol. 1, p. 433
Pack, Robert	Dec 18, 1932	Mar 15, 1997	Hunerwadel Cem.; Son of Mary K. Pack; addition to Cemeteries of Grundy Co., Vol. 1, p. 346
Pack, Thomas G.	Jan 15, 1930	Apr 10, 2013	Harrison Cem.; Son of James Cecil & Ella (Parson) Pack; m. Ann Elizabeth Pack

Name	Birth	Death	Notes
Paden, Thelma Irene (Burford)	Jun 18, 1912	Nov 06, 1995	Cumberland Heights Cem.; Dau. of Ohley B. & Manerva M. (Beane) Burford; m. Cecil Allen Paden; addition to Cemeteries of Grundy Co., Vol. 1, p. 197
Pando, Orlando	Jul 13, 1976	Dec 21, 2010	Plainview Cem.; Son of Mario & Arcilia Pando, Sr.
Pang, Duksoo	Dec 02, 1926	May 28, 2017	Cumberland Heights Seventh Day Adventist Cem.; from Korea
Pangelinan, Irma (McCoy)	Mar 14, 1947	Sep 30, 2020	Riverside National Cem., California; Dau. of Arthur & Martha (Layne) McCoy; m. George Pangelinan
Parham, Nell Virginia (Crabtree)	Jul 10, 1924	Jan 10, 2020	Franklin Memorial Gardens Cem.; Dau. of Rufus Quincy Crabtree & Ava Anna Cooper
Parker, Anna Mary	Jan 30, 1917	Aug 25, 2015	Monteagle Cem.; Dau. of William Overall & Esther (Francis) Parker
Parker, George Washington	1852	1929	Monteagle Cem.; Son of William McClelland & Sarah M. (Bonner) Parker; m. 1) Martha Ann Paty 2) Laura Lee Thomas; correction to Cemeteries of Grundy Co., Vol. 1, p.397
Parker, Krystal Michelle (Williams)	1985	Apr 23, 2019	Hillsboro Presbyterian Church Cem.; Dau. of Jimmy & Paula Williams
Parker, Laura Lee (Thomas)	1868	1937	Monteagle Cem.; Dau. of John Burkley & Rebecca Emeline (Knight) Thomas; correction to Cemeteries of Grundy County, Vol. 1, p. 397
Parker, William Thomas	Jun 13, 1845	Mar 21, 1912	Wesley Chapel Cem; Son of William McClelland & Sarah M. Parker; m. Esta Lee Berry Sep. 27, 1866; CSA Pvt. Co H, 11th TN Cavalry; addition to Cemeteries of Grundy Co., Vol. 2, p. 980
Parks, Betty Jo	Nov 15, 1931	Jun 09, 2016	Coalmont Cem.; Dau. of Hobert M. & Bessie May (Parmley) Grooms; m. J.T. Parks
Parks, Billee Fay (London)	Jan 18, 1931		Warren "Red Hill" Cem.; Dau. of James & Ruby (Duke) London; m. Fred Basil "Pink" Parks; addition
Parks, Child			Caldwell Cem.; Child of Robert & Nannie Parks buried beside parents; no stone
Parks, Christy Carol	Jun 11, 1970	Jan 12, 2020	Rose Hill Memorial Gardens; Dau. of George Grundy Parks & Edna Virginia Brothers
Parks, Edna Frances	Sep 20, 1920	Jan 02, 2016	Warren "Red Hill" Cem.; Dau. of Edgar Harold & Nannie Elizabeth (Rieder) Parks
Parks, Fred Basil "Pink"	May 19, 1929	Sep 05, 2015	Warren "Red Hill" Cem.; Son of Frederick Allen & Grace (Payne) Parks; m. Billee Fay London on Jun 10, 1950; addition
Parks, James	Jul 9, 1796	Jul 6, 1875	Coulson/Wesley Chapel Church Cem.

Name	Birth	Death	Details
Parks, Paul Keith	Oct 01, 1927	Mar 06, 2013	Warren "Red Hill" Cem.; Parks Section; Son of Frederick Allen & Grace (Payne) Parks; m. 1) Willie Mae Nunley 2) Abby (Nunley) Layne; US Army
Parmley, Harry Lewis	Sep 02, 1952	Nov 30, 2017	Cremated; Son of Harry Leslie & Dorothy Lee Hale Parmley; m. Dorraine Hamby
Parmley, Judith E. (Charles)	Dec 04, 1940	Jul 21, 2012	Orange Hill Cem.; Dau. of Robert & Anna Virginia (Roddy) Charles; m. Robert S. Parmely; addition to Cemteries of Grundy Co., Vol. 2, p. 549
Parmley, Nancy Lou	Jun 23, 1939	Apr 05, 2020	Cremated; Dau. of John Leonard Grooms & Katherine Clemetine Patton; m. Haskel Benny Parmley
Parmley, Robert S.	May 21, 1939	Nov 24, 2002	Orange Hill Cem.; Son of Haskel "Jack" & Rachel (Carrick) Parmley; m. Judith E. Charles; addition to Cemeteries of Grundy Co., Vol. 2, p. 549
Parmley, Ruby (Evans)	Sep 30, 1936	Jul 24, 2001	Coalmont Cem.; Dau. of Marvin Baxter & Bertha T. (Howard) Evans; m. Harry L. Parmley
Parson, Bessie Allen	May 05, 1925	Jun 06, 2017	Bonny Oak Cem.; Dau. of George & Mary (Kelly) Bennett; m. Johnny Parson
Parson, Christine (Adams)	Sep 24, 1926	Apr 07, 2021	Dau. of Chris Edwin & Velma Louise (Copeland) Adams; m. Lee A. Parson
Parson, Claude	Jun 06, 1931	Jul 20, 2018	Altamont Cem.; Son of Thomas F Parson & Lula Patrick; m. Ophelia Lawson; US Air Force
Parson, Craigory Dale	Aug 08, 1969	Apr 18, 2018	Clouse Hill Cem.; Son of Carl Junior Parson & Sharon Shrum
Parson, Enda (Scott)	Mar 18, 1905	Jun 14, 1905	Plainview Cem.; Dau. of Robert & Emma Thomas; m. Thomas Millard Parson; addition to Cemeteries of Grundy Co., Vol. 2, p. 664
Parson, Garland Eugene "Roho"	Jul 25, 1931	Dec 07, 2008	Clouse Hill Cem.; Son of Millard & Enda Parson; m; Mary Christine Melton; FHM; addition to Cemeteries of Grundy Co., Vol. 2, p. 151
Parson, Isaac Franklin	Apr 28, 1942	Mar 02, 2022	Cremated; Son of Robert & Flora (Foster) Parson; m. Wanda Sue Parson
Parson, Janice (Thomas)	Sep 22, 1950	Aug 30, 2020	Clouse Hill Cem.; Dau. of Hamp & Tressie Thomas; m. William Randell
Parson, Melvin E	Jun 12, 1945	Mar 28, 2020	Clouse Hill Cem.; Son of Andrew Jackson Parson & Ruby Pearl Smartt; m. Jettie Parson
Parson, Ruby Margaret (Pickett)	Dec 21, 1917	Sep 06, 1981	Bonny Oak Cem.; Dau. of John Allen & Emma D. (Childers) Pickett; m. Tommie Howard Parson; addition to Cemeteries of Grundy Co., Vol. 1, p. 90
Parson, Shirley Ann	Nov 13, 1947	Mar 05, 2018	Bonny Oak Cem.; Dau. of Johnn & Bessie (Allen) Bennett

Name	Birth	Death	Details
Parson, Thomas Millard	1899	1973	Plainview Cem.; Son of Calvin & Mary "Molly" (Church) Parson; m. Enda Scott; correction of spelling of Parson and addition to Cemeteries of Grundy Co. Vol. 2, p. 664
Parsons, Danny Ray	Apr 10, 1947	Nov 29, 2017	Cremated; Son of Isaac Wilber "Jakie" & Hazel Mildred (Thomas) Parsons; lived in Tracy City; m.1) Linda Sinnacle 2) Janet Ketchum
Parsons, Dolly Ann (Ellis)	Aug 01, 1873	Aug 03, 1947	Fall Creek Cem.; Dau of George & Julia Ellis m. William Joe Parsons
Parsons, Ella Naomi (Henley)	Dec 07, 1925	Jan 31, 1996	Palmer Cem.; Dau. of William Jonathan "Wes Willie" & Tennessee "Tennie" (Henley) Parsons; addition to Cemeteries of Grundy Co., Vol. 2, p. 559
Parsons, Elmer	Apr 14, 1908	Mar 01, 1992	Plainview Cem.; Son of Jesse Canova & Lilly Ann (Campbell) Parsons; m. Mozell Hampton; addition to Cemeteries of Grundy Co., Vol. 2, p. 683
Parsons, Enda (Scott)	1904	1994	Plainview Cem.; Dau. of Robert & Emma (Thomas) Scott; correction to Cemeteries of Grundy Co., Vol. 2, p. 664
Parsons, Naydean (Nunley)	Sep 26, 1931	Sep 03, 2016	Plainview Cem.; Dau. of Frank P. & Jennie Mae (Bess) Nunley; m. Lee Upton "Red" Parsons; addition to Cemeteries of Grundy Co., Vol. 2, p.664
Parsons, William Joe	Aug 12, 1872	May 09, 1958	Fall Creek Cem.; Son of Lewis & Mary Adeline (Boland) Parsons; m. Dolly Ann Ellis
Parsons, William Randell	Apr 22, 1949	Sep 30, 2019	Clouse Hill Cem.; Son of Howard & Rachel Parsons; m. Janice Thomas
Partain, John David	May 28, 1967	Feb 05, 2021	Palmer Cem.; Son of Arvol Ladell & Mary Maxey Partain; m. Ann Turner
Partin, Grady Ward	Mar 31, 1942		Swiss Colony Cem.; Son of Grady Edward & Georgia Violet (Schild) Partin; m. Jaquelin "Jackie" Mai Layne; Our sons: Stan, Curt, Daniel
Partin, Hester (Nunley)	Apr 27, 1945	Mar 22, 2022	Palmer Cem.; Dau. of Wesley & Bertha (Layne) Nunley; m. Larry Partin
Partin, Jackie Mae	Sep 29, 1942		Swiss Colony Cem.; Dau. of Cleveland & Clara Mae (Meeks) Layne; m. Grady Ward Partin, Jul 11, 1960; Our sons: Stan, Curt, Daniel
Partin, James Bobo	Feb 17, 1926	Apr 15, 2022	Brown's Chapel Cem.; Son of Benjamin Franklin & Ollie Jackson (Cagle) Partin; m. Marion Hattey; U.S. Army
Partin, Jimmie Ruth	ca1934	Oct 11, 2016	Rose Hill Memorial Gardens; Dau. of Andrew & Rebecca (Wilson) Jackson; m. 1) John W. Thomes 2) Edward Partin

Name	Birth	Death	Details
Partin, John A.	Sep 9, 1814	Mar 1896	Orange Hill Cem.; Son of Elisha & Sarah Partin; m. Thomas Etta Dove; no tombstone; information from descendants
Partin, Joseph Derrick "Jody"	Sep 25, 1989	Apr 23, 2016	Palmer Cem.; Son of Donald & Lisa Darlene (Davis) Partin
Partin, Marion Louise	Feb 12, 1925	Nov 28, 2015	Brown's Chapel Cem.; Dau. of Leslie & Dorothy Avril Hattey; m. James B. Partin
Partin, Stanley Ewing	Jun 06, 1939	Sep 17, 2019	Palmer Cem.; Son of Alvin Partin & Agnes Morrison; m. Clara Hart
Partin, Thomasetta "Etta" (Dove)	Oct 1, 1852	May 10, 1941	Orange Hill Cem.; Dau. of John Louis "Jim" & Nancy (Ridge) Dove; m. 1) John A. "Barney" Partin 2)__Shadrick; no tombstone; information from death certificate
Partin, Tracy Arlene (Thompson)	Nov 03, 1977	Mar 13, 2021	Fall Creek Cem.; Dau. of Charles & Frances (Roden) Thompson; m. Larry "Tykie" Partin, Jr.
Parton, Lori Angela	Jan 12, 1980	Dec 07, 2013	Homeland Acres Cem.; Grand Dau. of Jeannine & Hank Scullin
Parton, Patricia Anita (Long) "Patsy"	Aug 18, 1950	Jun 02, 2021	Cremated: Dau. of James David & Dorothy (Redfern) Long; m. J.A. Parton
Patrick, Arena (Jones)	Jul 16, 1858	Jul 19, 1939	Philadelphia Cem.; Dau of Abraham Benjamin & Clarissa (Adams) Jones; m. John Isaac Patrick
Patrick, David Franklin	Jan 22, 1951	Feb 16, 2013	Clouse Hill Cem.; Son of Elmer Franklin & Martha Flora Patrick
Patrick, Elcaney	Sep 06, 1920	Mar 17, 2017	Watson North Memorial Park Cem in Winchester; Son of William "Billy" M. & Elizabeth (Scott) Parker; m. Mary Louise Morgan; US Army WWII
Patrick, John Isaac	Aug 17, 1862	Dec 06, 1949	Philadelphia Cem.; Son of William "Billy" M. & Elizabeth (Scott) Patrick; m. Easter Arrena Jones
Patrick, Joseph A	Apr 04, 1945	Oct 10, 2018	Cremated; Son of Richard A. Patrick and Bettye Stanley Guffey; Rosa Nunley, caregiver is named in his obituary as a survivor.
Patrick, William P.	Mar 30, 1838	Apr 12, 1866	Philadelphia Cem.; Son of Moses Edward & Mary (Levan) Fitzpatrick; m. Margarete "Peggy" Wanamaker, Jan 29, 1859; addition to Cemeteries of Grundy Co., Vol. 2, p. 628
Patterson, Betty Christine (Henry)	May 25, 1944	Aug 17, 2021	Palmer Cem.; Dau. of Hubert & Gladys (Davis) Henry; m. Austin Patterson
Patterson, Billy Charles "Pat"	Apr 20, 1927	Aug 06, 2020	Cremated; Son of Harlon & Jennie Louise (Merrell) Patterson; m. Joyce Howard; Navy veteran
Patterson, Carolyn Anderson	Apr 02, 1928	Jun 03, 2016	Plainview Cem.; Dau. of Andrew Jackson Anderson & Allie Tate; m. Emmett F. Patterson

Name	Birth	Death	Notes
Patterson, Daniel B.	1886	1949	Warren "Red Hill" Cem.; Son of John & Margaret (Smith) Patterson; m. 1) Rose Ellen Conry 2) Elvie Aylor; addition to Cemeteries of Grundy Co., Vol 2, p. 937
Patterson, Geneva G (Oliver)	Nov 05, 1927	Feb 27, 2015	Warren "Red Hill" Cem.; Dau. of Cheatom & Irene (Phipps) Oliver; m. Dillon Patterson on Apr 24, 1943; children- Eddie Martin, Theresa J. Patterson; addition to Cemeteries of Grundy Co., Vol. 2, p. 955
Patterson, Vernon Ray	Jul 02, 1952	Feb 11, 2014	Warren "Red Hill" Cem.; Son of John Alton & Martha Grace (Bennett) Patterson; m. Glenda Sue Brown
Patterson, William	Nov 08, 1941	Jan 16, 2018	Gardens of Memory Cem.; Son of John Alton Patterson & Martha Patterson; m. Sharon White
Patton, Berta (Flanery)	Dec 20, 1908	Sep 23, 1998	Fall Creek Cem.; Dau.of Nathaniel H Flanery & Susie Shoupe
Patton, Harlan	Ca. Sep 1914	Nov 01, 1914	Patton Cem (probably) Pelham Church of Christ Cem.; Son of George Patton; Source *Grundy County Times*, Nov 19, 1914, child "died last week"
Patton, James Harris, Sr.	Jan 1834	Dec 12, 1921	Patton I Cem.; Son of Alexander Edgar & Salina Zora Bell (Hollingsworth) Patton; m. Susan "Sue" Woodlee, Corp, Co A 1st TN Infantry CSA; addition to Cemeteries of Grundy Co., Vol. 2, p. 586
Patton, Mary Louise	Feb 24, 1866	Jun 26, 1938	Tate Cem.; Dau. of Thomas & Selina (Reynolds) Willis; m. Joe Kirk Patton
Patton, Salina Zora Belle (Hollingsworth)	Jan 11, 1815	Aug 9, 1849	Patton I Cem.; Dau. of James & Mary "Polly" (Jones) Hollingsworth; m. Alexander Edgar Patton; addition to Cemeteries of Grundy Co., Vol. 2, p. 586
Patton, Sheila (Long)	Jun 09, 1936	May 20, 2019	Pelham Church of Christ Cem.; Dau. of Carl & Helen (Long) Long; m. Dennis Wayne Patton; addition to Cemeteries of Grundy Co., Vol. 2, p. 611
Paulk, Christopher Michael	Oct 24, 1987	Sep 29, 2014	Plainview Cem.; Son of Michael Paulk & Melissa White; fiance Nicole Haynes
Payne and/or Sanders possibly, Unidentified			Payne, George Conn & wife Almeda Sanders's homeplace; US Hwy 41 in Pelham next to the factory where the Pelham Water tank is located; 4 graves thought be Payne and/or Sanders related; Per descendant George Frank Wilson, there was nothing found to exhume when the property was sold for development
Payne, Annie Bell (Hill)	1779	ca 1860	Payne's Cove Cem.; Dau. of Samuel Hill possibly; m. Poindexter Payne; memorial stone; addition to Cemeteries of Grundy Co.

Name	Birth	Death	Notes
Payne, Benjamin Franklin	1804	1879	Payne's Cove Cem.; Son of Poindexter & Annie Bell (Hill) Payne; m. Elizabeth "Betsy" Conn; memorial stone, addition to Cemeteries of Grundy Co., Vol. 2, p. 600
Payne, Carl Bailey "Carley"	Aug 23, 1943	Aug 17, 2021	Fall Creek Cem.; ashes buried between parents; Son of Upton Bell "Buddy" & Lucy (Green) Payne; m. 1) Juanita Sue Payne 2) Janice Sharon Layne 3) Terry L. Kendall Kroushur; addition to Cemeteries of Grundy Co., Vol. 1
Payne, Carl Benton	Sep 28, 1929	Oct 18, 2017	Lynchburg Cem.; Son of Jospeh & Eva (Parks) Payne; m. Bobbie Jo Warren; US Air Force; Korea
Payne, Elizabeth "Betsy" (Conn)	1825	Jun 18, 1880	Payne's Cove Cem.; Dau of Josiah J., Jr. & Elizabeth (Townsend) Conn; memorial stone; m. Benjamin Franklin Payne
Payne, Frances Loretta	Ca 1934	Mar 05, 2017	Cremated; Carl H. & Mary Alberta (Pratt) Kilby; m. James Everett Payne
Payne, George Washington	Oct 1818	Sep 1883	Payne, George Washington Gravesite; Son of Poindexter & Annie Bell (Hill) Payne; m. Susannah Key Davis; addition to Cemeteries of Grundy Co., Vol. 2, p. 589
Payne, Jesse Willard	Apr 15, 1921	May 12, 2004	Altamont Cem.; Son of Elisha & Pearl (Sinks) Payne; m. Jessie Ruth Bess; PFC US ARMY WWII; addition to Cemeteries of Grundy Co., Vol. 1, p. 20
Payne, Leonard Elson	Nov 12, 1874	Nov 27, 1941	Tracy City Cem.; Son of Samuel W. & Mary (Foster) Payne; m. Danie Campbell; Correction to Cemeteries of Grundy Co. Vol. 2, p. 842
Payne, Louise (Watts)	Nov 21, 1930	Mar 05, 2006	Coalmont Cem.; Dau of Parker & Hazel (Levan) Watts; m. Herschel Payne; correction to Cemeteries of Grundy Co., Vol. 1, p. 184
Payne, Paul Edward	Nov 08, 1937	Jun 20, 2018	Sequatchie Valley Memorial Gardens Cem.; Son of Garland Payne & Ara Stewart; m. Tracy Payne.
Payne, Poindexter	1775	1826	Payne's Cove Cem.; Son of Thomas & Annie Bell (Hill) Payne; gave Payne's Cove its name; memorial stone addition to Cemeteries of Grundy Co., Vol. 2, p. 600
Payne, Rita F.	Jul 03, 1949	May 20, 2021	Cremated; Dau. of Charles & Mary (Barrells) Payne. Rita was the granddaughter of Upton Bell "Buddy" & Lucy Green of Laager.
Payne, Samuel William	Apr 4. 1845	Jun 08, 1938	Tracy City Cem; Son of George Washington & Susannah Key (Davis) Payne; m. Dec 26, 1872, to Mary Caroline Foster; correction to Susannah's last name & addition to Cemeteries of Grundy Co., Vol. 2, p. 842

Payne, Susannah Key (Davis)	Ca 1822	Feb 12, 1905	Payne, George Washington gravesite at her home in Tracy City; b. in VA. m. George Washington Payne; addition to Cemeteries of Grundy Co., Vol. 2, p. 589
Pearce, Madelyn F. (Hasty)	Jun 12, 1912	Jul 31, 2007	Cumberland Heights Cem.; Dau. of John W. & Mary E. (Ferguson) Hasty; m. C. W. Pearce; addition to Cemeteries of Grundy Co., Vol. 1, p. 196.
Pease, Fannie Idella (Meeks)	Feb 01, 1949	Aug 26, 2013	Hunerwadel Cem.; Dau. of William Thomas & Myrtle (Sanders) Meeks; m. Claudie Lee Pease; addition to Cemeteries of Grundy Co., Vol. 1, p. 343
Pease, Jess Prince	Aug 11, 1946	Feb 20, 2014	King Cem.; Son of Claude & Ollene Grace (King) Pease
Pease, Sharon Alvina (Adams)	Jnn 15, 1953	Feb 18, 2011	King Cem.; m. Jess Prince Pease; from OH
Peck, Bessie Edyth	Dec 23, 1902	Dec 01, 1998	Cumberland Heights Cem.; Dau. of Amos E. & Angelina (Rider) Peck; Brick sized stone with only the word Lela on it is at the head of her grave; addition to Cemeteries of Grundy Co., Vol. 1, p. 198
Peck, Ernestine "Susie" (Layne)	Dec 26, 1932	Aug 06, 2016	Watson North Memorial Park; Dau. of Robert Wilson "Bob" & William Edward "Willie" *female* (Thomas) Layne; m. John Milton Peck
Peck, Ethel Hayward	Jun 19, 1910	Sep 29, 2001	Cumberland Heights Cem.; Dau. of Amos E. & Angelina (Rider) Peck; addition to Cemeteries of Grundy Co., Vol. 1, p. 198
Pemberton, Carl Milton "Cotton"	Jan 19, 1945	Jun 26, 2001	Brown's Chapel Cem.; Son of Clarence Milton, Sr. & Geneva Lucille (Blaylock) Pemberton; m. 1) Carolyn Haskett 2) Margie Lynn Morgan; addition to Cemeteries of Grundy Co., Vol. 1, p. 109
Pemberton, Carl Milton, Jr.	Jul 09, 1967	Aug 01, 2005	Brown's Chapel Cem.; Son of Carl Milton "Cotton" & Carolyn (Haskett) Permberton; addition to Cemeteries of Grundy Co., Vol. 1, p. 109
Pemberton, Clarence Milton, Sr.	Apr 03, 1922	May 26, 2002	Brown's Chapel Cem.; Son of A. Burn & Marry Helen (Moore) Pemberton; m. Geneva Lucille Blaylock on Nov 4, 1939; addition to Cemeteries of Grundy Co., Vol. 1, p. 109
Pemberton, Geneva Lucille	Jan 16, 1926	Sep 29, 2007	Brown's Chapel Cem.; Dau. of Robert & Allie C. (Cagle) Blaylock; m. Clarence Milton Pemberton, Sr.; addition to Cemeteries of Grundy Co., Vol. 1, p. 109 I
Pemberton, Margie Lynn	Oct 26, 1947	Sep 25, 2107	Brown's Chapel Cem.; Dau. of Floyd & Arquilla June (Ledford) Bennett; m. Carl Milton "Cotton" Pemberton; addition to Cemeteries of Grundy Co., Vol. 1, p. 109

Name	Born	Died	Notes
Penley, Delilah Ross	1826	1872	Ross Mountain Cem.; Dau. of John & Nancy (Tabor) Ross; m. Carl Penley; She is said to be Cherokee; addition from informant to Cemeteries of Grundy Co., Vol. 2, p. 735
Pennell, Era (Northcutt)	Apr 06, 1905	Oct 21, 2015	Cremated; Dau. of Vernon Northcutt; m. John S. Pennell
Pennington, Ellis	Jan 10, 1944	Mar 05, 2022	Cremated; Son of Edgil & Mary (Johnson) Pennington; m. Carra Marie Crill
Pennington, Norman	May 08, 1934	Jan 16, 2019	Caraway Cem.; Son of Isaac Bertram Pennington & Pamelia Mae Chambers; m. Joyce Phillips
Perkins, Bobby Louis	Nov 28, 1959	Feb 2, 2017	Watson -North Memorial Park Cem.
Perry, C.T.	Feb 01, 1911	Mar 01, 1911	Unidentified Cem.; Source death Certificate
Perry, Colby Lee	Sep 30, 1965	Sep 23, 2013	Summerfield Cem.; Son of Kenneth Perry & Mary Elizabeth Ludwig; fiancé Beverly Patterson
Perry, Dorothy Mae (Shadrick)	Feb 13, 1922	Oct 22, 2001	Plainview Cem.; Dau. of William & Thelma (Ellis) Shadrick; m. James William Perry; addition to Cemeteries of Grundy Co., Vol. 2, p. 668
Perry, Eva May (McDonald)	Jun 10, 1905	Feb 20, 1992	Palmer Cem.; Dau. of Ben & Esther (Mosley) McDonald per birth certificate; m. William Washington Perry; addition to Cemeteries of Grundy Co., Vol. 2, p. 553
Perry, George Washington	Sep 24, 1917	Feb 22, 1995	Plainview Cem.; Son of John Thomas & Sarah Alice (Barnes) Perry; m. Alice Irene Nunley; S Sgt. US ARMY WWII; addition to Cemeteries of Grundy Co., Vol. 2, p. 689
Perry, Helen Louise (Meeks)	Feb 12, 1943	Sep 19, 2021	Orange Hill Cem.; Dau. of Wiley Clinton & Alma (Smartt) Meeks;
Perry, James Blaine	Ca 1925	Nov 15, 2017	Palmer Cem.; Son of Paul Wilson & Rosamond Margaret Doolittle Perry; m. Mary Perry; US Army - Korea
Perry, Joe Hayes "Hazel"	May 24, 1906	Aug 22, 1992	Bonny Oak Cem.; Son of Joe S. & Allie Belle (Meeks) Perry; m. Ethel Headrick; addition to Cemeteries of Grundy Co., Vol. 1, p. 92
Perry, John Henry	Jun 25, 1931	Jan 02, 1996	Palmer Cem.; Son of Manuel, Sr. & Hannah (James) Perry; m. Mary L. Pendergrass; addition to Cemeteries of Grundy Co., Vol. 2, p. 553
Perry, Joyce (Bonner)	Nov 01, 1940	Apr 02, 2008	Franklin Memorial Gardens; Dau. of Glenn E. & Rose (Howard) Bonner; m. Albert Leo Perry
Perry, Kenneth Ray	Feb 21, 1938	Mar 11, 2017	Cremated; Son of Albert E. & Olga Myrtle (Houge) Perry; m. Dion Jane Marquess; US Navy
Perry, Lewis Alton	Sep 02, 1940	Feb 21, 2019	Bonnie Oaks Cem.; Son of Isaac Perry & Berthina King; m. Dean Perry

Name	Born	Died	Notes
Perry, Malcolm Lee	Feb 04, 1950	Nov 10, 2016	Hill's Creek Cem.; Son of John W. & Alvida (King) Perry
Perry, Mary Elizabeth (Perry)	Sep 14, 1936	Dec 27, 2021	Palmer Cem.; Dau. of William "Horse Fly" & Eva (McDonald) Perry; m. James Blaine Perry
Perry, Mary L. (Pendergrass)	Jul 31, 1927	Jun 23, 2007	Palmer Cem.; Dau. of Andy & Clydie (Wells) Pendergrass; m. John Henry Perry; addition to Cemeteries of Grundy Co., Vol. 2, p. 553
Perry, Mildred	Jun 21, 1934	Sep 10, 2016	Hills Creek Cem.; Dau. of John & Gladys (Pickett) Nolan; m. Robert E. Perry, Sr.
Perry, Patsy Ann	Apr 28, 1905	Jun 29, 2014	Palmer Cem.; Dau of William Perry & Eva McDonald
Perry, Robert Edward "Buck", Sr.	Apr 24, 1929	Jan 19, 2014	Hill's Creek Cem in Warren Co.; Son of Joe Wheeler Perry & Lela Brown; m. Mildred Nolan
Perry, Robert Edward, Jr.	Aug 25, 1956	Feb 10, 2016	Fall Creek Cem.; Son of Robert E. & Mildred (Nolan) Perry
Perry, William	Ca 1865	Apr 05, 1916	Hobbs Hill Cem.; m. Sadie Perry; from *Mrs. Grundy* Apr 6, 1916; addition to Cemeteries of Grundy Co., Vol. 1, p.339
Perry, William Washington "Horsefly"	Nov 19, 1880	Jul 29, 1956	Palmer Cem.; Son of George Washington & Peggy Jane (Wells) Perry; m. Eva May McDonald; addition to Cemeteries of Grundy Co., Vol. 2, p. 553
Petty, Edna Mae (Meeks)	Aug 06, 1928	Jun 16, 2018	Summerfield Cem.; Dau. of Clarence Meeks & Vestie "Bo" Nunley; m. 1) Buddy Meeks 2) Lawrence Petty
Petty, J.R.	Jul 5, 1859	Sep 19, 1888	Oak Grove Cem.; living in Marion Co, with wife Kazia in 1880 Census; Correction to name. It was J.B. in original book, & addition to Cemeteries of Grundy Co., Vol. 1, p. 504
Petty, Mary Caroline (Uselton)	May 26, 1871	Jan 04, 1954	Plainview Cem.; Dau. of Richard A & Julia C. (Lambert) Uselton; m. William J. Petty; addition to Cemeteries of Grundy Co., Vol. 2, p. 682
Phelps, Linda Ann (Watley)	May 01, 1905	Mar 08, 2021	Cremation; Dau. of Grady & Thelma (Meeks) Watley
Phillips, David Foster	Dec 29, 1927	Nov 22, 2002	Palmer Cem.; Son of Jim & Mary (Griffith) Phillips; m. Rubie Nell Davis; addition to Cemeteries of Grundy Co., Vol. 2, p. 569
Phillips, James David	Dec 21, 1942	Feb 26, 1988	Altamont Cem.; Son of Marie Gertrude Phillips Ellis and step-father, Nolan Ellis; m. Barbara Ann Bromley; died in Michigan
Phillips, Jerry Lee	Jan 30, 1948	Apr 02, 2016	Palmer Cem.; Son of David & Rubie Nell (Davis) Phillips; m. Mary L. Phillips.
Phillips, Rubie Nell (Davis)	Apr 16, 1908	Jul 22, 1974	Palmer Cem.; Dau. of Walter Lee & Florence Ruth (Fults) Davis; m. David Foster Phillips; addition to Cemeteries of Grundy Co., Vol. 2, p. 569

Name	Birth	Death	Notes
Phillips, Timothy Edward	Mar 10, 1964	Jan 29, 2014	Palmer Cem.; Son of Billy Ed Phillips & Mildred McDaniel
Philpot, Loretta Ann (Hammers)	Mar 17, 1948	Aug 02, 2021	Palmer Cem.; Dau. of Hubert & Rosa Nell (Scruggs) Hammers
Phipps, Amanda "Mandy" (Spencer)	Apr 29, 1846	Aug 23, 1907	Old Baptist Cem.; Dau. of Zachariah Jarvis & Missouri Caroline (Crocker) Spencer; m. James Knox Polk "Jim" Phipps
Phipps, Bobbie D.	Aug 15, 1888	Oct 22, 1952	Bonny Oak Cem.; Son of Margaret Phipps; Correction of parent's name in Cemeteries of Grundy Co., Vol. 1, p. 84
Phipps, Brandon Lee	May 23, 1982	Mar 04, 2013	Bethel Cem.; Son of Keith & Cindy (Clouse) Phipps
Phipps, Charlie	1875		Bonny Oak Cem.; Son of David & Elizabeth (Sweeton) Phipps; addition to Cemeteries of Grundy Co., Vol. 1, missed in 2012 survey
Phipps, David	Jan 1, 1812	1890	Bonny Oak Cem.; Son of John & Mary (Sanders) Phipps; m. Elizabeth Sweeton; addition to Cemeteries of Grundy Co., Vol. 1. From Find A Grave
Phipps, Edward Clarence	child	Jul 17, 1914	Tracy City Cem. probably; Son of Henry & Flora (Armstrong) Phipps; from *Mrs. Grundy*
Phipps, Infant	1909	1909	Hobbs Hill Cem.; Infant of Henry & Lelia (Parsons) Phipps; Cemeteries of Grundy County Co., Vol. 1, p. 339; addition from *Mrs Grundy* newspaper
Phipps, Jackson	Aug 11, 1872	Feb 01, 1921	Bonny Oak Cem.; Son of David & Elizabeth (Sweeton) Phipps; addition to Cemeteries of Grundy Co.; missed in 2012 survey
Phipps, James David	1870	Nov 21, 1932	Bonny Oak Cem.; Son of David & Elizabeth (Sweeton) Phipps; addition to Cemeteries of Grundy Co.; missed in 2012 survey
Phipps, Jo Ann (Gipson)	May 22, 1948	Apr 07, 2019	Monteagle Cem.; Dau. of Charles J. Gipson & Ailene Henley; m. Larry Phipps
Phipps, John	1860		Bonny Oak Cem.; Son of David & Elizabeth (Sweeton) Phipps; addition to Cemeteries of Grundy Co; missed in 2012 survey
Phipps, Lutishey (Layne)	Jun 11, 1883	Feb 10, 1905	Old Baptist Cem.; Dau. of Jackson Charles & Mary Menda (Kilgore) Layne; m. William L "Bill" Phipps Jun 18, 1897 in Grundy Co.; addition to Cemeteries of Grundy Co. Vol. 2, p. 515
Phipps, Margaret Elizabeth	Oct 1850	May 22, 1933	Oak Grove Cem.; Dau. of David Jackson & Elizabeth (Sweeton) Phipps; never married but had two sons; addition to Cemeteries of Grundy Co., Vol. 1; from death certificate

Name	Birth	Death	Details
Phipps, Martha (Dickerson)	Mar 9, 1855	Jul 03, 1928	Hobbs Hill Cem.; Dau. of Buckey & Elmyra (Meeks) Dickerson; m. John D. Phipps, Jun 25, 1873; addition to Cemeteries of Grundy Co., Vol. 1, p. 329
Phipps, Mary Ann	1856	1918	Bonny Oak Cem.; Dau. of David & Elizabeth (Sweeton) Phipps; addition to Cemeteries of Grundy Co., Vol. 1; missed in the 2012 survey
Phipps, Sarah "Sally" (Smith)	1822	Aug 23, 1907	Old Baptist Cem.; Dau. of Thomas Alexander & Elizabeth Abigail (Emery) Smith m. Jackson Phipps; addition to Cemeteries of Grundy Co., Vol. 2, p. 515
Phipps, Shirley (VanHooser)	Mar 20, 1943	Dec 19, 2016	Plainview Cem.; Dau. of Sam Harley & Etta Sutton "Sut" (Boyd) VanHooser; m. Jack Phipps; addition of Cemeteries of Grundy Co., Vol. 2, p. 679
Pickett, Allan	1856	Jun 13, 1923	Bonny Oak Cem.; Son of John B. & Margaret Frances (Hoodenpile) Pickett; m. Ellen K. Bryant; addition to Cemeteries of Grundy Co., Vol. 1, p. 96
Pickett, Bailey A.	Jan 10, 1943	Aug 01, 2018	Fall Creek Cem.; Son of John L. & Helen B. (Caldwell) Pickett; m. Barbara J. Bonar
Pickett, Brenda (Ross)	Apr 02, 1941	Nov 21, 2015	Fall Creek Cem.; Dau. of Edwin & Mildred (Layne) Ross; m. Bailey Pickett
Pickett, Don Elton	Oct 05, 1954	Jul 31, 2005	Fall Creek Cem.; Son of Earl & Willie (Braden) Pickett; m. Deborah Kay Borne
Pickett, Ellen K. (Bryant)	Nov 23, 1858	Jan 22, 1918	Bonny Oak Cem.; Dau. of William & Rebecca Elizabeth Bryant; m. Alan Monroe Pickett; addition to Cemeteries of Grundy Co., Vol. 1, p. 75
Pickett, Frances Almeda	Apr 15, 1934	Aug 19, 1989	Cumberland Heights Cem.; Dau. of Ernest Buford & Thelma (Latham) Pickett; addition to Cemeteries of Grundy Co., Vol. 1, p. 196
Pickett, Gladys Marie (White)	Jun 29, 1930	Dec 14, 2019	Fall Creek Cem.; Dau. of Robert White & Maude Land; m. Jack Lloyd Pickett
Pickett, Jack William	Dec 25, 1944	Feb 11, 2013	Bonny Oak Cem.; Son of Elmer & Irene (Johnson) Pickett; m. Robbie Eletta Durham; US Army
Pickett, James Anthony	Sep 05, 1946	May 21, 1965	Fall Creek Cem.; Son of J. Harvey & Louise Kathleen (McHone) Pickett
Pickett, James Franklin	Feb 18, 1937	Aug 15, 2021	Altamont Cem.; Son of Vernon & Lassie (Taylor) Pickett; m. Shirley Ann Sanders
Pickett, James Lloyd	Dec 13, 1943	Mar 01, 2013	Bethel Cem in Ashland City; Son of John Bert & Jeanetta (Ward) Pickett; m. Debra Pickett; US Navy
Pickett, Jesse	1850	1924	Fall Creek Cem.; Son of Merideth & Milly Pickett; m. Martha Turner
Pickett, Jewell D. (Layne)	May 29, 1927	May 06, 2019	Fall Creek Cem.; Dau. of Pat Layne & Cleo Sanders; m. Clint Pickett

Name	Born	Died	Notes
Pickett, Martha (Turner)	1854	1901	Fall Creek Cem.; Dau. of Jessie & Lidy (Williams) Turner; m. Jesse Pickett
Pickett, Mary Elizabeth	May 28, 1876	Oct 02, 1963	Fall Creek Cem.; Dau. of Jesse & Martha (Turner) Pickett; addition to Cemeteries of Grundy Co., Vol. 1, p. 208
Pickett, Melvin	Jul 10, 1946	Mar 27, 2020	Center Hill Cem.; Son of Vernon Lester Pickett & Lassie Marilda Taylor; U.S. Army - Vietnam
Pierce, Esther L.	Dec 31, 1904	Oct 20, 1983	Cumberland Heights Cem: Dau. of Charles Franklin & Lula Carolina (Wright) Pierce; addition to Cemeteries of Grundy Co., Vol. 1, p. 198
Pierce, Ethel (Stotts)	Aug 24, 1932	Sep 01, 2020	Wesley Chapel Cem.; Dau. of Leonidas "Lon" Stotts & Oma Fults; m. Art Pierce
Pierce, Lelar Mae (Wilburn)	Feb 24, 1950	Sep 12, 2020	Private family Cem.; Dau. of Harry & Rita Mae Wilburn;
Pirtle, James August	Aug 05, 1929	Feb 23, 2015	Tracy City Cem.; Son of William & Melinda Pirtle; m. Margaret Frances Lewis
Pirtle, Julia Elizabeth	Sep 04, 1931	Oct 12, 2016	Monteagle Cem.; Dau. of Dave & Gleenie (Schaerer) Thomas; m. Alvin T. Pirtle
Pirtle, Margaret Frances (Lewis)	Apr 14, 1905	Apr 23, 2022	Tracy City Cem.; Dau. of George Herbert & Della Anna (Brown) Lewis; m. James Pirtle
Pistol, Fay (Green)	Apr 15, 1905	Aug 12, 2021	Cremated; m: 1) ____ Woodlee 2) ____ Pistol
Pittman, John William	Jan 12, 1935	Aug 30, 2020	Palmer Cem.; Son of Virgil Bolton Pittman & Mattie Cargile; m. Betty Lyda Pittman.
Pittmann, Richard Alfred, Jr.	May 14, 1962	Jan 08, 2022	Cremation; Son of Richard A. & Susan (Doleto) Pittmann; m. Cathy Hartsel
Pitts, Lana Carol (Stiefel)	Apr 16, 1959	Jan 05, 2017	Plainview Cem.; Dau. of Roy & Dorothy (Harris) Stiefel
Plantz, Alex Steven	Jan 09, 1990	Oct 31, 2013	Cremated; lived in Unionville, TN.
Pleasant, Rhonda Lynn (Meeks)	Jun 29, 1967	Feb 23, 2015	Pelham Church of Christ Cem.; Dau. of Ralph C. & Helen (Medley) Meeks; m. Albert Eugene Pleasant
Pocus, Jerry M.	Dec 11, 1938	Oct 16, 2015	Cremated; Son of George & Millie (Henry) Pocus; m. Joan Wilson; US Air Force
Pocus, Joann	Jul 18, 1943	Apr 17, 2008	Bonny Oak Cem.; Dau. of Sam & Orine (Blaylock) Hill; m. Jack Pocus; addition to Cemeteries of Grundy Co., Vol. 1, p. 94
Pocus, Laura	Ca 1884	May 26, 1933	Tracy City Cem.; from death certificate; Dau. of Alex Bunch; m. Joe Pocus; addition to Cemeteries of Grundy Co., Vol. 2
Pocus, Roger Samuel	Oct 23, 1964	Jan 13, 1974	Bonny Oak Cem.; Son of Jackie Sanders & Joann (Hill) Pocus; addition to Cemeteries of Grundy Co., Vol. 1, p. 91
Pocus, Thelma (Layne)	Aug 03, 1940	Sep 17, 2017	Palmer Cem.; Dau. of Henry C. & Betty (Crisp) Layne; m. Robert H. Pocus

Name	Born	Died	Details
Poe, Dora Evelyn (Nunley)	May 25, 1925	Aug 18, 2015	King Cem.; Dau. of Will & Lee G. (McGuffey) Nunley; m. Stanford Poe; addition to Cemeteries of Grundy Co., Vol. 1, p. 353
Pointer, Zilpha Ann (Terry)	Feb 1854	Jan 15, 1923	Wesley Chapel Cem.; Dau. of James Washington & Harriet Ann (Dowell) Terry; m. S.D. Pointer; addition to Cemeteries of Grundy Co., Vol. 2, p. 969
Ponder, Jerry M.	Jan 6, 1854	Jan 07, 1930	Tracy City Cem; Son of Malachil & Nancy Ann (Price) Ponder; m. Mary Ellen McCullough; addition to Cemeteries of Grundy Co., Vol. 2, p. 899
Ponder, Mary Ellen (McCullough)	May 14, 1859	Sep 03, 1928	Tracy City Cem.; Dau. of Allen N. & Sarah (Layne) McCullough; m. Jerry M. Ponder; addition to Cemeteries of Grundy Co., Vol. 2, p. 899
Porter, Alice Mabel (Coe)	Feb 23, 1885	Mar 25, 1965	Hunerwadel Cem.; Dau. of Samuel Augustus & Julia Jane (Whitney) Coe; m. Ford Davis Porter; addition to Cemeteries of Grundy Co., Vol. 1, p. 344
Potts, Bertha (Campbell)	Apr 25, 1932	Sep 14, 2013	Palmer Cem.; Dau. of Louie Howard & Mazie Hilda (Graham) Campbell; m. Marion John Potts, Jr.; addition to Cemeteries of Grundy Co., Vol. 2, p. 554
Potts, Billy Gerald "Ricky"	Dec 14, 1957	Feb 20, 2020	Palmer Cem.; Son of Rod & Norma Mae Campbell
Potts, Charles Gordon	Sep 04, 1952	Jul 20, 2019	Cremated; Son of Charles Ransom Potts & Rebecca Louise Sutherland
Powell, Buford Alvin, Sr.	Jul 31, 1936	Mar 15, 2005	Oak Grove Cem.; Son of Lou Ellen Powell; m. Claudia Mae Keel; addition to Cemeteries of Grundy Co., Vol. 1, p. 511
Powell, Charles Ray	Jul 15, 1961	Aug 19, 2015	Plainview Cem.; Son of Robert & Rachel Powell; m. Wendy Castoire; US Army
Powell, John Peyton	Mar 19, 1866	Jul 15, 1946	Tracy City Cem.; Son of Jerome B. & Mary I. (Gilley) Powell, correction to Cemeteries of Grundy Co., Vol. 2, p. 873
Powell, Nicole "Clyde"	Jun 18, 1905	Sep 23, 2018	Coalmont Cem.; Dau. of Jerome & Chrissy Powell
Powell, Robert A.	Jul 21, 1970	Jul 22, 1970	Bonny Oak Cem.; Son of Jerry & Charlotte (Meeks) Powell; addition to Cemeteries of Grundy Co., Vol. 1, p. 86
Prater, Bruce Wayne	Mar 29, 1953	Jun 06, 2019	Plainview Cem.; Son of Arble L. Prater & Dorothy Johnson
Prater, Dorothy E.	May 31, 1924	Mar 25, 2014	Plainview Cem.; Dau. of William Andrew & Anna Ruth (McDonald) Johnson; m. Arble Prater
Presley, Geneva (Starling)	Jun 18, 1928	Jun 21, 1994	Orange Hill Cem.; Dau. of Scott & Delia Mae (Tate) Starling; addition to Cemeteries of Grundy Co., Vol. 2, p. 524

Name	Birth	Death	Notes
Pressley, Paul Eugene	Nov 03, 1950	Mar 14, 1951	Monteagle Cem.; Son of James R. & Geneva (Starling) Pressley.
Price, Billie Jo	1946	May 23, 2022	Cremated; Dau. of Hyman "Lucky" & Velma Carlene (Brown) Price; m. Wright
Price, Lena Marie	Oct 24, 1943	Jun 08, 2015	Grace Chapel Cem.; Dau. of Carlene Brown & Hyman "Lucky" Price; funeral home marker only
Price, Lois May (Coppinger)	Jun 16, 1925	Jun 01, 2015	Gregg Cem.; Dau. of Clarence G. & Margaret E. "Maggie" (Meadows) Coppinger m. Roy Haskel Price, Sr.
Price, Neil Eugene	Nov 10, 1953	Jun 19, 2020	Gregg Cem.; Son of Roy Haskel Price, Sr. & Lois Coppinger;
Price, Roy Haskel Jr.	Sep 30, 1942	Jan 31, 2019	Gregg Cem.; Son of Roy Haskel Price, Sr. & Lois Coppinger; m. Peggy Haskel
Price, Trisha Kay	Mar 17, 1974	Feb 16, 2022	Cremated; Dau. of Steven B. Price & Marta Lynn Gilbert; m. Marshall Wilson
Prince, Dixie (Lawrence)	Jul 8, 1888	Sep 19, 1961	Bonny Oak Cem.; Dau. of Jason & Barbara (Luttrell) Lawrence; m. Thomas Leroy Prince
Prince, Larry Hawkins	Oct 20, 1931	Oct 09, 2020	Cremated; Son of J.D. & Irene (Hawkins) Prince; m. Ruth Meeks; U.S. Air Force`
Prince, Mabel (Hatfield)	Mar 09, 1906	Jun 16, 1947 per death cert. stone says 1946	Bonny Oak; Dau. of J.H. & Dixie (Lawrence) Hatfield; m. Toy Sweeton
Prince, Mansel R.	Jul 19, 1919	May 29, 2015	Franklin Memorial Gardens Cem.; Son of John & Betty (Garner) Prince; m. Ernestine Kelly; US Army
Prince, Samuel Thomas Leroy	1912	1941	Bonny Oak Cem.; Son of Thomas Leroy & Deola Lee (Towell) Prince; m. Edith Louise Bone; correction of maternal parent's name; addition to Cemeteries of Grundy Co., Vol, 1, p. 78
Prince, Thomas Leroy	1878	1958	Bonny Oak Cem.; Son of W.R. Prince & Elizabeth McGowan; m. Dixie Iowa Lawrence; addition to Cemeteries of Grundy Co., Vol. 1, p. 79
Pritchett, Ollie Beatrice (Perry)	Feb 03, 1942	Mar 18, 2020	Center Hill Cem.; Dau. of Issac Perry & Berthina King; m. Everett Pritchett
Privett, Elizabeth Ruth (Henry)	Aug 12, 1940	Aug 05, 2018	Palmer Cem.; Dau. of Hubert Henry & Gladys Davis; m. James Stephen Privett
Privett, George Herman	Aug 31, 1934	Apr 05, 1993	Palmer Cem.; Son of Franklin Turner & Katherine Elizabeth (Harveston) Privett; addition to Cemeteries of Grundy Co., Vol. 2, p. 578
Pruitt, Betty Ruth	Sep 27, 1947	Oct 17, 2015	Burns Cem.; Dau. of Richard & Velma Jean (Mann) Massey; m. Robert Pruitt

Pugh, Arvel Delano	Jan 20, 1935	Aug 20, 2009	Homeland Acres Cem.; Son of Arthur Allen & Maymie E. (Ryals) Pugh; m. Adina Dokum; addition to Cemeteries of Grundy Co., Vol. 1, p. 340
Pyburn, Carrie (O'Barr)	Mar 24, 1882	Apr 08, 1967	Plainview Cem.; Dau. of Larkin & Edna Jane (Cook) O'Barr; m. Thomas Love "Mug" Pyburn
Pyburn, Corbett	Jul 11, 1912	Jan 30, 1953	Plainveiw Cem.; Son of Thomas Love & Carrie (O'Barr) Pyburn per death certificate; addition to Cemeteries of Grundy Co.
Pyburn, Hugh	1840	Dec 16, 1924	Gregg Cem.; Son of Thomas Love & Rebecca (Lowry) Pyburn
Pyburn, Mary Catherine "Molly" (Anderson)	Ca 1869	May 26, 1933	Gregg Cem.; Dau. of Peter & Rebecca "Becky' (Pyburn) Anderson; m. William Pyburn
Pyburn, Mollie (Anderson)	Ca 1869	May 26, 1933	Gregg Cemetery; Dau. of Peter & Becky R. (Brown) Anderson; m. W.M. Pyburn; no marker, death certificate; addition to Cemeteries of Grundy County, Vol 1.
Pyburn, William	Jan 23, 1868	Dec 29, 1937	Gregg Cem.; Son of John & Mary (Johnson) Pyburn; m. Frances Pyburn.
Qualls, Albert Devander	Aug 27, 1938	Feb 21, 2017	Wesley Chapel Cem.; Son of Ralph Alford & Hazel (Anthony) Qualls; m. Esther Yvonne Stephens; addition to Cemeteries of Grundy Co., Vol. 2, p. 990
Qualls, Doretha Marie (Moore)	Jul 22, 1937	Mar 10, 2015	Wesley Chapel Cem.; Dau. of Samuel & Anna Mary (Pennington) Moore; m. Clarence E. Qualls; addition to Cemeteries of Grundy Co, Vol. 2, p. 967
Qualls, Esther Yvonne (Stephens)	Jun 10, 1941	Feb 17, 2017	Wesley Chapael Cem.; Dau. of Ores Elvert & Bessie May Stephens; m. Albert Devander Qualls; addition to Cemeteries of Grundy Co., Vol. 2, p. 990
Qualls, Izetta Inez	Mar 18, 1936	Jul 22, 2019	Wesley Chapel Cem.; Dau. of James Hollis & Pearly Mae (Fults) Qualls; addition to Cemeteries of Grundy Co., Vol, 2, p. 989
Quinn, Katherine	Jan 06, 1943	Jul 25, 2015	Taylor Cem, Vienna, IL; Dau. of Joe & Bethel (Simmons) Potts; m. Jerry Quinn
Rackar, John Steve	Nov 11, 1911	Dec 30, 1991	Coalmont Cem.; Son of John & Mary (Habat) Rackar; m. Evie Frances Woodlee; correction to Cemeteries of Grundy Co., Vol. 1, p. 179
Rakauskas, Shelby Francis "Rocky"	Jan 05, 1941	Feb 27, 2021	Cremated: Son of Fran & Mary Rakauskas; m. Inez Rakauskas
Ramirez, Christeena G.	Jun 19, 1976	Apr 10, 2016	Cremated; Dau. of Conrad & Chyrell (Davis) Bishop
Ramsey, Debbie Tyler		Mar 21, 2018	Cremated; Monteagle; Dau. of Sue Bennett

Name	Birth	Death	Notes
Ramsey, Karen Alvada	May 29, 1944		Summerfield Cem Dau. of Alvin Owen & Dava Audrey (Stephens) Gilliam; m. Marvin Edward Ramsey; addition to Cemeteries of Grundy Co., Vol. 2, p. 763
Ramsey, Marvin Edward	Sep 12, 1934	Jun 24, 1993	Summerfield Cem.; Son of Burr Edward & Willie Nellie Ramsey
Rankin, Rhoda Tabatha	Jun 14, 1923	Jan 06, 2016	Swiss Cem.; Dau. of William Carroll & Lila Jane (Smith) King; m. Murphy David Rankin
Raper, Harvey Mack	Aug 14, 1928	Nov 27, 2021	Cremated; Son of Mac & Bessie (McDowell) Raper; m. Marie Liddle; US Navy, WWII
Raper, Marie (Liddle)	Noc 8, 1929	Apr 05, 2011	Cremated; Dau. of Harold & Bessie Liddle; m. Harvey Mack Raper
Raulston, Linda (Morrison)	Jun 02, 1948	Jan 20, 2011	Swiss Colony Cem.; Dau. of Tammie Layne & mother of Tanya & Tammy
Raulston, Marion Greer "Fod"	Jan 01, 1930	Aug 01, 1985	Body donated to Emory University; Son of Jefferson Jones "Jonas" & Mary Orme (Sayles) Raulston; died in Atlanta; never married
Raulston, Mary Orme (Sayles)	Nov 24, 1902	Feb 15, 1965	Monteagle Cem.; Dau of Gilbert Sayles & Mary Kathryn Payne; m. J J Raulston; correction to Cemeteries of Grundy Co., Vol. 1, p. 417
Ray, Kenneth Paul	Sep 15, 1935	Mar 09, 2005	Altamont Cem.; Son of Homer Ernest & Nan (Spurrier) Ray; m. Mary Ellen Hobbs; addition to Cemeteries of Grundy Co., Vol. 1, p. 19
Reagon, Clyde Estes	Nov 22, 1923	Jan 07, 1999	Swiss Colony Cem; Son of Thomlin & Annie Myrtle (Ward) Reagon; m. Hallie M. Slatton; addition to Cemeteries of Grundy Co., Vol. 2, p. 797
Rector, Michael Kent	Nov 27, 1960	Sep 14, 2017	Pryor Ridge Cem.; Son of Marvin & Pauline Rector; m. Rhonda Rector
Redwine, Garrett Maxwell	Oct 05, 2012	Jul 04, 2015	Unidentified Cem.; Son of Jacob & Terri (Reep) Redwine
Reece, Larry Craig	Feb 22, 1980	Feb 08, 2016	New Prospect Cem.; Son of Larry & Annette Reece; m. Lindsey Reece.
Reed, Della (Lowe)	Jan 12, 1876	Aug 09, 1940	Payne's Cove Cem.; Dau. of James L & Martha A (Loyd) Lowe; m. Joseph S. Reed; addition to Cemeteries of Grundy Co., Vol. 2, p. 594
Reed, Emma Louella "Lou" (England)	Feb 12, 1905	Apr 14, 1905	Wesley Chapel Cem.; Dau. of Alexander Calvin & Mary M. (Purcell) England; m. Rollie Reed; addition to Cemeteries of Grundy Co., Vol. 2, p. 980
Reed, Henry Edgar	1909	1959	Tracy City Cem; Son of William Claude & Delila (Smith) Reed; m. Virginia Harrison on Dec 14, 1940; addition to Cemeteries of Grundy Co., Vol. 2, p. 847

Name	Birth	Death	Details
Reed, Joseph S.	1862	Oct 06, 1928	Payne's Cove Cem.; Son of William M. & Nancy Jane (Woosley) Reed; m. Della Lowe; addition to Cemeteries of Grundy Co., Vol. 2, p. 594; death cert says he was a peddler found shot – no physician.
Reed, Marvin Alf "Mac"	Aug 20, 1952	Feb 06, 2021	Monteagle Sunday School Assembly Cem.; Son of Henry "Minge" & Ruth (Coleman) Reed; m. Catherine Drennon
Reed, Raymond Earl	1964	1965	Tracy City Cem; Son of Clifford Lee & Henrietta (Reed) Tayse; addition to Cemeteries of Grundy Co., Vol. 2, p. 847
Reed, Samuel L. "Sam"	Feb 08, 1966	Dec 20, 2020	Hobbs Hill Cem.; Son of Samuel P. Reed & Geneva (Bateman) Wilhite
Reeves, Bonnie Faye (Cox)	1953	Sep 03, 2019	Swiss Colony Cem.; Dau. of James W. Cox & Elizabeth Hale
Reeves, Curtis L.	Jun 10, 1959	Nov 09, 1996	Swiss Colony Cem; Son of Robert Lavaughn & Nancy Reeves; addition to Cemeteries of Grundy Co., Vol. 2, p. 798
Reeves, Douglas Ralph	Dec 08, 1948	Feb 16, 2016	Cremated; Son of Louis Herbert & Mary Louise (McGuire) Reeves
Reeves, Edward David	May 05, 1947	Jul 08, 2013	Swiss Colony Cem.; Son of Robert & Viola (West) Reeves; m. Stella Cox
Reeves, James Franklin	Sep 23, 1879	Dec 19, 1946	Hobbs Hill Cem; Son of William Calvin & Nancy (Stewart) Reeves; m. Della Cunningham; addition to Cemeteries of Grundy Co. Vol. 1, p. 336
Reeves, Nancy	Mar 2, 1855	Sep 05, 1909	Hobbs Hill Cem.; Dau. of William "Willie" & Vernetea Stewart
Reeves, Robert Lavaughn	Apr 15, 1935	Nov 25, 2020	Swiss Colony Cem.; Son of Robert & Viola (West) Reeves; m. Nancy Blevins
Reeves, Shirley (Butner)	Jan 3, 1949	Jul 26, 2014	Cremated; Dau of Jim Ed Butner & Nell Couch; m. Douglas Reeves
Reeves, Viola (West)	May 15, 1918	Jun 30, 2007	Swiss Colony Cem.; Dau. of Jackson W. & Frances Louvenia (Avans) West; m. Robert Lee Reeves; addition to Cemeteries of Grundy Co., Vol. 2, p. 798
Reeves, William Calvin	1850	1900	Hobbs Hill Cem.; Son of William W. & Elizabeth (Norris) Reeves; addition to Cemeteries of Grundy Co., Vol. 1, p. 336
Reider, William Jonas	Sep 14, 1976	Jan 20, 2014	Warren "Red Hill" Cem.; Son of Don & Mary Rieder
Reinhard, Lessie Lee (Carter)	Mar 11, 1905	May 14, 1982	Cumberland Herights Cem.; Dau. of Asa G. & Kate E. (Rollins) Carter; m. Roy Edwin Reinhard; addition to Cemeteries of Grundy Co., Vol. 1, p. 195

Name	Born	Died	Details
Reinhard, Roy Edwin	May 03, 1906	Jun 29, 1989	Cumberland Heights Cem.; Son of Edward Edwin & Alice (Squires) Reinhard; m. 1) Lessie Lee Carter 2) Ellen Zenith Ley on Dec 3, 1982; addition to Cemeteries of Grundy Co., Vol, 1, p. 195
Releford, Oliver Alfred	Nov 22, 1922	Feb 13, 1983	Monteagle Cem.; Son of Alex & Maude (Coker) Jennings Brinkley Releford; m. Myrtle Brannan; grandson of Oliver Alfred Jennings; addition to Cemeteries of Grundy Co., Vol. 1, p. 423
Releford, Raymond Aarol, Sr.	Apr 15, 1924	May 01, 1977	Monteagle Cem.; Son of Alex & Maude (Coker) Releford; m. Virginia Byers; PVT US ARMY WWII
Reyes, Amelia Molly	May 05, 1984	Mar 23, 2014	Little Johnny Myers Cem.; Dau. of Frances (Martinez) Acevedo, m. Louis Alberto Reyes
Reynolds, Charlie	Feb 28, 1953	May 05, 2016	Little Johnny Myers Cem.; Son of Herman & Geneva (Dodson) Reynolds; m. Versie Reynolds
Reynolds, George Thomas	Jul 03, 1946	Aug 24, 2021	Welker Cem. in New Union, Coffee Co.; Son of Arthur & Lillian Reynolds; m. Anna "Frankie" Reynolds; U.S. Air Force
Rhea, Forrest Edgar	Jun 10, 1918	Aug 26, 1978	Bonny Oak Cem.; Son of Edward W & Mattie B (Savage) Rhea; m. Veola Mae Sweeton; PVT US Army; addition to Cemeteries of Grundy Co., Vol. 1, p. 84
Rhea, James Calvin	Jan 14, 1938	Dec 11, 2019	Wesley's Chapel Cem.; Son of Claude Calvin Rhea & Gladys Marie Adams; m. Linda J. Shafter; U.S. Air Force
Rhea, Mary Ruth (Lowe)	Jun 25, 1940	Mar 01, 2017	Plainview Cem.; Dau. of Carl & Louise (Pattie) Lowe; m. Eddie Rhea
Rhea, Maudie Lee	Apr 10, 1919	Apr 10, 1992	Bonny Oak Cem.; Dau. of Harvey & Maggie Caldwell; m. Willie Nephi Rhea; addition to Cemeteries of Grundy Co., Vol. 1, p. 84
Rhea, Raymond H.	Sep 05, 1924	Jan 04, 1945	Henri-Chapelle American Cem. & Memorial Cem in Liege, Belgium, Plot E, Row 13, Grave 10; Son of Edgar Witt Rhea & Martha Belle Savage; 347 Infantry Regiment 87th Infantry Division; KIA, purple heart from Altamont, TN.
Rhea, Tony Lynn	Aug 16, 1953	May 26, 2019	Northcutt Cove Cem.; Son of Felton Lerris & Melba Nadine Taylor; m. Nancy Boyd
Rhea, Veola Mae (Sweeton)	Feb 03, 1925	Dec 01, 1990	Bonny Oak Cem.; Dau. of Arthur Lee & Myrtle (Nunley) Sweeton; m. Forrest E. Rhea; addition to Cemeteries of Grundy Co., Vol. 1, p. 84
Rhoads, Vera June (Meeks)	Oct 04, 1920	May 29, 2018	Hillsboro Memorial Gardens Cem. Brandon, FL; Dau. of Jim Meeks & Zora Parks; m. Frank Hulon Rhoads

Name	Birth	Death	Notes
Rhodes, Marie Juanita (Basile)	Dec 24, 1939	Dec 17, 2017	Cremated; Dau. of Stephen & Mildred Basile
Rice, Gwendolyn Maxine (Ledford)	Dec 17, 1954	Mar 16, 2015	Cremated; Plainview Cem.; Dau. of George Samuel & Oma Ruth (Graham) Ledford; m. 1) Ronald Sherman Kelly in 1974, Tampa, FL. 2) E.L. Rice in 1991 in FL
Rice, Hazel Parsons	May 24, 1935	May 18, 2018	Plainview Cem.; Dau. of Glen & Katherine (Brookman) Parsons; addition to Cemeteries of Grundy Co., Vol. 2, p. 680
Richard, Willie Kate (Campbell)	Jun 29, 1936	Dec 07, 2018	Coalmont Cem.; Dau. of Oddist Campbell & Kate Nunley; m. Howard Eugene Richard, Jr.
Richards, Bobby Lee	Oct 16, 1938	Feb 08, 2021	Plainview Cem.; Son of Dorris Lee & Alma (Knighton) Richards; m. Diane McFarland; U.S. Army
Richardson, Clarence Glenn	Oct 05, 1940	Aug 21, 2020	Fults Cem.; Son of Clarence Richardson & Oma Bouldin; m. Wanda Farless
Richardson, Clayta Jean (Tate)	Oct 13, 1954	Mar 18, 2015	Richardson Family Cem.; Dau. of Everett Slatton & Abbie (King) Tate; m. Everett Richardson
Richardson, Everett Labrawn	Feb 02, 1952	Sep 30, 2021	Richardson Family Cem.; Son of Lemma Hazel Richardson; m. 1) Clayta Richardson 2) Donna Huntley
Richardson, Frank Joseph	Nov 30, 1906	Dec 02, 1980	Monteagle Cem.; Son of Isabelle Agnes Richardson; m. Emma Castella Hargis; US Navy WWII, Korea; addition to Cemeteries of Grundy Co., Vol. 1, p. 439
Richardson, George Franklin	Nov 19, 1933	Nov 01, 2017	Fults Cem.; Son of Jesse Herman & Lillian Edna (Scott) Richardson; m. Evelyn Faye McGee; US Army
Richardson, Lemma Hazel	Mar 23, 1931	Apr 11, 2015	Richardson Family Cem.; Dau. of McKinley & Elease (Walker) Richardson; children listed on tombstone Everett, Bertha, Marsha
Richardson, Lemma Hazel	Mar 23, 1931	Apr 11, 2015	Richardson Cem.; Dau. of McKinley & Elease (Walker) Richardson
Richardson, Morris Earl	Nov 28, 1957	Apr 11, 2021	Hunerwadel Cem.; Son of Clarence & Oma (Bouldin) Richardson
Richardson, Raymond	Dec 11, 1946	Aug 18, 2005	Fults Cem. Northcutt's Cove; Son of Richard Henry & Annie Myrtle (Richardson) Childers; addition to Cemeteries of Grundy Co,. Vol. 1, p. 284
Richmond, James Aubrey	Aug 12, 1896	Sep 24, 1978	Monteagle Cem.; Son of Josepn Atticus & Irene (Schaffer) Richmond; m. Sarah Margaret Parker, Jun 27, 1917. correction to Cemeteries of Grundy Co., Vol. 1, p. 40
Riddle, Billy Reid	Jan 31, 1938	Jun 16, 2019	Warren "Red Hill" Cem.; Son of Cordel Riddle & Amy Graven; m. 1) Jacqueline Kaye Riddle 2) Jayne Carolyn Patterson; U.S. Air Force; lived in Huntsville, AL

Name	Birth	Death	Details
Riddle, Jayne (Patterson)	Jun 27, 1938	Nov 19, 2014	Warren "Red Hill" Cem.; Dau. of Claude & Dorothy (Sanders) Patterson; m. Billy Reid Riddle on Aug 30, 1975; lived in Huntsville, AL
Riddle, Timothy Brian	Jul 02, 1960	Jan 18, 2019	Warren "Red Hill" Cem.; Son of Billy Reid & Jacqueline Kaye Riddle & stepson of Jayne Carolyn (Patterson) Riddle; lived in Huntsville, AL.
Ridley, Marion Berton, Dr	Nov 14, 1956	Jul 01, 2018	Pine Grove Cem. Jasper TN; Son of Billy Joe Ridley & Bonnie Lynn Cagle; m. Mark Lee Lundy
Rieben, Alfred Roy	Nov 06, 1936	May 29, 2015	Cremated; Son of Fritz & Rose Etta (Bass) Rieben; m. Joy Prince; lived in Franklin Co.; bro. of Ralph Rieben of Altamont
Rieben, Bonnie Sue (Fults)	Mar 07, 1941	Jan 06, 2010	Altamont Cem.; Dau of Malcolm A. & Willie Mae (Lusk) Fults; m., 1) ___ Wilkerson 2) Ralph E. Rieben
Rieben, Ralph E.	Jun 21, 1934	Sep 09, 2022	Altamont Cem.; Son of Fritz & Rosa Etta (Bass) Rieben; m. 1) Janice Marie Prince 2) Bonnie Sue (Fults) Wilkerson; addition to Cemeteries of Grundy Co., Vol. 1, p. 29
Rieder, Anna Pauline	Dec 14, 1909	May 18, 1913	Clouse Hill Cem.; Dau. of Albert Daniel & Minerva (Bennett) Rieder; source is *Mrs. Grundy, May 22, 1913*
Rieder, Georgia Fay (Garner)	1922	Mar 13, 2016	Warren "Red Hill" Cem.; Dau. of Lou Allen & Mary Catherine (Haynes) Garner; m. Lloyd H. Rieder
Rieder, Irma Jean (Gipson)	Apr 24, 1931	Jun 08, 2019	Warren "Red Hill"; Dau. of Clayborn Gipson & Gertrude Garner; m. William Jonas Rieder, Jr.
Rieder, John Henry	Sep 27, 1891	Nov 26, 1967	Warren "Red Hill" Cem.; Son of Francis Marion & Malinda Abigail (Parks) Rieder; m. Lillie Moran; Recent date of death engraving states death was Nov. 26, 1969, but his will was probated in Dec. of 1968; addition to Cemeteries of Grundy Co., Vol. 2, p. 938
Rieder, male child			Hargis Cem.; Son of John Henry & Lillie (Moran) Rieder
Rieder, William Jonas "Bill", Jr.	Aug 26, 1928	Dec 17, 2015	Warren "Red Hill" Cem.; Son of William Jonas, Sr., & Verna Rhea (Floyd) Rieder; m. Irma Jean Gipson
Riese, Therma Faye	Aug 15, 1916	Mar 14, 2003	Cumberland Heights Cem.; Dau. of William Nelson & Mattie V. (Beeson) McDowell; m. Theodore Alfred "Pete" Riese; addition to Cemeteries of Grundy Co., Vol, 1, p. 195
Rigsby, George Lee	Spe 12, 1924	Apr 25, 2019	Shockley Cem.; Son of Ewin Oliver Rigsby & Lara May Pack; m. Dortha Lee Brock

Name	Born	Died	Details
Rigsby, Nancy (Roberts) Cleek	Nov 27, 1923	May 11, 2016	Fall Creek Cem.; Dau. of Henry & Oda (James) Roberts; m. 1) Woodrow Cleek 2) John Lesser, 3) Earl Rigsby
Risko, Geneva (Dickerson)	Apr 20, 1923	Feb 21, 2013	Altamont Cem.; Dau. of Jim & Nina (Givens) Dickerson; m. John Risko
Risley, William F.	Jul 27, 1921	Jan 08, 2015	Cremated/Summerfield Cem.; Son of William H. & Mable (Smith) Risley; m. Pauline Rollins; WWII vet
Rives, Lucinda W.	Sep 12, 1838	Sep 1, 1877	Wesley Chapel Cem.; Dau. of Henry Smith & Evaline Rebecca (Rives) Thomas; m. Edmund Harrison Rives on Feb 2, 1854; addition to Cemeteries of Grundy Co., Vol, 2, p. 974
Roach, Dennis Scott	Nov 22, 1976	Apr 27, 2019	Cremated; Son of Dennis Dean Roach & Claudia Gower
Robbins, Elliot LeRoy	Jun 04, 1938	Jan 14, 2018	Cremated: Son of Elliot Kenneth Robbins & Athleen Bateman; m. Sally Ann Athey; US Army
Roberge, Diana Marie	Feb 03, 1956	Jul 20, 2020	Palmer Cem.; Dau. of Kenneth Wayne Trent & Thelma Lorene Lindsey; m. Michel Pierre Roberge
Roberts Robinson, Jeannette Julie (Blondelet)	Feb 24, 1926	Feb 24, 2018	Philadelphia Cem.; Dau. of Jules & Julia (Beulin) Blondelet; m. 1) Sherman Dewey Roberts 2) Albert Lee Robinson, Sr. addition to Cemeteries of Grundy Co., Vol. 2, p. 616
Roberts, James Arthur II	Sep 13, 1918	Feb 10, 2003	Burns Cemetery; Son of James Roberts & Sina M. Anderson; m. Mildred J. Roberts.; Army, WWII He has a tombstone in Fall Creek, but is actually buried in Burns Cem;
Roberts, Betty (Scott)	Jun 27, 1956	May 09, 2015	Coalmont Cem.; Dau. of Junior & Maxine Scott; m. Benton Roberts
Roberts, Donna "Donnie" Louise (Meeks)	Sep 07, 1942	May 23, 2017	Roberts Cem.; Dau. of Everett & Emma (Magouirk) Meeks; m. Billy Hagan Roberts on May 9, 1959; no tombstone
Roberts, Doris Ophelia (Caldwell)	1925	Apr 14, 2018	Burns Cem.; Dau. of Stanley Caldwell & Millie Morgan; m. Arville E. Roberts
Roberts, Elene	Feb 18, 1939	Feb 18, 1939	Roberts Cem.; Dau. of France & Maggie (Fults) Roberts, twin to Ernestine Roberts Gilbert
Roberts, Ernest Arnold, Sr.	Oct 29, 1906	Aug 11 1986	Cumberland Heights Cem.; Son of Edward & Alice (Hunter) Roberts; m. 1) Helen Mundy 2) Florence L. Parmeter; addition to Cemeteries of Grundy Co., Vol. 1, p. 198
Roberts, Etta Leona (Madewell)	Feb 27, 1929	Nov 09, 2018	Shellsford Cem.; Dau. of Albert Madewell & Allie Jennings; m. Marshal Roberts
Roberts, Evelyn (King)	Feb 08, 1936	Aug 08, 2019	King Cem.; Dau. of Henry King & Minnie Etta Sanders; m. Clyde Roberts

Roberts, Everett Bryan	Aug 15, 1934	Jul 31, 2015	Chattanooga Memorial Park Cem.; Son of Everett & Perry Leah (Stone) Roberts; m. Vivian Harmon; US Army
Roberts, Faye	May 10, 1957	Aug 18, 2021	Shiloh Cem.; Dau. of Jessie Dreadmon & Annie Betty Bouldin Roberts
Roberts, Fealy Mae	Mar 02, 1934	Oct 30, 1991	Brown's Chapel Cem.; Dau. of Jody W., Sr & Bell (King) Green; addition to Cemeteries of Grundy Co., Vol. 1, p. 106
Roberts, Florence L. (Parmeter)	Dec 27, 1913	Jan 03, 1997	Cumberland Heights Cem.; Dau. of William E. & Viola Mae (Straight) Parmeter; m. 1) Elder Louis Cornelius 2) Ernest Arnold Roberts, Sr.; addition to Cemeteries of Grundy Co., Vol. 1, p.198
Roberts, Geraldine (Grizzle)	Apr 29, 1957	Mar 20, 2017	Shiloh Cem.; Dau. of Rex & Louise (Hawkins) Grizzle; m. Jerry Roberts
Roberts, Julia (Brewer)	Apr 30, 1942	May 19, 2015	Fall Creek Cem.; Dau. of Frank & Ruth (Melton) Brewer; m. Harold Roberts
Roberts, Lee	Aug 02, 1917	Dec 29, 1993	Brown's Chapel Cem.; m. Fealy Mae Green; addition to Cemeteries of Grundy Co., Vol. 1, p. 106
Roberts, Lewis Elmer	Aug 24, 1921	Mar 26, 2016	Wesley's Chapel Cem in Hardin Co. TN; Son of Wiley Crawford & Fannie V. (Basim) Roberts; m. Lola Austin; US Army WWII
Roberts, Lewis G., Jr.	Apr 04, 1945	Nov 06, 2013	Altamont Cem.; Son of Lewis G., Sr. & Tennie (Boulder) Roberts
Roberts, Linda (Meeks)	Nov 02, 1942	Sep 28, 2015	Cremated; Dau. of Stanley & Eva (Phipps) Meeks; m. Kenneth Roberts
Roberts, Louis Shane "Bull"	Nov 20, 1970	Oct 01, 2013	Roberts Cem.; Son of Billy Hagan & Donna "Donnie" (Meeks) Roberts; no tombstone; never married
Roberts, M Louise	Feb 20, 1932	Mar 23, 2018	Tracy City Cem.
Roberts, Mary Betty	Nov 05, 1938	Mar 28, 2016	Mountain View Cem. In McMinnville, TN; Dau. of Lewis & Tennie (Bouldin) Roberts
Roberts, Mildred J	1918	1980	Fall Creek Falls Cem.; m. Arthur Roberts
Roberts, Monroe, Jr.	Mar 31, 1930	Sep 03, 2021	Palmer Cem.; Son of Monroe & Vergie (Shrum) Roberts, Sr.; m. Lucy Crabtree; U.S. Army - Korea
Roberts, Olline (Parson)	Mar 7, 1045	Sep 08, 2018	Bonnie Oaks Cem.; Dau. of Hershel Parson & Berta Sanders; m. Carl Wilson Roberts
Roberts, Phyllis Diane (Dotson)	Jul 19, 1951	Aug 27, 2017	Altamont Cem.; Dau. of William Clyde & Della Mae (Bagwell) Dotson; m. Roger Roberts
Roberts, Ralph Earl "Curley"	Aug 31, 1946	Jan. 1, 2018	Mt. Zion Cem.; Son of Jessie Roberts & Annie Bouldin; US Army

Name	Birth	Death	Notes
Roberts, Randall K.	Sep 26, 1936	May 04, 2013	Palmer Cem.; Son of Elmo & Alice (Ray) Roberts; m. Sylvia Ann (Dishroon) Oct 21, 1950; military veteran; correction & addition to Cemeteries of Grundy Co., Vol. 2, p.552
Roberts, Roger	Jun 07, 1949	Sep 23, 2021	Altamont Cem.; Son of Herschel & Lillie (Rollins) Roberts; m. Phyllis Dotson
Roberts, Stephen M	Dec 29, 1951	Jan 09, 2012	Tracy City Cem.; Son of Mark & Mary Elizabeth (Church) Roberts
Robertson, Bessie Anna Lee (Box)	May 31, 1898	Sep 23, 1987	Palmer Cem. according to some info, but other say Lovell Cem. in Lovell, WY; Dau. of William Wiley Box & Mary Etta Lee Harris; m. Lawrence Lafayette Robertson
Robertson, Martha J (Harris)	1885	Oct 19, 1941	Gregg Cem.; Dau. of Jesse Miles Harris & Nancy Jane Woody; m. James Robertson
Robertson, William A.	Sep 01, 1930	Apr 05, 2013	Chattanooga National Cem.; Son of Paul & Desse Robertson; m. Norma Mae Tate; US Army
Robison, Regina (Smith)	Aug 21, 1938	Apr 24, 2020	Cremated; Dau. of Wesley & Modena Smith & Hawell Owens, step-father; m. Barton F. Robison
Roddy, Billie Ruth	Sep 15, 1937	Nov 30, 2017	Plainview Cem.; Dau. of George Washington & Lillie Eleanor Scruggs Gipson; m. Robert Bradford Roddy, Sr.
Roddy, Franklin P.	May 13, 1889	Sep 22, 1916	Tracy City Cem.; Son of Albert D. & Paralee (Bailey) Rodddy
Roddy, Helen Beryl	Ca 1928	Dec 13, 2017	Tracy City Cem.; Dau. of Burge S., Sr. & Maude Roddy
Roddy, Lewis Wilson	Feb 27, 1897	Jan 14, 1949	Tracy City Cem.; Son of James Robert & Sarah "Sallie" (Stubblefield) Roddy; source death certificate
Roddy, Robert, Jr.	Jan 14, 1957	Dec 10, 2020	Cremated; Son of Robert & Billie Ruth Roddy
Roddy, Sarah "Sallie"	1867	Oct 13, 1918	Tracy City Cem; Dau of Harris & Mary (Caldwell) Stubblefield; m. James Robert Roddy
Roddy, Sue	ca 1901	Oct 28, 1914	Tracy City Cem.; Dau of James Robert & Sarah "Sallie" (Stubblefield) Roddy; source death certificate
Roden, Evelyn Pauline Wilson (Short)	Jun 09, 1924	Jun 27, 1999	Coalmont Cem.; Dau. of Raymond D & Florence (Cox) Short
Roden, Gary Wayne	Jan 24, 1961	Jan 07, 2016	Cremated; Son of Thurman & Etta Mae Roden; m. Cathy Porter
Rodrigues, Frank Anthony	Mar 04, 1949	Aug 06, 2006	Plainview Cem.; Son of Joseph & Bernice Reta (Ramos) Rodrigus
Rogers, Benjamin Hade	Jun 17, 1950	Nov 24, 2018	Palmer Cem.; Son of Benjamin Hade Rogers & Pauline Ward; m 1) Geraldine Layne Rogers 2) Patricia McHone

Name	Birth	Death	Notes
Rogers, Calvin Houston	Jan 28, 1948	Sep 14, 2021	Cremated; Son of Joe Harley & Ruby (Reed) Rogers; found deceased in his house 5 days after the fact. Calvin was from Payne's Cove.
Rogers, Clifford	Mar 03, 1942	Nov 27, 2003	Payne's Cove Cem.; Son of Henry H & Ida (Oliver) Rodgers; m. Candy Schaen; correction of spelling of Schaen to Cemeteries of Grundy Co., Vol. 2, p. 592; Parents did spell surname as Rodgers.
Rogers, David Earl	Oct 31, 1937	Jun 11, 2020	Mt. Zion Cem.; Son of Hervey Thomas Rogers & Lassie J. Smartt; m. Mary Reed; U.S. Navy
Rogers, George Houston	Oct 12, 1947	May 25, 2021	Payne's Cove Cem.; Son of Henry & Ida (Oliver) Rogers; m. Faye Morris
Rogers, James Alvin	Mar 17, 1932	May 15, 1993	Coalmont Cem.; Son of Hubert Benjamin & Elvie (Lockhart) Rogers; m. Eileen Margaret Tucker; correction to Cemeteries of Grundy Co., Vol. 1, p. 178
Rogers, James Alvin, Jr.	Mar 08, 1957	Nov 02, 2021	Coalmont Cem.; Son of James & Eileen Rogers; m. Ellen Rogers
Rogers, Maggie	Jul 1, 1878	Mar 21, 1966	Altamont Cem.; Dau. of Pleasant & Elizabeth Rogers; correction to Cemeteries of Grundy Co., Vol. 1. p. 10
Rogers, Margaret Eileen (Tucker)	Jun 23, 1934	Jan 08, 2021	Coalmont Cem.; Dau. of David & Leila Lucille (Kitchen) Tucker of MI; m James Alvin Rogers; addition to Cemeteries of Grundy Co., Vol. 1, p. 178
Rogers, Maurine (Green)	Sep 22, 1920	Aug 22, 2015	Wesley Chapel Cem.; Dau. of John Freeland & Stella (Webb) Green. m. J.G. Rogers; addition to Cemeteries of Grundy Co., Vol. 2, p. 964
Rogers, Pauline Marie (Ward)	Apr 06, 1925	Feb 21, 2012	Palmer Cem.; Dau. of Oscar Lee & Gertrude Leona (Mitchell) Ward; m. Benjamin Hade Rogers; addition to Cemeteries of Grundy Co., Vol. 2, p. 573
Rogers. Gene O. "Eyeballs"	Mar 17, 1936	Oct 24, 2014	Coalmont Cem.; Son of Hubert Rogers & Elvie Lockhart; m. Nellene Brown; Army
Roller, Clara (Argo)	Sep 23, 1926	Dec 30, 2018	Webb Cem.; Dau. of Howary Argo & Jennie Hobbs; m. Everette Roller
Rollings, Abner "Duck"	1844	1911	Warren "Red Hill" Cem.; Son of Benjamin Franklin & Louisa (Tate) Rollins; brother of Rebecca Rollins Clepper; correction of relationship & addition to Cemeteries of Grundy Co., Vol. 2, p. 930
Rollings, Melba Jean (Tate)	Jul 31, 1940	Jun 01, 2001	Altamont Cem.; Dau. of Hascal & Ada Mai (Scruggs) Tate; m. Alolphus Rollings; correction to Cemeteries of Grundy Co., Vol. 1, page 13
Rollings, Terry Keith "Quiver"	Dec 15, 1955	Jun 17, 2019	Cremated; Son of Adolphus Franklin Rollings & Melba Jean Tate

Name	Birth	Death	Details
Rollins, Bufford Cleston	Mar 24, 1930	Mar 11, 1995	Brown's Chapel Cem.; Son of James Franklin & Mary Agnes (Thompson) Rollins; m. Rachel Marie Nunley; addition to Cemeteries of Grundy Co., Vol. 1, p. 105
Rollins, Carolyn Jean (Layne)	Apr 21, 1905	Jul 13, 2013	Cremated; Dau. of Robert & Willie E. (Thomas) Layne; m. Edward Rollins
Rollins, Charles Matthew	Dec 12, 1942	Aug 10, 2017	Cremated; Son of Virgil & Vera Rollins; m. Norma Rollins
Rollins, Clara Belle (Ladd)	Dec 25, 1905	Dec 09, 1968	Monteagle Cem; Dau of John William Ladd & Lizzie McBee; m. 1) William Columbus Castle 2) Robert Jackson Rollins
Rollins, Dennis Edward	Feb 11, 1956	Jan 16, 2015	Palmer Cem.; Son of Richard E. & Dorothy Marlee (Gholston) Rollins; addition to Cemeteries of Grundy Co., Vol. 2, p. 555
Rollins, Dorothy Marie (Gholston)	Jun 20, 1937	Jan 16, 2013	Palmer Cem.; Dau. of Ralph Eugene & Marlee (Campbell) Gholston; m. Richard E. Rollins; addition to Cemeteries of Grundy Co., Vol. 2, p. 555
Rollins, John Thomas	Sep 13, 1919	Jan 01, 1976	Monteagle Cem.; Son of James "Jim" & Mary (Lemons) Rollins; m. Aline Johnson; He is buried beside his sister Lula (Rollins) Haynes even though her tombstone has her maiden name as her last name; addition to Cemeteries of Grundy Co., Vol. 1, p. 459
Rollins, Luevina "Lou"	Aug 07, 1921	May 03, 2014	Palmer Cem.; Dau of Theo Sanders & Liza Meeks; m. Walter "Smokey" Rollins
Rollins, Margie Ruth	May 18, 1935	Jun 22, 2016	Fall Creek Cem.; Dau. of Clell & Mary (Sanders) Layne; m. Hershel Rollins
Rollins, Marlon Marie (Greene)	May 20, 1954	Feb 07, 2021	Palmer Cem.; Dau. of Claude & Mary (Garner) Greene; m. Phillip Rollins
Rollins, Matthew Thomas "Math"	Dec 25, 1877	Nov 02, 1959	Monteagle Cem.; Son of William Jackson Rollins & Dicie Jane Trussell; m. 1) Katherine Summers 2) Louise Starling
Rollins, Michael Thomas	Mar 11, 1975	Sep 06, 2018	Cremated; Son of Michael R. Rollins & Marcie Nolan; companion, Mandy Allman
Rollins, Paul, Jr.	Nov 21, 1954	Apr 12, 2021	Summerfield Cem.; Son of Paul & Thelma Rollins; m. Mary Ruth Bennett
Rollins, Paula Lynette	Apr 01, 1959	Jun 19, 2022	Cremated; Dau of Paul & Dimple (Bouldin) Rollins; m. 1) Jody Morgan 2) Sammy Armstrong
Rollins, Rebecca (Mrs. Thomas W. Clepper)	1842	1917	Warren "Red Hill" Cem.; Dau. of Benjamin Franklin & Louisa (Tate) Rollins; sister of Abner "Duck" Rollins; m. Thomas W. Clepper on Jul 12, 1887, in Marion Co; corrections & addition to Cemeteries of Grundy Co., Vol. 2, p. 930
Rollins, Thelma	Jan 08, 1931	Jul 06, 2016	Summerfield Cem.; Dau. of Will & Pearl Nunley

Name	Born	Died	Notes
Rorer, Quentin Orion	Oct 09, 1998	May 07, 2016	Monteagle Cem.; Son of Charles "Chuck" & Amber (Layne) Rorer
Rose, Andrew Richard	Mar 10, 1987	Mar 26, 2019	Franklin Memorial Gardens Cem.; Son of Michael & Janis Rose; m. Erica Rose
Rose, Elizabeth Geneva (Green)	May 13, 1930	Mar 28, 2019	Franklin Memorial Gardens Cem.; Dau. of John Wesley Green & Lilly Sutherland; m. Melvin A. Rose
Rose, Melvin Wayne	Dec 11, 1953	Mar 26, 2019	Asbury Methodist Cem.; Son of Melvin A. Rose & Elizabeth Geneva Green; m. Jelina Allison Rose
Rose, Thomas J.	1867	Jul 29, 1922	Tracy City Cem.; Son of Solomon C & Lucinda (Lynch) Rose; according to death certificate buried in Tracy City Cem, but obituary in *Mrs Grundy* says burial at Clouse Hill; m. Mary Meeks on Mar 13, 1904 – no tombstone
Ross, Becky	Jun 18, 1962	Jan 04, 2022	Wesley Chapel Cem.; Dau. of Tommy D & Betty Jean (Campbell) Sweeton; m. Richard Allen Ross
Ross, Dianna Lynn	Jul 01, 1947	Dec 14, 2019	Armstrong Cem.; Dau. of Jerrel Woodlee & Peggy Evelyn Hutchins; m.1) _____Butcher 2) Kelly Austin Ross
Ross, Eugene	Apr 02, 1942	Oct 29, 2020	Watson - North Cem.; Son of William Herbert Robert & Louise Beth (Dykes) Ross; U.S. Army - Vietnam
Ross, George "Dobber"	Jul 16, 1933	Dec 25, 2021	Cermated; Son of Isaac & Winnie Ross; brother of Gary Ross.
Ross, Gladys Allene (Tate)	Apr 22, 1937	Jan 03, 2021	Palmer Cem.; Dau. of Ernold Eugene & Mary Lou (Fults) Tate; m. John C. Ross
Ross, James Harrison	Dec 11, 1922	Nov 11, 2006	Palmer Cem.; Son of Isaac & Winnie (Lockhart) Ross; US Army, addition to Cemeteries of Grundy Co., Vol 2, p. 551
Ross, John Carroll	Feb 09, 1929	Aug 07, 2013	Coalmont Cem.; Son of William Herbert & Louise (Dykes) Ross; US Navy
Ross, John Jacob "Hunky"	Sep 10, 1930	Jun 30, 2014	Coalmont Cem.; Son of Albert P & Nancy (Dykes) Ross; m. Addie F
Ross, John Wesley	Feb 19, 1873	Feb 13, 1947	Altamont Cem.; Son of Job & Delitha (Speegle) Ross; m. Nannie May Stump; Correction to Cemeteries of Grundy Co., Vol. 1, p. 13
Ross, Larry	Feb 25, 1926	Aug 05, 2002	Coalmont Cem.; Son of Albert P & Nancy Ross; correction to Cemeteries of Grundy Co., Volume 1, p. 180
Ross, Leon	Apr 01, 1907	Dec 23, 1926	Ross Cem.; Son of John Edward & Nellie (Nunley) Ross; addition to Cemeteries of Grundy Co., Vol. 2, p. 725

Name	Born	Died	Notes
Ross, Martha (Ramsey)	Jul 22, 1855	Apr 18, 1931	Ross Mountatin Cem.; Dau. of John & Julia Ramsey; m. James M. Ross; info. from death certificate
Ross, Myrtle		Apr 16, 1914	Orange Hill Cem
Ross, Nadine (Meeks)	Jun 24, 1928	May 07, 2015	Palmer Cem.; Freddie & Agnes (Henley) Cannon; m. James Ross Meeks
Ross, Nancy Tabor		Ca 1850	Ross Mountain Cem.; Nancy is thought to be buried here. No tombstone
Ross, Nannie May (Stump)	Feb 28, 1880	May 02, 1907	Altamont Cem.; Dau. of William M. & Linticia (Overturff) Stump; m. John Wesley Ross; addition to Cemeteries of Grundy Co, Vol. 1, p. 13
Ross, Nellie Gertrude (Nunley)	Dec 04, 1884	Jun 29, 1911	Ross Cem.; Dau. of John H. & Rhoda Jane (Allen) Nunley; m. Samuel Ross, died in childbirth with twins
Ross, Samuel	Jan 21, 1874	Apr 12, 1931	Ross Mountain Cem.; Son of John Edward & Nancy Ellen (Brown) Ross; m. 1) Nellie Gertrude Nunley 2) Belle Nunley; addition to Cemeteries of Grundy County; Vol. 2, p. 272
Roysdon, Nona Fay (Shadrick)	Jul 26, 1942	Jan 03, 2014	Terry Cem. Jamestown, TN; Dau. of Cecil & Flora (Mills) Shadrick; m. J.C. Roysdon
Rozell, Nellie Ruth (Winton)	Jun 26, 1931	Sep 21, 2019	Rose Hill Memorial Gardens; Dau. of Yancie Winton & Ada Sherrill; m. Delbert Rozell
Rubley, Charles H., Sr.	May 01, 1844	Jun 29, 1919	Tracy City Cem.; born in Switzerland; m. Elizabeth Keller
Rubley, Edward	Apr 02, 1891	Mar 23, 1916	Tracy City Cem.; Son of Charles H. Sr. & Elizabeth (Keller) Rubley; m Becky Layne
Ruch, Afra	Nov 10, 1836	May 26, 1915	Tracy City Cem.; Dau. of Gilg & Afra (Schiesser) Schaenberger; addition to Cemeteries of Grundy Co., Vol. 2, p. 895
Ruch, Elizabeth "Lisette"	Jun 24. 1842	Mar 16, 1920	Swiss Colony Cem.; Dau. of Jacob & Elizabeth (Linker) Ruch; addition to Cemeteries of Grundy Co., Vol. 2, p. 787
Rudd, Christine	Mar 04, 1942	Apr 23, 2015	Pleasant Hill Cem. in Fayetteville, TN; Dau. of Cam & Kathleine (Guthrie) Meeks; m. Johnny Rudd
Ruehling, Clarissa Davina (Mitchell)	1964	Jan 25, 2021	White Cem.; Dau. of James David and Clara Elizabeth (Caldwell) Mitchell; m. Ronnie Darrell Ruehling
Ruehling, Marvlee	Jan 05, 1928	Aug 12, 2017	Fall Creek Cem.; Son of John H & Allie (Blaylock) Ruehling; m. Dorothy Ward; US Navy
Ruehling, Willie Mae (Woodlee)	Oct 06, 1922	Jan 04, 2014	Fall Creek Cem.; Dau. of Jess & Lucy (Meeks) Woodlee; m. Hurl Ruehling
Rumsey, Jerry L.	Aug 17, 1939	Dec 10, 1998	Monteagle Cem.; Son of Lloyd, Jr., & Beula (Pound) Rumsey; m. Betty Jane McKee; addition to Cemeteries of Grundy Co., Vol. 1, p. 448.

Name	Birth	Death	Details
Russell, Velvie Lee	Mar 08, 1936	Jun 07, 2016	Shockley Cem.; Spencer, TN; Dau of Lee & Icy Lou (Fults) Kenner; m. Daniel Russell
Rust, Cynthia Rose	Nov 08, 1951	Feb 04, 2016	Coalmont Cem.; Dau. of Howard Allen & Martha Sue (Crabtree) Brown; m. Ricky Rust
Rust, Howell Bryan	May 30, 1960	Oct 21, 2017	Cremated; Son of Henry & Barbara (Maze) Rust
Rust, Ida Mae (Nunley)	Jul 27, 1893	Sep 07, 1970	Bonny Oak Cem.; Dau. of Francis Marion & Martha Elizabeth (Campbell) Nunley; addition to Cemeteries of Grundy Co., Vol. 1, p. 84
Rust, Mae (Childers)	ca 1894		Oak Grove Cem: Dau. of Frank & Adaline Childers; m. Lawrence Rust; no tombstone; addition to Cemeteries of Grundy Co., Vol. 1, p. 512
Rust, Newborn	Apr 29, 1884	Nov 09, 1906	Oak Grove Cem.; Son of S.R. Rust; no tombstone; source newspaper
Rust, Virginia R.	Jul 08, 1922	Mar 18, 2014	New Providence Cem in Maryville, TN; Dau of Claude G. Alexander & Connie VanSlyck; m.1) Lt. Howard Wood 2) Ambrose "Rusty" Rust
Rutledge, Ruth (Willis)	Feb 23, 1875	Apr 15, 1949	Tate Cem.; Dau. of Thomas & Selina (Reynolds) Willis; m Frank Rutledge
Rutschmann, Jakob	Jun 4, 1842	Mar 04, 1904	Swiss Colony Cem.; Son of Heinrich & Elisabeth (Keller) Rutschmann; m. Pauline Siegrist; addition to Cemeteries of Grundy Co., Vol. 2, p. 785
Ryberg, Johannah Sophia (Sorling)	May 9, 1885	Jan 07, 1982	Altamont Cem.; Dau. of Anders Gustaf & Maria (Persdotter) Sorling; m. Bernhard E. Ryberg; from Sweden; addition to Cemeteries of Grundy Co., Vol. 1, p. 16
Rymer, James Robert "Jim Bob"	Jul 26, 1978	Nov 09, 2018	Airview Cem.; Son of Steve & Linda Rymer
Rymer, Kenneth	Feb 01, 1932	Apr 21 2019	Airview Cem.; Son of Noah & Margaret (Howard) Rymer; m. Alvada Miller
Rymer, Maude Bell (Scoggins)	Jan 31, 1896	Jan 20, 1972	Airview Cem.; Dau. of David & Mary R. (Dabney) Scoggins; m. James Harvey Rymer; addition to Cemeteries of Grundy Co., Vol. 1, p. 7
Sabados, Martha Jane (Harris)	Jan 15, 1941	Apr 14, 2014	Burns Cem.; Dau. of Ben & Nina (Bouldin) Harris; m. Steve Sabados; US Army
Sabados, Steven Charles	Mar 28, 1948	Sep 28, 2017	Cremated; Son of Emil Sabados & Virginia Jacobs; m. 1) Martha Harris, 2) Lori Sabados; US Air Force
Sage, Rosalee (Foster)	Mar 01, 1935	Jun 01, 2020	Burns Cem.; Dau. of Orville Lester Foster & Velma Ann Bailey; m. Albert D. Sage
Sain James Murry, Jr. "Jimmy"	Nov 26, 1951	Sep 02, 2015	Wesley Chapel Cem.; Son of James Murry, Sr. & Alma Louise (Gilbert) Sain; m. 1) Deborah Ashby 2) Pamela Mayberry Stacy; addition to Cemeteries of Grundy Co., Vol. 2, p. 988

Name	Birth	Death	Details
Sain, Dolores "Doe" (Stubblefield)	Apr 15, 1931	Oct 02, 2019	Mt. Zion Cem.; Dau. of Hance Stubblefield & Josephine Davis; m. 1) Ben Wright 2) William R. Sain
Sain, Mary E. (Purcell)	Nov 10, 1872	Nov 26, 1908	Wesley Chapel Cem.; Dau. of Elbert Brabson & Mary Elizabeth (Adams) Purcell; m. Alfred Smartt "Dick" Sain; addition to Cemeteries of Grundy Co., Vol. 2, p. 975
Salyers, Darlene Sue	Feb 01, 1951	Sep 10, 2014	Burns Cem.; Dau of Landon Howard & Alka Thompson; companion, Tim Morgan
Samples, David M.	May 04, 1945	Dec 13, 2019	Plainview Cem.; Son of William Samples & Mary I. Pruitt
Sampley, Charles, Jr. "Chuck"	Dec 19, 1944	Jan 06, 2018	Cremated: Son of Charles Wilburn & Josephine (Rogers) Sampley; m. Beverly Ann Eslick
Sampley, William Richard		Oct 10, 2020	Cremated: Son of James & Minnie Ruth Sampley; m. Angela Leigh Short
Samson, Helena J (Miller)	Oct 04, 1901	Apr 24, 1985	Coalmont Cem.; Dau. of Rudolph C & Helena Jenny (Jones) Miller; m. Adam John Samson; correction to Cemeteries of Grundy Co., Vol. 1, p. 182
Sanders, 3 Infants			Infants of James & Catherine (Walker) Sanders) at the Sanders homeplace off Summerfield Rd.
Sanders, Adrian	1862	Dec 13, 1937	Clouse Hill Cem.; Son of Louis & Nancy (Cope) Sanders; m. Anna Sophronie "Fronie" Meeks; source death certificate; grandfather of Wallace "Jr" Sanders
Sanders, Alexander, Mrs.	Jun 19, 1882	Mar 17, 1959	Orange Hill Cem.; Dau of Wiley Meeks & Mary Baker per death certificate, but other info. says that the mother's name may not be listed correctly. No tombstone; m. Alexander Sanders
Sanders, Allie Jean "Shorty" (Worley)	Jul 02, 1933	Oct 15, 2018	Palmer Cem.; Dau. of Paul Worley & Jessie Thompson; m. James E. "Sham" Sanders
Sanders, Andrew "Andy "Jacob	1813	Aug 24, 1921	Clouse Hill Cem.; Son of J.K. Sanders; died at 108 years per his death certificate; His obit states he was 113 at his passing
Sanders, Anita Jean	Feb 23, 1963	Aug 11, 2014	Summerfield Cem.; Dau of Robert & Annette Patterson
Sanders, Anna Sophronie "Fronie" (Meeks)	Mar 01, 1855	Before Dec 1937	Clouse Hill Cem.; Dau of Riley Meeks & Hettie "Hassey" Jane Cope; m. Adrian Stephen Sanders on Oct 3, 1876, in Franklin Co, TN
Sanders, Anthony Edward	Dec 13, 1953	Oct 27, 2020	Fall Creek Cem.; Son of Elzie & Myrtle (Braden) Sanders; m. Darlene Bivens

Sanders, Arthur Milton	Sep 28, 1931	Oct 23, 1988	Plainview Cem.; Son of Albert Sidney Johnson & Willie Mae (Myers) Sanders; PVT US ARMY Korea; m. Elsie Juanita Dykes; addition to Cemeteries of Grundy Co., Vol. 2, p. 688
Sanders, Betty (King)	Jan 22, 1936	Nov 10, 2015	Orange Hill Cem.; Dau. of Raymond & Jessie (Graham) King; m. Jessie H. Sanders
Sanders, Brenda May (Gibson)	1954	Feb 05, 2019	Cremated; Dau. of Ben B. Davis & Annie Gibson; m. Larry H. Sanders
Sanders, Casper	Nov 01, 1902	Jan 01, 1903	Payne's Cove; Son of William Lee & Elizabeth (Ogle) Sanders; age 2 months; addition to Cemeteries of Grundy Co., Vol. 2, p. 595
Sanders, Charles Ray	Jun 02, 1930	Nov 07, 1993	Airview Cem: Son of Thomas Oscar, & Lethia (Meeks) Sanders; m. Dorothy Collins; 1st Sgt US Army Vietnam; addition and correction of death date for Cemeteries of Grundy Co., Vol. 1, p. 5
Sanders, Charles Ray	Jan 18, 1900	Dec 02, 1950	Bonnie Oak Cem.; Son of Crawford Sanders
Sanders, Charles Ray	Jun 02, 1930	Nov 07, 1993	Airview Cem: Son of Thomas Oscar & Lethia (Meeks) Sanders; m. Dorothy Collins;1st Sgt US Army Vietnam; addition and correction of death date for Cemeteries of Grundy Co., Vol. 1, p. 5
Sanders, Child			Clouse Hill Cem.; Child of John Russell & Selena Evalina (Goodman) Sanders
Sanders, Cleo Elizabeth (Campbell)	Jul 18, 1935	Dec 13, 2018	Plainview Cem.; Dau. of Robert Clency & Burtia (Cox) Campbell; m. Garlon Sanders; addition to Cemeteries of Grundy Co., Vol. 2, p. 703
Sanders, David	Apr 11, 1956	Feb 20, 2007	Burkett's Chapel Cem.; Son of Benjamin W. & Vera Elizabeth (Cribbs) Sanders, Sr. & son-in-law of Herbert W. & Annie Bell (Borne) King; addition to Cemeteries of Grundy Co., Vol. 1, p. 124
Sanders, Deidre Jane (Moore) "Dee"	Jan 16, 1965	Apr 10, 2022	Plainview Cem.; Dau. of Ray & Jean (Merriman) Moore; m. Glen Ed Sanders
Sanders, Dennis Ray	Nob 9, 1960	Aug 31, 2014	Swiss Colony Cem.; Son of Albert, Jr. & Helen Sanders; m. Connie Sanders
Sanders, Dorothy "Dottie" Juanita	Aug 31, 1945	May 09, 2015	Monteagle Cem.; Dau. of Herman & Wrenn (Wallace) Sanders
Sanders, Dorothy Mae (Collins)	Oct 21, 1936	Sep 22, 2018	Airview Cem.; Dau. of Eunice Collins & Girlie Sims; m. Charles R. Sanders
Sanders, Earl R., Jr.	Feb 09, 1930	Mar 25, 1931	Bonny Oak Cem.; Son of Earl R. & Louise (Meeks) Sanders; addition to Cemeteries of Grundy Co., Vol. 1, p. 71
Sanders, Edward Mark	Apr 09, 1978	Apr 09, 1978	Clouse Hill Cem.; Son of Daniel Mark & Glenda Faye (Gorman) Sanders

Name	Birth	Death	Notes
Sanders, Elizabeth "Betty" (Ogle)	Jul 13, 1881	Nov 27, 1967	Payne's Cove Cem.; Dau. of Wyatt McDaniel & Rebecca Emeline (Breadwell) Ogle; m. William Lee Sanders on Jul 6, 1902, in Grundy Co, addition to Cemeteries of Grundy Co., p. 595
Sanders, Elsie Juanita (Dykes)	Sep 12, 1938	Jul 23, 2015	Plainview Cem.; Dau. of David Leslie & Minnie Lee (Campbell) Dykes; m. Arthur Milton Sanders; addition to Cemeteries of Grundy Co., Vol. 2, p. 688
Sanders, Emma Ellen "Nenie"	Jul 1910 Death certificate says Aug 18, 1910	Nov 05, 1918	Payne's Cove Cem.; Dau. of William Lee & Elizabeth "Betty" (Ogle) Sanders; correction and addition to Grundy Co. Cemeteries, Vol. 2, p. 595
Sanders, Eugene P.	Jan 21, 1867	Apr 12, 1943	Summerfield Cem.; Son of John R & Selina (Goodman) Sanders; m. Lou Sanders
Sanders, Geneva L.	May 13, 1928	Aug 18, 1928	Palmer Cem.; Dau. of John Annis & Martha J. (Henley) Sanders; addition to Cemeteries of Grundy Co., Vol. 2, p. 558.
Sanders, George Carroll "Uncle Dick"	May 24, 1821	May 28, 1911	Dick Sanders/Sanders School House Cem.; Son of Thomas & Mary "Polly" (Roberts) Sanders; m. Melissa E. Phipps; no tombstone; addition to Cemeteries of Grundy Co., Vol. 2, p. 731; Source *Mrs Grundy*, Jun 1, 1911; States School House was built 30-40 years earlier.
Sanders, Giles Haston	Dec 16, 1849	Mar 19, 1905	Sanders Cem at Sanders Big Spring; Son of Jordan & Julia (Smith) Sanders; no stone, but thought to be buried here
Sanders, Ginger LoLetta	Jan 17, 1957	Feb 08, 1960	Oak Grove Cem: Dau. of Dillard & Lillian Virginia (Smartt) Sanders; addition to Cemeteries of Grundy Co., Vol. 1. p. 510
Sanders, Gregory Wallace	Jun 11, 1965	Feb 08, 2013	Plainview Cem.; Son of William Wallace, Jr. & Gabriel (Spiegel) Sanders
Sanders, Grover Carl	Mar 24, 1921	Jul 02, 1976	Coalmont Cem.; Son of Matthew & Mary J. (Meeks) Sanders; m. Mable Marie Meeks; correction to Cemeteries of Grundy Co., Vol. 1, p. 176
Sanders, Harrison "Harris"	1854	May 09, 1900	Sanders Cem at Sanders' Big Spring Payne's Cove; Son of Jordan & Julia (Smith) Sanders; m. Lydia Judith Parmley, had a tombstone in 1977, but not found in 2011; Correction to Cemeteries of Grundy Co., Vol. 2, p. 728
Sanders, Helen L. "Phoebe"	Nov 29, 1923	Oct 08, 2020	Plainview Cem.; Dau. of Roy Hillman "Judd" & Esther Elizabeth "Beth" Thomas; m. H.D. "Mutt" Sanders; addition to Cemeteries of Grundy Co., Vol. 2, p. 703
Sanders, Helen Ozell (Layman)	Jan 07, 1934	May 26, 2022	Swiss Colony Cem.; Dau. of Werner & Annie (Layne) Layman; m. Albert Sanders, Jr.

Name	Birth	Death	Details
Sanders, Homer Clinton	Jun 11, 1945	Oct 17, 2020	Orange Hill Cem.; Son of Dillard & Lillian Sanders; m. Wanda C. Bray; U.S. Army
Sanders, Houston "Hugh"	Nov 1860	Dec 27, 1938	Payne's Cove Cem.; Son of Wesley & Mary (Meeks) Sanders, per death certificate; m. 1) Lucinda Jane "Lucy" Payne 2) Martha Ann Adams; no tombstone
Sanders, Howard	Jun 16, 1948	Mar 20, 2015	Hillsboro Memorial Cem.; Son of Harold Woodrow & Z. Janie (Brock) Sanders; m. Patricia Elaine Forsythe
Sanders, Howard "Buck"	Nov 03, 1926	Sep 08, 2015	Plainview Cem.; Son of Rose Burr & Minnie (James) Sanders; m. Dorothy Sanders
Sanders, Infants (3 individual graves)			Sanders homeplace burial; Infant of James & Catherine (Walker) Sanders who lived off Summerfield Rd.
Sanders, James Darrell	May 03, 1953	Jan 02, 2017	Palmer Cem.; Son of James E. "Sham" & Allie J. "Shorty" Sanders; m. Valerie Burrows
Sanders, James Henry	Jun 11, 1939	Aug 16, 1997	Palmer Cem.; Son of Henry James & Ethel Maybell (Scott) Sanders; m. Judith Ann Sanders; addition to Cemeteries of Grundy Co., Vol. 2, p. 578
Sanders, James Kelly	Mar 07, 1960	Feb 02, 2020	Griffith Cem.; Son of Alta Odell (Greene) Sanders Smartt; m. Sharon Norris
Sanders, James Otho	Dec 29, 1914	Jun 18, 2005	Monteagle Cem.; Son of James A. & Ardelia Pauline "Delia" (Gossett) Sanders m. Blanche Lolita Gilland; addition to Cemeteries of Grundy Co., Vol 1, p. 415
Sanders, James Ray	Oct 24, 1939	Apr 30, 2018	Monteagle Cem.; Son of James Herman Sanders & Wrenn Carlene Wallace; m. Carol Kay Witt
Sanders, Joan Katherine (Ross)	Jun 12, 1936	Aug 22, 2019	Palmer Cem.; Isaac Ross & Winnie Lockhart; m. Earl "Bud" Sanders
Sanders, John	Jul 28, 1873	Dec 30, 1962	Fall Creek Cem.; Son of Harrison & Lidia (Parmley) Sanders; m. Elizabeth Bone on Nov 27, 1906
Sanders, John Emmett	Apr 12, 1888	Jul 26, 1932	Oak Grove Cem.; Son of Stephen Cope & Sarah Ellen (Dyer) Sanders; m. Allie Mae Morgan, addition to Cemeteries of Grundy Co., Vol. 1, p. 492
Sanders, John Russell	Aug 11, 1834	Dec 17, 1918	Clouse Hill Cem.; Son of Thomas & Mary (Robert) Sanders; m. Selena Evaline Goodman on Dec 31, 1856
Sanders, Josephine	Sep 29, 1934	Sep 29, 1934	Clouse Hill Cem.; Dau. of Thomas & Lethia (Meeks) Sanders; Source death certificate – Dates given are burial date; Child lived only 1 ½ hours; no tombstone
Sanders, Larry Michael	Apr 25, 1956	Jun 14, 2019	Swiss Memorial Cem.; Son of Albert & Helen (Layman) Sanders; addition to Cemeteries of Grundy Co., Vol. 2, p. 791

Name	Birth	Death	Details
Sanders, Lillian Virginia	Mar 07, 1923	May 25, 1994	Oak Grove Cem.; Dau. of Frank & Myrtle (Nolan) Smartt, m. Dillard D. Sanders; addition to Cemeteries of Grundy Co., Vol. 1, p. 510
Sanders, Louis	Jun 15, 1959	Jul 15, 2020	Plainview Cem.; Son of Garlan & Cleo Sanders
Sanders, Lucinda Jane "Lucy"	Feb 25, 1847	Jul 17, 1941	Payne's Cove Cem.; Dau. of Benjamin Franklin & Elizabeth (Conn) Payne; m. Houston "Hugh" Sanders; addition to Cemeteries of Grundy Co., Vol. 2; unmarked grave – info. from death certificate
Sanders, Lynette Nicloe "Nikki" (Ross)	Sep 06, 1971	Oct 03, 2014	Palmer Cem; Dau of Greg Ross & Rosemary Partin; m. Troy Sanders
Sanders, Mahlon Nelson	Dec 26, 1959	Mar 22, 2010	Oak Grove Cem.; Son of Dillard D. & Lillian Virginia (Smartt) Sanders; addition to Cemeteries of Grundy Co., Vol. 1, p. 510
Sanders, Margaret Anna Dell (Nunley)	Oct 15, 1930	Mar 12, 2021	Western Reserve Mem. Gardens, OH; Dau. of Lish & Mildred (Kilgore) Nunley; m. Wayne Stanley Sanders
Sanders, Margaret Kathleen (Parsons)	Sep 17, 1944	Dec 17, 2018	Plainview Cem.; Dau. of Elmer & Mozella Parsons; m. Gary Dale Sanders
Sanders, Matthew "Matt"	Jun 8, 1838	Oct 01, 1903	Sanders Cem.; Son of Jordan & Julia (Smith) Sanders; m. Emma Garner; no tombstone, but thought to be buried here.
Sanders, Matthew "Matt"		May 22, 1926	Parsons' Cem, now part of Bonny Oak Cem.; Son of Wheeler Sanders; *Chattanooga Times* Article, May 27, 1926, stated he died at Fork Ridge by being jammed between two coal cars
Sanders, Mattie J. (Henley)	Oct 1, 1886	Mar 22, 1946	Palmer Cem.; Dau. of John Henry "Jack" & Sarah Tennessee "Tennie" (Partin) Henley; m. John Annis Sanders; addition to Cemeteries of Grundy Co., Vol. 2, p. 558
Sanders, Micah Habakkuk	Jan 12, 1969	Oct 24, 2021	Cremated; Son of Garlan & Cleo (Campbell) Sanders
Sanders, Nancy (Cope)	Nov 17, 1832	Sep 14, 1919	Bonny Oak Cem.; Dau. of Stephen Payne & Comfort (Bowlin) Cope; m. Lewis Bradford Sanders; addition to Cemeteries of Grundy Co., Vol. 1, p. 96
Sanders, Navine	Sep 29, 1934	Sep 29, 1934	Clouse Hill Cem.; Dau. of Thomas & Lethia (Meeks) Sanders; per death cert; lived 1 1/2 hrs.
Sanders, Ninnie Emma Ellen	Aug 18, 1910	Nov 05, 1918	Payne's Cove Cem.; Dau. of William Lee & Elizabeth "Betty" (Ogles) Sanders; correction to Cemeteries of Grundy Co., Vol. 2, p. 595; source death certificate
Sanders, Pauline	Apr 02, 1934	Dec 26, 2019	Palmer Cem.; Dau. of Alford Henry, Sr. & Jossie Pearl (Norris) Jones; m Melvin Sanders; addition to Cemeteries of Grundy Co., Vol. 2, p. 567

Name	Birth	Death	Notes
Sanders, Randy Lee	May 11, 1905	Nov 28, 2014	Cremated; Son of Patrick Sanders & Helen Watson; companion Kimberly Cantrell
Sanders, Ruby Marie (Rollings)	Jan 17, 1923	Oct 16, 2014	Wesley Chapel Cem.; Son of John Robert & Mary Jane (Jones) Rollings; m. William Sanders
Sanders, Sarah Elizabeth	Apr 23, 1905	Jun 15, 2021	Hobbs Hill Cem. Dau of Andrew Campbell & Juanita Hargis; m. Ralph Sanders
Sanders, Selena Evalina (Goodman)	Nov 30, 1843	Jul 07, 1905	Clouse Hill Cem.; Dau. of Anderson Sanders & Evalina (Payne) Reed Goodman on Dec 31, 1856; source *Mrs. Grundy, May 22, 1913*
Sanders, Shelby Jean	1936	1937	Bonny Oak Cem.; Dau. of Ralph & Ola (Dykes) Sanders; no stone; information from family
Sanders, Sonya Dee		Mar 20, 2016	King Cem.; Tommy & Margie Layne; m. Jeremy Sanders - companion
Sanders, Sue Ellen	May 16, 1952	May 15, 2012	Tracy City Cem.; Dau. of Leonard Sanders & Carrie Campbell
Sanders, Suzette (Nunley)	Jun 26, 1958	Jun 04, 2015	Palmer Cem.; Dau. of Blenn & Jimmie Ruth (Finch) Nunley; m. Darrell Sanders
Sanders, Terry Lee	Jun 24, 1950	Jul 24, 2016	Cremated; Son of Ralph Sanders & Marie Pass; m. Judy Sanders; US Army
Sanders, William Asbury	Ca 1870	Apr 02, 1948	Monteagle Cem.; Son of Mitchell & Amanda (Thompson) Sanders
Sanders, William Grant	Nov 16, 1934	Nov 16, 1934	Buried at home near the west bank of Plainview Lake; Son of William Wallace, Sr. & Hester (Gibbs) Sanders; twin to William Wallace Sanders, Jr.
Sanders, William Houston	Oct 01, 1978	Feb 19, 1998	Dykes, Woodrow Wilson Gravesite; Son of Walter William & Audrey Lola (Jones) Sanders; grandson of Gordon & Audrey C. Jones; correction to Cemeteries of Grundy Co., Vol. 1, p. 177
Sanders, William Lee	May 13, 1957	Nov 13, 2015	Fall Creek; Son of Phillip & Virgie Jane (Wallace) Sanders
Sanders, Zora	ca. 1880	Jun 18, 1963	Fall Creek Cem.; Dau of Walter & Zora Stubblefield; m. Andrew Jackson Sanders; correction to Cemeteries of Grundy Co.,Vol. 1, p. 211
Sanderson, James W. Sr.	Dec 07, 1914	Aug 16, 1989	Homeland Acres Cem.; Son of Sam & Essie (Morgan) Sanderson; m. Mary Lorraine Conelly; PVT US Army Air Corps, WWII; addition to Cemeteries of Grundy Co., Vol. 1, p. 342
Sanderson, Mary Lorraine	Aug 27, 1918	Jan 28, 1999	Homeland Acres Cem.; Dau. of Frederick & Virginia (Russell) Conelly; m. James W. Sanderson; addition to Cemeteries of Grundy Co., Vol. 1, p. 342

Sargent, Doris Viola (Bunch)	Sep 21, 1924	Mar 04, 2010	Lappin Cem.; Dau. of Warren Otto & Gladie Marguerite (Walter) Bunch; m. James "Jim" Lappin Sargent; Funeral Home Marker; addition to Cemeteries of Grundy Co., Vol. 1, p. 359
Sargent, James Lappin	Sep 30, 1914	Mar 01, 2013	Lappin Cem.; Son of Samuel Arnold & Annie Olive (Lappin) Sargent; US Army
Sargent, Josephine (Meeks)	Apr 01, 1935	Mar 20, 2015	Eastern Star Cem.; Dau. of Bill & Bonnie (Campbell) Meeks; m. George M. Sargent
Sargent, Samuel Edward	Apr 10, 1923	Nov 18, 2013	Lappin Cem.; Son of Samuel A. & Annie Olive (Lappin) Sargent; m. Maxine Partlow; addition to Cemeteries of Grundy Co., Vol. 1, p. 359
Sartain-Sharp, Mary	Feb 01, 1932	Oct 08, 2017	Bethel Cem.; Dau. of M. Edison & Lida Mae (Fults) Sartain; m. Jack Sharp; addition to Cemeteries of Grundy Co., Vol. 1, p. 57
Sartain, Austin	Jan 28, 1923	Mar 12, 1983	Plainview Cem.; Son of Isaac Washington & Grace May (Thomas) Sartain; m. Mary Louise Stanley; US NAVY WWII; addition to Cemeteries of Grundy Co., Vol. 2, p. 691
Sartain, Democrates "Mock"	Sep 29, 1869	Jan 13, 1940	Bonny Oak Cem area; Son of Heraclitus Harrison "Jack" & Mary "Sarah Jane (Winton) Sartain; Mock was buried in his yard behind the Bonny Oak Cemetery in Coalmon according to local history.
Sartain, Donnie Wayne	May 21, 1951	May 19, 2020	Bethel Cem.; Son of Joe Sartain & Waldean Givens
Sartain, Frank	Dec 12, 1921	Jul 06, 1944	Bethel Cem.; Son of James & Alma May (Meeks) Sartain; PFC 330 Inf. 83 Inf Div. WWII; correction of mother's name to Cemeteries of Grundy Co., Vol. 1, p. 54
Sartain, Frank	ca. 1862	May 17, 1917	Old Baptist Cemetery; Son of Hamp & Sarah Nevills; m. Susan Charles; no marker, Known as Uncle Frank, lived in Burrows' Cove; took his surname from the Sartain family for whom he worked.
Sartain, Infants			Solomon Dickerson Family Graveyard in Burrows' Cove; Infants of Lewis & Bettie (Dickerson) Sartain, no markers, information from family.
Sartain, Jacqueline (Klinski)	Jan 13, 1931	Jun 14, 2019	Sartain Cem.; Dau. of Walter Klinski & Ella Mae O'Keefe; m. Gerald Ray Sartain
Sartain, James Brent	Jun 10, 1940	Jan 07, 2018	Sartain Cem.; Son of James Alfred Sartain & Rosa Alberta Phipps; m. 1) Jewell Rogers 2) Brenda Sherriell
Sartain, Jay D.	Jul 21, 1941	Feb 18, 2014	Cremains at Plainview Cem.; Son of J.D. & Myrtle (Nolan) Sartain
Sartain, L.D.	Feb 11, 1929	Dec 18, 2015	Warren "Red Hill" Cem.; Son of Herbert & Maymie (Hawk) Sartain; m. Reba Jo Bennett

Name	Born	Died	Notes
Sartain, Reba Jo (Bennett)	Dec 17, 1940	Jan 11, 2021	Warren "Red Hill" Cem.; Dau. of Dave & Almagene (Goodman) Bennett; m. L D Sartain
Sartain, Robert Elliott	Feb 28, 1876	Apr 17, 1909	Hobbs Hill Cem.; Son of Loke Adherable & Sarah Louise (Cope) Sartain; m. Mary Geary on Sep. 19, 1899; murdered by Rosetta Sweeton per death certificate; no tombstone
Sartain, Sterling Emerald	Apr 02, 1881	Dec 05, 1921	Hobbs Hill Cem.; Son of Loke Adherable & Sarah Louise (Cope) Sartain; m. Allie I. Dodson; no tombstone
Sartin, John L.	Feb 28, 1849	May 25, 1892	Oak Grove Cem.; Son of Calvin & Lennie Sartain; m. Sarah "Sallie" J (Dodd); addition to Cemeteries of Grundy Co., Vol. 1, p. 503
Sartin, Sarah "Sallie" J. (Dodd)	Jul 2, 1854	Aug 11, 1891	Oak Grove Cem.; Dau. of Hiram Cornelius Franklin & Martha Jane (Stone) Dodd; m. John L. Sartin; addition to Cemeteries of Grundy Co., Vol. 1, p. 503
Sasser, John Howard	Jan 06, 1942	Feb 12, 2020	Chattanooga National Cem.; Son of Johnny F. Sasser & Iola Johnson; m. Margaret Sasser
Savage, Donald Earl	Jun 17, 1933	Dec 03, 2013	Brown's Chapel Cem.; Son of Jessee Lawson & Pearl (Stockwell) Savage m. Marian Vogt
Savage, Dorothy Mae (Brown)	Sep 27, 1922	May 02, 2016	Fall Creek Cem.; Dau. of George W. & Nora (Dent) Brown; m. Nelmon Savage
Savage, Glenn	Apr 17, 1997	Aug 09, 2016	Old Sewanee Baptist Church Cem.; Son of James & Stephanie Savage
Savage, James Freddie	Oct 02, 1944	Jul 31, 2021	Shockley Cem.; Son of Marael Samuel & Lola (Simmons) Savage; m. Patsy Smith
Savage, Jerry Franklin	Dec 09, 1947	Aug 27, 2019	Philadelphia Cem.; Son of Osbon Savage & Willie Nunley; m. Ann Savage
Savage, Richard Preston	Feb 17, 1930	Sep 29, 2021	Brown's Chapel Cem.; Son of Jesse Lawson & Pearl (Stockwell) Savage; m. Anna Ross Swafford; U.S. Army
Sawyer, John Mitchell, Rev.	May 06, 1922	Feb 20, 2015	Rose Hill Cem.; Son of Zery Norman & Byrd Alice (Kilgore) Sawyer; m. Etta Lois Stewart; U.S. Navy
Saynes, Mildred Irene "Peg"	Aug 17, 1919	Sug 20, 2013	Tracy City Cem.; Dau. of Barney William & Pearl Lilie (Orange) Johnson; m. James E. Saynes
Schaerer, Bryan Hillis	May 26, 1957	May 16, 2020	Tracy City Cem.; Son of Sam Schaerer & Marie Pfeifer; m. Cheryl Schaerer
Schaerer, Elsie Louisa	Sep 14, 1912	Jun 16, 1918	Unidentified Cem.; Dau. of J.R. & Lettie (Kilgore) Schaerer
Schaerer, John Werner	Jul 18, 1942	Mar 28, 2022	Brainerd United Methodist Church Cem.; Son of Emil Tucker & Dorothy Schaerer; m. Barbara Schaerer
Schaerer, Sam Henry	Aug 31, 1920	Jan 21, 2016	Tracy City Cem.; Son of William Henry & Ethel (Hillis) Crawford, but adopted by Solomon E. & Georgia (Hillis) Schaerer; m. Marie Pfeifer; US Navy, WWI

Name	Birth	Death	Notes
Schauman, Toni Juanita (Davis)	Aug 01, 1981	Feb 21, 1967	Fall Creek Cem.; Dau. of Brenda Gail (Davis) Moffitt; m. Michael Schauman
Schell, Herman Ernest Robert	Aug 19, 1881	Feb 24, 1980	Altamont Cem.; Son of Emil Johann Heinrich & Maria Schell; m. Hazel Olive Mote; born in Germany; addition to Cemeteries of Grundy Co., Vol. 1, p. 17
Schiesser, Barbara	Mar 12, 1849	Jan 19, 1926	Swiss Colony Cem.; possible Dau. of Abraham & Katrina Constinoble/ Knobel; m. Peter Schiesser; addition to Cemeteries of Grundy Co., Vol. 2, p. 790
Schiesser, Peter	Feb 18, 1846	Aug 26, 1901	Swiss Colony Cem.; Son of Gabriel & Susanna (Knobel) Schieser; m. Barbara Constinoble; addition to Cemeteries of Grundy Co., Vol. 2, p. 784
Schiesser, Wilheminie "Minnie" E.	Mar 12, 1775	Jun 07, 1912	Swiss Colony Cem.; Dau. of Peter & Barbara (Knobel) Schiesser; m. Michael Schiesser; addition to Cemeteries of Grundy Co. Vol. 2, p. 784
Schild, Hildegard (Koehn)	Aug 31, 1917	Oct 26, 1993	Swiss Colony Cem.; Dau. of William August & Magdalena C. (Hahn) Koehn; m. John A. Schild; addition to Cemeteries of Grundy Co, Vol. 2, p. 795
Schild, Jerry Wayne	Mar 10, 1942	Apr 20, 2018	Plainview Cem.; Son of William Martin Schild & Audrey Lucille McGovern
Schild, Kaspar	Oct 24, 1833	Nov 28, 1905	Swiss Colony Cem.; Son of Johannes & Elisabeth (Sooder) Schild; m. Maragaretha Taennler; addition to Cemeteries of Grundy Co., Vol. 2.
Schild, Margaritha geb (Ruef)	Jul 28, 1833	Feb 1, 1890	Swiss Colony Cem.; Dau. of Ulrich & Anne Ruef; m. Peter Schild; addition and correction to maiden name, Cemeteries of Grundy Co., Vol. 2, p. 785
Schild, Wilma B.	Jun 08, 1926	Aug 23, 2015	Cremated; Dau of Audrey & Hazel (Walker) Black; m. 1) James W. Elliott 2) ____ Schild
Schlageter, Annie K.	Oct 23, 1874	Jun 24, 1957	Fall Creek Cem.; Dau. of Ignatz & Rosina (Laager) Schlageter
Schlageter, Jacob J.	Dec 28, 1875	Mar 18, 1957	Fall Creek Cem.; Son of Ignatz & Rosina (Laager) Schlageter
Schlageter, Linda Sue (Ellis)	Oct 09, 1956	Feb 17, 2007	Fall Creek Cem.; Dau of Thomas Ellis & Betty Jo Rush; m. Glenn David Schlageter on Jul 24, 1976
Schlageter, Marion Marie (James)	Oct 20, 1930	Feb 17, 2007	Fall Creek Cem.; Dau. of Fred Jackson James & Elizabeth Rosa Schoenmann; m. Glenn Schlageter

Name	Birth	Death	Details
Schlageter, Rosina geb (Laager)	Dec 14, 1838	Jul 5, 1883	Swiss Colony Cem.; Dau. of Meinard & Regula (Blesi) Laager; Died in the 44th year of her life; b. Switzerland; m. Ignatz Schlageter; Correction of birthdate & addition of information to Cemeteries of Grundy Co., Vol. 2, p. 785
Schmiedt, Balth	Jan 8, 1821	Jul 18, 1887	Swiss Colony Cem.; m. Kath geb Pfeffer; addition to Cemeteries of Grundy Co. Vol. 2, p. 785
Schoenmann, Alvin	Aug 24, 1932	Jun 24, 2016	Cremated; Son of Walter & Annie (McCarver) Schoenmann; m. Barbara Seibern
Schoenmann, Glenn Shely	Nov 12, 1930	Dec 29, 1950	Brown's Chapel Cem.; Son of William Elbert & Minnie Agnes (Tate) Schoenmann; US Army; KIA North Korea; Recovered body buried Dec. 29, 2013
Schoenmann, Raymond Jackson	May 06, 1932	Dec 14, 2013	Plainview Cem.; Son of William Elbert & Minnie (Tate) Schoenmann; addition to Cemeteries of Grundy Co., Vol. 2, p. 689
Schoenmann, Raymond Jackson	May 06, 1932	Dec 14, 2013	Plainview Cem.; Son of William Elbert & Minnie Agnes (Tate) Schoenmann; m. Mary Jo Thomas; US Army
Schoenmann, Walter Lannie	Sep 16, 1964	Jul 05, 2020	Son of Alvin T. Schoenmann & Argie Earlene Gilliam; m. Maryjane Vollmar
Scholer, Helen Faye (Crank)	Dec 15, 1923	Dec 08, 1986	Swiss Colony Cem.; Dau. of Bascom & Bertha (Mills) Crank; m. Johnnie Edwin Scholer; correction of maiden name and addition to Cemeteries of Grundy Co., Vol. 2, p. 789
Scissom, Billy Ray	Jan 02, 1945	Jun 13, 2013	Cremated; Son of Henry & Maudie Frances (Campbell) Scissom; m. Faye Scissom
Scissom, Dola Clarene (Tate)	Jul 06, 1929	Jul 22, 2020	Fall Creek Cem.; Dau. of Harley Tate & Bessie Brady; m. Roy Dale Scissom
Scissom, Gregory Garland	Feb 23, 1962	Sep 24, 2021	Palmer Cem.; Son of Chester & Lucille (Campbell) Scissom
Scissom, Sarah Ann (Steele)	Mar 8, 1848	Jan 05, 1919	Hobbs Hill Cem.; Dau. of Lewis & Catherine (Blevins) Steele; m. M.G. Thomas Scissom; addition to Cemeteries of Grundy Co., Vol. 1, p. 327
Scissom, Tina Dianna	Sep 27, 1964	Jan 16, 2015	Cremated; Dau. of Kenneth & Mary (Parks) Scissom
Scissom, Tom P	Jul 27, 1881	Jan 18, 1964	Coalmont Cem.; Son of George Thomas & Sarah Ann (Steele) Scissom; correction to Cemeteries of Grundy Co., Vol. 1, p. 186
Scoggin, Mary Evelyn (Singleton)	Jan 01, 1928	Feb 07, 2020	Cremated; Dau. of Silas Singleton & Hester Hale; m. Wilson "Sput" Scoggin
Scott, Ada (Harper)	Feb 18, 1890	Feb 09, 1965	Bonny Oak Cem.; Dau. of Lot Erwin & Savannah (Burgess) Harper; m. Barney Scott; addition to Cemeteries of Grundy Co., Vol. 1, p. 87

Name	Born	Died	Notes
Scott, Aileen (Burrows)	Jul 30, 1920	Apr 11, 2018	Coalmont Cem.; Dau. of Garnett Burrows & Carrie Nunley; m. Gerald Scott
Scott, Brandy Chavaughn (Reeves)	Apr 09, 1979	Oct 19, 2007	Swiss Colony Cem.; Dau. of Curtis Lavaughn Reeves; addition to Cemeteries of Grundy Co, Vol. 2, p. 798
Scott, Charles F. Sr.	Jan 24, 2019	Nov 22, 2013	Monteagle Cem.; Son of Charles M. & Ora Scott
Scott, Charlotte Lawana (Adams)	Aug 25, 1929	Aug 18, 2004	Plainview Cem.; Dau. of Charles W. & Maxie (Cleek) Adams; Cemeteries of Grundy Co., Vol. 2, p. 673; remove vertical line connection her with the Dove/Perry couple
Scott, Dorothy M. (Hammers)	Sep 08, 1916	Jan 23, 2015	Fall Creek Cem.; Dau. of Alec Levi & Suzie (Meeks) Hammers; m. Hubert H. Scott, Jr.
Scott, Edith Evelyn	Mar 25, 1932	Mar 02, 1911	Plainview Cem.; Dau. of Robert Riley & Lillie Mae (Sanders) Smith; m. Walter Scott; addition to Cemeteries of Grundy Co., Vol. 2, p. 686
Scott, Emma Casine (Thomas)	Jul 30, 1879	Aug 08, 1917	Monteagle Cem.; Dau. of William Franklin & Margaret Ellen (Crabtree) Thomas; correction to Cemeteries of Grundy Co., Vol. 1, p. 407
Scott, Frank Edward	1941	Mar 27, 2021	Wesley Chapel Cem.; Son of Edward Brown & Inez (Winton) Scott; m. Barbara June Ferrill
Scott, H. B.	Feb 13, 1930	Apr 13, 2017	Philadelphia Cem.; Son of Benjamin Franklin & Mary A. (Killian) Scott; m. Linda Joyce Rhea; addition to Cemeteries of Grundy Co., Vol. 2, p. 629
Scott, James Richard	Jul 2, 1873	Apr 20, 1951	Bonny Oak Cem.; Son of Stephen & Elen E. (Childers) Scott; m. Mary Etta Missouri Campbell; correction to spouse's name & addition to Cemeteries of Grundy Co., Vol, 1, p. 87
Scott, Jerry Benjamin	Mar 02, 1970	Apr 03, 2022	Homeland Acres Cem.; Son of Odous & Lottie (King) Scott
Scott, Karen (Bailey)	May 31, 1905	Aug 29, 2014	Cremated: Dau of Ronald Leon Bailey & Connie Yates Warner; m. Travis Scott
Scott, Korey Alan	Jan 19, 2018	Jan 19, 2018	Airview Cem.; Son of Korey Steven Scott & Samantha Lee Sanders
Scott, Lee	Jan 11, 1933	Oct 19, 1987	Monteagle Cem.; Son of Rather & Minnie Lee (Kirk) Scott; m. Mary A. Tate; addition to Cemeteries of Grundy Co., Vol. 1, p.456
Scott, Levice Edwin	Mar 27, 1933	Jan 22, 1997	Bonny Oak Cem.; Son of Elda J. & Nellie Gray (Clendenon) Scott; m. Florence Nunley; PFC US ARMY; addition to Cemeteries of Grundy Co., Vol. 1, p. 91
Scott, Lewis Earl	Feb 04, 1924	May 17, 2014	Warren "Red Hill" Cem.; Son of James Daniel & Frankie (Cox) Scott; m. Jean Partin; WWII vet

Name	Born	Died	Details
Scott, Linda Joyce (Rhea)	Sep 17, 1939	Sep 22, 2015	Philadelphia Cem.; Dau. of Oscar & Laura Ethel (Scott) Rhea; m. H.B. Scott Aug 12, 1960 in Logan, UT; addition to Cemeteries of Grundy Co., Vol. 2, p. 629
Scott, Margaret Ann	Dec 28, 1936	Dec 11, 2015	Monteagle Cem.; Dau. of William P. & Magabelle (Gaither) Barnes; m. Charles F. Scott, Sr.
Scott, Martha A	Nov 18, 1945	Dec 20, 1945	Palmer Cem.; Dau. of Glen & Elizabeth (Roberts) Scott; addition to Cemeteries of Grundy Co., Vol. 2, p. 562
Scott, Martha Melissa Jane (Dyer)	Feb 04, 1905	Feb 27, 1939	Summerfield Cem.; Dau. of James Albert & Elizabeth Dyer; m. William J.C. Scott; no tombstone
Scott, Mary A (Tate)	Oct 24, 1938	Mar 17, 2017	Monteagle Cem.; Dau. of Milton & Flossie Mae (Wise) Tate; m. Lee Scott; addition to Cemeteries of Grundy Co., Vol. 1, p. 456
Scott, Mary Etta Missouri (Campbell)	Aug 1, 1868	Mar 29, 1958	Bonny Oak Cem.; Dau. of Hugh & Elizabeth "Betty" (Nunley) Campbell; m. James Richard Scott, correction to last name and addition of information to Cemeteries of Grundy Co., Vol. 1, p. 87
Scott, Michael Hughes	Jan 16, 1957	Jan 07, 2017	New Hope Cem.; Son of George Hughes & Lorene (Smith) Scott; m. Gina Kennemore
Scott, Minnie V. (Kilgore)	Mar 09, 1944	Jan 20, 1998	Brown's Chapel Cem.; Dau. of R.G. & Alpha Neoma (McWain) Kilgore; m. Ralph Scott; addition to Cemeteries of Grundy Co., Vol. 1, p. 115
Scott, Patricia Sue	Nov 13, 1941	May 24, 2013	Swiss Cem.; Dau. of Claude & Hazel (Hargis) Scott; m. 1) Tommy Waymon Fults 2) Robert T. Schmidt
Scott, Priceford	May 11, 1934	Mar 26, 2021	Philadelphia Cem.; Son of Benjamin Franklin & Mary A. (Killian) Scott; m. Dorothy Emily Stoner on May 11, 1961; addition to Cemeteries of Grundy Co., Vol. 2, p. 648
Scott, Rachel Louise (Higgins)	Jan 16, 1945	Apr 02, 2021	Swiss Colony Cem.; Dau. of Ace & Stella Irene (Schiesser) Higgins; m. Abidine Scott
Scott, Rocky Lamar	Aug 06, 1960	Nov 06, 2013	Cremation; Son of Dexter & Marie Scott; m. Vickie Butler
Scott, Sidney	Mar 18, 1905	Ca 1920	Summerfield Cem.; Son of William J.C. & Martha Melissa Jane (Dyer) Scott; kicked by a mule; no tombstone
Scott, Sr., Michael Hughes	Jan 16, 1957	Jan 07, 2017	New Hope Cem.; Son of George Hughes Scott; m. Gina Kennemore
Scott, Walter	Nov 06, 1919	Jan 04, 2004	Plainview Cem.; Son of Guy "Ivey" Franklin & Katie Evelyn (Smith) Scott; m. Edith Mildred Smith; CPL US Army WWII; addition to Cemeteries of Grundy Co, Vol. 2, p. 686

Name	Birth	Death	Details
Scott, William J.C.	ca. 1923	Oct 11, 1933	Summerfield Cem.; Son of Samuel Scott and Keziah Stills m. Feb. 20,1886 to Martha Melissa Jane (Dyer)
Scott, William Thomas	Nov 11, 1932	Nov 24, 2018	Shiloh Cem.; Son of Charlie Scott & Nannie Myers; m. Wanda Womack; U.S. Navy
Scruggs, James T.	Jun 9, 1870	Mar 12, 1907	Oak Grove Cem.; Son of William M. & Julia M. (Gwinn) Hargis Scruggs; addition to Cemeteries of Grundy Co., Vol. 1, p. 506
Scruggs, John Wilson	Mar 18, 1930	Feb 08, 2018	Fall Creek Cem.; Son of Jim Scruggs & Lola Sanders; m. Willie Mae Argo
Scruggs, Kimberly Michell	Jul 12, 1976	Jan 20, 2021	Fall Creek Cem.; Dau. of James & Elfa (Hobbs) Scruggs
Scullin, Alda Mae (Franke)	Nov 18, 1920	Feb 10, 2016	Homeland Acres Cem: Dau of Val & Florence Franke; m, George Clifton Scullin
Scullin, George Clifton	Dec 02, 1915	Apr 06, 2015	Homeland Acres Cem.; Son of George Clements Scullin & Margaret Fern Hobensack m. Alda Mae Franke
Scullin, Lorraine H.	May 23, 1902	Nov 27, 1986	Homeland Acres Cem.; Dau. of Homer Leroy & Grace L. Holcomb; Cemeteries of Grundy Co., Vol, 1. p. 342
Seagroves, Aaron, Sr.	Apr 10, 1900	Feb 06, 1939	White Cem.; Son of William Henry "Bill" & Alice (Hamilton) Seagroves; m. Ada White; addition to Cemeteries of Grundy Co., Vol. 2, p. 1010
Seagroves, Alvin	Sep 20, 1946	Feb 09, 2015	Coalmont Cem.; Son of Lawrence & Effie Mae (Short) Seagroves
Seagroves, Billy Joe	Jun 01, 1951	Aug 01, 2015	Cremated; Son of Lynn W. Hargis & Vida Mae Seagroves; m. 1) Wilma Jean Rheal 2) Abby Dianne Totherow
Seagroves, Carl Junior	Nov 10, 1946	Sep 02, 2020	Tracy City Cem.; Son of Carl & Viola Seagroves
Seagroves, Dola T. (Dishroon)	Oct 16, 1935	Sep 16, 2019	Summerfield Cem.; Dau. of Fred D Dishroon & Letha D Morrison; m. Charles Herschel Seagroves
Seagroves, Franklin "Gabe"	Mar 18, 1934	Mar 05, 2022	Hobbs Hill Cem.; Son of Lawrence Dee & Effie Mae (Short) Seagroves; m. Doris Seagroves
Seagroves, Gladys	Sep 02, 1932	Dec 06, 2017	Plainview Cem.; Dau. of Lacy Samuel & Ethel Watson; m. Cecil Seagroves
Seagroves, Joshua Dee	Oct 15, 1982	Jun 28, 2013	Coalmont Cem.; Son of Arthur Neal "Yogi" & Lila Ann (Campbell) Seagroves
Seagroves, Mae Omillie (Kilgore)	Oct 02, 1924	Jul 31, 1996	Plainview Cem.; Dau. of Lewis & Martha N (Meeks) Kilgore; m. William "Bill" Seagroves; addition to Cemeteries of Grundy Co., Vol. 2, p. 669
Seagroves, Mary Eunice	Aug 17, 1928	Apr 21, 2014	Palmer Cem.; Dau of Jim Shrum & Rose Ellen Tate; m. 1) Rex Magouirk 2) James Seagroves

Name	Birth	Death	Details
Seagroves, Neoma Alice (Hamilton)	Mar 25, 1876	Sep 22, 1912	Brown's Chapel Cem.; Dau. of Wiley & Eliza Hamilton; m. William Henry Seagroves; addition to Cemeteries of Grundy Co., Vol. 1, p. 107
Seagroves, Roger Cecil	Oct 12, 1963	Sep 16, 2021	Cremated; Son of Cecil & Gladys (Watson) Seagroves; m. Wendy Hawkins
Seagroves, Sara Irena			Plainview Cem.; Dau. of Douglas & Ella Lois (Nunley) Seagroves
Seagroves, Shirley (Campbell)	1939	Feb 02, 2020	Plainview Cem.; Dau. of Brosie Campbell & Lillian Nunley; m. James Seagroves
Seagroves, Susie Bell (Fults)	Jul 07, 1934	Oct 23, 2021	Altamont Cem.; Dau. of Charlie & Susie (Fitch) Fults); m. Wiley Andrew Seagroves
Seagroves, Tammy M.	Mar 08, 1971	Jan 11, 2015	Plainview Cem.; Dau. of Cecil & Gladys Seagroves
Seagroves, Wiley Anderson	May 21, 1873	Mar 27, 1959	Tracy City Cem.; Son of Joshua & Charlotte "Lottie" (Blythe) Seagroves; m. 1) Fannie Bell Kilgore 2) Nancy Bell Sanders; addition to Cemeteries of Grundy Co., Vol. 2, p. 855
Seagroves, William "Doug"	Mar 16, 1943	Sep 13, 2016	Plainview Cem.; Son of William & Mae Seagroves; m. Lois Nunley
Seagroves, William Henry	Sep 14, 1872	Jan 17, 1962	Brown's Chapel Cem.; Son of Joshua Jackson & Lottie (Blythe) Seagroves; m. Neoma Alice Hamilton; addition to Cemeteries of Grundy Co., Vol. 1, p. 107
Seagroves, Willie Marie Sara Irene	Jan 02, 1941	May 04, 1941	Tracy City Cem.; Dau. of William & Mary (Kilgore) Seagroves
Seagroves, Willie Marie Sarah Irene	Jan 12, 1941	Mar 14, 1941	Trussell, Kilgore, Ladd Cem.; Dau. of William & Mae Omilee (Kilgore) Seagroves; from death certificate; no tombstone; addition to Cemeteries of Grundy Co., Vol, 2, p. 915
Seale, Roy Glenn	Jul 03, 1959	Aug 04, 2014	Stevenson, AL, City Cem.; Son of Carl Seale & Hazel Kirk; special friend Jackie Parker
Seely, George	Jan 28, 1905	Apr 16, 1823	Monteagle Cem.; Son of George Seeley & father of Mrs. Charles Metcalf; Source: *Mrs. Grundy*, Apr 19, 1923 & death certificate
Segroves, Pete	Jul 05, 1930	Apr 03, 1931	White Cem at Palmer; Son of Otis & Betty (Watley) Segroves; from death certificate; no tombstone
Sehorne, James M	Nov 20, 1867	Mar 17, 1925	Fall Creek Cem.; Son of Isham & Parlie Sehorne
Sehorne, Max	Jan 21, 1935	Dec 15, 2021	Chattanooga National Cem.; Son of Byron Cal & Irene Sehorne; m. Glenda Boak; U.S. Air Force
Seigrist, Heinrich	Jul 8, 1828	Dec 13, 1892	Swiss Colony Cem.; Son of Heinrich Siegrist Von Wel ZH & Barbara Muller; m. Katharina geb Heller; addition to Cemeteries of Grundy Co., Vol. 2, p. 783

Name	Birth	Death	Details
Sekulich, Alex Junior	Feb 01, 1931	Mar 29, 2019	Hillsboro United Methodist Church Cem.; Son of Alex Sekulich & Mary Oakich; m. 1) Caroline Sue Sekulich, 2) Myrtle Ellen Webb; U.S. Marines
Self, Edward Quincy	Aug 9, 1885	Jun 10, 1963	Wesley Chapel Cem.; Son of Robert Linford & Lila Armentha (Tatum) Self; m. Robbie Pearl Wooten; addition to Cemeteries of Grundy Co., Vol. 2, p. 978
Sellers, Roberta Jean (Reeves)	Feb 25, 1949	Aug 21, 2021	Swiss Colony Cem.; Dau. of Robert Lee & Anna Viola (West) Reeves; m. Sam Sellers
Sells, Carolyn Grace	Sep 09, 1940	Mar 25, 2015	Warren "Red Hill" Cem.; Dau. of Donald W. & Bernice Vance; m. George A. Sells
Sells, George A.	Feb 10, 1941		Warren "Red Hill" Cem.; Son of Elbert & Anna Allenen Sells; m. Carolyn Grace Vance
Sells, James Clifton	Feb 18, 1943	Mar 11, 2018	Warren "Red Hill" Cem.; Son of Elbert & Anna Allene Sells; m. Leah Dell Meeks; parents of Debbie Sells Turner & Jeff Sells; also listed is Cammie (Jenkins) Sells, former daughter-in-la;. addition to Cemeteries of Grundy Co., Vol. 2, p. 957
Sells, Verna Louise "Vernie" (Barnes)	Dec 20, 1951	Mar 28, 2014	Gager Lime Cem.; Dau. of William Woodrow & Mary E. (Haney) Barnes m. Steve Anthony Sells
Serio, Dorothy Betty Jane (Dove)	Sep 03, 1932	Sep 11, 2017	Kenosha, Wisconsin; Dau. of Avery, Sr & Callie Estil (Sweeton) Dove; m. Pasqual S. Serio; Betty Jane (Dove) Serio, originally thought to be buried in the Dove Cemetery, is not buried here; correction to Cemeteries of Grundy Co., Vol. 1, p. 202
Seymore, James Martin II	Dec 01, 1971	Jul 28, 2005	Palmer Cem.; Son of James S. & Glenda S (Leitsinger) Seymore, m. Jessica Renee Seymore; addition to Cemeteries of Grundy Co., Vol. 2, p. 555
Seymore, Jessica Renee (James)	Dec 29, 1981	Oct 31, 2017	Palmer Cem.; Dau. of Paul David & Sheila Renee (Singleton) James; m. James Martin Seymore II; addition to Cemeteries of Grundy Co., Vol. 2, p. 555
Shadrick, Charles Layden	1931	1966	Oak Grove Cem.; Son of Alvin Lawrence & Ola Beatrice (Shrum) Shadrick; addition to Cemeteries of Grundy Co., Vol. 1, p. 494.
Shadrick, Chester Willis	May 18, 1921	Aug 07, 1990	White Cem.; Son of Gilliam Edgar & Ina (Worley) Shadrick; m. Gertrude Lavonne Cookston; addition to Cemeteries of Grundy Co., Vol. 2, p. 1009
Shadrick, Cora Lee (Hammers)	Aug 29, 1921	Jun 20, 2003	White Cem.; Dau. of Robert Lee & Pearl Mae (Erwin) Hammers; m. Barney Paul Shadrick; addition to Cemeteries of Grundy Co., Vol. 2, p. 1009

Name	Born	Died	Notes
Shadrick, Dollie (Dyer)	Oct 01, 1939	May 25, 2013	Sequatchie Valley Memorial Cem.; Dau. of Thomas & Willie Mae (Anderson) Dyer; m. James David Shadrick
Shadrick, Gilliam Edgar	Nov 4, 1899	Apr 11, 1977	White Cem.; Son of Rufus & Rosalea Gay (Honea) Shadrick; m. Ina Worley; addition to Cemeteries of Grundy Co., Vol. 2, p. 1008.
Shadrick, Joseph Carl "Joe"	Mar 11, 1941	Apr 25, 2003	Palmer Cem.; Son of Carl A. & Gracie Mae (Green) Shadrick; m. Patricia A. Johnson; addition to Cemeteries of Grundy Co. Vol. 2, p. 568
Shadrick, Mary Ruth (Phillips)	Jan 28, 1951	Mar 05, 2021	Palmer Cem.; Dau. of David Foster & Rubie Nell (Davis) Phillips; m. Mike Shadrick
Shadrick, Osbin Wayne	Mar 23, 1947	Oct 29, 1994	White Cem.; Son of Chester Willis & Gertrude Lavonne (Cookston) Shadrick; US Army Vietnam; addition to Cemeteries of Grundy Co. Vol. 2, p. 1009
Sharkey, Conrad Griffith	Jun 12, 1953	Jan 13, 1963	Tracy City Cem.; Son of Rev. William Lawrence & Constance (Griffith) Sharkey
Sharkey, Mary Constance (Griffith)	Aug 04, 1922	May 10, 2018	Tracy City Cem.; Dau. of Thomas & Dalta Griffith; m. William Lawrence Sharkey
Sharkey, Sally Robbins	Jun 29, 1947	Jul 02, 1947	Tracy City Cem.; Dau. of Rev. William Lawrence & Constance (Griffith) Sharkey; correction of parenthesis around Robbins which indicated maiden name; this child was obviously never married. Cemeteries of Grundy Co., Vol. 2, p. 833
Sharp, Joan (Patterson)	Ca 1931	Jan 20, 2022	Hamilton Memorial Gardens; Dau. of William Harlon & Jennie Louise Patterson; m. Russell Johnson Sharp; Harlon Patterson was born and raised in Providence
Sharpe, Charles Gertner	Jul 23, 1887	May 30, 1962	Swiss Colony Cem.; Son of Howard James & Jean Gertrude Sharpe; m. Helen Catherine Stearns; addition to Cemeteries of Grundy Co., Vol. 2, p. 788
Sharpe, Helen Catherine	1888	1961	Swiss Colony Cem.; Dau. of Charles William & Helen (Bryant) Stearns; m: Charles Gerner Sharpe; death certificate says death was Jan 21, 1960; addition to Cemeteries of Grundy C.o, Vol. 2, p. 788
Shaun, Kevin Smith	Jan 04, 1979	Jul 26, 2020	Walker Cem.; Son of J.L. Smith & Patricia Childers
Shelton, Burna D.	Sep 11, 1951	May 17, 2017	Chattanooga National Cem (cremains); Dau. of Robert & Theida Jo Johnson; m. Billy R. Shelton; US Army
Shelton, Debra Sue	Jul 18, 1963	Mar 31, 1988	Bonny Oak Cem.; Dau. of William Howard "Bill" Shelton; addition to Cemeteries of Grundy Co., Vol. 1, p. 87

Name	Birth	Death	Notes
Shelton, Martha Tennessee "Tennie" (Henegar)	Aug 19, 1861	Jul 15, 1924	White Cem.; Dau. of Thomas Kirby & Annie J. (Ledbetter) Henegar; m. Elijah Coleman Shelton on Oct 16, 1890, Dade Co, GA; addition to Cemeteries of Grundy Co., Vol. 2, p. 1006
Shelton, Pleas Meyers			Robert Soward Meyers farm; two graves are at this location. They were found on a boundary drawing of Meyers land grant of Jan 29, 1845. Only Pleas Meyers Shelton was named on the drawing. It is thought that Soward Meyers might also be buried on the land sinc he has not been found elsewhere or with his wife.
Shepherd, Gavin Tristan	Jan 26, 1932	Feb 26, 2004	Plainview Cem.; Son of Cord & Susan Elizabeth (Mavesty) Shepherd
Sheridan, Martina Short	Jun 07, 1929	Dec 11, 2017	O'Dear Cem.; Dau. of James & Faye Goff Short; m. Joe Sheridan
Sherman, Bernard Sherman	Dec 11, 1944	Jul 01, 2019	Cagle-Mount Pleasant Cem.; Son of I.B. Sherman & Bertha Pauline King; m. Barbara Scissom; U.S. Army
Sherman, Tomothy Kirk	May 24, 1905	May 21, 2014	Swiss Colony Cem.; Son of Bernard Sherman & Barbara Jean Scissom; m. Katie Stocker
Sherrill, Andrew Jackson, Jr.	Sep 17, 1924	Feb 11, 2014	Warren "Red Hill" Cem.; Son of Andrew Jackson, Sr. & Lillian Mae (Phipps) Sherrill; m. Tomye Mae Henson
Sherrill, Andrew Mason	Apr 28, 1984	Jun 19, 2020	Cremated; ashes at Warren "Red Hill" Cem.; Son of Charles Sherrill & Jeanne Mason
Sherrill, Barbara Jean (Evett)	Jul 16, 1935	Apr 26, 1963	Providence Methodist Cem.; Dau. of John & Alice Bell (Temples) Evett; m. James Hershel Sherrill; addition to Cemeteries of Grundy Co., Vol. 2, p. 712
Sherrill, Clea Allen	Mar 13, 1963	May 10, 2015	Eastern Star Cem.; Son of James William & Cleo (Dotson) Sherrill
Sherrill, James William	June, 1930	Jan 17, 2019	Eastern Star Cem. Sewanee; Son of James Patty Sherrill & Juan Bowers; m. Cleo Dotson
Sherrill, Tomye (Henson)	Jum 8, 1926	Jul 08, 2017	Warren "Red Hill" Cem.; Dau. of Oscar & Willie Mae (Willis) Henson; m. Andrew J. Sherrill, Jr.
Shied, Margaret Elizabeth	Aug 4, 1848	Oct 27, 1854	Patton I Cem.; Dau. eldest of Henry S. & Mary E. Shied; age 6 yrs, 2 mo, 23 days; addition to Cemeteries of Grundy Co., Vol. 2, p. 58
Shields, Bill	Oct 06, 1937	Oct 09, 2015	Providence Cem.; Son of Lonnie & Clara Shields
Shipley, Jessie Len	Mar 08, 1968	Jun 25, 2021	Palmer Cem.; Son of J.P. & Diana (Darnell) Shipley
Shirlen, Clay	May 06, 1905	Jan 12, 2000	Altamont Cem.; Son of Jeff R & Margaret Shirlen of Dover, Del; died of brain aneurism; addition to Cemeteries of Grundy Co., Vol. 1, p. 14

Name	Birth	Death	Notes
Shirley, Edith Layne (Hill)	Oct 30, 1911	Apr 25, 2014	Cremated; Dau of William T. "Bill" Hill & Hattie Partin; m. 1) Abraham "Little Abe" Layne 2) Robert Hudson "Bob" Shirley, lived in Layne's Cove
Shirley, Hudson Robert "Bob"	Oct. 1, 1915	Apr 26, 1995	Summerfield Cem.; Son of Talton Taylor & Fannie Catherine (Hankins) Shirley; m. 1) Violet M Saverivein 2) Edith Irene (Hill) Layne; US ARMY WWII; addition to Cemeteries of Grundy Co., Vol. 2, p. 768
Shoenman, Jacob	May 5, 1823	Oct 8, 1899	Swiss Colony Cem.; b. in Switzerland; m. Elizabeth Anna Mueller who was the daughter of Grossman Muellerin 1844 in Niederbipp, Bern, Switzerland; addition to Cemeteries of Grundy Co., Vol. 2, p. 783.
Sholey, Vickie (Hawkins)	Mar 21, 1936	Jun 14, 2021	Eastern Star Cem.; Dau. of Jack Horace & Katherine (Mooney) Hawkins; m. Dwight Sholey
Short, Kenneth Eugene "Rooster"	Jan 31, 1945	Jun 12, 2013	Bailey-Short Family Cem.; Son of Jim and Faye (Short) Bailey; m. 1) Geraldine Barnett on Jun 25, 1973 in Marion Co. 2) Joy Short.
Short, Lucy Irene (Rose)	Dec 02, 1919	May 13, 2015	Monteagle Cem.; Dau. of David Martin & Vesta Ann Rose; m. James Albert Short
Short, Maxine	Aug 23, 1954	Oct 28, 2015	Coalmont Cem.; Dau. of Raymond & Zada Short
Short, Robert Mitchell "Pop"	May 26, 1944	Jul 24, 2017	Coalmont Cem.; Son of Johnny William & Ida Mae Edith Short; m. Virginia Carol Nunley
Short, Robert Mord	Oct 30, 1926	Nov 10, 2019	Cremated; Son of Mord Puryear Short & Jennie Fyfe
Short, Ruby Ella (Anderson)	Nov 04, 1920	Jul 09, 2005	Coalmont Cem.; Dau. of George P & Willie A (Reed) Anderson; m. Raymond D Short; correction to Cemeteries of Grundy Co., Vol. 1, p. 175
Short, Virginia C.	Oct 04, 1945	Feb 27, 2014	Coalmont Cem.; Dau. of Herbert & Nellie Nunley; m. Robert "Pop" Short
Shoulders, Ann Elizabeth "Libby" (McCarley)	May 20, 1923	Mar 30, 2019	Monteagle Assembly Cem.; Dau. of Theodore Trimmier & Sarah Elder (Hamm) McCarley; m. 1) Clifton E. Greer, Jr. 2) Dr. Harrison H. Shoulders, Jr.
Shoultz, Bonnie L.	Oct 27, 1948	Jan 04, 2014	Wesley Chapel Cem.; Dau. of Hershel Glenn & Hazel Louise (Caldwell) Brady; m. Edward R. Shoultz, Jr.
Shrum, Andrew Jackson	1905	Sep 13, 1936	Clouse Hill Cem.; Son of Moses & Sherilda Jane (Simpson) Shrum; m. Della Mae Gibbs; correction of death date to Cemeteries of Grundy Co., Vol. 1, p. 161
Shrum, Andrew Jackson, Jr.	Dec 27, 1930	Nov 06, 2014	Hamilton Memorial Gardens; Son of Andrew Jackson Shrum, Sr. & Della Mae Gibbs; m. Joyce Nix

Name	Born	Died	Notes
Shrum, Anna Bell (Meeks)	Feb 24, 1885	Sep 09, 1962	Hobbs Hill Cem.; Dau. of Elijah Keys & Kathryn Veoger "Kitt" (Irvin) Meeks; m. Richard Shrum on Feb 14, 1904; addition to Cemeteries of Grundy Co., Vol. 1, p. 327
Shrum, Beryl Rebecca (Allen)	May 17, 1922	Jul 21, 2014	Burns Cem.; Dau. of David Murphy & Josephine (Bentley) Allen; m. m. Rev. James Roy Shrum; Dec 24, 1938; addition to Cemeteries of Grundy Co., Vol. 1, p. 129
Shrum, Betty Mae	Sep 27, 1934	Nov 06, 2019	Burns Cem.; Dau. of Oscar Shrum & Sarah Caldwell
Shrum, Billy Gene	Mar 10, 1950	Jul 27, 1970	Oak Grove Cem.; Son of Charles Andrew & Jennie Olene (Haynes) Shrum; addition to Cemeteries of Grundy Co., Vol. 1, p. 510
Shrum, Brandon Andrew "Boo"	Jul 07, 1992	Jan 01, 2018	Coalmont Cem.; Son of Shawn Shrum & Paula Tate
Shrum, Carolyn (Nunley)	1955	Apr 10, 2021	Pryor Ridge Cem.; Dau. of Howard & Elsie Nunley; m. Jerry Shrum
Shrum, Charles Andrew	May 17, 1924	May 05, 1987	Pryor Ridge Cem.; Son of Sherman Andrew Shrum & Mary Edna Way; m. Jenni Olene Harris
Shrum, Charles Edward	May 16, 1935	Jan 31, 2013	Cumberland View Cem, Kimball, TN; Son of Walden M. & Mabel (Nolan) Shrum; m. Peggy Merrell
Shrum, Doris (Maddox)	May 13, 1936	Mar 16, 2008	Palmer Cem.; Dau. of Howard McKay & Emma (Bearden) Maddox; m. Howard Edward "Sonny" Shrum; addition to Cemeteries of Grundy Co., Vol. 2, p. 552
Shrum, Ernest Donald, Jr.	Jul 04, 1941	Oct 03, 2018	Coalmont Cem.; Son of Taylor Shrum & Julia Harris
Shrum, Evie Vernie	1901	1925	Ross Mountain Cem.; Dau. of Mose & Serilda Jane Shrum; addition to Cemeteries of Grundy Co., Vol, 2, p. 726
Shrum, Fred L.	Feb 11, 1926	May 04, 2015	Shrum Family Cem.; Son of Sherman & Millie Shrum; m. Sarah E. Sweeton; addition to Cemeteries of Grundy Co., Vol. 2, p. 745
Shrum, Howard "Blue"	Mar 14, 1911	Feb 21, 1984	Palmer Cem.; Son of Joe David & Bessie Leona (Almany) Shrum; addition to Cemeteries of Grundy Co., Vol. 2, p. 551
Shrum, Howard Edward "Sonny"	Mar 23, 1938	Sep 10, 2014	Palmer Cem.; Son of Howard W. & Opal (Crabtree) Shrum; m. Doris E. Maddox; addition to Cemeteries of Grundy Co., Vol. 2, p. 552
Shrum, Howell Franklin "Pinky"	Dec 16, 1940		Palmer Cem.; Son of Howard "Blue" & Opal Shrum; m. 1) Nancy Shrum 2) Evelyn Ruth Randler Oct 19, 1974; missing since March 1987; addition to Cemeteries of Grundy Co., Vol. 2, p. 551

Name	Birth	Death	Details
Shrum, Jeffrey Alan	May 15, 1963	Jan 27, 2017	Palmer Cem.; Son of Carl Bailey Shrum & Frances Maria (Zingale) Thomas; m. Cindy White
Shrum, Jerry Allen	Sep 24, 1952	Mar 20, 2018	Palmer Cem.; Son of Howard Shrum & Opal Crabtree; m. Anne Miller; US Navy
Shrum, Juanita (Green)	Jan 13, 1935	Jul 05, 2018	Eastern Star Cem.; Dau. of Wesley Green & Lillie Mae Southerland; m. Mose Shrum
Shrum, Kathy	Jul 21, 1953	Aug 05, 2015	Coalmont Cem.; Dau. of James & Dorothy Smith; m. Mike Shrum
Shrum, Kevin Russell	Oct 28, 1976	Dec 01, 2013	Coalmont Cem.; Son of Donald & Ginger Shrum
Shrum, Lloyd Ray	Sep 25, 1937	Dec 19, 2021	Lakewood Memory Gardens, South; Son of Lawrence & Nora B. (Kilgore) Shrum; m. Mildred Shrum
Shrum, Mamie Magdalene	Jan 19, 1925	Oct 06, 1925	White Cem.; Dau. of Joe David & Bessie (Almany) Shrum; addition to Cemeteries of Grundy Co., Vol. 2, p. 1007
Shrum, Marie (Nunley)	Oct 27, 1936	Mar 21, 2015	Palmer Cem.; Dau. of Arthur & Pearl (Meeks) Nunley; m.1) Ronnie Nunley 2) John Shrum
Shrum, Martha (Campbell)	Sep 06, 1936	Mar 19, 1994	Swiss Colony Cem.; Dau. of Raymond & Hazel (Dishroom) Campbell; m. Billie Jo Shrum; addition to Cemeteries of Grundy Co.,Vol. 2, p. 793
Shrum, Moses Walden	Mar 25, 1900	Aug 28, 1989	Plainview Cem.; Son of Moses Shrum & Sherilda Jane Simpson; m. 1) Cora Lee Gibbs 2) Maybell Nolan
Shrum, Norma Joyce (Nix)	Mar 15, 1934	Feb 10, 2022	Hamilton Memorial Gardens; Dau. of Luther & Nina Mae Nix; m. Andrew Shrum
Shrum, Peggy J.	Jul 30, 1941	Jul 25, 2013	Cumberland View Cem in Kimball; Dau. of James Merell & Barbara Grace Nunley m. Charles Edward Shrum
Shrum, Ralph Eugene	May 02, 1948	May 02, 1948	Palmer Cem.; Son of Henry & Marie (Nunley) Shrum; tombstone present; addition to Cemeteries of Grundy Co., Vol. 2, p.562
Shrum, Ray	May 09, 1938	Jan 27, 2017	Plainview Cem.; Son of Taylor & Julie (Harris) Shrum; m. Dola Gibbs; addition to Cemeteries of Grundy Co., Vol. 2, p. 682
Shrum, Rev. Stanley	Mar 17, 1926	Dec 26, 2012	Burns Cem.; Son of John Lawrence & Nora B. (Kilgore) Shrum; m. Katie Mae Nunley; addition to Cemeteries of Grundy Co., Vol, 1, p.134
Shrum, Roger C	Jul 08, 1954	Nov 13, 2020	Burns Cem.; Son of Stanle E. & Katie May (Nunley) Shrum
Shrum, Ruby Jewell (Nunley)	Apr 04, 1943	Jan 11, 2022	Pryor Ridge Cem.; Dau. of Howard & Elsie (Dykes) Nunley; m. John E. Shrum
Shrum, Steven McKay	Mar 07, 1978	Mar 07, 1978	Palmer Cem.; Son of Howard Edward "Sonny" & Doris (Maddox) Shrum; addition to Cemeteries of Grundy Co., Vol. 2; p. 552

Name	Birth	Death	Details
Shrum, Teresa Ann (Fults)	Jan 11, 1964		Brown's Chapel Cem.; Dau. of Wanda Fults; m. Rev Joe David "Jody" Shrum; addition to Cemeteries of Grundy Co., Vol. 1, p. 102
Shrum, Thomas A.	Nov 21, 1937	Mar 28, 2016	Burns Cem.; Son of Oscar & Louella Shrum; m. Carol Brown
Sides, Carrie Sue (Marler)	Oct 24, 1924	Jun 01, 2015	Plainview Cem.; Dau. of Joseph Pascal & Adaline "Addie" Lee (Green) Marler; m. Jack Kirby Sides; addition to Cemeteries of Grundy Co., Vol. 2, p. 667
Sides, Jack Kirby	Jun 24, 1917	May 09, 1997	Plainview Cem: Son of Fred & Lizzie (Allen) Sides; Lt. Col USAF WWII, Korea, Vietnam, Distinguished Flying Cross Air Medal; m. Carrie Sue Marler; addition to Cemeteries of Grundy Co., Vol. 2, p. 667
Siegrist, Heinrich	Jul 8, 1828	Dec 13, 1892	Swiss Colony Cem.; Son of Hans & Anna Barbara (Degen) Siegrist; m. 1) Ursula Bitterlin 2) Katherina geb Heller; addition to Cemeteries of Grundy Co., Vol. 2, p. 783
Silcox, Peggy Ann	Sep 02, 1946	May 07, 2023	Warren "Red Hill" Cem.; Dau of Ardell & Dolly (Kelly) Adams; m. Thomas Silcox
Siler, June Brewer (Hart)	Apr 21, 1925		Cumberland Heights Cem.; Dau. of Roy P. & Ada (Murr) Hart; m. Paul Maurice Siler in 1985; addition to Cemeteries of Grundy Co., Vol. 1, p. 197
Simer, Herman Everett	Nov 04, 1920	Mar 26, 1996	Palmer Cem.; Son of James E. & Dora Dean (Phillips) Simer; m. Delores Lorene Howell; addition to Cemeteries of Grundy Co., Vol. 2, p. 576
Simer, Ronald E.	Mar 01, 1947	Mar 07, 1995	Palmer Cem.; Son of Herman E. & Deloris Lorene (Howell) Simer; m. Laureen Gay Ross; addition to Cemeteries of Grundy Co, Vol. 2, p. 576
Simmons, Joe Allen	Jun 16, 1949	Apr 1983	Mountain View Cem in Franklin Co.; Son of James E. & Iva L. Simmons; m. Sandra Lou Hays; USMC, Vietnam
Simmons, Mary Elizabeth (Young)	Apr 10, 1905	Sep 12, 2015	Mt. Garner Cem. in Decherd; Dau. of Joseph & Effie (McKnight) Young; m. J.D. Simmons
Simmons, Matthew James	Mar 04, 1917	Aug 10, 2002	Airview Cem.; Son of Dan & Elizabeth (Bondurant) Simmons; never married; addition to Cemeteries of Grundy Co. Vol. 1, p. 6
Simmons, Richard	Feb 10, 1941	Mar 26, 2014	Mt. View Cem.; Son of Richard & Christine (Shetters) Simmons; m. 1) Elizabeth Coker 2) Willie Mae Caldwell
Simmons, Salinda (Cain)	Dec 26, 1812	Sep 28, 1887	Wesley Chapel Cem.; Dau. of John & Rebecca Cain; m. William Simmons; addition to Cemeteries of Grundy Co., Vol. 2, p. 970
Simmons, Sandra Lou	May 03, 1948	Nov 20, 2018	Providence Cem. (assumed since obit says Bell's Mill Rd.); Dau of Homer & Martha Smith; m. Joe Allen Simmons

Simmons, William	Mar 23, 1807	Jun 26, 1889	Wesley Chapel Cem.; Son of James & Elizabeth (Allen) Simmons; m. Salinda Cain; addition to Cemeteries of Grundy Co, Vol. 2, p. 970
Simon, June Marie Simon	Jun 15, 1936	Feb 16, 2013	Fall Creek Cem.; Dau. of Charlie & Viola (Perry) Sitz; m. John Simon
Simpson, Roy Lee	Aug 14, 1941	Dec 30, 1996	Clouse Hill Cem.; Son of Clarence & Anna (East) Simpson; m, Nancy J. Stanfield; addition to Cemeteries of Grundy Co., Vol. 1, p. 159
Sims, Carolyn Thelma (Pease)	Feb 10, 1949	Nov 21, 2022	King Cem.; Dau of Claudie Pease & Oline Grace King; m. Wayne Douglas Sims
Singelton, Albert "Frankie"	Dec 20, 1960	Feb 11, 2014	Cremated: Son of Jackson C. Singleton & Nellie Burnett; m. Tammy Lynn Johnson; Army & National Guard
Singleton, Mildred (Harris)	Aug 06, 1915	Jan 15, 1996	Oak Grove Cem.; Dau. of Albert Calloway Jackson & Bertha Jane (Nolan) Harris; m. 1) Albert Houston Singleton 2) Grant Wooden; addition to Cemeteries of Grundy Co., Vol. 1, p. 489,
Singleton, Sandra (Sanders)	Dec 11, 1951	Jan 04, 2022	Swiss Colony Cem.; Dau. of Albert, Jr. & Helen (Layman) Sanders; m. Willie Singleton
Sisk, Terry Wayne	Dec 13, 1960	Jan 02, 2020	Cremated; Son of George Pratt & Jeannette Ford per obituary
Sissom, Argie Earlene	Sep 25, 1936	Oct 08, 2017	Fults Cem.; Dau. of Lannie & Winifred (Sherrill) Gilliam; m. Stanley Sissom
Sissom, Dan Jack	Dec 24, 1938	May 14, 2015	Palmer Cem.; Son of Pascal F. Sr. & Mildred (Byers) Sissom; m. Winnie Gertrude Lockhart, Jan 15, 1960; addition to Cemeteries of Grundy Co, Vol. 2, p. 552
Sissom, Elsie Marie	Jun 26, 1928	Dec 09, 1997	Coalmont Cem.; Dau. of John William & Gertrude (Hobbs) Sissom; m. 1) James Alford Smith 2) Donald H. Bernard – information from John Sissom- no tomb stone
Sissom, George Thomas	Mar 1847	Jan 09, 1906	Pull Tight also called Blowing Springs Cem.; Son of Henry & Eliza Sissom; m. Sarah Ann Steele in GA ca 1872 per researcher John D. Sissom; correction and addition to Cemeteries of Grundy Co, Vol. 2, p. 719
Sissom, Glenn	Dec 31, 1945	Aug 22, 1969	Fall Creek Cem.; Son of Pascal Lafayette & Mildred Kathleen (Byers) Sissom
Sissom, James F.	Oct 7, 1880	Nov 19, 1956	Fall Creek Falls Cem.; Son of George T. & Sarah (Steel) Sissom; m. Ardena Sissom; Grundy County Cemetery Book Vol 1, p. 233
Sissom, Rosa Nell (Sweeton)	Oct 08, 1926	Sep 13, 2011	Palmer Cem.; Dau. of Albert "Hatchet" & Alice Mae (Sanders) Sweeton; m. J.C. "Tom" Sissom; addition to Cemeteries of Grundy Co. Vol. 2, p. 553

Name	Birth	Death	Notes
Sissom, Sarah Ann Steele	Mar 28, 1848	Jan 05, 1919	Hobbs Hill Cem.; b. in GA; m. George Thomas Sissom
Sitten-Davis, Barbara (Lowery)	May 03, 1937	Jul 20, 2020	Forest Home Cem., Boaz, AL; Son of Joe & Carrie Lowery
Sitz, Alvin Leon	1939	Dec 29, 2014	Tracy City Cem.; Son of Charlie Sitz & Viola Perry
Sitz, Bessie (Green)	Aug 08, 1902	Jun 17, 1930	Oak Grove Cem.; Dau. of Dan & Mary (Shrum) Green; addition to Cemeteries of Grundy Co. Vol. 1, p; 502
Sitz, Carl Houston	Oct 06, 1943	May 07, 2013	Meeks Family Cemetery at Flat Branch: Son of James H. & Thelma (Coppinger) Sitz; m. Geneva Jean Frederick on Apr 15, 1980
Sitz, Dan Wiley	Jan 16, 1960	Oct 27, 1987	Oak Grove Cem.; Son of Robert B. Sitz, addition to Cemeteries of Grundy Co, Vol. 1, p. 504
Sitz, David	Jul 28, 1943	Feb 10, 1997	Fall Creek Cem.; Son of Albert E. & Martha L. (Smith) Sitz
Sitz, Earl Mitchel	Jul 12, 1927	Oct 06, 2013	Oak Grove Cem.; Son of Robert & Bessie (Green) Sitz; U.S. Army
Sitz, Flora (Roberts)	Sep 26, 1915	Mar 04, 2003	Plainview Cem.; Dau. of Arthur & Lola (Brigance) Roberts; m. Charles F. Sitz; addition to Cemeteries of Grundy Co, Vol. 2, p. 692
Sitz, Gary Lee	Sep 19, 1955	Feb 07, 2014	O'Dear Cem.; Son of Charles & Flora (Roberts) Sitz; m. Janet Johnson; US Navy
Sitz, Geneva Jean (Frederick)	Feb 28, 1960		Meeks Family Cem. at Flat Branch; Dau of Pat Frederick; m Carl Houston Sitz
Sitz, Joanna Lee	Jun 13, 1981	Jul 13, 2014	Meeks Family Cem. at Flat Branch;
Sitz, Mattie Ruth (Guthrie)	Nov 12, 1912	Nov 10, 1985	Fall Creek Cem.; Dau. of James & Stacie (Levan) Guthrie; m. Frank Ernest Sitz
Sitz, Myrtle	Feb 04, 1913	Dec 24, 1998	Fall Creek Cem.; Dau. of Albert E. & Martha L. (Smith) Sitz
Sitz, Nancy Pearl	Oct 01, 1940	Mar 31, 2016	Cremated; Dau. of James Franklin & Lucille (Seagroves) McDaniel; m. R.B. Sitz
Sitz, Virgil Henry	Feb 18, 1896	Nov 13, 1956	Fall Creek Cem.; Son of Howard & Mattie (Smith) Sitz; m. Maggie Lou Levan; Cemeteries of Grundy Co., Vol 1, p. 246
Sitz, William "Tubby"	Feb 15, 1932	Oct 24, 2019	Whitwell Memorial Cem.; Son of Francis Benson & Martha Irene Rector; m. Shirley Rollins; U.S. Army – Korean Conflict
Sitz/Sits, Nella aka Nellie Ellender B. Choate	1801	Jan 15, 1866	Fall Creek Cem.; Dau of Native Americans; m. William Bost Sits; oldest DOB in this cem.
Sitz/Sits, William Bost	1802	Mar 17, 1872	Fall Creek Cem.; Son of Andrew Sitz & Mary Magdalene Bost; m: Nella/Nellie Ellender B. Choate; Donated the land for the original Fall Creek Cemetery

Name	Birth	Death	Details
Skelton, Arnold Lee	Sep 26, 1946	Sep 14, 2006	Summerfield Cem.; Son of James Franklin & Ola (Bowman) Skelton; m 1) Elizabeth Jane Heltzel 2) Elizabeth H. Darling: US ARMY VIETNAM;
Slatton, Fred, Jr.	Nov 15, 1936	Nov 19, 2013	Palmer Cem.; Son of Fred, Sr. & Bertha (Fults) Slatton; m Mary Frances Nolan; addition to Cemeteries of Grundy Co, Vol. 2, p. 575
Slatton, Horace Ray	Aug 23, 1943	Mar 18, 2021	Palmer Cem.; Son of Huke & Bertha (Kilgore) Slatton; m. Zella Fults
Slatton, Lewis E.	Jun 30, 1944	Jun 30, 1944	Oak Grove Cem.; Son of Gilbert & Ader Hazel (Layne) Slatton; addition to Cemeteries of Grundy Co, Vol. 1, p. 500
Slatton, Ricky Allen	Dec 27, 1955	Apr 23, 2018	Chattanooga National Cem.; Son of Cecil Slatton & Polly Layne; m. Charlotte Slatton; US Army
Slatton, Scottie E.	1988	Mar 28, 2014	Fall Creek Cem.; Son of Harold & Betty Jo Slatton
Slave graves			Nunley Cemetery in Northcutt's Cove; oral data only that there are 40 to 50 slave graves with no names in this cemetery
Slave graves			Known to be located in Hargis Cemetery in Valley Home, Patton Cemetery in Pelham, Tracy City Cemetery & High School Hill in Tracy City, Stockade near Tracy City, Payne's Cove Cemetery, Old Baptist Cemetery in Pelham, Milton Lockhart Homeplace in Tracy City, on Butch & Linda (Dykes) Goodman's homeplace which was formerly the Moran Place on Goodman Lane in Valley Home, and Tate Cemetery on Betsy Willis Rd. in edge of Coffee Co.
Sloan, Ernest	Mar 07, 1900	Jan 01, 1986	Griffith's Creek Church Cem.; Son of Bob Sloan & Mattie Meeks; m. Maggie Yarworth
Sloan, Howard Edward "Bouncy"	Aug 25, 1918	Oct 19, 2017	Coalmont Cem.; Son of Clarence & Lillie Mae Sloan
Sloan, Maggie (Yarworth)	Jul 06, 1907	Aug 19, 1997	Griffith's Creek Church Cem.; Dau of Orville Yarworth & Della Downum; m. Ernest Sloan
Sloan, Scott Jon	Nov 22, 1947	Jan 12, 2017	University Cem.; Son of George & Lillian (Berger) Solomon; m. Virginia Beard; Vietnam Vet
Small, Frances Austin	1911	Dec 17, 2013	Mulberry Cem.; Dau of Robert Austin & Effie J. Bateman; m. Urban Shofner Small, Jr.
Small, Urban Shofner, Jr.	Dec 27, 1905	Jan 19, 1964	Mulberry Cem.; Son of Urban Shofner, Sr. & Nora Small; m. Fances Austin Bateman
Smallwood, Henry "Hank"	May 12, 1932	Sep 25, 2013	Freedonia Cem in Coffee County; Son of Russell Lee & Mary Nina (Hill) Smallwood; m. Margaret Joyce Coffelt; US Army

Name	Birth	Death	Notes
Smallwood, Henry Lee	Oct 18, 1961	Jun 03, 2017	Fall Creek Cem.; Son of Henry S. & Margaret (Coffelt) Smallwood m. Cheyl Cawley; US Army
Smart, Elijah Ferris "Uncle Shine"	Jun 10, 1896	Feb 01, 1977	Bonny Oak Cem.; Son of John & Mary Estella (Sanders) Smart; addition to Cemeteries of Grundy Co., Vol. 1, p. 94
Smartt Steve A	Ar 30, 1869	Mar 13, 1948	Clouse Hill Cem.; Son of Ezekiel & Effie (Cope) Smartt; death cert # 7879
Smartt, Linda	Nov 09, 1950	Jul 17, 2017	Armstrong Cem.; James William & Emma Jane (Richardson) Daniel; m. Dale Smartt
Smartt, Amanda Denise	Jul 04, 1982	Jun 02, 2018	Northcutts Cove Cem.; Dau. of Glenn & Nellie Gladys King
Smartt, Barbara Allen (Meeks)	Sep 16, 1907	Feb 27, 1996	Clouse Hill Cem.; Dau. of George Cope "Banty" Meeks & Mary Elizabeth "Lizzie" Sanders; m. Lawrence Smartt, Apr 3, 1927
Smartt, Bill	Nov 24, 1946	Dec 15, 2021	Plainview Cem.; Son of Marvin & Beccie (Parsons) Smartt; m. Janice Smartt
Smartt, Billy Eugene	Sep 22, 1938	Jul 03, 2019	Swiss Colony Cem.; Son of Louie Smartt & Martha Pickett; m. Dottie Thomas; U.S. Army
Smartt, Cathy Marie (Shrum)	Jun 22, 1959	Jun 16, 2006	Walker Cem.; Dau. of Carl Bailey & Frances Marie (Zingale) Shrum; m. 1) Paul David Smartt 2) Robert Riley Roberts; addition to Cemeteries of Grundy Co., Vol. 2, p. 918
Smartt, Doris Ann	Jul 06, 1954	Mar 02, 2016	Pryor Ridge Cem.; Dau. of Dillard & Lilian (Smartt) Sanders; m. Lester "Punk" Smartt
Smartt, Ether (Bess)	Aug 09, 1884	Jun 07, 1964	Bess Cem.; Dau of Rufus Doak Bess & Margaret Green; m. Henry C. Smartt; correction to spelling of given name from Esther to Ether. Cemeteries of Grundy Co. Vol. 1, p. 30
Smartt, Geneva "Bluie"	Apr 20, 1921	Jul 24, 2015	Franklin Memorial Gardens; Dau. of Silas Samuel & Mattie (Thomas) Gregory; m. 1) Ernest Glenn Lautzenheiser 2) William Elliott
Smartt, Gregory Wakeman	Jun 06, 1943	Jun 30, 2014	Altamont Cem.; Son of Vester & Lorene (Woodlee) Smartt; m. Clara Mae Myers; addition to Cemeteries of Grundy Co. Vol. 1, p. 22
Smartt, James	Jul 08, 1930	Aug 01, 2015	Cremated; Son of Lawrence & Barbara (Meeks) Smartt; m. Thula Smartt
Smartt, Janie E.	Dec 07, 1939	Feb 07, 2016	Coalmont Cem.; Dau. of James "Mutt" & Mary "Duck" Nunley; m. 1) Phillip D Nunley 2) Wayne "Thick" Smartt
Smartt, Lawrence	1905	1938	Clouse Hill Cem.; Son of Stephen Adam & Lucy (Nunley) Smartt; m. Barbara Allen Meeks on Apr 3, 1937
Smartt, Lawrence Marie	Aug 01, 1937	Jun 05, 1938	Clouse Hill Cem.; Infant Dau. of Lawrence & Barbara Allen (Meeks) Smartt; per death certificate – died of malnuntrition.

Name	Birth	Death	Details
Smartt, Linda	Nov 09, 1950	Jul 17, 2017	Armstrong Cem.; James William & Emma Jane (Richardson) Daniel; m. Dale Smartt
Smartt, Lucy Belle	Jul 03, 1878	Dec 22, 1956	Clouse Hill Cem.; Dau. of jesse & Jane (Smartt) Nunley; m. Stephen A. Smartt; no marker, information from death certificate
Smartt, Margie Frances	1935	Mar 07, 2022	Clouse Hill Cem.; Dau. of Clyde Ransom & Lula Myrtle (Meeks) Smartt
Smartt, Martha Lee (Pickett)	Aug 03, 1918	Jan 29, 2018	Swiss Colony Cem.; Dau. of Leck Pickett & Lou Davis; m. Louie H Smartt
Smartt, Mary Estella "Stella" (Sanders)	Aug 28, 1879	Oct 12, 1940	Bonny Oak Cem.; Dau. of Joseph Charles & Mary Cyntina (Sweeton) Sanders; m. John De Baptist Smartt on Nov 4, 1895; twin to Louella Sanders; addition to Cemeteries of Grundy Co. Vol. 1, p. 78
Smartt, Nickie Dwayne	Nov 22, 1953	Feb 01, 2022	Northcutt Cove Cem.; Son of R.T. and Sammy Faye (Northcutt) Smartt; m. Linda Seibers
Smartt, Ralph Blaine	Apr 05, 1942	Mary 7, 2019	Fults Cem.; Son of Sidney James Smartt & Sally Hazel Fults; m. Bettie Killian
Smartt, Robert Henry	Aug 19, 1916	Oct 01, 2001	Plainview Cem.; Son of Stephen A & Lucy Belle (Nunley) Smarttt; addition to Cemeteries of Grundy Co. Vol. 2, p. 684
Smartt, Roger Dale	Oct 12, 1945	Apr 25, 2018	Manchester City Cem.; Son of Elmer Hubert Fults & Irene Smartt; m. Margaret Barrett
Smartt, Ronald "Beaver"	Jul 01, 1960	Jul 24, 2015	Altamont Cem.; Son of Tommy & Linda (Tate) Smartt; never married
Smartt, Saylor Hope Diamond	Aug 20, 2019	Aug 21, 2019	Brown's Chapel Cem.; Dau. of Danny Aaron Smartt & Bretney Nicole Floyd
Smartt, Steve A.	Apr 30, 1869	Mar 13, 1958	Clouse Hill Cem.; Son of Ezekiel & Effie (Cope) Smartt; Death Cert #7879 – no tombstone found
Smartt, Terry	Aug 24, 1957	Jan 07, 2013	Cremated; Son of Marvin D. & Doris B (Meadows) Smartt
Smartt, Theodore	Mar 25, 1947	Apr 19, 2020	Altamont Cem.; Son of Little Vester Smartt & Lydia Mae Fitch; m. Daisy M. Smartt
Smartt, Tommie Melvin	Sep 15, 1933	Dec 26, 2017	Northcutts Cove Cem.; Son of Marcus & Lillie Smartt
Smartt, Wallace	ca 1920		Altamont Cem.; Son of William & Louise (Fults) Smartt; US Navy; addition to Cemeteries of Grundy Co. Vol. 1, p. 36
Smartt, Wallace H.	Oct 14, 1915	Jun 08, 1986	Bess Cem.; Son of Henry C. Smartt & Ether Bess; m. Erma Azylene Bess, Apr 11, 1944; US Army; correction of mother's name, Cemeteries of Grundy Co. Vol 1, p. 44
Smartt, Wayne Ladue	Jul 28, 1950	Jul 05, 2023	Coalmont Cem.; Son of Thomas Winford Smart & Joyce Florence Short m. Janie Elizabeth Nunley
Smartt. Gina Lynn	Oct 31, 1973	Nov 09, 2014	Altamont Cem.; Dau of Reuben Smartt, Sr. & Lola (Tate) Harding

Name	Born	Died	Details
Smedley, George Washington	Feb 11, 1905	Nov 30, 1966	Palmer Cem.; Son of Christopher Columbus & Martha (Taylor) Smedley; m. Hazel Morgan; addition to Cemeteries of Grundy Co, Vol, 2, p. 562
Smedley, Hazel (Morgan)	Sep 22, 1909	Jan 03, 1979	Palmer Cem.; Dau. of Mose Allen & Mary Ella (Pearson) Morgan; m. George Washington Smedley; addition to Cemeteries of Grundy Co, Vol. 2, p. 562
Smedley, Jack Clayton	Jan 17, 1930	Jan 11, 2017	Philadelphia Cem.; Son of George & Hazel (Morgan) Smedley; m. Lodema Marie Clendenon on Apr 23, 1958; addition to Grundy Cemeteries, Vol. 2, p. 633
Smedley, Randall Dean	Feb 26, 1937	Dec 19, 2021	Hamilton Memorial Gardens; Son of George & Hazel Smedley; m. Billie Jo Daughtrey; U.S. Army
Smiley, Buford Ray	Dec 30, 1930	Sep 08, 2015	Cremated; Ashes to Battle Grove Cem. In KY; Son of Cecil & Mildred Florence Smiley; m. Bertha White; US Air Force
Smith Phyllis Gay (Rutledge)	Aug 16, 1962	Nov 16, 2018	Friendship Cem., Campaign; Dau. of Russell Lee Rutledge & Hazel Gladys King;
Smith, Alice Correne	Nov 17, 1943	Sep 13, 2017	Palmer Cem.; Dau. of Leroy & Ollie (Grayson) Sanders
Smith, Andrew C.	1818	1887	Hinton-Guinn Cem.; Son of Jeremiah & Margaret (Bradshaw) Smith; m. Sarah "Sally" Thomas on Apr 5, 1853, in Grundy Co. addition to Cemeteries of Grundy Co., Vol. 1, p. 322
Smith, Anna Carol Smith (Gilliam)	Feb 18, 1939	Aug 07, 2020	Warren "Red Hill" Cem.; Dau. of Martin Grady Gilliam & Anna Ruth Reider; m. Charles Smith
Smith, Betty Carlee (Meeks)	Jun 25, 1929	Dec 15, 2017	Bethel Cem.; Dau. of William Francis "France" & Bettie Izabelle (Sartain) Meeks; m. James Smith; children, James, Teery, Diane, Michelle; addition to Cemeteries of Grundy Co., Vol. 1, p. 67
Smith, Beverly (Johnson)	Jul 24, 1962	Jan 01, 2021	Gregg Cem.; Dau. of Carl & Joyce Johnson; m. Hayden Smith
Smith, Carol Sue	Apr 01, 1962	Sep 15, 2001	Palmer Cem.; Dau. of James Franklin & Shirley Ann (Sanders) Pickett; addition to Cemeteries of Grundy Co. Vol. 2, p. 563
Smith, Charles Dawes, OBGYN	1925	Jun 26, 2013	Fall Creek Cem.; Son of Charles & Minnie (Fults) Smith; Companion-Sue Britnell; USMC
Smith, Claud Everett	Feb 24, 1943	Sep 25, 2020	Brady Keener Family Cem.; Son of Elmer & Gladys (Blaylock) Smith; m. Treva Keener
Smith, David Hulon	Feb 09, 1943	May 26, 2018	Warren "Red Hill" Cem.; Son of John Hulon Smith & Lucille Patterson; m. Katherine Ann Magouirk

Name	Born	Died	Notes
Smith, Della Mai (Pickett)	Dec 31, 1940	Apr 14, 2022	Donated to science; Dau. of Elmer & Irene (Johnson) Pickett; m. Willie Smith
Smith, Dola (Smith)	Oct 21, 1871	Dec 17, 1912	Tracy City Cem.; Dau. of Peter & Irena (Williams) Smith; m. James William "Billie" Smith; addition to Cemeteries of Grundy Co. Vol. 2, p. 850
Smith, Doris F (Sweeton)	Nov 21, 1931	Aug 22, 2020	Dau. of Leonard Lyle Sweeton & Helen Pauline Shrum; m. Carl S. Smith
Smith, Dorothy	May 27, 1929	Feb 26, 2013	Coalmont Cem.; Dau. of Bill & Fannie (Nunley) Myers; m. James O. Smith
Smith, Dorothy Lee (Davis)	Jan 09, 1941	Oct 07, 2021	Altamont Cem.; Dau. of Clarence Edward & Altha Bell (Sims) Davis; m. Franklin Leroy Smith
Smith, Elvie Josie (Norman)	Apr 03, 1900	Oct 27, 1982	Bonny Oak Cem.; Dau. of William Dillard & Rosie (Reed) Norman; m. Loney Leroy Smith; addition to Cemeteries of Grundy Co. Vol. 1, p. 80
Smith, Frank Hayden, Jr.	Mar 19, 1960	Feb 13, 2015	Cremated; Son of Frank & Lorene Smith; m. Beverly Hayden
Smith, Franklin Leroy	Oct 10, 1949	Mar 05, 2018	Altamont Cem.; Son of Cleo Edward Smith & Betty Jane; m. Dorothy Lee Davis; US Army
Smith, Freddie Eugene	Feb 02, 1956	Jul 31, 2016	Fall Creek Cem.; Son of Elvin Franklin Smith & Beulah Bell Robertson
Smith, George Robert	Dec 04, 1954	Feb 16, 2015	Cremated; Son of George and Thelma (Jordan) Smith; m. Vicki Trussell
Smith, Gladys Luella (Blaylock)	Nov 30, 1909	Dec 21, 1988	Fall Creek Cem.; Dau. of William Nathaniel & Sarah Harrison (Savage) Blaylock; m. Elmer Elbert Smith
Smith, Harlie Ophelia	Jun 06, 1903	Jan 30, 1963	Plainview Cem.; Dau. of Bailey & Lou Ada (Myers) Haynes; m. Polete Smith; addition to Cemeteries of Grundy Co, Vol. 2, p. 697
Smith, Helen Melton	Dec 28, 1941	Nov 11, 1996	Clouse Hill Cem.; Dau. of Henry W. & Lucille A. (Smith) Melton; m. Bobby Smith; addition to Cemteries of Grundy Co, Vol. 1, p. 153
Smith, Henry L.	Nov 12, 1851	Jul 08, 1926	Bonny Oak Cem.; Son of Davis S. & Lucy (McDaniel) Smith; m. Nancy Ann Williams, Nov 26, 1872; addition to Cemeteries of Grundy Co. Vol. 1, p. 80
Smith, J. T.	Mar 4, 1877	Mar 22, 1951	Coalmont Cem.; Son of John Wesley & Martha H. (Patterson) Smith; m. Rebecca Seagroves
Smith, James Alfred	Mar 07, 1924	Jul 16, 1967	Coalmont Cem.; Son of James Francis & Halle (Parsons) Smith
Smith, James Francis	Jul 27, 1900	Oct 18, 1955	Hobbs Hill Cem.; Son of Virgil & "Maggie" Mary M. (Phipps) Smith; m. Hallie Marie Parsons; no tombstone; information from death certificate.

Smith, James O.	Aug 29, 1926	Nov 06, 2017	Coalmont Cem.; Son of Oscar & Thelma (Meeks) Smith; m. Dorothy Smith
Smith, James Oscar	Jun 19, 1902	Oct 18, 1967	Coalmont Cem.; Son of James Thomas & Rebecca Eller (Seagroves) Smith; m. Thelma Meeks; correction to Cemeteries of Grundy County, Vol. 1, p. 175
Smith, James William "Billie"	Mar 10, 1858	Jul 29, 1923	Tracy City Cem.; Son of John & Mary (Berry) Smith; m. Dola Smith; addition to Cemeterites of Grundy Co. Vol. 2, p. 850
Smith, Janie Ellen (Tate)	Jun 27, 1904	Mar 23, 1958	Monteagle Cem.; Dau. of Elijah Duncan "Dunk" & Mary Kelly (Bible) Tate; m. Thomas Jefferson Smith, Sr.; addition to Cemeteries of Grundy Co, Vol. 1, p. 446
Smith, Jasper Stephens	ca 1847	Jan 14, 1931	Summerfield Cem.; Son of John & Elizabeth (Davidson) Smith; father born in Missouri; no tombstone
Smith, Jimmy Ray	Mar 08, 1935	Apr 06, 2014	Providence Cem: Son of John Hulon & Lucille (Patterson) Smith; m. Jackie Sanders
Smith, Joseph Wayne	Apr 20, 1941	Mar 31, 2017	Plainview Cem.; Son of Herman & Betty Smith; m. Lucy Ola Hobbs
Smith, Josephine Flora Mae "Josie" (Sargent)	Feb 13, 1882	Mar 21, 1953	Monteagle Cem.; Dau. of George & Melinda (McBee) Sargent; m. William Augustus "Will" Smith; addition to Cemeteries of Grundy Co. Vol. 1, p. 463
Smith, Kathleen L (Sweeton)	Aug 20, 1924	Nov 27, 2017	Palmer Cem.; Dau. of Albert "Hatchet" & Alice Mae (Sanders) Sweeton; m. Richard Benson Smith; addition to Cemeteries of Grundy Co. Vol. 2, p. 553
Smith, Ken	Apr 09, 1945	Jun 24, 2016	Hunerwadel Cem.; Son of Vernon & Catherine (Reece) Smith; m. Judy King
Smith, Lewis Lincoln	Nov 05, 1919	Jan 26, 1967	Fall Creek Cem.; Son of Frank & Beulah Bell (Black) Smith; m. Hazel Bell Tate
Smith, Lillie Kathleen	Aug 20, 1924	Nov 27, 2017	Palmer Cem.; Dau. of Albert & Alice Mae Sanders Sweeton; m. Richard Benson Smith
Smith, Margaret	Feb 28, 1920	Mar 23, 2008	Swiss Colony Cem: Dau. of Victor Lee & Ruby (Jones) Swindell Smith; m. Henry Stampfli; She is actually buried in White Co. TN; addition to Cemeteries of Grundy Co. Vol. 2, p. 785
Smith, Margaret Jane Spearman	Ca 1850	Sep 27, 1938	Monteagle Cem.; Dau. of Joseph & Martha (Aylor) Bradshaw; from death certificate; no monument. Addition to Cemeteries of Grundy County, Vol II.
Smith, Mary Clementine "Tine" (Gallagher)	Jul 09, 1926	Aug 13, 2020	Franklin Memorial Gardens; Dau. of Joseph Edmund Gallagher & Aubrey Patton; m. Roy W. Smith, Jr.

Name	Birth	Death	Details
Smith, Mary Magdalene "Maggie" (Phipps)	1877		Hobbs Hill Cem.; Dau. of John & Martha (Dickerson) Phipps; m. Virgil L. Smith on Dec 25, 1895; addition to Cemeteries of Grundy Co., Vol. 1, p. 337
Smith, Mildred Ann (Gass)	Sep 10, 1934	Mar 12, 2013	Warren "Red Hill" Cem.; Dau. of Jerry & Bessie Gass m.1) Charles D. Knott 2) George Alex Smith
Smith, Minnie Colleen	May 03, 1959	Sep 03, 2017	Altamont Cem (cremated); Dau. of Vernie Prater Smith & Lydia (Jones) Smith Tate; m. Michael Childers
Smith, Otto Wilson	Sep 11, 1911	Apr 22, 1991	Palmer Cem.; Son of John Wesley & Manerva "Minnie" (Nunley) Smith; m. Mattie Lillian Anderson; addition to Cemeteries of Grundy Co. Vol. 2, p. 563
Smith, Rosa Lawrence	Oct 12, 1878	Dec 8, 1899	Laxson Cem.; Dau. of John Elijah M. & Nancy Catheriene (Braadshaw) Smith; remove "probably" from entry; Vol. 1, p. 360
Smith, Roy William III	Jul 07, 1947	Apr 04, 2022	Franklin Memorial Gardens Cem.; Son of Roy William, Jr. & Mary Clementine "Tine" (Gallagher) Smith
Smith, Russell Wayne	Oct 25, 1967	Oct 02, 2020	Swiss Colony Cem.; Son of Herbert Chester & Wanda (Borne) Smith
Smith, Sam Charles	May 20, 1929	Oct 11, 2020	Warren "Red Hill" Cem: Son of Sam & Thelma (Patterson) Smith; m. Nelena Gunn; addition to Cemeteries of Grundy Co. Vol. 2, p. 955
Smith, Samuel	Jul 10, 1944	Mar 31, 2021	Fall Creek Cem.; Son of Elvin & Beulah (Robinson) Smith; m. Wanda Faye Anderson
Smith, Sarah "Sally" (Thomas)	1836	1882	Hinton-Guinn Cem.; Dau. of James & Marinda (Walker) Thomas; See Hinton-Guinn Cem.; Cemeteries of Grundy Co. Vol. 1, p. 322
Smith, Steven Dee	Jul 07, 1978	Apr 05, 2003	Orange Hill Cem.; Son of William D. & Debra L. (Hargis) Guyear Smith; correction to Cemeteries of Grundy Co., Vol. 2, p. 523
Smith, Susan Ann (Kirby)	Oct 30, 1950	Aug 16, 2017	Armstrong Cem.; Dau. of E.B. & Rebecca (Woodlee) Smith; m. James B. Smith
Smith, Taylor V.	1874	Sep 30, 1909	Tracy City; Killed by falling slate in mine at Flat Branch– newspaper Son of James & Susan Smith
Smith, Thelma (Patterson)	Jan 15, 1906	Jun 13, 1987	Warren "Red Hill" Cem.; Dau. of Daniel M. & Annie (Jacobs) Patterson; m. Sam Smith; addition to Cemeteries of Grundy Co, Vol. 2, p. 945
Smith, Thelma Jewel "Nana" (Shipley)	Mar 11, 1942	Oct 18, 2003	Palmer Cem.; Dau. of Elmer T. & Velma L. (Higgins) Shipley; m. C. Leroy Smith; addition to Cemeteries of Grundy Co., Vol. 2, p. 568

Name	Born	Died	Details
Smith, Thomas Jefferson, Sr.	Mar 27, 1903	Apr 15, 1966	Monteagle Cem.; Son of John Wesley "West" & Annie Gay (Rollins) Smith; m. Janie Ellen Tate; addition to Cemeteries of Grundy Co. Vol. 1, p. 446
Smith, Vaughn W.	May 23, 1917	Aug 15, 1997	Cumberland Heights Cem.; Son of Clyde I & Hazel (Cribbs) Smith; Cpl US Army WWII; addition to Cemeteries of Grundy Co. Vol. 1, p. 197
Smith, Wayne "Speedy"	Oct 09, 1935	Aug 30, 2017	Cremated; Son of Thomas Lee "Polite" & Harlie Ophelia (Haynes) Smith
Smith, Willard T	May 16, 1942	Sep 09, 2013	Cremated/Tate Family Cem. Martin Springs; Son of Thomas & Jane Ellen (Tate) Smith; m. Reta Smith; US Army
Smith, William Dee "Buster"	May 31, 1946	Mar 10, 2015	Monteagle Cem.; Son of William Douglas & Beatrice Smith; m. Audrey Lola Smith; U.S. Army
Smoker, Katie Lapp	Jul 06, 1917	May 19, 2017	Cumberland Memonite Fellowship Cem.; Dau of Reuben & Anna (Lapp) Smoker
Snider, Pernell	Jun 14, 1962	Aug 01, 2020	Clouse Hill Cem.; Son of Harvey & Ruth Dodd; m. Tina Snider
Snowberger, Robby	Dec 30, 1965	Feb 01, 2020	Cremated; Son of Robert & Marie Snowberger
Sons, Mary Ann (Griffin)	Jan 08, 1946	Jan 09, 2017	Cremated: Dau. of Ples Hugh & Wanda Lee (Daniel) Griffin; m. Floyd Eugene Sons
Speegle, Alfred Newton, Jr.	1931	1947	Pigeon Springs Cem.; Son of Alfred Newton, Sr. & Bessie (Birdwell) Speegle
Speegle, Bonell	1928	1929	Pigeon Springs Cem.; Son of Alfred Newton, Sr. & Bessie (Birdwell) Speegle
Speegle, Donald Lyle	Jul 24, 1957	Jan 18, 2020	Monteagle Cem.; Son of Kenneth Speegle & Betty Kilgore
Spence, Billie (Thomas)	Aug 09, 1926	Jun 28, 2013	Cremated; Dau. of Victor J. & Lois (Smith) Thomas; m. Jack Spence, Jr.
Spencer, Atisha Darlene (Roberts)	Aug 12, 1971	Dec 07, 2020	Altamont Cem.; Dau. of Roger & Phyllis Diane (Dotson) Roberts; m. Roger Dale Spencer
Spencer, Lizzie (Adcock)	Feb 05, 1905	Apr 12, 1923	Hobbs Hill Cem.; Dau. of William & Louise J. Adcock; no tombstone
Spry, Gladys B (Dalt)	Dec 07, 1948	Jan 29, 2021	Cremated: Dau of Timothy Dalt & Lois Brymer; m. 1) Raymond Lawson 2) Michael Spry, Sr.
Stampfli, Elise (Stebler)	ca 1899	May 11, 1932	Swiss Colony Cem.; Dau. of Rudolf & Elisabeth (Kenti) Stebler; m. Ernest Stampfli; addition to Cemeteries of Grundy Co. Vol. 2, p. 788
Stampfli, Ernest	Sep 24, 1889	Jan 30, 1959	Swiss Colony Cem.; Son of Christian & Marie (Aeschlimann) Stampfli; m. 1) Elise Stebler 2) Julia Cleo Luchsinger

Name	Birth	Death	Notes
Stampfli, Linda (Brashears)	Feb 04, 1945		Swiss Colony Cem.; Dau. of Hazel Brashears; m. Stephen H. Stampfli
Stark, Jeremy Lindell (Brown)	Sep 23, 2021	Dec 18, 2021	Coalmont Cem.; Son of Katy Lynn Stark and Jeremy Brown
Starling, Alexander	Ca 1938	Before 1910	Monteagle Cem.; Son of John & Celia (Long) Starling; m. Margaret Turner on Nov 21, 1857; no stone
Starling, Margaret (Turner)	Ca 1938	Feb 14, 1915	Monteagle Cem.; Dau. of David & Elizabeth Turner; m, Alexander Starling; no stone
Starling, Roy Venson	Apr 28, 1930	Jan 07, 1963	Monteagle Cem.; Son of Scott & Della Mae (Tate) Starling; m. Esther Shrum; correction to Cemeteries of Grundy Co., Vol. 1, p. 412
Starr, Robert Allen	Feb 24, 1965	May 22, 2015	Starr Family Cem.; Son of Robert & Laura Starr; m. Brandie Starr
Statler, Catherine (Spencer)	Dec 19, 1938	Feb 11, 2000	Hunerwadel Cem.; Dau. of Ernest & Floy (Fyke) Spencer; m. 1) David Clark Statler 2) Anthony Trabue Statler; buried elsewhere; addition to Cemeteries of Grundy Co., Vol. 1, p. 344
Statler, David Clark, Sr.	Dec 17, 1893	May 16, 1987	Hunerwadel Cem.; Son of Lowry W. & Jessica (DeCamp) Statler; m. Lucinda Bryan Trabue, 1924 in Beersheba Springs; addition to Cemeteries of Grundy Co. Vol. 1, p. 344
Statler, Lucinda Bryan (Trabue)	1902	1985	Hunerwadel Cem.; Dau. of William D. & Lucinda (O'Bryan) Trabue; m. David Clark, Sr. Statler; addition to Cemeteries of Grundy Co., Vol. 1, p. 344
Stearns, Helen Lucretia (Bryant)	1860	Apr 27, 1937	Swiss Colony Cem.; Dau. of Seth S. & Catherine (Annin) Bryant; m. Charles W.A. Stearns; addition to Cemeteries of Grundy Co. Vol. 2, p. 788
Steele, Edna Loretta	Dec 05, 1931	Feb 22, 1993	Bonny Oak Cem.; Dau. of Lillard & Gladys E. (Caldwell) Sweeton; m. 1) Robert Wayne Steele 2) Carl C. Pyburn; addition to Cemeteries of Grundy Co. Vol. 1, p. 83
Steele, Justin "Butch"	Jan 07, 1963	Apr 25, 2013	Summerfield Cem.; Son of Loretta Sweeton; m. Connie Steele
Steele, Michael Phillip	Sep 24, 1951	Jul 28, 2021	Cremated; Son of Roland Edwin & Louise Marie (Miller) Steele
Steele, W. Della	Mar 04, 1930	Jun 21, 2008	Altamont Cem.; Dau. of James Ricey & Maggie (Smith) Price; m. Donald P. Steele; addition to Cemeteries of Grundy Co, Vol. 1, p. 15
Steen, Paul David	Mar 06, 1931	Nov 05, 2005	Cumberland Heights Cem.; Son of James Daniel & Wilma Esther (Lilliebridge) Steen; US Army; addition to Cemeteries of Grundy Co, Vol. 1, p. 198

Name	Born	Died	Notes
Stegemoller, Marlys Annette	May 24, 1952	Oct 24, 2017	Cremated; Dau. of Delno & Carrie Bolinger; m. 1) Steven Wayne Melton 2) _____ Stegemoller
Steiner, Cynthia Louise (Littell)	Nov 15, 1958	Jun 24, 2014	Plainview Cem.; Dau of Dr. Charles & Sue Littell; m. Eric Steiner
Steiner, Max	Dec 01, 1904	Jan 15, 2003	Hunerwadel Cem.; b.in Arbon, Switzerland; m. Alice Hunerwadel on Dec. 13, 1931; addition to Cemeteries of Grundy Co. Vol. 1, p. 344
Stephens, Betty (Scott)	Mar 15, 1892	Mar 26, 1969	Summerfield Cem.; Dau. of William & Jane Scott; correction to Cemeteries of Grundy County, Vol. 2, p. 763
Stephens, Mollie Clarise (Thurman)	May 31, 1935	Jan 12, 2016	Bailey Cem.; Dau. of James & Ruby (Spears) Thurman; m. 1) Grover Evans 2) Mancel Eugene Stephens
Stevens, Billy Ray	Jul 17, 1954	Sep 22, 2020	Cowan Montgomery Cem.; Son of Billy & Virginia (Elliott) Stevens; m. Patricia Stevens
Stevens, Bruce Howard, Jr. "Tadpole"	Dec 05, 1977	Sep 05, 2013	Altamont Cem.; Son of Bruce Howard, Sr. & Donna (Tate) Stevens; m. Christy Guire
Stevens, Elise (Campbell)	1954	Feb 03, 2022	Dau. of Cedric & Ruth (Walker) Campbell; m. 1) Larry Carrick 2) Sam Stevens
Stevens, Foster	Mar 05, 1905	Dec 01, 1991	Oak Grove Cem.; Son of Ab & Belle Stevens; m. Ethel Crowe; Feb 29, 1926; addition to Cemeteries of Grundy Co., Vol. 1, p. 511
Stevens, Henry Taylor	Dec 13, 1926	Mar 18, 2016	Cremated; Son of Foster & Ethel (Crowe) Stevens
Stevens, Hollie Maria (Johnson)	Sep 30, 1982	Jan 21, 2021	Coalmont Cem.; Dau. of Milton L "Rudy" & Jan Johnson; m. Willy Stephens
Stevens, Kathryn (Buckout)	Dec 12, 1921	Oct 14, 2013	Cumberland Heights Memorial Gardens; Dau. of John and Dorothy (Perry) Buckout; m. George Sheldon Stevens
Stevens, Lawandel Celina	Nov 05, 1974	Jun 09, 1976	Altamont Cem.; Dau. of Bruce Howard & Donna Ruth (Tate) Stevens; addition to Cemeteries of Grundy Co., Vol. 1, p. 24
Stevens, Mary Jean (Nunley)	Feb 12, 1933	Jul 11, 1997	Bonny Oak Cem.; Dau. of Alvin Murphy & Esther (Lockhart) Nunley; addition to Cemeteries of Grundy Co., Vol. 1, p. 87
Stevens, Nellie (Disheroon)	Jun 07, 1915	Jul 04, 1995	Bonny Oak Cem.; Dau. of Holis & Edna (Haynes) Disheroon; m. William Howard Shelton; addition to Cemeteries of Grundy Co. Vol. 1, p. 87
Stevens, Sam	1959	Nov 15, 2015	Summerfield Cem.; Son of Susie Stevens; m.1) Georgia Lee Stevens 2. Elise Stevens
Stevenson, James	ca 1841	May 13, 1873	Tracy City Cem.; Son of James & Hannah (Thompson) Stevenson; m. Mary E. Leeman in Nov of 1869; addition to Cemeteries of Grundy Co, Vol. 2, p. 905

Name	Birth	Death	Details
Stewart, Anton Galus	Jul 24, 1951	Oct 27, 2013	Altamont Cem.; Son of Anton Adam and Nadine (Brookshire) Stewart; US Air Force
Stewart, Bennie Frances (Hill)	Sep 16, 1929	Mar 19, 2017	Hunerwadel Cem.; Dau. of Marcus & Robbye (Hobbs) Hill
Stewart, Edna Marie	Dec 11, 1930	Dec 22, 1952	Fall Creek Cem.; Dau. of Harvey & Flora Mae (Glisson) Stewart
Stewart, Jesse Lafayette	Apr 28, 1852	Feb 12, 1906	Tracy City Cem.; Son of Absolom C. & Evaline (Dewitt) Stewart; m. Mary Louise Ashley; addition to Cemeteries of Grundy Co. Vol. 2, p. 839
Stewart, John William	May 13, 1926	Jun 18, 2021	Palmer Cem.; Son of Harvey & Flora Mae (Glisson) Stewart; m. Johnnie Ruth Smith; U.S. Army
Stewart, Johnnie Ruth	Feb 11, 1930	Jan 17, 2017	Palmer Cem.; Dau. of Rev. John & Minnie (Nunley) Smith; m. J.W. Stewart
Stewart, Linsey Kevin	Feb 01, 1953	Mar 29, 2016	Hunerwadel Cem.; Son of Frank & Allene (Ames) Stewart; m. Regina Knight
Stewart, Mildred Jewell (Nunley)	Jan 30, 1931	Jan 26, 2020	Fall Creek Cem.; Dau. of Charles E. Nunley & Carrie Parson; m. Harvey Stewart
Stiefel, Alma Jewel (Haynes)	Jan 29, 1928	Jan 07, 2019	Plainview Cem.; Dau. of Carl E. Haynes & Martha Ethel Meeks; m. Eule Stiefel
Stiefel, Barry Keith	Sep 18, 1951	Feb 11, 2020	Plainview Cem.; Son of Eule & Alma Stiefel; m. Nelda Carrick
Stiefel, Betty Louise (Christian)	May 01, 1945	Mar 15, 2022	Plainview Cem.; Dau. of Otto & Katherine (King) Christian; m. Billy Stiefel
Stiefel, Dorothy Louise (Harris)	Jun 10, 1936	Jul 04, 2014	Plainview Cem.; Dau of Robert Edward Harris, Sr. & Ella Ada Manley; m. Roy L. Stiefel
Stiefel, Eddie Brian	Nov 09, 1978	Feb 22, 1997	Burns Cem.; Son of Eddie Darnell & Donna (Harris) Stiefel
Stiefel, Eule Henry	Jun 10, 1923	Feb 19, 2019	Plainview Cem.; Son of H.A. Stiefel & Vircie Yates; m. Alma Jewel Haynes
Stiefel, Helen Ruth (Sanders)	Apr 02, 1928	Jan 03, 2019	Plainview Cem.; Dau. of William Wallace Sanders & Bobbie Hester Gibbs; m. Ray Stiefel
Stiefel, Roy Leonard	Feb 14, 1934	Jan 25, 2022	Plainview Cem.; Son of Harvey A. & Vircie (Yates) Stiefel; m. Dorothy Stiefel
Stiefel, Wendell	Oct 20, 1953	Sep 09, 2016	Burkett's Chapel; Son of Eule & Alma Stiefel; Kathy Bivens
Stocker, James Earl	Dec 07, 1937	Dec 31, 2019	Son of Alfred & Norma Stocker; m. Betty Scott
Stocker, Joseph	Mar 19. 1843	Nov 18, 1908	Swiss Colony Cem.; Son of Joseph & Anna Maria Josepha (Meyer) Stocker; m. Maria "Mary" Amacher or Ackermann (appears both spellings in records); US Army & served as a musician; correction & addition to Cemeteries of Grundy Co, Vol. 2, p. 785

Name	Birth	Death	Notes
Stocker, Joseph Albert	Apr 23, 1899	Oct 2, 1970	Fall Creek Cem.; Son of Joseph Jacob & Katherine (Andregg) Stocker; m. Irma Weaver
Stocker, Joseph Jacob	Jun 17, 1870	Feb 16, 1955	Fall Creek Cem.; Son of Joseph & Maria (Amacher or Ackerman) Stocker; m. Katherine Andregg
Stocker, Leon, Sr.	Oct 2, 1832	Mar 9, 1887	Swiss Colony Cem.; Son of Joseph & Anna Maria Josepha (Meyer) Stocker; m. Philomena Myers; addition to Cemeteries of Grundy Co, Vol. 2, p. 785
Stocker, Lewis Russell	May 02, 1944	May 20, 2018	Fall Creek Cem.; Son of Alfred Louis Stocker & Norma Sitz
Stocker, Maria "Mary" (Ackerman)	Aug 15, 1844	Apr 31, 1883	Swiss Colony Cem.; Dau. of Joseph Leone Carl & Maria Anna (Thurig) Ackerman; m Joseph Stocker; correction and addition to Cemeteries of Grundy Co, Vol. 2, p. 785
Stocker, Norma Mae (Sitz)	Apr 24, 1915	Apr 04, 2013	Fall Creek Cem.; Dau. of Eddie & Margie Lee (Fletcher) Sitz; m. Alfred Louis Stocker
Stocker, Philomena (Meyer)	Jun 22, 1843	May 21, 1905	Swiss Colony Cem.; Dau. of Joseph & Anna Maria Josepha Meyer; addition and correction of last name to Cemeteries of Grundy Co, Vol. 2, p. 785
Stockton, Hubert O'Neal	Jun 15, 1946	Aug 29, 2007	Coalmont Cem.; Son of James Wesley & Carrie Louellen (Jones) Stockton
Stockwell, Lewis Calvin	Sep 1, 1861	Jun 17, 1903	Unidentified Cem.; source *Mrs. Grundy Jun 25, 1903*
Stockwell, Linda Kay (Meeks)	May 11, 1948	Feb 02, 2015	Stockwell Cem.; Dau. of Buford & Nadine (Meeks) Ross; m. David Stockwell
Stoglin, Barbara Francine	Mar 24, 1958	Mar 24, 2019	Plainview Cem.; Dau. of Clyde Stoglin & Barbara A. Nunley
Stoker, Jacob	1844	1916	Swiss Colony Cem.; Son of Joseph Stocker (spelled this way); m. Margaret Brechtelabauer; addition to Cemeteries of Grundy Co, Vol. 2, p.784
Stone, Bentley Randolph	Apr 19, 1882	Sep 01, 1966	Altamont Cem.; Son of John & Nancy Stone; m. Brittanie Tanner; addition to Cemeteries of Grundy Co. Vol. 1, p. 27
Stone, Beulah Jane (Cupp)	May 02, 1923	Aapr 23, 2011	Altamont Cem.; Dau. of Henry Elbert & Beulah Frances (Patterson) Cupp; m. Banster Lee Stone, Jul 4, 1945; addition to Cemeteries of Grundy Co., Vol. 1, p. 22
Stone, Linda Jean (Hobbs)	Nov 01, 1949	May 17, 2020	Fults Cem.; Dau. of Dorsey Hobbs & Lois Joean Walker
Stoner, Andrew J.	Jun 12, 1886	Apr 16, 1895	Stoner Cem at Stella Bottom/Dry Shave; Son of John & Susan (Nunley) Stoner; struck by lightning

Name	Birth	Death	Notes
Stoner, John	1847	Jan 31, 1890	Stoner Cem at Stella Bottom; Son of William Houston "Bud" & Sarah Stoner; m. Susan A. Nunley; according to death records he is buried in Stoner Cemetery, and we believe this one at Stella Bottom to be the one.
Stoner, Lavina "Vina"	Sep 9, 1800	Jun 24, 1886	Stoner Cem at Stella Bottom/Dry Shave; Dau. of Henry, Jr. & Elizabeth (Wilson) Stoner
Stoner, Samuel M. "Sam"	Apr 1850	Jun 19, 1905	Stoner Cem. at Stella Bottom/Dry Shave; Son of William Houston "Bud" & Sarah "Sally" (Nunley) Stoner; m. Nancy Jane Patrick (1865-1942)
Stoner, William Houston "Bud"	1822	Before 1891	Rural Cem between Cal Place & Easter Knob; near Warren County line; Son of Peter Countiss & Lavinia Stoner
Stotts, Edgar	Jun 3, 1893	Jun 9, 1898	Hobbs Hill Cem.; Son of Monroe & Dea (Fults) Stotts; addition to Cemeteries of Grundy Co. Vol. 1, p. 334
Stotts, Hazel Kathleen	Aug 10, 1928	May 12, 2017	Fall Creek Cem.; Dau. of Calvin B. & Mae (Nunley) Caldwell; m. Sam Leroy Stotts
Stotts, Margie Lou	Mar 14, 1932	Mar 05, 1933	Bonny Oak Cem.; Dau. of Speaker Douglas & Maude Hayes (Hobbs) Stotts; addition to Cemteries of Grundy Co. Vol. 1, p. 79
Stotts, Speaker Douglas	Sep 18, 1894	May 26, 1985	Bonny Oak Cem.; Son of Benjamin Franklin & Rose Anna (Nunley) Stotts; **USMC, WWI**; addition to Cemeteries of Grundy Co. Vol. 1, p. 83
Stranahan, Richard "Squeak" Gipson, Jr.	Jan 03, 1954	Aug 10, 2015	Cremated; Son of Robert Carl Webster & Doris Webster per obituary
Tate, Lloyd Eugene	Jan 24, 1929	Jan 05, 2001	Warren "Red Hill" Cem.; cremated; Son of Lloyd Eugene & Stella Gertrude (Gephart) Tate, Sr.; m. Anna Dell Warren; died in NH.
Stubblefield, Walter	Jul 18, 1867	May 13, 1962	Fall Creek Cem.; Son of Parry Stubblefield & Nancy Davis; m. Zora Stubblefield; no tombstone; information from death certificate
Studer, August	Jul 29, 1852	Oct 20, 1881	Swiss Colony Cem.; Son of Benedict & Elisabeth (Gruetter) Studer; m. 1) Mary Agatha Studer 2) possibly Rebecca F. Douglas; correction of birth & death dates & addition to Cemeteries of Grundy Co. Vol. 2, p. 784
Stump, May	Feb 19, 1873	Feb 13, 1947	Altamont Cem.; page 13 Grundy County Cemetery book addition per informant
Stump, William Michael	May 23, 1858	Oct 24, 1942	Oak Grove Cem.; Son of Michael G. & Susanah (Armstrong) Stump; m.1) Luticia Overturf 2) Senie Tate; addition to Cemeteries of Grundy Co, Vol. 1, p. 504
Sublett, Patrick M.	Jan 18, 1952	Feb 09, 2022	Cremated; Son of R. B. & Avis Elizabeth (Gilliam) Sublett, Jr.; m. Megan M. Campbell

Name	Birth	Death	Notes
Sullivan, Martha Laverne (Keener)	Jul 04, 1940	Sep 13, 2013	Brown's Chapel Cem.; Dau. of Lee Henderson & Icie Lou (Fults) Keener; m. 1) Carl Edward Borne 2) Sammy Sullivan
Sullivan, Nelma (McGee)	May 18, 1929	Dec 01, 2013	Philadelphia Cem.; Dau. of William Beecher & Ollie (Coppinger) Wanamaker
Summers, Eugene P.	Jan 21, 1867	Apr 12, 1943	Summerfield Cem.; Son of John R. & Selina (Goodman) Sanders; m. Lou Summers; addition; per death certificate
Summers, James Allen	Mar 31, 1890	Sep 30, 1963	Plainview Cem.; Son of John Calvin & Linnie (Ray) Summers; m. Sarah Louise Nunley; TN CPL COHII INFT 5 DIV WWI; addition to Cemeteries of Grundy Co., Vol. 2, p. 686
Summers, Laura Sue (Church)	Ca 1936	Dec 21, 2015	Plainview Cem.; Dau. of John K. & Dosia (Meeks) Church; m. Ray Summers
Summers, Leota	Jun 22, 1938	Dec 11, 2015	Palmer Cem.; Dau. of Robert & Gladys (Barnett) Summers
Summers, Mary E. (Leeman) Stevenson	Jul 15, 1847	May 14, 1891	Tracy City Cem.; wife of 1) James Stevenson 2) M.F. Summers; addition to Cemeteries of Grundy Co. Vol. 2, p. 905
Summers, Sarah Louise (Nunley)	Nov 24, 1913	Sep 17, 2007	Plainview Cem.; Dau. of Lee & Hattie (Meeks) Nunley; m. James Allen Summers; addition to Cemeteries of Grundy Co, Vol. 2, p. 686
Summers, Tony Eugene	Jul 23, 1947	Dec 02, 2021	Palmer Cem. ashes; Son of Robert & Gladys (Barnett) Summers; m. Lana Roberts
Sumner, Albert "Bill" III	Sep 10, 1949	Jun 05, 2021	Cremated: Son of Albert William Sumner II & Beverly Sumner; m. Kathleen Sumner
Suter, Helen (Bond)	Nov 04, 1921	Oct 28, 1991	Swiss Colony Cem.; Dau. of Ora Vincent & Essie M (Baggett) Bond; m. Jacob George Suter; addition to Cemeteries of Grundy Co, Vol. 2, p. 791
Suter, Helen Lucille (Bond)	Nov 04, 1921	Oct 28. 1991	Swiss Cemetery; Dau. of Ora Vincent & Essie Mae (Baggett) Bond; m. Jacob George Suter
Suter, Mary (Ley)	Mar 5, 1887	Dec 27, 1957	Fall Creek Cem.; Dau. of William & Merlin Maria (Venhorst) Ley; m. Leonhard Suter
Sutherland, Catherine Patricia (Brown)	1957	Oct 07, 2017	Cremated; Dau. of John & Janie Brown; m. Mike Sutherland
Sutherland, Jackie Ray "Shotgun"	ca 1947	Feb 11, 2013	Cremated; Son of Eli & Maggie Ball per obituary; m. Debbie Sutherland
Sutherland, Linda Carolyn (King)	Apr 06, 1948	Jan 17, 2019	Cremated: Dau. of Eugene King & Ovie Martin; m. Gary Sutherland
Swallen, Lloyd Calvin	Apr 2, 1891	Apr 16, 1975	Monteagle Cem.; Son of Albert & Martha (Magnus) Swallen; m. Bessie A. Cotton; correction to Cemeteries of Grundy County, Vol. 1, p. 446

Swaney, Barry Ray	Jan 02, 1979	Jan 02, 1979	Altamont Cem.; Son of Richard & Cynthia (Sanders) Swaney rather than Harold Moore & Anna M. (Garland) Swaney who are the grandparents; Correction of parents' names in Cemeteries of Grundy Co, Vol. 1, p. 16
Swaney, Harold Monroe	Sep 16, 1930	Sep 02, 2002	Altamont Cem.; Son of Charlie & Nora (Costner) Swaney; m. Anna M. Garland; correction to middle name & addition to Cemeteries of Grundy Co, Vol. 1, p. 16
Sweeton, Abbie D. (Brown)	Mar 10, 1881	Jul 15, 1957	Hobbs Hill Cem.; Dau. of Russell Lester & Elizabeth (Tate) Brown
Sweeton, Allen	No dates	Infant burial	Bonny Oak Cem.; Son of Anthony "Yant" & Ruth (Richmond) Sweeton; no marker; information from family
Sweeton, Bessie	Oct 1898	Auag 2, 1918	Bonny Oak Cem.; Dau. of J.K. & Minerva Nunley; m. Will Sweeton; no marker; addition to Cemeteries of Grundy Co., Vol. 1, p. 96
Sweeton, Betty Jean (Campbell)	Aug 05, 1939	Jul 21, 2014	Wesley Chapel Cem.; Dau. of Orville & Johnnie Ruth (Robinson) Campbell; m. Elmer Rolston Sweeton; addition death date to Cemeteries of Grundy Co, p. 963
Sweeton, Beverly Ann (Tate)	Jul 28, 1937	Jan 22, 2020	Monteagle Cem: Dau. of Ransom Tate & Mary Emma Sampley; m. Danville Sweetona
Sweeton, Bobby Clark	Jun 09, 1957	Oct 03, 2012	Wesley Chapel Cem.; Son of Elmer Rolston & Betty Jean (Campbell) Sweeton; addition to Cemeteries of Grundy Co., Vol. 2, p. 985
Sweeton, Carl Wayne	Feb 05, 1939	Jan 04, 2022	Red Hill Cemetery; Son of Albery Flury & Alice Mae Sweeton; m. Barbara Colston
Sweeton, Charles Parker	Nov 3, 1873	Jan 26, 1942	Hobbs Hill Cem.; Son of William Howard & Tampico (Nunley) Sweeton; m. Abbie D. Brown
Sweeton, Cynthia Elizabeth	May 13, 1910	Apr 19, 1972	Hobbs Hill Cem.; Dau. of Charles Parker Sweeton & Abigail D. Brown
Sweeton, Danville Milton	Mar 01, 1934	Feb 05, 2016	Cremated; Son of Anthony Emmett Yancy & Ruth (Anders) Sweeton; m. Beverly Sweeton; US Air Force
Sweeton, Dottie (Cunningham)	Jun 25, 1934	Dec 25, 1984	Plainview Cem.; Dau. of Edward Cunningham & Carolyn (Rager) Thompson; m. J.C. Sweeton; addition to Cemeteries of Grundy Co., Vol. 2, p. 690
Sweeton, Ed Wilson	Sep 15, 1928	Sep 03, 2013	Plainview Cem.; Son of Albert F. & Alice Mae (Sanders) Sweeton; m. Virginia Ruth Terry
Sweeton, Edd	1869	1964	Bonny Oak Cem.; Son of Isaac & Mary Jane "Polly" (Sanders) Sweeton; m. Victoria Salina "Vic" Crabtree; addition to Cemeteries of Grundy Co. Vol. 1, p. 83

Name	Born	Died	Details
Sweeton, Edith "Tabby" (Layne)	Feb 15, 1918	Nov 02, 2013	Altamont Cem.; Dau. of Hence & Rosa (Fults) Layne; m. Ernest Sweeton; addition to Cemeteries of Grundy Co., Vol, 1, p.22
Sweeton, Francis Moses "Frank"	Oct 09, 1849	Nov 08, 1918	Bonny Oak Cem: Son of Greenberry & Mosley Minerva (Sullivan) Sweeton; m. Martha Ann Elizabeth Baswell Dau. of John & Mary Caroline (Capehart) Baswell; Francis is a twin to William Sweeton.
Sweeton, Harvey Morgan	Nov 25, 1933	Dec 22, 2013	Coalmont Cem.; Son of Lawrence & Margie (Burnett) Sweeton
Sweeton, Helen Marie (Oliver)	Sep 18, 1926	Feb 10, 2019	Chattanooga Memorial Park; Dau. of Emmett & Bessie Oliver; m. Byron Jefferson Sweeton
Sweeton, Irene J. (Shirkey)	Jul 29, 1926	Jan 15, 2010	Bonny Oak Cem: Dau. of Clarence Hampton & Minna Bertha Mathilde (Schroeder) Shirkey; m. 1) Buford Yancy "Dick" Sweeton 2) Roland Elroy Smith; addition to Cemeteries of Grundy Co., Vol. 1, p. 82
Sweeton, Isaac	Jan 12, 1843	Jan 12, 1901	Tracy City Cem.; Son of Robert Isaac & Mary M. (Myers) Sweeton; m. Mary Ann Sanders on Jan 30, 1856; addition to Cemeteries of Grundy Co, Vol. 2, p. 898
Sweeton, James Alton	Mar 23, 1942	Apr 07, 2021	Coalmont Cem.; Son of Lawrence & Margie (Burnett) Sweeton; m. Alice Borne
Sweeton, James Kelvin	Nov 17, 1955	Feb 21, 2015	Hill's Creek Cem.; Son of James Sweeton & Essie Jane Henderson; m. Carolyn Ann Fults
Sweeton, Jerry "Dude"	Sep 07, 1953	Jan 08, 2021	Pryor Ridge Cem.; Son of Byron & Helen Sweeton; m. Tami Sweeton
Sweeton, Jicie (Pendergraff)	May 2, 1881	Apr 13, 1974	Coalmont Cem.; Dau. of Mathy & Mary (Riddle) Pendergraff; correction to Cemeteries of Grundy County, Vol. 1, p. 185
Sweeton, John Henry	Jun 30, 1940	Oct 15, 2012	Bonny Oak Cem.; Son of Robert Bee & Besselene/Bessie Lee (Meeks) Sweeton; m. 1) Bonnie R Sweeton 2) Joyce Stairett
Sweeton, Joseph	Mar 02, 1929	Dec 28, 1881	Altamont Cem.; Son of Robert Isaac & Margaret Sweeton; addition to Cemeteries of Grundy Co. Vol. 1, p. 26
Sweeton, K. Elizabeth (Adams)	Apr 14, 1911	Mar 02, 1997	Hobbs Hill Cem.; Dau. of Charles Francis & Dorothey "Dollie" (Tate) Adams; m. J. Marshall Sweeton; addition to Cemeteries of Grundy Co., Vol. 1, p. 331
Sweeton, Linda Gail (Nunley)	Mar 02, 1948	Oct 01, 2019	Rose Hill Memorial Gardens Cem.; Dau. of Lawrence & Dorothy Nunley; m. John E. Sweeton
Sweeton, Linda K. (Campbell)	Mar 26, 1942	Nov 29, 2019	Cremated; Dau. of Ernest "Pib" Campbell & Jewell Van Hooser; m. Card David Sweeton
Sweeton, Mabel (Hatfield)	Mar 09, 1906	Jun 16, 1947	Bonny Oak Cem.; Dau. of J.H. & Dixie (Lawrence) Hatfield; m. Toy Sweeton

Name	Birth	Death	Details
Sweeton, Martha Ann Elizabeth "Eliza"	Sep 19, 1860	Dec 15, 1945	Grace Chapel Cem.; Dau. of John & Mary Caroline (Capehart) Baswell; m. Francis "Frank" Moses Sweeton who is buried at Bonny Oak. Heavy snow prevented her from being buried at Bonny Oak.
Sweeton, Rachel	No dates	Infant burial	Bonny Oak Cem.; Dau. of Anthony "Yant" & Ruth (Richmond) Sweeton; no stone; information from family
Sweeton, Reba Jane (Smartt)	Feb 17, 1945	Oct 16, 2020	Walker Cem.; Dau. of Aubrey Alfred & Annie Lee (Richardson) Smartt; m. James Avery Sweeton
Sweeton, Regina C. "Reggie"	May 22, 1937		Palmer Cem.; Dau of Vincent & Nellie Kazar from NY; M. Delbert E. Sweeton; addition to Cemeteries of Grundy Co. Vol. 2, p.553
Sweeton, Richard Anthony	Sep 30, 1922	May 08, 2001	Oak Grove Cem.; Son of Anthony "Yant" & Ruth (Richmond) Sweeton; addition to Cemeteries of Grundy Co., Vol. 1
Sweeton, Ronald Lee	May 31, 1956	May 26, 2020	Hobbs Hill Cem.; Son of Carl Wilson Sweeton & Winona McNeese
Sweeton, Ruth (Richmond)	Feb 15, 1893	Feb 11, 1978	Bonny Oak Cem.; Dau. of Masion B. & Harriet Ellen Richmond; m. 1) Jordan "Jerd" Sanders 2) Anthony E. "Yant" Sweeton; addition to Cemeteries of Grundy Co., Vol. 1, p. 82
Sweeton, Samuel Jerry	Dec 16, 1951	Dec 24, 2018	Altamont Cem.; Son of Ernest Sweeton & Edith "Tabby" Layne; m. Jeweldean Bess
Sweeton, Will	1889	Oct 07, 1971	Bonny Oak Cem.; Son of Francis "Frank" Moses & Martha Ann (Baswell) Sweeton; m. Bessie Nunley, June 13, 1916; Cemeteries of Grundy Co.,Vol. 1, p. 77 correction to birth year; twin of Francis Sweeton
Talley, Sadie Irene (Meeks)	Dec 13, 1927	Mar 01, 1980	Coalmont Cem.; Dau. of William H & Hilda (Smith) Meeks
Tankersley, Jerry Clayton	1943	Aug 18, 2018	Rose Hill Memorial Gardens Cem.; Son of Clayton Tankersley & Lena May Scott; m. Melvina Tankersly
Tanner, Rinnia (Turley)	May 19, 1953	Feb 03, 2020	Airview Cem.; Dau. of Ray & Rose (Edwards) Turley; m 1) Luther Farrell Baugh 2) William Lee Tanner; addition to Cemeteries of Grundy Co, Vol. 1, p. 8
Tanner, William Lee	Apr 16, 1939	May 06, 2005	Airview Cem.; Son of Roy & Lois (Wallace) Tanner; addition to Cemeteries of Grundy Co, Vol. 1, p. 8
Tate, Abbie Lillian	Mar 08, 1929	Sep 10, 2019	Richardson Family Cem.; Dau. of Alexander & Mary L. (Tate) King; m. 1) Everett Slatton 2) Roy Rex Tate; children listed on tombstone are Juanita, Clayta, Carl, Howard

Name	Birth	Death	Details
Tate, Alma Jean (Nunley)	Apr 04, 1938	Dec 17 2020	Orange Hill Cem.; Dau. of James & Elva Nunley; m. Bobby Tate
Tate, Alma Lee (Brannon)	Jun 15, 1936	Mar 01, 1990	Fall Creek Cem.; Dau. of Andrew & Martha Brannon
Tate, Anna Dell (Warren)	Mar 15, 1925	Apr 24, 2017	Warren "Red Hill" Cem.; cremated; Dau. of Maurice & Cora (Haynes) Warren; m. Lloyd Eugene Tate; died in Merrimack, NH.
Tate, Annie Frances (Sanders)	Apr 25, 1942	Jul 24, 2022	Philadelphia Cem.; Dau. of Mildred Sanders; m. Morton Willard Tate, Oct 26, 1962; There is a double tombstone for her and her husband; addition to Cemeteries of Grundy Co, Vol. 2, p. 613
Tate, Anthony Lydell	Mar 30, 1958	Nov 04, 2019	Palmer Cem.; Son of Johnny Vernon Tate & Margie King; m. Telsa Turner
Tate, Ben Franklin	Oct 05, 1919	Jan 02, 2006	Palmer Cem.; Son of William & Stella Mae (Hix) Tate; m. Marie Lankford; addition to Cemeteries of Grundy Co., Vol. 2, p. 554
Tate, Bessie Frances (Brown)	Jan 21, 1887	Sep 25, 1970	White Cem.; Dau. of Hezekiah Wesley & Fannie Louise (Smith) Brown; m. George Washington Tate; addition to Cemeteries of Grundy Co. Vol. 2, p. 1008.
Tate, Beulah (Pearson)	Nov 9, 1884	Oct 13, 1960	Cumberland Heights Cem.; Dau. of Roy P. & Ada (Murr) Hart; Paul Maurice Siler in 1985; addition to Cemeteries of Grundy Co. Vol. 1, p. 197
Tate, Billy Ray	Jan 11, 1949	Feb 11, 2020	Bonnie Oak Cem.; Son of Wilford Lynn Clyde Tate & Irene Nunley
Tate, Buford Linuel	Oct 16, 1942	Jan 26, 2021	Fults Cem.; Son of Buford & Sarah (Scott) Tate; m. Mildred Smartt
Tate, Carrie Mary	Oct 16, 1886	Mar 16, 1933	Burkett Chapel Cem.; Dau. of Sam & Elizabeth Catherine (Richmond) Grimes; m. Sam M. Tate; correction of her maiden name; addition to Cemeteries of Grundy Co., Vol. 1, p. 121
Tate, Catherine (Pittman)	Jul 18, 1934	Dec 07, 1990	Palmer Cem.; Dau. of Ralph & Susan (Cock) Pittman; m. Charles A. Tate; b. Labrador, Newfoundland, Canada; addition to Cemeteries of Grundy Co, Vol. 2, p. 555
Tate, Charlene "Nay Nay" (Nunley)	Sep 14, 1964	Aug 20, 2020	Plainview Cem.; Dau. of Louis Nunley & Edna Meeks
Tate, Charles A.	Aug 29, 1934	Jun 30, 1993	Palmer Cem.; Son of Arthur D. "Doc" & Mary J. (Knox) Tate; m. Catherine Pitman; T Sgt. US Air Force in Korea & Vietnam; addition to Cemeteries of Grundy Co, Vol. 2, p. 555
Tate, Child	ca 1904	Feb 21, 1911	Tracy City Cem.; Son of Susannah (Layne) Kitts; source *Mrs. Grundy*, Mar 2, 1911, cause of death, brain fever

Name	Birth	Death	Details
Tate, Clara Ruth	1931	Jun 12, 2016	Tracy City Cem.; Dau. of Graham & Sarah (Cannon) Nunley; m. Bill Holt Tate
Tate, Danny Lee	Mar 08, 1944	Sep 10, 2016	Cremated; Son of Andrew Jackson & Francis (Sitz) Tate; m. Shirley J. Tate
Tate, Darlene Lynda	1958	Nov 19, 2015	Fall Creek Cem.; Dau. of Alton & Elizabeth Tate; m. ____ Little
Tate, David Arthur	Nov 28, 1961	Jan 04, 2017	Cremated; Son of Joe David & Joy Carole (Beam) Tate; m. Julia Tate; US Air Force
Tate, David Edward	Apr 09, 1946	Feb 27, 2022	Clouse Hill Cem.; Son of Buford & Sarah Tate; m. Kathy Tate
Tate, Don Samuel	Aug 15, 1941	Dec 24, 2019	Coalmont Cem.; Son of Harley Tate & Ruby Omalee Meeks; m. Jennie Lee Brown
Tate, Evelyn	Jan 21, 1945	Nov 16, 2019	Cremated; Dau. of Lloyd Tate & Eudora Smart; _____Northcutt
Tate, Florence Hazel "Dolly"	Ca 1930	Sep 15, 2017	Coalmont Cem.; Dau. of Drew & Bessie (Roberts) Campbell; m. Clifford Tate
Tate, Gary Eugene	Jun 02, 1941	Jun 30, 2018	Philadelphia Cem.; Son of Joe Bradford & Katherine Iola Tate
Tate, George W.	Mar 24, 1878	Nov 03, 1948	White Cem in Palmer; Son of Marlon & Mary Tate; m. Bessie F. Tate; correction to Cemeteries of Grundy Co., Vol. 2, p. 1008
Tate, George Washington	Mar 24, 1878	Nov 03, 1948	White Cem.; Son of Francis Marion & Mary Minerva (Burton) Tate; m. Bessie Frances Brown; correction & addition to Cemeteries of Grundy Co, Vol. 2, p. 1008.
Tate, Gerald Wayne	Dec 04, 1957	Jan 02, 2016	Fall Creek Cem.; Son of Harley Cleveland & Joan (Licht) Tate
Tate, Harley Cleveland "H.C."	Aug 08, 1932	Feb 05, 2013	Fall Creek Cem.; Son of Harley & Bessie (Brady) Tate; m. Joan (Fletcher) Licht; US Navy
Tate, James Morton	Mar 19, 1948	Apr 19, 2009	Hunerwadel Cem.; Son of Jasper Joe & Wilsie E. (Hobbs) Tate; correction; m. Nancy Fults-only married to Nancy Fults and not to Elsie Fults as listed in Vol. 1, p. 348
Tate, Jeffery Leon	Sep 12, 1959	Mar 30, 2016	Palmer Cem.; Son of Leon & Willie Mae (Flynn) Tate; m. Patty Reiser
Tate, Jennie Lee (Brown)	May 07, 1948	Feb 24, 2022	Coalmont Cem.; Dau. of Rudolph & Clara Mae (Shadrick) Brown; m. Don Samuel Tate
Tate, Jerry Leavern	Oc 12, 1955	Nov 02, 2021	Hunerwadel Cem.; Son of Juanita Tate Smartt
Tate, Jerry Kenneth	Oct 25, 1943	Aug 02, 2016	Cremated; Son of Jewell & Geraldine (Roberts) Tate; m. Brenda Meeks
Tate, Jerry Leavern, Jr.	Mar 28, 1976	Nov 06, 2020	Cremated; Son of David Glenn & Freda Fay Ward; m. Amanda Tate
Tate, Joe David	Jul 28, 1932	Jan 21, 2015	Palmer Cem.; Son of Arthur D. & Mary J. (Knox) Tate; m. Glenda Sue Tate; U.S. Army Korea

Name	Born	Died	Details
Tate, Kenneth "Tim"	Jun 30, 1949	Jun 02, 2015	O'Dear Cem.; Son of Carl Norwood & Flossie Mae (Wise) Barlund; m. Lisa Tate
Tate, Laura Bell (Layne)	Jun 14, 1940	Dec 06, 2022	Palmer Cem.; Dau. of Franklin Parks & Dixie Lee (Nunley) Layne, Sr.; m. James Wayne Tate; addition to Cemeteries of Grundy Co., p. 574
Tate, Lisa Jane	Oct 30, 1969	Oct 28, 2013	O'Dear Cem.; Du of Thomas Preston King & Mary Elizabeth O'Dear; m. Tim Tate
Tate, Lloyd Eugene	Jan 24, 1929	Jan 05, 2001	Warren "Red Hill" Cem.; cremated; Son of Lloyd Eugene & Stella Gertrude (Gephart) Tate, Sr.; m. Anna Dell Warren; died in NH.
Tate, Marie (Lankford)	Sep 02, 1928	Mar 30, 1978	Palmer Cem.; Dau. of Jacob Henry & Mamie Lee (Cope) Lankford; addition to Cemeteries of Grundy Co., Vol. 2, p. 554
Tate, Mark Anthony	Sep 17, 1965	Sep 04, 2019	Cremated; Son of Alton Tate & Mary Elizabeth Sledge
Tate, Mary Ruth (Smalley)	Jun 14, 1934	Dec 24, 2021	Cremated: Dau. of Ules Lester & Maggie (Powell) Smalley; m. John D "Dink" Tate
Tate, Melissa Ann	maybe 1929	1929 9 mos old	Hobbs Hill; Dau of Sexton Tate & Nora Lee McGown
Tate, Melissa Ann			Fall Creek Cem; no information
Tate, Morton Harrison	Feb 1, 1889	Seo 27, 1909	Hobbs Hill Cem.; Son of Joseph Smith & Susan (Reno) Tate; m. Pearl Parsons; addition to Cemeteries of Grundy Co., Vol. 1, p. 331
Tate, Nancy Catherine (Morrison)	Apr 1, 1860	Feb 19, 1910	Oak Grove Cem.; Dau. of _____; m. Rev. Laden Farrel Tate; addition to Cemeteries of Grundy Co. Vol. 1, p. 501
Tate, Nannie O. (Watts)	Feb 13, 1888	Oct 24, 1946	White Cem.; Dau. of Isham C. & Mary F. (Embry) Watts; m. Walter Hoyt Tate; addition to Cemeteries of Grundy Co. Vol. 2, p. 1007
Tate, Nathaniel J.	1944	1999	Brown's Chapel Cem.; Son of Maudie R. Tate; addition to Cemeteries of Grundy Co. Vol. 1, p. 103
Tate, Ollie "Bug" (Griffith)	Jun 20, 1923	Apr 07, 2020	Griffith Creek Cem.; Dau. of Albert Lee & Maude Bell Griffith; m. Troy H. Tate
Tate, Patsy James (Killian)	Mar 27, 1945	Aug 16, 2019	Schild-Tate Cem.; Dau. of James Henry Killian & Velma Leona Jennings; m. George Lloyd Tate
Tate, Pricilla Christine (Knight)	Jul 29, 1958	Oct 25, 2021	Hunerwadel Cem.; Dau. of William Dennis & Georgia (Nunley) Knight; m. Jerry L. Tate
Tate, Retha Faye	May 30, 1945		Bonnie Oak Cem.; Dau. of John William Jasper & Precious Pearly (Mitchell) Nance; m. 1) Roy Fults 2) Raymond Tate; addition to Cemeteries of Grundy Co. Vol. 1, p. 88
Tate, Richard	Jan 16, 1941	Jan 14, 2021	Fall Creek Cem.; Son of Buford & Sarah (Scott) Tate

Tate, Richard Arlen	Jan 14, 1955	Dec 22, 2011	Little Johnny Myers Cem.; Son of Paul Henderson & Hazel Louise (Campbell) Tate; PVT US Army; addition to Cemeteries of Grundy Co., Vol. 1, p. 367
Tate, Richard Freeman	Jan 16, 1941	Jan 16, 2021	Fall Creek Cem.; Son of Buford & Sarah (Scott) Tate; m. Christine Land
Tate, Roy Evan	Jun 25, 1971		Coalmont Cem.; Son of Clinton Duane & Wanda Louise (Garrard) Tate; m. Oct 24, 1994, Kimberly Rose Johnson; correction to Cemeteries of Grundy Co., Vol. 1, p. 171
Tate, Sallie	Feb 3, 1891	Jul 9, 1891	Burkett Chapel Cem.; Dau. of Preston & Marsilar (Long) Tate; addition to Cemeteries of Grundy Co, Vol. 1, p. 118
Tate, Scottie Dewayne	Apr 21, 1972	Nov 21, 2020	Fall Creek Cem.; Son of Richard & Mary Christine (Land) Tate
Tate, Sharon Lee	Jul 18, 1948	Aug 07, 2013	Altamont Cem.; Dau. of John Robert & Clara Bell (Brown) Tate
Tate, Sheila Kay (Short)	Sep 27, 1954	Oct 11, 2014	Franklin Memorial Gardens; Dau of Billy Ray Short & Beulah Mae Sells; m. Murrell Allen Tate
Tate, Sherman M.	Mar 26, 1950	Sep 22, 2016	Cremated; Son of Buford & Sarah (Scott) Tate; m. Carla Smith
Tate, Wallace Alton	Dec 02, 1929	Mar 20, 2021	Son of Will & Della Mae (Smith) Tate; m. Mary Elizabeth Sledge
Tate, Wallace Brannon	Sep 13, 1906	Mar 01, 1960	Hobbs Hill Cem.; Son of Morton Harrison & Pearl (Parsons) Tate; m. Irene Levean; correction to Cemeteries of Grundy Co. Vol. 1, p. 331
Tate, Willie Mae (Flynn)	Nov 14, 1934	Jun 20, 2015	Palmer Cem.; Dau. of Tony & Mildred (Nunley) Flynn; m. Leon Tate
Taulbee, Eula O'Dessa	Jan 05, 1902	Oct 28, 1986	Plainview Cem.; Dau. of Geroge B. & Arra E. (Dickerson) Highfield; m. Andrew Homer Taulbee; addition to Cemeteries of Grundy Co. Vol. 2, p. 678
Taylor, America Edna	May 15, 1920	Apr 29, 2016	Fall Creek Cem.; Dau. of Francis & Margaret (Bess) Taylor
Taylor, Billy Wade	Sep 07, 1947	Jul 22, 2017	Taylor Family Cem.; Son of Everett Waymon & Martha Edna (Caldwell) Taylor; m. Kim Hill; US Army - Vietnam
Taylor, David Richard	Jun 16, 1944	Aug 06, 2023	Warren "Red Hill" Cem.; Son of Dewey Herbert & Ruby Nell (McCombs) Taylor; m. Janelle (Layne) Coats; Children - Cassandra, Geoffrey, Wesley Taylor; Sgt. US Army; addition and correction to Cemeteries of Grundy Co. Vol. 2, p. 924
Taylor, Easter	1891	Apr 14, 1918	Tracy City Cem.; She was married and was a cook

Name	Birth	Death	Details
Taylor, Grover Gene	Oct 26, 1943	Oct 23, 2018	Rose Hill Memorial Gardens Cem.; Son of Woodrow Wilson Taylor & Dixie Mae Allen; m. Patricia Ann Dickerson; U.S. Army
Taylor, Malcolm Robert	Oct 24, 1913	Jul 14, 1952	Fall Creek Cem.; Son of George & Betty Taylor
Taylor, Patricia Ann	Mar 23, 1946	Nov 30, 2017	Rose Hill Cem.; Dau. of Solly Dee & Eva Ruth Dickerson; m. Gene Taylor
Taylor, Rhonda Fae	Dec 08, 1970	Apr 01, 2022	Cremated, Dau. of Robert Eugene & Rita Taylor; Memorial Services in McMinnville, TN
Taylor, Robert Dean	Aug 25, 1960	Apr 12, 2019	Cremated; Son of Russell Dean Taylor & Juanita Green Shrum; m. Celestine Taylor
Taylor, Virgie		Aug 17, 2013	No information found
Taylor, Waymon Harty "Sonny"	Aug 11, 1941	Oct 05, 2017	Taylor Family Cem.; Son of Everett Waymon & Martha Edna (Caldwell) Taylor; m. Doris Jean Layman
Tell, Tillie Joy	Jul 10, 1948	Nov 13, 2018	Franklin Memorial Gardens Cem.; Dau. of James & Florence Tucker; m. Thomas Tell
Terrill, Billie Faye (Thomas)	Sep 22, 1945	Feb 15, 2021	Cremated: Dau. of Bill & Charline Thomas; m. Billy Terrill
Terrill, Freeland Roy "Coonie"	Aug 17, 1956	Dec 06, 2018	Cremation; Son of Freeland Roy & Irene Terrill; m. Denise Terrill
Terrill, Geraldine (Hill)	Jun 17, 1919	Mar 30, 2014	Eastern Star Cem.; Dau. of Allen & Elizabeth Hill; m. Clyde Terrill
Terry, Bobby Ray, Jr.	Sep 17, 1970	Mar 15, 2021	Pryor Ridge Cem.; Son of Bobby & Sue Terry; m. Lisa Cantrell
Tharp, Mrs. Frank		Sep 21, 1913	Tracy City Cem.; m. Frank Tharp; died at sanatorium in Tracy City; from Mrs. Grundy, Sep. 25, 1913; from *Mrs. Grundy*
Thomas, Alvirn (Dickerson)	Jun 13, 1929	May 01, 2013	Summerfield Cem.; Dau. of Alvin & Elizabeth (Brandon) Dickerson; m. Douglas Thomas
Thomas, Billy French	Feb 14, 1933	Oct 01, 2015	Cremated; Son of Herschel & Ruby (French) Thomas; m. Ann Glover; US Army, Korea
Thomas, Brianna Alisha	Mar 19, 2017	Mar 19, 2017	Monteagle Cem.; Dau. of Chad Thomas & Melissa Jean Henderson
Thomas, Danny Lee	Oct 11, 1960	Jul 06, 2013	Fall Creek Cem.; Son of Mack W. & Hazel Mae Thomas
Thomas, Danny Ray	Mar 23, 1949	Sep 17, 2014	Cremated; Son of Douglas Thomas, Sr. & Marie Dent
Thomas, David William	Apr 26, 1929	Dec 14, 2015	Monteagle Cem.; Son of Charles & Nettie (Holder) Thomas; m. 1) Midge Lockhart 2) Brenda Tucker
Thomas, Donnie Ray	1949	Sep 30, 2017	Clouse Hill Cem.; Son of Charles Ed & Rosa Lee (Kilgore) Thomas; m. Mary Thomas; US Army Vietnam

Name	Born	Died	Notes
Thomas, Frances Marie	Feb 07, 1938	Nov 12, 2017	Palmer Cem.; Dau. of Thomas & Mary Zingale; m. 1) Carl Bailey Shrum 2) Bill Thomas
Thomas, Frank	Oct 02, 1956	Nov 23, 2015	Cumberland View Cem. in Kimball, TN; Son of Robert & Emma (Lockhart) Thomas
Thomas, Hazel Mae (Turner)	Sep 16, 1938	Jul 03, 2018	Fall Creek Cem.; Dau. of Warner Turner & Jessie R. McCormick; m. Mack W. Thomas
Thomas, Helen Ruth	Oct 06, 1942	Oct 07, 1942	Monteagle Cem.; Dau. of Taylor Sam & Marjorie (Meeks) Thomas; Twin to Nannie Ruth Thomas; no stone
Thomas, Jackie Ray	Nov 25, 1953	Sep 03, 2017	Bean's Creek Cem.; Son of Charles & Betty (Brown) Thomas
Thomas, James Arnold	Jan 26, 1909	Oct 01, 1977	Summerfield Cem.; Son of Alan t & Sarah Ann (Trussell) Thomas; addition to Cemeteries of Grundy Co, Vol, 2, p. 765
Thomas, James Carlton	Jul 21, 1922	Nov 30, 2016	Monteagle Cem.; Charlie & Nettie (Holder) Thomas; m. 1) Mae Pearl King 2) June Thomas; Veteran
Thomas, James Carlton	Jul 31, 1922	Nov 30, 2016	Monteagle Cem.; Son of Charlie & Nettie (Holder) Thomas; m.1) Mae Pearl King 2) June Thomas
Thomas, James William "Buddy"	May 18, 1939	Mar 20, 2021	Summerfield Cem.; Son of Robert Jackson & Hazel Mae (Messick) Thomas; m. Patricia Myers
Thomas, Jeff	Apr 21, 1945	Aug 06, 2015	Clouse Hill Cem.; Son of Hamp & Tressie (Meeks) Thomas
Thomas, Jessica F. (Williams)	1913	1971	Summerfield Cem.; Dau. of Pace William & Annie Mae (Linn) Williams; m. James Arnold Thomas on May 27, 1930; addition to Cemeteries of Grundy Co, Vol. 2, p. 765
Thomas, Joshua	Feb 02, 1927	Oct 27, 2019	Sunset Memorial Gardens; Son of Lawrence Thomas; m. Anne Morefield; U.S. Army
Thomas, Junior Boyd	Jun 09, 1933	Aug 20, 2015	Summerfield Cem.; Son of Clarence & Ida E (Layne) Thomas; m. Ava Thomas
Thomas, Katherine (Elliott)	May 15, 1926	Jul 15, 1994	Monteagle Cem.; Dau. of John Witt, Jr. & Flossie (Smith) Elliott; correction of surname & addition to Cemeteries of Grundy Co. Vol. 1, p. 447
Thomas, Kenneth "Pee Wee"	Nov 29, 1945	Aug 10, 2013	Tracy City Cem.; Son of Roy Hilman & Esther Elizabeth Thomas; m. Margaret Ann Bowden
Thomas, Leroy	May 19, 1940	Feb 10, 2019	City Cemetery; Son of Roy Hilman & Esther Elizabeth Thomas; m. Margaret Dunwoody
Thomas, Nancy C	Aug 28, 1934	Mar 29, 2012	Tracy City Cem. Dau of Lydia Sue Roddy; m. Billy H. Thomas
Thomas, Nannie Ruth	Oct 06, 1942	Oct 09, 1942	Monteagle Cem.; Dau. of Taylor Sam & Marjorie (Meeks) Thomas; twin to Helen Ruth Thomas; no stone

Name	Birth	Death	Notes
Thomas, Sarah A. (Trussell)	Aug 15, 1888	Dec 05, 1974	Summerfield Cem.; Dau. of James Henry & Martha Carolina (McFarland) Trussell; Cemeteries of Grundy County, Vol. 2, p. 765 correction
Thomas, Teddie (Audie Lee Holmes is her real name)	Mar 04, 1927	Aug 13, 2010	Monteagle Cem.; Dau of Cora (Holmes) McCreary; m. 1) Leonard Grooms 2) Robert Charles Thomas; addition to Cemeteries of Grundy Co., Vol. 1, p. 435
Thomas, Virgil C.	Oct 21, 1912	May 11, 2012	Sequatchie Valley Memorial Gardens; Dau. of John William & Katherine (Hunt) Thomas; m. Mary Ellen Thomas
Thomason, Mamie B. (Kizer)	May 29, 1893	Nat 17, 1980	Homeland Acres Cem.; Dau. of John Kizer; correction of surname spelling & addition to Cemeteries of Grundy Co, Vol. 1, p. 341
Thompson, Bobbie Franklin	Ca 1928	Oct 16, 2015	Cremated; Son of Frank & Lula Thompson; m. Susan thompson; US Army, WWII
Thompson, Christopher Dewayne	Dec 20, 1976	May 18, 2020	Cagle Mount Pleasant Cem.; Son of James Anthony "Toby" & Willie Mae Thompson
Thompson, Dessie (Byars)	May 13, 1897	Mar 16, 1943	Gregg Cem.; Dau. of Joab Lambirth & Minda A. (Teague) Byars; Cemeteries of Grundy Co., Vol. 1, p. 306 correction
Thompson, Ralph Edward	Jun 27, 1947	Feb 10, 2017	Cremated; Son of Elmer & Isabell (Scruggs) Thompson; m. Susan Simpson
Thompson, Rita D	Jul 05, 1941	Aug 04, 2016	Tracy City Cem.; Dau. of Homer Lewis Layne & Wilma Mae Haynes; m. Albert J. "Jack" Thompson
Thompson, Sally (Hansford)	Aug 01, 1874	after 1940 census	White Cem.; Dau. of William & Sarah (Turpin) Hansford; m Jesse J. Thompson; addition to Cemeteries of Grundy Co., Vol. 2, p.1006
Thorpe, Francis Austin	ca. 1932	Mar 20, 2018	Cremated probably, no cemetery stated in obit.; Son of Austin Thorpe & Susie Guyer; m. Dorothy Ayre Sutherland
Thrasher, Skeyler Forrestt	Aug 09, 1993	Nov 14, 2019	Cremated.; Son of Johnny Wayne Thrasher & Victoria Lynn Hill Goode; U.S. Army
Throneberry, Bertha E. (Smith)	Sep 13, 1917	Aug 07, 2014	Providence Methodist Cem.; Dau. of John William & Mary Melinda (Long) Smith; m. David Ray Throneberry; addition to Cemeteries of Grundy Co. Vol. 2, p. 714
Throneberry, David Ray	Jul 06, 1917	May 27, 1974	Tracy City Cem.; no marker; Son of John Edward & Charlotte Edna (Steed) Throneberry; m. Bertha Estelle Smith; addition to Cemeteries of Grundy Co. Vol. 2, p. 853
Thurman, Charlie Anderson	Aug 01, 1925	Nov 19, 1886	Altamont Cem.; Son of Frederick Walter & Jane (Carnahan) Thurman; addition to Cemeteries of Grundy Co., Vol. 1, p. 28

Thurman, John Thomas	Mar 4, 1870	Jan 22, 1897	Altamont Cem.; Son of Charles Anderson, Sr. & Margaret Elizabeth (McDonald) Thurman; addition to Cemeteries of Grundy Co, Vol. 1, p. 28
Thurston, Mary Frances (Yokley)	Mar 03, 1937	May 14, 2010	Lappin Cem.; Dau. of Samuel B. & Eunice S. Yokley; m. William Thurston; correction of spelling of maiden surname
Tidman, Amos	Jan 28, 1905	Mar 25, 1905	Tracy City Cem.; Son of William & Anna (Beal) Tidman; m. Kishire Sutton; addition to Cemeteries of Grundy Co., Vol. 2, p. 857
Tidman, John	Feb 27, 1844	Jun 27, 1910	Tracy City Cem.; Son of William & Anna (Beal) Tidman; m. Susan Hunt; addition to Cemeteries of Grundy Co. Vol. 2, p. 899
Tidman, Susan (Hunt)	Sep 30, 1844	Dec 31, 1892	Tracy City Cem.; Dau. of Thomas & Sarah Hunt; m. John Tidman; addition to Cemeteries of Grundy Co., Vol. 2, p. 899
Tidwell, Leonard A., Jr.	Feb 11, 1941	Jun 16, 2020	Bonny Oak Cem.; Son of Leonard A. Tidwell, Sr. & Lula Mae Garton; m. Doris Pickett; U.S. Army - Vietnam
Tigert, Nancy K (Rollings)	Mar 30, 1942		Altamont Cem.; Dau. of Frank E. & Timmie L. Scruggs Rollings; m. Samuel Crawford Tigert; correction to Cemeteries of Grundy Co., Vol. 1, p. 24
Tigue, Dorothy Helen	Jul 08, 1919	Jan 18, 1982	Plainview Cem.; Dau. of Severt J & Helene Caroline (Iverson) Hagen; m. John Wilson Tigue; addition to Cemeteries of Grundy Co. Vol. 2, p. 699
Tinder, Barbara Jean Clark	Oct 04, 1938	Mar 08, 2019	Cremated; m. Carlton David Tinder
Tiney, Eloise Case	Nov 5, 1894	Jan 05, 1974	Altamont Cem.; Dau. of Arthur Wesley & Alma May (Lamberton) Case; m. John Henry Tiney, Jr.; addition to Cemeteries of Grundy Co, Vol. 1, p. 16
Tiney, John Henry, Jr.	Jul 15, 1892	Sep 20, 1979	Altamont Cem.; Son of John Henry, Sr. & Evalina Augusta (Edwards) Tiney; m. Eloise Case; addition to Cemeteries of Grundy Co. Vol. 1, p. 16
Tipps, Edna Louise (Crabtree)	Dec 22, 1929	Aug 04, 2017	Franklin Memorial Gardens; Dau of Rufus Quincy Crabtree & Ava Anna Cooper; m. Roy Tipps
Tipton, Charles L	Feb 14, 1953	Dec 28, 2019	Coalmont Cem.; Son of Tinsley & Margie (Sweeton) Tipton; m. Kris Tipton
Tipton, Harvey Ray	Apr 05, 1947	Jul 25, 2017	Cremated; Son of Tinsley & Margie (Sweeton) Tipton
Tipton, Margaret Ann (Geary) "Sissy"	Sep 08, 1935	Mar 06, 2022	Plainview Cem.; Dau. of Alton & Beatrice (Crabtree) Geary; m. Oscar "Big Boy" Tipton
Tipton, Oscar T. "Bib Boy"	Apr 18, 1905	Sep 20, 2014	Plainview Cem.; Son of Oscar Tipton, Sr. and Lillie Belle Gates; m. Margaret Ann "Sissy" Tipton

Name	Birth	Death	Notes
Tipton, Stephen Palmer, Capt	Feb 6, 1832	Jan 20, 1864	Altamont Cem.; Son of Jonathan & Jemima (Northcutt) Tipton; m. Louisa Griswold; Union Vidette Cavalry, Co. E, killed in Civil War; correction of middle name & addition to Cemeteries of Grundy Co,. Vol. 1, p. 11
Tipton, Tennie Bell	Jan 31, 1905	Feb 11, 1905	Altamont Cem.; Dau. of Stephen Palmer & Louisa (Griswold) Tipton; correction of father's middle name; Cemeteries of Grundy Co. Vol. 1, p. 11
Tipton, Tinsley Woodrow	Aug 01, 1917	Mar 22, 1993	Bonny Oak Cem.; Son of Oscar Thurston & Lily (Bates) Tipton, m. Margie E. Sweeton, Nov 24, 1945; addition to Cemeteries of Grundy Co. Vol. 1, p. 87
Tipton, Wilma J. "Ms. Wilma" (Crabtree)	Jul 24, 1939	Mar 14, 2020	Plainview Cem.; Dau. of Malcolm & Beryl (Lockhart) Crabtree; m. Arthur C. "Little Boy" Tipton; addition to Cemeteries of Grundy Co. Vol. 2, p. 702
Todd, Emma Diane	Mar 01, 1958	May 31, 2020	Ragsdale Cem.; Dau. of Gilbert Todd & Patricia Poff; m. Lynwood Gilbert
Totherow, Betty (Brown)	Dec 11, 1934	Jan 26, 2001	Swiss Colony Cem.; Dau. of James M. & Gladys M (Scarboro) Brown; m. Charles V. Totherow; addition to Cemeteries of Grundy Co, Vol. 2, p.794
Totherow, Dwight Vernon	Jan 20, 1948	Mar 02, 2021	Cremated: Son of Hugh & Georgia (Johnson) Totherow; m. Diane Totherow
Totherow, Herbert Roddie	Oct 01, 1950	Jun 05, 2019	Coalmont Cem.; Son of Maudie Lee Shrum; m. Gloria Velvedean Campbell
Totherow, Kenneth Howell	Feb 25, 1949	Mar 07, 2015	Cremated Totherow Cem.; Son of Maudie Shrum Lay; m. Leda Totherow
Totherow, Tommie Lee	Jun 26, 1969	Jul 31, 2021	Totherow Family Cem.; Son of Kenneth Howell & Leda (Nunley) Totherow; m. Teresa Totherow; U.S. Army
Towell, Barbara M (Luttrell)	Jun 27, 1870	Nov 09, 1932	Bonny Oak Cem.; Dau of Thomas Luttrell & Nancy Hartness; m. Marion C. "Lum" Towell per death certificate; She is one of 6 people listed on the Prince tombstone. addition to Cemeteries of Grundy Co. Vol. 1, p. 78
Travis, Charley	Apr 20, 1801	May 31, 1868	Tracy City Cem.; Son of William Henry & Sarah Ellen Travis; m. Mary Ann (Willis) Coursey; addition to Cemeteries of Grundy Co, Vol. 2, p. 902
Treat, Sarah Jane (Reagan)	Jun 15, 1930	Apr 23, 2020	Clouse Hill Cem.; Dau. of Frank & Josie (Maples) Reagan; addition to Cemeteries of Grundy Co., Vol. 1, p. 160
Treat, William Cefus	Sep 26, 1926	Oct 04, 2006	Clouse Hill Cem.; Son of John S & Frances Cordelia (Treat) Treat; m. Sara Jane Ragan; correction to parents' names Cemeteries of Grundy Co., Vol. 1, p. 160

Trent, Thelma Lorene	Jun 16, 1930	Dec 02, 2013	Palmer Cem.; Dau. of Raymond L. & Josephine M. (Grantham) Lindsey
Trickler, Kenneth Dean	Sep 09, 1929	Dec 13, 2018	Cremated; Son of Miller Shelton Trickler & Elva Marie Shiveley; m. Joan Walker
Trickler, Stephen J.	Feb 21, 1958	Sep 21, 2019	Cremated: Son of Kenneth D. Trickler & Joan Walker
Troglin, Lisa	Mar 05, 1968		Palmer Cem.; Dau. of William Harold & Betty M (Grimes) Kilgore; addition to Cemeteries of Grundy Co. TN, Vol. 2, p. 564
Troglin, Tony Dale	Aug 18, 1962	Mar 01, 2017	Palmer Cem.; Son of Buster & Ruby (Keener (Troglin; m. Lisa Kilgore
Trombulak, Jessie Marie (McKnight)	Sep 14, 1918	Feb 05, 2000	Cumberland Heights Cem.; Dau. of George & Bertha (Brown) McKnight; m. Rudolph Trombulak; addition to Cemeteries of Grundy Co, Vol. 1, p. 197
Trussell-Carrick, Jessie B.	Aug 13, 1919	Dec 02, 2010	Summerfield Cem.; Dau. of Henry Bryan & Clara (Woodlee) Trussell; m. 1) Gordon Nunley 2) Edward Blatnik 3) Henry Thomas Carrick; correction and addition to Cemeteries of Grundy Co. Vol. 2, p. 770
Trussell, Blanche L. (Wright)	Sep 18, 1921	Nov 05, 1993	Oak Grove Cem.; Dau. of Frank & Malinda (Morgan) Wright; m. Leon Trussell, addition to Cemeteries of Grundy Co. Vol. 1, p. 494
Trussell, Carl Hudson	Aug 14,1924	May 15,1955	Warren "Red Hill" Cem.; Son of James Wesley & Eugenia "Jean" (Gilliam) Trussell; p. 951 addition to Cemeteries of Grundy Co.,Vol. 2
Trussell, Elbert Ward	Apr 22, 1926	Sep 15, 1943	Warren "Red Hill" Cem.; Son of James Wesley & Eugenia "Jean" (Gilliam) Trussell; addition to Cemeteries of Grundy Co., Vol. 2, p. 951
Trussell, Gary Frank	Feb 01, 1951	Jun 16, 2014	Oak Grove Cem: Son of Leon & Blanche (Wright) Trussell; buried right beside his mother; m. 1. Diana Henley 2. Charlene (Henley) Sherrill
Trussell, Glen Edward	Nov 12, 1927	Nov 23, 2020	Memorial Park Cem.; Son of Oscar Clayton & Clara (Cope) Trussell; m. 1) Evyline Trussell 2) Lenora Trussell
Trussell, James Homer	Nov 14, 1912	Mar 23, 2013	Franklin Memorial Gardens Cem.; Son of James Wesley & Eugenia (Gilliam) Trussell; m. Lucille Rose 1915-1999
Trussell, James Wesley	Mar 23, 1890	Apr 08, 1969	Summerfield Cem.; Son of James Henry "Jim" & Martha Carolina (McFarland) Trussell; m. 1) Eugenia Bell Gilliam 2) Eileen (Wilson) Cook; addition to Cemeteries of Grundy Co., Vol. 2, p. 772

Name	Born	Died	Notes
Trussell, John M.	Aug 20, 1848	Jun 9, 1897	Tracy City Cem.; Son of Andrew Jackson & Mary "Polly" (Rawlings) Trussell; m. Melvina Summers on Jul 18, 1877; addition to Cemeteries of Grundy Co, Vol, 2, p. 895
Trussell, Katherine Elizabeth (Manley)	Apr 25, 1927	Nov 03, 2020	Burns Cem.; Dau. of Wiley Almany & Mamie Manley; m. Jack Trussell
Trussell, Lora Alvada	Apr 06, 1945	Jan 20, 2016	Pleaseant Ridge Cem Huntland, TN; Dau. of Eddy & Ida (Taylor) Mears; m. Eddie Trussell
Trussell, Maxie Bruce	Apr 06, 1946	Jul 16, 1967	Oak Grove Cem.; Son of Leon & Blanche (Wright) Trussell; addition to Cemeteries of Grundy Co., Vol. 1, p. 494
Trussell, Robert Wendell	Dec 31, 1971	Jul 06, 2017	Blanton Chapel Cem. in Coffee County; Son of George Wendell & Wanda (Puckett) Trussell; m. Jessica Trussell
Trussell, Virgil Ray	Oct 06, 1946	Sep 15, 2018	Summitville Cem.; Son of Aaron Trussell & Mary Ellen Johnson; m. Brenda Hodge
Trussell, William Allen "Will"	Mar 20, 1891	Jan 17, 1960	Summerfield Cem.; Son of James Henry "Jim" & Martha Carolina (McFarland) Trussell; m. Bessie Partin; correction to Grundy County Cemeteries, Vol. 2, p. 771
Tuck-Gorby, Joyce Elois (Myers)	Aug 29, 1943	Apr 12, 2015	Prairie Plains Church of Christ Cem.; Dau. of William Floyd & Eloise Iva Heane (Campbell) Myers; m. 1) Charles Tuck 2) Ken Gorby
Tucker, Alexander		Dec 25, 1888	Unknown Cem.; m. Martha Tucker. Newspaper notice
Tucker, Anna Elizabeth	Feb 26, 1905	May 19, 1905	Monteagle Cem.; Dau. of George Lee Ortwin; m. Fred Tucker; addition to Cemeteries of Grundy Co, Vol. 1, p. 392
Tucker, Annie Mae (McFarland)	Mar. 18, 1906	Apr. 13, 1984	Monteagle Cem.; Dau. of George Carter and Ella Mae (Cox) McFarland
Tucker, Baby		Feb 13, 1909	Unidentified Cem.; Son of Bud Hence Tucker
Tucker, Edward E.	Mar 08, 1926	Jul 13, 2013	Eastern Star Cem.; Son of Samuel & Nellie (Mooney) Tucker
Tucker, Frank		Aug 01, 1903	Monteagle Cem. Probably; Son of David "Dan" Tucker; brakeman on train, thrown off and run over by 23 cars; source *Murder, Mayhem & More Vol. 1;* no stone
Tucker, Haskel	Mar 01, 1905	Mar 24, 1905	Monteagle Cem.; Son of Frances Almeda Tucker; addition to Cemeteries of Grundy Co., Vol. 1, p. 398
Tucker, Sally Ann	Sep 15, 1925	May 01, 2014	Eastern Star Cem.; Dau of George McPheren & Etta Mae Gipson; m. Edward Eugene Tucker
Tucker, Silas Leon	Mar 4, 1850	Apr 20, 1919	Monteagle Cem.; Son of Samuel & Jane (Meeks) Tucker; m. 1) Orpha Levan 2) Frances Almeda Sherrill
Turley, Michael Anthony	Mar 27, 1972	Mar 02, 2018	Hobbs Hill Cem.; Son of William Turley, Jr. & Elizie Faye Bateman

Name	Born	Died	Notes
Turley, Sandra Kay	1967	Nov 18, 2021	Hobbs Hill Cem.; Dau. of William & Eliza Turley; companion Theron Gross
Turley, William	Sep 05, 1964	Mar 10, 2013	Hobbs Hill Cem.; Son of William & Eliza Fay Turley
Turley, William, Jr.	Feb 26, 1928	May 13, 2014	Hobbs Hill Cem.; Son of William Turley, Sr. of Whitwell, TN; m. Eliza Fay Bateman; addition to Cemeteries of Grundy Co., Vol. 1, p. 331
Turner, Alma Marie	Dec 31, 1927	May 30, 2016	Orange Hill Cem.; Dau. of Lewis & Bessie Yarworth; m. William Ray Turner
Turner, Annetta (Layman)	May 16, 1951	Mar 06, 2022	Fall Creek Cem.; Dau. of Werner & Annie (Layne) Laymen; m. Ernie Lee Turner
Turner, Betty Sue	May 24, 1950	Oct 21, 2016	Altamont Cem.; Dau. of Lynn Clyde & Irene (Nunley) Tate; m. 1) Charlie Nunley 2) Clayburn Turner
Turner, Bobby Gene	May 16, 1939	May 31, 2016	Coalmont Cem.; Son of Marlin & Margie Tipton; m. Judy K. Fults
Turner, Carmella Ann	Mar 03, 1961	Mar 22, 1961	Fall Creek Cem.; Dau. of Allen & Mabelle (King) Turner
Turner, Carolyn Ruth	Sep 03, 1954	Apr 28, 2013	Swiss Cem.; Dau. of Clay & Edith (Bone) McDaniel; companion Mike Withorne
Turner, Dorothy Irene (Layman)	Aug 21, 1951		Brown's Chapel Cem.; Dau. of Dorothy (Pry) Layman; m. Homer L. Turner, Jr.; addition to Cemeteries of Grundy Co. Vol. 1, p. 106
Turner, Edna Jean (Killian)	Oct 07, 1927	Jun 01, 2014	Altamont Cem.; Dau. of J.B. & Dora Ann (Nunley) Killian
Turner, Evelyn (Finney) Gilmer	Apr 25, 1905	Jan 22, 2022	New Brick Church Cem.; Dau of Ruben & Dimple (Weddington) Finney; m. 1) Jim Gilmer 2) Junior Turner
Turner, Glen Lonas	Mar 16, 1923	Jul 13, 2001	Oak Grove Cem.; Son of James Noah & Leah Armenda (Nolan) Turner; addition to Cemeteries of Grundy Co., Vol. 1, p. 486
Turner, Ike		Aug 11, 1910	Killed at Reed Hill Mine by falling slate; newspaper account
Turner, Inalee (Turner)	Jul 03, 1924	Aug 23, 1991	Fall Creek Cem.; Dau. of Henry Clay & Flora Belle Turner; m. William R. Turner
Turner, Jessie	Aug 30, 1933	Jan 03	Fall Creek Cem.; m. Lidy Williams
Turner, Joe Edgar	Mar 02, 1942	Jun 10, 2018	Palmer Cem.; Son of Edgar Turner & Mattie Cleo Meeks; m. Mary Anderson; US Army
Turner, John Robert	May 05, 1923	Apr 12, 2009	Altamont Cem.; Son of James & Eoda (Bess) Turner; m. Stella Mae Lockhart; Navy, WWII
Turner, Johnathan Kyle	Apr 30, 1987	Feb 17, 2020	Bess-Whitman-King Cem.; Son of ___ Turner & Michell Barks; m. Sheena Turner.
Turner, Joseph Weatherton	Jan 26, 1905	Apr. 1925	Tracy City Cem.; Son of John & ____ (Barton) Turner; m. Pagen Ellander "Ellen" Watley; addition to Cemeteries of Grundy Co. Vol. 2, p. 902

Name	Birth	Death	Details
Turner, Judy K.	Oct 04, 1959	Jun 02, 2013	Coalmont Cem; Dau. of Willie Carl & Beatrice (Nunley) Fults; m. Bobby Gene Turner
Turner, Lewis	Dec 24, 1952	Oct 10, 1969	Fall Creek Cem.; Son of Edgar L & Mattie Cleo (Tate) Turner
Turner, Linda Lou	Oct 11, 1946	Jan 12, 2016	Orange Hill Cem.; Dau. of Thomas Chester & Etta Lee (Nunley) Carrick
Turner, Lois (Ruehling)	Sep 13, 1918	Mar 25, 2014	Fall Creek Cem.; Dau. of John H. & Allie E. (Blaylock) Ruehling; m. Alvers "Bud" Turner on Oct 10, 1942
Turner, Mae Bell	Feb 02, 1930	Aug 27, 1913	Fall Creek Cem.; Dau. of John Wesley & Sarah Ellen (Dennis) King; m. Glenn Turner
Turner, Marie (Yarworth)	Dec 03, 1927	May 30, 2016	Orange Hill Cem.; Dau. of Lewis & Bessie (Johnson) Yarworth; m May 29, 1947, to William Ray Turner
Turner, Mary Eleen	Mar 17, 1936	May 04, 1936	Wesley Chapel Cam; Dau. of Werner & Jesse Turner
Turner, Mary Ester (Morrison)	Jun 21, 1901	Jul 21, 1978	Fall Creek Cem.; Dau. of William T & Sarah (Layne) Morrison; m. William Robert Turner
Turner, Mildred Lois (Ruehling)	Sep 13, 1918	Mar 25, 2014	Fall Creek Cem.; Dau. of Johnny & Allie (Blaylock) Ruehling; m. 1) Alvers Brown 2) Bud Turner
Turner, Rinnia Jean (Turley)	May 19, 1953	Feb 04, 2020	Airview Cem.; Dau. of Roy Turley & Rosa Bell Edwards; m. William Tanner
Turner, Robert A.	Oct 22, 1947	Jun 30, 1978	Fall Creek Cem.; Son of William R & Inalee Turner
Turner, Robert Earl "Bob"	Nov 19, 1949	Sep 20, 1973	Altamont Cem.; Son of Robert Eston & Edna Jean (Killian) Turner; addition to Cemeteries of Grundy Co. Vol. 1, p. 19
Turner, Robert Eston	Jun 30, 1925	May 11, 2014	Altamont Cem.; Son of Charlie Woods & Flora Elizabeth (Fults) Turner; m. Jean Killian
Turner, Sandra Ann	Apr 24, 1959	Apr 15, 2018	Dau. of Edward & Lillian Turner
Turner, Stella Mae (Lockhart)	Sep 22, 1927	Oct 08, 2020	Altamont Cem.; Dau. of Allen & Octa (Whitman) Lockhart; m. John Robert Turner
Turner, Tony Lester	Jun 02, 1957	Jan 08, 2022	Cremated; Son of James W. & Geraldine (Fultz) Turner; m. Nettie Jones
Turner, William B.	Dec 29, 1948	Dec 29, 1948	Brown's Chapel Cem.; Son of Homer D. & Della D. (Green) Turner; addition to Cemeteries of Grundy Co., Vol. 1, p. 106
Turner, William Edward	Jun 13, 1932	Nov 14, 2019	Bascom Cem.; Son of Oscar Earl Turner & Willie Everett Hurtt; m. Josephine Turner
Turner, William Jackson, Jr.	Oct 22, 1940	Mar 04, 1982	Fall Creek Cem.; Son of Edgar L & Mattie Cleo (Tate) Turner
Turner, William Ray	Feb. 1, 1926	Jun 12, 2016	Orange Hill Cem.; Son of James W. & Annie McCreary Turner; m. Marie Yarworth on May 29, 1947; addition to Cemeteries of Grundy Co, Vol. 2, p. 526

Name	Born	Died	Notes
Turney, Paul Samuel	Jan 08, 1948	Nov 18, 2021	Cremated: Son of Fred & Alberta (McGraw) Turney; m. Rose Nunley
Twitty, James Leslie	Feb 10, 1942	Jan 05, 2021	Cremated: Son of Layle & Ruth Twitty; m. Marsha Clark
Tylor, Dola (Schild)	Feb. 5, 1915	Nov 10, 2015	Dau. of Peter & Ethel (Tate) Schild; m. Richard "Dick" Tylor; buried Hamilton Memorial Gardens in Hixson, TN
Ulrich, Charles Henry	Mar 24, 1884	Nov 15, 1957	Altamont Cem.; Son of Adolph C. & Elizabeth (Umbach) Ulrich; m. Louise E. Bleuer; addition to Cemeteries of Grundy Co., Vol, 1, p. 31
Ulrich, Louise E.	Jul 29, 1901	May 12, 1992	Altamont Cem.; Dau. of John & Mary (Pfalfmann) Bleuer; m. Charles Henry Ulrich; addition to Cemeteries of Grundy Co., Vol. 1, p. 31
Umbarger, Bethany *(Davaney)	Dec 30, 1820	Apr 15, 1890	Wesley Chapel Cem.; *Bethany is name on tombstone, but Barthenia in other records; m. John Umbarger; addition to Cemeteries of Grundy Co. Vol. 2, p. 975
Umthun, Mary E. (Sitz)	Feb 25, 1903	Jun 29, 1989	Fall Creek Cem.; Dau.ghter of Albert E. & Martha L. (Smith) Sitz; m. Joseph G. Umthun
Underhill, Anna Nell (Layman)	Jan 19, 1946	Aug 22, 2021	Palmer Cem.; Dau. of Werner & Annie (Layne) Layman
Underhill, Jimmy Troy, Jr.	Nov 14, 1946	Jan 25, 2021	Hunerwadel Cem.; Son of Jimmy Troy & Ruby Mae (King) Underhill
Unidentified			Skymont, on Ann Sweeny's property on Soldier Rd.
Unidentified			Phipps, David homeplace in 1850; 3 unmarked graves on the right going out Bonnie Oak Cemetery Rd. GPS 35.20.173N and 85. 43. 340 W; Directions coming from Tracy City – Turn left off Hwy 56 at Lockhart Town Rd. Go 1.5 mi and stay left at Sweeton Hill Church: Go .1 mi- graves noticeable on right only by taller sedge grasses where Old Phipps house used to be located.
Unidentified			Skymont burials; near Earl Hobbs' home on Soldier Rd – 4 fieldstone markers
Unidentified			Skymont burials; near Earl Hobbs' home on Soldier Rd – 4 fieldstone markers
Unidentified graves			4 fieldstone markers near Earl Hobbs's place at Skymont Soldier Rd.
Unidentified graves			3 unmarked graves on the 1850 David Phipps homeplace on right going out Bonny Oak Cemetery Rd. GPS reading 35.20.173 N 85.43.340 W located off Lockhart Town Rd. Stay left at Sweeton Hill Church - graves noticeable on right only by taller sedge grasses where old Phipps house used to be located.

Name	Born	Died	Notes
Unidentified graves			4-6 graves on the old Elbert Patrick place toward bluff off Clouse Hill Rd. Owned by Gibbs now
Unidentified graves			Graves thought to be near the large power line going through Coalmont near the bluff. Family of Virginia Vincent Gibbs' family who drank lemonade from a zinc pan and died
Unknown			Monteagle Cem.; possible child of Elbert & Viola (Brown) McFarland; possible dates b. Apr 20, 1933, d. May 28, 1935; correction to Cemeteries of Grundy Co.,Vol. 1, p. 402
Unknown			Monteagle Cem.; possible child of Elbert & Viola (Brown) McFarland; possible dates b. Apr 20, 1933, d. May 28, 1935; correction to Cemeteries of Grundy Co.,Vol. 1, p. 402
Uselton, Jimmy Franklin	Sep 27, 1932	Sep 28, 2016	Whitwell Memorial Cem.; Son of Alton & Octie (Hobbs) Uselton; US Army, Korea
Valentine, Genie (Rollings)	May 16, 1925	Nov 25, 2006	Altamont Cem.; Dau. of James & Eva (Walker) Rollings; m. William Valentine; addition to Cemeteries of Grundy Co. Vol. 1, p. 23
Van Hooser, H. Wayne	Dec 03, 1947	Dec 06, 2020	Cremated; Son of J.B. & Mary (Ledbetter) Van Hooser
Van Hooser, Lewis Coleman	1950	Jul 10, 2019	Spring City Memorial Gardens Cem.; Son of J.B. Van Hooser & Mary Nell Sullivan; m. 1) Sharon Van Hooser 2) Donna Cawood
Van Hooser, Mary Lou "Tiny" (Parsons)	Jan 24, 1937	Jan 29, 2019	Plainview Cem.; Dau. of Glenn Parsons & Katherine Brookman
Van Hoosier, Nora Treva	Nov 09, 1945	Jun 19, 2016	Fall Creek Cem.; Dau. of Isaac & Nora (Layne) VanHoosier
Vandergriff, Harold Loyd	May 10, 1946	May 16, 2015	L & L Family Cem.; Son of Spearman & Ella (Smith) Vandergriff; m. 1) Carma Nell (Wideman) Anderson 2) Loretta Shrum
Vandergriff, Mildred L. (White)	Dec 28, 1928	Feb 10, 2013	White Cem.; Dau. of Robert N. & Maude (Land) White; m. Russell Hubert Vandergriff; addition to Cemeteries of Grundy Co., Vol. 2, p. 1011
Vandergriff, Russell Hubert	Aug 2. 1924	Jun 10, 1990	White Cem.; Son of Andrew Jackson & Annie Mae (Grayson) Vandergriff; m. Mildred White; addition to Cemeteries of Grundy Co. Vol. 2, p. 1011
VanDyke, Bonnie Evelyn (Caldwell)	Dec 26, 1942	Jul 09, 2020	Burns Cem.; Dau. of Stanley & Millie Caldwell; m. Kenneth Cambridge VanDyke, II
VanHooser, Becky	May 23, 1954	Jul 07, 1971	Hobbs Hill Cem.; Dau of John "Junior" & Juanita (Nunley) VanHooser; correction to Cemeteries of Grundy Co. Vol 1, p. 333, where she was labeled as their son.

Name	Born	Died	Notes
VanHooser, Jossie Pearl (Norris) Jones	Apr 03, 1905	Oct 06, 1981	Palmer Cem; Dau of John Wesley & Eliza Gillen (Mathis) Norris; m. 1) Alford H. Jones 2) ____VanHooser
VanHooser, Juanita	Oct 16, 1926	Nov 17, 2017	Hobbs Hill Cem.; Dau of Marvin & Rebecca Katherine (Geary) Nunley; m. Sam VanHooser
Varnell, Kathryn Gilbert (Graves)	Oct 03, 1917	Dec 20, 2018	Sewanee Cem.; Dau. of T. Graves & Lottie Everett; m. Lon Gilbert
Vaughn, Henry Mattison	Apr 23, 1878	Jan 01, 1936	Fall Creek Cem; Son of William M. & Sarah (Jonas) Vaughn; m. Minnie Worley; addition to Cemeteries of Grundy Co., Vol 1, p. 212
Vaughn, Lula Frances	Dec 18, 1937	Aug 16, 2016	Rose Hill Memorial Gardens; Dau. of Roy & Dama Magdeline (Meeks) Wimberly; m. Charles Edwin Vaughn
Vaughn, Pearl Elizabeth	Oct 06, 1928	Sep 01, 2007	Plainview Cem.; Dau. of William M & Mattie (Young) Vaughn; addition to Cemeteries of Grundy Co, Vol. 2, p. 707
Vaughn, Sarah (Jonas)	Aug 8, 1833	Apr 12, 1886	Tracy City Cem.; m. William Vaughn; addition to Cemeteries of Grundy Co. Vol. 2, p. 889
Ventura, Rose Ann Livingston	Aug 03, 1955	Feb 04, 2014	Chattanooga National Cem.; Dau of W. J. Livingston & Ina Muncey
Vogel, Alfred	Apr15, 1891	Feb 01, 1971	Altamont Cem.; born in Latvia; correction of birth date according to Social Security records; m. Beda Maria Johanson; correction & addition to Cemeteries of Grundy Co. Vol. 1, p. 33
Vogel, Beda Maria (Johanson)	1889		Altamont Cem.; born in Germany; Possible Dau of Eric Johanson; m. Alfred Vogel; addition to Cemeteries of Grundy Co., Vol, 1, p. 33
Vogel, Ingeborg Elenora	Aug 14, 1921	Jul 05, 1956	Altamont Cem.; Dau. of Alfred & Beda Maria (Johanson) Vogel; born in Sweden; addition to Cemeteries of Grundy Co. Vol, 1, p. 33
Vunkannon, Cline John	Feb 19. 1916	Jan 24, 1995	Plainview Cem.; Son of George Washington & Flora H (Broyles) Vunkannon; m. Nellie Christine (Nunley) Heubi; Correction and addition to Cemeteries of Grundy Co, Vol. 2, p. 659
Waggoner, Annie (Smith)	May 20, 1823	Mar 19, 1915	Monteagle Cem.; Dau of Elias "Lige" & Charity (Walker) Smith; m. 1) James H. Bennett who died in Civil War in 1862, 2) Solomon Waggoner on Aug 9, 1869; addition & correction to Cemeteries of Grundy Co, Vol. 1, p. 464
Wagner, Nancy Fults	Mar 8, 1882	Dec 10, 1904	Swiss Colony Cem.; Dau. of Adrian & Drucilla (Tate) Fults; m. Herman Wagner (1875-1934) in Feb 1901; addition to Cemeteries of Grundy Co. Vol. 2, p. 783

Name	Birth	Death	Details
Wakeland, Violet Blanche (Schlasner)	Mar 23, 1907	Mar 07, 1998	Monteagle Cem.; Dau. of August & Mary (Koch) Schlasner; m. 1) Blaine E. Roberts, 25 Feb 1926 in Wabasha, MN 2) Aesel Ray Wakeland; addition to Cemeteries of Grundy Co. Vol, 1, p. 427
Walden, James, Jr.	1940	Jul 24, 2020	Western Reserve Memorial Gardens in Chesterland, OH; Son of James Alton Walden & Edna Douglas; m. Myrlene Myers
Walden, Myrlene (Myers)	1930	Mar 21, 2011	Western Reserve Memorial Gardens in Chesterland, OH: Dau. of James & Vela Myers; m. James Walden, Jr.
Walden, Timothy Eugene	Aug 18, 1969	Dec 17, 2007	Swiss Memorial Cem.; Son of Benny Raymond & Shirley June (Garner) Walden; addition to Cemeteries of Grundy Co, Vol. 2, p. 791
Walker, Gregory Eugene	Aug 24, 1982	Jul 13, 2019	Catoosa Memorial Gardens Cem.; Son of Gene Walker & Darlene Walker
Walker, Herbert Glen, Sr.	Feb 14, 1936	Nov 26, 2021	Walker Cem.; Son of Elijah Andrew & Rosa Mae (Dickey) Walker; m. Nell Wanamaker; addition
Walker, Iris Nell	May 01, 1940	Jan 29, 2017	Walker Cem.; Dau. of Osborn Conard & Bessie (Tate) Wanamaker; m. Herbert G. Walker
Walker, James	Aug 18, 1771	Feb 4, 1860	Philadelphia Cem.; m. Mary "Polly" Campbell, Dec 18, 1800; no tombstone
Walker, James B. "Jimmy"	Apr 27, 1946	Mar 08, 2016	Hamilton Memorial Gardens; Son of James & Kat Walker
Walker, James Lawson "Jimmy"	Apr 27, 1944	Jul 16, 2018	Fults Cem.; Son of Charles Jefferson Walker & Lillian Smartt
Walker, Johnnie (Mason)	Oct 02, 1911	Jun 30, 2013	Philadelphia Cem.; Dau. of Cannon Eaton & Buelah Ann (Womack) Mason; m. John James Walker; addition to Cemeteries of Grundy Co, Vol. 2, p. 626
Walker, Johnnie Gene (Beene)	Oct 07, 1946	Dec 16, 2021	Cremated; Dau. of John & Dixie (Smith) Beene
Walker, Martha (Banks)	Apr 25, 1905	Sep 13, 1996	Brown's Chapel Cem.; Dau. of James Lafayette & Mary Levisa Banks; m. 1) George Seagroves 2) Clyde Scott on Sep. 21, 1928; correction of maiden name and addition to Cemeteries of Grundy Co., Vol. 1, p. 113
Walker, Mary "Polly" (Campbell)	Jul 1, 1785	Nov 11, 1865	Philadelphia Cem.; Dau. of Hugh & Ann Hannah Campbell; m. James Walker, Dec 18, 1900, no tombstone
Walker, Sara Ann (Hobbs)	Jul 16, 1924	Jun 27, 2014	Hunerwadel Cem.; Dau. of Herman M. & Carlena (Rubley) Hobbs; m. Leonard Parker Walker; addition of death date to Cemeteries of Grundy Co., Vol. 1, p. 348

Walker, Viola (King)	Jul 13, 1929	Aug 22, 2019	Palmer Cem.; Dau. of Willing King & Lila Smith; m. James Earl Walker
Wallace, James Laney	Ca 1898	Mar 06, 1928	Monteagle Cem.; Son of Marion Allen "Allie" & Martha Ida (Starling) Wallace; m. Theola Speegle
Wallace, Mark David	Apr 20, 1958	Feb 28, 2013	No cemetery found; Son of Robert Wallace of KY probably; m. Celina Kay Dees in 1977 in Coffee Co, TN
Waller, Charles Foster, Dr.	Mar 21, 1888	May 26, 1956	Monteagle Cem.; Son of Rev. W.T. & Katie (Bonner) Waller; m. Willa Roma (Shaver) MacDonald; addition to Cemeteries of Grundy Co., Vol. 1, p. 429
Walls, David Stephen	Jul 23, 1932	Jul 23, 2011	Coalmont Cem.; Born in WV, m: 1) Edna Frances Brown 2) Dollye Kinney; addition to Cemeteries of Grundy County, Vol. 1, p. 185
Walls, Fred W.	Aug 23. 1968	Jun 05, 1997	Altamont Cem.; Son of William Vaughn & Mary Lona (Denison) Walls; addition to Cemeteries of Grundy Co. Vol. 1, p. 31
Walls, Renaye Darnell	Dec 20, 1962	Jul 11, 2020	Mt. Garner Cem.; Dau. of Horace Thomas Walls & Edith Ann Darnell; m. Dale Walls
Walsingham, Goldie Marie (Bivens)	Jun 12, 1930	Jan 04, 2022	Fall Creek Cem.; Dau. of Harn & Bessie (Meeks) Bivens; m. 1) Dillard Taylor 2) Thomas Walsingham
Walston, Richard Lamar	Jul 13, 1951	Nov 25, 2018	Lakewood Memory Gardens South; Son of Charles J. Walston & Miriam Hickey; U.S. Navy
Walters, Linda Gail (Anderson)	Mar 19, 1939	Mar 20, 2020	Cremated; Dau. of Sherman & Cleo (Phipps) Anderson; m. John F. Walters, Jr.
Walton, Dora Ruth	Nov 12, 1918	Aug 21, 1998	Homeland Acres Cem.; Dau. of John R. & Mamie B. (Kizer) Thomason; addition to Cemeteries of Grundy Co, Vol. 1, p. 341
Walton, Randall Rex	May 22, 1922	Jan 15, 2014	Homeland Acres Cem.; Tech 4 US Army WWII 46th Tank Battalion, 13th Armored Div.
Walton, Viola Margaret (Marten)	Aug 01, 1916	Jul 10, 1988	Homeland Acres Cem.; Dau. of William A. & Lydia D. (Weiss) Marten; m. Lowell Mahlon Walton on Oct 5, 1940; addition to Cemeteries of Grundy Co. Vol. 1, p. 341
Wanamaker, Dock Bennett	Feb 08, 1941	Apr 17, 2019	Philadelphia Cem.; Son of Malcolm Ray & Mae Emma (Coppinger) Wanamaker; m. 1) Anita Caldwell 2) Earline Smartt; addition to Cemeteries of Grundy Co., Vol. 2, p. 649
Wanamaker, Evelyn Ann Griffith	Nov 26, 1935	Nov 10, 2021	Philadelphia Cem.; Dau. of James Hubert & Alta (Johnson) Griffith; m. Joe Frederick Wanamaker
Wanamaker, Hazel Annette (Phillips)	Jun 08, 1937	Aug 07, 2019	Shiloh Cem.; Dau. of John Phillips & Beulah Pearson; m. Carl Cantrell Wanamaker

Name	Birth	Death	Details
Wanamaker, Janice M. (Green)	Jan 20, 1974	Nov 28, 2013	Philadelphia Cem.; Dau. of Kelsie & Mary (Long) Green; m. Michael J. Wanamaker
Wanamaker, Jewel Dean (Nunley)	May 14, 1944		Philadelphia Cem.; Dau. of James C. & Frances S. Nunley; m. Alvin Felix Wanamaker Dec 23, 1961; correction and addition to Cemeteries of Grundy Co, Vol. 2, p. 654
Wanamaker, Joe Frederick	Jun 04, 1934	Aug 01, 2020	Philadelphia Cem.; Son of Spiegle Wanamaker & Mae Merriman; m. Evelyn Ann Griffith
Wanamaker, Joyce Levon (Brady)	Mar 10, 1946	Feb 25, 2019	Philadelphia Cem.; Dau. of Clyde Brady & Novela Nunley; m. Michael Joe Wanamaker
Wanamaker, Kenneth David	Jun 19, 1963	Sep 07, 2013	Philadelphia Cem.; Son of Jerry David & Edna Ruth (Ware) Wanamaker; addition to Cemeteries of Grundy Co, Vol. 2, p. 651
Wanamaker, M. Elizabeth	Jun 02, 1934	Jun 25, 1934	Philadelphia Cem.; Dau. of Willie "Aubry" and Bertha "Helen" (Gross) Wanamaker; addition to Cemeteries of Grundy Co, Vol. 2, p. 625
Wanamaker, Michael Joe	Oct 30, 1942	Apr 14, 2019	Philadelphia Cem.; Son of Osborn Conard Wanamaker & Bessie Tate; m. Joyce Brady
Wannamaker, James	Apr 15, 1830	1892	Burkett's Chapel Cem.; Son of Johann "Mowan" Wannamaker & Moriah Nancy Wannamaker; m. 1) Didama Patrick 2) Martha Ann (Abernathy) Cochran; CO11 10th TN Inf. US
Ward, Oscar Lee, Jr.	Oct 12, 1942	Feb 05, 2014	Chattanooga National Cem.; Son of Oscar Lee, Sr. & Gertrude (Mitchell) Ward; US Army, Vietnam
Ward, Reda (Hobbs)	Dec 18, 1956	Oct 12, 2019	Morrison Cem.; Dau. of Louis Paul Hobbs & Bessie Belle Graham; m. David Glen Ward
Ward, Willie Franklin	Feb 13, 1930	Feb 13, 1930	White Cem.; Son of Oscar Lee & Gertrude Leona (Dobbs) Ward; addition to Cemeteries of Grundy Co. Vol. 2, p. 1006
Wardell, George Francis	Dec 11, 1940	Sep 09, 2000	Coalmont Cem.; Son of Chester Lewis & Hazel Elizabeth (Lochhead) Wardell; m. Sheila Gae Spencer; U.S. Navy; correction to Cemeteries of Grundy Co. Vol. 1, p. 179
Wardell, Sheila Gae	Jul 21, 1945	Feb 19, 1996	Coalmont Cem.; Dau. of Glen Daniel & Donna Mae (Daley) Spencer; m. George Francis Wardell; correction to Cemeteries of Grundy Co. Vol. 1, p. 179
Ware, John William	Oct 14, 1944	Aug 26, 2019	Coalmont Cem.; Son of John Ware & Lucille Brown; m. JoAnn Ware
Warren, Anna Dell	Mar 15, 1925	Apr 24, 2017	Warren "Red Hill" Cem.; Dau. of Maurice & Cora (Haynes) Warren; m. 1) John McDerman 2) Lloyd E. Tate
Warren, Joe C.	Jun 16, 1939	Jun 24, 2018	Wesley Chapel Cem.; Son of Charles Thurman Warren & Vera Rogers; m. Peggy Warren

Name	Birth	Death	Notes
Warren, Mary Evelyn (Bryant)	Jun 01, 1913	Jul 04, 2014	Plainview Cem.; Dau. of Oscar Bryant & Mamie Ponder
Warren, Mildred (McCormick)	Oct 03, 1941	Dec 14, 2020	Centertown Cem.; Dau. of James & Minnie Lee (Sanders) McCormick; m. 1) Ed Thomas Adams 2) David Paul Warren
Warren, Susannah Rebecca "Susie" (Wallace)	1842	1927	Tracy City Cem.; Dau. of Benjamin & Martha Agnes (Sudberry) Wallace; m. Samuel A. Warren; addition to Cemeteries of Grundy Co. Vol. 2, p. 908
Watley, Louis Leo	May 19, 1943	Jan 24, 2019	Little Johnny Myers Cem.; Son of Louis Lavon Watley & Lucille Keene; m. Refa Smith
Watson, Alice (Bivens)	May 26, 1926	Apr 24, 2012	Fall Creek Cem.; Dau. of Harm & Bessie N. (Meeks) Bivens
Watson, Eunice Angele (Stoner)	Nov 19, 1935	May 11, 2022	Mount View Cem.; Dau. of Robert Clinton & Leida (Wanamaker) Stoner; m. Morris Vinson Watson
Watson, Joyce Darden	Aug 21, 1933	May 23, 1998	Bonny Oak Cem.; Dau. of Calvert E. "Cal" & Beatrice Elizabeth (Barnard) Watson; addition to Cemeteries of Grundy Co. Vol. 1, p. 93; Joyce is listed a second time on p. 95. The second listing is an error.
Watson, Kevin Mitchell	Jul 01, 1964	May 13, 1999	Brown's Chapel Cem.; Son of Clark Patrick & Minnie Doris (Stockwell) Watson; addition to Cemeteries of Grundy Co. Vol. 1, p. 112
Watson, Lethia (Jacobs)	May 25, 1933	Aug 07, 2017	Monteagle Assembly Cem.; Dau. of Elmer Pruitt & Geneva (Given) Jacobs; m. Herman A. Watson, Jr.
Watson, Thomas		Mar 04, 1908	Oak Grove Cem.; no tombstone; shot by George Nelson; no records found; source-newspaper
Watts, Bonnie Juanita	Jan 19, 1941	Dec 07, 2016	Palmer Cem.; Dau. of Lester & Beatrice (Frizzell) Smith; m. Parker Watts
Watts, Edward Earl	Jul 31, 1924	Oct 19, 1985	Summerfield Cem.; Son of Eddie & Odell (Kilgore) Watts; m. Patsy Ruth Womack; US ARMY WWII; correction of death date per tombstone and addition to Cemeteries of Grundy Co. Vol. 2, p. 779
Watts, Mary Francis	Oct 14, 1862	Dec 19, 1932	White Cem.; Dau. of George & Elizabeth (Sutton) Emery; m. Isham C. Watts; addition to Cemeteries of Grundy Co. Vol. 2, p. 1007
Watts, Patsy Ruth (Womack)	May 25, 1935	Jan 28, 1998	Summerfield Cem.; Dau. of Governor H. & Virgie (Bond) Womack; m. Edward Earl Watts; funeral home marker; addition to Cemeteries of Grundy Co. Vol. 2, p. 779
Wead, Marilyn Marie (Osmonson)	Jun 16, 1936	Mar 15, 2018	Cremated with burial in MN; Dau. of Rufus & Valda Osmonson; m. David Wead

Name	Born	Died	Notes
Weaver, Amy Lou (Brewer)	May 29, 1924	Apr 07, 2021	Fall Creek Cem.; Dau. of Walter & Dona (Cagle) Brewer; m. William Bedford Weaver
Weaver, Annie (Bedford)	May 17, 1890	Sep 05, 1963	Fall Creek Cem.; Dau of Terry Bradford & Ida Weaver; m. Andrew Jackson Weaver; addition to Cemeteries of Grundy Co. Vol 1, p. 207
Weaver, Billie Marie (Brinkley)	Feb 01, 1935	Sep 16, 2020	Cremated; Dau. of Raymond & Evelyn Brinkley; m. Jimmie Don Weaver
Weaver, Bonnie Marie (Schlageter)	Jul 08, 1939	Jun 11, 2020	Fall Creek Cem.; Dau. of William Carl Schlageter & Frances Lillian Johnson; m. Austin Eugene Weaver
Weaver, Carrie	Jul 02, 1900	Dec 01, 1982	Monteagle Cem.; Dau. of Dempsie Albert & Zora (Smith) Weaver; died in Bolivar, TN; addition to Cemeteries of Grundy Co. Vol. 1, p. 391
Weaver, Ernest Alton	Jul 04, 1910	Apr 13, 1975	Palmer Cem.; Son of Robert McManus & Nellie Mae (Burns) Weaver; m. Ella Mae Bone; addition to Cemeteries of Grundy Co. Vol. 2, p. 552
Weaver, Florence A. (Burroughs)	Jan 28, 1905	Feb 12, 1923	Tracy City Cem.; Dau. of Deck & Martha J. Burroughs; m. Thomas F. Weaver
Weaver, Jimmie Don	Feb 26, 1930	Oct 05, 2020	Cremated; Son of Emory & Jessie L. Weaver; m. Billie Marie Brinkley; U.S. Navy
Weaver, Julie A.	Jun 01, 1961	May 27, 2020	Rose Hill Memorial Gardens Cem.; Dau. of James H. Weaver & Ellen Mary Traynier
Weaver, Linda Faye (Long)	Jul 15, 1949	May 07, 2021	Cremated; Dau. of Elaine May Long Bradford
Weaver, Martin Dale	Nov 04, 1957	Aug 10, 2015	Fall Creek Cem.; Son of William B. & Amy Lou (Brewer) Weaver; m. Shirley Estes; US Army
Weaver, Matthew Ottis	Oct 20, 1971	Aug 04, 2021	Private Service - no cemetery stated; Son of Coy & Betty Weaver; m. Sabrina Weaver
Weaver, Myrtle Evelyn	Feb 10, 1913	Dec 25, 1948	Fall Creek Cem.; Dau of Andrew Jackson Weaver & Annie Bedford
Weaver, Thomas F.	Feb 06, 1905	Jul 07, 1919	Tracy City Cem.; Son of Harriet Weaver-Possibly; m. Florence A. Burroughs
Webster, Doris Marie (Green)	Jul 21, 1933	Aug 28, 2014	Cremated; Dau. of Kenneth & Elsie (Long) Green; m. Robert Carlton Webster
Webster, Robert Carlton	Aug 17, 1930	Jul 27, 2017	Cremated; Son of Vernon & Grace Webster; m. Doris Marie (Green) Webster; USAF
Weddington, Mary Elizabeth (Campbell)	Dec 09, 1973		Bethel Cem.; Dau. of Paul & Willene (Nunley) Campbell; m. John Weddington; addition and change of last name because of marriage to Cemeteries of Grundy Co. Vol. 1, p. 67
Weir, Lola Bell (Norris)	Feb 07, 1925	Dec 04, 2020	Altamont Cem.; Dau. of William Lester & Grace Louis (King) Norris; m. Thomas J. Weir

Name	Birth	Death	Details
Weir, Thomas Jacob	Sep 11, 1927	Jul 16, 2005	Altamont Cem.; Son of Paul Henry & Marie Antoinette (Flowers) Weir; m. Lola Bell Norris; m. Oct 4, 1952; US Navy, Tech 6; US Army WWII; addition to Cemeteries of Grundy Co. Vol. 1, p. 23
Welch, Gene Maurice	Apr 20, 1940	Mar 18, 2021	Asbury Cem.; Son of James Hewel & Katie Pearl Welch; m. Mary Elizabeth Freeze; U. S. Air Force
Wells, Alton Edsel, Sr.	Apr 28, 1938		Brown's Chapel Cem.; Son of Charles Richard & Alpha (Hatfield) Wells; addition to Cemeteries of Grundy Co. Vol. 1, p. 112
Wells, Bernard E.	Mar 01, 1915	Nov 18, 1977	Oak Grove Cem.; Son of Tom & Laura (Morris) Wells; addition to Cemeteries of Grundy Co. Vol. 1, p. 505
Wells, John Neel	1952	Mar 02, 2020	Cremated; Son of Dotson & Susan Wells; m. Mickey Wells
Welsh, Jessie Belle	Mar 17, 1866	Jun 20, 1955	Altamont Cem.; Dau. of Isaac & Phoebe (Osborn) Welsh; addition to Cemeteries of Grundy Co. Vol. 1, p. 18
Welsh, Teresa Lynn	Dec 24, 1963	Dec 04, 2017	Bethel Cem.; Dau. of James R. & Francis (Harris) Arp; m. Jeff Welsh
Wemberly, Therisa (Trussell)	May 19, 1947	Aug 06, 1975	Oak Grove Cem.; Dau. of Leon & Blanche L. (Wright) Trussell; m. John Randall Wimberly; addition to Cemeteries of Grundy Co. Vol. 1, p. 494
Werner, Samuel Herbert, Sr.	Aug 23, 1832	Jun 08, 1901	Tracy City Cem.; Son of Jacob & Annie (Bendel) Werner; born in Switzerland; m. 1854 to Elizabeth Kramer; addition to Cemeteries of Grundy Co. Vol. 2, p. 891
West, Bessie M.	Jul 20, 1890	Feb 07, 1973	Altamont Cem.; Dau. of Nelson Schuyler & Ada Jane (Bradbury) West; addition to Cemeteries of Grundy Co. Vol. 1, p. 31
Western, Jo Ann (Jacobs)	Jun 27, 1933	Feb 21, 2015	Cremated; Dau. of Clyde & Barbara Louise (Rollings) Jacobs; m. 1) Charles Leland Cunningham 2) Jesse Western
White, Bobby Leon	Mar 12, 1939	Apr 10, 2015	Brown's Chapel Cem.; Son of Allen Leo Bryant & Pearl (Glisson) White Bennett; USMC
White, Charles Christopher	Apr 21, 1963	Jun 23, 2019	Palmer Cem.; Son of John White & Louise Caldwell; m. Teresa Slatton
White, Charles David	Apr 08, 1918	May 20, 2000	White Cem.; Son of Charles Logan & Rachel Louisa (Hennessee) White; m. Louise Elizabeth Shrum; addition to Cemeteries of Grundy Co. Vol. 2, p. 1008

Name	Birth	Death	Details
White, Charles Emmett "Jack"	Jun 03, 1940		Warren "Red Hill" Cem.; Son of Emmette & Elsie (Haynes) White; m. Janice Burnett; USAF; back of tombstone lists children; Dr. Lydia Ann White, Dr. Lisa Marie White Griffith, Dr. Carol Lynette White Justice; See Janice (Burnett) White for more info.
White, Flora Lee	May 20, 1946	Jan 18, 2016	White Cem.; Dau. of Leroy & Ollie (Grayson) Sanders; m. Everette White
White, Glenda Sue	Oct 03, 1981	Oct 17, 2014	Burkett's Chapel Cem.; Dau. of Glenn White & Sue (Layne) Lake; Companion 1) Allon Caldwell, Companion 2) Jeremy Louis Braden
White, Harold Eugene	Jul 05, 1933	Oct 10, 2019	Plainview Cem.; Son of Noah & Clercie White; m. Estella White
White, Hazel Bernice (Smith)	Oct 04, 1909	Feb 03, 1994	White Cem.; Dau. of James Foster & Sarah Elizabeth (Hobbs) Smith; m. Roy Lee Smith, Sr.; addition to Cemeteries of Grundy Co. Vol. 2, p. 1010
White, Henry Junior	Nov 08, 1959	Apr 12, 2018	Keener Hill Cem.; Son of Henry Junior White & Hettie Delores Keener; m. Tammie Callahan; US Marines
White, Janice (Burnett)	Nov 21, 1951		Warren "Red Hill" Cem.; Daughter of Jim & Louvina (Meeks) Burnett; m. Charles Emmett "Jack" White; children: Dr. Lydia Ann White, b. Mar 19, 1980, Dr. Lisa Marie White Griffith, b. Mar 19, 1980, Dr. Carol Lynette White Justice, b, Oct 15, 1982
White, John T.	Feb 04, 1909	Jul 31, 1982	White Cem.; Son of Charlie Logan & Rachel Louise (Hennessee) White; m. Pearl Glisson; addition to Cemeteries of Grundy Co. Vol. 2, p. 1010
White, Kathleen "Kat" (Long)	Jan 07, 1924	Jul 13, 1974	White Cem.; Dau. of Maloy & Laura Lela "Belle" (Hamilton) Long; m. Grady L. White; addition to Cemeteries of Grundy Co. Vol. 2, p. 1012
White, Laura Ann	Dec 12, 1924	Apr 05, 2014	Warren "Red Hill" Cem.; Dau. of Henry Hall & Sallie Clara (Brashear) White
White, Lucille - no tombstone, rock marker only			Monteagle Cem.; possible grave of Lucille White; Dau. of J.W. & Fannie Della (Armstrong) White; correction to Cemeteries of Grundy Co. Vol. 1, p. 404
White, Malinda	Apr 13, 1870	Oct 30, 1881	Sims Cem.; Dau. of Robert Gilbert & Nancy Ann (Nevill) White, Jr.; addition to Cemeteries of Grundy Co. Vol. 2, p. 747
White, Malinda (Lowe)	Jan 04, 1807	Jan 22, 1860	Caldwell Cem.; Dau. of Charles Finley & Mary Elizabeth (Sutton) Lowe; m. Robert Gilbert White, Sr., Feb 8, 1925; addition to Cemeteries of Grundy Co. Vol. 1, p. 141

Name	Birth	Death	Details
White, Mamie Lula (Tate)	Jul 21, 1890	Oct 03, 1971	White Cem.; Dau. of Joseph S. & Flora (Layne) Tate; m. Willie Blane White; addition to Cemeteries of Grundy Co. Vol. 2, p. 1011
White, Pamela Jo	Jan 30, 1954	Feb 26, 2019	Palmer Cem.; Dau. of Jarvis D. & Fay (Smith) Dent; m. 1) Steven Eugene Scissom 2) Jimmy Carlton White, Sr. 3) Gene Caldwell; addition to Cemeteries of Grundy Co. Vol. 2, p. 572
White, Pearl (Glisson)	Dec 01, 1918	Oct 05, 1992	White Cem.; Dau. of John & Nannie (Seals) Glisson; m. John T. White; addition to Cemeteries of Grundy Co. Vol. 2, p. 1010
White, Rachel Louisa (Hennessee)	Jun 29, 1890	Jan 03, 1970	White Cem.; Dau. of Andrew Jackson & Martha (Gillentine) Hennessee; m. Charlie Logan White on Dec 21, 1907; addition to Cemeteries of Grundy Co. Vol. 2, p. 1010
White, Robert Gilbert, Jr.	Dec 16, 1837	Feb 12, 1899	Sims Cem.; Son of Robert Gilbert, Sr. & Malinda (Lowe) White; m. Nancy Ann (Nevill); addition to Cemeteries of Grundy Co. Vol. 2, p. 747
White, Robert Hatton	Oct 14, 1856	Oct 25, 1906	Warren "Red Hill" Cem.; Son of Charles Walter & Lydia Armenda (Summers) White; correction of birth year and addition to Cemeteries of Grundy Co. Vol. 2, p. 927
White, Robert Newton	Feb 08, 1901	Mar 21, 1939	White Cem.; Son of Robert Jackson & Lorena A. (Hatfield) White; m. Maude Land; addition to Cemeteries of Grundy Co. Vol. 2, p. 1011
White, Teresa Ann (Slatton)	Dec 03, 1967	Jun 08, 2020	Palmer Cem.; Dau. of Horace Ray Slatton & Zella Fults; m. Chris White
Whited, Jackie Ray	Jan 18, 1948	Aug 23, 2017	Pine Hill Cem.; Son of Rev. Howell & Mildred Opal (Bryant) Whited; m. Loretta Minton; USMC
Whitfield, Frances Nadine (Bennett)	Mar 23, 1936	Dec 06, 2015	Western Reserve Memorial Gardens, OH; Dau. of David & Almajean (Goodman) Bennett; m. Thomas Whitfield
Whitman, Adam Elmo	Jan 09, 1924	Sep 16, 2012	Whitman-King-Bess Cem.; Son of Louis & Mamie (Myers) Whitman; m. Frances Novella Tate; addition to Cemeteries of Grundy Co. Vol. 1, p. 45
Whitman, Alfred B.	Jan 03, 1935	Jan 22, 2015	Whitman-King-Bess Cem.; Son of Louis & Nellie (Smartt) Whitman; m. Jeweldene Campbell
Whitman, Danny	1954	Dec 17, 2018	Altamont Cem.; Son of Lecil Whitman & Sarah Jane Anderson; m. Helen Bratcher
Whitman, Frances Novella (Tate)	Mar 24, 1930	May 02, 2015	Whitman-King-Bess Cem.; Dau. of Arnold & Mary Lou (Fults) Tate; m. Elmo Whitman; addition to Cemeteries of Grundy Co. Vol. 1, p. 45
Whitman, JayShun McCrea	Jul 30, 2013	Jul 30, 2013	Cremated; Son of Bridgett Michelle Whitman

Name	Birth	Death	Details
Whitman, John	Feb 1822	Mar 26, 1899	Philadelphia Cem.; m. Matilda Fults; no tombstone; Civil War 1st TN Vidette Cal. Co. E
Whitman, Melissa Ann (Layman)	Jun 06, 1971	Sep 05, 2021	Palmer Cem.; Dau. of Tommy & Molly O'Day (Keener) Layman, Jr.; m. Stephen Whitman
Whitman, Patricia Ann	Feb 13, 1937	Mar 03, 2015	Hunerwadel Cem.; Dau. of Oscar & Martha Jane (Napier) Taylor; m. Lyndon "Pete" Whitman
Whitman, Stanley "Ransie"	Aug 23, 1972	Apr 04, 2014	Gregg Cem.; Son of Stanley L. & William Jonah (Campbell) Whitman Sanders & Stepfather William Sanders; m. Holly L. Whitman.
Whitmore, Henson	Jun 19, 1921	Nov 20, 2006	Plainview Cem.; Son of Allie (Sinks) Whitmore
Whitt, Beatrice Elizabeth	Dec 15, 1910	Sep 08, 2001	Altamont Cem.; Dau. of William & Bessie (Seigler) Langford; m. Charlie Whitt; addition to Cemeteries of Grundy Co. Vol. 1, p. 18
Whitt, Douglas Woodrow	May 25, 1936	Aug 10, 2013	Cremated; Son of James Carl & Mary E. (Balch) Whitt
Wichser, Fred, Sr.	Feb 16, 1844	Jan 13, 1929	Swiss Colony Cem.; Son of Johann Jakob Wichser; m. 1) Elizabeth Flury 2) Barbara Wild
Wideman, Gary Manuel	Jan 24, 1943	Jan 05, 2016	Brown's Chapel Cem.; Son of Manuel H. Wideman & Margaret (Andrews) Blaylock; m. Dawn Wideman
Wideman, James Howard	May 04, 1976	Jan 11, 2015	Wideman Cem.; Son of Dennis & Carol Wideman
Wiesener, Infant son	Feb 21, 1914	Feb 21, 1914	Tracy City Cem.; Son of E.B. & Florence Alma (Berry) Wiesener; addition to Cemeteries of Grundy Co. Vol. 2, p.875, from *Mrs. Grundy* Feb 26, 1914
Wiggins, John Wesley	Mar 02, 1942	Feb 18, 2022	Bonny Oak Cem.; Son of Robert & Louvenia (Wiggins) Byers; m. Martha Jewell Meeks
Wilburn, Wayne Thomas	Sep 10, 1951	Dec 20, 2020	Fall River Cem. in Fall River, TN; Son of James & Ivorene Wilburn
Wilcher, James Howard	Aug 20, 1941	Jul 10, 2005	Airview Cem.; Son of Howard Venus & Hattie J (Ogle) Wilcher; m. Gloria Jean Cline; addition to Cemeteries of Grundy Co. Vol. 1, p. 8
Wilcox, Walter	1878	Feb 16, 1907	Oak Grove Cem.; Son of Commodore Archibald & Sarah (Stephens) Wilcox; killed by falling slate in East Fork mine in Tracy City; wife died of grief the next day; no tombstone; source: newspaper article & Ancestry
Wilder, Billy Wayne	Jul 09, 1941	Sep 17, 2013	Monteagle Cem.; Son of Elbert & Esther (Church) Wilder; m. Lee Gilliam

Name	Born	Died	Notes
Wiley, James D.	Aug 30, 1853	Ca. 1924	Tracy City Cem.; the only name on the large stone is Wiley, but this is probably who is buried here. His wife Ellen (Farrell) Wiley is buried beside this grave.; Son of Thomas Alexander & Elizabeth (Harrison) Wiley; addition to Cemeteries of Grundy Co. Vol. 2, p. 890
Wiley, James Henry Newsom	1900	May 01, 1918	Tracy City Cem.; Son of Jefferson Davis & Paralee (O'Dear) Wiley
Wiley, William "Willie" H.	Aug 27, 1885	Aug 10, 1903	Tracy City Cem.; Son of Jefferson Davis & Paralee (O'Dear) Wiley
Wilhelm, Mae Pearl (King) Thomas	Apr 29, 1926	Sep 04, 2013	Monteagle Cem.; Dau. of Buford & Eva Bell (Layne) King; m. 1) Carlton Thomas 2) Paul Joseph Wilhelm; addition to Cemeteries of Grundy Co. Vol. 1, p. 436
Wilhite, Geneva (Bateman)	1944	Jan 19, 2021	Hobbs Hill Cem.; Dau. of Vester & Julia Elizabeth (Nunley) Bateman; m. 1) Sam P. Reed 2) Raymond Wilhite
Willems, Mary Marguerite	May 04, 1946	Apr 04, 2013	Cremated; Dau. of John D. & Frances Julia (Pleasant) McKendrick; m. Bob Willems
Williams Knott, Myrtle Katherine (Rollins)	Jul 02, 1924	Jul 20, 2015	Clouse Hill Cem.; Dau. of Robert Jackson & Lee Vester (Thomas) Rollins; m. 1) Manley Eugene "Gene" Williams 2) Francis Knott; addition to Cemeteries of Grundy Co. Vol. 1, p. 153
Williams, Artie Lula Ellen (Basham)	Feb 06, 1899	Aug 14, 1976	Fall Creek Cem.; Dau. of Melville Eakin & Mary Ann (Bastian) Basham; m. Roscoe Clifford Williams
Williams, Aylene	Apr 29, 1930	May 05, 2016	Fall Creek Cem.; Dau. of Ophelia Green Walker; m. James Edgar Williams
Williams, Cynthia Catherine	Dec 18, 2001	Jun 02, 2020	Monteagle Sunday School Assembly Cem.; Dau. of Stephen W. Williams & Anne Hudgins
Williams, Garrett Delane	Oct 02, 1995	Apr 08, 2021	Cremated; Son of Kenneth Delane & Elizabeth (Layne) Williams
Williams, Howard Baker	Sep 04, 1900	Jun 05, 1989	Altamont Cem.; Son of Charles Archard & Mariae "Mittie" Alice (Baker) Williams; m. Willie Mae Greeter; correction & addition to Cemeteries of Grundy Co. Vol. 1, p. 34
Williams, James "J. B."	1888	May 28, 1912	Tate Cem.; Son of George & Josephine (Southern) Williams; m. Gertrude (Willis) Kennerly
Williams, Kyle Garvis	May 08, 1926	Oct 20, 2009	Monteagle Cem.; Son of Charles & Mary Susan (Mullins) Williams; m. Nellie Louise Pack; PFC US ARMY WWII; addition to Cemeteries of Grundy Co. Vol. 1, p. 433

Name	Born	Died	Details
Williams, Mary Burton (Lockhart)	Nov 07, 1862	Sep 15, 1947	Philadelphia Cem.; Dau. of Holman Lincoln & Nancy Frances "Nannie" (Hunter) Lockhart; m. Lawson Brown Williams, Jan 27, 1879; She is actually buried at Greenwood Memorial Park in Phoenix, AZ; Correction by family to Cemeteries of Grundy Co. Vol. 2, p. 636
Williams, Sandra Fay (Buckner)	Mar 16, 1948	Feb 04, 2022	Rose Hill Memorial Gardens; Dau. of Clay & Rosetta (Lindsey) Buckner; m. Clyde Wesley Williams
Williams, Tammy Ann (Fults)	May 21, 1971	Dec 07, 2018	Airview Cem.; Dau. of Jeff & Margie Fults; m. Stacy Williams
Williams, Willie Mae (Greeter)	Feb 05, 1913	Oct 15, 1984	Altamont Cem.; Dau. of John George & Anna (Stocker) Greeter; m. Howard Baker Williams; correction & addition to Cemeteries of Grundy Co. Vol. 1, p. 34
Willie, Ruby Allison (Hill)	Dec 09, 1940	Mar 15, 2016	Hunerwadel Cem.; Dau. of Marcus & Robby Etta (Hobbs) Hill, Sr.
Willis, Anderson Charles	1859	1934	Tate Cem near Betsy Willis; Son of Thomas C. & Selina (Reynolds) Willis
Willis, Andrew	Apr 16, 1940	Jun 20, 2019	Mt. Zion Cem.; Son of Farmer Jack Willis & Ruth Esther McDowell; m. Sherry Lee Longenecker; U.S. Army
Willis, Jerry Newton	Jul 31, 1944	Apr 07, 2015	Cremated; Son of Bill & Pearl (Dotson) Willis; m. Bea Clark
Willis, John Franklin "Jack"	Dec 17, 1924	May 28, 2013	Hillsboro Methodist Memeorial Cem.; Son of John & Maggie Bell (Henley) Willis; m. Elizabeth Carr
Willis, Tennie	Feb 5, 1870	Dec 30, 1947	Tate Cem.; Dau. of Thomas C. & Selina (Reynolds) Willis
Willis, Velma Inez (Church)	Jan 20, 1942	Dec 14, 2021	Hunerwadel Cem.; Dau. of Clarence & Jenny Annie Lee (Lawson) Church; m. Ralph Houston Willis
Wilson, Coleman Clay	Apr 19, 1940	Feb 08, 2014	Cremated; Son of Coleman C. & Birdie Alma Wilson of Tarrant Co., TX; m. Sandra L. Lindsey
Wilson, Elsie "Bobbie" Lea (Sutherland)	May 24, 1937	Nov 21, 2016	Pelham Church of Christ Cem.; Dau. of Albert & Ruby Sutherland; m. Billy Wade Wilson
Wilson, Juanita (Kilby)	Jan 24, 1928	Jun 04, 1976	Plainview Cem.; Dau. of Carl Harvery & Mary Alberta (Pratt) Kilby; m. James C. Wilson; addition to Cemeteries of Grundy Co. Vol. 2, p. 694
Wilson, Lurto Jackson	Feb 03, 1904	Feb 12, 1968	Altamont Cem.; Son of Frank Swift & Minnie (Cresclious) Wilson; addition to Cemeteries of Grundy Co.Vol. 1, p. 16
Wilson, Narcia Mae (Brazile)	Aug 01, 1929	Apr 23, 2017	Warren "Red Hill" Cem.; Dau. of William Norris "Bee" & Biddie Sophia (Kilgore) Brazile; m. Wayne Kenneth Wilson; addition to Cemeteries of Grundy Co. Vol. 2, p. 929

Name	Born	Died	Notes
Wilson, Nina (Barry)	Jul 04, 1953	Oct 28, 2011	Lappin Cem.; Dau. of William Edward & Thelma Juanita (Martin) Barry; m. James Christopher Wilson
Wilson, Paul Bradley	Jan 26, 1973	Mar 31, 1991	Clouse Hill Cem.; Raised by his uncle & aunt: Harley "Buddy" & Cheryl (Yaneze) Layne; no tombstone. He was Cheryl's nephew.
Wilson, William Thurston "Thad"	Jul 22, 1949	Mar 16, 2017	Cremated; Son of William Ernest & Lydia Love (Sentell) Wilson; US Navy
Wimberly, Dama Magdaline (Meeks)	Aug 09, 1909	Sep 01, 1985	Rose Hill Memorial Gardens; Dau. of Hence & Thursie (Hamby) Meeks; m. Roy Wimberly
Wimberly, Margie (Reed)	Apr 14, 1932	Oct 02, 1952	Payne's Cove Cem.; Dau. of Sam & Flora (Meeks) Reed; m. Lynn Carden "Carty" Wimberly; addition to Cemeteries of Grundy Co. Vol. 2, p. 594
Wimberly, Virgie L. (Smith)	May 11, 1929	May 24, 2014	Philadelphia Cem.; Dau. of Clyde & Annie (Perry) Smith; m. 1) Oscar Junior Wimberly 2) Emit Earl Bishop; addition to Cemeteries of Grundy Co. Vol. 2, p. 635
Wimpy, William Forrest "Bill"	Apr 22, 1932	Apr 10, 2019	Plainview Cem.; Son of James Wilburn Wimpy & Mary Jane Parmley; m. Eleanor Wimpy
Windham, Patricia	Dec 26, 1937	Feb 29, 2016	Coalmont Cem.; Dau. of Coy & Georgie (Thomas) Ellis; m. Jack Windham
Winton, Cora	born when mother died in childbirth in 1917	Feb 19, 1918	Tracy City Cem.; Dau of Jesse James & Cora (Bouldin) Winton
Winton, Cora (Bouldin)	Ca. 1895	Oct 18, 1917	Tracy City Cem.; Dau. of Irvin & Callie (Holt) Bouldin; m. Jesse James Winton
Winton, David L.	Aug 15, 1963	Sep 15, 2021	Cremated; Son of Yancie C. & Joyce Marie (Carter) Winton
Winton, Dylan Matthew	Nov 24, 1981	Feb 25, 2017	Cremated; Son of Gary Winton & Lisha Sullivan
Winton, Elizabeth "Libba" (King)	Jun 14, 1920	Mar 16, 2015	Bethel Cem.; Dau. of Robert P. & Annie Mae King; m. Marshall Winton
Winton, Frankie (Bailey)	Jan 29, 1908	Dec 29, 2014	Wesley Chapel Cem.; Dau. of John & Betty (Layne) Bailey; m. Ralph E. Winton; addition to Cemeteries of Grundy Co. Vol. 2, p. 980
Winton, Gary Lynn	Jun 29, 1951	Dec 19, 2013	Coalmont Cem.; Son of Jamie & Jean (Jacobs) Winton
Winton, Harold David	Dec 12, 1948	Feb 07, 2003	Warren "Red Hill" Cem.; Son of Paul David Winton & Edna Mae (Oliver) Crowell; m. Mary Jane Stubblefield
Winton, Howard T.	Sep 21, 1933	Aug 11, 2017	Coalmont Cem.; Son of Leonard & Nina (Campbell) Winton; m 1) Frankie Braseel 2) Mary Ann Linely
Winton, Inez (Carden)	May 06, 1926	May 13, 2022	Warren "Red Hill" Cem.; Dau. of Lynn Abbott & Gladys (Conry) Carden; m. Lewie Winton

Name	Birth	Death	Details
Winton, James Lawrence	Dec 01, 1946	Apr 27, 2015	Coalmont Cem.; Son of James E. & Ola Jean (Jacobs) Winton
Winton, John Leonard "Jay"	Jun 06, 1934	Aug 14, 2022	Warren "Red Hill" Cem.; Son of Claude & Nell (Sartain) Winton; m. Verna Ruth Hawk
Winton, Kelly	Jan 16, 1940	Oct 27, 2017	Bethel Cem.; Son of Claude & Nell (Sartain) Winton; m. Patricia Hirsch
Winton, Leon Larson	Oct 15, 1929	Apr 08, 2011	Payne's Cove Cem.; Son of Larson & Della (Oliver) Winton; m. Mary Frances Franks
Winton, Mary Ann (Linley)	Dec 23, 1934	Jan 21, 2020	Coalmont Cem.; Dau. of William C. Linkley & Sara Lutes; m. Russell Baldwin
Winton, Mary Frances (Franks)	Aug 21, 1930	Feb 06, 2018	Payne's Cove Cem.; Dau. of Lawrence & Stella (White) Franks; m. Leon Larson Winton; addition to Cemeteries of Grundy Co. Vol. 2, p. 593
Winton, Mary Jane Stubblefield	Mar 13, 1950	Nov 23, 2017	Warren "Red Hill" Cem.; Dau. of William "Bill" & Addie (Stewart) Stubberfield; m. Harold David Winton; children: Paul David Winton, David Alan Winton
Winton, Robert Gene	Jul 28, 1936	Nov 24, 2021	Christ Church Cem.; Monteagle; Son of James & Lucille (Jones) Winton; m. Julia Bright
Winton, Ruby (Crabtree)	Feb 03, 1927	Feb 04, 2013	Coalmont Cem.; Dau. of Wilson & Lydia (Scruggs) Crabtree; m. Jim Winton
Winton, Sue (Duke)	Jul 22, 1921	Mar 07, 2014	Wesley Chapel Cem.; Dau. of John A. & Willie Dora (Smith) Duke; m. Fred T. Winton; addition of death date to Cemeteries of Grundy Co. Vol. 2, p. 1001
Winton, Timothy Dean	Nov 13, 1964	Jan 23, 2017	Bethel Cem.; Son of Carl Breedlove & Frankie Winton; m. Teresa Winton
Winton, Verna Ruth (Hawk)	May 15, 1936	Sep 12, 2018	Warren "Red Hill" Cem.; Dau. of Dillon Hawk & Ruby Rieder; m. John L. "Jay" Winton
Winton, William Jonathan	Aug 08, 1988	Mar 04, 2013	Little Johnny Myers Cem.; Son of Dale Winton & Gail Hobbs
Wirz, Fritz	Apr 09, 1837	Mar 27, 1920	Swiss Colony Cem.; Son of Abraham & Anna Maria (Hunziker) Wirz; m. Elizabeth Schneider (1837-1910); addition to Cemeteries of Grundy Co. Vol. 2, p. 787
Wise, Billy Don	Oct 04, 1969	Jun 08, 2020	Fall Creek Cem.; Son of Charles Wise & Peggy Shrum
Wise, Jack Robert	Dec 25, 1937	Jul 01, 2018	Wise Cem.; Son of John Ollie & Sarah Ann (Pack) Wise; US Army - Korea
Wise, James Harris "Jesse"	Aug 10, 1939	Oct 08, 2004	Coalmont Cem.; Son of John Ollie & Sarah Anne (Pack) Wise; m. Brenda S. Burnett on Feb 17, 1979
Wise, Peggy Diane	Jul 29, 1952	Jun 10, 2014	Fall Creek Cem.; Dau of Charles Andrew Shrum & Jennie Olene Haynes; m. Charles Wise

Name	Born	Died	Notes
Wiser, Linda Ruth (Bohanon)	1946	May 04, 2018	Cremated; Dau. of Isaiah Columbus Bohanon & Eva Mae Wylie; m. 1) Larry Haynes 2) Horace Wiser
Witbeck, Rodger Dale	May 28, 1952	Feb 04, 2020	Cremated; Mother's surname was Ridge. Born in Orange Co, CA; married Carmelit R. Perez in Riverside, CA on Aug 25, 1974; worked as a lumberjack in OR; divorced May 13, 1985, in Douglas, OR; died at Haven of Rest in Tracy City of cancer; Claimed to have no family; Ashes were scattered by Stan Partin.
Wockasen, Earl Anthony	Oct 14, 1941	Nov 28, 2018	Airview Cem.; Son of Earl W. Wockasen & Anna M. Pinto; m. Doris Earline Parker; U.S. Army
Womack, Governor Hodley	1892	Sep 24, 1948 per death cert.	Oak Grove Cem.; Son of George & ____ (Ballan) Womack; m. Virgie Bond; addition and correction to Cemeteries of Grundy Co. Vol. 1, p. 510
Womack, Virgie (Bond)	Oct 17, 1899	May 22, 1963	Oak Grove Cem: Dau. of Charles T. & Leirtha (Reed) Bond; m. Governor Hodley Womack, addition to Cemeteries of Grundy Co. Vol. 1, p. 510
Womack, William	Aug 14, 1938	Mar 10, 2013	Middle Tennessee Veterans Cem.; Son of Junus Vernon & Alice (Gilliam) Womack; US Army
Woodall, James Larry	Nov 15, 1946	Aug 04, 2018	Mt. Garner Cem.; Son of Albert Dewey Woodall & Johnnie Estella Whitaker; m. Faye Brown; US Army
Woodall, Patsy Virginia (Payne)	Oct 03, 1934	Jul 11, 2018	Franklin Memorial Gardens Cem.; Dau. of Joe Payne & Eva Lee Parks; m. Charles Woodall
Woodard, Ike B.	Ca 1870	Feb 02, 1915	Buried in front yard on Beersheba St. in Tracy City; Son of J. Fletcher Woodard; m. Rosa Lee Pocus
Woodlee, Alma L. (Crabtree)	Jun 04, 1925	Oct 05, 2015	Bethel Cem.; Dau. of Wilson & Lydia (Scruggs) Crabtree; m. Frank Cecil Woodlee; addition to Cemeteries of Grundy Co. Vol. 1, p. 68
Woodlee, Aubrey Eugene	Jun 25, 1932	Sep 15, 2019	Armstrong Cem.; Son of Franklin Christopher & Iva Lee Woodlee; m. Joan Lamb; US Air Force
Woodlee, C.L.	1924	Dec 22, 1928	Bethel Cem.; Son of William Hobart "Hobe" & Una (Ray) Woodlee; addition to Cemeteries of Grundy Co. Vol. 1, p. 55
Woodlee, Charlene (Dye)	Mar 02, 1937	Jul 08, 2020	Armstrong Cem.; Dau. of William & Mattie Dye; m. Gordon Woodlee
Woodlee, Douglas	1930	1932	Grace Chapel Cem.; Son of Carrol & Mamie (Sweeton) Woodlee, Sr.; addition to Cemeteries of Grundy Co. Vol. 1, p. 298

Name	Birth	Death	Details
Woodlee, Dwite David	Jul 06, 1944	Mar 02, 2020	Armstrong Cem.; Son of Andrew Beecher Woodlee, Jr. & Pauline Fults; m. Evelyn Ruth Harris
Woodlee, Elizabeth Marie (Jacobs)	Jan 14, 1969	Sep 07, 2019	Pelham Church of Christ Cem.; Dau. of Clyde "Jack" Jacobs & Karen Carroll; m. Marty Woodlee
Woodlee, Hardy Harrison	Jun 24, 1959	Jan 13, 2018	Armstrong Cem.; Son of Edwin Harrison Woodlee & Betty Massar
Woodlee, James B.	Aug 05, 1856	Jun 15, 1881	Altamont Cem.; Son of Enoch & Mary Ann (Reed) Woodlee; m. Mary Thompson; addition to Cemeteries of Grundy Co. Vol. 1, p. 26
Woodlee, Kenneth Morris	May 23, 1955	Sep 20, 2021	Walker Cem.; Son of Carroll & Thelma (McGee) Woodlee, Jr.; m. Paulette Fincher
Woodlee, Linda Nadyne (Wanamaker)	Mar 20, 1944	Apr 25, 2013	Wanamaker Annex Cem.; Dau. of Woodrow & Martha Layne (Merriman) Wanamaker; m. Robert Dale Woodlee; grand ch: Casey, Ryan, Derek, Rickie, Cristie, Mitchell, Alli, Blake, Damon; correction of birth year and addition to Cemeteries of Grundy Co. Vol. 2, p. 922
Woodlee, Maggie (Tate)	Feb 25, 1905	Dec 18, 1921	Tracy City Cem.; Dau of James S. & Susan (Layne) Tate; m. Harris B. Woodlee
Woodlee, Mamie Minerva (Sweeton)	Oct 23, 1895	Nov 15, 1979	Bonny Oak Cem.; Dau. of Francis Moses & Martha Ann Elizabeth (Baswell) Sweeton; m. 1) Carroll Woodlee 2) Hence Meeks; correction of Cemeteries of Grundy County, Vol. 1, p. 79
Woodlee, Margaret Louise (Anderson)	Aug 28, 1937	Aug 05, 2020	Fall Creek Cem.; Dau. of James Neil Anderson & Maude Shrum; m. Leonard "Hill" Woodlee; addition to Cemeteries of Grundy Co. Vol, 1, p. 272
Woodlee, Robert Dale	Nov 13, 1934	Jan 19, 2021	Philadelphia Cem.; Son of Andrew Beecher & Pauline (Fults) Woodlee; m. Nadyne Wanamaker; US Army
Woodlee, Wilma Sue (Sweeton)	Mar 27, 1950	Dec 31, 2019	Coalmont Cem.; Dau. of Lawrence Sweeton & Margie Burnett; m. Ray Woodlee
Woods, Gary Wayne	Jul 03, 1938	Aug 31, 2021	Cremated; Son of Carl & Norine Woods of West Virginia; m. Bunny Reed; addition to Cemeteries of Grundy Co. Vol. 1. They lived in Monteagle for a time, but lived in Manchester when Gary died.
Woods, Samantha Joan (Gipson)	May 22, 1940	Jan 04, 2021	Moore Cem, Huntand, TN; Dau. of Elbert & Harley (Gilliam) Gipson; m. Walter "Pete" Woods
Wooten, Cynthia Jane (Lawson)	Feb 13, 1880	Nov 06, 1971	Monteagle Cem.; 2nd wife of Benjamin Franklin Wooten
Wooten, Howard Mack	Mar 22, 1905	Oct 11, 1936	Monteagle Cem.; Son of Benjamin Franklin Wooten

Name	Birth	Death	Details
Wooten, Melody Chrystal "Sam"	Jun 04, 1962	May 16, 2022	Fall Creek Cem.; Dau. of E.H. & Willie Mae (McDaniel) Wooten
Wooten, Willie (McDaniel)	May 01, 1937	Sep 05, 2001	Fall Creek Cem.; Dau. of Frank & Lela (Banks) McDaniel
Worley, Dorothy Mae (Layne) "Dot"	May 22, 1937	Oct 12, 2020	Griffith's Creek Cem.; Dau. of Harlie & Roxie (Graham) Layne; m. Jim Worley
Worley, Ella Mable (Bone)	Nov 07, 1915	May 20, 2005	Palmer Cem.; Dau. of William Kasper & Rosa Bell (Caldwell) Bone; m. 1) Ernest Alton Weaver on Nov 12, 1949, 2) Elton Worley; addition to Cemeteries of Grundy Co. Vol. 2, p. 552
Worley, Herbert Stanley	Jan 17, 1939	Aug 22, 1992	White Cem.; Son of Raymond Rastus & Thelma Mae (Hobbs) Worley; addition to Cemeteries of Grundy Co. Vol. 2, p. 1008
Worley, Infant	Apr 01, 1921	May 23, 1921	Tracy City Cem.; Infant of Henry & Maggie (Shrum) Worley
Worley, Jack Donald		Feb 10, 1914	Tracy City Cem.; Infant of Henry & Maggie (Shrum) Worley
Worley, James Ed	Sep 30, 1940	Apr 23, 2016	Monteagle Cem.; Son of James William & Margaret "Sue" (Guess) Worley; m. Melessie Jo Falls, US Army
Worley, Mable (Bone) Weaver	Nov 17, 1915	May 20, 2005	Palmer Cem.; Dau. of William Kasper & Rosa Bell (Caldwell) Bone; m. 1) Ernest A. Weaver 2) Elton Worley; addition to Cemeteries of Grundy Co. Vol. 2, p. 552
Worley, Mable (Crabtree)	1917	1987	Palmer Cem.; Dau. of William Henry Crabtree, Sr.; m. 1) Lonnie Harold Morrison 2) ____ Worley; addition to Cemeteries of Grundy Co. Vol. 2, p. 569
Worley, Martha	Apr 12, 1929	Oct 18, 2018	Franklin Memorial Gardens Cem.; Dau. of Fate & Rhoda (O'Dear) Condra; m. Ershel Worley
Worley, Michael David	Mar 14, 1964	Mar 23, 2013	Griffith Creek Cem.; Son of Jim & Dot (Layne) Worley
Worley, Ronnie Lee	Jul 30, 1953	Nov 16, 2015	Monteagle Cem.; Son of James & Sue (Guess) Worley; m. Lisa Worley
Worley, Ruth P.	Oct 10, 1926	Feb 20, 1927	White Cem.; Dau. of Paul & Jessie (Thompson) Worley; addition to Cemeteries of Grundy Co. Vol. 2, p. 1997
Worley, Steve Michael	Nov 19, 1956	Jul 11, 2017	Monteagle Cem.; Son of James & Margaret "Sue" (Guess) Worley; never married
Worley, Thelma Mae (Hobbs)	Nov 17, 1909	not known	White Cem.; Dau. of John David & Nora Bell (Gibbs) Hobbs; m. Raymond Rastus Worley; addition to Cemeteries of Grundy Co. Vol. 2, p. 1008
Worley, Treva Lou	1941	Oct 16, 2009	White Cem.; Dau. of Osbin Worley; Treva is actually buried at Fall Creek, but has a stone at White Cem.

Name	Born	Died	Details
Wright, Douglas Eugene, Sr.	Mar 30, 1942	Nov 22, 2017	Middle TN Veterans Cem.; Son of Mark & Irene Wright; m. Linda Sue Bowman; US Army - Vietnam
Wright, Wanda Imogene	Aug 19, 1956	Mar 26, 2017	Park Cem.; Dau. of Crawford & Kate (Grimes) Hobbs; m. Dave Wright
Wyche, Ina M.	Jan 28, 1919	Mar 22, 2006	Palmer Cem.; Dau. of Jacob Henry & Mammie Lee (Cope) Lankford; m. 1) Jeff Pollard 2) ___ Wyche; addition to Cemeteries of Grundy Co. Vol. 2, p. 554
Yak, Edna Nell	Nov 13, 1928	Jan 11, 2018	Grace Chapel Cem.; Dau. of Morris & Frances Tate; m. ___ Melton
Yarber, Infant	Nov 31, 1913	Nov 31, 1913	Warren "Red Hill" Cem.; Son of Arthur Yarber; from *Grundy Co. Times*; Dec 3, 1913
Yarworth, Chester Carlton "Carl"	Jan 30, 1950	Dec 28, 2015	Orange Hill Cem.; Son of Lewis F. & Bessie (Johnson) Yarworth; m. Vicki Sue Garner
Yarworth, Della (Downum)	1882	1926	Hobbs Hill Cem.; Dau. of Daniel B. & Eliza (Statum) Downum; m. O.H. Yarworth; addition to Cemeteries of Grundy Co. Vol. 1, p. 325
Yarworth, Mildred (Tate) Cox	Mar 04, 1926	Aug 20, 2013	Palmer City Cem.; Dau. of Samuel & Carrie Mae (Stewart) Tate
Yarworth, Stanley	May 09, 1930	Jun 29, 2016	Plainview Cem.; Son of Lewis & Bessie Yarworth; m. 1) Ruth Harris 2) Arveta Yarworth
Yates-Nolan, Teresa Ann	Nov 04, 1971	Feb 20, 2021	Eastern Star Cem.; Dau. of Margaret Yates; m. Danny Wayne Nolan
Yates, Claudia Irene	Jan 14, 1921	May 04, 2016	Eastern Star Cem.; Dau. of Claude & Irene (Long) Young Taylor; m. Leesul Richard Yates
Yates, Douglas Jeffries	Apr 17, 1937		Hunerwadel Cem.; Son of Marvin Franklin & Mary Elizabeth (Askew) Yates; m. Julie Trabue; addition to Cemeteries of Grundy Co. Vol. 1, p. 345
Yates, Julie (Trabue)	Dec 17, 1938	Apr 26, 1989	Hunerwadel Cem.; Dau. of Charles Clay & Julie Mina (Ritzius) Trabue; m. Douglas Jeffries Yates; addition to Cemeteries of Grundy Co. Vol. 1, p. 345
Yates, Lonnie Wilson	Jul 08, 1940	Sep 11, 2016	Cremated; Son of Leesul & Claudia "Jay" Yates; m. Elizabeth Yates
Yates, Norma Jean (Burks)	Dec 04, 1929	Oct 20, 2019	Eastern Star Cem.; Dau. of John Clay Burks & Emma Jane Williams; m. Jackson "Bucky" Yates
Yates, Thomas Allen	Jun 27, 1945	Apr 10, 2014	Cremated; Son of Thomas McCord Yates & Lucia Adair Green; US Army
Yell, Catherine Laverne	May 22, 1944	Sep 24, 2007	Brown's Chapel Cem.; Dau. of Howard & Pauline Bennett; m. Joseph Alfred Yell, Sr. on Jan 15, 1966; addition to Cemeteries of Grundy Co. Vol. 1, p. 106

Name	Born	Died	Notes
Yell, Joseph Alfred, Sr.	Sep 17, 1941		Brown's Chapel Cem.; Son of Ples & Dora (Green) Yell; m. Catherine Laverne Bennett; addition to Cemeteries of Grundy Co. Vol. 1, p. 105
Yenny, Marie "Mary" (Maurer)	May 09, 1841	Oct 24, 1916	Tracy City Cem.; Dau. of ___ Maurer; m. Samuel Yenny; born in Stein, Switzerland; addition to Cemeteries of Grundy County, Vol. 2, p. 892, Source, *Mrs. Grundy*, Nov 2, 1916
Yokley, Harmon W.	Oct 24, 1925	Jul 09, 1977	Lappin Cem.; Son of William & Martha "Mattie" (Lappin) Yokley; TEC 5 US ARMY WWII; correction of spelling of surname
Yokley, Jeffery Nathan "Petee"	Dec 05, 1982	Dec 25, 2002	Coalmont Cem.; Son of Danny & Tina (Scissom) Yokley; correction to Cemeteries of Grundy County, Vol. 1, p. 177
Yokley, Jerry Donald	Feb 01, 1939	Sep 25, 2020	Fall Creek Cem.; Son of Herbert Lee & Betty May (Taylor) Yokley; m. Virginia Fay Cleek
Yokley, Lucille Eunice (Smith)	May 12, 1916	May 16, 1988	Lappin Cem.; Dau. of Rease & Frances Caroline "Carrie" (Lappin) Smith; m. Samuel Bert Lappin; correction of spelling of surname
Yokley, Martha Eveline "Mattie" (Lappin)	Oct 29, 1853	May 02, 1976	Lappin Cem.; Dau. of Jesse Morrell & Martha Eveline (Hopkins) Lappin; m. William Yokley; correction of spelling of surname
Yokley, Samuel Bert	Aug 24, 1910	Dec 31, 1981	Lappin Cem.; Son of Dallas Allen & Luella (Meeks) Yokley; m. Lucille Eunice Smith; correction of spelling of surname
Yokley, Virginia Fay (Cleek)	Jun 06, 1938	Jan 21, 2020	Fall Creek Cem.; Dau. of John Cleek, Jr. & Lizzie (Shrum) Cleek; m. Jerry Yokley
Young, Bobby	Apr 25, 1939	Oct 25, 2017	Maplewood Cem.; Son of Marty & Goldie (Lockhart) Young; US Army
Young, Hester Myers	Aug 22, 1936	Aug 29, 2021	Young Cem in DeKalb County; Dau. of Luther & Deamie (Fults) Myers; m. Charles Linberg Young
Young, Jeff Thomas, Jr.	Mar 13, 1935	May 24, 2010	Plainview Cem.; Son of Jeff Thomas, Sr. & Nezzie B. Young; addition to Cemeteries of Grundy Co. Vol. 2, p. 707
Young, Timothy Glynn	Feb 11, 1968	Jun 22, 2017	Altamont Cem.; Son of Berry & Daisy (Smartt) Young; never married
Zahn, Christi (Nunley)	Jul 02, 1968	Nov 04, 2021	Bethel Cem.; Dau. of Joseph Carl & Pamela (Ogelvie) Gould Nunley
Zdanowski, Frances Virginia	Mar 08, 1946	Jun 19, 2014	Coalmont Cem.; Dau. of James Carl Hogwood & Hallie Marie Rector; m. 1) James Steven Wynn 2) Michael Stephen Zdanowski
Zophi, Katherine (Zimmermann)	Jul 04, 1827	Feb 29, 1892	Swiss Colony Cem.; Dau. of David & Katharina (Knobel) Zimmermann; m. 1) Johan Georg Kunzle 2) Kaspar Zophi, Sr. (b. 1824); addition to Cemeteries of Grundy Co. Vol. 2, p. 784

Zwald, Katharina geb (Naegeli)   Apr 03, 1826   May 27, 1897   Swiss Colony Cem.; Dau. of Kasper & Barbara (Leuthold) Naegeli; m. Melchoir Zwald, Jr.; addition to Cemeteries of Grundy Co. Vol. 2, p.785

Name	Page
Abernathy, Martha Ann	289
Abrahamson, Doris Ann	1
Acevedo, Antonio	1
Acevedo, Frances	220
Acevedo, Francis	1
Acevedo, Steven	1
Ackerman, Joseph Leone Carl	265
Ackerman, Robert	201
Ackermann, Maria "Mary"	264
Adam, Christine	61
Adams, Aaron Matthew	1
Adams, Albert Dewey	1
Adams, Alford A.	1
Adams, Alfred	1
Adams, Alfred Thompson, Jr.	1
Adams, Alfred Thompson, Sr.	1
Adams, Alice Carrie (Pack)	1
Adams, Allie	95
Adams, Ardell	251
Adams, B.H.	1
Adams, Barney	1
Adams, Benjamin Harrison	1
Adams, Charles Allison Woodville	2
Adams, Charles F.	1
Adams, Charles Francis	38, 269
Adams, Charles W.	241
Adams, Charles Wesley	2
Adams, Chris Edwin	204
Adams, Clarissa	206
Adams, David Porterfield	1
Adams, David Porterfield, Jr.	1, 2
Adams, Ed Thomas	290
Adams, Emma (Smith)	1
Adams, Franklin D	1
Adams, Gladys Marie	220
Adams, Helen Maxine	6
Adams, Henry	1
Adams, Jefferson Fabian "Jeff"	2
Adams, John	1
Adams, John H.	1
Adams, Karin Hughes	1
Adams, Levina J. (Lindsey)	1
Adams, Lewis D	1
Adams, Lewis Davis	2
Adams, Lloyd	1
Adams, Lou Ann	1
Adams, Madeline (Reynolds)	2
Adams, Martha Ann	234
Adams, Mary	99
Adams, Mary Ann	47
Adams, Mary Elizabeth	231
Adams, Myrtis	1
Adams, Pherbia (Nunley)	2
Adams, Pink	2
Adams, Richard Lambert	2
Adams, Ruby Corin	1
Adams, Samuel Henry	1
Adams, William Edward	2
Adcock, Louise	261
Adcock, William	261
Adkins, Orlena Marie	2
Adkins, Robert	2
Aebi, Regina	104
Aebi, Russell	104
Aeschlimann, Marie	261
African American Cem.	v
Agan, Kitty Estelle	1
Agee, Kimberly Diane (Terry)	2
Agee, Steve	2
Ahlstrom, Ellen	145
Ahlstrom, Klas Emil Andersson	145
Akins, Sheila Regina	67
Akins, Allen	67
Akins, Allen S	2
Akins, Kara	2
Akins, Kenneth W.	2
Akins, Lorene Nannie (Holt)	2
Akins, Tabitha	2
Akins, Whitney Kala	2
Albritton, Charles Ray	2
Albritton, Daniel Lake	2, 8
Albritton, Etta Lee (Morgan)	2
Albritton, John Thomas	2
Albritton, Mary Ruth	8
Albritton, Ruby Jo (McCuiston)	2
Albritton, Ruth	8
Alexander, Allen Chester, Sr.	2
Alexander, Allen Crockett	2
Alexander, Bessie Lee	145
Alexander, Claude G.	230
Alexander, Johnny	3
Alexander, Mary	14
Alexander, Mary Rosetta Roop	2
Alexander, Neva June (Sherrill)	3
Alexander, William Robert	3
Allan, Henry Stanley	3
Allan, James Millard	3
Allen, Amanda	3
Allen, Ashley Karan	3
Allen, Bessie	204
Allen, Carol	3
Allen, Carol Olive	3
Allen, Courtney Rebeccah	3
Allen, David Murphy	249

Name	Page
Allen, Dessie Mae	162
Allen, Dixie Mae	275
Allen, Elizabeth	252
Allen, Geneva (Meeks)	3
Allen, Howard C.	3
Allen, Iulus	3
Allen, Jennifer	3
Allen, John Edward	3
Allen, Kobe Bryant	3
Allen, Lizzie	251
Allen, Margie Faith (Fulfer)	3
Allen, Rhoda Jane	229
Allen, Unis	24
Allison, Henry O.	137
Allison, Nannie Mae	137
Allman, Mandy	227
Allred, Charles Edward	3
Allred, Tava Lucille	3
Allred, Tava N.	3
Allred, Treava L	3
Allred, William Curtis	3
Almany, Bessie	250
Almany, Bessie Leona	124
Almany, Bessie Leona	249
Almany, F.M.	3
Almany, James Francis	3
Almany, Margarita	71
Almany, Nathan	3
Almany, Wiley	281
Almany, Wiley Francis Marion	3
Altamont, TN	vii
Amacher or Ackerman, Maria	265
Amacher, Maria "Mary"	264
Ames, Allene	264
Andelson, Bonny Johnson	3
Andelson, Robert Vernon	3
Anders, Isabel	121
Anders, Ruth	268
Anderson, A.P.	6
Anderson, Abb	6
Anderson, Agnes Inez	3
Anderson, Alf	104
Anderson, Alvin T. "Tom"	5
Anderson, Alvin Thomas	6
Anderson, Amos Phillip	4
Anderson, Andrew Jackson	206
Anderson, Billie	198
Anderson, C. L.	4, 5
Anderson, Carl Edward	4
Anderson, Carma Nell	285
Anderson, Carol	4
Anderson, Carter Hayden Elisha	4
Anderson, Charles E.	4
Anderson, Charles W.	5, 6
Anderson, Charlie	48
Anderson, Christine	34
Anderson, Clara	32
Anderson, Claude Leon	4
Anderson, Dale	4
Anderson, David Ray	4, 5
Anderson, Dennis	6
Anderson, Dorothy	4, 6
Anderson, Douglas Elisha	4
Anderson, Edd F.	6
Anderson, Elbert Hubert	4
Anderson, Eldred	66
Anderson, Elisha	4, 6
Anderson, Emily Elizabeth Paige	4
Anderson, Ernest R.	5
Anderson, Estelle	134
Anderson, Evalena "Inez"	4
Anderson, Evelyn	32
Anderson, Fannie (Caldwell)	4
Anderson, Faye	27
Anderson, Flora	101
Anderson, Floy	4
Anderson, Floyd Ray	4
Anderson, Frances Lee "Buster"	6
Anderson, Freda Louise	80
Anderson, George Allen	4
Anderson, George P	32, 248
Anderson, George Washington	4, 19
Anderson, George Washington "Wash"	4, 129
Anderson, Gertrude	169
Anderson, Gladys Margaret	4
Anderson, Guy Richard	4
Anderson, Herbert	5
Anderson, Herschel	66
Anderson, Hershel	5
Anderson, Hershel Eugene	4
Anderson, Hezekiah Carr	21
Anderson, Howell Edward	4
Anderson, Infant	4
Anderson, Infant	4
Anderson, Jacob Lee	4, 5
Anderson, James Henry "Q Ball"	4
Anderson, James L.	5
Anderson, James Mitchell "Rust"	5
Anderson, James Neely "Nelia"	5
Anderson, James Neil	301
Anderson, James Richard "Ricky"	5
Anderson, James Robert	4
Anderson, James Robert "Bo"	5
Anderson, James Thomas	5

Name	Page
Anderson, Jean	62
Anderson, Jerry Don	5
Anderson, Jo Anne	147
Anderson, John	4
Anderson, John Henry	5
Anderson, Joseph Dewey	4
Anderson, Judith	170
Anderson, Judy (Geary)	5
Anderson, Justin Don	5
Anderson, Kate	95
Anderson, Katie Fay	94
Anderson, Kenitha M.	5
Anderson, Kirsten Fults	4
Anderson, Larry	1
Anderson, Larry W	5
Anderson, Leonard Edward	5
Anderson, Leslie	5
Anderson, Leslie Raymond	5
Anderson, Linda	20
Anderson, Linda Ann (Layne)	5
Anderson, Lois	59
Anderson, Loulene (Thomas)	5
Anderson, Mary	5, 114
Anderson, Mary Ann (Crocker)	5
Anderson, Mary E.	6
Anderson, Mary Elizabeth	5
Anderson, Mary Jo (Parsons)	5
Anderson, Mary Marie	116
Anderson, Mattie Lillian	260
Anderson, Maude	127
Anderson, Minnie	178
Anderson, Mollie	45
Anderson, Morris	34
Anderson, Nadine	162
Anderson, Nolan	5
Anderson, Otsie June (Partin)	5
Anderson, Pamela Rose (Meeks)	5
Anderson, Peter	217
Anderson, Rachael	27, 96
Anderson, Ramie	6
Anderson, Ray	5
Anderson, Raymond Leslie	5
Anderson, Ricky Leon	6
Anderson, Robert	4
Anderson, Robert Kenneth	6
Anderson, Robert Lee	6
Anderson, Robert Nelson, Sr.	6
Anderson, Roy L.	3
Anderson, Ruby	113
Anderson, Sam	5, 6
Anderson, Sam Watson	6
Anderson, Sam Watson, Jr.	6
Anderson, Sandra Dee	6
Anderson, Sarah Agnes	165, 166, 170
Anderson, Sarah Jane	73, 294
Anderson, Sherman	288
Anderson, Sina	223
Anderson, Sylvia Kay	4
Anderson, T.A.	6
Anderson, Tabitha Louvisa "Bicie"	21
Anderson, Tasha	6
Anderson, Teresia (Irvin)	6
Anderson, Tom	4
Anderson, Ubert Tony	6
Anderson, Virgie Lee (Meeks)	6
Anderson, Virginia	103
Anderson, Wanda Faye	260
Anderson, Wash	4
Anderson, William Riley	4
Anderson, William Simon Doss	5
Anderson, Willie	246
Anderson, Willie Mae	47
Anderson, Willie Mae (Fults)	6
Anderton, Ellen Priscilla	39
Andregg, Katherine	265
Andrews, Margaret Elizabeth	17
Andrews, Elizabeth	57
Andrews, Jesse Richard	17
Andrews, Stella	67
Andy, Leo Leonard, Jr.	6
Andy, Leo Leonard, Sr.	6
Anglian, John Huston	6
Anglin, Adrian Thomas	6
Anglin, J.D.	7
Anglin, Jonathan	7
Anglin, Pearl	197
Annin, Catherine	262
Anstey, Phyllis	45
Anthony, Amzi	7
Anthony, Hazel	217
Anthony, Nancy	7
Aplanalp, Jacob	152
Aplanalp, Katharina	152
Arbuckle, Alice	94
Arbuckle, Jasper William	69
Archer, Lawson Timothy	93
Archey, Beatrice	7
Archey, Kelly Jo	7
Argo or Rhea children possibly, Unidentified	7
Argo, Abner "Dock"	7
Argo, Ada (Scott)	7
Argo, Arcy Lee	8
Argo, Barbara Ann	57
Argo, Beuna Vista (Fults)	7
Argo, Bunia Lee	159

Name	Page
Argo, Carrol	7, 8
Argo, Dean	7
Argo, Dewey Barney	7
Argo, Dewey Doston	7, 8
Argo, Dillard Henry	7
Argo, Dillie Ann	191
Argo, Doston	120, 155
Argo, Earl	7, 8
Argo, Elma (Perry)	7
Argo, Evaline	147
Argo, Evelyn Gearlean	8
Argo, Fannie (Madewell)	8
Argo, Hettie (Frazier)	8
Argo, Hiram	7
Argo, Irving	8
Argo, Jack Willis	7
Argo, Jennie	7, 183
Argo, John	79
Argo, John Josiah	7, 8
Argo, Loyd	8
Argo, Lucy B.	v, 79
Argo, Melchizedek "Dick"	8
Argo, Melvin	8
Argo, Melvin J	8
Argo, Ollie	99
Argo, Ruth (Albritton)	8
Argo, Sallie	v, 79
Argo, Sarah Elizabeth	73
Argo, Thomas Dale	8
Argo, Thomas Ervin	8
Argo, Thomas Melvin	8
Argo, Twins (Earl & Estella)	8
Argo, William John "Bill"	8
Argo, Willie Mae	243
Argo, Willis	8
Argo, Willis Mae	94
Armentrout, Donald Smith	8
Armentrout, Sue Ellen (Gray)	8
Armstrong, Edward	126
Armstrong, Edward E.	4
Armstrong, Fannie Della	293
Armstrong, Flora	102, 212
Armstrong, Jane	20
Armstrong, Laura	191
Armstrong, Martha	157, 187
Armstrong, Sammy	227
Armstrong, Susanah	266
Arnet, Gladys Creighton	8
Arnet, Robert	8
Arnold, Anthony Lynn	8
Arnold, Bunn Francis	94
Arnold, Harriet Elizabeth	89
Arnold, Riley Hershel, Sr.	8
Aroyo, Julia	41
Arp, Eddie Glenn	8
Arp, James R.	292
Arp, Paul	8
Arp, Rose	8
Arp, Wanda Sue Marilyn	182
Arthur, Alice	55
Arthur, Francis Douglas	55
Ashburn, Carol Dannette	8
Ashburn, Joe	86
Ashburn, Shirley Faye	56
Ashby, Deborah	230
Ashby, Leatrice	9
Ashby, Robert Wilson	53
Ashby, Yancy Barton	9
Ashby, Yancy Barton, Jr.	9
Ashby, Yancy Barton, Sr.	9
Asher, Edward Clay, Jr.	9
Asher, Edward Clay, Sr.	9
Ashley, Bertha (Shulze)	9
Ashley, Joe	9
Ashley, Mary Louise	264
Ashlin, Martha Matilda	1
Askew, Mary Elizabeth	303
Atha, Betty Sue (Scott)	9
Atha, Earl J	9
Athey, Sally Ann	223
Auld, Emma Alice	199
Austell, Jane (Petty)	9
Austell, William	9
Austin, Adam	9
Austin, Helen Elizabeth	40
Austin, James W	24
Austin, Joseph Adam	9
Austin, Lola	224
Austin, Rachael	72
Avans, Frances	219
Avent, James	184
Ax, Clarence "Jum"	9
Ax, Clarence W.	119
Ax, Hazel Elva Belle (Duncan)	9
Ax, Karen	128
Ayers, Earl	9
Ayers, Marilyn Kay (Clendenon)	9
Aylor, Boyd	9
Aylor, Clyde	9
Aylor, Elvie	207
Aylor, Elwanda Louise	47
Aylor, Emmett	9
Aylor, Martha	259
Aylor, Priscilla Ruth	9
Aylor, Sylvester "Bud"	39
Aylor, Verdie	107
Aylore, Oscar Franklin	47
Babineau III, Charles L.	9
Babineau, Louise (Green)	9

Name	Page
Baerg, "Betty Jo" Elizabeth Joanne (Gaitens)	9
Baerg, Freberin Parker "Bernie"	9
Baggenstoss, Albert	9
Baggenstoss, Ann Edwene	9
Baggenstoss, Charles W.	9
Baggenstoss, Pauline (Brawley)	9
Baggett, Essie	267
Bagwell, Della Mae	224
Bailey, Allen Pickett	9
Bailey, Henry	10
Bailey, Jim	248
Bailey, John	10, 199, 298
Bailey, Michael Shane "Mikey"	10
Bailey, Paralee	225
Bailey, Ronald Leon	241
Bailey, Sarah A. (Turner)	10
Bailey, Shannon Gay	10
Bailey, Unk	144, 145
Bailey, Velma Ann	230
Bain, Frank	80
Bain, James Frank	10
Bain, Marie	127
Bain, Ova Mae	80
Bain, Willadean (Gilliam)	10
Baker, Annette (Crittenden)	10
Baker, Billy	10
Baker, Carrie Melinda	26
Baker, Christine	10
Baker, Clyde	10
Baker, Curtis	10
Baker, David	10
Baker, Deborah	10
Baker, Frances Juanita (Rhea)	10
Baker, Jesse Edward	10
Baker, Jessica Susan	10
Baker, Johnnie Mae (Garner) Bonner	10
Baker, Leona	10
Baker, Lori	169
Baker, Malcolm Jackson, Sr.	10
Baker, Mariae "Mittie" Alice	296
Baker, Mary	231
Baker, Mary Frances	189
Baker, Michael Vernon	10
Baker, Ninnie Pauline	53
Baker, Robert	10
Baker, Sarah	70
Baker, Sarah Ann	86
Baker, Sarah Rhevena	71
Baker, Sarah Rhevena	165
Baker, Thomas Gene	10
Baker, Vernon Crownover	10
Baker, William Hardin	10
Baker, William Hardin	10
Balch, Mary E.	295
Baldwin, Russell	299
Bale, Annie	10
Balkenende, Christine	10
Balkenende, Robert	10
Balkenende, William	10
Ball, Eli	267
Ball, Maggie	267
Ballan, Unknown	300
Ballew, Teresa	10
Balsiger, Magdalena	130
Balsiger, Margritha "Margaret"	130
Baly, Jane	143
Banholzer, Andreas	11
Banholzer, Katherina geb (Von Bergen)	11
Banker, Lois Deborah	202
Banks, Agnes	113, 131
Banks, Dollie	101
Banks, Gordon Lee	112
Banks, James L.	11, 112
Banks, James Lafayette	287
Banks, Leila	158
Banks, Lela	302
Banks, Lela	187
Banks, Mary Levisa	287
Banks, Richard Harrison	11
Bankston, Robert	11
Bankston, Vivian Lee (Shepherd)	11
Barbee, Lily Oneida	145
Barillaro, Carmel	58
Barker, Elizabeth "Betey" (Hudson)	11
Barker, Flavius	11
Barker, Gilliam B.	11
Barker, Howel B.	11
Barker, Howell	11
Barker, Naomi (Miller)	11
Barks Cemetery	v
Barks, Daryl Ray	v
Barks, James Ed	11
Barks, Michell	282
Barks, Phillip Harold	11
Barksdale, Julin Wallace	11
Barksdale, Virginia Hyman (Hoosier)	11
Barlund, Carl Norwood	273
Barnard, Beatrice Elizabeth	290
Barnard, Donald Howard	11
Barnard, Elsie (Scissom)	11
Barnard, Howard Russell	11
Barnes, Alvin Lee	11
Barnes, Doris	1
Barnes, Fred	70
Barnes, Georgia	11

Name	Page
Barnes, Grady "Buck"	11
Barnes, Harry Richard	11
Barnes, James	11
Barnes, Jesse	11
Barnes, Karen	76, 171
Barnes, Laura	109
Barnes, Martha Ann	64
Barnes, Rhonda Denise	11
Barnes, Sarah	210
Barnes, Thomas Bruce	11
Barnes, William P.	242
Barnes, William Woodrow	245
Barnett, David	11
Barnett, Elsie Holt (Ramsey-Wright)	11
Barnett, Geraldine	248
Barnett, Gladys	51, 267
Barnett, James L.	11
Barnett, Lafayette G.	12
Barnett, Lafayette George, Jr. "Pepe"	12
Barnett, Lorna Mae	12
Barnett, William W.	12
Barney, Dewey Barney	7
Barrells, Mary	208
Barrett, Alford Ray	12
Barrett, Charles	118
Barrett, Charles Thomas	12
Barrett, Chasity Britton	23
Barrett, Chastity A. (Cunningham)	12
Barrett, Cord Montana	12
Barrett, Deanny Marie (Hawk)	12
Barrett, Ethridge	166
Barrett, Fay	170
Barrett, Irene (Kelly)	12
Barrett, Jack	12
Barrett, Jackie	12
Barrett, James Thomas	12
Barrett, Jarron	23
Barrett, Jarron G.	12
Barrett, Jeff	12
Barrett, Jeff	12
Barrett, Jo	12
Barrett, Keith	12
Barrett, Lorene (Fitch)	12
Barrett, Mae (Myers)	12
Barrett, Mamie Ione	12
Barrett, Margaret	256
Barrett, Marvin Eugene	12
Barrett, Ola Jo (Hampton)	12
Barrett, Thelma	115
Barrett, Thomas	12
Barrett, Twilla Nichole	12
Barrett, Wayne	12
Barrett, William	12
Barrett., Joseph Leo, Jr.	12
Barry, Arthur C.	112
Barry, Arthur Collier	12, 13
Barry, Ross Thomas	12
Barry, Sarah Ann	112
Barry, Thelma Juanita (Martin)	13
Barry, William Edward	13
Barry, William Edward	13, 298
Bartle, Fred Wilcox	28
Bartle, Mary Emmogene	28
Bartlett, Stella Stoner	ix
Barton, Betsy	183
Barton, Unk	282
Barwick, Lillian	181
Basham, Linda	68
Basham, Melville Eakin	296
Basham, Patsy Ann	13
Basham, Shona	143
Basham, Tommy	3, 13
Basile, Mildred	221
Basile, Stephen	221
Basim, Fannie	224
Bass, Helen	197
Bass, Rosa	222
Bass, Rose Etta	222
Bastian, Mary Ann	296
Baswell, John	269, 270
Baswell, Martha Ann	270
Baswell, Martha Ann Elizabeth	269, 301
Bateman, Athleen	223
Bateman, Effie	254
Bateman, Eliza Fay	282
Bateman, Elizie Faye	281
Bateman, Fances Austin	254
Bateman, Geneva	219
Bateman, Robert Austin	254
Bateman, Vester	296
Baters, Lucy Viola	190
Bates, Charles	182
Bates, Clarence	74
Bates, John William	194
Bates, Lily	279
Baugh, Luther Farrell	270
Bauldauf, DeVera	68
Bawel, Esther	109
Baxter, Don Houston	13
Baxter, Kathy	13
Bazile, Henrietta	202
Beaird, Cora Lee	151
Beal, Anna	278
Beam, Joy Carole	272
Beamer, John	17
Beamer, Lilah A.	17
Beamer, Minnie	17
Bean, Annie Katherine	13
Bean, Benjamin Franklin	13
Bean, Clyde	13, 127
Bean, David	102

Name	Page
Bean, Jackie	13
Bean, James Edward	13
Bean, Jay Boyd	13
Bean, Joe Lloyd	13
Bean, John William	13
Bean, Leonard Owne	13
Bean, Lillie (Meeks)	13
Bean, Lloyd	13
Bean, Lloyd Owen	13
Bean, Lucy	168
Bean, Mary Elizabeth	163, 169
Bean, Mary Ethelene	95
Bean, Mildred	13
Bean, Mildred (Campbell)	13
Bean, Raymond	13
Bean, Raymond, Jr.	13
Bean, Ronnie	13
Bean, Stanford	13
Bean, Tina	158
Bean, William Matthew	13
Bean, Willie	95
Bean, Wilma	13
Beane, Manerva	203
Beard, Delores	83
Beard, Fannie Mae	145
Beard, Virginia	254
Bearden, Emma	249
Beasley, Candyce Lynn	33
Beasley, Marion Catherin (Goedjen)	13
Beasley, William Boddie Rogers, Jr.	13
Beazilius, Helen	111
Beazilius, Louis Miller	111
Beazley, Charles	202
Beck, Dorothy	26
Becker, Elizabeth	87
Becker, Leon R.	13
Becker, Mannie (Smith)	13
Becker, Raymond Earl	25
Becker, Raymond Earl, Sr.	13
Beckman, Anna Elizabeth	115
Bedford, Annie	68, 117, 291
Bedwell, Virgie	201
Beebe, Walter	78
Beech, Betty Frances	136
Beene, Darlene	141
Beene, John	287
Beene, Rhonda	31
Beersheba Springs, TN	v
Beeson, Mattie	222
Beetch, Charles	13
Beetch, Dorothy Mae (Roeder)	13
Beitia, Cosme	41
Beitia, Rachel	41
Bekurs, Henry Gray	14
Bekurs, Suzanne (Walden)	14
Bell, Aletha	144
Bell, Cathleen (Harris)	14
Bell, Chassity	vi
Bell, Eugene R	14
Bell, Fannie	244
Bell, Harrison "Harris"	14
Bell, James F., Sr.	14
Bell, James Franklin	14
Bell, James Frederick, Jr.	14
Bell, Lisa Kay	14
Bell, Maxine	14
Bell, Sarah	14, 16
Bell, William	14
Bellflower, Bill	67
Bendel, Annie	292
Bender, Elder Urbanus	14
Bender, Nana (Rothwell)	14
Bendyna, Alexander, Sr.	14
Bendyna, George	14
Bennett, Ad Young	14
Bennett, Alma Jean	14
Bennett, Becky	14
Bennett, Cadwaldar Price	57
Bennett, Catherine Laverne	304
Bennett, Charles Jackson	14
Bennett, Clara B.	14
Bennett, Clyde William	15
Bennett, Daisy Katherine	14
Bennett, Dave	14, 238
Bennett, David	294
Bennett, David Darl	14
Bennett, Dorthy Leslie	14
Bennett, Eli Harlan	89
Bennett, Ella Adea	14
Bennett, Elsie Levona	141
Bennett, Floyd	209
Bennett, George	204
Bennett, George W.	14
Bennett, Howard	303
Bennett, James H.	286
Bennett, James W., Sr.	14
Bennett, John	14
Bennett, Johnn	204
Bennett, Joseph	130
Bennett, Lillian	57
Bennett, Luz	14
Bennett, Lynda Kay	14
Bennett, Mack	14
Bennett, Mack C.	3
Bennett, Mack Stephen	14
Bennett, Martha Grace	207
Bennett, Mary Kathleen	154
Bennett, Mary Ruth	227
Bennett, Minerva	222
Bennett, Pauline	303

Name	Page
Bennett, Pearl (Glisson) White	292
Bennett, Reba Jo	237
Bennett, Robert	14
Bennett, Ruth Carlie (Shoemake)	15
Bennett, Sue	217
Benson, Effie (Brendle)	15
Benson, Ira Nisbitte "Benny"	15
Benson, Unk	94
Bentley, Josephine	249
Benton, Lot markers	15
Benton, Mary Megan	iii, 142
Benton, Riley Warren	iii, 142
Benton, Ryan Layne	142
Bentz, Marie	110
Bergen, Johannes	11
Berger, Lillian	254
Bergholt, Edward Sanford	15
Bergholt, Edward Sanford, Sr.	15
Bernard, Donald H	252
Bernard, Laura	167, 171
Bernard, Raymond	168
Bernard, Rose	168
Berry, Charles Leroy	15, 128
Berry, Charlie	15
Berry, Erma Faye	11
Berry, Esta Lee	203
Berry, Florence Alma	295
Berry, Glenn Hampton	15
Berry, Henry Edward	15
Berry, Marcella Mildred	15
Berry, Mary	259
Berry, Rebecca	98
Berry, Sue	15
Berry, Velma	187
Bess, Anna Christine (Borne)	15
Bess, Aubrey	15
Bess, Basil	15, 16
Bess, Charlie	16
Bess, Charlie	15
Bess, Clayton Gerald	15
Bess, Clifford	16
Bess, Clifford Iola	15, 16
Bess, Clint Bodie	15
Bess, Dale	16
Bess, Debbie	12
Bess, Dusty Cole "Korn"	15
Bess, Edgar L	15
Bess, Eli	16
Bess, Elizabeth Louise (Phillips)	15
Bess, Eoda	282
Bess, Erma Azylene	256
Bess, Ether	256
Bess, George Cope	15
Bess, Gladys	16
Bess, Heber Earl	15
Bess, Homer Douglas	16
Bess, Jennie Mae	205
Bess, Jenny Mae	124
Bess, Jessie Ruth	208
Bess, Jeweldean	270
Bess, John Henry	16
Bess, John Henry "Nookum"	16
Bess, Joyce Avis	158
Bess, Margaret	274
Bess, Mary Elizabeth "Shorty" (Lockhart)	16
Bess, Oliver	16
Bess, Roger Dale	16
Bess, Rufus Doak	255
Bess, Sandra Jean (Nunley)	16
Bess, Sarah Bell	16
Bess, Therisa Gladys	15, 16
Bess, Venus	15
Bess Town Road	vii
Bess, Wiley	16
Bess, Woodrow Coleman	16
Betzel, John Hallberg "Jack"	91
Beulin, Julia	223
Bezoid, Mildred Pauline (Wise)	16
Bible, Mary Kelly	259
Bice, Billy	5
Bice, Billy Ronald	16
Bice, Oscar	16
Bice, Sarah Penny	16
Bickford, Frances Carol	56
Billingsly, Martha Jane	187
Binkley, Louisa	58
Birdwell, Bessie	261
Birdwell, Kendra Lynette	16
Birdwell, Laude Leonard	16
Birdwell, Mose	16
Birdwell, Roy Lee	16
Birdwell, Walter David	16
Birdwell, Willie Mae	62
Bishop, Charlene Grace	16
Bishop, Charles Edwin	16
Bishop, Conrad	217
Bishop, Emit Earl	298
Bishop, Gary	16
Bishop, Jacob Monroe, Jr.	16
Bishop, James Lafayette	16
Bishop, Juanita Marie (Patrick)	16
Bisop, Gladys	103
Bitterlin, Ursula	251
Bivens, Brenda	16
Bivens, Charles	16
Bivens, Darlene	231
Bivens, Donald Eugene	16

Name	Page
Bivens, Elizabeth Fay (Nance)	16
Bivens, Evelyn Denise (O'Brien)	16
Bivens, Harm	290
Bivens, Harn	288
Bivens, Jonathan	17
Bivens, Kathy	264
Bivens, Mae Arlene	17
Bivens, Mae Ellen	69
Bivens, Marshall	17
Bivens, Ottis Preston	132
Bivens, Willene	132
Bivens, William T.	16, 17, 132
Black, Audrey	239
Black, Beulah Bell	259
Black, Carol Bernice	43
Black, Celende (Taylor)	17
Black, Charles Loyd	17
Black, Elizabeth	65
Blackburn, Carolyn Janet (Pack)	17
Blackwell, Marian Louise	17
Blackwell, Nicholas Officer	17
Blackwood, Clara Etta (Wooten)	17
Blackwood, James Thomas	17
Blaine, James	211
Blake, Ethel	175
Blake, Lilah A.	17
Blake, Owen A.	17
Blake, Owen Andrew	17
Blake, Walter	17
Blakley, Darrell	17
Blakley, Deborah (Hobbs)	17
Blanton, Anna (Lowe)	17
Blanton, Doshia	169
Blassingame, Max	38
Blatnik, Edward	280
Blaylock K.M.	17
Blaylock, Allie	229, 283
Blaylock, Betty	18
Blaylock, Betty C. (White)	17
Blaylock, Geneva	152
Blaylock, Geneva Lucille	209
Blaylock, Gladys	257
Blaylock, Gladys Louella	171
Blaylock, James Echerd "Eck"	17
Blaylock, James Nimrod	17
Blaylock, James Robert	18
Blaylock, Jim	18
Blaylock, John Henry	18
Blaylock, K.M.	17
Blaylock, Kathryn C.	17
Blaylock, Margaret (Andrews)	295
Blaylock, Margaret Elizabeth (Andrews) Wideman	17
Blaylock, Mary	181
Blaylock, Nathaniel William Andrew	17
Blaylock, Nora (Prater)	17
Blaylock, Ollie (Prater)	18
Blaylock, Orine	214
Blaylock, Robert	209
Blaylock, Robert "Bob"	18
Blaylock, Robert H.	18
Blaylock, Robert Hal	17
Blaylock, Una Mae (Walker)	18
Blaylock, William Nathaniel	258
Blaylock, William Nathaniel "Blue"	18
Blesi, Regula	240
Bleuer, John	284
Bleuer, Louise E.	284
Blevins, Catherine	240
Blevins, Ike	18
Blevins, John Truman	18
Blevins, Martha E.	179
Blevins, Nancy	219
Blondelet, Jules	223
Bloodworth, Barbara Ann	202
Blum, Eva Jeannette (Johnson)	18
Blum, James Edgar	18
Blumer, Anna	151
Blythe, Charlotte	244
Blythe, Lottie	244
Boak, Glenda	244
Bobo, Mary	120
Bogart, Roberta Ellen	107
Boggess, Cecil Woodrow	18
Boggess, Leo Edward	18
Boggs, Cora (Pearson)	18
Boggs, Myrtle	31
Boggs, Pleasant D.	18
Boggs, William Simms	18
Bohannan, Linda	100
Bohannon, Mattie	116
Bohanon, Isaiah Columbus	300
Bohr, Dagmar (Plumacher)	18
Bohr, Fred	18
Boland, Mary Adaline	42
Boland, Mary Adeline	205
Bolen, Franklin	39
Bolen, Matilda Belle	39, 151
Bolin, Carolyn	175
Bolinger, Carrie	98, 263
Bolinger, Carrie Lee (Magness)	18
Bolinger, Delno	98, 263
Bolinger, Delno Leeotis "Dale"	18
Bolinger, Emily Dell	98

Name	Page
Bolinger, John Neal	18
Bolinger, Milburn Paris	18
Bonar, Barbara J.	213
Bond, Charles T	300
Bond, Martha	36
Bond, Ora Vincent	267
Bond, Virgie	290, 300
Bondurant, Elizabeth	97, 251
Bone, Duke "Sam"	18
Bone, Edith	33, 282
Bone, Edith Louise	30, 158, 216
Bone, Elizabeth	234
Bone, Janie	60, 126, 291
Bone, Janie A.	164
Bone, Male stillborn	18
Bone, Martin Luther	18, 19
Bone, Martin Luther Bone, Sr.	19
Bone, Mary Ann	190
Bone, Mary Elizabeth (Owens)	19
Bone, Mary Eva	19
Bone, Sammy Duke Sr.	19
Bone, Sammy Duke, Jr.	19
Bone, Samuel	18, 19, 134
Bone, Sharon	19
Bone, Will	187
Bone, William Kasper	302
Bonner, Charlie Vernon	92
Bonner, Clifton	19
Bonner, Faye Church	iii
Bonner, Glenn E.	210
Bonner, Glenn William	10
Bonner, Kate	41
Bonner, Katie	288
Bonner, Morgan Haskel	19, 27
Bonner, Rachel	179
Bonner, Sarah	203
Bonner, Wayne Oddist	19
Booker, Carl	19
Booker, Carl Frank	19
Booker, Ode H	82
Booker, Rochelle	19
Bookman, Willie D. "Bill"	32
Bookout, Cecil C.	19
Bookout, Lizzie R.	19
Bookout, Marylou	11
Boot, Betty Jean	187
Bordenet, Anna Bernadine	121
Boren, George	19
Boren, Judy Ann (Tate)	19
Boring, Thenia	161
Born, Charles	10
Born, Fred	19
Born, Frederick Theodore	19
Borne, Abbie Mary Ellen (Anderson)	19
Borne, Alice	269
Borne, Annie Bell	128, 232
Borne, Bonnie Lorrine (Sweeton)	19
Borne, Carl Edward	19, 267
Borne, Deborah Kay	213
Borne, George Washington	19
Borne, Howard	19
Borne, Jessie Arthur	144
Borne, June	79
Borne, Kathy	50
Borne, Labrina Kay (McDaniel)	19
Borne, Lawrence	15, 137
Borne, Lonnie	19
Borne, Melvin "Snood"	19
Borne, Mesha	25
Borne, Virgil Marie (Green)	19
Borne, Wanda	260
Borrensen, Anna	133
Borrensen, June Mildred	133
Borrensen, Olaf	133
Borwn, Robert McKenzie	13
Boscaino, Vincent Frank	19
Boscanino, Vincinzo Francisco	19
Bost, Mary Magdalene	253
Bost, Mary Sarah	194
Bost, Rachel Arkansas	92
Bost, Sarah Louise	26
Bostain, James M	146
Boston, Barbara Nell (Mowdry)	20
Boston, Bill	20
Boswell, Charles William	20
Boswell, Mary Nell "Nello"	20
Boulder, Tennie	224
Bouldin, Andrew Westman	120
Bouldin, Annie	224
Bouldin, Annie Betty	224
Bouldin, Cora	298
Bouldin, Dimple	227
Bouldin, Elizabeth	42
Bouldin, Elizabeth Ann (Schoenmann)	20
Bouldin, Esther L	15
Bouldin, Gary Lee	20
Bouldin, Irvin	298
Bouldin, James Allan	20
Bouldin, James Larry	20
Bouldin, James Parker	20
Bouldin, Leander	20
Bouldin, Nina	140, 230
Bouldin, Oma	221
Bouldin, Orphia Carlee	150
Bouldin, Ralph E.	20
Bouldin, Reba Rust	190

Name	Page
Bouldin, Roy Lyn	20
Bouldin, Tennie	224
Bouldin, Wade Crawford	20
Bouldin, Willard	20
Bouldin, Zada Elizabeth	21
Boulton, Robert	38
Bourne, Walter	192
Bowden, Margaret Ann	276
Bower, Bessie	150
Bowers, Anna Evelyn	24
Bowers, Juan	247
Bowles, Margaret	120
Bowlin, Comfort	235
Bowling, Elmer Earnest	20
Bowling, Ralph Richard	20
Bowman, Frances	140
Bowman, Kenneth Walton	76
Bowman, Linda Sue	303
Bowman, Ola	254
Bowman, Roger Wilson	20
Box, Cox	50
Box, William Wiley	225
Boyd, Attie Lee (Higdon)	20
Boyd, Clyde	147
Boyd, Clyde	147
Boyd, David	20
Boyd, Elizabeth	59
Boyd, Etta Sutton	213
Boyd, Fannie Ardella	20
Boyd, George Dibrell	20
Boyd, Martha Sue (Thorpe)	20
Boyd, Nancy	220
Boyd, Oma Lee	147
Boyer, Malcolmb Emmet	20
Boyer, Margaret Neil (Brooksher)	20
Boyette, Barbara Ann (Givens)	20
Boyette, Clyde	20
Boyles, Lois	83
Braadshaw, Nancy Catherine	260
Bradbury, Ada Jane	292
Braden, Araminda	4
Braden, Araminda "Mindy"	129
Braden, Bell	166, 167
Braden, Bessie	156
Braden, Billy	171
Braden, Buster	21
Braden, Claude Hobart	20
Braden, Denver Wayne	20
Braden, Dora Lee	180
Braden, Geneva Edna	20
Braden, Harley	20
Braden, Hester Mae (James)	20
Braden, Irene "Renie"	141
Braden, Isaac Michael	21
Braden, James Mitchell	21
Braden, Jeremy Louis	21, 293
Braden, Kirk	21
Braden, Margie Marie (Layne)	21
Braden, Mary	164
Braden, Mary Louise	170
Braden, Myrtle	231
Braden, Pauline	54
Braden, Randy	21
Braden, Richard Lee	21
Braden, Rosa Lee	6
Braden, Tabitha "Bicie" Louvisa	21
Braden, Tommy Eugene	21
Braden, William	156
Braden, Willie	213
Bradford, Georgia Lee	39
Bradford, Quinton	21
Bradford, Quinton, Jr.	21
Bradford, Terry	291
Bradley, Jane	48
Bradley, Lois	87
Bradshaw, Joseph	259
Bradshaw, Margaret	257
Brady, Bessie	240, 272
Brady, Betty Sue	182
Brady, Billiefaye Lee (Burnette)	21
Brady, Bonnie	186
Brady, Clyde	21
Brady, Clyde	289
Brady, Hazel Louise (Campbell)	21
Brady, Hershel Glenn	21, 33, 248
Brady, Hershell Glenn	21
Brady, James Colonel	21
Brady, James Mitchell	63
Brady, Johnny	21
Brady, Joyce	289
Brady, Kevin	21
Brady, Minnie	99
Braly, June Gloria	181
Bramblett, Emma	102
Bramblett, Emma	135
Branch, Michael	28
Brandon, Carl Jack	175
Brandon, Elizabeth	275
Brandon, Nancy O'Neal	42
Brandon, Naomi	175
Brandon, O'Neal	42
Brandt, Josephine	88
Brandt, Julius	88
Brannan, Cindy	30
Brannan, Evelyn	92
Brannan, Helen Joyce (Partin)	21
Brannan, Johnny C.	21
Brannan, Johnsie Katherine	21

Name	Page
Brannan, Marvin	21
Brannan, Marvin, Rev.	21
Brannan, Mary Ann E. (Hessey)	21
Brannan, Mike	30
Brannan, Myrtle	220
Brannon, Andrew	271
Brannon, Marshall	91
Brannon, Martha	271
Brannon, Sherrie Ellen	91
Brannon, Sol	21
Braseel-Davis, Imojean (Nunley)	21
Braseel, Clyde "C.L."	56
Braseel, Clyde Leo	21
Braseel, Ethridge "Bud"	116, 117
Braseel, Frankie	298
Braseel, Selma Joyce (King)	22
Braseel, Teresa Carol	187
Braseel, Tommy Ray	22
Brashear, Alma	102, 103
Brashear, Sallie Clara	293
Braswell, Nellie	127
Bratcher, Helen	294
Bratcher, Rose Marie	109
Brawley, J.D.	22
Brawley, Norman	9
Brawley, Vera Jean (Sartin)	22
Braxton, James	22
Braxton, Lacy	22
Bray, Clarice Virginia	22
Bray, Epps	22
Bray, Jerome	22
Bray, Wanda C.	234
Braziel, James Franklin	167
Braziel, Joann	164
Brazier, Berry Luke	22, 23
Brazier, Chad	22
Brazier, Danny Lee	22
Brazier, Ethel	47
Brazier, Gary	22
Brazier, Jona Mae	22
Brazile, Edna	47
Brazile, James Franklin	183
Brazile, William Norris "Bee"	297
Brazille, Leona	93
Breadwell, Rebecca Emeline	233
Brechtelabauer, Margaret	265
Breedlove, Carl	299
Brendle, Jon Harmon	15
Breshears, Hazel	262
Bretz, Jaxson Case	22
Bretz, John	22
Bretz, John Walker	22
Bretze, Hilda Grace	111
Brewer, Amy Lou	291
Brewer, Bernice "Bones"	20
Brewer, Burnes E. "Tooter Bill"	109
Brewer, Charles	22
Brewer, Clifford H. "Buck"	22
Brewer, Clifford Howell "Buck"	23
Brewer, Doris	23
Brewer, Earl	169
Brewer, Edna (Layne)	22
Brewer, Eugene N.	22
Brewer, Evelyn Dean (Taylor)	22
Brewer, Frank	224
Brewer, Grady	22, 23
Brewer, J. Ronny	22
Brewer, James Echerd	22
Brewer, Jesse L.	22
Brewer, Kenneth	22
Brewer, Linda F. "Little Red" (Murphy)	22
Brewer, Mark Dwain	22
Brewer, Mary Catherine (Coffelt)	23
Brewer, Pearlie Alma	202
Brewer, Ralph Otto	23
Brewer, Randall Ralph	23
Brewer, Rosa Nell	44
Brewer, Terry Ernest	23
Brewer, Walter	22, 52, 54, 66, 291
Brewer, Willette	16
Bridgers-Carlos, Jane Bennett	23
Bridgers, Ben	23
Bridgers, Sue Ellen	23
Brigance, Lola	253
Bright, Julia	299
Brinkley, Billie Marie	291
Brinkley, Evelyn	291
Britnell, Sue	257
Brittin, Patsy Joan	99
Britton, Buddie	23
Britton, Chasten Ryean	23
Britton, Gilliam Ernest	23
Britton, Glenda	97
Britton, Hilda (Brazier)	23
Britton, J. Raymond	23
Britton, Tony Britton	23
Britton, Wilson "Shorty"	23
Brock, Dortha Lee	222
Brock, Hobert	201
Brock, James Alton	23
Brock, John	23
Brock, Lucille	61
Brock, Marzella Marcie (Morrison)	23
Brock, Sarah	23
Brock, Walter	23
Brock, Z. Janie	234
Brodt, Andrew	23

Name	Page
Brodt, Andrew Jacob	23
Bromley, Barbara Ann	211
Bronstetter, Ruth	23
Bronstetter, Walton Lee	23
Bronstetter, William Eli	23
Brookman, Allen	23
Brookman, Andrew Jackson	23
Brookman, Jennie E. (Downam)	23
Brookman, Katherine	221, 285
Brookman, Keith Allen	23
Brookman, Mary Erma	144
Brookman, Shirley (Smith)	23
Brooks, Charles Bailey	23
Brooks, Charles Eugene	23
Brooks, James	23
Brooks, James Albert	23
Brooks, James Calvin "Flop"	23
Brooks, Louis	102
Brooks, Thelma	99
Brooks, Walter W.	24
Brooks, William Lyndal	23
Brooksher, Audie Lee	20
Brookshire, Nadine	90, 264
Brothers, Edna Virginia	203
Brothers, Elsie Harlan	24
Brothers, Fred Newton	24
Brothers, James Robert "Bob"	24
Brothers, Matthew Talley	24
Brown, Abbie D.	268
Brown, Abigail	268
Brown, Alexander William	72
Brown, Allan	24
Brown, Alvers	283
Brown, Amanda	53
Brown, Anthony Lynn	24, 25
Brown, B. Marvin	26
Brown, Becky	217
Brown, Ben Tilman	25
Brown, Bertha	280
Brown, Bessie Frances	272
Brown, Bessie Lee (Burnett)	24
Brown, Betty	276
Brown, Bettye	19
Brown, Bill	24
Brown, Buford, Sr.	24
Frederick, Burt Brown	26
Brown, Burton	41
Brown, Carl R.	24
Brown, Carlene	216
Brown, Carol	251, 252
Brown, Clara	24
Brown, Clara Bell	274
Brown, Clarence "Tobe"	26
Brown, Claude	25
Brown, Connie Darlene (Paradise)	24
Brown, Daniel Wade	51
Brown, Darrell Hembry	25
Brown, David	26
Brown, Deborah Marie (Campbell)	24
Brown, Della	147
Brown, Della Anna	214
Brown, Dillard Dee Tillman	38
Brown, Doc	169
Brown, Doris	95
Brown, Dwight Lee	24
Brown, Edgar Louis	24
Brown, Edna Frances	62, 288
Brown, Edward H.	74
Brown, Eleanor Elizabeth (Brooks)	24
Brown, Elmer	28
Brown, Elmer Benson	24
Brown, Estell	145
Brown, Ethleen Gladys	52
Brown, Faye	300
Brown, Flona Lee	29
Brown, Florence	104
Brown, Florence Margaret	65
Brown, Frank	24
Brown, George Daryl	24
Brown, George W.	238
Brown, Gladys	185
Brown, Glenda Sue	207
Brown, Harvey E.	25
Brown, Hazel (Floyd)	24
Brown, Helen E.	24, 25
Brown, Hembree	30
Brown, Henry L	25
Brown, Herman	49
Brown, Hershel	17
Brown, Hershel Douglas	24
Brown, Hezekiah Wesley	271
Brown, Howard Allen	230
Brown, Ida	54
Brown, Ida Pearl (Johnson)	25
Brown, Isaac Sanford	52
Brown, J.B.	30
Brown, James Albert, Jr. "Chief Brown"	25
Brown, James Albert, Sr.	25
Brown, James Allen	25
Brown, James Knox Polk	24
Brown, James M.	279
Brown, James William	25
Brown, Jane Roberta (O'Neal)	25
Brown, Janie	267
Brown, Jenna Mae	34
Brown, Jennie Lee	272
Brown, John	25, 267

Brown, John B.	25	Brown, Nancy Elizabeth (Gross)	26	Brown, Velma Carlene	216
Brown, John H.	25	Brown, Nancy Ellen	229	Brown, Viola	285
Brown, John R.	26	Brown, Nellene	226	Brown, Violet I.	26
Brown, Josephine	74	Brown, Norris B.	160	Brown, Virginia Mae	104
Brown, Joshua Darrell	25	Brown, Paul David	26	Brown, Wade Stanley	112
Brown, Juanita (Layne)	25	Brown, Paul David	25	Brown, William	26, 34
Brown, Katy Lynn	262	Brown, Paul Douglas "Tree"	26	Brown, William Almond	26
Brown, Kelley	25	Brown, Penelope "Neppie or P.J." (Saint)	26	Brown, William Almond "W.A."	26
Brown, Leander Virgil	25	Brown, Phyllis (Tate)	26	Brown, William Cecil	25
Brown, Lela	211	Brown, Preston	25	Brown, William Duke	26
Brown, Leona M. (McCubbins)	25	Brown, Prudence	136	Brown, William Robert "Bob"	26
Brown, Lewis Wayne	25	Brown, Quinton Silas	26	Brown, William Sanford	26
Brown, Lewis Wayne	24	Brown, Robert	25	Brown, Willie May	144
Brown, Lindsay Leonard	26	Brown, Robert McKenzie	24	Brown, Willis Eston	25
Brown, Louis Bud	24	Brown, Roddy	25	Brownell, Walter	27
Brown, Lucille	181	Brown, Rosa (Meyer)	26	Brownell, Ross Thomas	27
Brown, Lucille	289	Brown, Rose	28	Broyles, Flora	286
Brown, Luella	47	Brown, Roy E.	24	Brugger, Anna Marie	101
Brown, Lula (Wooten)	25	Brown, Rudolph	24, 272	Brunett, Jennifer	127
Brown, Mae	16	Brown, Russell	63	Bryan, Carl Ellis	143
Brown, Mannie Becker (Smith)	25	Brown, Russell Lester	268	Bryan, Dale McGregor	27
Brown, Marilena	25	Brown, Sarah	191	Bryan, Lorene (Gilliam)	27
Brown, Marilenea	24	Brown, Sarah Jane	74, 149	Bryan, Oakley Willis	27
Brown, Marshall E.	25	Brown, Silas James	26	Bryan, Thelma "Jane"	27
Brown, Martha D	180	Brown, Spencer Burton	42	Bryan, Thomas M	27
Brown, Martha Josephine (Johnson)	25	Brown, Stanley Wade "Stan"	26	Bryant, Abbye	53
Brown, Marvin Stanley	26	Brown, Stephen	24	Bryant, Allen Leo	292
Brown, Mary	157	Brown, Sula	160	Bryant, Anna	197
Brown, Mary (Fults)	26	Brown, Tammy Lee	26	Bryant, Cindy	27
Brown, Mary Sophrona	126	Brown, Thomas	144	Bryant, Clara	183
Brown, Mildred Irene	160	Brown, Thomas H.	59	Bryant, Ellen K.	213
Brown, Mildred T (Dyer)	26	Brown, Thomas Richard	26	Bryant, Elmer Jackson	27
Brown, Mollie Pearl	3	Brown, Ulysses	29	Bryant, Ethel	27
Brown, Mollie Pearl	174	Brown, Ulysses Grant	24	Bryant, Eva (Sinks)	27
Brown, Myrtle	107	Brown, Ulysses S.	26	Bryant, Garret	27
Brown, Myrtle Edith	52	Brown, Ulysses S. Grant, Jr.	26	Bryant, George Ferrell	27
				Bryant, Harriet	141

Name	Page
Bryant, Hazel Edith (Thomas)	27
Bryant, Helen	246
Bryant, Jerry William	27
Bryant, Jesse Lawrence	27
Bryant, Laura Elizabeth	151
Bryant, Mildred Opal	294
Bryant, Millie (Smith)	27
Bryant, Oscar	290
Bryant, Pat	27
Bryant, Rebecca Elizabeth	213
Bryant, Seth S.	262
Bryant, Troy	27
Bryant, W.R.	27
Bryant, Whitney	27
Bryant, William	213
Bryant, William "Houston"	27
Brymer, Lois	261
Buchan, John Russell	184
Buckholz, Wilhelmina	185
Buckner, Allie Mae (Hawk)	27
Buckner, Benjamin Franklin "B.F."	27
Buckner, Carl	27
Buckner, Carl Junior	27
Buckner, Clay	297
Lindsey, Clayton Buckner	27
Buckner, Dennis Wade	27
Buckner, Dustin Wade	27
Buckner, Finis	27
Buckner, Finis "Randy"	27
Buckner, Howard Don	27
Buckner, Jean	94
Buckner, Jean Ann (Gallagher)	27
Buckner, Joe	27, 28, 94
Buckner, Mary	27
Buckner, Mary Opal (Bonner)	27
Buckner, Terri Jane (Chambers)	27
Buckner, William Bluford	28
Buckout, Dorothy	263
Buckout, John	263
Buddy, Upton Bell	208
Buehler, Alton J	28
Buehler, Jack Alton	28
Buffington, Martha Louise "Marty"	28
Buffington, Ronald Paul	28
Bullard, Amanda Jane	27
Bullard, Eliza	83
Bunch, Alex	214
Bunch, Doris	108
Bunch, Tracy Laverne (Sartain)	28
Bunch, Warren Otto	108, 237
Bunde, Lynetta	104
Bunde, Marvin	28
Bunde, Matthew Wayne	28
Burdett, Sarah Jane	174
Burdick, Alfred Burnell	28
Burdick, Alfred William	28
Burdick, Mary Emmogene	28
Burford, Ohley B.	203
Burge, Martha (Page)	28
Burge, Rev. John E	28
Burgess, Julia Ann	88
Burgess, Savannah	240
Burgos, Barbara Lee	126
Burkhalter, Emma (Lyda)	28
Burkhalter, James C.	28
Burks, John Clay	303
Burnet, David	28
Burnet, William Bromwell II	28
Burnett, Albert Cleveland	29
Burnett, Amanda Jean	28
Burnett, Angela A. "Angie"	28
Burnett, Ann	48
Burnett, Barbara Ann	28
Burnett, Bette	120
Burnett, Betty (Meeks)	28
Burnett, Billy Garner	29
Burnett, Brenda S.	299
Burnett, Carl David	21, 29
Burnett, Carlton H.	28
Burnett, Carlton H.	29
Burnett, Carol Lynn	88
Burnett, Charles Benny	29
Burnett, Clara Louise	79
Burnett, Claudia "Sissy"	113
Burnett, Diane	21
Burnett, Edna Jewell (White)	29
Burnett, Edward Melvin	29
Burnett, Elisha	29, 37
Burnett, Elisha "Lish"	29
Burnett, Etta Mae	171
Burnett, Evelyn Marie (Nix)	29
Burnett, Frank Savage	29
Burnett, Frankie E.	29
Burnett, Grover Cleveland	29
Burnett, James	28
Burnett, Janice	293
Burnett, Jim	293
Burnett, John	29
Burnett, John David "J.D.".	29
Burnett, John Francis	24
Burnett, Karen	141
Burnett, Kim	29
Burnett, Leburn Hoyt "L.H."	29
Burnett, Lucy	72
Burnett, Lula Mae (Corn)	29

Name	Page
Burnett, Margaret W. (Coffelt)	29
Burnett, Margie	269
Burnett, Margie	301
Burnett, Mary (Byers)	29
Burnett, Mary Ethel	119
Burnett, Melvin	117
Burnett, Morgan	111
Burnett, Nancy	198
Burnett, Nancy Jane	177
Burnett, Nathaniel Hoyt	28
Burnett, Nellie	252
Burnett, Ophelia	6
Burnett, Ralph Edwin	29
Burnett, Rose	202
Burnett, Virginia	54
Burnett, Walter R.	29
Burnett, Willie	29, 119
Burnette, Brittany Aaron	29
Burnette, Flona Lee (Brown)	29
Burnette, James C	150
Burnette, Jeffery Allen	30
Burnette, John David "J.D."	29
Burnette, Johnny	30
Burnette, Melody	29
Burnette, Tommy Harmon	29
Burney, Gene	30
Burney, Linda (Matheson)	30
Burns, Mary Ann	86
Burns, Nellie Mae	291
Burr, Jno.	30
Burr, Norris, Rev.	25
Burrel, Kelly	179
Burrell, Dorothey (Ward)	30
Burrough's Cove Road	vii
Burroughs, Deck	291
Burroughs, Fannie	172
Burroughs, Florence A.	291
Burroughs, Martha J.	291
Burroughs/Burrows, Josie Josephine (Campbell)	30
Burrows, Garnett	241
Burrows, J.	30
Burrows, Jack	30
Burrows, Jack	30
Burrows, Kathleen	30
Burrows, Mary Rebecca	21
Burrows, Melvin	57
Burrows, Rachel	51
Burrows, Scott Brannon	30
Burrows, Shelby Jean (Brown)	30
Burrows, Stanley	30
Burrows, Valerie	234
Burrows, Wanda	57
Burton, Mary Minerva	272
Bush, Betty Jean (Finch)	30
Bush, Ruby Lee	104
Bush, Wayne	105
Bush, William H,	30
Bush, William Miller	30
Bush, William Miller "Bill"	30
Bussard, Casey	30
Bussard, Christy	30
Bussell, Lillie Mae	20
Butcher, Unk	228
Butler, George Parker	30
Butler, Claude	30
Butler, David	53
Butler, Emily	53
Butler, Marjorie Claudette	30
Butler, Pearl	30
Butler, Sharon	30
Butler, Timothy Joseph	30
Butler, Vickie	242
Butler, Walter, Sr.	30
Butler, William	30
Butner, Clarentine T. (Green)	30
Butner, Jim Ed	219
Butner, Noah	30
Byars, "Joe" William	30
Byars, "Joe" William Joab	31
Byars, Annie Frances (McDaniel)	30
Byars, Archie D. "Oscar"	31
Byars, Cecil Udell	162
Byars, Donald Wayne	31
Byars, Floyd Mitchell	31
Byars, George David	30
Byars, Herbert Henry	31
Byars, Infant	31
Byars, Jacob Lambirth	31
Byars, Joab Lambirth	31, 162, 277
Byars, John W.	31
Byars, John Wayne	31, 171
Byars, Malinda A. (Teague)	31
Byars, Marie	31
Byars, Nina	185
Byars, Nina Mae	185
Byars, Oscar	31
Byars, Sarah Morgan	172
Byars, William J.	31
Byars/Byers, Joe William "Joab"	63
Byers, Mary	32
Byers, Augusta (Smith)	31
Byers, Barbara	32
Byers, Bill	31, 107
Byers, Billy	32
Byers, Charles	32
Byers, Charles Frank	37
Byers, Charles Frank "Charlie"	31

Name	Page
Byers, Charles William	32
Byers, Charles William "Frosty"	31
Byers, Daniel	32
Byers, Donald Wayne	31
Byers, Donna Jo	31
Byers, Dustin "Big Country"	31
Byers, Floyd Mitchel	31
Byers, G.C.	31
Byers, George	128
Byers, George David	32
Byers, Grace Evelyn	32
Byers, Hattie Mae	31
Byers, James	32
Byers, James William	32
Byers, Jason	32
Byers, Jimmy Ray	32
Byers, Joab Lambirth	30
Byers, Joe William	32
Byers, John	32
Byers, John	114
Byers, John Berry	32
Byers, John Wayne	32, 62
Byers, Johnnie B.	32
Byers, Johnny Billy	32
Byers, Lena	128
Byers, Lena Rivers (Stump)	32
Byers, Lisa Ellen (Fredrick)	32
Byers, Mary	31, 37
Byers, Mary Ann	32
Byers, Mary Ellen	29
Byers, Maude Elizabeth (Taylor)	32
Byers, Mildred	252
Byers, Mildred Kathleen	252
Byers, Payton Elizabeth Clarity	32
Byers, Robert	295
Byers, Rodney	32
Byers, Verna	5
Byers, Verna Louise	66
Byers, Virginia	220
Byers, Vivian	104
Byers, William	32
Byers, William E.	31
Byers, William Monroe	29, 31, 32
Byers, William Morrison	32
Byers. Myrtle Ellen Fults	75
Bynum, Callie	2
Byrd, Anna Ruth	32
Byrd, Beatrice	49
Byrd, Georgia	109
Byrd, Jeffrey Lee	32
Byrd, Tabitha	32
Byrd, Zola	165, 171
Cabereras, Delphenia	1
Cagle, Albert A.	33
Cagle, Allie	18
Cagle, Allie	209
Cagle, Allie C.	18
Cagle, Billy R.	32
Cagle, Billy Ray	33
Cagle, Bonnie Lynn	222
Cagle, David Wade	32
Cagle, Dexter	33
Cagle, Dona	22
Cagle, Dona	52
Cagle, Dona	54
Cagle, Dona	291
Cagle, Donna	66
Cagle, Donnie Ray	32
Cagle, Gladys Marie	33
Cagle, James	32
Cagle, James	33
Cagle, James	33
Cagle, James A	33
Cagle, James A.	33
Cagle, James A.	33
Cagle, James Larry "Jim"	33
Cagle, Jerry Albert	33
Cagle, Larry Randall	33
Cagle, Lula Mae	194
Cagle, Mary	112
Cagle, Mary L.	11
Cagle, Michael Douglas	33
Cagle Mountain	vi
Cagle, Myrtle Marie	162
Cagle, Ollie	5
Cagle, Ollie Jackson	205
Cagle, Wavie Lillie Mae (Layne)	33
Cain, Grace	88
Cain, John	251
Cain, Rebecca	251
Cain, Salinda	252
Cal Place	viii
Caldwell, Allie White	47
Caldwell, Allon	293
Caldwell, Alton	33
Caldwell, Amanda	198
Caldwell, Amanda	199
Caldwell, Amanda	198
Caldwell, Andrew	66
Caldwell, Anita	36
Caldwell, Anita	288
Caldwell, Billy Eugene	33
Caldwell, Billy Ray	34
Caldwell, Brenda Lorene (Woodward)	33
Caldwell, Bruce Wayne	33
Caldwell, Calvin B.	34
Caldwell, Calvin B.	266
Caldwell, Carl	34
Caldwell, Carl Junior	33
Caldwell, Carolyn	33

Name	Page
Caldwell, Carrie Etta (Layne)	33
Caldwell, Charles Edward, Jr.	34
Caldwell, Charles Edward, Sr.	34
Caldwell, Charles T, "Chick"	33
Caldwell, Christine	33
Caldwell, Clara Elizabeth	229
Caldwell, Clara Elvia Marie	123
Caldwell, Craig Alton	33
Caldwell, Cynthia K.	85
Caldwell, Della	66
Caldwell, Denise Linette (Long)	33
Caldwell, Elvia	123
Caldwell, Erica	44
Caldwell, Ethel Virginia	177
Caldwell, Frank H.	33
Caldwell, Gene	34
Caldwell, Gene	294
Caldwell, Geneva	56
Caldwell, Geneva	182
Caldwell, Gladys	116
Caldwell, Gladys	262
Caldwell, Grace E. (McDaniel)	33
Caldwell, Grover H.	34
Caldwell, Harvey	220
Caldwell, Hazel L.	21
Caldwell, Hazel Louise	248
Caldwell, Hazel Louise (Campbell)	33
Caldwell, Helen	213
Caldwell, Helen	43
Caldwell, Helen Beatrice	9
Caldwell, Helen Dean (Hayes)	34
Caldwell, Helen Lena (Knowlan)	34
Caldwell, Herbert	34
Caldwell, Herbert Edward	34
Caldwell, Hilda Naomi (Meeks)	34
Caldwell, Hillard	33
Caldwell, Jessie	134
Caldwell, Jim	34
Caldwell, Joyce	33
Caldwell, Kenneth Ray	34
Caldwell, Larry Dean	34
Caldwell, Lee Franklin	33
Caldwell, Leonard	21
Caldwell, Lillie Mae (Sanders)	34
Caldwell, Louella	53
Caldwell, Louise	292
Caldwell, Mae Dean	192
Caldwell, Maggie	47
Caldwell, Maggie	220
Caldwell, Marcus	33
Caldwell, Marsha	37
Caldwell, Martha Edna	274
Caldwell, Martha Edna	275
Caldwell, Mary	225
Caldwell, Melvin Ray	147
Caldwell, Millie	285
Caldwell, Ophelia (Myers)	34
Caldwell, Ophelia Della	116
Caldwell, Oscar Shrum	53
Caldwell, Pamela Jo (Dent)	34
Caldwell, Patricia Ann (Anderson)	34
Caldwell, Patricia Sue	103
Caldwell, Paul Henderson	33
Caldwell, Polly Ann (Brown)	34
Caldwell, Rhonda	145
Caldwell, Ricky	33
Caldwell, Rosa	187
Caldwell, Rosa Bell	302
Caldwell, Ruth Sarah (Jackson)	34
Caldwell, Sandra Sue	45
Caldwell, Sarah	249
Caldwell, Sherri Lynn	184
Caldwell, Stanley	223
Caldwell, Stanley	285
Caldwell, Stanley, Jr.	34
Caldwell, Stephen Edward	34
Caldwell, Tammy	140
Caldwell, Unk	34
Caldwell, William	4
Caldwell, William Howard "Soll"	34
Caldwell, Willie Mae	251
Caldwell, Willis Alton	33
Calhoun, William	92
Callahan, Tammie	293
Cameron, Ruby	97
Camp , Noel Loner	56
Camp, Martha Frances	128
Camp, Martha Frances	128
Camp, Martha Frances	129
Campbell , Frances	190
Campbell, Adell	73
Campbell, Adell	74
Campbell, Alex	34
Campbell, Alexander W.	164
Campbell, Alexander W.	35
Campbell, Alexander W.	36
Campbell, Alexander William	63
Campbell, Alice	182
Campbell, Allen	36
Campbell, Andrew	236
Campbell, Andrew Jackson	72, 177
Campbell, Ann Hannah	287
Campbell, Anna Faye	185
Campbell, Arch H.	37

Campbell, Arizona	167	Campbell, Eloise Iva	281	Campbell, Lanny	54
Campbell, Betty	161	Campbell, Elsie	183	Campbell, Larry	35
Campbell, Betty Jean	228, 268	Campbell, Ernest "Pib"	269	Campbell, Lemuel	30
Campbell, Betty Ray	85	Campbell, Estes	187	Campbell, Lemuel J., Sr.	37
Campbell, Bird	125	Campbell, Frances Sue	187	Campbell, Lila Ann	243
Campbell, Bob Alton	34	Campbell, Gail	61	Campbell, Lillard	36
Campbell, Bonnie	237	Campbell, Gertrude	54	Campbell, Lillian	36
Campbell, Bonnie Mae	164, 172	Campbell, Gloria Velvedean	279	Campbell, Lilly Ann	205
Campbell, Brosie	36, 37, 244	Campbell, Harris	36, 82	Campbell, Lisa Meeks	v
Campbell, Brossie	36	Campbell, Harrison James	157	Campbell, Lorene	178
Campbell, Buffy Lynn	85			Campbell, Louie	158
Campbell, Buford Hollis	21	Campbell, Harry Damon	36	Campbell, Louie Howard	215
Campbell, Carrie	236	Campbell, Hazel	35		
Campbell, Catherine	34	Campbell, Hazel Louise	274	Campbell, Louisa/Louiza (Phipps)	35
Campbell, Cedric	263	Campbell, Henrietta	170	Campbell, Lucille	240
Campbell, Celo	117	Campbell, Hilda Hazel	42	Campbell, Lucille "Lucy" Bell	35
Campbell, Cerena D.	36	Campbell, Hollis	35	Campbell, Lucille (Stacy)	35
Campbell, Charles Wayne	34	Campbell, Hollis Buford	33		
		Campbell, Hugh	34, 35, 242, 287	Campbell, Lucretia	76
Campbell, Clara Evangeline	75			Campbell, Lucy (Smith)	35
		Campbell, James "Peanut"	156	Campbell, Mae Ellen	56, 109, 191
Campbell, Cleo	235				
Campbell, Danie	208	Campbell, James C.	34	Campbell, Malcolm "Dickie"	35
Campbell, Della	13, 34, 193	Campbell, James Enoch "Jim"	36		
Campbell, Delores	139			Campbell, Marlee	227
Campbell, Dianne	34	Campbell, James M.	36	Campbell, Martha	51, 107, 113
Campbell, Dorothy	34	Campbell, James William	194		
Campbell, Douglas John	35			Campbell, Martha Elizabeth	230
Campbell, Drew	30	Campbell, Jean Ellen	32		
Campbell, Drew	272	Campbell, Jenny	30	Campbell, Martin	35
Campbell, Edward	13, 34, 193	Campbell, Jeremy	192	Campbell, Mary "Polly"	287
Campbell, Edward "Duxie"	200	Campbell, Jeweldene	294	Campbell, Mary Etta "Missouri"	241
		Campbell, John Homer	36	Campbell, Maudie Frances	240
Campbell, Edward, Jr.	36	Campbell, John W.	iii		
Campbell, Elizabeth	124	Campbell, Johnny	35	Campbell, May Ellen	21
Campbell, Elizabeth "Betty" (Nunley)	34	Campbell, Johnny	36	Campbell, Megan	266
		Campbell, Juanita	85	Campbell, Melvin	35, 36
Campbell, Ella	4	Campbell, Kara	141	Campbell, Melvin F.	35
Campbell, Elloise	182	Campbell, Kate	158	Campbell, Melvin Franklin	148
Campbell, Eloise	83	Campbell, Katie	158	Campbell, Mildred	13
		Campbell, Lades	42	Campbell, Minnie Lee	14, 63, 233

Name	Page
Campbell, Moss	35, 36
Campbell, Myrtle (Reynolds)	35
Campbell, Nancy	75, 184
Campbell, Nancy Ann	142
Campbell, Naomi	200
Campbell, Naomi (Meeks)	35
Campbell, Nellie	62
Campbell, Nina	298
Campbell, Norma Mae	215
Campbell, Norris Martin	35
Campbell, Norris Martin, Jr.	35
Campbell, Oddist	35, 221
Campbell, Ola	72
Campbell, Ola May	35
Campbell, Orville	268
Campbell, Patrick Claiborne	35
Campbell, Paul	291
Campbell, Paula Marie (Perry)	35
Campbell, Randolph	35
Campbell, Raymond	88, 250
Campbell, Robert Clency	232
Campbell, Robert Roscoe	36
Campbell, Rocky Dwight	36
Campbell, Rod	24, 215
Campbell, Roger Vaughn	36
Campbell, Ronald Lee	36
Campbell, Roxanne	11
Campbell, Sarah Ann (Scott)	36
Campbell, Shawn Edward	36
Campbell, Sheila Marie (Westman)	36
Campbell, Shirley	36
Campbell, Shirley "Sherry" (Nunley)	36
Campbell, Stacey	36
Campbell, Stanley	37
Campbell, Stanley A.	36
Campbell, Steve	36
Campbell, Steven	36
Campbell, Susan Matilda (DeLeeuw)	36
Campbell, Sylvia Beatrice	35
Campbell, Sylvia Beatrice (Jones) Frisbee	36
Campbell, Taft	81
Campbell, Tammy	174
Campbell, Terri Yvonne	156
Campbell, Thomas "Bud"	36
Campbell, Tierra E. (Nunley)	36
Campbell, Timothy Lee	36
Campbell, Tom	37
Campbell, Tom Albert	100
Campbell, Tony Lamar	36
Campbell, Vance "Toby"	36
Campbell, Vernice Mae	81
Campbell, Violet H.	36
Campbell, Virginia Juanita (Stevens)	36
Campbell, Wade Preston	36
Campbell, Watson	35
Campbell, Willene Nunley	iii
Campbell, William Deloe	37
Campbell, William Enoch	35
Campbell, William Frank	37
Campbell, William Harrison	37
Campbell, William Howard	37
Campbell, William Jonah	295
Campbell, William Oscar	37
Campbell, William Ray "Pudgy"	37
Campbell, William Wayne	37
Campbell, Willie Kate	181
Campbell, Winnie Ella	51
Campbell, Zora	118
Canfield, Jan Rulison	ii, iii
Cannon, Archie D. "Oscar"	37
Cannon, Buena	174
Cannon, Ella	99
Cannon, Faye "Perkie"	87
Cannon, Freddie	229
Cannon, Freddie Morgan	37, 169
Cannon, Howard G.	37
Cannon, James M.	68
Cannon, Jerry	37
Cannon, Lavator	100
Cannon, Leon	37
Cannon, Levator	99
Cannon, Louise	73, 95
Cannon, Lucretia Sissy	140
Cannon, Margie	108
Cannon, Martha (Burnette)	37
Cannon, Nadine	164
Cannon, Oma Lee	84
Cannon, Rebecca	83
Cannon, Rosalyn	131
Cannon, Sarah	95, 189, 272
Cannon, Scott	87
Cannon, Taylor Lavator	37
Cannon, Theodore L.	37
Cannon, Venova	43
Cantrell-Daly, Elizabeth	37
Cantrell, Alice	187
Cantrell, Alice "Allie" (Sweeton)	37
Cantrell, Alvin	169
Cantrell, Arlie Parker	37
Cantrell, Billie Marie (Jones)	37

Name	Page
Cantrell, Claude J. "C.J."	38
Cantrell, Claude Jackson "C.J."	37
Cantrell, Claudia Seals Roberts	37
Cantrell, Cluade Meeks	100
Cantrell, Ernest Lee	38
Cantrell, Freda	106
Cantrell, George Washington	37
Cantrell, Georgia H. (Adams)	38
Cantrell, Herbert	141
Cantrell, Jackson Venus	38
Cantrell, James	37
Cantrell, James Erskine	38
Cantrell, Kimberly	236
Cantrell, Lisa	141, 275
Cantrell, Margaret Emily (Stone)	38
Cantrell, Mary "Meme"	38
Cantrell, Mary Louise	100
Cantrell, Mary Louise "Ladybug"	165
Cantrell, Nelda Jodi	76
Cantrell, Nellie	37
Cantrell, Newton "Nute"	37
Cantrell, Unk	37
Cantrell, Walter	37
Capehart, Mary Caroline	270
Capel, Virginia Anne (Boulton)	38
Carden, James T.	38
Carden, Lynn Abbott	298
Carden, Lynn Adolphus, Dr.	38
Carden, Roy W	38
Carden, Thelma E. (McClendon)	38
Cargile, Mattie	214
Carlson, David	38
Carlson, Marie Ann (Myers)	38
Carman, Ernest E.	173
Carnahan, Jane	277
Carpenter, Ambrose	38
Carpenter, April Renee	38
Carpenter, Clay	38
Carpenter, Joy Lee	75
Carpenter, LeAnn	26
Carpenter, Velma Pauline "Polly" (Gass)	38
Carr, Elizabeth	297
Carr, Felix	57
Carr, Josephine	38, 200, 201
Carr, Patrick	38
Carr, Patrick	201
Carrick, Benny	38
Carrick, Betty	157
Carrick, Beulah	195
Carrick, Beulah Sidney	118, 122, 124
Carrick, Bob	100
Carrick, Charles Mariman	38
Carrick, Doris	16
Carrick, Doris	17
Carrick, Edith	192
Carrick, Henry Thomas	280
Carrick, Herman	38
Carrick, Joe Wheeler	38
Carrick, Judy	30
Carrick, Larry	263
Carrick, Naomi M.	38
Carrick, Nelda	264
Carrick, Patricia "Patsy" (Lambert)	38
Carrick, Phyllis J (Sitz)	38
Carrick, Rachel	204
Carrick, Rebecca Charles	90
Carrick, Robert	180
Carrick, Robert Jackson	38
Carrick, Sally Marie	202
Carrick, Sylvia	100
Carrick, Thomas Chester	283
Carrick, Vilda	100
Carrick, Winnie Davis	78
Carrie, a baby	ix
Carroll, Delphia	123
Carroll, Karen	301
Carter, Arthur Richmond	39
Carter, Asa G.	219
Carter, C.D.	39
Carter, Casto	39
Carter, Grace (Tucker)	38
Carter, Harold Gordon	39
Carter, Joyce Marie	298
Carter, Julia	86
Carter, Lessie Lee	220
Carter, Mary Elizabeth (Gober)	39
Carter, Richmond	39
Carter, Ruby	20
Carter, Shirley	188
Case, Arthur Wesley	278
Case, Eloise	278
Cash, Billy Joe	39, 189
Cash, David Binkley	39
Cash, Faye	39, 144
Cash, Jenna	141
Cash, Lou Alma	150
Cashen, John	39
Cashen, Nancy Jane (Dove) Shadrick	39
Cashion, James	39
Cashion, Melvin G.	39
Caskett, Estelle	81
Casseday, Lynn Hampton	39
Casseday, Roy Dale	39
Cassidy, Brenda	5
Cassidy, Brenda Gail	16
Cassidy, Christopher James	39

Name	Page
Castle, William Columbus	227
Castleberry, Cynthia Ann	84
Castleberry, William	84
Castleman, Dennis	148
Castoire, Wendy	215
Castro, Rosie	110
Cates, Ray A.	28
Cates, Virginia	71
Catildo, Richard	39
Catildo, Robert Francis	39
Catildo, Theresa	39
Caudill, Gloria	49
Caudle, John Fulton	39
Caudle, Mike	39
Causey, John W.	39
Causey, Mary Alice	157
Causey, Rose H. (Hayes)	39
Cauthen, Coy	39
Cauthen, Mary Elizabeth (Aylor)	39
Cawley, Charles Raymond	39
Cawley, Charles Robert	39
Cawley, Cheyl	255
Cawood, Donna	285
Cawthorn, Deborah	104
Cecil, Charles Walter	39, 151
Cecil, Elbert Bisson	39
Cecil, Matilda Belle (Bolen)	39
Cemeteries of Grundy Co.	iv
Chambers, Alma (Fults)	39
Chambers, Barbara Jean (Meeks)	39
Chambers, Johnny Wayne	27
Chambers, Pamelia mae	210
Chambers, Unk	39
Chambers, William W.	39
Champion, Benjamin	40
Champion, Danny Ray	40
Champion, Gordon	40
Champion, Jimmy	40
Champion, Ruth	40
Champion, Scott	40
Champion, William	40
Chancey, Marian	96
Chapin, Margaret	134
Chapman, John Rosco	40
Chapman, Maurine	40
Chapman, William R.	40
Charles, Jennings	71
Charles, Judith E.	204
Charles, Niccoa Ann	77
Charles, Robert	204
Charles, Susan	237
Chatham, Sharan Claudette (Riddle)	40
Chatham, Steve	40
Cheek, Elizabeth Jane	138
Cheek, Eric Carter	40
Cheek, James	40
Cheek, Martha Elizabeth	115, 118
Cheek, William	117
Cherry, Dianne	149
Chesser, Shannon	131
Chester, Rose	8
Chester, Samuel Hall, Jr. (born III)	40
Chester, Samuel Hall, Sr.	40
Chester, Temperance Ransom Hudson	40
Childe, Golan	41
Childers, Adaline	230
Childers, Alton Thomas	40
Childers, Annie Myrtle (Richardson)	40
Childers, Bill	40
Childers, Charles Edwin	40
Childers, Darlene	173
Childers, Ed	41, 131
Childers, Edna May (Smith)	40
Childers, Elen	241
Childers, Ellen	115
Childers, Emma	204
Childers, Frank	230
Childers, George S.	40
Childers, Glenda	40
Childers, Golan	41
Childers, Gordon	40
Childers, Infant	40
Childers, Irene (Hodges)	40
Childers, Jack	40
Childers, James Eric	40
Childers, Jason Roland	40
Childers, Lois	40
Childers, Louis Woodrow	41
Childers, Mae	40
Childers, Maggie (Henley)	41
Childers, Marguerite (Dickerson)	41
Childers, Martha	41
Childers, Michael	260
Childers, Patricia	246
Childers, Pearly Mae	145
Childers, Perry	41
Childers, Raymond L.	40
Childers, Richard Gwinn	41
Childers, Richard Henry	41, 221
Childers, Susie M. (Brown)	41
Childers, Synthia A.	41
Childers, Thomas Edward	41
Childers, Veda	40
Childers, William Rufus, Sr.	41
Childers/Childress, George	41
Childers/Childress, Ida	41

Name	Page
Childress or Childers, Infant	41
Choat, Nellie Ellender B	253
Christa, Jesse	151
Christian, Cyndi Bess	15
Christian, David	41
Christian, Doyle Worth	41
Christian, Linda Mae	41
Christian, Lisa Dawn (King)	41
Christian, Lois	129
Christian, Mitchell	41
Christian, Otto	264
Christian, Rachel B. (Beitia)	41
Christian, Robert Lynn	15
Christian, Susan L.	145
Christian, Vaughn Worth	41
Christman, Earl	41
Christman, Kate	41
Christman, William Melvin	41
Christy, Mary	95
Church, Bobby	152
Church, Cindy	152
Church, Clarence	297
Church, Desmer	143
Church, Esther	295
Church, Ethel Mae	104
Church, Iva Jean	42
Church, John Henry O	42, 197
Church, John K.	267
Church, John Kenneth "Buc"	42
Church, Jr., Martin	41
Church, Linda	19
Church, Martin, Jr.	41
Church, Mary "Molly"	205
Church, Mary Elizabeth	225
Church, Mary Jane "Molly"	40
Church, Mary Sue	139
Church, Nervie Louisa Adaline Jane (Parsons)	42
Church, Sydney (Layne)	42
Church, Teresa	152
Church., Martin, Jr.	42
Cincotta, Catherine	19
Civil War	v
Clardy, Irene O'Dea	185
Clark, Ada Florence (Leak)	42
Clark, Allie	42
Clark, Bea	297
Clark, Brenda Joyce (Johnson)	42
Clark, Catherine Jane	5
Clark, Claude	42
Clark, Cordie Belle	88
Clark, Diana	188
Clark, Donald R.	42
Clark, Doris (Pearson)	42
Clark, Earl Wayne	42
Clark, Gerald "Jerry" Wayne	42
Clark, H.	42
Clark, James	42
Clark, James L	108
Clark, James William	42
Clark, John Overton	42
Clark, John Ray	42
Clark, Kathleen	30
Clark, Logan James Brock	42
Clark, Marsha	284
Clark, Martin B.	42
Clark, Nancy O'Neal (Brandon)	42
Clark, Riley	42
Clark, Susan	97
Clark, Thurman	105
Claus, Barbara	78
Claus, Jordan	78
Clay, Charles	67
Clay, Deloris	42
Clay, Elston	43
Clay, Elston	43
Clay, Frank Emmett	92
Clay, Garnett	42
Clay, George Harris "G.H.", Sr.	42
Clay, George Harris, Jr.	42
Clay, Kenneth Ray	42
Clay, Margaret "Peggy"	22
Clay, Ralph C	42
Clay, Selby (Henley)	43
Clay, Wayne	43
Clay, Wayne	42
Clayton, Michael J.R.	45
Cleek , Virginia Fay	103
Cleek, Alpha Gay (Dishroon)	43
Cleek, Amie	75
Cleek, Arnold	43
Cleek, Arnold	143
Cleek, Bill Falls	43
Cleek, Charles Clayton	43
Cleek, Charles Dakota	43
Cleek, Dee	52
Cleek, Gene	43, 150
Cleek, Hazel Ruth (Crisp)	43
Cleek, Hearl	43, 97
Cleek, Hearl F.	43
Cleek, Horace Ann	84
Cleek, John	43
Cleek, John, Jr.	43, 304
Cleek, Joyce Olean	139
Cleek, Kollins Ryann	43
Cleek, Leon Carl	43
Cleek, Lonnie	43
Cleek, Maxie	241
Cleek, Melanie Ann	43
Cleek, Mitchell	84

Name	Page
Cleek, Paul	72
Cleek, Shelva Jean	147
Cleek, Sherry Kay	130
Cleek, Tammy Lou (Dent)	43
Cleek, Virginia Fay	304
Cleek, Woodrow	223
Clemens, Pat	43
Clemens, Patricia Faye "Pati" (Wolford)	43
Clements, Emma	91
Clements, Ernest B.	43
Clements, Paul	121
Clements, Paul Raymond	43
Clements, Paula Rae	121
Clements, Vera Ruth (Houpert)	43
Clemmons, Effie Eugenia Bell	14
Clemmons, Florence	86
Clemons, Cindy (Rackar)	43
Clemons, James	43
Clemons, James Benjamin	180
Clemons, Jerry Wayne	43
Clemons, Leslie Clay	43
Clendenen, Minnie Belle	105
Clendenon, James Wiley	ix, 44
Clendenon, Harlie Everett	9
Clendenon, J.W.	44
Clendenon, Jerry	44
Clendenon, Junior	44
Clendenon, Lassie	200
Clendenon, Lodema Marie	257
Clendenon, Lucille (Sanders)	44
Clendenon, Minnie Bell	105
Clendenon, Nellie Gray	241
Clendenon, Ova Wiser	44
Clepper, Rebecca "Beck"	44
Clepper, Rebecca Rollins	226
Clepper, Thomas W.	44
Cleveland, Richard	44
Cleveland, Susan Joyce (Douglas)	44
Click, Carolyn	154
Click, Pamela Sue	44
Click, Paul Ronald	44
Cline, Gloria Jean	295
Cline, Mary	82
Clouse, Cindy	212
Coalmont, TN	v, viii
Coalson, David	44, 103
Coalson, Sarah (Cox)	44
Coats, Janelle	274
Coats, Thomas Eugene, Jr.	15, 44, 142
Coble, Liby	78
Cochran, Martha Ann	289
Cock, Susan	271
Coe, Samuel Augustus	215
Cofer, Mary Helen (Garrett)	44
Coffee County	v
Coffelt, Amos	45
Coffelt, Amos Henry	45, 106
Coffelt, Angela	188
Coffelt, Bessie Ann	44
Coffelt, Betty Ruth (Creighton)	44
Coffelt, Bob	45
Coffelt, Bruce	44
Coffelt, Christina Leigh Danelle	44
Coffelt, Crip Wesley	44, 45
Coffelt, Daniel	44
Coffelt, Dorcas (Shadrick)	44
Coffelt, Ellen Nellie	69
Coffelt, Ervine	89
Coffelt, Francis Marvin Lee "Leck"	44
Coffelt, Frankie Mae	44
Coffelt, Gail	44
Coffelt, James Allen	44
Coffelt, James H. "Cork"	45
Coffelt, James Jackson	69
Coffelt, John Henry	44
Coffelt, John Wesley	29
Coffelt, Judith	106
Coffelt, Louie Hershel	45
Coffelt, Luelda	45
Coffelt, Margaret	255
Coffelt, Margaret Joyce	254
Coffelt, Marvin Lee Leck	44
Coffelt, Mary Catherine	22
Coffelt, Mattie (Roberts)	45
Coffelt, Nancy	188
Coffelt, Patricia Ann "Pat" (Shaffer)	45
Coffelt, Robbie Wayne	45
Coffelt, Robert Edward	45
Coffelt, Violet (Smith)	45
Coffelt, Walter	23
Coffey, Barbara Amelia	5
Coggins, Bessie	47
Coggle, Judy Tessa	45
Coggle, Kenneth	45
Coker, Elizabeth	251
Coker, Julia A.	56
Coker, Maude	220
Coker, Maude	220
Coldwell, Annie	152
Cole, Ada	45
Cole, Arthur Carman, DD	45
Cole, Daniel H.	45
Cole, George	106
Cole, Joan	106
Cole, Latienne	157
Cole, Mae Belle	53

Name	Page
Coleman, Mattie	175
Coleman, Ruth	219
Coll, Albert George	45
Coll, Hugh Aloysius	45
Collier, Joan	45
Collier, Rosa Beatrice (Rosendaul)	45
Collier, Roscoe Ivan	45
Collier, Ruth Ann	45
Collier, Wiley Carter, Jr.	45
Collings, Daniel	45
Collings, Joshua David	45
Collins, Annie	46
Collins, Carl Leon	45
Collins, Carol	46
Collins, Daniel	46
Collins, David Browning	46
Collins, Della Faye	65
Collins, Della Frances	19
Collins, Dorothy	4, 232, 6
Collins, Edward Rayburn, Sr.	45
Collins, Eunice	45, 46, 65, 232
Collins, Girlie (Sims)	46
Collins, Harold	104
Collins, Harold Lee	46
Collins, Isaac M.	46
Collins, James Lionell "Hard Knot"	46
Collins, James Ray	46
Collins, Jeffery Glenn	46
Collins, Jennifer Rae	46
Collins, Jewel "Judy" (James)	46
Collins, John	46
Collins, John B.	45
Collins, John Clinton	85
Collins, John E.	46
Collins, John M.	53
Collins, John W.	134
Collins, Johnny B	46
Collins, Johnny Ray	46
Collins, Joshua David	46
Collins, Linda "Sue"	46
Collins, Maryon Virginia	46
Collins, Sarah	46, 110
Collins, Thomas C.	46
Collins, William	110
Collins, William D	46
Collins, William H.	46
Colston, Barbara	268
Colvin, Mary Agnes	28
Comer, Ray	46
Comer, Shelby LeAnn	46
Comfort, James	46
Comfort, Lola Mae	46
Comfort, Misty Carol	46
Comfort, William	46
Comfort, William Conway	46
Comstock, Harriet June (Hagelbarger)	46
Comstock, Lester Ray	46
Comstock, Lewis Raymond	46
Conatser, Martie	18
Condra, Alvin D.	46
Condra, Carl Eugene	47
Condra, Charles	47
Condra, Edward Lafayette "Fate"	47
Condra, Fate	302
Condra, Grace	47
Condra, John Douglas	46
Condra, Thurman Eugene	47
Conelly, Frederick	236
Conelly, Mary Lorraine	236
Conn, A.M. "Jack"	47
Conn, Elizabeth	235
Conn, Elizabeth "Betsy"	208
Conn, Josiah J., Jr.	208
Conn, Mark G	47
Connell, Carolyn	14
Connell, Earl Stanley	47
Connell, Thomas Nathaniel	47
Conner, Elzora	47
Conner, Frank	47
Conner, Whitt	47
Conry, Allie	47
Conry, Anna Grace Rieder	51
Conry, Bessie	47
Conry, Cam	146
Conry, Carl Eugene	47
Conry, Carl William	47
Conry, Carolyn	154
Conry, Conald	184
Conry, Daniel Campbell "Cam"	47
Conry, Danny Brice	47
Conry, Duncan	47
Conry, Ernest James, Sr.	47
Conry, Ernest, Jr.	47
Conry, Genevieve	82
Conry, Gladys	298
Conry, James Polk	51
Conry, James R.	47
Conry, Mary	151
Conry, Mike	47
Conry, Mike E., Jr.	47
Conry, Mike Emmett	47
Conry, Rosa Ellen	181, 207
Conry, Tammy Jo	47
Constinoble, Barbara	239
Cook, Bonnie	34
Cook, Charles	47
Cook, Cleopatra	38
Cook, Edna Jane	217
Cook, Eileen	280

Name	Page
Cook, Elizabeth	99
Cook, Ethel	58
Cook, Flora	147
Cook, Henry C.	47
Cook, Paul	58
Cook, Sara Josephine (Sain)	47
Cook, Thelma	105
Cook, Wanda Lee (Nunley)	47
Cooke, Arthur	47
Cooke, Edna	47
Cooke, Paul Gene	47
Cooke, Thomas F.	69
Cooksey, Gracie	95
Cookston, Allice	1
Cookston, Emmett Kelly	48
Cookston, George Washington	48, 246
Cookston, Gertrude Lavonne	245, 246
Cookston, Leonard	48, 115
Cookston, Opal (Rogers)	48
Cookston, Sonya J.	181
Cookston, William Stone "Buck"	48
Cooper, Alex	48
Cooper, Ava Anna	203, 278
Cooper, Barry Bradley	48
Cooper, Danny	48
Cooper, Donnie Edwin "Duck"	48
Cooper, Herbert Chris, Jr.	48
Cooper, Herbie	48
Cooper, J.W.	48
Cooper, Jannie D. (Dickinson)	48
Cooper, Jerry Wayne	48
Cooper, John Nathan	48
Cooper, Molt B.	48
Cope, Clara	280
Cope, Comfort	170
Cope, Effie	255, 256
Cope, Elizabeth	80
Cope, Hatty "Hessie"	172
Cope, Hettie "Hassey"	231
Cope, Hetty Jane	172
Cope, Louisa W.	171
Cope, Mamie Lee	153, 273
Cope, Mammie Lee	303
Cope, Martin	48
Cope, Nancy	231
Cope, Roda Lee	125
Cope, Sarah Louise	238
Cope, Sophonia Ann	73
Cope, Stephen	170
Cope, Stephen Payne	235
Cope, William	48
Copeland, Archie	48
Copeland, Bill	48
Copeland, Campbell Washington	48
Copeland, Charlotte Darlene (O'Neal)	48
Copeland, Jamie	48
Copeland, Jason Lee	48
Copeland, Jim	48
Copeland, John M.	49
Copeland, Lillie Mae (Parsons)	48
Copeland, Nora (White)	48
Copeland, Ronnie	48
Copeland, Rose	48
Copeland, Sheila	48
Copeland, Skyler Gauge	48
Copeland, Velma Louisa	204
Copeland, Walter Garfield	49
Coppinger, Agnes Lillian	172
Coppinger, Albert	66
Coppinger, Benny Eugene	49
Coppinger, Bobby	49
Coppinger, Clarence G.	216
Coppinger, Clarence G.	49
Coppinger, David	49
Coppinger, Dollie Etta (Foster)	49
Coppinger, Faye	49
Coppinger, Faye (Johnson)	49
Coppinger, Frank Marshall, Jr.	49
Coppinger, Gene	49
Coppinger, George	49
Coppinger, George A Willard	49
Coppinger, George Anthony	49
Coppinger, James Paul	49
Coppinger, Lassie	44
Coppinger, Lois	216
Coppinger, Lois	216
Coppinger, Mae Emma	288
Coppinger, Margaret	141
Coppinger, Margaret E. "Maggie" (Meadows)	49
Coppinger, Mary "Molly" (Purdom)	49
Coppinger, Mary Ann	126
Coppinger, Ollie	267
Coppinger, Ollie Mary	160
Coppinger, Rose Edna	63
Coppinger, Thelma	38
Coppinger, Thelma	253
Coppinger, Wanda L	49
Corbaley, Ida M. (Garner)	49
Corbin, Charles Washington	56
Corbisier, Melissa	140
Cordell, Charles Clifford	49
Cordell, Elizabeth	103
Cordell, Joe Laster	49
Cordell, John A.	93
Cordell, John Cross	49

Name	Page
Cordell, Johnnie Ruth	93
Cordell, Joyce	49
Cordell, Pauline	114
Cordov, Thomas	49
Cordova, April Dawn (Guess)	49
Corley, Myrtle Ann	188
Corliss, John Orr	88
Corn, James	29
Corn, William	29
Cornelison, James Paul	181
Cornelison, Malvina	25
Cornelius, Elder Louis	224
Cornett, Sandra	88
Costa, Richard Da	55
Costner, Nora	268
Cotham, Nancy Mae	36
Cotton, Agnes	91
Cotton, Bessie A.	267
Cotton, Louisa Ann "Lucy"	150
Cottrell, Kenneth F. "Ken"	49
Couch, Nell	219
Coulson, Alexander	49
Coulson, David C	49
Coulson, James	44
Coulston, Catherine Ellis	34
Countiss, IV, Peter	viii, ix, 183
County Farm Road	vii
Coursey, Mary Ann	279
Courtney, Bruce	118
Courtney, Vallery Griffith Shannon	118
Coutu, Euclid	50
Coutu, Richard Brian	50
Cowan, Ed Pratt	94
Cowan, Francis	50
Cowan, Leland	50
Cowan, Marsha	50
Cowan, Michael, DDS	50
Cowan, Ola Ann	194
Cowan, Peggy Rose	94
Cowin, June	56
Cox, Amanda M.	50
Cox, Anna Corene	140
Cox, Avery Jordan, Sr.	50
Cox, Betsy	28
Cox, Bonnie	50
Cox, Burtia	232
Cox, Carol Ann	50
Cox, Carolyn Sue Morrison	50
Cox, Charles Daniel	50
Cox, Charles E.	50
Cox, Cleo	163
Cox, Corene	139
Cox, Daisy Mae (Crabtree)	50
Cox, Eddie Junior "Dickie"	50
Cox, Elizabeth	104
Cox, Ella Mae	159, 281
Cox, Elsie (McCormack)	50
Cox, Estil Kelly (Dove)	50
Cox, Ferrell Dean	50
Cox, Florence	225
Cox, Frank Vestal	50
Cox, Frankie	241
Cox, George William	50
Cox, Grady Lockhart	50
Cox, Hallie Mae (Doss)	50
Cox, Herman Dallas	162
Cox, Howard	104
Cox, Hoyt	51
Cox, James	50
Cox, James Alex "Jamie"	50
Cox, James Arnold	50
Cox, James W.	219
Cox, Jeffery Thomas	50
Cox, John Edward	50
Cox, John Hardy	50
Cox, Josephine	173
Cox, Lizzy Mae	10
Cox, Lucille (Henley)	50
Cox, Mary	50
Cox, Mary Albertine (Richmond)	51
Cox, Mary E. (Sanders)	51
Cox, Patricia	143
Cox, Peggy Cleo	35, 191
Cox, Rhonda	186
Cox, Sarah	44, 49, 103
Cox, Shirley May	21
Cox, Stella	219
Cox, Wiley	50
Cox, William	50
Cox, William D	44
Cox, William Rush	51
Cox, William Warfield	50
Crabtree, Alfred Edman	51
Crabtree, Anita	184
Crabtree, Anita June (Finch)	51
Crabtree, Beatrice	278
Crabtree, Bessie	131
Crabtree, Bruce	51
Crabtree, Charles Edman	51
Crabtree, Charles W.	51
Crabtree, Duck	50
Crabtree, Edna Marie	22, 23
Crabtree, Elizabeth	117
Crabtree, Gabriela (Gomez)	ii, iii, 51
Crabtree, Gladys	29
Crabtree, Grace (Smartt)	51
Crabtree, Henry	114
Crabtree, Henry Simpson	51

Name	Page
Crabtree, Isaac	164
Crabtree, Janie	113
Crabtree, Jerome Wilson	51
Crabtree, Joan	134
Crabtree, Johnny S.	51
Crabtree, Kirby Earl	iii, 51
Crabtree, L.B.	184
Crabtree, Lela Mae	184
Crabtree, Louella	155
Crabtree, Lucy	224
Crabtree, Malcolm	279
Crabtree, Margaret (Summers)	51
Crabtree, Margaret Ellen	241
Crabtree, Marie	22
Crabtree, Martha Sue	230
Crabtree, Mary	167
Crabtree, Opal	249, 250
Crabtree, Opal	250
Crabtree, Rebecca	113
Crabtree, Rebecca Jane	112
Crabtree, Roxanne	51
Crabtree, Rue Cassander	160
Crabtree, Rufus Quincy	203, 278
Crabtree, Rufus Quincy	278
Crabtree, Sarah Jane Rebecca	113
Crabtree, Victoria Saline "Vic"	268
Crabtree, Vinnie	46
Crabtree, Violet	133
Crabtree, Walter Earl	51
Crabtree, Walter Reed	51
Crabtree, William "Jip"	51
Crabtree, William E.	51
Crabtree, William Henry, Sr.	51, 302
Crabtree, William Simpson, Sr.	51
Crabtree, Wilson	299, 300
Craig, Nellie	9
Craigmiles, Mary	58
Craigmiles, William H.	58
Crank, Bascom	240
Crawford, James Lee "Jim"	52
Creasman., Jane	60
Creek, Frances	130
Creighton, Anna Polk	51
Creighton, Barbara Mae (Meeks)	52
Creighton, Betty Ruth	44
Creighton, Billy Jo	52
Creighton, Danny Steven	52
Creighton, Darla	52
Creighton, Dick	52
Creighton, Earl Franklin	51
Creighton, Elizabeth	8, 172
Creighton, Ernestine "Tine" (Ross)	52
Creighton, Ethleen Gladys (Brown)	52
Creighton., Frank Earl	52
Creighton, John	52
Creighton, John A.	44, 52
Creighton, John Isaiah	52
Creighton, Juanita Joan	52
Creighton, Keith	52
Creighton, Leona	52
Creighton, Loretta (Sanders)	52
Creighton, Lydia Leona (Brewer)	52
Creighton, Margaret L. (Cleek)	52
Creighton, Mary	52
Creighton, Morgan	8, 52
Creighton, Nicky Mason	52
Creighton, Patsy	104
Creighton, Ralph Taylor	52
Creighton, Robert Asa	52
Creighton, Sherry Lois (Dills)	52
Creighton, Stacy D.	52
Creighton, Tom	52
Creighton, Vernie	112
Creighton, Wanda	52
Creighton, William David	52
Creighton, William Morton	52
Creselious, Minnie	297
Cribbs, Hazel	261
Cribbs, James	52
Cribbs, Mollie (Meeks)	52
Cribbs, Vera Elizabeth	232
Crichlow, Elizabeth	64
Crick, Clara	159
Crick, Jocob Powell	53
Crick, Mary C. (Butler)	53
Crick, Meddie	36
Crill, Carra Marie	210
Crisp, Amelia (Stone)	53
Crisp, Bertha Elizabeth (Shrum)	53
Crisp, Bettie	141
Crisp, Betty	214
Crisp, Carl "Squat"	53
Crisp, Frankie	53
Crisp, Fred	43
Crisp, Green Benny	53
Crisp, Haskel	71
Crisp, Jennie	53
Crisp, Leon	100
Crisp, Linda Carol	53
Crisp, Lloyd	53
Crisp, Marion Mitchell	43
Crisp, Ophelia	64
Crisp, Theresa Darlene	100
Crisp, Thomas	53
Crisp, Thomas William	53
Crisp, W. Leon	53
Crittenden, Harry Blake	53
Crittenden, James	10

Name	Page
Crittenden, James Crittenden	53
Crittenden, Rendy	10, 53
Critz, Tillman Rosamond	24
Crocker, J.C.	5
Crocker, Lillian Louise	8
Crocker, Missouri Caroline	212
Cronan, Vickie Rae	53
Crossland, Elizabeth	1
Crosslin, Amy Celeste	53
Crosslin, Dennis	53
Crosslin, Elizabeth	1
Crosslin, Hoyt Cleve	53
Crosslin, Melanie Joyce	53
Crosslin, Nancy	1
Crosslin, Richard	53
Crosslin, Ronald	53
Crouch, Betty Lynn	53
Crouch, Easter Mosley	53
Crouch, Elizabeth "Betty" (White)	53
Crouch, Feraby	53
Crouch, Isaac	153
Crouch, Orin White, Sr.	53
Crouch, Robert Lee	53
Crouch, William	53
Crowe, Ethel	156
Crowe, Ethel	263
Crowe, Isabell	29
Crowe, Mary	144
Crowe, Robert	143
Crowe, Sallie	107
Crowell, Edna Mae (Oliver)	298
Crowell, Melonee	20
Crowell, Rilla Mae	58, 82
Crownover, Carl Edward	53
Crownover, Clara Bell	21
Crownover, Malone Elizabeth	2
Crownover, Mary Anita "Ann"	53
Crozier, George	53
Crozier, Walter	53
Crutchfield, Joan "Bunny" (Nunley)	53
Crutchfield, Nettie	9
Crutchfield, Ward	53
Culbertson, Edith	84
Culbertson, Robert	84
Cullender, Henry	54
Cullinder, George D., Dr.	54
Cullinder, Mary C.	54
Cullom, Robert Martin	54
Cullum, John	54
Cumberland Baptist Church	vii
Cumberland Funeral Home	iii
Cummings, Ethel Amy	94
Cuningham, Emmett	54
Cunningham, Allen Howard	54
Cunningham, Ann	24
Cunningham, Brandy Lynn	54
Cunningham, Cecil	54
Cunningham, Cecil	78
Cunningham, Cecil W.	54
Cunningham, Charles Leland	292
Cunningham, Della	196, 219
Cunningham, Dorothy	143
Cunningham, Geneva	54
Cunningham, Infant	54
Cunningham, Jane	141
Cunningham, Mary	134
Cunningham, Mary Louise	158
Cunningham, Minnie (Murray)	54
Cunningham, Nettie	110
Cunningham, Phyllis	58
Cunningham, Porter	54
Cunningham, Rick	12
Cunningham, Shirley	54
Cunningham, Toby James	54
Cunningham, Webb	54
Cupp, Beulah Jane	145
Cupp, Henry Elbert	265
Curtis, Arthur	55
Curtis, Arthur David	54
Curtis, Arthur Roy	54
Curtis, Audra Jewel (Brewer)	54
Curtis, Bessie Mae	54
Curtis, Betty Jean	36
Curtis, Charlie	54
Curtis, Darrell Gregory	54
Curtis, David Wesley	54
Curtis, Dee	54, 55, 186
Curtis, Edwene	9
Curtis, Frances	54
Curtis, Fred	55
Curtis, Haley Denise	54
Curtis, Herschel	55
Curtis, Hershel	54
Curtis, Jackie Wade	54
Curtis, James Henry	54
Curtis, James Mitchell	54, 55
Curtis, James Ray	54
Curtis, Jeremiah	55
Curtis, Jerry	55
Curtis, Jerry Dewitt	54
Curtis, Jimmy	54
Curtis, John David	55
Curtis, Juanita Carol	55
Curtis, Kate	55
Curtis, Kaye	141
Curtis, Linda Faye	55
Curtis, Linda Gail	55

Name	Page
Curtis, Lola Bell (Keener)	55
Curtis, Mattie	54, 55, 186
Curtis, Minnie	55
Curtis, Mitchell	54
Curtis, Noah Chase	55
Curtis, Patricia	195
Curtis, Paul Wesley	54, 55
Curtis, Robert Alan	55
Curtis, Robert Kelly	55
Curtis, Ruby Jewel	183
Curtis, Shannon	54
Curtis, Steven Jeffery	55
Curtis, Virginia	55
Curtis, Virginia S.	54
Curtis, Will	52, 55
Curtis, William Harold	55
Curtis, William Howard	55
Curtis, William R.	55
Curtis, William Robert	55
Curtiss, Barbara Jean (Grayson)	55
Curtiss, Fred Neal	55
Curtiss, Fred Neil	55
Custer, Margaret	55
Custer, Nora	55, 64
Custer, Silas	64
Custer, Silas Lafayette	55
Custer, Silas Lafayette, Jr.	55
Da Costa, Gloria (Martin)	55
Dabney, Mary	230
Dahler, Sara	11
Dailey, Oddie	46
Daily, Anita	55
Daily, Terry	55
Daily, Timothy S.	55
Dale, Lavinia	83
Daley, Angela Marie (Arthur)	55
Daley, Donna Mae	289
Dalt, Timothy	261
Daly, Elizabeth	67
Daly, Lavern E.	37
Daniel, Ester	142
Daniel, Glenn Willis, Sr.	55
Daniel, James William	255, 256
Daniel, Sanada Elizabeth	55
Daniel, Wanda	161
Daniel, Wanda Lee	261
Daniels, Esther	56
Danilesdotter, Marie Kajsa	145
Danzey, Charlotte Rebecca	88
Darby, Angela Griffith	197
Darland, Eugene Dale	56
Darland, Mary (Myers)	56
Darling, Elizabeth H	254
Darnell, Diana	247
Darnell, Edith Ann	288
Darnell, Harold	56
Darnell, Miriam Catherine "Kay"	56
Darter, Betty	10
Daughtrey, Billie Jo	257
Daum, Ethel May	71
Davenport, Barbara LaVergne	28
Davenport, Harriet	4
David, Nancy Elain	13
Davidson, Donna	188
Davidson, Elizabeth	46, 259
Davidson, Louella	92
Davidson, Margaret Jane (Hudson)	56
Davidson, Thomas Jefferson	56
Davis, Alfred B.	56
Davis, Andrew	21
Davis, Andrew	56
Davis, Benjamin	56
Davis, Burt	56
Davis, Chyrell	217
Davis, Clarence Edward	258
Davis, Clementine	57
Davis, Dorothy Lee	258
Davis, Dorothy Orleen (Taylor)	56
Davis, Edith Griffy "Edie"	56
Davis, Ethel	114
Davis, Evelyn	91
Davis, G. W.	132
Davis, George Washington	56
Davis, Gladys	111, 206, 216
Davis, Gladys Irene	103
Davis, Grady Lester "Lurch"	56
Davis, Ida	2
Davis, Imojean "Jean" (Nunley)	56
Davis, John Pershing	56
Davis, John R.	183, 184
Davis, Josephine	231
Davis, Joyce	112
Davis, Katie Maggie	132
Davis, Lawrence M.	57
Davis, Linda Irene (Fults)	56
Davis, Lisa	57
Davis, Lisa Darlene	206
Davis, Lou	256
Davis, Lucinda	84
Davis, Margaret	25
Davis, Martha "Mattie"	13
Davis, Mary Caroline	133
Davis, Mary Jane	132
Davis, Matt Scott	56
Davis, Mattie Ethel	32
Davis, Miles Benson	133
Davis, Minnie	137

Name	Page
Davis, Nancy	266
Davis, Nancy Sue (Camp)	56
Davis, Nellie Irene	11
Davis, Nola Magdalene	139
Davis, Norman	56
Davis, Odell Jackson	56
Davis, Reba Mae	56
Davis, Rebecca Lynn (Green)	56
Davis, Roy Levan	56
Davis, Rubie Nell	211, 246
Davis, Ruth	57
Davis, Shelby	135
Davis, Sr., Amuel T	56
Davis, Susannah Key	208
Davis, Walter Lee	211
Davis, Wanda (Hart)	56
Davis, William	56, 84
Davis, William Levi	56
Davis, Willis Polk Macklin, Sr.	57
Dawson, Johnny Theodore	57
Dawson, Samuel Benner	57
Dean, Patrick	iii
Dean, Virginia Lee	57
DeBoer, Marie Elizabeth	172
DeBruyn, Addren	57
DeBruyn, Leonard Gary, Sr.	57
Debusschere, Juliana	28
DeCamp, Jessica	262
Deen, Edna	161
Dees, Celina Kay	288
Degen, Anna	251
Deitz, Sophia	29
Deitz, Zelda	108
Delaney, Alice	38
Delaney, Ralph Herman	108
Delong, Gladys	39
DeMaranville, Katie	147
Demo, Grace	186
Dempsey, Hubert	57
Dempsey, James Ray	57
Dempsey, Robert Lee	57
Dempsey, Sariah Louise	57
Dempsey, Sherry	22
Dempsy, Mary Imogene "Jean"	20
DenBesten, Clara	57
DenBesten, Gilbert	57
DenBesten, John	57
DenBesten, John	57
DenBesten, Lillian (Fugate)	57
Dendy, Lois	12, 93
Dendy, Lois Elizabeth	12
Denison, Mary Lona	288
Dennis, Edith	8
Dennis, Harriet Ellen	99
Dennis, Rita	19
Dennis, Sarah Ellen	128, 283
Dent, J.D.	34, 43, 108
Dent, Jarvis D.	294
Dent, Marie	275
Dent, Nora	238
Dent, Phyllis	iii
Dent, Sarah Annette	174
Dent, Scotty Walter	57
Denton, Kermit Ray	183
Denton, Lillian Lucille	79
DePriest, Jessie	193
Derosett, Shawn	162
Derry, Doris (Meadows)	57
Derryberry, George	57
Derryberry, John Eddie	57
Desmarais, Wallace	57
Desmarias, Raymond "Skip"	57
Desmaris, Raymond Skip	57
Desmaris, Wanda (Burrows)	57
Devine, Cora	24
Devine, Sarah "Sally"	57
DeWitt, Daniel	57
DeWitt, Danielle Elizabeth	57
DeWitt, Elizabeth	57
Dewitt, Evaline	264
Dick, Malcom	108
Dickerson, Alvin	275
Dickerson, Ame	41, 161
Dickerson, Ame David	78, 153
Dickerson, Arra	274
Dickerson, Bettie	237
Dickerson, Betty	136
Dickerson, Betty (Sherman)	57
Dickerson, Buckey	213
Dickerson, Bunia	80
Dickerson, Clarence L	58
Dickerson, Clifford	57
Dickerson, Dorothy Eva Ruth (Hutchison)	58
Dickerson, Doug	68
Dickerson, Estella	123, 124
Dickerson, Estie	123
Dickerson, Ethel	68
Dickerson, Eva Ruth	275
Dickerson, Harriette	84
Dickerson, Jim	75, 223
Dickerson, John	58
Dickerson, Joseph Carl	58
Dickerson, Marguerite	41
Dickerson, Martha	191
Dickerson, Martha	260
Dickerson, Mary Elizabeth	58
Dickerson, Marzee	40
Dickerson, Mint	57

Name	Page
Dickerson, Patricia	144
Dickerson, Patricia Ann	275
Dickerson, Robert Allen	57, 58
Dickerson, Solie Dee	58
Dickerson, Solly Dee	275
Dickerson, Soloman	58
Dickerson, Tom	157
Dickerson, Victoria	44
Dickey, John David	58
Dickey, John William	58
Dickey, Rosa Mae	287
Dickinson, Arthur	58
Dickinson, Barbara	58
Dickinson, Donna	58
Dickinson, Jamie	48
Dickinson, Joe	48
Dickinson, Rick Lee	58
Dickson, Elizabeth Ann (Yates)	58
Dickson, Thomas L.	58
Diebold, Hazel	196
Diebold, Marie	196
Diebold, Peter	196
Dies, Janette (Givens)	58
Dies, Wayne	58
Dillon, Daniel D.	58
Dillon, Mary Craigmiles	58
Dillon, Rebecca	58
Dillon, William George	58
Dills, Phillip Wayne	58
Dills, Buddy Ray	52
Dills, Mary	52
Dills, Philip Wayne Dills	171
Dills, Unk	176
Dills, Woodrow	58
Disheroon, Ella	80, 111
Disheroon, George E.	58
Disheroon, Georgia Tate	69
Disheroon, Herschel	69
Disheroon, Holis	263
Disheroon, Imogene Elizabeth (Schoenmann)	58
Disheroon, James	80
Disheroon, Jimmie Lee (Sanders)	58
Disheroon, Preston	58
Dishman, Ted	165, 171
Dishroom, Benny Hayes	58
Dishroom, Ernest	58
Dishroom, Fred	58, 59, 80
Dishroom, Freddy	179
Dishroom, Hazel	58, 250
Dishroom, Hollis S.	59
Dishroom, Jack Jones	41
Dishroom, John Wayne	58
Dishroom, Judith E. "Judy"	191
Dishroom, Letha	80
Dishroom, Pat	58
Dishroon, Alpha Gay	43
Dishroon, Bill D.	59
Dishroon, Elizabeth	129
Dishroon, Ernest B.	43
Dishroon, Esper	111
Dishroon, Fred D	59, 243
Dishroon, Georgia Fletcher (Tate)	59
Dishroon, Grace Leona	78, 113
Dishroon, Hazel	88
Dishroon, Herschel	59
Dishroon, James Everette	193
Dishroon, Jim	59
Dishroon, John Wayne	59
Dishroon, Louann Mary (Farmer)	59
Dishroon, Margaret Irene (Simpson)	59
Dishroon, Mari Ida	37
Dishroon, Myrtle	56
Dishroon, Ruth Ann	59
Dishroon, Sylvia Ann	225
Dixon, Annie	59
Dixon, Arnold Lee "Fat"	59
Dixon, Billy Joe	59
Dixon, Hilda Louise	59
Dixon, Juanita Jones (Roberts)	59
Dixon, Newton	59
Dixon, Texas	78
Dixon, Vernon Newton	59
Doak, Anna Marie	59
Doak, Christian Calvin	59
Doak, E. Dale	59
Dobbs, Gertrude Leona	175, 289
Dobbs, James D.	175
Dobbs, Samantha	175
Dobroff, Mike	59
Dockery, Carrie	106
Dockham, Lucille	2
Dockum, John Sinclair	185
Dodd, F.L. "Hokey"	155
Dodd, Harvey	59, 261
Dodd, Harvey, Jr.	59
Dodd, Hiram Cornelius Franklin	238
Dodd, Jr., Harvey	59
Dodd, Ruth	261
Dodd, Ruth M. (Meeks)	59
Dodd, Sarah J "Sallie"	238
Dodge, Richard	50
Dodson, Allie I,	238
Dodson, Barbara Joette (Pickett)	59
Dodson, Caroll "Toby"	59
Dodson, Eliza Catherine	127, 128
Dodson, Geneva	220
Dodson, Samuel	59
Doepel, Dorma	144
Dokum, Adina	217
Dolar, Jack	88

Name	Page
Doleto, Susan	214
Donaker, Genevieve	94
Donaker, John Martin	94
Doney, Eliza Mary	21
Donham, Murtle	13
Donohue, John T.	201
Dooley, Berry Lee	59
Dooley, Berry Lee, Jr.	59
Dooley, Rosemary Patty	59
Doran, John David	59
Doran, Phillip	59
Doran, Phyllis	59
Doss, Clyde A.	60
Doss, Fred	60
Doss, Hayden Edward	60
Doss, Margie Janie (Kilgore)	60
Doss, Mary Katherine (King)	60
Doss, Pearlie	21, 25
Doss, Sydney	50
Dotson, Cinthia Melvina "Molly" (Meeks)	60
Dotson, Cleo	81, 247
Dotson, Earnest	81
Dotson, George Edward "Buddy"	60
Dotson, George Edward, Jr.	60
Dotson, Krista	60
Dotson, Margaret	81
Dotson, Nicholas M.A. "Nick"	60
Dotson, Pearl	297
Dotson, Phyllis	225
Dotson, Phyllis Diane	261
Dotson, William Clyde	224
Douglas, Charles Mitchell	44
Douglas, Edna	287
Douglas, Pete	60
Douglas, Rebecca F	266
Douglas, Robert "Bob"	60
Dove, Annie	6
Dove, Arnold	60
Dove, Avery	61
Dove, Avery Sr.	60, 245
Dove, Benjamin	60
Dove, Bertha Fay	19
Dove, Calllie Estil	50
Dove, Charles Edward	60
Dove, Charles Robert, Jr.	61
Dove, Clarence Roscoe	60
Dove, Clayton Dean	60
Dove, David	60
Dove, Emma	60
Dove, Estil Kelly	50
Dove, James	39, 61
Dove, James Willard	60
Dove, John David	60, 61
Dove, John Louis "Jim"	206
Dove, Johnny	60
Dove, Jordan	125
Dove, Jordan B.	61
Dove, Lola (Howard)	61
Dove, Margaret	61
Dove, Mary Nell	150
Dove, Mavis Lillian (Shrum)	61
Dove, Nancy	61, 149
Dove, Pearly	121
Dove, Sally Ann (Sanders)	61
Dove, Susie	60
Dove, Thomas	60
Dove, Thomas Etta	186, 206
Dove, Thomasetta	107
Dove, Virginia	124
Dove, Walter Clayton	61
Dove, Willard	61
Dove, William Henry	61
Dove, Willie Carl	61
Dowell, Harriet Ann	215
Downam, Daniel B.	23
Downing, Ella P.	145
Downum, Daniel B.	303
Downum, Daniel Boone	87
Downum, Della	254
Downum, Mary Frances	87
Drake, Berry	61
Drake, Laura A. (Parsons)	61
Drake, Lillie	189
Drake, Louise	139
Drennon, Catherine	219
Drinkard, Keith	61
Driver, Evelyn Donna (Tate)	61
Driver, Kathryn Iola	61
Dry Shave Mountain Cemetery	vi
Dry Shave, TN	viii
Ducker, Mary	100
Ducker, Mary Etta	192
Dude, Alexander Benson	143
Dudley, Charles Edward	61
Dudley, Ed	61
Dudley, Elizabeth Pearl (Weaver)	61
Dudley, Homer F.	61
Dudley, Margaret	61
Dugger, Paul	61
Dugger, Tommie Mae (Parks)	61
Duke, Diane (Winton)	61
Duke, John A.	299
Duke, Ruby	203
Duncan, Harry E.	9
Duncan, Hazel	119
Duncan, Max	197
Duncan, Robert S.	156
Dunlap, TN	vi

Name	Page
Dunn, Carmen	61
Dunn, Josephine	84
Dunn, Laura Jean	61
Dunn, Mary	68
Dunn, Melvin Eugene	61
Dunn, Ronald Joseph	61
Dunn, William	61
Dunwoody, Georgie E. (Meeks)	61
Dunwoody, Jim	61, 62
Dunwoody, Margaret	276
Dunwoody, William Thatcher	62
Dupree, Clara	171
Durham, Robbie Eletta	213
Durham, Roy Ellis, Jr.	12
Dutton, Henry Griffith	62
Dutton, Joel Marion	62
Dycus, Nina G. (Sanders) Tate	62
Dycus, Unk	62
Dye, Ben	62
Dye, Mattie	300
Dye, Michael Sean	62
Dye, William	300
Dyer, Anita Louise	62
Dyer, Barbara	62
Dyer, Elizabeth	242
Dyer, George Tate	59
Dyer, George Winfield	26
Dyer, Harold	62
Dyer, Henry "Buck", Jr.	62
Dyer, Henry, Sr.	62
Dyer, J.C.	62
Dyer, James	62
Dyer, James Albert	242
Dyer, Juanita	4
Dyer, Margaret	26, 59, 109
Dyer, Margaret Katherine	69
Dyer, Martha Melissa Jane	242, 243
Dyer, Sarah	234
Dyer, Thomas	246
Dyke, Frank	66
Dykes, Andy	62
Dykes, Anna	82
Dykes, Anna Belle	89
Dykes, Arnold	62
Dykes, Beatrice G. (Yarworth)	62
Dykes, Bennie	62
Dykes, Byrtle M. (Byers)	62
Dykes, Calvin	63
Dykes, Carl Elmer	62
Dykes, Charles W.	62
Dykes, Claudene (McDaniel)	62
Dykes, Clfford Eugene	62, 63
Dykes, Clinton	62
Dykes, Clinton	63
Dykes, David A	63
Dykes, David Leslie	14, 63, 233
Dykes, Delores	62
Dykes, Delores (Byers)	63
Dykes, Dolly	63
Dykes, Edna	63, 77
Dykes, Elsie	169, 178, 250
Dykes, Elsie Juanita	232
Dykes, Elsie W (Williams)	63
Dykes, Gilbert Preston	96
Dykes, Grady	63
Dykes, Helen Marie (Parson)	63
Dykes, Hoyt G.	63
Dykes, J (Possibly John Dykes)	63
Dykes, Jody	63
Dykes, Lewis	63
Dykes, Lonnie	63
Dykes, Louise	228
Dykes, Louise Beth	228
Dykes, Martin	63
Dykes, Marvin L. Roberts	63
Dykes, Melissa G. (Brady)	63
Dykes, Minnie Lee (Campbell)	63
Dykes, Myrtle	139
Dykes, Nancy	26, 62, 228
Dykes, Nellie	93
Dykes, Ola	236
Dykes, Oma Lee	105
Dykes, Patricia	36
Dykes, Pearlie	95
Dykes, Robert J.	63, 178
Dykes, Sally	138
Dykes, Samantha Marie (Brown)	63
Dykes, Stanley Franklin "Bowzer"	63
Dykes, Susie	63
Dykes, Taylor Rosalee	63
Dykes, Thomas	63
Dykes, Virginia	60, 61, 125
Eads, Mary	70
Early, Albert	63
Early, Glenn Dale	63
Early, Jeanette	63
Early, Patricia Lynn	63
Earps, Cora	111
Earthman, Ellen D.	28
East, Anna	252
Easter Knob	viii
Eastridge, Barbara Joan	9, 59
Echols, Martin Eugene "Gene"	115
Eckard, Gail P.	174
Eckard, Gail Philbrook	63
Eckard, Vida (Williams)	63
Eckles, Georgia	74

Name	Page
Edge, Elizabeth	93
Edmister, Arthur Leon	64
Edmister, Elfa Irene (Lillie)	64
Edmister, Mattie Ann (Jessee)	64
Edmister, Wilfred Homer	64
Edwards, Dorothy Amy	68
Edwards, Evalina Augusta	278
Edwards, Floyd A.	74
Edwards, Genevive	56
Edwards, Juanita (Garner)	64
Edwards, Lena	160
Edwards, Michael H.	56
Edwards, Richard	68
Edwards, Rosa Bell	283
Edwards, Rose	270
Eldridge, Carlene (Haynes)	64
Eldridge, Carlene Hayes	88
Eldridge, Herschel	64
Eldridge, Stephan Wayne	64
Elizabeth, Ann	202
Elkins, James	72
Eller, Cherie	70
Eller, Martha "Mattie" (McCurdy)	64
Eller, Wiley Harrison	64
Elliot, Mary Ellen	1
Elliott, Bill	136
Elliott, James W.	239
Elliott, John Thomas	81
Elliott, John Witt	108
Elliott, Martha Alice (Wooten)	64
Elliott, Mickey	64
Elliott, Shirley	188
Elliott, Virginia	263
Elliott, William	255
Elliott, William Estill	160
Ellis, Coy	298
Ellis, Daisy Jo (Custer)	64
Ellis, David F.	64
Ellis, Dolly Ann	85, 205
Ellis, Eula Mae (Layne)	64
Ellis, Jr., John	276
Ellis, Lou (Sanson)	64
Ellis, Mary Gertrude	211
Ellis, Nolan	211
Ellis, Reva	94
Ellis, Thelma	210
Ellis, Thomas	239
Ellis, William	64
Ellison, Earl Austin, Sr.	64
Ellison, Walter Lee	64
Elsea, Carrie	30
Embry, Mary	273
Emery, Elizabeth Abigail	213
Emery, George	290
Ende, Arlyn Ruth	150
Engdahl, Eugene R	64
Engdahl, Hazel Ann	64
Engdahl, Herbert	64
England, Alexander Calvin	64, 218
England, Landy Holloway	64
Engle, Elzie Lee "Brown"	64
Engle, Joseph Edgar	64
Erwin, Pearl Mae	245
Esser, Stanley Earl	106
Estep, Carrie	126
Estes, Shirley	291
Eubanks, Glenda Mae (Huntley)	65
Eubanks, Josephine (King)	65
Eubanks, Raymond Carl, Sr	65
Eubanks, William Drobesh	65
Evans, Ada (Fisher)	65
Evans, Alfred	65
Evans, Bobby Franklin	65
Evans, Charles Edward	65
Evans, Deborah Ann	65
Evans, Della Faye (Collins)	65
Evans, Dorothy "Dot" (Hiett)	65
Evans, Grover	263
Evans, John Ernest	65
Evans, Joyce Jean (Miller)	65
Evans, Martha	65
Evans, Marvin Baxter	204
Evans, Simon C.	16
Evans, Stephen Michael	65
Evans, Walter Lee	65
Evans, Wirt Thomas	65
Everett, Bonnie Angalee	65
Everett, Lottie	286
Everett, Lucy S	65
Everett, T. Graves	286
Evett, John	247
Faharry, James	65
Fales, Varsal	174
Falls, Daniel	110
Falls, Melessie Jo	302
Fanshaw, Caleb G.	65
Fanshaw, Hazel Marie (Hunziker)	65
Farless, Wanda	221
Farmer, Belmont "Belle" (Wilbanks)	65
Farmer, Oscar Lloyd	59
Farmer, Samuel	66
Farmer, William Henry	66
Farmer, William Henry Bill	65
Farr, Carl Allen "Jack"	66

Name	Page
Farr, Effie Cordelia (Tanner)	66
Farr, Jackie	66
Farr, Joseph	66
Farrar, Geraldine	150
Farrar, Janice Ruth (Anderson)	66
Farrar, Neil	66
Farrell, Patrick	154
Farris, George H.	66
Farris, Lena Grace (Brewer)	66
Faucett, Martha Rebecca	20
Fehr, Emily	103
Feldman, Adolf	66
Feldman, Ronald A.	66
Felton, Henry Paul	66
Felton, Margie E. (Johnson)	66
Ferguson, Alexandria Ann	66
Ferguson, Celia Naomi	66
Ferguson, James	66
Ferguson, Mary	209
Fero, Fred	66
Fero, June Irene	66
Ferrell, Alma Jean	66
Ferrell, Brandon	42
Ferrell, Larry "Dude"	66
Ferrell, Steven Joe	66
Ferrell, Vance	70
Ferrell, William	66
Ferrill, Barbara June	241
Ferriss, Maria Judson	66
Finch, Benjamine	67
Finch, Betty Jean	30
Finch, Bonnie	143
Finch, Charles E., Sr.	67
Finch, Etta Mae	128
Finch, George Elbert	67
Finch, George M.	67
Finch, Herschel	67
Finch, Herschel Lee	30, 67
Finch, Herschel, Jr.	67
Finch, Hershel	51, 193
Finch, Jeff	137
Finch, Jeffrey Thomas "Jeff"	67
Finch, Jimmie Ruth	236
Finch, Jimmy Dale	67
Finch, John Henry	127
Finch, L.B. "Noel"	51
Finch, Larry Thomas	67
Finch, Leona	128, 129
Finch, Margie Joan	67
Finch, Maria	67
Finch, Mary Etta	67
Finch, Ronnie	67
Finch, Sandra Lee	67
Finch, Sheila Regina (Akins)	67
Finch, Tecia Laverne (Bellflower)	67
Fincher, Allen G	67
Fincher, Allen Gussie	67
Fincher, Hubert Allen	67
Fincher, Paul David	67
Fincher, Paulette	301
Fincher, Ruth	98
Fincher, Virgel	98
Finchum, Jessie may	67
Finchum, John H.	67
Finchum, John Robert	67
Finchum, Mary Evelyn (Geary)	67
Finchum, Roland	67
Finchum, Troy Allen	67
Finnell, Le Alice (Clay)	67
Finnell, Lewis Roscoe	67
Finney, Evelyn	163
Finney, Henry	67
Finney, Herbert G.	67
Finney, Richard G.	67
Finney, Ruben	282
Finney, Sammie June	60
Fish, Sarah LaVerna	178
Fisher, Adalphash	68
Fisher, Carolyn Sue	72
Fisher, Clara Matilda	49
Fisher, Dorothy Amy (Edwards)	68
Fisher, Ophelia W.	68
Fisher, Richard Leroy, Jr.	68
Fisher, Robert Taylor	68
Fisher, Samuel	65
Fisher, Wilma Dovie	73
Fitch, Bernice Margaret (Schreiber)	68
Fitch, Douglas	68
Fitch, Ethel	68
Fitch, Floyd	12, 68
Fitch, Henry Harris	68
Fitch, John Wilson	68
Fitch, Lela	183
Fitch, Lewis	68
Fitch, Lydia Mae	256
Fitch, Michael Stephen	68
Fitch, Ronald Dean	68
Fitch, Shirley Jean (Turner)	68
Fitch, Stephen	68
Fitch, Susie	244
Fitch, Susie (Cannon)	68
Fitch, Teresa Ann (Johnson)	68
Fitzgerald, Ethel	198
Fitzgerald, Frank	198
Fitzpatrick, Moses Edward	206
Flake, Ethel Loraine	50
Flanagan, James	68
Flanagan, John D	68

Name	Page
Flanagan, Mary (Dunn)	68
Flanagan, William P.	68
Flanders, Florence	57
Flanery, Nathaniel H Flanery	207
Flat Branch Spur Road	vii
Fleming, Patricia Riley	1
Fletcher Disheroon, Georgia (Tate)	69
Fletcher, Alvin	59
Fletcher, Alvin L	69
Fletcher, Charles Marion	69
Fletcher, Dale Ray	69
Fletcher, James Henry	194
Fletcher, John Reese "Renzi"	69
Fletcher, Kyle Ray	69
Fletcher, Lana	69
Fletcher, Margie Lee	265
Fletcher, Preston Eugene	69
Fletcher, Reece	107
Flint, Stella	161
Flippin, Hudson Melroy	14
Flowers, Marie Antoinette	292
Floyd, Amos A.	69
Floyd, Betty	69
Floyd, Bretney Nicole	256
Floyd, Charles	69
Floyd, Douglas Andrew	69
Floyd, Elsie Irene	24
Floyd, Hester (Slatton)	69
Floyd, Hugh E	69
Floyd, Hugh Ellis	69
Floyd, Hugh Ellis "Bit"	69
Floyd, June C.	67
Floyd, L.B.	24
Floyd, Mary M.	69
Floyd, Minnie C.	69
Floyd, Nancy	69
Floyd, Silas Preston	69
Floyd, Stanley	145
Floyd, Verna	222
Floyd, Virgie V.	69
Floyd, Wendell Charles	69
Flury, Catherine Bell	69
Flury, Elizabeth	295
Flury, Elizabeth (Von Rohr)	69
Flury, Frances	95
Flury, Frances (Arbuckle)	69
Flury, Frank J	69
Flury, Fritz L.	69
Flury, Henrich J "Henry"	69
Flury, Henry	69, 95
Flury, Henry Stocker	69
Flury, Mary Elwyn (Reid)	70
Flury, Sammy Louis	70
Flynn, Addie Mae	84
Flynn, Charles	84
Flynn, Elizabeth "Eliza" (Keeling)	70
Flynn, George	70
Flynn, George Walter	70
Flynn, Georgia	174
Flynn, Grace Sherbonne (Barnes)	70
Flynn, James Henry	70
Flynn, John	70
Flynn, Michael	70
Flynn, Michael "Mike", Sr.	70
Flynn, Michael Joseph, Sr.	70
Flynn, Michael R	70
Flynn, Patrick Sheehan	70
Flynn, Rena Ann	34
Flynn, Sr., Michael "Mike"	70
Flynn, Tony	274
Flynn, William Henry "Red"	70
Flynn, Willie Mae	272
Flynn, Willie Myrtle (Meeks)	70
Fogle, Alan	70
Fogle, Linda Roxanne (Ferrell)	70
Foley, Rita Josephine	135
Force, Rosetta Annetta	96
Ford, Ella Faye (Knox)	70
Ford, Jeannette	252
Ford, John R.	70
Ford, Nellie	25
Ford, Russell	70
Ford, Sherman	70
Ford, William R.	70
Foreman, Mary Elizabeth	64
Forrest, Elizabeth	199
Forsyth, Arter Clinton	70
Forsyth, Emma	67
Forsyth, J.T.	165
Forsyth, James Robert	71
Forsyth, Joseph Thomas	70, 71
Forsyth, Jr., Roy G	71
Forsyth, Vanessa Kay (Green)	71
Forsythe, Patricia Elaine	234
Fossett, Eula	176
Foster, Amada	58
Foster, Bertha A.	173
Foster, Bettye Jean (Charles)	71
Foster, Flora	204
Foster, James F.	49
Foster, John Robert	71
Foster, Lillie	96
Foster, Mary	208
Foster, Mary Caroline	208
Foster, Mary Frances (Magouirk)	71

Name	Page
Foster, Mary Jane	95
Foster, Mary Leota	175
Foster, Nellie	2
Foster, Orville Lester	230
Foster, Richard	71
Foster, Robert	71
Foster, Robert Hill	71
Foster, Ruth	3
Foster, William	71
Fothergill, Bell	119
Foutch, Agnes	95
Foutch, Carolyn Fay (Crisp)	71
Foutch, Garland	71
Foute, Francis Adeline	58
Fowler, Gwennie Estella Mae	32
Fowler, Jerry Lynn	71
Fowler, Melvin G	71
Fox, Sally Virginia (Willis)	71
Fox, Thomas W.	71
Frakenfield, Lydia	146
Frame, George Abner	71
Frame, George W.	71
Francis, Celia	45
Francis, Esther	203
Francis, Hazel	60
Francis, Zella	119
Franconi, Ursula	199
Franke, Alda	91, 98
Franke, Alda Mae	243
Franke, Florence	243
Franke, George	91
Franke, Val	243
Franklin, James Rodman	71
Franklin, Janice	71
Franklin, K.R.	71
Franklin, Kenneth Jason	71
Franklin, Marion Isaac	119
Franklin, Selmon T	71
Franklin, Tammy May	71
Franks, Lawrence	171
Franks, Lawrence	299
Franks, Mary Frances	299
Franks, Shirley	170
Franks, Stella	171
Frazier, Frank	8
Frazier, Lillie	8
Frederick, Carol Tressie	188
Frederick, Cecil Nortn	71
Frederick, Edward "Pat"	71
Frederick, Ernest "Pat"	166
Frederick, Geneva	253
Frederick, Geneva Jean	253
Frederick, Hazel	166
Frederick, Howell Jeffrey	71
Frederick, Isaac Jessie	71
Frederick, Jean	168
Frederick, John William	201
Frederick, Kathy	71
Frederick, Mary E.	71
Frederick, Mary Kathleen "Bet"	71
Frederick, Nellie	26, 41
Frederick, Pat	253
Frederick, Stella	200
Fredrick, Edward Ernest "Pat"	71
Fredrick, Jessie	71
Fredrick, John Dewey	71
Fredrick, Mary Kathleen "Bet" (Nunley)	71
Fredrick, Nellie	42
Fredrick, Paul Austin	32
Freeman, Martha	7
Freemont Road	viii
Freeze, Mary Elizabeth	292
French, Earldene Metcalfe	71
French, Edgar	71
French, Ruby	275
French, Violet O. "Vi"	71
Frisbee, Crimson Wade	72
Frisbee, Harvey Lee	36, 72
Frisbee, James Ray	72
Frisbee, William H "Bill"	72
Frisbee, Willow Brooke	72
Frizell, Iva	108
Frizinger, Muriel	83
Frizzell, Beatrice	290
Frost, Mattie Coleman	175
Fry, Dan J.	72
Fry, John	72
Frye, Frank Edward	89
Frye, Herbert "Louis"	148
Fugate, Amanda	57
Fugate, Bruce	57
Fulfer, Bill Sam	3
Fulfer, Houston	113
Fulghum, Harley	79
Fuller, Matilda	39
Fulton, Danice N. Pierce	72
Fulton, Geneva Jane	162
Fulton, Irene "Reenie" Lewisy Bean	72
Fults - Kilgore, Mary Jo	72
Fults, Adell (Campbell)	72
Fults, Adrian	286
Fults, Albert Hannar	73
Fults, Alfred	26, 102
Fults, Alkie Scott	73
Fults, Amy Lou	72
Fults, Andrew Jackson "Andy"	75
Fults, Andrew Lee	76
Fults, Anna	26
Fults, Anna Viola "Annie" (Oliver)	72

Name	Page
Fults, Annie	39
Fults, Annie Beatrice (Elkins)	72
Fults, Barbara June	127
Fults, Bertha	254
Fults, Betty (Rollins)	72
Fults, Bob	74
Fults, Bonnie Sue	222
Fults, Boyd	72, 74
Fults, Boyd Stanton	73, 76
Fults, Brenda Corean	72
Fults, Brenda Newby	76
Fults, Caroline Brown	72
Fults, Carolyn Ann	269
Fults, Carolyn Denise (Hill)	72
Fults, Charlie	73, 95, 244
Fults, Chester Lawrence	74
Fults, Clara Marie (Tate)	72
Fults, Clarence Fults	72
Fults, Clay	74
Fults, Clifford	73, 76
Fults, Cynthia Joan	73
Fults, Daisy Lee	73
Fults, Daniel	26, 147
Fults, Dave	73, 74
Fults, David	74
Fults, Dea	266
Fults, Deamie	38, 304
Fults, Dock	6
Fults, Dorothy Jean (Tate)	73
Fults, Earl F.	73
Fults, Edith Jane	76
Fults, Edith Jane (Whitman)	73
Fults, Edna	4
Fults, Edwin	75
Fults, Elihu	73
Fults, Ella Rose	2
Fults, Estelle	126
Fults, Ether	74
Fults, Ether Loren	72, 75
Fults, Ferlin James "Archie"	73, 74
Fults, Flora	192
Fults, Flora Elizabeth	283
Fults, Florence Ruth	211
Fults, France Hill	74
Fults, Fred A., Jr.	74
Fults, Fred, Jr.	75
Fults, George	73
Fults, Gordon	73
Fults, Helen Ruth	73
Fults, Hester Mae (Meeks)	73
Fults, Hollis Macdonald	75
Fults, Hollis McDonald "Mack"	73
Fults, Hoyt	72, 75
Fults, Hugh Willard "Dutch"	72
Fults, Icie Lou	267
Fults, Icy Lou	230
Fults, Ida	195
Fults, Ida Mai	107
Fults, Infant	73
Fults, Irean	73, 74
Fults, James	73
Fults, James E	73
Fults, James Marvin	73
Fults, James O	72
Fults, Jan	73
Fults, Jannie Robin (Edwards)	74
Fults, Jay	72, 73
Fults, Jay F	74
Fults, Jeff	297
Fults, Jefferson Davis	39
Fults, Jenny	156
Fults, Jesse	vii, 75
Fults, Joe Monroe	74
Fults, Joe Willard	74
Fults, John	74
Fults, John Bell	73
Fults, John Carroll	74
Fults, John Mason	74
Fults, John Wesley	76
Fults, Johnnie	183
Fults, Johnny	72
Fults, Johnny Earl	73, 74
Fults, Joseph	156
Fults, Josephine E. (Brown)	74
Fults, Joyce Marie (Nunley)	74
Fults, Judy K.	282
Fults, Julie A. (McCormick)	74
Fults, Kenneth Dale	74
Fults, Kenny	73
Fults, Kent	72
Fults, Kermit R.	75
Fults, Kermit Ray	195
Fults, Larry Parker	73
Fults, Lawrence	75
Fults, Lawson	74
Fults, Lawson F	72
Fults, Lida Mae	237
Fults, Lillie	139
Fults, Lillie Carlyon (Bates)	74
Fults, Linda	119
Fults, Linda Joyce (VanHooser)	74
Fults, Linda Wallace	73
Fults, Lisa	108
Fults, Lola Mae	46
Fults, Louise	256
Fults, Luther Don	74
Fults, Lydia	49
Fults, Lydia Mae	151

Name	Page
Fults, Mabel	116
Fults, Mable	116
Fults, Maggie	80, 223
Fults, Maggie Marie	75
Fults, Malcolm A.	222
Fults, Margaret	197
Fults, Margie	297
Fults, Margret	73
Fults, Margret Lucille	74
Fults, Marjorie (Gardner)	74
Fults, Marke Kevin	75
Fults, Martha Jane (King)	75
Fults, Martha Myrtle	74
Fults, Martin VanBuren Jackson	73, 74
Fults, Mary	8, 228
Fults, Mary A. Haskins	vii
Fults, Mary Jo	123
Fults, Mary Lou	19, 294
Fults, Matilda	295
Fults, Melissa Ann	75
Fults, Melvin	76
Fults, Melvin Levern	75
Fults, Michael Dale	75
Fults, Minnie	257
Fults, Myrtle	32
Fults, Nancy	8, 272
Fults, Nola Jean	75
Fults, Oma	214
Fults, Ophelia (Dickerson)	75
Fults, Ora	8
Fults, Oris	73, 76
Fults, Ovie	130
Fults, Parthenia L. (McHone)	75
Fults, Pauline	301
Fults, Pearl Layne	76
Fults, Pearly Mae	217
Fults, Perrie	76
Fults, Perrie Ula (Myers)	75
Fults, Perry	166
Fults, Randy	75
Fults, Ray	75
Fults, Ray Jackson	75, 174
Fults, Raymond "Cotton"	73
Fults, Richard W.	75
Fults, Rita	121
Fults, Robert Lee "Bob"	76
Fults, Ronald Dean	75
Fults, Rosa	269
Fults, Roy	273
Fults, Ruben	56, 72
Fults, Ruth	87
Fults, Ruthie Jane	vii, 26
Fults, Ruthy Jane	75
Fults, Sallie	156
Fults, Sally Hazel	256
Fults, Sara Bonita	127, 128
Fults, Sarah	53
Fults, Sarah Louise (Scott)	75
Fults, Sheryl Lynn "Sherri" (Sherwood)	75
Fults, Shirley C.	136
Fults, Smith	118
Fults, Sue	196
Fults, Tade	75, 76
Fults, Tammy	75
Fults, Tennessee	76, 117
Fults, Tennessee Palestine	118
Fults, Theron	74
Fults, Theron Elmore	74
Fults, Thomas Bryan	76
Fults, Tiffany Rhea	76
Fults, Tim	114, 117
Fults, Timmie	146
Fults, Tom	73
Fults, Tommy Waymon	242
Fults, Tresa Gail	76
Fults, Tressie	167
Fults, Vernon Lee	76
Fults, Violet Faye (VanHooser)	76
Fults, Virginia Lucille "Susie"	76
Fults, Wanda	251
Fults, Wayne "Smiley"	76
Fults, Wendell Edward	76
Fults, Wesley	72, 75, 119
Fults, Wesley A.	75
Fults, Wesley Earl	73
Fults, Willie Carl	74, 243
Fults, Willie Mae	89
Fults, Zella	254, 294
Fultz, Charley Jesse	76
Fultz, Edna Mae	93
Fultz, Geraldine	283
Fultz, Hester Mae	76
Fultz, Johnny L.	76
Fultz, Raymond "Cotton"	76
Fultz, Thomas Edward	76
Fultz, Willie Mae (Patrick)	76
Funglie, Alice	15
Furlong, Helen Jeanette	50
Fyfe, Jennie	248
Fyke, Floy	262
Gaitens, Anna Pearl (Hartwell)	76
Gaitens, James C.	9
Gaitens, James Clyde	76
Gaitens, Rae Clyde	76
Gaither, Magabelle	242
Gallagher, Benton Clay	76, 122
Gallagher, Dorothy	70
Gallagher, Jerry Dale	76, 171

Name	Page
Gallagher, John	105
Gallagher, Joseph Clark	76
Gallagher, Joseph Edmond	77
Gallagher, Joseph Edmund	259
Gallagher, Mary Clementine	260
Gallagher, Mary Ethel	42
Gallagher, Mary Frances (Prince)	76
Gallagher, Tom	27
Gallagher, Tressie Jo	122
Gallagher, Willodean "Dean"	77
Galligan, Jean	177
Gamble, Carrie Grace	77
Gamble, John J	77
Gamble, Orby	77
Gammons, Nicholas Anthony	7
Gardner, Frank Threlfell	74
Gardner, Lissa	33
Garland, Anna	268
Garland, Anna M.	268
Garner, Adeline	134
Garner, Bertha Mae	77
Garner, Berthe	150
Garner, Betty	134, 216
Garner, Billy Douglas	77, 111
Garner, Billy Ed	77
Garner, Clarence W	77
Garner, David Smith	49
Garner, Dennis	77
Garner, Don Carlos	77
Garner, Dorothy	77
Garner, Ed Monroe	77
Garner, Eleanor	97
Garner, Emma	235
Garner, Fay (Moran)	77
Garner, Flora Mae	154
Garner, Floyd	77
Garner, Georgia Fay	155
Garner, Gertrude	222
Garner, Henry	77
Garner, Herbert	77
Garner, Hobert	64, 149
Garner, Jeffrey Douglas "Pottsie"	77
Garner, John	10
Garner, Katie Helen	120
Garner, Lauren	72
Garner, Lauren Rochelle	72, 77
Garner, Lottie	10
Garner, Lou Allen	222
Garner, Louis Stanley	77
Garner, Marcia	77
Garner, Margaret	102
Garner, Martha Lee	77
Garner, Mary	227
Garner, Mary Elizabeth	166
Garner, Matthew	77
Garner, Maude	81
Garner, Ora	77
Garner, Oscar S.	77
Garner, Shirley June	287
Garner, Vicki Sue	303
Garner, Virginia	147
Garner, Wanda Faye (Nunley)	77
Garner, William F.	134
Garrard, Wanda Louise	274
Garret, Faye	36
Garretson, Frances	77
Garretson, Frances A	77
Garretson, Isaac	77
Garretson, Mary E	77
Garretson, Robert W	77
Garrett, Jean	iii
Garrett, Mary Jo	109
Garrett, Olvy J.	44
Garton, Lula Mae	278
Garza, Graciela	51
Gasaway, Dessie	25
Gass, Bessie	260
Gass, Jay C.	38
Gass, Jerry	260
Gaston, Ann Margaret	161
Gates, Fred	77
Gates, Johnnie Marler	96
Gates, Lilly Belle	278
Gates, Roy Leon	77
Gates, Sandra	77
Gates, Susan	77
Gatewood, Guy Percy	77
Gatewood, Joseph Rodney	77
Gattis, Betty (Roberts)	77
Gattis, C.F.	78
Gattis, Charles	77
Gattis, Nell (Dickerson)	78
Geary, Alton	278
Geary, Alvin Oats	78
Geary, Carl T.	5
Geary, Carson Dennis	78
Geary, Clayton	78
Geary, Dennis	78
Geary, Dennis Clayton	78
Geary, Everett	78
Geary Family Gravesite	v
Geary, Ima Jean (Shrum)	78
Geary, Johnnie Marie (Johnson)	78
Geary, Joseph S.	142
Geary, LaNea	40
Geary, Linda	23
Geary, Louise	94, 141, 144
Geary, Maria Patsy R	31
Geary, Mary	67, 238
Geary, Mary Louise	139

Name	Page
Geary, Max Douglas, Sr.	78
Geary, Nellie Dee	5
Geary, Rebecca	25, 192
Geary, Rebecca Katherine	286
Geary, Robert Lee	78
Geary, Roy Clayton	78
Geary, Thelma Arlean (Shrum)	78
Geary, Thomas	78
Geary, Thomas Jaefferson	78
Geary, William Robert "W.R."	78
Geary, Willie Hayes	67
Geary, Willie Mae (Thomas)	78
Geier, Mae	66
Geil, Elizabeth geb (Claus)	78
Geil, Jacob	78
Gentry, Madella (Beebe)	78
Gephart, Stella Gertrude	266
Gholston, Dorothy Marlee	227
Gholston, Ralph Eugene	227
Gholston, Sam	79
Gholston, Sam, Jr.	79
Gibbons, Tommy Louis	79
Gibbons, Walton Lee	79
Gibbs Bend Family Cemetery	v, vi
Gibbs, Annie Lee	54, 79
Gibbs, Adam	v
Gibbs, Audrey	79
Gibbs, Bobbie Hester	
Gibbs, Cora Lee	264
Gibbs, Della Mae	250
Gibbs, Dola	248
Gibbs, Eliza	250
Gibbs, Everett R.	115
Gibbs, Frances Cordelia "Puss"	79
Gibbs, Gordon H.	79
Gibbs, G. W.	v
Gibbs, Hanna	v
Gibbs, Hester	79
Gibbs, Homer, Jr.	171, 236
Gibbs, James	v
Gibbs, James Odom	v, 79
Gibbs, John	v
Gibbs, Johnny Dillard	79
Gibbs, Kelly	v
Gibbs, Lindel Joseph	79
Gibbs, Lois Lindsay	79
Gibbs, Lou Ella "Yell"	171
Gibbs, Louise	106
Gibbs, Lucy B. (Argo)	71
Gibbs, Luke	79
Gibbs, Luke Grady	79
Gibbs, Maria	79
Gibbs, Mary "Polly"	v
Gibbs, Nancy	v, 160
Gibbs, Nell Rose	79
Gibbs, Nora Bell	79
Gibbs, Paul	302
Gibbs, Rev. Lilian	79
Gibbs, Tedd K.	101
Gibbs, Virginia Vincent	79
Gibbs, William J.	v
Giblin, Sandi Diane	79, 285
Gibson, Alene	79
Gibson, Annie	118, 122
Gibson, Annie Lee	232
Gibson, Ben B. Davis	39
Gibson, John William	232
Gibson, Linda	173
Gibson, Martha Ann (Newman)	139
Gibson, William Dean	79
Gifford, Gary E. Gifford, Jr.	79
Gifford, Gary Eugene III	79
Gifford, Hannah (James)	79
Gifford, Ruby	79
Gifford, Ruby	51
Gifford, Ruby Lee	67
Gifford, Tammy Dale	30, 193
Gilbert, Alma Louise	79
Gilbert, Ernestine (Roberts)	230
Gilbert, John Thomas	80
Gilbert, Lon	80
Gilbert, Marta Lynn	286
Gilbert, Stephanie	216
Gill, Doris	103
Gilland, Blanche Lolita	113
Gillentine, Martha	234
Gillespie, David Daniel	294
Gillespie, David Wayne	80
Gillespie, Gordon R	80
Gillespie, James Ray	80
Gillespie, Soeldad	80
Gillespie, Thomas E.	80
Gillespie, William Harold	80
Gilley, Benjamin	80
Gilley, Benjamin Franklin	80
Gilley, Ella (Disheroon)	80
Gilley, Mary	80
Gilley, Mollie	215
Gilley, William H.	48
Gilley, William Henry	111
Gilliam, Dana	iii
Gilliam, Edna Jane	80
Gilliam, Alice	80
Gilliam, Alma Christine (Williams)	300
Gilliam, Alvin Owen	80
Gilliam, Ann	218
Gilliam, Argie Earlene	190

Name	Page
Gilliam, Austin	240
Gilliam, Autumn	154
Gilliam, Avis Elizabeth	27
Gilliam, Barbara "Bobbie" (Graves)	266
Gilliam, Beulah May	80
Gilliam, Bobbie	17
Gilliam, Bunia (Nunley)	46
Gilliam, Burwell	80
Gilliam, Charles E	80
Gilliam, Charles Hayden, Sr.	80
Gilliam, Charles Henry	80
Gilliam, Cordell	80
Gilliam, Cordell Hull	109
Gilliam, Denny Martin	81
Gilliam, Elbert Gipson	80
Gilliam, Eugenia	81
Gilliam, Eugenia Bell	280
Gilliam, Frank	280
Gilliam, George	81
Gilliam, Gerald Edward "Bud"	155
Gilliam, Glen A.	80
Gilliam, Gordon	80
Gilliam, Harley	80
Gilliam, Harris	81, 301
Gilliam, Huetta	81
Gilliam, Huetta "Etta"	142, 198
Gilliam, James H Cox	141, 142
Gilliam, James Harold	105
Gilliam, James William "Billy"	80
Gilliam, Jimmy	27
Gilliam, John Grady	80
Gilliam, L.M.	80
Gilliam, Lancen	105
Gilliam, Lannie	27
Gilliam, Lansing	252
Gilliam, Lanson O'Dell "Dellie"	121
Gilliam, Lee	152
Gilliam, Lewis Wright	295
Gilliam, Lorene	80
Gilliam, Lula Mae	121
Gilliam, Margie Mae (Bain)	105
Gilliam, Martha Jane	80
Gilliam, Martin Grady	44
Gilliam, Mary Ann	257
Gilliam, Minnie	80
Gilliam, Minnie Pearl (Elliott)	81
Gilliam, Nancy M.	81
Gilliam, Pauline (Privett) Harris	81
Gilliam, Robert	81
Gilliam, Robert "Bob Mitch"	80
Gilliam, Robert Gilliam, Jr.	80, 81
Gilliam, Robert, Jr.	81
Gilliam, Samuel	81
Gilliam, Sandy	81
Gilliam, Thelma (Turner)	80
Gilliam, Wilson	81
Gilliland, Sarah	10
Gilmer, Jim	109
Gilmer, Roy	163, 282
Gipson, Albert Preston	121
Gipson, Alene	123
Gipson, Beatrice	116
Gipson, Charles J.	123
Gipson, Charles Ray	212
Gipson, Clayborn	99
Gipson, Deborah	222
Gipson, Edna	5
Gipson, Elbert	51
Gipson, Elmer	301
Gipson, Etta Mae	114
Gipson, Eugene Burdith	281
Gipson, Franklin Delano Roosevelt	81
Gipson, George Washington	81
Gipson, Huetta	225
Gipson, Hugh	175
Gipson, Irma Jean	175
Gipson, James Elbert	222
Gipson, Joe C.	81
Gipson, Joshua Kane	81
Gipson, Keith	81
Gipson, Lillie Eleanor	3
Gipson, Linda	225
Gipson, Lucille	10
Gipson, Manerva	175
Gipson, Mary (Sherrill)	37
Gipson, Michael Anthony	81
Gipson, Pamela	81
Gipson, Paul Collis	81
Gipson, Richard	81
Gipson, Robert Lee, Sr.	81
Gipson, Ruth	81
Gipson, Sally	199
Gipson, Sarah	46
Gipson, Stanley	54
Gipson, Verna Mae	81
Gipson, Vernice Mae (Campbell)	180
Gipson, William Oscar	81
Given, Geneva	79
Givens, Alma Jean	290
Givens, Carlene	150
Givens, Dorothy Cleo	95
Givens, Eliza A. (Nichols)	131, 132
Givens, Helen K.	81
Givens, Hershel O	81
Givens, Hershel Owen	58
Givens, Howard L.	82
Givens, Ines	20

Name	Page
Givens, James Ralph	20
Givens, Jeffery Rodney "Bogart"	34, 81
Givens, Joann	82
Givens, Mamie Lee	34
Givens, Martha Cleo	196
Givens, Nina	25
Givens, Ralph	75, 223
Givens, Rona Lee	82
Givens, Rondal Owen	167
Givens, Sallie	82
Givens, Sally	153, 161
Givens, Waldean	41, 78
Givens, William Anderson	237
Glaus, Nicholas	81
Glisson, Addie	78
Glisson, Flora Mae	179
Glisson, John	264
Glisson, John W.	294
Glisson, Pearl	178
Glisson, Pearl Bryant	293
Glover, Ann	17
Glowner, Sophronia	275
Gnagey, Arminta Estella	164
Goad, Nancy Jane	45
Gober, Alfred	61
Gober, Alice	39
Godfrey, Tammy	39
Godsby, Lizzie	34
Godsby, Sarah Elizabeth	46
Goedjen, Albert J	45
Goedjen, Eugenie	13
Goehler, Kevin J.	13
Goff, Faye	67
Goff, Mary Iva	197
Goforth, Emma Lorene	65
Goforth, Anna (Griswold)	23
Gohl, Hampas Fritsof	82
Gohl, Inga Thuridor	148
Goins, Clarence	148
Goins, Clarence, Jr.	82
Goins, Hattie Louise (Bombailey)	82
Goins, Linda	82
Goins, Starnes Frederick	82
Goldey, Bobby Elizabeth (Singleton)	82
Goletz, Eva Nancy	82
Golston, Barton	134
Golston, Josie	82
Golston, Laden	82, 194
Golston, Louis Donald	29
Golston, Tampico	82
Gomez, Gabriela	29
Gomez, Gregorio	51
Good, Hattie & Mattie (twins)	51
Good, Lewis B.	82
Good, Sabrah Ann	82
Goode, Victoria Lynn	199
Goodman Lane	vi
Goodman, Alace	277
Goodman, Allie Blair	82
Goodman, Allison	21
Goodman, Almagene	177
Goodman, Almajean	238
Goodman, Annie	294
Goodman, Butch	vi
Goodman, Cliff	67
Goodman, Dorothy Nell	83
Goodman, Elbert	82
Goodman, Eula Gaynell (Booker)	176
Goodman, Evalina	82
Goodman, Harold Franklin	236
Goodman, James "Butch"	82
Goodman, James Elbert	254
Goodman, James Ralph	82
Goodman, James Tolbert	82
Goodman, Jewell (Hamby)	82
Goodman, Julia	82
Goodman, Lillard Harleth	82, 83
Goodman, Linda	83
Goodman, Lude Carroll	82, 83
Goodman, Mark Andrew	82
Goodman, Martha A	82
Goodman, Martha Irene	82
Goodman, Robert Harleth	70
Goodman, Sally Carole	83
Goodman, Selena Evalina	83
Goodman, Selena Evaline	232
Goodman, Selina	234
Goodman, Solomon	233, 267
Goodman, Solomon P.	83
Goodman, Thomas S.	82
Goodman, W.M.	83
Goodman, Ward	83
Goodman, William L.	83
Goodman, William Larry	82, 83
Goodman/Moran Cemetery	vi
Goodpasture, Mildred	83
Goodrich, Mary	1
Goodson, Ewing Marshall, II, Dr.	110
Goodson, Robert Jerome	83
Goodwin, Francis Marion	83
Goodwin, Mildred	83
Goodwin, Myrtle Virgil "Mirtie"	121
Goodwin, Richard Jackson	70
Goolsby, Marie (Wooten)	83
Goolsby, William Alex	83
Gorby, Joyce (Myers) Tuck	83

Name	Page
Gorby, Ken	83
Gordon, Arthur A.	281
Gordon, Robert Louis	83
Gorman, Glenda Faye	83
Gosnell, Heather	232
Goss, Johann	88
Goss, Sophia Christine	83
Gossett, Anna	83
Gossett, Anna Lee	151
Gossett, Ardelia Pauline	90
Gowen, Harriet	234
Gower, Claudia	7
Graham, Bessie Belle	223
Graham, Delia	289
Graham, Donna Gayle (Watley)	176
Graham, Earl	83
Graham, Earl William	83
Graham, Elizabeth	83
Graham, George William James	84
Graham, Hazel	159
Graham, Homer	43
Graham, Homer, Jr.	83
Graham, Homer, Sr.	83
Graham, Irene	83
Graham, James Homer	84
Graham, James Walter	109
Graham, Jessie	83
Graham, John H.	232
Graham, Margie	84
Graham, Martha "Patsy" (Stamback)	122
Graham, Martha Jane "Mattie" (Davis)	84
Graham, Mary Susan	84
Graham, Mazie	172
Graham, Mazie Hilda	158
Graham, Oma Ruth	215
Graham, Ralph J.	221
Graham, Ralph James	84
Graham, Renice	84
Graham, Rhoda Jane	83
Graham, Roxie	56
Graham, Simmon Peter	143, 302
Graham, Susan	84
Graham, Susie	15
Granlee, Lucille Mae	172
Grant, Charlestine F. (Flynn)	120
Grant, James S.	84
Grantham, Cynthia Ann (Castleberry)	84
Grantham, John	84
Grantham, Josephine	84
Grantham, Pleasant A.	280
Gratigny, Frances E. (Sitz)	84
Gratigny, Melvin	84
Graven, Amy	84
Graves, Dannie Ella	221
Graves, James	142
Graves, Lillian	80
Graves, Mignone	101
Gravitt, Audrey	80
Gray, Horace Ann (Cleek)	16
Gray, Bill	84
Gray, Daniel Clifford	84
Gray, Jane Lorraine	84
Gray, Jimmy Wayne	90
Gray, Joe D.	84
Gray, Nell	84
Gray, William H.	103
Grayson, Annie Mae	8
Grayson, Ollie	285
Grayson, Walter Crawford	257, 293
Green, Adaline	55
Green, Anita Celeste (Culbertson)	251
Green, Anna Cleo	84
Green, Anna Mae	124
Green, Barbara Jo	85
Green, Beatrice	84
Green, Bertha	123
Green, Bessie	80
Green, Bethel	253
Green, Benton J.	30
Green, Beuna	85
Green, Billy Ray	84, 85
Green, Carrie Grace	84
Green, Charles	77
Green, Charles "Tony"	86
Green, Charles Edward	84
Green, Charles Wesley, Sr.	84
Green, Clyde	85
Green, Columbus	85
Green, Columbus James	85, 161
Green, Creasie Eldridge	85
Green, Daisy Irene	170
Green, Dan	85
Green, Daniel Wesley	85, 214, 253
Green, Dave	177
Green, Dave Wesley	111
Green, Debra	85
Green, Della	85
Green, Dora	283
Green, Doris Marie	304
Green, Dortha	291
Green, E. Iola	84, 85, 86, 165
Green, Elizabeth Geneva	126, 127
Green, Elmer L.	228
Green, Eva	85
Green, Fannie	107
Green, Fealy Mae	194
Green, Floye	224
Green, George Earl	147
Green, Glenda	71

Name	Page
Green, Gloria Willene (Collins)	86
Green, Gracie Mae	85
Green, Hallie	44, 246
Green, Harold	163
Green, Hayes	32
Green, Henry Cleston	86
Green, Ina Ruth	85
Green, James	132
Green, James A.	85
Green, James Alexander	85
Green, James Arthur	85
Green, James Arthur, Jr.	132
Green, James Author	143
Green, James E. Gilliam	85
Green, James Frank	80
Green, James "Bill", Jr.	86
Green, Jean	85
Green, Jimmy Ray	112
Green, Joanie	85
Green, Jody W., Sr.	57
Green, John David	224
Green, John Harold	86
Green, John Wesley	85
Green, John William	228
Green, Juanita	86
Green, Juanita	275
Green, Katie E.	33
Green, Kelsey Lynn	85
Green, Kelsie	85
Green, Kenneth	289
Green, Lee	85, 291
Green, Lena Mae	77
Green, Leona Marie	85
Green, Lillian	85
Green, Lilly Artie Mishie	158
Green, Lucia Adair	85
Green, Lucy	303
Green, Margaret	208
Green, Marie (Parsons)	255
Green, Martha Rose	85
Green, Mary	54
Green, Mary "Jane"	30
Green, Mary C.	86
Green, Mary Elizabeth (Haynes)	85
Green, Mila	85
Green, Mildie	123
Green, Millie L. (Melton)	86
Green, Minnie	86
Green, Mordica	4
Green, Nancy	86
Green, Nellie	86
Green, Norman "Wesley"	120
Green, Norman L.	86
Green, Norman Lemuel	86, 172
Green, Ola Iowa	85
Green, Ophelia	86
Green, Parker H.	127
Green, Parker I	84, 86
Green, Paul	86
Green, Paul L.	86
Green, Paul Lesley	85
Green, Paul Richard	86
Green, Phyllis	86
Green, Rachel	85
Green, Ralph Edward	195, 197, 198
Green, Rebecca Lynn	86
Green, Richard Lee	56
Green, Robert Jackson	85
Green, Sally	86
Green, Samuel	85
Green, Scott	86, 196
Green, Shirley F. "Shirl"	84, 86
Green, Shirley Faye	86
Green, Shirley Jeanette (Jones)	86
Green, Teddy Estel	86
Green, Thomas	85
Green, Thomas Haywood	136
Green, Veller	86
Green, Velma	9
Green, Virgil	33
Green, Virginia	19
Green, Virginia	172
Green, Virginia Pearl	195
Green, W.C.	167
Green, Wesley	85
Green, William "Red"	250
Green, William A.	56
Green, William Alexander "Red"	77
Green, William Ernest	86
Green, William George	9
Green, William Jody, Sr.	86
Green, William Red	85
Green, Willie	86
Greene, Alta Odell	147
Greene, Billy Ray	234
Greene, Bobby Lloyd	86
Greene, Claborn	87
Greene, Claude	87
Greene, Clayborn William	227
Greene, Dorothy Elizabeth (Park)	87
Greene, Fay "Perkie" (Cannon)	87
Greene, Joseph Charles	87
Greene, Julia Virginia (Williams)	87
Greene, Karla	87
Greene, Lensia (Rhea)	38
Greene, Lillian	87
Greene, Peter L.	149
Greene, Virgil Franklin	87

Name	Page
Greenlee, Henderson	87
Greenlee, Mary Frances (Downum)	87
Greenlee, William James	87
Greer, Clifton E	87
Greeter, Christine (Worley)	248
Greeter, Elizabeth	87
Greeter, Harvey	87
Greeter, Jacob	87
Greeter, John George	87
Greeter, John J.	297
Greeter, John W.	87
Greeter, Joyce	87
Greeter, Marguerite (Walker)	102
Greeter, Werner E.	88
Greeter, Willie	88
Greeter, Willie Mae	90
Gregory, Abel Landers	296
Gregory, Aurella Dell	88
Gregory, Cecil	88
Gregory, Lucy	104
Gregory, Lula Virginia (Corliss)	187
Gregory, Marion	88
Gregory, Mattie	104
Gregory, Silas	88
Gregory, Silas Samuel	88
Gregory, Sylvia	136, 255
Gregory, Vivian Marie (Ladd)	104
Grein, Jamie	88
Griffin, Andrew V.	27
Griffin, Clara	88
Griffin, Don Edwin	12
Griffin, Floyd	88
Griffin, Gertie Mae (Rogers)	88
Griffin, Perry	88
Griffin, Ples Hugh	88
Griffis, Martha (Brandt)	261
Griffith, Albert Lee	88
Griffith, Alvis	273
Griffith, Billy Ray	125
Griffith, Clara	88
Griffith, Constance	86
Griffith, Dalta	246
Griffith, Elsie	246
Griffith, Evelyn Ann	138
Griffith, Fran	289
Griffith, George David	108
Griffith, James	138
Griffith, James Hubert	88
Griffith, Janice Faye (Layne)	288
Griffith, Jeanette	88
Griffith, Jesse	151
Griffith, Juanita Marjorie (Grimes)	184
Griffith, Kay (Eldridge)	88
Griffith, Larry Dean	88
Griffith, Mary	88
Griffith, Dr. Lisa Marie (White)	211
Griffith, Maude Bell	293
Griffith, Maxie Leann	273
Griffith, Michael	88
Griffith, Nancy Ann "Susie" (Campbell)	88
Griffith, Rachel (Slatton)	88
Griffith, Thomas	88
Griffith, William	246
Griffith, William, Jr.	88, 187
Griffith, William, Jr.	88
Griffith, William, Sr.	88
Grimes, Alene	88
Grimes, Betty	139
Grimes, Betty	280
Grimes, Brenda Rogers	126
Grimes, Charles P.	88
Grimes, Claudette	88
Grimes, Dale	89
Grimes, Earl Wesley	88
Grimes, Elouise	88, 89
Grimes, Eunice	89
Grimes, Fred	89
Grimes, Fred	123
Grimes, Gregory Lee	123
Grimes, Herbert	89
Grimes, Herbert Lee Grimes	69
Grimes, Herschel	89
Grimes, Hershel	89
Grimes, James Edward	88
Grimes, James William	88
Grimes, Kate	89
Grimes, Robert	303
Grimes, Robert "Bud", Jr.	187
Grimes, Robert, Sr.	89
Grimes, Sam	89
Grimm, Mary Elizabeth	271
Grimm, Richard	89
Grissom, Bennie Kay	89
Grissom, Harry	150
Grissom, Shawn Cameron	89
Griswold, Anna	89
Griswold, David M	177
Griswold, David Murphy	82
Griswold, Ellene	89
Griswold, Erier	89
Griswold, G.G.	199
Griswold, George Gilbert	89
Griswold, Jennie Lee	89
Griswold, Louisa	182
Griswold, Martha "Mattie"	279
Griswold, Martha Jane	89
Griswold, Mary Ann Susannah	89
Griswold, Mattie	187

Name	Page
Griswold, Rena	182
Griswold, Willie	11
Grizzle, Rex	89
Grodzicki, Mara	224
Groh, Franziska Margareta	159
Grooms, Elbert	173
Grooms, Elbert B.	89
Grooms, Elbert Ronald "Lad"	89
Grooms, Hobert M.	89
Grooms, John Leonard	203
Grooms, Keith "Budge"	204
Grooms, Keith Jackson "Budge"	121
Grooms, Leonard	89
Grooms, Lou	277
Grooms, Mary	121
Grooms, Ola	137
Grooms, Ola Rebecca	29
Gross, Asa	29
Gross, Della Mae	26
Gross, Floyd Lawson	31
Gross, Frank Marshall	89
Gross, Fred Cleveland	49
Gross, John Cleveland	89
Gross, Johnny Floyd	89
Gross, Leonard Floyd	89
Gross, Lillie Mae (Smith)	89
Gross, Margaret Ann	89
Gross, Ollie Bell	73
Gross, Ruth Clydene	72
Gross, Stanley Uvohn	44
Gross, Stella Margie	89
Gross, Theron	49
Gruetter, Elisabeth	282
Grutter, Jacob	266
Gudger, Pressie	87
Guess, Charlene	38
Guess, Ed Gullie	112
Guess, Leon	49
Guess, Margaret "Sue"	112
Guess, Martha Elizabeth	302
Guess, Mildred "Mickie"	149
Guess, Ricky Darrell	49
Guess, Rita	89
Guess, Sue	89
Guess, Thomas	302
Guess, Una	89
Guffey, Bettye Stanley	89
Guffey, Billy Carl	206
Guffey, Minnie	89
Guffy, Rebecca (Coffelt)	50
Gugliemotto, Anna Fay (King)	89
Gugliemotto, Joseph Jack	89
Guin, Gene	89
Guin, Matthew Allen	90
Guin, Terry	90
Guinn, Hobert N.	90
Guinn, Tennie	90
Guire, Christy	90
Gulas, Anton Adams	263
Gulas, Stewart Anton "Stu"	90
Gunn, Bernard M.	90
Gunn, Nelena	90
Gunn, Patricia Ann (Lowrie)	260
Gunn, Roscoe	90
Gunn, Thomas Edgar	90
Gunnels, Selina Vestina	90
Gunter, Mary	48
Gustafsdotter, Amelia	95
Guthrie, James	148
Guthrie, Kathleine	253
Guy, Margaret Estel	229
Guyear, Catherine Jane	90
Guyear, Margaret	90
Guyear, Marion	23
Guyear, Marion Phillip	90
Guyear, Mary	90
Guyear, Nancy (Stanback)	175
Guyear, Paul Newton	90
Guyear, Susan Catherine	90
Guyear, Willie Ray	90
Guyer, Susie	90
Guyer, Thomas	277
Gwinn, Julia	90
Habat, Mary	243
Hackworth, Geraldine	217
Haddon, Lana	39
Hagelbarger, Harriet June	108
Hagelbarger, Walter J.	46
Hagen, Severt J	46
Hagewood, Bertie Mae	278
Haggenmacher, Mary	84
Hagman, Anna	194
Hahn, Magdalena	101
Hain, Adela A.	239
Hale, Aubrey F.	90
Hale, Bessie Lou	90
Hale, Callie	4
Hale, Callie Dora	127
Hale, Elizabeth	65
Hale, Fred C.	219
Hale, Georgia Mae	90
Hale, Hester	131
Hale, Ida Lee	240
Hale, Richard	22
Hale, Silas Singleton	97
Haley, Jimmy Paul	240
Haley, Unk.	109
Halfacre, Virginia	82
Hall, Alton Floyd	33

Name	Page
Hall, Arthur L.	90
Hall, Benjamin Franklin "Bee"	185
Hall, Bruce Cullen	91
Hall, Carrie Ola (McWain)	90
Hall, Charlie	90
Hall, Dena	90, 91
Hall, Drusilla	93
Hall, Eddie Dean	118
Hall, Edward E.	91
Hall, Elbert H.	91
Hall, Elinor	91
Hall, Glenn H.	90
Hall, Harold	91
Hall, Harvey	12
Hall, Howard E.	91
Hall, James N.	91
Hall, James O. "Red"	91
Hall, John Douglas	91
Hall, John Solomon	91
Hall, Josie	91
Hall, Kimberly Renae (Melton)	82
Hall, Larry	91
Hall, Lina Caroline	90
Hall, Linna	70
Hall, Lucille (Kilgore)	70
Hall, Margaret	91
Hall, Marlon "Marty"	91
Hall, Michael	91
Hall, Myrtle	160
Hall, Myrtle (Hall) Cain	91
Hall, Ola	55
Hall, Ola Mae	91
Hall, Prudance	121
Hall, Ray Edward	12
Hall, Sherrie Ellen (Brannon)	91
Hall, Twilla Nichole	91
Hall, Van	12
Hall, Vivian Inez	91
Hall, Willis Robert	91
Hallbert, Madeleine (Slaick)	91
Hallman, James Samuel	91
Hallman, Mark Omar	91
Halstead, Edna	91
Halterman, Joann	45
Hamby, Billy Mitchell	154
Hamby, Billy Wayne "Blue"	92
Hamby, Catherine (Calhoun)	92
Hamby, David	92
Hamby, Dorraine	92
Hamby, Doyle	204
Hamby, Eli Washington	92
Hamby, Eli William	92
Hamby, Elizabeth Dianne	92
Hamby, Ephraim L.	92
Hamby, Ernestine (Meeks)	92
Hamby, Grady	92
Hamby, Grover Cleveland	92
Hamby, Grover Cleveland "Cleve"	107
Hamby, Horace	82
Hamby, Horace Mitchell	160
Hamby, Jesse Ransom	92
Hamby, Jo Ann	92
Hamby, Martha Jane	92
Hamby, Mary Leona (Johnson)	92
Hamby, Robert	92
Hamby, Robert Lee	92
Hamby, Sarah Lewis	92
Hamby, Thursa	92
Hamby, Thursie	188
Hamilton, Alice	298
Hamilton, Brenda (Bonner)	243
Hamilton, Carrie	92
Hamilton, Eliza	33
Hamilton, Emma Jeanette	244
Hamilton, James Gordon	92
Hamilton, Judith (Holiday)	92
Hamilton, Laura Lela "Belle"	92
Hamilton, Neoma Alice	293
Hamilton, Paul	244
Hamilton, Sally	92
Hamilton, Wiley	148
Hamilton, William John	244
Hamlin, Nicholas Allen	92
Hamlin, Ricky	92
Hamm, Sarah Elder	92
Hammers, Alec Levi	248
Hammers, Alex L	241
Hammers, Hubert	121
Hammers, Huey Dale	92, 212
Hammers, Kathy Jane	92
Hammers, Myrtle	92
Hammers, Robert Lee	111
Hammers, Rosal Nell	245
Hammond, Beatrice Arlene	92
Hammond, Charles Edward	60
Hammond, Elvin Wayne, Sr.	93
Hammond, James Hines	92
Hammond, Mittie Jane	92
Hammons, Arvile Edward	93
Hammons, Nannie	93
Hammons, Robert L	93
Hampton, Beatrice Ann (Archey)	93
Hampton, Ben C., Sr.	93
Hampton, Betty J.	36

Name	Page
Hampton, Betty Jean	130
Hampton, Billie Fay	93
Hampton, Charles Edward "Buck"	183
Hampton, Christopher Shane	93
Hampton, Connie	93
Hampton, Cora (Womble)	93
Hampton, David	93
Hampton, Deborah	93
Hampton, Dennis Rheal	54
Hampton, Edna Mae	7
Hampton, Elizabeth	188
Hampton, Eugene	93
Hampton, Eugene Dalvern	12, 93
Hampton, Fines H.	12
Hampton, George H	93
Hampton, Glenn "Rip", Jr.	182
Hampton, Glenn, Sr.	93
Hampton, Helen Marie (Nunley)	93
Hampton, J.C.	93
Hampton, James Andrew	93
Hampton, Jennie	97
Hampton, Jennie Elizabeth	97
Hampton, Johnnie Ruth	93
Hampton, Kathy	93
Hampton, Ketherine	93
Hampton, Lula Emma (Taylor)	106
Hampton, Mark C.	93
Hampton, Martha Lou	93
Hampton, Melvin	13
Hampton, Melvin C. "Bud"	93
Hampton, Milton	93, 172
Hampton, Mozell	93
Hampton, Mozella	205
Hampton, Nadine	48
Hampton, Otis	188
Hampton, Phinas "Finas"	93
Hampton, Rachel	93, 97
Hampton, Smartt L	93
Hampton, Thomas E.	93
Hampton, Veola	93
Hampton, Violet	16
Hampton, William H.	37
Hancock, Wagner Warren	93
Hancock, Warren O'Dell	93
Hand, Betty L. "Nell"	93
Haney, Mary	196
Hankins, Fannie Catherine	245
Hankins, Horace B.	248
Hankins, John William	94
Hankins, Peggy Rose C.	94
Hanna, Earl Mark	94
Hannah, Carolyn (Arnold)	94
Hannah, James Edward	94
Hannah, Jim	94
Hannah, Lula	94
Hanner, Mary Lou	94
Hanner, Thomas H.	94
Hanner, Thomas Huel	94
Hanner, Thomas Jeffery	94
Hansel, Martha "Mattie"	94
Hansen, Karen	91
Hansford, William	20
Hanson, Donald	277
Hanson, Earle	94
Hanson, Howard Sidney	42
Hanson, Margaret (Layne)	94
Hanson, Shirley	94
Hanson, Sidney R.	97
Harbolt, Byron David, Dr.	94
Harbolt, Byron David, MD	94
Harbolt, Genevieve L. (Donaker)	94
Harbolt, Willima Henry "Hallie"	94
Harbutt, Charles, Jr.	94
Harbutt, Sr., Charles	94
Hardbarger, Lydeth	94
Harden, Elisha T.	1
Hardie, Hannah Aldridge	94
Hardin, Dickie Lee "Buckey"	201
Hardin, Henry	94
Hardin, Joe Allen Pack	94
Hardin, Peter	94
Harding, Lola	94
Hardiwood, Myrtle	256
Hardy, Carrie (Buckner)	118
Hardy, Unk	94
Hargis, Alfred	94
Hargis, Alfreda "Susie"	176
Hargis, Allen R	94
Hargis, Anna (Adkins)	95
Hargis, Billy	95
Hargis, Carmon	95
Hargis, Carol Anne (Isaac)	95
Hargis, Claude	95
Hargis, Clayton	94
Hargis, Clayton D.	95
Hargis, Clayton Ray	95
Hargis, Debra	95
Hargis, Delbert Lee	260
Hargis, Doris Allene (Nunley)	95
Hargis, Dorothy (Wiggins)	95
Hargis, Emma	95
Hargis, Emma Castella	150
Hargis, Glenn "Bill"	221
Hargis, Hazel	95

Name	Page
Hargis, James	242
Hargis, James Gable, Jr.	95
Hargis, Jimmy	95
Hargis, Juanita	95
Hargis, Julia (Kirk)	236
Hargis, Kathy	95
Hargis, Larry Dale	157
Hargis, Lora Lee	95
Hargis, Louisa Jane	144
Hargis, Lynn W.	62
Hargis, Margaret	243
Hargis, Margaret Joyce (Roberts)	47
Hargis, Mary Ann	95
Hargis, Mary Ethlene	24
Hargis, Minnie Frances (Fults)	95
Hargis, Robert	95
Hargis, Thomas	95, 121
Hargis, William	95
Hargis, William Lee	95
Hargis, William Raymond	95
Harlan, B.B.	95
Harlan, Elsie	24
Harlan, Friend S.	24
Harlan, Herschel	181
Harless, Chester Thomas	55
Harless, James "Jim" Ronald	95
Harlow, Mary Kelly	95
Harmon, Vivian	154
Harper, Lot Erwin	224
Harrell, Jerry Oscar	240
Harrell, Luther	95
Harrell, Winona Elizabeth (Flury)	92
Harriman, Linda	95
Harriman, Marion	95
Harriman, Michael	95
Harriman, Paul	95
Harris, Thomas	95
Harris, Albert Calloway Jackson	97
Harris, Anna Selina	96, 252
Harris, Barbara Gail	73
Harris, Ben	95
Harris, Ben Easley Wilson, Sr.	230
Harris, Bonnie	95
Harris, Charles R	196
Harris, Charlie Edward	96
Harris, Donna	95
Harris, Donnie Edward	264
Harris, Dorothy	96
Harris, Earlene	214
Harris, Earline	8
Harris, Elbert L.	142
Harris, Elic	96
Harris, Ellen (Dykes)	96
Harris, Evelyn Ruth	96
Harris, Foster	301
Harris, Francis	96
Harris, Gilbert B.	292
Harris, Harold Edsel	81, 96
Harris, Helen Caroline (Kruzewski)	96
Harris, Herbert Spencer	96
Harris, Howard	96
Harris, Inez	96, 190
Harris, James W	96
Harris, Jay C.	96
Harris, Jay Cleveland	14
Harris, Jenni Olene	96
Harris, Jessie Miles	249
Harris, John Bradford	95, 96, 225
Harris, Johnnie	96
Harris, Julia	14
Harris, Julie	184, 249
Harris, Kathryn "Kate"	250
Harris, Lana	96
Harris, Lorenza B.	136
Harris, Margaret	96
Harris, Margaret (Thomas)	96
Harris, Martha	96
Harris, Martin	230
Harris, Mary (Sitz)	95
Harris, Mary Etta Lee	96
Harris, Mildred	225
Harris, Minnie	82
Harris, Minnie	124
Harris, Minnie Ada	124
Harris, Nat	97
Harris, Pauline	97
Harris, Rhonda	80
Harris, Robert	96
Harris, Robert E., Sr.	96
Harris, Ruth	264
Harris, Sadie	303
Harris, Samuel J	110
Harris, Sherry Dene (Layne)	96
Harris, Sory E.	97
Harris, Stella	96
Harris, Unk	138
Harris, Wendell	114, 117
Harris, William Carroll	95
Harris, William Edwin, Sr.	96
Harris, Willis Franklin	96
Harrison, Alma	97
Harrison, Alma	116
Harrison, Christine "Tina"	117
Harrison, Clarence	164
Harrison, Doris "Dosie"	97
Harrison, Dorothy Jean	170
Harrison, Elizabeth	57
Harrison, Hayes	296
Harrison, Hershel	97

Name	Page
Harrison, James Andrew	97
Harrison, Jennie (King)	97
Harrison, Jennie Elizabeth	97
Harrison, Jerri D.	97
Harrison, Lillie	37
Harrison, Lillie Bell	97
Harrison, Lillie Belle	93
Harrison, Nancy (Pack)	97
Harrison, Thomas	97
Harrison, Virginia	97
Harrison, William Randal	218
Harshman, Dale Lee	97
Harshman, Glenn	97
Harshman, Timothy Ray	97
Hart, Alice	97
Hart, Clara	33
Hart, J.B.	188, 206
Hart, O'lean	97
Hart, Renee	97
Hart, Roy P.	156
Hart, Roy Rainey	251, 271
Hartness, Nancy	56
Hartsel, Cathy	279
Hartsel, Doris	214
Hartsel, Thomas	97
Hartsel, Wolbun (Chang) "Joanne"	97, 98
Hartwell, Anna P	98
Hartwell, Anna Pearl	9
Hartwell, Beverly	76
Hartwell, Cleta Ione	98
Hartwell, Herbert Clifton	98
Hartwell, Russell Vernon	76
Hartwell, Vernon Dwight	98
Hartzell, Leona Ellen	98
Harveston, Katherine	200
Harvey, Bonnie	216
Haskel, Peggy	61
Haskett, Carolyn	216
Haskins, Abe	209
Haskins, Franz	98
Haskins, Joseph	98
Haskins, Manerva	196
Haskins, Mary A	193, 197
Haskins, Minerva	75
Haskins, Nervie	193
Hassebrock, Fermenda (Hill)	196
Hassebrock, Fred	98
Hassebrock, Freddie Wayne	98
Hassebrock, Margaret Loretta	98
Hastings, Billy Wayne	144
Hastings, Nelda	98
Hastings, Robert	98
Haston, Dorthena	98
Haston, Herbert L	155
Haston, Jerry Dean	98
Haston, Lillie Mae	98
Haston, Maudie	122
Hasty, John W.	122
Hatfield, Alpha	209
Hatfield, Curt	292
Hatfield, Emily Dell (Bolinger)	98
Hatfield, Ida	98
Hatfield, J.H.	98
Hatfield, Lorena A.	216, 269
Hatfield, Martin	294
Hatfield, Mary Ethel	98
Hatfield, Matilda	98
Hatfield, Perry Shelton	135, 136
Hatfield, Sarah Louise	98
Hattey, Dorothy Avril	190
Hattey, Leslie	206
Hattey, Marion	206
Hattfield, Lettie Jane	205
Havens, Jesse	192
Havens, Walter Sherman	98
Havner, Carrie	98
Hawes, Al	106
Hawes, Rosie Gearldean (Shrum)	98
Hawk, Bethie	98
Hawk, Bethie Dillon	19
Hawk, D. C.	27
Hawk, Dillon	156
Hawk, Emma Jean	98, 299
Hawk, Hubert	121
Hawk, Hubert Arvin	27
Hawk, Mary "Mary Jess"	12
Hawk, Maymie	92
Hawk, Ruby (Rieder)	237
Hawk, Vela Lucille	98
Hawk, Verna Ruth	183
Hawkings, Jeannine	299
Hawkins Ernestine P. (Peyton)	98
Hawkins, A.J.	98
Hawkins, Annie	98
Hawkins, Deborah	154
Hawkins, Glen H.	98
Hawkins, Hazek	99
Hawkins, Irene	98
Hawkins, Jack Horace	76, 216
Hawkins, James Marshall, Sr.	98, 248
Hawkins, John Ross	98
Hawkins, Kathryn	98
Hawkins, Louise	98
Hawkins, Marion Inez	224
Hawkins, Ricky	99
Hawkins, Velma	98
Hawkins, Wendy	49
Hay, Robert Donald	244

Name	Page
Hay, Sarah Barnwell Elliot (Howe)	99
Hayden, Beverly	99
Hayes, A.H.	258
Hayes, Arrie	39
Hayes, Betty Joann Veal	102
Hayes, Charlene	66
Haynes, Joe	122
Hayes, Holly Lisbeth	85
Hayes, John P.	27
Hayes, Lelia	99
Hayes, Martha "Mattie"	198
Hayes, Maybelle	201
Hayes, Ruby	100
Hayes, William	186
Hayes, William W	34
Hayes, Willie	99
Haynes, Alma Jewel	100
Haynes, Anna M	264
Haynes, Bailey	100
Haynes, Betty	258
Haynes, Bobby Edwin, Jr.	140
Haynes, Bobby Edwin, Sr.	99
Haynes, Carl E.	99
Haynes, Carlene	264
Haynes, Cheryl	64
Haynes, Cora	100
Haynes, Cora	271
Haynes, Diane Marie (Brittin)	289
Haynes, Donald D	99
Haynes, Doris Ophelia	99
Haynes, Dorothy	99
Haynes, Edna	30
Haynes, Eli	59, 64, 100, 263
Haynes, Elizabeth Orme (Raulston)	99
Haynes, Elsie	99
Haynes, Ephraim Madison	293
Haynes, Ernest Alfred	99
Haynes, Ernest Joel	99
Haynes, Eugene "Gene"	99
Haynes, George	99
Haynes, George Holbert	99
Haynes, George Holbert "Big George" III	99
Haynes, George Holbert II	99
Haynes, George Holbert III	99
Haynes, George Holbert IV	99
Haynes, Harlie Ophelia	99
Haynes, Harvey Chester	23, 33, 261
Haynes, Henry	99
Haynes, Henry Francis	99
Haynes, Hettie Juanita (Lockhart)	99
Haynes, Holbert	99
Haynes, Howard	100
Haynes, Huch Allen	99
Haynes, James Buford	99
Haynes, James Hollingsworth	100
Haynes, James Hollinsworth "Jim"	99
Haynes, Jennie Olene	99
Haynes, John W.	249, 299
Haynes, Joseph Bailey	100
Haynes, Julia	159
Haynes, Kenneth	99
Haynes, Larry	100
Haynes, Larry Lewis	100, 300
Haynes, Lena Mae	100
Haynes, Lula (Rollins)	138
Haynes, Martha	100, 227
Haynes, Mary	100
Haynes, Mary (Meeks)	222
Haynes, Nicole	100
Haynes, Ophelia (Cannon)	207
Haynes, Paul	100
Haynes, Paul Edward	99, 100
Haynes, Perry Lee	100
Haynes, Rachel N. (Campell)	100
Haynes, Randale	100
Haynes, Randall E.	100
Haynes, Ruby	100
Haynes, Sonya	186
Haynes, Sylvia (Carrick)	99
Haynes, Terry Blake	100
Haynes, Terry Dee	100
Haynes, Theona	100
Haynes, Theresa Darlene	69, 123
Haynes, Vernon	100
Haynes, Vernon C.	64, 100
Haynes, Vernon E.	100
Haynes, Vesta	99, 100
Haynes, Virginia Marie (Lewis)	99
Haynes, Wilma	100
Haynes, Wilma Mae	112
Haynes., Elizabeth Raulston	277
Hayostek, Alton	99
Hayostek, Andrew	100
Hayostek, Betty	100
Hayostek, Sondra	100
Hays, Permelia Ann	100
Hays, Sandra Lou	18
Hayse, Tericia	251
Hayse, Vernon "Gabby"	100
Haywood, Harriet E.	100
Hazen, Brooke	14
Hazen, Harold Russell	100
Hazen, Sherry Fay (Mayes)	101
Hazen, William R.H.	101
Hazen, William R.H. "Bill"	100, 101

Name	Page
Headrick, Ethel	101
Headrick, James Edward	210
Headrick, Lemuel J.	101
Headrick, Louella	101
Headrick, Louisa "Liza" (Anderson)	91
Headrick, Mary Ella	101
Headrick, Nancy	60
Headrick, Sarah	4
Headrick, Thomas	101
Headrick, William Henry	101
Headrick, William R	101
Heard, Harriet	101
Hedge, Susan	115
Hedges, Earlene	154
Hedges, Joseph B. W.	101
Hedges, Milford	101
Hedges, Milton Leland, Jr.	101
Hedges, Susan	101
Hedges, Sydney	101
Hediger, Arnold	101
Heer, Heinrich "John Henry"	101
Heer, Hilarius	101
Hefner, Sarah	101
Hefner, Sarah Catherine	94
Helenthal, Margaret	94
Heller, Katharina geb	86
Helmuth, Lydia	244, 251
Heltzel, Elizabeth Jane	72
Henderlight, Doris	254
Henderlight, James David	111
Henderson, Albert	111
Henderson, Charles E.	101
Henderson, Charley	101
Henderson, Dana	101
Henderson, Essie Jane	69
Henderson, Frances	269
Henderson, George	101
Henderson, Jasper	101
Henderson, John	101
Henderson, Linda	101
Henderson, Mary Juanita	68
Henderson, Melissa Jean	52
Henderson, Rosa (McGovern)	275
Henderson, Virginia	101
Henderson, Willie Lee	187
Hendrickson, Conrad	101
Hendrickson, Loda Jean	101
Henegar, Emma E.	101
Henegar, Marion	176
Henegar, Thomas Kirby	176
Henely, Claude C.	247
Henley, Mary	102
Henley, Adolphis	12
Henley, Adolphus	101
Henley, Agnes	102
Henley, Agnes Marguerite	229
Henley, Ailene	37, 169
Henley, Allen C.	212
Henley, Beckye	102
Henley, Bill	102
Henley, Bobby	102
Henley, Boris Stephen	58
Henley, Buford	102
Henley, Clarence H.	102
Henley, Claude Willis	43
Henley, Diana	102
Henley, Dorothy "Dottie" Jean (Keller)	280
Henley, Dorothy Mae (Fults)	102
Henley, Elizabeth	102
Henley, Evelyn (Russell)	197
Henley, General Joe	102
Henley, General Joseph	101
Henley, Hester	102
Henley, Horace	83
Henley, Jacob	102, 103
Henley, James "Jim"	50
Henley, James Campbell	102
Henley, John Burwell	41, 102
Henley, John Edward	102
Henley, John Edward, Jr.	102
Henley, John Henry "Jack"	102
Henley, John Lewis	235
Henley, John Patrick	102
Henley, Lillian	102
Henley, Lou Ermine	102
Henley, Lucille	9
Henley, Mabel	50, 83
Henley, Maggie Bell	150
Henley, Martha	297
Henley, Marvin F.	233
Henley, Marvin L.	102
Henley, Millie	102
Henley, Nora Agnes (Armstrong)	102
Henley, Parker Dean	102
Henley, Robert	102
Henley, Rosa Hobbs Jackson	176
Henley, Selby	102
Henley, Sybil Lee (Partin)	43
Henley, Tennessee	102
Henley, Thelma Corrine (Woodlee)	205
Henley, Unk	102
Henley, Vivian	102
Henley, William Brooks "Buddy"	74, 77
Henley, William Everett "Bill"	102
Henley, William Samuel	103
Hennessee, Andrew Jackson	102

Name	Page
Hennessee, Berry Gwenel	294
Hennessee, Grover	103
Hennessee, Rachel Louisa	103
Henninger, Frances E.	175, 292, 293
Henninger, Marcus Aurelius	103
Henry, Billie	103
Henry, Douglas	133
Henry, Douglas Selph	103
Henry, George D.	103
Henry, Georgia Ruth	85
Henry, Herman "Whick"	103
Henry, Hubert	103
Henry, Hubert H.	206, 216
Henry, John	103, 111
Henry, Johnnie Ruth	211
Henry, Kathryn	167
Henry, Leona Marie	103
Henry, Loiette "Lolly" (Hume)	86
Henry, Marion Alexander	103
Henry, Martha Belle	103
Henry, Millie	23
Henry, Mollie	214
Henry, Oscar	103
Henry, Pamela	103
Henry, Pearl	165
Henry, Pearl	70
Henry, Rodney	183
Henry, Roy Lee	103
Henry, Sylvia	168, 178
Henshaw, Peggy Carol	93
Henson, Oscar	42
Henson, Tomye Mae	247
Hereford, Kenneth Michael	247
Hereford, Richard Kenneth	103
Herington, Julia	103
Herman, Carol	202
Herman, William	103
Hernandes, Eva L.	103
Herriford, John	99
Herriford, Sarah (Coalson)	103
Hess, Elizabeth	103
Hess, Glyn	110
Hess, Nellie Mae	103
Hessey, Robert Hatton	103
Hester, Gregory "A.J."	21
Heubi, Austin Hayden	3
Heubi, Jeremiah	103
Heubi, John Jacob	103
Heubi, Ryan Austin	103
Hiatt, DeLaura	103
Hickey, Brenda Lee (Yokley)	37
Hickey, Donald E.	103
Hickey, John Sterling	103
Hickey, John Wesley	103
Hickey, Miriam	103, 110
Hickman, Ada Emiley	288
Hicks, Ada	74
Hicks, George	49
Hicks, Glendon Farrell	103
Hicks, Isaac	104
Hicks, James Martin	103
Hicks, Sarah	104
Hiers, Kathleen (Veal)	3
Hiers, Tony	104
Hiett, Marion	104
Hiett, Melinda	104
Hiett, Wallace	188
Hiett, Wallace Samuel, Sr.	104
Hiett, William	65
Hiett, William Eugene	104
Higdon, Joe	104
Higdon, Louise Elizabeth	20
Higdon, Mildred	179
Higginbotham, James Robert	48
Higginbotham, Jane	104
Higgins, Ace	104
Higgins, Ann	242
Higgins, Carrie Layne	191
Higgins, Daniel	104
Higgins, Donnie Ellen (Shrum)	104
Higgins, Katie	104
Higgins, Kelly Amos	145
Higgins, Lena Belle	104
Higgins, Mable Marie	87
Higgins, Rena	165, 168
Higgins, Velma	19
Higgins, Wiley Amos	260
Highfield, Geroge B.	104
Hilburn, Frances	274
Hill, Josephine C.	56
Hill, Aaron	104
Hill, Allen	104
Hill, Annie Bell	275
Hill, Barbara Anne	208
Hill, Benjamin J.	202
Hill, Benjamin Jefferson	105
Hill, Bertha	105
Hill, Billy Joe	156
Hill, Brenda Ann	104
Hill, C.D. "Big Don"	104
Hill, Charles D. "Big Don", Sr.	105
Hill, Charles Edward "Charlie"	104
Hill, Edith	104
Hill, Edith Irene	144
Hill, Elizabeth	248
Hill, Ferminda	275
Hill, Francis	98

Name	Page
Hill, Grover	105
Hill, Helen	104
Hill, Herbert	80
Hill, James Franklin	92
Hill, James Marvin "Slick"	104
Hill, Joann	104
Hill, Joe Lannie	214
Hill, John "Jack"	104, 173
Hill, Johnnie Morgan	104
Hill, Kim	30
Hill, Larry	274
Hill, Linda Lee	105
Hill, Lucille	104
Hill, Lucy Jane (Sears)	175
Hill, Malinda	104
Hill, Marcus	156
Hill, Marcus Hayes	264
Hill, Marcus Hayes, Jr.	104
Hill, Marcus, Sr.	104
Hill, Marvin Dennis	297
Hill, Marvin Wilson	72
Hill, Mary Louise "Lula"	104
Hill, Mary Nina	177
Hill, Mattie May	254
Hill, Morris Richard	27
Hill, Nancy Pauline (Shetters)	104
Hill, Nellie Katherine	105
Hill, Norma Marie	105
Hill, Rayburn	105
Hill, Reba Evelyn	105
Hill, Richard Harding	105
Hill, Ruby Lee (Bush)	104, 105
Hill, Sam	105
Hill, Samuel	214
Hill, Sr., Charles D.	207
Hill, Susan Pauline	105
Hill, Sylvia Jane	105
Hill, Unk	154
Hill, William T. "Bill"	191
Hill, Virginia Louise (Cox)	248
Hill, Will	105
Hill, William	104
Hill, William Hamilton "Hamp"	98, 117
Hill, William Thomas "Bill"	105
Hillard, Caroly Faye (Clark)	139
Hillard, Stanley Gene "Duke"	105
Hillis, Audrey B.	105
Hillis, Edwin Carroll "E.C."	105
Hillis, Ethel	105
Hillis, Hershel Leon	238
Hillis, J.D.	105
Hillis, Julia	186
Hillis, Linda "Kaye" (Johnson)	116
Hillis, Willie Hazel	105
Hindman, Joseph B	105
Hindman, Marjorie (Stockwell)	105
Hinerman, Sharon (Katona) "Sherry"	105
Hines, Janie Belle (Gallagher)	105
Hines, Raymond Glenn "Ray"	105
Hinkle, Charles L.	105
Hinkle, Ruby Inez (Gilliam)	105
Hinton, Emma Cotnam	105
Hintz, Johann Herman	14
Hirsch, Patricia	199
Hix, Stella Mae	299
Hoagland, Mary Ann	271
Hoback, Charles, Jr	170
Hoback, Claudia L.	105
Hoback, Donna Jo	105
Hoback, Dorothy Louvinia (Sisk)	106
Hoback, Grace	105
Hoback, Johnny Wendell	190
Hoback, Robert Lee	106
Hobbs, Abraham	105, 106
Hobbs, Alvin E.	106
Hobbs Hill	v
Hobbs, Amy	106
Hobbs, Billy	66
Hobbs, Billy Charles	106
Hobbs, Bobby Franklin	106
Hobbs, Bryan	106
Hobbs, Carl	106
Hobbs, Christopher	98
Hobbs, Clemmie	107
Hobbs, Clyne Alan	10
Hobbs, Crawford	106
Hobbs, Danny Lee	303
Hobbs, Delbert	106
Hobbs, Doc Albert	17
Hobbs, Dorsey	106
Hobbs, Earl	265
Hobbs, Earl Edward	284
Hobbs, Eddie L.	106
Hobbs, Eddie Leon	106
Hobbs, Elfa	106
Hobbs, Elmer Frances	243
Hobbs, Elmer Francis	106
Hobbs, Emma	13
Hobbs, Frankie Mae	126
Hobbs, Franklin Eugene	57
Hobbs, Gail	106
Hobbs, Gary Adam	299
Hobbs, Gertrude	106
Hobbs, Grace	252
Hobbs, Helen Virgina "Sue"	17, 182
Hobbs, Henry Haskell	106
Hobbs, Henry Haskell, Jr.	106

Name	Page
Hobbs, Herman	106
Hobbs, Herman M.	111
Hobbs, Horton	287
Hobbs, Howary Argo	195
Hobbs, Imogene	226
Hobbs, Infant	155
Hobbs, J.N.	106, 107
Hobbs, James	vi, 106
Hobbs, Jay	106
Hobbs, Jennie	200
Hobbs, Jerry Frances	226
Hobbs, Jimmy Lester	106
Hobbs, John	106
Hobbs, John David	72
Hobbs, Judith Marcella	302
Hobbs, Linda	106
Hobbs, Linda Sue	49
Hobbs, Louis Paul	40
Hobbs, Louvenia	289
Hobbs, Louvenia E.	21, 35
Hobbs, Lucy Ola	33
Hobbs, Mable	259
Hobbs, Manerva	44, 52
Hobbs, Martha Jane	132
Hobbs, Mary Ellen	200
Hobbs, Maude Hayes	218
Hobbs, Mildred	266
Hobbs, Nancy	116
Hobbs, Odie	75
Hobbs, Oma Lee	106, 117, 183, 285
Hobbs, Opal Faye	106
Hobbs, Patricia Irene (Ooley)	193
Hobbs, Patsy	106
Hobbs, Robby Etta	3
Hobbs, Robbye	297
Hobbs, Robbye Etta	264
Hobbs, Roger	104
Hobbs, Ruby Corin	106
Hobbs, Sally Sarah	1
Hobbs, Sandra D. (Cole)	8
Hobbs, Sarah	106
Hobbs, Sarah Elizabeth	7, 106
Hobbs, Sharon Denise	293
Hobbs, Thelma Mae	107
Hobbs, Thomas William "Tom"	302
Hobbs, Wesley J. "Scat"	vi, 107
Hobbs, William Douglas	107
Hobbs, William Horton	107
Hobbs, Willie	107
Hobbs, Wilsie	112
Hobensack, Margaret Fern	272
Hodge, Brenda	243
Hodge, Brenda Ann	281
Hodge, Harmon	4
Hodge, Lilly Mae	107
Hodge, Louise	61
Hodge, M. Janice (infant dau)	4
Hodges, Gurna Daniel	107
Hoffman, Bill	40
Hoffman, Doris Elaine	107
Hoffman, Evelyn	107
Hoffman, J.C.	175
Hoffman, Joseph Durward	107
Hoffman, Sherry	107
Hoffman, William Graham "Red"	107
Hoffmann, Helen	107
Hoffs, Hester Orange	5
Hoffs, W.L. "Willie"	107
Hogan, Harry D. Francis	107
Hogan, Harry D. Francis	107
Hogan, Harry III	107
Hogan, Traci Ann	107
Hogwood, James Carl	107
Holcomb, Grace	304
Holcomb, Homer Leroy	243
Holder, Edward H.	243
Holder, Elmer	107
Holder, Mary "Molly"	202
Holder, Melrose (Hamby)	157
Holder, Nettie	107
Holiday, Eva Cecile	151, 275, 276
Holiday, LaDue	67
Holland, Alexander	92
Holland, Caril Preston	107
Holland, Dean Murray	107
Holland, Dorothy (Fletcher)	107
Holland, Flora Ella	107
Holland, Juanita	173
Holland, Margaret	67
Holland, Steve Allan	181
Holland, William M.	107
Hollars, Nellie Laura	107
Hollingsworth, James	40
Hollingsworth, Salina Zora Bell	207
Hollis, Gilmer	207
Hollon, Charles O., Sr.	157
Hollon, Charles O., Jr. "Bones"	107
Holloway, Ada Mae	107
Holmes, Earl A	55
Holmes, Elizabeth	108
Holmes, Minnie Mae	183, 184
Holt, Arvis Milburn	108
Holt, Callie	108
Holt, Charles	298
Holt, David S.	108
Holt, Emma B.	182
Holt, Granville	183
Holt, James Earl "Bud"	108
Holt, John	108

Name	Page
Holt, John Milburn	69
Holt, Leona	108
Holt, Lorene	165, 170
Holt, Mary Lou	67
Holt, Michael	108
Holt, Oscar Lee	108
Holt, Patricia	2
Holt, Sam	41
Holt, Sherry Lynn	11
Holt, Ula Alvia	189
Holt, William	108
Holt, William Bennett	193
Honea, Rosalea Gay	194
Honey, Ada	246
Hood, Andrea F.	114
Hood, Bob	108
Hoodenpile, Margaret Frances	108
Hookey, Ruth (Bunch)	213
Hookey, Ted	108
Hooper, Bobby Gene	108
Hooper, Martha	108
Hooper, Nora Lee	174
Hooper, Zach	15
Hoosier, Billy Ray	108
Hoosier, Fay (Smith) Dent	108
Hoosier, Faye Dent	108
Hoosier, J.D. Dent	57
Hoosier, Jones	57
Hoosier, Linda Van	108
Hoosier, Mildred	72
Hoosier, Nell Rose	11
Hoosier, Scotty Ray	108
Hoosier, Tom	108
Hooten, Estell (Dick)	11
Hooten, Roy	108
Hopkins, Claude	108
Hopkins, Elizabeth	105
Hopkins, Martha Eveline	139, 154
Hopkins, Michael John	304
Hopkins, Myrtle	108
Hopkins, William John	105
Hopper, Troy L.	108
Hopper, Troy Lee, Jr.	108
Horn, Edith	108
Hornbuckle, Carl Douglas	2
Hornbuckle, Charles	108
Hornbuckle, Hazel Irene (Roberts)	108
Horst, Amanda	108
Horst, Corinne	153
Horton, Anna Mae (Nunley)	154
Horton, David	109
Horton, David Allen	109
Horton, Hallie O'Neal	109
Horton, Irena	109
Horton, Kathleen Marie (Smail)	109
Horton, Mordica Pinkney "Pink"	109
Horton, William	109
Horton, Wilston T.	109
Hoskins, Emma	109
Hostetler, Daniel	39
Hostetler, Nancy	109
Hostetler, Thomas Daniel	109
Houge, Olga Myrtle	109
Houpert, Henry C.	210
Houpert, Vera Ruth	43
Houppert, Vera	43
House, James	121
House, Mattie Loraine	175
Housley, Phyllis	175
Hovey, Mary Camilla	151
Howard, Allie May (Haley)	28
Howard, Amos	109
Howard, Bertha	69
Howard, Bertha Lee	204
Howard, Emily	57
Howard, John Gilliland	163
Howard, John Phillip	109
Howard, Joyce	109
Howard, Landon	206
Howard, Margaret	231
Howard, Mary Daisy	230
Howard, Mary Daisy	9
Howard, Noah	138
Howard, Rena	61
Howard, Rose	103
Howe, Raymond Reed	210
Howell, Delores Lorene	99
Howell, Edna	251
Howell, Harvey	143
Howell, Harvey L.	156
Howell, Mary Elizabeth	109
Howell, Reba	109
Huber, Margritha	53
Huckabee, Edna	120
Huckabee, Virgil	181
Hudgins, Anne	161
Hudson, Elizabeth	296
Hudson, John	11
Hudson, John	11
Huelbig, Martin Gerald	56
Huelbig, Martin Keith	109
Huffar, Elvah	109
Huffine, Dorothy Irene	10
Huffman, Darlene	194
Huffmaster, Bonnie Ree	23
Hughes, Doris Emily (Graham)	3
Hughes, Fred O	109
Hughes, Herschel	81
Hughes, John Arlington	109
Hughes, Karin	119

Name	Page
Hughes, Martha	1
Hughes, Martha L.	119
Hughes, Paul D.	119
Huie, Mary Myrtle	145
Huling, Arthur Mourfield	129
Huling, Walter, Dr.	109
Hull, Joshua Cly	109
Hull, Rodney	109
Hull, Susan Ann	109
Hume, Foster	109
Hume, Loiette "Lolly"	103
Humphrey, Mary	103
Humphreys, Judy Elaine (Brewer)	200
Hunerwadel, Alexander P	109
Hunerwadel, Alice	109
Hunerwadel, Beulah Mae (Turner)	263
Hunerwadel, Olga Marie	109
Hunerwadel, Robert Alexander	18
Hunt, Abraham Lincoln	109
Hunt, Elwood Mark	109
Hunt, Katherine	110
Hunt, Mary Jane (Metcalf)	277
Hunt, Richard Mark	109
Hunt, Sarah	110
Hunt, Susan	278
Hunt, Thomas	278
Hunter, Alice	278
Hunter, Elizabeth	223
Hunter, Nancy Frances "Nannie"	149
Hunter, Squire	297
Huntley, Clara	149
Huntley, Donna	196
Huntley, Edward	158, 221
Huntley, George "Peck"	65
Huntley, George Alvin, Jr.	110
Huntley, Glenda	110
Huntley, Hayley	65
Huntley, William Drobesh	180
Hunziker, Andreas Andrew	65
Hunziker, Anna Maria	110
Hunziker, Dorothy Rita (Torres)	299
Hunziker, Edward J	110
Hunziker, Emma	65
Hunziker, Jacob	9
Hunziker, James D.	110
Hunziker, Jr., Edward John "E.J."	110
Hunziker, Mary Cella "Boots"	110
Hunziker, Sr., Edward John	110
Hunziker, Susie (Swann)	110
Hunziker, Thomas	65, 110
Hurst, Arbie Inez (Falls)	125
Hurst, Helena "Lennie"	110
Hurst, Sharon	39
Hurst, William Sterling	185
Hurt, Retha Mae	110
Hurtt, Willie Everett	119
Hutchins, Orbin Latton	283
Hutchins, Peggy Evelyn	110
Hutchins, Peggy Evelyn (Tate)	228
Hutchinson, Kate	110
Hutchison, Howard Bennett	104
Hutchison, William H.	110
Hutchison, William Henry	58
Ikard, Betty Wiles (Lucas)	87, 110
Ikard, J.L.	110
Ikard, Lannie	110
Ikard, Lannie Looney	110
Illsey, Edward	110
Illsey, Emma	147
Ingle, Jack	147
Ingle, Newton Dowell	110
Ingle, Roger Neal	110
Ingle, Tabitha Anabel	110
Ingman, Dorothy	17
Ingram, Argie	175
Inman, David Andrew	183
Inman, Lela Mae (Hickey)	110
Irvin, Betty Ann (Collins)	110
Irvin, Carl David	110
Irvin, Carl David "Copie"	6
Irvin, Clabe	111
Irvin, David E	111
Irvin, Dorothy Jewel (Hobbs)	111
Irvin, Freeman	111
Irvin, Gail Evelyn	111
Irvin, George	111
Irvin, George Eugene	111
Irvin, Jack	111
Irvin, Jane (Payne)	110
Irvin, Jim	111
Irvin, Joe	111
Irvin, Johnny	111
Irvin, Katherine Elaine	111
Irvin, Kathryn Veoger	111
Irvin, Kirb	249
Irvin, Mary	111
Irvin, Mike	76, 169
Irvin, Myrtle	111
Irvin, Ophelia (Burnett) "Totsie"	111
Irvin, Paul	111
Irvin, Robert Clark	111
Irvin, Russell	111
Irvin, Tabitha	111
Irvin, Tabitha	2
Irvin, Wanda Jane (Garner)	2

Irvin, William	111	
Irwin, Kenneth	111, 129	
Isaac, George Isaac	111	
Isbell, Larry	95	
Isbell, Wanda Carol (Thomas)	111	
Ishcum, Pauline	111	
Isom, Lucy	23	
Ison, Aliene Frances	115	
Ito, Yoshiko	111	
Iverson, Helene Caroline	132	
Jablonski, Edith (Gilley)	278	
Jablonski, John	111	
Jacks, James K, Sr.	111	
Jacks, Reatha (Henry)	111	
Jackson Florence I. (Miller)	111	
Jackson, Andrew	111	
Jackson, Andrew David	205	
Jackson, Annie Edith	111	
Jackson, Billie	104	
Jackson, Charles Thomas	111	
Jackson, Charles W.	111	
Jackson, Charles William	111	
Jackson, David	34	
Jackson, Donna	111	
Jackson, Doris "Dot" (Owens)	111	
Jackson, Elizabeth	112	
Jackson, Harold	112	
Jackson, James Lincoln Reed	112	
Jackson, Jamie Ray	112	
Jackson, Joey	112	
Jackson, John William	46	
Jackson, Martha Helen M.	112	
Jackson, Miriah Donielle	62	
Jackson, Myrtle	112	
Jackson, Paul	105	
Jackson, Paul Andrew	112	
Jackson, Regina Kay	112	
Jackson, Rosa Hobbs	153	
Jackson, Ruthie Jane	102	
Jackson, Ruthie Jane	108	
Jackson, Samuel L.	108	
Jackson, Sharon	111	
Jackson, Tommy	111	
Jackson, William	112	
Jaco, Maudie Earline	111, 112	
Jacobs, Angela	37	
Jacobs, Annie	112	
Jacobs, Bertha Louise	182, 260	
Jacobs, Charles	112	
Jacobs, Clyde	179	
Jacobs, Clyde "Jack"	292	
Jacobs, Clyde E.	301	
Jacobs, Don	112	
Jacobs, Elmer Pruitt	112	
Jacobs, Evelyn Ann (Barry)	290	
Jacobs, Gary Wayne	112	
Jacobs, Jean	112	
Jacobs, Jim	298	
Jacobs, Joyce (Layne)	112	
Jacobs, Ola Jean	112	
Jacobs, Sally	299	
Jacobs, Shirley	161	
Jacobs, Virginia	152	
Jacobs, Virginia Ann	230	
James, Jeanne (Roberts)	55	
James, Paul David, Sr.	112	
James, Agnes A. (Banks)	113	
James, Albert	112	
James, Alexander James	113	
James, Amanda Opal	126	
James, Arnold	112	
James, Arnold E.	113	
James, Carl	112	
James, Christopher Columbus	112	
James, Christopher Columbus "Lum"	113	
James, Edna Parthenia	112	
James, Elbert	112	
James, Fred	112	
James, Fred J.	137	
James, Fred Jackson	143	
James, Gordon Lee	112, 114	
James, Hallie	113, 131	
James, Hannah	131	
James, Jean	210	
James, Jeffery Harold	120, 121	
James, Jerel "Judy"	112	
James, Jessie Jackson "Jack"	45	
James, Johnny E.	113	
James, Josh Logan	113	
James, Kenneth D.	113	
James, Lum Christopher Columbus	114	
James, Madge A. (Tate)	113	
James, Malery Eugene	113	
James, Marshall F.	113	
James, Martha	113	
James, Marvin	113	
James, Marvin D.	46	
James, Marvin D. "Red"	113	
James, Mary Lou (Fulfer)	114	
James, Mattie	113	
James, Melvin	169, 170	
James, Minnie	113	
James, Nancy Dee (Nunley)	234	
James, Oda	113	
James, Oscar Howell	95, 223	
James, Pamela Jane (Kurtsinger)	112, 113, 114	
James, Patrick	113	
James, Paul David	112	

James, Phoeba Ann	112, 245	Jenness, Reba Bernice	110	Johnson, Billy Levon	25
James, Ralph	131	Jennings, Allie	147	Johnson, Boyd	115
James, Randel Hoyt	20	Jennings, Frances	223	Johnson, Brenda Joyce	115
James, Richard	113	Jennings, James Berger	27	Johnson, Buena	201
James, Richard M. "Dick"	131	Jennings, Margaret	114	Johnson, Byrtle Arminda Way Echols	86, 165
James, Ruby Nell (Shrum)	112, 113	Jennings, Mary	185	Johnson, Carl	115
James, Ruth (Vandergriff)	113	Jennings, Mary E.	32	Johnson, Carolyn	257
James, Shelvy	114	Jennings, Velma Leona	114	Johnson, Christine	134
James, Steven Howell	114	Jennings, Wendell Ward	273	Johnson, Claude	177
James, Thelma	114	Jensen, Jacob V.	114	Johnson, Cody Garrett	42, 117, 120
James, Thomas	112	Jensen, Mary	173	Johnson, Daniel Seigfried	115
James, Vinnie L. (Crabtree)	113	Jensen, Ozzie M	114	Johnson, Danny Timothy "Tim"	115
James, Will	114	Jensen, Roger Eric	114	Johnson, David Jerome "Buckey"	115
James, William "Bill"	114	Jervis, Jean (McKee)	114	Johnson, David Walter	115
James, William E.	79, 124	Jervis, Oliver Wheeler	114	Johnson, Delbert Wayne	115
James, William Eli "Jesse"	112	Jessee, Henry Dobbin	114	Johnson, Della Ophelia	115
James, William Emmett	161	Jessee, Ruby Marie	64	Johnson, Dennis Clayton "Butch"	117
James, William Emmett "Floose"	113, 120	Jessing, Shirley "Susie" (Teeters)	62	Johnson, Dora S.	117
Jane, Betty	114	J. O. Hollow	v	Johnson, Dorothy	115
Jarrell, Ed	258	Johanson, Beda Maria	114	Johnson, Dustin Cody Boyd	215
Jarrell, Ruby Louise (Owen)	114	Johanson, Eric	286	Johnson, Eddie M.	115
Jarrett, Talley Davis	114	Johansson, Wilhelm	286	Johnson, Elbert S.	116
Jarrett, Tommy D.	114	John Richardson Road	vii	Johnson, Elsie Lee	118
Jarvis, Mary V.	114	Johnson Harris, Lassie Arizona	115	Johnson, Embrey	179
Jassels, Hannah	176	Johnson, Aaron Huling	114	Johnson, Emma	92, 117
Jaynes, Sue Ellen	7	Johnson, Albert	114	Johnson, Emma	17
Jean, Barbara	12	Johnson, Alfred	116	Johnson, Ethel	18
Jean, Carl R	55	Johnson, Aline	118	Johnson, Frances "Frank" J.	52
Jean, Carl Reese	114	Johnson, Allie Angeline (Cookston) Smith	227	Johnson, Frances Lillian	118
Jean, Margaret Elizabeth (Pollack)	114	Johnson, Alta	115	Johnson, Francis "Frank" Clarke	291
Jean, Thomas Kurtis	114	Johnson, Alton "Bear"	288	Johnson, Francis "Frank" J.	115
Jenkins, Julia Catherine (Gipson)	114	Johnson, Annie (Scott)	117	Johnson, Francis J. "Frank"	115
Jenkins, Margaret	114	Johnson, Barney William	115	Johnson, Gene	117
Jenne, Anita Lillian	154	Johnson, Bessie	3, 78, 238	Johnson, George Morgan	116
		Johnson, Betty Joyce	283, 303		
		Johnson, Bill	116		

Name	Page
Johnson, Georgia	118, 122, 124, 195
Johnson, Geraldine (O'Dear) Nunley	279
Johnson, Gladys Lee	115
Johnson, Grace	99
Johnson, Grady Eugene	106
Johnson, Hammon Val	115
Johnson, Harvey	116
Johnson, Hazel	116
Johnson, Hazel Lorene (Sweeton)	49, 57
Johnson, Heidi	116
Johnson, Henry Frank	102
Johnson, Hilda Daphine (Roberts)	116
Johnson, Huling Eugene "Buddy"	116
Johnson, Ida Pearl	114, 116
Johnson, Infant	26
Johnson, Iola	116
Johnson, Irene	238
Johnson, Ivor Lee	213, 258
Johnson, Jeff	143
Johnson, James	116
Johnson, James Calvin	115, 116
Johnson, James Franklin	116
Johnson, James Freeman	116
Johnson, James K	105
Johnson, James R.	116
Johnson, Jan	116
Johnson, Janet	263
Johnson, Janice	253
Johnson, Jarvis	85
Johnson, Jerlene "Jerry" (Braseel)	115, 118
Johnson, Jess	116
Johnson, Jesse H.	116
Johnson, Jimmy Ray	90, 114, 117
Johnson, Joan	116
Johnson, JoAnne	115
Johnson, John	121
Johnson, John Albert	116
Johnson, John Clark	118
Johnson, John James	115
Johnson, John T.	115
Johnson, John Wesley	115, 117
Johnson, Johnnie	116
Johnson, Johnnie Marie	117
Johnson, Jonathan Tolliver	54
Johnson, Joseph M.	25
Johnson, Josephine	117
Johnson, Joyce	160
Johnson, Joyce Ann (Burnett)	257
Johnson, Jr., John T "Jack"	117
Johnson, Julie Travis	117
Johnson, Kimberly Rose	117
Johnson, L. Jerelene "Jerry" (Braseel)	274
Johnson, Lassie Arizona Harris	117
Johnson, Lee	117
Johnson, Leo	18
Johnson, Leon	115
Johnson, Lewis B.	115
Johnson, Lillian	116
Johnson, Loma Lea	62
Johnson, Louise	115
Johnson, Loyd Richard	30
Johnson, Loys	117
Johnson, Loys Leo	170
Johnson, Luther Bryan	118
Johnson, Mabel Ruth (Hobbs)	66, 116, 117
Johnson, Mae	117
Johnson, Mae Arlene	133
Johnson, Margaret Elizabeth (Summers)	132
Johnson, Martha Elizabeth "Mattie" (Cheek)	117
Johnson, Mary	117
Johnson, Mary "Mary Jess"	117, 210, 217
Johnson, Mary (Thomas)	92
Johnson, Mary Ellen	117
Johnson, Mary Lee (Hill)	281
Johnson, Mary M.	117
Johnson, Maxie Ray	117
Johnson, May Magdalene "Duck"	117
Johnson, Mildred	188, 192
Johnson, Mildred M.	143
Johnson, Miles	117
Johnson, Milton L "Rudy"	118
Johnson, Minnie	263
Johnson, Mona	17
Johnson, Morgan "Jack"	117
Johnson, Ora	118
Johnson, Pascal	115
Johnson, Pat	115, 116
Johnson, Patricia A.	115
Johnson, Pauline	246
Johnson, Pauline (Sanders)	68
Johnson, Pearl Dollie (Powers)	118
Johnson, Phillip	118
Johnson, Phinis	115
Johnson, Polly	118
Johnson, Robert	106
Johnson, Roxann	115, 246
Johnson, Roy	116
Johnson, Ruth	49
Johnson, Sally (Kilgore)	115
Johnson, Samuel Clay	118
Johnson, Samuel Green	118
Johnson, Sara Hall	118
Johnson, Sarah	118
Johnson, Shannon	21, 159
Johnson, Steve Allan	115

Name	Page
Johnson, Susan	118
Johnson, Tammy Lynn	115
Johnson, Tennessee Palestine (Fults)	252
Johnson, Theida Jo	118
Johnson, Thelma Pauline (Barrett)	246
Johnson, Theresa	118
Johnson, Thomas	116
Johnson, Vernon Eugene	118
Johnson, Violet	118
Johnson, Virginia	72
Johnson, Wayne Clark	115
Johnson, Will	118
Johnson, William	116
Johnson, William Andrew	117
Johnson, William Henry	215
Johnson, William Riley	115
Johnson, Willie	118
Johnson, Wilma Mari	179
Johnson, Zelma	122
Johnson/Johnston, William Walter	99
Johnston, Patience	116
Jonas, Sarah	68
Jones, Abraham Benjamin	286
Jones, Adelbert Ira	206
Jones, Alford H.	119
Jones, Alford Henry, Sr.	286
Jones, Annilee (McDonald)	235
Jones, Arlington "Bumpus"	118
Jones, Arlington Boyd "Bumps"	119
Jones, Audrey	119
Jones, Audrey C.	236
Jones, Beatrice (Franklin)	236
Jones, Boyd	119
Jones, Carrie Louellen	119
Jones, Clarence	265
Jones, Connie (Keel)	36
Jones, Connie (Sweeton)	119
Jones, Donna	119
Jones, Easter Arrena	144
Jones, Evan B.	206
Jones, Evola	119
Jones, Floyd Burton	3
Jones, Freda	119
Jones, Gordon	154
Jones, Hattie	236
Jones, Helena Jenny	15
Jones, Herbert	231
Jones, J. Rucker	141
Jones, Jack	120
Jones, James Paul	59, 119
Jones, Jay Rucker Fathergill	131
Jones, Jeriah Beatrice	118, 119
Jones, Kathy	192
Jones, L.J.	6
Jones, LeAnne	119
Jones, Linda Marie	89
Jones, Lucille	119
Jones, Lydia	299
Jones, Marshall	260
Jones, Martha (Hughes)	119
Jones, Mary	119
Jones, Mary Ethel (Burnett)	207
Jones, Mary Jane	119
Jones, Naomi Ruth	236
Jones, Nettie	119
Jones, Pauline	283
Jones, Ronald Evan	165
Jones, Ruby	119
Jones, Sarah Elizabeth	259
Jones, Sylvester	76
Jones, Sylvia	119
Jones, Thurman	72
Jones, Timothy Boyd	119
Jones, Twila	119
Jones, Wesley Born	119
Jones, Willard Coleman	37
Jones, William Arthur	119
Jones, William Clarence	86
Jones, William Emmett	22
Jones, William Kenneth	120
Jones, William Wilbur	120
Jones, Willie Lee	119
Jordan, Deborah Sue	59
Jordan, Emmett	20
Jordan, Jimmy	120
Jordan, John A.	88
Jordan, Louise	120
Jordan, Marcella	85
Jossi, Ulrich	88
Jossi, William James	120
Jossi, William Lecil	120
Judge, Katie Mae (Johnson)	120
Judge, Kenneth	120
Judson, Nettie	120
Justice, Carol Lynette (White)	66
Kaldaras - Parks, Adeline (Argo)	293
Kaldaras, Unk	120
Kalmar, Dorothy	120
Kalmar, Jenoe	120
Kalmar, Joshua Lee	120
Kania, Paul	120
Kania, Ralph R.	120
Kashola, Ernest R., Sr.	120
Kashola, Ernest Ralph, Jr.	120
Katona, Alida	120
Katona, William	105
Kazar, Nellie	105

Name	Page
Kazar, Vincent	270
Ke, Ani	270
Kearn, Daniel Leroy	98
Keel, Betty	120
Keel, Claudia Mae	120
Keel, Florence	215
Keel, Frances Pauline	120
Keel, Jake	55
Keel, James Bell	120
Keel, Jean (James)	188
Keel, Jean James	120
Keel, Josephine E	119
Keel, Mildred Marie	42
Keel, Pascal	120
Keel, Pauline	90, 120, 121
Keel, Randal	54
Keel, Ronnie	120
Keel, Ruth Lourine	120
Keel, William F.	120
Keele, Amarilla Sullivan	119, 120, 121
Keele, Dorothy Jean	121
Keele, Hon. Robert Levi	121
Keele, Marvin E.	121
Keele, Robert Larry	121
Keeling, Elizabeth	121
Keeling, James Lowery	70
Keene, Lucille	70
Keener, Calvin	290
Keener, Clayton Casto	121
Keener, Dakota "Cody"	121
Keener, Dellene	121
Keener, Ervin Pete	17
Keener, Gracie Lea (Kilgore)	121
Keener, Hettie Delores	121
Keener, Joann	293
Keener, Lee Henderson	121
Keener, Lola Bell	267
Keener, Luther	55
Keener, Luther C.	121
Keener, Mary	55, 121
Keener, Molly O'Day	40
Keener, Randy Keener	295
Keener, Ricky Lewis	121
Keener, Rita Faye (Roles)	121
Keener, Rosie Virginia (Hammers)	121
Keener, Ruby	121
Keener, Treva	280
Keener, Wilburn "Bud"	257
Keeregan, Mary	121
Keever, Linda Gail	68
Keever, Ray	121
Keller, Daniel Crawford	121
Keller, David	102
Keller, Elisabeth	121
Keller, Elizabeth	230
Keller, Harold	229
Keller, Harold A.	121
Keller, William Albert	121
Kelley, Dennis	121
Kelley, Dennis Eugene	121
Kelley, Dora Edith	121
Kelley, Dorothy	121
Kelley, James	109
Kelley, Judy	121
Kelley, Judy Ann (Morrison)	121
Kelley, Michael Wayne	121
Kelley, Noah A.	121
Kellog, Julia	121
Kelly, Dolly	198
Kelly, Elford	251
Kelly, Ernestine	12
Kelly, Hattie Mae	216
Kelly, Johnny Foy	150
Kelly, Mary	150
Kelly, Mary Jane	204
Kelly, Ronald Sherman	14
Kelso, James Moffitt	221
Kelso, Jimmy Ray	121
Kelso, Paula R.	121
Kemmerly, Dr. Paul C	121
Kemmerly, Virginia Maxine	122
Kennedy, Charles Wesley	122
Kennedy, Delitha Jennie (Scissom)	122
Kennedy, John Charles	122
Kennedy, Maggie	122
Kennedy, Mary Magdalene	100
Kennedy, Tressie Jo	99
Kennedy, Walter	122
Kennemore, Gina	122
Kenner, Betty Marie	242
Kenner, Lee	186
Kenner, Lou	230
Kennerly, Darlene	89
Kennerly, Gertrude (Willis)	178
Kennerly, John	296
Kennerly, Ora Lee	122
Kent, Herbert Leo	122
Kenti, Elisabeth	122
Kerley, Joshua	261
Kerley, Mary Elizabeth (Smith)	122
Kerley, Thomas Newton	122
Kern, David Daniel	122
Kern, Jeffrey Allen	120
Kern, Jim	122
Kern, Marsha	122
Ketchum, Janet	122
Ketola, Shirley	205
Keylon, Peggy Joyce	189
Keyt, Edith	1
Kikuchi, Aiko	10

Name	Page
Kilby, C.H.	80
Kilby, Carl H.	122
Kilby, Carl Harvery	208
Kilby, John Edward	297
Kilby, Maudie Bell (Lewis)	122
Kilgor, Andrew	122
Kilgor, Martha	124
Kilgore Pearlie Mae (Nunley)	124
Kilgore, Abba Jean	122
Kilgore, Allen Richard	123
Kilgore, Amos	122
Kilgore, Andrew	124
Kilgore, Andrew Elmer	123
Kilgore, Ann	125
Kilgore, Arla Sue (North)	125
Kilgore, Barney	122
Kilgore, Barney Glenn	123
Kilgore, Bertha	123
Kilgore, Bertie	88, 122, 254
Kilgore, Betty	122
Kilgore, Betty (Grimes)	261
Kilgore, Biddie Sophia	123
Kilgore, Bill	297
Kilgore, Billy Jackson	124
Kilgore, Billy Joe "Flashlight"	123, 126
Kilgore, Blanton	123
Kilgore, Byrd Alice	123
Kilgore, Calvin	238
Kilgore, Calvin Calhoun	125
Kilgore, Carl H.	121
Kilgore, Carl P.	123
Kilgore, Cecelia Fay (Watson)	123
Kilgore, Charles Wesley	123
Kilgore, Clarence E.	125
Kilgore, Clarence Edward, Jr.	69, 123
Kilgore, Cora	123
Kilgore, Craven	162
Kilgore, Daniel	122, 160
Kilgore, Danny Ray "Skinny"	123
Kilgore, David C	123
Kilgore, Debbie	123, 125
Kilgore, Dora	125
Kilgore, Dortha	198
Kilgore, Earl	83
Kilgore, Edith	60, 126
Kilgore, Edna	99. 100
Kilgore, Edna (Schoenmann)	10
Kilgore, Edward	123
Kilgore, Elizabeth	123
Kilgore, Elizabeth (Gipson)	3
Kilgore, Emmitt	123
Kilgore, Erlene	123, 124
Kilgore, Ernest	123
Kilgore, Ernest Ray	125
Kilgore, Essel	123
Kilgore, Evelyn	123
Kilgore, Frances	157
Kilgore, Frank	122, 125
Kilgore, Frank Emmitt	123
Kilgore, George C.	123, 125
Kilgore, George Washington	123
Kilgore, Gertrude	111
Kilgore, Glen Ernest "Lucky 7"	142
Kilgore, Grace	124
Kilgore, Gracie Lea	121
Kilgore, Harold	55
Kilgore, Harold E	122
Kilgore, Harold Wayne	124
Kilgore, Hazel	124
Kilgore, Hershel Franklin "Frank"	53
Kilgore, Hobart Lee	124
Kilgore, Houston	124
Kilgore, Houston "Uncle Gab"	135
Kilgore, J.W.	125
Kilgore, James Alton	125
Kilgore, James Olen	186
Kilgore, James Riley	124
Kilgore, Jane Katherine "Katie" (Shrum)	125
Kilgore, Janice	124
Kilgore, Jeanne	123
Kilgore, Jerry E.	125
Kilgore, Jewell Yvonne (Nunley)	123
Kilgore, Jim	124
Kilgore, JoAnn	123
Kilgore, Joe Anner	125
Kilgore, Joe E.	124
Kilgore, John	124
Kilgore, John E.	123
Kilgore, John W.	190
Kilgore, Joseph Elishey	186
Kilgore, Joseph G.	124, 126
Kilgore, Josie	122
Kilgore, Joy Alfreda	64
Kilgore, Jr., Clarence	122
Kilgore, Katherine Fults (Thomas)	72
Kilgore, Kenneth	124
Kilgore, Kethley	102
Kilgore, Larry	124
Kilgore, LaVoy	112
Kilgore, Leon	126
Kilgore, Leonard	125
Kilgore, Lettie	124
Kilgore, Levi Marion	238
Kilgore, Lewis	124, 125
Kilgore, Linda Sue (Reel)	243
Kilgore, Lisa	124
Kilgore, Lou Rebecca (Starling)	280

Name	Page
Kilgore, Louise Kathleen	124
Kilgore, Lucille	91
Kilgore, Mae Omilee	91
Kilgore, Maggie Mae (James)	244
Kilgore, Margaret (probably maiden named Scott)	124
Kilgore, Margie	125
Kilgore, Margie Janie	67
Kilgore, Martha Myrtle (Meeks)	60
Kilgore, Mary	125
Kilgore, Mary E. (Griffith)	244
Kilgore, Mary Evelyn	125
Kilgore, Mary Magalene (Meeks)	157
Kilgore, Mary Menda	125
Kilgore, Matison Monroe "Mat"	212
Kilgore, Maxine	125
Kilgore, Mildred	64
Kilgore, Mildred Mae (Myers)	77, 189, 235
Kilgore, Mittie	125
Kilgore, Mittie Rutellie	141
Kilgore, Nancy	151
Kilgore, Nancy Elizabeth "Liz"	141, 155
Kilgore, Nancy Jean	125
Kilgore, Nora	186
Kilgore, Odell	250
Kilgore, Oma Lee	290
Kilgore, Orin Winfred	167
Kilgore, Para Lee	125
Kilgore, Patricia Ann	20
Kilgore, Patrick	123
Kilgore, Pauline H. "Polly"	125
Kilgore, Pearlie Mae	125
Kilgore, Pearly (Dove)	124
Kilgore, R.G.	125
Kilgore, Ramon	242
Kilgore, Richard Joseph "Bud"	125
Kilgore, Robbie Crawford	125
Kilgore, Roger Dale	125
Kilgore, Ronnie Eugene	125
Kilgore, Rosa Lee	158
Kilgore, Roy	275
Kilgore, Roy "Moe"	125, 171
Kilgore, Roy Laverne	122, 125
Kilgore, Rufus	125
Kilgore, Ruth	123
Kilgore, Ruth Ann	129
Kilgore, Sarah	158
Kilgore, Scottie Dale	118
Kilgore, Serena	124
Kilgore, Shane Leon "Gory"	123
Kilgore, Spence	125
Kilgore, Stacy	124
Kilgore, T. Cora	82
Kilgore, Thomas	126
Kilgore, Timothy Mark	124
Kilgore, Tiny Ann	126
Kilgore, Tom	186
Kilgore, Valerie	64
Kilgore, Walter B	125
Kilgore, Walter Benjamin	91, 125
Kilgore, Wanda Turner	iii
Kilgore, Wash	124
Kilgore, Washington Monroe	123
Kilgore, Wesley Earl	126
Kilgore, William Allen	123
Kilgore, William Eugene	126
Kilgore, William Harold	126
Kilgore, Willie Ruth	123, 126, 280
Killian, Alene	123
Killian, Arthur	35, 36
Killian, Arthur D.	126
Killian, Bettie	126
Killian, Betty Sue	256
Killian, Burl	ix
Killian, Chad	126
Killian, Dora	126
Killian, Edna Jean	126
Killian, George W.	283
Killian, J.B.	126
Killian, J.B. "Babe"	282
Killian, James Henry	126
Killian, Jean	273
Killian, Jeremiah	283
Killian, Jeremian Daniel	126
Killian, Jerry	126
Killian, Jesse	126
Killian, Lear	126
Killian, Martha	16
Killian, Mary	48
Killian, Paul Raymond	241, 242
Killian, Scotty	126
Killian, Stanley Earl "Snip"	126
Killian, Susan	126
Killian, Unk	52
Killian, Vera Mildred	87
Killian, Vernon Frank	126
Killian, Waynie Morris	126
Killian, Wilber	126
Killian, Willie Morris	126
Killman, Rosa	126
Kim, Pok Cha	115, 198
Kimble, Jessie Mae	41
Kimble, Ray	126
Kimming, Charles Eugene, Sr.	126
Kinary, Doris Laverna (James)	178
King, Billy Dione, Rev.	126
King, Abbie	129
King, Alexander	221

King, Alice (Orange)	270	King, Elmer Cline	61	King, Isabelle Margaret	127, 128
King, Allen Anthony	127	King, Eloise	127	King, Jennifer Ann (Byers)	128
King, Alma Lorene (Lockhart)	127	King, Elsie Ailene (Anderson)	127	King, Jeremy Wayne	128
King, Almeda	127	King, Elzie Martin	127	King, Jerry King	128
King, Alton	130	King, Emma Rose	127	King, Jess	128
King, Alvilda	152	King, Emmett Edward	139	King, Jesse Stokes	127, 128
King, Annalee	127, 211	King, Emmett Edwin	127, 128	King, Jessica Lee (Pickett)	128, 129
King, Annie D.	59	King, Esther	127	King, Jim	128
King, Annie Mae	127	King, Ethelene	131	King, Jimmy Dean	181
King, Arminda	298	King, Etta Mae (Finch)	110	King, Jodie	128
King, Aubrey Hill	127	King, Eugene	127	King, John Wesley	129
King, Barbara	65, 127	King, Euphema	130, 267	King, Josephine	128, 283
King, Bell	127	King, Fernando "Tony"	11	King, Judy	65
King, Bertha Pauline	85, 224	King, Fernando Edward "Tony"	129	King, Katherine	259
King, Berthina	57, 247	King, Frances	127	King, Lee Rev.	264
King, Bessie	210, 216	King, Frank C.	89	King, Lena	128
King, Bill Monroe	130	King, Fred	129	King, Leroy	41
King, Billy H.	127	King, Gary Richard	199	King, Leroy Venus	128
King, Billy Joe	127	King, George	127	King, Lillie	130
King, Brenda	127	King, Glema Ann (Sailors)	97	King, Lois	64
King, Buford	70	King, Glen	127	King, Loretta M (Minton)	9
King, Byron	296	King, Glenn	129	King, Lottie	128
King, Calbert Lee	60	King, Glenn Edward	255	King, Lucille	241
King, Carmen Ford	127	King, Grace Louis	128	King, Mabel	128
King, Carolyn	127	King, Harvey	291	King, Mabelle	25
King, Carrie Louise	108	King, Hazel Gladys	183	King, Mae Pearl	282
King, Charles	71	King, Henry	257	King, Mamie (Martin)	276
King, Clarence Glenn	129	King, Herbert W	223	King, Margie	129
King, Daisy	130	King, Herbert William	232	King, Marlene	140, 271
King, Dale	198	King, Herbert William, Jr.	128	King, Marshall O	129
King, Derek Edward	129	King, Herbert William, Sr.	128	King, Martha	126, 127
King, Dillard	127	King, Hershel Coy	128	King, Mary Edith	66, 72, 74, 127
King, Dwight	129	King, Hester (Orange)	89	King, Mary Ellen	129
King, Eddie Lee	41	King, Heual Denzil	128	King, Melanie Jean (Smith)	5, 6
King, Edna Jean	127	King, Houston	128	King, Michael Allen	129
King, Edna Ruth	127	King, Ira L.	130	King, Michael Alton	129
King, Elizabeth Bess	127				
King, Elizzabeth	129				

Name	Page
King, Minnie Emaline Payne (Anderson)	128
King, Minnie Lee	129
King, Monroe	129
King, Morris	127, 128
King, Morris E.	127
King, Nellie Gladys	129
King, Newton	129, 255
King, Newton Everett	129
King, Nora	129
King, Norman Lee	129
King, Oline Grace	129
King, Ollene Grace	252
King, Oma Lee	209
King, Opal	178
King, Ora (Mitchell)	197
King, Oscar B	129
King, Patsy	129
King, Paul Edward	129
King, Percy Glenn	129
King, Ray E.	129
King, Raymond	129
King, Reba Evelyn	232
King, Regina G. (Irvin)	104
King, Rena J	129
King, Rev. Lee	99
King, Richard	129
King, Richard H.	105
King, Richard Howell	22
King, Rickie Lee	129
King, Ricky E.	129
King, Robert	129
King, Robert E.	128
King, Robert P.	129
King, Ronald L "Bud"	298
King, Rosalee	128
King, Roy Douglas	129
King, Roy Lee	129
King, Ruby Mae	130
King, Sandra Leigh (Bennett)	284
King, Sandy	130
King, Sarah	127
King, Shirley	128
King, Stanley Thomas	127
King, Stephen N.	130
King, Steve A.	127
King, Steve Allen	130
King, Steven Shane	130
King, Teddy Ray	130
King, Thelma S. (Perry)	129
King, Thomas	130
King, Thomas Preston	75
King, Tom	273
King, Tomothy Jacob "Voo Doo"	129
King, Velma Irene	130
King, Violet	56, 72
King, W.L. "Willie"	24
King, Walter	127
King, Wilborn Ray	127, 130
King, William	130
King, William Carroll	129
King, Willing	218
Kinney, Dollye	288
Kinsey, Aleta Lee (Thomas)	288
Kinsey, Jr., Bennie	130
Kirby, Audia Mae	130
Kirby, Louis	130
Kirby, Robert Ray	130
Kirk, Charles "Buddy"	130
Kirk, Eliza Belle (Stephens)	130
Kirk, Georgia Helen (Tate)	130
Kirk, Hazel	130
Kirk, Helen Myers	244
Kirk, James B	130
Kirk, Minnie Lee	130
Kirk, Pauline	241
Kirk, Rufus L.	34
Kirk, Tom Ed	130
Kirk, Vilda Corinne	130
Kirk, Willie	180
Kirkendoll, Deborah	95
Kissinger, Donnabelle	147
Kissling, Johann	174
Kissling, Margritha "Margaret" (Balsiger)	130
Kitchen, Leila Lucille	130
Kitchens, Alex Shields	226
Kitchens, Sterling Bert	130
Kitts, Isabella	130
Kitts, Reason O.	131
Kitts, Susannah Layne	131
Kizer, John	271
Kizer, Mamie B.	277
Klien, Irmgard	288
Klingel, Fredia	116
Klinski, Walter	173
Knapp, Sally	237
Knight, Albert	50
Knight, Albert "Hooty"	131
Knight, Anna	131
Knight, Bruce Edward	145
Knight, Charles Raymond	131
Knight, Charles Raymond "Babe"	131
Knight, Charles Ronnie	132
Knight, Clifford Wayne	131
Knight, Della	131
Knight, Dennis	108
Knight, Edwin	131
Knight, Elton	131
Knight, Florence	131
Knight, George William	161
Knight, Georgia	131

Name	Page
Knight, Georgia N. (Nunley)	190
Knight, George William	131
Knight, Gus	145
Knight, Hallie	131
Knight, Hallie F. (James)	131
Knight, Hassie	131
Knight, Horace	129
Knight, Horace E "Gid"	131
Knight, Horace Newton, Jr.	131
Knight, Horace Newton, Sr.	131
Knight, Jack B.	131
Knight, Jimmie Carolyn (Jones)	131
Knight, Levander	131
Knight, Lizzie	131
Knight, Lucille	69
Knight, Mahaley "Haley" (O'Rear)	22, 105
Knight, Mary Melinda	131
Knight, Pearly Mae (Childers)	28
Knight, Phoeba Ann (James)	131
Knight, Randel	131
Knight, Rebecca	106
Knight, Regina	203
Knight, Robert	264
Knight, Ronald Colby	131
Knight, Starling	131
Knight, Timothy Randall	131, 132
Knight, Vernie	132
Knight, William Dennis	86
Knight, William Harris	273
Knighton, Alma	132
Knobel, Abraham	221
Knobel, Agatha	239
Knobel, Barbara	146
Knobel, Katharina	239
Knobel, Katrina	304
Knobel, Susanna	239
Knott, Alfred A.	239
Knott, Charles D.	132
Knott, Francis	260
Knott, Francis Lee	296
Knott, Katherine (Rollins)	132
Knott, Manuel Melvin	132
Knott, Mary	132
Knott, Oscar Luck	132
Knott, Willis	132
Knowlan, Annie (Davis)	132
Knowlan, Charles Ray	132
Knowlan, Fate	132
Knowlan, Fred	34, 81
Knowlan, John Lafayette "Fate"	132
Knowlan, Maggie	132
Knowlan, Margaret Fay	34, 81
Knowlan, Mitchel Nance	16
Knowlan, Ottis Preston	16
Knowlan, Troas	132
Knowlan, Willene (Bivens)	142
Knowlan, Yoshiko (Ito)	132
Knowland, Fate	132
Knowland, Franklen Hershel	132
Knowland, Ina Ruth (Green)	132
Knowland, Martha	132
Knowland, Martha M.	112, 114
Knox, Albert Edward	113
Knox, Ella Faye	132, 133
Knox, Fred Earl	70
Knox, George Leonard	70, 133, 183
Knox, Georgia	132
Knox, Mabel (Meeks)	182, 183
Knox, Mary	133
Knox, Mary Jane	271, 272
Knox, Pearl M. (Henry)	130, 140
Koch, Mary	133
Koehn, William August	287
Koeppel, Emma Catherine (Schlageter)	239
Koeppel, John Severin	133
Koger, Brenda J.	133
Koger, Willie Arvell	140
Kopek, Arlene	139
Kopek, Larry	133
Kopek, Lawrence David	133
Kopnitsky, Hedwig	133
Kopp, Elizabeth (Fults) Winton	161
Kopp, William Hayes	133
Korpits, Joseph	133
Kosack, Roberta Virginia	161
Kostiverejac, Fatima	133
Kovacs, Irene (Myers)	118
Kovacs, Samuel	133
Kraft, Ralph	133
Kraft, Virginia Ann (Roberts)	133
Krahenbuhl, Jacob W.	133
Krahenbuhl, Samuel	133
Kramer, Elizabeth	133
Kropp, Karl	292
Kroushur, Terry L Kendall	180
Krueger, Katie	208
Kruzewski, Adrew	87
Kubli, Gabriel	96
Kubli, Margaret	146
Kubli, Mary Magdalenen	146
Kundert, Anna Susanna	146
Kunz, Homer Bernard	101
Kunz, John	133
Kunz, Joyce	133
Kunz, June Mildred (Borrensen)	134
Kunzle, George	133
Kunzle, Johan Georg	133

Name	Page
Kurtsinger, Michael	304
Kurtzenger, Pamela Jane	113
Kustos, Rafael "Ralph"	112
Kuzak, Hattie	133
Laager, Burkhardt	171
Laager, Johann Jacob	133
Laager, Meinard	133
Laager, Regula	240
Laager, Rosina	133
Lacy, Alice Pauline (Smith) "Polly"	239
Lacy, Virgil Ward	134
Ladd, Betty Louise	134
Ladd, Charles Dwight	134
Ladd, Delbert Lamar	134
Ladd, Estelle (Anderson)	134
Ladd, Fannie Della (Armstrong) no tombstone, rock marker only	134
Ladd, George	134
Ladd, George W.	88
Ladd, Gwendolyn Kay	134
Ladd, James Bufford	134
Ladd, Jo	134
Ladd, John David	134
Ladd, John Henry	134
Ladd, John W	134
Ladd, John William	134
Ladd, Lawrence	227
Ladd, Patricia Sue (Rector)	134
Ladd, Virginia	134
Ladd, Virginia Lucille	180
Ladd, William "Willie" Kennetth	134
Ladewig, Bettie Mae (Sanders)	134
Ladewig, George William	134
Ladewig, John G.	134
Lafary, Ruth	134
LaFollette, Ivan Kermit	28
Lake, Sue (Layne)	136
Lamb, Joan	293
Lamb, Mary Emma	300
Lamb, Ruby	200
Lambert, Ginger	200
Lambert, John	38
Lambert, Julia	38
Lamberton, Alma May	211
Lamz, Denise	278
Lamz, Jonathan Troy	134
Lamz, Kylee Leanna	134
Lamz, Larry	134
Land, Arthur	134
Land, Christine	150
Land, Doug "Monk"	274
Land, Howard Willard	134
Land, Jesse Jane	134
Land, Lena May	134
Land, Mary	132, 143
Land, Mary Christine	187
Land, Maude	274
Land, Ruby	213, 285, 294
Land, William Bishop	85
Landon, Clara Augusta (Bone)	134
Landon, George	134
Landrum, Barbara Jane (Partin)	134
Lane, Clemit	135
Lane, John Franklin III	135
Lane, Margaret L.	135
Lanford-Simmons, James A.	135
Lanford, William Davis "Bill"	135
Lanford, William Henry	135
Lang, Edward Joseph	135
Lang, Edward William	135
Langer, Larry Joe, Jr.	135
Langer, Larry Joe, Sr.	135
Langford, William	135
Lankford, Albert Lee	295
Lankford, Albert Lee Levi	135, 136
Lankford, Albert Lee Levi	135
Lankford, Beersheba B. (Thompson)	135
Lankford, Charles Douglas	135
Lankford, Charles Rogers	135
Lankford, Earl L.	135
Lankford, Elsie (Kilgore)	135
Lankford, Elsie Iona	135
Lankford, Gilliam	135
Lankford, Harley D	135
Lankford, Herbert Newell	135
Lankford, Jacob Henry	135
Lankford, James Henry	273, 303
Lankford, James Loyd "Bub"	153
Lankford, James W "Bo John", Sr.	136
Lankford, James Wesley	135
Lankford, Jennifer	136
Lankford, Leslie	135
Lankford, Marie	136
Lankford, Neutra	271
Lankford, Newton Johnston	136
Lankford, Reta Beth (LaFollette)	135
Lankford, Robert Mark DeWitt	136
Lankford, Thomas Benjamin	135
Lankford, Vachel (Mrs.)	135
Lanoie, Melanie Jean	136
Lapp, Anna	135
Lappin, Alberta	261
Lappin, Annie Olive	145
Lappin, Bertha Emma	237

Name	Page
Lappin, Charles	13
Lappin, Frances Caroline "Carrie"	136
Lappin, Frances Caroline (Seeley)	304
Lappin, J. B.	136
Lappin, Jesse Morrell	136
Lappin, Martha "Mattie"	304
Lappin, Martha Sue	304
Lappin, Nell Beauty (Sartain)	136
Lappin, Ralph, Sr.	136
Lappin, Robert	136
Lappin, Roger	136
Lappin, Samuel Bert	136
Lappin, Wellington William	304
Laramore, Mary Alice	136
Large, Maxine	92
Lasater, David C.	42
Lasater, Randy E.	136
Lasater, Ruth	136
Laskowske, Otto Ernest	182
Laskowske, Phillip William	136
Latham, Lou	136
Latham, Thelma	91
Lathrum, Emma	213
Lathum, Jennie "June"	144
Lathum, John	136
Lathum, John G.	136
Lautzenhauser, Miriam	136
Lautzenheiser, Elliott, Geneva Bell "Bluie" (Gregory)	29
Lautzenheiser, Ernest Glen "Hunkie"	136
Lautzenheiser, Ernest Glenn	136
Lautzenheiser, Miriam	255
Lautzenhouser, Miriam	26
Laverne, Kaity	24
Laviner, Henry Thomas, Jr.	125
Laviner, Henry Thomas, Sr.	136
Law, Fannie	136
Lawhorn, Jess	18
Lawhorn, Mary Ann	136
Lawhorn, Willie Edward	136
Lawrence, Ameda	136
Lawrence, Dixie	47
Lawrence, Dixie Iowa	216, 269
Lawrence, Jason	216
Lawrence, Maude	216
Lawrence, Misty Shea (Layne)	64
Lawson, Allan	137
Lawson, Andrew	137
Lawson, Carrie Francis (Layne)	137
Lawson, Charles A.	137
Lawson, Charles A., Jr.	137
Lawson, Charles Alfred, Jr.	137
Lawson, Coy "Gene"	137
Lawson, Coy Washington	137
Lawson, Cynthia	137
Lawson, Henry Jackson	17
Lawson, Janice	137, 194
Lawson, Jenny Annie Lee	191
Lawson, Kenneth Wayne	297
Lawson, Lester	137
Lawson, Martha	137
Lawson, Mildred	137
Lawson, Mildred Annette (Allison)	137
Lawson, Missouri Cordelia	137
Lawson, Ophelia	46
Lawson, Phillip A.	204
Lawson, Phillip Oscar	137
Lawson, Phillip Oscoe	137
Lawson, Raymond	137
Lawson, Rubye Lee (Robinson)	261
Lawson, Samuel W. "Sammy"	137
Lawson, Sarah	137
Lawson, William	201
Lawyer, Unk	137, 197
Laxson, Charles "Josh"	181
Laxson, Charles Edwin "Josh"	137
Laxson, Clara Mildred	137
Laxson, Herbie	102
Laxson, Jessie Cecil	137
Laxson, John Guinn	137
Laxson, Rachel	137
Laxson, Sandra Lee (Griggs)	14
Lay, Alma Jean (Borne)	137
Lay, Clifford, Jr.	137
Lay, Maudie Shrum	137
Lay, Peter Edgar	279
Lay, William Leslie	137
Layman, Alton E.	137
Layman, Alicia Cheyenne	137
Layman, Alton E.	137
Layman, Arrietta Elois (James)	138
Layman, Billy Ray	137
Layman, Bo	137
Layman, Brenda	24
Layman, Charles Vernon	6
Layman, Clyde	138
Layman, David Allen "Big Al"	138
Layman, Doris Jean	138
Layman, Dorothy Irene	275
Layman, Dorothy Pry	138
Layman, Edna (Scott)	282
Layman, Elsie Griffith	138
Layman, Elsie Marie (Griffith)	138
Layman, Everett	138

Name	Page
Layman, Everett J.	137
Layman, George Washington	138
Layman, Helen	138
Layman, Homer	234, 252
Layman, J. C.	138
Layman, James Clyde	138
Layman, Joe Ray	138
Layman, John	138
Layman, John Adam	138
Layman, Mitchell Michael	138
Layman, Molly O.	138
Layman, Myra Jeanetta	138
Layman, Nancy	33
Layman, Pam	138
Layman, Pamela Kay	137
Layman, Ralph	138
Layman, Tom	137
Layman, Tommy Leon	138
Layman, Tommy Leon, Jr.	138
Layman, Tommy, Jr.	138
Layman, Virgie (Layne)	295
Layman, Werner	138
Laymon, George Washington	233, 282, 284
Laymon, Homer	138
Laymon, Homer W.	138
Laymon, Percy Ezell	138
Layne - Shirley, Edith Irene (Hill)	138
Layne child	139
Layne Funeral Home	iii
Layne, Abba Jean	139
Layne, Abby	190
Layne, Aberham	204
Layne, Abraham	139
Layne, Abraham "Little Abe"	139
Layne, Abraham K. "Little Abe", Jr.	248
Layne, Abraham Kelly "Little Abe"	144
Layne, Ader Hazel	139
Layne, Albert	254
Layne, Alexander Benson "Dude"	139
Layne, Alfred L	139
Layne, Alfred Leemon	140, 142
Layne, Alice	139
Layne, Almedia	33, 158, 180
Layne, Alyene	141
Layne, Amber	156
Layne, Amos	228
Layne, Andrew	88
Layne, Andrew Jackson	144
Layne, Annie	138
Layne, Arthur Alexander	152, 233, 282, 284
Layne, Aylor	139
Layne, Aylor "A.J."	22, 139
Layne, Barney	139
Layne, Barney H.	1
Layne, Bartley	142
Layne, Bass	141
Layne, Becky	21, 25
Layne, Bell	229
Layne, Benjamin Etwell	145
Layne, Bertha	142
Layne, Betty	123, 205
Layne, Betty J	298
Layne, Betty Jean	142
Layne, Beulah	139
Layne, Billie	141
Layne, Billie Evelyn	54
Layne, Billy	55
Layne, Billy Ray	66
Layne, Birtia	139
Layne, Bobby Joe	189
Layne, Bradford	139
Layne, Brenda J.	144
Layne, Carl David	139
Layne, Charles	144
Layne, Charles "Boy"	142
Layne, Charles D "Steamboat"	139
Layne, Charles Doyle	143
Layne, Charles Edward	139
Layne, Charlotte	139, 141
Layne, Chester Earl	172
Layne, Clara Irene	139
Layne, Clara Mai	71, 117
Layne, Clara O'Dell	155
Layne, Claude	144
Layne, Claude Elmer	140
Layne, Clell	139
Layne, Clell Lendon	227
Layne, Cleveland	140
Layne, Clyde	155, 205
Layne, Coleman	141, 143, 198
Layne, Cora	97, 139, 140
Layne, Daisie	169
Layne, Daniel Leander	80
Layne, Daniel Leander, Rev.	144
Layne, Danny Lee	195
Layne, Darrell	76, 140
Layne, Dauntie Elizabeth	140
Layne, David Stephen	81
Layne, Deborah	139, 144
Layne, Dereda Joyce	66
Layne, Devin James	140
Layne, Dillard H. "Dill"	140
Layne, Dillard H., Sr.	139
Layne, Dillard Harold, Jr.	140
Layne, Donna Jo	139, 140
Layne, Doris	6

Layne, Dorothy Arlene (Mainord)	152
Layne, Dorothy L. (Rollins)	140
Layne, Dot	140
Layne, Douglas Dewayne	302
Layne, E.W.	140
Layne, Earline (O'Neal)	140
Layne, Edd	140
Layne, Edith "Tabby"	141
Layne, Edith Irene	270
Layne, Elizabeth	248
Layne, Elizabeth Bertha Louise	296
Layne, Emiel Dewey	186
Layne, Emma	142
Layne, Emma Jean (Meeks)	73, 76, 138
Layne, Enoch	140
Layne, Ernest	140
Layne, Etta (Slatton)	142
Layne, Eva Bell	140
Layne, Fannie Clair	296
Layne, Fay	140
Layne, Flora	103, 104
Layne, Floyd Benjamin	294
Layne, Ford Ray	139, 144
Layne, Frank	143
Layne, Frank McKinley	33, 140, 142
Layne, Frank Parks	140
Layne, Franklin Parks	164
Layne, Franklin Parks, Jr.	143, 273
Layne, Franklin Parks, Sr.	140
Layne, Fred	140
Layne, Fred Anthony	141, 151
Layne, George Coleman	141
Layne, Gertrude	141
Layne, Gilbert	33
Layne, Grace	141
Layne, Grace Marie	102
Layne, Grady	101
Layne, Harley	141, 144
Layne, Harley "Buddy"	143
Layne, Harlie	298
Layne, Harold Franklin	302
Layne, Harold Wayne	141
Layne, Harvey Raymond	137
Layne, Hence	143
Layne, Henry	269
Layne, Henry C.	141
Layne, Henry Miller	214
Layne, Hester	140
Layne, Hilda	88
Layne, Homer	144
Layne, Homer Lewis	112
Layne, Ida	97, 277
Layne, Ida Ellen (Cantrell)	276
Layne, Ike	141
Layne, Ila Lee	139
Layne, Imogene (Jones)	109, 169
Layne, Irene	141
Layne, Isaac "Doc"	117
Layne, Isier	139
Layne, Jack	140
Layne, Jack Watson	141
Layne, Jackie	141
Layne, Jackson Charles	141, 143
Layne, Jackson Reid	212
Layne, James	141
Layne, James Duane "Jim"	140
Layne, James Ed Layne	141
Layne, James Walter	141
Layne, Janelle	141
Layne, Janice Sharon	44, 274
Layne, Jaquelin Mai "Jackie"	208
Layne, Jason	205
Layne, Jay Hugh	141
Layne, Jennie	144
Layne, Jennifer Leann (Roddy)	59
Layne, Jerry Hayes	141
Layne, Jim Washington	141
Layne, Jimmy	141, 142
Layne, Jo Ann	6
Layne, Joe C.	139
Layne, Joe Edward	142
Layne, Joe T.	141
Layne, John	142
Layne, John Dave	139
Layne, John Franklin "Squirrel"	iii
Layne, John Henry	141
Layne, John Henry, Jr.	141
Layne, John Jacob	141
Layne, John Wesley	140
Layne, John William "Johnny"	142
Layne, Johnathan	140
Layne, Johnnie	141
Layne, Johnny Ray	142
Layne, Joseph Elbert	142
Layne, Joyce	15, 142, 173
Layne, Joyce (Kilgore)	1, 158
Layne, Judy Ann	142
Layne, Judy Lynn	54
Layne, Karon	142
Layne, Katherine	144
Layne, Kenneth Owen	141
Layne, Kent A. "Bear"	142
Layne, Kimberly Michelle	142
Layne, Larry Dean	142
Layne, Leander	142
Layne, Leonard	42
Layne, Leora Merritt	142
Layne, Lila (Melton)	104

Name	Page
Layne, Lillie May	142
Layne, Linda Ann	127
Layne, Linda Darlene	5
Layne, Linda Janelle	139
Layne, Lisa	142
Layne, Lonnie	21
Layne, Louise (Geary)	140, 142
Layne, Margaret	142
Layne, Margaret Aleene (Turner)	141
Layne, Margie	142
Layne, Margie Elizabeth (Green)	82, 236
Layne, Mark	143
Layne, Mark Anthony	145
Layne, Martha	143
Layne, Martin Eugene	203
Layne, Mary	143
Layne, Mary (Crowe)	10, 170
Layne, Mary Beulah	143
Layne, Mary E.	141
Layne, Mary Edith	103
Layne, Mary Elizabeth	127
Layne, Mary Kathleen	110
Layne, Mary M. (Lockhart)	151
Layne, Mary Sue (Church)	143
Layne, Matieal/Margaret	143
Layne, Mattie	139
Layne, Maudie	181
Layne, Maxine	139
Layne, Melinda Carol "Lindy"	155
Layne, Mildred	143
Layne, Mildred Pollard (Johnson)	213
Layne, Misty Lawrence	143
Layne, Nan Ruth (Magouirk)	67
Layne, Nancy	143
Layne, Nancy Ann	125
Layne, Nellie Irene	184
Layne, Nellie Ruth	3
Layne, Nelson	143
Layne, Nicholas Cole "Bird"	143
Layne, Nora	143
Layne, Novella	74, 76, 285
Layne, Oliver D.	143
Layne, Oliver Dentrell "O.D."	135
Layne, Oscar F.	5
Layne, Patricia Carole (Vangaasbeck)	143, 155, 213
Layne, Paul Edward	143
Layne, Pearl	143
Layne, Ples	179
Layne, Polly	64
Layne, Preston Franklin	47, 254
Layne, R.D.	139, 154
Layne, Raymond	162
Layne, Rex Allen	144
Layne, Rick Layne	140
Layne, Rickey Gene	143
Layne, Ricky	143
Layne, Rita Faye	143
Layne, Robert	144
Layne, Robert Bradford	141, 144, 227
Layne, Robert Dewitt	144
Layne, Robert Earl, Sr.	140
Layne, Robert Joe	144
Layne, Robert Overton	139
Layne, Robert Wilson "Bob"	143
Layne, Rodney Gerald	209
Layne, Ronnie Dwayne	144
Layne, Rosie	144
Layne, Roy	50
Layne, Roy D.	137
Layne, Roy David	141
Layne, Russell	94, 139, 142, 144
Layne, Ruth	141
Layne, Samuel	55
Layne, Sarah	143
Layne, Scottie Douglas	124, 142, 215, 283
Layne, Shannon Gay	140, 142
Layne, Sherman	10
Layne, Simeon Glover	144
Layne, Spencer	144
Layne, Stephen	144
Layne, Susan	141
Layne, Susannah	301
Layne, Tammie	131
Layne, Tammy E.	218
Layne, Tennessee	144
Layne, Thelma	146
Layne, Thomas Jackson	144
Layne, Timmie	140
Layne, Tommy	140
Layne, Tootsie	236
Layne, Virgie	153
Layne, Virgie	138
Layne, W.T.	138
Layne, Wanda Sue	141
Layne, Wavie	174
Layne, William Anderson	32
Layne, William Harrison	142
Layne, William Harrison "Little Britches"	33
Layne, William Kinnard "Kenny"	141, 142, 144, 198
Layne, William Lee	144
Layne, William Leonard	144
Layne, William Virgil	144
Layne, William Wayne	144
Layne, Willie	144
Layne, Willie Mae (Borne)	141
Layne, Willie Mae (Brown)	144
Layne, Wilma	144

Name	Page
Layne, Yancie	97
Lea Bailey, Mary Anna (Knight)	144
Lea, Dan	145
Lea, Gerald Dean	145
Lea, Gerald Dean "Poppie"	145
Leach, Henry Grady	145
Leach, Henry Grady, Sr.	145
Leaderman, Unk	145
Leaird, Alfred	112
Leak, Ada Florence	145
Leak, George	42
Leak, Mary	42
LeCroy, Beatrice	9
Lecroy, Donna Elizabeth (Shadrick)	88
Lecroy, Jeffrey "Darin"	145
Lecroy, Larry T.	145
Lecroy, Larry Thomas	145
Lecroy, Lorene	145
LeCroy, Mamie Kathleen (Layne)	119
LeCroy, Patricia	145
LeCroy, Samuel Duke	108
Ledbetter, Annie	145
Ledbetter, Billy J.	247
Ledbetter, Margaret	145
Ledbetter, Mary	145
Ledbetter, Virgil	130, 285
Ledford, Arquilla June	145
Ledford, Billy Ray	209
Ledford, George Samuel	145
Ledford, Judith	221
Ledford, Thomas Franklin	24
Lee, B.L.	145
Lee, Banster	145
Lee, Ellen (Ahlstrom)	145
Lee, Harold Ellsworth	145
Lee, Nancy Clay	145
Lee, Paul R.	145
Lee, Peter Elbert	145
Leedy, Harold S. III	145
Leedy, Harold S. Jr.	145
Leeman, Mary E.	145
Leenn, Joseph	263
LeFevers, Theonia Ruth	61
Lehman, Annie	48
Leiderman, Charlene Leiderman	201
Leiderman, Homer Mitchell	145
Leiderman, Hoyt	145
Leiderman, Mitchell Bryan	145
Leiderman, Mitchell Hoyt	145
Leiderman, Nita "Granny"	145
Leitseinger, Johann Heinrich	145
Leitsinger, Gabriel	146
Leitsinger, Glenda	146
Leitsinger, Henry	245
Leitsinger, Lydia Margaret (Smith)	146
Leitsinger, Margaret (Kubli)	146
Leitzel, Bessie	146
Leitzel, Donald	146
Leitzel, Jan	146
Leitzel, Jessie Robert	146
LeMasters, Emma Theodosia	146
Lemons, George H.	181
Lemons, Mary	56
Lemons, Mary	100
Lennox, John Gordon	227
Lenox, Betty (Rollings)	146
Lenox, G. Merrill	146
Lenox, John Gordon	146
Lenox, Stephen Rollings	146
Lentz, Bill	146
Lentz, Geraldine (Conry)	146
Leon, Barbara Jean	146
Leon, Theodore	185, 186
Leonard, Floyd James "Nehi"	186
Leonard, Joyce Inez (Upchurch)	146
Lerris, Felton	146
Lese, Unk.	220
Lesser, John	201
Leuthold, Barbara	223
Leuzi, Verena	305
Levan, Annie	151
Levan, Arizona	146
Levan, Celia "Sis"	90
Levan, Charles Oscar	146
Levan, Daniel	146
Levan, Fannie Elizabeth (Tate)	146
Levan, Frances (Bostain)	146
Levan, Hazel	146
Levan, Helen	208
Levan, Hence	5
Levan, James	114, 117, 146, 147
Levan, James Alton	146
Levan, James Alton, Sr.	146, 165, 168
Levan, Maggie	146
Levan, Maggie Lou	84
Levan, Martin E.	161
Levan, Mary	146
Levan, Orpha	206
Levan, Ressie Paul (Turner)	159, 281
Levan, Stacie	146
Levan, Timmie (Fults)	253
Levean, Irene	147
Leverton, Ellen	274
Leverton, Mary	67
Lewis, Allison	37
Lewis, Billy Wayne	100

Name	Page
Lewis, Bobbie Jean	147
Lewis, Carlos Everett	189
Lewis, Cheryl Lynn (Shook)	147
Lewis, Danny "Jughead"	147
Lewis, Dovie Mae	147
Lewis, Dudley	59
Lewis, Edward	122
Lewis, Francine	147
Lewis, George Herbert	147
Lewis, George Washington	147, 214
Lewis, Gloria	147
Lewis, Hayden	147
Lewis, Hobart	147
Lewis, Howard Creig	147
Lewis, Hubert W.	147
Lewis, Jean	147
Lewis, Jimmy Don	92
Lewis, Joe A	147
Lewis, Joe Allison	147
Lewis, Joe Allison, Jr.	192
Lewis, Laurie Allison	147
Lewis, Margaret Frances	6
Lewis, Oma Lee (Boyd)	214
Lewis, Phillip	147
Lewis, Phillip S.	147
Lewis, Priscilla Fay (Caldwell)	147
Lewis, Sarah	147
Lewis, Susie	92
Lewis, Thomas Howard	147
Lewis, Tim Joe	147
Lewis, Timothy Dan	147
Lewis, William	147
Lewis, William Austin	92
Lewis, William Howard	147
Lewisy, Dorothea	147
Lewisy, George	72
Ley, Ellen Zenith	72
Ley, William	220
Licht, Joan	267
Liddle, Bessie	272
Liddle, Harold	218
Liftin, Joan	218
Lile, Nancy	94
Lillie, Catherine Ellen	117
Lillie, Charles Phelps	147
Lilliebridge, Wilma Esther	64, 147
Lincoln, Alexander Benton	262
Lincoln, Miriam Illsey	147
Lind, Hilding	147
Lind, John Hilding	148
Linder, Una	148
Lindermann, Bertha	136
Lindsay, Mary Elizabeth	26
Lindsey, Raymond L.	1
Lindsey, Rosetta	280
Lindsey, Sandra L.	27, 297
Lindsey, Thelma Lorene	297
Lindsey, William David	223
Linely, Mary Ann	1
Linker, Elizabeth	298
Linkley, William C.	229
Linkous, Anna J.	299
Linkous, Brenda Sue	148
Linkous, Robert Leo	148
Linley, Annie	148
Linn, Annie Mae	34
Linton, Charles Jones	276
Linton, Mary Elizabeth	148
Littell, Dr. Charles	11
Littell, Sue	263
Little, James	263
Little, Patricia Ann (Campbell)	148
Little, Unk	148
Livingston, W. J.	272
Ljungblad, Carl August	286
Ljungblad, Inga Thuridor (Gohl)	148
Ljungblad, Jonas Emanuel	148
Lobdell, Frank W.	148
Lobdell, Minnie Catherine	148
Lochhead, Hazel Elizabeth	148
Locke, Emma Clara (Wooten)	289
Locke, William Setliffe	148
Lockhart, William Henry	148
Lockhart, Alice	148
Lockhart, Allen	121
Lockhart, Alta Josephine	148, 149, 283
Lockhart, Andy	148, 149
Lockhart, Beryl	148
Lockhart, Bettie	279
Lockhart, Bobby Eugene	148
Lockhart, Buford William	148
Lockhart, Della	148
Lockhart, Earl	6
Lockhart, Edgar Monroe	99, 149
Lockhart, Elizabeth "Bettie" (Summers)	149
Lockhart, Elvie	149
Lockhart, Emma	226
Lockhart, Esther	276
Lockhart, Flora	189, 191, 193, 263
Lockhart, Fred	179
Lockhart, George C.	16
Lockhart, Goldie	149
Lockhart, Grady	304
Lockhart, Hazel	164
Lockhart, Hester (Ross)	181
Lockhart, Hettie Juanita	149
Lockhart, Holman Lincoln	99
Lockhart, Irene	297

Name	Page
Lockhart, James Edward	63
Lockhart, James Leonard	93
Lockhart, James Leonard "Sandy"	127
Lockhart, James Monroe	149
Lockhart, Jason Wallice	149
Lockhart, Jerry	149
Lockhart, John Willie	149
Lockhart, Joseph S.	149
Lockhart, Leanna Lettie	149
Lockhart, Lucy (Hunter)	26
Lockhart, Margaret (McCutchen)	149
Lockhart, Mary	149
Lockhart, Mary Elizabeth	12
Lockhart, May Belle (Shadrick)	15, 16
Lockhart, Melton	149
Lockhart, Midge	63
Lockhart, Milton Dixon	275
Lockhart, Minnie (Nunley)	149
Lockhart, Minnie Bell	149
Lockhart, Nancy	67
Lockhart, Nancy	107
Lockhart, Nancy Jane	127, 128
Lockhart, Oscar	200, 201
Lockhart, Paul Eugene	149
Lockhart, Sabrina	148, 149
Lockhart, Sarah	196
Lockhart, Shirley	149
Lockhart, Stephen Allen	170
Lockhart, Toby Bradford	149
Lockhart, Troy	149
Lockhart, Violet Marie (Garner)	149
Lockhart, William	149
Lockhart, William Condit	143
Lockhart, William E.	148
Lockhart, Willie "Elder"	150
Lockhart, Willie Condit	149
Lockhart, Winnie	149
Lockhart, Winnie Gertrude	228, 234
Logan, Bobby Lee	252
Lohman, Evelyn M. (Smith)	150
Lohman, Melvin	150
London, Billee Fay	150
London, James	203
Long Bradford, Elaine May	203
Long, Abram Wallace	291
Long, Alma	150
Long, Bill D.	80
Long, Carl	150
Long, Carol Lee (Meeks)	207
Long, Carrie	150
Long, Celia	132
Long, Charles Edward	262
Long, Charlotte	150
Long, Colleene "Cookie" (Burnette)	37, 192
Long, Cornelius	150
Long, Ella	150, 153
Long, Elsie	77
Long, Harry	291
Long, Helen	33
Long, Irene	207
Long, James David	303
Long, James E "Jim"	206
Long, James Riley	150
Long, Joyce Winona	150
Long, June Ann (Smith)	150
Long, Kelso	150
Long, Kenneth	150
Long, Lloyd Raymond	150
Long, Lou Ann	150
Long, Lula Ann "Lou"	1
Long, Maloy	150
Long, Margaret Pearson (Marks)	293
Long, Marilyn N.	150
Long, Marsilar	102
Long, Mary	274
Long, Mary Melinda	289
Long, Myrtle Ova (Owen)	277
Long, Rebecca	150
Long, Sarah	79
Long, Sarah Ann	85
Long, Sarah Elizabeth	12, 13
Long, Sue Ann	85
Long, Theodore	150
Long, Theodore Lindley, Jr.	143
Long, Unknown	143, 150
Long, William	291
Long, William Albro	150
Long, William Bertram	150
Long, William Houston	150
Longendyke, Mary Delores	150
Longenecker, Sherry Lee	154
Longley, Linda	297
Looney, Gladys May	58
Lovelace, Elizabeth	110
Lovelace, Eunice Estelle	153
Lovett, Joseph William, Jr.	135
Lovett, Mark William	150
Lovlace, Genice Estell	150
Low, Jessie	136
Lowe, Agnes	34
Lowe, Bertha	39
Lowe, Carl	184
Lowe, Charles Finley	220
Lowe, Della	293
Lowe, James L	219
Lowe, John Wesley	218
Lowe, Kenny	150

Name	Page
Lowe, Lucinda	150
Lowe, Lucindy	107
Lowe, Maggie Ann	107
Lowe, Malinda	103
Lowe, Malines	294
Lowe, Mildred "Mickey"	53
Lowe, Mildred "Mickie"	173
Lowe, Velma (Turner) "Little Un"	91
Lowe, William E	150
Lowe, William Patterson	17
Lowery, Carrie	150
Lowery, Joe	253
Lowery, Nellie	253
Lowhorn, Bessie	202
Lowrie, Charlene A. (Thomas)	145
Lowrie, Charlie	151
Lowrie, Harold	151
Lowrie, Harold Lappin	90
Lowrie, James William	151
Lowrie, Patricia	151
Lowry, Rebecca	90
Loyd, Cecil	217
Loyd, Jack Williams "Bill Jack"	151
Loyd, Martha	151
Lucas, Betty	218
Lucas, William Orville	110
Luchsinger, Fannie	110
Luchsinger, Hilarius	151
Luchsinger, Hilbrey	151
Luchsinger, Jackob	151
Luchsinger, John B.	151
Luchsinger, Julia Cleo	151
Luchsinger, Kaspar	261
Luchsinger, Verena (Leuzi)	151
Ludwig, Alfred II "Big Al"	151
Ludwig, Mary	151
Ludwig, Mary Elizabeth	151
Ludwig, Tom	210
Ludwig, Veda	151
Luebeck, Lucille	151
Lundy, Mark Lee	94
Lungblad, Josefa Christina	222
Lusk, Amos	148
Lusk, Bessie Bolen (Cecil)	199
Lusk, Byron Hugh	151
Lusk, Clarron Delton	151
Lusk, Earl T.	151
Lusk, Opal (McCuiston)	151
Lusk, Sarah Lorene	151
Lusk, Sarah Lorene	199
Lusk, Thomas Clinton	199
Lusk, Willie Mae	151
Lutes, Sara	222
Luttrel, Dorothy	299
Luttrell, Barbara	154
Luttrell, Linda Faye	216
Luttrell, Thomas	80
Lyda, Virgil	279
Lyle, Sadie Anastasia	28
Lyle, Sarah	151
Lyle, Steven Matt	151
Lynch, Annie Elizabeth	151
Lynch, Earl	105
Lynch, Earl Edison	153
Lynch, Ella Virginia "Dolly"	151
Lynch, Justice James Gable	153
Lynch, Lucinda	151
Lynch, Mary Kathleen (Layne)	228
Lynn, Clark	151
Lynn, Dorcus	151
Lynn, Helen Northcutt	184
Machen, James	151
Machen, Nina (Christa)	151
Maddox, Doris	151
Maddox, Doris E.	250
Maddox, Howard McKay	249
Maddox, Mary Ann	249
Madewell, Albert	110
Madewell, Elbert	223
Madewell, James	151
Madewell, Ray	8
Madewell, Robert	151
Madewell, Taskah L.	173
Mae, Betty	173
Maeder, Elizabeth	129
Maeder, Jacob	152
Magnes, Carrie Lee	152
Magness, Carrie Lee	18
Magnus, Bettie	18
Magnus, L.P.	18
Magnus, Martha	18
Magouirk, Annie Alberta "Bertie"	267
Magouirk, Bertie Mae	152
Magouirk, Cindy	152
Magouirk, D J	152
Magouirk, DJ, Jr.	152
Magouirk, Don Allen	152
Magouirk, Dorcie Allen	152
Magouirk, Edna E	152
Magouirk, Ellen	152
Magouirk, Emma	166
Magouirk, Francis	223
Magouirk, George Washington	152
Magouirk, James Leonard "Jim"	152
Magouirk, James William	160
Magouirk, James William, Jr.	71, 152
Magouirk, James William, Sr.	152

Magouirk, Jerry	152	Malone, Edith M.	152	Marion County	ix
Magouirk, Joey	152	Mancroft, Mina	153	Markham, Alice	279
Magouirk, John	122	Manders, Ellen	197	Marks, Felix	38
Magouirk, Katherine Ann	152	Manders, John	153	Marler, Carrie Sue	150
Magouirk, Kenneth	257	Manders, NJ	153	Marler, Joseph Pascal	251
Magouirk, Kenneth Wayne	119	Manders, Solomon W.	153	Marlow, Thomas	251
Magouirk, Martha	152	Manders, Young	153	Marquess, Dion Jane	105
Magouirk, Mary Etta	152	Mankin, Brown	153	Marr, Amanda	210
Magouirk, Nacole Church	71	Mankin, Brown H	153	Marshall, Dorothy	80
Magouirk, Nan Ruth	152	Mankin, Mrs. Erp	153	Marten, William A.	48
Magouirk, Otis	141	Mankin, Sarah Jane (Long) "Sallie"	153	Martin, Aaron H.	288
Magouirk, Ozella	108	Manley, Dennis W.	153	Martin, Amanda Roseann	153
Magouirk, Paul V.	133	Manley, Ella	153	Martin, Christine	32
Magouirk, Paula	152	Manley, Ella Virginia "Dolly" (Lynch)	264	Martin, Corinne H.	23
Magouirk, Ray	vii	Manley, Hayden Francis	153	Martin, Elijah Depew "Lige"	153
Magouirk, Rex	92	Manley, Ilene Louise	153	Martin, Eliza	55
Magouirk, Rex	143	Manley, James	96	Martin, Eliza Caroline	201
Magouirk, Ruth (Pemberton)	243	Manley, James Galen "Shim"	3	Martin, Estie (Crouch)	38
Magouirk, Thermon B.	152	Manley, James H. "Son"	153	Martin, Evan	153
Magourik Family "Boots Garden" Cemetery	vi	Manley, James Henry	153	Martin, Frances Peronneau	154
Magourik, Betty Sue (Thompson)	vi, 152	Manley, Mamie	153	Martin, Halson Wooten	28
Magourik, Ray	152	Manley, Mamie Beatrice	281	Martin, Hilda Marie (Nunley)	154
Magourik, Tammy Jeanice	vi, 152	Manley, Nancy	3	Martin, Irene	154
Mahaffey, Ashley	152	Manley, Robert Ray	58	Martin, Isaac Eby	101
Mahan, Charlcie	22	Mann, Velma Jean	153	Martin, Jack Andrew	154
Mahan, Fay	12	Manning, Benny	216	Martin, James Isham	154
Mahan, James	18	Manning, Marie (Dickerson)	153	Martin, James Phillip	129
Mainord, Louis Waymond	57	Mansfield, Jemima	153	Martin, Lehman	143, 154
Mainord, Tegan Brooke	140	Mansfield, Jerry	117	Martin, Mary	153, 154
Mainord, Terra	152	Mansfield, John William	153	Martin, Mildred (Ray)	154
Mainord, Trinton	152	Mansfield, Jonathan "Noodle"	153	Martin, Ovie	154
Malde, Bhanu	152	Mansfield, Laura (Smith)	153	Martin, Patricia C. (Van Gaasbek)	267
Malde, Lakha Jerual	152	Mansfield, William	153	Martin, Rosa	154
Malde, Lathi Ladhiben	152	Manus, Gene	201	Martin, Samson	31, 37
Malde, Motichand	152	Manus, Wilma Tate	153	Martin, Samuel Cecil	69
		Maples, Josie	153	Martin, Serena	13

Name	Page	Name	Page	Name	Page
Martin, Stephen	69	Maurer, Unknown	176	McAmis, Clyde James	155
Martin, Thelma Juanita	154	Mavesty, Susan Elizabeth	304	McAmis, Jean Hobbs	155
Martin, Thomas	13, 298	Maxwell, Lowanda	247	McBee, Alma Jean	155
Martin, Thomas A.	154	May, Beverly Marcus	137	McBee, Aylene L. (Layne)	33
Martin, Vickie Lynn	154	May, Ernest R.	169	McBee, Bertha Mae	155
Martin, Wanda K. (Gilliam)	48	May, Judy	155	McBee, Charllie	111
Martin, William James	154	Mayes, Billy	155	McBee, Churchwell	188
Martin, Willis Edwin	154	Mayes, Blantford	155	McBee, Doris O.	156
Martinez, Frances	154	Mayes, Blantford "B.F."	101, 155	McBee, Edgar William	29
Masingill, Charles Edward	220	Mayes, Diane M (Meeks)	155	McBee, Etta Mae (Braden)	156
Masingill, William	154	Mayes, Gary W.	155	McBee, Frances Louise (Pace)	156
Mason, Barbara Reave	154	Mayes, Glenn	155	McBee, Gary Edward	156
Mason, Cannon Eaton	154	Mayes, Glenn A.	155	McBee, James David "Jim Dave"	106
Mason, Daniel	287	Mayes, Johnnie Maxine (Layne)	155	McBee, James Edward	156
Mason, Howard Price	154	Mayes, Kenneth	155	McBee, James N.	156
Mason, Jeanne	154	Mayes, Kenneth L	155	McBee, Jim Dave	156
Mason, Jerry Q	247	Mayes, Linda Gayle (Rieder)	155	McBee, John Henry	155
Mason, Nancy Jane (Farrell)	154	Mayes, Roy	155	Mcbee, Julie Ann	3
Mason, Thurman Lee	154	Mayes, Sherry Fay	155	McBee, Lawrence	156
Mason, Walter Ballard	154	Mayfield, Wanda	100	McBee, Leona (Rose) Hawk	156
Mason, Walter Scott	68	Maynard, Kendrick	121	McBee, Lizzie	156
Mason, Waymon	154	Maynard, Ova (Moore)	155	McBee, Mary Grace	227
Massar, Betty	154	Maynard, Waymon L.	155	McBee, Melinda	58
Massey, Bessie Mae (Layne)	301	Mays, Chris	155	McBee, Nellie Layne	259
Massey, George	154	Mays, Martha	193	McBee, Paul	3
Massey, Richard	154	Maze, Barbara	129	McBee, Rosa Lee	156
Matherly, Linda	216	Maze, Nora Lee	230	McBee, Terrell Keith	37
Matheson, Kenneth	175	Mc Daniel, Bunia Lee (Argo)	15	McBee, Virginia	156
Mathews, Bill	30	Mc Farland, Lillie Myrtle "Daisy" (Tucker)	155	McBee, William Edward	130
Mathews, Steve Allen	154	Mc Govern, Phillip H.	155	McCallie, Edna	156
Mathis, Eliza Gillen	154	McAfee, Danny	155	McCampbell, Jaime Elizabeth	82
Matney, Issic Lee	286	McAfee, Sharon (Dodd)	155	McCanless, Paulette	156
Matney, Jeffery Lee	155	McAlexander, Daisy	155	McCanless, William Edward	156
Matthews, Annette	155	McAlpine, Davis A.	103	McCanless, Willie Earl	156
Matthews, Opal	178	McAlpine, Susan (Gilliam)	155	McCann, Dallas Porter	156
Matthews, Unk	60				

Name	Page
McCann, Elizabeth (Duncan)	156
McCann, Hazel	156
McCarley, Theodore Trimmier	196
McCarty, Peggie L	248
McCarver, Annie	181
McCarver, David	58, 240
McCarver, Edna	156
McCarver, Rosie Nell	118
McCeney, Benjamin	156
McClain, Charles Edward	160
McClain, Richard Lee	156
McClearen, Charlie	156
McClearen, Pauline	196
McClellan, Evora	196
McClendon, Thelma E.	61
McClure, Bertha	38
McClure, Fannie	16
McClure, James	156
McClure, James Madison	156
McClure, Sallie (Fults)	156
McClure, William	156
McCombs, Ruby Nell	156
McCord, Anna (Smith)	274
McCord, Samuel B.	157
McCormack, Tommie Lester	157
McCormick, Ann (Rhea)	50
McCormick, Bransford Levander	157
McCormick, Clifford L.	157
McCormick, Clifford Levander	157
McCormick, James	157
McCormick, Jessie	290
McCormick, Jim	68, 276
McCormick, Mildred	157
McCormick, Nelson Wayne	71
McCormick, Raymond E.	157
McCormick, Raymond Earl	157
McCormick, Rosie Della (Dickerson)	157
McCormick, Wiliam B.	157
McCormick, William Ace	74
McCown, Malena	157
McCoy, Arlis Wayne	32
McCoy, Arthur	157
McCoy, Brenda Mai (Hollis)	203
McCoy, Caroline	157
McCoy, Sally Ann	157
McCoy, Sherman	157
McCraw, Susan Laura	157
McCraw, William	157
McCraw, William	157
McCreary, Bessie Lea	187
McCreary, Cora A Holmes	117
McCreary, Mae Ellen	277
McCubbins, Charlie	18, 19
McCubbins, Jessie	25
McCuiston, Ralph	25
McCullough, Allen N.	2
McCullough, Danny L.	215
McCullough, Danny Lavaughn	157
McCullough, Mary Ellen	157
McCurdy, Evelyn	215
McCurdy, William Alexander	92
McCurry, Barney	64
McCurry, Carleton G., Sr.	157, 197
McCurry, Charles W.	157
McCurry, Fan Jordan	157
McCurry, Gerald	157
McCurry, Jewarl Louis	19
McCurry, Kathryn	157
McCurry, Mae Ellen	157
McCurry, Mae Elvin (Nunley)	19
McCurry, Shirley	157
McCuston, Ralph	3
McCuston. Mary Snyder	151
McCutchen, Merzy	2
McCutcheon, Edward Troy	149
McCutcheon, Margaret	158
McCutcheon, Mersey	149
McDaniel, Mildred	158
McDaniel, Adeline	212
McDaniel, Anna Lee	185
McDaniel, Anna Ruth	158
McDaniel, Annie Frances	158
McDaniel, Bill	32
McDaniel, Carl Ladue	62
McDaniel, Charles	158
McDaniel, Charles	19
McDaniel, Charles Ray	158
McDaniel, Claudine	158
McDaniel, Clay	62
McDaniel, Crawford	33, 158, 282
McDaniel, Eddie L.	159
McDaniel, Eulice	158
McDaniel, Frank	158
McDaniel, Grace	158, 302
McDaniel, Henry Clay	33
McDaniel, Henry Clay "Reggie"	30
McDaniel, Horace G	158
McDaniel, Jack	158
McDaniel, James	158
McDaniel, James Carlton, Sr.	158
McDaniel, James Franklin	158
McDaniel, James Franklin "Buzz"	253

Name	Page
McDaniel, Jamey Mae (Kilgore)	158
McDaniel, Jimmy Dewayne	158
McDaniel, Katie Mae (Campbell)	158
McDaniel, Linda (Ruehling)	158
McDaniel, Lucy	158
McDaniel, Melissa M (White)	258
McDaniel, Mildred	158
McDaniel, Nadine P.	43
McDaniel, Oscar Howell	158
McDaniel, Randall	158
McDaniel, Randall "Buck"	158
McDaniel, Randy Carl	158
McDaniel, Richard Lee	158
McDaniel, Rickey Dewayne "Gomer"	158
McDaniel, Rita	158
McDaniel, Rose Ann (Rogers)	158
McDaniel, Tammy	158
McDaniel, Tressie	140
McDaniel, Wanda J	62
McDaniel, William Eugene	158
McDaniel, Willie Mae	155, 159
McDaris, Anna	31, 302
McDerman, John	193
McDole, Cathy	289
McDole, Kirstin	193
McDonald, Anna Lee	195
McDonald, Anna Ruth	120
McDonald, Annilee	215
McDonald, Ben	119
McDonald, Eva	210
McDonald, Eva May	211
McDonald, John S.	211
McDonald, Margaret Elizabeth	159
McDonald, Melissa Carlie (Montgomery)	278
McDonald, William Wilbur	159
McDowell, Bessie	118
McDowell, Brian	218
McDowell, Ciela	159
McDowell, David	159
McDowell, Ruth Esther	159
McDowell, William Nelson	297
McDuffie, Marjorie	222
McElderry, Mary Ann	115
McElhaney, Georgia (Snyder)	89
McElhaney, Leoni Kate	159
McElhaney, Maude	159
McElhaney, Nathan Thomas	159
McElhenie, Norman M	159
McEwan, Helen Stewart	159
McFalls, R.M.	76
McFarland, Alice	181, 197
McFarland, Angie Marie	96
McFarland, Daisy (Tucker)	159
McFarland, Diane	159
McFarland, Edith	221
McFarland, Elbert	109
McFarland, Elijah	285
McFarland, Ester	159
McFarland, Fred	145
McFarland, George Carter	159
McFarland, James B. "JB"	159, 281
McFarland, James Cecil	159
McFarland, James Cecil "JC"	159
McFarland, James N.	159
McFarland, James Washington Lafayette Benjamin	155
McFarland, John	159
McFarland, Karen Renee	159
McFarland, Kate	159
McFarland, Lillie Myrtle "Daisy" (Tucker)	183
McFarland, Margaret	159
McFarland, Margaret Louise	159
McFarland, Martha Caroline	134
McFarland, Myrtle	277, 280, 281
McFarland, R.C.	150
McFarland, Thomas Edgar "Ed"	183
McFarland, Tressie	160
McFarland, William E. "Scooter Bill"	9
McFarland, William Edward	159
McFarland, William Henry	160
McGee, Edith	160
McGee, Eva Rosy (Hamby)	110
McGee, Evelyn Faye	160
McGee, G.W.	221
McGee, Hubert	160
McGee, Josh	160
McGee, Loyd	160
McGee, Melba	160
McGee, Nelma Dean (Wanamaker)	65
McGee, Stephanie Leigh-Ann (Hall)	160
McGee, Thelma	160
McGee, Thelma Ruth (Tate)	301
McGhee, Martha Jewell	160
McGill, Nettie Mae	160
McGinnis, Patsy Ruth (Meeks)	3
McGovern, Alice (Brown)	160
McGovern, Audrey Lucille	160
McGovern, Betty E. (Elliott)	239
McGovern, Bill	160
McGovern, Charles L.	160

Name	Page
McGovern, Elizabeth "Lizzie"	160
McGovern, James	187
McGovern, James	101
McGovern, John	155, 160
McGovern, Minnie	155, 160
McGovern, Nancy (Kilgroe)	105
McGovern, Pete	160
McGovern, Phillip H.	160
McGovern, Rosa	160
McGovern, Thomas B.	101
McGowan, Elizabeth	160
McGowan, Mattie	216
McGown, Nora Lee	88, 187
McGraw, Alberta	273
McGraw, Charlotte	284
McGraw, Dorothy Louise (Stucker)	70
McGraw, Elizabeth	161
McGraw, Samuel B	185
McGregor, Jesse Howard	161
McGregor, Sarah (Green)	161
McGregor, Vernice	161
McGuffey, Lee	27
McGuffey, Lue	215
McGuire, Mary Louise	193
McHone, Billy	219
McHone, Edward	161
McHone, Elsie	161
McHone, Emma	142
McHone, Harley	75
McHone, Louise Kathleen	75
McHone, Parthenia	213
McIntire, Unk	72, 75, 119
McIntosh, Ernest John	161
McIntosh, Floyd C.	161
McIntyre, Susan (Raney)	161
McIntyre, William Henry	161
McKee, Betty Jane	161
McKee, Wallace F	229
McKendrick, John D.	114
McKenzie, Estel Guthrie	296
McKenzie, Harold F.	161
McKenzie, John W.	161
McKnigh, Lois Ann (Ondrizek)	161
McKnight, Effie	161
McKnight, Frieda Lucille (Dickerson)	251
McKnight, George	161
McKnight, Grady H.	280
McKnight, Katherine K.	161
McKnight, Melvin Theodore	161
McKnight, Ronald Leroy	161
McLain, Charles Edward	161
McLain, Richard Lee	161
McLeard, Elva	161
McLeard, William	145
McMahan, Wanda	145
McMahan, Willie Mae	54
McMahon, Catharine	117
McMillan, Beulah Jean	94
McMillan, Henry Samuel	137
McNabb, Ethleen	137
McNabb, Obid Marion "Soap"	161
McNabb, Oma Louise (James)	161
McNabb, Thomas Crawford	161
McNabb, William Crandel	161
McNabb, William Crandle	161
McNeece, Edna M. (Huckabee)	161
McNeece, John	161
McNeece, Virgil N	161
McNeese, Winona	181
McNeil, Lela Dixie	270
McNew, Elvira Jane	20
McPheren, George	132
McPherson, Arnold	281
McPherson, Arnold M, Sr.	162
McPherson, Arnold M., Jr.	162
McPherson, Mamie Lee (Cox)	162
McQuiston, Clarence W.	162
McQuiston, Joseph Emery	162
McRae, John D.	162
McRae, Ruby (Layne)	162
McTaggart, Jerry	162
McWain, Alpha Neoma	138
McWain, Benjamin Franklin	242
McWain, Benjamin Franklin "Frank"	186
McWain, Buford	90
McWain, Buford Larry	162
McWain, Carrie Ola	162
McWain, Flora	90
McWain, Flora Mae	76, 166
McWain, Frank	73, 170
McWain, Hazel (Sloan)	187
McWain, Ola	162
McWain, Thomas Franklin	91
McWhirter, Amanda	162
McWilliams, James E	87
McWilliams, Melinda	162
McWilliams, William	162
Meade, Conley	162
Meade, Norman Cline	162
Meadows, Babette	162
Meadows, Cecil Udell (Byers)	162
Meadows, Charlie	162
Meadows, Daphine Posie	162

Name	Page
Meadows, Doris B.	162
Meadows, Ida Mae	256
Meadows, Jewell, Rosanell "Ann"	162
Meadows, John Mitchell	177
Meadows, Judy Dianne	162
Meadows, Lloyd Edward "George"	102
Meadows, Lloyd Ray	162
Meadows, Margaret	162
Meadows, Thomas Eugene, Jr. "Red"	216
Meadows, Thomas Eugene, Sr.	162
Meadows, Thomas Jefferson	162
Meadows, Tina Michelle	57
Meadows, Tommy Eugene	5
Meadows, Virginia	162
Meadows, William H.	162
Meadows, William Henry	162
Meadows, William Henry "Bill"	49
Meadows, William Henry Harrison "Hatton", Jr.	162
Meadows, William Henry Harrison, Sr.	162
Mears, Eddy	162
Medley, Albert J	281
Medley, Angela	163
Medley, Anna	162
Medley, Claude "Pork Chop"	25
Medley, Danny Pascal	162
Medley, Deborah Kaye (Gilmer)	162, 163
Medley, Edward	163
Medley, Edward Lee "Edd"	162, 163
Medley, Gladys	163
Medley, Helen	80
Medley, Helen Ruth	214
Medley, Isaac	170
Medley, James Isaac	163
Medley, John Albert	163
Medley, Johnny "Shorty"	163
Medley, Margie Ruth (Tucker)	12
Medley, Nancy Louise	163
Medley, Pascal	71
Medley, Pascal "Pack"	163
Medley, Patricia "Patti"	162
Medley, Rufus Emmett "Dock"	12
Medley, Willie Jo	163
Medlin, Ora	163
Meek, Marvin Vester, Rev.	28
Meeks, Thomas "Tommie"	163
Meeks, Walter Felix, Jr.	163
Meeks, "Denny" Mitchell	169
Meeks, Adam Shane	163
Meeks, Agnes	163
Meeks, Agnes Jane (Sanders)	168
Meeks, Aileen	163
Meeks, Alace	183
Meeks, Alfred D.	125
Meeks, Alfred James	171
Meeks, Alice	172
Meeks, Alice Ladean	169
Meeks, Allen	163
Meeks, Allene	163, 168
Meeks, Allie	85
Meeks, Allie (Smartt)	59
Meeks, Allie Belle	163
Meeks, Alma	210
Meeks, Alma (Smartt)	169
Meeks, Alma Jean	163
Meeks, Alma May	172
Meeks, Alvin "Jack"	237
Meeks, Amanda Gail	166
Meeks, Anna Dorean	109
Meeks, Anna Mae	164
Meeks, Anna Sophronie "Fronie"	196
Meeks, Annie	231
Meeks, Arthur	3
Meeks, Arthur Edward	6, 166, 168
Meeks, Barbara	163
Meeks, Barbara Allen	47, 255
Meeks, Baxter	255
Meeks, Becky	34
Meeks, Belle	32
Meeks, Benton	164
Meeks, Besselene/Bessie	169
Meeks, Bessie	269
Meeks, Betty	82, 107, 288, 290
Meeks, Bill	137
Meeks, Billie Jean	237
Meeks, Billie Louie "Bill"	7
Meeks, Billy	164
Meeks, Billy Leonard	170
Meeks, Birdie	165
Meeks, Bobby Dewayne	163
Meeks, Bobby Levoid	164
Meeks, Bonnie	164
Meeks, Bonnie Mae (Campbell)	36
Meeks, Bradford	164
Meeks, Bradford Orion	164
Meeks, Brady Wayne	164
Meeks, Brenda	164
Meeks, Buddy	272
Meeks, Buford E.	164, 211
Meeks, Buford Eldridge	164
Meeks, Buford Howard "Mousey"	164, 169
Meeks, Cam	164
Meeks, Carl David	229
Meeks, Carol	169
Meeks, Cecil Thomas	143

Name	Page
Meeks, Chandra Gayle	170
Meeks, Charles E.	164
Meeks, Charles Martin	164
Meeks, Charlie	164
Meeks, Charlotte	167
Meeks, Charlotte Main (Layne)	215
Meeks, Cheatom Clinton	164
Meeks, Cheatum Clinton	169
Meeks, Chester "Bug", Jr.	170
Meeks, Chester "Chet"	164, 167
Meeks, Child	164
Meeks, Clara	164
Meeks, Clara Louise	32
Meeks, Clara Mae	192
Meeks, Clarence Meeks	205
Meeks, Clarsie Mae	211
Meeks, Claude	80
Meeks, Claude, Sr.	165, 170
Meeks, Cleracy	169
Meeks, Clercie Mae	165
Meeks, Clercy "Sis"	80
Meeks, Clouse L	81
Meeks, Clyde	195
Meeks, Clyde Junior	165, 167
Meeks, Connie (Levan)	165, 168
Meeks, Creasie Eldridge (Green)	165
Meeks, Crede	165
Meeks, Cretty	171
Meeks, Dalpha	125
Meeks, Dalpha	83
Meeks, Dama Magdeline	47
Meeks, Danny F	286
Meeks, Danny Ray	165
Meeks, Dave	168
Meeks, David	164, 165
Meeks, David Jerome Wiley	165
Meeks, David's little son	165
Meeks, Dellia Emma	165
Meeks, Delma Inez (Forsyth)	172
Meeks, Diana M.	165
Meeks, Diane	165
Meeks, Diane (Sanders)	15
Meeks, Dollie	165
Meeks, Donald Henderson	167
Meeks, Donald Ray	160
Meeks, Donna	165
Meeks, Donna Lou	112, 224
Meeks, Dora Kay (Treat)	129
Meeks, Dorothy	165
Meeks, Dosia	101, 155, 190, 193
Meeks, Douglas	267
Meeks, Earnest	165, 171
Meeks, Earnest Dwayne	140
Meeks, Eddie Wayne	165
Meeks, Edgar	172
Meeks, Edna	61
Meeks, Edna "Eddie" (Scott)	5, 16, 0271
Meeks, Edwene	165
Meeks, Elihugh	115
Meeks, Elijah	v, vii
Meeks, Elijah Keys	150, 172
Meeks, Ellis	249
Meeks, Elmyra	171
Meeks, Elsie	213
Meeks, Erman	141, 143, 181, 198
Meeks, Ernest R.	3
Meeks, Ernie Sue (Dishman)	165
Meeks, Ethel Aileen	165
Meeks, Eula Mae	184
Meeks, Eva Bell	39
Meeks, Evelyn	10
Meeks, Evelyn Bell (Meeks)	170
Meeks, Everett	165
Meeks, Faye Barrett	223
Meeks, Felicia Lynn	vii, 166
Meeks, Flora	166
Meeks, Floyd Clayton	298
Meeks, France	166
Meeks, Frances H	171, 182
Meeks, Francis "France"	167, 168
Meeks, Francis Lee	165
Meeks, Frank Ray	166
Meeks, Fred	166, 168
Meeks, Fronie	155
Meeks, George	124
Meeks, George C.	133, 166, 167
Meeks, George C. "Banty"	125, 168
Meeks, George Cope	255
Meeks, George Cope "Banty"	163
Meeks, George Mac	166, 168, 172
Meeks, George Mack	163, 169
Meeks, Georgia	125
Meeks, Georgia Mae (Nunley)	62
Meeks, Geroge Cope "Banty"	166
Meeks, Gladys Faye	163
Meeks, Glenda Sue (Nunley)	166
Meeks, Gordon Vince	166
Meeks, Harvey Sonny	166
Meeks, Hattie	166
Meeks, Hazel Darlene (Frederick)	267
Meeks, Hence	166
Meeks, Henry Benton	298, 301
Meeks, Hollis	166, 169
Meeks, Hollis Melton	28
Meeks, Homer "Cotton"	166, 272

Name	Page
Meeks, Horace David	172
Meeks, Infant	163
Meeks, Irene	166, 167
Meeks, J.T.	19
Meeks, Jack	172
Meeks, Jackie	168
Meeks, Jackson	8
Meeks, Jackson Hiles	167
Meeks, Jackson Hiles "Jack" Meeks, Sr.	163
Meeks, Jackson Hiles, Sr.	191
Meeks, James	35
Meeks, James "Danny"	164, 166, 195
Meeks, James "Jim" Houston	168
Meeks, James A.	170
Meeks, James Britton	166
Meeks, James Buford	172
Meeks, James David	5
Meeks, James Dee	167
Meeks, James Donald	167
Meeks, James Donald "Don"	171
Meeks, James Edward	52
Meeks, James Frank	167
Meeks, James Frank	167
Meeks, James Gregory	169, 180
Meeks, James Isaac	167
Meeks, James L.	165, 168, 170
Meeks, James Lee	172
Meeks, James Leonard	167
Meeks, James Malcolm	167, 172
Meeks, James Ross	167
Meeks, Jane	229
Meeks, Jason Peter	281
Meeks, Jeffrey L.	167
Meeks, Jerry Riley	167
Meeks, Jess	164
Meeks, Jessie	164
Meeks, Jewell Virginia "Sissy"	170
Meeks, Jim	167
Meeks, Jincy Jane	220
Meeks, Joann (Braziel)	37
Meeks, JoAnn L.	167
Meeks, Joe Lester	172
Meeks, Joe Vernon	167
Meeks, John	169
Meeks, John "Crip John"	39, 59, 164, 168, 172
Meeks, John Henderson	170
Meeks, John K. "Buck"	167
Meeks, John T. Sr.	181
Meeks, John Vester	168
Meeks, John Vester, Jr.	163, 167
Meeks, John Vester, Sr.	165, 168
Meeks, John Wesley	168
Meeks, John William	168
Meeks, John, Jr.	170
Meeks, Johnny R. (Henry)	163
Meeks, Josephine	168
Meeks, Joyce	85, 167
Meeks, Joyce Charlene	172
Meeks, Judy Ann (Levan)	168
Meeks, Kathleen M.	168
Meeks, Kathy	168
Meeks, Kenneth Marshal	164
Meeks, Kenneth O	169
Meeks, Kitt	v, vii
Meeks, Larry	168
Meeks, Larry B.	164
Meeks, Laura	166
Meeks, Laura (Nelson)	168
Meeks, Laura M. (Bernard)	168
Meeks, Leah Dell	168
Meeks, Lee	245
Meeks, Lethia	3, 174
Meeks, Lillie Mae	232, 234, 235
Meeks, Linda	117
Meeks, Lisa	168
Meeks, Liza	28
Meeks, Lizzie (Sanders)	227
Meeks, Lois Elizabeth	168
Meeks, Lorene (Nunley)	168
Meeks, Lottie	168
Meeks, Louise	42, 43
Meeks, Louise "Bumble"	232
Meeks, Louvina	11
Meeks, Lucy	293
Meeks, Luella	35, 80, 229
Meeks, Lula Myrtle	304
Meeks, Mabel	256
Meeks, Mable Marie	132
Meeks, Margaret	233
Meeks, Margaret (Rose)	41
Meeks, Margaret Louise	168
Meeks, Margie	165, 168, 170
Meeks, Marjorie	191
Meeks, Marlee	276
Meeks, Mart Clinton	155
Meeks, Martha	52
Meeks, Martha Ellen (Shortridge)	243
Meeks, Martha Ethel	168
Meeks, Martha Faye "Willie"	264
Meeks, Martha Jewell	177
Meeks, Martha Myrtle	295
Meeks, Rev. Martin Vester	122
Meeks, Marvin A.	163
Meeks, Marvin H	168
Meeks, Marvin Vester, Rev.	167
Meeks, Mary	169, 170
Meeks, Mary Agnes	140, 228, 233, 234

Name	Page
Meeks, Mary Cathrine (May)	47
Meeks, Mary Elizabeth "Lizzie" (Sanders)	169
Meeks, Mary Ellen	169
Meeks, Mary Helen	169
Meeks, Mary Jo	99
Meeks, Mary Louise	164, 169
Meeks, Mary Magdalene	169
Meeks, Mary Myrtle	169
Meeks, Mary Ruth (Nunley)	72
Meeks, Mary Savannah	169
Meeks, Mattie	169
Meeks, Mattie Cleo	254
Meeks, Melinda	96, 282
Meeks, Melissa Faye (Brewer)	122
Meeks, Melvin Frank	169
Meeks, Michael Anthony	169
Meeks, Mickey Virgil	169
Meeks, Monte	169
Meeks, Nadine	171
Meeks, Nadine (Cannon)	265
Meeks, Nancy	169
Meeks, Nancy "Dollie"	90, 166, 186, 187
Meeks, Nancy Jo	163, 168
Meeks, Nancy L.	169
Meeks, Nancy Ocie Olla	169
Meeks, Naomi	44
Meeks, Nathan	36
Meeks, Newt	172
Meeks, Newt A.	76, 171
Meeks, Newt A.	73
Meeks, Newton Alexander	166
Meeks, Norman	170
Meeks, Norman M.	169
Meeks, Norman, Jr. "Junebug"	164, 165
Meeks, Norman, Sr.	169
Meeks, Ola	170
Meeks, Ola Idella	194
Meeks, Oma	73
Meeks, Orpha	168
Meeks, Oscar Franklin	108
Meeks, Pamela	165, 169
Meeks, Pascal	5
Meeks, Pat	171
Meeks, Paul	16
Meeks, Paul David	163
Meeks, Paul Ray	169
Meeks, Paulette (Johnson)	170
Meeks, Pearl	170
Meeks, Pearl M. (Tate)	250
Meeks, Peggy Sue	170
Meeks, Phillip Douglas	170
Meeks, Phillip Doyle	170
Meeks, Polly (Cope)	170
Meeks, Quarrels Sutton	170
Meeks, Ralph	170
Meeks, Ralph Adams	170
Meeks, Ralph C.	170
Meeks, Ralph Clinton	214
Meeks, Randall E.	170
Meeks, Randall, Jr.	vii
Meeks, Randall, Sr.	vii
Meeks, Ray	166
Meeks, Ray Edward	165, 170
Meeks, Rebecca "Becky"	170
Meeks, Rhonda	32
Meeks, Richard	144
Meeks, Richard N.	165, 166
Meeks, Ricky Allen	170
Meeks, Riley	170
Meeks, Riley	169, 172
Meeks, Riley D. "Dee"	231
Meeks, Robert Franklin "Bobby"	170
Meeks, Robert Franklin "Bobby"	171
Meeks, Robert James	170
Meeks, Roberta Jo (Dills)	167, 169
Meeks, Rochelle	171
Meeks, Ronald F.	77
Meeks, Rosa Lee (Kilgore)	167, 168, 171
Meeks, Rose	171
Meeks, Roxanne	86
Meeks, Ruby Omalee	85
Meeks, Ruth	272
Meeks, Ruth Hazel	59, 167, 216
Meeks, Sally R.	176
Meeks, Sam	171
Meeks, Samuel James	165, 170
Meeks, Sarah Agnes (Anderson)	193, 194
Meeks, Sarah Charlotte "Lottie"	171
Meeks, Sarah J. (Morgan) Byars	171
Meeks, Shalonda (Gallagher)	171
Meeks, Shane	171
Meeks, Shanna	156
Meeks, Sherry Oleta	30
Meeks, Shirley (Meeks)	171
Meeks, Shirley M. (Franks)	171
Meeks, Shirley Mae (Gibbs)	171
Meeks, Shirley Ruth	171
Meeks, Siebert	46
Meeks, Stanley	171
Meeks, Steven Darrell	224
Meeks, Sue	165
Meeks, Sue E. (Dishman)	164
Meeks, Susie	171
Meeks, Suzie	121
Meeks, Taylor	241
Meeks, Thelma	166, 167

Name	Page
Meeks, Thelma Lucille	83, 193, 211, 259
Meeks, Theresa (Robak) Mayo	173
Meeks, Thomas	171
Meeks, Thomas "Tommie"	164, 171, 172
Meeks, Thomas Tommie	172
Meeks, Tom	165
Meeks, Tommy	164
Meeks, Tressie	164
Meeks, Tressie Mae	276
Meeks, Uliss	5
Meeks, Unk	168
Meeks, Vance Myers	171
Meeks, Vester	183
Meeks, Vincy Lee	172
Meeks, Viney Sarah	102
Meeks, Virginia Carol	166
Meeks, Virginia Louise (Nunley)	172
Meeks, Virginia Pearl (Green)	172
Meeks, W. D. "Jack"	172
Meeks, W.D.	166
Meeks, Wanda June (Hampton)	92
Meeks, Wiley	172
Meeks, Wiley C.	166, 169
Meeks, Wiley Clinton	163
Meeks, Wiley D.	166, 210
Meeks, Wiley	170, 171, 172
Meeks, Will	231
Meeks, William	15, 170
Meeks, William Allan	166, 172, 189
Meeks, William C.	172
Meeks, William E.	169, 172
Meeks, William F.	171
Meeks, William Francis "France"	167
Meeks, William Grover	166, 257
Meeks, William H	164, 172
Meeks, William Ray "Billy"	270
Meeks, William Ray C	172
Meeks, William Thomas	172
Meeks, Willie "Tate"	209
Meeks, Willie Dee	172
Meeks, Willie Mae	164, 172
Meeks, Willie Myrtle	90
Meeks, Willis Benson	70
Meeks, Wilson Alexander	70
Meeks, Zach	vii
Meeksor, Colleen	172
Meenen, Peter Martin, Jr.	163
Meenen, Peter Martin, Sr.	172
Meimbresse, Carol	172
Meimbresse, Frederick	173
Meleen, Eric Martin	173
Meleen, Evelyn Estella (Gibson) Carman	173
Mell, George Washington	173
Mell, Hildegard Margaret (Jensen)	173
Mell, Lorenda	173
Mellen, Jacqueline	159
Melson, Tina	53
Melton, Bertha Louise	40
Melton, Betsy	182
Melton, Bill	86
Melton, Bryan Uriah	173
Melton, C.D.	173
Melton, Carl David	173
Melton, Connie Marie (Parsons)	173
Melton, Dave	173
Melton, Dawn Marie	142, 173
Melton, Delbert Carlton "Bolley"	173
Melton, Dyke H	91, 173
Melton, Floyd C	173
Melton, Harvey E	173
Melton, Harvey Houston	173
Melton, Hattie	173
Melton, Helen Louise	173
Melton, Henry "Bud"	173
Melton, Henry W.	168
Melton, Jack Foster	258
Melton, Lila	173
Melton, Mary Christine	141
Melton, Michael	204
Melton, Millie	173
Melton, Rice	86
Melton, Ruth	86
Melton, Steven Wayne	224
Melton, Tom	263
Melton, Unknown	173
Melton, Wiley B.	303
Merell, James	173
Merett, Sarah	250
Merrell, Albert E.	71
Merrell, Hassie M. "Pebbles" (Hill)	173
Merrell, Jennie Louise	173
Merrell, Jimmy	206
Merrell, Juanita	173
Merrell, Peggy	173
Merriman, Jean	249
Merriman, JoAnne	232
Merriman, Mae	185
Merriman, Martha Layne	289
Merritt, Wanda	301
Messer, Anna Mae	162
Messer, Doc Lewis	174
Messick, Hazel Mae	174
Metcalf, Barbara	276
Metcalf, Charles, Mrs.	62
Metcalfe, Barbara	244
Metcalfe, John	62

Name	Page
Metcalfe, Joseph Maurice	95
Metcalfe, Kerry	71
Metcalfe, Stephen	32
Metrolis, George Eric	109
Metrolis, George J.	173
Meyer, Alma Rosaline Christina	173
Meyer, Anna Maria	26
Meyer, Anna Maria	264
Meyer, Herman Eduard	265
Meyer, John H.	173
Meyer, Joseph	26
Meyers, Robert Soward	265
Middlebrock, Arizona	247
Middleton, Vicki	15
Milbrath, Mary Lou Shook	123
Milbrath, Ralph E.	174
Miles, Florence	174
Miller, Alden	151
Miller, Alvada	174
Miller, Anna Mae (Messer)	230
Miller, Anne	174
Miller, Bernice	10, 250
Miller, Billy Wayne	131
Miller, Cathy	174
Miller, Cecil	174
Miller, Charles Winchester	93
Miller, Clinton	17
Miller, Colton James	174
Miller, Don	174
Miller, Esther Alice	174
Miller, Frankie	86, 196
Miller, Goldie Lee (Meeks)	174
Miller, Harry R.	174
Miller, Helen M.	174
Miller, Henry L.	17
Miller, Jacob Thomas	174
Miller, Joyce	174
Miller, Lee	107
Miller, Louetta	174
Miller, Louise Marie	161
Miller, Marie	262
Miller, Marie A (Fales)	174
Miller, Marvin	174
Miller, Michael D.	174
Miller, Naomi	174
Miller, Pamela	11
Miller, Peter A.	73
Miller, R.E.	148
Miller, Randall "Randy"	11
Miller, Robert G, Jr.	174
Miller, Robert G. Sr.	174
Miller, Ronald "Ronney" Campbell	174
Miller, Roy Alton	174
Miller, Royal	174
Miller, Ruby May	65
Miller, Rudolph C	3
Miller, Ruth	231
Miller, Ruth (Eckard)	148
Miller, Sallie Mae (Young)	174
Miller, Tammy Rae (Fults)	174
Miller, Ulys Clayton	174
Miller, Virginia Katherine	119
Miller, Willie Mae	164
Millirons, Robert R.	3
Millirons, Robert Raymond	174
Millirons, Tammy	174
Millraney, Tennie Sue	174
Millrany, Wayne	174
Mills, Bertha	174
Mills, Flora	240
Millsaps, Larry Newton	229
Millsaps, Ruby Mae	175
Millsaps, Silas	175
Milner, Joseph Hartwell	175
Milner, Naomi (Brandon)	175
Milner, Oscar Allen	175
Milner, Patty	175
Milstead, Charlie	153
Milstead, Forrest Eugene	175
Mince, James Earl	175
Mince, Jimmy M.	175
Minkler, April	175
Minkler, Jackson Dwight	175
Minkler, Ray Ingman	175
Minor, Donald Eugene "Gene", Sr.	175
Minor, Donald Eugene, Sr.	175
Minor, Euless Mose	175
Minor, Huetta Jean	175
Minton, Edith Turner	175
Minton, Josephine	72
Minton, Loretta	128
Minton, S.T.	294
Mitchell, Emmett Estle	128
Mitchell, Gertrude	175
Mitchell, Gertrude Leona	289
Mitchell, Gertrude Leona (Dobbs)	226
Mitchell, H. Mattie (House)	175
Mitchell, Henry Newton	175
Mitchell, James David	129, 175
Mitchell, John	229
Mitchell, Kelsey H.	175
Mitchell, Mary	175
Mitchell, Mattie (White)	13, 95
Mitchell, Paige	175
Mitchell, Pasgal Marvin	125
Mitchell, Precious Pearly	175
Mitchell, Willie B.	273
Modschiedler, John	175

Name	Page
Modschiedler, Larry L.	176
Modschiedler, Leslie	176
Moffett, Abigail	79
Moffitt, Brenda Gail Davis	189
Molissee, Josephine	239
Moneyheffer, Bertha (Henegar)	39
Moneyheffer, William H.	176
Montgomery, Malissa	176
Montomery, John A.	118
Moody, Fanny Ann	159
Moon, Annie Sue	122
Moon, Austin D.	14
Moon, Frances Marie	176
Mooney, Albert Lucis	176
Mooney, Buddy	176
Mooney, Flora	176
Mooney, Georgia Goodman	177
Mooney, Gladys	176
Mooney, James	136
Mooney, Joe	176
Mooney, Juanita	162, 176
Mooney, Katherine	153
Mooney, Lillian	248
Mooney, Nellie	18, 19, 134
Mooney, Paul W.	281
Mooney, Willie Belle	176
Mooneyham, Douglas E. Sr.	176
Mooneyham, Douglas E., Jr.	176
Moore Cortner Funeral Home	iii
Moore, Burlin Lee	176
Moore, Charles Donald	176
Moore, Darthula	176
Moore, Dorothy	155
Moore, Elizabeth	176
Moore, Ethel Theodosia	192
Moore, Flora Louise	2
Moore, George W.	44
Moore, Gertie	155
Moore, Grace	70
Moore, J. Horace, Jr.	122
Moore, James Willard	176
Moore, Jane	176
Moore, Janet Lou (Sternkopf)	161
Moore, Jessy Howard	176
Moore, John Carroll	176
Moore, Lynwood	176
Moore, Marry Helen	176
Moore, Novella (Hargis)	209
Moore, Ova	176
Moore, Ray	155
Moore, Rebecca	232
Moore, Ruthie Jane	171
Moore, Samuel	179
Moore, Silas Alton "Tom"	217
Moore, Terry Lee	176
Moore, Thomas	176
Moore, Thomas Davis, Jr.	176
Moorehead, Stephanie	176
Moran Place	176
Moran, Bessie Elizabeth "Bet"	254
Moran, Bridgett	177
Moran, Faye	177
Moran, Franklin Peter	77
Moran, James	177
Moran, Jerri	177
Moran, Karen	177
Moran, Lillie	177
Moran, Lillie	98
Moran, Mark II	222
Moran, Mark III	177
Moran, Mark Wilson	177
Moran, Patrick Ellis	177
Moran, Peter	177
Moran, Terri	177
Moran, Tom	177
Moran, Wiley	177
Morefield, Anne	77
Moreland, Karl Phillip	276
Moreland, Mona Griswold (Sweeton)	177
Morgan, Allie Mae	177
Morgan, Appielona O'Neal	234
Morgan, Bertie	177
Morgan, Betty	178
Morgan, Betty Jean "Mary Lou"	177
Morgan, Charles	177
Morgan, Charles J.	178
Morgan, Charles William	178
Morgan, Craig Franklin	177
Morgan, David Garvin	177
Morgan, David Jackson	177
Morgan, Dorothy Mae	177
Morgan, Edmund	177
Morgan, Edna	2
Morgan, Edna Vera	188, 194
Morgan, Essie	71
Morgan, Ethel	236
Morgan, Etta Lee	177
Morgan, Franklin	2, 8
Morgan, Franklin D.	177
Morgan, George W.	177
Morgan, George Washington "Judge"	177
Morgan, Hazel	177
Morgan, J.T.	257
Morgan, Jackie Ray	178
Morgan, Jody	177
Morgan, John A.	227
Morgan, John Lonzo	177

Name	Page
Morgan, Lorene (Campbell)	177
Morgan, Malinda	177
Morgan, Margie Lynn	280
Morgan, Mary Louise	209
Morgan, Mildred Frances	206
Morgan, Millie	191
Morgan, Mose Allen	223
Morgan, Nell (Nunley)	257
Morgan, Nellie	178
Morgan, Patsy Louise	196
Morgan, Phyllis Ann	178
Morgan, Rose Marie "Rosie" (Dykes)	178
Morgan, Rudy Lee	178
Morgan, Sarah J.	178
Morgan, Shawn Lisa	31
Morgan, Thomas A.	178
Morgan, Tim	178
Morgan, Tom Ray	231
Morgan, Walter Orene	178
Morgan, William M.	177, 178
Morgan, Zac	171
Morgan, Zeb	178
Morris, Barbara	178
Morris, Bessie	178
Morris, Caldonia "Callie"	112
Morris, Christopher	64
Morris, Ed Jackson	178
Morris, Edy	112
Morris, Elbert T	80
Morris, Faye	178
Morris, Franklin Taylor	226
Morris, Jessie	178
Morris, Johnny Lee	178
Morris, Kenneth	178
Morris, Kim	178
Morris, Laura	178
Morris, Lee Roy	292
Morris, Mary Elizabeth (Henry)	178
Morris, Maymie	178
Morris, Melissa	178
Morris, Minnie Mae	178
Morris, Rita T.	107
Morris, Timothy Wade	178
Morris, Wanda	178
Morrison, Adam Theodore Mitchell	178
Morrison, Agnes	178
Morrison, Alfred	206
Morrison, Alfred, Jr.	180
Morrison, Allen Eugene	179, 180
Morrison, Allie Edith (Glisson)	178
Morrison, Arnold T.	178
Morrison, Arnold Theodore	179
Morrison, Ben	178
Morrison, Ben Jr.	77, 179
Morrison, Benjamin H.	121
Morrison, Betty Jean (Dishroom)	179
Morrison, Billy Keith	179
Morrison, Carolyn Sue	179
Morrison, Charlene "Char" (Jacobs)	50
Morrison, Claude Edward	179
Morrison, Claude Wesley	179
Morrison, Cyrus	23, 179
Morrison, Dan Stanford	180
Morrison, Danny Ray	179, 180
Morrison, David Alfred	179
Morrison, Delores	179
Morrison, Edith Cordelia	189
Morrison, Elsia (Nolan)	69
Morrison, Elsie Lee (Johnson)	179
Morrison, Ester	179
Morrison, Ethel	146
Morrison, George	178
Morrison, Glenda	179
Morrison, Hazel	22
Morrison, Huch Elmer	142
Morrison, Hugh L	179
Morrison, Hunter Hobbs	180
Morrison, Isom Moses	179
Morrison, Jamie	179
Morrison, Jerry E.	63
Morrison, Jerry R.	179
Morrison, John C.	179
Morrison, Johnny Kenneth	179
Morrison, Jr., Ben	179
Morrison, Kathleen (Nunley)	179
Morrison, Kathy	179
Morrison, Lee Robert	129, 178
Morrison, Letha	179
Morrison, Linda	58, 59, 179, 243
Morrison, Lonnie	144
Morrison, Lonnie Harold	178
Morrison, Lonnie Norman	180, 302
Morrison, Mandy	179
Morrison, Martin Charles	179
Morrison, Mary	179, 180
Morrison, Maudie	201
Morrison, Mitchell	22
Morrison, Nellie D.	179
Morrison, Oma Lee (Meeks)	180
Morrison, Ozia Bonnal "O.B."	180
Morrison, Patti	180
Morrison, Paul	192
Morrison, Phyllis	179
Morrison, Randy	192
Morrison, Rene	179

Morrison, Ricky	77	Mott, Linda Rose (Ware)	181	Murray, Gladys	181
Morrison, Robert Lee	129, 178	Mott, Tommy	181	Murray, Joseph	181
Morrison, Ronald	180	Mottern, Jack Henderson	181	Murray, Keith Allen, Sr.	181
Morrison, Ruthie Jane	180	Mottern, Lorene (Patterson)	181	Murray, Lydia Ellen	181
Morrison, Stephany	180	Mounts, Lionel Moise	181	Murray, Mattie M. (Layne)	147
Morrison, Teresa (Stevens)	180	Mounts, Maryon	46	Murray, Minnie	181
Morrison, William "Bill"	180	Mowdry, Mamie	46	Murray, Opal R. (Meeks)	54
Morrison, William Daniel	179	Mowdry, Mike	20	Murray, Sharon	181
Morrison, William T	180	Mueller, Elizabeth Anna	20	Murray, Thomas	181
Morrison, Wilma Grace	283	Mullens, Lois	248	Murvin, Theoren	54
Morrison, Zachary Taylor	180	Muller, Barbara	101	Murvin, Theoren J., Jr.	181
Morrow, Betty (Carrick)	179	Mullican, Arthur Gyle	244	Muse, Mary	181
Morrow, Willie Edward "Bill"	180	Mullican, James Arthur	181	Musgrove, Margaret Inez	56
Morton, Edith	180	Mullins, Mary Susan	181	Muthling, Waldermar Friedrich	14
Moser, Brandy	140, 142	Mullins, Phyllis Ann	296	Myers, Altalene "Tiny" (Sissom)	181
Moses, Marlene	134	Muncey, Ina	110	Myers, Alton	182
Mosier, Charles	141	Mundy, Helen	286	Myers, Annie	183
Mosier, Raymond	180	Murphy, Crista Jane (Cornelison)	223	Myers, Barbara Mooney	ii,iii
Mosley, Esther	180	Murphy, Dorothy Ella (McNeece)	181	Myers, Benson	30
Mosley, Mildred Christine (O'Neal) Sanders	210	Murphy, Floyd	181	Myers, Bernie Robert	184
Mosley, Unk	180	Murphy, III, Charles Austin	22	Myers, Bettie	182
Moss, Gisela Alwine Karla (Kropp)	180	Murphy, Juanita Carol (Harlan)	181	Myers, Betty	125
Moss, Gislea A.	180	Murphy, Morris V.	181	Myers, Bill	196
Moss, James David	180	Murphy, Paul Silas	181	Myers, Billie Faye (Hampton)	183, 258
Moss, John Grover	180	Murphy, Robert	181	Myers, Bonnie Ozell (Patterson)	182
Moss, Mary Shilo	180	Murr, Ada	55, 181	Myers, Brent	182
Moss, Thomas Wesbury	180	Murr, Ada Ellen	251, 271	Myers, Buddy	182
Moss, Virginia A.	180	Murr, Albert Bailey	56	Myers, Calvin	183
Moss, William Asa	180	Murray, Adam Troy "Scoobie"	199	Myers, Carmon	56, 182
Moss, William Lee	180	Murray, Bill	181	Myers, Carmon Ernest, Sr	182
Moss, William Lee, Jr.	180	Murray, Brenda	181	Myers, Cebert C.	182
Moss., Jr., William Lee	180	Murray, Clyde	54	Myers, Celia	182
Mote, Hazel Olive	180	Murray, David	181	Myers, Charles	165
Mott, Claudie	239	Murray, David Vincent	181	Myers, Charlie	21
Mott, Floyd	181	Murray, Faye	181	Myers, Cheatum	182
		Murray, George	181		

Myers, Christopher C.	125	
Myers, Clara Mae	126	
Myers, Claude	255	
Myers, Claude Eugene	183	
Myers, Cleo	182	
Myers, Clifton	61	
Myers, David	182, 184	
Myers, David Allen	182	
Myers, Debra	182	
Myers, Delbert "Delva"	182	
Myers, Denver	182	
Myers, Denver Alton	202	
Myers, Donald "Catfish"	183	
Myers, Donald Edward "Donnie"	182	
Myers, Donald Ray	182	
Myers, Edgar	182	
Myers, Eliza Jane	182	
Myers, Emma	160	
Myers, Emma B. (Holt)	137	
Myers, Ethel Aileen (Meeks)	182	
Myers, Evelyn D (Bates)	182	
Myers, Everette B.	182	
Myers, Floyd	34	
Myers, Franklin S.	182	
Myers, Gene D	182	
Myers, Georgia M. (Knox)	182	
Myers, Glenn Hardy	183	
Myers, Henry Clay	184	
Myers, Ina Myers	184	
Myers, Jacob	183	
Myers, James	184	
Myers, James Herman	183, 287	
Myers, James Lee	183	
Myers, James Merrell	183	
Myers, James W.	183	
Myers, Jeana	182, 183	
Myers, Jim W	182	
Myers, John	184
Myers, John J.	182
Myers, John K.	183
Myers, John Kenneth "Duck"	182
Myers, John Will	183
Myers, Johnny	ix, 182, 183
Myers, Julie	183
Myers, Katherine	49
Myers, Kathy	202
Myers, Keith R.	182
Myers, Kenneth Dewayne	183
Myers, Lavina "Vina" (Stoner)	183
Myers, Leonard	183
Myers, Lettie Lucille	106, 183
Myers, Lillie	183
Myers, Lillie Frances (Davis)	78
Myers, Lillie May	183
Myers, Lonnie	21
Myers, Lou Ada	182
Myers, Louisa	258
Myers, Lucy	12
Myers, Luther	106
Myers, Lyda	38, 304
Myers, Lydia	106, 117
Myers, Mae Wanda (McFarland)	183
Myers, Mamie	183
Myers, Mancel Perry	294
Myers, Mancil Perry	184
Myers, Margaret Abigail	183
Myers, Margie Ann	49
Myers, Marshall E.	198
Myers, Martha Jane	183
Myers, Martha Katherine (Tigue) Brazile	75
Myers, Mary	183
Myers, Mary	12
Myers, Mary Belle (King)	269
Myers, Mary Catherine "Kate"	183
Myers, Mary Elisabeth	3
Myers, Mary Ellen "Toodie" (Hobbs)	21
Myers, Michael Hardy	183
Myers, Mildred	184
Myers, Mildred Jewel	123
Myers, Mitchel	182
Myers, Mollie (Davis)	184
Myers, Myles Benson	184
Myers, Myrlene	75
Myers, Nannie	287
Myers, Orpha Jean (Griffith)	243
Myers, Pamela G. (Conry)	184
Myers, Pascal	184
Myers, Patricia	183
Myers, Paul Jacob	75, 276
Myers, Perrie Ula	184
Myers, Philomena	73
Myers, Renice	265
Myers, Robert Elijah	109
Myers, Ruby	196
Myers, Ruby Eleanor	55, 124, 195
Myers, Ruby Jewel	192, 194
Myers, Rudy Wendell	184
Myers, Speeker	184
Myers, Stanley	183
Myers, T. Cora	184
Myers, Teresa Ann	124
Myers, Thomas L.	184
Myers, Thomas Snoddy	184
Myers, Tressie	187
Myers, Vance	157
Myers, Vance "Tubby"	182
Myers, Vela	184
Myers, Vernon	287

Myers, Vina Stoner	ix	Neal, Mildred Ada	184	Newson, Charles Wilkie	126
Myers, Waldo	12, 183	Neal, Roy	121	Newson, Laura Jean (Willoughby)	185
Myers, Wendell	184	Neal, Sally	185	Newson, Tonny W.	185
Myers, Wendell Matthew	184	Neal, William	184	Newson, Tonny Wilkie	185
Myers, William	184	Nearn, Mansfield Lafayette	184	Nichols, Ed	185
Myers, William Cecil	184	Nearn, Mary L.	185	Nichols, Flossie	12
Myers, William Douglas	183	Nearn, Nellie P.	185	Nichols, Pearl	23
Myers, William Floyd	183	Needham, Katina	185	Nichols, William	185
Myers, Willie Mae	83, 281	Neighbors, Lucy	130	Nicholson, James L, III	81
Myrick, Dorothy	232	Nelson, Dennis	195	Nicholson, James. Jr.	185
Nabors, Mary	176	Nelson, George	185	Nigg, Joseph	185
Naegeli, Kasper	46	Nelson, George Edward	290	Nivison, LeRoy	185
Nance, Brenda	305	Nelson, Harvey	185	Nivison, Leroy N.	185
Nance, Curtis	111	Nelson, Jeanette	185	Nivison, Lois Leta Rutherford	185
Nance, John Lafayette	184	Nelson, John	184	Nivison, Wilhelmina (Weber)	185
Nance, John William Jasper	184	Nelson, Theodore Ray	168	Nix, Evelyn Mae	185
Nance, Katie	273	Nester, Harvey Wilson	185	Nix, George Ray	117
Nance, Kayla Leigh Ann	184	Nester, Honor Eda Nettie (Dockum)	185	Nix, Henry Joel	185
Nance, Leonard Curtis	184	Nevill, Martha Jane	185	Nix, Infant	186
Nance, Lonnie B.	184	Nevill, Nancy Ann	28	Nix, Irmgard	185
Nance, Margaret Fay	184	Nevill, Sarah Lucinda	293, 294	Nix, Joyce	185
Nance, Mayna Rose (Avent)	184	Nevills, Hamp	109	Nix, Luther	248
Nance, Mitchel G.	184	Nevills, Sarah	237	Nix, Luther G.	185, 250
Nance, Sue	184	Newbern, Helen	237	Nix, Mildred L. (Smartt)	185
Nance, Walter	85	Newby, Rhonda	185	Nix, Nina Mae	186
Nancy, Michael Lonnie	184	Newcomb, Ruby Lillian	177	Nix, William Bedford	250
Napier, Frances	184	Newman, Eddie Clara	14	Nixon, John Edwin	29
Napier, Martha Jane	166	Newman, Fannie Belle	160	Nixon, Martha Louise (Kilgore)	186
Nasso, Joan Bishop	ii, iii	Newman, George Martin	190	Nodine, Rachel E.	186
Neal, Alice Elizabeth	295	Newman, John W.	79	Noel, Cynthia Lee (White)	23
Neal, Fred	22, 23	Newman, Unk	160	Noel, Dean	186
Neal, James David	185	Newsome, Almedia	161	Nolan, Alfred "Buddy"	186
Neal, James Robert	184	Newsome, Buford Eugene	141	Nolan, Alpha Neoma (Meeks)	187
Neal, Jerry W.	184	Newsome, Charles A.	185	Nolan, Annie Ruth	186
Neal, John Wilburn, Sr.	184	Newsome, Grover W	185	Nolan, Barbara Jean (Leon)	186
Neal, Lily Mae	177	Newsome, James Henry	185		
Neal, Lizzie	185	Newsome, Serena	185		

Name	Page
Nolan, Bertha Jane	186
Nolan, Charcie Dean	96, 252
Nolan, Christine	93
Nolan, Claude	186
Nolan, Clyde	186
Nolan, Clyde Allen	186
Nolan, Clyde Allen	186
Nolan, Dale	186
Nolan, Dale Baxter	187
Nolan, Danny Wayne	186
Nolan, Dee Jay	303
Nolan, Donna	186
Nolan, Donna Beth	186
Nolan, Donnie	39
Nolan, E. Ster	186
Nolan, Edna	193
Nolan, Edward Louis	115, 116
Nolan, Elsie (Nunley)	186
Nolan, Elsie Harriet	186
Nolan, Elvie Ellen	178
Nolan, Eugene "Rudy"	5
Nolan, Freeman Doug	186
Nolan, Freeman Douglas	187
Nolan, Gaberial (Hillis)	186
Nolan, Gilliam	186
Nolan, Gilliam Baxter	186
Nolan, Harvey	171, 186
Nolan, Helen	103
Nolan, Herman	82
Nolan, James	186
Nolan, James Jerome	179
Nolan, James Willoughby	186
Nolan, Jimmy	185
Nolan, Jimmy Dale	186
Nolan, Jimmy Leefayette	186
Nolan, Joey	186
Nolan, John	39
Nolan, John Jerome	186, 211
Nolan, Katherine Lucille (Kilgore)	186
Nolan, Laura Frances	186
Nolan, Leah	140
Nolan, Loretta	282
Nolan, Mabel	128
Nolan, Maggie Marie (Curtis)	249
Nolan, Mamie Esther	186
Nolan, Marcella	162
Nolan, Marcie	106
Nolan, Marvin	227
Nolan, Mary Frances	186
Nolan, Mary Louise "Molley" (Partin)	254
Nolan, Maybell	186
Nolan, Milda Mary	250
Nolan, Mildie	85
Nolan, Mildred	172
Nolan, Myrtle	211
Nolan, Naomi (McWain)	235, 237
Nolan, Ola Mae	187
Nolan, Oscar Edward	186
Nolan, Raymond Charleston	186
Nolan, Shelia Faye (Campbell)	186
Nolan, Shirley Jean (Ward)	187
Nolan, Sr., Alvin Lee	187
Nolan, Stone Garrett	187
Nolan, Sudonna	187
Nolan, Thelma	187
Nolan, William Edward "Ed"	187
Norman, Christine	186
Norman, Dwayne Fulton	187
Norman, Henry	187
Norman, Newton	187
Norman, William Dillard	187
Norman, William Franklin, Rev.	258
Norris, Arene	187
Norris, Arwin Eugene	187
Norris, Billy J.	187
Norris, Bobby Eugene	187
Norris, Clarence E.	187
Norris, Edith	187
Norris, Elizabeth	187
Norris, Elmer Lee	219
Norris, John Wesley	187
Norris, Jossie Pearl	286
Norris, Lena Mae	235
Norris, Lola Bell	143
Norris, Louella (Grimes)	292
Norris, Melissa Carol (Prater)	187
Norris, Sam	187
Norris, Sharon	187
Norris, Velma Louise	234
Norris, William Lester	185
North, John Lee	291
North, Vera	122
Northcut, Fannie Louise (McCraw)	122
Northcut, Harris Bradford	187
Northcut, Lawson Hill	187
Northcut, Mary Elizabeth (Myers)	187
Northcut, Stephen Adrian	187
Northcut, William E.	187
Northcut, William Elihu	187
Northcutt, Alice	187
Northcutt, Angela A.	170
Northcutt, Clarence	29
Northcutt, Crystal Eddie	151
Northcutt, Edith Blondell	188
Northcutt, Edward Fultz	148
Northcutt, Felicia	188
Northcutt, George Benson	55
Northcutt, George Stanley	188

Name	Page
Northcutt, Grady W.	188
Northcutt, Hunter Andrew	28
Northcutt, James Claudie	188
Northcutt, Jemima	9
Northcutt, Jim	279
Northcutt, Jo Nathan	102
Northcutt, Joseph	188
Northcutt, Lynngail	188
Northcutt, Marty	188
Northcutt, Mrs. Spencer	188
Northcutt, Nadine (Hampton)	188
Northcutt, Robby Dwayne	188
Northcutt, Sammy Faye	188
Northcutt, Spencer	256
Northcutt, Stanley	188
Northcutt, Unk	188
Northcutt, Vernon	272
Northcutt, William Earl	210
Northcutt, Willie	188
Northcutt, Willie Mae (Payne)	188
Northcutt's Cove Road	vi
Northstine, Ida Faye M.	188
Norwood, Donald Wade	43
Norwood, James "Jim"	188
Norwood, Lizzie (Keel)	188
Norwood, Rosie Lee	188
Norwood, Samuel Henry, Sr.	134
Norwood, Wilburn C.	188
Novak, Pauline	188
Nunely, Carolyn	30
Nuncly, Mary Elizabeth	195
Nunley Oaks Cemetery	vii
Nunley, Lizzie	188
Nunley Smartt, Janie Elizabeth (Nunley)	53
Nunley, Abby	188
Nunley, Ada	204
Nunley, Ada Bell	178, 190, 198
Nunley, Albert Carroll	144
Nunley, Albert Douglas	178, 190, 198
Nunley, Alice Irene	188
Nunley, Alma Lee	210
Nunley, Alvin	183
Nunley, Alvin Murphy	47, 189, 194
Nunley, Amelia Faith	191, 193, 263
Nunley, Ann	188
Nunley, Ann Higgins	vii
Nunley, Anthony Dean	193
Nunley, Arthur	188
Nunley, Audrey Lea (McBee)	250
Nunley, Avery Willis	188
Nunley, Bailey	197
Nunley, Barbara	191
Nunley, Barbara Grace	265
Nunley, Barbara Jean (Roberts)	250
Nunley, Barney	188, 189
Nunley, Barney Jasper	188
Nunley, Barton	189
Nunley, Beatrice	194
Nunley, Beatrice (Whitt)	283
Nunley, Beatrice Franklikn	189
Nunley, Belle	74
Nunley, Berta	229
Nunley, Bessie	189
Nunley, Betty	193, 270
Nunley, Betty Lou Saint	68, 172
Nunley, Betty Loulene "Tarp" (Short)	197
Nunley, Beverly Jo	189
Nunley, Biddie	189
Nunley, Billy D.	98
Nunley, Billy Earl	189
Nunley, Billy Joe	189
Nunley, Billy Ray	189
Nunley, Blenn	189
Nunley, Bob	236
Nunley, Bobby Allen	189, 192
Nunley, Bobby C.	189
Nunley, Bobby D.	189
Nunley, Bobby Gene "Bob"	189
Nunley, Bobby Joe "Jody"	189
Nunley, Bonaill B.	192
Nunley, Bonell	189
Nunley, Bonnie	195
Nunley, Brenda Gayle	27
Nunley, Brooke	6
Nunley, Bruce Edward	195
Nunley, Buford	189
Nunley, Bunia	189
Nunley, C Carroll	142
Nunley, Caldonia (Bost)	189
Nunley, Carl David	189
Nunley, Carl Dewayne	193
Nunley, Carl Ed	195
Nunley, Carl Edward	192
Nunley, Carl Edward, Jr.	189
Nunley, Carol	189
Nunley, Carrie	189, 197
Nunley, Carrie Bell (Parsons)	241
Nunley, Catherine	190
Nunley, Celia	158
Nunley, Charles	184
Nunley, Charles D.	179, 190
Nunley, Charles E.	191
Nunley, Charles Edward	264
Nunley, Charles N. "Shot"	190
Nunley, Charles William	190
Nunley, Charley	192, 194, 196, 197
Nunley, Charlie	194, 197

Name	Pages
Nunley, Charlie D	282
Nunley, Charlie, Jr.	189, 190, 191, 193
Nunley, Christeen (Ruckweed)	190
Nunley, Christine	190
Nunley, Clarence	48
Nunley, Clarence Edward	190, 194, 195, 198
Nunley, Clark	195
Nunley, Clifford Leroy	197
Nunley, Clytus	190
Nunley, Connie Ray	190, 197
Nunley, Cora Elizabeth	190
Nunley, Cora Jean (Kilgore)	76
Nunley, Cory	190
Nunley, Daisy	188
Nunley, Danny James	124
Nunley, Daryl G.	195
Nunley, David	190
Nunley, David Abraham	191
Nunley, Deloris Janie May (Harris)	190
Nunley, Dillie	190
Nunley, Dixie	197
Nunley, Dixie Lee	273
Nunley, Donald Ray	140, 143, 164
Nunley, Donna	188
Nunley, Donnie Lee	196
Nunley, Dora	190
Nunley, Dora Ann	13
Nunley, Dorothy	282
Nunley, Earl Dean	269
Nunley, Earnest	190
Nunley, Ed	198
Nunley, Edna	192, 195
Nunley, Edna Allene	36, 105
Nunley, Edna Josephine (Meeks)	200
Nunley, Edna Mae	191
Nunley, Edwin	191
Nunley, Elaine	191
Nunley, Elias	190
Nunley, Elizabeth	197
Nunley, Elizabeth Betty	35, 106, 107, 192, 242
Nunley, Elizabeth Jane (Sanders)	34
Nunley, Ella Lois	191
Nunley, Elsie	244
Nunley, Elsie Kathleen	193, 198, 249
Nunley, Elva	23
Nunley, Emaline (Phipps)	271
Nunley, Emanuel	191
Nunley, Emma	34
Nunley, Ernest	142
Nunley, Ernest	192
Nunley, Etta Bea	191
Nunley, Etta Lee	9
Nunley, Eula Augusta	283
Nunley, Fannie	93
Nunley, Faye (Hill)	6, 189, 190, 191, 193, 258
Nunley, Florence	191
Nunley, Frances	241
Nunley, Francis Marion	289
Nunley, Frank P.	113, 230
Nunley, Freddy	124, 205
Nunley, Freddy Allen	193
Nunley, George	vii, 191
Nunley, George Edward	172, 191
Nunley, George Franklin	191
Nunley, Georgia	131
Nunley, Geraldine	92, 273
Nunley, Gilliam	165, 169
Nunley, Gordon	197
Nunley, Grace Josephine (Sartain)	74, 280
Nunley, Graham	191
Nunley, Harley Dee	21, 56, 95, 109, 189, 191, 272
Nunley, Harriett (Smith)	191
Nunley, Harvey	191
Nunley, Hattie	71, 105, 188, 194
Nunley, Hattie Demetro	166
Nunley, Helen	8
Nunley, Helen Marie	107
Nunley, Henderson Pleasant	191
Nunley, Henry	189
Nunley, Henry Gordon	192
Nunley, Henry Howard	192
Nunley, Henry Newton	189
Nunley, Henry Newton Nunley	192
Nunley, Herbert	192
Nunley, Herbert	196, 248
Nunley, Hiram	248
Nunley, Hiram Russell	193
Nunley, Hollis	195
Nunley, Houston	197
Nunley, Howard	192
Nunley, Ida Mae	169, 193, 249, 250
Nunley, Infant	34, 118
Nunley, Irene	192
Nunley, Isaac Murphy	139, 189, 271, 282
Nunley, J.K.	192
Nunley, J.L.	268
Nunley, Jack	ix
Nunley, Jacqueline Patricia (Sanders)	190
Nunley, James	192
Nunley, James "Mutt"	190, 191, 271
Nunley, James C.	255
Nunley, James Calvin	289
Nunley, James D.	190, 194

Nunley, James David	193	Nunley, John Henry	229	Nunley, Leona (Holt)	193
Nunley, James Douglas	192	Nunley, John W.	196	Nunley, Leona Holt	193
Nunley, James H.	189, 195	Nunley, Joseph Carl	193	Nunley, Leonard "Pood"	194
Nunley, James Hobart "Mutt"	195	Nunley, Josie	304	Nunley, Leonard Norton	193, 194
Nunley, James Howard	188, 192, 197	Nunley, Joyce Smith	177	Nunley, Leslie H.	195
Nunley, James Howard "Red"	196	Nunley, Jr., Charlie	33	Nunley, Lewis	194, 197
Nunley, James Mattison/Madison	192	Nunley, Jr., Kenneth Douglas Nunley, Jr.	191	Nunley, Lewis Jefferson "Jeff"	36
Nunley, James Oscar	195	Nunley, Juanita	194	Nunley, Lillian	196
Nunley, Jane	192, 194, 195, 196	Nunley, Judith "Judy" Elaine	193, 285	Nunley, Lillie	37, 244
Nunley, Janie Elizabeth	118	Nunley, Julia Elizabeth	193	Nunley, Lilly Belle	34, 93, 116
Nunley, Jason Edward	192, 256	Nunley, Justin	296	Nunley, Linda Sue (Sanders)	73, 74
Nunley, Jay C.	192	Nunley, Kate	194	Nunley, Lish	194
Nunley, Jean (Lewis)	192	Nunley, Katherine Marie	35, 221	Nunley, Lloyd Allen, Sr.	189, 235
Nunley, Jean Miller	viii	Nunley, Kathleen	158	Nunley, Lois	194
Nunley, Jeffery Lynn	192	Nunley, Kathryn	178	Nunley, Lora Louise	244
Nunley, Jeffery Newton	192	Nunley, Katie Mae	190	Nunley, Lorene	167
Nunley, Jennie Sophronia	192	Nunley, Katie May	250	Nunley, Louis	163
Nunley, Jeremy	194	Nunley, Keith	250	Nunley, Louis A.	271
Nunley, Jeri Lynn	192	Nunley, Keith Alan	192	Nunley, Louis Donald "Grey Fox"	195
Nunley, Jerry Louise (Spencer)	192	Nunley, Kelley	188	Nunley, Louis Jefferson	194
Nunley, Jesse	192	Nunley, Kelly	193	Nunley, Louise	80
Nunley, Jessie	192, 256	Nunley, Kelly Carroll	196, 197	Nunley, Lucy	43, 54
Nunley, Jim	5	Nunley, Kelly Greenberry	193	Nunley, Lucy Belle	163, 255
Nunley, Jimmie "Boots" (Finch)	192	Nunley, Kelly Leon	193	Nunley, Lucy Viola (Bates)	256
Nunley, Jimmy	193	Nunley, Kenneth	193	Nunley, Lydia (Woodlee)	194
Nunley, Jimmy Allen	192	Nunley, Kenneth Douglas	197	Nunley, Lydia Sue	194
Nunley, Joe	193	Nunley, Kenneth Paul	193	Nunley, Mable Sandra	131
Nunley, Joe Allen	149, 193, 194	Nunley, Kermit Ray	193	Nunley, Mae	194
Nunley, Joe Bailey	122	Nunley, Kirstin Nicole (McDole)	193	Nunley, Mae Dean	35, 266
Nunley, Joe Edwin, Jr.	190	Nunley, Lavonna	193	Nunley, Mae Elvin	192
Nunley, John	193	Nunley, Lawrence	193	Nunley, Magdalene (Lawson)	157
Nunley, John Beecher	196	Nunley, Lawrence Edward, Sr.	269	Nunley, Magdaline A. "Dale"	194
Nunley, John Franklin	53	Nunley, Lawson	190, 193	Nunley, Maggie	189
Nunley, John H.	190	Nunley, Leda	190	Nunley, Maggie Hazel	52
		Nunley, Lee	279	Nunley, Mamie Florene (Campbell)	38
		Nunley, Lee Roy	267		

Name	Page
Nunley, Manerva "Minnie"	194
Nunley, Marcus D.	260
Nunley, Marcus DeShawn	197
Nunley, Margaret	194
Nunley, Margie	5, 173
Nunley, Marie	72
Nunley, Mark Douglas	158, 250
Nunley, Mark Howard	194
Nunley, Martha Ada (Tate)	188
Nunley, Marvin	194
Nunley, Marvin "Mark"	286
Nunley, Mary	192
Nunley, Mary "Duck"	189
Nunley, Mary Alyce (Fletcher)	255
Nunley, Mary Emaleene (Sanders)	194
Nunley, Mary Emma	195
Nunley, Mary Kathleen	93
Nunley, Mary Lillian	166
Nunley, Mary Lillie "Lil"	36
Nunley, Mary Magdalene "Duck" Johnson	195
Nunley, Matt	195
Nunley, Matthew Dean	192
Nunley, Maxie Bruce	193, 195
Nunley, Melissa Ann	189
Nunley, Melvia Ruth	195
Nunley, Melvin Reece	97
Nunley, Michael	197
Nunley, Michael "Mody"	195
Nunley, Michael William	195
Nunley, Mildred	195
Nunley, Mildred "Millie"	274
Nunley, Minerva	195
Nunley, Minnie	268
Nunley, Minnie Lee	45, 264
Nunley, Mrs. Roy	99
Nunley, Murph	195
Nunley, Murphy	122
Nunley, Myrtle	157, 195
Nunley, Nadine	220
Nunley, Nancy Ann Matilda (Ward)	183
Nunley, Nancy D	195
Nunley, Nancy Dee	114
Nunley, Nancy Louisa	161
Nunley, Naomi Ruth (Layne)	195
Nunley, Neal Edward	195
Nunley, Nellie	195
Nunley, Nellie Christine	228, 248
Nunley, Nellie Gertrude	103, 286
Nunley, Nevaeh	229
Nunley, Nila	195
Nunley, Noah	76
Nunley, Novela	189
Nunley, Novella	289
Nunley, Opal Faye (Hobbs)	21
Nunley, Otsie (Tigue)	195
Nunley, Ovie	195
Nunley, Patricia	163, 198
Nunley, Patricia Page	195
Nunley, Patti	194
Nunley, Patty Laverne (McClearen)	145
Nunley, Paul Louis	196
Nunley, Paula	16, 191
Nunley, Pauline	137
Nunley, Pearl	19
Nunley, Pearl (Reeves)	85, 111, 189, 227
Nunley, Phillip	196
Nunley, Phillip D.	192
Nunley, Rachel	188, 255
Nunley, Rachel (Green)	77
Nunley, Rachel Marie	196
Nunley, Randil E.	227
Nunley, Rev Gilliam	196
Nunley, Rhoda Allen	191
Nunley, Rita	196
Nunley, Robert	193
Nunley, Robert E.	190, 197
Nunley, Robert Eugene	196
Nunley, Robert G.	194
Nunley, Robert K.	196
Nunley, Robert Kelly	196
Nunley, Robert Vernon	93
Nunley, Robin B	196
Nunley, Roger Dale	196
Nunley, Roger William	196
Nunley, Ronnie	196
Nunley, Ronnie "Bud"	250
Nunley, Rosa	189
Nunley, Rose (Diebold)	37, 206, 266, 284
Nunley, Roy Wayne	196
Nunley, Ruby Eleanor (Myers)	196
Nunley, Russell	196
Nunley, Ruth	168
Nunley, Sally	27, 189
Nunley, Sally Ann	183
Nunley, Sally M. (Haskins)	7, 8, 120, 155
Nunley, Samuel	196
Nunley, Sarah	193, 196
Nunley, Sarah Louise	115, 266
Nunley, Sarah "Sally"	viii
Nunley, Sealie	267
Nunley, Sharon Maxine (Duncan)	157, 197
Nunley, Sheila Jean (McFalls)	197
Nunley, Shirley	197
Nunley, Shirley (Short)	188, 189, 194, 196
Nunley, Simon	197

Name	Page
Nunley, Sonja Gail (Lawson)	197
Nunley, Stanley	197
Nunley, Stella F. (Scaggs)	190, 191
Nunley, Stephen Chad	197
Nunley, Susan	197
Nunley, Susan A.	265
Nunley, Susie Ann	266
Nunley, Tampico	111
Nunley, Taylor	268
Nunley, Ted Allen	166
Nunley, Teddy Reece	197
Nunley, Thelma	197
Nunley, Thomas Jefferson	vii, ix
Nunley, Tierra Elizabeth	127
Nunley, Tierra Ellizabeth	63
Nunley, Tommye Sue	164
Nunley, Tracy Scott	197
Nunley, Valentine (Church)	197
Nunley, Vernon N.	197
Nunley, Vestie "Bo"	196
Nunley, Violet	211
Nunley, Virginia Carol	194
Nunley, W.H.	248
Nunley, Webster	191
Nunley, Wesley	196
Nunley, Wesley Earl	76, 205
Nunley, Wilburn Haggard	186
Nunley, Wilford	197
Nunley, Will	195, 196, 197, 198
Nunley, Willene	197, 215, 227
Nunley, William	viii, 291
Nunley, William A	193, 196, 197
Nunley, William Carol	193
Nunley, William Carroll	154
Nunley, William Charles	36, 190, 197
Nunley, William E.	198
Nunley, William Edward	194
Nunley, William Elihu	188
Nunley, William Grady	191, 198
Nunley, William L	189
Nunley, William Norman	196
Nunley, William Perry	190
Nunley, Willie	189
Nunley, Willie Mae	238
Nunley, Yancy	194, 204
Nunn, Novella (Layne)	135, 179, 189, 196
Nunnley, Myrtle	198
Nussbaum, Alice Mae	76
Nussbaum, Francis Richard	36
Nussbaum, Henry	198
Nussbaum, Minnie	198
O'Barr, Carrie	67
O'Barr, Larkin	217
O'Brien, Aileen (Fitzgerald)	217
O'Brien, Carlotta Leigh (Yarrington)	198
O'Brien, Marshall	198
O'Brien, Pamela	16
O'Bryan, Lucinda	88
O'Dear, Dennis W.	262
O'Dear, Elbert	198
O'Dear, Esther Louise (Sitz)	198
O'Dear, Herman	198
O'Dear, James Herman	115, 198
O'Dear, Lydeth	198
O'Dear, Mary	1
O'Dear, Mary (Nunley)	170
O'Dear, Mary Elizabeth	198
O'Dear, Paralee	273
O'Dear, Rhoda	296
O'Dear, Rhoda Lee	302
O'Dear, Tammy	47
O'Keefe, Ella Mae	63
O'Neal, Amanda	237
O'Neal, Amanda Matilda "Mandy"	85
O'Neal, Bettie Sue	177
O'Neal, Charles	48
O'Neal, Early	198
O'Neal, Early Peyton	140
O'Neal, Elbert	198
O'Neal, Elbert Willis	48
O'Neal, Hazel Rurh	180
O'Neal, Helen	198
O'Neal, Helen Frankie	153
O'Neal, Infant	153
O'Neal, J.D.	198
O'Neal, Jane Roberta	198
O'Neal, Jim	24
O'Neal, John	198
O'Neal, John King	198, 199
O'Neal, John Wilburn	74
O'Neal, John Wilburn, Jr.	198
O'Neal, Johnny	198
O'Neal, Jonathan Corbett, Jr. "Jay"	25
O'Neal, Kenneth	198
O'Neal, Kenny	198
O'Neal, Lawrence	198
O'Neal, Linda	198
O'Neal, Marlene (Layne)	198
O'Neal, Nancy	198
O'Neal, Robert B.	63
O'Neal, Stella	199
O'Neal, Veola Christine	199
O'Neal, William P "Sonny"	148
O'Neal, William Perry	199
O'Neal, Sr., Jonathan Corbett	199

Name	Page
O'Rear, Calvin	198
Oakich, Mary	131
Oblander, Ada Hart	245
Oblander, John Fred	199
Oblander, Rosamond Rachel (Hintz)	199
Odom, Anna Bell (King)	199
Odom, Joe	199
Oehlert, Wendy	199
Ogelvie, Cynthia Caroline (Bailey)	1
Ogelvie, Essie Mae (Thomas)	199
Ogelvie, John Washington	199
Ogelvie, Maty	199
Ogelvie, Maybelle	18
Ogelvie, Pamela	11
Ogle, Elizabeth	304
Ogle, Elizabeth "Betty"	232
Ogle, Hattie J.	233
Ogle, Wyatt McDaniel	295
Ogles, Elizabeth	233
Oklahoma	ix
Okuly, Mary	235
Olgiati, Annie (Wichser)	108
Olgiati, Pietro Rodolfo	199
Olgiati, Roman A.	199
Olgiati, Roman Anton	199
Olin, Anna Elizabeth	199
Olinger, Cheryl	115
Olinger, Elbert	199
Olinger, Leroy Elbert	199
Olinger, Sarah Lorene (Lusk)	199
Oliver, Alfred	199
Oliver, Altha	200
Oliver, Arthur Lee "Yock"	199
Oliver, Asa	199, 200
Oliver, Bessie	199
Oliver, Cheatom	269
Oliver, Danita Renea (Campbell)	207
Oliver, Della	200
Oliver, Emmett	299
Oliver, George	269
Oliver, Ida	200
Oliver, Ida	226
Oliver, John	226
Oliver, Johnny	199
Oliver, Juanita	200
Oliver, Martha Jane (Hobbs)	183
Oliver, Nancy	200
Oliver, Nell Ruth	200
Oliver, Paul	182
Oliver, Paul William	200
Oliver, Robert "Bob"	200
Oliver, Ruben Eugene	72
Olmstead, Earl LeVant	200
Olmstead, James G.	200
Olmstead, James Glenwood	200
Olmstead, Olive Alda (Peterson)	200
Olney, Arthur Cain	200
Olney, Arthur Hamilton	200
Olney, Mary Emma	200
Ona, Hattie Lou	200
Ondrizek, Joseph	93
Oneal, Amanda	161
Ooley, James Bert	214
Ooley, Martha	106
Orange, Alvin Lee	152
Orange, Buford	200
Orange, Edward Ray	200
Orange, Emmett Sylvester	200
Orange, Fred George	200, 201
Orange, George Stanford	200
Orange, James	200
Orange, James Douglas "Big O"	200
Orange, James Emmett	200
Orange, John William	201
Orange, John William Frederick	107, 127, 128, 200
Orange, Johnnie Mae	200
Orange, Josephine (Carr)	200
Orange, Lillie Pearl	201
Orange, Pearl Lilie	78
Orange, Pearl Lilly	238
Orange, Rosa (Lese)	3
Orange, Samuel Emmett	201
Orange, William	38, 200, 201
Orr, John W	201
Orr, Margaret (Donohue)	201
Orrell, Royce A	201
Ortel, Carol	201
Ortiz, Evalardo "Joe"	66
Ortwin, George Lee	42, 201
Osborn, John	281
Osborn, Mattie	201
Osborn, Phoebe	125
Osborne, Emma Glenn	292
Osborne, Martha Ann (Mansfield)	135
Osmonson, Rufus	201
Osmonson, Valda	290
Ostertag, Madison Miller	290
Ostertag, Michael	201
Ottinger, Luster Beatrice	201
Overby, Lily	136
Overton, Louise	65
Overturf, Clifton	145
Overturf, Crystal	201
Overturf, Edgar	33
Overturf, Gilbert	201
Overturf, Henry Clifton	138
Overturf, Jerry Edward	201
Overturf, Junior	201
Overturf, Luticia	201

Name	Page
Overturf, Mary Magdelene (Smith)	266
Overturf, Nellie C.	201
Overturf, Oscar Darrell	89
Overturf, Williadean Brock	201
Overturff, Ben H.	201
Overturff, Edwin Lee	202
Overturff, Linticia	201
Overturff, Mary Virginia	229
Overturff, William B.	202
Owen, Alice Faye	201
Owen, Laura Louella	189
Owen, Mary Alice	182
Owen, Myrtle Ova	17
Owenby, Dorothy L.	150
Owenby, Edward J.	202
Owenby, Lawrence R.	202
Owenby, Lawrence Robert	202
Owenby, Mary Lee	202
Owens, Alma Brewer	72
Owens, David	112
Owens, Doris "Dot"	202
Owens, Elsie	26
Owens, Henrietta (Myers) "Tiny"	202
Owens, James Harvey	202
Owens, John Savage	19
Owens, Lorraine	150
Owens, Mary Elizabeth	42
Owens, Roy Allen	18, 19
Owens, Thomas Earl	202
Owens, Tressie Leona	112, 202
Owens, William	202
Owens, William George	202
Owens, William Robert	202
Owens, William Thomas	202
Owings Family Plot	202
Owings, Jon Michael	202
Oyler, Ralph	202
Pace, Henry	55
Pace, Irene	156
Pace, Malda	156
Pack, Alice Carrie	18
Pack, Allan Foster	2
Pack, Brooks Kennedy Hayes	202
Pack, Donna Mae	202
Pack, Edward David "Edd"	202
Pack, Ernest William	202
Pack, James Cecil	17
Pack, Jefferson Davis	202
Pack, Jesse	202
Pack, Jesse Earl, Jr.	202
Pack, John	202
Pack, Lara May	1
Pack, Mary Ellen	222
Pack, Mary K	1
Pack, Nancy	202
Pack, Nellie Louise	97
Pack, Ortense W.	296
Pack, Robert	202
Pack, Sarah Ann	202
Pack, Sarah Anne	299
Pack, Thomas G.	299
Pack, Willie Mae	202
Paden, Cecil Allen	202
Paden, Thelma Irene (Burford)	203
Page, Luther E.	203
Pando, Arcilia	28
Pando, Mario	203
Pando, Orlando	203
Pang, Duksoo	203
Pangelinan, George	203
Pangelinan, Irma (McCoy)	203
Panter, Maggie Myrtle	203
Paradise, James	64
Paradise, Louvenia	24
Parham, Nell Virginia (Crabtree)	24
Paris, Daisy L.	203
Park, T. Blake	185
Parker, Allie Jean	87
Parker, Anna Mary	198
Parker, Doris Earline	203
Parker, George Washington	300
Parker, Jackie	203
Parker, Krystal Michelle (Williams)	244
Parker, Laura Lee (Thomas)	203
Parker, Lucille	203
Parker, Mary Jane	141
Parker, Sarah	130
Parker, Sarah Margaret	203
Parker, William "Billy" M.	221
Parker, William McClelland	206
Parker, William Overall	203
Parker, William Thomas	203
Parkinson, James McKamey	203
Parks, Amanda "Mandy"	109
Parks, Betty Jo	7
Parks, Billee Fay (London)	203
Parks, Child	203
Parks, Christy Carol	203
Parks, Doris	203
Parks, Edgar Harold	174
Parks, Edna Frances	203
Parks, Estella	203
Parks, Eva	41
Parks, Eva Lee	208
Parks, Fred Basil "Pink"	300
Parks, Frederick Allen	203

Name	Page
Parks, George Grundy	61, 203, 204
Parks, J.T.	203
Parks, James	203
Parks, Jane	203
Parks, Jonas H.	96
Parks, Malinda Abigail	120
Parks, Mary	222
Parks, Nannie	240
Parks, Paul Keith	203
Parks, Robert	204
Parks, Sarah Rebecca	203
Parks, Zora	28
Parks, Zora Belle	220
Parks, Zora Elizabeth	170
Parmely, Robert S.	13
Parmeter, Florence L	204
Parmeter, William E.	223
Parmley, Bessie May	224
Parmley, Delilah Mary	203
Parmley, Dorothy Lee Hale	200
Parmley, Harry L.	204
Parmley, Harry Leslie	204
Parmley, Harry Lewis	204
Parmley, Haskel "Jack"	204
Parmley, Haskel Benny	204
Parmley, Ingram	204
Parmley, Judith E. (Charles)	83
Parmley, Leddy	204
Parmley, Lidia	168
Parmley, Lydia "Leddy"	234
Parmley, Lydia Judith	169
Parmley, Mary Jane	233
Parmley, Nancy Lou	298
Parmley, Robert S.	204
Parmley, Ruby (Evans)	204
Parrott, Sue Bouldin	iii
Parson, Amanda Elizabeth	204
Parson, Andrew Jackson	2
Parson, Berta "Birdie"	204
Parson, Bessie Allen	63
Parson, Betty	204
Parson, Calvin	5
Parson, Carl Junior	205
Parson, Carrie	204
Parson, Christine (Adams)	264
Parson, Claude	204
Parson, Craigory Dale	204
Parson, Ella	204
Parson, Enda	202
Parson, Enda (Scott)	204
Parson, Garland Eugene "Roho"	204
Parson, Helen	204
Parson, Hershel	63
Parson, Isaac Franklin	63, 224
Parson, Janice (Thomas)	204
Parson, Jessie Pauline	204
Parson, Jettie	173
Parson, Johnny	204
Parson, Lee A.	204
Parson, Melvin E	204
Parson, Millard	204
Parson, Robert	204
Parson, Ruby Margaret (Pickett)	204
Parson, Shirley Ann	204
Parson, Thomas F	204
Parson, Thomas Millard	204
Parson, Tommie Howard	204, 205
Parson, Wanda Sue	204
Parson, Whitney	204
Parsons, Beccie	149
Parsons, Clara	255
Parsons, Danny Ray	5
Parsons, Dolly Ann (Ellis)	205
Parsons, Ella Naomi (Henley)	205
Parsons, Elmer	205
Parsons, Enda (Scott)	48, 205, 235
Parsons, George	205
Parsons, Glen	205
Parsons, Glenn	221
Parsons, Halle	285
Parsons, Hallie Marie	258
Parsons, Howard	258
Parsons, Isaac	205
Parsons, Isaac Wilber "Jakie"	190
Parsons, Janice	205
Parsons, Jess	173
Parsons, Jesse Canova	61
Parsons, Jessie	205
Parsons, Jessie Beatrice	79
Parsons, Julia Ellis	79
Parsons, Lee Upton "Red"	205
Parsons, Lelia	205
Parsons, Lewis	212
Parsons, Lewis Elsbery	205
Parsons, Lillie Mae	42
Parsons, Lucy Emeline "Bell"	48
Parsons, Lydia Parelee	190
Parsons, Mary Jo	36
Parsons, Minerva Louise Aseltine	4
Parsons, Mozella	197
Parsons, Naydean (Nunley)	235
Parsons, Nila	205
Parsons, Pearl	160
Parsons, Pearl	274
Parsons, Rachel	273
Parsons, Randel	205
Parsons, Roy	173

Parsons, Ruth Hazel	5	Partin, John A.	206	Patrick, Lula	206
Parsons, William Joe	176	Partin, John Louis	206	Patrick, Martha Flora	204
Parsons, William Jonathan "Wes Willie"	205	Partin, Joseph Derrick "Jody"	186	Patrick, Millard Fletcher	206
Parsons, William Joseph	205	Partin, June	206	Patrick, Nancy Jane	76
Parsons, William Randell	85	Partin, Larry	6	Patrick, Richard A	266
Partain, Arvol Ladell	205	Partin, Larry "Tykie", Jr.	205	Patrick, Sue	206
Partain, John David	205	Partin, Lloyd "Dean" Palmer Long	206	Patrick, Veola	126
Partain, Mary Maxey	205	Partin, Marion Louise	150	Patrick, William "Billy" M.	155
Partin, Alvin	205	Partin, Orville Patrick Partin	206	Patrick, William P.	206
Partin, Arlene	206	Partin, Reba	21	Patten, Cora	206
Partin, Barney	103	Partin, Rosemary	197	Patterson, Annette	120
Partin, Benjamin	176	Partin, Ruby Anna Mae	235	Patterson, Austin	231
Partin, Benjamin Franklin	5	Partin, Sarah	150	Patterson, Bertha	206
Partin, Bessie	205	Partin, Sarah Tennessee	206	Patterson, Betty Christine (Henry)	161
Partin, Bessie Lee	281	Partin, Stan	235	Patterson, Beulah Frances	206
Partin, Bryan	127	Partin, Stanley Ewing	205	Patterson, Beverly	265
Partin, Carrie	102, 135	Partin, Thomasetta "Etta" (Dove)	206	Patterson, Billy Charles "Pat"	210
Partin, Charlotte	127	Partin, Tracy Arlene (Thompson)	206	Patterson, Bonnie	206
Partin, Curt	14	Partlow, Maxine	206	Patterson, Carolyn Anderson	182
Partin, Daniel	205	Parton, J.A.	237	Patterson, Claude	206
Partin, Donald	205	Parton, Lori Angela	206	Patterson, Daniel B.	222
Partin, Edward	206	Parton, Patricia Anita (Long) "Patsy"	206	Patterson, Daniel M.	181, 207
Partin, Elisha	205	Pass, Marie	206	Patterson, Dillon	182, 260
Partin, Grady Edward	206	Paterson, Daniel S.	236	Patterson, Emmett F.	207
Partin, Grady Ward	205	Pathfinder	iv	Patterson, Geneva G (Oliver)	206
Partin, Hattie	205	Patrick, Arena (Jones)	200	Patterson, Harlon	207
Partin, Hattie Huetta "Etta"	98, 117, 248	Patrick, Arminta	206	Patterson, Ida	206
Partin, Helen Joyce	139	Patrick, Charles Francis	74	Patterson, Jayne Caroline	46
Partin, Hester (Nunley)	21	Patrick, David Franklin	16	Patterson, Jayne Carolyn	40
Partin, Jackie Layne	iii	Patrick, Didama	206	Patterson, Jennie Louise	221, 222
Partin, Jackie Mae	205	Patrick, Elbert	289	Patterson, Joan	246
Partin, James B.	205	Patrick, Elcaney	20, 285	Patterson, John	53
Partin, James Bobo	206	Patrick, Elmer Franklin	206	Patterson, John Alton	207
Partin, Jean	205	Patrick, Helen Louise	206	Patterson, Lela	207
Partin, Jimmie Ruth	241	Patrick, John Isaac	197	Patterson, Lucille	9
Partin, John A "Barney"	205	Patrick, Joseph A	206		

Name	Page
Patterson, Martha	257, 259
Patterson, Robert	258
Patterson, Thelma	231
Patterson, Vernon Ray	260
Patterson, William	207
Patterson, William Harlon	207
Pattie, Frankie Jean	ii, iii
Pattie, Louise	246
Pattie, Mary Ellen	220
Patton, Alexander Edgar	10
Patton, Aubrey	207
Patton, Aubrey Lellis	259
Patton, Belle	77
Patton, Berta (Flanery)	105
Patton, Cora	207
Patton, Dennis Wayne	112, 114
Patton, Edmonia "Mona"	207
Patton, George	102
Patton, Harlan	207
Patton, James Harris, Sr.	207
Patton, Joe Kirk	207
Patton, Johnnie Vera	207
Patton, Katherine Clemetine	29, 119
Patton, Mary Louise	204
Patton, Rona Lee	207
Patton, Salina Zora Belle (Hollingsworth)	167
Patton, Sheila (Long)	207
Paty, Martha Ann	207
Paulk, Christopher Michael	203
Paulk, Michael	207
Paulsen, Lori Jo	207
Pavlak, Lottie Lena	20
Payne and/or Sanders possibly, Unidentified	196
Payne, Amelia	207
Payne, Andrew Bass	152
Payne, Anna Bell	178
Payne, Annie Bell (Hill)	13
Payne, Barbara	207
Payne, Benjamin Franklin	147
Payne, Bertha	208, 235
Payne, Carl Bailey "Carley"	132
Payne, Carl Benton	208
Payne, Charles	208
Payne, Elisha	208
Payne, Elizabeth "Betsy" (Conn)	208
Payne, Evalina	208
Payne, Frances Loretta	236
Payne, Garland	208
Payne, George Conn	208
Payne, George Washington	207
Payne, Georgia	208, 209
Payne, Goldie	56
Payne, Grace	42, 117, 120
Payne, Herschel	61, 203, 204
Payne, J.L.	208
Payne, James Everett	105
Payne, Jesse Willard	208
Payne, Joe	208
Payne, Jospeh	300
Payne, Juanita Sue	208
Payne, Leonard Elson	208
Payne, Louise (Watts)	208
Payne, Lucinda Jane "Lucy"	208
Payne, Margaret	234
Payne, Mary Elsie	84
Payne, Mary Kathryn	15, 142
Payne, Paul Edward	218
Payne, Pearl	208
Payne, Poindexter	74
Payne, Rachel	207, 208
Payne, Rita F.	29
Payne, Samuel W.	208
Payne, Samuel William	208
Payne, Stella Mae	208
Payne, Susannah Key (Davis)	199, 200
Payne, Thomas	209
Payne, Tracy	208
Payne, Upton Bell "Buddy"	208
Payne, Vergie	208
Payne, Willie Wilson "Will"	27
Pearce, C. W.	188
Pearce, Madelyn F. (Hasty)	209
Pearsall, Katharine	209
Pearson, Bennie	83
Pearson, Beulah	42
Pearson, Catherine	288
Pearson, Cora	18
Pearson, Mary Ella	18
Pease, Catherine	257
Pease, Claude	98
Pease, Claudie	209
Pease, Claudie Lee	252
Pease, Fannie Idella (Meeks)	209
Pease, Jess Prince	209
Pease, Sharon Alvina (Adams)	209
Peat, Amarillys	209
Peck, Amos E.	31
Peck, Bessie Edyth	209
Peck, Ernestine "Susie" (Layne)	209
Peck, Ethel Hayward	209
Peck, John Milton	209
Peden, Susie	209
Peeks, Rebecca	59
Pelham, Sarah	43, 180
Pemberton, A. Burn	79, 124
Pemberton, Carl Milton "Cotton"	209

Name	Page
Pemberton, Carl Milton, Jr.	209
Pemberton, Clarence	209
Pemberton, Clarence Milton, Sr.	152, 209
Pemberton, Geneva Lucille	209
Pemberton, Margie Lynn	209
Pemberton, Wilma	209
Pendergraff, Mathy	18
Pendergrass, Andy	269
Pendergrass, Mary L.	211
Pendergrass, Nancy	210
Penley, Carl	168
Penley, Delilah Ross	210
Pennell, Era (Northcutt)	210
Pennell, John S.	210
Pennington, Anna Mary	210
Pennington, Edgil	217
Pennington, Ellis	210
Pennington, Isaac Bertram	210
Pennington, Norman	210
Pennington, Tennessee	210
Perez, Carmelit R.	160
Perkins, Bobby Louis	300
Perkins, Lawrence Merrill	210
Perkins, Ruby	148
Perry, Albert E.	197
Perry, Albert Leo	210
Perry, Annie	210
Perry, Arvilla	298
Perry, Betty May	135
Perry, C.T.	143
Perry, Charlene	210
Perry, Colby Lee	192
Perry, Dean	210
Perry, Dora	210
Perry, Dorothy Mae (Shadrick)	127, 128
Perry, Edna Jean	210
Perry, Elizabeth	127
Perry, Elsie	52
Perry, Ester	126
Perry, Esther Mae	76
Perry, Esther May	73
Perry, Eva May (McDonald)	73
Perry, George	210
Perry, George Washington	35
Perry, Helen Louise (Meeks)	210, 211
Perry, Isaac	210
Perry, James Blaine	210, 216
Perry, James William	210
Perry, Joe Hayes "Hazel"	210
Perry, Joe S.	210
Perry, Joe Wheeler	210
Perry, John Henry	211
Perry, John Thomas	210
Perry, John W.	210
Perry, Johnny Wesley	211
Perry, Joyce (Bonner)	127, 130
Perry, Kenneth	210
Perry, Kenneth Ray	210
Perry, Lewis Alton	210
Perry, Malcolm Lee	210
Perry, Manuel	211
Perry, Manuel, Sr.	7, 79
Perry, Margie Frances	210
Perry, Mary	89
Perry, Mary Elizabeth (Perry)	210
Perry, Mary L. (Pendergrass)	211
Perry, Mildred	211
Perry, Patsy Ann	211
Perry, Paul Wilson	211
Perry, Peggy	210
Perry, Robert E, Sr.	101
Perry, Robert E.	211
Perry, Robert Edward "Buck", Sr.	211
Perry, Robert Edward, Jr.	211
Perry, Rosamond Margaret	211
Perry, Sadie	210
Perry, Sarah Catherine	211
Perry, Theopolis	127
Perry, Vennie A.	101
Perry, Viola	173
Perry, Virginia	252, 253
Perry, William	35
Perry, William Washington	211
Perry, William Washington "Horsefly"	210
Perry, Zula	211
Persdotter, Maria	92
Peterson, Olive Alda	230
Petterson, Martha	200
Pettit, Mearl "Minnie"	207
Pettit, Millie	22
Petty, Charles	36
Petty, Edna Mae (Meeks)	9
Petty, Hetie	211
Petty, J.R.	15
Petty, James	211
Petty, Kazia	185
Petty, Lawrence	211
Petty, Mary Caroline (Uselton)	211
Petty, Olivia "Livy"	211
Petty, William J.	2
Peyton, Dorcas	211
Peyton, Ernest	98
Pfalfmann, Mary	98
Pfeffer, Kath geb	284
Pfeifer, Marie	240
Pfeifer, Marie	238
Phelps, Linda Ann (Watley)	238

Name	Page
Phelps, Nancy Eglatine	211
Philbrick, Catherine Ellen	87
Philbrick, William F.	64
Phillips, Bessie Elizabeth	147
Phillips, Billy Ed	177
Phillips, Carl	43
Phillips, David	177
Phillips, David Foster	211
Phillips, Dora Dean	211, 246
Phillips, Ed	251
Phillips, James David	212
Phillips, Jerry Lee	211
Phillips, Jim	211
Phillips, Joe	211
Phillips, John	15
Phillips, Josephine Floyd	288
Phillips, Joyce	119
Phillips, Mary L.	210
Phillips, Melvin Richard	211
Phillips, Rubie Nell (Davis)	158
Phillips, Rufus	211
Phillips, Timothy Edward	174
Phillips, Willene	212
Phillips, Willie Jane	35, 148
Philpot, Loretta Ann (Hammers)	6
Phipps, Amanda "Mandy" (Spencer)	212
Phipps, Bobbie D.	212
Phipps, Brandon Lee	212
Phipps, Charlie	212
Phipps, Cleo	212
Phipps, David	288
Phipps, David Jackson	35, 212, 213, 284
Phipps, Edward Clarence	212
Phipps, Elizabeth	212
Phipps, Eva	80
Phipps, Henry	224
Phipps, Infant	212
Phipps, Irene	212
Phipps, Irene Holt	207
Phipps, Jack	197
Phipps, Jackson	213
Phipps, James David	212
Phipps, James Knox Polk "Jim"	212
Phipps, Jo Ann (Gipson)	212
Phipps, John	212
Phipps, John D.	191, 212, 260
Phipps, Keith	213
Phipps, Larry	212
Phipps, Lillian Mae	212
Phipps, Lutishey (Layne)	247
Phipps, Margaret	212
Phipps, Margaret Elizabeth	212
Phipps, Martha (Dickerson)	212
Phipps, Mary "Maggie"	213
Phipps, Mary Ann	258
Phipps, Melissa E.	213
Phipps, Mollie	233
Phipps, Rosa Alberta	191
Phipps, Sally	237
Phipps, Sarah "Sally" (Smith)	3
Phipps, Shirley (VanHooser)	213
Phipps, Thomas Alexander	213
Phipps, William L "Bill"	213
Pickett, Alan Monroe	212
Pickett, Allan	213
Pickett, Bailey	213
Pickett, Bailey A.	213
Pickett, Bailey Allen	213
Pickett, Brenda (Ross)	59
Pickett, Brenda Faye	213
Pickett, Clint	63
Pickett, Cristal	213
Pickett, Darlene	48
Pickett, Debra	164
Pickett, Don Elton	213
Pickett, Donnie	213
Pickett, Doris	128
Pickett, Earl	278
Pickett, Ellen K. (Bryant)	213
Pickett, Elmer	213
Pickett, Ernest Buford	213, 258
Pickett, Eula A.	213
Pickett, Frances Almeda	196
Pickett, Gladys	213
Pickett, Gladys Marie (White)	186, 211
Pickett, Gladys Tennessee	213
Pickett, Ida	186
Pickett, J. Harvey	40
Pickett, Jack Lloyd	213
Pickett, Jack William	213
Pickett, James Anthony	213
Pickett, James Franklin	213
Pickett, James Lloyd	213, 257
Pickett, Jesse	213
Pickett, Jewell D. (Layne)	213, 214
Pickett, John Allen	213
Pickett, John B.	204
Pickett, John Bert	213
Pickett, John L.	213
Pickett, John Lillard	213
Pickett, Leck	9
Pickett, Martha	256
Pickett, Martha (Turner)	140, 255
Pickett, Mary	214
Pickett, Mary Elizabeth	128
Pickett, Mary L.	214

Name	Page
Pickett, Melvin	196
Pickett, Merideth	214
Pickett, Milly	213
Pickett, Nancy Lucinda	213
Pickett, Shea Ashlyn	76
Pickett, Vernon	9
Pickett, Vernon Lester	213
Pierce, Art	214
Pierce, Charles	214
Pierce, Charles Franklin	61
Pierce, Esther L.	214
Pierce, Ethel (Stotts)	214
Pierce, Lelar Mae (Wilburn)	214
Pierce, Mary	214
Pile, Mary Jane	61
Pinto, Anna M.	54
Pirtle, Alvin T.	300
Pirtle, James	214
Pirtle, James August	214
Pirtle, Julia Elizabeth	214
Pirtle, Leda	214
Pirtle, Lucyle	121
Pirtle, Margaret Frances (Lewis)	93
Pirtle, Melinda	214
Pirtle, William	214
Pistol, Fay (Green)	214
Pitman, Catherine	214
Pittman, Betty Lyda	271
Pittman, John William	214
Pittman, Ralph	214
Pittman, Virgil Bolton	271
Pittmann, Richard Alfred, Jr.	214
Pittmann, Richard A.	214
Pitts, Lana Carol (Stiefel)	214
Plantz, Alex Steven	214
Player, Edith	214
Pleasant, Albert Eugene	174
Pleasant, Frances Julia	214
Pleasant, Rhonda Lynn (Meeks)	296
Plumacher, Eugene H.	214
Pocus, Corine	18
Pocus, Corinne	107
Pocus, George	69
Pocus, Jack	214
Pocus, Jackie Sanders	214
Pocus, Jerry M.	214
Pocus, Joann	214
Pocus, Joe	214
Pocus, Laura	214
Pocus, Robert H.	214
Pocus, Roger Samuel	214
Pocus, Rose Lee	214
Pocus, Sue	25, 300
Pocus, Thelma (Layne)	52
Poe, Dora Evelyn (Nunley)	214
Poe, Stanford	215
Poff, Nellie Pearl	215
Poff, Patricia	81
Pohlman, Ruth	279
Pointer, S.D.	114
Pointer, Zilpha Ann (Terry)	215
Pollack, Ellen	215
Pollack, John	114
Pollard, Clarine	114
Pollard, Clarine	23
Pollard, Doris	179
Pollard, Jeff	137
Polston, Mary Ann	303
Pomrenting, Minnie	182
Ponder, Jerry	66
Ponder, Jerry M.	215
Ponder, Malachil	215
Ponder, Mamie	215
Ponder, Mary Ellen (McCullough)	290
Pool, Nathan Deon	215
Poole, Ina Elvina	109
Pope, Martha Kathleen	28
Porter, Alice Mabel (Coe)	39
Porter, Cathy	215
Porter, Ford Davis	225
Porter, Freida	215
Porter, Jr., James Walter	55
Poteet, Mattie M.	55
Potts, Bertha (Campbell)	176
Potts, Billy Gerald "Ricky"	215
Potts, Charles Gordon	215
Potts, Charles Ransom	215
Potts, Joe	215
Potts, Marion John, Jr.	217
Poulton, Rosalea Regina	215
Pound, Beula	119
Powell, Buford Alvin, Sr.	229
Powell, Charles Ray	215
Powell, Chrissy	215
Powell, Jerome	215
Powell, Jerome B.	215
Powell, Jerry	215
Powell, John Peyton	215
Powell, Lou Ellen	215
Powell, Maggie	215
Powell, Nicole "Clyde"	273
Powell, Noma Beatrice	215
Powell, Rachel	22
Powell, Robert	215
Powell, Robert A.	215
Powell, Robert Lee Childers	215
Powell, Tressie	40
Powers, Granville	40
Powers, Lisa	118

Name	Page
Powers, Lula Mae	48
Prater, Arble	92
Prater, Arble L.	215
Prater, Arthur Young	215
Prater, Bruce Wayne	17
Prater, Bytha	215
Prater, Dorothy E.	55
Prater, Mary A.	215
Prater, Melvin	17
Prater, Simps	187
Prater, Tracey	18
Pratt, George	115
Pratt, Mary	252
Pratt, Mary Alberta	122, 208
Pray, Ethel	297
Pray, Ethel M.	128
Presley, Geneva (Starling)	15
Presley, Minnie Lou	215
Pressley, James R.	81
Pressley, Paul Eugene	216
Price, Billie Jo	216
Price, Ethel	216
Price, Grace O	165, 171, 182
Price, Hyman "Lucky"	190
Price, James Ricey	216
Price, Julia Ann	262
Price, Lena Marie	158
Price, Lois May (Coppinger)	216
Price, Minnie Belle	216
Price, Nancy Ann	159
Price, Neil Eugene	215
Price, Rhonda	216
Price, Roy Haskel Jr.	91
Price, Roy Haskel, Sr.	216
Price, Seabert	216
Price, Steven B.	50
Price, Trisha Kay	216
Prince, Dixie (Lawrence)	216
Prince, J.D.	216
Prince, Janice Marie	76, 216
Prince, John	222
Prince, Joy	216
Prince, Larry Hawkins	222
Prince, Mabel (Hatfield)	216
Prince, Mansel R.	216
Prince, Samuel Thomas Leroy	216
Prince, Thomas Leroy	216
Prince, W.R.	216
Pritchett, Bonnie	216
Pritchett, Ollie Beatrice (Perry)	147
Privett, Dorothy	216
Privett, Dorothy Carol	179
Privett, Elizabeth Ruth (Henry)	180
Privett, Franklin Turner	216
Privett, George Herman	216
Privett, Harley	216
Privett, James Stephen	81
Privett, Pauline	216
Proudfoot, Claire	iii
Pruitt, Betty Ruth	96
Pruitt, Mary	216
Pruitt, Robert	231
Pruitt, Ruby	216
Pry, Dorothy Irene	55
Pry, Taylor W.	138
Pryor, Dorothy Irene	138
Puckett, Wanda	138
Puckette, Isabelle	281
Pugh, Arthur Allen	99
Pugh, Arvel Delano	217
Purcell, Elbert Brabson	217
Purcell, Mary	231
Purcell, Mary	218
Purdom, Wilson	64
Pyburn, Carl C	49
Pyburn, Carrie (O'Barr)	262
Pyburn, Corbett	217
Pyburn, Frances	217
Pyburn, Hugh	217
Pyburn, John	217
Pyburn, Linda Faye	217
Pyburn, Mary Catherine "Molly" (Anderson)	147
Pyburn, Mollie (Anderson)	217
Pyburn, Rebecca	217
Pyburn, Thomas Love	217
Pyburn, Thomas Love "Mug"	217
Pyburn, W. M.	217
Pyburn, William	217
Q Switch Road	viii
Qualls, Albert Devander	217
Qualls, Clarence E.	217
Qualls, Doretha Marie (Moore)	217
Qualls, Esther Yvonne (Stephens)	217
Qualls, Izetta Inez	217
Qualls, James Hollis	217
Qualls, Ralph Alford	217
Quinn, Jerry	217
Quinn, Katherine	217
Rackar, John	217
Rackar, John Steve	217
Rader, Lora	43, 217
Ragan, Sara Jane	43
Rager, Carolyn	279
Ragsdale, Isabelle	268
Ragsdale, Nancy	155, 159
Rakauskas, Fran	70
Rakauskas, Inez	217
Rakauskas, Mary	217
Rakauskas, Shelby Francis "Rocky"	217
Ramey, Sarah Virginia	217

Name	Page
Ramirez, Christeena G.	116
Ramos, Bernice Reta	217
Ramsey-Wright, Elbert	225
Ramsey-Wright, Mary	11
Ramsey, Burr Edward	11
Ramsey, Debbie Tyler	218
Ramsey, John	217
Ramsey, Julia	229
Ramsey, Karen Alvada	229
Ramsey, Marvin Edward	218
Ramsey, Virginia	218
Ramsey, Willie Nellie	69
Randell, William	218
Randler, Evelyn Ruth	204
Raney, William Andrew	249
Rankhorn, Beverly Irene Brown	161
Rankin, Murphy David	138
Rankin, Rhoda Tabatha	218
Rankin, Sue	218
Ransome, Minnie	173
Raper, Harvey Mack	181
Raper, Mac	218
Raper, Marie (Liddle)	218
Raulston, J J	218
Raulston, Jefferson Jones	218
Raulston, Jefferson Jones "Jonas"	99
Raulston, Linda (Morrison)	218
Raulston, Marion Greer "Fod"	218
Raulston, Mary Orme (Sayles)	218
Rawlings, Mary "Polly"	218
Ray, Alice	281
Ray, Dorothy	225
Ray, Hobert	102
Ray, Homer Ernest	154
Ray, Jacob Floyd	218
Ray, Johnnie	117
Ray, Kenneth Paul	200
Ray, Linnie	218
Ray, Una	267
Rayback, Michilena	300
Reader, Etta Lena	14
Reagan, Agnes	200
Reagan, Clyde	106, 107
Reagan, Frank	50
Reagan, Sarah Jane	279
Reagon, Clyde Estes	165
Reagon, Thomlin	218
Reaves, Louisa Jane	218
Rector, Francis Benson	109
Rector, Hallie Marie	253
Rector, Martha Irene	304
Rector, Marvin	253
Rector, Michael Kent	218
Rector, Pauline	218
Rector, Rhonda	218
Red Hill Cemetery	i
Redfern, Dorothy	218
Rediker, Nellie Blanche	206
Redwine, Garrett Maxwell	30
Redwine, Jacob	218
Reece, Annette	218
Reece, Catherine	218
Reece, Larry	259
Reece, Larry Craig	218
Reece, Lindsey	218
Reed, Bessie Jane	218
Reed, Bunny	184
Reed, Della (Lowe)	301
Reed, Elizabeth Jane "Elsie"	218
Reed, Emma Louella "Lou" (England)	86
Reed, Emma Mae	218
Reed, Henrietta	167, 169, 180
Reed, Henry "Minge"	219
Reed, Henry Edgar	219
Reed, Joseph S.	218
Reed, Leirtha	218, 219
Reed, Marvin Alf "Mac"	300
Reed, Mary	219
Reed, Mary Ann	226
Reed, Nancy	301
Reed, Nannie J.	81
Reed, Pauline	178
Reed, Raymond Earl	174
Reed, Rollie	219
Reed, Rosie	218
Reed, Ruby	258
Reed, Sam	226
Reed, Sam P.	298
Reed, Samuel L. "Sam"	296
Reed, Samuel P.	219
Reed, Verdie Marie	219
Reed, William Claude	74
Reed, William M.	218
Reed, Willie A.	219
Reel, Ira	248
Reep, Terri	124
Rees, Frances	218
Reeves, Bonnie Faye (Cox)	163
Reeves, Curtis L.	219
Reeves, Curtis Lavaughn	219
Reeves, Douglas	241
Reeves, Douglas Ralph	219
Reeves, Edward David	219
Reeves, James Franklin	219
Reeves, Lily	196, 219
Reeves, Louis Herbert	193
Reeves, Nancy	219
Reeves, Robert	219
Reeves, Robert Lavaughn	219

Name	Page
Reeves, Robert Lee	219
Reeves, Shirley (Butner)	219, 245
Reeves, Viola (West)	219
Reeves, William Calvin	219
Reeves, William W.	219
Reggio, Claire	219
Reid, Robert Caldwell	150
Reid, Willie Ann	70
Reider, Anna Ruth	32
Reider, William Jonas	257
Reimers, Johanne	219
Reinhard, Edward Edwin	180
Reinhard, Lessie Lee (Carter)	220
Reinhard, Roy Edwin	219
Reiser, Patty	219, 220
Releford, Alex	272
Releford, Oliver Alfred	220
Releford, Raymond Aarol, Sr.	220
Reno, Susan	220
Rever, Elizabeth	273
Reyes, Amelia Molly	24
Reyes, Louis Alberto	220
Reynolds, Anna "Frankie"	220
Reynolds, Arthur	220
Reynolds, Charlie	220
Reynolds, Edith Horn	220
Reynolds, George Thomas	2
Reynolds, Herman	220
Reynolds, John	220
Reynolds, John Rook	35
Reynolds, Lillian	2
Reynolds, Selina	220
Reynolds, Vera Louise	207, 230, 297
Rhea, Claude Calvin	155
Rhea, Edgar Witt	220
Rhea, Edward W	220
Rhea, Forrest E.	220
Rhea, Forrest Edgar	220
Rhea, Frances Juanita	220
Rhea, James Calvin	10
Rhea, Linda Joyce	220
Rhea, Mae	241
Rhea, Mary	vi
Rhea, Mary Ruth (Lowe)	157
Rhea, Maudie Lee	220
Rhea, Oscar	220
Rhea, Raymond H.	10, 242
Rhea, Robert	220
Rhea, Rosey	87
Rhea, Russ	24
Rhea, Tony Lynn	157
Rhea, Veola Mae (Sweeton)	220
Rhea, Willie Nephi	220
Rheal, Wilma Jean	220
Rhinehart, Ruth	243
Rhoads, Frank Hulon	14
Rhoads, Vera June (Meeks)	220
Rhodes, Marie Juanita (Basile)	220
Rice, Gwendolyn Maxine (Ledford)	221
Rice, Hazel Parsons	221
Rich, Ora	221
Richard, Jr., Howard Eugene	66
Richard, Willie Kate (Campbell)	221
Richards, Bobby Lee	221
Richards, Dorris Lee	221
Richardson Cemetery in Beersheba Springs	vii
Richardson, Annie Lee	221
Richardson, Annie Myrtle	270
Richardson, Bertha	41, 221
Richardson, Clarence	221
Richardson, Clarence Glenn	221
Richardson, Clayta	221
Richardson, Clayta Jean (Tate)	221
Richardson, Cleo	221
Richardson, Dean	20
Richardson, E.J.	67
Richardson, Elease	106
Richardson, Emma Jane	221
Richardson, Everett	255, 256
Richardson, Everett Labrawn	221
Richardson, Frank Joseph	221
Richardson, George Franklin	221
Richardson, Isabelle Agnes	221
Richardson, Jesse Herman	221
Richardson, Lemma Hazel	221
Richardson, Marsha	221
Richardson, McKinley	221
Richardson, Morris Earl	40, 221
Richardson, Raymond	221
Richie, David	221
Richie, Mary	91
Richmond, Elizabeth Catherine	90
Richmond, Harriet Ellen	271
Richmond, James Aubrey	270
Richmond, James H	221
Richmond, Josepn Atticus	51
Richmond, Masion B.	221
Richmond, Ruth	270
Richmond, Sarah Jane	268, 270
Richner, Lydia	96
Ricketts, Sylvia Ann	101
Rickman, Ruby	12
Riddle, Billy Reid	108
Riddle, Billy Reid	221

Name	Page
Riddle, Cordel	40, 222
Riddle, Jacqueline Kaye	221
Riddle, Jayne (Patterson)	221, 222
Riddle, Jayne Carolyn	222
Riddle, Mary	222
Riddle, Sharon Claudette	269
Riddle, Timothy Brian	40
Rider, Angelina	222
Ridge, Nancy	209
Ridge, Nancy	39
Ridge, Unknown	206
Riding, Fanny	300
Ridley, Billy Joe	202
Ridley, Marion Berton, Dr	222
Rieben, Alfred Roy	222
Rieben, Bonnie Sue (Fults)	222
Rieben, Fritz	222
Rieben, Ralph E.	iii, 222
Ried, Judy	222
Rieder, Albert Daniel	134
Rieder, Anna Pauline	222
Rieder, Don	222
Rieder, Francis Marion	219
Rieder, Georgia Fay (Garner)	222
Rieder, Henrietta	222
Rieder, Henrietta	55
Rieder, Henry J.	55
Rieder, Irma Jean (Gipson)	98
Rieder, John Henry	222
Rieder, Linda Gayle	222
Rieder, Lloyd	155
Rieder, Lloyd H.	155
Rieder, male child	222
Rieder, Mary	222
Rieder, Nannie Elizabeth	219
Rieder, Ruby	203
Rieder, Sandra	299
Rieder, William Jonas "Bill", Jr.	90
Rieder, William Jonas, Jr.	222
Rieder, William Jonas, Sr,	222
Riese, Theodore Alfred "Pete"	222
Riese, Therma Faye	222
Rigsby, Earl	222
Rigsby, Ewin Oliver	223
Rigsby, George Lee	222
Rigsby, Nancy (Roberts) Cleek	222
Rigsby, Shirley Jean	223
Rinehart, Judy	151
Risko, Geneva (Dickerson)	130
Risko, John	223
Risley, William F.	223
Risley, William H.	223
Risner, Lena	223
Ritchie, Tina Marie	125
Ritzius, Julie Mina	129
Rives, Edmund Harrison	303
Rives, Evaline Rebecca	223
Rives, Lucinda W.	223
Roach, Connie	223
Roach, Dennis Dean	89
Roach, Dennis Scott	223
Roach, Lillie Irene	223
Roark, Shirley	148
Robak, Ralph	174
Robbins, Elliot Kenneth	171
Robbins, Elliot LeRoy	223
Roberge, Diana Marie	223
Roberge, Michel Pierre	223
Roberson, Ethel	223
Roberson, Malinda	87
Robert, Mary	34
Robert, Willis	234
Roberts Robinson, Jeannette Julie (Blondelet)	91
Roberts, James Arthur II	223
Roberts, Agnes	223
Roberts, Amos	89
Roberts, Anna Lee	45
Roberts, Annie Betty	160
Roberts, Arthur	224
Roberts, Arvill Elihue	224, 253
Roberts, Arville E	109
Roberts, Barbara Jean	223
Roberts, Benton	189
Roberts, Bessie	223
Roberts, Betty	30, 272
Roberts, Betty (Scott)	38
Roberts, Billy Hagan	223
Roberts, Blaine E.	112, 223, 224
Roberts, Carl Wilson	133, 287
Roberts, Charlie Bradford	224
Roberts, Clyde	116
Roberts, Donna "Donnie" Louise (Meeks)	223
Roberts, Doris Ophelia (Caldwell)	223
Roberts, Edward	223
Roberts, Elene	223
Roberts, Elizabeth	223
Roberts, Elmo	242
Roberts, Emma	225
Roberts, Ernest Arnold, Sr.	106
Roberts, Etta Leona (Madewell)	223, 224
Roberts, Evelyn (King)	223
Roberts, Everett	223
Roberts, Everett Bryan	224
Roberts, Faye	224
Roberts, Fealy Mae	224
Roberts, Flora	224

Name	Page
Roberts, Florence L. (Parmeter)	188, 189, 253
Roberts, France	224
Roberts, Francis	223
Roberts, Francis M.	75
Roberts, George	80
Roberts, Geraldine	37
Roberts, Geraldine (Grizzle)	272
Roberts, Gertie	224
Roberts, Harold	175
Roberts, Hazel	224
Roberts, Henry	108
Roberts, Herschel	95, 189, 223
Roberts, Hother	225
Roberts, Isham	74
Roberts, James	108
Roberts, Jeanne	188, 223
Roberts, Jerry	113
Roberts, Jessie	224
Roberts, Jessie Dreadmon	224
Roberts, Joyce	224
Roberts, Julia (Brewer)	95, 182
Roberts, Kenneth	224
Roberts, Lana	224
Roberts, Lee	267
Roberts, Lewis	224
Roberts, Lewis Elmer	224
Roberts, Lewis G., Jr.	224
Roberts, Lewis G, Sr.	224
Roberts, Linda (Meeks)	224
Roberts, Lola	224
Roberts, Louie	75, 153
Roberts, Louis Shane "Bull"	116
Roberts, M Louise	224
Roberts, Maggie Marie Fults	vii
Roberts, Mark	224
Roberts, Marshal	225
Roberts, Marvin	223
Roberts, Mary "Polly"	77
Roberts, Mary Betty	233
Roberts, Mattie	224
Roberts, Maude	29, 44, 45
Roberts, Mildred J.	24
Roberts, Minnie P.	223, 224
Roberts, Monroe, Jr.	178
Roberts, Nora Evelyn	224
Roberts, Olline (Parson)	189
Roberts, Phyllis Diane (Dotson)	224
Roberts, Ralph Earl "Curley"	224
Roberts, Randall K.	224
Roberts, Robert Riley	225
Roberts, Roger	255
Roberts, Sally	224, 225, 261
Roberts, Sherman Dewey	18
Roberts, Sr., Monroe	223
Roberts, Stephen M	224
Roberts, Susan	225
Roberts, Susan Elizabeth	175
Roberts, Susannah	175
Roberts, Susannah Elizabeth	129
Roberts, Tilda	175
Roberts, Tom	23
Roberts, Vera	59
Roberts, Wiley Crawford	80
Robertson, Bessie Anna Lee (Box)	224
Robertson, Beulah Bell	225
Robertson, Desse	258
Robertson, James	225
Robertson, Lawrence Lafayette	225
Robertson, Martha J (Harris)	225
Robertson, Matt	225
Robertson, Nancy C. Bell	96
Robertson, Paul	6
Robertson, Rachel Elizabeth	225
Robertson, Rachel Oma	3
Robertson, William A.	167
Robinson, Albert Lee, Sr.	225
Robinson, Beulah	223
Robinson, Charlie	260
Robinson, Dorothy Lee	202
Robinson, Hebron	202
Robinson, Johnnie Ruth	137
Robinson, Nina Mae	268
Robinson, Rose Lee	137
Robison, Barton F.	120
Robison, Martha	225
Robison, Regina (Smith)	115
Rodddy, Albert D.	225
Roddy, Anna	225
Roddy, Anna Virginia	71
Roddy, Billie Ruth	204
Roddy, Burge S., Sr.	225
Roddy, Franklin P.	225
Roddy, Harris	225
Roddy, Helen Beryl	225
Roddy, Henry Jackson	225
Roddy, James Robert	137
Roddy, Joseph	225
Roddy, Lewis Wilson	141
Roddy, Lydia Sue	225
Roddy, Margaret Sue	276
Roddy, Maude	137
Roddy, Rhonda Kay	173, 225
Roddy, Robert	149
Roddy, Robert Bradford, Sr.	225
Roddy, Robert, Jr.	225
Roddy, Sarah "Sallie"	225

Name	Page
Roddy, Sue	225
Roden, Etta Mae	225
Roden, Evelyn Pauline Wilson (Short)	225
Roden, Frances	225
Roden, Gary Wayne	206
Roden, Thurman	225
Rodgers, Henry H	225
Rodrigues, Frank Anthony	226
Rodrigus, Joseph	225
Roeder, John William	225
Rogers, Benjamin Hade	13
Rogers, Bert B.	88, 225, 226
Rogers, Bobbie Lee	48
Rogers, Brenda	110
Rogers, Calvin Houston	89
Rogers, Charlestine	226
Rogers, Clifford	50
Rogers, David Earl	226
Rogers, Eileen	226
Rogers, Elizabeth	226
Rogers, Ellen	226
Rogers, Gary Joel	226
Rogers, George Daniel	158
Rogers, George Houston	88
Rogers, Geraldine Layne	226
Rogers, Gertie Mae	225
Rogers, Henry	88
Rogers, Hervey Thomas	226
Rogers, Hubert	226
Rogers, Hubert Benjamin	226
Rogers, James	226
Rogers, James Alvin	226
Rogers, James Alvin, Jr.	226
Rogers, Jewell	226
Rogers, Joe Harley	237
Rogers, John Freeland	226
Rogers, Josephine	226
Rogers, Lelon	231
Rogers, Linda Carol	137
Rogers, Louisa "Eliza"	178
Rogers, Maggie	159
Rogers, Margaret Eileen (Tucker)	226
Rogers, Marie	226
Rogers, Maurine (Green)	156, 161
Rogers, Melissa "Missy"	226
Rogers, Melva	145
Rogers, Nadine	166, 169
Rogers, Nora	105
Rogers, Pauline Marie (Ward)	192
Rogers, Pleasant	226
Rogers, Vera	226
Rogers. Gene O. "Eyeballs"	289
Roles, Mollie	226
Roles, Morris Hugh Arrington	121
Roller, Clara (Argo)	121
Roller, Everette	226
Rollings, Abner "Duck"	226
Rollings, Adolphus	226
Rollings, Barbara Louise	226
Rollings, Betty	292
Rollings, Frank E.	146
Rollings, James	146, 278
Rollings, John Robert	285
Rollings, Melba Jean (Tate)	236
Rollings, Terry Keith "Quiver"	226
Rollings, Thelma Ruth	226
Rollings, Timmie	104, 105
Rollins, Abner "Duck"	278
Rollins, Annie Gay	227
Rollins, Benjamin Franklin	261
Rollins, Betty	226, 227
Rollins, Bob	73
Rollins, Bufford Cleston	132
Rollins, Carolyn Jean (Layne)	227
Rollins, Charles Matthew	227
Rollins, Christie	227
Rollins, Clara Belle (Ladd)	184
Rollins, Dennis Edward	227
Rollins, Dicie Jane	227
Rollins, Dorothy Marie (Gholston)	114
Rollins, Frances Marie	227
Rollins, Hershel	134
Rollins, James	227
Rollins, James "Jim"	72
Rollins, James Franklin	100, 227
Rollins, John Thomas	227
Rollins, Kate	100, 227
Rollins, Kate Emma	219
Rollins, Leta	200
Rollins, Lillie	71
Rollins, Luevina "Lou"	225
Rollins, Margie Ruth	227
Rollins, Marlon Marie (Greene)	227
Rollins, Matthew Thomas "Math"	227
Rollins, Michael R.	227
Rollins, Michael Thomas	227
Rollins, Nina Sue	227
Rollins, Norma	141
Rollins, Paul	227
Rollins, Paul, Jr.	227
Rollins, Paula Lynette	227
Rollins, Pauline	227
Rollins, Phillip	223
Rollins, Rebecca (Mrs. Thomas W. Clepper)	227
Rollins, Richard E.	227
Rollins, Robert Jackson	227

Name	Page
Rollins, Shirley	140, 227, 296
Rollins, Thelma	253
Rollins, Vera	227
Rollins, Virgil	227
Rollins, Walter "Smokey"	227
Rollins, William Jackson	227
Roop, Mary Rosetta	227
Root, Hope	2
Roper, Judy	74
Rorer, Charles "Chuck"	91
Rorer, Quentin Orion	228
Rosa, Jerrie Jeanette	228
Rose, Andrew Richard	57
Rose, Clara Louise	228
Rose, Cullie Agnes	135
Rose, David Martin	94
Rose, Dick	248
Rose, Elizabeth	156
Rose, Elizabeth Geneva (Green)	97
Rose, Emma	228
Rose, Erica	156
Rose, Janice	228
Rose, Janis	121
Rose, Jelina Allison	228
Rose, Lucille	228
Rose, Margaret	280
Rose, Melvin A.	168, 172
Rose, Melvin Wayne	228
Rose, Michael	228
Rose, Solomon C	228
Rose, Thomas J.	228
Rose, Vesta Ann	228
Rosendaul, Albert Ellsworth	21, 29, 228
Ross, Addie F.	45
Ross, Albert P	228
Ross, Becky	228
Ross, Buford	228
Ross, Dianna Lynn	265
Ross, Edwin	228
Ross, Eleanor	213
Ross, Elizabeth	152
Ross, Essie	92
Ross, Eugene	123
Ross, Gary	228
Ross, George "Dobber"	228
Ross, Gladys	228
Ross, Gladys Allene (Tate)	165
Ross, Gladys Tate	228
Ross, Greg	170
Ross, Isaac	235
Ross, James	228, 234
Ross, James Harrison	229
Ross, Job	228
Ross, John	228
Ross, John C.	210
Ross, John Carroll	228
Ross, John Edward	228
Ross, John Jacob "Hunky"	228, 229
Ross, John Wesley	228
Ross, John William "Bill"	228, 229
Ross, Kelly Austin	52
Ross, Larry	228
Ross, Laureen Gay	228
Ross, Leon	251
Ross, Lillie	228
Ross, Martha (Ramsey)	43, 97
Ross, Myrtle	229
Ross, Nadine (Meeks)	229
Ross, Nancy	229
Ross, Nancy Tabor	228
Ross, Nannie May (Stump)	229
Ross, Nellie Gertrude	229
Ross, Nellie Gertrude (Nunley)	149
Ross, Richard Allen	229
Ross, Samuel	228
Ross, True Ernestine	149, 229
Ross, Vernon	52
Ross, William Herbert	53
Ross, William Herbert Robert	228
Ross, Winnie	228
Rothwell, William Willis	228
Rowe, Roberta Pike	14
Rowe, Ruby	130
Rowe, Sarah	200
Rowland, Stephanie	14
Royal, Bessie Myrtle	45, 46
Roysden, Marie	82
Roysdon, J.C.	162
Roysdon, Nona Fay (Shadrick)	229
Rozell, Delbert	229
Rozell, Nellie Ruth (Winton)	229
Rubley, Carlena	229
Rubley, Charles H., Sr.	111, 287
Rubley, Edward	229
Ruch, Afra	229
Ruch, Elizabeth "Lisette"	229
Ruch, Elizabeth Lisette	229
Ruch, Jacob	19
Ruckweed, Christopher	229
Rudd, Christine	190
Rudd, Johnny	229
Ruef, Anne	229
Ruef, Ulrich	239
Ruehling, Brenda Sanders	iii
Ruehling, Clarissa Davina (Mitchell)	239
Ruehling, Hurl	229
Ruehling, Hurl G	229

Name	Page
Ruehling, John H	158
Ruehling, Johnny	229, 283
Ruehling, Marvlee	283
Ruehling, Ronnie Darrell	229
Ruehling, Willie Mae (Woodlee)	229
Rumsey, Jerry L.	229
Rumsey, Lloyd, Jr,	229
Rundquist, Gladys Violet	229
Runge, Leonard Benedict	148
Runion, Melinda	22
Rural Cemetery at Easter Knob	viii
Rush, Betty Jo	28
Russell, Alice	239
Russell, Billie	137
Russell, Daniel	102
Russell, Fred	230
Russell, Iva Michelle	102
Russell, John Henry	201
Russell, Leona	72
Russell, Velvie Lee	96
Russell, Virginia	230
Rust, Ambrose "Rusty"	236
Rust, Cynthia Rose	230
Rust, Ella	230
Rust, Ella Mae	4
Rust, Hattie	19
Rust, Henry	101
Rust, Howell Bryan	230
Rust, Ida Mae (Nunley)	230
Rust, Lawrence	230
Rust, Lillie Bell	230
Rust, Mae (Childers)	171
Rust, Newborn	230
Rust, Rebha	230
Rust, Ricky	96
Rust, S. R.	230
Rust, Virginia Isabel	230
Rust, Virginia R.	163
Rutherford, Edgar L	230
Rutherford, Martha	185
Rutledge Hill	v
Rutledge, Frank	142
Rutledge, Russell Lee	230
Rutledge, Ruth (Willis)	257
Rutschmann, Heinrich	230
Rutschmann, Jakob	230
Ryals, Maymie	230
Ryan, Jimmy	217
Ryan, Nora	158
Ryberg, Bernhard E.	26
Ryberg, Johannah Sophia (Sorling)	230
Rymer, James Harvey	230
Rymer, James Robert "Jim Bob"	230
Rymer, Kenneth	230
Rymer, Linda	230
Rymer, Maude Bell (Scoggins)	230
Rymer, Mildred	230
Rymer, Noah	166
Rymer, Steve	230
Sabados, Emil	230
Sabados, Lori	230
Sabados, Martha Jane (Harris)	230
Sabados, Steve	230
Sabados, Steven Charles	230
Sage, Albert D.	230
Sage, Rosalee (Foster)	230
Sailors, Oscar	230
Sain James Murry, Jr. "Jimmy"	127
Sain, Alfred Smartt "Dick"	230
Sain, Dolores "Doe" (Stubblefield)	231
Sain, James Murry, Sr.	231
Sain, Mary E. (Purcell)	230
Sain, Thomas Finneran	231
Sain, William R	47
Saint, Penelope	231
Saint, Unk	26
Salas, Rosita	26
Sales, Elizabeth	25
Salyers, Darlene Sue	159
Samples, David M.	231
Samples, William	231
Sampley, Charles Wilburn	231
Sampley, Charles, Jr. "Chuck"	231
Sampley, James	231
Sampley, Mary Emma	231
Sampley, Minnie Ruth	268
Sampley, William Richard	231
Samson, Adam John	231
Samson, Helena J (Miller)	231
Samuel, Lacy	231
Sanders, 3 Infants	243
Sanders, Adrian	231
Sanders, Adrian Stephen	231
Sanders, Agnes Jane	231
Sanders, Albert	163, 169, 170
Sanders, Albert Jr.	234
Sanders, Albert Sanders, Jr.	252
Sanders, Albert Sidney Johnson	233
Sanders, Albert, Jr.	232
Sanders, Alex Houston	232
Sanders, Alexander	163
Sanders, Alexander, Mrs.	231
Sanders, Alice Mae	231
Sanders, Allie J. "Shorty"	252, 259, 268
Sanders, Allie Jean "Shorty" (Worley)	234

Name	Page
Sanders, Almeda	231
Sanders, Alta Odell	207
Sanders, Anderson	234
Sanders, Andrew "Andy" Jacob	236
Sanders, Andrew Jackson	231
Sanders, Andrew Jacob	236
Sanders, Anita Jean	171
Sanders, Anna Sophronie "Fronie" (Meeks)	231
Sanders, Anthony Edward	231
Sanders, Arthur	231
Sanders, Arthur Lee	10
Sanders, Arthur Milton	191
Sanders, Benjamin W., Sr.	232, 233
Sanders, Bernice	232
Sanders, Berta	156, 161
Sanders, Bettie Mae	224
Sanders, Betty (King)	134
Sanders, Brenda May (Gibson)	232
Sanders, Candace	232
Sanders, Casper	78
Sanders, Charles R.	232
Sanders, Charles Ray	232
Sanders, Child	232
Sanders, Cleo	232
Sanders, Cleo Elizabeth (Campbell)	155, 213, 235
Sanders, Connie	232
Sanders, Cora Jean	232
Sanders, Crawford	184
Sanders, Daniel Mark	232
Sanders, Darrell	232
Sanders, David	236
Sanders, Deidre Jane (Moore) "Dee"	232
Sanders, Delia	232
Sanders, Delilah Jane	164, 166
Sanders, Dennis Ray	179
Sanders, Dessie	232
Sanders, Dillard	43
Sanders, Dillard D.	57, 233, 234, 235, 255
Sanders, Dorie	235
Sanders, Doris	27
Sanders, Dorothy	142
Sanders, Dorothy "Dottie" Juanita	222, 234
Sanders, Dorothy Mae (Collins)	232
Sanders, Earl "Bud"	232
Sanders, Earl R.	234
Sanders, Earl R., Jr.	232
Sanders, Eda	232
Sanders, Edna Mae	178
Sanders, Edward Mark	192
Sanders, Elizabeth	232
Sanders, Elizabeth "Betty" (Ogle)	124
Sanders, Elizabeth Janie	233
Sanders, Ella Louise	190
Sanders, Elsie Juanita (Dykes)	196
Sanders, Elzie	233
Sanders, Emma Ellen "Nenie"	231
Sanders, Emmitt	233
Sanders, Ernest Milton	192
Sanders, Eugene P.	194
Sanders, Frank	233
Sanders, Fronia Novella	235
Sanders, Fronie	71
Sanders, Garlan	71
Sanders, Garlon	235
Sanders, Gary Dale	232
Sanders, Geneva L.	235
Sanders, George Carroll "Uncle Dick"	233
Sanders, Giles Haston	233
Sanders, Ginger LoLetta	233
Sanders, Glen Ed	233
Sanders, Gregory Wallace	232
Sanders, Grover Carl	233
Sanders, H.D. "Mutt"	233
Sanders, Hallie	233
Sanders, Harold Woodrow	62
Sanders, Harrison	234
Sanders, Harrison "Harris"	168, 169, 234
Sanders, Helen	233
Sanders, Helen L. "Phoebe"	232
Sanders, Helen Ozell (Layman)	233
Sanders, Henry James	233
Sanders, Herman	44, 51, 234
Sanders, Homer Clinton	232
Sanders, Houston "Hugh"	234
Sanders, Howard	234, 235
Sanders, Howard "Buck"	234
Sanders, Infants (3 individual graves)	234
Sanders, J. K.	234
Sanders, Jackie	231
Sanders, James	259
Sanders, James A.	231, 234
Sanders, James Darrell	234
Sanders, James E "Sham"	234
Sanders, James Henry	231, 234
Sanders, James Herman	234
Sanders, James Kelly	234
Sanders, James Otho	234
Sanders, James Ray	234
Sanders, Jennie	234
Sanders, Jeremy	58
Sanders, Jessie H.	236
Sanders, Jewelene	232
Sanders, Jo Ann	184

Name	Page
Sanders, Joan Katherine (Ross)	104
Sanders, Joe Reggie	234
Sanders, John	180
Sanders, John Annis	234
Sanders, John Emmett	233, 235
Sanders, John R	234
Sanders, John Russell	233, 267
Sanders, John William	232, 234
Sanders, Jordan	34
Sanders, Jordan "Jerd"	233, 235
Sanders, Joseph Charles	270
Sanders, Josephine	256
Sanders, Judith Ann	234
Sanders, Judy	234
Sanders, Katherine	236
Sanders, Kathryn	138
Sanders, Larry H.	75, 137
Sanders, Larry Michael	232
Sanders, Leonard	234
Sanders, Leonard "Little Red"	236
Sanders, Leroy	62
Sanders, Lewis Bradford	257, 293
Sanders, Lillian	235
Sanders, Lillian Virginia	234
Sanders, Lillie Mae	235
Sanders, Lizzie	241
Sanders, Lloyd	163
Sanders, Lola	61
Sanders, Lorene	129, 243
Sanders, Loretta	200
Sanders, Lou	52
Sanders, Lou Ella	233
Sanders, Louella	76
Sanders, Louis	61
Sanders, Lucinda Jane "Lucy"	231, 235
Sanders, Lynette Nicloe "Nikki" (Ross)	235
Sanders, Mahlon Nelson	235
Sanders, Mandy	235
Sanders, Margaret	61
Sanders, Margaret Anna Dell (Nunley)	36
Sanders, Margaret Kathleen (Parsons)	235
Sanders, Martha	235
Sanders, Martha "Mattie"	114
Sanders, Mary	51
Sanders, Mary Ann	212, 227, 268
Sanders, Mary Elizabeth	269
Sanders, Mary Elizabeth "Lizzie"	79, 125, 163, 166, 168, 255
Sanders, Mary Estella	172
Sanders, Mary Estells Estora	255
Sanders, Mary Jane	51
Sanders, Matthew	63
Sanders, Matthew "Matt"	233
Sanders, Mattie J. (Henley)	235
Sanders, Maude Josephine	235
Sanders, Maudie	162
Sanders, Melvin	49, 162
Sanders, Micah Habakkuk	165, 235
Sanders, Mildred	235
Sanders, Mina	271
Sanders, Minnie	69, 200
Sanders, Minnie Etta	157, 200
Sanders, Minnie Lee	223
Sanders, Mitchell	290
Sanders, Myrtle	236
Sandcrs, Nancy (Cope)	209
Sanders, Nancy Bell	235
Sanders, Navine	244
Sanders, Ninnie Emma Ellen	235
Sanders, Ollie Faye	235
Sanders, Patrick	12, 68
Sanders, Pauline	236
Sanders, Phillip	88, 170, 235
Sanders, Piney Angeline	236
Sanders, Ralph	48
Sanders, Randy Lee	236
Sanders, Rebecca Idella Eudors	236
Sanders, Rose Burr	137
Sanders, Ruby Marie (Rollings)	234
Sanders, Sally	236
Sanders, Samantha Lee	60
Sanders, Sarah Ann	241
Sanders, Sarah Elizabeth	25
Sanders, Sarah Lottie	236
Sanders, Secil	52
Sanders, Selena Evalina (Goodman)	52
Sanders, Shelby Jean	236
Sanders, Shirley Ann	236
Sanders, Sonya Dee	213, 257
Sanders, Southerland	236
Sanders, Stanley L.	195
Sanders, Stephen Cope	295
Sanders, Sue Ellen	234
Sanders, Suzette (Nunley)	236
Sanders, Terry Lee	236
Sanders, Theo	236
Sanders, Thomas	58, 227
Sanders, Thomas Oscar	233, 234, 235
Sanders, Tinny	232
Sanders, Troy	118
Sanders, Vina	235
Sanders, Wallace	155
Sanders, Walter William	171
Sanders, Wayne Stanley	236
Sanders, Wesley	235
Sanders, Wheeler	234

Name	Page
Sanders, William	235
Sanders, William Asbury	236, 295
Sanders, William Grant	236
Sanders, William H.	236
Sanders, William Houston	191
Sanders, William Lee	236
Sanders, William Wallace	232, 233, 235, 236
Sanders, William Wallace, Jr.	264
Sanders, William Wallace, Sr.	233, 236
Sanders, Willie Edward	236
Sanders, Willie James	134
Sanders, Zora	118
Sanderson, James W.	236
Sanderson, James W. Sr.	236
Sanderson, Mary Lorraine	236
Sanderson, Sam	236
Sanson, Green F.	236
Sargent, Doris Viola (Bunch)	64
Sargent, George	237
Sargent, George M.	259
Sargent, James Lappin	237
Sargent, James Lappin "Jim'	237
Sargent, Josephine (Meeks)	237
Sargent, Samuel A.	237
Sargent, Samuel Arnold	237
Sargent, Samuel Edward	237
Sartain-Sharp, Mary	237
Sartain, Austin	237
Sartain, Bettie	237
Sartain, Bettie Isabel	257
Sartain, Calvin	166
Sartain, Charles Harold	238
Sartain, Democrates "Mock"	28
Sartain, Donnie Wayne	237
Sartain, Frank	237
Sartain, Gerald Ray	237
Sartain, Hazel	237
Sartain, Heraclitus Harrison "Jack"	12, 27
Sartain, Herbert	237
Sartain, Hope	237
Sartain, Ike Washington	188
Sartain, Infants	191
Sartain, Isaac Washington	237
Sartain, J.D.	237
Sartain, Jacqueline (Klinski)	237
Sartain, James	237
Sartain, James Alfred	237
Sartain, James Brent	237
Sartain, Jay D.	237
Sartain, Jennie	237
Sartain, Jennie Earmie	13
Sartain, Joe	13
Sartain, L.D.	237
Sartain, Lennie	237, 238
Sartain, Lewis	238
Sartain, Loke Adherable	237
Sartain, Louis	238
Sartain, M. Edison	136
Sartain, Marguerite	237
Sartain, Nell	29
Sartain, Pauline	299
Sartain, Rachel Arkansas	22
Sartain, Reba Jo (Bennett)	92
Sartain, Robert Elliott	238
Sartain, Stella	238
Sartain, Sterling Emerald	7, 8
Sartain, Susan Harrison	238
Sartin, Hervie Lee	97
Sartin, John L.	22
Sartin, Sarah "Sallie" J. (Dodd)	238
Sarver, Roy Jack	238
Sasser, John Howard	147
Sasser, Johnny F.	238
Sasser, Margaret	238
Savage Cove Creek	viii
Savage, Ann	238
Savage, Anna Bell	238
Savage, Donald Earl	25
Savage, Dorothy Mae (Brown)	238
Savage, Glenn	238
Savage, James	238
Savage, James Freddie	238
Savage, Jerry Franklin	238
Savage, Jesse Lawson	238
Savage, Jessee Lawson	238
Savage, Marael Samuel	238
Savage, Martha Belle	238
Savage, Martha Jane "Jennie"	220
Savage, Mattie	165
Savage, Nelmon	220
Savage, Osbon	238
Savage, Richard Preston	238
Savage, Sally Ann	238
Savage, Sally H. Westfall	18
Savage, Sarah Harrison	17
Savage, Stephanie	258
Saverivein, Violet M	238
Saville, Malinda	248
Sawyer, John Mitchell, Rev.	37
Sawyer, Zery Norman	238
Sayles, Gilbert	238
Sayles, Mary Orme	218
Saylor, Elizabeth "Teat"	99, 218
Saylor, Johnnie	60
Saynes, James E.	61
Saynes, Mildred Irene "Peg"	238

Name	Page
Scaggs, Robert Thomas	238
Scaggs, Stella F.	197
Scantland, Ruby	190
Scarboro, Gladys	146
Schaen, Candy	279
Schaenberger, Gilg	226
Schaerer, Barbara	229
Schaerer, Bryan Hillis	238
Schaerer, Cheryl	238
Schaerer, Dorothy	238
Schaerer, Elsie Louisa	238
Schaerer, Emil Tucker	238
Schaerer, Gleenie	238
Schaerer, Henry	214
Schaerer, J.R.	153
Schaerer, John Werner	238
Schaerer, Sam	238
Schaerer, Sam Henry	238
Schaerer, William Henry	238
Schaffer, Irene	238
Schauman, Michael	221
Schauman, Toni Juanita (Davis)	239
Scheisser, Barbara Grace	239
Schell, Emil Johann Heinrich	154
Schell, Herman Ernest Robert	239
Schell, Maria	239
Schieser, Etheleen	239
Schieser, Gabriel	140
Schiesser, Abbie	239
Schiesser, Afra	182, 184
Schiesser, Barbara	229
Schiesser, Frances	193, 239
Schiesser, Michael	191
Schiesser, Peter	239
Schiesser, Stella Irene	239
Schiesser, Wilheminie "Minnie" E.	242
Schild, Anna	239
Schild, Anna Margaret	20
Schild, Elizabeth	20
Schild, Georgia Violet	133
Schild, Hildegard (Koehn)	205
Schild, Jerry Wayne	239
Schild, Johannes	239
Schild, John A.	239
Schild, Kaspar	239
Schild, Margaritha geb (Ruef)	239
Schild, Peter	239
Schild, Unk	239, 284
Schild, William Martin	239
Schild, Wilma B.	239
Schiller, Linda	239
Schlageter, Annie K.	131
Schlageter, Glenn	239
Schlageter, Glenn David	239
Schlageter, Ignatz	239
Schlageter, Ignatz	133
Schlageter, Jacob J.	239, 240
Schlageter, Linda Sue (Ellis)	239
Schlageter, Marion Marie (James)	239
Schlageter, Rosina geb (Laager)	239
Schlageter, William Carl	240
Schlasner, August	291
Schlasner, Violet Blanche	287
Schmidt, Robert T	133
Schmiedt, Balth	242
Schmitt, Susan	240
Schnebly, Nancy Ann	136
Schneider, Robert	11
Schneider, Elizabeth	133
Schoenemann, Elisabeth	299
Schoenmann, Alvin	69
Schoenmann, Alvin T	240
Schoenmann, Alvin Tony	240
Schoenmann, Edna	20
Schoenmann, Elizabeth Rosa	126
Schoenmann, Fred Jackson James	239
Schoenmann, Glenn Shely	239
Schoenmann, Jacob	240
Schoenmann, Raymond Jackson	10
Schoenmann, Rosa	240
Schoenmann, Walter	114, 137, 143
Schoenmann, Walter Douglas	240
Schoenmann, Walter Lannie	58
Schoenmann, William Elbert	240
Scholer, Helen Faye (Crank)	123, 240
Scholer, Johnnie Edwin	240
Scholer, Rosina	240
Schonemann, Rosa	198
Schreiber, John	112
Schroeder, Lydia	68
Schroeder, Minna Bertha	13
Schultz, Bonnie	269
Schulze, Oscar	186
Schwante, Karen	9
Scissom, Argie Earlene	121
Scissom, Barbara	20
Scissom, Barbara Jean	247
Scissom, Billy Ray	247
Scissom, Carolyn	240
Scissom, Chester	74
Scissom, Deb	iii
Scissom, Dola Clarene (Tate)	240
Scissom, Elsie Marie	240
Scissom, Faye	11
Scissom, George Thomas	240

Name	Page
Scissom, Gregory Garland	122, 240
Scissom, Hazel	240
Scissom, Henry	153
Scissom, Kenneth	240
Scissom, M.G. Thomas	240
Scissom, Patricia Marie	240
Scissom, Roy Dale	43
Scissom, Sarah Ann (Steele)	240
Scissom, Steven Eugene	240
Scissom, Tina	294
Scissom, Tina Dianna	304
Scissom, Tom P	240
Scissom, Wanda	240
Scissom, Wanda Sue	75
Scissom, Willie Mae	174
Scoggin, Mary Evelyn (Singleton)	97
Scoggin, Wilson "Sput"	240
Scoggins, David	240
Scoggins, Virginia Jo	230
Scott, Abidine	102
Scott, Ada	242
Scott, Ada (Harper)	7, 8
Scott, Aileen (Burrows)	240
Scott, Alma	241
Scott, Amos J.	58
Scott, Annie	165
Scott, Barney	117
Scott, Benjamin Franklin	240
Scott, Betty	241, 242
Scott, Brandy Chavaughn (Reeves)	264
Scott, Bridgett B.	241
Scott, Charles F. Sr.	134
Scott, Charles M.	241, 242
Scott, Charlie	241
Scott, Charlotte Lawana (Adams)	243
Scott, Claude	241
Scott, Clyde	242
Scott, Dexter	287
Scott, Dorothy M. (Hammers)	242
Scott, Edith Evelyn	241
Scott, Edna	241
Scott, Edna "Eddie"	138
Scott, Edward Brown	163, 172
Scott, Elda J.	241
Scott, Elizabeth	241
Scott, Emma Casine (Thomas)	206
Scott, Enda	241
Scott, Eta Pearl	205
Scott, Ethel	74
Scott, Ethel Mae	51
Scott, Ethel Maybell	44
Scott, Evelyn	234
Scott, Frank Edward	49
Scott, George Hughes	241
Scott, Gerald	242
Scott, Glen	241
Scott, Grace Estella	242
Scott, Guy "Ivey" Franklin	42
Scott, H. B.	242
Scott, Harlie	241, 242
Scott, Hazel	62
Scott, Helen	197
Scott, James Daniel	28
Scott, James Richard	241
Scott, Jane	241, 242
Scott, Jerry Benjamin	263
Scott, John	241
Scott, Joyve	viii
Scott, Jr., Hubert H	36, 75
Scott, Julia Elizabeth	241
Scott, Julie	96
Scott, Junior	176
Scott, Karen (Bailey)	223
Scott, Korey Alan	241
Scott, Korey Steven	241
Scott, Laura Ethel	241
Scott, Laura Ether	242
Scott, Lee	10
Scott, Lena Mae	241, 242
Scott, Leslie Jane	146, 165, 168, 270
Scott, Levice Edwin	25
Scott, Lewis Earl	241
Scott, Lillian Edna	241
Scott, Linda Joyce (Rhea)	221
Scott, Margaret	242
Scott, Margaret Ann	135
Scott, Marie	242
Scott, Martha A	242
Scott, Martha Melissa Jane (Dyer)	242
Scott, Mary A (Tate)	242
Scott, Mary Etta Missouri (Campbell)	242
Scott, Maxine	242
Scott, Michael Hughes	223
Scott, Minnie V. (Kilgore)	242
Scott, Odous	242
Scott, Ollie	241
Scott, Ora	177
Scott, Patricia Sue	241
Scott, Price	viii, ix
Scott, Priceford	242
Scott, Rachel Louise (Higgins)	242
Scott, Ralph	242
Scott, Rather	242
Scott, Robert	241
Scott, Rocky Lamar	205
Scott, Rose	242
Scott, Samuel	50
Scott, Sarah	243

Name	Page
Scott, Sidney	73, 160, 271, 273, 274
Scott, Spuder	242
Scott, Sr., Michael Hughes	7
Scott, Stephen	242
Scott, Steve	241
Scott, Susanah "Annie"	115
Scott, Travis	12
Scott, Walter	241
Scott, William	241, 242
Scott, William Bryan	263
Scott, William J.C.	9, 138
Scott, William Thomas	242, 243
Scruggs, Ada	243
Scruggs, Ada Mai	110
Scruggs, Ella	226
Scruggs, Isabell	100
Scruggs, James	277
Scruggs, James T.	243
Scruggs, Jim	243
Scruggs, John Wilson	243
Scruggs, Kimberly Michell	243
Scruggs, Lydia	243
Scruggs, Lydia Frances	299, 300
Scruggs, Minnie Lee	51
Scruggs, Nancy Jane	89
Scruggs, Sarah Almeda	121
Scruggs, Timmie	89
Scruggs, William M.	146
Scullin, Alda Mae (Franke)	243
Scullin, George	243
Scullin, George Clements Scullin	98
Scullin, George Clifton	243
Scullin, Hank	243
Scullin, Jeannine	206
Scullin, Lorraine H.	206
Seagroves Cemetery	viii
Seagroves, Aaron, Sr.	243
Seagroves, Alvin	243
Seagroves, Arthur Neal "Yogi"	243
Seagroves, Billy Joe	243
Seagroves, Carl	243
Seagroves, Carl Junior	243
Seagroves, Cecil	243
Seagroves, Charles Herschel	243, 244
Seagroves, Connie Lousie	243
Seagroves, Cynthia	viii
Seagroves, Dola T. (Dishroon)	108
Seagroves, Doris	243
Seagroves, Douglas	243
Seagroves, Dovie	244
Seagroves, Franklin "Gabe"	123
Seagroves, George	243
Seagroves, Gladys	287
Seagroves, James	243, 244
Seagroves, Joe	243, 244
Seagroves, Joshua	48
Seagroves, Joshua Dee	244
Seagroves, Joshua Jackson	243
Seagroves, Kenny	244
Seagroves, Lawrence	31
Seagroves, Lawrence Dee	243
Seagroves, Lucille	243
Seagroves, Mae	253
Seagroves, Mae Omillie (Kilgore)	244
Seagroves, Mary Eunice	243
Seagroves, Neoma Alice (Hamilton)	243
Seagroves, Rebecca	244
Seagroves, Rebecca Eller	258
Seagroves, Roger Cecil	259
Seagroves, Sara Irena	244
Seagroves, Shirley (Campbell)	244
Seagroves, Stella Lucille	244
Seagroves, Susie Bell (Fults)	158
Seagroves, Tammy M.	244
Seagroves, Vida Mae	244
Seagroves, Viola	243
Seagroves, Wiley Anderson	243
Seagroves, Wiley Andrew	244
Seagroves, William	244
Seagroves, William "Bill"	244
Seagroves, William "Doug"	243
Seagroves, William Henry	244
Seagroves, William Henry "Bill"	244
Seagroves, Willie Marie Sara Irene	243
Seale, Carl	244
Seale, Roy Glenn	244
Seals, Nannie	244
Searcy, Doyle	294
Sears, Buddy	62
Sears, Elsie	104
Seeley, George	104
Seeley, Jesse	244
Seely, George	136
Segroves, Otis	244
Segroves, Pete	244
Segroves, Stella Lucilld	244
Sehorne, Byron Cal	158
Sehorne, Irene	244
Sehorne, Isham	244
Sehorne, James M	244
Sehorne, Maudie	244
Sehorne, Max	49
Sehorne, Parlie	244

Name	Page
Seibern, Barbara	244
Seibers, Linda	240
Seigler, Bessie	256
Seigrist, Heinrich	295
Seipp, Mary	244
Sekulich, Alex	136
Sekulich, Alex Junior	245
Sekulich, Caroline Sue	245
Self, Edward Quincy	245
Self, Robert Linford	245
Sellars, Martha	245
Sellers, Roberta Jean (Reeves)	49
Sellers, Sam	245
Sells, Anna Allenen	245
Sells, Beulah Mae	245
Sells, Carolyn Grace	274
Sells, Elbert	245
Sells, George A.	245
Sells, James Clifton	245
Sells, Steve Anthony	245
Sells, Verna Louise "Vernie" (Barnes)	245
Sentell, Lydia Love	245
Sequatchie County	vi
Sergent, Eva	298
Serio, Dorothy Betty Jane (Dove)	35
Serio, Pasqual S.	245
Servidia, Unk.	245
Sevier, Ludora	201
Seweeton, Mary Savannah	48
Sewanee, TN	ix
Seymore, James Martin II	167
Seymore, James S.	245
Seymore, Jessica Renee	245
Seymore, Jessica Renee (James)	245
Shaddoack, Ruth	245
Shaddock, Ruth	136
Shadrick, Alvin Lawrence	182
Shadrick, Anderson	245
Shadrick, Barney	39, 149
Shadrick, Barney Paul	145
Shadrick, Carl A.	245
Shadrick, Carl Alton	246
Shadrick, Cecil	44
Shadrick, Charles Layden	229
Shadrick, Chester Willis	245
Shadrick, Clara Mae	245, 246
Shadrick, Cora Lee (Hammers)	272
Shadrick, Dollie (Dyer)	245
Shadrick, Donna Elizabeth	246
Shadrick, Gilliam Edgar	145
Shadrick, James David	245, 246
Shadrick, Joseph Carl "Joe"	246
Shadrick, Lila	246
Shadrick, Lyla	172
Shadrick, Mary Ruth (Phillips)	131
Shadrick, Matilda	246
Shadrick, Mike	123
Shadrick, Osbin Wayne	246
Shadrick, Roy Lee	246
Shadrick, Rufus	149
Shadrick, Tammy	246
Shadrick, Unk	139
Shadrick, William	206
Shaffer, Harley Wayne	210
Shaffer, Patricia Ann	45
Shafter, Linda J.	45
Sharkey, Conrad Griffith	220
Sharkey, Mary Constance (Griffith)	246
Sharkey, Sally Robbins	246
Sharkey, William Lawrence	246
Sharp, Jack	246
Sharp, Joan (Patterson)	237
Sharp, Russell Johnson	246
Sharp, Sandy	246
Sharpe, Charles Gerner	173
Sharpe, Charles Gertner	246
Sharpe, Helen Catherine	246
Sharpe, Howard James	246
Sharpe, Jean Gertrude	246
Shaun, Kevin Smith	246
Shaver, Willa Roma	246
Sheehan, Kathleen	288
Sheeks, Pat	70
Sheeley, Katherine	59
Sheeley, Kathryn	143
Shell, Dorothy	154
Shell, Dortha Jean "Dot"	195
Shell, Juanita	189
Shelnut, Jill	23
Shelton, Billy R.	154
Shelton, Burna D.	246
Shelton, Debra Sue	246
Shelton, Elijah Coleman	246
Shelton, Martha Tennessee "Tennie" (Henegar)	247
Shelton, Pleas Meyers	247
Shelton, William Howard	247
Shelton, William Howard "Bill"	263
Shepherd, Claria	246
Shepherd, Cord	48
Shepherd, Edward Freeman	247
Shepherd, Gavin Tristan	11
Sheppard, Justin Wayne	247
Sheridan, Joe	134
Sheridan, Martina Short	247
Sherman, Bernard	247
Sherman, Betty	247
Sherman, I.B	58

Name	Page
Sherman, Joyce	57, 247
Sherman, Tomothy Kirk	139, 141
Sherriell, Brenda	247
Sherrill, Ada	237
Sherrill, Andrew Jackson, Jr.	229
Sherrill, Andrew Jackson, Sr.	247
Sherrill, Andrew Mason	247
Sherrill, Anna Jean	247
Sherrill, Barbara Jean (Evett)	19
Sherrill, Charlene Henley	247
Sherrill, Charles	280
Sherrill, Clea Allen	247
Sherrill, Frances	247
Sherrill, Frances Almeda	38
Sherrill, Howard	281
Sherrill, Ida May	3
Sherrill, James Hershel	112
Sherrill, James Patty	247
Sherrill, James William	247
Sherrill, Jr., Andrew J	81, 247
Sherrill, Lora Bertha	247
Sherrill, Tomye (Henson)	156
Sherrill, Verbie	247
Sherrill, Virginia O.	3
Sherrill, Winifred	156
Sherwood, James Robert	252
Shetters, Christine	75
Shetters, Elijah, Sr.	251
Shetters, James "Punkin"	105
Shied, Henry S.	156
Shied, Margaret Elizabeth	247
Shied, Mary	247
Shield, Montyne	247
Shields, Bill	130
Shields, Clara	247
Shields, Lonnie	247
Shields, Marilyn	247
Shimmin, Raymond	59
Shimmin, Sherry (Mayes)	101
Shipley, Elmer T.	101
Shipley, J.P.	260
Shipley, Jessie Len	247
Shiriever, Dorothea	247
Shirkey, Clarence Hampton	84
Shirlen, Clay	269
Shirlen, Jeff R	247
Shirlen, Margaret	247
Shirley, Edith Layne (Hill)	247
Shirley, Hudson Robert "Bob"	248
Shirley, Talton Taylor	139, 248
Shiveley, Elva Marie	248
Shoemake, George Washington	280
Shoemake, Mattie	15
Shoemaker, Eunice Ann	75
Shoemaker, Shirley	104
Shoenman, Jacob	135
Shofner, Urban, Sr.	248
Sholey, Dwight	254
Sholey, Vickie (Hawkins)	248
Shook, Alan	248
Shook, Cheryl Lynn	174
Shook, Helen Jewel	147
Shook, Leonard Clint	181
Short, Angela Leigh	147
Short, Annie Esther	231
Short, Billy Ray	85
Short, Effie Mae	274
Short, Effie Mae	243
Short, Faye Goff	243
Short, George	247
Short, Geraldine	189
Short, Ida	12
Short, James	248
Short, James Albert	247
Short, James Reuben	248
Short, Jim	197
Short, Johnny William	197
Short, Joy	248
Short, Joyce Florence	248
Short, Kenneth Eugene "Rooster"	256
Short, Lucy Irene (Rose)	248
Short, Maxine	248
Short, Mord Puryear	248
Short, Raymond	248
Short, Raymond D	248
Short, Robert Mitchell "Pop"	225, 248
Short, Robert Mord	248
Short, Ruby Ella (Anderson)	248
Short, Virginia C.	248
Short, Zada	248
Shortridge, Granville	248
Shoulders, Harrison H. Jr.	168
Shoulders, Ann Elizabeth "Libby" (McCarley)	248
Shoultz, Bonnie L.	248
Shoultz, Jr., R	248
Shoupe, Susie	248
Shrum, Albert	207
Shrum, Andrew	96
Shrum, Andrew Jackson	250
Shrum, Andrew Jackson, Jr.	248
Shrum, Andrew Jackson, Sr.	248
Shrum, Anna Bell (Meeks)	248
Shrum, Beryl Rebecca (Allen)	249
Shrum, Betty Mae	249
Shrum, Billie Jo	249
Shrum, Billy Gene	250

Name	Page
Shrum, Brandon Andrew "Boo"	249
Shrum, Brenda	249
Shrum, Carl Bailey	119
Shrum, Carolyn (Nunley)	250, 255, 276
Shrum, Charles A.	249
Shrum, Charles Andrew	59
Shrum, Charles Edward	249, 299
Shrum, Donald	249, 250
Shrum, Doris (Maddox)	250
Shrum, Ernest Donald, Jr.	249
Shrum, Esther	249
Shrum, Evie Vernie	262
Shrum, Fred	249
Shrum, Fred L.	104
Shrum, Fred Lee	249
Shrum, Gearldean	61
Shrum, Ginger	98
Shrum, Helen Pauline	250
Shrum, Henry	258
Shrum, Howard	250
Shrum, Howard "Blue"	250
Shrum, Howard Edward "Sonny"	249
Shrum, Howard W.	249, 250
Shrum, Howell Franklin "Pinky"	249
Shrum, James	249
Shrum, James Roy, Rev.	78
Shrum, Jeffrey Alan	249
Shrum, Jerry	250
Shrum, Jerry Allen	249
Shrum, Jessie	250
Shrum, Jim	150
Shrum, Joe David	134, 243
Shrum, Rev. Joe David "Jody"	124, 249, 250
Shrum, John	251
Shrum, John E.	250
Shrum, John Lawrence	250
Shrum, Rev. Joe Bailey	250
Shrum, Joseph Bailey	78
Shrum, Juanita (Green)	113
Shrum, Kathy	250
Shrum, Katie	250
Shrum, Kevin Russell	91, 98, 125
Shrum, Lawrence	250
Shrum, Lizzie	250
Shrum, Lloyd Ray	43, 304
Shrum, Loretta	250
Shrum, Louella	285
Shrum, Louise Elizabeth	251
Shrum, Louvine Elizabeth	292
Shrum, Lucille Worley	43
Shrum, Maggie	53
Shrum, Mamie Magdalene	302
Shrum, Marie (Nunley)	250
Shrum, Martha (Campbell)	250
Shrum, Mary	250
Shrum, Mary Christine	253
Shrum, Mary Eunice	195
Shrum, Maude	143
Shrum, Maude L.	173, 301
Shrum, Maudie Lee Shrum	5
Shrum, Mavis L.	279
Shrum, Mike	60
Shrum, Mildred	250
Shrum, Millie	250
Shrum, Mose	115, 249
Shrum, Moses	249, 250
Shrum, Moses Walden	248, 250
Shrum, Nancy	250
Shrum, Nelda	249
Shrum, Nellie	98
Shrum, Norma Joyce (Nix)	24
Shrum, Ola Beatrice	250
Shrum, Opal	245
Shrum, Oscar	249
Shrum, Paul	249, 251
Shrum, Peggy	98
Shrum, Peggy J.	299
Shrum, Ralph Eugene	250
Shrum, Ray	250
Shrum, Rena J	250
Shrum, Richard	99
Shrum, Roger C	249
Shrum, Rosie	250
Shrum, Ruby	86
Shrum, Ruby Edna	4
Shrum, Ruby Jewell (Nunley)	143
Shrum, Sarah	250
Shrum, Serilda Jane	104
Shrum, Sharon	249
Shrum, Shawn	204
Shrum, Sherman	249
Shrum, Sherman Andrew	249
Shrum, Stanle E.	249
Shrum, Stanley E., Rev.	250
Shrum, Rev. Stanley	98
Shrum, Steven McKay	250
Shrum, Sue	250
Shrum, Taylor	32
Shrum, Teresa Ann (Fults)	249, 250
Shrum, Thomas A.	251
Shrum, Vergie	251
Shrum, Walden M.	224
Shultz, Bunny Stiefel	249
Shultz, Jackie	120
Sides, Carrie Sue (Marler)	120
Sides, Fred	251
Sides, Jack Kirby	251
Siegrist Von Wel ZH, Heinrich	251

Name	Page
Siegrist, Hans	244
Siegrist, Heinrich	251
Siegrist, Pauline	251
Silcox, Peggy Ann	230
Silcox, Thomas	251
Siler, June Brewer (Hart)	251
Siler, Paul Maurice	251
Simer, Herman E.	251, 271
Simer, Herman Everett	251
Simer, James E.	251
Simer, Ronald E.	251
Simmons, Allen	251
Simmons, Bethel	135
Simmons, Dan	217
Simmons, Gladys	97, 251
Simmons, Iva	151
Simmons, J.D.	251
Simmons, James	251
Simmons, James E.	252
Simmons, Jennifer Lanford	251
Simmons, Joe Allen	135
Simmons, Lola	251
Simmons, Mary Elizabeth (Young)	238
Simmons, Matthew James	251
Simmons, Minnie Ada	251
Simmons, Minnie Ruth	97
Simmons, Richard	181
Simmons, Salinda (Cain)	251
Simmons, Sandra Lou	251
Simmons, William	251
Simon, John	251, 252
Simon, June Marie Simon	252
Simpson, Albert Benton	252
Simpson, Clarence	59
Simpson, Margaret	252
Simpson, Roy Lee	41, 119
Simpson, Sherilda Jane	252
Simpson, Susan	248, 250
Sims, Altha Bell	277
Sims, Carolyn Thelma (Pease)	258
Sims, Girlie	252
Sims, James Albert	46, 65, 232
Sims, Myrtle	46
Sims, Rececca	168
Sims, Wayne Douglas	68
Singelton, Albert "Frankie"	252
Singleton, Albert	252
Singleton, Albert Houston	82
Singleton, Cynthia	252
Singleton, Jackson C	10
Singleton, Mildred (Harris)	252
Singleton, Nellie	252
Singleton, Sandra (Sanders)	155
Singleton, Sheila Renee	252
Sinks, Pearl	245
Sinks, William M	208
Sinnacle, Linda	27
Sisk, Dorothy Louvinia	205
Sisk, James Clayton	106
Sisk, Joseph	200
Sisk, Terry Wayne	105
Sisk, Unk	252
Sissom, Alton	97
Sissom, Ardena	182
Sissom, Argie Earlene	252
Sissom, Dan Jack	252
Sissom, Eliza	252
Sissom, Elsie Marie	252
Sissom, George T.	252
Sissom, George Thomas	252
Sissom, Glenn	252, 253
Sissom, Henry	252
Sissom, J.C. "Tom"	252
Sissom, James F.	252
Sissom, Jessie Ruth	252
Sissom, John William	98
Sissom, Myrtle	252
Sissom, Pascal F. Sr.	64, 149
Sissom, Pascal Lafayette	252
Sissom, Rosa Nell (Sweeton)	252
Sissom, Sarah Ann Steele	252
Sissom, Stanley	253
Sitten-Davis, Barbara (Lowery)	252
Sitz, Albert E.	253
Sitz, Alvin Leon	253, 284
Sitz, Andrew	253
Sitz, Bessie (Green)	253
Sitz, Carl H	253
Sitz, Carl Houston	168
Sitz, Carolyn	253
Sitz, Charles	154
Sitz, Charles F.	253
Sitz, Charles Harvey	253
Sitz, Charlie	198
Sitz, Dan	252, 253
Sitz, Dan Wiley	163
Sitz, David	253
Sitz, Earl Mitchel	253
Sitz, Eddie	253
Sitz, Ethleen	265
Sitz, Faithy	161
Sitz, Flora (Roberts)	150
Sitz, Francis	253
Sitz, Frank Ernest	272
Sitz, Gary Lee	253
Sitz, Geneva Jean (Frederick)	253
Sitz, George Washington	253
Sitz, Gerald	iii

Sitz, Howard	96	Slatton, Huke	254, 294	Smartt Steve A	256
Sitz, James	253	Slatton, Kathleene	88, 254	Smartt, Linda	255
Sitz, James H	38	Slatton, Lewis E.	161	Smartt, Alma	255
Sitz, Joanna Lee	253	Slatton, Louise Kathleen	254	Smartt, Alva	53, 166, 210
Sitz, Mattie Ruth (Guthrie)	253	Slatton, Luther	91	Smartt, Amanda Denise	182
Sitz, Myrtle	253	Slatton, Nornia Mae	69	Smartt, Aubrey Alfred	255
Sitz, Nancy Pearl	253	Slatton, Rachel	24	Smartt, Barbara Allen (Meeks)	270
Sitz, Norma	253	Slatton, Ricky Allen	88	Smartt, Belle	255
Sitz, R.B.	265	Slatton, Robert	254	Smartt, Bill	73
Sitz, Robert	253	Slatton, Scottie E.	50	Smartt, Billy Eugene	255
Sitz, Robert B.	253	Slatton, Teresa	254	Smartt, Carl David	255
Sitz, Virgil	253	Slave graves	292	Smartt, Cathy Marie (Shrum)	186
Sitz, Virgil Henry	84	Sledge, Mary Elizabeth	254	Smartt, Cheryl	255
Sitz, William "Tubby"	161, 253	Slick, Ruth	273, 274	Smartt, Clyde Ransom	91
Sitz, Willie Jo	253	Sloan, Bob	97	Smartt, Daisy	256
Sitz/Sits, Nella aka Nellie Ellender B. Choate	162	Sloan, Clarence	254	Smartt, Daisy M.	304
		Sloan, Ernest	254	Smartt, Dale	256
Sitz/Sits, William Bost	253	Sloan, Howard Edward "Bouncy"	254	Smartt, Danny Aaron	255, 256
Skelton, Arnold Lee	253	Sloan, Lillie Mae	254	Smartt, Deborah Annette	256
Skelton, James Franklin	254	Sloan, Maggie (Yarworth)	254	Smartt, Dennis	ix
Skillin, Lourany	254	Sloan, Mattie	254	Smartt, Doris Ann	148
Skinner, Diane	150, 153	Sloan, Robert	162	Smartt, Earline	255
Slaick, John	72	Sloan, Scott Jon	162	Smartt, Elmer Hubert Fults	288
Slaick, Madeline	91	Smail, Herbert	254	Smartt, Ether (Bess)	256
Slater, Reba Ann	91	Small, Nora	109	Smartt, Ezekiel	255
Slatton, Betty Jo	77	Small, Frances Austin	254	Smartt, Geneva "Bluie"	255, 256
Slatton, Cecil	254	Small, Urban Shofner, Jr.	254	Smartt, Georgia Lee	255
Slatton, Charlotte	254	Smalley, Ules Lester	254	Smartt, Geraldine	81
Slatton, Clair	254	Smallwood, Henry "Hank"	273	Smartt, Gladys Marie	126
Slatton, Ella	4	Smallwood, Henry Lee	254	Smartt, Grace	189
Slatton, Essie	142	Smallwood, Russell Lee	255	Smartt, Gregory Wakeman	51
Slatton, Everett	123	Smallwood, Henry S.	254	Smartt, Hassie	255
Slatton, Fred, Jr.	270	Smart, Elijah Ferris "Uncle Shine"	255	Smartt, Hassie L.	168
Slatton, Fred, Sr.	254	Smart, Eudora	255	Smartt, Henry C	166
Slatton, Gilbert	254	Smart, John	272	Smartt, Imogene	255, 256
Slatton, Hallie	254	Smart, Thomas Winford	255	Smartt, Irene	131
Slatton, Harold	218				
Slatton, Horace Ray	254				

Name	Page
Smartt, James	256
Smartt, Jane	51, 255
Smartt, Janice	256
Smartt, Janie E.	255
Smartt, John C.	255
Smartt, John DeBaptist	163
Smartt, Judy	256
Smartt, Lassie	190, 195
Smartt, Lawrence	226
Smartt, Lawrence Marie	255
Smartt, Leonard	vi, ix
Smartt, Lester "Punk"	255
Smartt, Lilian	255
Smartt, Lillian	255
Smartt, Lillian Virginia	287
Smartt, Lillie	57, 233, 235
Smartt, Linda	256
Smartt, Little Vester	256
Smartt, Loretta	256
Smartt, Lottie	ix
Smartt, Louie	140
Smartt, Louie H	255
Smartt, Lucy Belle	256
Smartt, Maggie Myrtle	256
Smartt, Marcus	125
Smartt, Margaret	256
Smartt, Margie Frances	120
Smartt, Martha Lee (Pickett)	256
Smartt, Marvin	256
Smartt, Marvin D.	255
Smartt, Mary	256
Smartt, Mary Estella "Stella" (Sanders)	7, 73, 101
Smartt, Mildred	256
Smartt, Nellie	271
Smartt, Nickie Dwayne	294
Smartt, Paul David	256
Smartt, R. T.	255
Smartt, Ralph Blaine	256
Smartt, Rebecca Faye	256
Smartt, Rita	187
Smartt, Robert Henry	51
Smartt, Roger Dale	256
Smartt, Ronald "Beaver"	256
Smartt, Ruby Pearl	256
Smartt, Sarah	204
Smartt, Saylor Hope Diamond	75
Smartt, Shelia	256
Smartt, Sidney James	202
Smartt, Sr., Reuben	256
Smartt, Stephen A.	256
Smartt, Stephen Adam	256
Smartt, Steve A.	255
Smartt, Steven A.	256
Smartt, Susie	163
Smartt, Susie Ellen	141
Smartt, Terry	141
Smartt, Theodore	256
Smartt, Thula	256
Smartt, Tommie Melvin	255
Smartt, Tommy	256
Smartt, Vernon	256
Smartt, Vester	71
Smartt, Virginia	255
Smartt, Wallace	199
Smartt, Wallace H.	256
Smartt, Wayne "Thick"	256
Smartt, Wayne L	255
Smartt, Wayne Ladue	188
Smartt, William	256
Smartt. Gina Lynn	256
Smedley, Christopher Columbus	256
Smedley, George	257
Smedley, George Washington	257
Smedley, Hazel	257
Smedley, Hazel (Morgan)	257
Smedley, Jack Clayton	257
Smedley, Margaret "Maggie"	257
Smedley, Randall Dean	5
Smiley, Buford Ray	257
Smiley, Cecil	257
Smiley, Mildred Florence	257
Smith Phyllis Gay (Rutledge)	257
Smith, Alexander H.	257
Smith, Alice Correne	134
Smith, Allie Angeline	257
Smith, Alonzo	116
Smith, Anderson	201
Smith, Andrew C.	191
Smith, Anna Carol Smith (Gilliam)	257
Smith, Audrey Lola	257
Smith, Beatrice	261
Smith, Bertha	261
Smith, Bertha Estelle	57
Smith, Betty	277
Smith, Betty Carlee (Meeks)	259
Smith, Beverly (Johnson)	257
Smith, Bobby	257
Smith, C. Leroy	258
Smith, Carl S.	260
Smith, Carla	258
Smith, Carol Sue	274
Smith, Charles	257
Smith, Charles	257
Smith, Charles Dawes, OBGYN	257
Smith, Claud Everett	257
Smith, Cleo Edward	257
Smith, Clyde	258
Smith, Clyde I	298
Smith, Cora Della	261

Smith, David Hulon	68
Smith, Davis S.	257
Smith, Delila	258
Smith, Della Mae	218
Smith, Della Mai (Pickett)	274
Smith, Dixie	258
Smith, Dola	287
Smith, Dola (Smith)	259
Smith, Doris F (Sweeton)	258
Smith, Dorothy	258
Smith, Dorothy Lee (Davis)	250, 258, 259
Smith, E.B.	258
Smith, Edith Mildred	260
Smith, Elias "Lige"	242
Smith, Elizabeth	286
Smith, Ella	24, 169
Smith, Elmer	114, 285
Smith, Elmer Elbert	257
Smith, Elvie Josie (Norman)	171, 258
Smith, Elvin	258
Smith, Elvin Franklin	260
Smith, Ernest Hoyt	258
Smith, Ethel	88
Smith, Fannie Ellen	22
Smith, Fannie Louise	35
Smith, Fay	271
Smith, Faye	294
Smith, Florence	34
Smith, Flossie	76, 171
Smith, Frank	108, 276
Smith, Frank Hayden, Jr.	258, 259
Smith, Franklin Leroy	258
Smith, Freddie Eugene	258
Smith, George	258
Smith, George Alex	150, 258
Smith, George Preston	260
Smith, George Robert	129
Smith, Gladys Luella (Blaylock)	258
Smith, Gladys Marie	258
Smith, Harlie Ophelia	33
Smith, Harriett	258
Smith, Hayden	198
Smith, Helen	257
Smith, Helen Melton	168
Smith, Henry	258
Smith, Henry Clay	1
Smith, Henry L	115
Smith, Herbert Chester	35, 258
Smith, Herman	260
Smith, Hilda	259
Smith, Homer	270
Smith, J. T.	251
Smith, J.L.	258
Smith, James	246
Smith, James Albert	86, 250, 257, 260
Smith, James Alford	157
Smith, James Alfred	11, 252
Smith, James B.	258
Smith, James Foster	260
Smith, James Francis	293
Smith, James O.	258
Smith, James Oscar	258, 259
Smith, James Thomas	259
Smith, James William "Billie"	259
Smith, Janie Ellen (Tate)	258, 259
Smith, Jasper Stephens	259
Smith, Jeremiah	259
Smith, Jimmy Ray	257
Smith, John	259
Smith, Rev. John	45, 259
Smith, John Calvin	264
Smith, John Elijah M.	89
Smith, John Hulon	260
Smith, John Lewis	257, 259
Smith, John Wesley	103
Smith, John Wesley "West"	258, 260
Smith, John William	261
Smith, Johnnie Ruth	277
Smith, Joseph Wayne	264
Smith, Josephine Flora Mae "Josie" (Sargent)	259
Smith, Josie Evelina	259
Smith, Julia	201
Smith, Kathleen L (Sweeton)	233, 235
Smith, Katie	259
Smith, Katie Evelyn	156
Smith, Ken	242
Smith, Laura	259
Smith, Laura Mae	201
Smith, Lena	142
Smith, Lester	152
Smith, Lester B.	290
Smith, Lewis Lincoln	108
Smith, Lila	259
Smith, Lila Jane	288
Smith, Lillie Kathleen	218
Smith, Lois	259
Smith, Loney Leroy	261
Smith, Lorene	258
Smith, Lorene Jo	242, 258
Smith, Lucille	94
Smith, Lucille Eunice	258
Smith, Mable	304
Smith, Magdaline	223
Smith, Maggie	201
Smith, Mannie	262
Smith, Margaret	13
Smith, Margaret Jane Spearman	184, 207, 259
Smith, Martha	259
Smith, Martha Tennessee	115, 251, 253, 284

Name	Page
Smith, Mary	103
Smith, Mary Clementine "Tine" (Gallagher)	170
Smith, Mary Elizabeth	259
Smith, Mary J.	122, 164, 165
Smith, Mary Lee	144
Smith, Mary Lou	26
Smith, Mary Magdalene "Maggie" (Phipps)	26
Smith, Mary Polly	260
Smith, Mary Sue	86
Smith, Mattie	193
Smith, May	253
Smith, Merrill	51
Smith, Mildred Ann (Gass)	150
Smith, Mildred Louise	260
Smith, Minnie Colleen	60
Smith, Modena	260
Smith, Nancy	225
Smith, Nelson Faye	21
Smith, Neva Joyce	43
Smith, Oscar	113
Smith, Otha Dale	259
Smith, Otto Wilson	44
Smith, Patsy	260
Smith, Peter	238
Smith, Polete	258
Smith, Rease	258
Smith, Rebecca	304
Smith, Refa	153
Smith, Richard Benson	290
Smith, Robert Riley	259
Smith, Robert Taylor	241
Smith, Roland Elroy	40
Smith, Rosa Lawrence	269
Smith, Roy Lee, Sr.	260
Smith, Roy W, Jr.	293
Smith, Roy William III	259
Smith, Roy William, Jr.	260
Smith, Russell Wayne	260
Smith, Sally Ruth	260
Smith, Sam	186
Smith, Sam Charles	260
Smith, Samuel	260
Smith, Sarah	31, 260
Smith, Sarah "Sally" (Thomas)	109
Smith, Savannah	260
Smith, Shirley	132
Smith, Simon Peter	23
Smith, Sissan	146
Smith, Sr., Thomas Jefferson	18
Smith, Steven Dee	259
Smith, Susan	260
Smith, Susan Ann (Kirby)	260
Smith, Susie Eller	260
Smith, Taylor V.	50
Smith, Thelma (Patterson)	260
Smith, Thelma Jewel "Nana" (Shipley)	260
Smith, Thomas	260
Smith, Thomas Jefferson, Sr.	261
Smith, Thomas Lee "Polite"	261
Smith, Timmie	23, 33, 261
Smith, Vaughn W.	26
Smith, Verise Virginia	261
Smith, Vernie Prater	104
Smith, Vernon	260
Smith, Victor Lee	259
Smith, Violet	259
Smith, Violet Lucille	106
Smith, Virgil	45
Smith, Virgil L.	258
Smith, Virginia	260
Smith, Virginia Edith	180
Smith, Wayne "Speedy"	176
Smith, Wesley	261
Smith, Willard T	225
Smith, Willialm Augustus "Will"	261
Smith, William	259
Smith, William D.	27
Smith, William Dee "Buster"	260
Smith, William Douglas	261
Smith, Willie	261
Smith, Willie Beckham	258
Smith, Willie Dora	13
Smith, Willis	299
Smith, Zora	25
Smoker, Katie Lapp	291
Smoker, Reuben	261
Snavely, Helen Virginia	261
Sneed, Diane	176
Snider, Pernell	89
Snider, Tina	261
Snowberger, Marie	261
Snowberger, Robby	261
Snowberger, Robert	261
Snyder, John	261
Snyder, Joseph	159
Snyder, Mary	117
Soape, Percy C.	2, 151
Sobczak, Frances Elizabeth	93
Sok, Chang J	64
Solomon, George	98
Sons, Alma	254
Sons, Floyd Eugene	147
Sons, Mary Ann (Griffin)	261
Sons, Tonya	261
Sooder, Elisabeth	82
Sorling, Anders Gustaf	239
South Pittsburg Mountain Road	ix

Name	Page
Southerland, Lillie Mae	230
Southern, Josephine	250
Soward, Virginia	296
Spears, Leora Patra	185
Spears, Ruby	22
Speegle, Alfred N. Sr.	263
Speegle, Alfred Newton, Jr.	261
Speegle, Bonell	261
Speegle, Delitha	261
Speegle, Donald Lyle	228
Speegle, Kenneth	261
Speegle, Theola	261
Speer, Earlene Y.	288
Spence, Billie (Thomas)	92
Spence, Jr., Jack	261
Spencer, Atisha Darlene (Roberts)	261
Spencer, Ernest	261
Spencer, Glen Daniel	262
Spencer, Jese David	289
Spencer, Lizzie (Adcock)	192
Spencer, Roger Dale	261
Spencer, Sheila Gae	261
Spencer, Zachariah Jarvis	289
Spiegel, Gabriel	212
Spithaler, Joan	233
Spray, Clarice	143
Sprears, Edith	81
Spreiht, Marie C.	87
Spry, Gladys B (Dalt)	120
Spry, Michael, Sr.	261
Spurrier, Nan	261
Squires, Alice	218
Stacey, Nellie Elizabeth	220
Stacy, Lawson	45
Stacy, Pamela Mayberry	35
Stairett, Joyce	230
Stamback, Benjamin	269
Stamm, Marie Magdaline	84
Stampfli, Christian	133
Stampfli, Elise (Stebler)	261
Stampfli, Ernest	261
Stampfli, Henry	261
Stampfli, Linda (Brashears)	259
Stampfli, Minnie	262
Stampfli, Stephen H.	47
Standifer, Patricia Laeria	262
Standridge, Christopher C.	173
Stanfield, Nancy J.	176
Stanley, Audrey Pearl	252
Stanley, Mary Louise	88
Stark, Jeremy Lindell (Brown)	237
Starling, Alexander	262
Starling, Geneva	262
Starling, George	216
Starling, John	124
Starling, Margaret (Turner)	262
Starling, Martha Ida	262
Starling, Roy Venson	288
Starling, Scott	262
Starr, Brandie	215, 262
Starr, Laura	262
Starr, Robert	262
Starr, Robert Allen	262
Statler, Anthony Trabue	262
Statler, Catherine (Spencer)	262
Statler, David Clark	262
Statler, David Clark, Sr.	262
Statler, Lowry W.	262
Statler, Lucinda Bryan (Trabue)	262
Statler, Sr., David Clark	262
Statum, Eliza	262
Statum, Eliza Jane	23, 303
Steaman, Asbury Phoebe Anders	87
Stearns, Charles W.A.	51
Stearns, Charles William	262
Stearns, Helen Catherine	246
Stearns, Helen Lucretia (Bryant)	246
Stebler, Elise	262
Stebler, Rudolf	261
Steed, Charlotte Edna	261
Steedley, Beth	277
Steel, Gracie	182
Steel, Sarah	11
Steele, Connie	252
Steele, Donald P.	262
Steele, Edna Loretta	262
Steele, Justin "Butch"	262
Steele, Lewis	262
Steele, Mary "Polly" Mayhew	240
Steele, Michael Phillip	139
Steele, Robert Wayne	262
Steele, Roland Edwin	262
Steele, Sarah Ann	262
Steele, W. Della	122, 240, 252
Steen, James Daniel	262
Steen, Paul David	262
Stegemoller, Marlys Annette	262
Stegemoller, Unk	263
Steiner, Cynthia Louise (Littell)	263
Steiner, Eric	263
Steiner, Max	263
Stella Bottom	viii, ix
Stephens, Arcadia Jane	263
Stephens, Bessie May	177
Stephens, Betty (Scott)	217
Stephens, Dava Audrey	263
Stephens, Eliza Belle	218

Name	Page
Stephens, Esther	130
Stephens, Esther Yvonne	139, 144
Stephens, Irene	217
Stephens, Mancel Eugene	98
Stephens, Mollie Clarise (Thurman)	263
Stephens, Ores Elvert	263
Stephens, Samuel	217
Stephens, Sarah	130
Stephens, Willy	295
Stephenson, Opal	263
Sternkopf, Janet Lou	79
Sternkopf, Robert Henry	176
Stevens, Ab	176
Stevens, Angelia	263
Stevens, Belle	174
Stevens, Billy	263
Stevens, Billy Ray	263
Stevens, Bruce Howard	263
Stevens, Bruce Howard, Jr. "Tadpole"	263
Stevens, Bruce Howard, Sr.	263
Stevens, Elise	263
Stevens, Elise (Campbell)	263
Stevens, Foster	263
Stevens, George Sheldon	156, 263
Stevens, Georgia Lee	263
Stevens, Harold James	263
Stevens, Henry Taylor	180
Stevens, Hollie Maria (Johnson)	263
Stevens, Irene	263
Stevens, John Clark	36
Stevens, Kathryn (Buckout)	36
Stevens, Kathy	263
Stevens, Lawandel Celina	134
Stevens, Mary Jean (Nunley)	263
Stevens, Nellie (Disheroon)	263
Stevens, Patricia	263
Stevens, Paulette	263
Stevens, Sam	156
Stevens, Susie	263
Stevens, Teresa	263
Stevenson, Catherine	179
Stevenson, James	50
Steves, Alberta	263, 267
Stewart, Absolom C.	94
Stewart, Addie	264
Stewart, Anton Adam	299
Stewart, Anton Galus	264
Stewart, Ara	264
Stewart, Bennie Frances (Hill)	208
Stewart, Carrie Mae	264
Stewart, Edna Marie	303
Stewart, Elizabeth	264
Stewart, Etta Lois	136
Stewart, Frank	238
Stewart, Harvey	264
Stewart, Irene Stella	264
Stewart, J.W.	77
Stewart, Jesse Lafayette	264
Stewart, John William	264
Stewart, Johnnie Ruth	264
Stewart, Linsey Kevin	264
Stewart, Mildred Jewell (Nunley)	264
Stewart, Nancy	264
Stewart, Vernetea	219
Stewart, William "Willie"	219
Stiefel, Alma	219
Stiefel, Alma Jewel (Haynes)	264
Stiefel, Barry Keith	264
Stiefel, Betty Louise (Christian)	264
Stiefel, Billy	264
Stiefel, Dorothy	264
Stiefel, Dorothy Louise (Harris)	264
Stiefel, Eddie Brian	264
Stiefel, Eddie Darnell	264
Stiefel, Eule	264
Stiefel, Eule Henry	264
Stiefel, H.A.	264
Stiefel, Harvey A.	264
Stiefel, Helen Ruth (Sanders)	264
Stiefel, Ray	264
Stiefel, Roy	264
Stiefel, Roy L.	214
Stiefel, Roy Leonard	264
Stiefel, Wendell	264
Stiehl, Mary	264
Stiltner, Ocie Ruth	68
Stocker, Alfred	35
Stocker, Alfred Louis	264
Stocker, Almeta	265
Stocker, Anna	16
Stocker, James Earl	297
Stocker, Joseph	264
Stocker, Joseph	264
Stocker, Joseph Albert	264, 265
Stocker, Joseph Jacob	265
Stocker, Katie	265
Stocker, Leon, Sr.	247
Stocker, Lewis Russell	265
Stocker, Maria "Mary" (Ackerman)	265
Stocker, Norma	265
Stocker, Norma Mae (Sitz)	264
Stocker, Philomena (Meyer)	265
Stockton, Hubert O'Neal	265
Stockton, James Wesley	265
Stockwell, David	265
Stockwell, John Willard	265

Stockwell, Lewis Calvin	105	Stoner, Stella	viii	Stump, May	32
Stockwell, Linda Kay (Meeks)	265	Stoner, Vicki	iii	Stump, Michael G.	266
Stockwell, Minnie Doris	265	Stoner, William Houston "Bud"	viii, ix, 266	Stump, Nannie May	266
Stockwell, Pearl	290	Stotts, Benjamin Franklin	266	Stump, William M.	228
Stoglin, Barbara Francine	238	Stotts, Edgar	266	Stump, William Michael	229
Stoglin, Clyde	265	Stotts, Hazel Kathleen	266	Sublett, Jr., R. B.	32, 266
Stoker, Jacob	265	Stotts, Leonidas "Lon"	266	Sublett, Patrick M.	266
Stokes, Minnie	265	Stotts, Margie Lou	214	Sudberry, Martha Agnes	266
Stone, Banster Lee	195	Stotts, Mary Emeline	266	Sue, Mary	290
Stone, Bentley Randolph	265	Stotts, Monroe	6	Sullivan, Bannie	26
Stone, Beulah Jane (Cupp)	265	Stotts, Sam Leroy	266	Sullivan, Bridget	22
Stone, Fletcher Richardson	265	Stotts, Speaker Douglas	266	Sullivan, Dean	70
Stone, John	38	Stoup, Linda Darlene	266	Sullivan, Eddie	24
Stone, Linda Jean (Hobbs)	265	Straight, Viola Mae	93	Sullivan, Isaac Washington, Jr.	76
Stone, Margaret Emily	265	Stranahan, Richard "Squeak" Gipson, Jr.	224	Sullivan, Lisha	32
Stone, Martha Jane	37	Street, Elva Arlene	266	Sullivan, Martha Laverne (Keener)	298
Stone, Melissa	238	Street, Ida Mae	113	Sullivan, Mary Nell	267
Stone, Nancy	130	Street, Maudie	53	Sullivan, Mosley Minerva	285
Stone, Perry	265	Strick, Patricia	168	Sullivan, Nelma (McGee)	269
Stone, Ruth	224	Strong, Mary Magdalene	190	Sullivan, Sammy	267
Stone, Tullulah Mae	11	Stubberfield, William "Bill"	17	Summers, Clarence Walden	267
Stone, William	38	Stubblefield, Hance	299	Summers, Elizabeth	117
Stoner Cemetery at Stella Bottom	viii	Stubblefield, Mary Jane	231	Summers, Ethel Gordon	148
Stoner, Andrew J.	ix, 53	Stubblefield, Parry	298	Summers, Eugene P.	69
Stoner, Dorothy Emily	265	Stubblefield, Sarah	266	Summers, James Allen	267
Stoner, Henry, Jr.	242	Stubblefield, Walter	225	Summers, John Calvin	267
Stoner, John	ix, 183, 266	Stubblefield, Zora	236, 266	Summers, John W.	267
Stoner, Kenneth	iii	Stucker, Samuel	236, 266	Summers, Josephine	149
Stoner, Lavina "Vina"	265, 266	Studer, Anna Mary	161	Summers, Katherine	144
Stoner, Lavinia	viii, ix, 266	Studer, August	19	Summers, Keon Shiann	227
Stoner, Peter Countiss	266	Studer, Benedict	266	Summers, Laura Sue (Church)	43
Stoner, Robert Clinton	266	Studer, Fidel "Fred"	266	Summers, Leota	267
Stoner, Sally Nunley	viii, ix	Studer, Mary Agatha	69	Summers, Lou	267
Stoner, Samuel M. "Sam"	ix, 290	Stugeon, Hattie	266	Summers, Lydia Armenda	267
Stoner, Sarah	266	Stump, Lena	126	Summers, M.F.	294
		Stump, Lena Rivers	31		

Name	Page
Summers, Martha Naomi	267
Summers, Mary E. (Leeman) Stevenson	25
Summers, Melvina	267
Summers, Nancy	281
Summers, Ray	195
Summers, Robert	267
Summers, Robert T.	267
Summers, Sarah Louise (Nunley)	51
Summers, Tony Eugene	267
Sumner II, Albert William	267
Sumner, Albert "Bill" III	267
Sumner, Beverly	267
Sumner, Kathleen	267
Suter, Helen (Bond)	267
Suter, Helen Lucille (Bond)	267
Suter, Jacob George	267
Suter, Leonhard	267
Suter, Mary (Ley)	267
Sutherland, Albert	267
Sutherland, Catherine Patricia (Brown)	297
Sutherland, Debbie	267
Sutherland, Dorothy Ayre	267
Sutherland, Gary	277
Sutherland, Jackie Ray "Shotgun"	267
Sutherland, Lilly	267
Sutherland, Linda Carolyn (King)	228
Sutherland, Mike	267
Sutherland, Rebecca Louise	267
Sutherland, Ruby	215
Suttle, Emma	297
Suttle, John	73
Sutton, Elizabeth	73
Sutton, Kishire	290
Sutton, Mary Elizabeth	278
Sutton, Winnie	293
Suwalski, Felicia	149
Swafford, Anna Ross	96
Swain, Bernice	238
Swain, Jerry	122
Swallen, Albert	122
Swallen, Lloyd Calvin	267
Swaney, Barry Ray	267
Swaney, Charlie	268
Swaney, Harold Monroe	268
Swaney, Harold Moore	268
Swaney, Richard	268
Swann, John Wesley	268
Swearengen, Ethel	110
Sweeton Hill	v
Sweeny, Ann	20
Sweeton, Abbie D. (Brown)	284
Sweeton, Albert	268
Sweeton, Albert "Hatchet"	259
Sweeton, Albert F.	252, 259
Sweeton, Albery Flury	268
Sweeton, Alice Mae	268
Sweeton, Allen	259, 268
Sweeton, Anthony "Yant"	268
Sweeton, Anthony E "Yant"	268, 270
Sweeton, Anthony Emmett Yancy	270
Sweeton, Arthur Lee	268
Sweeton, Bessie	220
Sweeton, Betty Jean (Campbell)	268
Sweeton, Betty Mae	268
Sweeton, Beverly	27
Sweeton, Beverly Ann (Tate)	268
Sweeton, Bobby Clark	268
Sweeton, Bonnie R	268
Sweeton, Buford Yancy "Dick"	269
Sweeton, Byron	269
Sweeton, Byron Jefferson	269
Sweeton, Callie	269
Sweeton, Callie Estil	60
Sweeton, Card David	60, 245
Sweeton, Carl	269
Sweeton, Carl P	82
Sweeton, Carl Wayne	177
Sweeton, Carl Wilson	268
Sweeton, Carolyn	270
Sweeton, Charles Parker	169, 175
Sweeton, Cynthia Elizabeth	268
Sweeton, Danville Milton	268
Sweeton, Delbert E.	268
Sweeton, Dottie	270
Sweeton, Dottie (Cunningham)	119
Sweeton, Doug	268
Sweeton, Ed Wilson	150
Sweeton, Edd	268
Sweeton, Edith "Tabby" (Layne)	268
Sweeton, Elizabeth	269
Sweeton, Elmer Rolston	35, 212, 213
Sweeton, Elsie	268
Sweeton, Ernest	195
Sweeton, Estil	269, 270
Sweeton, Ferby	60
Sweeton, Francis "Frank" Moses	78
Sweeton, Francis Moses	270
Sweeton, Francis Moses "Frank"	301
Sweeton, Greenberry	269, 270
Sweeton, Harvey Morgan	269
Sweeton, Helen	269
Sweeton, Helen Marie (Oliver)	269
Sweeton, Irene J. (Shirkey)	269

Name	Page
Sweeton, Isaac	269
Sweeton, J. Marshall	268, 269
Sweeton, J.C.	269
Sweeton, J.D.	119, 268
Sweeton, James	19
Sweeton, James Alton	269
Sweeton, James Avery	269
Sweeton, James Kelvin	270
Sweeton, Jerry "Dude"	269
Sweeton, Jicie (Pendergraff)	269
Sweeton, John	269
Sweeton, John E.	37, 41
Sweeton, John Henry	269
Sweeton, Joseph	269
Sweeton, Joyce	269
Sweeton, K. Elizabeth (Adams)	39
Sweeton, Lafayette	269
Sweeton, Lawrence	169
Sweeton, Leonard Lyle	269, 301
Sweeton, Lillard	258
Sweeton, Linda Gail (Nunley)	116, 262
Sweeton, Linda K. (Campbell)	269
Sweeton, Loretta	269
Sweeton, Lucille	262
Sweeton, Mabel (Hatfield)	35
Sweeton, Maggie	269
Sweeton, Mamie	34
Sweeton, Margaret	300
Sweeton, Margie	269
Sweeton, Margie E.	81, 150, 278
Sweeton, Martha Ann Elizabeth "Eliza"	279
Sweeton, Mary Cyntina	270
Sweeton, Mary Etta	256
Sweeton, Mona	25
Sweeton, Myrtle	176
Sweeton, Nora	119
Sweeton, Pearl	36, 82
Sweeton, Rachel	117
Sweeton, Reba Jane (Smartt)	270
Sweeton, Regina C. "Reggie"	270
Sweeton, Richard Anthony	270
Sweeton, Robert Bee	270
Sweeton, Robert Eugene	269
Sweeton, Robert Isaac	34
Sweeton, Ronald Lee	269
Sweeton, Rosetta	270
Sweeton, Ruth (Richmond)	238
Sweeton, Samuel Jerry	270
Sweeton, Sarah	270
Sweeton, Sarah E.	61
Sweeton, Synthia	249
Sweeton, Tami	41, 131
Sweeton, Tommy D	269
Sweeton, Toy	228
Sweeton, Unk	216, 269
Sweeton, Veola Mae	84
Sweeton, Will	220
Sweeton, William Howard	268, 270
Sweetona, Danville	268
Swingle, Ada	268
Tabernacle of the Lord Cemetery	v
Tabor, Minnie	63
Tabor, Nancy	33
Tabors, Martha Josephine	210
Taennler, Maragaretha	167
Tallent, Mary	239
Talley, Ethel	74
Talley, Sadie Irene (Meeks)	105
Tankersley, Clayton	270
Tankersley, Jerry Clayton	270
Tankersly, Melvina	270
Tanner, Brittanie	270
Tanner, Effie	265
Tanner, Effie Cordelia	66
Tanner, Kenneth Eugene	66
Tanner, Rinnia (Turley)	151
Tanner, Roy	270
Tanner, William	270
Tanner, William Lee	66, 283
Tarzi, Janice	270
Tate, Lynn Clyde III	71
Tate, Abbie Lillian	270
Tate, Allie	270
Tate, Alma Jean (Nunley)	206
Tate, Alma Lee (Brannon)	271
Tate, Alton	271
Tate, Alvin	272, 273
Tate, Amanda	69
Tate, Andrew Jackson	272
Tate, Anna Dell (Warren)	272
Tate, Annie Frances (Sanders)	271
Tate, Annie Mae	271
Tate, Anthony Lydell	129
Tate, Arnold	271
Tate, Arnold Eugene	294
Tate, Arthur	19
Tate, Arthur D.	130, 140
Tate, Arthur D. "Doc"	272
Tate, Ben Franklin	271
Tate, Bessie	271
Tate, Bessie F.	108, 110, 287, 289
Tate, Bessie Frances (Brown)	272
Tate, Beulah (Pearson)	271
Tate, Bill Holt	271

Tate, Billy Ray	272	
Tate, Bobby	271	
Tate, Buford	271	
Tate, Buford Linuel	73, 160, 271, 272, 273, 274	
Tate, Carrie	271	
Tate, Carrie Mary	67	
Tate, Catherine (Pittman)	271	
Tate, Cecil Etheleen	271	
Tate, Charlene "Nay Nay" (Nunley)	184	
Tate, Charles A.	271	
Tate, Chester M	271	
Tate, Child	2	
Tate, Clara Belle	271	
Tate, Clara Ruth	14	
Tate, Clifford	272	
Tate, Clinton Duane	272	
Tate, Danny Charles	274	
Tate, Danny Lee	10	
Tate, Darlene Lynda	272	
Tate, David Arthur	272	
Tate, David Edward	272	
Tate, Davidson	272	
Tate, Debbie	170	
Tate, Delia Mae	93	
Tate, Della Mae	215	
Tate, Diane	262	
Tate, Dolly	89	
Tate, Don Samuel	1	
Tate, Donna	272	
Tate, Donna Ray	263	
Tate, Donna Ruth	200	
Tate, Dorothey "Dollie"	263	
Tate, Dorothy	269	
Tate, Drucilla	38	
Tate, Elijah Duncan "Dunk"	286	
Tate, Elizabeth	259	
Tate, Elsie Jean	156, 268, 272	
Tate, Ernold Eugene	154	
Tate, Ethel	228	
Tate, Evelyn	284	
Tate, Everett Slatton	188, 272	
Tate, Florence Hazel "Dolly"	221	
Tate, Floyd	272	
Tate, Frances	158	
Tate, Frances Novella	303	
Tate, Francis	294	
Tate, Francis Marion	42	
Tate, Gary Eugene	194, 272	
Tate, George	272	
Tate, George Lloyd	109	
Tate, George W.	273	
Tate, George Washington	272	
Tate, George Winfield	271, 272	
Tate, Gerald Wayne	69	
Tate, Glenda Sue	272	
Tate, Grace	272	
Tate, Harley	46	
Tate, Harley Cleveland	26, 240, 272	
Tate, Harley Cleveland "H.C."	272	
Tate, Hascal	272	
Tate, Haskell	226	
Tate, Hazel	110	
Tate, Hazel Ann	185, 195	
Tate, Hazel Bell	144	
Tate, Ida	259	
Tate, Ida Mae	28	
Tate, James M.	166, 172	
Tate, James Morton	110	
Tate, James S.	272	
Tate, James Wayne	301	
Tate, Jane Ellen	273	
Tate, Janie Ellen	261	
Tate, Jasper Joe	261	
Tate, Jeanetta	272	
Tate, Jeffery Leon	67	
Tate, Jennie Lee (Brown)	272	
Tate, Jerry Leavern	272	
Tate, Jerry Kenneth	272	
Tate, Jerry L.	272	
Tate, Jerry Leavern, Jr.	273	
Tate, Jessie	272	
Tate, Jessie Lee	121	
Tate, Jewell	179	
Tate, Joe Bradford	272	
Tate, Joe David	61, 272	
Tate, John D "Dink"	272	
Tate, John Harrison	273	
Tate, John Robert	113	
Tate, Johnny Vernon	274	
Tate, Joseph S.	271	
Tate, Joseph Smith	294	
Tate, Julia	273	
Tate, Katherine Iola	153, 272	
Tate, Kathy	272	
Tate, Kenneth "Tim"	272	
Tate, Laden Farrel, Rev.	273	
Tate, Laura Bell (Layne)	273	
Tate, Lela	273	
Tate, Leo	16, 147	
Tate, Leon	72	
Tate, Linda	272, 274	
Tate, Lisa	116, 256	
Tate, Lisa Jane	273	
Tate, Lloyd	273	
Tate, Lloyd E.	272	
Tate, Lloyd Eugene	289	
Tate, Lola	271, 273	
Tate, Lorrine	256	
Tate, Lou	197	
Tate, Loucinda	126	

Name	Page
Tate, Louisa	25
Tate, Lynn Clyde	226, 227
Tate, Lynn Clyde III	282
Tate, Lynn Clyde Tate "Junior"	273
Tate, Lynn Clyde, Jr.	270
Tate, Mable Venear	273
Tate, Marie (Lankford)	104
Tate, Marilyn	273
Tate, Mark Anthony	164
Tate, Marlon	273
Tate, Martha Ada	272
Tate, Mary	188
Tate, Mary A.	23, 124, 272
Tate, Mary Catherine	241
Tate, Mary Ellen	49
Tate, Mary Isabella	78
Tate, Mary L.	33
Tate, Mary Ruth (Smalley)	270
Tate, Mattie Cleo	273
Tate, Maudie R	283
Tate, Melba Jean	273
Tate, Melinda	226
Tate, Melissa Ann	126
Tate, Milton	273
Tate, Minnie	242
Tate, Minnie Agnes	240
Tate, Morris	123
Tate, Morton Harrison	303
Tate, Morton Willard	273, 274
Tate, Murrell Allen	271
Tate, Myrna	274
Tate, Myrtle	41
Tate, Nancy Catherine (Morrison)	29
Tate, Nannie O. (Watts)	273
Tate, Nathaniel	273
Tate, Nathaniel J.	75, 153
Tate, Neal Richard	273
Tate, Nellie D.	113
Tate, Norma Mae	179
Tate, Ollie "Bug" (Griffith)	225
Tate, Omalee	273
Tate, Pat	26
Tate, Patsy James (Killian)	57
Tate, Paul	273
Tate, Paul Henderson	21
Tate, Paula	33, 274
Tate, Preston	249
Tate, Preston Lee	274
Tate, Pricilla Christine (Knight)	96
Tate, Ransom Tate	273
Tate, Raymond	268
Tate, Retha Faye	273
Tate, Rhonda	273
Tate, Richard	270, 273
Tate, Richard Arlen	273, 274
Tate, Richard Freeman	274
Tate, Roger Dwight	274
Tate, Rose Ellen	62
Tate, Rosie	243
Tate, Roy Evan	134
Tate, Roy Rex	274
Tate, Rupert	270
Tate, Sallie	2
Tate, Sam	274
Tate, Samuel	271
Tate, Sandra	303
Tate, Sarah	103
Tate, Scottie Dewayne	272
Tate, Senie	274
Tate, Sexton Tate	32, 66
Tate, Sharon Lee	273
Tate, Sheila Kay (Short)	274
Tate, Sherman M.	274
Tate, Shirley J.	274
Tate, Tim	272
Tate, Troy H.	273
Tate, Wallace Alton	273
Tate, Wallace Brannon	274
Tate, Walter Hoyt	274
Tate, Wilford Lynn Clyde	273
Tate, Will	271
Tate, William	274
Tate, Willie Mae (Flynn)	108, 271
Tatum, Lila Armentha	274
Tatum, Lula Permelia	245
Taulbee, Andrew Homer	16
Taulbee, Eula O'Dessa	274
Taulbee, Helen June	274
Tavares, Josephine Darlene	78
Taylor, Alberta	23
Taylor, America Edna	29
Taylor, Betty	274
Taylor, Betty May	275
Taylor, Bevley B.	304
Taylor, Billy Wade	32
Taylor, Bob	274
Taylor, Celestine	93
Taylor, Claude	275
Taylor, Corbett	303
Taylor, David Richard	22
Taylor, Dewey Herbert	142, 274
Taylor, Dillard	274
Taylor, Easter	288
Taylor, Eliza Jane	274
Taylor, Emory W.	112, 113
Taylor, Everett Waymon	56, 142
Taylor, Fannie	274, 275
Taylor, Francis	178
Taylor, Gene	274
Taylor, George	275

Name	Page
Taylor, Grover Gene	275
Taylor, Ida	275
Taylor, Janelle	i, ii, iii
Taylor, Jon Monson	281
Taylor, Judy Lynn	17
Taylor, Lassie	140
Taylor, Lassie Marilda	213
Taylor, Linda	214
Taylor, Lula Emma	74
Taylor, Malcolm Robert	93
Taylor, Martha	275
Taylor, Maude	257
Taylor, Maude E.	31
Taylor, Maude Elizabeth	30
Taylor, Melba Nadine	31, 62, 63
Taylor, Oscar	220
Taylor, Patricia Ann	295
Taylor, Rhonda Fae	275
Taylor, Rita	275
Taylor, Robert Dean	275
Taylor, Robert Eugene	275
Taylor, Rose M	275
Taylor, Russell Dean	114
Taylor, Virgie	275
Taylor, Waymon Harty "Sonny"	275
Taylor, Woodrow Wilson	275
Tayse, Clifford Lee	275
Teague, Amanda	219
Teague, Henry	31
Teague, Minda	31
Teague, Minda A.	31, 162, 277
Teague, Otsia	30
Teal, Mary Frances	189
Tedder, Hazel	26
Teeters, Eugenia	30
Teeters, Gordon	114
Tell, Thomas	114
Tell, Tillie Joy	275
Temples, Alice Bell	275
Tennis, Bobbye	247
Terrill, Billie Faye (Thomas)	73
Terrill, Billy	275
Terrill, Clyde	275
Terrill, Freeland Roy	275
Terrill, Freeland Roy "Coonie"	275
Terrill, Geraldine (Hill)	275
Terrill, Irene	275
Terrill, Tana	275
Terry, Bobby	151
Terry, Bobby Ray, Jr.	275
Terry, Earl	275
Terry, James Washington	2
Terry, Rena	215
Terry, Sue	2
Terry, Virginia Ruth	275
Thacker, Gertrude	268
Tharp, Frank	82
Tharp, Mrs. Frank	275
Thebault, Mary	275
Thomas, Alan T	50
Thomas, Alvirn (Dickerson)	276
Thomas, Ava	275
Thomas, Barbara	276
Thomas, Bettie Martin	130
Thomas, Bill	40
Thomas, Billy French	275, 276
Thomas, Billy H.	275
Thomas, Bonnie Gaynell	276
Thomas, Brianna Alisha	64
Thomas, Carlton	275
Thomas, Carrie John	296
Thomas, Catherine Laviner	20
Thomas, Cathy	136
Thomas, Chad	98
Thomas, Charles	275
Thomas, Charles E.	275, 276
Thomas, Charles Ed	111
Thomas, Charles Thomas	275
Thomas, Charlie	277
Thomas, Charline	276
Thomas, Clarence	275
Thomas, Danny Lee	276
Thomas, Danny Ray	275
Thomas, Dave	275
Thomas, David William	214
Thomas, Debra Jane	275
Thomas, Diana	182
Thomas, Donnie Ray	85
Thomas, Dottie	275
Thomas, Douglas	255
Thomas, Elizabeth	275
Thomas, Emma	69
Thomas, Erma Colleen	204, 205
Thomas, Esther Elizabeth	126
Thomas, Ezella	27, 78, 233, 276
Thomas, Frances Marie	92
Thomas, Frank	276
Thomas, Georgia Evelin	276
Thomas, Georgie	202
Thomas, Glenn	298
Thomas, Grace	33
Thomas, Grace May	191
Thomas, Hamp	237
Thomas, Hamp Bernest	204, 276
Thomas, Hazel Mae	5
Thomas, Hazel Mae (Turner)	275
Thomas, Hazel Mildred	276
Thomas, Helen Ruth	205
Thomas, Henry Smith	276

Name	Page
Thomas, Herschel	223
Thomas, Ida Mae	275
Thomas, Jackie Ray	79
Thomas, James	276
Thomas, James Arnold	260
Thomas, James Carlton	276
Thomas, James Earl "Jim Earl"	276
Thomas, James Herman	117
Thomas, James William "Buddy"	124
Thomas, Janice	276
Thomas, Jeff	205
Thomas, Jessica F. (Williams)	276
Thomas, Jim Earl	276
Thomas, John Burkley	71, 117
Thomas, John William	203
Thomas, Joshua	277
Thomas, June	276
Thomas, Junior Boyd	276
Thomas, Katherine (Elliott)	276
Thomas, Kenneth "Pee Wee"	276
Thomas, Laura Lee	276
Thomas, Lawrence	203
Thomas, Lee Vester	276
Thomas, Leroy	140, 296
Thomas, Levester	276
Thomas, Linda	132
Thomas, Lucretia	163
Thomas, Mack W.	51
Thomas, Marvin W	275, 276
Thomas, Mary	96
Thomas, Mary Ellen	56, 275
Thomas, Mary Jo	277
Thomas, Mattie	240
Thomas, Minnie Mae	136, 255
Thomas, Myrtle	37, 100
Thomas, Nancy C	15
Thomas, Nannie Ruth	276
Thomas, Odell	276
Thomas, Opal	111
Thomas, Robena	1
Thomas, Robert	32, 152
Thomas, Robert Jackson	204, 276
Thomas, Roy	276
Thomas, Roy Dunn	27
Thomas, Roy Hillman "Judd"	199
Thomas, Roy Hilman	78, 233
Thomas, Sarah "Sally"	276
Thomas, Sarah A. (Trussell)	257
Thomas, Sr., Douglas	277
Thomas, Taylor Sam	275
Thomas, Teddie (Audie Lee Holmes is her real name)	276
Thomas, Tressie	277
Thomas, Vandrene Ezella	204
Thomas, Victor J.	92
Thomas, Virgil C.	261
Thomas, William Edward	277
Thomas, William Franklin	209
Thomas, William Mae	241
Thomas, Willie	78
Thomas, Willie Mae	227
Thomason, John R.	78
Thomason, Mamie B. (Kizer)	288
Thomasson, Charlene	277
Thomes, John W.	185
Thompson, Albert J "Jack"	205
Thompson, Alka	277
Thompson, Amanda	231
Thompson, Ann	236
Thompson, Berniect	93
Thompson, Betty	152
Thompson, Bobbie Franklin	152
Thompson, Charles	277
Thompson, Christopher Dewayne	206
Thompson, Dessie (Byars)	277
Thompson, Edward Cunningham	277
Thompson, Elizabeth	268
Thompson, Elmer	80
Thompson, Frank	277
Thompson, Hannah	277
Thompson, Irene	263
Thompson, James Anthony "Toby"	14
Thompson, Jesse J.	277
Thompson, Jessie	277
Thompson, Joann	191, 231, 302
Thompson, Loadema	34
Thompson, Louise	102
Thompson, Lula	101
Thompson, Malinda	277
Thompson, Mark	102
Thompson, Mary	88
Thompson, Mary Agnes	60, 301
Thompson, Minnie	227
Thompson, Ora	140
Thompson, Paul Worley	201
Thompson, Ralph Edward	231
Thompson, Rita D	277
Thompson, Sally (Hansford)	277
Thompson, Sarah	277
Thompson, Susan	66
Thompson, Wilburn	42, 277
Thompson, Willie	152
Thorpe, Austin	277
Thorpe, Catherine	277
Thorpe, Edwin Austin	20
Thorpe, Francis Austin	20

Name	Page	Name	Page	Name	Page
Thorpe, Leota "Lee"	277	Tigue, Unk	193	Todd, Gilbert	199
Thorpe, Maude	19	Tigue, Vivian	39	Tolar, Tracy Yvette	279
Thrasher, Johnny Wayne	54	Tilghman, Ruth	169	Tollett, Barbara	120
Thrasher, Skeyler Forrestt	277	Tinder, Barbara Jean Clark	145	Tolman, Janice Jane	11
Threehouse, Ethel	277	Tinder, Carlton David	278	Tooney, Renee	17
Throneberry, Bertha E. (Smith)	126	Tiney, Eloise Case	278	Torres, Quintin	34
Throneberry, David Ray	277	Tiney, John Henry, Jr.	278	Totherow, Abby Dianne	110
Throneberry, John Edward	277	Tiney, John Henry, Sr.	278	Totherow, Betty (Brown)	243
Thurig, Maria Anna	277	Tipps, Edna Louise (Crabtree)	278	Totherow, Charles V.	279
Thurman, Charles Anderson, Sr.	265	Tipps, Roy	278	Totherow, Diane	279
Thurman, Charlie Anderson	278	Tipton, Arthur C "Little Boy"	278	Totherow, Dwight Vernon	279
Thurman, Frederick Walter	277	Tipton, Charles L	279	Totherow, Herbert Roddie	279
Thurman, James	277	Tipton, Harvey Ray	278	Totherow, Hugh	279
Thurman, John Thomas	263	Tipton, Jonathan	278	Totherow, Jennifer Lynn	279
Thurman, Martha	278	Tipton, Kris	279	Totherow, Kenneth Howell	136
Thurman, Sarah J	191	Tipton, Margaret Ann (Geary) "Sissy"	278	Totherow, Leda	279
Thurmon, Eliza Emmaline	4	Tipton, Margie	278	Totherow, Teresa	279
Thurston, Mary Frances (Yokley)	103	Tipton, Marlin	282	Totherow, Tommie Lee	279
Thurston, William	278	Tipton, Mary Ann	282	Totherow, William Martin	279
Tidman, Amos	278	Tipton, Oscar "Big Boy"	175	Towell, Barbara M (Luttrell)	86
Tidman, John	278	Tipton, Oscar T. "Bib Boy"	278	Towell, Deola Lee	279
Tidman, Susan (Hunt)	278	Tipton, Oscar Thurston	278	Towell, Marion C "Lum"	216
Tidman, William	278	Tipton, Oscar, Sr.	279	Townsend, Elizabeth	279
Tidwell, Leonard A. Sr.	278	Tipton, Sabrina "Sabra"	278	Trabue, Charles Clay	208
Tidwell, Leonard A., Jr.	278	Tipton, Shirley	7	Trabue, Julie	303
Tidwell, Rachel	278	Tipton, Stephen Palmer	172	Trabue, Lucinda Bryan	303
Tigert, Nancy K (Rollings)	144	Tipton, Stephen Palmer, Capt	279	Trabue, William D.	262
Tigert, Samuel Crawford	278	Tipton, Tennie Bell	279	Travis, Charley	262
Tigue, Daisy Bell	278	Tipton, Tinsley	279	Travis, Sarah Ellen	279
Tigue, Dorothy Helen	183	Tipton, Tinsley Woodrow	278	Travis, William Henry	279
Tigue, John Wilson	278	Tipton, Wilma J. "Ms. Wilma" (Crabtree)	279	Traynier, Ellen Mary	279
Tigue, Leonard Norton	278	Tittsworth, Mary Ruth Argo	279	Treat, Frances Cordelia	291
Tigue, Martha Katherine	183	Todd, Emma Diane	8	Treat, John S	279
Tigue, Otsie Naomi	167	Todd, Frances	279	Treat, Sarah Jane (Reagan)	279
				Treat, William Cebis	279

Name	Page
Treat, William Cefus	165
Trees, Lee	279
Trent, Kenneth Wayne	65
Trent, Thelma Lorene	223
Tressler, Jimmy	280
Tribble, Dorothy	4
Trickler, Kenneth D.	186
Trickler, Kenneth Dean	280
Trickler, Miller Shelton	280
Trickler, Stephen J.	280
Tripp, Lugina Lazina	280
Troglin, Buster	22
Troglin, Lisa	280
Troglin, Tony Dale	280
Trombulak, Jessie Marie (McKnight)	280
Trombulak, Rudolph	280
Trotter, Kathy Ilene	280
Troutman, Sally	81
Troxler, Irene	133
Troxler, Thelma	176
Troxler, Warner	95
Trumpy, Barbara	103
Truner, Marllin	151
Trussell-Carrick, Jessie B.	150
Trussell, Aaron	280
Trussell, Amanda Caroline	281
Trussell, Andrew Jackson	159
Trussell, Blanche L. (Wright)	281
Trussell, Carl Hudson	280
Trussell, Dicie Jane	280
Trussell, Eddie	227
Trussell, Elbert Ward	281
Trussell, Evyline	280
Trussell, Gary Frank	280
Trussell, George Wendell	280
Trussell, Glen Edward	281
Trussell, Henry Bryan	280
Trussell, Jack	280
Trussell, James Henry	281
Trussell, James Henry "Jim"	277
Trussell, James Homer	280, 281
Trussell, James Wesley	280
Trussell, Jessica	280
Trussell, Jessie	281
Trussell, John M.	74, 192
Trussell, Katherine Elizabeth (Manley)	281
Trussell, Lenora	281
Trussell, Leon	280
Trussell, Lora Alvada	280, 280, 281, 292
Trussell, Maxie Bruce	281
Trussell, Oscar Clayton	281
Trussell, Robert Wendell	280
Trussell, Sarah Ann	281
Trussell, Vicki	276
Trussell, Virgil Ray	258
Trussell, William Allen "Will"	281
Tuck-Gorby, Joyce Elois (Myers)	281
Tuck, Charles	281
Tucker, Alexander	83, 281
Tucker, Anna Elizabeth	281
Tucker, Annie Mae (McFarland)	281
Tucker, Baby	281
Tucker, Brenda	281
Tucker, Bud Hence	275
Tucker, Daisy	281
Tucker, David	159
Tucker, David "Dan"	226
Tucker, David Thomas "Dan"	281
Tucker, Edward E.	155, 159
Tucker, Edward Eugene	281
Tucker, Eileen Margaret	281
Tucker, Elizabeth	226
Tucker, Elizabeth Margaret	137
Tucker, Florence	59
Tucker, Frances Almeda	275
Tucker, Frank	281
Tucker, Fred	281
Tucker, Haskel	281
Tucker, James	281
Tucker, Johnnie	275
Tucker, Lillie Myrtle	163
Tucker, Lottie	159
Tucker, Margie Ruth	163
Tucker, Maria Patsy R	163
Tucker, Martha	31
Tucker, Mary	281
Tucker, Mary Alice	105
Tucker, Orpha Gertrude "Gertie"	83
Tucker, Ruth	160
Tucker, Sally Ann	162
Tucker, Samuel	281
Tucker, Silas	281
Tucker, Silas Leon	38
Tucker, Susie	159, 281
Tucker, William	52
Tucker, Willie Winton	82
Tucker, Wilson James	155
Turley, Eliza Fay	20
Turley, Jr., William	282
Turley, Judy	281
Turley, Michael Anthony	32
Turley, Ray	281
Turley, Roy	270
Turley, Sandra Kay	283
Turley, William	282
Turley, William	282
Turley, William, Jr.	282
Turley, William, Sr.	282

Name	Page
Turner, Allen	282
Turner, Alma Marie	282
Turner, Andrea	282
Turner, Ann	137
Turner, Anna	205
Turner, Annetta (Layman)	122
Turner, Annie McCreary	282
Turner, Barbara Joe	283
Turner, Betty	86
Turner, Betty Sue	176
Turner, Beulah Mae	282
Turner, Bobby Gene	109
Turner, Bud	282, 283
Turner, Carmella Ann	283
Turner, Carolyn Ruth	282
Turner, Charlie Woods	282
Turner, Clayburn	283
Turner, Daisy Dean	282
Turner, David	6
Turner, Diane	262
Turner, Dorothy Irene (Layman)	89
Turner, Edgar	282
Turner, Edgar L	282
Turner, Edna Earl	283
Turner, Edna Jean (Killian)	42
Turner, Edward	282
Turner, Elizabeth	283
Turner, Ellen Beatrice	262
Turner, Ernie Lee	79
Turner, Ethel Tresie	282
Turner, Evelyn (Finney) Gilmer	179
Turner, Flora Belle	282
Turner, Glen Lonas	282
Turner, Glenn	282
Turner, Henry Clay	283
Turner, Homer D.	282
Turner, Homer L, Jr.	283
Turner, Howard	282
Turner, Ike	84
Turner, Inalee	282
Turner, Inalee (Turner)	283
Turner, James	282
Turner, James Noah	282
Turner, James W.	282
Turner, Jessie	283
Turner, Jewel	214, 282, 283
Turner, Joe Edgar	190
Turner, John	282
Turner, John Robert	282
Turner, Johnathan Kyle	282, 283
Turner, Joseph Weatherton	282
Turner, Josephine	282
Turner, Jr., Homer L	283
Turner, Judy K.	283
Turner, Junior	283
Turner, Lewis	282
Turner, Lillian	283
Turner, Linda Lou	283
Turner, Lois (Ruehling)	283
Turner, Louise	283
Turner, Mae Bell	155
Turner, Margaret	283
Turner, Marie (Yarworth)	262
Turner, Mark T.	283
Turner, Martha	109
Turner, Mary Eleen	213, 214
Turner, Mary Ester (Morrison)	283
Turner, Mildred Lois (Ruehling)	283
Turner, Opal	283
Turner, Oscar Earl	84
Turner, Rinnia Jean (Turley)	283
Turner, Robert	283
Turner, Robert A.	146
Turner, Robert Earl "Bob"	283
Turner, Robert Eston	283
Turner, Sandra Ann	283
Turner, Sarah	283
Turner, Sarah A.	199
Turner, Sheena	10
Turner, Stella Mae (Lockhart)	282
Turner, Telsa	283
Turner, Tony Lester	271
Turner, Unk	283
Turner, Warner	282
Turner, Wernr	68, 276
Turner, William B.	283
Turner, William Edward	283
Turner, William Jackson, Jr.	283
Turner, William Polk	283
Turner, William R	142
Turner, William Ray	283
Turner, William Robert	282, 283
Turney, Fred	283
Turney, Paul Samuel	284
Turpin, Sarah	284
TVA	v
Twitty, James Leslie	277
Twitty, Layle	284
Twitty, Ruth	284
Tyler, Elma	284
Tylor, Dola (Schild)	39
Tylor, Richard "Dick"	284
Ulrich, Adolph C.	284
Ulrich, Charles Henry	284
Ulrich, Louise E.	284
Umbach, Elizabeth	284
Umbarger, Barthenia	284
Umbarger, Bethany *(Davaney)	284

Name	Page
Umbarger, Genevea Ruth	284
Umbarger, John	93
Umthun, Joseph G.	284
Umthun, Mary E. (Sitz)	284
Underhill, Anna Nell (Layman)	284
Underhill, Jimmy Troy	284
Underhill, Jimmy Troy, Jr.	284
Unidentified	284
Unidentified	284
Unidentified graves	284
Unknown	284, 185
Upchurch, Charlie	285
Uselton, Alton	146
Uselton, Jimmy Franklin	285
Uselton, Richard A	285
Utz, Theresa Gilliam	iii
Valentine, Genie (Rollings)	211
Valentine, William	285
Valley Home Community	vi
Van Hooser, H. Wayne	285
Van Hooser, J.B.	285
Van Hooser, Jewell	285
Van Hooser, Lewis Coleman	269
Van Hooser, Mary Lou "Tiny" (Parsons)	285
Van Hoosier, Nora Treva	285
Van Meter, Iva	285
Vance, Bernice	107
Vance, Carolyn Grace	245
Vance, Donald W.	245
Vandergriff, Andrew Jackson	245
Vandergriff, Harold Loyd	285
Vandergriff, Mildred L. (White)	285
Vandergriff, Russell Hubert	285
Vandergriff, Spearman	285
Vandergriff, Spearman	114
VanDyke, Bonnie Evelyn (Caldwell)	285
VanDyke, Kenneth Cambridge, II	285
Vangaasbeck, James Burton	285
VanGaasbek, James Burton	143
Vangaasbek, Patricia C.	154
VanHooser, Becky	154
VanHooser, Isaac	285
VanHooser, John "Junior"	74, 76
VanHooser, Jossie Pearl (Norris) Jones	285
VanHooser, Juanita	286
VanHooser, Sam Harley	286
VanHooser, Sam, Jr.	213
VanHooser, Sharon	286
VanHooser, Unk	285
VanHoosier, Isaac	115, 286
VanHoosier, Violet Faye	285
VanMeter, Iva	75
VanSlyck, Connie	107
Varnell, Kathryn Gilbert (Graves)	230
Vaughn, Charles Edwin	286
Vaughn, Ethel	286
Vaughn, Ethel Juanita	88, 89
Vaughn, Henry Mattison	89
Vaughn, Lula Frances	286
Vaughn, Mary Ellizabeth	286
Vaughn, Pearl Elizabeth	113
Vaughn, Sarah (Jonas)	286
Vaughn, Susan Anna	286
Vaughn, William	148
Vaughn, William M	71, 286
Veal, Opal Pauline	286
Veal, Robert	58
Veit, Lloyd	104
Veit, Margaret	108
Venhorst, Merlin Maria	108
Ventura, Rose Ann Livingston	267
Verde, Rose	286
Vest, Frances Maries	168
Viez, Franck	106
Vinson, Elma/Elmo Lee	20
Vogel, Alfred	52
Vogel, Beda Maria (Johanson)	286
Vogel, Ingeborg Elenora	286
Vogt, Marian	286
Vollmar, Maryjane	238
Von Rohr, Elizabeth	240
Von Rohr, Leonhard	69
Vunkannon, Cline John	69
Vunkannon, George Washington	286
Waggoner, Annie (Smith)	286
Waggoner, Solomon	286
Wagner, Herman	286
Wagner, Nancy Fults	286
Wakeland, Aesel Ray	286
Wakeland, Violet Blanche (Schlasner)	287
Walden, Benny Raymond	287
Walden, Charles	287
Walden, James Alton	14
Walden, James, Jr.	287
Walden, Myrlene (Myers)	287
Walden, Timothy Eugene	287
Waldo, Debbie Ann	287
Walker, Catherine	157
Walker, Charity	231, 234
Walker, Charles Jefferson	286
Walker, Daisy Meeks	287
Walker, Darlene	116
Walker, Elease	287

Name	Page
Walker, Elijah Andrew	40, 221
Walker, Ella Pearl	287
Walker, Eva	53
Walker, Gene Walker	285
Walker, Grace Katherine	287
Walker, Gregory Eugene	38
Walker, Grover H.	287
Walker, Hazel	18
Walker, Herbert G.	239
Walker, Herbert Glen, Sr.	287
Walker, Howard	287
Walker, Iris Nell	81
Walker, James	287
Walker, James B. "Jimmy"	287
Walker, James Earl	287
Walker, James Lawson "Jimmy"	288
Walker, Jewel Dean	287
Walker, Joan	94
Walker, John James	280
Walker, Johnnie (Mason)	287
Walker, Johnnie Gene (Beene)	287
Walker, Kat	287
Walker, Leonard Parker	287
Walker, Lois Joean	287
Walker, Loretta	265
Walker, Marinda	89
Walker, Martha (Banks)	260
Walker, Mary "Polly" (Campbell)	287
Walker, Mary Edna	287
Walker, Mary Jane	84, 86
Walker, Nora	148
Walker, Ophelia Green	109
Walker, Ruth	296
Walker, Sam	263
Walker, Sara Ann (Hobbs)	127
Walker, Viola (King)	287
Walker, William	288
Wall, Martha	88
Wallace, Benjamin	49
Wallace, James Laney	290
Wallace, Laura	288
Wallace, Lois	64
Wallace, Marion Allen "Allie"	270
Wallace, Mark David	288
Wallace, Patricia	288
Wallace, Robert	4
Wallace, Sarah	288
Wallace, Virgie Jane	81
Wallace, Wrenn	236
Wallace, Wrenn Carlene	232
Waller, Charles Foster, Dr.	234
Waller, W.T., Rev.	288
Walls, Dale	288
Walls, David Stephen	288
Walls, Fred W.	288
Walls, Horace Thomas	288
Walls, Renaye Darnell	288
Walls, Vickie	288
Walls, William Vaughn	136
Walsingham, Goldie Marie (Bivens)	288
Walsingham, Thomas	288
Walston, Charles J.	288
Walston, Richard Lamar	288
Walter, Buelah Edna	288
Walter, Eula Edna	137
Walter, Gladie Marguerite	194
Walters, John F, Jr.	108, 237
Walters, Linda Gail (Anderson)	288
Walters, Vanessa Sue	288
Walton, Dora Ruth	23
Walton, Jean	288
Walton, Lowell Mahlon	138
Walton, Randall Rex	288
Walton, Viola Margaret (Marten)	288
Wanamaker, Alvin Felix	288
Wanamaker, Anthony	vi
Wanamaker, Beecher	289
Wanamaker, Boyce	iii
Wanamaker, Carl Cantrell	160
Wanamaker, Dock Bennett	288
Wanamaker, Evelyn Ann Griffith	288
Wanamaker, Gail	288
Wanamaker, Hazel Annette (Phillips)	9
Wanamaker, Janice M. (Green)	288
Wanamaker, Jerry David	289
Wanamaker, Jewel Dean (Nunley)	289
Wanamaker, Joe Frederick	289
Wanamaker, Joyce Levon (Brady)	288, 289
Wanamaker, Kenneth David	289
Wanamaker, Leida	289
Wanamaker, M. Elizabeth	290
Wanamaker, Malcolm Ray	289
Wanamaker, Margarete "Peggy"	288
Wanamaker, Michael J.	206
Wanamaker, Michael Joe	289
Wanamaker, Nadyne	289
Wanamaker, Nell	301
Wanamaker, Osborn Conard	287
Wanamaker, Spiegle	287, 289
Wanamaker, William Beecher	289
Wanamaker, Willie "Aubry"	267
Wanamaker, Woodrow	289

Wannamaker, James	301	Warren, Charles Thurman	208	Watts, Bonnie Juanita	290
Wannamaker, Johann "Mowan" Wannamaker	289	Warren, David Paul	289	Watts, Eddie	290
Wannamaker, Moriah Nancy	289	Warren, Joe C.	290	Watts, Edward Earl	290
Ward, Annie Myrtle	289	Warren, Lloyd Eugene, 'Sr.	289	Watts, Isham C.	290
Ward, David Glenn	218	Warren, Mary Evelyn (Bryant)	266	Watts, Katie	273, 290
Ward, Dorothy	272, 289	Warren, Maurice	290	Watts, Mary Francis	128
Ward, Freda Fay	30, 127, 229	Warren, Mildred (McCormick)	271, 289	Watts, Parker	290
Ward, Gertrude Leona	30, 127, 229,	Warren, Peggy	290	Watts, Patsy Ruth (Womack)	208, 290
Ward, Jeanetta	175	Warren, Samuel A.	271, 289	Way, Charles Hayes	290
Ward, Lily Ann	213	Warren, Susannah Rebecca "Susie" (Wallace)	290	Way, Ethel	115
Ward, Luther D.	162			Way, Ethel	178
Ward, Myra Maria	30	Watley, Arthur	290	Way, Josie Lee	178
Ward, Nancy	9	Watley, Aubrey	15	Way, Mary Edna	179
Ward, Oscar Lee	168	Watley, Betty	16	Wead, David	249
Ward, Oscar Lee, Jr.	175, 226	Watley, Grady	244	Wead, Marilyn Marie (Osmonson)	290
Ward, Oscar Lee, Sr.	289	Watley, Louis Lavon	83, 193, 211	Weathers, Ruby Lee	290
Ward, Pauline	289	Watley, Louis Leo	290	Weatherup, Candy	16
Ward, Pauline Marie	225	Watley, Mary Etta	290	Weaver, Amy Lou (Brewer)	169
Ward, Reda (Hobbs)	88	Watley, Pagen Ellander "Ellen"	152	Weaver, Andrew Jackson	291
Ward, William F.	289	Watson, Alice (Bivens)	282	Weaver, Andrew Jackson	68
Ward, William Hudson	187	Watson, Calvert E. "Cal"	290	Weaver, Annie (Bedford)	117, 291
Ward, Willie Franklin	195	Watson, Clark Patrick	290	Weaver, Austin Eugene	291
Wardell, Chester Lewis	289	Watson, Ethel	290	Weaver, Betty	291
Wardell, George Francis	289	Watson, Eunice Angele (Stoner)	243	Weaver, Billie Marie (Brinkley)	291
Wardell, Sheila Gae	289	Watson, Gladys	290	Weaver, Bonnie Marie (Schlageter)	291
Ware, Edna Ruth	289	Watson, Helen	244	Weaver, Carrie	291
Ware, JoAnn	289	Watson, Helen	123	Weaver, Coy	291
Ware, John	289	Watson, Jr., Herman A	236	Weaver, Dempsie Albert	291
Ware, John William	181, 289	Watson, Herman A, Jr.	290	Weaver, Elizabeth Pearl	291
Ware, Linnie Lee	289	Watson, Kevin Mitchell	290	Weaver, Emory	61
Warner, Connie Yates	126	Watson, Lethia (Jacobs)	290	Weaver, Ernest A.	291
Warner, Henry Herbert	241	Watson, Marti	290	Weaver, Ernest Alton	302
Warren Cemetery	i	Watson, Morris Vinson	192	Weaver, Florence A. (Burroughs)	291
Warren County	vi, viii	Watson, Roy	290		
Warren, Anna Dell	61	Watson, Thomas	25	Weaver, Harriet	291
Warren, Bobbie Jo	289				

Name	Page
Weaver, Ida	291
Weaver, Irma	291
Weaver, James H.	265
Weaver, Jessie L.	291
Weaver, Jimmie Don	291
Weaver, Julie A.	291
Weaver, Linda Faye (Long)	291
Weaver, Martin Dale	291
Weaver, Mary Elizabeth "Eliza"	291
Weaver, Matthew Ottis	1
Weaver, Myrtle Evelyn	291
Weaver, Ophelia	291
Weaver, Raymond	68
Weaver, Robert McManus	291
Weaver, Sabrina	291
Weaver, Thomas F.	291
Weaver, William B.	291
Weaver, William Bedford	291
Webb, Eda	291
Webb, Myrtle Ellen	131
Webb, Stella	245
Webb, Tennessee	226
Weber, Ernest	16
Weber, Verena	185
Webster, Doris	151
Webster, Doris Marie (Green)	266
Webster, Grace	291
Webster, Robert Carl Webster	291
Webster, Robert Carlton	266
Webster, Vernon	291
Weddington, Dimple	291
Weddington, John	282
Weddington, John Roy	291
Weddington, Mary Elizabeth (Campbell)	37
Weems, Betsy	291
Weibert, Brad	28
Weir, Lennie Bell	121
Weir, Lola Bell (Norris)	43
Weir, Paul Henry	291
Weir, Thomas Jacob	292
Weiss, Lydia	291, 292
Welch, Gene Maurice	288
Welch, James Hewel	292
Welch, Katie Pearl	292
Wells, Alton Edsel, Sr.	292
Wells, Bernard E.	292
Wells, Charles Richard	292
Wells, Clydie	292
Wells, Dotson	211
Wells, John Neel	292
Wells, Mickey	292
Wells, Peggy Jane	292
Wells, Susan	211
Wells, Tom	292
Welsh, Isaac	292
Welsh, Jeff	292
Welsh, Jessie Belle	292
Welsh, Teresa Lynn	292
Wemberly, Therisa (Trussell)	292
Werner, Eliza "Ettie"	292
Werner, Jacob	101
Werner, Samuel Herbert, Sr.	292
Werren, Sophie	292
Wesley, Carolyn Jane	133
Wessner, Howard	47
West, Agnes McClung	161
West, Angelia	28
West, Anna Viola	200
West, Annie Rose	245
West, Bessie M.	5
West, Jackson W.	292
West, Mary Christine	219
West, Mary Melinda	20
West, Nelson Schuyler	28
West, Viola	292
Westerfield, Johnny Bear	219
Westerfield, Virginia Lucille	134
Western, Jesse	134
Western, Jo Ann (Jacobs)	292
Westfall, Mildred	292
Westman, Andrew	105
Westman, Margaret	36
Whaley, Louthenia Caldonia	36
Wheeler, Tippie Louise	174
Whitaker, Dewey	175
Whitaker, Johnnie Estella	122
Whitaker, Lottie	300
White, Ada	122
White, Alice	243
White, Bertha	138
White, Bobby Leon	257
White, Charles Christopher	292
White, Charles David	292
White, Charles Emmett "Jack"	292
White, Charles Logan	293
White, Charles Walter	175, 292
White, Charlie Logan	294
White, Chris	175, 292, 294
White, Christopher C.	294
White, Cindy	48
White, Clercie	250
White, Dock	293
White, Edna Jewell	29
White, Edna Jo	29
White, Emmette	134
White, Essie	293
White, Estella	158

Name	Page
White, Everette	293
White, Flora	293
White, Flora Lee	147
White, Glenda Sue	293
White, Glenn	293
White, Grady L.	293
White, Hallie Gean	21, 293
White, Harold Eugene	135
White, Hazel Bernice (Smith)	293
White, Henry Hall	293
White, Henry Junior	293
White, J.T.	293
White, J.W.	17
White, Janice (Burnett)	134, 293
White, Jessie	293
White, Jimmy Carlton, Sr.	57, 98
White, John	294
White, John T.	292
White, Kathleen "Kat" (Long)	293, 294
White, Laura Ann	293
White, Lucille - no tombstone, rock marker only	293
White, Dr. Lydia Ann	293
White, Malinda	293
White, Malinda (Lowe)	293
White, Mamie Lula (Tate)	293
White, Margaret Jane	294
White, Mattie Loraine	156
White, Melissa	175
White, Nina Faye	207
White, Noah	139
White, Ola	293
White, Ola H.	48, 293
White, Pamela Jo	138
White, Pearl (Glisson)	294
White, R.L.	294
White, Rachel Louisa (Hennessee)	158
White, Reba	294
White, Robert	176
White, Robert Gilbert	213
White, Robert Gilbert, Jr.	53
White, Robert Gilbert, Sr.	293, 294
White, Robert Hatton	293, 294
White, Robert Jackson	294
White, Robert N.	294
White, Robert Newton	285
White, Sharon	294
White, Shirley	207
White, Stella	129
White, Teresa Ann (Slatton)	299
White, Velma Louise	294
White, Willie Blane	87
Whited, Jackie Ray	294
Whited, Rev. Howell	294
Whitehead, Elizabeth	294
Whitfield, Frances Nadine (Bennett)	146
Whitfield, Thomas	294
Whitlock, Lucille	294
Whitman, Adam Elmo	8
Whitman, Alfred B.	294
Whitman, Bridget Michelle	294
Whitman, Charity	294
Whitman, Danny	187
Whitman, Elmo	294
Whitman, Frances Novella (Tate)	294
Whitman, Holly L.	294
Whitman, Janice	295
Whitman, JayShun McCrea	91
Whitman, Joann	294
Whitman, John	27
Whitman, Lecil	295
Whitman, Lettie	73, 294
Whitman, Louis	15
Whitman, Lyndon "Pete"	294
Whitman, Melissa Ann (Layman)	295
Whitman, Octa	295
Whitman, Patricia Ann	148, 149, 283
Whitman, Shirley	295
Whitman, Stanley "Ransie"	183
Whitman, Stephen	295
Whitmore, Allie (Sinks)	295
Whitmore, Henson	295
Whitney, Julia Jane	295
Whitt, Beatrice Elizabeth	215
Whitt, Charlie	295
Whitt, Douglas Woodrow	295
Whitt, George Mack	295
Whitt, James Carl	189
Wichser, Anna	295
Wichser, Fred, Sr.	199
Wichser, Frederic	295
Wichser, Johann Jakob	199
Wichser, Rose	295
Wideman, Carma Nell	95
Wideman, Carmenell	285
Wideman, Carol	5
Wideman, Carolyn Ann	295
Wideman, Dawn	4
Wideman, Dennis	295
Wideman, Gary Manuel	295
Wideman, Howard	295
Wideman, James Howard	67
Wideman, Manuel	295
Wideman, Manuel H.	17
Wideman, Margaret Andrews	295
Wideman, Margaret Elizabeth	149

Name	Page
Wierik, Mary	17
Wiersma, Francine	173
Wiesener, E.B.	172
Wiesener, Infant son	295
Wiggins, Dot	295
Wiggins, John Wesley	95
Wiggins, Louvenia	295
Wiggins, Robert	295
Wilbanks, Belmont "Belle"	95
Wilbanks, Charlotta	66
Wilbanks, William Henry	65
Wilburn, Harry	65
Wilburn, Ivorene	214
Wilburn, James	295
Wilburn, Rita Mae	295
Wilburn, Wayne Thomas	214
Wilcher, Howard Venus	295
Wilcher, James Howard	295
Wilcox, Commodore Archibald	295
Wilcox, Walter	295
Wild, Barbara	295
Wilder, Billy Wayne	199, 295
Wilder, Elbert	295
Wiles, Lena Rivers	295
Wiley, Cornelia Mae	110
Wiley, Ellen (Farrell)	20
Wiley, James D.	296
Wiley, James Henry Newsom	296
Wiley, Jefferson Davis	296
Wiley, Thomas Alexander	296
Wiley, William "Willie" H.	296
Wilhelm, Mae Pearl (King) Thomas	296
Wilhelm, Paul Joseph	296
Wilhite, Geneva (Bateman)	296
Wilhite, Raymond	296
Wilhoit, Maudie	296
Wilhoite, Maude	25
Wilkerson, Bonnie Sue	13
Wilkerson, Kelli Lea	222
Wilkerson, Unk	170
Willems, Bob	222
Willems, Mary Marguerite	296
William Donaldson	296
William, Pace	67
Williams Knott, Myrtle Katherine (Rollins)	276
Williams, Artie Lula Ellen (Basham)	296
Williams, Aylene	296
Williams, Charles	296
Williams, Charles Archard	296
Williams, Charlotte	296
Williams, Christopher Columbus	63
Williams, Clyde Wesley	20
Williams, Cynthia Catherine	297
Williams, Daniel	296
Williams, Emma Jane	63
Williams, Esther	303
Williams, Eva	151
Williams, Fannie Mai	199
Williams, Frank	157
Williams, Garrett Delane	63
Williams, Gene	296
Williams, George	132
Williams, Howard Baker	296
Williams, Irena	296, 297
Williams, Irene Jane	258
Williams, James "J. B."	146
Williams, James Edgar	296
Williams, Jimmy	296
Williams, Julia Virginia	203
Williams, Julius Bennett	58, 110
Williams, Kenneth Delane	87
Williams, Kyle Garvis	296
Williams, Lawson Brown	296
Williams, Lidy	297
Williams, Manley Eugene "Gene"	214, 282
Williams, Margaret	296
Williams, Mary Alice	159
Williams, Mary Burton (Lockhart)	157
Williams, Nancy Ann	297
Williams, Paula	258
Williams, Pauline	203
Williams, Roscoe Clifford	96
Williams, Sandra Fay (Buckner)	296
Williams, Stacy	297
Williams, Stephen W.	297
Williams, Tammy Ann (Fults)	296
Williams, Vida Margaret	297
Williams, Walter	174
Williams, Willie Mae (Greeter)	80
Willie, Ruby Allison (Hill)	297
Willis, Anderson Charles	297
Willis, Andrew	297
Willis, Bill	297
Willis, Fannie	297
Willis, Farmer Jack	102
Willis, Jerry Newton	297
Willis, John	297
Willis, John Franklin "Jack"	297
Willis, Linda	297
Willis, Nancy	53
Willis, Ralph Houston	94
Willis, Tennie	297
Willis, Thomas	297
Willis, Thomas C.	230

Name	Page
Willis, Velma Inez (Church)	207, 230
Willis, Willie Mae	297
Willoughby, Laura	247
Wilson, Addie	185
Wilson, Alta Cordelia	21
Wilson, Amy Eugenia	53
Wilson, Billy Wade	68
Wilson, Birdie Alma	297
Wilson, Cleora	297
Wilson, Coleman C.	76, 122
Wilson, Coleman Clay	297
Wilson, Dorothy	297
Wilson, Eileen	198
Wilson, Elizabeth	280
Wilson, Elsie "Bobbie" Lea (Sutherland)	183, 266
Wilson, Frank Swift	297
Wilson, George Leonard	297
Wilson, Georgia	202
Wilson, Georgia Ann	30, 90
Wilson, Hulda Ellen	134
Wilson, James C.	185
Wilson, James Christopher	297
Wilson, Jennie	298
Wilson, Joan	29
Wilson, Juanita (Kilby)	214
Wilson, Lorene	297
Wilson, Lurto Jackson	47, 146
Wilson, Marshall	297
Wilson, Martha	216
Wilson, Mary	67
Wilson, Morris Anderson	70
Wilson, Narcia Mae (Brazile)	134
Wilson, Nina (Barry)	297
Wilson, Orphie	298
Wilson, Ortense	95
Wilson, Paul Bradley	202
Wilson, Rebecca	298
Wilson, Susan	112, 205
Wilson, Susannah	112
Wilson, Wayne Kenneth	84
Wilson, William Ernest	297
Wilson, William Thurston "Thad"	298
Wimberly, Dama Magdaline (Meeks)	298
Wimberly, John Randall	298
Wimberly, Lynn Carden "Carty"	292
Wimberly, Margie (Reed)	298
Wimberly, Martha	298
Wimberly, Oscar Junior	74
Wimberly, Roy	298
Wimberly, Virgie L. (Smith)	286, 298
Wimpy, Eleanor	298
Wimpy, James Wilburn	298
Wimpy, William Forrest "Bill"	298
Windham, Jack	298
Windham, Patricia	298
Winton, Marshal, Colonel	298
Winton, Bill	61
Winton, Claude	160
Winton, Cora	299
Winton, Cora (Bouldin)	298
Winton, Dale	298
Winton, David Alan	299
Winton, David L.	299
Winton, Dylan Matthew	298
Winton, Elizabeth "Libba" (King)	298
Winton, Frankie	298
Winton, Frankie (Bailey)	299
Winton, Fred T.	298
Winton, Gary	299
Winton, Gary Lynn	298
Winton, Harold David	298
Winton, Howard T.	298, 299
Winton, Inez	298
Winton, Inez (Carden)	241
Winton, James	298
Winton, James E.	299
Winton, James Lawrence	299
Winton, Jamie	299
Winton, Jesse James	298
Winton, Jim	298
Winton, John L. "Jay"	299
Winton, John Leonard "Jay"	299
Winton, Kelly	299
Winton, Larson	299
Winton, Leon Larson	299
Winton, Leonard	299
Winton, Leonard Dale	298
Winton, Lewie	133
Winton, Marshall	298
Winton, Mary "Sarah" Jane	298
Winton, Mary Ann (Linley)	237
Winton, Mary Frances (Franks)	299
Winton, Mary Jane Stubblefield	299
Winton, Patricia	299
Winton, Patty	129
Winton, Paul David	153
Winton, Ralph E.	299
Winton, Robert Gene	298
Winton, Ruby (Crabtree)	298, 299
Winton, Sarah	299
Winton, Sue (Duke)	187
Winton, Teresa	299
Winton, Timothy Dean	299
Winton, Verna Ruth (Hawk)	299
Winton, William Jonathan	299
Winton, Yancie	299

Name	Page
Winton, Yancie C.	229
Wintrow, Emma Crystal	298
Wirz, Abraham	79
Wirz, Fritz	299
Wise, Billy Don	299
Wise, Charles	299
Wise, Charles	299
Wise, Flossie	299
Wise, Flossie Mae	242
Wise, Jack Robert	273
Wise, James Harris "Jesse"	299
Wise, John Ollie	299
Wise, Kevin	299
Wise, Kristi	54
Wise, Peggy Diane	32
Wise, Tom Norris	299
Wiser, Horace	16
Wiser, Linda Ruth (Bohanon)	300
Witbeck, Rodger Dale	300
Withorne, Mike	300
Witt, Albert Michael	282
Witt, Carol Kay	107
Wockasen, Earl Anthony	234
Wockasen, Earl W.	300
Wolff, Judith	300
Wolford, Orville William	182
Womack, Buelah Ann	43
Womack, Elisa Ophia	287
Womack, George	50
Womack, Governor H.	300
Womack, Governor Hodley	290
Womack, Junus Vernon	300
Womack, Patsy Ruth	300
Womack, Virgie (Bond)	290
Womack, Wanda	300
Womack, William	243
Womble, Benjamin	300
Womble, Lynn	93
Wood, Esther	54
Wood, Howard, Lt.	130
Wood, Loretta Kay	230
Woodall, Albert Dewey	183
Woodall, Charles	300
Woodall, James Larry	300
Woodall, Patsy Virginia (Payne)	300
Woodard, Ike B.	300
Woodard, J. Fletcher	300
Wooden, Grant	300
Woodlee, Alma L. (Crabtree)	252
Woodlee, Andrew Beecher	300
Woodlee, Andrew Beecher, Jr.	301
Woodlee, Aubrey Eugene	301
Woodlee, Bettye Claire	300
Woodlee, C.L.	98
Woodlee, Carrol, Sr.	300
Woodlee, Carroll	300
Woodlee, Carroll, Jr.	301
Woodlee, Charlene (Dye)	301
Woodlee, Clara	300
Woodlee, Douglas	280
Woodlee, Dwite David	300
Woodlee, Edwin Harrison	301
Woodlee, Elizabeth Marie (Jacobs)	301
Woodlee, Enoch	301
Woodlee, Esper	301
Woodlee, Estella	140, 162
Woodlee, Evie	54
Woodlee, Evie Frances	43
Woodlee, Frank Cecil	217
Woodlee, Franklin Christopher	300
Woodlee, Gladys	300
Woodlee, Gordon	116
Woodlee, Hardy Harrison	300
Woodlee, Harris B.	301
Woodlee, Ida	301
Woodlee, Iva Lee	37
Woodlee, James B.	300
Woodlee, Jerrel	301
Woodlee, Jess	228
Woodlee, Kenneth Morris	229
Woodlee, Leonard "Hill"	301
Woodlee, Leonard Patton	301
Woodlee, Liddy	194
Woodlee, Linda Nadyne (Wanamaker)	193
Woodlee, Lorene	301
Woodlee, Lydia	255
Woodlee, Maggie (Tate)	149
Woodlee, Mamie Minerva (Sweeton)	301
Woodlee, Margaret Louise (Anderson)	301
Woodlee, Marty	301
Woodlee, Maude	301
Woodlee, Maude Victoria	137
Woodlee, Nancy	15
Woodlee, Nancy "Nannie"	192
Woodlee, Ray	157
Woodlee, Rebecca	301
Woodlee, Robert Dale	260
Woodlee, Susan "Sue"	301
Woodlee, Unk.	207
Woodlee, William Hobart "Hobe"	214
Woodlee, Willie	300
Woodlee, Wilma Sue (Sweeton)	158
Woods, Carl	301
Woods, Dorothy	301

Name	Page
Woods, Gary Wayne	111
Woods, Lucinda	301
Woods, Mildred	108
Woods, Norine	173
Woods, Samantha Joan (Gipson)	301
Woods, Walter "Pete"	301
Woodson, Nera	301
Woodward, Kitty	104
Woodward, Richard	171
Woody, Nancy Jane	33
Woody, Nannie	225
Woosley, Nancy Jane	95
Wooten, Benjamin Anderson	219
Wooten, Benjamin Franklin	25
Wooten, Bettye Lou	17, 301
Wooten, Carrie Leigh	75
Wooten, Clariss Eveline "Clercy"	34
Wooten, Clarissa Evaline	99
Wooten, Cynthia Jane (Lawson)	99
Wooten, Dessie	301
Wooten, E.H.	9
Wooten, Edna Mae	302
Wooten, Howard Mack	59
Wooten, Hughie, Sr.	301
Wooten, Lois	64
Wooten, Melody Chrystal "Sam"	83
Wooten, Robbie Pearl	302
Wooten, Thomas Benton	245
Wooten, Willie (McDaniel)	148
Workman, Cora Jane	302
Worley, Christine	46
Worley, Clara	87
Worley, Daisy Bell	135, 179, 189, 196
Worley, Dorothy Mae (Layne) "Dot"	195
Worley, Ella Mable (Bone)	302
Worley, Elton	302
Worley, Emma Jean	302
Worley, Ershel	74
Worley, Henry	302
Worley, Herbert Stanley	302
Worley, Ina	302
Worley, Infant	245, 246
Worley, Jack Donald	302
Worley, James	302
Worley, James Ed	302
Worley, James William	302
Worley, Jim	302
Worley, Lisa	302
Worley, Mable (Bone) Weaver	302
Worley, Mable (Crabtree)	302
Worley, Martha	302
Worley, Michael David	302
Worley, Minnie	302
Worley, Mona Lee	286
Worley, Osbin	79
Worley, Paul	302
Worley, Pearl	191, 302
Worley, Peggy Joyce	147
Worley, Raymond Rastus	81
Worley, Ronnie Lee	302
Worley, Ruby	302
Worley, Ruth P.	33
Worley, Steve Michael	302
Worley, Thelma Mae (Hobbs)	302
Worley, Treva Lou	302
Worley, Unk	302
Worley, Unknown	87
Wright, Bea	302
Wright, Ben	9
Wright, Blanche	231
Wright, Blanche L.	280, 281
Wright, Dave	292
Wright, Douglas Eugene, Sr.	303
Wright, Floyd	303
Wright, Frank	9
Wright, Irene	280
Wright, Laura Bell	303
Wright, Leatrice	10
Wright, Lula Carolina	9
Wright, Mark	214
Wright, Thelma	303
Wright, Wanda Imogene	6
Wrisner, Oma Lee	303
Wyche, Ina M.	13
Wyche, Unknown	303
Wylie, Eva Mae	303
Wynn, James Steven	300
Wynn, Mary	304
Yak, Edna Nell	176
Yaneze, Cheryl	303
Yarber, Arthur	298
Yarber, Infant	303
Yarrington, Alfred	303
Yarworth, Arveta	198
Yarworth, Bessie	303
Yarworth, Chester Carlton "Carl"	282, 303
Yarworth, Della (Downum)	303
Yarworth, Denver	303
Yarworth, Edward John	75
Yarworth, Lewis	62
Yarworth, Lewis F.	282, 283, 303
Yarworth, Maggie	303
Yarworth, Marie	254
Yarworth, Mildred (Tate) Cox	283
Yarworth, Mildred Tate Yarworth	303
Yarworth, O.H.	50

Name	Page
Yarworth, Orville	303
Yarworth, Stanley	254
Yarworth, William Paul Cox	303
Yates-Nolan, Teresa Ann	50
Yates, B.F.	303
Yates, Claudia "Jay"	73
Yates, Claudia Irene	303
Yates, Douglas Jeffries	303
Yates, Edward	303
Yates, Elizabeth	58
Yates, Florence Laurene	99, 303
Yates, Jackson "Bucky"	194
Yates, Julie (Trabue)	303
Yates, Leesul	303
Yates, Leesul Richard	303
Yates, Lonnie Wilson	303
Yates, Margaret	303
Yates, Marvin Franklin	303
Yates, Norma Jean (Burks)	303
Yates, Thomas Allen	303
Yates, Thomas McCord	303
Yates, Vircie	303
Yell, Catherine Laverne	264
Yell, Joseph Alfred, Sr.	303
Yell, Ples	303, 304
Yenny, Marie "Mary" (Maurer)	304
Yenny, Samuel	304
Yokley Family Cemetery	ix
Yokely, Alva Pauline	304
Yokley, Dallas Allen	49
Yokley, Danny	304
Yokley, Eunice	304
Yokley, Harmon W.	278
Yokley, Herbert Lee	304
Yokley, Imogene	304
Yokley, Jeffery Nathan "Petee"	35
Yokley, Jerry	304
Yokley, Jerry Donald	304
Yokley, Lucille Eunice (Smith)	103, 304
Yokley, Martha Eveline "Mattie" (Lappin)	304
Yokley, Samuel B.	304
Yokley, Samuel Bert	278
Yokley, Virginia Fay (Cleek)	304
Yokley, William	304
Young, Benjamin Franklin	304
Young, Berry	174
Young, Bettye	304
Young, Bobby	79
Young, Charles Linberg	304
Young, Edna Earl	304
Young, Hester Myers	56
Young, Jeff Thomas, Jr.	304
Young, Jeff Thomas, Sr.	304
Young, Joseph	304
Young, Katherine	251
Young, Marty	55
Young, Mattie	304
Young, Nancy Southdown	286
Young, Nezzie B.	118
Young, Sallie Mae	304
Young, Timothy Glynn	174
Zahn, Christi (Nunley)	304
Zdanowski, Frances Virginia	304
Zdanowski, Michael Stephen	304
Zeman, Dennis	304
Zimmermann, David	107
Zingale, Frances Maria	304
Zingale, Frances Marie	250
Zingale, Mary	255
Zingale, Thomas	276
Zopfi, Kaspar, Sr.	276
Zopfi, Katherine	304
Zophi, Katherine (Zimmermann)	133
Zwald, Katharina geb (Naegeli)	304
Zwald, Melchoir, Jr.	305
	305